WRITING SAMPLES

Writing samples in this book show you representative types of writing about literature—from initial notes to a revised, final research paper. Reading these samples along with their commentary should help you understand what is expected when your instructor asks you to write about the literature you are reading.

CRITICAL APPROACHES

This short guide to important critical approaches briefly explains the tools that professional critics and theorists employ when they write about literature.

THE NORTON INTRODUCTION TO
Literature

PORTABLE THIRTEENTH EDITION

Kelly J. Mays

UNIVERSITY OF NEVADA, LAS VEGAS

W. W. NORTON & COMPANY
New York, London

W. W. Norton & Company has been independent since its founding in 1923, when William Warder Norton and Mary D. Herter Norton first published lectures delivered at the People's Institute, the adult education division of New York City's Cooper Union. The firm soon expanded its program beyond the Institute, publishing books by celebrated academics from America and abroad. By midcentury, the two major pillars of Norton's publishing program—trade books and college texts—were firmly established. In the 1950s, the Norton family transferred control of the company to its employees, and today—with a staff of four hundred and a comparable number of trade, college, and professional titles published each year—W. W. Norton & Company stands as the largest and oldest publishing house owned wholly by its employees.

Editor: Sarah Touborg
Assistant Editor: Madeline Rombes
Editorial Assistant: Emma Peters
Project Editor: Maura Gaughan
Production Manager: Ashley Horna
Media Editor: Carly Fraser Doria, Sarah Rose Aquilina
Media Project Editor: Cooper Wilhelm
Assistant Media Editor: Alexander Lee
Ebook Production Manager: Danielle Lehmann
Marketing Manager, Literature: Kimberly Bowers
Design Director: Lissi Sigillo
Photo Editor: Ted Szczepanski
Permissions Manager: Megan Schindel
Composition: Westchester Publishing Services
Manufacturing: LSC Communications

Copyright © 2020, 2017, 2014, 2011, 2006 by W. W. Norton & Company, Inc.

Permission to use copyrighted material is included in the permissions acknowledgments section of this book, which begins on page A25.

Library of Congress Cataloging-in-Publication Data

Names: Mays, Kelly J., editor.
Title: The Norton introduction to literature / [edited by] Kelly J. Mays.
Description: Portable thirteenth edition. | New York : W. W. Norton & Company, [2020] | Includes bibliographical references and index.
Identifiers: LCCN 2018040216 | ISBN 9780393674002 (pbk.)
Subjects: LCSH: Literature—Collections.
Classification: LCC PN6014 .N67 2020 | DDC 808.8—dc23 LC record available at https://lccn.loc.gov/2018040216

W. W. Norton & Company, Inc., 500 Fifth Avenue, New York, N. Y. 10110

www.wwnorton.com

W. W. Norton & Company, Ltd., 15 Carlisle Street, London W1D 3BS

1 2 3 4 5 6 7 8 9 0

Contents

UNDERSTANDING THE TEXT   428

The Sonnet: An Album 567

READING MORE POETRY 583

PART THREE Drama

18 Drama: Reading, Responding, Writing   650

UNDERSTANDING THE TEXT   676

19 Elements of Drama   676

READING MORE DRAMA   787

PART FOUR Writing about Literature

Contents Arranged by Topic

DEATH/MORTALITY/MOURNING

EDUCATION/SCHOOLING

GENDER

Preface for Instructors

Like its predecessors, this Portable Thirteenth Edition of *The Norton Intro-duction to Literature* offers in a single volume a complete course in reading literature and writing about it. A teaching anthology focused on the actual tasks, challenges, and questions typically faced by students and instructors, *The Norton Introduction to Literature* offers practical advice to help students transform their first impressions of literary works into fruitful discussions and meaningful crit-ical essays, and it helps students and instructors together tackle the complex ques-tions at the heart of literary study.

The Norton Introduction to Literature has been revised with an eye to providing a book that is as flexible and as useful as possible—adaptable to many different teaching styles and individual preferences—and that also conveys the excitement at the heart of literature itself.

NEW TO THE PORTABLE THIRTEENTH EDITION

Twenty-nine new selections

This lucky Thirteenth Edition of *The Norton Introduction to Literature* features six new stories, over twenty new poems, and one new play. These include new selections from popular and canonical writers including A. S. Byatt, Ralph Ellison, George Saunders, and Quiara Alegría Hudes (in Fiction and Drama), Emily Dickinson, Joy Harjo, and Claude McKay (in Poetry). But you will also find here work by exciting new authors such as Cathy Song, A. E. Stallings, and Pulitzer Prize winner Tracy K. Smith. Prompting the reintroduction of John Crowe Ransom's "Bells for John White-side's Daughter," which it appears alongside, Hai-Dang Phan's moving "My Father's 'Norton Introduction to Literature,' Third Edition (1981)" reminds us just how much new works and new voices renew and reanimate, rather than replace, classic ones.

Improved writing pedagogy

Recent editions of *The Norton Introduction to Literature* greatly expanded and improved the resources for student writers, including thorough introductions to each genre, broadened online materials, and new student writing. The Thirteenth Edition offers an enlarged and revamped chapter on "Quotation, Citation, and Documenta-tion." In keeping with the latest (8th edition) MLA guidelines, it explains the elements that comprise the works-cited entry and the principles by which any entry is assem-bled rather than presenting a dizzying menu of entry types for student writers to pore through and copy. Here, as throughout "Writing about Literature," we demonstrate with brief examples, often drawn from the work of student or professional writers. A new student comparative essay on Nathaniel Hawthorne's "The Birth-Mark" and A. S. Byatt's "The Thing in the Forest" brings the total of complete writing samples to fifteen, including notes, response papers, essays analyzing one work or comparing several, and research essays exploring critical and/or historical contexts. As always, by including more and more lengthy extracts from published literary criticism than any other textbook of its kind, *The Norton Introduction to Literature* offers student writers both a trove of sources to draw on in articulating their own responses to particular works and models of the sorts of questions, strategies, and "moves" that power effective reading and writing about literature.

A new design and expanded photo program

A contemporary new design invites greater enjoyment and even greater use of the book's many special features. The photo program has been enriched and expanded with new author photos throughout as well as contextual illustrations, such as an advertising poster for Buffalo Bill alongside the poem by E. E. Cummings, a photograph of Hai-Dang Phan's father's annotated *Norton Introduction to Literature* to accompany his poem in the Introduction, and many more.

Enhanced and updated Shakespeare

To make Shakespeare more accessible and enjoyable, every page of *Hamlet* features new in-line glossing of challenging words or allusions. The version of the play is adopted from the acclaimed new third edition of *The Norton Shakespeare*, edited by Stephen Greenblatt.

New combined glossary and index

A new combined Glossary and Index makes it easier for students to review key literary terms and find examples within the book.

Unmatched support for students, with new close reading workshops

New to our popular LitWeb (digital.wwnorton.com/lit13portable) site are twenty-five Close Reading Workshops. Providing step-by-step guidance in literary analysis and interpretation drawing on works in the anthology, many of which are enhanced with audio, these interactive workshops help students learn how to observe, contextualize, analyze, and create an argument based on a close reading of text. The workshops are easily assignable with class reports that allow you to see how students' close reading skills improve over the course of the semester.

Unmatched support for instructors

The new Interactive Instructor's Guide by Jason Snart features hundreds of teaching resources in one searchable, sortable site to help you enrich your classes and save course-prep time, including:

- Teaching notes, discussion questions, and suggestions for writing
- Hundreds of downloadable images for in-class presentation
- The Writing about Literature video series
- Lecture PowerPoints for the most-taught works in the anthology

HALLMARK FEATURES OF *THE NORTON INTRODUCTION TO LITERATURE*

Although this Portable Thirteenth Edition contains much that is new or refashioned, the essential features of the text have remained consistent over many editions:

Diverse selections with broad appeal

Because readings are the central component of any literature class, my most important task has been to select a rich array of appealing and challenging literary works. Among the 41 stories, 203 poems, and 8 plays in *The Norton Introduction to Literature*, readers will find selections by well-established and emerging voices alike, representing a broad range of times, places, cultural perspectives, and styles. The readings are excitingly diverse in terms of subject and style as well as authorship and national origin. In selecting and presenting literary texts, my top priorities continue to be quality as well as pedagogical relevance and usefulness. I have integrated the new with the old and the experimental with the canonical, believing that contrast and variety help students recognize and respond to the unique features of any literary work. In this way, I aim to help students and instructors alike approach the unfamiliar by way of the familiar (and vice versa).

Helpful and unobtrusive editorial matter

As always, the instructional material before and after each selection avoids dictating any particular interpretation or response, instead highlighting essential terms and concepts in order to make the literature that follows more accessible to student readers. Questions and writing suggestions help readers apply general concepts to specific readings in order to develop, articulate, refine, and defend their own responses. As in all Norton anthologies, I have annotated the works with a light hand, seeking to be informative but not interpretive.

An introduction to the study of literature

To introduce students to fiction, poetry, and drama is to open up a complex field of study with a long history. The Introduction addresses many of the questions that students may have about the nature of literature as well as the practice of literary criticism. By exploring some of the most compelling reasons for reading and writing about literature, much of the mystery about matters of method is cleared away, and I provide motivated students with a sense of the issues and opportunities that lie ahead as they study literature. As in earlier editions, I encourage student engagement with individual authors and their perspectives in "Authors on Their Work" features as well as single-author chapters and albums.

Thoughtful guidance for writing about literature

The Portable Thirteenth Edition integrates opportunities for student writing at each step of the course, highlighting the mastery of skills for students at every level. "Reading, Responding, Writing" chapters at the beginning of each genre unit offer students concrete advice about how to transform careful reading into productive and insightful writing. Sample questions for each work or about each element (e.g., "Questions about

Character") provide exercises for answering these questions or for applying new concepts to particular works, and examples of student writing demonstrate how a student's notes on a story or poem may be developed into a response paper or an organized critical argument. New examples of student writing bring the total number to nineteen.

The constructive, step-by-step approach to the writing process is thoroughly demonstrated in the "Writing about Literature" section. As in the chapters introducing concepts and literary selections, the first steps presented in the writing section are simple and straightforward, outlining the basic formal elements common to essays—thesis, structure, and so on. Following these steps encourages students to approach the essay both as a distinctive genre with its own elements and as an accessible form of writing with a clear purpose. From here, I walk students through the writing process: how to choose a topic, gather evidence, and develop an argument; the methods of writing a research essay; and the mechanics of effective quotation and responsible citation and documentation. Also featured is a sample research essay that has been annotated to call attention to important features of good student writing.

Even more resources for student writers, including Close Reading Workshops and Pause & Practice exercises, are available on the LitWeb site (digital.wwnorton.com /lit13portable).

A comprehensive approach to the contexts of literature

The Portable Thirteenth Edition not only offers expanded resources for interpreting and writing about literature but also extends the perspectives from which students can view particular authors and works. One of the greatest strengths of *The Norton Introduction to Literature* has been its exploration of the relation between literary texts and a variety of contexts. "Author's Work as Context," "Cultural and Historical Contexts," and "Critical Contexts" chapters serve as mini-casebooks containing a wealth of material for in-depth, context-focused reading and writing assignments.

The "Critical Approaches" section provides an overview of contemporary critical theory and its terminology and is useful as an introduction, a refresher, or a preparation for further exploration.

A sensible and teachable organization

The accessible format of *The Norton Introduction to Literature*, which has worked so well for teachers and students for many editions, remains the same. Each genre is approached in three logical steps. Fiction, for example, is introduced by the chapter "Fiction: Reading, Responding, Writing," which treats the purpose and nature of fiction, the reading experience, and the steps one takes to begin writing about fiction. This feature is followed by the six-chapter section called "Understanding the Text," which concentrates on the genre's key elements. Appearing throughout are albums that build on the chapters they follow, inviting students to compare stories narrated by protagonists whom others deem monsters, featuring initiation plots or futuristic settings, and so on. The third section, "Exploring Contexts" suggests ways to embrace a work of literature by considering various literary, temporal, and cultural contexts. "Reading More Fiction," the final component in the Fiction section, is a reservoir of additional readings for independent study or a different approach. The Poetry and Drama sections, in turn, follow exactly the same organizational format as Fiction.

The book's arrangement allows movement from narrower to broader frameworks, from simpler to more complex questions and issues, and mirrors the way people read—wanting to learn more as they experience more. At the same time, I have worked hard to ensure that no section, chapter, or album depends on any other, allowing individual teachers to pick and choose which to assign and in what order.

ACKNOWLEDGMENTS

In working on this book, I have been guided by teachers and students in my own and other English departments who have used this textbook and responded with comments and suggestions. Thanks to such capable help, I am hopeful that this book will continue to offer a solid and stimulating introduction to the experience of literature.

This project continually reminds me why I follow the vocation of teaching literature, which after all is a communal rather than a solitary calling. Since its inception, *The Norton Introduction to Literature* has been very much a collaborative effort. I am grateful for the opportunity to carry on the work begun by the late Carl Bain and Jerome Beaty, whose student I will always be. And I am equally indebted to my wonderful former co-editors Paul Hunter and Alison Booth. Their wisdom and intelligence have had a profound effect on me, and their stamp will endure on this and all future editions of this book. I am thankful to Alison especially for the erudition, savvy, grace, and humor she brought to our partnership. Their intelligence, erudition, grace, and humor have had a profound effect on me, and their stamp will endure on this and all future editions of this book.

So, too, will that of Spencer Richardson-Jones, my Norton editorial partner on the last two (eleventh and twelfth) editions. For the wisdom and wit he brought to that partnership, for the all-new life he breathed into this book, and for his laser-like attention to—and indefatigable championship of—it, I am forever grateful. The book's new in-house editor, Sarah Touborg, has proved a worthy successor under much less than ideal circumstances. And I am thankful—as I think all users of the Thirteenth Edition will be—for the new perspective and insight she has brought to this project. With admirable skill and great energy, assistant editor Madeline Rombes managed myriad manuscript details. I am grateful to project editors Christine D'Antonio and Maura Gaughan, editorial assistant Emma Peters, and copyeditor Rebecca Caine, photo editor Ted Szczepanski and researcher Julie Tesser, production managers Ashley Horna and Stephen Sajdak, and media editor Carly Frasier Doria who brought together the innovative array of web resources and other pedagogical tools. Huge, heartfelt thanks, too, to Kimberly Bowers, the very best, brightest, and most tireless of marketing managers.

In putting together the Thirteenth Edition, I have accrued debts to many friends and colleagues including Frederic Svoboda, of the University of Michigan–Flint; his student, Megan Groeneveld; and other users of the Twelfth Edition who generously reached out to point out its errors, as well as successes. Special thanks to Darren Lone-Fight, for introducing me to the work of Indigenous Futurist Steven Paul Judd; to Jane Hafen, Molly O'Donnell, Emily Setina, and Anne Stevens, for sage advice on literary selections and much else; to my sister, Nelda Mays, and to my UNLV students, whose open-mindedness, strong-mindedness, perseverance, and passion inspire me every day; and, as always, to Hugh Jackson, my in-house editor in the most literal of senses.

The Norton Introduction to Literature continues to thrive because so many teachers and students generously take the time to provide valuable feedback and suggestions. Thank you to all who have done so. This book is equally your making.

At the beginning of planning for the Twelfth Edition, my editors at Norton solic-
ited the guidance of hundreds of instructors via in-depth reviews and a Web-hosted
survey. The response was impressive, bordering on overwhelming; it was also
immensely helpful. Thank you to those who provided extensive written commentary:
Julianne Altenbernd (Cypress College), Troy Appling (Florida Gateway College),
Christina Bisirri (Seminole State College), Jill Channing (Mitchell Community
College), Thomas Chester (Ivy Tech), Marcelle Cohen (Valencia College), Priscilla,
Glanville (State College of Florida), Julie Gibson (Greenville Tech), Christina
Grant (St. Charles Community College), Lauren Hahn (City Colleges of Chicago),
Zachary Hyde (Valencia College), Brenda Jernigan (Methodist University), Mary
Anne Keefer (Lord Fairfax Community College), Shari Koopman (Valencia Col-
lege), Jessica Rabin (Anne Arundel Community College), Angela Rasmussen
(Spokane Community College), Britnee Shandor (Lanier Technical College), Heidi
Sheridan (Ocean County College), Jeff Tix (Wharton Jr. College), Bente Videbaek
(Stony Brook University), Patrice Willaims (Northwest Florida State College), and
Connie Youngblood (Blinn College).

Thanks also to everyone who responded to the survey online for the Thirteenth Edition:

Beth Anish (Community College of Rhode Island), Eric Ash (Wayland Baptist
University), Matthew Ayres (County College of Morris), Suzanne Barnett (Francis
Marion University), Stuart Bartow (SUNY Adirondack), Jon Brooks (Northwest Flor-
ida State College), Akilah Brown (Santa Fe College), Rachel Brunner (Sauk Valley
Community College), Lisa Buchanan (Northeast State Community College), David
Clark (Suffolk County Community College), Jim Compton (Muscatine Community
College), Susan Dauer (Valencia College), Alexandra DeLuise (University of New
Haven), Amber Durfield (Citrus College), Michelle Fernandes (Paramus High
School), Africa Fine (Palm Beach State College), Christine Fisher (Trinity Valley
Community College), Jeffrey Foster (University of New Haven), James Glickman
(Community College of Rhode Island), Kathy Harrison (Alief Independent School
District, Kerr High School), Joan Hartman (William Paterson University), Spring
Hyde (Lincoln College), Tina Iraca (Dutchess Community College), Jack Kelnhofer
(Ocean County College), Ellen Knodt (Pennsylvania State University–Penn State
Abington), Liz Langemak (La Salle University), Rachel Luckenbill (Southeastern
University), Sarah Maitland (Bryant University), Cassandra Makela (Concordia
University), Brtini Mastria (Ocean County College), Marion McAvey (Becker Col-
lege), Lizzie McCormick (Suffolk County Community College), Deborah Nester
(Northwest Florida State College), Amy Oneal-Self (Wor-Wic Community College),
Keith O'Neill (Dutchess Community College), Natala Orobello (Florida South-
Western State College), Michele Oster (Suffolk County Community College),
Matthew Parry (Bishop England High School), Barri Piner (University of North
Carolina Wilmington), Joshua Rafael Rodriguez (East Los Angeles College), Kathy
Romack (University of West Florida), Shelbey Rosengarten (St. Petersburg College),
Jennifer Royal (Santa Rosa Junior College), John Sauls (East Arkansas Community
College), Richard Sears (Oklahoma State University–Stillwater), Bonnie Spears
(Chaffey College), Camilla Stastny (SouthLake Christian Academy), Jason Stuff
(Alfred State College), Donna Jane Terry (St. Johns River State College), Filiz Turhan
(Suffolk County Community College), Roger Vaccaro (St. Johns River State College),
Tammy Verkamp (Arkansas Tech University–Ozark), Bente Videbaek (Stony Brook
University), Stephanie Webster (Ivy Tech Community College), and Kelli Wilkes
(Columbus Technical College).

Introduction

In the opening chapters of Charles Dickens's novel *Hard Times* (1854), the aptly named Thomas Gradgrind warns the teachers and pupils at his "model" school to avoid using their imaginations. "Teach these boys and girls nothing but Facts. Facts alone are wanted in life," exclaims Mr. Gradgrind. To press his point, Mr. Gradgrind asks "girl number twenty," Sissy Jupe, the daughter of a circus performer, to define a horse. When she cannot, Gradgrind turns to Bitzer, a pale, spiritless boy who "looked as though, if he were cut, he would bleed white." A "model" student of this "model" school, Bitzer gives exactly the kind of definition to satisfy Mr. Gradgrind:

> Quadruped. Graminivorous. Forty teeth, namely, twenty-four grinders, four eye-teeth, and twelve incisive. Sheds coat in spring; in marshy countries, sheds hoofs.

Anyone who has any sense of what a horse is rebels against Bitzer's lifeless picture of that animal and against the "Gradgrind" view of reality. As these first scenes of *Hard Times* lead us to expect, in the course of the novel the fact-grinding Mr. Gradgrind learns that human beings cannot live on facts alone; that it is dangerous to stunt the faculties of imagination and feeling; that, in the words of one of the novel's more lovable characters, "People must be amused." Through the downfall of an exaggerated enemy of the imagination, Dickens reminds us why we like and even *need* to read literature.

What Is Literature?

But what is literature? Before you opened this book, you probably could guess that it would contain the sorts of stories, poems, and plays you have encountered in English classes or in the literature section of a library or bookstore. But why are some written works called *literature* whereas others are not? And who gets to decide? *The American Heritage Dictionary of the English Language* offers a number of definitions for the word *literature*, one of which is "imaginative or creative writing, especially of recognized artistic value." In this book, we adopt a version of that definition by focusing on fictional stories, poems, and plays—the three major kinds (or **genres**)[1] of "imaginative or creative writing" that form the heart of literature as it has been taught in schools and universities for over a century. Many of the works we have chosen to include are already ones "of recognized artistic value" and thus belong to what scholars call the **canon**, a select, if much-debated and ever-evolving, list of the most highly and widely esteemed works. Though quite a few of the literary texts we include are too new to have earned that status, they, too, have already drawn praise, and some have even generated controversy.

Certainly it helps to bear in mind what others have thought of a literary work. Yet one of this book's primary goals is to get you to think for yourself, as well as

---

1. Throughout this book, terms included in the glossary appear in bold font.

communicate with others, about what "imaginative writing" and "artistic value" are or might be and thus about what counts as literature. What makes a story or poem different from an essay, a newspaper editorial, or a technical manual? For that matter, what makes a published, canonical story like Herman Melville's BARTLEBY, THE SCRIVENER[2] both like and unlike the sorts of stories we tell each other every day? What about so-called *oral literature*, such as the fables and folktales that circulated by word of mouth for hundreds of years before they were ever written down? or published works such as comic strips and graphic novels that rely little, if at all, on the written word? or Harlequin romances, television shows, and the stories you collaborate in making when you play a video game? Likewise, how is Shakespeare's poem MY MISTRESS' EYES ARE NOTHING LIKE THE SUN both like and unlike a verse you might find in a Hallmark card or even a jingle in a mouthwash commercial?

Today, literature departments offer courses in many of these forms of expression, expanding the realm of literature far beyond the limits of the dictionary definition. An essay, a song lyric, a screenplay, a supermarket romance, a novel by Toni Morrison or William Faulkner, and a poem by Walt Whitman or Emily Dickinson—each may be read and interpreted in *literary ways* that yield insight and pleasure. What makes the literary way of reading different from pragmatic reading is, as scholar Louise Rosenblatt explains, that it does not focus "on what will remain [. . .] *after* the reading—the information to be acquired, the logical solution to a problem, the actions to be carried out," but rather on "what happens *during* [. . .] reading." The difference between pragmatic and literary reading, in other words, resembles the difference between a journey that is only about reaching a destination and one that is just as much about fully experiencing the ride.

In the pages of this book, you will find cartoons, song lyrics, folktales, and stories and plays that have spawned movies. Through this inclusiveness, we do not intend to suggest that there are no distinctions among these various forms of expression or between a good story, poem, or play and a bad one; rather, we want to get you thinking, talking, and writing both about what the key differences and similarities among these forms are and what makes one work a better example of its genre than another. Sharpening your skills at these peculiarly intensive and responsive sorts of reading and interpretation is a primary purpose of this book and of most literature courses.

Another goal of inclusiveness is to remind you that literature doesn't just belong in a textbook or a classroom, even if textbooks and classrooms are essential means for expanding your knowledge of the literary terrain and of the concepts and techniques essential to thoroughly enjoying and analyzing a broad range of literary forms. You may or may not be the kind of person who always takes a novel when you go to the beach or writes a poem about your experience when you get back home. You may or may not have taken literature courses before. Yet you already have a good deal of literary experience and even expertise, as well as much more to discover about literature. A major aim of this book is to make you more conscious of how and to what end you might use the tools you already possess and to add many new ones to your tool belt.

What Does Literature Do?

One quality that may well differentiate stories, poems, and plays from other kinds of writing is that they help us move beyond and probe beneath abstractions by giving us concrete, vivid particulars. Rather than talking *about* things, they bring them to life for us by *representing* experience, and so they *become* an experience for us—one that engages our emotions, our imagination, and all of our senses, as well as our intellects. As the British poet Matthew Arnold put it more than a century ago, "The interpretations of science do not give us this intimate sense of objects as the interpretations of poetry give it; they appeal to a limited faculty, and not to the whole man. It is not Linnaeus [. . .] who gives us the true sense of animals, or water, or plants, who seizes their secret for us, who makes us participate in their life; it is Shakespeare [. . .] Wordsworth [. . .] Keats."

To test Arnold's theory, compare the *American Heritage Dictionary*'s rather dry definition of *literature* with the following poem, in which John Keats describes his first encounter with a specific literary work—George Chapman's translation of the *Iliad* and the *Odyssey*, two **epics** by the ancient Greek poet Homer.

JOHN KEATS
On First Looking into Chapman's Homer[3]

Much have I traveled in the realms of gold,
And many goodly states and kingdoms seen;
Round many western islands have I been
Which bards in fealty to Apollo[4] hold.
5 Oft of one wide expanse had I been told
That deep-browed Homer ruled as his demesne;
Yet did I never breathe its pure serene[5]
Till I heard Chapman speak out loud and bold:
Then felt I like some watcher of the skies
10 When a new planet swims into his ken;[6]
Or like stout Cortez[7] when with eagle eyes
He stared at the Pacific—and all his men
Looked at each other with a wild surmise—
Silent, upon a peak in Darien.

1816

Keats makes us *see* literature as a "wide expanse" by greatly developing this **metaphor** and complementing it with **similes** likening reading to the sighting of a "new planet" and the first glimpse of an undiscovered ocean. More important, he shows us what literature means and why it matters by allowing us to share with him the subjective experience of reading and the complex sensations it inspires— the dizzying exhilaration of discovery; the sense of power, accomplishment, and pride that comes of achieving something difficult; the wonder we feel in those rare moments when a much-anticipated experience turns out to be even greater than we had imagined it would be.

It isn't the definitions of words alone that bring this experience to life for us as we read Keats's poem, but also their sensual qualities—the way the words look, sound, and even feel in our mouths because of the particular way they are put together on the page. The sensation of excitement—of a racing heart and mind—is reproduced *in* us as we read the poem. For example, notice how the lines in the middle run into each other, but then Keats forces us to slow down at the poem's end—stopped short by that dash and comma in the poem's final lines, just as Cortez and his men are when they reach the edge of the known world and peer into the vastness that lies beyond.

What Are the Genres of Literature?

The conversation that is literature, like the conversation about literature, invites all comers, requiring neither a visa nor a special license of any kind. Yet literary

3. George Chapman's were among the most famous Renaissance translations of Homer; he completed his *Iliad* in 1611, his *Odyssey* in 1616. Keats wrote the sonnet after being led to Chapman by a former teacher and reading the *Iliad* all night long.
4. Greek god of poetry and music. *Fealty*: literally, the loyalty owed by a vassal to his feudal lord.
5. Atmosphere.
6. Range of vision; awareness.
7. Actually, Balboa; he first viewed the Pacific from Darien, in Panama.

studies, like all disciplines, has developed its own terminology and its own systems of classification. Helping you understand and effectively use both is a major purpose of this book.

Some essential literary terms are common, everyday words used in a special way in the conversation about literature. A case in point, perhaps, is the term *literary criticism*, as well as the closely related term *literary critic*. Despite the usual connotations of the word *criticism*, literary criticism is called *criticism* not because it is negative or corrective but rather because those who write criticism ask searching, analytical, "critical" questions about the works they read. Literary criticism is both the process of interpreting and commenting on literature and the result of that process. If you write an essay on the play HAMLET, the poetry of John Keats, or the development of the short story in the 1990s, you engage in literary criticism. By writing the essay, you've become a literary critic.

Similarly, when we classify works of literature, we use terms that may be familiar to you but have specific meanings in a literary context. All academic disciplines have systems of classification, or taxonomies, as well as jargon. Biologists, for example, classify all organisms into a series of ever-smaller, more specific categories: *kingdom*, *phylum* or *division*, *class*, *order*, *family*, *genus*, and *species*. Classification and comparison are just as essential in the study of literature. We expect a poem to work in a certain way, for example, when we know from the outset that it *is* a poem and not, say, a factual news report or a short story. And—whether consciously or not—we compare it, as we read, to other poems we've read. If we know, further, that the poem was first published in eighteenth-century Japan, we expect it to work differently from one that appeared in the latest *New Yorker*. Indeed, we often choose what to read, just as we choose what movie to see, based on the "class" or "order" of book or movie we like or what we are in the mood for that day—horror or comedy, action or science fiction.

As these examples suggest, we generally tend to categorize literary works in two ways: (1) on the basis of contextual factors, especially historical and cultural context—that is, when, by whom, and where it was produced (as in *nineteenth-century literature, the literature of the Harlem Renaissance, American literature*, or *African American literature*)—and (2) on the basis of formal textual features. For the latter type of classification, the one we focus on in this book, the key term is *genre*, which simply means, as the *Oxford English Dictionary* tells us, "A particular style or category of works of art; esp. a type of literary work characterized by a particular form, style, or purpose."

Applied rigorously, *genre* refers to the largest categories around which this book is organized—**fiction, poetry,** and **drama** (as well as **nonfiction** prose). The word *subgenre* applies to smaller divisions within a genre, and the word *kind* to divisions within a subgenre. *Subgenres* of fiction include the **novel,** the **novella,** and the **short story.** *Kinds* of novels, in turn, include the **bildungsroman** and the epistolary novel. Similarly, important subgenres of nonfiction include the essay, as well as **biography** and autobiography; a memoir is a particular kind of autobiography, and so on.

However, the terms of literary criticism are not so fixed or so consistently, rigorously used as biologists' are. You will often see the word *genre* applied both much more narrowly—referring to the novel, for example, or even to a kind of novel such as the historical novel.

The way we classify a work depends on which aspects of its form or style we concentrate on, and categories may overlap. When we divide fiction, for example, into the subgenres novel, novella, and short story, we take the length of the works as the salient aspect. (Novels are much longer than short stories.) But other fictional subgenres—detective fiction, **gothic fiction**, **historical fiction**, science fiction, and even **romance**—are based on the types of **plots**, **characters**, **settings**, and so on that are customarily featured in these works. These latter categories may include works from all the other, length-based categories. There are, after all, gothic novels (think Stephenie Meyer), as well as gothic short stories (think Edgar Allan Poe).

A few genres even cut across the boundaries dividing poetry, fiction, drama, and nonfiction. A prime example is **satire**—any literary work (whether poem, play, fiction, or nonfiction) "in which prevailing vices and follies are held up to ridicule" (*Oxford English Dictionary*). Examples of satire include poems such as Alexander Pope's *Dunciad* (1728); plays, movies, and television shows, from Molière's *Tartuffe* (1664) to Stanley Kubrick's *Dr. Strangelove* (1964) to *South Park*; works of fiction like Jonathan Swift's *Gulliver's Travels* (1726) and Voltaire's *Candide* (1759); and works of nonfiction such as Swift's "A Modest Proposal" (1729) and Ambrose Bierce's *The Devil's Dictionary* (1906). Three other major genres that cross the borders between fiction, poetry, drama, and nonfiction are **parody**, **pastoral**, and romance.

Individual works can thus belong simultaneously to multiple generic categories or observe some **conventions** of a genre without being an example of that genre in any simple or straightforward way. The Old English poem *Beowulf* is an **epic** and, because it's written in verse, a poem. Yet because (like all epics) it narrates a story, it is also a work of fiction in the more general sense of that term.

Given this complexity, the system of literary genres can be puzzling, especially to the uninitiated. Used well, however, classification schemes are among the most essential and effective tools we use to understand and enjoy just about everything, including literature.

Why Read Literature?

Because there has never been and never will be absolute agreement about where exactly the boundaries between one literary genre and another should be drawn or even about what counts as literature at all, it might be more useful from the outset to focus on *why* we look at particular forms of expression.

Over the ages, people have sometimes dismissed *all* literature or at least certain genres as a luxury, a frivolous pastime, even a sinful indulgence. Plato famously banned poetry from his ideal republic on the grounds that it tells beautiful lies that "feed and water our passions" rather than our reason. Thousands of years later, the influential eighteenth-century philosopher Jeremy Bentham decried the "magic art" of literature as doing a good deal of "mischief" by "stimulating our passions" and "exciting our prejudices." One of Bentham's contemporaries—a minister—blamed the rise of immorality, irreligion, and even prostitution on the increasing popularity of that particular brand of literature called the novel.

Today, many Americans express their sense of literature's insignificance by simply not reading it: According to a 2016 National Endowment for the Arts (NEA) report, only 43% of U.S. adults read at least one work of imaginative literature in the previous year, the lowest percentage since NEA began its yearly surveys in 1982. Though the report also demonstrates that women are significantly more likely to read literature than men, as are college graduates, the drops in the literary reading rate occurred across the board, among people of all ages, races, and educational levels. Even if they very much enjoy reading on their own, many contemporary U.S. college students nonetheless hesitate to study or major in literature for fear that their degree won't provide them with marketable credentials, knowledge, or skills.

Yet millions of people continue to find both reading literature and discussing it with others to be enjoyable, meaningful, even essential activities. English thrives as a major at most colleges and universities, almost all of which require undergraduates majoring in other areas to take at least one course in literature. (Perhaps that's why you are reading this book!) Schools of medicine, law, and business are today *more* likely to require their students to take literature courses than they were in past decades, and they continue to welcome literature majors as applicants, as do many corporations. (As former Google and Twitter executive Santosh Jayaram told the *Wall Street Journal* in 2012, "English majors are exactly the people I'm looking for.") So why do so many people read and study literature, and why do schools encourage and even require students to do so? Even if we know what literature is, what does it *do* for us? What is its value?

There are, of course, as many answers to such questions as there are readers. For centuries, a standard answer has been that imaginative literature provides a unique brand of "instruction and delight." John Keats's On First Looking into Chapman's Homer illustrates some of the many forms such delight can take. Some kinds of imaginative writing offer us the delight of immediate escape, but imaginative writing that is more difficult to read and understand than a Harry Potter or Twilight novel offers escape of a different and potentially more instructive sort, liberating us from the confines of our own time, place, and social milieu, as well as our habitual ways of thinking, feeling, and looking at the world. In this way, a story, poem, or play can satisfy our desire for broader experience—including the sorts of experience we might be unable or unwilling to endure in real life. We can learn what it might be like to grow up on a Canadian fox farm or to party-hop with a model. We can travel back into the past, experiencing war from the perspective of a soldier watching his comrade die or of prisoners suffering in a Nazi labor camp. We can journey into the future or into universes governed by entirely different rules than our own. Perhaps we yearn for such knowledge because we can best come to understand our own identities and outlooks by leaping over the boundaries that separate us from other selves and worlds.

Keats's friend and fellow poet Percy Bysshe Shelley argued that literature increases a person's ability to make such leaps, to "imagine intensely and comprehensively" and "put himself in the place of another and of many othe[r]" people as one has to in order "to be greatly good." Shelley meant "good" in a moral sense, reasoning that the ability both to accurately imagine and to truly *feel* the human consequences of our actions is the key to ethical behavior. Numerous recent studies by cognitive psychologists and neuroscientists endorse and expand on Shelley's argument, demonstrating that while we read our brains respond to fictional events and characters precisely as they would to real ones. Perhaps as a result, readers—particularly of literary, as opposed to popular, fiction or nonfiction—perform better on tests measuring their ability to infer or even predict, to understand, and to empathize with others' thoughts and emotions. Reading a poem, as opposed to a prose translation, sparks more activity in more areas of the brain, including those associated with personal memory and emotion, as well as language. As a result, scientists posit, poetry triggers "reappraisal mechanisms," making us reflect and rethink our own experiences. Reading literature of various genres thus, as one review of a decade's worth of research concludes, "enables us to better understand people, better cooperate with them."

Such abilities have great pragmatic and even economic, as well as personal, moral, even political value. In virtually any career you choose, you will need to interact positively and productively with both coworkers and clients, and in today's increasingly globalized world, you will need to learn to deal effectively and empathetically with people vastly different from yourself. At the very least, literature written by people from various backgrounds and depicting various places, times, experiences, and feelings will give you some understanding of how others' lives and worldviews may differ from your own—and how very much the same they may be. Such understanding is ever more in demand in an age when business success— according to many a venture capitalist, marketing consultant, and Silicon Valley entrepreneur—often depends less on technical know-how than on both a grasp of the whys and hows of human behavior within and across cultures (markets), and the ability to tell compelling stories to potential funders and consumers alike.

Similarly, our rapidly changing world and economy require intellectual flexibility, adaptability, and ingenuity, making ever more essential the human knowledge, general skills, and habits of mind developed through the study of literature. Literature explores issues and questions relevant in any walk of life. Yet rather than offering us neat or comforting solutions and answers, literature enables us to experience difficult situations and human conundrums in all their complexity and to look at them from various points of view. In so doing, it invites us sometimes to question conventional thinking and sometimes to see the wisdom of such thinking, even as it helps us imagine altogether new possibilities.

Finally, literature awakens us to the richness and complexity of language—our primary tool for engaging with, understanding, and shaping the world around us. As we read more and more, seeing how different writers use language to help us feel others' joy, pain, love, rage, or laughter, we begin to recognize the vast range of possibilities for expression. Writing and discussion in turn give us invaluable practice in discovering, expressing, and defending our own nuanced, often contradictory thoughts about both literature and life. The study of literature enhances our command of language and our sensitivity to its effects and meanings in every form or medium, providing interpretation and communication skills especially crucial in our information age. By learning to appreciate and articulate what the language of a story, a poem, a play, or an essay does to us and by considering how it affects others, we also learn much about what we can do with language.

What We Do with Literature: Three Tips

1. *Take a literary work on its own terms.* Adjust to the work; don't make the work adjust to you. Be prepared to hear things you do not want to hear. Not all works are about your ideas, nor will they always present emotions you want to feel. But be tolerant and listen to the work first; later you can explore the ways you do or don't agree with it.
2. *Assume there is a reason for everything.* Writers do make mistakes, but when a work shows some degree of verbal control it is usually safest to assume that the writer chose each word carefully; if the choice seems peculiar, you may be missing something. Try to account for everything in a work, see what kind of sense you can make of it, and figure out a coherent pattern that explains the text as it stands.

3. *Remember that literary texts exist in time and that times change.* Not only the meanings of words, but whole ways of looking at the universe vary in different ages. Consciousness of time works two ways: Your knowledge of history provides a context for reading the work, even as the work may modify your notion of a particular age.

Why Study Literature?

You may already feel the power and pleasure to be gained from a sustained encounter with challenging reading. Then why not simply enjoy it in solitude, on your own time? Why take a course in literature? Literary study, like all disciplines, has developed its own terminology and its own techniques. Some knowledge and understanding of both can greatly enhance our personal appreciation of literature and our conversations with others about it. Literature also has a context and a history, and learning something about them can make all the difference in the amount and kind of pleasure and insight you derive from literature. By reading and discussing different genres of literature, as well as works from varied times and places, you may well come to appreciate and even love works that you might never have discovered or chosen to read on your own or that you might have disliked or misunderstood if you did.

Most important, writing about works of literature and discussing them with your teachers and other students will give you practice in analyzing literature in greater depth and in considering alternative views of both the works themselves and the situations and problems the works explore. A clear understanding of the aims and designs of a story, poem, or play never falls like a bolt from the blue. Instead, it emerges from a process that involves trying to put into words *how* and *why* this work had such an effect on you and, just as important, responding to what others say or write about it. Literature itself is a vast, ongoing, ever-evolving conversation in which we most fully participate when we enter into actual conversation with others.

As you engage in this conversation, you will notice that interpretation is always variable, always open to discussion. A great diversity of interpretations might suggest that the discussion is pointless. On the contrary, that's when the discussion gets most interesting. Because there is no single, straight, paved road to an understanding of a literary text, you can explore a variety of blazed trails and less traveled paths. In sharing your own interpretations, tested against your peers' responses and guided by your instructor's or other critics' expertise, you will hone your skills at both interpretation and communication. After the intricate and interactive process of interpretation, you will find that the work has changed when you read it again. What we do with literature alters what it does to us.

To help you think further about how literature operates as a vast, never-ending, ever-expanding conversation that outlives—even as it invites and potentially works through and on—all of us, we close this chapter with two poems, Hai-Dang Phan's MY FATHER'S "NORTON INTRODUCTION TO LITERATURE," THIRD EDITION (1981) and BELLS FOR JOHN WHITESIDE'S DAUGHTER, by another American poet, John Crowe Ransom. Phan's 2015 poem responds in a wonderfully personal way to an array of literary texts published decades, even centuries, before his own birth (in 1980), including Ransom's **elegy** and a Shakespeare play that elegy echoes. But as his title suggests, Phan responds to these texts by means of another one—the traces of his own still-living father's responses to them, as recorded many years ago on the pages of his father's copy of an earlier edition of the very book *you* are now reading and, we hope, literally leaving your own distinctive marks on. What answers might these poems offer to the questions *Why read literature? Why study it?*

HAI-DANG PHAN

My Father's "Norton Introduction to Literature," Third Edition (1981)

Certain words give him trouble: *cannibals, puzzles, sob,*
bosom, martyr, deteriorate, shake, astonishes, vexed, ode . . .
These he looks up and studiously annotates in Vietnamese.
Ravish means *cướp đoạt; shits* is like when you have to *đi ỉa;*
5   *mourners* are those whom we say are full of *buồn rầu.*
For "even the like precurse of feared events"[8] think *báo trước.*

Its thin translucent pages are webbed with his marginalia,
graphite ghosts of a living hand, and the notes often sound
just like him: "All depend on how look at thing," he pencils
10 after "I first surmised the Horses' Heads / Were toward Eternity—"[9]
His slanted handwriting is generally small, but firm and clear.
His pencil is a No. 2, his preferred Hi-Liter, arctic blue.

I can see my father trying out the tools of literary analysis.
He identifies the "turning point" of "The Short and Happy Life
15 of Francis Macomber"; underlines the simile in "Both the old man
and the child stared ahead <u>as if</u> they were awaiting an apparition."[1]
My father, as he reads, continues to notice relevant passages
and to register significant reactions, but increasingly sorts out

his ideas in English, shaking off those Vietnamese glosses.
20 1981 was the same year we *vượt biển*[2] and came to America,
where my father took Intro Lit ("for fun"), Comp Sci ("for job").
"Stopping by Woods on a Snowy Evening,"[3] he murmurs
something about the "dark side of life how awful it can be"
as I begin to track silence and signal to a cold source.

25 Reading Ransom's "Bells for John Whiteside's Daughter,"
a poem about a "young girl's death," as my father notes,
how could he not have been "<u>vexed</u> at her brown study /
Lying so primly propped," since he never properly observed
(I realize this just now) his own daughter's wake.
30 *Lấy làm ngạc nhiên về* is what it means to be astonished.

8. *Hamlet* 1.1.121 (p. 906); the line (spoken by Horatio) immediately precedes the second appearance of Hamlet's father's ghost.
9. Final lines (23–24) of Emily Dickinson's "Because I could not stop for Death—" (p. 492).
1. From Flannery O'Connor's short story "The Artificial Nigger" (1955). "The Short and Happy Life of Francis Macomber": short story (1936) by Ernest Hemingway. *Turning point*: see chapter 1.
2. Crossed the border (Vietnamese).
3. Poem (1923) by Robert Frost (p. 604).

Experiencing Poetry 545

The lazy geese, like a snow cloud
Dripping their snow on the green grass,   10
Tricking and stopping, sleepy and proud,
Who cried in goose, Alas,

For the tireless heart within the little
Lady with rod that made them rise
From their noon apple-dreams and scuttle   15
Goose-fashion under the skies!

But now go the bells, and we are ready,
In one house we are sternly stopped
To say we are vexed at her brown study,
Lying so primly propped.   20

1924

After an opening stanza that introduces the basic contrast between
activity and stillness and between life and death, the center of the
poem concentrates on one vivid scene in the dead girl's life, a moment
when she played Mother Goose to her world and created a colorful,

Hai-Dang Phan's father's annotations in his *Norton Introduction to Literature*

Her name was Đông Xưa, Ancient Winter, but at home she's Bebe.
"There was such speed in her little body, / And such lightness
in her footfall, / It is no wonder her brown study / Astonishes
us all." In the photo of her that hangs in my parents' house
she is always fourteen months old and staring into the future.   35
In "reeducation camp"[4] he had to believe she was alive

because my mother on visits "took arms against her shadow."
Did the memory of those days sweep over him like a leaf storm
from the pages of a forgotten autumn? Lost in the margins,
I'm reading the way I discourage my students from reading.   40
But this is "how we deal with death," his black pen replies.
Assume there is a reason for everything, instructs a green asterisk.[5]

Then between pp. 896–97, opened to Stevens' "Sunday Morning,"[6]
I pick out a newspaper clipping, small as a stamp, an old listing
from the 404-Employment Opps State of Minnesota, and read: 45
For current job opportunities dial (612) 297-3180. Answered 24 hrs.
When I dial, the automated female voice on the other end
tells me I have reached a non-working number.

2015

4. Prison camp used for the indoctrination or ideological retraining of political dissidents; such
camps were common in Communist-ruled postwar Vietnam (1975–86).
5. See "What We Do with Literature: Three Tips (p. 8)."
6. Poem (1915, 1923) by Wallace Stevens.

• What does Phan's poem suggest about what his father gained from reading and studying literature? about how his father's practices as a reader shaped what literature did for him? What does the **speaker** seem to gain from reading the traces of his own father's reading experiences?

AUTHORS ON THEIR WORK

HAI-DANG PHAN (b. 1980)

From *The Best American Poetry 2016* (2016)*

["My Father's 'Norton Introduction to Literature,' Third Edition (1981)" i]s a found poem, artifice meets accident, sourced from the literary works and reader's notes of my father's textbook. I wanted to convey the uniquely tactile, sensuous, and material experience of reading and responding to a printed book, alongside the intimate thrill of handwriting. It's a poem-quilt made of well-worn texts [. . .]. It's a capsule biography, a portrait of my father (who served during the war as an officer in the South Vietnamese Navy, mostly on a small patrol boat unit in the Mekong Delta); as an immigrant trying to learn the language and literature of his adopted country; as a father trying to come to terms with the loss of his first child, whom he only ever saw alive once, and while he was in reeducation camp. I feel compelled to note that it's my mother's grief, briefly acknowledged and secreted inside a borrowed metaphor, which haunts the margins of the poem when I return to it now. After all, she was the one who had to deal with the death of her daughter while her husband was imprisoned, her private sorrow its own prison house. It's also a self-portrait because my life is bound up with this family trauma, and the historical trauma surrounding it. Insofar as I grapple with these legacies, as a writer I'm interested in the formal problems and possibilities they pose. Given the intense emotional response my father's marginalia provoked in me and what became the concerns of the poem, I needed a distancing strategy to combat the threat of cheap sentiment, false immediacy, and unknowing appropriation. Hence, the professorial persona and voice of the detached academic. In October 2012, when I came across my father's *Norton* while visiting my parents in Wisconsin, I had just started teaching at Grinnell College and entered a period of uncertainty about the course of my writing life. It's a reconciliation between two selves, the poet and the professor, that I, too, often see as conflictual, not to mention the age-old wars between fathers and sons, the present and the past. It's my marginalia on his marginalia, a double-annotation and translation, of what words, memories, people, and events mean as they change contexts, of the unknowable. It's a record and reenactment of reading, between the lines, behind the words, for the lives we've missed, others' and our own.

* *The Best American Poetry 2016*. Edited by Edward Hirsch, Scribner Poetry, 2016, pp. 186–87. The Best American Poetry Series, edited by Dennis Lehman.

JOHN CROWE RANSOM
Bells for John Whiteside's Daughter

There was such speed in her little body,
And such lightness in her footfall,
It is no wonder her brown study[7]
Astonishes us all.

5 Her wars were bruited[8] in our high window.
We looked among orchard trees and beyond
Where she took arms against her shadow,[9]
Or harried unto the pond

The lazy geese, like a snow cloud
10 Dripping their snow on the green grass,
Tricking and stopping, sleepy and proud,
Who cried in goose, Alas,

For the tireless heart within the little
Lady with rod that made them rise
15 From their noon apple-dreams and scuttle
Goose-fashion under the skies!

But now go the bells,[1] and we are ready,
In one house we are sternly stopped
To say we are vexed at her brown study,
20 Lying so primly propped.

1924

> • What can you surmise from the poem about the speaker's relationship to
> the dead girl? Why might it matter that the poem uses the first-person plu-
> ral (we), not the singular (I)? that it never explicitly mentions death? Why
> exactly are "we [. . .] vexed" and "[a]stonishe[d]" (lines 19, 4)?

7. State of intense contemplation or reverie.
8. Heard, but also suggesting "noise," "clamor."
9. Compare *Hamlet* 3.1.56–60 (p. 948), in which Hamlet asks, "Whether 'tis nobler in the mind to suffer / The slings and arrows of outrageous fortune, / Or to take arms against a sea of troubles."
1. Perhaps alluding to John Donne's *Devotions upon Emergent Occasions*, Meditation 17 (1624): "Any Mans *death* diminishes *me*, because I am involved in *Mankinde*, And therefore never send to know for whom the *bell* tolls; It tolls for *thee*" (spelling original).

PART ONE Fiction

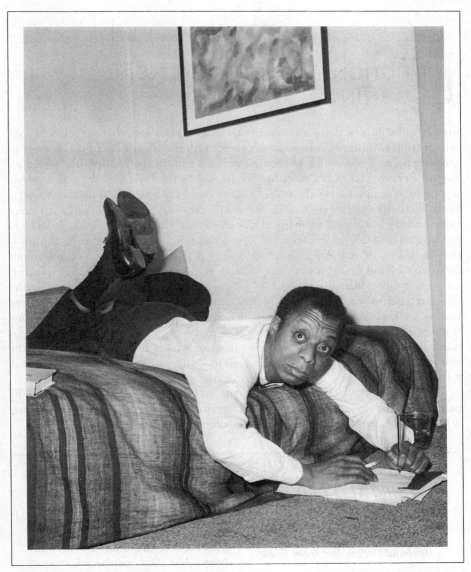

James Baldwin

1 | FICTION: READING, RESPONDING, WRITING

Stories are a part of daily life in every culture. Stories are what we tell when we return from vacation or survive an accident or illness. They help us make sense of growing up or growing old, of a hurricane or a war, of the country and world we live in. In conversations, a story may be invited by the listener ("What did you do last night?") or initiated by the teller ("Guess what I saw when I was driving home!"). We assume such stories are true, or at least that they are meant to describe an experience honestly. Of course, many of the stories we encounter daily, from jokes to online games to television sitcoms to novels and films, are intended to be **fiction**—that is, stories or narratives about imaginary persons and events. The difference between fact and fiction is obviously crucial. But every story, whether a news story, sworn testimony, idle gossip, or a fairy tale, is a version of events told from a particular perspective (or several) and is inevitably incomplete. As we listen to others' stories, we keep alert to the details, which make the stories rich and entertaining. But we also need to spend considerable time and energy making sure that we accurately interpret what we hear: We ask ourselves who is telling the story, why the story is being told, and whether we have all the information we need to understand it fully.

Even newspaper articles that tell true stories—the facts of what actually happened—may be open to such interpretation. Take as an example the following article, which appeared in the *New York Times* on January 1, 1920:

ACCUSED WIFE KILLS HER ALLEGED LOVER

Cumberland (Md.) Woman Becomes Desperate When Her Husband Orders Her from Home.

Special to The New York Times.

CUMBERLAND, Md., Dec. 31.—Accused by her husband of unfaithfulness, Mrs. Kate Uhl, aged 25, this morning stabbed to death Bryan Pownall, who she alleged was the cause of the estrangement with her husband, Mervin Uhl.

Mrs. Uhl, who is the mother of three children, denies her husband's charge of misconduct with Pownall, asserting that the latter forced his attentions on her by main physical strength against her will.

The stabbing this morning came as a dramatic sequel to the woman's dilemma after she had been ordered to leave her home. Mrs. Uhl summoned Pownall after her husband had gone to work this morning, and according to her story begged him to tell her husband that she, Mrs. Uhl, was not to blame. This Pownall refused to do, but again tried to make love to her, Mrs. Uhl said. When Pownall sought to kiss her Mrs. Uhl seized a thin-bladed butcher knife and stabbed the man to the heart, she admitted.

The report's appearance in a reliable newspaper; its identification of date, location, and other information; and the legalistic adjectives "accused" and "alleged" suggest that it strives to be accurate and objective. And it fundamentally is. But this news story is still a *story*. Note that certain points of view are better represented than others, and certain details are highlighted, just as in a work of fiction. The news item is based almost entirely on what Kate Uhl asserts, and even the subtitle, "Woman Becomes Desperate," plays up the "dramatic sequel to the woman's dilemma." We don't know what Mervin Uhl said when he allegedly accused his wife and turned her out of the house, and Bryan Pownall, the murdered man, obviously has no chance to speak in his own defense. Presumably, the article reports accurately the husband's accusation of adultery and the wife's accusation of rape, but we have no way of knowing whose accusations are true.

Our everyday interpretation of the stories we hear from various sources—including other people, the Internet, television, newspapers, and ads—has much in common with the interpretation of short stories such as those in this anthology. The processes of reading, responding to, and writing about stories are already somewhat familiar to you. Most readers already know, for instance, that they should pay close attention to seemingly trivial details; they should ask questions and find out more about any matters of fact that seem mysterious, odd, or unclear. Most readers are well aware that words can have several meanings and that there are alternative ways to tell a story. How would someone else have told the story? What are the storyteller's perspective and motives? What is the context of the tale—for instance, when is it supposed to have taken place and what was the occasion of its telling? These and other questions from our experience of everyday storytelling are equally relevant in reading fiction. Similarly, we can usually tell in reading a story or hearing it whether it is supposed to make us laugh, shock us, or provoke some other response.

TELLING STORIES: INTERPRETATION

Everyone has a unique story to tell. In fact, many stories are about this difference or divergence among people's interpretations of reality. Consider a well-known tale, "The Blind Men and the Elephant," a Buddhist story over two thousand years old. Like other stories that have been transmitted orally, this one exists in many versions. Here's one way of telling it:

The Elephant in the Village of the Blind

Once there was a village high in the mountains in which everyone was born blind. One day a traveler arrived from far away with many fine things to sell and many tales to tell. The villagers asked, "How did you travel so far and so high carrying so much?" The traveler said, "On my elephant." "What is an elephant?" the villagers asked, having never even heard of such an animal in their remote mountain village. "See for yourself," the traveler replied.

The elders of the village were a little afraid of the strange-smelling creature that took up so much space in the middle of the village square. They could hear it breathing and munching on hay, and feel its slow, swaying movements disturbing the air around them. First one elder reached out and felt its flapping ear. "An elephant is soft but tough, and flexible, like a leather fan." Another grasped its back leg. "An elephant is a rough, hairy pillar." An old woman took hold of a tusk and gasped, "An elephant is a cool, smooth staff." A young girl seized the tail and declared, "An elephant is a fringed rope." A boy took hold of the trunk and announced, "An elephant is a water pipe." Soon others were stroking its sides, which were furrowed like a dry plowed field, and others determined that its head was an overturned washing tub attached to the water pipe.

At first each villager argued with the others on the definition of the elephant, as the traveler watched in silence. Two elders were about to come to blows about a fan that could not possibly be a pillar. Meanwhile the elephant patiently enjoyed the investigations as the cries of curiosity and angry debate mixed in the afternoon sun. Soon someone suggested that a list could be made of all the parts: the elephant had four pillars, one tub, two fans, a water pipe, and two staffs, and was covered in tough, hairy leather or dried mud. Four young mothers, sitting on a bench and comparing impressions, realized that the elephant was in fact an enormous, gentle ox with a stretched nose. The traveler agreed, adding only that it was also a powerful draft horse and that if they bought some of his wares for a good price he would be sure to come that way again in the new year.

The different versions of such a tale, like the different descriptions of the elephant, alter its meaning. Changing any aspect of the story will inevitably change how it works and what it means to the listener or reader. For example, most versions of this story feature not an entire village of blind people (as this version does), but a small group of blind men who claim to be wiser than their sighted neighbors. These blind men quarrel endlessly because none of them can see; none can put together all the evidence of all their senses or all the elephant's various parts to create a whole. Such traditional versions of the story criticize people who are too proud of what they think they know; these versions imply that sighted people would know better what an elephant is. However, other versions of the tale, like the one above, are set in an imaginary "country" of the blind. This setting changes the emphasis of the story from the errors of a few blind wise men to the value and the insufficiency of *any* one person's perspective. For though it's clear that the various members of the community in this version will never agree entirely on one interpretation of (or story about) the elephant, they do not let themselves get bogged down in endless dispute. Instead they compare and combine their various stories and "readings" in order to form a more satisfying, holistic understanding of the wonder in their midst. Similarly, listening to others' different interpretations of stories, based on their different perspectives, can enhance your experience of a work of literature and your skill in responding to new works.

Just as stories vary depending on who is telling them, so their meanings vary depending on who is responding to them. In the elephant story, the villagers pay attention to what the tail or the ear feels like, and then they draw on comparisons to what they already know. But ultimately, the individual interpretations of the elephant depend on what previous experiences each villager brings to bear (of pillars, water pipes, oxen, and dried mud, for example), and also on where (quite literally) he or she stands in relation to the elephant. In the same way, readers participate in re-creating a story as they interpret it. When you read a story for the first time, your response will be informed by other stories you have heard and read as well as by your expectations for this kind of story. To grapple with what is new in any story, start by observing one part at a time and gradually trying to understand how those parts work together to form a whole. As you make sense of each new piece of the picture, you adjust your expectations about what is yet to come. When you have read and grasped it as fully as possible, you may share your interpretation with other readers, discussing different ways of seeing the story. Finally, you might express your understanding in writing—in a sense, telling *your* story about the work.

Questions about the Elements of Fiction

- Expectations: What do you expect?
  - from the title? from the first sentence or paragraph?
  - after the first events or interactions of characters?
  - as the **conflict** is resolved?
- What happens in the story? (See ch. 2.)
  - Do the characters or the situation change from the beginning to the end?
  - Can you summarize the **plot**? Is it a recognizable kind or **genre** of story?
- How is the story narrated? (See ch. 3.)
  - Is the **narrator** identified as a character?
  - Is it narrated in the past or present tense?
  - Is it narrated in the first, second, or third person?
  - Do you know what every character is thinking, or only some characters, or none?
- Who are the **characters**? (See ch. 4.)
  - Who is (or are) the **protagonist**(s) (hero, heroine)?
  - Who is (or are) the **antagonist**(s) (villain, opponent, obstacle)?
  - Who are the other characters? What is their role in the story?
  - Do your expectations change with those of the characters, or do you know more or less than each of the characters?
- What is the **setting** of the story? (See ch. 5.)
  - When does the story take place?
  - Where does it take place?
  - Does the story move from one setting to another? Does it move in one direction only or back and forth in time and place?
- What do you notice about how the story is written?
  - What is the **style** of the prose? Are the sentences and the vocabulary simple or complex?
  - Are there any **images**, **figures of speech**, or **symbols**? (See ch. 6.)
  - What is the **tone** or mood? Does the reader feel sad, amused, worried, curious?
- What does the story mean? Can you express its **theme** or themes? (See ch. 7.)
  - Answers to these big questions may be found in many instances in your answers to the previous questions. The story's meaning or theme depends on all its features.

READING AND RESPONDING TO FICTION

When imaginary events are acted out onstage or onscreen, our experience of those events is that of being a witness to them. In contrast, prose fiction, whether oral or written, is relayed to us by someone. Reading it is more like hearing what happened after the fact than witnessing it with our very eyes. The teller, or **narrator**, of fiction addresses a listener or reader, often referred to as the audience. How much or how little we know about the characters and what they say or do depends on what a narrator tells us.

You should read a story attentively, just as you would listen attentively to someone telling a story out loud. This means limiting distractions and interruptions; you should take a break from social media and obtrusive music. Literary prose, like poetry, works with the sounds as well as meanings of words, just as film works with music and sound as well as images. Be prepared to mark up the text and to make notes.

While reading and writing, you should always have a good college-level dictionary on hand or on screen so that you can look up any unfamiliar terms. One excellent resource is the *Oxford English Dictionary*, available in the reference section of most academic libraries or on their websites, which reveals the wide range of meanings words have had over time. Words in English always have a long story to tell because over the centuries so many languages have contributed to ours. It's not uncommon for meanings to overlap or even reverse themselves.

The following short short story is a contemporary work. As in THE ELEPHANT IN THE VILLAGE OF THE BLIND, this narrator gives us a minimal amount of information, merely observing the characters' different perceptions and interpretations of things they see during a cross-country car trip. As you read the story, pay attention to your expectations, drawing on your personal experience and such clues as the title; the characters' statements and behavior; specifics of setting (time and place); and any repetitions or changes. When and how does the story begin to challenge and change your initial expectations? You can use the questions above to guide your reading of any story and help you focus on some of its important features.

LINDA BREWER

20/20

By the time they reached Indiana, Bill realized that Ruthie, his driving companion, was incapable of theoretical debate. She drove okay, she went halves on gas, etc., but she refused to argue. She didn't seem to know how. Bill was used to East Coast women who disputed everything he said, every step of the way. Ruthie stuck to simple observation, like "Look, cows." He chalked it up to the fact that she was from rural Ohio and thrilled to death to be anywhere else.

She didn't mind driving into the setting sun. The third evening out, Bill rested his eyes while she cruised along making the occasional announcement.

"Indian paintbrush. A golden eagle."

Miles later he frowned. There was no Indian paintbrush, that he knew of, near Chicago.

The next evening, driving, Ruthie said, "I never thought I'd see a Bigfoot in 5 real life." Bill turned and looked at the side of the road streaming innocently out behind them. Two red spots winked back—reflectors nailed to a tree stump.

"Ruthie, I'll drive," he said. She stopped the car and they changed places in the light of the evening star.

"I'm so glad I got to come with you," Ruthie said. Her eyes were big, blue, and capable of seeing wonderful sights. A white buffalo near Fargo. A UFO above Twin Falls. A handsome genius in the person of Bill himself. This last vision came to her in Spokane and Bill decided to let it ride.

1996

·   ·   ·

SAMPLE WRITING: ANNOTATION AND NOTES ON "20/20"

Now re-read the story, along with the brief notes one reader made in the margins, based on the "Questions about the Elements of Fiction" that appear on page 19. The reader then expanded these annotations into longer, more detailed notes. These notes could be organized and expanded into a response paper on the story. Some of your insights might even form the basis for a longer essay on one of the elements of the story.

Like "20/20 hind-sight" or perfect vision? Also like the way Bill and Ruthie go 50/50 on the trip, and see things in two different ways.

Bill's doubts about Ruthie. Is he reliable? Does she "refuse" or not "know how" to argue? What's her view of him?

Bill's keeping score; maybe Ruthie's nicer, or has better eyesight. She notices things.

Repetition, like a folktale: 2nd sunset drive, 3rd time she speaks. Not much dialogue in story.

20/20

By the time they reached Indiana, Bill realized that Ruthie, his driving companion, was incapable of theoretical debate. She drove okay, she went halves on gas, etc., but she refused to argue. She didn't seem to know how. Bill was used to East Coast women who disputed everything he said, every step of the way. Ruthie stuck to simple observation, like "Look, cows." He chalked it up to the fact that she was from rural Ohio and thrilled to death to be anywhere else.

She didn't mind driving into the setting sun. The third evening out, Bill rested his eyes while she cruised along making the occasional announcement.

"Indian paintbrush. A golden eagle."

Miles later he frowned. There was no Indian paintbrush, that he knew of, near Chicago.

The next evening, driving, Ruthie said, "I never thought I'd see a Bigfoot in real life." Bill turned and looked at the side of the road

streaming innocently out behind them. Two red spots winked back—
reflectors nailed to a tree stump.

"Ruthie, I'll drive," he said. She stopped the car and they changed
places in the light of the evening star.

"I'm so glad I got to come with you," Ruthie said. Her eyes were big,
blue, and capable of seeing wonderful sights. A white buffalo near Fargo.
A UFO above Twin Falls. A handsome genius in the person of Bill himself. This last vision came to her in Spokane and Bill decided to let it ride.

Bill's only speech.
Turning point: Bill
sees something he
doesn't already
know.

Repetition, like a
joke, in 3 things
Ruthie sees.

Story begins and
ends in the middle
of things: "By the
time," "let it ride."

Initial Impressions

Plot: begins in the middle of action, on a journey. *Narration*: past tense, third
person. *Setting*: Indiana is a middling, unromantic place.

Paragraph 1

Narration and Character: Bill's judgments of Ruthie show that he prides himself
on arguing about abstract ideas; that he thinks Ruthie must be stupid; that they
didn't know each other well and aren't suited for a long trip together. Bill is from
the unfriendly East Coast; Ruthie, from easygoing, dull "rural Ohio." *Style*: The
casual language—"okay" and "etc."—sounds like Bill's voice, but he's not the
narrator. The vague "etc." hints that Bill isn't really curious about her. The
observation of cows sounds funny, childlike, even stupid. But why does he have
to "chalk it up" or keep score?

Paragraph 2

Plot and Character: This is the first specific time given in the story, the "third
evening": Ruthie surprises the reader and Bill with more than dull "observation."

Paragraph 4

Style, Character, Setting, and Tone: Dozing in the speeding car, Bill is too late to
check out what she says. He frowns (he doesn't argue) because the plant and the
bird can't be seen in the Midwest. Brewer uses a series of place names to indicate
the route of the car. There's humor in Ruthie's habit of pointing out bizarre sights.

Paragraph 5

Character and Setting: Bigfoot is a legendary monster living in Western forests.
Is Ruthie's imagination getting the better of Bill's logic? "Innocently" personifies
the road, and the reflectors on the stump wink like the monster; Bill is finally
looking (though in hindsight). The scenery seems to be playing a joke on him.

Paragraph 6

Plot and Character: Here the characters change places. He wants to drive (is she
hallucinating?), but it's as if she has won. The narration (which has been relying
on Bill's voice and perspective) for the first time notices a romantic detail of
scenery that Ruthie doesn't point out (the evening star).

Paragraph 7

Character and Theme: Bill begins to see Ruthie and what she is capable of. What they see *is* the journey these characters take toward falling in love, in the West where things become unreal. *Style*: The long "o" sounds and images in "A white buffalo near Fargo. A UFO above Twin Falls" (along with the words "Ohio," "Chicago," and "Spokane") give a feeling for the wildness (notice the Indian place names). The outcome of the story is that they *go far* to Fargo, see double and fall in love at Twin Falls—see and imagine wonderful things in each other. They end up with perfectly matched vision.

JULES FEIFFER

(b. 1929)

Superman

New Yorker Jules Feiffer got his professional start at age 16, assisting revered cartoonist Will Eisner, who reportedly thought little of Feiffer's drawing skills but came to respect his talent as a writer with a special gift for characterization and dialogue. After a stint in the army during the Korean War, Feiffer landed a job (initially unpaid) at the *Village Voice*, the nation's first alternative newspaper. Here his nationally syndicated, Pulitzer Prize–winning satirical strip appeared weekly for four decades, from 1956 to 1997, when the *New York Times* hired Feiffer as its first op-ed cartoonist. Also a playwright, screenwriter, children's book author, and book illustrator, whose credits include *The Phantom Tollbooth* (1961), Feiffer penned the first history of comic-book superheroes in 1965. Sometimes credited with helping to invent "graphic novels" with his "novel-in-pictures" *Tantrum* (1979), Feiffer himself reserves the label "graphic novels" for the noir trilogy he launched at age 85, with *Kill My Mother* (2014) and *Cousin Joseph* (2016). An illustrated memoir, *Backing into Forward*, appeared in 2010.

KEY CONCEPTS

As you read, respond to, and write about fiction, some key terms and concepts will be useful in comparing or distinguishing different kinds of stories. Stories may be oral rather than written down, and they may be of different lengths. They may be based on true stories or completely invented. They may be written in verse rather than prose, or they may be created in media other than the printed page.

1960

STORY AND NARRATIVE

Generally speaking, a *story* is a short account of an incident or series of incidents, whether actual or invented. The word is often used to refer to an entertaining tale of imaginary people and events, but it is also used in phrases like "the *story* of my life"—suggesting a true account. The term **narrative** is especially useful as a general concept for the substance rather than the form of what is told about persons and their actions. A story or a tale is usually short, whereas a narrative may be of any length.

Narratives in Daily Life

Narrative plays an important role in our lives beyond the telling of fictional stories. Consider the following:

- Today, sociologists and historians may collect *personal narratives* to present an account of society and everyday life in a certain time or place.
- Since the 1990s, the practice of *narrative medicine* has spread as an improved technique of diagnosis and treatment that takes into account the patient's point of view.
- There is a movement to encourage *mediation* rather than litigation in divorce cases. A mediator may collaborate with the couple in arriving at a shared perspective on the divorce; in a sense, they try to agree on the story of their marriage and how it ended.
- Some countries have attempted to recover from the trauma of genocidal ethnic conflict through *official hearings of testimony* by victims as well as defendants. South Africa's Truth and Reconciliation Commission is an example of this use of stories.

ORAL NARRATIVE AND TALES

We tend to think of stories in their written form, but many of the stories that we now regard as among the world's greatest, such as Homer's *Iliad* and the Old English epic *Beowulf*, were sung or recited by generations of storytellers before being written down. Just as rumors change shape as they circulate, oral stories tend to be more fluid than printed ones. Traditionally oral **tales** such as fairy tales or folktales may endure for a very long time yet take different forms in various countries and eras. And it's often difficult or impossible to trace such a story back to a single "author" or creator. In a sense, then, an oral story is the creation of a whole community or communities, just as oral storytelling tends to be a more communal event than reading.

Certain recognizable signals set a story or tale apart from common speech and encourage us to pay a different kind of attention. Children know that a story is beginning when they hear or read "Once upon a time . . . ," and traditional oral storytellers have formal ways to set up a tale, such as *Su-num-twee* ("Listen to me"), as Spokane storytellers say. "And they lived happily ever after," or simply "The End," may similarly indicate when the story is over. Such conventions have been adapted since the invention of printing and the spread of literacy.

FICTION AND NONFICTION

The word *fiction* comes from the Latin root *fingere* "to fashion or form." The earliest definitions concern the act of making something artificial to imitate something else. In the past two centuries, *fiction* has become more narrowly defined as "prose narrative about imaginary people and events," the main meaning of the word as we use it in this anthology.

Genres of Prose Fiction by Length

A **novel** is a work of prose fiction of about forty thousand words or more. The form arose in the seventeenth and early eighteenth centuries as prose romances and adventure tales began to adopt techniques of history and travel narrative as well as memoir, letters, and biography.

A **novella** is a work of prose fiction of about seventeen thousand to forty thousand words. The novella form was especially favored between about 1850 and 1950, largely because it can be more tightly controlled and concentrated than a long novel, while focusing on the inner workings of a character.

A **short story** is broadly defined as anywhere between one thousand and twenty thousand words. One expectation of a short story is that it may be read in a single sitting. The modern short story developed in the mid-nineteenth century, in part because of the growing popularity of magazines.

A **short short story**, sometimes called "flash fiction" or "micro-fiction," is generally not much longer than one thousand words and sometimes much shorter. There have always been very short fictions, including parables and fables, but the short short story is an invention of recent decades.

In contrast with *fiction*, **nonfiction** usually refers to *factual* prose narrative. Some major nonfiction genres are history, biography, and autobiography. In film, documentaries and "biopics," or biographical feature films, similarly attempt to represent real people, places, and events. The boundary between fiction and creative nonfiction is porous. So-called true crime novels such as Truman Capote's *In Cold Blood* (1966) and novelized biographies such as Colm Tóibín's *The Master* (2004), about the life of the novelist Henry James, use the techniques of fiction writing to narrate actual events. Graphic novels, with a format derived from comic books, have become an increasingly popular medium for memoirs. (Four famous examples are Art Spiegelman's *Maus* [1986, 1991], Marjane Satrapi's *Persepolis* [2003], Alison Bechdel's *Fun Home* [2006], and Congressman John Lewis's *March* [2013–16].) Some Hollywood movies and TV shows dramatize real people in everyday situations or contexts, or real events such as the assassination of President John F. Kennedy. In contrast, **historical fiction**, developed by Sir Walter Scott around 1815, comprises prose narratives that present history in imaginative ways.

Such works of prose fiction adhere closely to the facts of history and actual lives, just as many "true"-life stories are more or less fictionalized.

The fiction chapters in this volume present a collection of prose works—mostly short stories. Even as you read the short prose fiction in this book, bear in mind the many ways we encounter stories or narrative in everyday life, and consider the almost limitless variety of forms that fiction may take.

WRITING ABOUT FICTION

During your first reading of any story, you may want to read without stopping to address each of the questions on page 19. After you have read the whole piece once, re-read it carefully, using the questions as a guide. It's always interesting to compare your initial reactions with your later ones. In fact, a paper may focus on comparing the expectations of readers (and characters) at the beginning of a story to their later conclusions. Responses to fiction may come in unpredictable order, so feel free to address the questions as they arise. Looking at how the story is told and what happens to which characters may lead to observations on expectations or setting. Consideration of setting and style can help explain the personalities, actions, mood, and effect of the story, which can lead to well-informed ideas about the meaning of the whole. But any one of the questions, pursued further, can serve as the focus of more formal writing.

Following this chapter are three written responses to Raymond Carver's short story CATHEDRAL. First, read the story and make notes on any features that you find interesting, important, or confusing. Then look at the notes and response paper by Wesley Rupton and the essay by Bethany Qualls, which illustrate two different ways of writing about "Cathedral."

RAYMOND CARVER
(1938–88)

Cathedral

Born in the logging town of Clatskanie, Oregon, to a working-class family, Raymond Carver married at nineteen and had two children by the time he was twenty-one. Despite these early responsibilities and a lifelong struggle with alcoholism, Carver published his first story in 1961 and graduated from Humboldt State College in 1963. He published his first book, *Near Klamath*, a collection of poems, in 1968 and thereafter supported himself with visiting lectureships at the University of California at Berkeley, Syracuse University, and the Iowa Writer's Workshop, among other institutions. Described by the *New York Times* as "surely the most influential writer of American short stories in the second half of the twentieth century"; credited by others with "reviving what was once thought of as a dying literary form"; and compared to such literary luminaries as Ernest

Hemingway, Stephen Crane, and Anton Chekhov, Carver often portrays characters whom one reviewer describes as living, much as Carver long did, "on the edge: of poverty, alcoholic self-destruction, loneliness." The author himself labeled them the sort of "good people," "doing the best they could," who "filled" America. Dubbed a "minimalist" due to his spare style and low-key plots, Carver himself suffered an early death, of lung cancer, at age fifty. His major short-story collections include *Will You Please Be Quiet, Please?* (1976), *What We Talk about When We Talk about Love* (1983), and the posthumously published *Call If You Need Me* (2001).

This blind man, an old friend of my wife's, he was on his way to spend the night. His wife had died. So he was visiting the dead wife's relatives in Connecticut. He called my wife from his in-laws'. Arrangements were made. He would come by train, a five-hour trip, and my wife would meet him at the station. She hadn't seen him since she worked for him one summer in Seattle ten years ago. But she and the blind man had kept in touch. They made tapes and mailed them back and forth. I wasn't enthusiastic about his visit. He was no one I knew. And his being blind bothered me. My idea of blindness came from the movies. In the movies, the blind moved slowly and never laughed. Sometimes they were led by seeing-eye dogs. A blind man in my house was not something I looked forward to.

That summer in Seattle she had needed a job. She didn't have any money. The man she was going to marry at the end of the summer was in officers' training school. He didn't have any money, either. But she was in love with the guy, and he was in love with her, etc. She'd seen something in the paper: HELP WANTED—*Reading to Blind Man*, and a telephone number. She phoned and went over, was hired on the spot. She'd worked with this blind man all summer. She read stuff to him, case studies, reports, that sort of thing. She helped him organize his little office in the county social-service department. They'd become good friends, my wife and the blind man. How do I know these things? She told me. And she told me something else. On her last day in the office, the blind man asked if he could touch her face. She agreed to this. She told me he touched his fingers to every part of her face, her nose—even her neck! She never forgot it. She even tried to write a poem about it. She was always trying to write a poem. She wrote a poem or two every year, usually after something really important had happened to her.

When we first started going out together, she showed me the poem. In the poem, she recalled his fingers and the way they had moved around over her face. In the poem, she talked about what she had felt at the time, about what went through her mind when the blind man touched her nose and lips. I can remember I didn't think much of the poem. Of course, I didn't tell her that. Maybe I just don't understand poetry. I admit it's not the first thing I reach for when I pick up something to read.

Anyway, this man who'd first enjoyed her favors, the officer-to-be, he'd been her childhood sweetheart. So okay. I'm saying that at the end of the summer she let the blind man run his hands over her face, said goodbye to him, married her childhood etc., who was now a commissioned officer, and she moved away from Seattle. But they'd kept in touch, she and the blind man. She made the first contact after a year or so. She called him up one night from an Air Force base in Alabama. She wanted to talk. They talked. He asked her to send him a tape and tell him about her life. She did this. She sent the tape. On the tape, she told the blind man about her husband and about their life together in the military. She told the blind man she loved her husband but she didn't like it where they lived and she didn't like it that he was a part of the military-industrial thing. She told the blind man she'd written a poem and he was in it. She told him that she was writing a poem about what it was like to be an Air Force officer's wife. The poem wasn't finished yet. She was still writing it. The blind man made a tape. He sent her the tape. She made a tape. This went on for years. My wife's officer was posted to one base and then another. She sent tapes from Moody AFB, McGuire, McConnell, and finally Travis, near Sacramento, where one night she got to feeling lonely and cut off from people she kept losing in that moving-around life. She got to feeling she couldn't go it another step. She went in and swallowed all the pills and capsules in the medicine chest and washed them down with a bottle of gin. Then she got into a hot bath and passed out.

But instead of dying, she got sick. She threw up. Her officer—why should 5 he have a name? he was the childhood sweetheart, and what more does he want?—came home from somewhere, found her, and called the ambulance. In time, she put it all on a tape and sent the tape to the blind man. Over the years, she put all kinds of stuff on tapes and sent the tapes off lickety-split. Next to writing a poem every year, I think it was her chief means of recreation. On one tape, she told the blind man she'd decided to live away from her officer for a time. On another tape, she told him about her divorce. She and I began going out, and of course she told her blind man about it. She told him everything, or so it seemed to me. Once she asked me if I'd like to hear the latest tape from the blind man. This was a year ago. I was on the tape, she said. So I said okay, I'd listen to it. I got us drinks and we settled down in the living room. We made ready to listen. First she inserted the tape into the player and adjusted a couple of dials. Then she pushed a lever. The tape squeaked and someone began to talk in this loud voice. She lowered the volume. After a few minutes of harmless chitchat, I heard my own name in the mouth of this stranger, this blind man I didn't even know! And then this: "From all you've said about him, I can only conclude—" But we were interrupted, a knock at the door, something, and we didn't ever get back to the tape. Maybe it was just as well. I'd heard all I wanted to.

Now this same blind man was coming to sleep in my house.

"Maybe I could take him bowling," I said to my wife. She was at the draining board doing scalloped potatoes. She put down the knife she was using and turned around.

"If you love me," she said, "you can do this for me. If you don't love me, okay. But if you had a friend, any friend, and the friend came to visit, I'd make him feel comfortable." She wiped her hands with the dish towel.

"I don't have any blind friends," I said.

"You don't have *any* friends," she said. "Period. Besides," she said, "goddamn 10 it, his wife's just died! Don't you understand that? The man's lost his wife!"

I didn't answer. She'd told me a little about the blind man's wife. Her name was Beulah. Beulah! That's a name for a colored woman.

"Was his wife a Negro?" I asked.

"Are you crazy?" my wife said. "Have you just flipped or something?" She picked up a potato. I saw it hit the floor, then roll under the stove. "What's wrong with you?" she said. "Are you drunk?"

"I'm just asking," I said.

15   Right then my wife filled me in with more detail than I cared to know. I made a drink and sat at the kitchen table to listen. Pieces of the story began to fall into place.

Beulah had gone to work for the blind man the summer after my wife had stopped working for him. Pretty soon Beulah and the blind man had themselves a church wedding. It was a little wedding—who'd want to go to such a wedding in the first place?—just the two of them, plus the minister and the minister's wife. But it was a church wedding just the same. It was what Beulah had wanted, he'd said. But even then Beulah must have been carrying the cancer in her glands. After they had been inseparable for eight years—my wife's word, *inseparable*—Beulah's health went into a rapid decline. She died in a Seattle hospital room, the blind man sitting beside the bed and holding on to her hand. They'd married, lived and worked together, slept together—had sex, sure—and then the blind man had to bury her. All this without his having ever seen what the goddamned woman looked like. It was beyond my understanding. Hearing this, I felt sorry for the blind man for a little bit. And then I found myself thinking what a pitiful life this woman must have led. Imagine a woman who could never see herself as she was seen in the eyes of her loved one. A woman who could go on day after day and never receive the smallest compliment from her beloved. A woman whose husband could never read the expression on her face, be it misery or something better. Someone who could wear makeup or not—what difference to him? She could, if she wanted, wear green eye-shadow around one eye, a straight pin in her nostril, yellow slacks and purple shoes, no matter. And then to slip off into death, the blind man's hand on her hand, his blind eyes streaming tears—I'm imagining now—her last thought maybe this: that he never even knew what she looked like, and she on an express to the grave. Robert was left with a small insurance policy and half of a twenty-peso Mexican coin. The other half of the coin went into the box with her. Pathetic.

So when the time rolled around, my wife went to the depot to pick him up. With nothing to do but wait—sure, I blamed him for that—I was having a drink and watching the TV when I heard the car pull into the drive. I got up from the sofa with my drink and went to the window to have a look.

I saw my wife laughing as she parked the car. I saw her get out of the car and shut the door. She was still wearing a smile. Just amazing. She went around to the other side of the car to where the blind man was already starting to get out. This blind man, feature this, he was wearing a full beard! A beard on a blind man! Too much, I say. The blind man reached into the back seat and dragged out a suitcase. My wife took his arm, shut the car door, and, talking all the way, moved him down the drive and then up the steps to the front porch. I turned off the TV. I finished my drink, rinsed the glass, dried my hands. Then I went to the door.

My wife said, "I want you to meet Robert. Robert, this is my husband. I've told you all about him." She was beaming. She had this blind man by his coat sleeve.

The blind man let go of his suitcase and up came his hand.   20

I took it. He squeezed hard, held my hand, and then he let it go.

"I feel like we've already met," he boomed.

"Likewise," I said. I didn't know what else to say. Then I said, "Welcome. I've heard a lot about you." We began to move then, a little group, from the porch into the living room, my wife guiding him by the arm. The blind man was carrying his suitcase in his other hand. My wife said things like, "To your left here, Robert. That's right. Now watch it, there's a chair. That's it. Sit down right here. This is the sofa. We just bought this sofa two weeks ago."

I started to say something about the old sofa. I'd liked that old sofa. But I didn't say anything. Then I wanted to say something else, small-talk, about the scenic ride along the Hudson. How going *to* New York, you should sit on the right-hand side of the train, and coming *from* New York, the left-hand side.

"Did you have a good train ride?" I said. "Which side of the train did you sit   25
on, by the way?"

"What a question, which side!" my wife said. "What's it matter which side?" she said.

"I just asked," I said.

"Right side," the blind man said. "I hadn't been on a train in nearly forty years. Not since I was a kid. With my folks. That's been a long time. I'd nearly forgotten the sensation. I have winter in my beard now," he said. "So I've been told, anyway. Do I look distinguished, my dear?" the blind man said to my wife.

"You look distinguished, Robert," she said. "Robert," she said. "Robert, it's just so good to see you."

My wife finally took her eyes off the blind man and looked at me. I had the   30
feeling she didn't like what she saw. I shrugged.

I've never met, or personally known, anyone who was blind. This blind man was late forties, a heavy-set, balding man with stooped shoulders, as if he carried a great weight there. He wore brown slacks, brown shoes, a light-brown shirt, a tie, a sports coat. Spiffy. He also had this full beard. But he didn't use a cane and he didn't wear dark glasses. I'd always thought dark glasses were a must for the blind. Fact was, I wished he had a pair. At first glance, his eyes looked like anyone else's eyes. But if you looked close, there was something different about them. Too much white in the iris, for one thing, and the pupils seemed to move around in the sockets without his knowing it or being able to stop it. Creepy. As I stared at his face, I saw the left pupil turn in toward his nose while the other made an effort to keep in one place. But it was only an effort, for that eye was on the roam without his knowing it or wanting it to be.

I said, "Let me get you a drink. What's your pleasure? We have a little of everything. It's one of our pastimes."

"Bub, I'm a Scotch man myself," he said fast enough in this big voice.

"Right," I said. Bub! "Sure you are. I knew it."

He let his fingers touch his suitcase, which was sitting alongside the sofa. He   35
was taking his bearings. I didn't blame him for that.

"I'll move that up to your room," my wife said.

"No, that's fine," the blind man said loudly. "It can go up when I go up."

"A little water with the Scotch?" I said.

"Very little," he said.

40   "I knew it," I said.

He said, "Just a tad. The Irish actor, Barry Fitzgerald? I'm like that fellow. When I drink water, Fitzgerald said, I drink water. When I drink whiskey, I drink whiskey." My wife laughed. The blind man brought his hand up under his beard. He lifted his beard slowly and let it drop.

I did the drinks, three big glasses of Scotch with a splash of water in each. Then we made ourselves comfortable and talked about Robert's travels. First the long flight from the West Coast to Connecticut, we covered that. Then from Connecticut up here by train. We had another drink concerning that leg of the trip.

I remembered having read somewhere that the blind didn't smoke because, as speculation had it, they couldn't see the smoke they exhaled. I thought I knew that much and that much only about blind people. But this blind man smoked his cigarette down to the nubbin and then lit another one. This blind man filled his ashtray and my wife emptied it.

When we sat down at the table for dinner, we had another drink. My wife heaped Robert's plate with cube steak, scalloped potatoes, green beans. I buttered him up two slices of bread. I said, "Here's bread and butter for you." I swallowed some of my drink. "Now let us pray," I said, and the blind man lowered his head. My wife looked at me, her mouth agape. "Pray the phone won't ring and the food doesn't get cold," I said.

45   We dug in. We ate everything there was to eat on the table. We ate like there was no tomorrow. We didn't talk. We ate. We scarfed. We grazed that table. We were into serious eating. The blind man had right away located his foods, he knew just where everything was on his plate. I watched with admiration as he used his knife and fork on the meat. He'd cut two pieces of meat, fork the meat into his mouth, and then go all out for the scalloped potatoes, the beans next, and then he'd tear off a hunk of buttered bread and eat that. He'd follow this up with a big drink of milk. It didn't seem to bother him to use his fingers once in a while, either.

We finished everything, including half a strawberry pie. For a few moments, we sat as if stunned. Sweat beaded on our faces. Finally, we got up from the table and left the dirty plates. We didn't look back. We took ourselves into the living room and sank into our places again. Robert and my wife sat on the sofa. I took the big chair. We had us two or three more drinks while they talked about the major things that had come to pass for them in the past ten years. For the most part, I just listened. Now and then I joined in. I didn't want him to think I'd left the room, and I didn't want her to think I was feeling left out. They talked of things that had happened to them—to them!—these past ten years. I waited in vain to hear my name on my wife's sweet lips: "And then my dear husband came into my life"—something like that. But I heard nothing of the sort. More talk of Robert. Robert had done a little of everything, it seemed, a regular blind jack-of-all-trades. But most recently he and his wife had had an Amway distributorship, from which, I gathered, they'd earned their living, such as it was. The blind man was also a ham radio operator. He talked in his loud voice about conversations he'd had with fellow operators in Guam, in the Philippines, in Alaska, and even in Tahiti. He said he'd have a lot of friends there if he ever wanted to go visit those places. From time to time, he'd turn his blind face toward me, put his hand under his beard, ask me something. How long had I been in my present position? (Three years.) Did I like my work? (I didn't.) Was I going to stay with it? (What were the options?) Finally, when I thought he was beginning to run down, I got up and turned on the TV.

My wife looked at me with irritation. She was heading toward a boil. Then she looked at the blind man and said, "Robert, do you have a TV?"

The blind man said, "My dear, I have two TVs. I have a color set and a black-and-white thing, an old relic. It's funny, but if I turn the TV on, and I'm always turning it on, I turn on the color set. It's funny, don't you think?"

I didn't know what to say to that. I had absolutely nothing to say to that. No opinion. So I watched the news program and tried to listen to what the announcer was saying.

"This is a color TV," the blind man said. "Don't ask me how, but I can tell."   50

"We traded up a while ago," I said.

The blind man had another taste of his drink. He lifted his beard, sniffed it, and let it fall. He leaned forward on the sofa. He positioned his ashtray on the coffee table, then put the lighter to his cigarette. He leaned back on the sofa and crossed his legs at the ankles.

My wife covered her mouth, and then she yawned. She stretched. She said, "I think I'll go upstairs and put on my robe. I think I'll change into something else. Robert, you make yourself comfortable," she said.

"I'm comfortable," the blind man said.

"I want you to feel comfortable in this house," she said.   55

"I am comfortable," the blind man said.

After she'd left the room, he and I listened to the weather report and then to the sports roundup. By that time, she'd been gone so long I didn't know if she was going to come back. I thought she might have gone to bed. I wished she'd come back downstairs. I didn't want to be left alone with a blind man. I asked him if he wanted another drink, and he said sure. Then I asked if he wanted to smoke some dope with me. I said I'd just rolled a number. I hadn't, but I planned to do so in about two shakes.

"I'll try some with you," he said.

"Damn right," I said. "That's the stuff."

I got our drinks and sat down on the sofa with him. Then I rolled us two fat   60
numbers. I lit one and passed it. I brought it to his fingers. He took it and inhaled.

"Hold it as long as you can," I said. I could tell he didn't know the first thing.

My wife came back downstairs wearing her pink robe and her pink slippers.

"What do I smell?" she said.

"We thought we'd have us some cannabis," I said.

My wife gave me a savage look. Then she looked at the blind man and said,   65
"Robert, I didn't know you smoked."

He said, "I do now, my dear. There's a first time for everything. But I don't feel anything yet."

"This stuff is pretty mellow," I said. "This stuff is mild. It's dope you can reason with," I said. "It doesn't mess you up."

"Not much it doesn't, bub," he said, and laughed.

My wife sat on the sofa between the blind man and me. I passed her the number. She took it and toked and then passed it back to me. "Which way is this going?" she said. Then she said, "I shouldn't be smoking this. I can hardly keep my eyes open as it is. That dinner did me in. I shouldn't have eaten so much."

70   "It was the strawberry pie," the blind man said. "That's what did it," he said, and he laughed his big laugh. Then he shook his head.

"There's more strawberry pie," I said.

"Do you want some more, Robert?" my wife said.

"Maybe in a little while," he said.

We gave our attention to the TV. My wife yawned again. She said, "Your bed is made up when you feel like going to bed, Robert. I know you must have had a long day. When you're ready to go to bed, say so." She pulled his arm. "Robert?"

75   He came to and said, "I've had a real nice time. This beats tapes, doesn't it?"

I said, "Coming at you," and I put the number between his fingers. He inhaled, held the smoke, and then let it go. It was like he'd been doing it since he was nine years old.

"Thanks, bub," he said. "But I think this is all for me. I think I'm beginning to feel it," he said. He held the burning roach out for my wife.

"Same here," she said. "Ditto. Me, too." She took the roach and passed it to me. "I may just sit here for a while between you two guys with my eyes closed. But don't let me bother you, okay? Either one of you. If it bothers you, say so. Otherwise, I may just sit here with my eyes closed until you're ready to go to bed," she said. "Your bed's made up, Robert, when you're ready. It's right next to our room at the top of the stairs. We'll show you up when you're ready. You wake me up now, you guys, if I fall asleep." She said that and then she closed her eyes and went to sleep.

The news program ended. I got up and changed the channel. I sat back down on the sofa. I wished my wife hadn't pooped out. Her head lay across the back of the sofa, her mouth open. She'd turned so that her robe had slipped away from her legs, exposing a juicy thigh. I reached to draw her robe back over her, and it was then that I glanced at the blind man. What the hell! I flipped the robe open again.

80   "You say when you want some strawberry pie," I said.

"I will," he said.

I said, "Are you tired? Do you want me to take you up to your bed? Are you ready to hit the hay?"

"Not yet," he said. "No, I'll stay up with you, bub. If that's all right. I'll stay up until you're ready to turn in. We haven't had a chance to talk. Know what I mean? I feel like me and her monopolized the evening." He lifted his beard and he let it fall. He picked up his cigarettes and his lighter.

"That's all right," I said. Then I said, "I'm glad for the company."

85   And I guess I was. Every night I smoked dope and stayed up as long as I could before I fell asleep. My wife and I hardly ever went to bed at the same time. When I did go to sleep, I had these dreams. Sometimes I'd wake up from one of them, my heart going crazy.

Something about the church and the Middle Ages was on the TV. Not your
run-of-the-mill TV fare. I wanted to watch something else. I turned to the other
channels. But there was nothing on them, either. So I turned back to the first
channel and apologized.

"Bub, it's all right," the blind man said. "It's fine with me. Whatever you want
to watch is okay. I'm always learning something. Learning never ends. It won't
hurt me to learn something tonight. I got ears," he said.

We didn't say anything for a time. He was leaning forward with his head turned
at me, his right ear aimed in the direction of the set. Very disconcerting. Now
and then his eyelids drooped and then they snapped open again. Now and then
he put his fingers into his beard and tugged, like he was thinking about something he was hearing on the television.

On the screen, a group of men wearing cowls was being set upon and tormented by men dressed in skeleton costumes and men dressed as devils. The men
dressed as devils wore devil masks, horns, and long tails. This pageant was part of
a procession. The Englishman who was narrating the thing said it took place in
Spain once a year. I tried to explain to the blind man what was happening.

"Skeletons," he said. "I know about skeletons," he said, and he nodded.   90

The TV showed this one cathedral. Then there was a long, slow look at
another one. Finally, the picture switched to the famous one in Paris, with its
flying buttresses and its spires reaching up to the clouds. The camera pulled
away to show the whole of the cathedral rising above the skyline.

There were times when the Englishman who was telling the thing would
shut up, would simply let the camera move around over the cathedrals. Or else
the camera would tour the countryside, men in fields walking behind oxen. I
waited as long as I could. Then I felt I had to say something. I said, "They're
showing the outside of this cathedral now. Gargoyles. Little statues carved to
look like monsters. Now I guess they're in Italy. Yeah, they're in Italy. There's
paintings on the walls of this one church."

"Are those fresco paintings, bub?" he asked, and he sipped from his drink.

I reached for my glass. But it was empty. I tried to remember what I could
remember. "You're asking me are those frescoes?" I said. "That's a good question. I don't know."

The camera moved to a cathedral outside Lisbon. The differences in the   95
Portuguese cathedral compared with the French and Italian were not that great.
But they were there. Mostly the interior stuff. Then something occurred to
me, and I said, "Something has occurred to me. Do you have any idea what a
cathedral is? What they look like, that is? Do you follow me? If somebody says
cathedral to you, do you have any notion what they're talking about? Do you
know the difference between that and a Baptist church, say?"

He let the smoke dribble from his mouth. "I know they took hundreds of
workers fifty or a hundred years to build," he said. "I just heard the man say
that, of course. I know generations of the same families worked on a cathedral.
I heard him say that, too. The men who began their life's work on them, they
never lived to see the completion of their work. In that wise, bub, they're no different from the rest of us, right?" He laughed. Then his eyelids drooped again.
His head nodded. He seemed to be snoozing. Maybe he was imagining himself

in Portugal. The TV was showing another cathedral now. This one was in Germany. The Englishman's voice droned on. "Cathedrals," the blind man said. He sat up and rolled his head back and forth. "If you want the truth, bub, that's about all I know. What I just said. What I heard him say. But maybe you could describe one to me? I wish you'd do it. I'd like that. If you want to know, I really don't have a good idea."

I stared hard at the shot of the cathedral on the TV. How could I even begin to describe it? But say my life depended on it. Say my life was being threatened by an insane guy who said I had to do it or else.

I stared some more at the cathedral before the picture flipped off into the countryside. There was no use. I turned to the blind man and said, "To begin with, they're very tall." I was looking around the room for clues. "They reach way up. Up and up. Toward the sky. They're so big, some of them, they have to have these supports. To help hold them up, so to speak. These supports are called buttresses. They remind me of viaducts, for some reason. But maybe you don't know viaducts, either? Sometimes the cathedrals have devils and such carved into the front. Sometimes lords and ladies. Don't ask me why this is," I said.

He was nodding. The whole upper part of his body seemed to be moving back and forth.

100   "I'm not doing so good, am I?" I said.

He stopped nodding and leaned forward on the edge of the sofa. As he listened to me, he was running his fingers through his beard. I wasn't getting through to him, I could see that. But he waited for me to go on just the same. He nodded, like he was trying to encourage me. I tried to think what else to say. "They're really big," I said. "They're massive. They're built of stone. Marble, too, sometimes. In those olden days, when they built cathedrals, men wanted to be close to God. In those olden days, God was an important part of everyone's life. You could tell this from their cathedral-building. I'm sorry," I said, "but it looks like that's the best I can do for you. I'm just no good at it."

"That's all right, bub," the blind man said. "Hey, listen. I hope you don't mind my asking you. Can I ask you something? Let me ask you a simple question, yes or no. I'm just curious and there's no offense. You're my host. But let me ask if you are in any way religious? You don't mind my asking?"

I shook my head. He couldn't see that, though. A wink is the same as a nod to a blind man. "I guess I don't believe in it. In anything. Sometimes it's hard. You know what I'm saying?"

"Sure, I do," he said.

105   "Right," I said.

The Englishman was still holding forth. My wife sighed in her sleep. She drew a long breath and went on with her sleeping.

"You'll have to forgive me," I said. "But I can't tell you what a cathedral looks like. It just isn't in me to do it. I can't do any more than I've done."

The blind man sat very still, his head down, as he listened to me.

I said, "The truth is, cathedrals don't mean anything special to me. Nothing. Cathedrals. They're something to look at on late-night TV. That's all they are."

110   It was then that the blind man cleared his throat. He brought something up. He took a handkerchief from his back pocket. Then he said, "I get it, bub. It's

okay. It happens. Don't worry about it," he said. "Hey, listen to me. Will you do me a favor? I got an idea. Why don't you find us some heavy paper? And a pen. We'll do something. We'll draw one together. Get us a pen and some heavy paper. Go on, bub, get the stuff," he said.

So I went upstairs. My legs felt like they didn't have any strength in them. They felt like they did after I'd done some running. In my wife's room, I looked around. I found some ballpoints in a little basket on her table. And then I tried to think where to look for the kind of paper he was talking about.

Downstairs, in the kitchen, I found a shopping bag with onion skins in the bottom of the bag. I emptied the bag and shook it. I brought it into the living room and sat down with it near his legs. I moved some things, smoothed the wrinkles from the bag, spread it out on the coffee table.

The blind man got down from the sofa and sat next to me on the carpet.

He ran his fingers over the paper. He went up and down the sides of the paper. The edges, even the edges. He fingered the corners.

"All right," he said. "All right, let's do her."   115

He found my hand, the hand with the pen. He closed his hand over my hand. "Go ahead, bub, draw," he said. "Draw. You'll see. I'll follow along with you. It'll be okay. Just begin now like I'm telling you. You'll see. Draw," the blind man said.

So I began. First I drew a box that looked like a house. It could have been the house I lived in. Then I put a roof on it. At either end of the roof, I drew spires. Crazy.

"Swell," he said. "Terrific. You're doing fine," he said. "Never thought anything like this could happen in your lifetime, did you, bub? Well, it's a strange life, we all know that. Go on now. Keep it up."

I put in windows with arches. I drew flying buttresses. I hung great doors. I couldn't stop. The TV station went off the air. I put down the pen and closed and opened my fingers. The blind man felt around over the paper. He moved the tips of his fingers over the paper, all over what I had drawn, and he nodded.

"Doing fine," the blind man said.   120

I took up the pen again, and he found my hand. I kept at it. I'm no artist. But I kept drawing just the same.

My wife opened up her eyes and gazed at us. She sat up on the sofa, her robe hanging open. She said, "What are you doing? Tell me, I want to know."

I didn't answer her.

The blind man said, "We're drawing a cathedral. Me and him are working on it. Press hard," he said to me. "That's right. That's good," he said. "Sure. You got it, bub. I can tell. You didn't think you could. But you can, can't you? You're cooking with gas now. You know what I'm saying? We're going to really have us something here in a minute. How's the old arm?" he said. "Put some people in there now. What's a cathedral without people?"

My wife said, "What's going on? Robert, what are you doing? What's going   125
on?"

"It's all right," he said to her. "Close your eyes now," the blind man said to me.

I did it. I closed them just like he said.

"Are they closed?" he said. "Don't fudge."

"They're closed," I said.

130   "Keep them that way," he said. He said, "Don't stop now. Draw."

So we kept on with it. His fingers rode my fingers as my hand went over the paper. It was like nothing else in my life up to now.

Then he said, "I think that's it. I think you got it," he said. "Take a look. What do you think?"

But I had my eyes closed. I thought I'd keep them that way for a little longer. I thought it was something I ought to do.

"Well?" he said. "Are you looking?"

135   My eyes were still closed. I was in my house. I knew that. But I didn't feel like I was inside anything.

"It's really something," I said.

1983

SAMPLE WRITING: READING NOTES

Wesley Rupton wrote the notes below with the "Questions about the Elements of Fiction" in mind (p. 19). As you read these notes, compare them to the notes you took as you read CATHEDRAL. Do Rupton's notes reveal anything to you that you didn't notice while reading the story? Did you notice anything he did not, or do you disagree with any of his interpretations?

Notes on Raymond Carver's "Cathedral"

What do you expect?

- Title: The first words are "This blind man," and those words keep being repeated. Why not call it "The Blind Man" or "The Blind Man's Visit"?
- The threatening things the husband says made me expect him to attack the blind man. I thought the wife might leave her husband for the blind man, who has been nicer to her.
- When they talk about going up to bed, and the wife goes to "get comfortable" and then falls asleep, I thought there was a hint about sex.

What happens in the story?

- Not that much. It is a story about one evening in which a husband and wife and their guest drink, have dinner, talk, and then watch TV.
- These people have probably drunk two bottles of hard liquor (how many drinks?) before, during, and after a meal. And then they smoke marijuana.
- In the final scene, the two men try to describe and draw cathedrals that are on the TV show. Why cathedrals?
- The husband seems to have a different attitude at the end: He likes Robert and seems excited about the experience "like nothing else in my life up to now."

How is the story narrated?

- It's told in first person and past tense. The husband is the narrator. We never get inside another character's thoughts. He seems to be telling someone about the incident, first saying the blind man was coming, then filling in the background about his wife and the blind man, and then telling what happens after the guest arrives.
- The narrator describes people and scenes and summarizes the past; there is dialogue.
- It doesn't have episodes or chapters, but there are two gaps on the page, before paragraph 57 and before paragraph 88. Maybe time passes here.

Who are the characters?

- Three main characters: husband, wife, and blind man (the blind man's own wife has just died, and the wife divorced her first husband). I don't think we ever know the husband's or wife's names. The blind man, Robert, calls him "bub," like "buddy." They seem to be white, middle-class Americans. The wife is lonely and looking for meaning. The blind man seems sensitive, and he cares about the poetry and tapes.
- The husband is sort of acting out, though mostly in his own mind. Asking "Was his wife a Negro?" sounds like he wants to make fun of black or blind people. His wife asks, "Are you drunk?" and says that he has no friends; I thought he's an unhappy man who gets drunk and acts "crazy" a lot and that she doesn't really expect him to be that nice.
- It sounds like these people have plenty of food and things, but aren't very happy. They all sound smart, but the narrator is ignorant, and he has no religion. All three characters have some bad or nervous habits (alcohol, cigarettes, drugs; insomnia; suicide attempt; divorce).

What is the setting of the story?

- Mostly in the house the evening the blind man arrives. But after the intro there's a kind of flashback to the summer in Seattle ten years ago (par. 2). The story about the visit starts again in paragraph 6, and then the wife tells the husband more about the blind man's marriage—another flashback in paragraph 16. In paragraph 17, "the time rolled around" to the story's main event. After that, it's chronological.
- We don't know the name of the town, but it seems to be on the U.S. East Coast (five hours by train from Connecticut [par. 1]). It can't be too long ago or too recent either: they mention trains, audiotapes, color TV, no Internet. No one seems worried about food or health the way they might be today.
- I noticed that travel came up in the story. Part of what drives the wife crazy about her first husband is moving around to different military bases (par. 4). In paragraph 46, Robert tells us about his contact with ham radio operators in places he would like to visit (Guam, Alaska). The TV show takes Robert and the narrator on a tour of France, Italy, and Portugal.

What do you notice about how the story is written?

- The narrator is irritating. He repeats words a lot. He uses stereotypes. He seems to be informally talking to someone, as if he can't get over it. But then he sometimes uses exaggerated or bored-sounding phrases: "this man who'd first enjoyed her favors," "So okay. I'm saying . . . married her childhood etc." (par. 4). His style is almost funny.
- Things he repeats: Paragraphs 2 and 3: "She told me" (3 times), "he could touch her face . . . he touched his fingers to every part of her face . . ." (and later "touched her nose" (par. 3) and "they'd kept in touch" (par. 4)). "She even tried to write a poem . . . always trying to write a poem" (and 4 more times "poem"). The words "talk," "tape," "told" are also repeated.

What does the story mean? Can you express its theme or themes?

- The way the narrator learns to get along with the blind man must be important. The narrator is disgusted by blind people at first, and at the end he closes his eyes on purpose.

- I think it makes a difference that the two men imagine and try to draw a cathedral, not a flower or an airplane. It's something made by human beings, and it's religious. As they mention, the builders of cathedrals don't live to see them finished, but the buildings last for centuries. It's not like the narrator is saved or becomes a great guy, but he gets past whatever he's afraid of at night, and he seems inspired for a little while. I don't know why the wife has to be left out of this, but probably the husband couldn't open up if he was worrying about how close she is to Robert.

SAMPLE WRITING: RESPONSE PAPER

A response paper may use a less formal organization and style than a longer, more formal essay, but it should not just be a summary or description of the work. Indeed, a response paper could be a step on the way to a longer essay. You need not form a single thesis or argument, but you should try to develop your ideas and feelings about the story by making reference to some specifics. The point is to get your thoughts in writing without worrying too much about form and style.

Almost everything in the following response paper comes directly from the notes above, but notice how the writer has combined observations, adding a few direct quotations or details from the text to support claims about the story's effects and meaning. (For ease of reference, we have altered the citations in this paper to refer to paragraph numbers. Unless your instructor indicates otherwise, you should always follow convention by instead citing page numbers when writing about fiction.)

Wesley Rupton
Professor Suarez
English 170
6 January 2019

Response Paper on Raymond Carver's "Cathedral"

Not much happens in Raymond Carver's short story "Cathedral," and at first I wondered what it was about and why it was called "Cathedral." The narrator, the unnamed husband, seems to be telling someone about the evening that Robert, a blind friend of his wife, came to stay at their house, not long after Robert's own wife has died. After the narrator fills us in about his wife's first marriage and her relationship with the blind man, he describes what the three characters do that evening: they drink a lot of alcohol, eat a huge dinner that leaves them "stunned" (par. 46), smoke marijuana, and after the wife falls asleep the two men watch TV. A show about cathedrals leads the husband to try to describe what a cathedral looks like, and then the men try to draw one together. The husband seems to have a different attitude at the end: he likes Robert and seems excited about an experience "like nothing else in my life up to now" (par. 131).

The husband's way of telling the story is definitely important. He is sort of funny, but also irritating. As he makes jokes about stereotypes, you start to dislike or distrust him. When he hears about Robert's wife, Beulah, he asks,

"Was his wife a Negro?" (par. 12) just because her name sounds like a black woman's name to him. In three paragraphs, he flashes back to the time ten years ago when his wife was the blind man's assistant and the blind man

> asked if he could touch her face. . . . She told me he touched his fingers to every part of her face. . . . She even tried to write a poem about it. . . .
>
> . . . In the poem, she recalled his fingers . . . over her face. In the poem, she talked about what she had felt . . . when the blind man touched her nose and lips. (pars. 2-3)

The narrator seems to be going over and over the same creepy idea of a man feeling his wife's face. It seems to disgust him that his wife and the blind man communicated or expressed themselves, perhaps because he seems incapable of doing that. When his wife asks, "Are you drunk?" and says that he has no friends, I got a feeling that the husband is an unhappy man who gets drunk and acts "crazy" a lot and that his wife doesn't really expect him to be very nice (pars. 8-13). He's going to make fun of their guest (asking a blind man to go bowling). The husband is sort of acting out, though he's mostly rude in his own mind.

There's nothing heroic or dramatic or even unusual about these people (except that one is blind). The events take place in a house somewhere in an American suburb and not too long ago. Other than the quantity of alcohol and drugs they consume, these people don't do anything unusual, though the blind man seems strange to the narrator. The ordinary setting and plot make the idea of something as grand and old as a European cathedral come as a surprise at the end of the story. I wondered if part of the point is that they desperately want to get out of a trap they're in. I noticed that travel came up in the story. Part of what drove the wife crazy with her first husband was moving around to different military bases (par. 4). In paragraph 46, Robert tells us about his contact with ham radio operators in places he would like to visit (Guam, Alaska). The TV show takes Robert and the narrator on a tour of France, Italy, and Portugal.

The way the narrator changes from disliking the blind man to getting along with him must be important to the meaning of the story. After the wife goes up to "get comfortable," suggesting that they might go to bed, the story focuses on the two men. Later she falls asleep on the sofa between them, and the narrator decides not to cover up her leg where her robe has fallen open, as if he has stopped being jealous. At this point the narrator decides he is "glad for the company" of Robert (par. 84). The cooperation between the two men is the turning point. The narrator is disgusted by blind people at first, and at the end he closes his eyes on purpose. The two men try to imagine something and build something together, and Robert is coaching the narrator. Robert says, "let's do her," and then says, "*You're* doing fine" (pars. 115, 118; emphasis added). I think it makes a difference that they imagine and draw a cathedral, not a flower or a cow or an airplane. It's something made by human beings, and it's religious. I don't think the men are converted to believing in God at the end, but this narrow-minded guy gets past whatever he's afraid of at night and finds some sort of inspiring feeling. I don't know why the wife has to be left out, but probably the husband couldn't open up if he was worrying about how close she is to Robert.

Rupton 3

The ideas of communicating or being in touch and travel seem connected to me. I think that the husband tries to tell this story about the cathedral the way his wife tried to write a poem. The narrator has had an exciting experience that gets him in touch with something beyond his small house. After drawing the cathedral, the narrator says that he "didn't feel like I was inside anything" (par. 135). Though I still didn't like the narrator, I felt more sympathy, and I thought the story showed that even this hostile person could open up.

Rupton 4

WORK CITED

Carver, Raymond. "Cathedral." *The Norton Introduction to Literature*, edited by Kelly J. Mays, portable 13th ed., W. W. Norton, 2020, pp. 27–38.

SAMPLE WRITING: ESSAY

Because it focuses on both narration and character in Raymond Carver's CATHE-DRAL, the following essay would be an appropriate response to essay assignments involving either of these elements. More specifically, Bethany Qualls here tackles a series of interesting, interlinked questions: How does narration contribute to characterization in the story? How, if at all, might the story's central character develop over its course?

Read this essay as you would one of your peers' drafts, looking for opportunities for the writer to improve her argument and presentation in revision. How effectively does the draft answer the questions it poses? Are there claims that might be developed further? other evidence that should be considered? How might the conclusion be strengthened? (For one critique and revision of the conclusion, see ch. 31, "The Literature Essay.")

For ease of reference, we have altered the citations in this essay to refer to paragraph numbers. Unless your instructor indicates otherwise, you should always follow convention by instead citing page numbers when writing about fiction. For more on citation, see chapter 34.

Bethany Qualls
Professor Netherton
English 301
16 January 2019

A Narrator's Blindness in Raymond Carver's "Cathedral"

A reader in search of an exciting plot will be pretty disappointed by Raymond Carver's "Cathedral" because the truth is nothing much happens. A suburban husband and wife receive a visit from her former boss, who is blind. After the wife falls asleep, the two men watch a TV program about cathedrals and eventually try to draw one. Along the way the three characters down a few cocktails and smoke a little pot. But that's about as far as the action goes. Instead of focusing on plot, then, the story really asks us to focus on the characters, especially the husband who narrates the story. Through his words even more than his actions, the narrator unwittingly shows us why nothing much happens to him by continually demonstrating his utter inability to connect with others or to understand himself.

The narrator's isolation is most evident in the distanced way he introduces his own story and the people in it. He does not name the other characters or himself, referring to them only by using labels such as "this blind man," "His wife," "my wife" (par. 1), and "The man [my wife] was going to marry" (par. 2). Even after the narrator's wife starts referring to their visitor as "Robert," the narrator keeps calling him "the blind man." These labels distance him from the other characters and also leave readers with very little connection to them.

At least three times the narrator notices that this habit of not naming or really acknowledging people is significant. Referring to his wife's "officer," he asks, "why should he have a name? he was the childhood sweetheart, and what more does he want?" (par. 5). Moments later he describes how freaked out he was when he listened to a tape the blind man had sent his wife and "heard [his] own name in the mouth of this . . . blind man [he] didn't even know!" (par. 5). Yet once the blind man arrives and begins to talk with the wife, the narrator finds himself "wait[ing] in vain to hear [his] name on [his] wife's sweet lips" and disappointed to hear "nothing of the sort" (par. 46). Simply using someone's name suggests an intimacy that the narrator avoids and yet secretly yearns for.

Also reinforcing the narrator's isolation and dissatisfaction with it are the awkward euphemisms and clichés he uses, which emphasize how disconnected he is from his own feelings and how uncomfortable he is with other people's. Referring to his wife's first husband, the narrator says it was he "who'd first enjoyed her favors" (par. 4), an antiquated expression even in 1983, the year the story was published. Such language reinforces our sense that the narrator cannot speak in language that is meaningful or heartfelt, especially when he tries to talk about emotions. He describes his wife's feelings for her first husband, for example, by using generic language and then just trailing off entirely: "she was in love with the guy, and he was in love with her, etc." (par. 2). When he refers to the blind man and his wife as "inseparable," he points out that this is, in fact, his "wife's word," not one that he's come up with (par. 16). And even when he admits that he would like to hear his wife talk about him (par. 46), he speaks in language that seems to come from books or movies rather than the heart.

Once the visit actually begins, the narrator's interactions and conversations with the other characters are even more awkward. His discomfort with the very idea of the visit is obvious to his wife and to the reader. As he says in his usual deadpan manner, "I wasn't enthusiastic about his visit" (par. 1). During the visit he sits silent when his wife and Robert are talking and then answers Robert's questions about his life and feelings with the shortest possible phrases: "How long had I been in my present position? (Three years.) Did I like my work? (I didn't.)" (par. 46). Finally, he tries to escape even that much involvement by simply turning on the TV and tuning Robert out.

Despite Robert's best attempt to make a connection with the narrator, the narrator resorts to a label again, saying that he "didn't want to be left alone with a blind man" (par. 57). Robert, merely "a blind man," remains a category, not a person, and the narrator can initially relate to Robert only by invoking the stereotypes about that category that he has learned "from the movies" (par. 1). He confides to the reader that he believes that blind people always wear dark glasses, that they never smoke (par. 43), and that a beard on a blind man is "too much" (par. 18). It follows that the narrator is amazed about the connection his wife and Robert have because he is unable to see Robert as a person like any

Qualls 3

other. "Who'd want to go to such a wedding in the first place?" (par. 16), he asks rhetorically about Robert's wedding to his wife, Beulah.

Misconceptions continue as the narrator assumes Beulah would "never receive the smallest compliment from her beloved," since the compliments he is thinking about are physical ones (par. 16). Interestingly, when faced with a name that is specific (Beulah), the narrator immediately assumes that he knows what the person with that name must be like ("a colored woman," par. 11), even though she is not in the room or known to him. Words fail or mislead the narrator in both directions, as he's using them and as he hears them.

There is hope for the narrator at the end as he gains some empathy and forges a bond with Robert over the drawing of a cathedral. That process seems to begin when the narrator admits to himself, the reader, and Robert that he is "glad for [Robert's] company" (par. 84) and, for the first time, comes close to disclosing the literally nightmarish loneliness of his life. It culminates in a moment of physical and emotional intimacy that the narrator admits is "like nothing else in my life up to now" (par. 131)—a moment in which discomfort with the very idea of blindness gives way to an attempt to actually experience blindness from the inside. Because the narrator has used words to distance himself from the world, it seems fitting that all this happens only when the narrator *stops* using words. They have a tendency to blind him.

However, even at the very end it isn't clear just whether or how the narrator has really changed. He does not completely interact with Robert but has to be prodded into action by him. By choosing to keep his eyes closed, he not only temporarily experiences blindness but also shuts out the rest of the world, since he "didn't feel like [he] was inside anything" (par. 135). Perhaps most important, he remains unable to describe his experience meaningfully, making it difficult for readers to decide whether or not he has really changed. For example, he says, "It was like nothing else in my life up to now" (par. 131), but he doesn't explain why this is true. Is it because he is doing something for someone else? Because he is thinking about the world from another's perspective? Because he feels connected to Robert? Because he is drawing a picture while probably drunk and high? There is no way of knowing.

It's possible that not feeling "inside anything" (par. 135) could be a feeling of freedom from his own habits of guardedness and insensitivity, his emotional "blindness." But even with this final hope for connection, for the majority of the story the narrator is a closed, judgmental man who isolates himself and cannot connect with others. The narrator's view of the world is one filled with misconceptions that the visit from Robert starts to slowly change, yet it is not clear what those changes are, how far they will go, or whether they will last.

Qualls 4

WORK CITED

Carver, Raymond. "Cathedral." *The Norton Introduction to Literature*, edited by Kelly J. Mays, portable 13th ed., W. W. Norton, 2020, pp. 27–38.

Understanding the Text

2 | PLOT

At its most basic, every story is an attempt to answer the question *What happened?* In some cases, this question is easy to answer. J. R. R. Tolkien's *The Lord of the Rings* trilogy (1954–55) is full of battles, chases, and other heart-stopping dramatic action; Mark Twain's *Adventures of Huckleberry Finn* (1884) relates Huck and Jim's adventures as they travel down the Mississippi River. Yet if we ask what happens in other works of fiction, our initial answer might well be "Not much." In one of the most pivotal scenes in Henry James's novel *The Portrait of a Lady* (1881), for example, a woman enters a room, sees a man sitting down and a woman standing up, and beats a hasty retreat. Not terribly exciting stuff, it would seem. Yet this event ends up radically transforming the lives of just about everyone in the novel. "On very tiny pivots do human lives turn" would thus seem to be one common message—or **theme**—of fiction.

All fiction, regardless of its subject matter, should make us ask, *What will happen next?* and *How will all this turn out?* And responsive readers of fiction will often pause to answer those questions, trying to articulate what their expectations are and how the story has shaped them. But great fiction and responsive readers are often just as interested in questions about *why* things happen and about *how* the characters' lives are affected as a result. These *how* and *why* questions are likely to be answered very differently by different readers of the very same fictional work; as a result, such questions will often generate powerful essays, whereas mainly factual questions about what happens in the work usually won't.

PLOT VERSUS ACTION, SEQUENCE, AND SUBPLOT

The term **plot** is sometimes used to refer to the events recounted in a fictional work. But in this book we instead use the term **action** in this way, reserving the term *plot* for the way the author sequences and paces the events so as to shape our response and interpretation.

The difference between action and plot resembles the difference between ancient chronicles that merely list the events of a king's reign in chronological order and more modern histories that make a meaningful sequence out of those events. As the British novelist and critic E. M. Forster put it, "The king died and then the queen died" is not a plot, for it has not been "tampered with." "The queen died after the king died" describes the same events, but the order in which they are reported has been changed. The reader of the first sentence focuses on the king first, the reader of the second on the queen. The second sentence, moreover, subtly encourages us to speculate about *why* things happened, not just *what* happened and *when*: Did the queen die *because* her husband did? If so, was her death the result of her grief? Or was she murdered by a rival who saw the king's death as the perfect opportunity to get rid of her, too? Though our two sentences describe the same action, each has quite a different focus, emphasis, effect, and meaning thanks to its *sequencing*—the precise order in which events are related.

Like chronicles, many fictional works do relate events in chronological order, starting with the earliest and ending with the latest. Folktales, for example, have this sort of plot. But fiction writers have other choices; events need not be recounted in the order in which they happened. Quite often, then, a writer will choose to mix things up, perhaps opening a story with the most recent event and then moving backward to show us all that led up to it. Still other stories begin somewhere in the middle of the action or, to use the Latin term, ***in medias res*** (literally, "in the middle of things"). In such plots, events that occurred before the story's opening are sometimes presented in **flashbacks**. Conversely, a story might jump forward in time to recount a later **episode** or event in a **flashforward**. **Foreshadowing** occurs when an author merely gives subtle clues or hints about what will happen later in the story.

Though we often talk about *the* plot of a fictional work, however, keep in mind that some works, especially longer ones, have two or more. A plot that receives significantly less time and attention than another is called a **subplot**.

PACE

In life, we sometimes have little choice about how long a particular event lasts. If you want a driver's license, you may have to spend a boring hour or two at the motor vehicle office. And much as you might prefer to relax and enjoy your lunch, occasionally you have to scarf it down during your drive to campus.

One of the pleasures of turning experiences into a story, however, is that doing so gives a writer more power over them. In addition to choosing the order in which to recount events, the writer can also decide how much time and attention to devote to each. *Pacing*, or the duration of particular episodes—especially relative to each other and to the time they would take in real life—is a vital tool of storytellers and another important factor to consider in analyzing plots. In all fiction, pace as much as sequence determines focus and emphasis, effect and meaning. And though it can be very helpful to differentiate between "fast-paced" and "slow-paced" fiction, all effective stories contain both faster and slower bits. When an author slows down to home in on a particular moment and scene, often introduced by a phrase such as "Later that evening" or "The day before Maggie fell down," we call this a **discriminated occasion**. For example, the first paragraph of Linda Brewer's *20/20* quickly and generally refers to events that occur over three days. Then Brewer suddenly slows down, pinpointing an incident that takes place on "[t]he third evening out." That episode or discriminated occasion consumes four paragraphs of the story, even though the action described in those paragraphs accounts for only a few minutes of Bill and Ruthie's time. Next the story devotes two more paragraphs to an incident that occurs "[t]he next evening." In the last paragraph, Brewer speeds up again, telling us about the series of "wonderful sights" Ruthie sees between Indiana and Spokane, Washington.

CONFLICTS

Whatever their sequence and pace, all plots hinge on at least one **conflict**—some sort of struggle—and its resolution. Conflicts may be *external* or *internal*. External conflicts arise between characters and something or someone outside themselves.

Adventure stories and action films often present this sort of conflict in its purest form, keeping us poised on the edge of our seats as James Bond or Jason Bourne struggles to outwit and outfight an archvillain intent on world domination or destruction. Yet external conflicts can also be much subtler, pitting an individual against nature or fate, against a social force such as racism or poverty, or against another person or group of people with a different way of looking at things (as in "20/20"). The cartoon below presents an external conflict of the latter type and one you may well see quite differently than the cartoonist does. How would you articulate that conflict?

Internal conflicts occur when a character struggles to reconcile two competing desires, needs, or duties, or two parts or aspects of himself: His head, for instance, might tell him to do one thing, his heart another.

Often, a conflict is simultaneously external and internal, as in the following brief folktale, in which a woman seems to struggle simultaneously with nature, with mortality, with God, and with her desire to hold on to someone she loves versus her need to let go.

JACOB AND WILHELM GRIMM
The Shroud

There was once a mother who had a little boy of seven years old, who was so handsome and lovable that no one could look at him without liking him, and she herself worshipped him above everything in the world. Now it so happened that he suddenly became ill, and God took him to himself; and for this the mother could not be comforted, and wept both day and night. But soon afterwards, when the child had been buried, it appeared by night in the places where it had sat and played during its life, and if the mother wept, it wept also, and, when morning came, it disappeared. As, however, the mother would not stop crying, it came one night, in the little white shroud in which it had been laid in its coffin, and with its wreath of flowers round its head, and stood on the bed at her feet, and said, "Oh, mother, do stop crying, or I shall never fall asleep in my coffin, for my shroud will not dry because of all thy tears which fall upon it." The mother was afraid when she heard that, and wept no more. The next night the child came again, and held a little light in its hand, and said, "Look, mother, my shroud is nearly dry, and I can rest in my grave." Then the mother gave her sorrow into God's keeping, and bore it quietly and patiently, and the child came no more, but slept in its little bed beneath the earth.

1812

· · ·

THE FIVE PARTS OF PLOT

Even compact and simple plots, like that of THE SHROUD, have the same five parts or phases as lengthy and complex plots: (1) exposition, (2) rising action, (3) climax or turning point, (4) falling action, and (5) conclusion or resolution. The following diagram, named *Freytag's pyramid* after the nineteenth-century German scholar Gustav Freytag, maps out a typical plot structure:

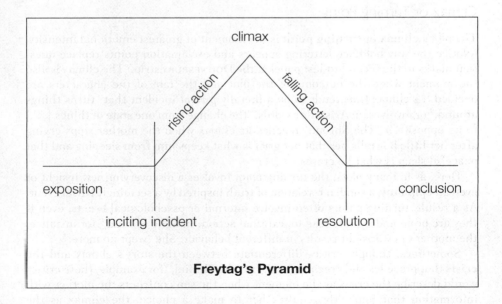

Freytag's Pyramid

Exposition

The first part of the plot, called the **exposition**, introduces the characters, their situations, and, usually, a time and place, giving us all the basic, background information we need to understand what is to come. In longer works of fiction, exposition may go on for paragraphs or even pages, and some exposition may well be deferred until later phases of the plot. But in our examples, the exposition is all up-front and brief: Trudeau's first panel shows us a teacher (or at least his words), a group of students, and a classroom; the Grimms' first sentence introduces a mother, her young son, and the powerful love she feels for him.

Exposition usually reveals some source or seed of potential conflict in the initial situation, of which the characters may be as yet unaware. In Trudeau's cartoon, the contrast between the talkative teacher, who expects "independent thought" from those in his class, and the silent, scribbling students suggests a conflict in the making. So, too, does the Grimms' statement that the mother "worshipped" her boy "above everything" else in a world in which nothing and no one lasts forever.

Rising Action

By suggesting a conflict, exposition may blend into the second phase of the plot, the **rising action**, which begins with an **inciting incident** or *destabilizing event*— that is, some action that destabilizes the initial situation and incites open conflict, as does the death of the little boy in the second sentence of "The Shroud." Typically, what keeps the action rising is a **complication**, an event that introduces a new conflict or intensifies an existing one. This happens in the third sentence of "The Shroud," when the mother begins to see her little boy every night, although he is dead and buried.

Climax or Turning Point

The plot's **climax** or **turning point** is the moment of greatest emotional intensity. (Notice the way boldface lettering appears and exclamation points replace question marks in the second-to-last panel of the DOONESBURY strip.) The climax is also the moment when the outcome of the plot and the fate of the characters are decided. (A climax thus tends to be a literally *pivotal* incident that "turns things around," or involves, in Aristotle's words, "the change from one state of things [. . .] to its opposite.") "The Shroud" reaches its climax when the mother stops crying after her little boy tells her that her grief is what keeps him from sleeping and that peaceful sleep is what he craves.

Here, as in many plots, the turning point involves a discovery or new insight or even an **epiphany**, a sudden revelation of truth inspired by a seemingly trivial event. As a result, turning points often involve internal or psychological events, even if they are prompted by, and lead to, external action. In "The Shroud," for instance, the mother's new insight results in different behavior: She "wept no more."

Sometimes, though, critics differentiate between the story's climax and the **crisis** that precedes and precipitates it. In "The Shroud," for example, these critics would describe the crisis as the moment when the son confronts the mother with information that implicitly requires her to make a choice, the climax as the moment when she makes it. This distinction might be especially helpful when you grapple with longer works of fiction in which much more time and action intervenes between crisis and climax.

Falling Action

The **falling action** brings a release of emotional tension and moves us toward the resolution of the conflict(s). This release occurs in "The Shroud" when the boy speaks for the second and last time, assuring his mother that her more peaceful demeanor is giving him peace as well.

In some works of fiction, resolution is achieved through an utterly unexpected twist, as in "Meanwhile, unknown to our hero, the marines were just on the other side of the hill," or "Susan rolled over in bed and realized the whole thing had been just a dream." Such a device is sometimes called a **deus ex machina**. (This Latin term literally means "god out of the machine" and derives from the ancient theatrical practice of using a machine to lower onto the stage a god who solves the problems of the human characters.)

Conclusion

Finally, just as a plot begins with a situation that is later destabilized, so its **conclusion** presents us with a new and at least somewhat stable situation—one that gives a sense of closure because the conflicts have been resolved, if only temporarily and not necessarily in the way we or the characters had expected. In "The Shroud," that resolution comes in the last sentence, in which the mother bears her grief "quietly and patiently" and the child peacefully sleeps his last sleep. The final *Doonesbury* panel presents us with a situation that is essentially the reverse of the one with which the strip begins—with the teacher silently slumped over his podium, his students suddenly talking to each other instead of scribbling down his words. Many plots instead end with a situation that outwardly looks almost identical to the one with which they began. But thanks to all that has happened between the story's beginning and its end, the final "steady state" at which the characters arrive can never be exactly the same as the one in which they started. A key question to ask at the end of a work of fiction is precisely why, as well as how, things are different.

Some fictional works may also include a final section called an **epilogue**, which ties up loose ends left dangling in the conclusion proper, updates us on what has happened to the characters since their conflicts were resolved, and/or provides some sort of commentary on the story's larger significance. (An epilogue is thus a little like this paragraph, which comes after we have concluded our discussion of the five phases of plot but still feel that there is one more term to deal with.)

A Note on *Dénouement*

In discussions of plot, you will very often encounter the French word **dénouement** (literally, "untying," as of a knot). In this anthology, however, we generally try to avoid using *dénouement* because it tends to be used in three different, potentially contradictory ways—as a synonym for *falling action*; as a synonym for *conclusion* or *resolution*; and even as a label for a certain kind of epilogue.

Plot Summary: An Example and an Exercise

Although any good **plot summary** should be a relatively brief recounting (or *synopsis*) of what happens in a work of fiction, it need not necessarily tell what happens in the same order that the work itself does. As a result, many a plot summary is in fact more like an action summary in the sense that we define the terms *action* and *plot* in this book. But unless you have a good reason for reordering events, it is generally a good idea to follow the plot. The following plot summary of Raymond Carver's CATHEDRAL does just that:

> The narrator is annoyed to learn that his wife's old friend Robert, a blind man who once employed her as a reader, is coming to visit the couple. The wife has corresponded with her friend for years via cassette tapes, describing the details of her early marriage, divorce, and remarriage to her husband, the narrator. Uncomfortable with the prospect of having a blind person in his home, the narrator is surprised by Robert's appearance and behavior: his booming voice and full beard are not what he expected, and he eats, drinks, and smokes marijuana with relish. After dinner the three watch television. After the narrator's wife has fallen asleep, a program about cathedrals begins. The narrator asks Robert if he knows what cathedrals look like or represent, and Robert, admitting that he does not, asks the narrator to draw one. With Robert's hand lying on top of his own, the narrator traces roofs, spires, arches, and even people. Eventually Robert instructs the narrator to close his eyes and continue drawing. The narrator reports that this experience was like nothing else in life up to now. (From "Raymond Carver: 'Cathedral.'" *Characters in Twentieth Century Literature*, book 2, Gale Research, 1995.)

Now try this yourself: Choose any of the stories in this anthology and write a one-paragraph plot summary. Then, in a paragraph or two, reflect on your choices about which details to include, which to omit, and how to order them (especially if you've deviated from the plot). What does your summary imply about the story's focus, meaning, and significance? Now repeat the exercise, summarizing the story in a different way and then reflecting on the significance and effect of the changes you've made.

Alternatively, try the same exercise with a friend who has also read the story: Each of you should write your own summary; then exchange them and (separately or together) write a few paragraphs comparing your summaries and reflecting on the significance of the similarities and differences.

COMMON PLOT TYPES

If most plots are essentially variations on the same five-part pattern, some plots have even more features in common. As you think back over the fiction you have read and the movies you have seen (not to mention the video games you have played), you might be surprised to discover just how many of their plots involve a quest—a character or characters' journey to find something or someone that seems, at least at first, of tremendous material or spiritual value. Traditionally, that requires a literal journey, the challenge being both to find and acquire the object and to return home with it. Such quests occur often in folktales and are a **convention** of chivalric **romance** and **epic**, in which the questing heroes are often men of high rank sent on their quests by someone with even greater power—a god, a wizard, a prophet, a king. And many works of modern fiction—from James Joyce's ARABY to Tolkien's *Lord of the Rings* to William Gibson's science-fiction classic *Neuromancer* (1984)—depend for their full effect on our knowledge of the conventions of traditional quest plots.

Many fictional works both ancient and modern also (or instead) follow patterns derived from the two most important and ancient forms (or subgenres) of drama—**tragedy** and **comedy**. Tragic plots, on the one hand, trace a downward movement centering on a character's fall from fortune into misfortune and isolation; they end unhappily, often with death. Comedic plots, on the other hand, tend to end happily, often with marriage or some other act of social integration and celebration.

• • •

As you read the stories in this chapter, or any other work of fiction, think about what sets each one apart when it comes to plot; how each uses variations on common plot conventions; how each generates, fulfills, and often frustrates our expectations about the action to come; and how each uses sequence, pace, and other techniques to endow action with both emotional charge and meaning. When it comes to action and plot, every good story holds its own surprises and offers a unique answer to the nagging question *What happened?*

Questions about Plot

- Read the first few paragraphs and then stop. What potential for conflict do you see here? What do you expect to happen in the rest of the story?
- What is the inciting incident or destabilizing event? How and why does this event destabilize the initial situation?
- How would you describe the conflict that ultimately develops? To what extent is it external, internal, or both? What, if any, complications or secondary conflicts arise?
- Where, when, how, and why does the story defy your expectations about what will happen next? What in this story—and in your experience of other stories—created these expectations?

- What is the climax or turning point? Why and how so?
- How is the conflict resolved? How and why might this resolution fulfill or defy your expectations? How and why is the situation at the end of the story different from what it was at the beginning?
- Looking back at the story as a whole, what seems especially significant and effective about its plot, especially in terms of the sequence and pace of the action?
- Does this plot follow any common plot pattern? Is there, for example, a quest of any kind? Or does this plot follow a tragic or comedic pattern?

RALPH ELLISON

(1914–94)

King of the Bingo Game

Named after nineteenth-century poet-essayist Ralph Waldo Emerson, Ralph Ellison lost his beloved father, a deliveryman and voracious reader, when he was only three. Ellison's mother thus had to raise her two sons by doing janitorial and domestic work, ensuring that the family endured "years of shabby rented rooms, hand-me-down clothing, second-rate meals, [and] sneers and slights from people better off," to quote biographer Arnold Rampersad. Oklahoma City nonetheless afforded Ellison opportunities he might not have had in the Jim Crow South, where his grandparents had once been slaves: He attended good schools; found mentors, both white and black; and learned to play the cornet. A jazz lover, Ellison studied classical music at Alabama's Tuskegee Institute, where he enrolled in 1933 in hopes of becoming a composer. When he headed to New York three years later, he meant to stay only long enough to make the money necessary to complete his studies. But with the encouragement of Langston Hughes and novelist Richard Wright, Ellison stayed put, publishing short stories, essays, book reviews, and then, in 1952, *Invisible Man*. The best-selling, National Book Award–winning novel is widely regarded as among the greatest of the twentieth century; it aims to reveal, said Ellison, "the human universals hidden within the plight of one who was both black and American." Thereafter, Ellison lectured and taught at various institutions, including New York University, and published *Shadow and Act* (1964), a collection of critical essays on the novelist's art. Upon his death from cancer in 1994, the literary world learned that he had been working steadily on a second major novel, begun in 1952, seemingly lost in a fire in 1967. The nearly completed manuscript was edited by Ellison's friend John F. Callahan and published as *Juneteenth* (1999).

The woman in front of him was eating roasted peanuts that smelled so good that he could barely contain his hunger. He could not even sleep and wished they'd hurry and begin the bingo game. There, on his right, two fellows were drinking wine out of a bottle wrapped in a paper bag, and he could hear soft gurgling in the dark. His stomach gave a low, gnawing growl. "If this was down South," he thought, "all I'd have to do is lean over and say, 'Lady, gimme a few of those peanuts, please ma'am,' and she'd pass me the bag and never think nothing of it." Or he could ask the fellows for a drink in the same way. Folks down South stuck together that way; they didn't even have to know you. But up here it was different. Ask somebody for something, and they'd think you were crazy. Well, I ain't crazy. I'm just broke, 'cause I got no birth certificate to get a job, and Laura 'bout to die 'cause we got no money for a doctor. But I ain't crazy. And yet a pinpoint of doubt was focused in his mind as he glanced toward the screen and saw the hero stealthily entering a dark room and sending the beam of a flashlight along a wall of bookcases. This is where he finds the trapdoor, he remembered. The man would pass abruptly through the wall and find the girl tied to a bed, her legs and arms spread wide, and her clothing torn to rags. He laughed softly to himself. He had seen the picture three times, and this was one of the best scenes.

On his right the fellow whispered wide-eyed to his companion, "Man, look ayonder!"

"Damn!"

"Wouldn't I like to have her tied up like that . . ."

"Hey! That fool's letting her loose!"

"Aw, man, he loves her."

"Love or no love!"

The man moved impatiently beside him, and he tried to involve himself in the scene. But Laura was on his mind. Tiring quickly of watching the picture he looked back to where the white beam filtered from the projection room above the balcony. It started small and grew large, specks of dust dancing in its whiteness as it reached the screen. It was strange how the beam always landed right on the screen and didn't mess up and fall somewhere else. But they had it all fixed. Everything was fixed. Now suppose when they showed that girl with her dress torn the girl started taking off the rest of her clothes, and when the guy came in he didn't untie her but kept her there and went to taking off his own clothes? *That* would be something to see. If a picture got out of hand like that those guys up there would go nuts. Yeah, and there'd be so many folks in here you couldn't find a seat for nine months! A strange sensation played over his skin. He shuddered. Yesterday he'd seen a bedbug on a woman's neck as they walked out into the bright street. But exploring his thigh through a hole in his pocket he found only goose pimples and old scars.

The bottle gurgled again. He closed his eyes. Now a dreamy music was accompanying the film and train whistles were sounding in the distance, and he was a boy again walking along a railroad trestle down South, and seeing the train coming, and running back as fast as he could go, and hearing the whistle blowing, and getting off the trestle to solid ground just in time, with the earth trembling

beneath his feet, and feeling relieved as he ran down the cinder-strewn embankment onto the highway, and looking back and seeing with terror that the train
had left the track and was following him right down the middle of the street,
and all the white people laughing as he ran screaming. . . .

10   "Wake up there, buddy! What the hell do you mean hollering like that? Can't
you see we trying to enjoy this here picture?"

He stared at the man with gratitude.

"I'm sorry, old man," he said. "I musta been dreaming."

"Well, here, have a drink. And don't be making no noise like that, damn!"

His hands trembled as he tilted his head. It was not wine, but whiskey. Cold
rye whiskey. He took a deep swoller, decided it was better not to take another,
and handed the bottle back to its owner.

15   "Thanks, old man," he said.

Now he felt the cold whiskey breaking a warm path straight through the
middle of him, growing hotter and sharper as it moved. He had not eaten all
day, and it made him light-headed. The smell of the peanuts stabbed him like a
knife, and he got up and found a seat in the middle aisle. But no sooner did he
sit than he saw a row of intense-faced young girls, and got up again, thinking,
"You chicks musta been Lindy-hopping[1] somewhere." He found a seat several
rows ahead as the lights came on, and he saw the screen disappear behind a
heavy red and gold curtain; then the curtain rising, and the man with the microphone and a uniformed attendant coming on the stage.

He felt for his bingo cards, smiling. The guy at the door wouldn't like it if
he knew about his having *five* cards. Well, not everyone played the bingo
game; and even with five cards he didn't have much of a chance. For Laura,
though, he had to have faith. He studied the cards, each with its different
numerals, punching the free center hole in each and spreading them neatly
across his lap; and when the lights faded he sat slouched in his seat so that
he could look from his cards to the bingo wheel with but a quick shifting of
his eyes.

Ahead, at the end of the darkness, the man with the microphone was pressing
a button attached to a long cord and spinning the bingo wheel and calling out the
number each time the wheel came to rest. And each time the voice rang out his
finger raced over the cards for the number. With five cards he had to move fast.
He became nervous; there were too many cards, and the man went too fast with
his grating voice. Perhaps he should just select one and throw the others away.
But he was afraid. He became warm. Wonder how much Laura's doctor would
cost? Damn that, watch the cards! And with despair he heard the man call three
in a row which he missed on all five cards. This way he'd never win. . . .

When he saw the row of holes punched across the third card, he sat paralyzed and heard the man call three more numbers before he stumbled forward,
screaming,

20   "Bingo! Bingo!"

"Let that fool up there," someone called.

"Get up there, man!"

---

1. Dancing the "Lindy" or "Lindy Hop," a popular form of the jitterbug that originated in Harlem.

He stumbled down the aisle and up the steps to the stage into a light so sharp and bright that for a moment it blinded him, and he felt that he had moved into the spell of some strange, mysterious power. Yet it was as familiar as the sun, and he knew it was the perfectly familiar bingo.

The man with the microphone was saying something to the audience as he held out his card. A cold light flashed from the man's finger as the card left his hand. His knees trembled. The man stepped closer, checking the card against the numbers chalked on the board. Suppose he had made a mistake? The pomade on the man's hair made him feel faint, and he backed away. But the man was checking the card over the microphone now, and he had to stay. He stood tense, listening.

"Under the O, forty-four," the man chanted. "Under the I, seven. Under the G, three. Under the B, ninety-six. Under the N, thirteen!" 25

His breath came easier as the man smiled at the audience.

"Yes sir, ladies and gentlemen, he's one of the chosen people!"

The audience rippled with laughter and applause.

"Step right up to the front of the stage."

He moved slowly forward, wishing that the light was not so bright. 30

"To win tonight's jackpot of $36.90 the wheel must stop between the double zero, understand?"

He nodded, knowing the ritual from the many days and nights he had watched the winners march across the stage to press the button that controlled the spinning wheel and receive the prizes. And now he followed the instructions as though he'd crossed the slippery stage a million prize-winning times.

The man was making some kind of joke, and he nodded vacantly. So tense had he become that he felt a sudden desire to cry and shook it away. He felt vaguely that his whole life was determined by the bingo wheel; not only that which would happen now that he was at last before it, but all that had gone before, since his birth, and his mother's birth and the birth of his father. It had always been there, even though he had not been aware of it, handing out the unlucky cards and numbers of his days. The feeling persisted, and he started quickly away. I better get down from here before I make a fool of myself, he thought.

"Here, boy," the man called. "You haven't started yet."

Someone laughed as he went hesitantly back. 35

"Are you all reet?"

He grinned at the man's jive talk, but no words would come, and he knew it was not a convincing grin. For suddenly he knew that he stood on the slippery brink of some terrible embarrassment.

"Where are you from, boy?" the man asked.

"Down South."

"He's from down South, ladies and gentlemen," the man said. "Where from? 40 Speak right into the mike."

"Rocky Mont," he said. "Rock' Mont, North Car'lina."

"So you decided to come down off that mountain to the U.S.," the man laughed. He felt that the man was making a fool of him, but then something cold was placed in his hand, and the lights were no longer behind him.

Standing before the wheel he felt alone, but that was somehow right, and he remembered his plan. He would give the wheel a short quick twirl. Just a touch of the button. He had watched it many times, and always it came close to double zero when it was short and quick. He steeled himself; the fear had left, and he felt a profound sense of promise, as though he were about to be repaid for all the things he'd suffered all his life. Trembling, he pressed the button. There was a whirl of lights, and in a second he realized with finality that though he wanted to, he could not stop. It was as though he held a high-powered line in his naked hand. His nerves tightened. As the wheel increased its speed it seemed to draw him more and more into its power, as though it held his fate; and with it came a deep need to submit, to whirl, to lose himself in its swirl of color. He could not stop it now. So let it be.

The button rested snugly in his palm where the man had placed it. And now he became aware of the man beside him, advising him through the microphone, while behind the shadowy audience hummed with noisy voices. He shifted his feet. There was still that feeling of helplessness within him, making part of him desire to turn back, even now that the jackpot was right in his hand. He squeezed the button until his fist ached. Then, like the sudden shriek of a subway whistle, a doubt tore through his head. Suppose he did not spin the wheel long enough? What could he do, and how could he tell? And then he knew, even as he wondered, that as long as he pressed the button, he could control the jackpot. He and only he could determine whether or not it was to be his. Not even the man with the microphone could do anything about it now. He felt drunk. Then, as though he had come down from a high hill into a valley of people, he heard the audience yelling.

45 "Come down from there, you jerk!"

"Let somebody else have a chance. . . ."

"Ole Jack thinks he done found the end of the rainbow. . . ."

The last voice was not unfriendly, and he turned and smiled dreamily into the yelling mouths. Then he turned his back squarely on them.

"Don't take too long, boy," a voice said.

50 He nodded. They were yelling behind him. Those folks did not understand what had happened to him. They had been playing the bingo game day in and night out for years, trying to win rent money or hamburger change. But not one of those wise guys had discovered this wonderful thing. He watched the wheel whirling past the numbers and experienced a burst of exaltation: This is God! This is the really truly God! He said it aloud, "This is God!"

He said it with such absolute conviction that he feared he would fall fainting into the footlights. But the crowd yelled so loud that they could not hear. These fools, he thought. I'm here trying to tell them the most wonderful secret in the world, and they're yelling like they gone crazy. A hand fell upon his shoulder.

"You'll have to make a choice now, boy. You've taken too long."

He brushed the hand violently away.

"Leave me alone, man. I know what I'm doing!"

The man looked surprised and held on to the microphone for support. And 55 because he did not wish to hurt the man's feelings he smiled, realizing with a sudden pang that there was no way of explaining to the man just why he had to stand there pressing the button forever.

"Come here," he called tiredly.

The man approached, rolling the heavy microphone across the stage.

"Anybody can play this bingo game, right?" he said.

"Sure, but . . ."

He smiled, feeling inclined to be patient with this slick looking white man 60 with his blue shirt and his sharp gabardine suit.

"That's what I thought," he said. "Anybody can win the jackpot as long as they get the lucky number, right?"

"That's the rule, but after all . . ."

"That's what I thought," he said. "And the big prize goes to the man who knows how to win it?"

The man nodded speechlessly.

"Well then, go on over there and watch me win like I want to. I ain't going to 65 hurt nobody," he said, "and I'll show you how to win. I mean to show the whole world how it's got to be done."

And because he understood, he smiled again to let the man know that he held nothing against him for being white and impatient. Then he refused to see the man any longer and stood pressing the button, the voices of the crowd reaching him like sounds in distant streets. Let them yell. All the Negroes down there were just ashamed because he was black like them. He smiled inwardly, knowing how it was. Most of the time he was ashamed of what Negroes did himself. Well, let them be ashamed for something this time. Like him. He was like a long thin black wire that was being stretched and wound upon the bingo wheel; wound until he wanted to scream; wound, but this time himself controlling the winding and the sadness and the shame, and because he did, Laura would be all right. Suddenly the lights flickered. He staggered backwards. Had something gone wrong? All this noise. Didn't they know that although he controlled the wheel, it also controlled him, and unless he pressed the button forever and forever and ever it would stop, leaving him high and dry, dry and high on this hard high slippery hill and Laura dead? There was only one chance; he had to do whatever the wheel demanded. And gripping the button in despair, he discovered with surprise that it imparted a nervous energy. His spine tingled. He felt a certain power.

Now he faced the raging crowd with defiance, its screams penetrating his eardrums like trumpets shrieking from a juke-box. The vague faces glowing in the bingo lights gave him a sense of himself that he had never known before. He was running the show, by God! They had to react to him, for he was their luck. This is *me*, he thought. Let the bastards yell. Then someone was laughing inside him, and he realized that somehow he had forgotten his own name. It was a sad, lost feeling to lose your name, and a crazy thing to do. That name had been given him by the white man who had owned his grandfather a long lost time ago down South. But maybe those wise guys knew his name.

"Who am I?" he screamed.

"Hurry up and bingo, you jerk!"

70   They didn't know either, he thought sadly. They didn't even know their own names, they were all poor nameless bastards. Well, he didn't need that old name; he was reborn. For as long as he pressed the button he was The-man-who-pressed-the-button-who-held-the-prize-who-was-the-King-of-Bingo. That was the way it was, and he'd have to press the button even if nobody understood, even though Laura did not understand.

"Live!" he shouted.

The audience quieted like the dying of a huge fan.

"Live, Laura, baby. I got holt of it now, sugar. Live!"

He screamed it, tears streaming down his face. "I got nobody but YOU!"

75   The screams tore from his very guts. He felt as though the rush of blood to his head would burst out in baseball seams of small red droplets, like a head beaten by police clubs. Bending over he saw a trickle of blood splashing the toe of his shoe. With his free hand he searched his head. It was his nose. God, suppose something has gone wrong? He felt that the whole audience had somehow entered him and was stamping its feet in his stomach and he was unable to throw them out. They wanted the prize, that was it. They wanted the secret for themselves. But they'd never get it; he would keep the bingo wheel whirling forever, and Laura would be safe in the wheel. But would she? It had to be, because if she were not safe the wheel would cease to turn; it could not go on. He had to get away, *vomit* all, and his mind formed an image of himself running with Laura in his arms down the tracks of the subway just ahead of an A train, running desperately *vomit* with people screaming for him to come out but knowing no way of leaving the tracks because to stop would bring the train crushing down upon him and to attempt to leave across the other tracks would mean to run into a hot third rail as high as his waist which threw blue sparks that blinded his eyes until he could hardly see.

He heard singing and the audience was clapping its hands.

> Shoot the liquor to him, Jim, boy!
> Clap-clap-clap
> Well a-calla the cop
> He's blowing his top!
> Shoot the liquor to him, Jim, boy!

Bitter anger grew within him at the singing. They think I'm crazy. Well let 'em laugh. I'll do what I got to do.

He was standing in an attitude of intense listening when he saw that they were watching something on the stage behind him. He felt weak. But when he turned he saw no one. If only his thumb did not ache so. Now they were applauding. And for a moment he thought that the wheel had stopped. But that was impossible, his thumb still pressed the button. Then he saw them. Two men in uniform beckoned from the end of the stage. They were coming toward him, walking in step, slowly, like a tap-dance team returning for a third encore. But their shoulders shot forward, and he backed away, looking wildly about. There was nothing to fight them with. He had only the long black cord which led to a plug somewhere back stage, and he couldn't use that because it operated the bingo wheel. He backed slowly, fixing the men with his eyes as his lips stretched over his teeth in a tight, fixed grin; moved toward the end of the stage and realizing that he couldn't go much further, for suddenly the cord became taut and he couldn't afford to break the cord. But he had to do something. The audience was howling. Suddenly he stopped dead, seeing the men halt, their legs lifted as in an interrupted step of a slow-motion dance. There was nothing to do but run in the other direction and he dashed forward, slipping and sliding. The men fell back, surprised. He struck out violently going past.

"Grab him!"

He ran, but all too quickly the cord tightened, resistingly, and he turned and 80
ran back again. This time he slipped them, and discovered by running in a circle before the wheel he could keep the cord from tightening. But this way he had to flail his arms to keep the men away. Why couldn't they leave a man alone? He ran, circling.

"Ring down the curtain," someone yelled. But they couldn't do that. If they did the wheel flashing from the projection room would be cut off. But they had him before he could tell them so, trying to pry open his fist, and he was wrestling and trying to bring his knees into the fight and holding on to the button, for it was his life. And now he was down, seeing a foot coming down, crushing his wrist cruelly, down, as he saw the wheel whirling serenely above.

"I can't give it up," he screamed. Then quietly, in a confidential tone, "Boys, I really can't give it up."

It landed hard against his head. And in the blank moment they had it away from him, completely now. He fought them trying to pull him up from the stage as he watched the wheel spin slowly to a stop. Without surprise he saw it rest at double-zero.

"You see," he pointed bitterly.

"Sure, boy, sure, it's O.K.," one of the men said smiling. 85

And seeing the man bow his head to someone he could not see, he felt very, very happy; he would receive what all the winners received.

But as he warmed in the justice of the man's tight smile he did not see the man's slow wink, nor see the bow-legged man behind him step clear of the swiftly descending curtain and set himself for a blow. He only felt the dull pain exploding in his skull, and he knew even as it slipped out of him that his luck had run out on the stage.

1944

QUESTIONS

1. Re-read the first paragraph of the story: What facts do we learn here about the protagonist, his background, and his situation? Why has he come to the theater, especially if he has already "seen the picture three times"? Does the paragraph introduce an actual or potential conflict?

2. What "wonderful thing" does the protagonist think he has "discovered" once he is onstage (par. 50)? Why can't or won't he let go of the button, even when the police arrive?

3. What is the effect of Ellison's choice not to give his protagonist a name? How might his namelessness shape your sense of what the story's central conflict is? What role does race play in that conflict?

JOYCE CAROL OATES
(b. 1938)
Where Are You Going, Where Have You Been?

A remarkably prolific writer of short stories, poems, novels, and nonfiction, Joyce Carol Oates was born in Lockport, New York. Daughter of a tool-and-die designer and his wife, she submitted her first novel to a publisher at fifteen and a few years later became the first person in her family to graduate from high school, later earning a BA from Syracuse University (1960) and an MA from the University of Wisconsin (1961). The recipient of countless awards, including a National Book Award for the novel *them* (1969), an O. Henry Special Award for Continuing Achievement (1970, 1986), a Pushcart Prize (1976), and at least four lifetime achievement awards, Oates taught for over thirty-five years at Princeton University, retiring in 2014. In addition to the novels *Mudwoman* (2012), *Daddy Love* (2013), *The Accursed* (2013), and *Carthage* (2014), Oates's recent works include the collections *Black Dahlia & White Rose* (2012) and *Evil Eye: Four Novellas of Love Gone Wrong* (2013), as well as the memoirs *A Widow's Story* (2011) and *The Lost Landscape: A Writer's Coming of Age* (2015).

For Bob Dylan

Her name was Connie. She was fifteen and she had a quick, nervous giggling habit of craning her neck to glance into mirrors or checking other people's faces to make sure her own was all right. Her mother, who noticed everything and knew everything and who hadn't much reason any longer to look at her own face, always scolded Connie about it. "Stop gawking at yourself. Who are you? You think you're so pretty?" she would say. Connie would raise her eyebrows at these familiar old complaints and look right through her mother, into a shadowy vision of herself as she was right at that moment: she knew she was pretty and that was everything. Her mother had been pretty once too, if you could believe those old snapshots in the album, but now her looks were gone and that was why she was always after Connie.

"Why don't you keep your room clean like your sister? How've you got your hair fixed—what the hell stinks? Hair spray? You don't see your sister using that junk."

Her sister, June, was twenty-four and still lived at home. She was a secretary in the high school Connie attended, and if that wasn't bad enough—with her in the same building—she was so plain and chunky and steady that Connie had to hear her praised all the time by her mother and her mother's sisters. June did this, June did that, she saved money and helped clean the house and cooked and Connie couldn't do a thing, her mind was all filled with trashy daydreams. Their father was away at work most of the time and when he came home he wanted supper and he read the newspaper at supper and after supper he went to bed. He didn't bother talking much to them, but around his bent head Connie's mother kept picking at her until Connie wished her mother was dead and she herself was dead and it was all over. "She makes me want to throw up sometimes," she complained to her friends. She had a high, breathless, amused voice that made everything she said sound a little forced, whether it was sincere or not.

There was one good thing: June went places with girl friends of hers, girls who were just as plain and steady as she, and so when Connie wanted to do that her mother had no objections. The father of Connie's best girl friend drove the girls the three miles to town and left them at a shopping plaza so they could walk through the stores or go to a movie, and when he came to pick them up again at eleven he never bothered to ask what they had done.

They must have been familiar sights, walking around the shopping plaza in their shorts and flat ballerina slippers that always scuffed on the sidewalk, with charm bracelets jingling on their thin wrists; they would lean together to whisper and laugh secretly if someone passed who amused or interested them. Connie had long dark blond hair that drew anyone's eye to it, and she wore part of it pulled up on her head and puffed out and the rest of it she let fall down her back. She wore a pullover jersey top that looked one way when she was at home and another way when she was away from home. Everything about her had two sides to it, one for home and one for anywhere that was not home: her walk, which could be childlike and bobbing, or languid enough to make anyone think she was hearing music in her head; her mouth, which was pale and smirking most of the time, but bright and pink on these evenings out; her laugh, which was cynical and drawling at home—"Ha, ha, very funny,"—but high-pitched and nervous anywhere else, like the jingling of the charms on her bracelet.

Sometimes they did go shopping or to a movie, but sometimes they went across the highway, ducking fast across the busy road, to a drive-in restaurant where older kids hung out. The restaurant was shaped like a big bottle, though squatter than a real bottle, and on its cap was a revolving figure of a grinning boy holding a hamburger aloft. One night in midsummer they ran across, breathless with daring, and right away someone leaned out a car window and invited them over, but it was just a boy from high school they didn't like. It made them feel good to be able to ignore him. They went up through the maze of parked and cruising cars to the bright-lit, fly-infested restaurant, their faces pleased and expectant as if they were entering a sacred building that loomed up out of the night to give them what haven and blessing they yearned for. They sat at the counter and crossed their legs at the ankles, their thin shoulders rigid with excitement, and listened to the music that made everything so good: the music was always in the background, like music at a church service; it was something to depend upon.

A boy named Eddie came in to talk with them. He sat backward on his stool, turning himself jerkily around in semicircles and then stopping and turning back again, and after a while he asked Connie if she would like something to eat. She said she would so she tapped her friend's arm on her way out—her friend pulled her face up into a brave, droll look—and Connie said she would meet her at eleven across the way. "I just hate to leave her like that," Connie said earnestly, but the boy said that she wouldn't be alone for long. So they went out to his car, and on the way Connie couldn't help but let her eyes wander over the windshields and faces all around her, her face gleaming with a joy that had nothing to do with Eddie or even this place; it might have been the music. She drew her shoulders up and sucked in her breath with the pure pleasure of being alive, and just at that moment she happened to glance at a face just a few feet away from hers. It was a boy with shaggy black hair, in a convertible jalopy[1] painted gold. He stared at her and then his lips widened into a grin. Connie slit her eyes at him and turned away, but she couldn't help glancing back and there he was, still watching her. He wagged a finger and laughed and said, "Gonna get you, baby," and Connie turned away again without Eddie noticing anything.

She spent three hours with him, at the restaurant where they ate hamburgers and drank Cokes in wax cups that were always sweating, and then down an alley a mile or so away, and when he left her off at five to eleven only the movie house was still open at the plaza. Her girl friend was there, talking with a boy. When Connie came up, the two girls smiled at each other and Connie said, "How was the movie?" and the girl said, "*You* should know." They rode off with the girl's father, sleepy and pleased, and Connie couldn't help but look back at the darkened shopping plaza with its big empty parking lot and its signs that were faded and ghostly now, and over at the drive-in restaurant where cars were still circling tirelessly. She couldn't hear the music at this distance.

Next morning June asked her how the movie was and Connie said, "So-so."

10   She and that girl and occasionally another girl went out several times a week, and the rest of the time Connie spent around the house—it was summer vacation—getting in her mother's way and thinking, dreaming about the boys she met. But all the boys fell back and dissolved into a single face that was not even a face but an idea, a feeling, mixed up with the urgent insistent pounding of the music and the humid night air of July. Connie's mother kept dragging her back to the daylight by finding things for her to do or saying suddenly, "What's this about the Pettinger girl?"

And Connie would say nervously, "Oh, her. That dope." She always drew thick clear lines between herself and such girls, and her mother was simple and kind enough to believe it. Her mother was so simple, Connie thought, that it was maybe cruel to fool her so much. Her mother went scuffling around the house in old bedroom slippers and complained over the telephone to one sister about the other, then the other called up and the two of them complained about the third one. If June's name was mentioned her mother's tone was approving, and if Connie's name was mentioned it was disapproving. This did not really mean she disliked Connie, and actually Connie thought that her mother preferred her to June just because she was prettier, but the two of them kept up a pretense of exasperation, a sense that they were tugging and struggling over something of little value to either of them. Sometimes, over coffee, they were almost friends,

---

1. Older car, often in poor condition.

but something would come up—some vexation that was like a fly buzzing suddenly around their heads—and their faces went hard with contempt.

One Sunday Connie got up at eleven—none of them bothered with church—and washed her hair so that it could dry all day long in the sun. Her parents and sister were going to a barbecue at an aunt's house and Connie said no, she wasn't interested, rolling her eyes to let her mother know just what she thought of it. "Stay home alone then," her mother said sharply. Connie sat out back in a lawn chair and watched them drive away, her father quiet and bald, hunched around so that he could back the car out, her mother with a look that was still angry and not at all softened through the windshield, and in the backseat poor old June, all dressed up as if she didn't know what a barbecue was, with all the running yelling kids and the flies. Connie sat with her eyes closed in the sun, dreaming and dazed with the warmth about her as if this were a kind of love, the caresses of love, and her mind slipped over onto thoughts of the boy she had been with the night before and how nice he had been, how sweet it always was, not the way someone like June would suppose but sweet, gentle, the way it was in movies and promised in songs; and when she opened her eyes she hardly knew where she was, the backyard ran off into weeds and a fencelike line of trees and behind it the sky was perfectly blue and still. The asbestos "ranch house"[2] that was now three years old startled her—it looked small. She shook her head as if to get awake.

It was too hot. She went inside the house and turned on the radio to drown out the quiet. She sat on the edge of her bed, barefoot, and listened for an hour and a half to a program called *XYZ Sunday Jamboree*, record after record of hard, fast, shrieking songs she sang along with, interspersed by exclamations from "Bobby King": "An' look here, you girls at Napoleon's—Son and Charley want you to pay real close attention to this song coming up!"

And Connie paid close attention herself, bathed in a glow of slow-pulsed joy that seemed to rise mysteriously out of the music itself and lay languidly about the airless little room, breathed in and breathed out with each gentle rise and fall of her chest.

After a while she heard a car coming up the drive. She sat up at once, star-   15
tled, because it couldn't be her father so soon. The gravel kept crunching all the way in from the road—the driveway was long—and Connie ran to the window. It was a car she didn't know. It was an open jalopy, painted a bright gold that caught the sunlight opaquely. Her heart began to pound and her fingers snatched at her hair, checking it, and she whispered, "Christ, Christ," wondering how she looked. The car came to a stop at the side door and the horn sounded four short taps, as if this were a signal Connie knew.

She went into the kitchen and approached the door slowly, then hung out the screen door, her bare toes curling down off the step. There were two boys in the car and now she recognized the driver: he had shaggy, shabby black hair that looked crazy as a wig and he was grinning at her.

"I ain't late, am I?" he said.

"Who the hell do you think you are?" Connie said.

"Toldja I'd be out, didn't I?"

---

2. Style of long, one-story houses common in suburban neighborhoods built between the 1940s and 1980s. *Asbestos*: fireproof building material once used in roofs and siding, but now known to be toxic.

20   "I don't even know who you are."

She spoke sullenly, careful to show no interest or pleasure, and he spoke in a fast, bright monotone. Connie looked past him to the other boy, taking her time. He had fair brown hair, with a lock that fell onto his forehead. His side-burns gave him a fierce, embarrassed look, but so far he hadn't even bothered to glance at her. Both boys wore sunglasses. The driver's glasses were metallic and mirrored everything in miniature.

"You wanta come for a ride?" he said.

Connie smirked and let her hair fall loose over one shoulder.

"Don'tcha like my car? New paint job," he said. "Hey."

25   "What?"

"You're cute."

She pretended to fidget, chasing flies away from the door.

"Don'tcha believe me, or what?" he said.

"Look, I don't even know who you are," Connie said in disgust.

30   "Hey, Ellie's got a radio, see. Mine broke down." He lifted his friend's arm and showed her the little transistor radio the boy was holding, and now Connie began to hear the music. It was the same program that was playing inside the house.

"Bobby King?" she said.

"I listen to him all the time. I think he's great."

"He's kind of great," Connie said reluctantly.

"Listen, that guy's *great*. He knows where the action is."

35   Connie blushed a little, because the glasses made it impossible for her to see just what this boy was looking at. She couldn't decide if she liked him or if he was a jerk, and so she dawdled in the doorway and wouldn't come down or go back inside. She said, "What's all that stuff painted on your car?"

"Can'tcha read it?" He opened the door very carefully, as if he were afraid it might fall off. He slid out just as carefully, planting his feet firmly on the ground, the tiny metallic world in his glasses slowing down like gelatine hardening, and in the midst of it Connie's bright-green blouse. "This here is my name, to begin with," he said. ARNOLD FRIEND was written in tarlike black letters on the side, with a drawing of a round, grinning face that reminded Connie of a pumpkin, except it wore sunglasses. "I wanta introduce myself. I'm Arnold Friend and that's my real name and I'm gonna be your friend, honey, and inside the car's Ellie Oscar, he's kinda shy." Ellie brought his transistor radio up to his shoulder and balanced it there. "Now, these numbers are a secret code, honey," Arnold Friend explained. He read off the numbers 33, 19, 17 and raised his eyebrows at her to see what she thought of that, but she didn't think much of it. The left rear fender had been smashed and around it was written, on the gleaming gold back-ground: DONE BY CRAZY WOMAN DRIVER. Connie had to laugh at that. Arnold Friend was pleased at her laughter and looked up at her. "Around the other side's a lot more—you wanta come and see them?"

"No."

"Why not?"

"Why should I?"

40   "Don'tcha wanta see what's on the car? Don'tcha wanta go for a ride?"

"I don't know."

"Why not?"

"I got things to do."

"Like what?"

"Things." 45

He laughed as if she had said something funny. He slapped his thighs. He was standing in a strange way, leaning back against the car as if he were balancing himself. He wasn't tall, only an inch or so taller than she would be if she came down to him. Connie liked the way he was dressed, which was the way all of them dressed: tight faded jeans stuffed into black, scuffed boots, a belt that pulled his waist in and showed how lean he was, and a white pullover shirt that was a little soiled and showed the hard small muscles of his arms and shoulders. He looked as if he probably did hard work, lifting and carrying things. Even his neck looked muscular. And his face was a familiar face, somehow; the jaw and chin and cheeks slightly darkened because he hadn't shaved for a day or two, and the nose long and hawklike, sniffing as if she was a treat he was going to gobble up and it was all a joke.

"Connie, you ain't telling the truth. This is your day set aside for a ride with me and you know it," he said, still laughing. The way he straightened and recovered from his fit of laughing showed that it had been all fake.

"How do you know what my name is?" she said suspiciously.

"It's Connie."

"Maybe and maybe not." 50

"I know my Connie," he said, wagging his finger. Now she remembered him even better, back at the restaurant, and her cheeks warmed at the thought of how she had sucked in her breath just at the moment she passed him—how she must have looked to him. And he had remembered her. "Ellie and I come out here especially for you," he said. "Ellie can sit in back. How about it?"

"Where?"

"Where what?"

"Where're we going?"

He looked at her. He took off the sunglasses and she saw how pale the skin 55 around his eyes was, like holes that were not in shadow but instead in light. His eyes were like chips of broken glass that catch the light in an amiable way. He smiled. It was as if the idea of going for a ride somewhere, to someplace, was a new idea to him.

"Just for a ride, Connie sweetheart."

"I never said my name was Connie," she said.

"But I know what it is. I know your name and all about you, lots of things," Arnold Friend said. He had not moved yet but stood still leaning back against the side of his jalopy. "I took a special interest in you, such a pretty girl, and found out all about you—like I know your parents and sister are gone somewheres and I know where and how long they're going to be gone, and I know who you were with last night, and your best girl friend's name is Betty. Right?"

He spoke in a simple lilting voice, exactly as if he was reciting the words to a song. His smile assured her that everything was fine. In the car Ellie turned up the volume on his radio and did not bother to look around at them.

60   "Ellie can sit in the backseat," Arnold Friend said. He indicated his friend with a casual jerk of his chin, as if Ellie did not count and she should not bother with him.

    "How'd you find out all that stuff?" Connie said.

    "Listen: Betty Schultz and Tony Fitch and Jimmy Pettinger and Nancy Pettinger," he said in a chant. "Raymond Stanley and Bob Hutter—"

    "Do you know all those kids?"

    "I know everybody."

65   "Look, you're kidding. You're not from around here."

    "Sure."

    "But—how come we never saw you before?"

    "Sure you saw me before," he said. He looked down at his boots, as if he was a little offended. "You just don't remember."

    "I guess I'd remember you," Connie said.

70   "Yeah?" He looked up at this, beaming. He was pleased. He began to mark time with the music from Ellie's radio, tapping his fists lightly together. Connie looked away from his smile to the car, which was painted so bright it almost hurt her eyes to look at it. She looked at that name, ARNOLD FRIEND. And up at the front fender was an expression that was familiar—MAN THE FLYING SAUCERS. It was an expression kids had used the year before but didn't use this year. She looked at it for a while as if the words meant something to her that she did not yet know.

    "What're you thinking about? Huh?" Arnold Friend demanded. "Not worried about your hair blowing around in the car, are you?"

    "No."

    "Think I maybe can't drive good?"

    "How do I know?"

75   "You're a hard girl to handle. How come?" he said. "Don't you know I'm your friend? Didn't you see me put my sign in the air when you walked by?"

    "What sign?"

    "My sign." And he drew an X in the air, leaning out toward her. They were maybe ten feet apart. After his hand fell back to his side the X was still in the air, almost visible. Connie let the screen door close and stood perfectly still inside it, listening to the music from her radio and the boy's blend together. She stared at Arnold Friend. He stood there so stiffly relaxed, pretending to be relaxed, with one hand idly on the door handle as if he was keeping himself up that way and had no intention of ever moving again. She recognized most things about him, the tight jeans that showed his thighs and buttocks and the greasy leather boots and the tight shirt, and even that slippery friendly smile of his, that sleepy dreamy smile that all the boys used to get across ideas they didn't want to put into words. She recognized all this and also the singsong way he talked, slightly mocking, kidding, but serious and a little melancholy, and she recognized the way he tapped one fist against the other in homage to the perpetual music behind him. But all these things did not come together.

    She said suddenly, "Hey, how old are you?"

    His smile faded. She could see then that he wasn't a kid, he was much older—thirty, maybe more. At this knowledge her heart began to pound faster.

80   "That's a crazy thing to ask. Can'tcha see I'm your own age?"

    "Like hell you are."

"Or maybe a coupla years older. I'm eighteen."

"Eighteen?" she said doubtfully.

He grinned to reassure her and lines appeared at the corners of his mouth. His teeth were big and white. He grinned so broadly his eyes became slits and she saw how thick the lashes were, thick and black as if painted with a black tar-like material. Then, abruptly, he seemed to become embarrassed and looked over his shoulder at Ellie. "*Him*, he's crazy," he said. "Ain't he a riot? He's a nut, a real character." Ellie was still listening to the music. His sunglasses told nothing about what he was thinking. He wore a bright-orange shirt unbuttoned halfway to show his chest, which was a pale, bluish chest and not muscular like Arnold Friend's. His shirt collar was turned up all around and the very tips of the collar pointed out past his chin as if they were protecting him. He was pressing the transistor radio up against his ear and sat there in a kind of daze, right in the sun.

"He's kinda strange," Connie said.   85

"Hey, she says you're kinda strange! Kinda strange!" Arnold Friend cried. He pounded on the car to get Ellie's attention. Ellie turned for the first time and Connie saw with shock that he wasn't a kid either—he had a fair, hairless face, cheeks reddened slightly as if the veins grew too close to the surface of his skin, the face of a forty-year-old baby. Connie felt a wave of dizziness rise in her at this sight and she stared at him as if waiting for something to change the shock of the moment, make it all right again. Ellie's lips kept shaping words, mumbling along with the words blasting in his ear.

"Maybe you two better go away," Connie said faintly.

"What? How come?" Arnold Friend cried. "We come out here to take you for a ride. It's Sunday." He had the voice of the man on the radio now. It was the same voice, Connie thought. "Don'tcha know it's Sunday all day? And honey, no matter who you were with last night, today you're with Arnold Friend and don't you forget it! Maybe you better step out here," he said, and this last was in a different voice. It was a little flatter, as if the heat was finally getting to him.

"No. I got things to do."

"Hey."   90

"You two better leave."

"We ain't leaving until you come with us."

"Like hell I am—"

"Connie, don't fool around with me. I mean—I mean, don't fool *around*," he said, shaking his head. He laughed incredulously. He placed his sunglasses on top of his head, carefully, as if he was indeed wearing a wig, and brought the stems down behind his ears. Connie stared at him, another wave of dizziness and fear rising in her so that for a moment he wasn't even in focus but was just a blur standing there against his gold car, and she had the idea that he had driven up the driveway all right but had come from nowhere before that and belonged nowhere and that everything about him and even about the music that was so familiar to her was only half real.

"If my father comes and sees you—"   95

"He ain't coming. He's at a barbecue."

"How do you know that?"

"Aunt Tillie's. Right now they're—uh—they're drinking. Sitting around," he said vaguely, squinting as if he was staring all the way to town and over to Aunt

Tillie's backyard. Then the vision seemed to get clear and he nodded energetically. "Yeah. Sitting around. There's your sister in a blue dress, huh? And high heels, the poor sad bitch—nothing like you, sweetheart! And your mother's helping some fat woman with the corn, they're cleaning the corn—husking the corn—"

"What fat woman?" Connie cried.

100 "How do I know what fat woman, I don't know every goddamn fat woman in the world!" Arnold Friend laughed.

"Oh, that's Mrs. Hornsby. . . . Who invited her?" Connie said. She felt a little light-headed. Her breath was coming quickly.

"She's too fat. I don't like them fat. I like them the way you are, honey," he said, smiling sleepily at her. They stared at each other for a while through the screen door. He said softly, "Now, what you're going to do is this: you're going to come out that door. You're going to sit up front with me and Ellie's going to sit in the back, the hell with Ellie, right? This isn't Ellie's date. You're my date. I'm your lover, honey."

"What? You're crazy—"

"Yes. I'm your lover. You don't know what that is but you will," he said. "I know that too. I know all about you. But look: it's real nice and you couldn't ask for nobody better than me, or more polite. I always keep my word. I'll tell you how it is, I'm always nice at first, the first time. I'll hold you so tight you won't think you have to try to get away or pretend anything because you'll know you can't. And I'll come inside you where it's all secret and you'll give in to me and you'll love me—"

105 "Shut up! You're crazy!" Connie said. She backed away from the door. She put her hands up against her ears as if she'd heard something terrible, something not meant for her. "People don't talk like that, you're crazy," she muttered. Her heart was almost too big now for her chest and its pumping made sweat break out all over her. She looked out to see Arnold Friend pause and then take a step toward the porch, lurching. He almost fell. But, like a clever drunken man, he managed to catch his balance. He wobbled in his high boots and grabbed hold of one of the porch posts.

"Honey?" he said. "You still listening?"

"Get the hell out of here!"

"Be nice, honey. Listen."

"I'm going to call the police—"

110 He wobbled again and out of the side of his mouth came a fast spat curse, an aside not meant for her to hear. But even this "Christ!" sounded forced. Then he began to smile again. She watched this smile come, awkward as if he was smiling from inside a mask. His whole face was a mask, she thought wildly, tanned down to his throat but then running out as if he had plastered makeup on his face but had forgotten about his throat.

"Honey—? Listen, here's how it is. I always tell the truth and I promise you this: I ain't coming in that house after you."

"You better not! I'm going to call the police if you—if you don't—"

"Honey," he said, talking right through her voice, "honey. I'm not coming in there but you are coming out here. You know why?"

She was panting. The kitchen looked like a place she had never seen before, some room she had run inside but that wasn't good enough, wasn't going to help her. The kitchen window had never had a curtain, after three years, and there were dishes in the sink for her to do—probably—and if you ran your hand across the table you'd probably feel something sticky there.

"You listening, honey? Hey?"

"—going to call the police—"

"Soon as you touch the phone I don't need to keep my promise and can come inside. You won't want that."

She rushed forward and tried to lock the door. Her fingers were shaking. "But why lock it," Arnold Friend said gently, talking right into her face. "It's just a screen door. It's just nothing." One of his boots was at a strange angle, as if his foot wasn't in it. It pointed out to the left, bent at the ankle. "I mean, anybody can break through a screen door and glass and wood and iron or anything else if he needs to, anybody at all, and specially Arnold Friend. If the place got lit up with a fire, honey, you'd come runnin' out into my arms, right into my arms an' safe at home— like you knew I was your lover and'd stopped fooling around. I don't mind a nice shy girl but I don't like no fooling around." Part of those words were spoken with a slight rhythmic lilt, and Connie somehow recognized them—the echo of a song from last year, about a girl rushing into her boyfriend's arms and coming home again—

Connie stood barefoot on the linoleum floor, staring at him. "What do you want?" she whispered.

"I want you," he said.

"What?"

"Seen you that night and thought, that's the one, yes sir. I never needed to look anymore."

"But my father's coming back. He's coming to get me. I had to wash my hair first—" She spoke in a dry, rapid voice, hardly raising it for him to hear.

"No, your daddy is not coming and yes, you had to wash your hair and you washed it for me. It's nice and shining and all for me. I thank you, sweetheart," he said with a mock bow, but again he almost lost his balance. He had to bend and adjust his boots. Evidently his feet did not go all the way down; the boots must have been stuffed with something so that he would seem taller. Connie stared out at him and behind him at Ellie in the car, who seemed to be looking off toward Connie's right, into nothing. Then Ellie said, pulling the words out of the air one after another as if he were just discovering them, "You want me to pull out the phone?"

"Shut your mouth and keep it shut," Arnold Friend said, his face red from bending over or maybe from embarrassment because Connie had seen his boots. "This ain't none of your business."

"What—what are you doing? What do you want?" Connie said. "If I call the police they'll get you, they'll arrest you—"

"Promise was not to come in unless you touch that phone, and I'll keep that promise," he said. He resumed his erect position and tried to force his shoulders back. He sounded like a hero in a movie, declaring something important. But he spoke too loudly and it was as if he was speaking to someone behind Connie. "I ain't made plans for coming in that house where I don't belong but just for you to come out to me, the way you should. Don't you know who I am?"

"You're crazy," she whispered. She backed away from the door but did not want to go into another part of the house, as if this would give him permission to come through the door. "What do you . . . you're crazy, you . . ."

115

120

125

"Huh? What're you saying, honey?"

130   Her eyes darted everywhere in the kitchen. She could not remember what it was, this room.

"This is how it is, honey: you come out and we'll drive away, have a nice ride. But if you don't come out we're gonna wait till your people come home and then they're all going to get it."

"You want that telephone pulled out?" Ellie said. He held the radio away from his ear and grimaced, as if without the radio the air was too much for him.

"I toldja shut up, Ellie," Arnold Friend said, "you're deaf, get a hearing aid, right? Fix yourself up. This little girl's no trouble and's gonna be nice to me, so Ellie keep to yourself, this ain't your date—right? Don't hem in on me, don't hog, don't crush, don't bird dog, don't trail me," he said in a rapid, meaningless voice, as if he were running through all the expressions he'd learned but was no longer sure which of them was in style, then rushing on to new ones, making them up with his eyes closed. "Don't crawl under my fence, don't squeeze in my chip-munk hole, don't sniff my glue, suck my Popsicle, keep your own greasy fingers on yourself!" He shaded his eyes and peered in at Connie, who was backed against the kitchen table. "Don't mind him, honey, he's just a creep. He's a dope. Right? I'm the boy for you and like I said, you come out here nice like a lady and give me your hand, and nobody else gets hurt, I mean, your nice old bald-headed daddy and your mummy and your sister in her high heels. Because listen: why bring them in this?"

"Leave me alone," Connie whispered.

135   "Hey, you know that old woman down the road, the one with the chickens and stuff—you know her?"

"She's dead!"

"Dead? What? You know her?" Arnold Friend said.

"She's dead—"

"Don't you like her?"

140   "She's dead—she's—she isn't here anymore—"

"But don't you like her, I mean, you got something against her? Some grudge or something?" Then his voice dipped as if he was conscious of a rudeness. He touched the sunglasses perched up on top of his head as if to make sure they were still there. "Now, you be a good girl."

"What are you going to do?"

"Just two things, or maybe three," Arnold Friend said. "But I promise it won't last long and you'll like me the way you get to like people you're close to. You will. It's all over for you here, so come on out. You don't want your people in any trouble, do you?"

She turned and bumped against a chair or something, hurting her leg, but she ran into the back room and picked up the telephone. Something roared in her ear, a tiny roaring, and she was so sick with fear that she could do nothing but listen to it—the telephone was clammy and very heavy and her fingers groped down to the dial but were too weak to touch it. She began to scream into the phone, into the roaring. She cried out, she cried for her mother, she felt her breath start jerking back and forth in her lungs as if it was something Arnold Friend was stabbing her with again and again with no tenderness. A noisy sorrowful wailing rose all about her and she was locked inside it the way she was locked inside this house.

After a while she could hear again. She was sitting on the floor with her wet   145
back against the wall.

Arnold Friend was saying from the door, "That's a good girl. Put the phone
back."

She kicked the phone away from her.

"No, honey. Pick it up. Put it back right."

She picked it up and put it back. The dial tone stopped.

"That's a good girl. Now, you come outside."   150

She was hollow with what had been fear but what was now just an empti-
ness. All that screaming had blasted it out of her. She sat, one leg cramped
under her, and deep inside her brain was something like a pin-point of light that
kept going and would not let her relax. She thought, *I'm not going to see my
mother again.* She thought, *I'm not going to sleep in my bed again.* Her bright-
green blouse was all wet.

Arnold Friend said, in a gentle-loud voice that was like a stage voice, "The
place where you came from ain't there anymore, and where you had in mind to go
is canceled out. This place you are now—inside your daddy's house—is nothing
but a cardboard box I can knock down anytime. You know that and always did
know it. You hear me?"

She thought, *I have got to think. I have got to know what to do.*

"We'll go out to a nice field, out in the country here where it smells so nice
and it's sunny," Arnold Friend said. "I'll have my arms tight around you so you
won't need to try to get away and I'll show you what love is like, what it does.
The hell with this house! It looks solid all right," he said. He ran his fingernail
down the screen and the noise did not make Connie shiver, as it would have the
day before. "Now, put your hand on your heart, honey. Feel that? That feels
solid too but we know better. Be nice to me, be sweet like you can because what
else is there for a girl like you but to be sweet and pretty and give in?—and get
away before her people get back?"

She felt her pounding heart. Her hand seemed to enclose it. She thought for   155
the first time in her life that it was nothing that was hers, that belonged to her,
but just a pounding, living thing inside this body that wasn't really hers either.

"You don't want them to get hurt," Arnold Friend went on. "Now, get up,
honey. Get up all by yourself."

She stood.

"Now, turn this way. That's right. Come over here to me.—Ellie, put that
away, didn't I tell you? You dope. You miserable creepy dope," Arnold Friend said.
His words were not angry but only part of an incantation. The incantation was
kindly. "Now, come out through the kitchen to me, honey, and let's see a smile,
try it, you're a brave, sweet little girl and now they're eating corn and hot dogs
cooked to bursting over an outdoor fire, and they don't know one thing about
you and never did and honey, you're better than them because not a one of them
would have done this for you."

Connie felt the linoleum under her feet; it was cool. She brushed her hair
back out of her eyes. Arnold Friend let go of the post tentatively and opened his
arms for her, his elbows pointing in toward each other and his wrists limp, to
show that this was an embarrassed embrace and a little mocking, he didn't want
to make her self-conscious.

160   She put out her hand against the screen. She watched herself push the door slowly open as if she was back safe somewhere in the other doorway, watching this body and this head of long hair moving out into the sunlight where Arnold Friend waited.

"My sweet little blue-eyed girl," he said in a half-sung sigh that had nothing to do with her brown eyes but was taken up just the same by the vast sunlit reaches of the land behind him and on all sides of him—so much land that Connie had never seen before and did not recognize except to know that she was going to it.

                                                                                    1966

QUESTIONS

1. At what specific points in the story do your expectations about "where you are going" change? Why and how so? How might these shifts in your expectations relate to Connie's?

2. To what extent is the major conflict in Oates's story external (between Connie and Arnold, Connie and her family, Connie and her milieu)? To what extent is it internal (within Connie herself)? Why might she act as she does at the story's end? What happens next, or does it matter?

3. Both Connie and Arnold Friend more than once suggest that he is, or should be, familiar to her. Aside from the fact she has seen him at least once before, why and how does he seem familiar? Why might that familiarity be significant, or how might it shape your sense of who Arnold is or what he might represent in the story?

3 | NARRATION AND POINT OF VIEW

When we read fiction, our sense of who is telling us the story is as important as what happens. Unlike drama, in which events are acted out in front of us, fiction is always mediated or represented to us by someone else, a **narrator**. Often a reader is very aware of the **voice** of a narrator telling the story, as if the words are being spoken aloud. Commonly, stories also reveal a distinct angle of vision or perspective from which the characters, events, and other aspects are viewed. Just as the verbal quality of narration is called the voice, the visual angle is called the **focus**. Focus acts much as a camera does, choosing the direction of our gaze, the framework in which we see things. Both voice and focus are generally considered together in the term **point of view**. To understand how a story is narrated, you need to recognize both voice and focus. These in turn shape what we know and care about as the plot unfolds, and they determine how close we feel to each character.

A story is said to be from a character's point of view, or a character is said to be a focal or focalizing character, if for the most part the action centers on that character, as if we see with that character's eyes or we watch that character closely. But the effects of narration certainly involve more than attaching a video camera to a character's head or tracking wherever the character moves. What about the spoken and unspoken words? In some stories, the narrator is a character, and we may feel as if we are overhearing his or her thoughts, whereas in other stories the narrator takes a very distant or critical view of the characters. At times a narrator seems more like a disembodied, unidentified voice. Prose fiction has many ways to convey speech and thought, so it is important to consider voice as well as focus when we try to understand the narration of a story.

Besides focus and voice, point of view encompasses more general matters of value. A story's narrator may explicitly endorse or subtly support whatever a certain character values, knows, or seeks, even when the character is absent or silent or unaware. Other narrators may treat characters and their interests with far more detachment. At the same time, the **style** and **tone** of the narrator's voice—from echoing the characters' feelings to mocking their pretentious speech or thoughts to stating their actions in formal diction—may convey clues that a character or a narrator's perspective is limited. Such discrepancies or gaps between vision and voice, intentions and understandings, or expectations and outcomes generate **irony**.

Sometimes the point of view shifts over the course of a narrative. Or the style of narration itself may change dramatically from one section to another. Bram Stoker's novel *Dracula* (1897), for example, is variously narrated through characters' journals and letters, as well as newspaper articles.

The point of view varies according to the narrator's position in the story and the grammatical person (for example, first or third) the narrative voice assumes.

These elements determine who is telling the story, whom it is about, and what information the reader has access to.

TYPES OF NARRATION

Third-Person Narration

A *third-person narrator* tells an unidentified listener or reader what happened, referring to all characters using the pronouns *he*, *she*, or *they*. Third-person narration is virtually always external, meaning that the narrator is not a character in the story and does not participate in its action. Even so, different types of third-person narration—omniscient, limited, and objective—provide the reader with various amounts and kinds of information about the characters.

An *omniscient* or *unlimited narrator* has access to the thoughts, perceptions, and experiences of more than one character (often of several), though such narrators usually focus selectively on a few important characters. A *limited narrator* is an external, third-person narrator who tells the story from a distinct point of view, usually that of a single character, revealing that character's thoughts and relating the action exclusively from his or her perspective. This focal character is also known as a **central consciousness**. Sometimes a limited narrator will reveal the thoughts and feelings of a small number of the characters in order to enhance the story told about the central consciousness. (Jane Austen's novel *Emma* [1815] includes a few episodes from Mr. Knightley's point of view to show what he thinks about Emma Woodhouse, the focal character, and her relationships.) Finally, an *objective narrator* does not explicitly report the characters' thoughts and feelings but may obliquely suggest them through the characters' speech and actions. Stories with objective narrators consist mostly of dialogue interspersed with minimal description.

First-Person Narration

Instead of using third-person narration, an author might choose to tell a story from the point of view of a *first-person narrator*. Most common is first-person singular narration, in which the narrator uses the pronoun *I*. The narrator may be a major or minor character within the story and therefore is an *internal narrator*. Notice that the first-person narrator may be telling a story mainly about someone else or about his or her own experience. Sometimes the first-person narrator addresses an **auditor**, a listener within the fiction whose possible reaction is part of the story.

One kind of narrator that is especially effective at producing irony is the *unreliable narrator*. First-person narrators may unintentionally reveal their flaws as they try to impress. Or narrators may make claims that other characters or the audience know to be false or distorted. Some fictions are narrated by villains, insane people, fools, liars, or hypocrites. When we resist a narrator's point of view and judge his or her flaws or misperceptions, we call that narrator unreliable. This does not mean that you should dismiss everything such a narrator says, but you should be on the alert for ironies.

Less common is the first-person plural, where the narrator uses the pronoun *we*. The plural may be used effectively to express the shared perspective of a community, particularly one that is isolated, unusually close-knit, and/or highly regulated. Elizabeth Gaskell's classic short novel *Cranford* (1853) is a good example. The narrator is a young woman who visits a community of genteel widows and spinsters in the English village of Cranford and describes their customs. At one point, a visitor arrives, Lady Glenmire, and all of Cranford society is in awe of her aristocratic rank and title. At an evening party, "We were all very silent at first. We were thinking what we could talk about, that should be high enough to interest My Lady. There had been a rise in the price of sugar, which, as preserving-time was near, was a piece of intelligence to all our housekeeping hearts, and would have been the natural topic if Lady Glenmire had not been by. But we were not sure if the Peerage ate preserves" (that is, whether aristocrats ate fruit jam). The high price of sugar doesn't seem "high enough" in another sense for a high-ranked guest to talk about.

The narrator of Cranford does sometimes refer to herself as "I" or address the reader as "you." So, too, does the narrator in Nobel Laureate Kazuo Ishiguro's *Never Let Me Go* (2005), another novel that portrays an isolated group that follows regulated customs. At a boarding school, a student, Polly, suddenly questions one of the rules: "*We* all went silent. Miss Lucy [the teacher] didn't often get cross, but when she did, *you* certainly knew about it, and we thought for a second Polly was for it [would be punished]. But then we saw Miss Lucy wasn't angry, just deep in thought. *I* remember feeling furious at Polly for so stupidly breaking the unwritten rule, but at the same time, being terribly excited about what answer Miss Lucy might give" (emphasis added). Ishiguro's narrator, like Gaskell's, resorts to different narrative perspectives and voices to represent the experience of both an entire community and one individual within it.

Second-Person Narration

Like narrators who refer to themselves as "we" throughout a work of fiction, *second-person narrators* who consistently speak to *you* are unusual. This technique has the effect of turning the reader into a character in the story. Jay McInerney, for example, in his novel *Bright Lights, Big City* (1984) employs the second-person voice, creating an effect similar to conversational anecdotes. But second-person narratives can instead sound much like instructional manuals or "how-to" books or like parents or other elders speaking to children.

TENSE

Along with the grammatical "person," the verb tense used has an effect on the narration of a story. Since narrative is so wrapped up in memory, most stories rely on the past tense. In contemporary fiction, however, the present tense is also frequently used. The present tense can lend an impression of immediacy, of frequent repetition, or of a dreamlike or magical state in which time seems suspended. An author might also use the present tense to create a conversational tone. Rarely, for a strange prophetic outlook, a narrator may even use the future tense, predicting what *will* happen.

NARRATOR VERSUS IMPLIED AUTHOR

As you consider how a story is being narrated, by whom, and from what point of view, how should you respond to the shifting points of view, tones of voice, and hints of critical distance or irony toward characters? Who is really shaping the story, and how do you know what is intended? Readers may answer the question

"Who is telling this story?" with the name of the author. It is more accurate and practical, however, to distinguish between the narrator who presents the story and the flesh-and-blood author who wrote it, even when the two are hard to tell apart. If you are writing an essay about a short story, you do not need to research the biography of the author or find letters or interviews in which the author comments on the work. This sort of biographical information may enrich your study of the story (it can be a good critical approach), but it is not *necessary* to an understanding of the text. And yet if you only consider the narrator when you interpret a story, you may find it difficult to account for the effects of distance and irony that come from a narrator's or a character's limitations. Many critics rely on the concept of the *implied author*, not to be confused with either the flesh-and-blood person who wrote the work or the narrator who relates the words to us. Most of the time, when we ask questions about the "author" of a work, we are asking about its implied author, the perspective and values that govern the whole work, including the narrator.

Why not ignore the idea of the narrator or the implied author? What's wrong with writing an essay about *Great Expectations* (1860–61) in which you refer only to the author, Charles Dickens? After all, his name is on the title page, and we know that this coming-of-age narrative has some autobiographical aspects. Yet from the first sentence of the novel it is clear that someone besides Charles Dickens is telling the story: Pip, the first-person narrator. "My father's family name being Pirrip, and my Christian name Philip, my infant tongue could make of both names nothing longer or more explicit than Pip. So, I called myself Pip, and came to be called Pip." The reader sympathizes with Pip, the focal character-narrator, as an abused child, but he is also flawed and makes mistakes, as Pip himself realizes when he has grown up and tells the story of his own life. The reader understands Pip's errors through the subtle guidance of the implied author who created the narrator and shaped the plot and other characters. How useful or accurate would it be to attribute Pip's character and experience to the real Charles Dickens? The facts of the flesh-and-blood author's life and his actual personality differ widely from the novel's character, which in turn may differ from what Charles Dickens himself consciously intended. Hence the value of referring to a narrator and an implied author of a work of fiction. In critical essays, these concepts help us discover what even the most detailed biography might never pin down: Who in fact was Charles Dickens, and what did he actually intend in *Great Expectations*?

Reading a story, we know that it consists of words on a page, but we imagine the narrator speaking to us, giving shape, focus, and voice to a particular history. At the same time, we recognize that the reader should not take the narrator's words as absolute truth, but rather as effects shaped by an implied author. The concept of the implied author helps keep the particulars of the real author's (naturally imperfect) personality and life out of the picture. But it also reminds us to distinguish between the act of writing the work and the imaginary utterance of "telling" the story: The narrator is *neither* the real nor the implied author.

Questions about Narration and Point of View

- Does the narrator speak in the first, second, or third person?
- Is the story narrated in the past or present tense? Does the verb tense affect your reading of it in any way?
- Does the narrator use a distinctive vocabulary, style, and tone, or is the language more standard and neutral?
- Is the narrator identified as a character, and if so, how much does he or she participate in the action?
- Does the narrator ever seem to speak to the reader directly (addressing "you") or explicitly state opinions or values?
- Do you know what every character is thinking, or only some characters, or none?
- Does the narrative voice or focus shift during the story or remain consistent?
- Do the narrator, the characters, and the reader all perceive matters in the same way, or are there differences in levels of understanding?

Because our responses to a work of fiction are largely guided by the designs and values implied in a certain way of telling the story, questions about narration and point of view can often lead to good essay topics. You might start by considering any other choices the implied author might have made and how these would change your reading of the story. As you read the stories in this chapter, imagine different voices and visions, different narrative techniques, in order to assess the specific effects of the particular types of narration and point of view. How would each story's meaning and effects change if its narrative voice or focus were different? Can you show the reader of your essay how the specific narration and point of view of a story contribute to its significant effects?

EDGAR ALLAN POE
(1809–49)
The Cask of Amontillado

Orphaned before he was three, Edgar Poe was adopted by John Allan, a wealthy Richmond businessman. Poe received his early schooling in Richmond and in England before a brief, unsuccessful stint at the University of Virginia. After serving for two years in the army, he was appointed to West Point in 1830 but expelled within the year for cutting classes. Living in Baltimore with his grandmother, aunt, and cousin Virginia (whom he married in 1835, when she was thirteen), Poe eked out a precarious living as an editor; his keen-edged reviews earned him numerous literary enemies. His two-volume *Tales of the Grotesque and Arabesque* received little critical attention when published in 1839, but his poem "The Raven" (1845) made him a literary celebrity. After his wife's death of tuberculosis in 1847, Poe, already an alcoholic, became increasingly erratic; two years later he died mysteriously in Baltimore.

The thousand injuries of Fortunato I had borne as I best could, but when he ventured upon insult I vowed revenge. You, who so well know the nature of my soul, will not suppose, however, that I gave utterance to a threat. *At length* I would be avenged; this was a point definitively settled—but the very definitiveness with which it was resolved precluded the idea of risk. I must not only punish but punish with impunity. A wrong is unredressed when retribution overtakes its redresser. It is equally unredressed when the avenger fails to make himself felt as such to him who has done the wrong.

It must be understood that neither by word nor deed had I given Fortunato cause to doubt my good will. I continued, as was my wont, to smile in his face, and he did not perceive that my smile *now* was at the thought of his immolation.

He had a weak point—this Fortunato—although in other regards he was a man to be respected and even feared. He prided himself upon his connoisseurship in wine. Few Italians have the true virtuoso spirit. For the most part their enthusiasm is adopted to suit the time and opportunity, to practice imposture upon the British and Austrian *millionaires*. In painting and gemmary, Fortunato, like his countrymen, was a quack, but in the matter of old wines he was sincere. In this respect I did not differ from him materially;—I was skilful in the Italian vintages myself, and bought largely whenever I could.

It was about dusk, one evening during the supreme madness of the carnival season, that I encountered my friend. He accosted me with excessive warmth, for he had been drinking much. The man wore motley. He had on a tight-fitting parti-striped dress,[1] and his head was surmounted by the conical cap and bells. I was so pleased to see him that I should never have done wringing his hand.

5   I said to him—"My dear Fortunato, you are luckily met. How remarkably well you are looking to-day. But I have received a pipe[2] of what passes for Amontillado, and I have my doubts."

"How?" said he. "Amontillado? A pipe? Impossible! And in the middle of the carnival!"

"I have my doubts," I replied; "and I was silly enough to pay the full Amontillado price without consulting you in the matter. You were not to be found, and I was fearful of losing a bargain."

"Amontillado!"

"I have my doubts."

10   "Amontillado!"

"And I must satisfy them."

"Amontillado!"

---

1. Fortunato wears a jester's costume (i.e., motley), not a woman's dress.
2. Large cask.

"As you are engaged, I am on my way to Luchresi. If any one has a critical turn it is he. He will tell me——"

"Luchresi cannot tell Amontillado from Sherry."

"And yet some fools will have it that his taste is a match for your own." 15

"Come, let us go."

"Whither?"

"To your vaults."

"My friend, no; I will not impose upon your good nature. I perceive you have an engagement. Luchresi——"

"I have no engagement;—come." 20

"My friend, no. It is not the engagement, but the severe cold with which I perceive you are afflicted. The vaults are insufferably damp. They are encrusted with nitre."[3]

"Let us go, nevertheless. The cold is merely nothing. Amontillado! You have been imposed upon. And as for Luchresi, he cannot distinguish Sherry from Amontillado."

Thus speaking, Fortunato possessed himself of my arm; and putting on a mask of black silk and drawing a *roquelaire*[4] closely about my person, I suffered him to hurry me to my palazzo.

There were no attendants at home; they had absconded to make merry in honour of the time. I had told them that I should not return until the morning, and had given them explicit orders not to stir from the house. These orders were sufficient, I well knew, to insure their immediate disappearance, one and all, as soon as my back was turned.

I took from their sconces two flambeaux,[5] and giving one to Fortunato, 25 bowed him through several suites of rooms to the archway that led into the vaults. I passed down a long and winding staircase, requesting him to be cautious as he followed. We came at length to the foot of the descent, and stood together upon the damp ground of the catacombs of the Montresors.

The gait of my friend was unsteady, and the bells upon his cap jingled as he strode.

"The pipe," said he.

"It is farther on," said I; "but observe the white web-work which gleams from these cavern walls."

He turned towards me, and looked into my eyes with two filmy orbs that distilled the rheum of intoxication.

"Nitre?" he asked, at length. 30

"Nitre," I replied. "How long have you had that cough?"

"Ugh! ugh! ugh!—ugh! ugh! ugh!—ugh! ugh! ugh!—ugh! ugh! ugh!—ugh! ugh! ugh!"

My poor friend found it impossible to reply for many minutes.

"It is nothing," he said, at last.

---

3. Potassium nitrate (saltpeter), a white mineral often found on the walls of damp caves and used in gunpowder.

4. Man's heavy, knee-length cloak.

5. That is, two torches from their wall brackets.

35   "Come," I said, with decision, "we will go back; your health is precious. You are rich, respected, admired, beloved; you are happy, as once I was. You are a man to be missed. For me it is no matter. We will go back; you will be ill, and I cannot be responsible. Besides, there is Luchresi——"

    "Enough," he said; "the cough is a mere nothing; it will not kill me. I shall not die of a cough."

    "True—true," I replied; "and, indeed, I had no intention of alarming you unnecessarily—but you should use all proper caution. A draught of this Medoc[6] will defend us from the damps."

    Here I knocked off the neck of a bottle which I drew from a long row of its fellows that lay upon the mould.

    "Drink," I said, presenting him the wine.

40   He raised it to his lips with a leer. He paused and nodded to me familiarly, while his bells jingled.

    "I drink," he said, "to the buried that repose around us."

    "And I to your long life."

    He again took my arm, and we proceeded.

    "These vaults," he said, "are extensive."

45   "The Montresors," I replied, "were a great and numerous family."

    "I forget your arms."

    "A huge human foot d'or,[7] in a field azure; the foot crushes a serpent rampant whose fangs are imbedded in the heel."

    "And the motto?"

    Nemo me impune lacessit.[8]

50   "Good!" he said.

    The wine sparkled in his eyes and the bells jingled. My own fancy grew warm with the Medoc. We had passed through long walls of piled skeletons, with casks and puncheons[9] intermingling, into the inmost recesses of the catacombs. I paused again, and this time I made bold to seize Fortunato by an arm above the elbow.

    "The nitre!" I said; "see, it increases. It hangs like moss upon the vaults. We are below the river's bed. The drops of moisture trickle among the bones. Come, we will go back ere it is too late. Your cough——"

    "It is nothing," he said; "let us go on. But first, another draught of the Medoc."

    I broke and reached him a flaçon of De Grâve. He emptied it at a breath. His eyes flashed with a fierce light. He laughed and threw the bottle upwards with a gesticulation I did not understand.

55   I looked at him in surprise. He repeated the movement—a grotesque one.

    "You do not comprehend?" he said.

    "Not I," I replied.

    "Then you are not of the brotherhood."

    "How?"

6. Like De Grâve (below), a French wine.
7. Of gold.
8. No one provokes me with impunity (Latin).
9. Large casks.

"You are not of the masons."[1]   60

"Yes, yes," I said; "yes, yes."

"You? Impossible! A mason?"

"A mason," I replied.

"A sign," he said, "a sign."

"It is this," I answered, producing from beneath the folds of my *roquelaire* a   65
trowel.

"You jest," he exclaimed, recoiling a few paces. "But let us proceed to the
Amontillado."

"Be it so," I said, replacing the tool beneath the cloak and again offering him
my arm. He leaned upon it heavily. We continued our route in search of the
Amontillado. We passed through a range of low arches, descended, passed on,
and descending again, arrived at a deep crypt, in which the foulness of the air
caused our flambeaux rather to glow than flame.

At the most remote end of the crypt there appeared another less spacious. Its
walls had been lined with human remains, piled to the vault overhead, in the
fashion of the great catacombs of Paris. Three sides of this interior crypt were
still ornamented in this manner. From the fourth side the bones had been
thrown down, and lay promiscuously upon the earth, forming at one point a
mound of some size. Within the wall thus exposed by the displacing of the
bones, we perceived a still interior crypt or recess, in depth about four feet, in
width three, in height six or seven. It seemed to have been constructed for no
especial use within itself, but formed merely the interval between two of the
colossal supports of the roof of the catacombs, and was backed by one of their
circumscribing walls of solid granite.

It was in vain that Fortunato, uplifting his dull torch, endeavoured to pry
into the depth of the recess. Its termination the feeble light did not enable us
to see.

"Proceed," I said; "herein is the Amontillado. As for Luchresi——"   70

"He is an ignoramus," interrupted my friend, as he stepped unsteadily forward, while I followed immediately at his heels. In an instant he had reached
the extremity of the niche, and finding his progress arrested by the rock, stood
stupidly bewildered. A moment more and I had fettered him to the granite. In
its surface were two iron staples, distant from each other about two feet, horizontally. From one of these depended a short chain, from the other a padlock.
Throwing the links about his waist, it was but the work of a few seconds to
secure it. He was too much astounded to resist. Withdrawing the key I stepped
back from the recess.

"Pass your hand," I said, "over the wall; you cannot help feeling the nitre.
Indeed, it is *very* damp. Once more let me *implore* you to return. No? Then I
must positively leave you. But I will first render you all the little attentions in my
power."

"The Amontillado!" ejaculated my friend, not yet recovered from his
astonishment.

"True," I replied; "the Amontillado."

---

1. Masons or Freemasons, an international secret society condemned by the Catholic Church. Montresor means by *mason* one who builds with stone, brick, etc.

75   As I said these words I busied myself among the pile of bones of which I have before spoken. Throwing them aside, I soon uncovered a quantity of building stone and mortar. With these materials and with the aid of my trowel, I began vigorously to wall up the entrance of the niche.

I had scarcely laid the first tier of the masonry when I discovered that the intoxication of Fortunato had in great measure worn off. The earliest indication I had of this was a low moaning cry from the depth of the recess. It was *not* the cry of a drunken man. There was then a long and obstinate silence. I laid the second tier, and the third, and the fourth; and then I heard the furious vibration of the chain. The noise lasted for several minutes, during which, that I might hearken to it with the more satisfaction, I ceased my labours and sat down upon the bones. When at last the clanking subsided, I resumed the trowel, and finished without interruption the fifth, the sixth, and the seventh tier. The wall was now nearly upon a level with my breast. I again paused, and holding the flambeaux over the mason-work, threw a few feeble rays upon the figure within.

A succession of loud and shrill screams, bursting suddenly from the throat of the chained form, seemed to thrust me violently back. For a brief moment I hesitated, I trembled. Unsheathing my rapier, I began to grope with it about the recess; but the thought of an instant reassured me. I placed my hand upon the solid fabric of the catacombs and felt satisfied. I reapproached the wall. I replied to the yells of him who clamoured. I re-echoed, I aided, I surpassed them in volume and in strength. I did this, and the clamourer grew still.

It was now midnight, and my task was drawing to a close. I had completed the eighth, the ninth and the tenth tier. I had finished a portion of the last and the eleventh; there remained but a single stone to be fitted and plastered in. I struggled with its weight; I placed it partially in its destined position. But now there came from out the niche a low laugh that erected the hairs upon my head. It was succeeded by a sad voice, which I had difficulty in recognizing as that of the noble Fortunato. The voice said—

"Ha! ha! ha!—he! he! he!—a very good joke, indeed—an excellent jest. We will have many a rich laugh about it at the palazzo—he! he! he!—over our wine—he! he! he!"

80   "The Amontillado!" I said.

"He! he! he!—he! he! he!—yes, the Amontillado. But is it not getting late? Will not they be awaiting us at the palazzo—the Lady Fortunato and the rest? Let us be gone."

"Yes," I said, "let us be gone."

"For the love of God, Montresor!"

"Yes," I said, "for the love of God!"

85   But to these words I hearkened in vain for a reply. I grew impatient. I called aloud—

"Fortunato!"

No answer. I called again—

"Fortunato!"

No answer still. I thrust a torch through the remaining aperture and let it fall within. There came forth in return only a jingling of the bells. My heart grew sick; it was the dampness of the catacombs that made it so. I hastened to make

an end of my labour. I forced the last stone into its position; I plastered it up.
Against the new masonry I re-erected the old rampart of bones. For the half of
a century no mortal has disturbed them. *In pace requiescat!*[2]

1846

QUESTIONS

1. What can the reader infer about Montresor's social position and character from
   hints in the text? What evidence does the story provide that Montresor is an unreliable narrator?
2. Who is the auditor, the "You," addressed in the first paragraph of THE CASK OF
   AMONTILLADO? When is the story being told? Why is it being told? How does your
   knowledge of the auditor and the occasion influence the story's effect?
3. What devices does Poe use to create and heighten the suspense in the story? Is the
   outcome ever in doubt?

GEORGE SAUNDERS

(b. 1958)

Puppy

When he described early twentieth-century American novelist Thomas Wolfe as "broken-hearted [. . .]
emotional, and in love with the world," George
Saunders might have been talking about himself. A
MacArthur "genius grant" recipient, Saunders is often
compared to Kurt Vonnegut for his extraordinary
ability to capture life's tragedy while simultaneously
making readers laugh. Saunders's fiction includes
intricately plotted social satires set in bizarre worlds. *The Brief and Frightening Reign of
Phil* (2005), for instance, takes place in Inner and Outer Horner, the former a place "so
small that only one Inner Hornerite at a time could fit inside." For all its fantastical,
humorous elements, however, his work often concerns a very down-to-earth issue: compassion and the lack thereof.

Born in Amarillo, Texas, Saunders recalls that his first story, written when he was in
third grade, depicted "a third-grade kid [. . .] who, in the face of an extreme manpower
shortage, gets drafted by the Marines and goes to fight in WWII." Despite such precocious
beginnings, Saunders took a circuitous path to his career as a writer, earning a degree in
geophysical engineering from the Colorado School of Mines (1981) and working as everything from a slaughterhouse knuckle-puller in Texas to an oil-exploration crewman in
Sumatra before entering the creative-writing program at Syracuse University (MA, 1988),
where he now teaches. This diverse experience informs the short stories, novellas, and
essays collected in *CivilWarLand in Bad Decline* (1996), *Pastoralia* (2000), *In Persuasion
Nation* (2006), *The Braindead Megaphone* (2007), and *Tenth of December* (2013). His first
novel is *Lincoln in the Bardo* (2017).

---

2. May he rest in peace (Latin).

Twice already Marie had pointed out the brilliance of the autumnal sun on the perfect field of corn, because the brilliance of the autumnal sun on the perfect field of corn put her in mind of a haunted house—not a haunted house she had ever actually seen but the mythical one that sometimes appeared in her mind (with adjacent graveyard and cat on a fence) whenever she saw the brilliance of the autumnal sun on the perfect etc. etc., and she wanted to make sure that, if the kids had a corresponding mythical haunted house that appeared in their minds whenever they saw the brilliance of the etc. etc., it would come up now, so that they could all experience it together, like friends, like college friends on a road trip, sans pot, ha ha ha!

But no. When she, a third time, said, "Wow, guys, check that out," Abbie said, "O.K., Mom, we get it, it's corn," and Josh said, "Not now, Mom, I'm Leavening my Loaves," which was fine with her; she had no problem with that, Noble Baker being preferable to Bra Stuffer, the game he'd asked for.

Well, who could say? Maybe they didn't even have any mythical vignettes in their heads. Or maybe the mythical vignettes they had in their heads were totally different from the ones she had in her head. Which was the beauty of it, because, after all, they were their own little people! You were just a caretaker. They didn't have to feel what *you* felt; they just had to be supported in feeling what *they* felt.

Still, wow, that cornfield was such a classic.

5   "Whenever I see a field like that, guys?" she said. "I somehow think of a haunted house!"

"Slicing Knife! Slicing Knife!" Josh shouted. "You nimrod machine! I chose that!"

Speaking of Halloween, she remembered last year, when their cornstalk column had tipped their shopping cart over. Gosh, how they'd laughed at that! Oh, family laughter was golden; she'd had none of that in her childhood, Dad being so dour and Mom so ashamed. If Mom and Dad's cart had tipped, Dad would have given the cart a despairing kick and Mom would have stridden purposefully away to reapply her lipstick, distancing herself from Dad, while she, Marie, would have nervously taken that horrid plastic Army man she'd named Brady into her mouth.

Well, in this family laughter was encouraged! Last night, when Josh had goosed her with his Game Boy, she'd shot a spray of toothpaste across the mirror and they'd all cracked up, rolling around on the floor with Goochie, and Josh had said, such nostalgia in his voice, "Mom, remember when Goochie was a puppy?" Which was when Abbie had burst into tears, because, being only five, she had no memory of Goochie as a puppy.

Hence this Family Mission. And as far as Robert? Oh, God bless Robert! There was a man. He would have no problem whatsoever with this Family Mission. She loved the way he had of saying "Ho HO!" whenever she brought home something new and unexpected.

10   "Ho HO!" Robert had said, coming home to find the iguana. "Ho HO!" he had said, coming home to find the ferret trying to get into the iguana cage. "We appear to be the happy operators of a menagerie!"

She loved him for his playfulness—you could bring home a hippo you'd put on a credit card (both the ferret and the iguana had gone on credit cards) and he'd just say "Ho HO!" and ask what the creature ate and what hours it slept and what the heck they were going to name the little bugger.

In the back seat, Josh made the *git-git-git* sound he always made when his Baker was in Baking Mode, trying to get his Loaves into the oven while fighting off various Hungry Denizens, such as a Fox with a distended stomach; such as a fey Robin that would improbably carry the Loaf away, speared on its beak, whenever it had succeeded in dropping a Clonking Rock on your Baker—all of which Marie had learned over the summer by studying the Noble Baker manual while Josh was asleep.

And it had helped, it really had. Josh was less withdrawn lately, and when she came up behind him now while he was playing and said, like, "Wow, honey, I didn't know you could do Pumpernickel," or "Sweetie, try Serrated Blade, it cuts quicker. Try it while doing Latch the Window," he would reach back with his non-controlling hand and swat at her affectionately, and yesterday they'd shared a good laugh when he'd accidentally knocked off her glasses.

So her mother could go right ahead and claim that she was spoiling the kids. These were not spoiled kids. These were *well-loved* kids. At least she'd never left one of them standing in a blizzard for two hours after a junior-high dance. At least she'd never drunkenly snapped at one of them, "I hardly consider you college material." At least she'd never locked one of them in a closet (a closet!) while entertaining a literal ditchdigger in the parlor.

Oh, God, what a beautiful world! The autumn colors, that glinting river, that 15 lead-colored cloud pointing down like a rounded arrow at that half-remodelled McDonald's standing above I-90 like a castle.

This time would be different, she was sure of it. The kids would care for this pet themselves, since a puppy wasn't scaly and didn't bite. ("Ho HO!" Robert had said the first time the iguana bit him. "I see you have an opinion on the matter!")

Thank you, Lord, she thought, as the Lexus flew through the cornfield. You have given me so much: struggles and the strength to overcome them; grace, and new chances every day to spread that grace around. And in her mind she sang out, as she sometimes did when feeling that the world was good and she had at last found her place in it, "Ho HO, ho HO!"

Callie pulled back the blind.

Yes. Awesome. It was still solved so *perfect*.

There was plenty for him to do back there. A yard could be a whole world, like 20 her yard when she was a kid had been a whole world. From the three holes in her wood fence she'd been able to see Exxon (Hole One) and Accident Corner (Hole Two), and Hole Three was actually two holes that if you lined them up right your eyes would do this weird crossing thing and you could play Oh My God I Am So High by staggering away with your eyes crossed, going "Peace, man, peace."

When Bo got older, it would be different. Then he'd need his freedom. But now he just needed not to get killed. Once they found him way over on Testament. And that was across I-90. How had he crossed I-90? She knew how. Darted. That's how he crossed streets. Once a total stranger called them from Hightown Plaza. Even Dr. Brile had said it: "Callie, this boy is going to end up dead if you don't get this under control. Is he taking the medication?"

Well, sometimes he was and sometimes he wasn't. The meds made him grind his teeth and his fist would suddenly pound down. He'd broken plates that way, and once a glass tabletop and got four stitches in his wrist.

Today he didn't need the medication because he was safe in the yard, because she'd fixed it so *perfect.*

He was out there practicing pitching by filling his Yankees helmet with pebbles and winging them at the tree.

25   He looked up and saw her and did the thing where he blew a kiss.

Sweet little man.

Now all she had to worry about was the pup. She hoped the lady who'd called would actually show up. It was a nice pup. White, with brown around one eye. Cute. If the lady showed up, she'd definitely want it. And if she took it Jimmy was off the hook. He'd hated doing it that time with the kittens. But if no one took the pup he'd do it. He'd have to. Because his feeling was, when you said you were going to do a thing and didn't do it, that was how kids got into drugs. Plus, he'd been raised on a farm, or near a farm anyways, and anybody raised on a farm knew that you had to do what you had to do in terms of sick animals or extra animals—the pup being not sick, just extra.

That time with the kittens, Jessi and Mollie had called him a murderer, getting Bo all worked up, and Jimmy had yelled, "Look, you kids, I was raised on a farm and you got to do what you got to do!" Then he'd cried in bed, saying how the kittens had mewed in the bag all the way to the pond, and how he wished he'd never been raised on a farm, and she'd almost said, "You mean near a farm" (his dad had run a car wash outside Cortland[3]), but sometimes when she got too smart-assed he would do this hard pinching thing on her arm while waltzing her around the bedroom, as if the place where he was pinching were like her handle, going, "I'm not sure I totally heard what you just said to me."

So, that time after the kittens, she'd only said, "Oh, honey, you did what you had to do."

30   And he'd said, "I guess I did, but it's sure not easy raising kids the right way."

And then, because she hadn't made his life harder by being a smart-ass, they had lain there making plans, like why not sell this place and move to Arizona and buy a car wash, why not buy the kids "Hooked on Phonics," why not plant tomatoes, and then they'd got to wrestling around and (she had no idea why she remembered this) he had done this thing of, while holding her close, bursting this sudden laugh/despair snort into her hair, like a sneeze, or like he was about to start crying.

Which had made her feel special, him trusting her with that.

So what she would love, for tonight? Was getting the pup sold, putting the kids to bed early, and then, Jimmy seeing her as all organized in terms of the pup, they could mess around and afterward lie there making plans, and he could do that laugh/snort thing in her hair again.

Why that laugh/snort meant so much to her she had no freaking idea. It was just one of the weird things about the Wonder That Was Her, ha ha ha.

35   Outside, Bo hopped to his feet, suddenly curious, because (here we go) the lady who'd called had just pulled up?

Yep, and in a nice car, too, which meant too bad she'd put "Cheap" in the ad.

---

3. City in upstate New York, between Binghamton and Syracuse.

Abbie squealed, "I love it, Mommy, I want it!," as the puppy looked up dimly from its shoebox and the lady of the house went trudging away and one-two-three-four plucked up four *dog turds* from the rug.

Well, wow, what a super field trip for the kids, Marie thought, ha ha (the filth, the mildew smell, the dry aquarium holding the single encyclopedia volume, the pasta pot on the bookshelf with an inflatable candy cane inexplicably sticking out of it), and although some might have been disgusted (by the spare tire *on the dining-room table*, by the way the glum mother dog, the presumed in-house pooper, was dragging its rear over the pile of clothing in the corner, in a sitting position, splay-legged, a moronic look of pleasure on her face), Marie realized (resisting the urge to rush to the sink and wash her hands, in part because the sink had *a basketball in it*) that what this really was was deeply sad.

Please do not touch anything, please do not touch, she said to Josh and Abbie, but just in her head, wanting to give the children a chance to observe her being democratic and accepting, and afterward they could all wash up at the half-remodelled McDonald's, as long as they just please please kept their hands out of their mouths, and God forbid they should rub their eyes.

The phone rang, and the lady of the house plodded into the kitchen, placing 40 the daintily held, paper-towel-wrapped turds *on the counter*.

"Mommy, I want it," Abbie said.

"I will definitely walk him like twice a day," Josh said.

"Don't say 'like,'" Marie said.

"I will definitely walk him twice a day," Josh said.

O.K., then, all right, they would adopt a white-trash dog. Ha ha. They could 45 name it Zeke, buy it a little corncob pipe and a straw hat. She imagined the puppy, having crapped on the rug, looking up at her, going, *Cain't hep it*. But no. Had she come from a perfect place? Everything was transmutable. She imagined the puppy grown up, entertaining some friends, speaking to them in a British accent: *My family of origin was, um, rather not, shall we say, of the most respectable* . . .

Ha ha, wow, the mind was amazing, always cranking out these—

Marie stepped to the window and, anthropologically pulling the blind aside, was shocked, so shocked that she dropped the blind and shook her head, as if trying to wake herself, shocked to see a young boy, just a few years younger than Josh, harnessed and chained to a tree, via some sort of doohickey by which—she pulled the blind back again, sure she could not have seen what she thought she had—

When the boy ran, the chain spooled out. He was running now, looking back at her, showing off. When he reached the end of the chain, it jerked and he dropped as if shot.

He rose to a sitting position, railed against the chain, whipped it back and forth, crawled to a bowl of water, and, lifting it to his lips, took a drink: a drink *from a dog's bowl*.

Josh joined her at the window. She let him look. He should know that the 50 world was not all lessons and iguanas and Nintendo. It was also this muddy simple boy tethered like an animal.

She remembered coming out of the closet to find her mother's scattered lingerie and the ditchdigger's metal hanger full of orange flags. She remembered waiting outside the junior high in the bitter cold, the snow falling harder, as she counted over and over to two hundred, promising herself each time that when she reached two hundred she would begin the long walk back—

God, she would have killed for just one righteous adult to confront her mother, shake her, and say, "You idiot, this is your child, your child you're—"

"So what were you guys thinking of naming him?" the woman said, coming out of the kitchen.

The cruelty and ignorance just radiated from her fat face, with its little smear of lipstick.

55   "I'm afraid we won't be taking him after all," Marie said coldly.

Such an uproar from Abbie! But Josh—she would have to praise him later, maybe buy him the Italian Loaves Expansion Pak—hissed something to Abbie, and then they were moving out through the trashed kitchen (past some kind of *crankshaft* on a cookie sheet, past a partial red pepper afloat *in a can of green paint*) while the lady of the house scuttled after them, saying, wait, wait, they could have it for free, please take it—she really wanted them to have it.

No, Marie said, it would not be possible for them to take it at this time, her feeling being that one really shouldn't possess something if one wasn't up to properly caring for it.

"Oh," the woman said, slumping in the doorway, the scrambling pup on one shoulder.

Out in the Lexus, Abbie began to cry softly, saying, "Really, that was the perfect pup for me."

60   And it was a nice pup, but Marie was not going to contribute to a situation like this in even the smallest way.

Simply was not going to do it.

The boy came to the fence. If only she could have said to him, with a single look, *Life will not necessarily always be like this. Your life could suddenly blossom into something wonderful. It can happen. It happened to me.*

But secret looks, looks that conveyed a world of meaning with their subtle blah blah blah—that was all bullshit. What was not bullshit was a call to Child Welfare, where she knew Linda Berling, a very no-nonsense lady who would snatch this poor kid away so fast it would make that fat mother's thick head spin.

Callie shouted, "Bo, back in a sec!," and, swiping the corn out of the way with her non-pup arm, walked until there was nothing but corn and sky.

65   It was so small it didn't move when she set it down, just sniffed and tumped over.

Well, what did it matter, drowned in a bag or starved in the corn? This way Jimmy wouldn't have to do it. He had enough to worry about. The boy she'd first met with hair to his waist was now this old man shrunk with worry. As far as the money, she had sixty hidden away. She'd give him twenty of that and go, "The people who bought the pup were super-nice."

Don't look back, don't look back, she said in her head as she raced away through the corn.

Then she was walking along Teallback Road like a sportwalker, like some lady who walked every night to get slim, except that she was nowhere near slim, she knew that, and she also knew that when sportwalking you did not wear jeans and unlaced hiking boots. Ha ha! She wasn't stupid. She just made bad choices. She remembered Sister Carol saying, "Callie, you are bright enough but you incline toward that which does not benefit you." *Yep, well, Sister, you got that right,* she said to the nun in her mind. But what the hell. What the heck. When things got easier moneywise, she'd get some decent tennis shoes and start walking and get slim. And start night school. Slimmer. Maybe medical technology. She was never going to be really slim. But Jimmy liked her the way she was, and she liked him the way he was, which maybe that's what love was, liking someone how he was and doing things to help him get even better.

Like right now she was helping Jimmy by making his life easier by killing something so he—no. All she was doing was walking, walking away from—

Pushing the words *killing puppy* out of her head, she put in her head the words *beautiful sunny day wow I'm loving this beautiful sunny day so much*— 70

What had she just said? That had been good. *Love was liking someone how he was and doing things to help him get better.*

Like Bo wasn't perfect, but she loved him how he was and tried to help him get better. If they could keep him safe, maybe he'd mellow out as he got older. If he mellowed out, maybe he could someday have a family. Like there he was now in the yard, sitting quietly, looking at flowers. Tapping with his bat, happy enough. He looked up, waved the bat at her, gave her that smile. Yesterday he'd been stuck in the house, all miserable. He'd ended the day screaming in bed, so frustrated. Today he was looking at flowers. Who was it that thought up that idea, the idea that had made today better than yesterday? Who loved him enough to think that up? Who loved him more than anyone else in the world loved him?

Her.

She did.

2007

QUESTIONS

1. At what point in PUPPY do you begin to realize that Saunders's third-person narrator might be speaking *like* or using the voice of his two main characters—first Marie, then Callie, and so on? How is your initial response and attitude to the characters different than it would be if one or both of these characters actually narrated the story (in the first person) or if the third-person narrator's voice were consistent throughout the story? What are the most distinctive features of each voice, and what do they tell us about the characters?

2. How does each of the subsequent shifts in both focus and voice affect the way you interpret and feel about the characters and their situations? What is the effect of Saunders's choice to end the story with Callie's point of view?

3. What is the effect of the way the narrator refers to real consumer products by using their brand names (Game Boy) and discusses (in some detail) entirely fictional ones like the games "Noble Baker" and "Bra Stuffer"? What do these details contribute to the story, especially in terms of our attitudes toward the various characters and their world (or our own)?

4 | CHARACTER

Robert Buss, *Dickens' Dream* (1870)

In the unfinished watercolor *Dickens' Dream*, the nineteenth-century writer peacefully dozes while above and around him float ghostly images of the hundreds of characters that people his novels and, apparently, his dreams. This image captures the undeniable fact that characters loom large in the experience of fiction, for both its writers and its readers. Speaking for the former, Elie Wiesel describes a novelist like himself as practically possessed by characters who "force the writer to tell their stories" because "they want to get out." As readers of fiction, we care about *what* happens and *how* mainly because it happens *to* someone. Indeed, without a "someone," it is unlikely that anything would happen at all.

It is also often a "someone," or the *who* of a story, that sticks with us long after we have forgotten the details of what, where, and how. In this way, characters sometimes seem to take on a life of their own, to float free of the texts where we first encounter them, and even to haunt us. You may know almost nothing about

Charles Dickens, but you probably have a vivid sense of his characters Ebenezer Scrooge and Tiny Tim from *A Christmas Carol* (1843).

A **character** is any personage in a literary work who acts, appears, or is referred to as playing a part. Though *personage* usually means a human being, it doesn't have to. Whole genres or subgenres of fiction are distinguished, in part, by the specific kinds of nonhuman characters they conventionally feature, whether alien species and intelligent machines (as in science fiction), animals (as in fables), or elves and monsters (as in traditional fairy tales and modern fantasy). All characters must have at least some human qualities, however, such as the ability to think, to feel pain, or to fall in love.

Evidence to Consider in Analyzing a Character: A Checklist

- the character's name
- the character's physical appearance
- objects and places associated with the character
- the character's actions
- the character's thoughts and speech, including
  - content (what he or she thinks or says)
  - timing (when he or she thinks or says it)
  - phrasing (how he or she thinks or says it)
- other characters' thoughts about the character
- other characters' comments to and about the character
- the narrator's comments about the character

HEROES AND VILLAINS VERSUS PROTAGONISTS AND ANTAGONISTS

A common term for the character with the leading male role is **hero**, the "good guy," who opposes the **villain**, or "bad guy." The leading female character is the **heroine**. Heroes and heroines are usually larger-than-life, stronger or better than most human beings, sometimes almost godlike. They are characters that a text encourages us to admire and even to emulate, so that the words *hero* and *heroine* can also be applied to especially admirable characters who do not play leading roles.

In most modern fiction, however, the leading character is much more ordinary, not so clearly or simply a "good guy." For that reason, it is usually more appropriate to use the older and more neutral terms **protagonist** and **antagonist** for the leading character and his or her opponent. These terms do not imply either the presence or the absence of outstanding virtue or vice.

The claim that a particular character either is or is not heroic might well make a good thesis for an essay, whereas the claim that he is or is not the protagonist generally won't. You might argue, for instance, that Montresor (in Poe's THE CASK

OF AMONTILLADO) or Ebenezer Scrooge (in Dickens's *A Christmas Carol*) is a hero, but most readers would agree that each is his story's protagonist. Like most rules, however, this one admits of exceptions. Some stories do leave open to debate the question of which character most deserves to be called the *protagonist*. In SONNY'S BLUES, for example, Sonny and his brother are equally central.

Controversial in a different way is a particular type of protagonist known as an **antihero**. Found mainly in fiction written since around 1850, an antihero, as the name implies, possesses traits that make him or her the opposite of a traditional hero. An antihero may be difficult to like or admire. One early and influential example of an antihero is the narrator-protagonist of Fyodor Dostoevsky's 1864 Russian-language novella *Notes from the Underground*—a man utterly paralyzed by his own hypersensitivity. More familiar and recent examples are Homer and Bart Simpson.

It would be a mistake to see the quality of a work of fiction as dependent on whether we find its characters likable or admirable, just as it would be wrong to assume that an author's outlook or values are the same as those of the protagonist. Often, the characters we initially find least likable or admirable may ultimately move and teach us the most.

MAJOR VERSUS MINOR CHARACTERS

The *major* or *main characters* are those we see more of over time; we learn more about them, and we think of them as more complex and, frequently, as more "realistic" than the *minor characters*, the figures who fill out the story.

Yet even though minor characters are less prominent and may seem less complex, they are ultimately just as indispensable to a story as major characters. Minor characters often play a key role in shaping our interpretations of, and attitudes toward, the major characters, and also in precipitating the changes that major characters undergo. For example, a minor character might function as a **foil**—a character that helps by way of contrast to reveal the unique qualities of another (especially main) character.

Questions about minor characters can lead to good essay topics precisely because such characters' significance to a story is not immediately apparent. Rather, we often have to probe the details of the story to formulate a persuasive interpretation of their roles.

FLAT VERSUS ROUND AND STATIC VERSUS DYNAMIC CHARACTERS

Characters that act from varied, often conflicting motives, impulses, and desires, and who seem to have psychological complexity, are said to be *round characters*; they can "surprise convincingly," as one critic puts it. Simple, one-dimensional characters that behave and speak in predictable or repetitive (if sometimes odd) ways are called *flat*. Sometimes characters seem round to us because our impression of them evolves as a story unfolds. Other times, the characters themselves—not just our impression of them—change as a result of events that occur in the story. A character that changes is *dynamic*; one that doesn't is *static*. Roundness and dynamism tend to go together. But the two qualities are distinct, and one does not require the other: Not all round characters are dynamic; not all dynamic characters are round.

Terms like *flat* and *round* or *dynamic* and *static* are useful so long as we do not let them harden into value judgments. Because flat characters are less complex than round ones, it is easy to assume they are artistically inferior; however, we need only think of the characters of Charles Dickens, many of whom are flat, to realize that this is not always the case. A truly original flat character with only one or two very distinctive traits or behavioral or verbal tics will often prove more memorable than a round one. Unrealistic as such characters might seem, in real life you probably know at least one or two people who can always be counted on to say or do pretty much the same thing every time you see them. Exaggeration can provide insight, as well as humor. Dickens's large gallery of lovable flat characters includes a middle-aged man who constantly pulls himself up by his own hair and an old one who must continually be "fluffed up" by others because he tends to slide right out of his chair. *South Park*'s Kenny is little more than a hooded orange snowsuit with a habit of dying in ever more outrageous ways only to come back to life over and over again.

STOCK CHARACTERS AND ARCHETYPES

Flat characters who represent a familiar, frequently recurring type—the dumb blond, the mad scientist, the inept sidekick, the plain yet ever-sympathetic best friend—are called *stock characters* because they seem to be pulled out of a stockroom of familiar, prefabricated figures. Characters that recur in the myths and literature of many different ages and cultures are instead called **archetypes**, though this term also applies to recurring elements other than characters (such as actions or symbols). One archetypal character is the trickster figure that appears in the guise of Brer Rabbit in the Uncle Remus stories, the spider Anansi in African and Afro-Caribbean folktales, the coyote in Native American folklore, and, perhaps, Bugs Bunny. Another such character is the **scapegoat**.

READING CHARACTER IN FICTION AND LIFE

On the one hand, we get to know characters in a work of fiction and try to understand them much as we do people in real life. We observe what they own and wear, what they look like and where they live, how they carry themselves and what expressions flit across their faces, how they behave in various situations, what they say and how they say it, what they don't say, what others say about them, and how others act in their presence. Drawing on all that evidence and on our own past experience of both literature and life, we try to deduce characters' motives and desires, their values and beliefs, their strengths and weaknesses—in short, to figure out what makes them tick and how they might react if circumstances changed. In our daily lives, being able to "read" other people in this way is a vital skill, one that, science suggests, we hone by reading fiction. The skills of observation and interpretation, the enlarged experience and capacity for empathy, that we develop in reading fiction can help us better navigate our real world.

On the other hand, however, fictional characters are not real people; they are imaginary personages crafted by authors. Fiction offers us a more orderly and expansive world than the one we inhabit every day—one in which each person, gesture, and word is a meaningful part of a coherent, purposeful design; one in which our responses to people are guided by a narrator and, ultimately, an author; one in which we can sometimes crawl inside other people's heads and know their thoughts; one in which we can get to know murderers and ministers, monsters and miracle workers—the sorts of people (or personages) we might be afraid, unwilling, or simply unable to meet or spend time with in real life.

In other words, fictional characters are the products not of nature, chance, or God, but of careful, deliberate **characterization**—the art and technique of representing fictional personages. In analyzing character, we thus need to consider not only who a character is and what precisely are his or her most important traits, motivations, and values, but also precisely how the text shapes our interpretation of, and degree of sympathy or admiration for, the character; what function the character serves in the narrative; and what the character might represent.

This last issue is important because all characters, no matter how individualized and idiosyncratic, ultimately become meaningful to us only if they represent something beyond the story, something bigger than themselves—a type of person, a particular set of values or way of looking at the world, a human tendency, a demographic group. When you set out to write about a character, consider how the story would be different without the character and what the author says or shows us through the character.

Direct and Indirect Characterization: An Example and an Exercise

The following conversation appears in the pages of a well-known nineteenth-century novel. Even without being familiar with this novel, you should be able to discern a great deal about the two characters that converse in this scene simply by carefully attending to what each says and how each says it. As you will see, one of the things that differentiates the two speakers is that they hold conflicting views of "character" itself:

"In what order you keep these rooms, Mrs Fairfax!" said I. "No dust, no canvas coverings: except that the air feels chilly, one would think they were inhabited daily."

"Why, Miss Eyre, though Mr Rochester's visits here are rare, they are always sudden and unexpected; and as I observed that it put him out to find everything swathed up, and to have a bustle of arrangement on his arrival, I thought it best to keep the rooms in readiness."

"Is Mr Rochester an exacting, fastidious sort of man?"

"Not particularly so; but he has a gentleman's tastes and habits, and he expects to have things managed in conformity to them."

"Do you like him? Is he generally liked?"

"O yes; the family have always been respected here. Almost all the land in this neighbourhood, as far as you can see, has belonged to the Rochesters time out of mind."

"Well, but leaving his land out of the question, do you like him? Is he liked for himself?"

"I have no cause to do otherwise than like him; and I believe he is considered a just and liberal landlord by his tenants: but he has never lived much amongst them."

"But has he no peculiarities? What, in short, is his character?"

"Oh! his character is unimpeachable, I suppose. He is rather peculiar, perhaps: he has travelled a great deal, and seen a great deal of the world, I should think. I daresay he is clever: but I never had much conversation with him."

"In what way is he peculiar?"

"I don't know—it is not easy to describe—nothing striking, but you feel it when he speaks to you: you cannot be always sure whether he is in jest or earnest, whether he is pleased or the contrary; you don't thoroughly understand him, in short—at least, I don't: but it is of no consequence, he is a very good master."

- What facts about the two speakers can you glean from this conversation? What do you infer about their individual outlooks, personalities, and values?
- What different definitions of the word *character* emerge here? How would you describe each speaker's view of what matters most in the assessment of character?

This scene—from Charlotte Brontë's *Jane Eyre* (1847)—demonstrates the first of the two major methods of presenting character—*indirect characterization* or showing (as opposed to *direct characterization* or telling). In this passage Brontë simply *shows* us what Jane (the narrator) and Mrs. Fairfax say and invites us to infer from their words who each character is (including the absent Mr. Rochester), how each looks at the world, and what each cares about.

Sometimes, however, authors present characters more directly, having narrators *tell* us what makes a character tick and what we are to think of him or her. Charlotte Brontë engages in both direct and indirect characterization in the paragraph of *Jane Eyre* that immediately follows the passage above. Here, Jane (the narrator) tells the reader precisely what she thinks this conversation reveals about Mrs. Fairfax, even as she reveals more about herself in the process:

> This was all the account I got from Mrs Fairfax of her employer and mine. There are people who seem to have no notion of sketching a character, or observing and describing salient points, either in persons or things: the good lady evidently belonged to this class; my queries puzzled, but did not draw her out. Mr Rochester was Mr Rochester in her eyes; a gentleman, a landed proprietor—nothing more: she inquired and searched no further, and evidently wondered at my wish to gain a more definite notion of his identity.

- How does Jane's interpretation of Mrs. Fairfax compare to yours?
- How and why might this paragraph corroborate or complicate your view of Jane herself?

Characters, Conventions, and Beliefs

Just as fiction and the characters that inhabit it operate by somewhat different rules than do the real world and real people, so the rules that govern particular fictional worlds and their characters differ from one another. As the critic James Wood argues,

> our hunger for the particular depth or reality level of a character is tutored by each writer, and adapts to the internal conventions of each book. This is how we can read W. G. Sebald one day and Virginia Woolf or Philip Roth the next, and not demand that each resemble the other. [. . . Works of fiction] tend to fail not when the characters are not vivid or "deep" enough, but when the [work] in question has failed to teach us how to adapt to its conventions, has failed to manage a specific hunger for its own characters, its own reality level.

Works of fiction in various subgenres differ widely in how they handle characterization. Were a folktale, for example, to depict more than a few, mainly flat, archetypal characters; to make us privy to its characters' thoughts; or to offer up detailed descriptions of their physiques and wardrobes, it would cease both to be a folktale and to yield the particular sorts of pleasures and insights that only a folktale can. By the same token, readers of a folktale miss out on its pleasures and insights if they expect the wrong things of its characters and modes of characterization.

But even within the same fictional subgenre, the treatment of character varies over time and across cultures. Such variations sometimes reflect profound differences in the way people understand human nature. Individuals and cultures hold conflicting views of what produces personality, whether innate factors such as genes, environmental factors such as upbringing, supernatural forces, unconscious impulses or drives, or some combination of these. Views differ as well as to whether character is simply an unchanging given or something that can change through experience, conversion, or an act of will. Some works of fiction tackle such issues head-on. But many others—especially from cultures or eras different from our own—may raise these questions for us simply because their modes of characterization imply an understanding of the self different from the one we take for granted.

We can thus learn a lot about our own values, prejudices, and beliefs by reading a wide array of fiction. Similarly, we learn from encountering a wide array of fictional characters, including those whose values, beliefs, and ways of life differ from our own.

The stories in this chapter vary widely in terms of the number and types of characters they depict and the techniques they use to depict them. In their pages, you will meet a range of diverse individuals—some complex and compelling, some utterly ordinary—struggling to make sense of the people around them just as you work to make sense of them and, through them, yourself.

Questions about Character

- Who is the protagonist, or might there be more than one? Why and how so? Which other characters, if any, are main or major characters? Which are minor characters?
- What are the protagonist's most distinctive traits, and what is most distinctive about his or her outlook and values? What motivates the character? What is it about the character that creates internal and/or external conflict?
- Which textual details and moments reveal most about this character? Which are most surprising or might complicate your interpretation of this character? How is your view of the character affected by what you *don't* know about him or her?
- What are the roles of other characters? Which, if any, functions as an antagonist? Which, if any, serves as a foil? Why and how so? How would the story as a whole (not just its action or plot) be different if any of these characters disappeared? What points might the author be raising or illustrating through each character?
- Which of the characters, or which aspects of the characters, does the text encourage us to sympathize with or to admire? to view negatively? Why and how so?
- Does your view of any character change over the course of the story, or do any of the characters themselves change? If so, when, how, and why?
- Does characterization tend to be indirect or direct in the story? What kinds of information do and don't we get about the characters, and how does the story tend to give us that information?

TONI MORRISON

(b. 1931)

Recitatif[1]

Born in Lorain, Ohio, a steel town on the shores of Lake Erie, Chloe Anthony Wofford was the first member of her family to attend college, graduating from Howard University in 1953 and earning an MA from Cornell. She taught at both Texas Southern University and at Howard before becoming an editor at Random House, where she worked for nearly twenty years. In such novels as *The Bluest Eye* (1969), *Sula* (1973), *Song of Solomon* (1977), *Beloved* (1987), *Paradise* (1998), *A Mercy* (2008), and *Home* (2012), Morrison traces the problems and possibilities faced by black Americans struggling with slavery and its aftermath in the United States. Morrison is also a gifted and influential critic and essayist: Her oft-cited *Playing in the Dark: Whiteness and the Literary Imagination* appeared in 1993, the same year she became the first African American author to win the Nobel Prize for Literature.

---

1. In classical music such as opera, a vocal passage that is sung in a speechlike manner.

My mother danced all night and Roberta's was sick. That's why we were taken to St. Bonny's. People want to put their arms around you when you tell them you were in a shelter, but it really wasn't bad. No big long room with one hundred beds like Bellevue.[2] There were four to a room, and when Roberta and me came, there was a shortage of state kids, so we were the only ones assigned to 406 and could go from bed to bed if we wanted to. And we wanted to, too. We changed beds every night and for the whole four months we were there we never picked one out as our own permanent bed.

It didn't start out that way. The minute I walked in and the Big Bozo introduced us, I got sick to my stomach. It was one thing to be taken out of your own bed early in the morning—it was something else to be stuck in a strange place with a girl from a whole other race. And Mary, that's my mother, she was right. Every now and then she would stop dancing long enough to tell me something important and one of the things she said was that they never washed their hair and they smelled funny. Roberta sure did. Smell funny, I mean. So when the Big Bozo (nobody ever called her Mrs. Itkin, just like nobody ever said St. Bonaventure)—when she said, "Twyla, this is Roberta. Roberta, this is Twyla. Make each other welcome." I said, "My mother won't like you putting me in here."

"Good," said Bozo. "Maybe then she'll come and take you home."

How's that for mean? If Roberta had laughed I would have killed her, but she didn't. She just walked over to the window and stood with her back to us.

5   "Turn around," said the Bozo. "Don't be rude. Now Twyla. Roberta. When you hear a loud buzzer, that's the call for dinner. Come down to the first floor. Any fights and no movie." And then, just to make sure we knew what we would be missing, *The Wizard of Oz.*"

Roberta must have thought I meant that my mother would be mad about my being put in the shelter. Not about rooming with her, because as soon as Bozo left she came over to me and said, "Is your mother sick too?"

"No," I said. "She just likes to dance all night."

"Oh," she nodded her head and I liked the way she understood things so fast. So for the moment it didn't matter that we looked like salt and pepper standing there and that's what the other kids called us sometimes. We were eight years old and got F's all the time. Me because I couldn't remember what I read or what the teacher said. And Roberta because she couldn't read at all and didn't even listen to the teacher. She wasn't good at anything except jacks, at which she was a killer: pow scoop pow scoop pow scoop.

We didn't like each other all that much at first, but nobody else wanted to play with us because we weren't real orphans with beautiful dead parents in the sky. We were dumped. Even the New York City Puerto Ricans and the upstate Indians ignored us. All kinds of kids were in there, black ones, white ones, even two Koreans. The food was good, though. At least I thought so. Roberta hated it and left whole pieces of things on her plate: Spam, Salisbury steak—even jello with fruit cocktail in it, and she didn't care if I ate what she wouldn't. Mary's idea of supper was popcorn and a can of Yoo-Hoo. Hot mashed potatoes and two weenies was like Thanksgiving for me.

---

2. Large New York City hospital best known for its psychiatric wards.

It really wasn't bad, St. Bonny's. The big girls on the second floor pushed us 10
around now and then. But that was all. They wore lipstick and eyebrow pencil and
wobbled their knees while they watched TV. Fifteen, sixteen, even, some of them
were. They were put-out girls, scared runaways most of them. Poor little girls who
fought their uncles off but looked tough to us, and mean. God did they look
mean. The staff tried to keep them separate from the younger children, but sometimes they caught us watching them in the orchard where they played radios and
danced with each other. They'd light out after us and pull our hair or twist our
arms. We were scared of them, Roberta and me, but neither of us wanted the
other one to know it. So we got a good list of dirty names we could shout back
when we ran from them through the orchard. I used to dream a lot and almost
always the orchard was there. Two acres, four maybe, of these little apple trees.
Hundreds of them. Empty and crooked like beggar women when I first came to
St. Bonny's but fat with flowers when I left. I don't know why I dreamt about that
orchard so much. Nothing really happened there. Nothing all that important, I
mean. Just the big girls dancing and playing the radio. Roberta and me watching.
Maggie fell down there once. The kitchen woman with legs like parentheses. And
the big girls laughed at her. We should have helped her up, I know, but we were
scared of those girls with lipstick and eyebrow pencil. Maggie couldn't talk. The
kids said she had her tongue cut out, but I think she was just born that way: mute.
She was old and sandy-colored and she worked in the kitchen. I don't know if she
was nice or not. I just remember her legs like parentheses and how she rocked
when she walked. She worked from early in the morning till two o'clock, and if
she was late, if she had too much cleaning and didn't get out till two-fifteen or so,
she'd cut through the orchard so she wouldn't miss her bus and have to wait
another hour. She wore this really stupid little hat—a kid's hat with ear flaps—
and she wasn't much taller than we were. A really awful little hat. Even for a
mute, it was dumb—dressing like a kid and never saying anything at all.
    "But what about if somebody tries to kill her?" I used to wonder about that.
"Or what if she wants to cry? Can she cry?"
    "Sure," Roberta said. "But just tears. No sounds come out."
    "She can't scream?"
    "Nope. Nothing."
    "Can she hear?"   15
    "I guess."
    "Let's call her," I said. And we did.
    "Dummy! Dummy!" She never turned her head.
    "Bow legs! Bow legs!" Nothing. She just rocked on, the chin straps of her baby-
boy hat swaying from side to side. I think we were wrong. I think she could hear
and didn't let on. And it shames me even now to think there was somebody in
there after all who heard us call her those names and couldn't tell on us.
    We got along all right, Roberta and me. Changed beds every night, got F's in 20
civics and communication skills and gym. The Bozo was disappointed in us,
she said. Out of 130 of us state cases, 90 were under twelve. Almost all were
real orphans with beautiful dead parents in the sky. We were the only ones
dumped and the only ones with F's in three classes including gym. So we got
along—what with her leaving whole pieces of things on her plate and being nice
about not asking questions.

I think it was the day before Maggie fell down that we found out our mothers were coming to visit us on the same Sunday. We had been at the shelter twenty-eight days (Roberta twenty-eight and a half) and this was their first visit with us. Our mothers would come at ten o'clock in time for chapel, then lunch with us in the teachers' lounge. I thought if my dancing mother met her sick mother it might be good for her. And Roberta thought her sick mother would get a big bang out of a dancing one. We got excited about it and curled each other's hair. After breakfast we sat on the bed watching the road from the window. Roberta's socks were still wet. She washed them the night before and put them on the radiator to dry. They hadn't, but she put them on anyway because their tops were so pretty—scalloped in pink. Each of us had a purple construction-paper basket that we had made in craft class. Mine had a yellow crayon rabbit on it. Roberta's had eggs with wiggly lines of color. Inside were cellophane grass and just the jelly beans because I'd eaten the two marshmallow eggs they gave us. The Big Bozo came herself to get us. Smiling she told us we looked very nice and to come downstairs. We were so surprised by the smile we'd never seen before, neither of us moved.

"Don't you want to see your mommies?"

I stood up first and spilled the jelly beans all over the floor. Bozo's smile disappeared while we scrambled to get the candy up off the floor and put it back in the grass.

She escorted us downstairs to the first floor, where the other girls were lining up to file into the chapel. A bunch of grown-ups stood to one side. Viewers mostly. The old biddies who wanted servants and the fags who wanted company looking for children they might want to adopt. Once in a while a grandmother. Almost never anybody young or anybody whose face wouldn't scare you in the night. Because if any of the real orphans had young relatives they wouldn't be real orphans. I saw Mary right away. She had on those green slacks I hated and hated even more now because didn't she know we were going to chapel? And that fur jacket with the pocket linings so ripped she had to pull to get her hands out of them. But her face was pretty—like always, and she smiled and waved like she was the little girl looking for her mother—not me.

25   I walked slowly, trying not to drop the jelly beans and hoping the paper handle would hold. I had to use my last Chiclet because by the time I finished cutting everything out, all the Elmer's was gone. I am left-handed and the scissors never worked for me. It didn't matter, though; I might just as well have chewed the gum. Mary dropped to her knees and grabbed me, mashing the basket, the jelly beans, and the grass into her ratty fur jacket.

"Twyla, baby. Twyla, baby!"

I could have killed her. Already I heard the big girls in the orchard the next time saying, "Twyyyyyla, baby!" But I couldn't stay mad at Mary while she was smiling and hugging me and smelling of Lady Esther dusting powder. I wanted to stay buried in her fur all day.

To tell the truth I forgot about Roberta. Mary and I got in line for the traipse into chapel and I was feeling proud because she looked so beautiful even in those ugly green slacks that made her behind stick out. A pretty mother on earth is better than a beautiful dead one in the sky even if she did leave you all alone to go dancing.

I felt a tap on my shoulder, turned, and saw Roberta smiling. I smiled back, but not too much lest somebody think this visit was the biggest thing that ever happened in my life. Then Roberta said, "Mother, I want you to meet my room-mate, Twyla. And that's Twyla's mother."

I looked up it seemed for miles. She was big. Bigger than any man and on her chest was the biggest cross I'd ever seen. I swear it was six inches long each way. And in the crook of her arm was the biggest Bible ever made.

Mary, simple-minded as ever, grinned and tried to yank her hand out of the pocket with the raggedy lining—to shake hands, I guess. Roberta's mother looked down at me and then looked down at Mary too. She didn't say anything, just grabbed Roberta with her Bible-free hand and stepped out of line, walking quickly to the rear of it. Mary was still grinning because she's not too swift when it comes to what's really going on. Then this light bulb goes off in her head and she says "That bitch!" really loud and us almost in the chapel now. Organ music whining; the Bonny Angels singing sweetly. Everybody in the world turned around to look. And Mary would have kept it up—kept calling names if I hadn't squeezed her hand as hard as I could. That helped a little, but she still twitched and crossed and uncrossed her legs all through service. Even groaned a couple of times. Why did I think she would come there and act right? Slacks. No hat like the grand-mothers and viewers, and groaning all the while. When we stood for hymns she kept her mouth shut. Wouldn't even look at the words on the page. She actually reached in her purse for a mirror to check her lipstick. All I could think of was that she really needed to be killed. The sermon lasted a year, and I knew the real orphans were looking smug again.

We were supposed to have lunch in the teachers' lounge, but Mary didn't bring anything, so we picked fur and cellophane grass off the mashed jelly beans and ate them. I could have killed her. I sneaked a look at Roberta. Her mother had brought chicken legs and ham sandwiches and oranges and a whole box of chocolate-covered grahams. Roberta drank milk from a thermos while her mother read the Bible to her.

Things are not right. The wrong food is always with the wrong people. Maybe that's why I got into waitress work later—to match up the right people with the right food. Roberta just let those chicken legs sit there, but she did bring a stack of grahams up to me later when the visit was over. I think she was sorry that her mother would not shake my mother's hand. And I liked that and I liked the fact that she didn't say a word about Mary groaning all the way through the service and not bringing any lunch.

Roberta left in May when the apple trees were heavy and white. On her last day we went to the orchard to watch the big girls smoke and dance by the radio. It didn't matter that they said, "Twyyyyyla, baby." We sat on the ground and breathed. Lady Esther. Apple blossoms. I still go soft when I smell one or the other. Roberta was going home. The big cross and the big Bible was coming to get her and she seemed sort of glad and sort of not. I thought I would die in that room of four beds without her and I knew Bozo had plans to move some other dumped kid in there with me. Roberta promised to write every day, which was really sweet of her because she couldn't read a lick so how could she write any-body. I would have drawn pictures and sent them to her but she never gave me her address. Little by little she faded. Her wet socks with the pink scalloped tops and her big serious-looking eyes—that's all I could catch when I tried to bring her to mind.

35   I was working behind the counter at the Howard Johnson's on the Thruway just before the Kingston exit. Not a bad job. Kind of a long ride from Newburgh,[3] but okay once I got there. Mine was the second night shift—eleven to seven. Very light until a Greyhound checked in for breakfast around six-thirty. At that hour the sun was all the way clear of the hills behind the restaurant. The place looked better at night—more like shelter—but I loved it when the sun broke in, even if it did show all the cracks in the vinyl and the speckled floor looked dirty no matter what the mop boy did.

It was August and a bus crowd was just unloading. They would stand around a long while: going to the john, and looking at gifts and junk-for-sale machines, reluctant to sit down so soon. Even to eat. I was trying to fill the coffee pots and get them all situated on the electric burners when I saw her. She was sitting in a booth smoking a cigarette with two guys smothered in head and facial hair. Her own hair was so big and wild I could hardly see her face. But the eyes. I would know them anywhere. She had on a powder-blue halter and shorts outfit and earrings the size of bracelets. Talk about lipstick and eyebrow pencil. She made the big girls look like nuns. I couldn't get off the counter until seven o'clock, but I kept watching the booth in case they got up to leave before that. My replacement was on time for a change, so I counted and stacked my receipts as fast as I could and signed off. I walked over to the booth, smiling and wondering if she would remember me. Or even if she wanted to remember me. Maybe she didn't want to be reminded of St. Bonny's or to have anybody know she was ever there. I know I never talked about it to anybody.

I put my hands in my apron pockets and leaned against the back of the booth facing them.

"Roberta? Roberta Fisk?"

She looked up. "Yeah?"

40   "Twyla."

She squinted for a second and then said, "Wow."

"Remember me?"

"Sure. Hey. Wow."

"It's been a while," I said, and gave a smile to the two hairy guys.

45   "Yeah. Wow. You work here?"

"Yeah," I said. "I live in Newburgh."

"Newburgh? No kidding?" She laughed then a private laugh that included the guys but only the guys, and they laughed with her. What could I do but laugh too and wonder why I was standing there with my knees showing out from under that uniform. Without looking I could see the blue and white triangle on my head, my hair shapeless in a net, my ankles thick in white oxfords. Nothing could have been less sheer than my stockings. There was this silence that came down right after I laughed. A silence it was her turn to fill up. With introductions, maybe, to her boyfriends or an invitation to sit down and have a Coke. Instead she lit a cigarette off the one she'd just finished and said, "We're on our way to the Coast. He's got an appointment with Hendrix." She gestured casually toward the boy next to her.

3. City on the Hudson River north of New York City.

"Hendrix? Fantastic," I said. "Really fantastic. What's she doing now?"

Roberta coughed on her cigarette and the two guys rolled their eyes up at the ceiling.

"Hendrix. Jimi Hendrix, asshole. He's only the biggest—Oh, wow. Forget it." 50

I was dismissed without anyone saying goodbye, so I thought I would do it for her.

"How's your mother?" I asked. Her grin cracked her whole face. She swallowed. "Fine," she said. "How's yours?"

"Pretty as a picture," I said and turned away. The backs of my knees were damp. Howard Johnson's really was a dump in the sunlight.

James is as comfortable as a house slipper. He liked my cooking and I liked his big loud family. They have lived in Newburgh all of their lives and talk about it the way people do who have always known a home. His grandmother is a porch swing older than his father and when they talk about streets and avenues and buildings they call them names they no longer have. They still call the A & P[4] Rico's because it stands on property once a mom and pop store owned by Mr. Rico. And they call the new community college Town Hall because it once was. My mother-in-law puts up jelly and cucumbers and buys butter wrapped in cloth from a dairy. James and his father talk about fishing and baseball and I can see them all together on the Hudson in a raggedy skiff. Half the population of Newburgh is on welfare now, but to my husband's family it was still some upstate paradise of a time long past. A time of ice houses and vegetable wagons, coal furnaces and children weeding gardens. When our son was born my mother-in-law gave me the crib blanket that had been hers.

But the town they remembered had changed. Something quick was in the 55 air. Magnificent old houses, so ruined they had become shelter for squatters and rent risks, were bought and renovated. Smart IBM[5] people moved out of their suburbs back into the city and put shutters up and herb gardens in their backyards. A brochure came in the mail announcing the opening of a Food Emporium. Gourmet food it said—and listed items the rich IBM crowd would want. It was located in a new mall at the edge of town and I drove out to shop there one day—just to see. It was late in June. After the tulips were gone and the Queen Elizabeth roses were open everywhere. I trailed my cart along the aisle tossing in smoked oysters and Robert's sauce and things I knew would sit in my cupboard for years. Only when I found some Klondike ice cream bars did I feel less guilty about spending James's fireman's salary so foolishly. My father-in-law ate them with the same gusto little Joseph did.

Waiting in the check-out line I heard a voice say, "Twyla!"

The classical music piped over the aisles had affected me and the woman leaning toward me was dressed to kill. Diamonds on her hand, a smart white summer dress. "I'm Mrs. Benson," I said.

"Ho. Ho. The Big Bozo," she sang.

4. Supermarket, part of a chain originally known as the Great Atlantic and Pacific Tea Company.
5. The International Business Machine Corporation, which had its executive headquarters in Poughkeepsie, New York.

For a split second I didn't know what she was talking about. She had a bunch of asparagus and two cartons of fancy water.

60   "Roberta!"

"Right."

"For heaven's sake. Roberta."

"You look great," she said.

"So do you. Where are you? Here? In Newburgh?"

65   "Yes. Over in Annandale."

I was opening my mouth to say more when the cashier called my attention to her empty counter.

"Meet you outside." Roberta pointed her finger and went into the express line.

I placed the groceries and kept myself from glancing around to check Roberta's progress. I remembered Howard Johnson's and looking for a chance to speak only to be greeted with a stingy "wow." But she was waiting for me and her huge hair was sleek now, smooth around a small, nicely shaped head. Shoes, dress, everything lovely and summery and rich. I was dying to know what happened to her, how she got from Jimi Hendrix to Annandale, a neighborhood full of doctors and IBM executives. Easy, I thought. Everything is so easy for them. They think they own the world.

"How long," I asked her. "How long have you been here?"

70   "A year. I got married to a man who lives here. And you, you're married too, right? Benson, you said."

"Yeah. James Benson."

"And is he nice?"

"Oh, is he nice?"

"Well, is he?" Roberta's eyes were steady as though she really meant the question and wanted an answer.

75   "He's wonderful, Roberta. Wonderful."

"So you're happy."

"Very."

"That's good," she said and nodded her head. "I always hoped you'd be happy. Any kids? I know you have kids."

"One. A boy. How about you?"

80   "Four."

"Four?"

She laughed. "Step kids. He's a widower."

"Oh."

"Got a minute? Let's have a coffee."

85   I thought about the Klondikes melting and the inconvenience of going all the way to my car and putting the bags in the trunk. Served me right for buying all that stuff I didn't need. Roberta was ahead of me.

"Put them in my car. It's right here."

And then I saw the dark blue limousine.

"You married a Chinaman?"

"No," she laughed. "He's the driver."

90   "Oh, my. If the Big Bozo could see you now."

We both giggled. Really giggled. Suddenly, in just a pulse beat, twenty years disappeared and all of it came rushing back. The big girls (whom we called gar girls—Roberta's misheard word for the evil stone faces described in a civics class) there dancing in the orchard, the ploppy mashed potatoes, the double weenies, the Spam with pineapple. We went into the coffee shop holding on to one another and I tried to think why we were glad to see each other this time and not before. Once, twelve years ago, we passed like strangers. A black girl and a white girl meeting in a Howard Johnson's on the road and having nothing to say. One in a blue and white triangle waitress hat—the other on her way to see Hendrix. Now we were behaving like sisters separated for much too long. Those four short months were nothing in time. Maybe it was the thing itself. Just being there, together. Two little girls who knew what nobody else in the world knew—how not to ask questions. How to believe what had to be believed. There was politeness in that reluctance and generosity as well. Is your mother sick too? No, she dances all night. Oh—and an understanding nod.

We sat in a booth by the window and fell into recollection like veterans.

"Did you ever learn to read?"

"Watch." She picked up the menu. "Special of the day. Cream of corn soup. Entrées. Two dots and a wriggly line. Quiche. Chef salad, scallops . . ."

I was laughing and applauding when the waitress came up. 95

"Remember the Easter baskets?"

"And how we tried to *introduce* them?"

"Your mother with that cross like two telephone poles."

"And yours with those tight slacks."

We laughed so loudly heads turned and made the laughter harder to suppress. 100

"What happened to the Jimi Hendrix date?"

Roberta made a blow-out sound with her lips.

"When he died I thought about you."

"Oh, you heard about him finally?"

"Finally. Come on, I was a small-town country waitress." 105

"And I was a small-town country dropout. God, were we wild. I still don't know how I got out of there alive."

"But you did."

"I did. I really did. Now I'm Mrs. Kenneth Norton."

"Sounds like a mouthful."

"It is." 110

"Servants and all?"

Roberta held up two fingers.

"Ow! What does he do?"

"Computers and stuff. What do I know?"

"I don't remember a hell of a lot from those days, but Lord, St. Bonny's is as 115 clear as daylight. Remember Maggie? The day she fell down and those gar girls laughed at her?"

Roberta looked up from her salad and stared at me. "Maggie didn't fall," she said.

"Yes, she did. You remember."

"No, Twyla. They knocked her down. Those girls pushed her down and tore her clothes. In the orchard."

"I don't—that's not what happened."

"Sure it is. In the orchard. Remember how scared we were?" 120

"Wait a minute. I don't remember any of that."

"And Bozo was fired."

"You're crazy. She was there when I left. You left before me."

"I went back. You weren't there when they fired Bozo."

125   "What?"

"Twice. Once for a year when I was about ten, another for two months when I was fourteen. That's when I ran away."

"You ran away from St. Bonny's?"

"I had to. What do you want? Me dancing in that orchard?"

"Are you sure about Maggie?"

130   "Of course I'm sure. You've blocked it, Twyla. It happened. Those girls had behavior problems, you know."

"Didn't they, though. But why can't I remember the Maggie thing?"

"Believe me. It happened. And we were there."

"Who did you room with when you went back?" I asked her as if I would know her. The Maggie thing was troubling me.

"Creeps. They tickled themselves in the night."

135   My ears were itching and I wanted to go home suddenly. This was all very well but she couldn't just comb her hair, wash her face and pretend everything was hunky-dory. After the Howard Johnson's snub. And no apology. Nothing.

"Were you on dope or what that time at Howard Johnson's?" I tried to make my voice sound friendlier than I felt.

"Maybe, a little. I never did drugs much. Why?"

"I don't know; you acted sort of like you didn't want to know me then."

"Oh, Twyla, you know how it was in those days: black—white. You know how everything was."

140   But I didn't know. I thought it was just the opposite. Busloads of blacks and whites came into Howard Johnson's together. They roamed together then: students, musicians, lovers, protesters. You got to see everything at Howard Johnson's and blacks were very friendly with whites in those days. But sitting there with nothing on my plate but two hard tomato wedges wondering about the melting Klondikes it seemed childish remembering the slight. We went to her car, and with the help of the driver, got my stuff into my station wagon.

"We'll keep in touch this time," she said.

"Sure," I said. "Sure. Give me a call."

"I will," she said, and then just as I was sliding behind the wheel, she leaned into the window. "By the way. Your mother. Did she ever stop dancing?"

I shook my head. "No. Never."

145   Roberta nodded.

"And yours? Did she ever get well?"

She smiled a tiny sad smile. "No. She never did. Look, call me, okay?"

"Okay," I said, but I knew I wouldn't. Roberta had messed up my past somehow with that business about Maggie. I wouldn't forget a thing like that. Would I?

Strife came to us that fall. At least that's what the paper called it. Strife. Racial strife. The word made me think of a bird—a big shrieking bird out of 1,000,000,000 B.C. Flapping its wings and cawing. Its eye with no lid always bearing down on you. All day it screeched and at night it slept on the rooftops. It woke you in the morning and from the *Today* show to the eleven o'clock news it kept you an awful company. I couldn't figure it out from one day to the next. I knew I was supposed to feel something strong, but I didn't know what, and James wasn't any help. Joseph was on the list of kids to be transferred from the junior high school to another one at some far-out-of-the-way place and I thought it was a good thing until I heard it was a bad thing. I mean I didn't know. All the schools seemed dumps to me, and the fact that one was nicer looking didn't hold much weight. But the papers were full of it and then the kids began to get jumpy. In August, mind you. Schools weren't even open yet. I thought Joseph might be frightened to go over there, but he didn't seem scared so I forgot about it, until I found myself driving along Hudson Street out there by the school they were trying to integrate and saw a line of women marching. And who do you suppose was in line, big as life, holding a sign in front of her bigger than her mother's cross? MOTHERS HAVE RIGHTS TOO! it said.

I drove on, and then changed my mind. I circled the block, slowed down, and 150 honked my horn.

Roberta looked over and when she saw me she waved. I didn't wave back, but I didn't move either. She handed her sign to another woman and came over to where I was parked.

"Hi."

"What are you doing?"

"Picketing. What's it look like?"

"What for?" 155

"What do you mean, 'What for?' They want to take my kids and send them out of the neighborhood. They don't want to go."

"So what if they go to another school? My boy's being bussed too, and I don't mind. Why should you?"

"It's not about us, Twyla. Me and you. It's about our kids."

"What's more us than that?"

"Well, it is a free country." 160

"Not yet, but it will be."

"What the hell does that mean? I'm not doing anything to you."

"You really think that?"

"I know it."

"I wonder what made me think you were different." 165

"I wonder what made me think you were different."

"Look at them," I said. "Just look. Who do they think they are? Swarming all over the place like they own it. And now they think they can decide where my child goes to school. Look at them, Roberta. They're Bozos."

Roberta turned around and looked at the women. Almost all of them were standing still now, waiting. Some were even edging toward us. Roberta looked at me out of some refrigerator behind her eyes. "No, they're not. They're just mothers."

"And what am I? Swiss cheese?"

"I used to curl your hair." 170

"I hated your hands in my hair."

The women were moving. Our faces looked mean to them of course and they looked as though they could not wait to throw themselves in front of a police car, or better yet, into my car and drag me away by my ankles. Now they surrounded my car and gently, gently began to rock it. I swayed back and forth like a sideways yo-yo. Automatically I reached for Roberta, like the old days in the orchard when they saw us watching them and we had to get out of there, and if one of us fell the other pulled her up and if one of us was caught the other stayed to kick and scratch, and neither would leave the other behind. My arm shot out of the car window but no receiving hand was there. Roberta was looking at me sway from side to side in the car and her face was still. My purse slid from the car seat down under the dashboard. The four policemen who had been drinking Tab in their car finally got the message and strolled over, forcing their way through the women. Quietly, firmly they spoke. "Okay, ladies. Back in line or off the streets."

Some of them went away willingly; others had to be urged away from the car doors and the hood. Roberta didn't move. She was looking steadily at me. I was fumbling to turn on the ignition, which wouldn't catch because the gearshift was still in drive. The seats of the car were a mess because the swaying had thrown my grocery coupons all over it and my purse was sprawled on the floor.

"Maybe I am different now, Twyla. But you're not. You're the same little state kid who kicked a poor old black lady when she was down on the ground. You kicked a black lady and you have the nerve to call me a bigot."

175   The coupons were everywhere and the guts of my purse were bunched under the dashboard. What was she saying? Black? Maggie wasn't black.

"She wasn't black," I said.

"Like hell she wasn't, and you kicked her. We both did. You kicked a black lady who couldn't even scream."

"Liar!"

"You're the liar! Why don't you just go on home and leave us alone, huh?"

180   She turned away and I skidded away from the curb.

The next morning I went into the garage and cut the side out of the carton our portable TV had come in. It wasn't nearly big enough, but after a while I had a decent sign: red spray-painted letters on a white background—AND SO DO CHILDREN ****. I meant just to go down to the school and tack it up somewhere so those cows on the picket line across the street could see it, but when I got there, some ten or so others had already assembled—protesting the cows across the street. Police permits and everything. I got in line and we strutted in time on our side while Roberta's group strutted on theirs. That first day we were all dignified, pretending the other side didn't exist. The second day there was name calling and finger gestures. But that was about all. People changed signs from time to time, but Roberta never did and neither did I. Actually my sign didn't make sense without Roberta's. "And so do children what?" one of the women on my side asked me. Have rights, I said, as though it was obvious.

Roberta didn't acknowledge my presence in any way and I got to thinking maybe she didn't know I was there. I began to pace myself in the line, jostling people one minute and lagging behind the next, so Roberta and I could reach the end of our respective lines at the same time and there would be a moment in our turn when we would face each other. Still, I couldn't tell whether she saw me and knew my sign was for her. The next day I went early before we were scheduled to assemble. I waited until she got there before I exposed my new creation. As soon as she hoisted her MOTHERS HAVE RIGHTS TOO I began to wave my new one, which said, HOW WOULD YOU KNOW? I know she saw that one, but I had gotten addicted now. My signs got crazier each day, and the women on my side decided that I was a kook. They couldn't make heads or tails out of my brilliant screaming posters.

I brought a painted sign in queenly red with huge black letters that said, IS YOUR MOTHER WELL? Roberta took her lunch break and didn't come back for the rest of the day or any day after. Two days later I stopped going too and couldn't have been missed because nobody understood my signs anyway.

It was a nasty six weeks. Classes were suspended and Joseph didn't go to anybody's school until October. The children—everybody's children—soon got bored with that extended vacation they thought was going to be so great. They looked at TV until their eyes flattened. I spent a couple of mornings tutoring my son, as the other mothers said we should. Twice I opened a text from last year that he had never turned in. Twice he yawned in my face. Other mothers organized living room sessions so the kids would keep up. None of the kids could concentrate so they drifted back to *The Price Is Right* and *The Brady Bunch.*[6] When the school finally opened there were fights once or twice and some sirens roared through the streets every once in a while. There were a lot of photographers from Albany. And just when ABC was about to send up a news crew, the kids settled down like nothing in the world had happened. Joseph hung my HOW WOULD YOU KNOW? sign in his bedroom. I don't know what became of AND SO DO CHILDREN ****. I think my father-in-law cleaned some fish on it. He was always puttering around in our garage. Each of his five children lived in Newburgh and he acted as though he had five extra homes.

I couldn't help looking for Roberta when Joseph graduated from high school, but I didn't see her. It didn't trouble me much what she had said to me in the car. I mean the kicking part. I know I didn't do that, I couldn't do that. But I was puzzled by her telling me Maggie was black. When I thought about it I actually couldn't be certain. She wasn't pitch-black, I knew, or I would have remembered that. What I remember was the kiddie hat, and the semicircle legs. I tried to reassure myself about the race thing for a long time until it dawned on me that the truth was already there, and Roberta knew it. I didn't kick her; I didn't join in with the gar girls and kick that lady, but I sure did want to. We watched and never tried to help her and never called for help. Maggie was my dancing mother. Deaf, I thought, and dumb. Nobody inside. Nobody who would hear you if you cried in the night. Nobody who could tell you anything important that you could use. Rocking, dancing, swaying as she walked. And when the gar girls pushed her down, and started roughhousing, I knew she wouldn't scream, couldn't—just like me—and I was glad about that.

We decided not to have a tree, because Christmas would be at my mother-in-law's house, so why have a tree at both places? Joseph was at SUNY New Paltz and we had to economize, we said. But at the last minute, I changed my mind. Nothing could be that bad. So I rushed around town looking for a tree, something small but wide. By the time I found a place, it was snowing and very late. I dawdled like it was the most important purchase in the world and the tree man was fed up with me. Finally I chose one and had it tied onto the trunk of the car. I drove away slowly because the sand trucks were not out yet and the streets could be murder at the beginning of a snowfall. Downtown the streets were wide and rather empty except for a cluster of people coming out of the Newburgh Hotel. The one hotel in town that wasn't built out of cardboard and Plexiglas. A party, probably. The men huddled in the snow

6. Television sitcom popular in the 1970s, as was the game show *The Price Is Right.*

were dressed in tails and the women had on furs. Shiny things glittered from underneath their coats. It made me tired to look at them. Tired, tired, tired. On the next corner was a small diner with loops and loops of paper bells in the window. I stopped the car and went in. Just for a cup of coffee and twenty minutes of peace before I went home and tried to finish everything before Christmas Eve.

"Twyla?"

There she was. In a silvery evening gown and dark fur coat. A man and another woman were with her, the man fumbling for change to put in the cigarette machine. The woman was humming and tapping on the counter with her finger-nails. They all looked a little bit drunk.

"Well. It's you."

190   "How are you?"

I shrugged. "Pretty good. Frazzled. Christmas and all."

"Regular?" called the woman from the counter.

"Fine," Roberta called back and then, "Wait for me in the car."

She slipped into the booth beside me. "I have to tell you something, Twyla. I made up my mind if I ever saw you again, I'd tell you."

195   "I'd just as soon not hear anything, Roberta. It doesn't matter now, anyway."

"No," she said. "Not about that."

"Don't be long," said the woman. She carried two regulars to go and the man peeled his cigarette pack as they left.

"It's about St. Bonny's and Maggie."

"Oh, please."

200   "Listen to me. I really did think she was black. I didn't make that up. I really thought so. But now I can't be sure. I just remember her as old, so old. And because she couldn't talk—well, you know, I thought she was crazy. She'd been brought up in an institution like my mother was and like I thought I would be too. And you were right. We didn't kick her. It was the gar girls. Only them. But, well, I wanted to. I really wanted them to hurt her. I said we did it, too. You and me, but that's not true. And I don't want you to carry that around. It was just that I wanted to do it so bad that day—wanting to is doing it."

Her eyes were watery from the drinks she'd had, I guess. I know it's that way with me. One glass of wine and I start bawling over the littlest thing.

"We were kids, Roberta."

"Yeah. Yeah. I know, just kids."

"Eight."

205   "Eight."

"And lonely."

"Scared, too."

She wiped her cheeks with the heel of her hand and smiled. "Well, that's all I wanted to say."

I nodded and couldn't think of any way to fill the silence that went from the diner past the paper bells on out into the snow. It was heavy now. I thought I'd better wait for the sand trucks before starting home.

210   "Thanks, Roberta."

"Sure."

"Did I tell you? My mother, she never did stop dancing."

"Yes. You told me. And mine, she never got well." Roberta lifted her hands from the tabletop and covered her face with her palms. When she took them away she really was crying. "Oh shit, Twyla. Shit, shit, shit. What the hell happened to Maggie?"

1983

QUESTIONS

1. At the end of Recitatif, how do Twyla's and Roberta's explorations of the "truth" of what they had seen at St. Bonny's many years earlier affect your sense of the "truth" of later episodes in the story? Is either Twyla or Roberta more reliable than the other?
2. At what point in the story do you first begin to make assumptions about the race and class of the two main characters, Twyla and Roberta? Why? Do you change your mind later in the story? When and why so—or not? What is the significance of Morrison's choice both to withhold information about the characters' race and class and to have Twyla narrate the story?
3. How does the relationship between Twyla and Roberta evolve over the course of the story?

AUTHORS ON THEIR WORK

TONI MORRISON (b. 1931)

From "Toni Morrison: The Art of Fiction CXXXIV" (1993)*

MORRISON: Faulkner in *Absalom, Absalom!* spends the entire book tracing race, and you can't find it. No one can see it, even the character who *is* black can't see it. [. . .] Do you know how hard it is to withhold that kind of information but hinting, pointing all of the time? And then to reveal it in order to say that it is *not* the point anyway? It is technically just astonishing. As a reader you have been forced to hunt for a drop of black blood that means everything and nothing. The insanity of racism.

MORRISON: [. . .] I wrote a story entitled "Recitatif," in which there are two little girls in an orphanage, one white and one black. But the reader doesn't know which is white and which is black. I use class codes, but no racial codes.

INTERVIEWER: Is this meant to confuse the reader?

MORRISON: Well, yes. But to provoke and enlighten. I did that as a lark. What was exciting was to be forced as a writer not to be lazy and rely on obvious codes. Soon as I say, "Black woman . . ." I can rest on or provoke predictable responses, but if I leave it out then I have to talk about her in a complicated way—as a person.

*"Toni Morrison: The Art of Fiction CXXXIV." Interview by Elisa Schappell with Claudia Brodsky Lacour. *The Paris Review*, no. 128, Fall 1993, www.theparisreview.org/interviews /1888/the-art-of-fiction-no-134-toni-morrison.

DAVID FOSTER WALLACE
(1962–2008)

Good People

Born in Ithaca, New York, to a philosophy professor and an English teacher, David Foster Wallace has been dubbed an "outrageously gifted novelist" and "the genius of his generation," as well as a "recovering smart aleck" and "a decent, decent man." A philosophy and English major at Amherst College, he contemplated a career in math before—at age twenty-four—earning an MFA from the University of Arizona and publishing his first novel, *The Broom of the System* (1987). His subsequent work includes short-story collections like *Brief Interviews with Hideous Men* (1999) and *Oblivion* (2006), as well as wide-ranging nonfiction, some of which appears in *A Supposedly Fun Thing I'll Never Do Again* (1997) and *Consider the Lobster and Other Essays* (2006). At over a thousand pages and with almost four hundred footnotes, his most famous novel, *Infinite Jest* (1996), intertwines several narratives set in a near future in which years are named by their corporate sponsors ("Year of the Whopper") and New England is a giant toxic-waste dump. Included on *Time's* list of the hundred best novels published since 1923, it also helped earn Wallace a MacArthur "genius grant."

Wallace described his own goal as "morally passionate, passionately moral fiction" that might help readers "become less alone inside." Though admired as much for its humor as for its bulk and complexity, his fiction often dwells on what he called "an ineluctable part of being a human"—"suffering." Though Wallace long battled depression, his 2008 suicide shocked and saddened fans and fellow writers around the world. The story "Good People," first published in 2007, ultimately became part of *The Pale King* (2011), the unfinished novel he left behind.

They were up on a picnic table at that park by the lake, by the edge of the lake, with part of a downed tree in the shallows half hidden by the bank. Lane A. Dean, Jr., and his girlfriend, both in bluejeans and button-up shirts. They sat up on the table's top portion and had their shoes on the bench part that people sat on to picnic or fellowship together in carefree times. They'd gone to different high schools but the same junior college, where they had met in campus ministries. It was springtime, and the park's grass was very green and the air suffused with honeysuckle and lilacs both, which was almost too much. There were bees, and the angle of the sun made the water of the shallows look dark. There had been more storms that week, with some downed trees and the sound of chainsaws all up and down his parents' street. Their postures on the picnic table were both the same forward kind with their shoulders rounded and elbows on their knees. In this position the girl rocked slightly and once put her face in her hands, but she was not crying. Lane was very still and immobile and looking past the bank at the downed tree in the shallows and its ball of exposed roots going all directions and the tree's cloud of branches all half in the water. The only other individual nearby was a dozen spaced tables away, by himself, standing upright. Looking at the torn-up hole in the ground there where the tree had gone over. It was still early yet and all the shadows wheeling right and shortening. The girl wore a thin old checked cotton shirt with pearl-colored snaps with the long sleeves down and always smelled very good and clean, like someone you could trust and care about even if you weren't in love. Lane Dean had liked the smell of her right away. His mother called her *down to earth* and liked her, thought she was good people, you could tell—she made this evident in little ways. The shallows lapped from different directions at the tree as if almost teething on it. Sometimes when alone and thinking or struggling to turn a matter over to Jesus Christ in prayer, he would find himself putting his fist in his palm and turning it slightly as if still playing and pounding his glove to stay sharp and alert in center. He did not do this now; it would be cruel and indecent to do this now. The older individual stood beside his picnic table—he was at it but not sitting—and looked also out of place in a suit coat or jacket and the kind of men's hat Lane's grandfather wore in photos as a young insurance man. He appeared to be looking across the lake. If he moved, Lane didn't see it. He looked more like a picture than a man. There were not any ducks in view.

One thing Lane Dean did was reassure her again that he'd go with her and be there with her. It was one of the few safe or decent things he could really say. The second time he said it again now she shook her head and laughed in an unhappy way that was more just air out her nose. Her real laugh was different. Where he'd be was the waiting room, she said. That he'd be thinking about her and feeling bad for her, she knew, but he couldn't be in there with her. This was so obviously true that he felt like a ninny that he'd kept on about it and now knew what she had thought every time he went and said it—it hadn't brought her comfort or eased the burden at all. The worse he felt, the stiller he sat. The whole thing felt balanced on a knife or wire; if he moved to put his arm up or touch her the whole thing could tip over. He hated himself for sitting so frozen. He could almost visualize himself tiptoeing past something explosive. A big stupid-looking tiptoe, like in a cartoon. The whole last black week had been this way and it was wrong. He knew it was wrong, knew something was required of him that was not this terrible frozen care and caution, but he pretended to himself he did not know what it was that was required. He pretended it had no name. He pretended that not saying aloud what he knew to be right and true was for her sake, was for the sake of her needs and feelings. He also worked dock and routing at UPS, on top of school, but had traded to get the day off after they'd decided together. Two days before, he had awakened very early and tried to pray but could not. He was freezing more and more solid, he felt like, but he had not thought of his father or the blank frozenness of his father, even in church, which had once filled him with such pity. This was the truth. Lane Dean, Jr., felt sun on one arm as he pictured in his mind an image of himself on a train, waving mechanically to something that got smaller and smaller as the train pulled away. His father and his mother's father had the same birthday, a Cancer. Sheri's hair was colored an almost corn blond, very clean, the skin through her central part pink in the sunlight. They'd sat here long enough that only their right side was shaded now. He could look at her head, but not at her. Different parts of him felt unconnected to each other. She was smarter than him and they both knew it. It wasn't just school—Lane Dean was in accounting and business and did all right; he was hanging in there. She was a year older, twenty, but it was also more—she had always seemed to Lane to be on good terms with her life in a way that age could not account for. His mother had put it that she *knew what it is she wanted*, which was nursing and not an easy program at Peoria Junior College, and plus she worked hostessing at the Embers and had bought her own car. She was serious in a way Lane liked. She had a cousin that died when she was thirteen, fourteen, that she'd loved and been close with. She only talked about it that once. He liked her smell and her downy arms and the way she exclaimed when something made her laugh. He had liked just being with her and talking to her. She was serious in her faith and values in a way that Lane had liked and now, sitting here with her on the table, found himself afraid of. This was an awful thing. He was starting to believe that he might not be serious in his faith. He might be somewhat of a hypocrite, like the Assyrians in Isaiah,[1] which would be a far graver sin than the appointment—he had decided he believed this. He was desperate to be good people, to still be able to feel he was good. He rarely before now had thought of damnation and Hell—that part of it didn't speak to his spirit—and in worship services he more just tuned himself out and tolerated Hell when it came up, the same way you tolerate the job you've got to have to save up for what it is you want. Her tennis shoes had little things doodled on them from sitting in her class lectures. She stayed looking down like that. Little notes or reading assignments in Bic in her neat round hand on the rubber elements around the sneaker's rim. Lane A. Dean, looking now at her inclined head's side's barrettes in the shape of blue ladybugs. The appointment was for afternoon, but when the doorbell had rung so early and his mother'd called to him up the stairs, he had known, and a terrible kind of blankness had commenced falling through him.

He told her that he did not know what to do. That he knew if he was the salesman of it and forced it upon her that was awful and wrong. But he was trying to understand—they'd prayed on it and talked it through from every different angle. Lane said how sorry she knew he was, and that if he was wrong in believing they'd truly decided together when they decided to make the appointment she should please tell him, because he thought he knew how she must have felt as it got closer and closer and how she must be so scared, but that what he couldn't tell was if it was more than that. He was totally still except for moving his mouth, it felt like. She did not reply. That if they needed to pray on it more and talk it through, then he was here, he was ready, he said. The appointment could get moved back; if she just said the word they could call and push it back to take more time to be sure in the decision. It was still so early in it—they both knew that, he said. This was true, that he felt this way, and yet he also knew he was also trying to say things that would get her to open up and say enough back that he could see her and read her heart and know what to say to get her to go through with it. He knew this without admitting to himself that this was what he wanted, for it would make him a hypocrite and liar. He knew, in some locked-up little part of him, why it was that he'd gone to no one to open up and seek their life counsel, not Pastor Steve or the prayer partners at campus ministries, not his UPS friends or the spiritual counselling available through his parents' old church. But he did not know why Sheri herself had not gone to Pastor Steve—he could not read her heart. She was blank and hidden. He so fervently wished it never happened. He felt like he knew now why it was a true sin and not just a leftover rule from past society. He felt like he had been brought low by it and humbled and now did believe that the rules were there for a reason. That the rules

---

1. Perhaps a reference to Isaiah 36, in which the Assyrians promise to save the kingdom of Judah if its king will trust and surrender to them rather than relying on God. Later chapters describe Assyria's fall as punishment for their hubris.

were concerned with him personally, as an individual. He promised God he had learned his lesson. But what if that, too, was a hollow promise, from a hypocrite who repented only after, who promised submission but really only wanted a reprieve? He might not even know his own heart or be able to read and know himself. He kept thinking also of 1 Timothy and the hypocrite therein who *disputeth over words.*[2] He felt a terrible inner resistance but could not feel what it was that it resisted. This was the truth. All the different angles and ways they had come at the decision together did not ever include it—the word—for had he once said it, avowed that he did love her, loved Sheri Fisher, then it all would have been transformed. It would not be a different stance or angle, but a difference in the very thing they were praying and deciding on together. Sometimes they had prayed together over the phone, in a kind of half code in case anybody accidentally picked up the extension. She continued to sit as if thinking, in the pose of thinking, like that one statue. They were right up next to each other on the table. He was looking over past her at the tree in the water. But he could not say he did: it was not true.

But neither did he ever open up and tell her straight out he did not love her. This might be his *lie by omission.* This might be the frozen resistance—were he to look right at her and tell her he didn't, she would keep the appointment and go. He knew this. Something in him, though, some terrible weakness or lack of values, could not tell her. It felt like a muscle he did not have. He didn't know why; he just could not do it, or even pray to do it. She believed he was good, serious in his values. Part of him seemed willing to more or less just about lie to someone with that kind of faith and trust, and what did that make him? How could such a type of individual even pray? What it really felt like was a taste of the reality of what might be meant by Hell. Lane Dean had never believed in Hell as a lake of fire or a loving God consigning folks to a burning lake of fire—he knew in his heart this was not true. What he believed in was a living God of compassion and love and the possibility of a personal relationship with Jesus Christ through whom this love was enacted in human time. But sitting here beside this girl as unknown to him now as outer space, waiting for whatever she might say to unfreeze him, now he felt like he could see the edge or outline of what a real vision of Hell might be. It was of two great and terrible armies within himself, opposed and facing each other, silent. There would be battle but no victor. Or never a battle—the armies would stay like that, motionless, looking across at each other, and seeing therein something so different and alien from themselves that they could not understand, could not hear each other's speech as even words or read anything from what their face looked like, frozen like that, opposed and uncomprehending, for all human time. Two-hearted, a hypocrite to yourself either way.

When he moved his head, a part of the lake further out flashed with sun—the water up close wasn't black now, and you could see into the shallows and see that all the water was moving but gently, this way and that—and in this same way he besought to return to himself as Sheri moved her leg and started to turn beside him. He could see the man in the suit and gray hat standing motionless now at the lake's rim, holding something under one arm and looking across at the opposite side where

2. See 1 Timothy 6.3–4: "If any man teach otherwise, and consent not to wholesome words, *even* the words of our Lord Jesus Christ, and to the doctrine which is according to godliness; He is proud, knowing nothing, but doting about questions and strifes of words, whereof cometh envy, strife, railings, evil surmisings."

a row of little forms on camp chairs sat in a way that meant they had lines in the water for crappie—which mostly only your blacks from the East Side ever did—and the little white shape at the row's end a Styrofoam creel. In his moment or time at the lake now just to come, Lane Dean first felt he could take this all in whole: everything seemed distinctly lit, for the circle of the pin oak's shade had rotated off all the way, and they sat now in sun with their shadow a two-headed thing in the grass before them. He was looking or gazing again at where the downed tree's branches seemed to all bend so sharply just under the shallows' surface when he was given to know that through all this frozen silence he'd despised he had, in truth, been praying, or some little part of his heart he could not hear had, for he was answered now with a type of vision, what he would later call within his own mind a vision or *moment of grace*. He was not a hypocrite, just broken and split off like all men. Later on, he believed that what happened was he'd had a moment of almost seeing them both as Jesus saw them—as blind but groping, wanting to please God despite their inborn fallen nature. For in that same given moment he saw, quick as light, into Sheri's heart, and was made to know what would occur here as she finished turning to him and the man in the hat watched the fishing and the downed elm shed cells into the water. This down-to-earth girl that smelled good and wanted to be a nurse would take and hold one of his hands in both of hers to unfreeze him and make him look at her, and she would say that she cannot do it. That she is sorry she did not know this sooner, that she hadn't meant to lie—she agreed because she'd wanted to believe that she could, but she cannot. That she will carry this and have it; she has to. With her gaze clear and steady. That all night last night she prayed and searched inside herself and decided this is what love commands of her. That Lane should please please sweetie let her finish. That listen—this is her own decision and obliges him to nothing. That she knows he does not love her, not that way, has known it all this time, and that it's all right. That it is as it is and it's all right. She will carry this, and have it, and love it and make no claim on Lane except his good wishes and respecting what she has to do. That she releases him, all claim, and hopes he finishes up at P.J.C. and does so good in his life and has all joy and good things. Her voice will be clear and steady, and she will be lying, for Lane has been given to read her heart. To see through her. One of the opposite side's blacks raises his arm in what may be greeting, or waving off a bee. There is a mower cutting grass someplace off behind them. It will be a terrible, last-ditch gamble born out of the desperation in Sheri Fisher's soul, the knowledge that she can neither do this thing today nor carry a child alone and shame her family. Her values blocked the way either way, Lane could see, and she has no other options or choice—this lie is not a sin. Galatians 4:16, *Have I then become your enemy?*[3] She is gambling that he is good. There on the table, neither frozen nor yet moving, Lane Dean, Jr., sees all this, and is moved with pity, and also with something more, something without any name he knows, that is given to him in the form of a question that never once in all the long week's thinking and division had even so much as occurred—why is he so sure he doesn't love her? Why is one kind of love any different? What if he has no

---

3. "Am I therefore become your enemy, because I tell you the truth?" (Gal. 4.16). Earlier in this letter, Paul exhorts the Galatians to understand that when they "knew not God," they inevitably served "them which by nature are no gods," but now that they know God such "bondage" is instead a choice. At the same time, he reminds them that he is, like them, fallible, and that despite that "temptation which was in my flesh ye despised [me] not, nor rejected."

earthly idea what love is? What would even Jesus do? For it was just now he felt her two small strong soft hands on his, to turn him. What if he was just afraid, if the truth was no more than this, and if what to pray for was not even love but simple courage, to meet both her eyes as she says it and trust his heart?

2007

QUESTIONS

1. How would you summarize or characterize Lane Dean, Jr.'s conflicts, both internal and external? How does his faith intensify or even create those conflicts and help him to resolve them?

2. How is your interpretation of Lane Dean, Jr.'s character and conflicts shaped by all that the story withholds from us, including dialogue; Sheri's point of view or thoughts; explicit information about the nature of Sheri's "appointment" or of the "it" he "wished [. . .] never happened" (par. 3); a description of what actually happens at the end rather than Lane Dean's "vision" of what would happen and/or his later "belie[f]" about what happened?

3. What different definitions of "good people" or of a "good person" are implied here, or how might Lane Dean, Jr.'s understanding of what it means to be "good people" change over the course of the story? What part does the idea of hypocrisy play in those definitions?

5 | SETTING

If plot and action are the way fictional works answer the question *What happened?* and characters are the *who*, **setting** is the *where* and *when*. All action in fiction, as in the real world, takes place in a context or setting—a time and place and a social environment or milieu.

TEMPORAL AND PHYSICAL, GENERAL AND PARTICULAR SETTING

The **time**—a work's *temporal setting* or *plot time*—can be roughly the same as that in which the work was written (its *author time*); or it can be much later, as in most science fiction; or much earlier, as in **historical fiction**. Especially in short stories, which tend not to cover as much time or space as novels do, time may be very restricted, involving only a few hours or even minutes. Yet even in short stories, the action may span years or even decades.

Similarly, the place—a work's *geographical* or *physical setting*—might be limited to a single locale, or it might encompass several disparate ones. Those places might be common and ordinary, unique and extraordinary, or fantastic and even impossible according to the laws of our world (as in modern **fantasy** or **magic realism**).

Even when a story's action takes place in multiple times and places, we still sometimes refer to its *setting* (singular). By this, we indicate what we might call the entire story's *general setting*—the year(s) and the region, country, or even world in which the story unfolds and which often provides a historical and cultural context for the action. The general setting of Margaret Mitchell's historical novel *Gone with the Wind* (1936), for instance, is the Civil War–era South. But this novel, like many, has numerous *particular settings*; it opens, for instance, on an April morning on the porch of a north Georgia mansion called Tara. To fully appreciate the nature and role of setting, we thus need to consider the specific time of day and year as well as the specific locales in which the action unfolds.

FUNCTIONS OF SETTING

Some stories merely offer hints about setting; others describe setting in great sensory detail. Especially in the latter case, we might be tempted to skim through what seems like mere "scenery" or "background information" to find out what happens next or how things turn out. But in good fiction, setting always functions as an integral part of the whole.

Fiction often relies on setting to establish mood, situation, and character. The first sentence of Edgar Allan Poe's short story "The Fall of the House of Usher" (1839), for example, quickly sets the **tone**:

> During the whole of a dull, dark, and soundless day in the autumn of the year, when the clouds hung oppressively low in the heavens, I had been passing alone, on horseback, through a singularly dreary tract of country; and at length found myself, as the shades of the evening drew on, within view of the melancholy House of Usher.

This sentence aims to instill in the reader the same fear, "melancholy," and "sense of insufferable gloom" the narrator feels. With it, Poe prepares the reader for the sad and eerie tale about to unfold. He also generates suspense and certain expectations about just what might happen, as well as empathy with the narrator-protagonist.

Here, as in other fiction, specific details prove crucial to setting's emotional effect and meaning precisely because, as Poe's narrator himself observes,

> there *are* combinations of very simple natural objects which have the power of thus affecting us [. . .]. It was possible, I reflected, that a mere different arrangement of the particulars of the scene, of the details of the picture, would be sufficient to modify [. . .] its [. . .] impression.

In addition to creating such emotional impressions, setting can reveal, even shape a character's personality, outlook, and values; it can occasionally be an actor in the plot; and it often prompts characters' actions. (Who might you become and what might you do if you lived in the isolated, gloomy House of Usher?) Descriptions of setting may even (as in the first "Example and Exercise" below) suggest a key **conflict** or **theme**. To gloss over descriptions of setting would thus mean not only missing much of the pleasure fiction affords but also potentially misreading its meanings. Setting is one of the many ways we learn about characters and the chief means by which characters and plots take on a larger historical, social, or even universal significance.

VAGUE AND VIVID SETTINGS

Not all stories, of course, rely as heavily on setting as Poe's does. In some works and in some subgenres, the general time, place, or both may be so vague as to seem, at first glance, unimportant. Many folktales and fairy tales take place in **archetypal** settings: "A long time ago," in "the forest" or "a village" or "a cottage," "in a land far, far away." By offering little, if any, specific information about their settings—neither locating the "forest" or "village" or faraway land in a place we can find on a map or a time we can identify on a calendar or clock, nor describing it in any detail—these works implicitly urge us to see the conflicts and aspects of human experience they depict (death, grief, a mother's relationship to her child, the danger and incomprehensibility of the unknown) as timeless and universal. Here, the very lack of attention to setting paradoxically turns out to be all-important.

At the opposite extreme are works and subgenres of fiction in which setting generates the conflicts, defines the characters, and gives the story purpose and meaning—so much so that there would be little, if any, story left if all the details about setting were removed or the characters and plot were somehow transported to a different time, place, and social milieu. Without their settings, what would remain of historical novels like *Gone with the Wind* or Nathaniel Hawthorne's *The Scarlet Letter* (1850)? An even more extreme example is Italo Calvino's fantasy novel *Invisible Cities*, which consists almost entirely of a series of descriptions of impossible, yet often hauntingly beautiful places like the following one.

ITALO CALVINO
From Invisible Cities

What makes Argia different from other cities is that it has earth instead of air. The streets are completely filled with dirt, clay packs the rooms to the ceiling, on every stair another stairway is set in negative, over the roofs of the houses hang layers of rocky terrain like skies with clouds. We do not know if the inhabitants can move about the city, widening the worm tunnels and the crevices where roots twist: the dampness destroys people's bodies and they have scant strength; everyone is better off remaining still, prone; anyway, it is dark.

From up here, nothing of Argia can be seen; some say, "It's down below there," and we can only believe them. The place is deserted. At night, putting your ear to the ground, you can sometimes hear a door slam.

1972

Most fiction, of course, occupies a middle ground between the extremes of Calvino's novel or historical fiction (with their highly particularized settings) versus folklore (with its generic, archetypal setting). Though all fiction may ultimately deal with some types of people, aspects of human experience, and conflicts that can crop up in some form or fashion anywhere or any time, much fiction also draws our attention to the way people, their experience, and their conflicts are twisted into a particular "form and fashion" by specific contexts.

TRADITIONAL EXPECTATIONS OF TIME AND PLACE

The effects and meanings evoked by setting depend on our traditional associations with, and often unconscious assumptions about, particular times, places, and even such factors as weather conditions—autumn, evening, a deserted country road, a house grand enough to have a name, a sky full of low and lowering clouds (to refer back to the Poe example).

Traditional associations derive, in part, from literature and myth, and some are culturally specific. (To someone unfamiliar with the Old Testament, an apple orchard would simply be an apple orchard, without any suggestion of evil or sin. Likewise, to someone who knows little about the U.S. Civil War, a big white house in the middle of a cotton field might seem like nothing more than a very beautiful place full of lucky, wealthy, happy people.) These associations also come from our learning, our experience, our own specific social and historical context, and even our primal instincts and physical condition as human beings. Almost all of us are more vulnerable in the dark and in inclement weather. And people do behave differently and expect different things to happen in different times and places—on a Saturday versus a Sunday versus a Monday, during spring break versus midsemester or midweek, at a posh beach resort we are just visiting versus the grocery store in our own neighborhood, and so on.

Often, however, authors draw on such associations precisely in order to reverse and question them. John Updike has said that he was initially inspired to write A & P because a suburban grocery store seemed just the sort of mundane place no reader would expect either heroism or a story to take place. ("Why don't you ever read a story set in an A & P?" he reportedly asked his wife.) By reversing expectations in this way, stories not only deepen their emotional effect but also encourage us to rethink our assumptions about particular times and places and the people who inhabit them.

• • •

Setting is key to each of the stories gathered in this chapter. Their settings range from the Western United States to China; from the early to the late twentieth century; from tiny towns to crowded, cosmopolitan cities. The stories take place in just about every season and all kinds of weather, but regardless of the specific setting each paints a revealing portrait of a time and place. Just as our own memories of important experiences include complex impressions of when and where they occurred—the weather, the shape of the room, the music that was playing, even the fashions or the events in the news back then—so stories rely on setting to evoke emotion and generate meaning.

Questions about Setting

General Setting

- What is the general temporal and geographical setting of this work of fiction? How do you know?
- How important does the general setting seem to be? In what ways is it important? What about the plot and characters would remain the same if they were transported to a different setting? What wouldn't? For example, how does the setting
  ◦ create or shape conflict?
  ◦ affect characters' personalities, outlooks, and actions?
  ◦ shape our impressions of who the characters are and what they represent?
  ◦ establish mood?

Particular Settings

- Does all the action occur in one time and place, or in more than one? If the latter, what are those times and places?
- What patterns do you notice regarding where and when things happen? Which characters are associated with each setting? How do different characters relate to the same setting? When, how, and why do characters move from one setting to another? Are there significant deviations from these patterns?
- Are particular settings described in detail, or merely sketched? If the former, what seems significant about the details? How might they establish mood, reveal character, and affect individual characters and their interactions with one another?

JAMES JOYCE
(1882–1941)
Araby

In 1902, after graduating from University College, Dublin, James Joyce left Ireland for Paris, returning a year later. In October 1904, he eloped with Nora Barnacle and settled in Trieste, where he taught English for the Berlitz school. Though he lived as an expatriate for the rest of his life, all of his fiction is set in his native Dublin. Joyce had more than his share of difficulties with publication and censorship. His short-story collection, *Dubliners*, completed in 1905, was not published until 1914. His novel *Portrait of the Artist as a Young Man*, dated "Dublin 1904, Trieste 1914," appeared first in America, in 1916. His great novel *Ulysses* (1921) was banned for a dozen years in the United States and as long or longer elsewhere. In addition, Joyce published a play, *Exiles* (1918); two collections of poetry, *Chamber Music* (1907) and *Pomes Penyeach* (1927); and the monumental, experimental, and puzzling novel *Finnegans Wake* (1939).

North Richmond Street, being blind,[1] was a quiet street except at the hour when the Christian Brothers' School set the boys free. An uninhabited house of two storeys stood at the blind end, detached from its neighbours in a square ground. The other houses of the street, conscious of decent lives within them, gazed at one another with brown imperturbable faces.

The former tenant of our house, a priest, had died in the back drawing-room. Air, musty from having been long enclosed, hung in all the rooms, and the waste room behind the kitchen was littered with old useless papers. Among these I found a few paper-covered books, the pages of which were curled and damp: *The Abbot*, by Walter Scott, *The Devout Communicant* and *The Memoirs of Vidocq*.[2] I liked the last best because its leaves were yellow. The wild garden behind the house contained a central apple-tree and a few straggling bushes under one of which I found the late tenant's rusty bicycle-pump. He had been a very charitable priest; in his will he had left all his money to institutions and the furniture of his house to his sister.

When the short days of winter came dusk fell before we had well eaten our dinners. When we met in the street the houses had grown sombre. The space of sky above us was the colour of ever-changing violet and towards it the lamps of the street lifted their feeble lanterns. The cold air stung us and we played till our

---

1. That is, a dead-end street.
2. The "memoirs" were probably *not* written by François Vidocq (1775–1857), a French criminal who became chief of detectives and died poor and disgraced for his part in a crime that he solved. *The Abbot*: The 1820 novel by Sir Walter Scott (1771–1834) is a romance about the Catholic Mary, Queen of Scots (1542–87), who was beheaded. *The Devout Communicant, or, Pious Meditations and Aspirations, for Three Days before and Three Days after Receiving the Holy Eucharist* (1813) is a Catholic religious tract.

bodies glowed. Our shouts echoed in the silent street. The career of our play brought us through the dark muddy lanes behind the houses where we ran the gantlet of the rough tribes from the cottages, to the back doors of the dark dripping gardens where odours arose from the ashpits,[3] to the dark odorous stables where a coachman smoothed and combed the horse or shook music from the buckled harness. When we returned to the street light from the kitchen windows had filled the areas. If my uncle was seen turning the corner we hid in the shadow until we had seen him safely housed. Or if Mangan's sister came out on the doorstep to call her brother in to his tea we watched her from our shadow peer up and down the street. We waited to see whether she would remain or go in and, if she remained, we left our shadow and walked up to Mangan's steps resignedly. She was waiting for us, her figure defined by the light from the half-opened door. Her brother always teased her before he obeyed and I stood by the railings looking at her. Her dress swung as she moved her body and the soft rope of her hair tossed from side to side.

Every morning I lay on the floor in the front parlour watching her door. The blind was pulled down to within an inch of the sash so that I could not be seen. When she came out on the doorstep my heart leaped. I ran to the hall, seized my books and followed her. I kept her brown figure always in my eye and, when we came near the point at which our ways diverged, I quickened my pace and passed her. This happened morning after morning. I had never spoken to her, except for a few casual words, and yet her name was like a summons to all my foolish blood.

Her image accompanied me even in places the most hostile to romance. On [5] Saturday evenings when my aunt went marketing I had to go to carry some of the parcels. We walked through the flaring streets, jostled by drunken men and bargaining women, amid the curses of labourers, the shrill litanies of shop-boys who stood on guard by the barrels of pigs' cheeks, the nasal chanting of street-singers, who sang a *come-all-you* about O'Donovan Rossa,[4] or a ballad about the troubles in our native land. These noises converged in a single sensation of life for me: I imagined that I bore my chalice safely through a throng of foes. Her name sprang to my lips at moments in strange prayers and praises which I myself did not understand. My eyes were often full of tears (I could not tell why) and at times a flood from my heart seemed to pour itself out into my bosom. I thought little of the future. I did not know whether I would ever speak to her or not or, if I spoke to her, how I could tell her of my confused adoration. But my body was like a harp and her words and gestures were like fingers running upon the wires.

One evening I went into the back drawing-room in which the priest had died. It was a dark rainy evening and there was no sound in the house. Through one of the broken panes I heard the rain impinge upon the earth, the fine incessant needles of water playing in the sodden beds. Some distant lamp or lighted window gleamed below me. I was thankful that I could see so little. All my senses seemed to desire to veil themselves and, feeling that I was about to slip from them, I pressed the palms of my hands together until they trembled, murmuring: *O love! O love!* many times.

---

3. Where fireplace ashes and other household refuse were dumped.
4. Jeremiah O'Donovan (1831–1915) was a militant Irish nationalist who fought on despite prison terms and banishment. *Come-all-you*: a song, of which there were many, that began "Come, all you Irishmen."

At last she spoke to me. When she addressed the first words to me I was so confused that I did not know what to answer. She asked me was I going to *Araby*.[5] I forget whether I answered yes or no. It would be a splendid bazaar, she said; she would love to go.

—And why can't you? I asked.

While she spoke she turned a silver bracelet round and round her wrist. She could not go, she said, because there would be a retreat[6] that week in her convent. Her brother and two other boys were fighting for their caps and I was alone at the railings. She held one of the spikes, bowing her head towards me. The light from the lamp opposite our door caught the white curve of her neck, lit up her hair that rested there and, falling, lit up the hand upon the railing. It fell over one side of her dress and caught the white border of a petticoat, just visible as she stood at ease.

10　　—It's well for you, she said.

—If I go, I said, I will bring you something.

What innumerable follies laid waste my waking and sleeping thoughts after that evening! I wished to annihilate the tedious intervening days. I chafed against the work of school. At night in my bedroom and by day in the classroom her image came between me and the page I strove to read. The syllables of the word *Araby* were called to me through the silence in which my soul luxuriated and cast an Eastern enchantment over me. I asked for leave to go to the bazaar on Saturday night. My aunt was surprised and hoped it was not some Freemason[7] affair. I answered few questions in class. I watched my master's face pass from amiability to sternness; he hoped I was not beginning to idle. I could not call my wandering thoughts together. I had hardly any patience with the serious work of life which, now that it stood between me and my desire, seemed to me child's play, ugly monotonous child's play.

On Saturday morning I reminded my uncle that I wished to go to the bazaar in the evening. He was fussing at the hallstand, looking for the hat-brush, and answered me curtly:

—Yes, boy, I know.

15　　As he was in the hall I could not go into the front parlour and lie at the window. I left the house in bad humour and walked slowly towards the school. The air was pitilessly raw and already my heart misgave me.

When I came home to dinner my uncle had not yet been home. Still it was early. I sat staring at the clock for some time and, when its ticking began to irritate me, I left the room. I mounted the staircase and gained the upper part of the house. The high cold empty gloomy rooms liberated me and I went from room to room singing. From the front window I saw my companions playing below in the street. Their cries reached me weakened and indistinct and, leaning my forehead against the cool glass, I looked over at the dark house where she lived. I may have stood there for an hour, seeing nothing but the brown-clad figure cast by my imagination, touched discreetly by the lamplight at the curved neck, at the hand upon the railings and at the border below the dress.

5. Charity bazaar billed as a "Grand Oriental Fete," Dublin, May 1894.
6. Period of withdrawal dedicated to prayer and religious study.
7. Freemasons—members of an influential, secretive, and highly ritualistic fraternal organization—were considered enemies of Catholics.

When I came downstairs again I found Mrs. Mercer sitting at the fire. She was an old garrulous woman, a pawnbroker's widow, who collected used stamps for some pious purpose. I had to endure the gossip of the tea-table. The meal was prolonged beyond an hour and still my uncle did not come. Mrs. Mercer stood up to go: she was sorry she couldn't wait any longer, but it was after eight o'clock and she did not like to be out late, as the night air was bad for her. When she had gone I began to walk up and down the room, clenching my fists. My aunt said:

—I'm afraid you may put off your bazaar for this night of Our Lord.

At nine o'clock I heard my uncle's latchkey in the halldoor. I heard him talking to himself and heard the hallstand rocking when it had received the weight of his overcoat. I could interpret these signs. When he was midway through his dinner I asked him to give me the money to go to the bazaar. He had forgotten.

—The people are in bed and after their first sleep now, he said. 20

I did not smile. My aunt said to him energetically:

—Can't you give him the money and let him go? You've kept him late enough as it is.

My uncle said he was very sorry he had forgotten. He said he believed in the old saying: *All work and no play makes Jack a dull boy.* He asked me where I was going and, when I had told him a second time he asked me did I know *The Arab's Farewell to his Steed.*[8] When I left the kitchen he was about to recite the opening lines of the piece to my aunt.

I held a florin[9] tightly in my hand as I strode down Buckingham Street towards the station. The sight of the streets thronged with buyers and glaring with gas recalled to me the purpose of my journey. I took my seat in a third-class carriage of a deserted train. After an intolerable delay the train moved out of the station slowly. It crept onward among ruinous houses and over the twinkling river. At Westland Row Station a crowd of people pressed to the carriage doors; but the porters moved them back, saying that it was a special train for the bazaar. I remained alone in the bare carriage. In a few minutes the train drew up beside an improvised wooden platform. I passed out on to the road and saw by the lighted dial of a clock that it was ten minutes to ten. In front of me was a large building which displayed the magical name.

I could not find any sixpenny entrance and, fearing that the bazaar would be 25 closed, I passed in quickly through a turnstile, handing a shilling to a weary-looking man. I found myself in a big hall girdled at half its height by a gallery. Nearly all the stalls were closed and the greater part of the hall was in darkness. I recognized a silence like that which pervades a church after a service. I walked into the centre of the bazaar timidly. A few people were gathered about the stalls which were still open. Before a curtain, over which the words *Café Chantant*[1] were written in coloured lamps, two men were counting money on a salver. I listened to the fall of the coins.

Remembering with difficulty why I had come I went over to one of the stalls and examined porcelain vases and flowered tea-sets. At the door of the stall a

8. Or *The Arab's Farewell to His Horse*, a sentimental nineteenth-century poem by Caroline Norton. The speaker has sold the horse.
9. A two-shilling piece, thus four times the "sixpenny entrance" fee.
1. Café with music (French).

young lady was talking and laughing with two young gentlemen. I remarked
their English accents and listened vaguely to their conversation.

—O, I never said such a thing!

—O, but you did!

—O, but I didn't!

30   —Didn't she say that?

—Yes. I heard her.

—O, there's a . . . fib!

Observing me the young lady came over and asked me did I wish to buy anything. The tone of her voice was not encouraging; she seemed to have spoken to
me out of a sense of duty. I looked humbly at the great jars that stood like eastern guards at either side of the dark entrance to the stall and murmured:

—No, thank you.

35   The young lady changed the position of one of the vases and went back to the
two young men. They began to talk of the same subject. Once or twice the
young lady glanced at me over her shoulder.

I lingered before her stall, though I knew my stay was useless, to make my
interest in her wares seem the more real. Then I turned away slowly and walked
down the middle of the bazaar. I allowed the two pennies to fall against the
sixpence in my pocket. I heard a voice call from one end of the gallery that the
light was out. The upper part of the hall was now completely dark.

Gazing up into the darkness I saw myself as a creature driven and derided by
vanity; and my eyes burned with anguish and anger.

1914

QUESTIONS

1. How do the first three paragraphs of ARABY characterize the environment in which
   the narrator lives? How might that environment inspire and shape his fascination
   with Mangan's sister? with Araby?
2. What kind of "vanity" does the narrator attribute to himself at the story's end? Why
   is he filled with "anguish and anger"?
3. How might ARABY work as a sort of quest narrative (see "Common Plot Types" in
   ch. 2)? In these terms, what is the significance of the narrator's reference to "romance,"
   his vision of himself carrying a "chalice safely through a throng of foes" (par. 5), and
   Araby's "Eastern" theme (par. 12)?

AMY TAN

(b. 1952)

A Pair of Tickets

Amy Tan was born in Oakland, California, just two
and a half years after her parents immigrated from
China. She received her MA in linguistics from San
Jose State University and has worked on programs for
disabled children and as a freelance writer. In 1987, at
age thirty-five, she visited China for the first time—
"As soon as my feet touched China, I became Chinese"—and returned to write her first

book, *The Joy Luck Club* (1989), a novel composed of stories told by four Chinese immigrant women and their American-born daughters. Tan has written more best-selling novels—including *The Kitchen God's Wife* (1991), *The Hundred Secret Senses* (1995), *The Bonesetter's Daughter* (2000), *Saving Fish from Drowning* (2006), and *The Valley of Amazement* (2013)—and has coauthored two children's books. Her first book of nonfiction, *The Opposite of Fate: A Book of Musings* (2003), explores lucky accidents, choice, and memory. Tan is also a backup singer for Rock Bottom Remainders, a rock band made up of fellow writers, including Stephen King and Dave Barry; they make appearances at benefits that support literacy programs for children.

The minute our train leaves the Hong Kong border and enters Shenzhen, China, I feel different. I can feel the skin on my forehead tingling, my blood rushing through a new course, my bones aching with a familiar old pain. And I think, My mother was right. I am becoming Chinese.

"Cannot be helped," my mother said when I was fifteen and had vigorously denied that I had any Chinese whatsoever below my skin. I was a sophomore at Galileo High in San Francisco, and all my Caucasian friends agreed: I was about as Chinese as they were. But my mother had studied at a famous nursing school in Shanghai, and she said she knew all about genetics. So there was no doubt in her mind, whether I agreed or not: Once you are born Chinese, you cannot help but feel and think Chinese.

"Someday you will see," said my mother. "It's in your blood, waiting to be let go."

And when she said this, I saw myself transforming like a werewolf, a mutant tag of DNA suddenly triggered, replicating itself insidiously into a *syndrome*, a cluster of telltale Chinese behaviors, all those things my mother did to embarrass me—haggling with store owners, pecking her mouth with a toothpick in public, being color-blind to the fact that lemon yellow and pale pink are not good combinations for winter clothes.

But today I realize I've never really known what it means to be Chinese. I am 5 thirty-six years old. My mother is dead and I am on a train, carrying with me her dreams of coming home. I am going to China.

We are going to Guangzhou, my seventy-two-year-old father, Canning Woo, and I, where we will visit his aunt, whom he has not seen since he was ten years old. And I don't know whether it's the prospect of seeing his aunt or if it's because he's back in China, but now he looks like he's a young boy, so innocent and happy I want to button his sweater and pat his head. We are sitting across from each other, separated by a little table with two cold cups of tea. For the first time I can ever remember, my father has tears in his eyes, and all he is seeing out the train window is a sectioned field of yellow, green, and brown, a narrow canal flanking the tracks, low rising hills, and three people in blue jackets riding an ox-driven cart on this early October morning. And I can't help myself. I also have misty eyes, as if I had seen this a long, long time ago, and had almost forgotten.

In less than three hours, we will be in Guangzhou, which my guidebook tells me is how one properly refers to Canton these days. It seems all the cities I have heard of, except Shanghai, have changed their spellings. I think they are saying China has changed in other ways as well. Chungking is Chongqing. And Kweilin is Guilin. I have looked these names up, because after we see my father's aunt in Guangzhou, we will catch a plane to Shanghai, where I will meet my two half-sisters for the first time.

They are my mother's twin daughters from her first marriage, little babies she was forced to abandon on a road as she was fleeing Kweilin for Chungking in 1944. That was all my mother had told me about these daughters, so they had remained babies in my mind, all these years, sitting on the side of a road, listening to bombs whistling in the distance while sucking their patient red thumbs.

And it was only this year that someone found them and wrote with this joyful news. A letter came from Shanghai, addressed to my mother. When I first heard about this, that they were alive, I imagined my identical sisters transforming from little babies into six-year-old girls. In my mind, they were seated next to each other at a table, taking turns with the fountain pen. One would write a neat row of characters: *Dearest Mama. We are alive.* She would brush back her wispy bangs and hand the other sister the pen, and she would write: *Come get us. Please hurry.*

10   Of course they could not know that my mother had died three months before, suddenly, when a blood vessel in her brain burst. One minute she was talking to my father, complaining about the tenants upstairs, scheming how to evict them under the pretense that relatives from China were moving in. The next minute she was holding her head, her eyes squeezed shut, groping for the sofa, and then crumpling softly to the floor with fluttering hands.

So my father had been the first one to open the letter, a long letter it turned out. And they did call her Mama. They said they always revered her as their true mother. They kept a framed picture of her. They told her about their life, from the time my mother last saw them on the road leaving Kweilin to when they were finally found.

And the letter had broken my father's heart so much—these daughters calling my mother from another life he never knew—that he gave the letter to my mother's old friend Auntie Lindo and asked her to write back and tell my sisters, in the gentlest way possible, that my mother was dead.

But instead Auntie Lindo took the letter to the Joy Luck Club and discussed with Auntie Ying and Auntie An-mei what should be done, because they had known for many years about my mother's search for her twin daughters, her endless hope. Auntie Lindo and the others cried over this double tragedy, of losing my mother three months before, and now again. And so they couldn't help but think of some miracle, some possible way of reviving her from the dead, so my mother could fulfill her dream.

So this is what they wrote to my sisters in Shanghai: "Dearest Daughters, I too have never forgotten you in my memory or in my heart. I never gave up hope that we would see each other again in a joyous reunion. I am only sorry it has been too long. I want to tell you everything about my life since I last saw you. I want to tell you this when our family comes to see you in China. . . ." They signed it with my mother's name.

15   It wasn't until all this had been done that they first told me about my sisters, the letter they received, the one they wrote back.

"They'll think she's coming, then," I murmured. And I had imagined my sisters now being ten or eleven, jumping up and down, holding hands, their pigtails bouncing, excited that their mother—*their* mother—was coming, whereas my mother was dead.

"How can you say she is not coming in a letter?" said Auntie Lindo. "She is their mother. She is your mother. You must be the one to tell them. All these years, they have been dreaming of her." And I thought she was right.

But then I started dreaming, too, of my mother and my sisters and how it would be if I arrived in Shanghai. All these years, while they waited to be found, I had lived with my mother and then had lost her. I imagined seeing my sisters at the airport. They would be standing on their tiptoes, looking anxiously, scanning from one dark head to another as we got off the plane. And I would recognize them instantly, their faces with the identical worried look.

"*Jyejye, Jyejye.* Sister, Sister. We are here," I saw myself saying in my poor version of Chinese.

"Where is Mama?" they would say, and look around, still smiling, two flushed and eager faces. "Is she hiding?" And this would have been like my mother, to stand behind just a bit, to tease a little and make people's patience pull a little on their hearts. I would shake my head and tell my sisters she was not hiding.

"Oh, that must be Mama, no?" one of my sisters would whisper excitedly, pointing to another small woman completely engulfed in a tower of presents. And that, too, would have been like my mother, to bring mountains of gifts, food, and toys for children—all bought on sale—shunning thanks, saying the gifts were nothing, and later turning the labels over to show my sisters, "Calvin Klein, 100% wool."

I imagined myself starting to say, "Sisters, I am sorry, I have come alone . . ." and before I could tell them—they could see it in my face—they were wailing, pulling their hair, their lips twisted in pain, as they ran away from me. And then I saw myself getting back on the plane and coming home.

After I had dreamed this scene many times—watching their despair turn from horror into anger—I begged Auntie Lindo to write another letter. And at first she refused.

"How can I say she is dead? I cannot write this," said Auntie Lindo with a stubborn look.

"But it's cruel to have them believe she's coming on the plane," I said. "When they see it's just me, they'll hate me."

"Hate you? Cannot be." She was scowling. "You are their own sister, their only family."

"You don't understand," I protested.

"What I don't understand?" she said.

And I whispered, "They'll think I'm responsible, that she died because I didn't appreciate her."

And Auntie Lindo looked satisfied and sad at the same time, as if this were true and I had finally realized it. She sat down for an hour, and when she stood up she handed me a two-page letter. She had tears in her eyes. I realized that the very thing I had feared, she had done. So even if she had written the news of my mother's death in English, I wouldn't have had the heart to read it.

"Thank you," I whispered.

The landscape has become gray, filled with low flat cement buildings, old factories, and then tracks and more tracks filled with trains like ours passing by in the opposite direction. I see platforms crowded with people wearing drab Western clothes, with spots of bright colors: little children wearing pink and yellow, red and peach. And there are soldiers in olive green and red, and old ladies in gray tops and pants that stop mid-calf. We are in Guangzhou.

Before the train even comes to a stop, people are bringing down their belongings from above their seats. For a moment there is a dangerous shower of heavy suitcases laden with gifts to relatives, half-broken boxes wrapped in miles of string to keep the contents from spilling out, plastic bags filled with yarn and vegetables and packages of dried mushrooms, and camera cases. And then we are caught in a stream of people rushing, shoving, pushing us along, until we find ourselves in one of a dozen lines waiting to go through customs. I feel as if I were getting on a number 30 Stockton bus in San Francisco. I am in China, I remind myself. And somehow the crowds don't bother me. It feels right. I start pushing too.

I take out the declaration forms and my passport. "Woo," it says at the top, and below that, "June May," who was born in "California, U.S.A.," in 1951. I wonder if the customs people will question whether I'm the same person as in the passport photo. In this picture, my chin-length hair is swept back and artfully styled. I am wearing false eyelashes, eye shadow, and lip liner. My cheeks are hollowed out by bronze blusher. But I had not expected the heat in October. And now my hair hangs limp with the humidity. I wear no makeup; in Hong Kong my mascara had melted into dark circles and everything else had felt like layers of grease. So today my face is plain, unadorned except for a thin mist of shiny sweat on my forehead and nose.

35   Even without makeup, I could never pass for true Chinese. I stand five-foot-six, and my head pokes above the crowd so that I am eye level only with other tourists. My mother once told me my height came from my grandfather, who was a northerner, and may have even had some Mongol blood. "This is what your grandmother once told me," explained my mother. "But now it is too late to ask her. They are all dead, your grandparents, your uncles, and their wives and children, all killed in the war, when a bomb fell on our house. So many generations in one instant."

She had said this so matter-of-factly that I thought she had long since gotten over any grief she had. And then I wondered how she knew they were all dead.

"Maybe they left the house before the bomb fell," I suggested.

"No," said my mother. "Our whole family is gone. It is just you and I."

"But how do you know? Some of them could have escaped."

40   "Cannot be," said my mother, this time almost angrily. And then her frown was washed over by a puzzled blank look, and she began to talk as if she were trying to remember where she had misplaced something. "I went back to that house. I kept looking up to where the house used to be. And it wasn't a house, just the sky. And below, underneath my feet, were four stories of burnt bricks and wood, all the life of our house. Then off to the side I saw things blown into the yard, nothing valuable. There was a bed someone used to sleep in, really just a metal frame twisted up at one corner. And a book, I don't know what kind, because every page had turned black. And I saw a teacup which was unbroken but filled with ashes. And then I found my doll, with her hands and legs broken, her hair burned off. . . . When I was a little girl, I had cried for that doll, seeing it all alone in the store window, and my mother had bought it for me. It was an American doll with yellow hair. It could turn its legs and arms. The eyes moved up and down. And when I married and left my family home, I gave the doll to my youngest niece, because she was like me. She cried if that doll was not with her always. Do you see? If she

was in the house with that doll, her parents were there, and so everybody was there, waiting together, because that's how our family was."

The woman in the customs booth stares at my documents, then glances at me briefly, and with two quick movements stamps everything and sternly nods me along. And soon my father and I find ourselves in a large area filled with thousands of people and suitcases. I feel lost and my father looks helpless.

"Excuse me," I say to a man who looks like an American. "Can you tell me where I can get a taxi?" He mumbles something that sounds Swedish or Dutch.

"Syau Yen! Syau Yen!" I hear a piercing voice shout from behind me. An old woman in a yellow knit beret is holding up a pink plastic bag filled with wrapped trinkets. I guess she is trying to sell us something. But my father is staring down at this tiny sparrow of a woman, squinting into her eyes. And then his eyes widen, his face opens up and he smiles like a pleased little boy.

"Aiyi! Aiyi!"—Auntie Auntie!—he says softly.

"Syau Yen!" coos my great-aunt. I think it's funny she has just called my 45 father "Little Wild Goose." It must be his baby milk name, the name used to discourage ghosts from stealing children.

They clasp each other's hands—they do not hug—and hold on like this, taking turns saying, "Look at you! You are so old. Look how old you've become!" They are both crying openly, laughing at the same time, and I bite my lip, trying not to cry. I'm afraid to feel their joy. Because I am thinking how different our arrival in Shanghai will be tomorrow, how awkward it will feel.

Now Aiyi beams and points to a Polaroid picture of my father. My father had wisely sent pictures when he wrote and said we were coming. See how smart she was, she seems to intone as she compares the picture to my father. In the letter, my father had said we would call her from the hotel once we arrived, so this is a surprise, that they've come to meet us. I wonder if my sisters will be at the airport.

It is only then that I remember the camera. I had meant to take a picture of my father and his aunt the moment they met. It's not too late.

"Here, stand together over here," I say, holding up the Polaroid. The camera flashes and I hand them the snapshot. Aiyi and my father still stand close together, each of them holding a corner of the picture, watching as their images begin to form. They are almost reverentially quiet. Aiyi is only five years older than my father, which makes her around seventy-seven. But she looks ancient, shrunken, a mummified relic. Her thin hair is pure white, her teeth are brown with decay. So much for stories of Chinese women looking young forever, I think to myself.

Now Aiyi is crooning to me: *"Jandale."* So big already. She looks up at me, at 50 my full height, and then peers into her pink plastic bag—her gifts to us, I have figured out—as if she is wondering what she will give to me, now that I am so old and big. And then she grabs my elbow with her sharp pincerlike grasp and turns me around. A man and a woman in their fifties are shaking hands with my father, everybody smiling and saying, "Ah! Ah!" They are Aiyi's oldest son and his wife, and standing next to them are four other people, around my age, and a little girl who's around ten. The introductions go by so fast, all I know is that one of them is Aiyi's grandson, with his wife, and the other is her granddaughter, with her husband. And the little girl is Lili, Aiyi's great-granddaughter.

Aiyi and my father speak the Mandarin dialect from their childhood, but the rest of the family speaks only the Cantonese of their village. I understand only Mandarin but can't speak it that well. So Aiyi and my father gossip unrestrained in Mandarin, exchanging news about people from their old village. And they stop only occasionally to talk to the rest of us, sometimes in Cantonese, sometimes in English.

"Oh, it is as I suspected," says my father, turning to me. "He died last summer." And I already understood this. I just don't know who this person, Li Gong, is. I feel as if I were in the United Nations and the translators had run amok.

"Hello," I say to the little girl. "My name is Jing-mei." But the little girl squirms to look away, causing her parents to laugh with embarrassment. I try to think of Cantonese words I can say to her, stuff I learned from friends in Chinatown, but all I can think of are swear words, terms for bodily functions, and short phrases like "tastes good," "tastes like garbage," and "she's really ugly." And then I have another plan: I hold up the Polaroid camera, beckoning Lili with my finger. She immediately jumps forward, places one hand on her hip in the manner of a fashion model, juts out her chest, and flashes me a toothy smile. As soon as I take the picture she is standing next to me, jumping and giggling every few seconds as she watches herself appear on the greenish film.

By the time we hail taxis for the ride to the hotel, Lili is holding tight onto my hand, pulling me along.

55   In the taxi, Aiyi talks nonstop, so I have no chance to ask her about the different sights we are passing by.

"You wrote and said you would come only for one day," says Aiyi to my father in an agitated tone. "One day! How can you see your family in one day! Toishan is many hours' drive from Guangzhou. And this idea to call us when you arrive. This is nonsense. We have no telephone."

My heart races a little. I wonder if Auntie Lindo told my sisters we would call from the hotel in Shanghai?

Aiyi continues to scold my father. "I was so beside myself, ask my son, almost turned heaven and earth upside down trying to think of a way! So we decided the best was for us to take the bus from Toishan and come into Guangzhou— meet you right from the start."

And now I am holding my breath as the taxi driver dodges between trucks and buses, honking his horn constantly. We seem to be on some sort of long freeway overpass, like a bridge above the city. I can see row after row of apartments, each floor cluttered with laundry hanging out to dry on the balcony. We pass a public bus, with people jammed in so tight their faces are nearly wedged against the window. Then I see the skyline of what must be downtown Guangzhou. From a distance, it looks like a major American city, with highrises and construction going on everywhere. As we slow down in the more congested part of the city, I see scores of little shops, dark inside, lined with counters and shelves. And then there is a building, its front laced with scaffolding made of bamboo poles held together with plastic strips. Men and women are standing on narrow platforms, scraping the sides, working without safety straps or helmets. Oh, would OSHA[1] have a field day here, I think.

---

1. The Occupational Safety and Health Administration, a division of the U.S. Department of Labor.

Aiyi's shrill voice rises up again: "So it is a shame you can't see our village, 60 our house. My sons have been quite successful, selling our vegetables in the free market. We had enough these last few years to build a big house, three stories, all of new brick, big enough for our whole family and then some. And every year, the money is even better. You Americans aren't the only ones who know how to get rich!"

The taxi stops and I assume we've arrived, but then I peer out at what looks like a grander version of the Hyatt Regency. "This is communist China?" I wonder out loud. And then I shake my head toward my father. "This must be the wrong hotel." I quickly pull out our itinerary, travel tickets, and reservations. I had explicitly instructed my travel agent to choose something inexpensive, in the thirty-to-forty-dollar range. I'm sure of this. And there it says on our itinerary: Garden Hotel, Huanshi Dong Lu. Well, our travel agent had better be prepared to eat the extra, that's all I have to say.

The hotel is magnificent. A bellboy complete with uniform and sharp-creased cap jumps forward and begins to carry our bags into the lobby. Inside, the hotel looks like an orgy of shopping arcades and restaurants all encased in granite and glass. And rather than be impressed, I am worried about the expense, as well as the appearance it must give Aiyi, that we rich Americans cannot be without our luxuries even for one night.

But when I step up to the reservation desk, ready to haggle over this booking mistake, it is confirmed. Our rooms are prepaid, thirty-four dollars each. I feel sheepish, and Aiyi and the others seem delighted by our temporary surroundings. Lili is looking wide-eyed at an arcade filled with video games.

Our whole family crowds into one elevator, and the bellboy waves, saying he will meet us on the eighteenth floor. As soon as the elevator door shuts, everybody becomes very quiet, and when the door finally opens again, everybody talks at once in what sounds like relieved voices. I have the feeling Aiyi and the others have never been on such a long elevator ride.

Our rooms are next to each other and are identical. The rugs, drapes, bed- 65 spreads are all in shades of taupe. There's a color television with remote-control panels built into the lamp table between the two twin beds. The bathroom has marble walls and floors. I find a built-in wet bar with a small refrigerator stocked with Heineken beer, Coke Classic, and Seven-Up, mini-bottles of Johnnie Walker Red, Bacardi rum, and Smirnoff vodka, and packets of M & M's, honey-roasted cashews, and Cadbury chocolate bars. And again I say out loud, "This is communist China?"

My father comes into my room. "They decided we should just stay here and visit," he says, shrugging his shoulders. "They say, Less trouble that way. More time to talk."

"What about dinner?" I ask. I have been envisioning my first real Chinese feast for many days already, a big banquet with one of those soups steaming out of a carved winter melon, chicken wrapped in clay, Peking duck, the works.

My father walks over and picks up a room service book next to a *Travel & Leisure* magazine. He flips through the pages quickly and then points to the menu. "This is what they want," says my father.

So it's decided. We are going to dine tonight in our rooms, with our family, sharing hamburgers, french fries, and apple pie à la mode.

70 Aiyi and her family are browsing the shops while we clean up. After a hot ride on the train, I'm eager for a shower and cooler clothes.

The hotel has provided little packets of shampoo which, upon opening, I discover is the consistency and color of hoisin sauce.[2] This is more like it, I think. This is China. And I rub some in my damp hair.

Standing in the shower, I realize this is the first time I've been by myself in what seems like days. But instead of feeling relieved, I feel forlorn. I think about what my mother said, about activating my genes and becoming Chinese. And I wonder what she meant.

Right after my mother died, I asked myself a lot of things, things that couldn't be answered, to force myself to grieve more. It seemed as if I wanted to sustain my grief, to assure myself that I had cared deeply enough.

But now I ask the questions mostly because I want to know the answers. What was that pork stuff she used to make that had the texture of sawdust? What were the names of the uncles who died in Shanghai? What had she dreamt all these years about her other daughters? All the times when she got mad at me, was she really thinking about them? Did she wish I were they? Did she regret that I wasn't?

75 At one o'clock in the morning, I awake to tapping sounds on the window. I must have dozed off and now I feel my body uncramping itself. I'm sitting on the floor, leaning against one of the twin beds. Lili is lying next to me. The others are asleep, too, sprawled out on the beds and floor. Aiyi is seated at a little table, looking very sleepy. And my father is staring out the window, tapping his fingers on the glass. The last time I listened my father was telling Aiyi about his life since he last saw her. How he had gone to Yenching University, later got a post with a newspaper in Chungking, met my mother there, a young widow. How they later fled together to Shanghai to try to find my mother's family house, but there was nothing there. And then they traveled eventually to Canton and then to Hong Kong, then Haiphong and finally to San Francisco. . . .

"Suyuan didn't tell me she was trying all these years to find her daughters," he is now saying in a quiet voice. "Naturally, I did not discuss her daughters with her. I thought she was ashamed she had left them behind."

"Where did she leave them?" asks Aiyi. "How were they found?"

I am wide awake now. Although I have heard parts of this story from my mother's friends.

"It happened when the Japanese took over Kweilin," says my father.

80 "Japanese in Kweilin?" says Aiyi. "That was never the case. Couldn't be. The Japanese never came to Kweilin."

"Yes, that is what the newspapers reported. I know this because I was working for the news bureau at the time. The Kuomintang[3] often told us what we could say and could not say. But we knew the Japanese had come into Kwangsi Province. We had sources who told us how they had captured the Wuchang-

2. Sweet brownish-red sauce made from soybeans, sugar, water, spices, garlic, and chili.
3. National People's Party, led by Generalissimo Chiang Kai-shek (1887–1975), which fought successfully against the Japanese occupation before being defeated militarily in 1949 by the Chinese Communist Party, led by Mao Zedong (1893–1976).

Canton railway. How they were coming overland, making very fast progress, marching toward the provincial capital."

Aiyi looks astonished. "If people did not know this, how could Suyuan know the Japanese were coming?"

"An officer of the Kuomintang secretly warned her," explains my father. "Suyuan's husband also was an officer and everybody knew that officers and their families would be the first to be killed. So she gathered a few possessions and, in the middle of the night, she picked up her daughters and fled on foot. The babies were not even one year old."

"How could she give up those babies!" sighs Aiyi. "Twin girls. We have never had such luck in our family." And then she yawns again.

"What were they named?" she asks. I listen carefully. I had been planning on 85 using just the familiar "Sister" to address them both. But now I want to know how to pronounce their names.

"They have their father's surname, Wang," says my father. "And their given names are Chwun Yu and Chwun Hwa."

"What do the names mean?" I ask.

"Ah." My father draws imaginary characters on the window. "One means 'Spring Rain,' the other 'Spring Flower,'" he explains in English, "because they born in the spring, and of course rain come before flower, same order these girls are born. Your mother like a poet, don't you think?"

I nod my head. I see Aiyi nod her head forward, too. But it falls forward and stays there. She is breathing deeply, noisily. She is asleep.

"And what does Ma's name mean?" I whisper. 90

"'Suyuan,'" he says, writing more invisible characters on the glass. "The way she write it in Chinese, it mean 'Long-Cherished Wish.' Quite a fancy name, not so ordinary like flower name. See this first character, it mean something like 'Forever Never Forgotten.' But there is another way to write 'Suyuan.' Sound exactly the same, but the meaning is opposite." His finger creates the brushstrokes of another character. "The first part look the same: 'Never Forgotten.' But the last part add to first part make the whole word mean 'Long-Held Grudge.' Your mother get angry with me, I tell her her name should be Grudge."

My father is looking at me, moist-eyed. "See, I pretty clever, too, hah?"

I nod, wishing I could find some way to comfort him. "And what about my name," I ask, "what does 'Jing-mei' mean?"

"Your name also special," he says. I wonder if any name in Chinese is not something special. "'Jing' like excellent *jing*. Not just good, it's something pure, essential, the best quality. *Jing* is good leftover stuff when you take impurities out of something like gold, or rice, or salt. So what is left—just pure essence. And 'Mei,' this is common *mei*, as in *meimei*, 'younger sister.'"

I think about this. My mother's long-cherished wish. Me, the younger sister 95 who was supposed to be the essence of the others. I feed myself with the old grief, wondering how disappointed my mother must have been. Tiny Aiyi stirs suddenly, her head rolls and then falls back, her mouth opens as if to answer my question. She grunts in her sleep, tucking her body more closely into the chair.

"So why did she abandon those babies on the road?" I need to know, because now I feel abandoned too.

"Long time I wondered this myself," says my father. "But then I read that letter from her daughters in Shanghai now, and I talk to Auntie Lindo, all the others. And then I knew. No shame in what she done. None."

"What happened?"

"Your mother running away—" begins my father.

100   "No, tell me in Chinese," I interrupt. "Really, I can understand."

He begins to talk, still standing at the window, looking into the night.

After fleeing Kweilin, your mother walked for several days trying to find a main road. Her thought was to catch a ride on a truck or wagon, to catch enough rides until she reached Chungking, where her husband was stationed.

She had sewn money and jewelry into the lining of her dress, enough, she thought, to barter rides all the way. If I am lucky, she thought, I will not have to trade the heavy gold bracelet and jade ring. These were things from her mother, your grandmother.

By the third day, she had traded nothing. The roads were filled with people, everybody running and begging for rides from passing trucks. The trucks rushed by, afraid to stop. So your mother found no rides, only the start of dysentery pains in her stomach.

105   Her shoulders ached from the two babies swinging from scarf slings. Blisters grew on the palms from holding two leather suitcases. And then the blisters burst and began to bleed. After a while, she left the suitcases behind, keeping only the food and a few clothes. And later she also dropped the bags of wheat flour and rice and kept walking like this for many miles, singing songs to her little girls, until she was delirious with pain and fever.

Finally, there was not one more step left in her body. She didn't have the strength to carry those babies any farther. She slumped to the ground. She knew she would die of her sickness, or perhaps from thirst, from starvation, or from the Japanese, who she was sure were marching right behind her.

She took the babies out of the slings and sat them on the side of the road, then lay down next to them. You babies are so good, she said, so quiet. They smiled back, reaching their chubby hands for her, wanting to be picked up again. And then she knew she could not bear to watch her babies die with her.

She saw a family with three young children in a cart going by. "Take my babies, I beg you," she cried to them. But they stared back with empty eyes and never stopped.

She saw another person pass and called out again. This time a man turned around, and he had such a terrible expression—your mother said it looked like death itself—she shivered and looked away.

110   When the road grew quiet, she tore open the lining of her dress, and stuffed jewelry under the shirt of one baby and money under the other. She reached into her pocket and drew out the photos of her family, the picture of her father and mother, the picture of herself and her husband on their wedding day. And she wrote on the back of each the names of the babies and this same message: "Please care for these babies with the money and valuables provided. When it is safe to come, if you bring them to Shanghai, 9 Weichang Lu, the Li family will be glad to give you a generous reward. Li Suyuan and Wang Fuchi."

And then she touched each baby's cheek and told her not to cry. She would go down the road to find them some food and would be back. And without looking back, she walked down the road, stumbling and crying, thinking only of this one last hope, that her daughters would be found by a kindhearted person who would care for them. She would not allow herself to imagine anything else.

She did not remember how far she walked, which direction she went, when she fainted, or how she was found. When she awoke, she was in the back of a bouncing truck with several other sick people, all moaning. And she began to scream, thinking she was now on a journey to Buddhist hell. But the face of an American missionary lady bent over her and smiled, talking to her in a soothing language she did not understand. And yet she could somehow understand. She had been saved for no good reason, and it was now too late to go back and save her babies.

When she arrived in Chungking, she learned her husband had died two weeks before. She told me later she laughed when the officers told her this news, she was so delirious with madness and disease. To come so far, to lose so much and to find nothing.

I met her in a hospital. She was lying on a cot, hardly able to move, her dysentery had drained her so thin. I had come in for my foot, my missing toe, which was cut off by a piece of falling rubble. She was talking to herself, mumbling.

"Look at these clothes," she said, and I saw she had on a rather unusual dress 115 for wartime. It was silk satin, quite dirty, but there was no doubt it was a beautiful dress.

"Look at this face," she said, and I saw her dusty face and hollow cheeks, her eyes shining black. "Do you see my foolish hope?"

"I thought I had lost everything, except these two things," she murmured. "And I wondered which I would lose next. Clothes or hope? Hope or clothes?"

"But now, see here, look what is happening," she said, laughing, as if all her prayers had been answered. And she was pulling hair out of her head as easily as one lifts new wheat from wet soil.

It was an old peasant woman who found them. "How could I resist?" the peasant woman later told your sisters when they were older. They were still sitting obediently near where your mother had left them, looking like little fairy queens waiting for their sedan to arrive.

The woman, Mei Ching, and her husband, Mei Han, lived in a stone cave. 120 There were thousands of hidden caves like that in and around Kweilin so secret that the people remained hidden even after the war ended. The Meis would come out of their cave every few days and forage for food supplies left on the road, and sometimes they would see something that they both agreed was a tragedy to leave behind. So one day they took back to their cave a delicately painted set of rice bowls, another day a little footstool with a velvet cushion and two new wedding blankets. And once, it was your sisters.

They were pious people, Muslims, who believed the twin babies were a sign of double luck, and they were sure of this when, later in the evening, they discovered how valuable the babies were. She and her husband had never seen rings and bracelets like those. And while they admired the pictures, knowing the babies came from a good family, neither of them could read or write. It was not until many months later that Mei Ching found someone who could read the writing on the back. By then, she loved these baby girls like her own.

In 1952 Mei Han, the husband, died. The twins were already eight years old, and Mei Ching now decided it was time to find your sisters' true family.

She showed the girls the picture of their mother and told them they had been born into a great family and she would take them back to see their true mother and grandparents. Mei Ching told them about the reward, but she swore she would refuse it. She loved these girls so much, she only wanted them to have what they were entitled to—a better life, a fine house, educated ways. Maybe the family would let her stay on as the girls' amah.[4] Yes, she was certain they would insist.

Of course, when she found the place at 9 Weichang Lu, in the old French Concession, it was something completely different. It was the site of a factory building, recently constructed, and none of the workers knew what had become of the family whose house had burned down on that spot.

125   Mei Ching could not have known, of course, that your mother and I, her new husband, had already returned to that same place in 1945 in hopes of finding both her family and her daughters.

Your mother and I stayed in China until 1947. We went to many different cities—back to Kweilin, to Changsha, as far south as Kunming. She was always looking out of one corner of her eye for twin babies, then little girls. Later we went to Hong Kong, and when we finally left in 1949 for the United States, I think she was even looking for them on the boat. But when we arrived, she no longer talked about them. I thought, At last, they have died in her heart.

When letters could be openly exchanged between China and the United States, she wrote immediately to old friends in Shanghai and Kweilin. I did not know she did this. Auntie Lindo told me. But of course, by then, all the street names had changed. Some people had died, others had moved away. So it took many years to find a contact. And when she did find an old schoolmate's address and wrote asking her to look for her daughters, her friend wrote back and said this was impossible, like looking for a needle on the bottom of the ocean. How did she know her daughters were in Shanghai and not somewhere else in China? The friend, of course, did not ask, How do you know your daughters are still alive?

So her schoolmate did not look. Finding babies lost during the war was a matter of foolish imagination, and she had no time for that.

But every year, your mother wrote to different people. And this last year, I think she got a big idea in her head, to go to China and find them herself. I remember she told me, "Canning, we should go, before it is too late, before we are too old." And I told her we were already too old, it was already too late.

130   I just thought she wanted to be a tourist! I didn't know she wanted to go and look for her daughters. So when I said it was too late, that must have put a terrible thought in her head that her daughters might be dead. And I think this possibility grew bigger and bigger in her head, until it killed her.

Maybe it was your mother's dead spirit who guided her Shanghai schoolmate to find her daughters. Because after your mother died, the schoolmate saw your sisters, by chance, while shopping for shoes at the Number One Department Store on Nanjing Dong Road. She said it was like a dream, seeing these two women who looked so much alike, moving down the stairs together. There was something about their facial expressions that reminded the schoolmate of your mother.

---

4. Maidservant or nurse.

She quickly walked over to them and called their names, which of course, they did not recognize at first, because Mei Ching had changed their names. But your mother's friend was so sure, she persisted. "Are you not Wang Chwun Yu and Wang Chwun Hwa?" she asked them. And then these double-image women became very excited, because they remembered the names written on the back of an old photo, a photo of a young man and woman they still honored, as their much-loved first parents, who had died and become spirit ghosts still roaming the earth looking for them.

At the airport, I am exhausted. I could not sleep last night. Aiyi had followed me into my room at three in the morning, and she instantly fell asleep on one of the twin beds, snoring with the might of a lumberjack. I lay awake thinking about my mother's story, realizing how much I have never known about her, grieving that my sisters and I had both lost her.

And now at the airport, after shaking hands with everybody, waving good-bye, I think about all the different ways we leave people in this world. Cheerily waving good-bye to some at airports, knowing we'll never see each other again. Leaving others on the side of the road, hoping that we will. Finding my mother in my father's story and saying good-bye before I have a chance to know her better.

Aiyi smiles at me as we wait for our gate to be called. She is so old. I put one arm around her and one arm around Lili. They are the same size, it seems. And then it's time. As we wave good-bye one more time and enter the waiting area, I get the sense I am going from one funeral to another. In my hand I'm clutching a pair of tickets to Shanghai. In two hours we'll be there.   135

The plane takes off. I close my eyes. How can I describe to them in my broken Chinese about our mother's life? Where should I begin?

"Wake up, we're here," says my father. And I awake with my heart pounding in my throat. I look out the window and we're already on the runway. It's gray outside.

And now I'm walking down the steps of the plane, onto the tarmac and toward the building. If only, I think, if only my mother had lived long enough to be the one walking toward them. I am so nervous I cannot even feel my feet. I am just moving somehow.

Somebody shouts, "She's arrived!" And then I see her. Her short hair. Her small body. And that same look on her face. She has the back of her hand pressed hard against her mouth. She is crying as though she had gone through a terrible ordeal and were happy it is over.

And I know it's not my mother, yet it is the same look she had when I was five and   140 had disappeared all afternoon, for such a long time, that she was convinced I was dead. And when I miraculously appeared, sleepy-eyed, crawling from underneath my bed, she wept and laughed, biting the back of her hand to make sure it was true.

And now I see her again, two of her, waving, and in one hand there is a photo, the Polaroid I sent them. As soon as I get beyond the gate, we run toward each other, all three of us embracing, all hesitations and expectations forgotten.

"Mama, Mama," we all murmur, as if she is among us.

My sisters look at me, proudly. *"Meimei jandale,"* says one sister proudly to the other. "Little Sister has grown up." I look at their faces again and I see no trace of my mother in them. Yet they still look familiar. And now I also see what part of me is Chinese. It is so obvious. It is my family. It is in our blood. After all these years, it can finally be let go.

My sisters and I stand, arms around each other, laughing and wiping the tears from each other's eyes. The flash of the Polaroid goes off and my father hands me the snapshot. My sisters and I watch quietly together, eager to see what develops.
145   The gray-green surface changes to the bright colors of our three images, sharpening and deepening all at once. And although we don't speak, I know we all see it: Together we look like our mother. Her same eyes, her same mouth, open in surprise to see, at last, her long-cherished wish.

1989

QUESTIONS

1. Why is the opening scene of A PAIR OF TICKETS—the train journey from Hong Kong to Guangzhou—an appropriate setting for June May's remark that she is "becoming Chinese" (par. 1)?
2. When June May arrives in Guangzhou, what are some details that seem familiar to her, and what are some that seem exotic? Why is she so preoccupied with comparing China to America?
3. June May says that she "could never pass for true Chinese" (par. 35), yet by the end of the story she has discovered "what part of [her] is Chinese" (par. 143). How does the meaning of "Chinese" evolve throughout the story?

JUDITH ORTIZ COFER
(1952–2016)
Volar[1]

Born in Hormigueros, Puerto Rico, Judith Ortiz Cofer just two years later moved with her family, first to New Jersey and later to Georgia, experiences that would inspire much of her later fiction and poetry. "How can you inject passion and purpose into your work if it has no roots?" she once asked, avowing that her own roots included a long line of women storytellers who "infected" her at a very early age with the desire to tell stories both on and off the page. After earning an MA at Florida Atlantic University (1977), Ortiz Cofer returned to Georgia, teaching at the University of Georgia for over 26 years. Among her numerous publications are the novels *The Line of the Sun* (1989), in which a young girl relates the history of her ne'er-do-well uncle's emigration from Puerto Rico, *The Meaning of Consuelo* (2003), and *Call Me Maria* (2006); the poetry collection *A Love Story Beginning in Spanish* (2005); and *The Latin Deli* (1993) and *The Year of Our Revolution* (1998), two collections that seamlessly interweave fiction, nonfiction, and poetry, thereby demonstrating, in Ortiz Cofer's words, "the need to put things together in a holistic way."

1. To fly (Spanish).

At twelve I was an avid consumer of comic books—*Supergirl* being my favorite. I spent my allowance of a quarter a day on two twelve-cent comic books or a double issue for twenty-five. I had a stack of *Legion of Super Heroes* and *Supergirl* comic books in my bedroom closet that was as tall as I am. I had a recurring dream in those days: that I had long blond hair and could fly. In my dream I climbed the stairs to the top of our apartment building as myself, but as I went up each flight, changes would be taking place. Step by step I would fill out: My legs would grow long, my arms harden into steel, and my hair would magically go straight and turn a golden color. Of course I would add the bonus of breasts, but not too large; Supergirl had to be aerodynamic. Sleek and hard as a supersonic missile. Once on the roof, my parents safely asleep in their beds, I would get on tiptoe, arms outstretched in the position for flight, and jump out my fifty-story-high window into the black lake of the sky. From up there, over the rooftops, I could see everything, even beyond the few blocks of our barrio;[2] with my X-ray vision I could look inside the homes of people who interested me. Once I saw our landlord, whom I knew my parents feared, sitting in a treasure-room dressed in an ermine coat and a large gold crown. He sat on the floor counting his dollar bills. I played a trick on him. Going up to his building's chimney, I blew a little puff of my superbreath into his fireplace, scattering his stacks of money so that he had to start counting all over again. I could more or less program my Supergirl dreams in those days by focusing on the object of my current obsession. This way I "saw" into the private lives of my neighbors, my teachers, and in the last days of my childish fantasy and the beginning of adolescence, into the secret room of the boys I liked. In the mornings I'd wake up in my tiny bedroom with the incongruous—at least in our tiny apartment—white "princess" furniture my mother had chosen for me, and find myself back in my body: my tight curls still clinging to my head, skinny arms and legs and flat chest unchanged.

In the kitchen my mother and father would be talking softly over a café con leche.[3] She would come "wake me" exactly forty-five minutes after they had gotten up. It was their time together at the beginning of each day and even at an early age I could feel their disappointment if I interrupted them by getting up too early. So I would stay in my bed recalling my dreams of flight, perhaps planning my next flight. In the kitchen they would be discussing events in the barrio. Actually, he would be carrying that part of the conversation; when it was her turn to speak she would, more often than not, try shifting the topic toward her desire to see her *familia* on the Island: *How about a vacation in Puerto Rico together this year, Querido?*[4] *We could rent a car, go to the beach. We could . . .* And he would answer patiently, gently, *Mi amor,*[5] *do you know how much it would cost for all of us to fly there? It is not possible for me to take the time off . . . Mi vida,*[6] *please understand. . . .* And I knew that soon she would rise from the table. Not abruptly. She would light a cigarette and look out the kitchen window. The view was of a dismal alley that was littered with refuse thrown from

2. Spanish-speaking neighborhood or district in the United States or any district in a Spanish-speaking country.
3. Coffee with milk (Spanish).
4. Beloved, dear (Spanish).
5. My love (Spanish).
6. My life (Spanish).

windows. The space was too narrow for anyone larger than a skinny child to enter safely, so it was never cleaned. My mother would check the time on the clock over her sink, the one with a prayer for patience and grace written in Spanish. A birthday gift. She would see that it was time to wake me. She'd sigh deeply and say the same thing the view from her kitchen window always inspired her to say: *Ay, si yo pudiera volar.*[7]

1993

QUESTIONS

1. VOLAR seems simultaneously vague about its general setting and detailed about its particular setting, at least when it comes to place (versus time). How does this combination of vagueness and specificity shape your response to the story and your sense of whom and what it is about?
2. What does the story suggest about how the characters have been shaped by their environment? about how they feel about it, and why?
3. What is the effect of the way Spanish is used both in the title and throughout the story? What might these uses of Spanish add to our understanding of the setting, the characters, and their conflicts?

7. Oh, if only I could fly (Spanish).

6 | SYMBOL AND FIGURATIVE LANGUAGE

A **symbol** is something that represents something else. Sometimes a symbol resembles or closely relates to what it represents, but often the association is arbitrary or subtle. Even so, through common usage, many symbols are instantly understood by almost everyone in a particular group. Although we rarely think of them as such, the letters of the English alphabet are themselves symbols, representing different sounds. We simply learn to recognize them, however, without thinking about whether there is any resemblance between what the symbols look like and what they represent. In other languages, one character may stand for an object or concept, such as the Chinese characters for "fire." Yet some symbols do help us by resembling what they stand for, such as the symbol for a fire alarm.

Similarly, abstractions may be represented by symbols that resemble things that are associated with them:

Although the smiley face can simply mean "Smile!" its meanings when used as an emoticon range from "I like this" to "Just joking." The skull and crossbones symbol is used on warning labels to indicate that the contents are poisonous, but it has also been associated with death, cemeteries, and pirates.

Other symbols are more arbitrary, having no literal connection with what they represent. Octagons and the color red have little to do with stopping a car, but

147

most Americans understand what a stop sign means. Such symbols, though not based on resemblances, elicit an unconscious and reflexive response from us. The meaning of a symbol is not always so concrete and practical, however. The U.S. national flag is an arbitrary symbol, having no direct resemblance to what it represents, but most people recognize its primary significance; the "stars and stripes" undoubtedly stands for the United States. Nevertheless, the flag differs from a traffic sign in that the flag evokes much more varied, complex, and even conflicting responses.

LITERARY SYMBOLISM

A symbol usually conveys an abstraction or cluster of abstractions, from the ideal to the imperceptible or the irrational, in a more concrete form. In a literary work, a symbol compares or puts together two things that are in some ways dissimilar. But literary symbolism rarely comes down to a simple equation of one thing to another. Unlike an arbitrary symbol such as a letter or traffic sign, a symbol in literature usually carries richer and more varied meanings, as does a flag or a religious image. And because of its significance, a symbol usually appears or is hinted at numerous times throughout the work. In reading literature, it may be challenging to recognize symbols, and readers may have good reasons to disagree about their interpretation, since literary works often incorporate symbolism for which there is no single "correct" interpretation. Reading a short story is not like a treasure hunt for some shiny symbol that clearly reveals all the hidden meanings; the complexity remains and requires further exploration even when we have recognized a symbol's significance. A literary symbol may be understood as an extended figure of speech that rewards further interpretation. (For one fiction writer's views of how literary symbolism works, see the excerpt from Flannery O'Connor's THE NATURE AND AIM OF FICTION.)

Traditional Symbols and Archetypes

Some symbols have been in use by many people for a long time (in which case they are known as *traditional symbols*); a white dove, for example, is a traditional symbol of peace and love. A rose can be a symbol of godly love, of romantic desire, of female beauty, of mortality (because the flower wilts), or of hidden cruelty (because it has thorns). The snake has traditionally been a symbol of evil, but in Rudyard Kipling's *The Jungle Book* (1894), the python Ka, while frightening, is on the side of law and order. A few symbolic character types, plots, objects, or settings—for example, the trickster, the quest, the garden—have become so pervasive and have recurred in so many cultures that they are considered **archetypes** (literary elements that recur in the literature and myths of multiple cultures). Fire, water, a flower, or a tree can all be considered archetypes because numerous cultures use them symbolically, often within their systems of religion or myth. Literary symbolism frequently borrows from the symbols and archetypes associated with such systems.

Allegory and Myth

A common literary form, especially in works written by and for religious believers, is the **allegory**, which may be regarded as an "extended" symbol or series of symbols that encompasses a whole work. In an allegory, concrete things and abstract concepts may be associated with each other across a narrative that consistently maintains at least two distinct levels of meaning. Because allegories set up series of correspondences, they usually help the reader translate these correspondences through the use of names that readily function as labels, often with obvious moral implications. In *The Pilgrim's Progress* (1678), the most famous prose allegory in English, the central character is named Christian; he is born in the City of Destruction and sets out for the Celestial City, passes through the Slough of Despond and Vanity Fair, meets men named Pliable and Obstinate, and so on. The point of an allegory is not to make us hunt for disguised meanings, so it is no defect if an allegory's intended meaning is clear. Instead, the purpose is to let us enjoy an invented world where everything is especially meaningful and everything corresponds to something else according to a moral or otherwise "correct" plan.

When an entire story is allegorical or symbolic, it is sometimes called a **myth**. *Myth* originally referred to a story of communal origin providing an explanation or religious interpretation of humanity, nature, the universe, or the relations among them. Sometimes we apply the term *myth* to stories associated with religions we do not believe in, and sometimes to literature that seeks to express experiences or truths that transcend any one location, culture, or time.

FIGURES OF SPEECH

Figures of speech, or **figurative language**, are similar to symbols in that they supplement or replace literal meaning, often by creating imaginative connections between our ideas and our senses. Sometimes referred to as *tropes* (literally, "turnings"), figures of speech could be described as *bending* the usual meaning of language and *shaping* our response to a work. Whether or not they have anything to do with spatial forms or "figures," or whether they rely on vision, such tropes contribute to what are called the **images** or **imagery** of a story. Many figures of speech are known by the Latin or Greek names used in classical Greek and Roman **rhetoric**, the art and science of speech and persuasion.

Just as you can enjoy gymnastics or diving competitions without knowing the names of the specific twists and turns, you can enjoy the figurative language in a story without identifying each figure of speech. Yet for the purposes of interpreting and writing about literature, it is important to learn some basic terms and distinctions so that you have access to a shared and economical language for describing your responses and the techniques that trigger them. The box below defines some of the most common figures of speech.

Key Figures of Speech

allegory   an extended association, often sustained in every element (character, plot, setting, etc.) and throughout an entire work, between two levels of meaning, usually literal and abstract. In *Animal Farm* (1945), for example, George Orwell uses an uprising of barnyard animals as an allegory for the Bolshevik revolution in Russia.

allusion   a reference, usually brief, to another text or some person or entity external to the work. Examples may range from a direct quotation of the Bible to the mention of a famous name.

irony   a meaning or outcome contrary to what is expected; in *verbal irony*, a speaker or narrator says one thing and means the reverse. When the intended meaning is harshly critical or mocking, it is called *sarcasm*. If a teenager says, "I just love it when my mom lectures me," she may well be using irony.

metaphor   a representation of one thing as if it were something else, without a verbal signal such as *like* or *as*. When Scout, in *To Kill a Mockingbird* (1960), remarks that she "inched sluggishly along the treadmill of the Maycomb County school system," she doesn't indicate what literally happened at school. She figuratively suggests how it felt by implicitly comparing the experience to being on a treadmill.

metonymy   using the name of one thing to refer to another thing associated with it. The common phrase *red tape* is a metonym for excessive paperwork and procedure that slows down an official transaction, based on the fact that such paperwork used to be tied up with red tape.

oxymoron   a combination of contradictory or opposite ideas, qualities, or entities, as in *wise fool*.

personification   sometimes called *anthropomorphism*, attributing human qualities to objects or animals. In THE OPEN BOAT, Stephen Crane personifies the birds who "sat comfortably in groups" and looked at the men with "unblinking scrutiny." He pushes personification to comic extreme in the shipwrecked men's thoughts: "If this old ninny-woman, Fate, cannot do better than this [. . . s]he is an old hen who knows not her intention." Here, "hen" is a metaphor for a silly woman, who in turn personifies the idea of destiny or fate.

simile   a representation of one thing as if it were something else, with an explicit verbal signal such as *like* or *as*. In *To Kill a Mockingbird*, Scout describes a teacher who "looked and smelled like a peppermint drop" and bored students "wriggling like a bucket of Catawba worms."

symbol   a person, place, object, or image that represents more than its literal meaning. A symbol is more than a passing comparison (such as a simile); instead, as in allegory, its meaning usually relates to most details and themes of the work. Unlike allegory, a symbol usually associates more than two entities or ideas and may be obscure or ambiguous in its meaning. Short stories (or poems) may refer to their central symbolic figure in the title, as in Raymond Carver's CATHEDRAL.

synecdoche   a form of metonymy (or name substitution) in which the part represents the whole (a *sail* refers to a ship, *wheels* to a car).

INTERPRETING SYMBOLISM AND FIGURATIVE LANGUAGE

The context of an entire story or poem or play can guide you in deciding how far to push your own "translation" of a figure of speech or whether a metaphor has the deeper significance of a symbol. It is best to read the entire story and note all of the figures of speech or imagery before you examine one as a symbol. Often, a symbol is a focal point in a story, a single object or situation that draws the attention of one or more characters.

In F. Scott Fitzgerald's *The Great Gatsby* (1925), for example, a faded billboard featuring a pair of bespectacled eyes takes on a central and multilayered significance, though there is no longstanding tradition of symbolic meaning for billboards or spectacles. Although the billboard is a purely realistic detail of setting (one can easily imagine seeing something like it along any highway today), it comes to function as a symbol, too, because of the number of times and specific ways it is discussed by the narrator and characters. When one character, George Wilson, looks up at the looming eyes and remarks, "God sees everything," it becomes pretty clear what the billboard symbolizes to him. Yet when another character immediately reminds Wilson that what he sees is only "an advertisement," we are forced to consider both what Wilson's interpretation might tell us about him and with what alternative or additional meanings the rest of the novel might invest this object. The symbol remains ambiguous and complex.

Effective symbols and figurative language cannot be extracted from the story they serve, but they can leave a lasting image of what the story is about. With guidance and practice, identifying and interpreting literary symbolism and other figurative language will begin to feel almost as familiar to you as reading the letter symbols on a page, though the meanings may be subtle, ambiguous, and far-reaching rather than straightforward.

Responding to Symbolism: Some Guidelines

- Read the story carefully, noting any details that seem to have exceptional significance, such as names, repeated actions or statements, recurring references to objects, peculiar places, allusions, or other figures of speech.
- Using your list of such possibly symbolic details, look back through the story to find the passages that feature these details. Are any of the passages connected to each other in a pattern? Do any of these interconnected details suggest themes?
- Note any symbols or images that you recognize from mythology, religion, or any other literature, art, or popular culture. Look again at the way the story presents such material. What are the signals that the fire is more than a fire, the tree is more than a tree, the ring is more than a ring? If the story invents its own symbol, find any words in the story that show how the characters see something meaningful in it.
- Once you have found a symbol—an aspect of the story that is a figure of speech, trope, image, or connection between literal and nonliteral; is extended beyond a few sentences; is more complicated than an allegory's one-to-one translation; and may be interpreted in multiple ways—review every aspect of the story, on the literal level, that relates to this symbol.
- As you write about the symbol or symbolism in a story, consider your claims about its meaning. Try not to narrow down the possible meanings of either the symbol or the story, but at the same time don't make overly grand claims

for their ability to reveal the meaning of life. When in doubt, refer back to the story and its characterization, plot, and setting.
• Remember to cite specific passages that will help your reader understand the symbol's significance. Your reader may suspect that you are reading too much into it or miscasting its meanings, so this evidence is crucial to explaining your interpretation and persuading your reader that it is reasonable.

NATHANIEL HAWTHORNE
(1804–64)

The Birth-Mark

Nathaniel Hawthorne was born in Salem, Massachusetts, a descendant of Puritan immigrants. Educated at Bowdoin College, he was agonizingly slow in winning recognition for his work and supported himself from time to time in government service—working in the customhouses of Boston and Salem and serving as the U.S. consul in Liverpool, England. His early collections of stories, *Twice-Told Tales* (1837) and *Mosses from an Old Manse* (1846), did not sell well, and it was not until the publication of his most famous novel, *The Scarlet Letter* (1850), that his fame spread beyond a discerning few. His other novels include *The House of the Seven Gables* (1851) and *The Blithedale Romance* (1852). Burdened by a deep sense of guilt for his family's role in the notorious Salem witchcraft trials over a century before he was born (one ancestor had been a judge), Hawthorne used fiction as a means of exploring the moral dimensions of sin and the human soul.

I n the latter part of the last century[1] there lived a man of science, an eminent proficient in every branch of natural philosophy,[2] who not long before our story opens had made experience of a spiritual affinity more attractive than any chemical one. He had left his laboratory to the care of an assistant, cleared his fine countenance from the furnace-smoke, washed the stain of acids from his fingers, and persuaded a beautiful woman to become his wife. In those days, when the comparatively recent discovery of electricity and other kindred mysteries of Nature seemed to open paths into the region of miracle, it was not unusual for the love of science to rival the love of woman in its depth and absorbing energy. The higher intellect, the imagination, the spirit, and even the heart might all find their congenial aliment in pursuits which, as some of their ardent votaries believed, would ascend from one step of powerful intelligence

---

1. That is, the eighteenth century; this story was first published in 1843.
2. The body of knowledge we now call science.

to another, until the philosopher should lay his hand on the secret of creative force and perhaps make new worlds for himself. We know not whether Aylmer possessed this degree of faith in man's ultimate control over nature. He had devoted himself, however, too unreservedly to scientific studies ever to be weakened from them by any second passion. His love for his young wife might prove the stronger of the two; but it could only be by intertwining itself with his love of science and uniting the strength of the latter to his own.

Such a union accordingly took place, and was attended with truly remarkable consequences and a deeply impressive moral. One day, very soon after their marriage, Aylmer sat gazing at his wife with a trouble in his countenance that grew stronger until he spoke.

"Georgiana," said he, "has it never occurred to you that the mark upon your cheek might be removed?"

"No, indeed," said she, smiling; but, perceiving the seriousness of his manner, she blushed deeply. "To tell you the truth, it has been so often called a charm, that I was simple enough to imagine it might be so."

"Ah, upon another face perhaps it might," replied her husband; "but never on 5 yours. No, dearest Georgiana, you came so nearly perfect from the hand of Nature, that this slightest possible defect, which we hesitate whether to term a defect or a beauty, shocks me, as being the visible mark of earthly imperfection."

"Shocks you, my husband!" cried Georgiana, deeply hurt; at first reddening with momentary anger, but then bursting into tears. "Then why did you take me from my mother's side? You cannot love what shocks you!"

To explain this conversation, it must be mentioned that in the center of Georgiana's left cheek there was a singular mark, deeply interwoven, as it were, with the texture and substance of her face. In the usual state of her complexion—a healthy though delicate bloom—the mark wore a tint of deeper crimson, which imperfectly defined its shape amid the surrounding rosiness. When she blushed it gradually became more indistinct, and finally vanished amid the triumphant rush of blood that bathed the whole cheek with its brilliant glow. But if any shifting motion caused her to turn pale there was the mark again, a crimson stain upon the snow, in what Aylmer sometimes deemed an almost fearful distinctness. Its shape bore not a little similarity to the human hand, though of the smallest pygmy size. Georgiana's lovers were wont to say that some fairy at her birth-hour had laid her tiny hand upon the infant's cheek, and left this impress there in token of the magic endowments that were to give her such sway over all hearts. Many a desperate swain would have risked life for the privilege of pressing his lips to the mysterious hand. It must not be concealed, however, that the impression wrought by this fairy sign-manual varied exceedingly according to the difference of temperament in the beholders. Some fastidious persons—but they were exclusively of her own sex—affirmed that the bloody hand, as they chose to call it, quite destroyed the effect of Georgiana's beauty and rendered her countenance even hideous. But it would be as reasonable to say that one of those small blue stains which sometimes occur in the purest statuary marble would convert the Eve of Powers[3] to a monster. Masculine observers, if the

3. Hiram Powers (1805–73), American sculptor and friend of Hawthorne, produced noted marble statues, including *Eve Tempted* and *Eve Disconsolate*.

birth-mark did not heighten their admiration, contented themselves with wishing it away, that the world might possess one living specimen of ideal loveliness without the semblance of a flaw. After his marriage—for he thought little or nothing of the matter before—Aylmer discovered that this was the case with himself.

Had she been less beautiful—if Envy's self could have found aught else to sneer at—he might have felt his affection heightened by the prettiness of this mimic hand, now vaguely portrayed, now lost, now stealing forth again and glimmering to and fro with every pulse of emotion that throbbed within her heart; but, seeing her otherwise so perfect, he found this one defect grow more and more intolerable with every moment of their united lives. It was the fatal flaw of humanity which Nature, in one shape or another, stamps ineffaceably on all her productions, either to imply that they are temporary and finite, or that their perfection must be wrought by toil and pain. The crimson hand expressed the ineludible gripe in which mortality clutches the highest and purest of earthly mould, degrading them into kindred with the lowest, and even with the very brutes, like whom their visible frames return to dust. In this manner, selecting it as the symbol of his wife's liability to sin, sorrow, decay, and death, Aylmer's somber imagination was not long in rendering the birth-mark a frightful object, causing him more trouble and horror than ever Georgiana's beauty, whether of soul or sense, had given him delight.

At all the seasons which should have been their happiest he invariably, and without intending it, nay, in spite of a purpose to the contrary, reverted to this one disastrous topic. Trifling as it at first appeared, it so connected itself with innumerable trains of thought and modes of feeling that it became the central point of all. With the morning twilight Aylmer opened his eyes upon his wife's face and recognized the symbol of imperfection; and when they sat together at the evening hearth his eyes wandered stealthily to her cheek, and beheld, flickering with the blaze of the wood-fire, the spectral hand that wrote mortality where he would fain[4] have worshipped. Georgiana soon learned to shudder at his gaze. It needed but a glance with the peculiar expression that his face often wore to change the roses of her cheek into a death-like paleness, amid which the crimson hand was brought strongly out, like a bas-relief of ruby on the whitest marble.

10   Late one night, when the lights were growing dim so as hardly to betray the stain on the poor wife's cheek, she herself, for the first time, voluntarily took up the subject.

"Do you remember, my dear Aylmer," said she, with a feeble attempt at a smile, "have you any recollection, of a dream last night about this odious hand?"

"None! none whatever!" replied Aylmer, starting; but then he added, in a dry, cold tone, affected for the sake of concealing the real depth of his emotion, "I might well dream of it; for, before I fell asleep, it had taken a pretty firm hold of my fancy."

"And you did dream of it?" continued Georgiana, hastily; for she dreaded lest a gush of tears should interrupt what she had to say. "A terrible dream! I wonder that you can forget it. Is it possible to forget this one expression?—'It is in her

4. Eagerly, preferably.

heart now; we must have it out!' Reflect, my husband; for by all means I would have you recall that dream."

The mind is in a sad state when Sleep, the all-involving, cannot confine her specters within the dim region of her sway, but suffers them to break forth, affrighting this actual life with secrets that perchance belong to a deeper one. Aylmer now remembered his dream. He had fancied himself with his servant Aminadab attempting an operation for the removal of the birth-mark; but the deeper went the knife, the deeper sank the hand, until at length its tiny grasp appeared to have caught hold of Georgiana's heart; whence, however, her husband was inexorably resolved to cut or wrench it away.

When the dream had shaped itself perfectly in his memory, Aylmer sat in his 15 wife's presence with a guilty feeling. Truth often finds its way to the mind close muffled in robes of sleep, and then speaks with uncompromising directness of matters in regard to which we practice an unconscious self-deception during our waking moments. Until now he had not been aware of the tyrannizing influence acquired by one idea over his mind, and of the lengths which he might find in his heart to go for the sake of giving himself peace.

"Aylmer," resumed Georgiana, solemnly, "I know not what may be the cost to both of us to rid me of this fatal birth-mark. Perhaps its removal may cause cureless deformity; or it may be the stain goes as deep as life itself. Again: do we know that there is a possibility, on any terms, of unclasping the firm gripe of this little hand which was laid upon me before I came into the world?"

"Dearest Georgiana, I have spent much thought upon the subject," hastily interrupted Aylmer. "I am convinced of the perfect practicability of its removal."

"If there be the remotest possibility of it," continued Georgiana, "let the attempt be made, at whatever risk. Danger is nothing to me; for life, while this hateful mark makes me the object of your horror and disgust—life is a burden which I would fling down with joy. Either remove this dreadful hand, or take my wretched life! You have deep science. All the world bears witness of it. You have achieved great wonders. Cannot you remove this little, little mark, which I cover with the tips of two small fingers? Is this beyond your power, for the sake of your own peace, and to save your poor wife from madness?"

"Noblest, dearest, tenderest wife," cried Aylmer, rapturously, "doubt not my power. I have already given this matter the deepest thought—thought which might almost have enlightened me to create a being less perfect than yourself. Georgiana, you have led me deeper than ever into the heart of science. I feel myself fully competent to render this dear cheek as faultless as its fellow; and then, most beloved, what will be my triumph when I shall have corrected what Nature left imperfect in her fairest work! Even Pygmalion,[5] when his sculptured woman assumed life, felt not greater ecstasy than mine will be."

"It is resolved, then," said Georgiana, faintly smiling. "And, Aylmer, spare me 20 not, though you should find the birth-mark take refuge in my heart at last."

Her husband tenderly kissed her cheek—her right cheek—not that which bore the impress of the crimson hand.

---

5. Pygmalion was a legendary artist of Cyprus who fell in love with the statue he made of a beautiful woman; in Ovid's *Metamorphoses*, she comes to life.

The next day Aylmer apprised his wife of a plan that he had formed whereby he might have opportunity for the intense thought and constant watchfulness which the proposed operation would require; while Georgiana, likewise, would enjoy the perfect repose essential to its success. They were to seclude themselves in the extensive apartments occupied by Aylmer as a laboratory, and where, during his toilsome youth, he had made discoveries in the elemental powers of Nature that had roused the admiration of all the learned societies in Europe. Seated calmly in this laboratory, the pale philosopher had investigated the secrets of the highest cloud-region and of the profoundest mines; he had satisfied himself of the causes that kindled and kept alive the fires of the volcano; and had explained the mystery of fountains, and how it is that they gush forth, some so bright and pure, and others with such rich medicinal virtues, from the dark bosom of the earth. Here, too, at an earlier period, he had studied the wonders of the human frame, and attempted to fathom the very process by which Nature assimilates all her precious influences from earth and air, and from the spiritual world, to create and foster man, her masterpiece. The latter pursuit, however, Aylmer had long laid aside in unwilling recognition of the truth—against which all seekers sooner or later stumble—that our great creative Mother, while she amuses us with apparently working in the broadest sunshine, is yet severely careful to keep her own secrets, and, in spite of her pretended openness, shows us nothing but results. She permits us, indeed, to mar, but seldom to mend, and, like a jealous patentee, on no account to make. Now, however, Aylmer resumed these half-forgotten investigations; not, of course, with such hopes or wishes as first suggested them; but because they involved much physiological truth and lay in the path of his proposed scheme for the treatment of Georgiana.

As he led her over the threshold of the laboratory Georgiana was cold and tremulous. Aylmer looked cheerfully into her face, with intent to reassure her, but was so startled with the intense glow of the birth-mark upon the whiteness of her cheek that he could not restrain a strong convulsive shudder. His wife fainted.

"Aminadab! Aminadab!" shouted Aylmer, stamping violently on the floor.

25   Forthwith there issued from an inner apartment a man of low stature, but bulky frame, with shaggy hair hanging about his visage, which was grimed with the vapors of the furnace. This personage had been Aylmer's underworker during his whole scientific career, and was admirably fitted for that office by his great mechanical readiness, and the skill with which, while incapable of comprehending a single principle, he executed all the details of his master's experiments. With his vast strength, his shaggy hair, his smoky aspect, and the indescribable earthiness that incrusted him, he seemed to represent man's physical nature; while Aylmer's slender figure, and pale, intellectual face, were no less apt a type of the spiritual element.

"Throw open the door of the boudoir, Aminadab," said Aylmer, "and burn a pastil."[6]

"Yes, master," answered Aminadab, looking intently at the lifeless form of Georgiana; and then he muttered to himself, "If she were my wife, I'd never part with that birth-mark."

6. Pastille, a lozenge or tablet of medicinal incense.

When Georgiana recovered consciousness she found herself breathing an atmosphere of penetrating fragrance, the gentle potency of which had recalled her from her death-like faintness. The scene around her looked like enchantment. Aylmer had converted those smoky, dingy, somber rooms, where he had spent his brightest years in recondite pursuits, into a series of beautiful apartments not unfit to be the secluded abode of a lovely woman. The walls were hung with gorgeous curtains, which imparted the combination of grandeur and grace that no other species of adornment can achieve; and, as they fell from the ceiling to the floor, their rich and ponderous folds, concealing all angles and straight lines, appeared to shut in the scene from infinite space. For aught Georgiana knew, it might be a pavilion among the clouds. And Aylmer, excluding the sunshine, which would have interfered with his chemical processes, had supplied its place with perfumed lamps, emitting flames of various hue, but all uniting in a soft, impurpled radiance. He now knelt by his wife's side, watching her earnestly, but without alarm; for he was confident in his science, and felt that he could draw a magic circle round her within which no evil might intrude.

"Where am I? Ah, I remember," said Georgiana, faintly; and she placed her hand over her cheek to hide the terrible mark from her husband's eyes.

"Fear not, dearest!" exclaimed he. "Do not shrink from me! Believe me, Georgiana, I even rejoice in this single imperfection, since it will be such a rapture to remove it." 30

"O, spare me!" sadly replied his wife. "Pray do not look at it again. I never can forget that convulsive shudder."

In order to soothe Georgiana, and, as it were, to release her mind from the burden of actual things, Aylmer now put in practice some of the light and playful secrets which science had taught him among its profounder lore. Airy figures, absolutely bodiless ideas, and forms of unsubstantial beauty came and danced before her, imprinting their momentary footsteps on beams of light. Though she had some indistinct idea of the method of these optical phenomena, still the illusion was almost perfect enough to warrant the belief that her husband possessed say over the spiritual world. Then again, when she felt a wish to look forth from her seclusion, immediately, as if her thoughts were answered, the procession of external existence flitted across a screen. The scenery and the figures of actual life were perfectly represented but with that bewitching yet indescribable difference which always makes a picture, an image, or a shadow so much more attractive than the original. When wearied of this, Aylmer bade her cast her eyes upon a vessel containing a quantity of earth. She did so, with little interest at first; but was soon startled to perceive the germ of a plant shooting upward from the soil. Then came the slender stalk; the leaves gradually unfolded themselves; and amid them was a perfect and lovely flower.

"It is magical!" cried Georgiana. "I dare not touch it."

"Nay, pluck it," answered Aylmer—"pluck it, and inhale its brief perfume while you may. The flower will wither in a few moments and leave nothing save its brown seed vessels; but thence may be perpetuated a race as ephemeral as itself."

But Georgiana had no sooner touched the flower than the whole plant suffered a blight, its leaves turning coal-black as if by the agency of fire. 35

"There was too powerful a stimulus," said Aylmer, thoughtfully.

To make up for this abortive experiment, he proposed to take her portrait by a scientific process of his own invention. It was to be affected by rays of light striking upon a polished plate of metal. Georgiana assented; but, on looking at the result, was affrighted to find the features of the portrait blurred and indefinable; while the minute figure of a hand appeared where the cheek should have been. Aylmer snatched the metallic plate and threw it into a jar of corrosive acid.

Soon, however, he forgot these mortifying failures. In the intervals of study and chemical experiment he came to her flushed and exhausted, but seemed invigorated by her presence, and spoke in glowing language of the resources of his art. He gave a history of the long dynasty of the alchemists, who spent so many ages in quest of the universal solvent by which the golden principle might be elicited from all things vile and base.[7] Aylmer appeared to believe that, by the plainest scientific logic, it was altogether within the limits of possibility to discover this long-sought medium. "But," he added, "a philosopher who should go deep enough to acquire the power would attain too lofty a wisdom to stoop to the exercise of it." Not less singular were his opinions in regard to the elixir vitae.[8] He more than intimated that it was at his option to concoct a liquid that should prolong life for years, perhaps interminably; but that it would produce a discord in Nature which all the world, and chiefly the quaffer of the immortal nostrum, would find cause to curse.

"Aylmer, are you in earnest?" asked Georgiana, looking at him with amazement and fear. "It is terrible to possess such power, or even to dream of possessing it."

40   "O, do not tremble, my love," said her husband. "I would not wrong either you or myself by working such inharmonious effects upon our lives; but I would have you consider how trifling, in comparison, is the skill requisite to remove this little hand."

At the mention of the birth-mark, Georgiana, as usual, shrank as if a red-hot iron had touched her cheek.

Again Aylmer applied himself to his labors. She could hear his voice in the distant furnace-room giving directions to Aminadab, whose harsh, uncouth, misshapen tones were audible in response, more like the grunt or growl of a brute than human speech. After hours of absence, Aylmer reappeared and proposed that she should now examine his cabinet of chemical products and natural treasures of the earth. Among the former he showed her a small vial, in which, he remarked, was contained a gentle yet most powerful fragrance, capable of impregnating all the breezes that blow across a kingdom. They were of inestimable value, the contents of that little vial; and, as he said so, he threw some of the perfume into the air and filled the room with piercing and invigorating delight.

"And what is this?" asked Georgiana, pointing to a small crystal globe containing a gold-colored liquid. "It is so beautiful to the eye that I could imagine it the elixir of life."

"In one sense it is," replied Aylmer; "or rather, the elixir of immortality. It is the most precious poison that ever was concocted in this world. By its aid I could apportion the lifetime of any mortal at whom you might point your finger.

7. Before the advent of modern chemistry, alchemists studied the properties of matter in a search for spiritual essences and the secret of transforming base metals into gold.
8. Literally, the drink or potion of life (Latin), imagined to give immortality.

The strength of the dose would determine whether he were to linger out years, or drop dead in the midst of a breath. No king on his guarded throne could keep his life if I, in my private station, should deem that the welfare of millions justified me in depriving him of it."

"Why do you keep such a terrific drug?" inquired Georgiana, in horror.   45

"Do not mistrust me, dearest," said her husband, smiling; "its virtuous potency is yet greater than its harmful one. But see! here is a powerful cosmetic. With a few drops of this in a vase of water, freckles may be washed away as easily as the hands are cleansed. A stronger infusion would take the blood out of the cheek, and leave the rosiest beauty a pale ghost."

"Is it with this lotion that you intend to bathe my cheek?" asked Georgiana, anxiously.

"O no," hastily replied her husband; "this is merely superficial. Your case demands a remedy that shall go deeper."

In his interviews with Georgiana, Aylmer generally made minute inquiries as to her sensations, and whether the confinement of the rooms and the temperature of the atmosphere agreed with her. These questions had such a particular drift that Georgiana began to conjecture that she was already subjected to certain physical influences, either breathed in with the fragrant air or taken with her food. She fancied likewise, but it might be altogether fancy, that there was a stirring up of her system—a strange, indefinite sensation creeping through her veins, and tingling, half painfully, half pleasurably, at her heart. Still, whenever she dared to look into the mirror, there she beheld herself pale as a white rose and with the crimson birth-mark stamped upon her cheek. Not even Aylmer now hated it so much as she.

To dispel the tedium of the hours which her husband found it necessary to   50 devote to the processes of combination and analysis, Georgiana turned over the volumes of his scientific library. In many dark old tomes she met with chapters full of romance and poetry. They were the works of the philosophers of the Middle Ages, such as Albertus Magnus, Cornelius Agrippa, Paracelsus, and the famous friar who created the prophetic Brazen Head.[9] All these antique naturalists stood in advance of their centuries, yet were imbued with some of their credulity, and therefore were believed, and perhaps imagined themselves to have acquired from the investigation of Nature a power above Nature, and from physics a sway over the spiritual world. Hardly less curious and imaginative were the early volumes of the Transactions of the Royal Society,[1] in which the members, knowing little of the limits of natural possibility, were continually recording wonders or proposing methods whereby wonders might be wrought.

But, to Georgiana, the most engrossing volume was a large folio from her husband's own hand, in which he had recorded every experiment of his scientific career, its original aim, the methods adopted for its development, and its final success or failure, with the circumstances to which either event was attributable.

9. The Brazen Head, a brass bust of a man, was supposed to be able to answer any question; the "famous friar" is Roger Bacon (c. 1214–94), an English natural philosopher, as scientists were then called. Albertus Magnus (1193/1206–80), Agrippa (1496–1535), and Paracelsus (1493–1541) were all European experimenters reputed to have near-magical powers in alchemy or astrology.
1. *The Philosophical Transactions of the Royal Society* is the oldest scientific journal in English, published since 1665.

The book, in truth, was both the history and emblem of his ardent, ambitious, imaginative, yet practical and laborious life. He handled physical details as if there were nothing beyond them; yet spiritualized them all, and redeemed himself from materialism by his strong and eager aspiration towards the infinite. In his grasp the veriest clod of earth assumed a soul. Georgiana, as she read, reverenced Aylmer and loved him more profoundly than ever, but with a less entire dependence on his judgment than heretofore. Much as he had accomplished, she could not but observe that his most splendid successes were almost invariably failures, if compared with the ideal at which he aimed. His brightest diamonds were the merest pebbles, and felt to be so by himself, in comparison with the inestimable gems which lay hidden beyond his reach. The volume, rich with achievements that had won renown for its author, was yet as melancholy a record as ever mortal hand had penned. It was the sad confession and continual exemplification of the shortcomings of the composite man, the spirit burdened with clay and working in matter, and of the despair that assails the higher nature at finding itself so miserably thwarted by the earthly part. Perhaps every man of genius, in whatever sphere, might recognize the image of his own experience in Aylmer's journal.

So deeply did these reflections affect Georgiana that she laid her face upon the open volume and burst into tears. In this situation she was found by her husband.

"It is dangerous to read in a sorcerer's books," said he with a smile, though his countenance was uneasy and displeased. "Georgiana, there are pages in that volume which I can scarcely glance over and keep my senses. Take heed lest it prove as detrimental to you."

"It has made me worship you more than ever," said she.

55   "Ah, wait for this one success," rejoined he, "then worship me if you will. I shall deem myself hardly unworthy of it. But come, I have sought you for the luxury of your voice. Sing to me, dearest."

So she poured out the liquid music of her voice to quench the thirst of his spirit. He then took his leave with a boyish exuberance of gayety, assuring her that her seclusion would endure but a little longer, and that the result was already certain. Scarcely had he departed when Georgiana felt irresistibly impelled to follow him. She had forgotten to inform Aylmer of a symptom which for two or three hours past had begun to excite her attention. It was a sensation in the fatal birth-mark, not painful, but which induced a restlessness throughout her system. Hastening after her husband, she intruded for the first time into the laboratory.

The first thing that struck her eye was the furnace, that hot and feverish worker, with the intense glow of its fire, which by the quantities of soot clustered above it seemed to have been burning for ages. There was a distilling-apparatus in full operation. Around the room were retorts, tubes, cylinders, crucibles, and other apparatus of chemical research. An electrical machine stood ready for immediate use. The atmosphere felt oppressively close, and was tainted with gaseous odors which had been tormented forth by the processes of science. The severe and homely simplicity of the apartment, with its naked walls and brick pavement, looked strange, accustomed as Georgiana had become to the fantastic elegance of her boudoir. But what chiefly, indeed almost solely, drew her attention, was the aspect of Aylmer himself.

He was pale as death, anxious and absorbed, and hung over the furnace as if it depended upon his utmost watchfulness whether the liquid which it was distilling should be the draught of immortal happiness or misery. How different from the sanguine and joyous mien that he had assumed for Georgiana's encouragement!

"Carefully now, Aminadab; carefully, thou human machine; carefully, thou man of clay," muttered Aylmer, more to himself than his assistant. "Now, if there be a thought too much or too little, it is all over."

"Ho! ho!" mumbled Aminadab. "Look, master! look!" 60

Aylmer raised his eyes hastily, and at first reddened, then grew paler than ever, on beholding Georgiana. He rushed towards her and seized her arm with a gripe that left the print of his fingers upon it.

"Why do you come hither? Have you no trust in your husband?" cried he, impetuously. "Would you throw the blight of that fatal birth-mark over my labors? It is not well done. Go, prying woman! go!"

"Nay, Aylmer," said Georgiana with the firmness of which she possessed no stinted endowment, "it is not you that have a right to complain. You mistrust your wife; you have concealed the anxiety with which you watch the development of this experiment. Think not so unworthily of me, my husband. Tell me all the risk we run, and fear not that I shall shrink; for my share in it is far less than your own."

"No, no, Georgiana!" said Aylmer, impatiently; "it must not be."

"I submit," replied she, calmly. "And, Aylmer, I shall quaff whatever draught 65 you bring me; but it will be on the same principle that would induce me to take a dose of poison if offered by your hand."

"My noble wife," said Aylmer, deeply moved, "I knew not the height and depth of your nature until now. Nothing shall be concealed. Know, then, that this crimson hand, superficial as it seems, has clutched its grasp into your being with a strength of which I had no previous conception. I have already administered agents powerful enough to do aught except to change your entire physical system. Only one thing remains to be tried. If that fail us we are ruined."

"Why did you hesitate to tell me this?" asked she.

"Because, Georgiana," said Aylmer, in a low voice, "there is danger."

"Danger? There is but one danger—that this horrible stigma shall be left upon my cheek!" cried Georgiana. "Remove it, remove it, whatever be the cost, or we shall both go mad!"

"Heaven knows your words are too true," said Aylmer, sadly. "And now, dear- 70 est, return to your boudoir. In a little while all will be tested."

He conducted her back and took leave of her with a solemn tenderness which spoke far more than his words how much was now at stake. After his departure Georgiana became rapt in musings. She considered the character of Aylmer, and did it completer justice than at any previous moment. Her heart exulted, while it trembled, at his honorable love—so pure and lofty that it would accept nothing less than perfection, nor miserably make itself contented with an earlier nature than he had dreamed of. She felt how much more precious was such a sentiment than that meaner kind which would have borne with the imperfection for her sake, and have been guilty of treason to holy love by degrading its perfect idea to the level of the actual; and with her whole spirit she prayed that, for a single moment, she might satisfy his highest and deepest conception. Longer than one moment she well knew it could not be; for his spirit was ever on the march, ever ascending, and each instant required something that was beyond the scope of the instant before.

The sound of her husband's footsteps aroused her. He bore a crystal goblet containing a liquor colorless as water, but bright enough to be the draught of immortality. Aylmer was pale; but it seemed rather the consequence of a highly wrought state of mind and tension of spirit than of fear or doubt.

"The concoction of the draught has been perfect," said he, in answer to Georgiana's look. "Unless all my science have deceived me, it cannot fail."

"Save on your account, my dearest Aylmer," observed his wife, "I might wish to put off this birth-mark of mortality by relinquishing mortality itself in preference to any other mode. Life is but a sad possession to those who have attained precisely the degree of moral advancement at which I stand. Were I weaker and blinder, it might be happiness. Were I stronger, it might be endured hopefully. But, being what I find myself, methinks I am of all mortals the most fit to die."

75   "You are fit for heaven without tasting death!" replied her husband. "But why do we speak of dying? The draught cannot fail. Behold its effect upon this plant."

On the window-seat there stood a geranium diseased with yellow blotches, which had overspread all its leaves. Aylmer poured a small quantity of the liquid upon the soil in which it grew. In a little time, when the roots of the plant had taken up the moisture, the unsightly blotches began to be extinguished in a living verdure.

"There needed no proof," said Georgiana, quietly. "Give me the goblet. I joyfully stake all upon your word."

"Drink, then, thou lofty creature!" exclaimed Aylmer, with fervid admiration. "There is no taint of imperfection on thy spirit. Thy sensible frame, too, shall soon be all perfect."

She quaffed the liquid and returned the goblet to his hand.

80   "It is grateful," said she, with a placid smile. "Methinks it is like water from a heavenly fountain; for it contains I know not what of unobtrusive fragrance and deliciousness. It allays a feverish thirst that had parched me for many days. Now, dearest, let me sleep. My earthly senses are closing over my spirit like the leaves around the heart of a rose at sunset."

She spoke the last words with a gentle reluctance, as if it required almost more energy than she could command to pronounce the faint and lingering syllables. Scarcely had they loitered through her lips ere she was lost in slumber. Aylmer sat by her side, watching her aspect with the emotions proper to a man, the whole value of whose existence was involved in the process now to be tested. Mingled with this mood, however, was the philosophic investigation characteristic of the man of science. Not the minutest symptom escaped him. A heightened flush of the cheek, a slight irregularity of breath, a quiver of the eyelid, a hardly perceptible tremor through the frame—such were the details which, as the moments passed, he wrote down in his folio volume. Intense thought had set its stamp upon every previous page of that volume; but the thoughts of years were all concentrated upon the last.

While thus employed, he failed not to gaze often at the fatal hand, and not without a shudder. Yet once, by a strange and unaccountable impulse, he pressed it with his lips. His spirit recoiled, however, in the very act; and Georgiana, out of the midst of her deep sleep, moved uneasily and murmured, as if in remonstrance. Again Aylmer resumed his watch. Nor was it without avail. The crimson hand, which at first had been strongly visible upon the marble paleness of Georgiana's cheek, now grew more faintly outlined. She remained not less pale than ever; but the birth-mark, with every breath that came and went, lost somewhat of its former distinctness. Its presence had been awful; its departure was more awful still. Watch the stain of the rainbow fading out of the sky, and you will know how that mysterious symbol passed away.

"By Heaven! it is wellnigh gone!" said Aylmer to himself, in almost irrepressible ecstasy. "I can scarcely trace it now. Success! success! And now it is like the faintest rose-color. The lightest flush of blood across her cheek would overcome it. But she is so pale!"

He drew aside the window-curtain and suffered the light of natural day to fall into the room and rest upon her cheek. At the same time he heard a gross, hoarse chuckle, which he had long known as his servant Aminadab's expression of delight.

"Ah, clod! ah, earthly mass!" cried Aylmer, laughing in a sort of frenzy, "you 85 have served me well! Matter and spirit—earth and heaven—have both done their part in this! Laugh, thing of the senses! You have earned the right to laugh."

These exclamations broke Georgiana's sleep. She slowly unclosed her eyes and gazed into the mirror which her husband had arranged for that purpose. A faint smile flitted over her lips when she recognized how barely perceptible was now that crimson hand which had once blazed forth with such disastrous brilliancy as to scare away all their happiness. But then her eyes sought Aylmer's face with a trouble and anxiety that he could by no means account for.

"My poor Aylmer!" murmured she.

"Poor? Nay, richest, happiest, most favored!" exclaimed he. "My peerless bride, it is successful! You are perfect!"

"My poor Aylmer," she repeated, with a more than human tenderness, "you have aimed loftily; you have done nobly. Do not repent that, with so high and pure a feeling, you have rejected the best the earth could offer. Aylmer, dearest Aylmer, I am dying!"

Alas! it was too true! The fatal hand had grappled with the mystery of life, 90 and was the bond by which an angelic spirit kept itself in union with a mortal frame. As the last crimson tint of the birth-mark—that sole token of human imperfection—faded from her cheek, the parting breath of the now perfect woman passed into the atmosphere, and her soul, lingering a moment near her husband, took its heavenward flight. Then a hoarse, chuckling laugh was heard again! Thus ever does the gross fatality of earth exult in its invariable triumph over the immortal essence which, in this dim sphere of half-development, demands the completeness of a higher state. Yet, had Aylmer reached a profounder wisdom, he need not thus have flung away the happiness which would have woven his mortal life of the self-same texture with the celestial. The momentary circumstance was too strong for him; he failed to look beyond the shadowy scope of time, and, living once for all in eternity, to find the perfect future in the present.

1843

QUESTIONS

1. What difference would it make if the mark on Georgiana's cheek were shaped like a fish, a heart, or an irregular oval? Why (and when) does the mark appear redder or more visible or faint? If the birthmark is explicitly a "symbol of imperfection" (par. 9), what *kinds* of imperfection does it represent?

2. Aylmer says to his wife, "Even Pygmalion, when his sculptured woman assumed life, felt not greater ecstasy than mine will be" (par. 19). How does this literary allusion to the myth of Pygmalion enhance the meaning of THE BIRTH-MARK? Is this allusion ironic, given what happens to Alymer's project to make his wife perfect?

3. Look closely at the specific settings of the story, from the laboratory to the boudoir. Note the similes, metaphors, and other figures of speech that help characterize these places. How do these different patterns of imagery contribute to the symbolism of the story? to an allegorical reading of the story?

A. S. BYATT
(b. 1936)

The Thing in the Forest

The oldest of four children (and half sister of novelist Margaret Drabble), Antonia Susan Byatt was born in Sheffield, England; graduated from Newnham College, Cambridge; and worked toward a PhD in English literature at Bryn Mawr College in Pennsylvania and at Oxford University. In the early 1960s Byatt began teaching at the University of London and published her first novel, *The Shadow of the Sun* (1964). By far the most successful of the numerous works that followed is *Possession: A Romance* (1990), the Booker Prize–winning best seller that inspired a 1996 film starring Gwyneth Paltrow. Interweaving the story of the unlikely romance between two Victorian poets reminiscent of Christina Rossetti and Robert Browning, on the one hand, with the tale of the two modern academics who uncover it, on the other, along with poems and tales ostensibly written by its protagonists, *Possession* is simultaneously a fascinating blend of literary genres—from detective and historical fiction to romance, fairy tale, and dramatic monologue—and a reflection *on* literature—how we use it to make sense of and thus "possess" our present and our past and why it often takes "possession" of us. In this, it resembles other Byatt novels such as *The Children's Book* (2009), the novellas in *Angels and Insects* (1992), and many of her short stories. Made a Dame Commander of the British Empire in 1999, Dame Byatt is also a distinguished literary critic who has written books on novelist Iris Murdoch and on poets William Wordsworth and Samuel Taylor Coleridge, as well as *Portraits in Fiction* (2001), a collection of biographical essays.

There were once two little girls who saw, or believed they saw, a thing in a forest. The two little girls were evacuees, who had been sent away from the city by train with a large number of other children.[1] They all had their names attached to their coats with safety pins, and they carried little bags or satchels, and the regulation gas mask. They wore knitted scarves and bonnets or caps, and many had knitted gloves attached to long tapes that ran along their sleeves, inside their coats, and over their shoulders and out, so that they could leave their ten woollen fingers dangling, like a spare pair of hands, like a scarecrow. They all had bare legs and scuffed shoes and wrinkled socks. Most had wounds on their knees in varying stages of freshness and scabbiness. They were at the age when children fall often and their knees were unprotected. With their suitcases, some of which were almost too big to carry, and their other impedimenta, a doll, a toy car, a comic, they were like a disorderly dwarf regiment, stomping along the platform.

The two little girls had not met before, and made friends on the train. They shared a square of chocolate, and took alternate bites at an apple. Their names were Penny and Primrose. Penny was thin and dark and taller, possibly older, than Primrose, who was plump and blond and curly. Primrose had bitten nails, and a velvet collar on her dressy green coat. Penny had a bloodless transparent paleness, a touch of blue in her fine lips. Neither of them knew where they were going, nor how long the journey might take. They did not even know why they were going, since neither of their mothers had quite known how to explain the danger to them. How do you say to your child, I am sending you away, because enemy bombs may fall out of the sky, but I myself am staying here, in what I believe may be daily danger of burning, being buried alive, gas, and ultimately perhaps a gray army rolling in on tanks over the suburbs? So the mothers (who did not resemble each other at all) behaved alike, and explained nothing—it was easier. Their daughters, they knew, were little girls, who would not be able to understand or imagine.

The girls discussed whether it was a sort of holiday or a sort of punishment, or a bit of both. Both had the idea that these were all perhaps not very good children, possibly being sent away for that reason. They were pleased to be able to define each other as "nice." They would stick together, they agreed.

The train crawled sluggishly farther and farther away from the city and their homes. It was not a clean train—the upholstery of their carriage had the dank smell of unwashed trousers, and the gusts of hot steam rolling backward past their windows were full of specks of flimsy ash, and sharp grit, and occasionally fiery sparks that pricked face and fingers like hot needles if you opened the window. It was very noisy, too, whenever it picked up a little speed. The windowpanes were both grimy and misted up. The train stopped frequently, and when it stopped they used their gloves to wipe rounds, through which they peered out at flooded fields, furrowed hillsides, and tiny stations whose names were carefully blacked out, whose platforms were empty of life.

The children did not know that the namelessness was meant to baffle or delude an invading army. They felt—they did not think it out, but somewhere inside them the idea sprouted—that the erasure was because of them, because

1. The story begins during the Blitz—that is, during the period (1940–41) when British cities were frequently bombed by German warplanes. Many children were evacuated from cities to safer locations in the countryside.

they were not meant to know where they were going or, like Hansel and Gretel, to find the way back. They did not speak to each other of this anxiety, but began the kind of conversation children have about things they really dislike, things that upset, or disgust, or frighten them. Semolina pudding with its grainy texture, mushy peas, fat on roast meat. Having your head held roughly back over the basin to have your hair washed, with cold water running down inside your liberty bodice. Gangs in playgrounds. They felt the pressure of all the other alien children in all the other carriages as a potential gang. They shared another square of chocolate, and licked their fingers, and looked out at a great white goose flapping its wings beside an inky pond.

The sky grew dark gray and in the end the train halted. The children got out, and lined up in a crocodile,[2] and were led to a mud-colored bus. Penny and Primrose managed to get a seat together, although it was over the wheel, and both of them began to feel sick as the bus bumped along snaking country lanes, under whipping branches, with torn strips of thin cloud streaming across a full moon.

They were billeted in a mansion commandeered from its owner. The children were told they were there temporarily, until families were found to take them. Penny and Primrose held hands, and said to each other that it would be wizard if they could go to the same family, because at least they would have each other. They didn't say anything to the rather tired-looking ladies who were ordering them about, because, with the cunning of little children, they knew that requests were most often counterproductive—adults liked saying no. They imagined possible families into which they might be thrust. They did not discuss what they imagined, as these pictures, like the black station signs, were too frightening, and words might make some horror solid, in some magical way. Penny, who was a reading child, imagined Victorian dark pillars of severity, like Jane Eyre's Mr. Brocklehurst, or David Copperfield's Mr. Murdstone. Primrose imagined—she didn't know why—a fat woman with a white cap and round red arms who smiled nicely but made the children wear sacking aprons and scrub the steps and the stove. "It's like we were orphans," she said to Penny. "But we're not." Penny said, "If we manage to stick together. . . ."

The great house had a double flight of imposing stairs to its front door, and carved griffins and unicorns on its balustrade. There was no lighting, because of the blackout. All the windows were shuttered. The children trudged up the staircase in their crocodile, and were given supper (Irish stew and rice pudding with a dollop of blood-red jam) before going to bed in long makeshift dormitories, where once servants had slept. They had camp beds (military issue) and gray shoddy blankets. Penny and Primrose got beds together but couldn't get a corner. They queued[3] to brush their teeth in a tiny washroom, and both suffered (again without speaking) suffocating anxiety about what would happen if they wanted to pee in the middle of the night. They also suffered from a fear that in the dark the other children would start laughing and rushing and teasing, and turn themselves into a gang. But that did not happen. Everyone was tired and anxious and orphaned. An uneasy silence, a drift of perturbed

2. Group of people lined up two by two.
3. Lined up.

sleep, came over them all. The only sounds—from all parts of the great dormitory, it seemed—were suppressed snuffles and sobs, from faces pressed into thin pillows.

When daylight came, things seemed, as they mostly do, brighter and better. The children were given breakfast in a large vaulted room, at trestle tables, porridge made with water, and a dab of the red jam, heavy cups of strong tea. Then they were told they could go out and play until lunchtime. Children in those days—wherever they came from—were not closely watched, were allowed to come and go freely, and those evacuated children were not herded into any kind of holding pen or transit camp. They were told they should be back for lunch at twelve-thirty, by which time those in charge hoped to have sorted out their provisional future lives. It was not known how they would know when it was twelve-thirty, but it was expected that—despite the fact that few of them had wristwatches—they would know how to keep an eye on the time. It was what they were used to.

Penny and Primrose went out together, in their respectable coats and laced 10
shoes, onto the terrace. The terrace appeared to them to be vast. It was covered with a fine layer of damp gravel, stained here and there bright green, or invaded by mosses. Beyond it was a stone balustrade, with a staircase leading down to a lawn. Across the lawn was a sculpted yew hedge. In the middle of the hedge was a wicket gate, and beyond the gate were trees. A forest, the little girls said to themselves.

"Let's go into the forest," said Penny, as though the sentence were required of her.

Primrose hesitated. Most of the other children were running up and down the terrace. Some boys were kicking a ball on the grass.

"O.K.," said Primrose. "We needn't go far."

"No. I've never been in a forest."

"Nor me." 15

"We ought to look at it, while we've got the opportunity," said Penny.

There was a very small child—one of the smallest—whose name, she told everyone, was Alys. With a "y," she told those who could spell, and those who couldn't, which surely included herself. She was barely out of nappies.[4] She was quite extraordinarily pretty, pink and white, with large pale-blue eyes, and sparse little golden curls all over her head and neck, through which her pink skin could be seen. Nobody seemed to be in charge of her, no elder brother or sister. She had not quite managed to wash the tearstains from her dimpled cheeks.

She had made several attempts to attach herself to Penny and Primrose. They did not want her. They were excited about meeting and liking each other. She said now, "I'm coming, too, into the forest."

"No, you aren't," said Primrose.

"You are too little, you must stay here," said Penny. 20

"You'll get lost," said Primrose.

"You won't get lost. I'll come with you," said the little creature, with an engaging smile, made for loving parents and grandparents.

4. Diapers.

"We don't want you, you see," said Primrose.

"It's for your own good," said Penny.

25   Alys went on smiling hopefully, the smile becoming more of a mask.

"It will be all right," said Alys.

"Run," said Primrose.

They ran; they ran down the steps and across the lawn, and through the gate, into the forest. They didn't look back. They were long-legged little girls. The trees were silent round them, holding out their branches to the sun.

Primrose touched the warm skin of the nearest saplings, taking off her gloves to feel the cracks and knots. Penny looked into the thick of the forest. There was undergrowth—a mat of brambles and bracken. There were no obvious paths. Dark and light came and went, inviting and mysterious, as the wind pushed clouds across the face of the sun.

30   "We have to be careful not to get lost," she said. "In stories, people make marks on tree trunks, or unroll a thread, or leave a trail of white pebbles—to find their way back."

"We needn't go out of sight of the gate," said Primrose. "We could just explore a little bit."

They set off, very slowly. They went on tiptoe, making their own narrow passages through the undergrowth, which sometimes came as high as their thin shoulders. They were urban, and unaccustomed to silence. Then they began to hear small sounds. The chatter and repeated lilt and alarm of invisible birds, high up, further in. Rustling in dry leaves. Slitherings, dry coughs, sharp cracks. They went on, pointing out to each other creepers draped with glistening berries, crimson, black, and emerald, little crops of toadstools, some scarlet, some ghostly pale, some a dead-flesh purple, some like tiny parasols—and some like pieces of meat protruding from tree trunks. They met blackberries, but didn't pick them, in case in this place they were dangerous or deceptive. They admired from a safe distance the stiff upright fruiting rods of the lords-and-ladies,[5] packed with fat red berries.

Did they hear it first or smell it? Both sound and scent were at first infinitesimal and dispersed. They gave the strange impression of moving in—in waves—from the whole perimeter of the forest. Both increased very slowly in intensity, and both were mixed, a sound and a smell fabricated of many disparate sounds and smells. A crunching, a crackling, a crushing, a heavy thumping, combining with threshing and thrashing, and added to that a gulping, heaving, boiling, bursting, steaming sound, full of bubbles and farts, piffs and explosions, swallowings and wallowings. The smell was worse, and more aggressive, than the sound. It was a liquid smell of putrefaction, the smell of maggoty things at the bottom of untended dustbins, blocked drains, mixed with the smell of bad eggs, and of rotten carpets and ancient polluted bedding. The ordinary forest smells and sounds were extinguished. The two little girls looked at each other, and took each other's hand. Speechlessly and instinctively, they crouched down behind a fallen tree trunk, and trembled, as the thing came into view.

5. Wild arum, a flowering perennial common to southern Britain.

Its head appeared to form, or first become visible in the distance, between the trees. Its face—which was triangular—appeared like a rubbery or fleshy mask over a shapeless sprouting bulb of a head, like a monstrous turnip. Its color was the color of flayed flesh, pitted with wormholes, and its expression was neither wrath nor greed but pure misery. Its most defined feature was a vast mouth, pulled down and down at the corners, tight with a kind of pain. Its lips were thin, and raised, like welts from whip-strokes. It had blind, opaque white eyes, fringed with fleshy lashes and brows like the feelers of sea anemones. Its face was close to the ground and moved toward the children between its forearms, which were squat, thick, powerful, and akimbo, like a cross between a washer-woman's and a primeval dragon's. The flesh on these forearms was glistening and mottled.

The rest of its very large body appeared to be glued together, like still wet ³⁵ papier-mâché, or the carapace of stones and straws and twigs worn by caddis flies underwater. It had a tubular shape, as a turd has a tubular shape, a provisional amalgam. It was made of rank meat, and decaying vegetation, but it also trailed veils and prostheses of man-made materials, bits of wire netting, foul dishcloths, wire-wool full of pan scrubbings, rusty nuts and bolts. It had feeble stubs and stumps of very slender legs, growing out of it at all angles, wavering and rippling like the suckered feet of a caterpillar or the squirming fringe of a centipede. On and on it came, bending and crushing whatever lay in its path, including bushes, though not substantial trees, which it wound between, awkwardly. The little girls observed, with horrified fascination, that when it met a sharp stone, or a narrow tree trunk, it allowed itself to be sliced through, flowed sluggishly round in two or three smaller worms, convulsed, and reunited. Its progress was apparently very painful, for it moaned and whined among its other burblings and belchings. They thought it could not see, or certainly could not see clearly. It and its stench passed within a few feet of their tree trunk, humping along, leaving behind it a trail of bloody slime and dead foliage.

Its end was flat and blunt, almost transparent, like some earthworms.

When it had gone, Penny and Primrose, kneeling on the moss and dead leaves, put their arms about each other, and hugged each other, shaking with dry sobs. Then they stood up, still silent, and stared together, hand in hand, at the trail of obliteration and destruction, which wound out of the forest and into it again. They went back, hand in hand, without looking behind them, afraid that the wicket gate, the lawn, the stone steps, the balustrade, the terrace, and the great house would be transmogrified, or simply not there. But the boys were still playing football on the lawn, a group of girls were skipping and singing shrilly on the gravel. They let go each other's hand, and went back in.

They did not speak to each other again.

The next day, they were separated and placed with strange families. Their stay in these families—Primrose was in a dairy farm, Penny was in a parsonage—did not in fact last very long, though then the time seemed slow-motion and endless. Later, Primrose remembered the sound of milk spurting in the pail, and Penny remembered the empty corsets of the Vicar's wife, hanging bony on the line. They remembered dandelion clocks, but you can remember those from anywhere, any time. They remembered the thing they had seen in the forest, on the contrary, in the way you remember those very few dreams—almost all nightmares—that have the quality of life itself. (Though what are dreams if not life itself?) They remembered too solid flesh, too precise a stink, a rattle and a soughing that thrilled the nerves and the cartilage of their growing ears. In the memory, as in such a dream, they felt, I cannot get out, this is a real thing in a real place.

40   They returned from evacuation, like many evacuees, so early that they then lived through wartime in the city, bombardment, blitz, unearthly light and roaring, changed landscapes, holes in their world where the newly dead had been. Both lost their fathers. Primrose's father was in the Army, and was killed, very late in the war, on a crowded troop carrier sunk in the Far East. Penny's father, a much older man, was in the Auxiliary Fire Service, and died in a sheet of flame in the East India Docks on the Thames, pumping evaporating water from a puny coil of hose. They found it hard, after the war, to remember these different men. The claspers of memory could not grip the drowned and the burned. Primrose saw an inane grin under a khaki cap, because her mother had a snapshot. Penny thought she remembered her father, already gray-headed, brushing ash off his boots and trouser cuffs as he put on his tin hat to go out. She thought she remembered a quaver of fear in his tired face, and the muscles composing themselves into resolution. It was not much what either of them remembered.

After the war, their fates were still similar and dissimilar. Penny's widowed mother embraced grief, closed her face and her curtains. Primrose's mother married one of the many admirers she had had before the ship went down, gave birth to another five children, and developed varicose veins and a smoker's cough. She dyed her blond hair with peroxide when it faded. Both Primrose and Penny were only children who now, because of the war, lived in amputated or unreal families. Penny was a good student and in due course went to university, where she chose to study developmental psychology. Primrose had little education. She was always being kept off school to look after the others. She, too, dyed her blond curls with peroxide when they turned mousy and faded. She got fat as Penny got thin. Neither of them married. Penny became a child psychologist, working with the abused, the displaced, the disturbed. Primrose did this and that. She was a barmaid. She worked in a shop. She went to help at various church crèches and Salvation Army gatherings, and discovered she had a talent for storytelling. She became Aunty Primrose, with her own repertoire. She was employed to tell tales to kindergartens and entertain at children's parties. She was much in demand at Halloween, and had her own circle of bright-colored plastic chairs in a local shopping mall, where she kept an eye on the children of burdened women, keeping them safe, offering them just a frisson of fear and terror, which made them wriggle with pleasure.

The house in the country aged differently. During this period of time—while the little girls became women—it was handed over to the nation, which turned it into a living museum. Guided tours took place in it, at regulated times. During these tours, the ballroom and intimate drawing rooms were fenced off with crimson twisted ropes on little brass one-eyed pedestals. The bored and the curious peered in at four-poster beds and pink silk fauteuils,[6] at silver-framed photographs

6. Armchairs.

of wartime royalty, and crackling crazing[7] Renaissance and Enlightenment portraits. In the room where the evacuees had eaten their rationed meals, the history of the house was displayed, on posters, in glass cases, with helpful notices and opened copies of old diaries and records. There was no mention of the evacuees, whose presence appeared to have been too brief to have left any trace.

The two women met in this room on an autumn day in 1984. They had come with a group, walking in a chattering crocodile behind a guide. They prowled around the room, each alone with herself, in opposite directions, each without acknowledging the other's presence. Their mothers had died that spring, within a week of each other, though this coincidence was unknown to them. It had made both of them think of taking a holiday, and both had chosen that part of the world. Penny was wearing a charcoal trouser suit and a black velvet hat. Primrose wore a floral knit long jacket over a shell-pink cashmere sweater, over a rustling long skirt with an elastic waist, in a mustard-colored tapestry print. Her hips and bosom were bulky. Both of them, at the same moment, leaned over an image in a medieval-looking illustrated book. Primrose thought it was a very old book. Penny assumed it was nineteenth-century mock-medieval. It showed a knight, on foot, in a forest, lifting his sword to slay something. The knight shone on the rounded slope of the page, in the light, which caught the gilding on his helmet and sword belt. It was not possible to see what was being slain. This was because, both in the tangled vegetation of the image and in the way the book was displayed in the case, the enemy, or victim, was in shadows.

Neither of them could read the ancient (or pseudo-ancient) black letter of the text beside the illustration. There was a typed description, under the book. They had to lean forward to read it, and to see what was worming its way into, or out of, the deep spine of the book, and that was how each came to see the other's face, close up, in the glass, which was both transparent and reflective. Their transparent reflected faces lost detail—cracked lipstick, pouches, fine lines of wrinkles—and looked both younger and grayer, less substantial. And that is how they came to recognize each other, as they might not have done, plump face to bony face. They breathed each other's names—Penny, Primrose—and their breath misted the glass, obscuring the knight and his opponent. I could have died, I could have wet my knickers, said Penny and Primrose afterward to each other, and both experienced this still moment as pure, dangerous shock. They read the caption, which was about the Loathly Worm, which, tradition held, had infested the countryside and had been killed more than once by scions of that house—Sir Lionel, Sir Boris, Sir Guillem. The Worm, the typewriter had tapped out, was an English worm, not a European dragon, and, like most such worms, was wingless. In some sightings it was reported as having vestigial legs, hands, or feet. In others it was limbless. It had, in monstrous form, the capacity of common or garden worms to sprout new heads or trunks if it was divided, so that two worms, or more, replaced one. This was why it had been killed so often, yet reappeared. It had been reported travelling with a slithering pack of young ones, but these may have been only revitalized segments.

Being English, they thought of tea. There was a tearoom in the great house, 45 in a converted stable at the back. There they stood silently side by side, clutching

7. Sealed with varnish that, with age, has cracked in patterns.

The Lambton Worm, as depicted in
Fairy-Gold: A Book of Old English Fairy Tales (1906)

floral plastic trays spread with briar roses, and purchased scones, superior raspberry jam in tiny jam jars, little plastic tubs of clotted cream. "You couldn't get cream or real jam in the war," said Primrose as they found a corner table. She said wartime rationing had made her permanently greedy, and thin Penny agreed it had—clotted cream was still a treat.

They watched each other warily, offering bland snippets of autobiography in politely hushed voices. Primrose thought Penny looked gaunt, and Penny thought Primrose looked raddled.[8] They established the skein of coincidences—dead fathers, unmarried status, child-caring professions, recently dead mothers. Circling like beaters,[9] they approached the covert thing in the forest. They discussed the great house, politely. Primrose admired the quality of the carpets. Penny said it was nice to see the old pictures back on the wall. Primrose said, Funny really, that there was all that history, but no sign that they, the children, that was, had ever been there. Funny, said Penny, that they should meet each other next to that book, with that picture. "Creepy," said Primrose in a light, light cobweb voice, not looking at Penny. "We saw that thing. When we went in the forest."

"Yes, we did," said Penny. "We saw it."

"Did you ever wonder," asked Primrose, "if we really saw it?"

"Never for a moment," said Penny. "That is, I don't know what it was, but I've always been quite sure we saw it."

50   "Does it change—do you remember all of it?"

8. Frazzled.
9. Hunters who beat the bushes to drive out game.

"It was a horrible thing, and yes, I remember all of it, there isn't a bit of it I can manage to forget. Though I forget all sorts of things," said Penny, in a thin voice, a vanishing voice.

"And have you ever told anyone of it, spoken of it?" asked Primrose more urgently, leaning forward.

"No," said Penny. She had not. She said, "Who would believe it?"

"That's what I thought," said Primrose. "I didn't speak. But it stuck in my mind like a tapeworm in your gut. I think it did me no good."

"It did me no good either," said Penny. "No good at all. I've thought about it," she said to the aging woman opposite, whose face quivered under her dyed goldilocks. "I think, I think there are things that are real—more real than we are—but mostly we don't cross their paths, or they don't cross ours. Maybe at very bad times we get into their world, or notice what they are doing in ours."

Primrose nodded energetically. She looked as though sharing was solace, and Penny, to whom it was not solace, grimaced with pain.

"Sometimes I think that thing finished me off," Penny said to Primrose, a child's voice rising in a woman's gullet, arousing a little girl's scared smile, which wasn't a smile on Primrose's face.

Primrose said, "It did finish her off, that little one, didn't it? She got into its path, didn't she? And when it had gone by—she wasn't anywhere," said Primrose. "That was how it was?"

"Nobody ever asked where she was or looked for her," said Penny.

"I wondered if we'd made her up," said Primrose. "But I didn't, we didn't."

"Her name was Alys."

"With a 'y.'"

There had been a mess, a disgusting mess, they remembered, but no particular sign of anything that might have been, or been part of, or belonged to, a persistent little girl called Alys.

Primrose shrugged voluptuously, let out a gale of a sigh, and rearranged her flesh in her clothes.

"Well, we know we're not mad, anyway," she said. "We've got into a mystery, but we didn't make it up. It wasn't a delusion. So it was good we met, because now we needn't be afraid we're mad, need we—we can get on with things, so to speak?"

They arranged to have dinner together the following evening. They were staying in different bed-and-breakfasts and neither of them thought of exchanging addresses. They agreed on a restaurant in the market square of the local town—Seraphina's Hot Pot—and a time, seven-thirty. They did not even discuss spending the next day together. Primrose went on a local bus tour. Penny took a long solitary walk. The weather was gray, spitting fine rain. Both arrived at their lodgings with headaches, and both made tea with the tea bags and kettle provided in their rooms. They sat on their beds. Penny's had a quilt with blowsy cabbage roses. Primrose's had a black-and-white checked gingham duvet. They turned on their televisions, watched the same game show, listened to the inordinate jolly laughter.

Seven-thirty came and went, and neither woman moved. Both, indistinctly, imagined the other waiting at a table, watching a door open and shut. Neither moved. What could they have said, they asked themselves, but only perfunctorily.

The next day, Penny thought about the wood, put on her walking shoes, and set off obliquely in the opposite direction. Primrose sat over her breakfast, which was English and ample. The wood, the real and imagined wood—both before and after she had entered it with Penny—had always been simultaneously a source of attraction and of discomfort, shading into terror. Without speaking to herself a sentence in her head—"I shall go there"—Primrose decided. And she went straight there, full of warm food, arriving as the morning brightened with the first busload of tourists, and giving them the slip, to take the path they had once taken, across the lawn and through the wicket gate.

The wood was much the same, but denser and more inviting in its new greenness. Primrose's body decided to set off in a rather different direction from the one the little girls had taken. New bracken was uncoiling with snaky force. Yesterday's rain still glittered on limp new hazel leaves and threads of gossamer. Small feathered throats above her whistled and trilled with enchanting territorial aggression and male self-assertion, which were to Primrose simply the chorus. She found a mossy bank, with posies of primroses, which she recognized and took vaguely as a good sign, a personal sign. She was better at flowers than birds, because there had been Flower Fairies in the school bookshelves when she was little, with the flowers painted accurately, accompanied by truly pretty human creatures, all children, clothed in the blues and golds, russets and purples of the flowers and fruits. Here she saw and recognized them, windflower and bryony, self-heal and dead nettle, and had—despite where she was—a lovely lapping sense of invisible, just invisible life swarming in the leaves and along the twigs.

70   She stopped. She did not like the sound of her own toiling breath. She was not very fit. She saw, then, a whisking in the bracken, a twirl of fur, thin and flaming, quivering on a tree trunk. She saw a squirrel, a red squirrel, watching her from a bough. She had to sit down, as she remembered her mother. She sat on a hummock of grass, rather heavily. She remembered them all, Nutkin and Moldywarp, Brock and Sleepy Dormouse, Natty Newt and Ferdy Frog. Her mother hadn't told stories and hadn't opened gates into imaginary worlds. But she had been good with her fingers. Every Christmas during the war, when toys, and indeed materials, were not to be had, Primrose had woken to find in her stocking a new stuffed creature, made from fur fabric, with button eyes and horny claws. There had been an artistry to them. The stuffed squirrel was the essence of squirrel, the fox was watchful, the newt was slithery. They did not wear anthropomorphic jackets or caps, which made it easier to invest them with imaginary natures. She believed in Father Christmas, and the discovery that her mother had made the toys, the vanishing of magic, had been a breathtaking blow. She could not be grateful for the skill and the imagination, so uncharacteristic of her flirtatious mother. The creatures continued to accumulate. A spider, a Bambi. She told herself stories at night about a girlwoman, an enchantress in a fairy wood, loved and protected by an army of wise and gentle animals. She slept banked in by stuffed creatures, as the house in the blitz was banked in by inadequate sandbags.

Primrose registered the red squirrel as disappointing—stringier and more rat-like than its plump gray city cousins. But she knew it was special, and when it took off from branch to branch, flicking its extended tail like a sail, gripping with its tiny hands, she set out to follow it. It would take her to the center, she thought. It could easily have leaped out of sight, she thought, but it didn't. She pushed through brambles into denser, greener shadows. Juices stained her skirts and skin. She began to tell herself a story about staunch Primrose, not giving up, making her way to "the center." Her childhood stories had all been in the third person. "She was not afraid." "She faced up to the wild beasts. They cowered." She laddered her tights and muddied her shoes and breathed heavier. The squirrel stopped to clean its face. She crushed bluebells and saw the sinister hoods of arum lilies.

She had no idea how far she had come, but she decided that the clearing where she found herself was the center. The squirrel had stopped, and was running up and down a single tree. There was a mossy mound that could have had a thronelike aspect, if you were being imaginative. So she sat on it. "She came to the center and sat on the mossy chair."

Now what?

She had not forgotten what they had seen, the blank miserable face, the powerful claws, the raggle-taggle train of accumulated decay. She had come neither to look for it nor to confront it, but she had come because it was there. She had known all her life that she, Primrose, had really been in a magic forest. She knew that the forest was the source of terror. She had never frightened the littluns she entertained, with tales of lost children in forests. She frightened them with slimy things that came up the plughole, or swarmed out of the U-bend in the lavatory, and were dispatched by bravery and magic. But the woods in her tales bred glamour. They were places where you used words like "spangles" and "sequins" for real dewdrops on real dock leaves. Primrose knew that glamour and the thing they had seen, brilliance and the ashen stink, came from the same place. She made both things safe for the littluns by restricting them to pantomime flats and sweet illustrations. She didn't look at what she knew, better not, but she did know she knew, she recognized confusedly.

Now what?

She sat on the moss, and a voice in her head said, "I want to go home." And she heard herself give a bitter, entirely grownup little laugh, for what was home? What did she know about home?

Where she lived was above a Chinese takeaway. She had a dangerous cupboard-corner she cooked in, a bed, a clothes-rail, an armchair deformed by generations of bottoms. She thought of this place in faded browns and beiges, seen through drifting coils of Chinese cooking steam, scented with stewing pork and a bubbling chicken broth. Home was not real, as all the sturdy twigs and roots in the wood were real. The stuffed animals were piled on the bed and the carpet, their fur rubbed, their pristine stare gone from their scratched eyes. She thought about what one thought was real, sitting there on the moss throne at the center. When Mum had come in, snivelling, to say Dad was dead, Primrose herself had been preoccupied with whether pudding would be tapioca or semolina, whether there would be jam, and, subsequently, how ugly Mum's dripping nose was, how she looked as though she were putting it on.[1] She remembered the semolina and the rather nasty blackberry jam, the taste and the texture, to this day. So was that real, was that home?

She had later invented a picture of a cloudy aquamarine sea under a gold sun, in which a huge fountain of white curling water rose from a foundering ship. It was very beautiful but not real. She could not remember Dad. She could remember the Thing in the Forest, and she could remember Alys. The fact that

1. Pretending.

the mossy tump had lovely colors—crimson and emerald—didn't mean she didn't remember the Thing. She remembered what Penny had said about "things that are more real than we are." She had met one. Here at the center, the spout of water was more real than the semolina, because she was where such things reign. The word she found was "reign." She had understood something, and did not know what she had understood. She wanted badly to go home, and she wanted never to move. The light was lovely in the leaves. The squirrel flirted its tail and suddenly set off again, springing into the branches. The woman lumbered to her feet and licked the bramble scratches on the back of her hands.

Penny walked very steadily, keeping to hedgerows and field-edge paths. She remembered the Thing. She remembered it clearly and daily. But she walked away, noticing and not noticing that her path was deflected by field forms and the lay of the land into a snaking sickle shape. As the day wore on, she settled into her stride and lifted her eyes. When she saw the wood on the horizon, she knew it was the wood, although she was seeing it from an unfamiliar aspect, from where it appeared to be perched on a conical hillock, ridged as though it had been grasped and squeezed by coils of strength. It was almost dusk. She mounted the slope, and went in over a suddenly discovered stile.[2]

80   Once inside, she moved cautiously. She stood stock-still, and snuffed the air for the remembered rottenness: she listened to the sounds of the trees and the creatures. She smelled rottenness, but it was normal rottenness, leaves and stems mulching back into earth. She heard sounds. Not birdsong, for it was too late in the day, but the odd raucous warning croak. She heard her own heartbeat in the thickening brown air.

It was no use looking for familiar tree trunks or tussocks. They had had a lifetime, her lifetime, to alter out of recognition.

She began to think she discerned dark tunnels in the undergrowth, where something might have rolled and slid. Mashed seedlings, broken twigs and fronds, none of it very recent. There were things caught in the thorns, flimsy colorless shreds of damp wool or fur. She peered down the tunnels and noted where the scrapings hung thickest. She forced herself to go into the dark, stooping, occasionally crawling on hands and knees. The silence was heavy. She found threadworms of knitting wool, unravelled dishcloth cotton, clinging newsprint. She found odd sausage-shaped tubes of membrane, containing fragments of hair and bone and other inanimate stuffs. They were like monstrous owl pellets, or the gut-shaped hairballs vomited by cats. Penny went forward, putting aside briars and tough stems with careful fingers. It had been here, but how long ago?

Quite suddenly, she came out at a place she remembered. The clearing was larger, the tree trunks were thicker, but the great log behind which they had hidden still lay there. The place was almost the ghost of a camp. The trees round about were hung with pennants and streamers, like the scorched, hacked, threadbare banners in the chapel of the great house, with their brown stains of earth or blood. It had been here, it had never gone away.

Penny moved slowly and dreamily round, looking for things. She found a mock-tortoiseshell hairslide, and a shoe button with a metal shank. She found a

2. Set of steps for climbing over a fence or hedge.

bird skeleton, quite fresh, bashed flat. She found ambivalent shards and several teeth, of varying sizes and shapes. She found—spread around, half hidden by roots, stained green but glinting white—a collection of small bones, finger bones, tiny toes, a rib, and finally what might be a brainpan and brow. She thought of putting them in her knapsack, and then thought she could not. She was not an anatomist. The tiny bones might have been badger or fox.

She sat down, with her back against the fallen trunk. She thought, Now I am watching myself as you do in a safe dream, but then, when I saw it, it was one of those dreams where you are inside and cannot get out. Except that it wasn't a dream.

It was the encounter with the Thing that had led her to deal professionally in dreams. Something that resembled unreality had lumbered into reality, and she had seen it. She had been the reading child, but after the sight of the Thing she had not been able to inhabit the customary and charming unreality of books. She had become good at studying what could not be seen. She took an interest in the dead, who inhabited real history. She was drawn to the invisible forces that moved in molecules and caused them to coagulate or dissipate. She had become a psychotherapist "to be useful." That was not quite accurate. The corner of the blanket that covered the unthinkable had been turned back enough for her to catch sight of it. She was in its world. It was not by accident that she had come to specialize in severely autistic children, children who twittered, or banged, or stared, who sat damp and absent on Penny's official lap and told her no dreams. The world they knew was a real world. Often Penny thought it was the real world, from which even their desperate parents were at least partly shielded. Somebody had to occupy themselves with the hopeless. Penny felt she could.

All the leaves of the forest began slowly to quaver and then to clatter. Far away, there was the sound of something heavy, and sluggish, stirring. Penny sat very still and expectant. She heard the old blind rumble, she sniffed the old stink. It came from no direction; it was all around; as though the Thing encompassed the wood, or as though it travelled in multiple fragments, as it was described in the old text. It was dark now. What was visible had no distinct color, only shades of ink and elephant.

Now, thought Penny, and just as suddenly as it had begun the turmoil ceased. It was as though the Thing had turned away; she could feel the tremble of the wood recede and become still. Quite rapidly, over the treetops, a huge disk of white gold mounted and hung. Penny remembered her father, standing in the cold light of the full moon, and saying wryly that the bombers would not come tonight, they were safe under a cloudless full moon. He had vanished in an oven of red-yellow roaring, Penny had guessed, or been told, or imagined. Her mother had sent her away before allowing the fireman to speak, who had come with the news. She had been a creep-mouse on stairs and in cubbyholes, trying to overhear what was being imparted. Her mother didn't, or couldn't, want her company. She caught odd phrases of talk—"nothing really to identify," "absolutely no doubt." He had been a tired, gentle man with ash in his trouser turnups. There had been a funeral. Penny remembered thinking there was nothing, or next to nothing, in the coffin his fellow-firemen shouldered. It went up so lightly. It was so easy to set down on the crematorium slab.

They had been living behind the blackout anyway, but her mother went on living behind drawn curtains long after the war was over.

90   The moon had released the wood, it seemed. Penny stood up and brushed leaf mold off her clothes. She had been ready for it, and it had not come. She felt disappointed. But she accepted her release and found her way back to the fields and her village along liquid trails of moonlight.

The two women took the same train back to the city, but did not encounter each other until they got out. The passengers scurried and shuffled toward the exit, mostly heads down. Both women remembered how they had set out in the war-time dark, with their twig legs and gas masks. Both raised their heads as they neared the barrier, not in hope of being met, for they would not be, but automatically, to calculate where to go and what to do. They saw each other's faces in the cavernous gloom, two pale, recognizable rounds, far enough apart for speech, and even greetings, to be awkward. In the dimness, they were reduced to similarity—dark eyeholes, set mouth. For a moment or two, they stood and simply stared. On that first occasion the station vault had been full of curling steam, and the air gritty with ash. Now the blunt-nosed sleek diesel they had left was blue and gold under a layer of grime. They saw each other through the black imagined veil that grief or pain or despair hangs over the visible world. Each saw the other's face and thought of the unforgettable misery of the face they had seen in the forest. Each thought that the other was the witness, who made the thing certainly real, who prevented her from slipping into the comfort of believing she had imagined it or made it up. So they stared at each other, blankly, without acknowledgment, then picked up their baggage, and turned away into the crowd.

Penny found that the black veil had somehow become part of her vision. She thought constantly about faces, her father's, her mother's, Primrose's face, the hopeful little girl, the woman staring up at her from the glass case, staring at her conspiratorially over the clotted cream. The blond infant Alys, an ingratiating sweet smile. The half-human face of the Thing. She tried to remember that face completely, and suffered over the detail of the dreadful droop of its mouth, the exact inanity of its blind squinnying.[3] Present faces were blank disks, shadowed moons. Her patients came and went. She was increasingly unable to distinguish one from another. The face of the Thing hung in her brain, jealously soliciting her attention, distracting her from dailiness. She had gone back to its place, and had not seen it. She needed to see it. Why she needed it was because it was more real than she was. She would go and face it. What else was there, she asked herself, and answered herself, nothing.

So she made her way back, sitting alone in the train as the fields streaked past, drowsing through a century-long night under the cabbage quilt in the B. and B. This time, she went in the old way, from the house, through the garden gate; she found the old trail quickly, her sharp eye picked up the trace of its detritus, and soon enough she was back in the clearing, where her cairn of tiny bones by the tree trunk was undisturbed. She gave a little sigh, dropped to her knees, and then sat with her back to the rotting wood and silently called the Thing. Almost immediately, she sensed its perturbation, saw the trouble in the branches, heard the lumbering, smelled its ancient smell. It was a grayish, unremarkable day. She closed her eyes briefly as the noise and movement grew stronger. When

3. Squinting.

it came, she would look it in the face, she would see what it was. She clasped her hands loosely in her lap. Her nerves relaxed. Her blood slowed. She was ready.

Primrose was in the shopping mall, putting out her circle of rainbow-colored plastic chairs. She creaked as she bent over them. It was pouring with rain outside, but the mall was enclosed like a crystal palace in a casing of glass. The floor under the rainbow chairs was gleaming dappled marble. They were in front of a dimpling fountain, with lights shining up through the greenish water, making golden rings round the polished pebbles and wishing coins that lay there. The little children collected round her: their mothers kissed them good-bye, told them to be good and quiet and listen to the nice lady. They had little transparent plastic cups of shining orange juice, and each had a biscuit in silver foil. They were all colors—black skin, brown skin, pink skin, freckled skin, pink jacket, yellow jacket, purple hood, scarlet hood. Some grinned and some whimpered, some wriggled, some were still. Primrose sat on the edge of the fountain. She had decided what to do. She smiled her best, most comfortable smile, and adjusted her golden locks. Listen to me, she told them, and I'll tell you something amazing, a story that's never been told before.

There were once two little girls who saw, or believed they saw, a thing in a forest. . . .   95

2000

QUESTIONS

1. Traditional fairy tales often rely on symbolic objects, actions, settings, or characters. How is THE THING IN THE FOREST like a fairy tale in this respect? How is it different? Are there figures of speech in this story that you would argue are not symbolic?

2. Is the "Loathly Worm" (par. 44) supernatural, imaginary, or real? Notice the description of its appearances. Can you identify different *kinds* of literal or physical traits that people see in it? Can you identify three or more concepts, feelings, or historical conditions that it might represent? Is it personified? Does it resemble other monsters in literature, art, or media?

3. Are "Penny" and "Primrose" allegorical names? How do the differences between the characters add to the symbolic meaning of the Thing? How do their different actions in the story help reveal its meanings?

SAMPLE WRITING: COMPARATIVE ESSAY

The essay below compares two stories by exploring the role symbolism plays in each. More specifically, it tackles questions posed in the fourth writing suggestion at the end of chapter 6: To what extent does anything within a story (or stories) become a symbol not only for readers but also for the characters themselves? What, for these characters, does the thing symbolize? What seems alike and different about how various characters perceive or interpret and respond to the same symbol? What is the significance and effect of their various perceptions and responses? As you read the essay, try to identify the specific strategies and techniques this student writer uses to tackle the single greatest challenge of the comparative essay—creating one coherent argument out of observations about two quite different literary texts. (For more on comparative essays, see 21.2.1.)

For ease of reference, we have altered the citations in this essay to refer to paragraph numbers. Unless your instructor indicates otherwise, you should follow convention by instead citing page numbers when writing about fiction.

Collins 1

Charles Collins
Dr. Mays
English 298
15 March 2019

Symbolism in "The Birth-Mark" and "The Thing in the Forest"

In "The Birth-Mark" by Nathaniel Hawthorne and A. S. Byatt's "The Thing in the Forest," the symbols of the birthmark and the Thing move the plots of the stories. Characters in both stories are compelled by these objects to act, though in different ways. In "The Birth-Mark," the main character, Aylmer, views his wife's birthmark as a flaw in her beauty, as well as a symbol of human imperfection, and tries to remove it. In "The Thing in the Forest," the protagonists, Penny and Primrose, react to the Thing both as a real thing and as a symbol. The characters' interpretation of these things is what creates conflict, and the stories are both shaped by the symbolic meanings that the characters ascribe to those things.

In "The Birth-Mark," Aylmer, a "natural philosopher," becomes obsessed with a birthmark in the shape of a small hand on his wife's face. The plot of the

---

story concerns his attempt to remove the mark, which results in the death of Georgiana, his wife. The reader finds out in the very beginning that Aylmer views Georgiana's birthmark as more than a mere birthmark. In fact, it is because he views the mark as symbolic that he becomes obsessed with it. He makes his thoughts clear when he says to his wife, in response to her stating that other people have found her birthmark attractive, "No, dearest Georgiana, you came so nearly perfect from the hand of Nature, that this slightest possible defect, which we hesitate whether to term a defect or a beauty, shocks me, as being the visible mark of earthly imperfection" (par. 5). Aylmer sees his wife as nearly perfect, so when he sees something that does not seem consistent with his idea of beauty, he is disturbed by it and begins to view it as having a greater meaning. The narrator later clarifies this point by saying, "In this manner, selecting it as the symbol of his wife's liability to sin, sorrow, decay, and death, Aylmer's somber imagination was not long in rendering the birth-mark a frightful object, causing him more trouble and horror than ever Georgiana's beauty, whether of soul or sense, had given him delight" (par. 8). Here the story explicitly states that Aylmer sees his wife's birthmark as more than a physical feature; to him, it is a symbol of all of the imperfect things about humans.

Though the narrator suggests that "[w]e know not whether Aylmer possessed this degree of faith in man's ultimate control over nature," such that "the philosopher should lay his hand on the secret of creative force and perhaps make new worlds for himself" (par. 1), Aylmer's actions throughout the story suggest that he does believe this. Once Aylmer sees the birthmark as a "frightful object," he becomes intent upon removing it. The birthmark to him symbolizes human imperfection, and so it is a challenge to him to conquer that imperfection and control the "defect" that Nature placed upon his wife. It is only because he views the birthmark as a symbol that it comes to have this level of control over him and to motivate his actions and thus the plot of the story.

Unfortunately for Aylmer, he does not realize the cost of getting rid of the birthmark. He succeeds in his plan, but by succeeding he ends up killing his wife. What he sees as a symbol of imperfection the reader can see as a symbol of life. In Aylmer's dream the birthmark is tied to Georgiana's heart, and he must remove her heart to remove the birthmark. Georgiana's heart and her birthmark are actually symbolic of the human spark of life that keeps her alive. Perhaps part of this spark involves imperfection, or perhaps it is "a charm (par. 4)," but either way Georgiana cannot live without it. Aminadab seems to understand this and remarks to himself that "[i]f she were my wife, I'd never part with that birth-mark" (par. 27).

However, both Aylmer and Georgiana are so horrified by what the birthmark represents that they are willing to take incredible risks to get rid of it. Georgiana even acknowledges that removing the birthmark might kill her, but says, "Danger is nothing to me; for life, while this hateful mark makes me the object of your horror and disgust . . . is a burden which I would fling down with joy" (par. 18). Because Aylmer and Georgiana view the birthmark as a mark of human imperfection, they are willing to try to remove it, so much so that Aylmer fails to see how the birthmark is tied to Georgiana's life and that Georgiana is willing to lose her life to be rid of it. Aylmer misinterprets the birthmark, thinking that it represents imperfection instead of life, and so he ends up losing his perfect wife.

The symbolism in "The Birth-Mark" is fairly straightforward. The characters openly acknowledge the power of the symbol, and the narrator of the story clearly states what meaning Aylmer finds in it. In "The Thing in the Forest" what the Thing represents is not as clear. Penny and Primrose, the story's main characters, do not view the Thing as symbolic, as Aylmer does the birthmark. Neither the narrator nor the characters directly say why the Thing is important to Penny and Primrose or even whether the Thing they see in the forest is the monster, the Loathly Worm, that they later read about in the book at the mansion. Instead of viewing the Thing as a symbol, Penny and Primrose view the Thing as real and physical. Penny says, "I think, I think there are things that are real—more real than we are—but mostly we don't cross their paths, or they don't cross ours" (par. 55). When Primrose returns to the forest she also realizes that the Thing is real, even more real than her everyday life at home. Penny and Primrose comfort each other by acknowledging that the Thing really exists, that they saw it, and that it "did finish [Alys] off" (par. 58). But despite their assertions that the Thing exists, they do not say what it is. Primrose says to Penny, "We've got into a mystery, but we didn't make it up. It wasn't a delusion" (par. 65). Though they reassure one another that the Thing is real, they recognize that what they saw is more mysterious than the mythical Loathly Worm.

Though they do not define the Thing, it motivates Penny and Primrose to act just as the birthmark causes Aylmer to act. However, each girl responds in a different way. On the one hand, Primrose, who makes her living telling fantastic stories to children, "had never frightened the littluns she entertained, with tales of lost children in forests" (par. 74). Primrose has avoided the Thing by entering a world of fairy tales where she speaks of the forest in unrealistic terms. After going to the forest and realizing "[s]he had understood something, and did not know what she had understood" (par. 78), she is able to continue with her life by finally telling the story of their encounter with the Thing as a fairy tale to children. She makes the Thing unreal and is therefore able to live with it.

Penny, on the other hand, tries to study the Thing because "[s]omething that resembled unreality had lumbered into reality, and she had seen it" (par. 86). After seeing the Thing, she becomes uninterested in fiction, like the stories Primrose told or like the novels she read as a child, and instead becomes a child psychologist who tries to scientifically study children who see things that are more real. Upon the death of her mother and her visit to the mansion and the forest, Penny feels compelled to confront the Thing, refusing to take it as a symbol. She goes into the forest to seek out the Thing, but it does not come to her. As time passes, she begins to see the darkness of the thing all around her, and so she goes back to the forest once again to confront the Thing, where presumably it finishes her off, as there is no account of her life after the encounter. When Penny goes to see the Thing for the final time, "she would look it in the face, she would see what it was. She clasped her hands loosely in her lap. Her nerves relaxed. Her blood slowed. She was ready" (par. 93). Penny treats the Thing as real, and so there are real consequences for her. Though the story does not state so explicitly, presumably the Thing kills Penny as it did Alys.

Though the characters in the story do not state what the Thing represents, the story suggests that it is a symbol of suffering and death, among other

Collins 4

things. The women's visits to the Thing correspond with the deaths of their parents. The first time the girls see the Thing is during the bombing of London during World War II, shortly before their fathers die. When they go to the mansion the second time, it is shortly after the deaths of their mothers. When the adult Primrose goes into the forest, instead of seeing the worm, she recognizes that the memory of her mother telling her about her father's death was "real" (par. 77), like the Thing. The Thing also looks and smells like something that has died, like "liquid . . . putrefaction" and "maggoty things at the bottom of untended dustbins" (par. 33), something that is decomposing. Furthermore, the characters believe that the Thing got Alys, that is, that she died. All of this suggests that the Thing is a symbol for death and that the story is about how different people handle death.

While symbolism is present in both "The Birth-Mark" and "The Thing in the Forest," it is handled in different ways. In "The Birth-Mark," on the one hand, Aylmer consistently views the birthmark as a symbol. He is obsessed with the birthmark because of what he thinks it represents. He has little concern for the birthmark as a physical, real thing. Penny and Primrose, on the other hand, are initially worried about the Thing as something real and physical. Penny never views the Thing as a symbol, but instead views it as a real thing, a monster, and presumably at the end of the story she faces it, and it kills her. Primrose, however, understands that the Thing is real, but chooses to make it a part of a fairy tale and thereby deals with it as a type of symbol, even though she does not understand what the Thing is a symbol of. By choosing to tell a story about the Thing, she makes it unreal, and it does not harm her. In both stories, the power given to symbolism or its rejection is what motivates the actions of the characters and determines the consequences they suffer.

Collins 4

WORKS CITED

Byatt, A. S. "The Thing in the Forest." Mays, pp. 164–79.
Hawthorne, Nathaniel. "The Birth-Mark." Mays, pp. 152–63.
Mays, Kelly J., editor. *The Norton Introduction to Literature*. Portable 13th ed., W. W. Norton, 2020.

7 | THEME

At some point, a responsive reader of any story or novel will inevitably ask, *Why does it all matter? What does it all mean? What's the point?* When we ask what a text means, we are inquiring, at least in part, about its **theme**—a general idea or insight conveyed by the work in its entirety. Theme is certainly not the only way fiction matters nor the only thing we take away from our experience of reading it. Nor is theme fiction's *point* in the sense of its sole "objective" or "purpose." Yet theme is a fictional work's *point* in the sense of its "essential meaning" (or meanings). And our experience of any work isn't complete unless we grapple with the question of its theme.

On rare occasions, we might not have to grapple hard or look far: A very few texts, such as **fables** and certain fairy tales and folktales, explicitly state their themes. To succeed, however, even these works must ultimately "earn" their themes, bringing a raw statement to life through their characters, plot, setting, symbols, and narration. The following fable, by Aesop, succinctly makes its point through a brief dialogue.

AESOP
The Two Crabs

One fine day two crabs came out from their home to take a stroll on the sand. "Child," said the mother, "you are walking very ungracefully. You should accustom yourself to walking straight forward without twisting from side to side."

"Pray, mother," said the young one, "do but set the example yourself, and I will follow you."

"EXAMPLE IS THE BEST PRECEPT."

* * *

In most literary works, all the elements work together to imply an unstated theme that usually requires re-reading to decipher. Even the most careful and responsive readers will likely disagree about just what the theme is or how best to state it. And each statement of a given theme will imply a slightly different view of what matters most and why.

THEME(S): SINGULAR OR PLURAL?

In practice, readers even disagree about the precise meaning of the term *theme* itself. One source of disagreement hinges on the question of whether any single work of fiction can convey more than one theme. On one side of the debate are those who use the word *theme* to refer only to the central or main idea of a work. On the other are those who use the term, as we generally do in this book, to refer to any idea a work conveys. While the former readers tend to talk about *the* theme, the latter instead refer to *a* theme in order to stress that each theme is only one of many. Regardless of whether we call all of the ideas expressed in a work *themes* or instead refer to some of them as *subthemes*, the essential points on which all agree are that a single literary work often expresses multiple ideas and that at least one of those ideas is likely to be more central or overarching and inclusive than others.

THE TWO CRABS demonstrates that even the most simple and straightforward of stories can convey more than one idea. This fable's stated theme, "Example is the best precept," emerges only because the little crab back talks to its mother, implicitly suggesting another theme: that children are sometimes wiser than their parents or even that we sometimes learn by questioning, rather than blindly following, authority. The fact that crabs naturally "twist from side to side"—that no crab *can* walk straight—certainly adds **irony** to the fable, but might it also imply yet another theme?

BE SPECIFIC: THEME AS IDEA VERSUS TOPIC OR SUBJECT

Often, you will see the term *theme* used very loosely to refer to a topic or subject captured in a noun phrase—"the wisdom of youth," "loss of innocence," "the dangers of perfectionism"—or even a single noun—"loss," "youth," "grief," or "prejudice." Identifying such topics—especially those specific enough to require a noun phrase rather than a single noun—can be a useful first step on the way to figuring out a particular story's themes and also to grouping stories together for the purpose of comparison.

For now, though, we urge you to consider this merely a first step on the path to interpreting a story. The truth is, we haven't yet said anything very insightful, revealing, or debatable about the meaning of an individual story until we articulate the idea it expresses *about* a topic such as love, prejudice, or grief. To state a theme in this much more restricted and helpful sense, you will need at least one complete sentence. Note, however, that a complete sentence is still not necessarily a statement of theme. For example, an online student essay begins with the less than scintillating sentence, "In Nathaniel Hawthorne's 'The Birth-Mark' the reader finds several themes—guilt, evil, love and alienation." One reason this sentence is both unexciting and unhelpful is that—despite its specific list of topics—we could in fact substitute for THE BIRTH-MARK almost any other story in this book. (Try it yourself.) Notice how much more interesting things get, however, when we instead articulate the story's particular insight about just one of these very general topics: "Nathaniel Hawthorne's 'The Birth-Mark' shows us that we too often destroy the very thing we love by trying to turn the good into the perfect."

DON'T BE TOO SPECIFIC: THEME AS *GENERAL* IDEA

Though a theme is specific in the sense that it is a complete idea or statement rather than a topic, it is nonetheless a *general* idea rather than one that describes the characters, plot, or settings unique to one story. Theme is a general insight illustrated *through* these elements rather than an insight *about* any of them. Look again at the statement above—"Nathaniel Hawthorne's 'The Birth-Mark' shows us that we too often destroy the very thing we love by trying to turn the good into the perfect." Now compare this statement with one such as this: "In Nathaniel Hawthorne's 'The Birth-Mark,' the scientist Aylmer kills his wife because he can't tolerate imperfection." Though both statements are valid, only the first of them is truly a statement of theme—of what the story shows us about love through Aylmer rather than what the story suggests about Aylmer himself.

THEME VERSUS MORAL

In some cases, a theme may take the form of a **moral**—a rule of conduct or maxim for living. But most themes are instead general observations and insights about how humans actually *do* behave, or about how life, the world, or some particular corner of it actually *is*, rather than moral imperatives about how people *should* behave or how life *should* ideally be. As one contemporary critic puts it, a responsive reader should thus "ask not *What does this story teach?* but *What does this story reveal?*" By the same token, we're usually on safer and more fertile ground if we phrase a theme as a statement rather than as a command. Hawthorne's "The Birth-Mark," for example, certainly demonstrates the dangers of arrogantly seeking a perfection that isn't natural or human. As a result, we might well be tempted to reduce its theme to a moral such as "Accept imperfection," "Avoid arrogance," or "Don't mess with Mother Nature." None of these statements is wholly inappropriate to the story. Yet each of them seems to underestimate the story's complexity and especially its implicit emphasis on all that humanity gains, as well as loses, in the search for perfection. As a result, a better statement of the story's theme might be "Paradoxically, both our drive for perfection and our inevitable imperfection make us human."

As you decipher and discuss the themes of the stories that follow, keep in mind that to identify a theme is not to "close the case" but rather to begin a more searching investigation of the details that make each story vivid and unique. Theme is an abstraction from the story; the story and its details do not disappear or lose significance once distilled into theme, nor could you reconstruct a story merely from a statement of its theme. Indeed, theme and story are fused, inseparable. Or, as Flannery O'Connor puts it, "You tell a story because a statement [alone] would be inadequate." Often difficult to put into words, themes are nonetheless the essential common ground that helps you care about a story and relate it to your own life—even though it seems to be about lives and experiences very different from your own.

Tips for Identifying Themes

Because theme emerges from a work in its entirety and from all the other elements working together, there is no "one-size-fits-all" method for identifying theme. Here, however, are some things to look for and consider as you read and re-read the work.

TIP	EXAMPLE
1. Pay attention to the title. A title will seldom spell out in full a work's main theme, but some titles do suggest a central topic or topics or a clue to theme. Probe the rest of the story to see what, if any, insights about that topic it ultimately seems to offer.	What might Bharati Mukherjee's "The Management of Grief," suggest about whether and how grief can be "managed"?
2. List any recurring phrases and words, especially those for abstract concepts (e.g., love, honor). Certain concrete terms (especially if noted in the title) may likewise provide clues; objects of value or potency might attract significant attention in the text (an heirloom, a weapon, a tree in a garden). Then probe the story to see how and where else it might implicitly deal with that concept or entity and what, if any, conclusions the story proposes.	Versions of the word *blind* occur six times in the relatively short first paragraph of Raymond Carver's "Cathedral," and the word recurs throughout the story. What different kinds of blindness does the story depict? What truth or insight about blindness might it ultimately offer?
3. Identify any statements that the characters or narrator(s) make about a general concept, issue, or topic such as human nature, the natural world, and so on. Look, too, for statements that potentially have a general meaning or application beyond the story, even if they refer to a specific situation in it. Then consider whether and how the story as a whole corroborates, overturns, or complicates any one such view or statement.	In A. S. Byatt's "The Thing in the Forest," one of the two protagonists observes, "I think there are things that are real—more real than we are—but mostly we don't cross their paths, or they don't cross ours. Maybe at very bad times we get into their world, or notice what they are doing in ours" (par. 55). How does the rest of the story both flesh out what these "things" might be and either corroborate or complicate this character's generalization about them?
4. If a character changes over the course of the story, articulate the truth or insight that he or she seems to discover. Then consider whether and how the story as a whole corroborates or complicates that insight.	The end of "The Thing in the Forest" implies that one of its protagonists has come to believe that even the most fantastic stories have an important function in real life. What is that function? Does the story as a whole confirm her conclusions?

TIP	EXAMPLE
5. Identify a conflict depicted in the work and state it in general terms or turn it into a general question, leaving out any reference to specific characters, situations, and so on. Then think about the insight or theme that might be implied by the way the conflict is resolved.	Through Sarty, William Faulkner's "Barn Burning" raises the question of how we should reconcile loyalty to our family with our own individual sense of right and wrong. In the end, the story implies that following our own moral code can sometimes be the more painful, as well as the more noble, option.

STEPHEN CRANE
(1871–1900)
The Open Boat

One of fourteen children, Stephen Crane and his family moved frequently before settling, after his father's death in 1880, in Asbury Park, New Jersey. Crane sporadically attended various preparatory schools and colleges without excelling at much besides baseball. Determined to be a journalist, he left school for good in 1891 and began contributing to New York newspapers. His city experiences led him to write *Maggie: A Girl of the Streets*, a realist social-reform novel published in 1893 at his own expense. His next novel, *The Red Badge of Courage* (1895), presented a stark picture of the Civil War and brought him widespread fame. Many of his stories were published in the collections *The Open Boat and Other Tales of Adventure* (1898) and *The Monster and Other Stories* (1899). Crane served as a foreign correspondent, reporting on conflicts in Cuba and Greece, and lived his last years abroad, dying of tuberculosis at the age of twenty-eight.

A Tale Intended to Be after the Fact:[1] Being the Experience of Four Men from the Sunk Steamer Commodore

I

None of them knew the color of the sky. Their eyes glanced level and were fastened upon the waves that swept toward them. These waves were of the hue of slate, save for the tops, which were of foaming white, and all of the men knew the colors of the sea. The horizon narrowed and widened, and dipped and rose,

---

1. Crane had an experience very like the one here re-created in fiction. His autobiographical account of his adventure at sea appeared in the *New York Press* on January 7, 1897.

and at all times its edge was jagged with waves that seemed thrust up in points like rocks.

Many a man ought to have a bathtub larger than the boat which here rode upon the sea. These waves were most wrongfully and barbarously abrupt and tall, and each froth-top was a problem in small-boat navigation.

The cook squatted in the bottom, and looked with both eyes at the six inches of gunwale which separated him from the ocean. His sleeves were rolled over his fat forearms, and the two flaps of his unbuttoned vest dangled as he bent to bail out the boat. Often he said, "Gawd! that was a narrow clip." As he remarked it he invariably gazed eastward over the broken sea.

The oiler, steering with one of the two oars in the boat, sometimes raised himself suddenly to keep clear of water that swirled in over the stern. It was a thin little oar, and it seemed often ready to snap.

The correspondent, pulling at the other oar, watched the waves and won- 5 dered why he was there.

The injured captain, lying in the bow, was at this time buried in that profound dejection and indifference which comes, temporarily at least, to even the bravest and most enduring when, willy-nilly, the firm fails, the army loses, the ship goes down. The mind of the master of a vessel is rooted deep in the timbers of her, though he command for a day or a decade; and this captain had on him the stern impression of a scene in the grays of dawn of seven turned faces, and later a stump of a topmast with a white ball on it, that slashed to and fro at the waves, went low and lower, and down. Thereafter there was something strange in his voice. Although steady, it was deep with mourning, and of a quality beyond oration or tears.

"Keep'er a little more south, Billie," said he.

"A little more south, sir," said the oiler in the stern.

A seat in his boat was not unlike a seat upon a bucking broncho, and by the same token a broncho is not much smaller. The craft pranced and reared and plunged like an animal. As each wave came, and she rose for it, she seemed like a horse making at a fence outrageously high. The manner of her scramble over these walls of water is a mystic thing, and, moreover, at the top of them were ordinarily these problems in white water, the foam racing down from the summit of each wave requiring a new leap, and a leap from the air. Then, after scornfully bumping a crest, she would slide and race and splash down a long incline, and arrive bobbing and nodding in front of the next menace.

A singular disadvantage of the sea lies in the fact that after successfully sur- 10 mounting one wave you discover that there is another behind it just as important and just as nervously anxious to do something effective in the way of swamping boats. In a ten-foot dinghy one can get an idea of the resources of the sea in the line of waves that is not probable to the average experience, which is never at sea in a dinghy. As each slaty wall of water approached, it shut all else from the view of the men in the boat, and it was not difficult to imagine that this particular wave was the final outburst of the ocean, the last effort of the grim water. There was a terrible grace in the move of the waves, and they came in silence, save for the snarling of the crests.

In the wan light the faces of the men must have been gray. Their eyes must have glinted in strange ways as they gazed steadily astern. Viewed from a balcony, the whole thing would, doubtless, have been weirdly picturesque. But the men in the boat had no time to see it, and if they had had leisure, there were other things to occupy their minds. The sun swung steadily up the sky, and they knew it was broad day because the color of the sea changed from slate to emerald-green streaked with amber lights, and the foam was like tumbling snow. The process of the breaking day was unknown to them. They were aware only of this effect upon the color of the waves that rolled toward them.

In disjointed sentences the cook and the correspondent argued as to the difference between a life-saving station and a house of refuge. The cook had said: "There's a house of refuge just north of the Mosquito Inlet Light, and as soon as they see us they'll come off in their boat and pick us up."

"As soon as who see us?" said the correspondent.

"The crew," said the cook.

15 "Houses of refuge don't have crews," said the correspondent. "As I understand them, they are only places where clothes and grub are stored for the benefit of shipwrecked people. They don't carry crews."

"Oh, yes, they do," said the cook.

"No, they don't," said the correspondent.

"Well, we're not there yet, anyhow," said the oiler, in the stern.

"Well," said the cook, "perhaps it's not a house of refuge that I'm thinking of as being near Mosquito Inlet Light; perhaps it's a life-saving station."

20 "We're not there yet," said the oiler in the stern.

II

As the boat bounced from the top of each wave the wind tore through the hair of the hatless men, and as the craft plopped her stern down again the spray slashed past them. The crest of each of these waves was a hill, from the top of which the men surveyed for a moment a broad tumultuous expanse, shining and wind-riven. It was probably splendid, it was probably glorious, this play of the free sea, wild with lights of emerald and white and amber.

"Bully good thing it's an on-shore wind," said the cook. "If not, where would we be? Wouldn't have a show."

"That's right," said the correspondent.

The busy oiler nodded his assent.

25 Then the captain, in the bow, chuckled in a way that expressed humor, contempt, tragedy, all in one. "Do you think we've got much of a show now, boys?" said he.

Whereupon the three were silent, save for a trifle of hemming and hawing. To express any particular optimism at this time they felt to be childish and stupid, but they all doubtless possessed this sense of the situation in their minds. A young man thinks doggedly at such times. On the other hand, the ethics of their condition was decidedly against any open suggestion of hopelessness. So they were silent.

"Oh, well," said the captain, soothing his children, "we'll get ashore all right."

But there was that in his tone which made them think; so the oiler quoth, "Yes! if this wind holds."

The cook was bailing. "Yes! if we don't catch hell in the surf."

Canton-flannel[2] gulls flew near and far. Sometimes they sat down on the 30
sea, near patches of brown seaweed that rolled over the waves with a movement
like carpets on a line in a gale. The birds sat comfortably in groups, and they
were envied by some in the dinghy, for the wrath of the sea was no more to them
than it was to a covey of prairie chickens a thousand miles inland. Often they
came very close and stared at the men with black bead-like eyes. At these times
they were uncanny and sinister in their unblinking scrutiny, and the men
hooted angrily at them, telling them to be gone. One came, and evidently
decided to alight on the top of the captain's head. The bird flew parallel to the
boat and did not circle, but made short sidelong jumps in the air in chicken
fashion. His black eyes were wistfully fixed upon the captain's head. "Ugly
brute," said the oiler to the bird. "You look as if you were made with a jackknife."
The cook and the correspondent swore darkly at the creature. The captain naturally wished to knock it away with the end of the heavy painter,[3] but he did not
dare do it, because anything resembling an emphatic gesture would have capsized this freighted boat; and so, with his open hand, the captain gently and
carefully waved the gull away. After it had been discouraged from the pursuit
the captain breathed easier on account of his hair, and others breathed easier
because the bird struck their minds at this time as being somehow gruesome
and ominous.

In the meantime the oiler and the correspondent rowed; and also they rowed.
They sat together in the same seat, and each rowed an oar. Then the oiler took
both oars; then the correspondent took both oars, then the oiler; then the correspondent. They rowed and they rowed. The very ticklish part of the business was
when the time came for the reclining one in the stern to take his turn at the oars.
By the very last star of truth, it is easier to steal eggs from under a hen than it
was to change seats in the dinghy. First the man in the stern slid his hand along
the thwart and moved with care, as if he were of Sèvres.[4] Then the man in the
rowing-seat slid his hand along the other thwart. It was all done with the most
extraordinary care. As the two sidled past each other, the whole party kept
watchful eyes on the coming wave, and the captain cried: "Look out, now!
Steady, there!"

The brown mats of seaweed that appeared from time to time were like
islands, bits of earth. They were travelling, apparently, neither one way nor the
other. They were, to all intents, stationary. They informed the men in the boat
that it was making progress slowly toward the land.

The captain, rearing cautiously in the bow after the dinghy soared on a great
swell, said that he had seen the lighthouse at Mosquito Inlet. Presently the
cook remarked that he had seen it. The correspondent was at the oars then, and
for some reason he too wished to look at the lighthouse; but his back was toward
the far shore, and the waves were important, and for some time he could not
seize an opportunity to turn his head. But at last there came a wave more gentle
than the others, and when at the crest of it he swiftly scoured the western
horizon.

2. Plain-weave cotton fabric.
3. Mooring rope attached to the bow of a boat.
4. Type of fine china.

"See it?" said the captain.

35   "No," said the correspondent, slowly; "I didn't see anything."

"Look again," said the captain. He pointed. "It's exactly in that direction."

At the top of another wave the correspondent did as he was bid, and this time his eyes chanced on a small, still thing on the edge of the swaying horizon. It was precisely like the point of a pin. It took an anxious eye to find a lighthouse so tiny.

"Think we'll make it, Captain?"

"If this wind holds and the boat don't swamp, we can't do much else," said the captain.

40   The little boat, lifted by each towering sea and splashed viciously by the crests, made progress that in the absence of seaweed was not apparent to those in her. She seemed just a wee thing wallowing, miraculously top up, at the mercy of five oceans. Occasionally a great spread of water, like white flames, swarmed into her.

"Bail her, cook," said the captain, serenely.

"All right, Captain," said the cheerful cook.

III

It would be difficult to describe the subtle brotherhood of men that was here established on the seas. No one said that it was so. No one mentioned it. But it dwelt in the boat, and each man felt it warm him. They were a captain, an oiler, a cook, and a correspondent, and they were friends—friends in a more curiously iron-bound degree than may be common. The hurt captain, lying against the water jar in the bow, spoke always in a low voice and calmly; but he could never command a more ready and swiftly obedient crew than the motley three of the dinghy. It was, more than a mere recognition of what was best for the common safety. There was surely in it a quality that was personal and heart-felt. And after this devotion to the commander of the boat, there was this comradeship, that the correspondent, for instance, who had been taught to be cynical of men, knew even at the time was the best experience of his life. But no one said that it was so. No one mentioned it.

"I wish we had a sail," remarked the captain. "We might try my overcoat on the end of an oar, and give you two boys a chance to rest." So the cook and the correspondent held the mast and spread wide the overcoat; the oiler steered; and the little boat made good way with her new rig. Sometimes the oiler had to scull sharply to keep a sea from breaking into the boat, but otherwise sailing was a success.

45   Meanwhile the lighthouse had been growing slowly larger. It had now almost assumed color, and appeared like a little gray shadow on the sky. The man at the oars could not be prevented from turning his head rather often to try for a glimpse of this little gray shadow.

At last, from the top of each wave, the men in the tossing boat could see land. Even as the lighthouse was an upright shadow on the sky, this land seemed but a long black shadow on the sea. It certainly was thinner than paper. "We must be about opposite New Smyrna,"[5] said the cook, who had coasted

5. Town on the Florida coast.

this shore often in schooners. "Captain, by the way, I believe they abandoned that life-saving station there about a year ago."

"Did they?" said the captain.

The wind slowly died away. The cook and the correspondent were not now obliged to slave in order to hold high the oar. But the waves continued their old impetuous swooping at the dinghy, and the little craft, no longer underway, struggled woundily over them. The oiler or the correspondent took the oars again.

Shipwrecks are *apropos* of nothing. If men could only train for them and have them occur when the men had reached pink condition, there would be less drowning at sea. Of the four in the dinghy none had slept any time worth mentioning for two days and two nights previous to embarking in the dinghy, and in the excitement of clambering about the deck of a foundering ship they had also forgotten to eat heartily.

For these reasons, and for others, neither the oiler nor the correspondent was 50 fond of rowing at this time. The correspondent wondered ingenuously how in the name of all that was sane could there be people who thought it amusing to row a boat. It was not an amusement; it was a diabolical punishment, and even a genius of mental aberrations could never conclude that it was anything but a horror to the muscles and a crime against the back. He mentioned to the boat in general how the amusement of rowing struck him, and the weary-faced oiler smiled in full sympathy. Previously to the foundering, by the way, the oiler had worked a double watch in the engine-room of the ship.

"Take her easy, now, boys," said the captain. "Don't spend yourselves. If we have to run a surf you'll need all your strength, because we'll sure have to swim for it. Take your time."

Slowly the land arose from the sea. From a black line it became a line of black and a line of white—trees and sand. Finally the captain said that he could make out a house on the shore. "That's the house of refuge, sure," said the cook. "They'll see us before long, and come out after us."

The distant lighthouse reared high. "The keeper ought to be able to make us out now, if he's looking through a glass," said the captain. "He'll notify the life-saving people."

"None of those other boats could have got ashore to give word of the wreck," said the oiler, in a low voice, "else the life-boat would be out hunting us."

Slowly and beautifully the land loomed out of the sea. The wind came again. 55 It had veered from the northeast to the southeast. Finally a new sound struck the ears of the men in the boat. It was the low thunder of the surf on the shore. "We'll never be able to make the lighthouse now," said the captain. "Swing her head a little more north, Billie."

"A little more north, sir," said the oiler.

Whereupon the little boat turned her nose once more down the wind, and all but the oarsman watched the shore grow. Under the influence of this expansion doubt and direful apprehension were leaving the minds of the men. The management of the boat was still most absorbing, but it could not prevent a quiet cheerfulness. In an hour, perhaps, they would be ashore.

Their backbones had become thoroughly used to balancing in the boat, and they now rode this wild colt of a dinghy like circus men. The correspondent thought that he had been drenched to the skin, but happening to feel in the top pocket of his coat, he found therein eight cigars. Four of them were soaked with sea-water; four were perfectly scatheless. After a search, somebody produced three dry matches; and thereupon the four waifs rode impudently in their little boat and, with an assurance of an impending rescue shining in their eyes, puffed at the big cigars, and judged well and ill of all men. Everybody took a drink of water.

IV

"Cook," remarked the captain, "there don't seem to be any signs of life about your house of refuge."

60   "No," replied the cook. "Funny they don't see us!"

A broad stretch of lowly coast lay before the eyes of the men. It was of low dunes topped with dark vegetation. The roar of the surf was plain, and some-times they could see the white lip of a wave as it spun up the beach. A tiny house was blocked out black upon the sky. Southward, the slim lighthouse lifted its little gray length.

Tide, wind, and waves were swinging the dinghy northward. "Funny they don't see us," said the men.

The surf's roar was here dulled, but its tone was nevertheless thunderous and mighty. As the boat swam over the great rollers the men sat listening to this roar. "We'll swamp sure," said everybody.

It is fair to say here that there was not a life-saving station within twenty miles in either direction; but the men did not know this fact, and in conse-quence they made dark and opprobrious remarks concerning the eyesight of the nation's life-savers. Four scowling men sat in the dinghy and surpassed records in the invention of epithets.

65   "Funny they don't see us."

The light-heartedness of a former time had completely faded. To their sharp-ened minds it was easy to conjure pictures of all kinds of incompetency and blindness and, indeed, cowardice. There was the shore of the populous land, and it was bitter and bitter to them that from it came no sign.

"Well," said the captain, ultimately, "I suppose we'll have to make a try for ourselves. If we stay out here too long, we'll none of us have strength left to swim after the boat swamps."

And so the oiler, who was at the oars, turned the boat straight for the shore. There was a sudden tightening of muscles. There was some thinking.

"If we don't all get ashore," said the captain—"if we don't all get ashore, I suppose you fellows know where to send news of my finish?"

70   They then briefly exchanged some addresses and admonitions. As for the reflections of the men, there was a great deal of rage in them. Perchance they might be formulated thus: "If I am going to be drowned—if I am going to be drowned—if I am going to be drowned, why, in the name of the seven mad gods who rule the sea, was I allowed to come thus far and contemplate sand and trees? Was I brought here merely to have my nose dragged away as I was about to nibble the sacred cheese of life? It is preposterous. If this old ninny-woman, Fate, cannot do better than this, she should be deprived of the management of men's fortunes. She is an old hen who knows not her intention. If she has

decided to drown me, why did she not do it in the beginning and save me all this trouble? The whole affair is absurd. . . . But no; she cannot mean to drown me. She dare not drown me. She cannot drown me. Not after all this work." Afterward the man might have had an impulse to shake his fist at the clouds. "Just you drown me, now, and then hear what I call you!"

The billows that came at this time were more formidable. They seemed always just about to break and roll over the little boat in a turmoil of foam. There was a preparatory and long growl in the speech of them. No mind unused to the sea would have concluded that the dinghy could ascend these sheer heights in time. The shore was still afar. The oiler was a wily surfman. "Boys," he said, swiftly, "she won't live three minutes more, and we're too far out to swim. Shall I take her to sea again, Captain?"

"Yes; go ahead!" said the captain.

This oiler, by a series of quick miracles and fast and steady oarsmanship, turned the boat in the middle of the surf and took her safely to sea again.

There was a considerable silence as the boat bumped over the furrowed sea to deeper water. Then somebody in gloom spoke: "Well, anyhow, they must have seen us from the shore by now."

The gulls went in slanting flight up the wind toward the gray, desolate east. 75
A squall, marked by dingy clouds and clouds brick-red, like smoke from a burning building, appeared from the southeast.

"What do you think of those life-saving people? Ain't they peaches?"

"Funny they haven't seen us."

"Maybe they think we're out here for sport! Maybe they think we're fishin'. Maybe they think we're damned fools."

It was a long afternoon. A changed tide tried to force them southward, but wind and wave said northward. Far ahead, where coast-line, sea, and sky formed their mighty angle, there were little dots which seemed to indicate a city on the shore.

"St. Augustine." 80

The captain shook his head. "Too near Mosquito Inlet."

And the oiler rowed, and then the correspondent rowed; then the oiler rowed. It was a weary business. The human back can become the seat of more aches and pains than are registered in books for the composite anatomy of a regiment. It is a limited area, but it can become the theatre of innumerable muscular conflicts, tangles, wrenches, knots, and other comforts.

"Did you ever like to row, Billie?" asked the correspondent.

"No," said the oiler. "Hang it."

When one exchanged the rowing-seat for a place in the bottom of the boat, he 85
suffered a bodily depression that caused him to be careless of everything save an obligation to wiggle one finger. There was cold sea-water swashing to and fro in the boat, and he lay in it. His head, pillowed on a thwart, was within an inch of the swirl of a wave-crest, and sometimes a particularly obstreperous sea came inboard and drenched him once more. But these matters did not annoy him. It is almost certain that if the boat had capsized he would have tumbled comfortably out upon the ocean as if he felt sure that it was a great soft mattress.

"Look! There's a man on the shore!"

"Where?"

"There! See 'im? See 'im?"

"Yes, sure! He's walking along."

90   "Now he's stopped. Look! He's facing us!"

"He's waving at us!"

"So he is! By thunder!"

"Ah, now we're all right! Now we're all right! There'll be a boat out here for us in half an hour."

"He's going on. He's running. He's going up to that house there."

95   The remote beach seemed lower than the sea, and it required a searching glance to discern the little black figure. The captain saw a floating stick, and they rowed to it. A bath towel was by some weird chance in the boat, and, tying this on the stick, the captain waved it. The oarsman did not dare turn his head, so he was obliged to ask questions.

"What's he doing now?"

"He's standing still again. He's looking, I think. . . . There he goes again—toward the house. . . . Now he's stopped again."

"Is he waving at us?"

"No, not now; he was, though."

100   "Look! There comes another man!"

"He's running."

"Look at him go, would you!"

"Why, he's on a bicycle. Now he's met the other man. They're both waving at us. Look!"

"There comes something up the beach."

105   "What the devil is that thing?"

"Why, it looks like a boat."

"Why, certainly, it's a boat."

"No; it's on wheels."

"Yes, so it is. Well, that must be the life-boat. They drag them along shore on a wagon."

110   "That's the life-boat, sure."

"No, by God, it's—it's an omnibus."

"I tell you it's a life-boat."

"It is not! It's an omnibus. I can see it plain. See? One of these big hotel omnibuses."

"By thunder, you're right. It's an omnibus, sure as fate. What do you suppose they are doing with an omnibus? Maybe they are going around collecting the life-crew, hey?"

115   "That's it, likely. Look! There's a fellow waving a little black flag. He's standing on the steps of the omnibus. There comes those other two fellows. Now they're all talking together. Look at the fellow with the flag. Maybe he ain't waving it!"

"That ain't a flag, is it? That's his coat. Why, certainly, that's his coat."

"So it is: it's his coat. He's taken it off and is waving it around his head. But would you look at him swing it!"

"Oh, say, there isn't any life-saving station there. That's just a winter-resort."

"What's that idiot with the coat mean? What's he signaling, anyhow?"

120   "It looks as if he were trying to tell us to go north. There must be a life-saving station up there."

"No; he thinks we're fishing. Just giving us a merry hand. See? Ah, there, Willie!"

"Well, I wish I could make something out of those signals. What do you suppose he means?"

"He don't mean anything; he's just playing."

"Well, if he'd just signal us to try the surf again, or to go to sea and wait, or go north, or go south, or go to hell, there would be some reason in it. But look at him! He just stands there and keeps his coat revolving like a wheel. The ass!"

"There come more people."   125

"Now there's quite a mob. Look! Isn't that a boat?"

"Where? Oh, I see where you mean. No, that's no boat."

"That fellow is still waving his coat."

"He must think we like to see him to do that. Why don't he quit? It don't mean anything."

"I don't know. I think he is trying to make us go north. It must be that there's   130
a life-saving station there somewhere."

"Say, he ain't tired yet. Look at 'im wave!"

"Wonder how long he can keep that up. He's been revolving his coat ever since he caught sight of us. He's an idiot. Why aren't they getting men to bring a boat out? A fishing boat—one of those big yawls—could come out here all right. Why don't he do something?"

"Oh, it's all right now."

"They'll have a boat out here for us in less than no time, now that they've seen us."

A faint yellow tone came into the sky over the low land. The shadows on the   135
sea slowly deepened. The wind bore coldness with it, and the men began to shiver.

"Holy smoke!" said one, allowing his voice to express his impious mood, "if we keep on monkeying out here! If we've got to flounder out here all night!"

"Oh, we'll never have to stay here all night! Don't you worry. They've seen us now, and it won't be long before they'll come chasing out after us."

The shore grew dusky. The man waving a coat blended gradually into this gloom, and it swallowed in the same manner the omnibus and the group of people. The spray, when it dashed uproariously over the side, made the voyagers shrink and swear like men who were being branded.

"I'd like to catch the chump who waved the coat. I feel like socking him one, just for luck."

"Why? What did he do?"   140

"Oh, nothing, but then he seemed so damned cheerful."

In the meantime the oiler rowed, and then the correspondent rowed, and then the oiler rowed. Gray-faced and bowed forward, they mechanically, turn by turn, plied the leaden oars. The form of the lighthouse had vanished from the southern horizon, but finally a pale star appeared, just lifting from the sea. The streaked saffron in the west passed before the all-merging darkness, and the sea to the east was black. The land had vanished, and was expressed only by the low and drear thunder of the surf.

"If I am going to be drowned—if I am going to be drowned—if I am going to be drowned, why, in the name of the seven mad gods who rule the sea, was I allowed to come thus far and contemplate sand and trees? Was I brought here merely to have my nose dragged away as I was about to nibble the sacred cheese of life?"

The patient captain, drooped over the water-jar, was sometimes obliged to speak to the oarsman.

145   "Keep her head up! Keep her head up!"

"Keep her head up, sir." The voices were weary and low.

This was surely a quiet evening. All save the oarsman lay heavily and list-lessly in the boat's bottom. As for him, his eyes were just capable of noting the tall black waves that swept forward in a most sinister silence, save for an occasional subdued growl of a crest.

The cook's head was on a thwart, and he looked without interest at the water under his nose. He was deep in other scenes. Finally he spoke. "Billie," he murmured, dreamfully, "what kind of pie do you like best?"

V

"Pie!" said the oiler and the correspondent, agitatedly. "Don't talk about those things, blast you!"

150   "Well," said the cook, "I was just thinking about ham sandwiches, and——"

A night on the sea in an open boat is a long night. As darkness settled finally, the shine of the light, lifting from the sea in the south, changed to full gold. On the northern horizon a new light appeared, a small bluish gleam on the edge of the waters. These two lights were the furniture of the world. Otherwise there was nothing but waves.

Two men huddled in the stern, and distances were so magnificent in the dinghy that the rower was enabled to keep his feet partly warm by thrusting them under his companions. Their legs indeed extended far under the rowing-seat until they touched the feet of the captain forward. Sometimes, despite the efforts of the tired oarsman, a wave came piling into the boat, an icy wave of the night, and the chilling water soaked them anew. They would twist their bodies for a moment and groan, and sleep the dead sleep once more, while the water in the boat gurgled about them as the craft rocked.

The plan of the oiler and the correspondent was for one to row until he lost the ability, and then arouse the other from his sea-water couch in the bottom of the boat.

The oiler plied the oars until his head drooped forward and the overpowering sleep blinded him; and he rowed yet afterward. Then he touched a man in the bottom of the boat, and called his name. "Will you spell me for a little while?" he said meekly.

155   "Sure, Billie," said the correspondent, awaking and dragging himself to a sitting position. They exchanged places carefully, and the oiler, cuddling down in the sea-water at the cook's side, seemed to go to sleep instantly.

The particular violence of the sea had ceased. The waves came without snarling. The obligation of the man at the oars was to keep the boat headed so that the tilt of the rollers would not capsize her, and to preserve her from filling when the crests rushed past. The black waves were silent and hard to be seen in the darkness. Often one was almost upon the boat before the oarsman was aware.

In a low voice the correspondent addressed the captain. He was not sure that the captain was awake, although this iron man seemed to be always awake. "Captain, shall I keep her making for that light north, sir?"

The same steady voice answered him. "Yes. Keep it about two points off the port bow."

The cook had tied a life-belt around himself in order to get even the warmth which this clumsy cork contrivance could donate, and he seemed almost stove-like when a rower, whose teeth invariably chattered wildly as soon as he ceased his labor, dropped down to sleep.

The correspondent, as he rowed, looked down at the two men sleeping under- 160
foot. The cook's arm was around the oiler's shoulders, and, with their fragmentary clothing and haggard faces, they were the babes of the sea—a grotesque rendering of the old babes in the wood.

Later he must have grown stupid at his work, for suddenly there was a growling of water, and a crest came with a roar and a swash into the boat, and it was a wonder that it did not set the cook afloat in his life-belt. The cook continued to sleep, but the oiler sat up, blinking his eyes and shaking with the new cold.

"Oh, I'm awful sorry, Billie," said the correspondent, contritely.

"That's all right, old boy," said the oiler, and lay down again and was asleep.

Presently it seemed that even the captain dozed, and the correspondent thought that he was the one man afloat on all the ocean. The wind had a voice as it came over the waves, and it was sadder than the end.

There was a long, loud swishing astern of the boat, and a gleaming trail of 165
phosphorescence, like blue flame, was furrowed on the black waters. It might have been made by a monstrous knife.

Then there came a stillness, while the correspondent breathed with open mouth and looked at the sea.

Suddenly there was another swish and another long flash of bluish light, and this time it was alongside the boat, and might almost have been reached with an oar. The correspondent saw an enormous fin speed like a shadow through the water, hurling the crystalline spray and leaving the long glowing trail.

The correspondent looked over his shoulder at the captain. His face was hidden, and he seemed to be asleep. He looked at the babes of the sea. They certainly were asleep. So, being bereft of sympathy, he leaned a little way to one side and swore softly into the sea.

But the thing did not then leave the vicinity of the boat. Ahead or astern, on one side or the other, at intervals long or short, fled the long sparkling streak, and there was to be heard the *whirroo* of the dark fin. The speed and power of the thing was greatly to be admired. It cut the water like a gigantic and keen projectile.

The presence of this biding thing did not affect the man with the same hor- 170
ror that it would if he had been a picnicker. He simply looked at the sea dully and swore in an undertone.

Nevertheless, it is true that he did not wish to be alone with the thing. He wished one of his companions to awake by chance and keep him company with it. But the captain hung motionless over the water-jar and the oiler and the cook in the bottom of the boat were plunged in slumber.

VI

"If I am going to be drowned—if I am going to be drowned—if I am going to be drowned, why, in the name of the seven mad gods who rule the sea, was I allowed to come thus far and contemplate sand and trees?"

During this dismal night, it may be remarked that a man would conclude that it was really the intention of the seven mad gods to drown him, despite the abominable injustice of it. For it was certainly an abominable injustice to drown a man who had worked so hard, so hard. The man felt it would be a crime most unnatural. Other people had drowned at sea since galleys swarmed with painted sails, but still——

When it occurs to a man that nature does not regard him as important, and that she feels she would not maim the universe by disposing of him, he at first wishes to throw bricks at the temple, and he hates deeply the fact that there are no bricks and no temples. Any visible expression of nature would surely be pelleted with his jeers.

175 Then, if there be no tangible thing to hoot, he feels, perhaps, the desire to confront a personification and indulge in pleas, bowed to one knee, and with hands supplicant, saying, "Yes, but I love myself."

A high cold star on a winter's night is the word he feels that she says to him. Thereafter he knows the pathos of his situation.

The men in the dinghy had not discussed these matters, but each had, no doubt, reflected upon them in silence and according to his mind. There was seldom any expression upon their faces save the general one of complete weariness. Speech was devoted to the business of the boat.

To chime the notes of his emotions, a verse mysteriously entered the correspondent's head. He had even forgotten that he had forgotten this verse, but it suddenly was in his mind.

> A soldier of the Legion lay dying in Algiers;
> There was lack of woman's nursing, there was dearth of woman's tears;
> But a comrade stood beside him, and he took the comrade's hand,
> And he said, "I never more shall see my own, my native land."[6]

In his childhood the correspondent had been made acquainted with the fact that a soldier of the Legion lay dying in Algiers, but he had never regarded it as important. Myriads of his schoolfellows had informed him of the soldier's plight, but the dinning had naturally ended by making him perfectly indifferent. He had never considered it his affair that a soldier of the Legion lay dying in Algiers, nor had it appeared to him as a matter for sorrow. It was less to him than the breaking of a pencil's point.

Now, however, it quaintly came to him as a human, living thing. It was no longer merely a picture of a few throes in the breast of a poet, meanwhile drinking tea and warming his feet at the grate; it was an actuality—stern, mournful, and fine.

180 The correspondent plainly saw the soldier. He lay on the sand with his feet out straight and still. While his pale left hand was upon his chest in an attempt

6. From "Bingen on the Rhine" by Caroline Norton (1808–77).

to thwart the going of his life, the blood came between his fingers. In the far Algerian distance, a city of low square forms was set against a sky that was faint with the last sunset hues. The correspondent, plying the oars and dreaming of the slow and slower movements of the lips of the soldier, was moved by a profound and perfectly impersonal comprehension. He was sorry for the soldier of the Legion who lay dying in Algiers.

The thing which had followed the boat and waited had evidently grown bored at the delay. There was no longer to be heard the slash of the cutwater, and there was no longer the flame of the long trail. The light in the north still glimmered, but it was apparently no nearer to the boat. Sometimes the boom of the surf rang in the correspondent's ears, and he turned the craft seaward then and rowed harder. Southward, some one had evidently built a watch-fire on the beach. It was too low and too far to be seen, but it made a shimmering, roseate reflection upon the bluff in back of it, and this could be discerned from the boat. The wind came stronger, and sometimes a wave suddenly raged out like a mountain-cat, and there was to be seen the sheen and sparkle of a broken crest.

The captain, in the bow, moved on his water-jar and sat erect. "Pretty long night," he observed to the correspondent. He looked at the shore. "Those life-saving people take their time."

"Did you see that shark playing around?"

"Yes, I saw him. He was a big fellow, all right."

"Wish I had known you were awake."

Later the correspondent spoke into the bottom of the boat. "Billie!" There was a slow and gradual disentanglement. "Billie, will you spell me?"

"Sure," said the oiler.

As soon as the correspondent touched the cold, comfortable sea-water in the bottom of the boat and had huddled close to the cook's life-belt he was deep in sleep, despite the fact that his teeth played all the popular airs. This sleep was so good to him that it was but a moment before he heard a voice call his name in a tone that demonstrated the last stages of exhaustion. "Will you spell me?"

"Sure, Billie."

The light in the north had mysteriously vanished, but the correspondent took his course from the wide-awake captain.

Later in the night they took the boat farther out to sea, and the captain directed the cook to take one oar at the stern and keep the boat facing the seas. He was to call out if he should hear the thunder of the surf. This plan enabled the oiler and the correspondent to get respite together. "We'll give those boys a chance to get into shape again," said the captain. They curled down and, after a few preliminary chatterings and trembles, slept once more the dead sleep. Neither knew they had bequeathed to the cook the company of another shark, or perhaps the same shark.

As the boat caroused on the waves, spray occasionally bumped over the side and gave them a fresh soaking, but this had no power to break their repose. The ominous slash of the wind and the water affected them as it would have affected mummies.

"Boys," said the cook, with the notes of every reluctance in his voice, "she's drifted in pretty close. I guess one of you had better take her to sea again." The correspondent, aroused, heard the crash of the toppled crests.

As he was rowing, the captain gave him some whiskey-and-water, and this steadied the chills out of him. "If I ever get ashore and anybody shows me even a photograph of an oar——"

195   At last there was a short conversation.

"Billie! . . . Billie, will you spell me?"

"Sure," said the oiler.

VII

When the correspondent again opened his eyes, the sea and the sky were each of the gray hue of the dawning. Later, carmine and gold was painted upon the waters. The morning appeared finally, in its splendor, with a sky of pure blue, and the sunlight flamed on the tips of the waves.

On the distant dunes were set many little black cottages, and a tall white windmill reared above them. No man, nor dog, nor bicycle appeared on the beach. The cottages might have formed a deserted village.

200   The voyagers scanned the shore. A conference was held in the boat. "Well," said the captain, "if no help is coming, we might better try a run through the surf right away. If we stay out here much longer we will be too weak to do anything for ourselves at all." The others silently acquiesced in this reasoning. The boat was headed for the beach. The correspondent wondered if none ever ascended the tall wind-tower,[7] and if then they never looked seaward. This tower was a giant, standing with its back to the plight of the ants. It represented in a degree, to the correspondent, the serenity of nature amid the struggles of the individual—nature in the wind, and nature in the vision of men. She did not seem cruel to him then, nor beneficent, nor treacherous, nor wise. But she was indifferent, flatly indifferent. It is, perhaps, plausible that a man in this situation, impressed with the unconcern of the universe, should see the innumerable flaws of his life, and have them taste wickedly in his mind, and wish for another chance. A distinction between right and wrong seems absurdly clear to him, then, in this new ignorance of the grave-edge, and he understands that if he were given another opportunity he would mend his conduct and his words, and be better and brighter during an introduction or at a tea.

"Now, boys," said the captain, "she is going to swamp sure. All we can do is to work her in as far as possible, and then when she swamps, pile out and scramble for the beach. Keep cool now, and don't jump until she swamps sure."

The oiler took the oars. Over his shoulders he scanned the surf. "Captain," he said, "I think I'd better bring her about and keep her head-on to the seas and back her in."

"All right, Billie," said the captain. "Back her in." The oiler swung the boat then, and, seated in the stern, the cook and the correspondent were obliged to look over their shoulders to contemplate the lonely and indifferent shore.

The monstrous inshore rollers heaved the boat high until the men were again enabled to see the white sheets of water scudding up the slanted beach. "We won't get in very close," said the captain. Each time a man could wrest his attention from the rollers, he turned his glance toward the shore, and in the expression of the eyes during this contemplation there was a singular quality. The

---

7. Watchtower for observing weather.

correspondent, observing the others, knew that they were not afraid, but the full meaning of their glances was shrouded.

As for himself, he was too tired to grapple fundamentally with the fact. He tried to coerce his mind into thinking of it, but the mind was dominated at this time by the muscles, and the muscles said they did not care. It merely occurred to him that if he should drown it would be a shame.

There were no hurried words, no pallor, no plain agitation. The men simply looked at the shore. "Now, remember to get well clear of the boat when you jump," said the captain.

Seaward the crest of a roller suddenly fell with a thunderous crash, and the long white comber came roaring down upon the boat.

"Steady now," said the captain. The men were silent. They turned their eyes from the shore to the comber and waited. The boat slid up the incline, leaped at the furious top, bounced over it, and swung down the long back of the wave. Some water had been shipped, and the cook bailed it out.

But the next crest crashed also. The tumbling, boiling flood of white water caught the boat and whirled it almost perpendicular. Water swarmed in from all sides. The correspondent had his hands on the gunwale at this time, and when the water entered at that place he swiftly withdrew his fingers, as if he objected to wetting them.

The little boat, drunken with this weight of water, reeled and snuggled deeper into the sea.

"Bail her out, cook! Bail her out!" said the captain.

"All right, Captain," said the cook.

"Now, boys, the next one will do for us sure," said the oiler. "Mind to jump clear of the boat."

The third wave moved forward, huge, furious, implacable. It fairly swallowed the dinghy, and almost simultaneously the men tumbled into the sea. A piece of life-belt had lain in the bottom of the boat, and as the correspondent went over-board he held this to his chest with his left hand.

The January water was icy, and reflected immediately that it was colder than he had expected to find it off the coast of Florida. This appeared to his dazed mind as a fact important enough to be noted at the time. The coldness of the water was sad; it was tragic. This fact was somehow mixed and confused with his opinion of his own situation, so that it seemed almost a proper reason for tears. The water was cold.

When he came to the surface he was conscious of little but the noisy water. Afterward he saw his companions in the sea. The oiler was ahead in the race. He was swimming strongly and rapidly. Off to the correspondent's left, the cook's great white and corked back bulged out of the water, and in the rear the captain was hanging with his one good hand to the keel of the overturned dinghy.

There is a certain immovable quality to a shore, and the correspondent wondered at it amid the confusion of the sea.

It seemed also very attractive; but the correspondent knew that it was a long journey, and he paddled leisurely. The piece of life-preserver lay under him, and sometimes he whirled down the incline of a wave as if he were on a hand-sled.

But finally he arrived at a place in the sea where travel was beset with difficulty. He did not pause swimming to inquire what manner of current had caught him, but there his progress ceased. The shore was set before him like a bit of scenery on a stage, and he looked at it and understood with his eyes each detail of it.

220   As the cook passed, much farther to the left, the captain was calling to him, "Turn over on your back, cook! Turn over on your back and use the oar."

"All right, sir." The cook turned on his back, and, paddling with an oar, went ahead as if he were a canoe.

Presently the boat also passed to the left of the correspondent, with the captain clinging with one hand to the keel. He would have appeared like a man raising himself to look over a board fence if it were not for the extraordinary gymnastics of the boat. The correspondent marvelled that the captain could still hold to it.

They passed on nearer to shore—the oiler, the cook, the captain—and following them went the water-jar, bouncing gaily over the seas.

The correspondent remained in the grip of this strange new enemy, a current. The shore, with its white slope of sand and its green bluff topped with little silent cottages, was spread like a picture before him. It was very near to him then, but he was impressed as one who, in a gallery, looks at a scene from Brittany or Algiers.

225   He thought: "I am going to drown? Can it be possible? Can it be possible? Can it be possible?" Perhaps an individual must consider his own death to be the final phenomenon of nature.

But later a wave perhaps whirled him out of this small deadly current, for he found suddenly that he could again make progress toward the shore. Later still he was aware that the captain, clinging with one hand to the keel of the dinghy, had his face turned away from the shore and toward him, and was calling his name. "Come to the boat! Come to the boat!"

In his struggle to reach the captain and the boat, he reflected that when one gets properly wearied drowning must really be a comfortable arrangement—a cessation of hostilities accompanied by a large degree of relief; and he was glad of it, for the main thing in his mind for some moments had been horror of the temporary agony; he did not wish to be hurt.

Presently he saw a man running along the shore. He was undressing with most remarkable speed. Coat, trousers, shirt, everything flew magically off him.

"Come to the boat!" called the captain.

230   "All right, Captain." As the correspondent paddled, he saw the captain let himself down to bottom and leave the boat. Then the correspondent performed his one little marvel of the voyage. A large wave caught him and flung him with ease and supreme speed completely over the boat and far beyond it. It struck him even then as an event in gymnastics and a true miracle of the sea. An overturned boat in the surf is not a plaything to a swimming man.

The correspondent arrived in water that reached only to his waist, but his condition did not enable him to stand for more than a moment. Each wave knocked him into a heap, and the undertow pulled at him.

Then he saw the man who had been running and undressing, and undressing and running, come bounding into the water. He dragged ashore the cook, and then waded toward the captain; but the captain waved him away and sent him to the correspondent. He was naked—naked as a tree in winter; but a halo was about his head, and he shone like a saint. He gave a strong pull, and a long drag, and a bully heave at the correspondent's hand. The correspondent, schooled in the minor formulae, said, "Thanks, old man." But suddenly the man cried, "What's that?" He pointed a swift finger. The correspondent said, "Go."

In the shallows, face downward, lay the oiler. His forehead touched sand that was periodically, between each wave, clear of the sea.

The correspondent did not know all that transpired afterward. When he achieved safe ground he fell, striking the sand with each particular part of his body. It was as if he had dropped from a roof, but the thud was grateful to him.

It seems that instantly the beach was populated with men with blankets, 235 clothes, and flasks, and women with coffee-pots and all the remedies sacred to their minds. The welcome of the land to the men from the sea was warm and generous; but a still and dripping shape was carried slowly up the beach, and the land's welcome for it could only be the different and sinister hospitality of the grave.

When it came night, the white waves paced to and fro in the moonlight, and the wind brought the sound of the great sea's voice to the men on the shore, and they felt that they could then be interpreters.

1898

QUESTIONS

1. When do you become aware that your view of events in THE OPEN BOAT is limited to things seen and heard by the four men in the boat? In what specific ways is that important to the story's effect? Where does the story's perspective "expand" to include larger reflections and generalizations? How are they justified by the narrative point of view?

2. Examine paragraphs 3–6; then differentiate the four men as fully as you can. What distinguishing features help you keep them straight as the narrative proceeds? What facts are provided later about each of the men? In which of the men do you become most interested as the story develops?

3. Which, if any, of the following seem like apt statements of the story's theme, and why? Which, if any, seems most central?

   a. All human beings are ultimately the same in that we are all equally powerless against nature.
   b. As the novelist George Eliot once said, "Character is destiny."
   c. In the face of disaster, people tend to become selfless, forgetting their differences and bonding together.
   d. Our individual fates are ultimately determined by forces beyond our control.
   e. We can never know the full truth; all we have is our own limited individual perspective.
   f. Pride is man's downfall.

YASUNARI KAWABATA

(1899–1972)

The Grasshopper and the Bell Cricket[1]

Born in Osaka, Japan, to a prosperous family, Yasunari Kawabata graduated from Tokyo Imperial University in 1924 and had his first literary success with the semiautobiographical novella *The Izu Dancer* (1926). He cofounded the journal *Contemporary Literature* in support of the Neosensualist movement, which had much in common with the European literary movements of Dadaism, Expressionism, and Cubism. His best-known works include *Snow Country* (1937), *Thousand Cranes* (1952), *The Sound of the Mountain* (1954), *The Lake* (1955), *The Sleeping Beauty* (1960), *The Old Capital* (1962), and the collection *Palm-of-the-Hand Stories* (translated in 1988). Kawabata was awarded the Nobel Prize for Literature in 1968. After long suffering from poor health, he committed suicide in 1972.

Walking along the tile-roofed wall of the university, I turned aside and approached the upper school. Behind the white board fence of the school playground, from a dusky clump of bushes under the black cherry trees, an insect's voice could be heard. Walking more slowly and listening to that voice, and furthermore reluctant to part with it, I turned right so as not to leave the playground behind. When I turned to the left, the fence gave way to an embankment planted with orange trees. At the corner, I exclaimed with surprise. My eyes gleaming at what they saw up ahead, I hurried forward with short steps.

At the base of the embankment was a bobbing cluster of beautiful varicolored lanterns, such as one might see at a festival in a remote country village. Without going any farther, I knew that it was a group of children on an insect chase among the bushes of the embankment. There were about twenty lanterns. Not only were there crimson, pink, indigo, green, purple, and yellow lanterns, but one lantern glowed with five colors at once. There were even some little red store-bought lanterns. But most of the lanterns were beautiful square ones which the children had made themselves with love and care. The bobbing lanterns, the coming together of children on this lonely slope—surely it was a scene from a fairy tale?

One of the neighborhood children had heard an insect sing on this slope one night. Buying a red lantern, he had come back the next night to find the insect. The night after that, there was another child. This new child could not buy a lantern. Cutting out the back and front of a small carton and papering it, he placed a candle on the bottom and fastened a string to the top. The number of children grew to five, and then to seven. They learned how to color the paper that they stretched over the windows of the cutout cartons, and to draw pictures

1. Translated by Lane Dunlop.

on it. Then these wise child-artists, cutting out round, three-cornered, and loz-enge leaf shapes in the cartons, coloring each little window a different color, with circles and diamonds, red and green, made a single and whole decorative pattern. The child with the red lantern discarded it as a tasteless object that could be bought at a store. The child who had made his own lantern threw it away because the design was too simple. The pattern of light that one had had in hand the night before was unsatisfying the morning after. Each day, with cardboard, paper, brush, scissors, penknife, and glue, the children made new lanterns out of their hearts and minds. Look at my lantern! Be the most unusually beautiful! And each night, they had gone out on their insect hunts. These were the twenty children and their beautiful lanterns that I now saw before me.

Wide-eyed, I loitered near them. Not only did the square lanterns have old-fashioned patterns and flower shapes, but the names of the children who had made them were cut out in squared letters of the syllabary. Different from the painted-over red lanterns, others (made of thick cutout cardboard) had their designs drawn onto the paper windows, so that the candle's light seemed to emanate from the form and color of the design itself. The lanterns brought out the shadows of the bushes like dark light. The children crouched eagerly on the slope wherever they heard an insect's voice.

"Does anyone want a grasshopper?" A boy, who had been peering into a bush 5 about thirty feet away from the other children, suddenly straightened up and shouted.

"Yes! Give it to me!" Six or seven children came running up. Crowding behind the boy who had found the grasshopper, they peered into the bush. Brushing away their outstretched hands and spreading out his arms, the boy stood as if guarding the bush where the insect was. Waving the lantern in his right hand, he called again to the other children.

"Does anyone want a grasshopper? A grasshopper!"

"I do! I do!" Four or five more children came running up. It seemed you could not catch a more precious insect than a grasshopper. The boy called out a third time.

"Doesn't anyone want a grasshopper?"

Two or three more children came over.   10

"Yes. I want it."

It was a girl, who just now had come up behind the boy who'd discovered the insect. Lightly turning his body, the boy gracefully bent forward. Shifting the lantern to his left hand, he reached his right hand into the bush.

"It's a grasshopper."

"Yes. I'd like to have it."

The boy quickly stood up. As if to say "Here!" he thrust out his fist that held 15 the insect at the girl. She, slipping her left wrist under the string of her lantern, enclosed the boy's fist with both hands. The boy quietly opened his fist. The insect was transferred to between the girl's thumb and index finger.

"Oh! It's not a grasshopper. It's a bell cricket." The girl's eyes shone as she looked at the small brown insect.

"It's a bell cricket! It's a bell cricket!" The children echoed in an envious chorus.

"It's a bell cricket. It's a bell cricket."

Glancing with her bright intelligent eyes at the boy who had given her the cricket, the girl opened the little insect cage hanging at her side and released the cricket in it.

20   "It's a bell cricket."

"Oh, it's a bell cricket," the boy who'd captured it muttered. Holding up the insect cage close to his eyes, he looked inside it. By the light of his beautiful many-colored lantern, also held up at eye level, he glanced at the girl's face.

Oh, I thought. I felt slightly jealous of the boy, and sheepish. How silly of me not to have understood his actions until now! Then I caught my breath in surprise. Look! It was something on the girl's breast which neither the boy who had given her the cricket, nor she who had accepted it, nor the children who were looking at them noticed.

In the faint greenish light that fell on the girl's breast, wasn't the name "Fujio" clearly discernible? The boy's lantern, which he held up alongside the girl's insect cage, inscribed his name, cut out in the green papered aperture, onto her white cotton kimono. The girl's lantern, which dangled loosely from her wrist, did not project its pattern so clearly, but still one could make out, in a trembling patch of red on the boy's waist, the name "Kiyoko." This chance interplay of red and green—if it was chance or play—neither Fujio nor Kiyoko knew about.

Even if they remembered forever that Fujio had given her the cricket and that Kiyoko had accepted it, not even in dreams would Fujio ever know that his name had been written in green on Kiyoko's breast or that Kiyoko's name had been inscribed in red on his waist, nor would Kiyoko ever know that Fujio's name had been inscribed in green on her breast or that her own name had been written in red on Fujio's waist.

25   Fujio! Even when you have become a young man, laugh with pleasure at a girl's delight when, told that it's a grasshopper, she is given a bell cricket; laugh with affection at a girl's chagrin when, told that it's a bell cricket, she is given a grasshopper.

Even if you have the wit to look by yourself in a bush away from the other children, there are not many bell crickets in the world. Probably you will find a girl like a grasshopper whom you think is a bell cricket.

And finally, to your clouded, wounded heart, even a true bell cricket will seem like a grasshopper. Should that day come, when it seems to you that the world is only full of grasshoppers, I will think it a pity that you have no way to remember tonight's play of light, when your name was written in green by your beautiful lantern on a girl's breast.

1924

QUESTIONS

1. Who might the narrator of this story be? What clues are provided in the story?
2. What might the grasshopper and the bell cricket each come to symbolize in the story?
3. Might the final three paragraphs of this story come close to stating its theme(s)? How would you state the theme(s)?

JUNOT DÍAZ
(b. 1968)

Wildwood

Aptly described by one British newspaper as "a truly all-American writer" and by himself as an "African diasporic, migrant, Caribbean, Dominican, Jersey boy," MIT professor and MacArthur Foundation "genius grant" winner Junot Díaz lived in the Dominican Republic until age six, when he and the rest of his family joined his father in the United States. While his mother worked on a factory assembly line and his father, a former military policeman, drove a forklift, Díaz and his four siblings navigated life in what he calls a "very black, very Puerto Rican and very poor" New Jersey neighborhood. Díaz supported himself through college, earning a BA in English from Rutgers and a Cornell MFA. A year after graduating, Díaz published *Drown* (1996), a collection of interrelated short stories. A decade later, his novel *The Brief Wondrous Life of Oscar Wao* (2007) won numerous prizes, including both a National Book Critics Circle Award and a Pulitzer. Hailed in a 2015 poll as the greatest novel of the twenty-first century (so far), *Oscar Wao* is a tale of a lovelorn and utterly lovable "ghetto nerd," who dreams of becoming the next J. R. R. Tolkien, and three generations of his Dominican American family. Díaz published a second short-story collection, *This Is How You Lose Her* (2012), and cofounded the pioneering Voices of Our Nations Arts Foundation to nurture the work of writers of color. "Wildwood," published almost simultaneously as both a short story and a chapter of *Oscar Wao*, is something of a departure for Díaz thanks to its female narrator-protagonist. But it is utterly characteristic in its creation of an entirely new fictional language to capture the unique voices, experiences, and outlooks of its funny, complicated, thoroughly all-American cast of characters.

I t's never the changes we want that change everything.

This is how it all starts: with your mother calling you into the bathroom. You will remember what you were doing at that precise moment for the rest of your life: you were reading "Watership Down"[1] and the bucks and their does were making the dash for the raft and you didn't want to stop reading, the book had to go back to your brother tomorrow, but then she called you again, louder, her I'm-not-fucking-around voice, and you mumbled irritably, Sí, señora.

She is standing in front of the medicine-cabinet mirror, naked from the waist up, her bra slung about her hips like a torn sail, the scar on her back as vast and inconsolable as the sea. You want to return to your book, to pretend you didn't hear her, but it is too late. Her eyes meet yours, the same big smoky eyes you

---

1. Richard Adams's classic novel (1972) about the adventures of a community of English rabbits who, inspired by the prophetic vision of one of their youngest and smallest members, flee their doomed warren and create a new home.

will have in the future. Ven acá,[2] she commands. She is frowning at something on one of her breasts.

Your mother's breasts are immensities. One of the wonders of the world. The only ones you've seen that are bigger are in nudie magazines or on really fat ladies. They're forty-two triple Ds and the areolas are as big as saucers and black as pitch and at their edges are fierce hairs that sometimes she plucks and sometimes she doesn't. These breasts have always embarrassed you and when you walk in public with her you are conscious of them. After her face and her hair, her tetas are what she is most proud of. Your father could never get enough of them, she always brags. But given the fact that he ran off on her after their third year of marriage it seemed in the end that he could.

5   You dread conversations with your mother. These one-sided dressing-downs. You figure that she has called you in to give you another earful about your diet. Your mom's convinced that if you only eat more plátanos you will suddenly acquire her extraordinary train-wrecking secondary sex characteristics. Even at that age you are nothing if not your mother's daughter. You are twelve years old and already as tall as her, a long slender-necked ibis of a girl. You have her straight hair, which makes you look more Hindu than Dominican, and a behind that the boys haven't been able to stop talking about since the fifth grade and whose appeal you do not yet understand. You have her complexion, too, which means you are dark as night. But for all your similarities the tides of inheritance have yet to reach your chest. You have only the slightest hint of breasts: from most angles you're flat as a board and you're thinking she's going to order you to stop wearing bras again because they're suffocating your potential breasts, discouraging them from popping out. You're ready to argue with her to the death, because you're as possessive of your bras as you are of the pads you now buy yourself.

But no, she doesn't say a word about eating more plátanos. Instead, she takes your right hand and guides you. Your mom is rough in all things, but this time she is gentle. You did not think her capable of it.

Do you feel that? she asks in her too familiar raspy voice.

At first all you feel is the density of the tissue and the heat of her, like a bread that never stopped rising. She kneads your fingers into her. You're as close as you've ever been and your breathing is what you hear.

Don't you feel that?

10   She turns toward you. Coño, muchacha,[3] stop looking at me and feel.

So you close your eyes and your fingers are pushing down and you're thinking of Helen Keller[4] and how when you were little you wanted to be her except more nunnish and then suddenly you do feel something. A knot just beneath her skin, tight and secretive as a plot. And at that moment, for reasons you will never quite understand, you are overcome by the feeling, the premonition, that something in your life is about to change. You become light-headed and you can feel a throbbing in your blood, a rhythm, a drum. Bright lights zoom through you like photon torpedoes, like comets. You don't know how or why you know this thing, but that you know it cannot be doubted. It is exhilarating. For as long as you've been alive

2. Come here (Spanish).
3. Damn, girl (Dominican Spanish).
4. Famously blind and deaf American author, activist, and lecturer (1880–1968).

you've had bruja[5] ways; even your mother will not begrudge you that much. Hija de Liborio, she called you after you picked your tía's[6] winning numbers for her and when you guessed correctly how old to the day she'd been when she left home for the U.S. (a fact she'd never told anyone). You assumed Liborio was a relative. That was before Santo Domingo, before you knew about the Great Power of God.

I feel it, you say, too loudly. Lo siento.[7]

And like that, everything changes. Before the winter is out the doctors remove that breast you were kneading and its partner, along with the auxiliary lymph nodes. Because of the operations, your mother will have trouble lifting her arms over her head for the rest of her life. Her hair begins to fall out and one day she pulls it all out herself and puts it in a plastic bag. You change, too. Not right away, but it happens. And it's in that bathroom that it all begins. That you begin.

A punk chick. That's what I became. A Siouxsie and the Banshees-loving[8] punk chick. The Puerto Rican kids on the block couldn't stop laughing when they saw my hair; they called me Blacula. And the morenos,[9] they didn't know what to say; they just called me devil-bitch. Yo, devil-bitch, yo, yo! My tía Rubelka thought it was some kind of mental illness. Hija, she said while frying pastelitos, maybe you need *help*. But my mother was the worst. It's the last straw, she screamed. The. Last. Straw. But it always was with her. Mornings when I came downstairs she'd be in the kitchen making her coffee in la greca and listening to Radio WADO[1] and when she saw me and my hair she'd get mad all over again, as if during the night she'd forgotten who I was.

My mother was one of the tallest women in Paterson[2] and her anger was just   15
as tall. It pincered you in its long arms, and if you showed any weakness you were finished. Que muchacha tan fea,[3] she said in disgust, splashing the rest of her coffee in the sink. Fea had become my name. It was nothing new, to tell the truth. She'd been saying stuff like that all our lives. My mother would never win any awards, believe me. You could call her an absentee parent: if she wasn't at work she was sleeping and when she wasn't sleeping all she did was scream and hit. As kids, me and Oscar were more scared of our mother than we were of the dark or el cuco.[4] She would hit us anywhere, in front of anyone, always free with the chanclas and the correa,[5] but now with her cancer there wasn't much she could do anymore. The last time she tried to whale on me it was because of

5. Witch (Spanish).
6. Aunt's (Spanish). *Hija de Liborio*: literally, child of Liborio (Spanish), an allusion to Olivorio Liborio Mateo (1876–1922), a peasant farmer turned messianic faith healer regarded by his followers as an incarnation of Christ; remnants of his once-powerful Liborista movement still survive.
7. I feel it (Spanish).
8. English rock band (1976–96) created and fronted by Siouxsie Sioux, hailed by the London *Times* as inventing "a form of post-punk discord [. . .] as influential as it was underrated."
9. Literally, browns (Spanish), a term for people with dark skin.
1. Spanish-language news and talk station owned by Univision. *La greca*: Italian-style aluminum stovetop espresso pot (Spanish).
2. New Jersey city in the New York metropolitan area, home to many Hispanic and Middle Eastern immigrants.
3. What an ugly girl (Spanish).
4. Mythical ghost-monster, a sort of Spanish-language "bogeyman."
5. Belt (Spanish). *Chanclas*: flip-flops (Spanish).

my hair, but instead of cringing or running I punched her hand. It was a reflex more than anything, but once it happened I knew I couldn't take it back, not ever, and so I just kept my fist clenched, waiting for whatever came next, for her to attack me with her teeth like she had this one lady in the Pathmark.[6] But she just stood there shaking, in her stupid wig and her stupid bata,[7] with two huge foam prostheses in her bra, the smell of burning wig all around us. I almost felt sorry for her. This is how you treat your mother? she cried. And if I could I would have broken the entire length of my life across her face, but instead I screamed back, And this is how you treat your daughter?

Things had been bad between us all year. How could they not have been? She was my Old World Dominican mother who had come alone to the United States and I was her only daughter, the one she had raised up herself with the help of nobody, which meant it was her duty to keep me crushed under her heel. I was fourteen and desperate for my own patch of world that had nothing to do with her. I wanted the life that I used to see when I watched "Big Blue Marble"[8] as a kid, the life that drove me to make pen pals and to borrow atlases from school. The life that existed beyond Paterson, beyond my family, beyond Spanish. And as soon as she became sick I saw my chance and I'm not going to pretend or apologize; I saw my chance and eventually I took it.

If you didn't grow up like I did then you don't know and if you don't know it's probably better you don't judge. You don't know the hold our mothers have on us, even the ones that are never around—*especially* the ones that are never around. What it's like to be the perfect Dominican daughter, which is just a nice way of saying a perfect Dominican slave. You don't know what it's like to grow up with a mother who never said anything that wasn't negative, who was always suspicious, always tearing you down and splitting your dreams straight down the seams. On TV and in books mothers talk to daughters, about life, about themselves, but on Main Street in Paterson mothers say not a word unless it's to hurt you. When my first pen pal, Tomoko, stopped writing me after three letters my mother was the one who said, You think someone's going to lose life writing to you? Of course I cried; I was eight and I had already planned that Tomoko and her family would adopt me. My mother, of course, saw clean into the marrow of those dreams and laughed. I wouldn't write to you, either, she said.

She was that kind of mother: who makes you doubt yourself, who would wipe you out if you let her. But I'm not going to pretend, either. For a long time I let her say what she wanted about me and, what was worse, for a long time I believed her. I was a fea, I was a worthless, I was an idiota. From ages two to thirteen I believed her and because I believed her I was the perfect hija. I was the one cooking, cleaning, doing the wash, buying groceries, writing letters to the bank to explain why a house payment was going to be late, translating. I had the best grades in my class. I never caused trouble, even when the morenas used to come after me with scissors because of my straight straight hair. I stayed at home and made sure my little brother Oscar was fed and everything ran right while she was

6. Grocery store, part of a chain owned (as A&P is) by the Great Atlantic and Pacific Tea Company.
7. Bathrobe (Spanish).
8. American television series for children (1974–83); featuring stories about children around the world, the show sponsored an international pen-pal club.

at work. I raised him and I raised me. I was the one. You're my hija, she said, that's what you're supposed to be doing. When that thing happened to me when I was eight and I finally told her what our neighbor had done she told me to shut my mouth and stop crying and I did exactly that, I shut my mouth and clenched my legs and my mind and within a year I couldn't have told you what he looked like or even his name. All you do is complain, she said to me, but you have no idea what life really is. Sí, señora.

When she told me that I could go on my sixth-grade sleepaway to Bear Mountain[9] and I bought a backpack with my own paper-route money and wrote Bobby Santos notes because he was promising to break into my cabin and kiss me in front of everyone I believed her and when on the morning of the trip she announced that I wasn't going and I said, But you promised, and she said, Muchacha del diablo,[1] I promised you nothing, I didn't throw my backpack at her or pull out my hair, and when it was Laura Saenz who ended up kissing Bobby Santos, not me, I didn't say anything, either. I just lay in my room with stupid Bear-Bear and sang under my breath, imagining where I would run away to when I grew up. To Japan maybe, where I would track down Tomoko, or to Austria, where my singing would inspire a remake of "The Sound of Music."

All my favorite books from that period were about runaways—"Watership Down," "The Incredible Journey," "My Side of the Mountain"[2]—and when Bon Jovi's "Runaway"[3] came out I imagined it was me they were singing about. No one had any idea. I was the tallest, dorkiest girl in school, the one who dressed up as Wonder Woman[4] every Halloween, the one who never said a word. People saw me in my glasses and my hand-me-down clothes and could not have imagined what I was capable of. And then when I was twelve I got that feeling, the scary witchy one, and before I knew it my mother was sick and the wildness that had been in me all along, that I had tried to tamp down with chores and with home-work and with promises that once I reached college I would be able to do whatever I pleased, burst out. I couldn't help it. I tried to keep it down, but it just flooded through all my quiet spaces. It was a message more than a feeling, a message that tolled like a bell: Change, change, change.

It didn't happen overnight. Yes the wildness was in me, yes it kept my heart beating fast all the long day, yes it danced around me while I walked down the street, yes it let me look boys straight in the face when they stared at me, yes it turned my laugh from a cough into a wild fever, but I was still scared. How could I not be? I was my mother's daughter. Her hold on me was stronger than love. And then one day I was walking home with Karen Cepeda, who at that time was my friend. Karen did the goth thing really well; she had spiky Robert

20

9. New York state park, located in the mountains along the Hudson River.
1. Devil girl (Spanish).
2. 1959 novel about the adventures of a twelve-year-old boy who flees his family's cramped New York City apartment and learns to survive on his own in the Catskill Mountains. *The Incredible Journey*: novel (1961) and, later, Disney movie (1963) about a bull terrier, a Siamese cat, and a Labrador retriever who trek through the Canadian wilderness searching for their human masters.
3. Earliest hit record by the rock band formed in New Jersey in 1983.
4. Fictional superhero featured in DC Comics since the 1940s and in an American television series (1975–79).

Smith[5] hair and wore all black and had the skin color of a ghost. Walking with her in Paterson was like walking with the bearded lady. Everybody would stare and it was the scariest thing and that was, I guess, why I did it.

We were walking down Main and being glared at by everybody and out of nowhere I said, Karen, I want you to cut my hair. As soon as I said it I knew. The feeling in my blood, the rattle, came over me again. Karen raised her eyebrow: What about your mother? You see, it wasn't just me—everybody was scared of Belicia de León.

Fuck her, I said.

Karen looked at me like I was being stupid—I never cursed, but that was something else that was about to change. The next day we locked ourselves in her bathroom while downstairs her father and uncles were bellowing at some soccer game. Well, how do you want it? she asked. I looked at the girl in the mirror for a long time. All I knew was that I didn't want to see her ever again. I put the clippers in Karen's hand, turned them on, and guided her hand until it was all gone.

25 So now you're punk? Karen asked uncertainly.

Yes, I said.

The next day my mother threw the wig at me. You're going to wear this. You're going to wear it every day. And if I see you without it on I'm going to kill you!

I didn't say a word. I held the wig over the burner.

Don't do it, she said as the burner clicked. Don't you dare—

30 It went up in a flash, like gasoline, like a stupid hope, and if I hadn't thrown it in the sink it would have taken my hand. The smell was horrible, like all the chemicals from all the factories in Elizabeth.[6]

That was when she slapped at me, when I struck her hand and she snatched it back, like I was the fire.

Of course everyone thought I was the worst daughter ever. My tía and our neighbors kept saying, Hija, she's your mother, she's dying, but I wouldn't listen. When I hit her hand, a door opened. And I wasn't about to turn my back on it.

But God how we fought! Sick or not, dying or not, my mother wasn't going to go down easy. She wasn't una pendeja.[7] I'd seen her slap grown men, push white police officers onto their asses, curse a whole group of bochincheras.[8] She had raised me and my brother by herself, she had worked three jobs until she could buy this house we lived in, she had survived being abandoned by my father, she had come from Santo Domingo all by herself, and as a young girl she'd been beaten, set on fire, left for dead. (This last part she didn't tell me, my tía Rubelka did, in a whisper, Your mother almost died, she almost died, and when I asked my mother about it at dinner she took my dinner and gave it to my brother.) That was my mother and there was no way she was going to let me go

---

5. Former Siouxsie and the Banshees guitarist (b. 1959) and (since 1976) lead singer-songwriter of the English rock band The Cure.
6. Elizabeth, New Jersey, is home to a major oil refinery consistently ranked as among the nation's worst polluters.
7. Dumbass, fool, pushover, or coward (Spanish).
8. Gossips (Spanish).

without killing me first. Figurín de mierda, she called me. You think you're someone, but you ain't nada.[9]

She dug hard, looking for my seams, wanting me to tear like always, but I didn't, I wasn't going to. It was that feeling I had that my life was waiting for me on the other side that made me fearless. When she threw away my Smiths and Sisters of Mercy posters—aquí yo no quiero maricones[1]—I bought replacements. When she threatened to rip up my new clothes I started keeping them in my locker and at Karen's house. When she told me that I had to quit my job at the Greek diner I explained to my boss that my mother was starting to lose it because of her chemo, and when she called to say I couldn't work there anymore he just handed me the phone and stared out at his customers in embarrassment. When she changed the locks on me—I had started staying out late, going to the Limelight because even though I was fourteen I looked twenty-five—I would knock on Oscar's window and he would let me in, scared because the next day my mother would run around the house screaming, Who the hell let that hija de la gran puta[2] in the house? Who? Who? And Oscar would be at the breakfast table stammering, I don't know, Mami, I don't.

Her rage filled the house, like flat stale smoke. It got into everything, into our hair and our food, like the fallout they told us about in school that would one day drift down soft as snow. My brother didn't know what to do. He stayed in his room, though sometimes he would lamely try to ask me what was going on. Nothing. You can tell me, Lola, he said, and I could only laugh. You need to lose weight, I told him. 35

In those final weeks I knew better than to go near my mother. Most of the time she just looked at me with the stink eye, but sometimes without warning she would grab me by my throat and hang on until I pried her fingers off. She didn't bother talking to me unless it was to make death threats: When you grow up you'll meet me in a dark alley when you least expect it and then I'll kill you and nobody will know I did it! Gloating as she said this.

You're crazy, I told her.

You don't call me crazy, she said, and then she sat down panting.

It was bad, but no one expected what came next. So obvious when you think about it.

All my life I'd been swearing that one day I would just disappear. 40

And one day I did.

I ran off, dique,[3] because of a boy.

What can I really tell you about him? He was like all boys: beautiful and callow and, like an insect, he couldn't sit still. Un blanquito[4] with long hairy legs who I met one night at the Limelight.

9. Nothing (Spanish). *Figurín de mierda*: literally, perhaps something like figure made of crap; figuratively, a phony, something that only looks refined (Spanish).

1. I don't want to have those fags here (Spanish). *Smiths* and *Sisters of Mercy*: influential British alternative rock bands of the 1980s, fronted by highly literary singer-songwriter Morrissey (who once described himself as "humasexual") and Andrew Eldritch, respectively.

2. Daughter of a bitch (Spanish).

3. Supposedly or so they say (Dominican Spanish).

4. Little white boy (Spanish).

His name was Aldo.

45   He was nineteen and lived down at the Jersey Shore with his seventy-four-year-old father. In the back of his Oldsmobile on University I pulled my leather skirt up and my fishnet stockings down and the smell of me was everywhere. I didn't let him go all the way, but still. The spring of my sophomore year we wrote and called each other at least once a day. I even drove down with Karen to visit him in Wildwood[5] (she had a license, I didn't). He lived and worked near the boardwalk, one of three guys who operated the bumper cars, the only one without tattoos. You should stay, he told me that night while Karen walked ahead of us on the beach. Where would I live? I asked, and he smiled. With me. Don't lie, I said, but he looked out at the surf. I want you to come, he said seriously.

He asked me three times. I counted, I know.

That summer my brother announced that he was going to dedicate his life to designing role-playing games, and my mother was trying to keep a second job for the first time since her operation. It wasn't working out. She was coming home exhausted, and since I wasn't helping, nothing around the house was getting done. Some weekends my tía Rubelka would help out with the cooking and cleaning and would lecture us both, but she had her own family to look after, so most of the time we were on our own. Come, he said on the phone. And then in August Karen left for Slippery Rock.[6] She had graduated from high school a year early. If I don't see Paterson again it will be too soon, she said before she left. Five days later, school started. I cut class six times in the first two weeks. I just couldn't do school anymore. Something inside wouldn't let me. It didn't help that I was reading "The Fountainhead" and had decided that I was Dominique and Aldo was Roark.[7] And finally what we'd all been waiting for happened. My mother announced at dinner, quietly, I want you both to listen to me: the doctor is running more tests on me.

Oscar looked like he was going to cry. He put his head down. And my reaction? I looked at her and said, Could you please pass the salt?

These days I don't blame her for smacking me across my face, but right then it was all I needed. We jumped on each other and the table fell and the sancocho[8] spilled all over the floor and Oscar just stood in the corner bellowing, Stop it, stop it, stop it!

50   Hija de tu maldita madre![9] she shrieked. And I said, This time I hope you die from it.

For a couple of days the house was a war zone, and then on Friday she let me out of my room and I was allowed to sit next to her on the sofa and watch novelas with her. She was waiting for her blood work to come back, but you would never have known her life was in the balance. She watched the TV like it was the only thing that mattered, and whenever one of the characters did something

---

5. Beachfront community on the Jersey shore; the town's population surges from around 5,000 in the off-season to over 200,000 in season.

6. University in Pennsylvania about fifty miles north of Pittsburgh.

7. Influential and controversial best seller (1943) by Ayn Rand; a celebration of individualism, it chronicles young architect Howard Roark's struggles to achieve success without compromising, even with the equally headstrong architect's daughter (Dominique Francon) with whom he falls in love.

8. Thick soup or stew common in South America and the Caribbean.

9. Child of a motherfucker, considered one of the worst possible insults in Dominican Spanish.

underhanded she would start waving her arms: Someone has to stop her! Can't they see what that puta[1] is up to?

I hate you, I said very quietly, but she didn't hear.

Go get me some water, she said. Put an ice cube in it.

That was the last thing I did for her. The next morning I was on the bus bound for the shore. One bag, two hundred dollars in tips, Tío[2] Rudolfo's old knife, and the only picture my mother had of my father, which she had hidden under her bed (she was in the picture, too, but I pretended not to notice). I was so scared. I couldn't stop shaking. The whole ride down I was expecting the sky to split open and my mother to reach down and shake me. But it didn't happen. Nobody but the man across the aisle noticed me. You're really beautiful, he said. Like a girl I once knew.

I didn't write them a note. That's how much I hated them. Her.   55

That night while Aldo and I lay in his sweltering kitty-litter-infested room I told him: I want you to do it to me.

He started unbuttoning my pants. Are you sure?

Definitely, I said grimly.

He had a long thin dick that hurt like hell, but the whole time I just said, Oh yes, Aldo, yes, because that was what I imagined you were supposed to say while you were losing your virginity to some boy you thought you loved.

It was like the stupidest thing I ever did. I was miserable. And so bored. But of 60
course I wouldn't admit it. I had run away, so I was happy! Happy!

Aldo had neglected to mention, all those times he asked me to live with him, that his father hated him like I hated my mother. Aldo, Sr., had been in the Second World War and he'd never forgiven the "Japs" for all the friends he had lost. My dad's so full of shit, Aldo said. He never left Fort Dix.[3] I don't think his father said nine words to me the whole time I lived with them. He was one mean vicjito[4] and even had a padlock on the refrigerator. Stay the hell out of it, he told me. We couldn't even get ice cubes out.

Aldo and his dad lived in one of the cheapest little bungalows on New Jersey Avenue, and me and Aldo slept in a room where his father kept the litter box for his two cats, and at night we would move it out into the hallway, but he always woke up before us and put it back in the room: I told you to leave my crap alone! Which is funny when you think about it. But it wasn't funny then. I got a job selling French fries on the boardwalk and between the hot oil and the cat piss I couldn't smell anything else. On my days off I would drink with Aldo or I would sit in the sand dressed in all black and try to write in my journal, which I was sure would form the foundation for a utopian society after we blew ourselves into radioactive kibble. Sometimes boys would walk up to me and throw lines at me like, Who fuckin' died? They would sit down next to me in the sand. You a good-looking girl, you should be in a bikini. Why, so you can rape me? Jesus Christ, one of them said, jumping to his feet. What the hell is wrong with you?

1. Whore (Spanish).
2. Uncle (Spanish).
3. U.S. military post just south of Trenton, New Jersey.
4. Old man (Spanish).

To this day I don't know how I lasted. At the beginning of October I was laid off from the French-fry palace; by then most of the boardwalk was closed up and I had nothing to do except hang out at the public library, which was even smaller than my high-school one. Aldo had moved on to working with his dad at his garage, which only made them more pissed off at each other and by extension more pissed off at me. When they got home they would drink Schlitz[5] and complain about the Phillies. I guess I should count myself lucky that they didn't decide to bury the hatchet by gangbanging me. I stayed out as much as I could and waited for the feeling to come back to me, to tell me what I should do next, but I was bone dry, bereft, no visions whatsoever. I started to think that maybe it was like in the books: as soon as I lost my virginity I lost my power. I got really mad at Aldo after that. You're a drunk, I told him. And an idiot. So what, he shot back. Your pussy smells. Then stay out of it! I will!

But of course I was happy! Happy! I kept waiting to run into my family posting flyers of me on the boardwalk—my mom, the tallest blackest chestiest thing in sight, Oscar looking like the Brown Blob, my tía Rubelka, maybe even my tío if they could get him off the heroin long enough—but the closest I came to any of that was some flyers someone had put up for a lost cat. That's white people for you. They lose a cat and it's an all-points bulletin, but we Dominicans lose a daughter and we might not even cancel our appointment at the salon.

65   By November I was so finished. I would sit there with Aldo and his putrid father and the old shows would come on the TV, the ones me and my brother used to watch when we were kids, "Three's Company," "What's Happening!!," "The Jeffersons,"[6] and my disappointment would grind against some organ that was very soft and tender. It was starting to get cold, too, and wind just walked right into the bungalow and got under your blankets or jumped in the shower with you. It was awful. I kept having these stupid visions of my brother trying to cook for himself. Don't ask me why. I was the one who cooked for us. The only thing Oscar knew how to make was grilled cheese. I imagined him thin as a reed, wandering around the kitchen, opening cabinets forlornly. I even started dreaming about my mother, except in my dreams she was young, my age, and it was because of those dreams that I realized something obvious: she had run away, too, and that was why we were all in the United States.

I put away the photo of her and my father, but the dreams didn't stop. I guess when a person is with you they're only with you when they're with you, but when they're gone, when they're really gone, they're with you forever.

And then at the end of November Aldo, my wonderful boyfriend, decided to be cute. I knew he was getting unhappy with us, but I didn't know exactly how bad it was until one night he had his friends over. His father had gone to

---

5. Notoriously cheap American beer.
6. Like *Three's Company* (1977–84) and *What's Happening!!* (1976–79), a popular American sitcom (1975–85). Where *What's Happening!!* features three working-class African American teens in Los Angeles, both *The Jeffersons* and *Three's Company* focus on the conflicts and humor arising from particular living arrangements: The former features a newly affluent African American family who move from working-class Queens into a luxurious Manhattan high-rise; in the latter, which has an all-Caucasian cast, two young women keep their apartment only by convincing their landlord that their male roommate is gay.

Atlantic City[7] and they were all drinking and smoking and telling dumb jokes and suddenly Aldo says, Do you know what Pontiac stands for? Poor Old Nigger Thinks It's A Cadillac. Who was he looking at when he told his punch line? He was looking straight at me.

That night he wanted me but I pushed his hand away. Don't touch me.

Don't get sore, he said, putting my hand on his cock. It wasn't nothing. And then he laughed.

So what did I do a couple days later—a really dumb thing. I called home. The first time no one answered. The second time it was Oscar. The de León residence, how may I direct your call? That was my brother for you. This is why everybody in the world hated his guts.

It's me, dumb-ass.

Lola. He was so quiet and then I realized he was crying. Where *are* you?

You don't want to know. I switched ears, trying to keep my voice casual. How is everybody?

Lola, Mami's going to *kill* you.

Dumb-ass, could you keep your voice down. Mami isn't home, is she?

She's working.

What a surprise, I said. Mami working. On the last minute of the last hour of the last day my mother would be at work. She would be at work when the missiles were in the air.

I guess I must have missed him real bad or I just wanted to see somebody who knew anything about me, or the cat piss had damaged my common sense, because I gave him the address of a coffee shop on the boardwalk and told him to bring my clothes and some of my books.

Bring me money, too.

He paused. I don't know where Mami keeps it.

You know, Mister. Just bring it.

How much? he asked timidly.

All of it.

That's a lot of money, Lola.

Just bring me the money, Oscar.

O.K., O.K. He inhaled deeply. Will you at least tell me if you're O.K. or not?

I'm O.K., I said, and that was the only point in the conversation where I almost cried. I kept quiet until I could speak again and then I asked him how he was going to get down here without our mother finding out.

You know me, he said weakly. I might be a dork, but I'm a resourceful dork.

I should have known not to trust anybody whose favorite books as a child were Encyclopedia Brown.[8] But I wasn't really thinking; I was so looking forward to seeing him.

By then I had this plan. I was going to convince my brother to run away with me. My plan was that we would go to Dublin. I had met a bunch of Irish guys on the boardwalk and they had sold me on their country. I would become a

---

7. Somewhat rundown New Jersey beach town renowned for its casinos.
8. Fictional series (1963–present) about the adventures of bookish boy detective Leroy ("Encyclopedia") Brown.

backup singer for U2[9] and both Bono and the drummer would fall in love with me, and Oscar could become the Dominican James Joyce.[1] I really believed it would happen, too. That's how deluded I was by then.

The next day I walked into the coffee shop, looking brand-new, and he was there, with the bag. Oscar, I said, laughing. You're so fat!

I know, he said, ashamed. I was worried about you.

We embraced for like an hour and then he started crying. Lola, I'm sorry.

It's O.K., I said, and that's when I looked up and saw my mother and my tía Rubelka and my tío Rudolfo boiling out of the kitchen.

Oscar! I screamed, but it was too late. My mother already had me in her hands. She looked so thin and worn, almost like a hag, but she was holding on to me like I was her last nickel, and underneath her red wig her green eyes were *furious.* I noticed, absently, that she had dressed up for the occasion. That was typical. Muchacha del diablo, she shrieked. I managed to haul her out of the coffee shop and when she pulled back her hand to smack me I broke free. I ran for it. Behind me I could feel her sprawling, hitting the curb hard with a crack, but I wasn't looking back. No—I was running. In elementary school, whenever we had field day I was always the fastest girl in my grade, took home all the ribbons; they said it wasn't fair, because I was so big, but I didn't care. I could even have beaten the boys if I'd wanted to, so there was no way my sick mother, my messed-up tíos, and my fat brother were going to catch me. I was going to run as fast as my long legs could carry me. I was going to run down the boardwalk, past Aldo's miserable house, out of Wildwood, out of New Jersey, and I wasn't going to stop. I was going to *fly.*

Anyway, that's how it *should* have worked out. But I looked back. I couldn't help it. It's not like I didn't know my Bible, all the pillars-of-salt stuff,[2] but when you're someone's daughter that she raised by herself with no help from nobody habits die hard. I just wanted to make sure my mom hadn't broken her arm or smashed open her skull. I mean, really, who the hell wants to kill her own mother by accident? That's the only reason I glanced back. She was sprawled on the ground, her wig had fallen out of reach, her poor bald head out in the day like something private and shameful, and she was bawling like a lost calf, Hija, hija! And there I was wanting to run off into my future. It was right then that I needed that feeling to guide me, but it wasn't anywhere in sight. Only me. In the end I didn't have the ovaries. She was on the ground, bald as a baby, crying, probably a month away from dying, and here I was, her one and only daughter. And there was nothing I could do about it. So I walked back and when I reached down to help her she clamped on to me with both hands. That was when I realized she hadn't been crying at all. She'd been faking! Her smile was like a lion's.

---

9. Wildly successful Irish rock band formed in Dublin in 1976 by frontman Bono, guitarist The Edge, bassist Adam Clayton, and drummer Larry Mullen, Jr.
1. Celebrated Dublin-born author (1882–1941) of books including the short-story collection *Dubliners* (1914), which includes "Araby" (p. 126).
2. In the book of Genesis, Lot and his wife flee the iniquitous Sodom at the behest of angels who warn them not to look back lest they share in that city's well-earned destruction; when Lot's wife ignores the warning, she turns into a pillar of salt.

Ya te tengo,[3] she said, jumping triumphantly to her feet. Te tengo.

And that is how I ended up in Santo Domingo.[4] I guess my mother thought it would be harder for me to run away from an island where I knew no one, and in a way she was right. I'm into my sixth month here and these days I'm just trying to be philosophical about the whole thing. I wasn't like that at first, but in the end I had to let it go. It was like the fight between the egg and the rock, my abuela[5] said. No winning.

I'm actually going to school, not that it's going to count when I return to Pat- 100
erson, but it keeps me busy and out of trouble and around people my own age. You don't need to be around us viejos all day, Abuela says. I have mixed feelings about the school. For one thing, it's improved my Spanish a lot. It's a private school, a Carol Morgan[6] wanna-be filled with people my tío Carlos Moya calls los hijos de mami y papi.[7] And then there's me. If you think it was tough being a goth in Paterson, try being a Dominican york in one of those private schools back in D.R. You will never meet bitchier girls in your whole life. They whisper about me to death. Someone else would have had a nervous breakdown, but after Wildwood I'm not so brittle. I don't let it get to me.

And the irony of all ironies? I'm on our school's track team. I joined because my friend Rosio, the scholarship girl from Los Mina,[8] told me I could win a spot on the team on the length of my legs alone. Those are the pins of a winner, she prophesied. Well, she must have known something I didn't, because I'm now our school's top runner in the four hundred metres and under. That I have talent at this simple thing never ceases to amaze me. Karen would pass out if she could see me running sprints out behind my school while Coach Cortés screams at us, first in Spanish and then in Catalán. Breathe, breathe, *breathe!* I've got like no fat left on me and the musculature of my legs impresses everyone, even me. I can't wear shorts anymore without causing traffic jams, and the other day when my abuela accidentally locked us out of the house she turned to me in frustration and said, Hija, just kick the door open. That pushed a laugh out of both of us.

So much has changed these last months, in my head, my heart. Rosio has me dressing up like a real Dominican girl. She's the one who fixes my hair and helps me with my makeup, and sometimes when I see myself in mirrors I don't even know who I am anymore. Not that I'm unhappy or anything. Even if I found a hot-air balloon that would whisk me straight to U2's house I'm not sure I would take it. (I'm still not talking to my traitor brother, though.) The truth is I'm even thinking of staying one more year. Abuela doesn't want me ever to leave—I'll miss you, she says so simply it can't be anything but true—and my mom has told me I can stay if I want to but that I would be welcome at home, too. Tía Rubelka tells me she's hanging tough, my mother, that she's back to two

3. Now I've got you (Spanish).
4. Capital city (founded in 1496) of the Dominican Republic, which, along with the Republic of Haiti, occupies Hispaniola Island.
5. Grandmother (Spanish).
6. Prestigious English-language school in Santo Domingo, founded in 1933 by U.S. missionaries Carol and Barney Morgan.
7. Spoiled kids, something like "Daddy's girls" and "Mommy's boys" (Spanish).
8. Neighborhood in Santo Domingo.

jobs. They sent me a picture of the whole family and Abuela framed it and I can't look at it without misting up. My mother's not wearing her fakies in it; she looks so thin I don't even recognize her.

Just know that I would die for you, she told me the last time we talked. And before I could say anything she hung up.

But that's not what I wanted to tell you. It's about that crazy feeling that started this whole mess, the bruja feeling that comes singing out of my bones, that takes hold of me the way blood seizes cotton. The feeling that tells me that everything in my life is about to change. It's come back. Just the other day I woke up from all these dreams and it was there, pulsing inside of me. I imagine this is what it feels like to have a child in you. At first I was scared, because I thought it was telling me to run away again, but every time I looked around our house, every time I saw my abuela the feeling got stronger, so I knew this was something different.

105   I was dating a boy by then, a sweet morenito[9] by the name of Max Sánchez, who I had met in Los Mina while visiting Rosio. He's short, but his smile and his snappy dressing make up for a lot. Because I'm from Nueba Yol[1] he talks about how rich he's going to become and I try to explain to him that I don't care about that, but he looks at me like I'm crazy. I'm going to get a white Mercedes-Benz, he says. Tú verás.[2] But it's the job he has that I love best, that got me and him started. In Santo Domingo two or three theatres often share the same set of reels for a movie, so when the first theatre finishes with the first reel they put it in Max's hands and he rides his motorcycle like crazy to make it to the second theatre and then he drives back, waits, picks up the second reel, and so on. If he's held up or gets into an accident the first reel will end and there will be no second reel and the people in the audience will throw bottles. So far he's been blessed, he tells me while kissing his San Miguel[3] medal. Because of me, he brags, one movie becomes three. I'm the man who puts together the pictures. Max is not from la clase alta,[4] as my abuela would describe it, and if any of the stuck-up bitches in school saw us they would just about die, but I'm fond of him. He holds open doors, he calls me his morena; when he's feeling brave he touches my arm gently and then pulls back.

Anyway I thought maybe the feeling was about Max, and so one day I let him take me to one of the love motels. He was so excited he almost fell off the bed, and the first thing he wanted was to look at my ass. I never knew my big ass could be such a star attraction, but he kissed it, four, five times, gave me goose bumps with his breath, and pronounced it a tesoro. When we were done and he was in the bathroom washing himself I stood in front of the mirror naked and looked at my culo for the first time. A tesoro,[5] I repeated. A treasure.

Well? Rosio asked at school. And I nodded once, quickly, and she grabbed me and laughed and all the girls I hated turned to look, but what could they do? Happiness, when it comes, is stronger than all the jerk girls in Santo Domingo combined.

---

9. Literally, *moreno* (brown) plus *-ito* (a diminutive suffix) equals "little brown" (Spanish), that is, a little brown-skinned boy.
1. New York City (Spanish).
2. You'll see (Spanish).
3. St. Michael (Spanish), leader of God's army and angel of death, who ensures the redeemed soul's safe passage to heaven.
4. The upper class (Spanish).
5. Treasure (Spanish). *Culo*: ass (Spanish).

But I was still confused. Because the feeling, it just kept getting stronger and stronger, wouldn't let me sleep, wouldn't give me any peace. I started losing races, which was something I never did.

You ain't so great, are you, gringa,[6] the girls on the other teams hissed at me, and I could only hang my head. Coach Cortés was so unhappy he just locked himself in his car and wouldn't say anything to any of us.

The whole thing was driving me crazy, and then one night I came home from 110 being out with Max. He had taken me for a walk along the Malecón[7]—he never had money for anything else—and we had watched the bats zigzagging over the palms and an old ship head into the distance. While I stretched my hamstrings, he talked quietly about moving to the U.S. My abuela was waiting for me at the living-room table. Even though she still wears black to mourn the husband she lost when she was young she's one of the most handsome women I've ever known. We have the same jagged lightning-bolt part, and when I saw her at the airport, the first time in ten years, I didn't want to admit it but I knew that things were going to be O.K. between us. She stood like she was her own best thing[8] and when she saw me she said, Hija, I have waited for you since the day you left. And then she hugged me and kissed me and said, I'm your abuela, but you can call me La Inca.[9]

Standing over her that night, her part like a crack in her hair, I felt a surge of tenderness. I put my arms around her and that was when I noticed that she was looking at photos. Old photos, the kind I'd never seen in my house. Photos of my mother when she was young, before she had her breasts. She was even skinnier than me! I picked the smallest photo up. Mami was standing in front of a bakery. Even with an apron on she looked potent, like someone who was going to be someone.

She was very guapa, I said casually.

Abuela snorted. Guapa soy yo. Your mother was a diosa. But so cabeza dura. When she was your age we never got along. She was cabeza dura and I was . . . exigente.[1] You and her are more alike than you think.

I know she ran away. From you. From Santo Domingo.

La Inca stared at me, incredulous. Your mother didn't run away. We had to 115 *send* her away. To keep her from being murdered. To keep us all from being murdered. She didn't listen and she fell in love with the wrong man. She didn't listen. Jesu Cristo, hija—

She was about to say something more and then she stopped.

And that's when it hit with the force of a hurricane. The *feeling*. My abuela was sitting there, forlorn, trying to cobble together the right words, and I could not move or breathe. I felt like I always did in the last seconds of a race, when I

6. English-speaking foreigner (Spanish).
7. Santo Domingo's world-famous oceanfront promenade.
8. Perhaps an allusion to Toni Morrison's novel *Beloved* (1987), in which a man works to convince his lover, a mother grieving for her children, that she, not they, is her "own best thing." In interviews, Díaz has referred to his "relationship with" Morrison's work as "the most sustained love of mine, the one that's carried me through all these years."
9. The Incan (Spanish), a noble, member, or follower of the Indian peoples who established, in what is now Peru, pre-Columbian America's largest empire (c. thirteenth century through 1572).
1. Demanding. *Guapa soy yo:* I am pretty or attractive. *Diosa:* goddess. *Cabeza dura:* hardheaded (all Spanish).

was sure that I was going to explode. She was about to say something and I was waiting for whatever she was going to give me. I was waiting to begin.

2007

QUESTIONS

1. WILDWOOD begins with Lola's observation that "[i]t's never the changes we want that change everything." How and why exactly does Lola change over the course of the story?
2. WILDWOOD ends with Lola's remark, "I was waiting to begin." Why do you think the story ends with reference to a beginning, or how does this line shape the way you understand the nature and significance of the changes Lola has undergone up to this point?
3. How do Díaz's specific ways of intermixing Spanish and English, as well as his frequent allusions (literary, musical, televisual, and biblical), help to flesh out the story's central conflicts and/or theme(s)?

SUGGESTIONS FOR WRITING

1. Choose any story in this chapter and write an essay exploring how character, point of view, setting, symbolism, or any recurring word or phrase contributes to the development of theme. Be sure to state that theme in a sentence.
2. Sometimes the theme in a work of literature can be expressed as a strong, clear statement: "A always follows from B," or "An X can never be a Y." More often, though, especially in modern literature, authors offer subtler, often ambiguous themes that deliberately undermine our faith in simple absolutes: "A doesn't necessarily always follow B," or "There are times when an X can be a Y." Write an essay in which you argue that one of the stories in this chapter has an "always" or "never" kind of theme, and contrast it to the more indeterminate theme of another story. Alternatively, use your essay to explain why we might be both tempted and wrong to see one of these stories as having an "always" or "never" theme. What is the overly simplistic version of the theme, and what is the more complex one?
3. Write an essay exploring how theme is developed through the juxtaposition of realistic detail and fantastic elements in A VERY OLD MAN WITH ENORMOUS WINGS, especially (but not exclusively) in the description of the winged man himself.
4. Though the main theme of WILDWOOD may well be a universal one (an insight that applies to all or most people), its major characters are all contemporary working-class Domican Americans. Write an essay exploring how the story characterizes their lives and how this characterization shapes the story's theme, perhaps giving the story a culturally and historically specific, as well as universal, resonance and relevance.
5. Write an essay comparing the way Stephen Crane's THE OPEN BOAT and Nathaniel Hawthorne's THE BIRTH-MARK portray the relationship between human beings and nature. What is similar and different about the nature-related themes of the two stories?
6. Write your own fable, perhaps reworking or modernizing one by Aesop. Be sure both to state the theme and to make sure it is demonstrated in the fable itself.

Reading More Fiction

JAMES BALDWIN
(1924–87)
Sonny's Blues

For much of his life, James Baldwin was a—perhaps even *the*—leading literary spokesman for civil rights and racial equality. Raised, with his eight younger siblings, in Depression-era Harlem—often, as he once put it, with a child in one hand and a book in the other—he would spend much of his adult life in France. Here, when he first arrived in late 1948, Baldwin would experience poverty so extreme that he had to sell his clothes and typewriter. But only here, he said, could he get "over—and a lot beyond [. . .] all the terms in which Americans identified me—in my own mind." He first attracted critical attention with two extraordinary novels, *Go Tell It on the Mountain* (1953), which draws on his past as a teenage preacher in the Fireside Pentecostal Church, and *Giovanni's Room* (1956), which deals with the anguish of being black and homosexual in a largely white and heterosexual society. In addition to his novels and the short-story collection *Going to Meet the Man* (1965), Baldwin also had a long flirtation with the theater; his play *Blues for Mister Charlie* (1964) is based partly on the real-life murder of Emmett Till (1955). But Baldwin is perhaps best remembered today for the essays collected in books such as *Notes of a Native Son* (1955) and the best-selling *The Fire Next Time* (1963). Here especially, as Nobel Laureate Toni Morrison avows, her beloved friend Jimmy "made American English honest," "reshap[ing] it until it was truly modern [. . .] , representative, humane," "un-gat[ing] it for black people so that in your wake we could enter it, occupy it, restructure it in order to accommodate [. . .] our intricate, difficult, demanding beauty, our tragic, insistent knowledge, our lived reality."

I read about it in the paper, in the subway, on my way to work. I read it, and I couldn't believe it, and I read it again. Then perhaps I just stared at it, at the newsprint spelling out his name, spelling out the story. I stared at it in the swinging lights of the subway car, and in the faces and bodies of the people, and in my own face, trapped in the darkness which roared outside.

It was not to be believed and I kept telling myself that, as I walked from the subway station to the high school. And at the same time I couldn't doubt it. I was scared, scared for Sonny. He became real to me again. A great block of ice got settled in my belly and kept melting there slowly all day long, while I taught my classes algebra. It was a special kind of ice. It kept melting, sending trickles of ice water all up and down my veins, but it never got less. Sometimes it hardened and seemed to expand until I felt my guts were going to come spilling out or that I was going to choke or scream. This would always be at a moment when I was remembering some specific thing Sonny had once said or done.

When he was about as old as the boys in my classes his face had been bright and open, there was a lot of copper in it; and he'd had wonderfully direct brown eyes, and great gentleness and privacy. I wondered what he looked like now. He had been picked up, the evening before, in a raid on an apartment downtown, for peddling and using heroin.

I couldn't believe it: but what I mean by that is that I couldn't find any room for it anywhere inside me. I had kept it outside me for a long time. I hadn't wanted to know. I had had suspicions, but I didn't name them, I kept putting them away. I told myself that Sonny was wild, but he wasn't crazy. And he'd always been a good boy, he hadn't ever turned hard or evil or disrespectful, the way kids can, so quick, so quick, especially in Harlem. I didn't want to believe that I'd ever see my brother going down, coming to nothing, all that light in his face gone out, in the condition I'd already seen so many others. Yet it had happened and here I was, talking about algebra to a lot of boys who might, every one of them for all I knew, be popping off needles every time they went to the head.[1] Maybe it did more for them than algebra could.

5   I was sure that the first time Sonny had ever had horse,[2] he couldn't have been much older than these boys were now. These boys, now, were living as we'd been living then, they were growing up with a rush and their heads bumped abruptly against the low ceiling of their actual possibilities. They were filled with rage. All they really knew were two darknesses, the darkness of their lives, which was now closing in on them, and the darkness of the movies, which had blinded them to that other darkness, and in which they now, vindictively, dreamed, at once more together than they were at any other time, and more alone.

When the last bell rang, the last class ended, I let out my breath. It seemed I'd been holding it for all that time. My clothes were wet—I may have looked as though I'd been sitting in a steam bath, all dressed up, all afternoon. I sat alone in the classroom a long time. I listened to the boys outside, downstairs, shouting and cursing and laughing. Their laughter struck me for perhaps the first time. It was not the joyous laughter which—God knows why—one associates with children. It was mocking and insular, its intent was to denigrate. It was disenchanted, and in this, also, lay the authority of their curses. Perhaps I was listening to them because I was thinking about my brother and in them I heard my brother. And myself.

One boy was whistling a tune, at once very complicated and very simple, it seemed to be pouring out of him as though he were a bird, and it sounded very cool and moving through all that harsh, bright air, only just holding its own through all those other sounds.

1. Lavatory.
2. Heroin.

I stood up and walked over to the window and looked down into the courtyard. It was the beginning of the spring and the sap was rising in the boys. A
teacher passed through them every now and again, quickly, as though he or she
couldn't wait to get out of that courtyard, to get those boys out of their sight and
off their minds. I started collecting my stuff. I thought I'd better get home and
talk to Isabel.

The courtyard was almost deserted by the time I got downstairs. I saw this
boy standing in the shadow of a doorway, looking just like Sonny. I almost called
his name. Then I saw that it wasn't Sonny, but somebody we used to know, a boy
from around our block. He'd been Sonny's friend. He'd never been mine, having
been too young for me, and, anyway, I'd never liked him. And now, even though
he was a grown-up man, he still hung around that block, still spent hours on the
street corners, was always high and raggy. I used to run into him from time to
time and he'd often work around to asking me for a quarter or fifty cents. He
always had some real good excuse, too, and I always gave it to him. I don't know
why.

But now, abruptly, I hated him. I couldn't stand the way he looked at me, 10
partly like a dog, partly like a cunning child. I wanted to ask him what the hell
he was doing in the school courtyard.

He sort of shuffled over to me, and he said, "I see you got the papers. So you
already know about it."

"You mean about Sonny? Yes, I already know about it. How come they didn't
get you?"

He grinned. It made him repulsive and it also brought to mind what he'd
looked like as a kid. "I wasn't there. I stay away from them people."

"Good for you." I offered him a cigarette and I watched him through the
smoke. "You come all the way down here just to tell me about Sonny?"

"That's right." He was sort of shaking his head and his eyes looked strange, as 15
though they were about to cross. The bright sun deadened his damp dark brown
skin and it made his eyes look yellow and showed up the dirt in his kinked hair.
He smelled funky. I moved a little away from him and I said, "Well, thanks. But
I already know about it and I got to get home."

"I'll walk you a little ways," he said. We started walking. There were a couple
of kids still loitering in the courtyard and one of them said goodnight to me and
looked strangely at the boy beside me.

"What're you going to do?" he asked me. "I mean, about Sonny?"

"Look. I haven't seen Sonny for over a year, I'm not sure I'm going to do anything. Anyway, what the hell *can* I do?"

"That's right," he said quickly, "ain't nothing you can do. Can't much help old
Sonny no more, I guess."

It was what I was thinking and so it seemed to me he had no right to say it. 20

"I'm surprised at Sonny, though," he went on—he had a funny way of talking,
he looked straight ahead as though he were talking to himself—"I thought
Sonny was a smart boy, I thought he was too smart to get hung."

"I guess he thought so too," I said sharply, "and that's how he got hung. And
how about you? You're pretty goddamn smart, I bet."

Then he looked directly at me, just for a minute. "I ain't smart," he said. "If I
was smart, I'd have reached for a pistol a long time ago."

"Look. Don't tell *me* your sad story, if it was up to me, I'd give you one." Then I felt guilty—guilty, probably, for never having supposed that the poor bastard *had* a story of his own, much less a sad one, and I asked, quickly, "What's going to happen to him now?"

25   He didn't answer this. He was off by himself some place.

"Funny thing," he said, and from his tone we might have been discussing the quickest way to get to Brooklyn, "when I saw the papers this morning, the first thing I asked myself was if I had anything to do with it. I felt sort of responsible."

I began to listen more carefully. The subway station was on the corner, just before us, and I stopped. He stopped, too. We were in front of a bar and he ducked slightly, peering in, but whoever he was looking for didn't seem to be there. The juke box was blasting away with something black and bouncy and I half watched the barmaid as she danced her way from the juke box to her place behind the bar. And I watched her face as she laughingly responded to something someone said to her, still keeping time to the music. When she smiled one saw the little girl, one sensed the doomed, still-struggling woman beneath the battered face of the semi-whore.

"I never *give* Sonny nothing," the boy said finally, "but a long time ago I come to school high and Sonny asked me how it felt." He paused, I couldn't bear to watch him, I watched the barmaid, and I listened to the music which seemed to be causing the pavement to shake. "I told him it felt great." The music stopped, the barmaid paused and watched the juke box until the music began again. "It did."

All this was carrying me some place I didn't want to go. I certainly didn't want to know how it felt. It filled everything, the people, the houses, the music, the dark, quicksilver barmaid, with menace; and this menace was their reality.

30   "What's going to happen to him now?" I asked again.

"They'll send him away some place and they'll try to cure him." He shook his head. "Maybe he'll even think he's kicked the habit. Then they'll let him loose"—he gestured, throwing his cigarette into the gutter. "That's all."

"What do you mean, that's *all*?"

But I knew what he meant.

"I *mean*, that's all." He turned his head and looked at me, pulling down the corners of his mouth. "Don't you know what I mean?" he asked, softly.

35   "How the hell *would* I know what you mean?" I almost whispered it, I don't know why.

"That's right," he said to the air, "how would *he* know what I mean?" He turned toward me again, patient and calm, and yet I somehow felt him shaking, shaking as though he were going to fall apart. I felt that ice in my guts again, the dread I'd felt all afternoon; and again I watched the barmaid, moving about the bar, washing glasses, and singing. "Listen. They'll let him out and then it'll just start all over again. That's what I mean."

"You mean—they'll let him out. And then he'll just start working his way back in again. You mean he'll never kick the habit. Is that what you mean?"

"That's right," he said, cheerfully. "*You* see what I mean."

"Tell me," I said at last, "why does he want to die? He must want to die, he's killing himself, why does he want to die?"

He looked at me in surprise. He licked his lips. "He don't want to die. He 40
wants to live. Don't nobody want to die, ever."

Then I wanted to ask him—too many things. He could not have answered, or
if he had, I could not have borne the answers. I started walking. "Well, I guess
it's none of my business."

"It's going to be rough on old Sonny," he said. We reached the subway station.
"This is your station?" he asked. I nodded. I took one step down. "Damn!" he
said, suddenly. I looked up at him. He grinned again. "Damn it if I didn't leave
all my money home. You ain't got a dollar on you, have you? Just for a couple of
days, is all."

All at once something inside gave and threatened to come pouring out of me.
I didn't hate him any more. I felt that in another moment I'd start crying like a
child.

"Sure," I said. "Don't sweat." I looked in my wallet and didn't have a dollar, I
only had a five. "Here," I said. "That hold you?"

He didn't look at it—he didn't want to look at it. A terrible, closed look came 45
over his face, as though he were keeping the number on the bill a secret from
him and me. "Thanks," he said, and now he was dying to see me go. "Don't
worry about Sonny. Maybe I'll write him or something."

"Sure," I said. "You do that. So long."

"Be seeing you," he said. I went on down the steps.

And I didn't write Sonny or send him anything for a long time. When I finally
did, it was just after my little girl died, and he wrote me back a letter which
made me feel like a bastard.

Here's what he said:

Dear brother, 50

    You don't know how much I needed to hear from you. I wanted to write
you many a time but I dug how much I must have hurt you and so I didn't
write. But now I feel like a man who's been trying to climb up out of some
deep, real deep and funky hole and just saw the sun up there, outside. I got to
get outside.

    I can't tell you much about how I got here. I mean I don't know how to
tell you. I guess I was afraid of something or I was trying to escape from
something and you know I have never been very strong in the head (smile).
I'm glad Mama and Daddy are dead and can't see what's happened to their
son and I swear if I'd known what I was doing I would never have hurt you
so, you and a lot of other fine people who were nice to me and who believed
in me.

    I don't want you to think it had anything to do with me being a musician.
It's more than that. Or maybe less than that. I can't get anything straight in
my head down here and I try not to think about what's going to happen to me
when I get outside again. Sometime I think I'm going to flip and *never* get
outside and sometime I think I'll come straight back. I tell you one thing,
though, I'd rather blow my brains out than go through this again. But that's
what they all say, so they tell me. If I tell you when I'm coming to New York
and if you could meet me, I sure would appreciate it. Give my love to Isabel

and the kids and I was sure sorry to hear about little Gracie. I wish I could be like Mama and say the Lord's will be done, but I don't know it seems to me that trouble is the one thing that never does get stopped and I don't know what good it does to blame it on the Lord. But maybe it does some good if you believe it.

Your brother,
Sonny

Then I kept in constant touch with him and I sent him whatever I could and I went to meet him when he came back to New York. When I saw him many things I thought I had forgotten came flooding back to me. This was because I had begun, finally, to wonder about Sonny, about the life that Sonny lived inside. This life, whatever it was, had made him older and thinner and it had deepened the distant stillness in which he had always moved. He looked very unlike my baby brother. Yet, when he smiled, when we shook hands, the baby brother I'd never known looked out from the depths of his private life, like an animal waiting to be coaxed into the light.

"How you been keeping?" he asked me.
55   "All right. And you?"
"Just fine." He was smiling all over his face. "It's good to see you again."
"It's good to see you."
The seven years' difference in our ages lay between us like a chasm: I wondered if these years would ever operate between us as a bridge. I was remembering, and it made it hard to catch my breath, that I had been there when he was born; and I had heard the first words he had ever spoken. When he started to walk, he walked from our mother straight to me. I caught him just before he fell when he took the first steps he ever took in this world.
"How's Isabel?"
60   "Just fine. She's dying to see you."
"And the boys?"
"They're fine, too. They're anxious to see their uncle."
"Oh, come on. You know they don't remember me."
"Are you kidding? Of course they remember you."
65   He grinned again. We got into a taxi. We had a lot to say to each other, far too much to know how to begin.
As the taxi began to move, I asked, "You still want to go to India?"
He laughed. "You still remember that. Hell, no. This place is Indian enough for me."
"It used to belong to them," I said.
And he laughed again. "They damn sure knew what they were doing when they got rid of it."
70   Years ago, when he was around fourteen, he'd been all hipped on the idea of going to India. He read books about people sitting on rocks, naked, in all kinds of weather, but mostly bad, naturally, and walking barefoot through hot coals and arriving at wisdom. I used to say that it sounded to me as though they were getting away from wisdom as fast as they could. I think he sort of looked down on me for that.

"Do you mind," he asked, "if we have the driver drive alongside the park? On the west side—I haven't seen the city in so long."

"Of course not," I said. I was afraid that I might sound as though I were humoring him, but I hoped he wouldn't take it that way.

So we drove along, between the green of the park and the stony, lifeless elegance of hotels and apartment buildings, toward the vivid, killing streets of our childhood. These streets hadn't changed, though housing projects jutted up out of them now like rocks in the middle of a boiling sea. Most of the houses in which we had grown up had vanished, as had the stores from which we had stolen, the basements in which we had first tried sex, the rooftops from which we had hurled tin cans and bricks. But houses exactly like the houses of our past yet dominated the landscape, boys exactly like the boys we once had been found themselves smothering in these houses, came down into the streets for light and air and found themselves encircled by disaster. Some escaped the trap, most didn't. Those who got out always left something of themselves behind, as some animals amputate a leg and leave it in the trap. It might be said, perhaps, that I had escaped, after all, I was a school teacher; or that Sonny had, he hadn't lived in Harlem for years. Yet, as the cab moved uptown through streets which seemed, with a rush, to darken with dark people, and as I covertly studied Sonny's face, it came to me that what we both were seeking through our separate cab windows was that part of ourselves which had been left behind. It's always at the hour of trouble and confrontation that the missing member aches.

We hit 110th Street and started rolling up Lenox Avenue. And I'd known this avenue all my life, but it seemed to me again, as it had seemed on the day I'd first heard about Sonny's trouble, filled with a hidden menace which was its very breath of life.

"We almost there," said Sonny.

"Almost." We were both too nervous to say anything more.

We live in a housing project. It hasn't been up long. A few days after it was up it seemed uninhabitably new, now, of course, it's already rundown. It looks like a parody of the good, clean, faceless life—God knows the people who live in it do their best to make it a parody. The beat-looking grass lying around isn't enough to make their lives green, the hedges will never hold out the streets, and they know it. The big windows fool no one, they aren't big enough to make space out of no space. They don't bother with the windows, they watch the TV screen instead. The playground is most popular with the children who don't play at jacks, or skip rope, or roller skate, or swing, and they can be found in it after dark. We moved in partly because it's not too far from where I teach, and partly for the kids; but it's really just like the houses in which Sonny and I grew up. The same things happen, they'll have the same things to remember. The moment Sonny and I started into the house I had the feeling that I was simply bringing him back into the danger he had almost died trying to escape.

Sonny has never been talkative. So I don't know why I was sure he'd be dying to talk to me when supper was over the first night. Everything went fine, the oldest boy remembered him, and the youngest boy liked him, and Sonny had remembered to bring something for each of them; and Isabel, who is really much nicer than I am, more open and giving, had gone to a lot of trouble about

75

dinner and was genuinely glad to see him. And she's always been able to tease Sonny in a way that I haven't. It was nice to see her face so vivid again and to hear her laugh and watch her make Sonny laugh. She wasn't, or, anyway, she didn't seem to be, at all uneasy or embarrassed. She chatted as though there were no subject which had to be avoided and she got Sonny past his first, faint stiffness. And thank God she was there, for I was filled with that icy dread again. Everything I did seemed awkward to me, and everything I said sounded freighted with hidden meaning. I was trying to remember everything I'd heard about dope addiction and I couldn't help watching Sonny for signs. I wasn't doing it out of malice. I was trying to find out something about my brother. I was dying to hear him tell me he was safe.

"Safe!" my father grunted, whenever Mama suggested trying to move to a neighborhood which might be safer for children. "Safe, hell! Ain't no place safe for kids, nor nobody."

80   He always went on like this, but he wasn't, ever, really as bad as he sounded, not even on weekends, when he got drunk. As a matter of fact, he was always on the lookout for "something a little better," but he died before he found it. He died suddenly, during a drunken weekend in the middle of the war, when Sonny was fifteen. He and Sonny hadn't ever got on too well. And this was partly because Sonny was the apple of his father's eye. It was because he loved Sonny so much and was frightened for him, that he was always fighting with him. It doesn't do any good to fight with Sonny. Sonny just moves back, inside himself, where he can't be reached. But the principal reason that they never hit it off is that they were so much alike. Daddy was big and rough and loud-talking, just the opposite of Sonny, but they both had—that same privacy.

Mama tried to tell me something about this, just after Daddy died. I was home on leave from the army.

This was the last time I ever saw my mother alive. Just the same, this picture gets all mixed up in my mind with pictures I had of her when she was younger. The way I always see her is the way she used to be on a Sunday afternoon, say, when the old folks were talking after the big Sunday dinner. I always see her wearing pale blue. She'd be sitting on the sofa. And my father would be sitting in the easy chair, not far from her. And the living room would be full of church folks and relatives. There they sit, in chairs all around the living room, and the night is creeping up outside, but nobody knows it yet. You can see the darkness growing against the windowpanes and you hear the street noises every now and again, or maybe the jangling beat of a tambourine from one of the churches close by, but it's real quiet in the room. For a moment nobody's talking, but every face looks darkening, like the sky outside. And my mother rocks a little from the waist, and my father's eyes are closed. Everyone is looking at something a child can't see. For a minute they've forgotten the children. Maybe a kid is lying on the rug, half asleep. Maybe somebody's got a kid in his lap and is absent-mindedly stroking the kid's head. Maybe there's a kid, quiet and big-eyed, curled up in a big chair in the corner. The silence, the darkness coming, and the darkness in the faces frighten the child obscurely. He hopes that the hand which strokes his forehead will never stop—will never die. He hopes that there will never come a time when the old folks won't be sitting around the living room, talking about where they've come from, and what they've seen, and what's happened to them and their kinfolk.

But something deep and watchful in the child knows that this is bound to end, is already ending. In a moment someone will get up and turn on the light. Then the old folks will remember the children and they won't talk any more that day. And when light fills the room, the child is filled with darkness. He knows that every time this happens he's moved just a little closer to that darkness outside. The darkness outside is what the old folks have been talking about. It's what they've come from. It's what they endure. The child knows that they won't talk any more because if he knows too much about what's happened to *them*, he'll know too much too soon, about what's going to happen to *him*.

The last time I talked to my mother, I remember I was restless. I wanted to get out and see Isabel. We weren't married then and we had a lot to straighten out between us.

There Mama sat, in black, by the window. She was humming an old church 85 song, *Lord, you brought me from a long ways off.* Sonny was out somewhere. Mama kept watching the streets.

"I don't know," she said, "if I'll ever see you again, after you go off from here. But I hope you'll remember the things I tried to teach you."

"Don't talk like that," I said, and smiled. "You'll be here a long time yet."

She smiled, too, but she said nothing. She was quiet for a long time. And I said, "Mama, don't you worry about nothing. I'll be writing all the time, and you be getting the checks. . . ."

"I want to talk to you about your brother," she said, suddenly. "If anything happens to me he ain't going to have nobody to look out for him."

"Mama," I said, "ain't nothing going to happen to you *or* Sonny. Sonny's all 90 right. He's a good boy and he's got good sense."

"It ain't a question of his being a good boy," Mama said, "nor of his having good sense. It ain't only the bad ones, nor yet the dumb ones that gets sucked under." She stopped, looking at me. "Your Daddy once had a brother," she said, and she smiled in a way that made me feel she was in pain. "You didn't never know that, did you?"

"No," I said, "I never knew that," and I watched her face.

"Oh, yes," she said, "your Daddy had a brother." She looked out of the window again. "I know you never saw your Daddy cry. But *I* did—many a time, through all these years."

I asked her, "What happened to his brother? How come nobody's ever talked about him?"

This was the first time I ever saw my mother look old. 95

"His brother got killed," she said, "when he was just a little younger than you are now. I knew him. He was a fine boy. He was maybe a little full of the devil, but he didn't mean nobody no harm."

Then she stopped and the room was silent, exactly as it had sometimes been on those Sunday afternoons. Mama kept looking out into the streets.

"He used to have a job in the mill," she said, "and, like all young folks, he just liked to perform on Saturday nights. Saturday nights, him and your father would drift around to different places, go to dances and things like that, or just sit around with people they knew, and your father's brother would sing, he had a fine voice, and play along with himself on his guitar. Well, this particular Saturday night, him and your father was coming home from some place, and they were both a little drunk and there was a moon that night, it was bright like day. Your father's brother was feeling kind of good, and he was whistling to himself, and he had his guitar slung over his shoulder. They was coming down a hill and beneath them was a road that turned off from the highway. Well, your father's brother, being always kind of frisky, decided to run down this hill, and he did, with that guitar banging and clanging behind him, and he ran across the road, and he was making water behind a tree. And your father was sort of amused at him and he was still coming down the hill, kind of slow. Then he heard a car motor and that same minute his brother stepped from behind the tree, into the road, in the moonlight. And he started to cross the road. And your father started to run down the hill, he says he don't know why. This car was full of white men. They was all drunk, and when they seen your father's brother they let out a great whoop and holler and they aimed the car straight at him. They was having fun, they just wanted to scare him, the way they do sometimes, you know. But they was drunk. And I guess the boy, being drunk, too, and scared, kind of lost his head. By the time he jumped it was too late. Your father says he heard his brother scream when the car rolled over him, and he heard the wood of that guitar when it give, and he heard them strings go flying, and he heard them white men shouting, and the car kept on a-going and it ain't stopped till this day. And, time your father got down the hill, his brother weren't nothing but blood and pulp."

Tears were gleaming on my mother's face. There wasn't anything I could say.

100   "He never mentioned it," she said, "because I never let him mention it before you children. Your Daddy was like a crazy man that night and for many a night thereafter. He says he never in his life seen anything as dark as that road after the lights of that car had gone away. Weren't nothing, weren't nobody on that road, just your Daddy and his brother and that busted guitar. Oh, yes. Your Daddy never did really get right again. Till the day he died he weren't sure but that every white man he saw was the man that killed his brother."

She stopped and took out her handkerchief and dried her eyes and looked at me.

"I ain't telling you all this," she said, "to make you scared or bitter or to make you hate nobody. I'm telling you this because you got a brother. And the world ain't changed."

I guess I didn't want to believe this. I guess she saw this in my face. She turned away from me, toward the window again, searching those streets.

"But I praise my Redeemer," she said at last, "that He called your Daddy home before me. I ain't saying it to throw no flowers at myself, but, I declare, it keeps me from feeling too cast down to know I helped your father get safely through this world. Your father always acted like he was the roughest, strongest man on earth. And everybody took him to be like that. But if he hadn't had me there—to see his tears!"

105   She was crying again. Still, I couldn't move. I said, "Lord, Lord, Mama, I didn't know it was like that."

"Oh, honey," she said, "there's a lot that you don't know. But you are going to find out." She stood up from the window and came over to me. "You got to hold on to your brother," she said, "and don't let him fall, no matter what it looks like is happening to him and no matter how evil you gets with him. You going to be evil with him many a time. But don't you forget what I told you, you hear?"

"I won't forget," I said. "Don't you worry, I won't forget. I won't let nothing happen to Sonny."

My mother smiled as though she was amused at something she saw in my face. Then, "You may not be able to stop nothing from happening. But you got to let him know you's *there*."

Two days later I was married, and then I was gone. And I had a lot of things on my mind and I pretty well forgot my promise to Mama until I got shipped home on a special furlough for her funeral.

And, after the funeral, with just Sonny and me alone in the empty kitchen, I   110
tried to find out something about him.

"What do you want to do?" I asked him.

"I'm going to be a musician," he said.

For he had graduated, in the time I had been away, from dancing to the juke box to finding out who was playing what, and what they were doing with it, and he had bought himself a set of drums.

"You mean, you want to be a drummer?" I somehow had the feeling that being a drummer might be all right for other people but not for my brother Sonny.

"I don't think," he said, looking at me very gravely, "that I'll ever be a good   115
drummer. But I think I can play a piano."

I frowned. I'd never played the role of the oldest brother quite so seriously before, had scarcely ever, in fact, *asked* Sonny a damn thing. I sensed myself in the presence of something I didn't really know how to handle, didn't under-stand. So I made my frown a little deeper as I asked: "What kind of musician do you want to be?"

He grinned. "How many kinds do you think there are?"

"Be *serious*," I said.

He laughed, throwing his head back, and then looked at me. "I *am* serious."

"Well, then, for Christ's sake, stop kidding around and answer a serious   120
question. I mean, do you want to be a concert pianist, you want to play classical music and all that, or—or what?" Long before I finished he was laughing again. "For Christ's *sake*, Sonny!"

He sobered, but with difficulty. "I'm sorry. But you sound so—*scared*!" and he was off again.

"Well, you may think it's funny now, baby, but it's not going to be so funny when you have to make your living at it, let me tell you *that*." I was furious because I knew he was laughing at me and I didn't know why.

"No," he said, very sober now, and afraid, perhaps, that he'd hurt me, "I don't want to be a classical pianist. That isn't what interests me. I mean"—he paused, looking hard at me, as though his eyes would help me to understand, and then gestured helplessly, as though perhaps his hand would help—"I mean, I'll have a lot of studying to do, and I'll have to study *everything*, but, I mean, I want to play *with*—jazz musicians." He stopped. "I want to play jazz," he said.

Well, the word had never before sounded as heavy, as real, as it sounded that afternoon in Sonny's mouth. I just looked at him and I was probably frowning a real frown by this time. I simply couldn't see why on earth he'd want to spend his time hanging around nightclubs, clowning around on bandstands, while people pushed each other around a dance floor. It seemed—beneath him, somehow. I had never thought about it before, had never been forced to, but I suppose I had always put jazz musicians in a class with what Daddy called "good-time people."

125   "Are you *serious*?"

"Hell, *yes*, I'm serious."

He looked more helpless than ever, and annoyed, and deeply hurt.

I suggested, helpfully: "You mean—like Louis Armstrong?"[3]

His face closed as though I'd struck him. "No. I'm not talking about none of that old-time, down-home crap."

130   "Well, look, Sonny, I'm sorry, don't get mad. I just don't altogether get it, that's all. Name somebody—you know, a jazz musician you admire."

"Bird."

"Who?"

"Bird! Charlie Parker![4] Don't they teach you nothing in the goddamn army?"

I lit a cigarette. I was surprised and then a little amused to discover that I was trembling. "I've been out of touch," I said. "You'll have to be patient with me. Now. Who's this Parker character?"

135   "He's just one of the greatest jazz musicians alive," said Sonny, sullenly, his hands in his pockets, his back to me. "Maybe *the* greatest," he added, bitterly, "that's probably why *you* never heard of him."

"All right," I said, "I'm ignorant. I'm sorry. I'll go out and buy all the cat's records right away, all right?"

"It don't," said Sonny, with dignity, "make any difference to me. I don't care what you listen to. Don't do me no favors."

I was beginning to realize that I'd never seen him so upset before. With another part of my mind I was thinking that this would probably turn out to be one of those things kids go through and that I shouldn't make it seem important by pushing it too hard. Still, I didn't think it would do any harm to ask: "Doesn't all this take a lot of time? Can you make a living at it?"

He turned back to me and half leaned, half sat, on the kitchen table. "Everything takes time," he said, "and—well, yes, sure, I can make a living at it. But what I don't seem to be able to make you understand is that it's the only thing I want to do."

140   "Well, Sonny," I said gently, "you know people can't always do exactly what they *want* to do—"

"*No*, I don't know that," said Sonny, surprising me. "I think people *ought* to do what they want to do, what else are they alive for?"

"You getting to be a big boy," I said desperately, "it's time you started thinking about your future."

"I'm thinking about my future," said Sonny, grimly. "I think about it all the time."

I gave up. I decided, if he didn't change his mind, that we could always talk about it later. "In the meantime," I said, "you got to finish school." We had

---

3. New Orleans–born trumpeter and singer (1901–71); by the 1950s, his music would have seemed old-fashioned to a jazz aficionado.
4. Charlie ("Bird") Parker (1920–55), brilliant saxophonist, jazz innovator, and narcotics addict; working in New York in the mid-1940s, he developed, with Dizzy Gillespie and others, the style of jazz called "bebop."

already decided that he'd have to move in with Isabel and her folks. I knew this wasn't the ideal arrangement because Isabel's folks are inclined to be dicty[5] and they hadn't especially wanted Isabel to marry me. But I didn't know what else to do. "And we have to get you fixed up at Isabel's."

There was a long silence. He moved from the kitchen table to the window. 145 "That's a terrible idea. You know it yourself."

"Do you have a *better* idea?"

He just walked up and down the kitchen for a minute. He was as tall as I was. He had started to shave. I suddenly had the feeling that I didn't know him at all.

He stopped at the kitchen table and picked up my cigarettes. Looking at me with a kind of mocking, amused defiance, he put one between his lips. "You mind?"

"You smoking already?"

He lit the cigarette and nodded, watching me through the smoke. "I just 150 wanted to see if I'd have the courage to smoke in front of you." He grinned and blew a great cloud of smoke to the ceiling. "It was easy." He looked at my face. "Come on, now. I bet you was smoking at my age, tell the truth."

I didn't say anything but the truth was on my face, and he laughed. But now there was something very strained in his laugh. "Sure. And I bet that ain't all you was doing."

He was frightening me a little. "Cut the crap," I said. "We already decided that you was going to go and live at Isabel's. Now what's got into you all of a sudden?"

"*You* decided it," he pointed out. "*I* didn't decide nothing." He stopped in front of me, leaning against the stove, arms loosely folded. "Look, brother. I don't want to stay in Harlem no more, I really don't." He was very earnest. He looked at me, then over toward the kitchen window. There was something in his eyes I'd never seen before, some thoughtfulness, some worry all his own. He rubbed the muscle of one arm. "It's time I was getting out of here."

"Where do you want to *go*, Sonny?"

"I want to join the army. Or the navy, I don't care. If I say I'm old enough, 155 they'll believe me."

Then I got mad. It was because I was so scared. "You must be crazy. You god-damn fool, what the hell do you want to go and join the *army* for?"

"I just told you. To get out of Harlem."

"Sonny, you haven't even finished *school*. And if you really want to be a musi-cian, how do you expect to study if you're in the *army*?"

He looked at me, trapped, and in anguish. "There's ways. I might be able to work out some kind of deal. Anyway, I'll have the G.I. Bill when I come out."

"*If* you come out." We stared at each other. "Sonny, please. Be reasonable. I 160 know the setup is far from perfect. But we got to do the best we can."

"I ain't learning nothing in school," he said. "Even when I go." He turned away from me and opened the window and threw his cigarette out into the nar-row alley. I watched his back. "At least, I ain't learning nothing you'd want me to learn." He slammed the window so hard I thought the glass would fly out, and turned back to me. "And I'm sick of the stink of these garbage cans!"

5. Snobbish, bossy.

"Sonny," I said, "I know how you feel. But if you don't finish school now, you're going to be sorry later that you didn't." I grabbed him by the shoulders. "And you only got another year. It ain't so bad. And I'll come back and I swear I'll help you do *whatever* you want to do. Just try to put up with it till I come back. Will you please do that? For me?"

He didn't answer and he wouldn't look at me.

"Sonny. You hear me?"

165 He pulled away. "I hear you. But you never hear anything *I* say."

I didn't know what to say to that. He looked out of the window and then back at me. "OK," he said, and sighed. "I'll try."

Then I said, trying to cheer him up a little, "They got a piano at Isabel's. You can practice on it."

And as a matter of fact, it did cheer him up for a minute. "That's right," he said to himself. "I forgot that." His face relaxed a little. But the worry, the thoughtfulness, played on it still, the way shadows play on a face which is staring into the fire.

But I thought I'd never hear the end of that piano. At first, Isabel would write me, saying how nice it was that Sonny was so serious about his music and how, as soon as he came in from school, or wherever he had been when he was supposed to be at school, he went straight to that piano and stayed there until suppertime. And, after supper, he went back to that piano and stayed there until everybody went to bed. He was at the piano all day Saturday and all day Sunday. Then he bought a record player and started playing records. He'd play one record over and over again, all day long sometimes, and he'd improvise along with it on the piano. Or he'd play one section of the record, one chord, one change, one progression, then he'd do it on the piano. Then back to the record. Then back to the piano.

170 Well, I really don't know how they stood it. Isabel finally confessed that it wasn't like living with a person at all, it was like living with sound. And the sound didn't make any sense to her, didn't make any sense to any of them—naturally. They began, in a way, to be afflicted by this presence that was living in their home. It was as though Sonny were some sort of god, or monster. He moved in an atmosphere which wasn't like theirs at all. They fed him and he ate, he washed himself, he walked in and out of their door; he certainly wasn't nasty or unpleasant or rude, Sonny isn't any of those things; but it was as though he were all wrapped up in some cloud, some fire, some vision all his own; and there wasn't any way to reach him.

At the same time, he wasn't really a man yet, he was still a child, and they had to watch out for him in all kinds of ways. They certainly couldn't throw him out. Neither did they dare to make a great scene about that piano because even they dimly sensed, as I sensed, from so many thousands of miles away, that Sonny was at that piano playing for his life.

But he hadn't been going to school. One day a letter came from the school board and Isabel's mother got it—there had, apparently, been other letters but Sonny had torn them up. This day, when Sonny came in, Isabel's mother showed him the letter and asked where he'd been spending his time. And she finally got it out of him that he'd been down in Greenwich Village, with musicians and other characters, in a white girl's apartment. And this scared her and she started to scream at him and what came up, once she began—though she denies it to this day—was what sacrifices they were making to give Sonny a decent home and how little he appreciated it.

Sonny didn't play the piano that day. By evening, Isabel's mother had calmed down but then there was the old man to deal with, and Isabel herself. Isabel says she did her best to be calm but she broke down and started crying. She says she just watched Sonny's face. She could tell, by watching him, what was happening with him. And what was happening was that they penetrated his cloud, they had reached him. Even if their fingers had been a thousand times more gentle than human fingers ever are, he could hardly help feeling that they had stripped him naked and were spitting on that nakedness. For he also had to see that his presence, that music, which was life or death to him, had been torture for them and that they had endured it, not at all for his sake, but only for mine. And Sonny couldn't take that. He can take it a little better today than he could then but he's still not very good at it and, frankly, I don't know anybody who is.

The silence of the next few days must have been louder than the sound of all the music ever played since time began. One morning, before she went to work, Isabel was in his room for something and she suddenly realized that all of his records were gone. And she knew for certain that he was gone. And he was. He went as far as the navy would carry him. He finally sent me a postcard from some place in Greece and that was the first I knew that Sonny was still alive. I didn't see him any more until we were both back in New York and the war had long been over.

He was a man by then, of course, but I wasn't willing to see it. He came by ₁₇₅ the house from time to time, but we fought almost every time we met. I didn't like the way he carried himself, loose and dreamlike all the time, and I didn't like his friends, and his music seemed to be merely an excuse for the life he led. It sounded just that weird and disordered.

Then we had a fight, a pretty awful fight, and I didn't see him for months. By and by I looked him up, where he was living, in a furnished room in the Village, and I tried to make it up. But there were lots of other people in the room and Sonny just lay on his bed, and he wouldn't come downstairs with me, and he treated these other people as though they were his family and I weren't. So I got mad and then he got mad, and then I told him that he might just as well be dead as live the way he was living. Then he stood up and he told me not to worry about him any more in life, that he *was* dead as far as I was concerned. Then he pushed me to the door and the other people looked on as though nothing were happening, and he slammed the door behind me. I stood in the hallway, staring at the door. I heard somebody laugh in the room and then the tears came to my eyes. I started down the steps, whistling to keep from crying, I kept whistling to myself, *You going to need me, baby, one of these cold, rainy days.*

I read about Sonny's trouble in the spring. Little Grace died in the fall. She was a beautiful little girl. But she only lived a little over two years. She died of polio and she suffered. She had a slight fever for a couple of days, but it didn't seem like anything and we just kept her in bed. And we would certainly have called the doctor, but the fever dropped, she seemed to be all right. So we thought it had just been a cold. Then, one day, she was up, playing, Isabel was in the kitchen fixing lunch for the two boys when they'd come in from school, and she heard Grace fall down in the living room. When you have a lot of children you don't always start running when one of them falls, unless they start screaming or something. And, this time, Gracie was quiet. Yet, Isabel says that when she heard that *thump* and then that silence, something happened to her to make her afraid. And she ran to the living room and there was little Grace on the floor, all twisted up, and the reason she hadn't screamed was that she couldn't get her breath. And when she did scream, it was the worst sound, Isabel says, that she'd ever heard in all her life, and she still hears it sometimes in her dreams. Isabel will sometimes wake me up with a low, moaning, strangling sound and I have to be quick to awaken her and hold her to me and where Isabel is weeping against me seems a mortal wound.

I think I may have written Sonny the very day that little Grace was buried. I was sitting in the living room in the dark, by myself, and I suddenly thought of Sonny. My trouble made his real.

One Saturday afternoon, when Sonny had been living with us, or anyway, been in our house, for nearly two weeks, I found myself wandering aimlessly about the living room, drinking from a can of beer, and trying to work up courage to search Sonny's room. He was out, he was usually out whenever I was home, and Isabel had taken the children to see their grandparents. Suddenly I was standing still in front of the living room window, watching Seventh Avenue. The idea of searching Sonny's room made me still. I scarcely dared to admit to myself what I'd be searching for. I didn't know what I'd do if I found it. Or if I didn't.

180   On the sidewalk across from me, near the entrance to a barbecue joint, some people were holding an old-fashioned revival meeting. The barbecue cook, wearing a dirty white apron, his conked[6] hair reddish and metallic in the pale sun, and a cigarette between his lips, stood in the doorway, watching them. Kids and older people paused in their errands and stood there, along with some older men and a couple of very tough-looking women who watched everything that happened on the avenue, as though they owned it, or were maybe owned by it. Well, they were watching this, too. The revival was being carried on by three sisters in black, and a brother. All they had were their voices and their Bibles and a tambourine. The brother was testifying[7] and while he testified two of the sisters stood together, seeming to say, amen, and the third sister walked around with the tambourine outstretched and a couple of people dropped coins into it. Then the brother's testimony ended and the sister who had been taking up the collection dumped the coins into her palm and transferred them to the pocket of her long black robe. Then she raised both hands, striking the tambourine against the air, and then against one hand, and she started to sing. And the two other sisters and the brother joined in.

It was strange, suddenly, to watch, though I had been seeing these meetings all my life. So, of course, had everybody else down there. Yet, they paused and watched and listened and I stood still at the window. *"'Tis the old ship of Zion,"* they sang, and the sister with the tambourine kept a steady, jangling beat, *"it has rescued many a thousand!"* Not a soul under the sound of their voices was hearing

6. Processed: straightened and greased.
7. Publicly professing belief.

this song for the first time, not one of them had been rescued. Nor had they seen much in the way of rescue work being done around them. Neither did they especially believe in the holiness of the three sisters and the brother, they knew too much about them, knew where they lived, and how. The woman with the tambourine, whose voice dominated the air, whose face was bright with joy, was divided by very little from the woman who stood watching her, a cigarette between her heavy, chapped lips, her hair a cuckoo's nest, her face scarred and swollen from many beatings, and her black eyes glittering like coal. Perhaps they both knew this, which was why, when, as rarely, they addressed each other, they addressed each other as Sister. As the singing filled the air the watching, listening faces underwent a change, the eyes focusing on something within; the music seemed to soothe a poison out of them; and time seemed, nearly, to fall away from the sullen, belligerent, battered faces, as though they were fleeing back to their first condition, while dreaming of their last. The barbecue cook half shook his head and smiled, and dropped his cigarette and disappeared into his joint. A man fumbled in his pockets for change and stood holding it in his hand impatiently, as though he had just remembered a pressing appointment further up the avenue. He looked furious. Then I saw Sonny, standing on the edge of the crowd. He was carrying a wide, flat notebook with a green cover, and it made him look, from where I was standing, almost like a schoolboy. The coppery sun brought out the copper in his skin, he was very faintly smiling, standing very still. Then the singing stopped, the tambourine turned into a collection plate again. The furious man dropped in his coins and vanished, so did a couple of the women, and Sonny dropped some change in the plate, looking directly at the woman with a little smile. He started across the avenue, toward the house. He has a slow, loping walk, something like the way Harlem hipsters walk, only he's imposed on this his own half-beat. I had never really noticed it before.

I stayed at the window, both relieved and apprehensive. As Sonny disappeared from my sight, they began singing again. And they were still singing when his key turned in the lock.

"Hey," he said.

"Hey, yourself. You want some beer?"

"No. Well, maybe." But he came up to the window and stood beside me, looking out. "What a warm voice," he said. 185

They were singing *If I could only hear my mother pray again!*

"Yes," I said, "and she can sure beat that tambourine."

"But what a terrible song," he said, and laughed. He dropped his notebook on the sofa and disappeared into the kitchen. "Where's Isabel and the kids?"

"I think they went to see their grandparents. You hungry?"

"No." He came back into the living room with his can of beer. "You want to come some place with me tonight?" 190

I sensed, I don't know how, that I couldn't possibly say no. "Sure. Where?"

He sat down on the sofa and picked up his notebook and started leafing through it. "I'm going to sit in with some fellows in a joint in the Village."

"You mean, you're going to play, tonight?"

"That's right." He took a swallow of his beer and moved back to the window. He gave me a sidelong look. "If you can stand it."

195   "I'll try," I said.

He smiled to himself and we both watched as the meeting across the way broke up. The three sisters and the brother, heads bowed, were singing *God be with you till we meet again.* The faces around them were very quiet. Then the song ended. The small crowd dispersed. We watched the three women and the lone man walk slowly up the avenue.

"When she was singing before," said Sonny, abruptly, "her voice reminded me for a minute of what heroin feels like sometimes—when it's in your veins. It makes you feel sort of warm and cool at the same time. And distant. And— and sure." He sipped his beer, very deliberately not looking at me. I watched his face. "It makes you feel—in control. Sometimes you've got to have that feeling."

"Do you?" I sat down slowly in the easy chair.

"Sometimes." He went to the sofa and picked up his notebook again. "Some people do."

200   "In order," I asked, "to play?" And my voice was very ugly, full of contempt and anger.

"Well"—he looked at me with great, troubled eyes, as though, in fact, he hoped his eyes would tell me things he could never otherwise say—"they *think* so. And *if* they think so—!"

"And what do *you* think?" I asked.

He sat on the sofa and put his can of beer on the floor. "I don't know," he said, and I couldn't be sure if he were answering my question or pursuing his thoughts. His face didn't tell me. "It's not so much to *play.* It's to *stand* it, to be able to make it at all. On any level." He frowned and smiled: "In order to keep from shaking to pieces."

"But these friends of yours," I said, "they seem to shake themselves to pieces pretty goddamn fast."

205   "Maybe." He played with the notebook. And something told me that I should curb my tongue, that Sonny was doing his best to talk, that I should listen. "But of course you only know the ones that've gone to pieces. Some don't—or at least they haven't *yet* and that's just about all *any* of us can say." He paused. "And then there are some who just live, really, in hell, and they know it and they see what's happening and they go right on. I don't know." He sighed, dropped the notebook, folded his arms. "Some guys, you can tell from the way they play, they on something *all* the time. And you can see that, well, it makes something real for them. But of course," he picked up his beer from the floor and sipped it and put the can down again, "they *want* to, too, you've got to see that. Even some of them that say they don't—*some*, not all."

"And what about you?" I asked—I couldn't help it. "What about you? Do *you* want to?"

He stood up and walked to the window and I remained silent for a long time. Then he sighed. "Me," he said. Then: "While I was downstairs before, on my way here, listening to that woman sing, it struck me all of a sudden how much suffering she must have had to go through—to sing like that. It's *repulsive* to think you have to suffer that much."

I said: "But there's no way not to suffer—is there, Sonny?"

"I believe not," he said and smiled, "but that's never stopped anyone from try-ing." He looked at me. "Has it?" I realized, with this mocking look, that there stood between us, forever, beyond the power of time or forgiveness, the fact that I had held silence—so long!—when he had needed human speech to help him. He turned back to the window. "No, there's no way not to suffer. But you try all kinds of ways to keep from drowning in it, to keep on top of it, and to make it seem—well, like *you*. Like you did something, all right, and now you're suffer-ing for it. You know?" I said nothing. "Well you know," he said, impatiently, "why *do* people suffer? Maybe it's better to do something to give it a reason, *any* reason."

"But we just agreed," I said, "that there's no way not to suffer. Isn't it better, then, 210 just to—take it?"

"But nobody just takes it," Sonny cried, "that's what I'm telling you! *Everybody* tries not to. You're just hung up on the *way* some people try—it's not *your* way!"

The hair on my face began to itch, my face felt wet. "That's not true," I said, "that's not true. I don't give a damn what other people do, I don't even care how they suffer. I just care how *you* suffer." And he looked at me. "Please believe me," I said, "I don't want to see you—die—trying not to suffer."

"I won't," he said flatly, "die trying not to suffer. At least, not any faster than anybody else."

"But there's no need," I said, trying to laugh, "is there? in killing yourself."

I wanted to say more, but I couldn't. I wanted to talk about will power and how 215 life could be—well, beautiful. I wanted to say that it was all within; but was it? or, rather, wasn't that exactly the trouble? And I wanted to promise that I would never fail him again. But it would all have sounded—empty words and lies.

So I made the promise to myself and prayed that I would keep it.

"It's terrible sometimes, inside," he said, "that's what's the trouble. You walk these streets, black and funky and cold, and there's not really a living ass to talk to, and there's nothing shaking, and there's no way of getting it out—that storm inside. You can't talk it and you can't make love with it, and when you finally try to get with it and play it, you realize *nobody's* listening. So *you've* got to listen. You got to find a way to listen."

And then he walked away from the window and sat on the sofa again, as though all the wind had suddenly been knocked out of him. "Sometimes you'll do *anything* to play, even cut your mother's throat." He laughed and looked at me. "Or your brother's." Then he sobered. "Or your own." Then: "Don't worry. I'm all right now and I think I'll *be* all right. But I can't forget—where I've been. I don't mean just the physical place I've been, I mean where I've *been*. And *what* I've been."

"What have you been, Sonny?" I asked.

He smiled—but sat sideways on the sofa, his elbow resting on the back, his 220 fingers playing with his mouth and chin, not looking at me. "I've been some-thing I didn't recognize, didn't know I could be. Didn't know anybody could be." He stopped, looking inward, looking helplessly young, looking old. "I'm not talking about it now because I feel *guilty* or anything like that—maybe it would be better if I did, I don't know. Anyway, I can't really talk about it. Not to you, not to anybody," and now he turned and faced me. "Sometimes, you know, and it was actually when I was most *out* of the world, I felt that I was in it, that I was *with* it, really, and I could play or I didn't really have to *play*, it just came out of me, it was there. And I don't know how I played, thinking about it now, but I know I did awful things, those times, sometimes, to people. Or it wasn't that I *did* anything to them—it was that they weren't real." He picked up the beer can; it was empty; he rolled it between his palms: "And other times—well, I needed a fix, I needed to find a place to lean, I needed to clear a space to *listen*—and I couldn't find it, and I—went crazy, I did terrible things to *me*, I was terrible *for* me." He began pressing the beer can between his hands, I watched the metal begin to give. It glittered, as he played with it like a knife, and I was afraid he would cut himself, but I said nothing. "Oh well. I can never tell you. I was all by myself at the bottom of something, stinking and sweating and crying and shaking, and I smelled it, you know? *my* stink, and I thought I'd die if I couldn't get away from it and yet, all the same, I knew that everything I was doing was just locking me in with it. And I didn't know," he paused, still flattening the beer can, "I didn't know, I still *don't* know, something kept telling me that maybe it was good to smell your own stink, but I didn't think that *that* was what I'd been trying to do—and—who can stand it?" and he abruptly dropped the ruined beer can, looking at me with a small, still smile, and then rose, walking to the window as though it were the lodestone rock. I watched his face, he watched the avenue. "I couldn't tell you when Mama died—but the reason I wanted to leave Harlem so bad was to get away from drugs. And then, when I ran away, that's what I was running from—really. When I came back, nothing had changed, *I* hadn't changed, I was just—older." And he stopped, drumming with his fingers on the windowpane. The sun had vanished, soon darkness would fall. I watched his face. "It can come again," he said, almost as though speaking to himself. Then he turned to me. "It can come again," he repeated. "I just want you to know that."

"All right," I said, at last. "So it can come again. All right."

He smiled, but the smile was sorrowful. "I had to try to tell you," he said.

"Yes," I said. "I understand that."

"You're my brother," he said, looking straight at me, and not smiling at all.

225   "Yes," I repeated, "yes. I understand that."

He turned back to the window, looking out. "All that hatred down there," he said, "all that hatred and misery and love. It's a wonder it doesn't blow the avenue apart."

We went to the only nightclub on a short, dark street, downtown. We squeezed through the narrow, chattering, jampacked bar to the entrance of the big room, where the bandstand was. And we stood there for a moment, for the lights were very dim in this room and we couldn't see. Then, "Hello, boy," said the voice and an enormous black man, much older than Sonny or myself, erupted out of all that atmospheric lighting and put an arm around Sonny's shoulder. "I been sitting right here," he said, "waiting for you."

He had a big voice, too, and heads in the darkness turned toward us.

Sonny grinned and pulled a little away, and said, "Creole, this is my brother. I told you about him."

Creole shook my hand. "I'm glad to meet you, son," he said, and it was clear 230
that he was glad to meet me *there*, for Sonny's sake. And he smiled, "You got a
real musician in *your* family," and he took his arm from Sonny's shoulder and
slapped him, lightly, affectionately, with the back of his hand.

"Well. Now I've heard it all," said a voice behind us. This was another musician, and a friend of Sonny's, a coal-black, cheerful-looking man, built close to
the ground. He immediately began confiding to me, at the top of his lungs, the
most terrible things about Sonny, his teeth gleaming like a lighthouse and his
laugh coming up out of him like the beginning of an earthquake. And it turned
out that everyone at the bar knew Sonny, or almost everyone; some were musicians, working there, or nearby, or not working, some were simply hangers-on,
and some were there to hear Sonny play. I was introduced to all of them and
they were all very polite to me. Yet, it was clear that, for them, I was only Sonny's brother. Here, I was in Sonny's world. Or, rather: his kingdom. Here, it was
not even a question that his veins bore royal blood.

They were going to play soon and Creole installed me, by myself, at a table in
a dark corner. Then I watched them, Creole, and the little black man, and
Sonny, and the others, while they horsed around, standing just below the bandstand. The light from the bandstand spilled just a little short of them and,
watching them laughing and gesturing and moving about, I had the feeling that
they, nevertheless, were being most careful not to step into that circle of light
too suddenly; that if they moved into the light too suddenly, without thinking,
they would perish in flame. Then, while I watched, one of them, the small black
man, moved into the light and crossed the bandstand and started fooling around
with his drums. Then—being funny and being, also, extremely ceremonious—
Creole took Sonny by the arm and led him to the piano. A woman's voice called
Sonny's name and a few hands started clapping. And Sonny, also being funny
and being ceremonious, and so touched, I think, that he could have cried, but
neither hiding it nor showing it, riding it like a man, grinned, and put both hands
to his heart and bowed from the waist.

Creole then went to the bass fiddle and a lean, very bright-skinned brown
man jumped up on the bandstand and picked up his horn. So there they were,
and the atmosphere on the bandstand and in the room began to change and
tighten. Someone stepped up to the microphone and announced them. Then
there were all kinds of murmurs. Some people at the bar shushed others. The
waitress ran around, frantically getting in the last orders, guys and chicks got
closer to each other, and the lights on the bandstand, on the quartet, turned
to a kind of indigo. Then they all looked different there. Creole looked about
him for the last time, as though he were making certain that all his chickens
were in the coop, and then he—jumped and struck the fiddle. And there they
were.

All I know about music is that not many people ever really hear it. And even
then, on the rare occasions when something opens within, and the music enters,
what we mainly hear, or hear corroborated, are personal, private, vanishing evoca-
tions. But the man who creates the music is hearing something else, is dealing
with the roar rising from the void and imposing order on it as it hits the air. What
is evoked in him, then, is of another order, more terrible because it has no words,

and triumphant, too, for that same reason. And his triumph, when he triumphs, is ours. I just watched Sonny's face. His face was troubled, he was working hard, but he wasn't with it. And I had the feeling that, in a way, everyone on the bandstand was waiting for him, both waiting for him and pushing him along. But as I began to watch Creole, I realized that it was Creole who held them all back. He had them on a short rein. Up there, keeping the beat with his whole body, wailing on the fiddle, with his eyes half closed, he was listening to everything, but he was listening to Sonny. He was having a dialogue with Sonny. He wanted Sonny to leave the shoreline and strike out for the deep water. He was Sonny's witness that deep water and drowning were not the same thing—he had been there, and he knew. And he wanted Sonny to know. He was waiting for Sonny to do the things on the keys which would let Creole know that Sonny was in the water.

235   And, while Creole listened, Sonny moved, deep within, exactly like someone in torment. I had never before thought of how awful the relationship must be between the musician and his instrument. He has to fill it, this instrument, with the breath of life, his own. He has to make it do what he wants it to do. And a piano is just a piano. It's made out of so much wood and wires and little hammers and big ones, and ivory. While there's only so much you can do with it, the only way to find this out is to try; to try and make it do everything.

And Sonny hadn't been near a piano for over a year. And he wasn't on much better terms with his life, not the life that stretched before him now. He and the piano stammered, started one way, got scared, stopped; started another way, panicked, marked time, started again; then seemed to have found a direction, panicked again, got stuck. And the face I saw on Sonny I'd never seen before. Everything had been burned out of it, and, at the same time, things usually hidden were being burned in, by the fire and fury of the battle which was occurring in him up there.

Yet, watching Creole's face as they neared the end of the first set, I had the feeling that something had happened, something I hadn't heard. Then they finished, there was scattered applause, and then, without an instant's warning, Creole started into something else, it was almost sardonic, it was Am I Blue.[8] And, as though he commanded, Sonny began to play. Something began to happen. And Creole let out the reins. The dry, low, black man said something awful on the drums, Creole answered, and the drums talked back. Then the horn insisted, sweet and high, slightly detached perhaps, and Creole listened, commenting now and then, dry, and driving, beautiful and calm and old. Then they all came together again, and Sonny was part of the family again. I could tell this from his face. He seemed to have found, right there beneath his fingers, a damn brand-new piano. It seemed that he couldn't get over it. Then, for a while, just being happy with Sonny, they seemed to be agreeing with him that brand-new pianos certainly were a gas.

Then Creole stepped forward to remind them that what they were playing was the blues. He hit something in all of them, he hit something in me, myself, and the music tightened and deepened, apprehension began to beat the air.

8. Jazz standard brilliantly recorded by Billie Holiday (1915–59).

Creole began to tell us what the blues were all about. They were not about any-thing very new. He and his boys up there were keeping it new, at the risk of ruin, destruction, madness, and death, in order to find new ways to make us listen. For, while the tale of how we suffer, and how we are delighted, and how we may triumph is never new, it always must be heard. There isn't any other tale to tell, it's the only light we've got in all this darkness.

And this tale, according to that face, that body, those strong hands on those strings, has another aspect in every country, and a new depth in every genera-tion. Listen, Creole seemed to be saying, listen. Now these are Sonny's blues. He made the little black man on the drums know it, and the bright, brown man on the horn. Creole wasn't trying any longer to get Sonny in the water. He was wishing him Godspeed. Then he stepped back, very slowly, filling the air with the immense suggestion that Sonny speak for himself.

Then they all gathered around Sonny and Sonny played. Every now and 240 again one of them seemed to say, amen. Sonny's fingers filled the air with life, his life. But that life contained so many others. And Sonny went all the way back, he really began with the spare, flat statement of the opening phrase of the song. Then he began to make it his. It was very beautiful because it wasn't hur-ried and it was no longer a lament. I seemed to hear with what burning he had made it his, and what burning we had yet to make it ours, how we could cease lamenting. Freedom lurked around us and I understood, at last, that he could help us to be free if we would listen, that he would never be free until we did. Yet, there was no battle in his face now, I heard what he had gone through, and would continue to go through until he came to rest in earth. He had made it his: that long line, of which we knew only Mama and Daddy. And he was giving it back, as everything must be given back, so that, passing through death, it can live forever. I saw my mother's face again, and felt, for the first time, how the stones of the road she had walked on must have bruised her feet. I saw the moonlit road where my father's brother died. And it brought something else back to me, and carried me past it, I saw my little girl again and felt Isabel's tears again, and I felt my own tears begin to rise. And I was yet aware that this was only a moment, that the world waited outside, as hungry as a tiger, and that trouble stretched above us, longer than the sky.

Then it was over. Creole and Sonny let out their breath, both soaking wet, and grinning. There was a lot of applause and some of it was real. In the dark, the girl came by and I asked her to take drinks to the bandstand. There was a long pause, while they talked up there in the indigo light and after awhile I saw the girl put a Scotch and milk on top of the piano for Sonny. He didn't seem to notice it, but just before they started playing again, he sipped from it and looked toward me, and nodded. Then he put it back on top of the piano. For me, then, as they began to play again, it glowed and shook above my brother's head like the very cup of trembling.[9]

1957

9. See Isaiah 51.17, 22–23: "Awake, awake, stand up, O Jerusalem, which hast drunk at the hand of the Lord the cup of his fury; thou hast drunken the dregs of the cup of trembling, and wrung them out. [. . .] Behold, I have taken out of thine hand the cup of trembling, even the dregs of the cup of my fury; thou shalt no more drink it again: But I will put it into the hand of them that afflict thee [. . .]."

TONI CADE BAMBARA
(1939–95)
The Lesson

Born in New York City, Toni Cade Bambara grew up in Harlem and Bedford-Stuyvesant, two of New York's poorest neighborhoods. She began writing as a child and took her last name from a signature on a sketchbook she found in a trunk belonging to her great-grandmother. (The Bambara are a people of northwest Africa.) After graduating from Queens College, she wrote fiction in "the predawn in-betweens" while studying for her MA at the City College of New York and working at a variety of jobs: dancer, social worker, recreation director, psychiatric counselor, college English teacher, literary critic, and film producer. Bambara began to publish her stories in 1962. Her fiction includes two collections of stories, *Gorilla, My Love* (1972) and *The Sea Birds Are Still Alive* (1977), as well as two novels, *The Salt Eaters* (1980) and *If Blessing Comes* (1987). Bambara also edited two anthologies, *The Black Woman* (1970) and *Stories for Black Folks* (1971).

Back in the days when everyone was old and stupid or young and foolish and me and Sugar were the only ones just right, this lady moved on our block with nappy[1] hair and proper speech and no makeup. And quite naturally we laughed at her, laughed the way we did at the junk man who went about his business like he was some big-time president and his sorry-ass horse his secretary. And we kinda hated her too, hated the way we did the winos who cluttered up our parks and pissed on our handball walls and stank up our hallways and stairs so you couldn't halfway play hide-and-seek without a goddamn gas mask. Miss Moore was her name. The only woman on the block with no first name. And she was black as hell, cept for her feet, which were fish-white and spooky. And she was always planning these boring-ass things for us to do, us being my cousin, mostly, who lived on the block cause we all moved North the same time and to the same apartment then spread out gradual to breathe. And our parents would yank our heads into some kinda shape and crisp up our clothes so we'd be presentable for travel with Miss Moore, who always looked like she was going to church, though she never did. Which is just one of the things the grown-ups talked about when they talked behind her back like a dog. But when she came calling with some sachet she'd sewed up or some gingerbread she'd made or some book, why then they'd all be too embarrassed to turn her down and we'd get handed over all spruced up. She'd been to college and said it was only right that she should take responsibility for the young ones' education, and she not even related by marriage or blood. So they'd go for it. Specially Aunt Gretchen. She was the main gofer in the family. You got some ole dumb shit foolishness you want somebody to go for, you send for Aunt Gretchen. She been screwed into the go-along for so long, it's a blood-deep natural thing with her. Which is how she got saddled with me and

---

1. Untreated and unstraightened, naturally curly or coiled.

Sugar and Junior in the first place while our mothers were in a la-de-da apartment up the block having a good ole time.

So this one day Miss Moore rounds us all up at the mailbox and it's pure-dee hot and she's knockin herself out about arithmetic. And school suppose to let up in summer I heard, but she don't never let up. And the starch in my pinafore scratching the shit outta me and I'm really hating this nappy-head bitch and her goddamn college degree. I'd much rather go to the pool or to the show where it's cool. So me and Sugar leaning on the mailbox being surly, which is a Miss Moore word. And Flyboy checking out what everybody brought for lunch. And Fat Butt already wasting his peanut-butter-and-jelly sandwich like the pig he is. And Junebug punchin on Q.T.'s arm for potato chips. And Rosie Giraffe shifting from one hip to the other waiting for somebody to step on her foot or ask her if she from Georgia so she can kick ass, preferably Mercedes'. And Miss Moore asking us do we know what money is, like we a bunch of retards. I mean real money, she say, like it's only poker chips or monopoly papers we lay on the grocer. So right away I'm tired of this and say so. And would much rather snatch Sugar and go to the Sunset and terrorize the West Indian kids and take their hair ribbons and their money too. And Miss Moore files that remark away for next week's lesson on brotherhood, I can tell. And finally I say we oughta get to the subway cause it's cooler and besides we might meet some cute boys. Sugar done swiped her mama's lipstick, so we ready.

So we heading down the street and she's boring us silly about what things cost and what our parents make and how much goes for rent and how money ain't divided up right in this country. And then she gets to the part about we all poor and live in the slums, which I don't feature. And I'm ready to speak on that, but she steps out in the street and hails two cabs just like that. Then she hustles half the crew in with her and hands me a five-dollar bill and tells me to calculate 10 percent tip for the driver. And we're off. Me and Sugar and Junebug and Flyboy hangin out the window and hollering to everybody, putting lipstick on each other cause Flyboy a faggot anyway, and making farts with our sweaty armpits. But I'm mostly trying to figure how to spend this money. But they all fascinated with the meter ticking and Junebug starts laying bets as to how much it'll read when Flyboy can't hold his breath no more. Then Sugar lays bets as to how much it'll be when we get there. So I'm stuck. Don't nobody want to go for my plan, which is to jump out at the next light and run off to the first bar-b-que we can find. Then the driver tells us to get the hell out cause we there already. And the meter reads eighty-five cents. And I'm stalling to figure out the tip and Sugar say give him a dime. And I decide he don't need it bad as I do, so later for him. But then he tries to take off with Junebug foot still in the door so we talk about his mama something ferocious. Then we check out that we on Fifth Avenue[2] and everybody dressed up in stockings. One lady in a fur coat, hot as it is. White folks crazy.

"This is the place," Miss Moore say, presenting it to us in the voice she uses at the museum. "Let's look in the windows before we go in."

---

2. Major Manhattan street famous for its expensive, exclusive shops.

5   "Can we steal?" Sugar asks very serious like she's getting the ground rules squared away before she plays. "I beg your pardon," say Miss Moore, and we fall out. So she leads us around the windows of the toy store and me and Sugar screamin, "This is mine, that's mine, I gotta have that, that was made for me, I was born for that," till Big Butt drowns us out.

"Hey, I'm goin to buy that there."

"That there? You don't even know what it is, stupid."

"I do so," he say punchin on Rosie Giraffe. "It's a microscope."

"Whatcha gonna do with a microscope, fool?"

10   "Look at things."

"Like what, Ronald?" ask Miss Moore. And Big Butt ain't got the first notion. So here go Miss Moore gabbing about the thousands of bacteria in a drop of water and the somethinorother in a speck of blood and the million and one living things in the air around us is invisible to the naked eye. And what she say that for? Junebug go to town on that "naked" and we rolling. Then Miss Moore ask what it cost. So we all jam into the window smudgin it up and the price tag say $300. So then she ask how long'd take for Big Butt and Junebug to save up their allowances. "Too long," I say. "Yeh," adds Sugar, "outgrown it by that time." And Miss Moore say no, you never outgrow learning instruments. "Why, even medical students and interns and," blah, blah, blah. And we ready to choke Big Butt for bringing it up in the first damn place.

"This here costs four hundred eighty dollars," say Rosie Giraffe. So we pile up all over her to see what she pointin out. My eyes tell me it's a chunk of glass cracked with something heavy, and different-color inks dripped into the splits, then the whole thing put into a oven or something. But for $480 it don't make sense.

"That's a paperweight made of semi-precious stones fused together under tremendous pressure," she explains slowly, with her hands doing the mining and all the factory work.

"So what's a paperweight?" asks Rosie Giraffe.

15   "To weigh paper with, dumbbell," say Flyboy, the wise man from the East.[3]

"Not exactly," say Miss Moore, which is what she say when you warm or way off too. "It's to weigh paper down so it won't scatter and make your desk untidy." So right away me and Sugar curtsy to each other and then to Mercedes who is more the tidy type.

"We don't keep paper on top of the desk in my class," say Junebug, figuring Miss Moore crazy or lyin one.

"At home, then," she say. "Don't you have a calendar and a pencil case and a blotter[4] and a letter-opener on your desk at home where you do your homework?" And she know damn well what our homes look like cause she nosys around in them every chance she gets.

"I don't even have a desk," say Junebug. "Do we?"

20   "No. And I don't get no homework neither," say Big Butt.

"And I don't even have a home," say Flyboy like he do at school to keep the white folks off his back and sorry for him. Send this poor kid to camp posters, is his specialty.

---

3. In the Bible three wise men travel from the East to visit the newborn Christ.
4. Framed sheet or pad of paper designed to protect a desktop from excess ink.

"I do," says Mercedes. "I have a box of stationery on my desk and a picture of my cat. My godmother bought the stationery and the desk. There's a big rose on each sheet and the envelopes smell like roses."

"Who wants to know about your smelly-ass stationery," say Rosie Giraffe fore I can get my two cents in.

"It's important to have a work area all your own so that . . ."

"Will you look at this sailboat, please," say Flyboy, cuttin her off and pointin to the thing like it was his. So once again we tumble all over each other to gaze at this magnificent thing in the toy store which is just big enough to maybe sail two kittens across the pond if you strap them to the posts tight. We all start reciting the price tag like we in assembly. "Handcrafted sailboat of fiberglass at one thousand one hundred ninety-five dollars."

"Unbelievable," I hear myself say and am really stunned. I read it again for myself just in case the group recitation put me in a trance. Same thing. For some reason this pisses me off. We look at Miss Moore and she lookin at us, waiting for I dunno what.

Who'd pay all that when you can buy a sailboat set for a quarter at Pop's, a tube of glue for a dime, and a ball of string for eight cents? "It must have a motor and a whole lot else besides," I say. "My sailboat cost me about fifty cents."

"But will it take water?" say Mercedes with her smart ass.

"Took mine to Alley Pond Park once," say Flyboy. "String broke, Lost it. Pity."

"Sailed mine in Central Park and it keeled over and sank. Had to ask my father for another dollar."

"And you got the strap," laugh Big Butt. "The jerk didn't even have a string on it. My old man wailed on his behind."

Little Q.T. was staring hard at the sailboat and you could see he wanted it bad. But he too little and somebody'd just take it from him. So what the hell. "This boat for kids, Miss Moore?"

"Parents silly to buy something like that just to get all broke up," say Rosie Giraffe.

"That much money it should last forever," I figure.

"My father'd buy it for me if I wanted it."

"Your father, my ass," say Rosie Giraffe getting a chance to finally push Mercedes.

"Must be rich people shop here," say Q.T.

"You are a very bright boy," say Flyboy. "What was your first clue?" And he rap him on the head with the back of his knuckles, since Q.T. the only one he could get away with. Though Q.T. liable to come up behind you years later and get his licks in when you half expect it.

"What I want to know is," I says to Miss Moore though I never talk to her, I wouldn't give the bitch that satisfaction, "is how much a real boat costs? I figure a thousand'd get you a yacht any day."

"Why don't you check that out," she says, "and report back to the group?" Which really pains my ass. If you gonna mess up a perfectly good swim day least you could do is have some answers. "Let's go in," she say like she got something up her sleeve. Only she don't lead the way. So me and Sugar turn the corner to where the entrance is, but when we get there I kinda hang back. Not that I'm scared, what's there to be afraid of, just a toy store. But I feel funny, shame. But what I got to be shamed about? Got as much right to go in as anybody. But somehow I can't seem to get hold of the door, so I step away for Sugar to lead. But she hangs back too. And I look at her and she looks at me and this is ridiculous. I mean, damn, I have never ever been shy about doing nothing or going nowhere. But then Mercedes steps up and then Rosie Giraffe and Big Butt crowd in behind and shove, and next thing we all stuffed into the doorway with only Mercedes squeezing past us, smoothing out her jumper and walking right down the aisle. Then the rest of us tumble in like a glued-together jigsaw done all wrong. And people lookin at us. And it's like the time me and Sugar crashed into the Catholic church on a dare. But once we got in there and everything so hushed and holy and the candles and the bowin and the handkerchiefs on all the drooping heads, I just couldn't go through with the plan. Which was for me to run up to the altar and do a tap dance while Sugar played the nose flute and messed around in the holy water. And Sugar kept givin me the elbow. Then later teased me so bad I tied her up in the shower and turned it on and locked her in. And she'd be there till this day if Aunt Gretchen hadn't finally figured I was lyin about the boarder[5] takin a shower.

Same thing in the store. We all walkin on tiptoe and hardly touchin the games and puzzles and things. And I watched Miss Moore who is steady watchin us like she waitin for a sign. Like Mama Drewery watches the sky and sniffs the air and takes note of just how much slant is in the bird formation. Then me and Sugar bump smack into each other, so busy gazing at the toys, 'specially the sailboat. But we don't laugh and go into our fat-lady bump-stomach routine. We just stare at that price tag. Then Sugar run a finger over the whole boat. And I'm jealous and want to hit her. Maybe not her, but I sure want to punch somebody in the mouth.

"Watcha bring us here for, Miss Moore?"

"You sound angry, Sylvia. Are you mad about something?" Givin me one of them grins like she tellin a grown-up joke that never turns out to be funny. And she's lookin very closely at me like maybe she plannin to do my portrait from memory. I'm mad, but I won't give her that satisfaction. So I slouch around the store bein very bored and say, "Let's go."

Me and Sugar at the back of the train watchin the tracks whizzin by large then small then gettin gobbled up in the dark. I'm thinkin about this tricky toy I saw in the store. A clown that somersaults on a bar then does chin-ups just cause you yank lightly at his leg. Cost $35. I could see me askin my mother for a $35 birthday clown. "You wanna who that costs what?" she'd say, cocking her head to the side to get a better view of the hole in my head. Thirty-five dollars could buy new bunk beds for Junior and Gretchen's boy. Thirty-five dollars and the whole household could go visit Granddaddy Nelson in the country. Thirty-five dollars would pay for the rent and the piano bill too. Who are these people that spend that much for performing clowns and $1,000 for toy sailboats? What kinda work they do and how they live and how come we ain't in on it? Where we are is who we are, Miss Moore always pointin out. But it don't nec-

5. Tenant in another person's house.

essarily have to be that way, she always adds then waits for somebody to say that poor people have to wake up and demand their share of the pie and don't none of us know what kind of pie she talkin about in the first damn place. But she ain't so smart cause I still got her four dollars from the taxi and she sure ain't gettin it. Messin up my day with this shit. Sugar nudges me in my pocket and winks.

Miss Moore lines us up in front of the mailbox where we started from, seem 45 like years ago, and I got a headache for thinkin so hard. And we lean all over each other so we can hold up under the draggy-ass lecture she always finishes us off with at the end before we thank her for borin us to tears. But she just looks at us like she readin tea leaves. Finally she say, "Well, what did you think of F.A.O. Schwarz?"[6]

Rosie Giraffe mumbles, "White folks crazy."

"I'd like to go there again when I get my birthday money," says Mercedes, and we shove her out the pack so she has to lean on the mailbox by herself.

"I'd like a shower. Tiring day," say Flyboy.

Then Sugar surprises me by sayin, "You know, Miss Moore, I don't think all of us here put together eat in a year what that sailboat costs." And Miss Moore lights up like somebody goosed her. "And?" she say, urging Sugar on. Only I'm standin on her foot so she don't continue.

"Imagine for a minute what kind of society it is in which some people can 50 spend on a toy what it would cost to feed a family of six or seven. What do you think?"

"I think," say Sugar pushing me off her feet like she never done before, cause I whip her ass in a minute, "that this is not much of a democracy if you ask me. Equal chance to pursue happiness means an equal crack at the dough, don't it?" Miss Moore is besides herself and I am disgusted with Sugar's treachery. So I stand on her foot one more time to see if she'll shove me. She shuts up, and Miss Moore looks at me, sorrowfully I'm thinkin. And somethin weird is goin on, I can feel it in my chest.

"Anybody else learn anything today?" lookin dead at me.

I walk away and Sugar has to run to catch up and don't even seem to notice when I shrug her arm off my shoulder.

"Well, we got four dollars anyway," she says.

"Uh hunh." 55

"We could go to Hascombs and get half a chocolate layer and then go to the Sunset and still have plenty money for potato chips and ice-cream sodas."

"Uh hunh."

"Race you to Hascombs," she say.

We start down the block and she gets ahead which is O.K. by me cause I'm goin to the West End and then over to the Drive to think this day through. She can run if she want to and even run faster. But ain't nobody gonna beat me at nuthin.

1972

6. Manhattan toy store (founded 1862), one of the world's largest and oldest, known for its expensive, one-of-a-kind offerings.

AUTHORS ON THEIR WORK

TONI CADE BAMBARA (1939–95)

From "How She Came by Her Name" (1996)*

I went to the library and read a bunch of [short-story] collections and noticed that the voice was consistent, but it was a boring and monotonous voice. Oh, your voice is supposed to be consistent in a collection, I figured. Then I pulled out a lot of stories that had a young protagonist-narrator because that voice is kind of consistent—a young, tough, compassionate girl.

The book [*Gorilla, My Love*] came out, and I never dreamed that such a big fuss would be made. "Oh, *Gorilla, My Love,* what a radical use of dialect! What a bold, political angle on linguistics!" At first I felt like a fraud. It didn't have anything to do with a political stance. I just thought people lived and moved around in this particular language system. It is also the language system I tend to remember childhood in. This is the language many of us speak. It just seemed polite to handle the characters in this mode.

*"How She Came by Her Name: An Interview with Louis Massiah." *Deep Sightings and Rescue Missions: Fiction, Essays, and Conversations,* edited by Toni Morrison, Pantheon Books, 1996, pp. 201–45.

RAY BRADBURY
(1920–2012)

The Veldt[1]

The only writer ever both to receive a National Medal of Arts (2004) and to have a lunar crater (1971) and a Mars rover landing site (2012) named in his honor, Ray Bradbury was born and raised mostly in Waukegan, Illinois, until 1934, when the Great Depression took his family to Los Angeles. Here he began publishing short stories in the "pulp" magazines that had first introduced him (at age eight) to science fiction. After winning his first O. Henry Award for "The Lake" (1942), Bradbury left off selling newspapers to become a full-time writer. He never looked back. Arguably the twentieth century's most widely read science-fiction/fantasy writer and the first to attract a mainstream audience, Bradbury is perhaps most famous for two books. More a collection of interlinked stories than a novel, *The Martian Chronicles* (1950) imagines the colonization of Mars circa 1999–2026, focusing on how the human colonists both interact with the planet's gentle, shape-shifting, telepathic inhabitants and project their own desires and cultural values onto their new home. The novel *Fahrenheit 451* (1953) features what novelist Kingsley Amis hailed as "the most skillfully drawn of all

1. Area of grassy land with scattered trees and shrubs, especially in southern (sub-Saharan) Africa.

science fiction's conformist hells"—a future in which reading is outlawed and firemen are tasked with burning books. In addition to other novels, including *Something Wicked This Way Comes* (1962) and *Farewell Summer* (2006), Bradbury wrote for both stage and screen, even featuring in his own television series, *The Ray Bradbury Theater*, from 1985 to 1992. First and foremost, however, Bradbury was a short-story writer; *The Stories of Ray Bradbury* (1980) and *Ray Bradbury Stories, Volume 2* (2009) gather some of his best.

"George, I wish you'd look at the nursery."
    "What's wrong with it?"
"I don't know."
"Well, then."
"I just want you to look at it, is all, or call a psychologist in to look at it."   5
"What would a psychologist want with a nursery?"
"You know very well what he'd want." His wife paused in the middle of the kitchen and watched the stove busy humming to itself, making supper for four.
"It's just that the nursery is different now than it was."
"All right, let's have a look."
They walked down the hall of their soundproofed, Happylife Home, which 10 had cost them thirty thousand dollars installed, this house which clothed and fed and rocked them to sleep and played and sang and was good to them. Their approach sensitized a switch somewhere and the nursery light flicked on when they came within ten feet of it. Similarly, behind them, in the halls, lights went on and off as they left them behind, with a soft automaticity.
"Well," said George Hadley.
They stood on the thatched floor of the nursery. It was forty feet across by forty feet long and thirty feet high; it had cost half again as much as the rest of the house. "But nothing's too good for our children," George had said.
The nursery was silent. It was empty as a jungle glade at hot high noon. The walls were blank and two dimensional. Now, as George and Lydia Hadley stood in the center of the room, the walls began to purr and recede into crystalline distance, it seemed, and presently an African veldt appeared, in three dimensions; on all sides, in colors reproduced to the final pebble and bit of straw. The ceiling above them became a deep sky with a hot yellow sun.
George Hadley felt the perspiration start on his brow.
"Let's get out of the sun," he said. "This is a little too real. But I don't see anything 15 wrong."
"Wait a moment, you'll see," said his wife.
Now the hidden odorophonics were beginning to blow a wind of odor at the two people in the middle of the baked veldtland. The hot straw smell of lion grass, the cool green smell of the hidden water hole, the great rusty smell of animals, the smell of dust like a red paprika in the hot air. And now the sounds: the thump of distant antelope feet on grassy sod, the papery rustling of vultures. A shadow passed through the sky. The shadow flickered on George Hadley's upturned, sweating face.

"Filthy creatures," he heard his wife say.

"The vultures."

20   "You see, there are the lions, far over, that way. Now they're on their way to the water hole. They've just been eating," said Lydia. "I don't know what."

"Some animal." George Hadley put his hand up to shield off the burning light from his squinted eyes. "A zebra or a baby giraffe, maybe."

"Are you sure?" His wife sounded peculiarly tense.

"No, it's a little late to be sure," he said, amused. "Nothing over there I can see but cleaned bone, and the vultures dropping for what's left."

"Did you hear that scream?" she asked.

25   "No."

"About a minute ago?"

"Sorry, no."

The lions were coming. And again George Hadley was filled with admiration for the mechanical genius who had conceived this room. A miracle of efficiency selling for an absurdly low price. Every home should have one. Oh, occasionally they frightened you with their clinical accuracy, they startled you, gave you a twinge, but most of the time what fun for everyone, not only your own son and daughter, but for yourself when you felt like a quick jaunt to a foreign land, a quick change of scenery. Well, here it was!

And here were the lions now, fifteen feet away, so real, so feverishly and startlingly real that you could feel the prickling fur on your hand, and your mouth was stuffed with the dusty upholstery smell of their heated pelts, and the yellow of them was in your eyes like the yellow of an exquisite French tapestry, the yellows of lions and summer grass, and the sound of the matted lion lungs exhaling on the silent noontide, and the smell of meat from the panting, dripping mouths.

30   The lions stood looking at George and Lydia Hadley with terrible green-yellow eyes.

"Watch out!" screamed Lydia.

The lions came running at them.

Lydia bolted and ran. Instinctively, George sprang after her. Outside, in the hall, with the door slammed, he was laughing and she was crying, and they both stood appalled at the other's reaction.

"George!"

35   "Lydia! Oh, my dear poor sweet Lydia!"

"They almost got us!"

"Walls, Lydia, remember; crystal walls, that's all they are. Oh, they look real, I must admit—Africa in your parlor—but it's all dimensional superreactionary, supersensitive color film and mental tape film behind glass screens. It's all odorophonics and sonics, Lydia. Here's my handkerchief."

"I'm afraid." She came to him and put her body against him and cried steadily. "Did you see? Did you *feel*? It's too real."

"Now, Lydia . . ."

40   "You've got to tell Wendy and Peter[2] not to read any more on Africa."

"Of course—of course." He patted her.

2. The Hadley children bear the same names as characters featured in the work of English author J. M. Barrie (1860–1937), including his play *Peter Pan, or the Boy Who Wouldn't Grow Up* (1904).

"Promise?"

"Sure."

"And lock the nursery for a few days until I get my nerves settled."

"You know how difficult Peter is about that. When I punished him a month 45
ago by locking the nursery for even a few hours—the tantrum he threw! And
Wendy too. They *live* for the nursery."

"It's got to be locked, that's all there is to it."

"All right." Reluctantly he locked the huge door. "You've been working too
hard. You need a rest."

"I don't know—I don't know," she said, blowing her nose, sitting down in a
chair that immediately began to rock and comfort her. "Maybe I don't have
enough to do. Maybe I have time to think too much. Why don't we shut the
whole house off for a few days and take a vacation?"

"You mean you want to fry my eggs for me?"

"Yes." She nodded.   50

"And darn my socks?"

"Yes." A frantic, watery-eyed nodding.

"And sweep the house?"

"Yes, yes—oh, yes!"

"But I thought that's why we bought this house, so we wouldn't have to do 55
anything?"

"That's just it. I feel like I don't belong here. The house is wife and mother
now and nursemaid. Can I compete with an African veldt? Can I give a bath
and scrub the children as efficiently or quickly as the automatic scrub bath can?
I can not. And it isn't just me. It's you. You've been awfully nervous lately."

"I suppose I have been smoking too much."

"You look as if you didn't know what to do with yourself in this house, either.
You smoke a little more every morning and drink a little more every afternoon
and need a little more sedative every night. You're beginning to feel unnecessary
too."

"Am I?" He paused and tried to feel into himself to see what was really there.

"Oh, George!" She looked beyond him, at the nursery door. "Those lions can't 60
get out of there, can they?"

He looked at the door and saw it tremble as if something had jumped against
it from the other side.

"Of course not," he said.

At dinner they ate alone, for Wendy and Peter were at a special plastic carnival
across town and had televised home to say they'd be late, to go ahead eating.
So George Hadley, bemused, sat watching the dining-room table produce warm
dishes of food from its mechanical interior.

"We forgot the ketchup," he said.

"Sorry," said a small voice within the table, and ketchup appeared.   65

As for the nursery, thought George Hadley, it won't hurt for the children to
be locked out of it awhile. Too much of anything isn't good for anyone. And it
was clearly indicated that the children had been spending a little too much time
on Africa. That sun. He could feel it on his neck, still, like a hot paw. And the
lions. And the smell of blood. Remarkable how the nursery caught the telepathic
emanations of the children's minds and created life to fill their every desire. The

children thought lions, and there were lions. The children thought zebras, and there were zebras. Sun—sun. Giraffes—giraffes. Death and death.

That last. He chewed tastelessly on the meat that the table had cut for him. Death thoughts. They were awfully young, Wendy and Peter, for death thoughts. Or, no, you were never too young, really. Long before you knew what death was you were wishing it on someone else. When you were two years old you were shooting people with cap pistols.

But this—the long, hot African veldt—the awful death in the jaws of a lion. And repeated again and again.

"Where are you going?"

70   He didn't answer Lydia. Preoccupied, he let the lights glow softly on ahead of him, extinguished behind him as he padded to the nursery door. He listened against it. Far away, a lion roared.

He unlocked the door and opened it. Just before he stepped inside, he heard a faraway scream. And then another roar from the lions, which subsided quickly.

He stepped into Africa. How many times in the last year had he opened this door and found Wonderland, Alice, the Mock Turtle, or Aladdin and his Magical Lamp, or Jack Pumpkinhead of Oz, or Dr. Doolittle, or the cow jumping over a very real-appearing moon[3]—all the delightful contraptions of a make-believe world. How often had he seen Pegasus[4] flying in the sky ceiling, or seen fountains of red fireworks, or heard angel voices singing. But now, this yellow hot Africa, this bake oven with murder in the heat. Perhaps Lydia was right. Perhaps they needed a little vacation from the fantasy which was growing a bit too real for ten-year-old children. It was all right to exercise one's mind with gymnastic[5] fantasies, but when the lively child mind settled on *one* pattern . . . ? It seemed that, at a distance, for the past month, he had heard lions roaring, and smelled their strong odor seeping as far away as his study door. But, being busy, he had paid it no attention.

George Hadley stood on the African grassland alone. The lions looked up from their feeding, watching him. The only flaw to the illusion was the open door through which he could see his wife, far down the dark hall, like a framed picture, eating her dinner abstractedly.

"Go away," he said to the lions.

75   They did not go.

He knew the principle of the room exactly. You sent out your thoughts. Whatever you thought would appear.

"Let's have Aladdin and his lamp," he snapped.

The veldtland remained; the lions remained.

"Come on, room! I demand Aladdin!" he said.

80   Nothing happened. The lions mumbled in their baked pelts.

"Aladdin!"

He went back to dinner. "The fool room's out of order," he said. "It won't respond."

3. Places and characters from famous works of children's literature, including Lewis Carroll's *Alice's Adventures in Wonderland* (1865); the Middle Eastern folktale "Aladdin and the Magic [or Wonderful] Lamp," about a young orphan and the genie of the lamp who grants his wishes; L. Frank Baum's novels, beginning with *The Wonderful Wizard of Oz* (1900); Hugh Lofting's Doctor Dolittle series (1920–52); and the nursery rhyme "Hey Diddle Diddle."
4. Flying horse of Greek myth.
5. Athletic.

"Or—"

"Or what?"

"Or it *can't* respond," said Lydia, "because the children have thought about 85
Africa and lions and killing so many days that the room's in a rut."

"Could be."

"Or Peter's set it to remain that way."

"*Set* it?"

"He may have got into the machinery and fixed something."

"Peter doesn't know machinery."   90

"He's a wise one for ten. That I.Q. of his—"

"Nevertheless—"

"Hello, Mom. Hello, Dad."

The Hadleys turned. Wendy and Peter were coming in the front door, cheeks
like peppermint candy, eyes like bright blue agate marbles, a smell of ozone on
their jumpers from their trip in the helicopter.

"You're just in time for supper," said both parents.   95

"We're full of strawberry ice cream and hot dogs," said the children, holding
hands. "But we'll sit and watch."

"Yes, come tell us about the nursery," said George Hadley.

The brother and sister blinked at him and then at each other. "Nursery?"

"All about Africa and everything," said the father with false joviality.

"I don't understand," said Peter.   100

"Your mother and I were just traveling through Africa with rod and reel; Tom
Swift[6] and his Electric Lion," said George Hadley.

"There's no Africa in the nursery," said Peter simply.

"Oh, come now, Peter. We know better."

"I don't remember any Africa," said Peter to Wendy. "Do you?"

"No."   105

"Run see and come tell."

She obeyed.

"Wendy, come back here!" said George Hadley, but she was gone. The house
lights followed her like a flock of fireflies. Too late, he realized he had forgotten
to lock the nursery door after his last inspection.

"Wendy'll look and come tell us," said Peter.

"She doesn't have to tell *me*. I've seen it."   110

"I'm sure you're mistaken, Father."

"I'm not, Peter. Come along now."

But Wendy was back. "It's not Africa," she said breathlessly.

"We'll see about this," said George Hadley, and they all walked down the hall
together and opened the nursery door.

There was a green, lovely forest, a lovely river, a purple mountain, high voices 115
singing, and Rima,[7] lovely and mysterious, lurking in the trees with colorful flights
of butterflies, like animated bouquets, lingering on her long hair. The African

6. Hero of a series of books launched in 1910 and relating adventures made possible by his ingenious
inventions.
7. South American forest-dwelling heroine of W. H. Hudson's *Green Mansions: A Romance of the
Tropical Forest* (1904).

veldtland was gone. The lions were gone. Only Rima was here now, singing a song so beautiful that it brought tears to your eyes.

George Hadley looked in at the changed scene. "Go to bed," he said to the children.

They opened their mouths.

"You heard me," he said.

They went off to the air closet, where a wind sucked them like brown leaves up the flue to their slumber rooms.

120   George Hadley walked through the singing glade and picked up something that lay in the corner near where the lions had been. He walked slowly back to his wife.

"What is that?" she asked.

"An old wallet of mine," he said.

He showed it to her. The smell of hot grass was on it and the smell of a lion. There were drops of saliva on it, it had been chewed, and there were blood smears on both sides.

He closed the nursery door and locked it, tight.

125   In the middle of the night he was still awake and he knew his wife was awake. "Do you think Wendy changed it?" she said at last, in the dark room.

"Of course."

"Made it from a veldt into a forest and put Rima there instead of lions?"

"Yes."

"Why?"

130   "I don't know. But it's staying locked until I find out."

"How did your wallet get there?"

"I don't know anything," he said, "except that I'm beginning to be sorry we bought that room for the children. If children are neurotic at all, a room like that—"

"It's supposed to help them work off their neuroses in a healthful way."

"I'm starting to wonder." He stared at the ceiling.

135   "We've given the children everything they ever wanted. Is this our reward—secrecy, disobedience?"

"Who was it said, 'Children are carpets, they should be stepped on occasionally'? We've never lifted a hand. They're insufferable—let's admit it. They come and go when they like; they treat us as if we were offspring. They're spoiled and we're spoiled."

"They've been acting funny ever since you forbade them to take the rocket to New York a few months ago."

"They're not old enough to do that alone, I explained."

"Nevertheless, I've noticed they've been decidedly cool toward us since."

140   "I think I'll have David McClean come tomorrow morning to have a look at Africa."

"But it's not Africa now, it's Green Mansions country and Rima."

"I have a feeling it'll be Africa again before then."

A moment later they heard the screams.

Two screams. Two people screaming from downstairs. And then a roar of lions.

145   "Wendy and Peter aren't in their rooms," said his wife.

He lay in his bed with his beating heart. "No," he said. "They've broken into the nursery."

"Those screams—they sound familiar."

"Do they?"

"Yes, awfully."

And although their beds tried very hard, the two adults couldn't be rocked to   150
sleep for another hour. A smell of cats was in the night air.

"Father?" said Peter.

"Yes."

Peter looked at his shoes. He never looked at his father any more, nor at his
mother. "You aren't going to lock up the nursery for good, are you?"

"That all depends."

"On what?" snapped Peter.   155

"On you and your sister. If you intersperse this Africa with a little variety—
oh, Sweden perhaps, or Denmark or China—"

"I thought we were free to play as we wished."

"You are, within reasonable bounds."

"What's wrong with Africa, Father?"

"Oh, so now you admit you have been conjuring up Africa, do you?"   160

"I wouldn't want the nursery locked up," said Peter coldly. "Ever."

"Matter of fact, we're thinking of turning the whole house off for about a
month. Live sort of a carefree one-for-all existence."

"That sounds dreadful! Would I have to tie my own shoes instead of letting the
shoe tier do it? And brush my own teeth and comb my hair and give myself a bath?"

"It would be fun for a change, don't you think?"

"No, it would be horrid. I didn't like it when you took out the picture painter   165
last month."

"That's because I wanted you to learn to paint all by yourself, son."

"I don't want to do anything but look and listen and smell; what else *is* there
to do?"

"All right, go play in Africa."

"Will you shut off the house sometime soon?"

"We're considering it."   170

"I don't think you'd better consider it any more, Father."

"I won't have any threats from my son!"

"Very well." And Peter strolled off to the nursery.

"Am I on time?" said David McClean.

"Breakfast?" asked George Hadley.   175

"Thanks, had some. What's the trouble?"

"David, you're a psychologist."

"I should hope so."

"Well, then, have a look at our nursery. You saw it a year ago when you dropped
by; did you notice anything peculiar about it then?"

"Can't say I did; the usual violences, a tendency toward a slight paranoia here   180
or there, usual in children because they feel persecuted by parents constantly,
but, oh, really nothing."

They walked down the hall. "I locked the nursery up," explained the father,
"and the children broke back into it during the night. I let them stay so they
could form the patterns for you to see."

There was a terrible screaming from the nursery.

"There it is," said George Hadley. "See what you make of it."

They walked in on the children without rapping.

185 The screams had faded. The lions were feeding.

"Run outside a moment, children," said George Hadley. "No, don't change the mental combination. Leave the walls as they are. Get!"

With the children gone, the two men stood studying the lions clustered at a distance, eating with great relish whatever it was they had caught.

"I wish I knew what it was," said George Hadley. "Sometimes I can almost see. Do you think if I brought high-powered binoculars here and—"

David McClean laughed dryly. "Hardly." He turned to study all four walls. "How long has this been going on?"

190 "A little over a month."

"It certainly doesn't *feel* good."

"I want facts, not feelings."

"My dear George, a psychologist never saw a fact in his life. He only hears about feelings; vague things. This doesn't feel good, I tell you. Trust my hunches and my instincts. I have a nose for something bad. This is very bad. My advice to you is to have the whole damn room torn down and your children brought to me every day during the next year for treatment."

"Is it that bad?"

195 "I'm afraid so. One of the original uses of these nurseries was so that we could study the patterns left on the walls by the child's mind, study at our leisure, and help the child. In this case, however, the room has become a channel toward—destructive thoughts, instead of a release away from them."

"Didn't you sense this before?"

"I sensed only that you had spoiled your children more than most. And now you're letting them down in some way. What way?"

"I wouldn't let them go to New York."

"What else?"

200 "I've taken a few machines from the house and threatened them, a month ago, with closing up the nursery unless they did their homework. I did close it for a few days to show I meant business."

"Ah, ha!"

"Does that mean anything?"

"Everything. Where before they had a Santa Claus now they have a Scrooge.[8] Children prefer Santas. You've let this room and this house replace you and your wife in your children's affections. This room is their mother and father, far more important in their lives than their real parents. And now you come along and want to shut it off. No wonder there's hatred here. You can feel it coming out of the sky. Feel that sun. George, you'll have to change your life. Like too many others, you've built it around creature comforts. Why, you'd starve tomorrow if something went wrong in your kitchen. You wouldn't know how to tap an egg. Nevertheless, turn everything off. Start new. It'll take time. But we'll make good children out of bad in a year, wait and see."

---

8. Miserly, hard-hearted protagonist of Charles Dickens's *A Christmas Carol* (1843).

"But won't the shock be too much for the children, shutting the room up abruptly, for good?"

"I don't want them going any deeper into this, that's all."   205

The lions were finished with their red feast.

The lions were standing on the edge of the clearing watching the two men.

"Now *I'm* feeling persecuted," said McClean. "Let's get out of here. I never have cared for these damned rooms. Make me nervous."

"The lions look real, don't they?" said George Hadley. "I don't suppose there's any way—"

"What?"   210

"—that they could *become* real?"

"Not that I know."

"Some flaw in the machinery, a tampering or something?"

"No."

They went to the door.   215

"I don't imagine the room will like being turned off," said the father.

"Nothing ever likes to die—even a room."

"I wonder if it hates me for wanting to switch it off?"

"Paranoia is thick around here today," said David McClean. "You can follow it like a spoor. Hello." He bent and picked up a bloody scarf. "This yours?"

"No." George Hadley's face was rigid. "It belongs to Lydia."   220

They went to the fuse box together and threw the switch that killed the nursery.

The two children were in hysterics. They screamed and pranced and threw things. They yelled and sobbed and swore and jumped at the furniture.

"You can't do that to the nursery, you can't!"

"Now, children."

The children flung themselves onto a couch, weeping.   225

"George," said Lydia Hadley, "turn on the nursery, just for a few moments. You can't be so abrupt."

"No."

"You can't be so cruel."

"Lydia, it's off, and it stays off. And the whole damn house dies as of here and now. The more I see of the mess we've put ourselves in, the more it sickens me. We've been contemplating our mechanical, electronic navels for too long. My God, how we need a breath of honest air!"

And he marched about the house turning off the voice clocks, the stoves, the   230 heaters, the shoe shiners, the shoe lacers, the body scrubbers and swabbers and massagers, and every other machine he could put his hand to.

The house was full of dead bodies, it seemed. It felt like a mechanical cemetery. So silent. None of the humming hidden energy of machines waiting to function at the tap of a button.

"Don't let them do it!" wailed Peter at the ceiling, as if he was talking to the house, the nursery. "Don't let Father kill everything." He turned to his father. "Oh, I hate you!"

"Insults won't get you anywhere."

"I wish you were dead!"

"We were, for a long while. Now we're going to really start living. Instead of   235 being handled and massaged, we're going to *live*."

Wendy was still crying and Peter joined her again. "Just a moment, just one moment, just another moment of nursery," they wailed.

"Oh, George," said the wife, "it can't hurt."

"All right—all right, if they'll only just shut up. One minute, mind you, and then off forever."

"Daddy, Daddy, Daddy!" sang the children, smiling with wet faces.

240   "And then we're going on a vacation. David McClean is coming back in half an hour to help us move out and get to the airport. I'm going to dress. You turn the nursery on for a minute, Lydia, just a minute, mind you."

And the three of them went babbling off while he let himself be vacuumed upstairs through the air flue and set about dressing himself. A minute later Lydia appeared.

"I'll be glad when we get away," she sighed.

"Did you leave them in the nursery?"

"I wanted to dress too. Oh, that horrid Africa. What can they see in it?"

245   "Well, in five minutes we'll be on our way to Iowa. Lord, how did we ever get in this house? What prompted us to buy a nightmare?"

"Pride, money, foolishness."

"I think we'd better get downstairs before those kids get engrossed with those damned beasts again."

Just then they heard the children calling, "Daddy, Mommy, come quick—quick!"

They went downstairs in the air flue and ran down the hall. The children were nowhere in sight. "Wendy? Peter!"

250   They ran into the nursery. The veldtland was empty save for the lions waiting, looking at them. "Peter, Wendy?"

The door slammed.

"Wendy, Peter!"

George Hadley and his wife whirled and ran back to the door.

"Open the door!" cried George Hadley, trying the knob. "Why, they've locked it from the outside! Peter!" He beat at the door. "Open up!"

255   He heard Peter's voice outside, against the door.

"Don't let them switch off the nursery and the house," he was saying.

Mr. and Mrs. George Hadley beat at the door. "Now, don't be ridiculous, children. It's time to go. Mr. McClean'll be here in a minute and . . ."

And then they heard the sounds.

The lions on three sides of them, in the yellow veldt grass, padding through the dry straw, rumbling and roaring in their throats.

260   The lions.

Mr. Hadley looked at his wife and they turned and looked back at the beasts edging slowly forward, crouching, tails stiff.

Mr. and Mrs. Hadley screamed.

And suddenly they realized why those other screams had sounded familiar.

"Well, here I am," said David McClean in the nursery doorway. "Oh, hello." He stared at the two children seated in the center of the open glade eating a little picnic lunch. Beyond them was the water hole and the yellow veldtland; above was the hot sun. He began to perspire. "Where are your father and mother?"

The children looked up and smiled. "Oh, they'll be here directly."

"Good, we must get going." At a distance Mr. McClean saw the lions fighting and clawing and then quieting down to feed in silence under the shady trees.

He squinted at the lions with his hand up to his eyes.

Now the lions were done feeding. They moved to the water hole to drink.

A shadow flickered over Mr. McClean's hot face. Many shadows flickered. The vultures were dropping down the blazing sky.

"A cup of tea?" asked Wendy in the silence. 270

1951

KATE CHOPIN

(1850–1904)

The Story of an Hour

Katherine O'Flaherty was born in St. Louis, Missouri, to a high-ranking Creole-Irish family. Her father died when she was four, and Kate was raised by her mother, grandmother, and great-grandmother. Well-read at a young age, she received her formal education at the St. Louis Academy of the Sacred Heart. In 1870, she married Oscar Chopin, a Louisiana businessman, and lived with him in Natchitoches Parish and New Orleans, where she became a close observer of Creole and Cajun life. Following her husband's sudden death in 1884, she returned to St. Louis, where she raised her six children and began her literary career. In slightly more than a decade she produced a substantial body of work, including the story collections *Bayou Folk* (1894) and *A Night in Acadie* (1897). Her classic novella *The Awakening* (1899) was greeted with a storm of criticism for its frank treatment of female sexuality.

K nowing that Mrs. Mallard was afflicted with a heart trouble, great care was taken to break to her as gently as possible the news of her husband's death.

It was her sister Josephine who told her, in broken sentences; veiled hints that revealed in half concealing. Her husband's friend Richards was there, too, near her. It was he who had been in the newspaper office when intelligence of the railroad disaster was received, with Brently Mallard's name leading the list of "killed." He had only taken the time to assure himself of its truth by a second telegram, and had hastened to forestall any less careful, less tender friend in bearing the sad message.

She did not hear the story as many women have heard the same, with a paralyzed inability to accept its significance. She wept at once, with sudden, wild abandonment, in her sister's arms. When the storm of grief had spent itself she went away to her room alone. She would have no one follow her.

There stood, facing the open window, a comfortable, roomy armchair. Into this she sank, pressed down by a physical exhaustion that haunted her body and seemed to reach into her soul.

5   She could see in the open square before her house the tops of trees that were all aquiver with the new spring life. The delicious breath of rain was in the air. In the street below a peddler was crying his wares. The notes of a distant song which some one was singing reached her faintly, and countless sparrows were twittering in the eaves.

There were patches of blue sky showing here and there through the clouds that had met and piled one above the other in the west facing her window.

She sat with her head thrown back upon the cushion of the chair, quite motionless, except when a sob came up into her throat and shook her, as a child who has cried itself to sleep continues to sob in its dreams.

She was young, with a fair, calm face, whose lines bespoke repression and even a certain strength. But now there was a dull stare in her eyes, whose gaze was fixed away off yonder on one of those patches of blue sky. It was not a glance of reflection, but rather indicated a suspension of intelligent thought.

There was something coming to her and she was waiting for it, fearfully. What was it? She did not know; it was too subtle and elusive to name. But she felt it, creeping out of the sky, reaching toward her through the sounds, the scents, the color that filled the air.

10   Now her bosom rose and fell tumultuously. She was beginning to recognize this thing that was approaching to possess her, and she was striving to beat it back with her will—as powerless as her two white slender hands would have been.

When she abandoned herself a little whispered word escaped her slightly parted lips. She said it over and over under her breath: "free, free, free!" The vacant stare and the look of terror that had followed it went from her eyes. They stayed keen and bright. Her pulses beat fast, and the coursing blood warmed and relaxed every inch of her body.

She did not stop to ask if it were or were not a monstrous joy that held her. A clear and exalted perception enabled her to dismiss the suggestion as trivial.

She knew that she would weep again when she saw the kind, tender hands folded in death; the face that had never looked save with love upon her, fixed and gray and dead. But she saw beyond that bitter moment a long procession of years to come that would belong to her absolutely. And she opened and spread her arms out to them in welcome.

There would be no one to live for her during those coming years; she would live for herself. There would be no powerful will bending hers in that blind persistence with which men and women believe they have a right to impose a private will upon a fellow-creature. A kind intention or a cruel intention made the act seem no less a crime as she looked upon it in that brief moment of illumination.

15   And yet she had loved him—sometimes. Often she had not. What did it matter! What could love, the unsolved mystery, count for in face of this possession

of self-assertion which she suddenly recognized as the strongest impulse of her being!

"Free! Body and soul free!" she kept whispering.

Josephine was kneeling before the closed door with her lips to the keyhole, imploring for admission. "Louise, open the door! I beg; open the door—you will make yourself ill. What are you doing, Louise? For heaven's sake open the door."

"Go away. I am not making myself ill." No; she was drinking in a very elixir of life through that open window.

Her fancy was running riot along those days ahead of her. Spring days, and summer days, and all sorts of days that would be her own. She breathed a quick prayer that life might be long. It was only yesterday she had thought with a shudder that life might be long.

She arose at length and opened the door to her sister's importunities. There was a feverish triumph in her eyes, and she carried herself unwittingly like a goddess of Victory. She clasped her sister's waist, and together they descended the stairs. Richards stood waiting for them at the bottom. 20

Some one was opening the front door with a latchkey. It was Brently Mallard who entered, a little travel-stained, composedly carrying his grip-sack and umbrella. He had been far from the scene of accident, and did not even know there had been one. He stood amazed at Josephine's piercing cry; at Richards' quick motion to screen him from the view of his wife.

But Richards was too late.

When the doctors came they said she had died of heart disease—of joy that kills.

1894

EDWIDGE DANTICAT
(b. 1969)
A Wall of Fire Rising

When she was twelve, Edwidge Danticat moved from Port-au-Prince, Haiti, to Brooklyn, New York, where her parents had relocated eight years before. Having grown up speaking only French and Creole, Danticat published her first writing in English at age fourteen, a newspaper article about her immigration to the United States that developed into her first novel, *Breath, Eyes, Memory* (1994). Danticat received a degree in French literature from Barnard College and an MFA from Brown University. *Krik? Krak!* (1991), a collection of short stories, was nominated for the National Book Award. Her second novel, *The Farming of Bones* (1998), is based on the 1937 massacre of Haitians at the border of the Dominican Republic. In 2002, Danticat published *After the Dance: A Walk through Carnival in Jacmel, Haiti*, an account of her travels. More recent publications include *The Dew Breaker* (2004), a collection of interlinked stories examining the life of a Haitian torturer; *Brother, I'm Dying* (2007), winner of the National Book Critics Circle Award for Autobiography; the essay collection *Create Dangerously: The Immigrant Artist at Work* (2010); and the novel *Claire of the Sea Light* (2013). Danticat's first young-adult novel, *Untwine*, debuted in 2015.

" Listen to what happened today," Guy said as he barged through the rattling door of his tiny shack.

His wife, Lili, was squatting in the middle of their one-room home, spreading cornmeal mush on banana leaves for their supper.

"Listen to what happened to *me* today!" Guy's seven-year-old son—Little Guy—dashed from a corner and grabbed his father's hand. The boy dropped his composition notebook as he leaped to his father, nearly stepping into the corn mush and herring that his mother had set out in a trio of half gourds on the clay floor.

"Our boy is in a play." Lili quickly robbed Little Guy of the honor of telling his father the news.

5   "A play?" Guy affectionately stroked the boy's hair.

The boy had such tiny corkscrew curls that no amount of brushing could ever make them all look like a single entity. The other boys at the Lycée Jean-Jacques[1] called him "pepper head" because each separate kinky strand was coiled into a tight tiny ball that looked like small peppercorns.

"When is this play?" Guy asked both the boy and his wife. "Are we going to have to buy new clothes for this?"

Lili got up from the floor and inclined her face towards her husband's in order to receive her nightly peck on the cheek.

"What role do you have in the play?" Guy asked, slowly rubbing the tip of his nails across the boy's scalp. His fingers made a soft grating noise with each invisible circle drawn around the perimeters of the boy's head. Guy's fingers finally landed inside the boy's ears, forcing the boy to giggle until he almost gave himself the hiccups.

10   "Tell me, what is your part in the play?" Guy asked again, pulling his fingers away from his son's ear.

"I am Boukman," the boy huffed out, as though there was some laughter caught in his throat.

"Show Papy your lines," Lili told the boy as she arranged the three open gourds on a piece of plywood raised like a table on two bricks, in the middle of the room. "My love, Boukman is the hero of the play."

The boy went back to the corner where he had been studying and pulled out a thick book carefully covered in brown paper.

"You're going to spend a lifetime learning those." Guy took the book from the boy's hand and flipped through the pages quickly. He had to strain his eyes to see the words by the light of an old kerosene lamp, which that night—like all others—flickered as though it was burning its very last wick.

---

1. Haiti is French speaking; Little Guy attends a *lycée* (school) named after Jean-Jacques Dessalines (1758–1806), founder of independent Haiti. A former slave, Dessalines was declared emperor Jacques I in 1804.

"All these words seem so long and heavy," Guy said. "You think you can do 15
this, son?"

"He has one very good speech," Lili said. "Page forty, remember, son?"

The boy took back the book from his father. His face was crimped in an
of-course-I-remember look as he searched for page forty.

"Bouk-man," Guy struggled with the letters of the slave revolutionary's
name as he looked over his son's shoulders. "I see some very hard words here,
son."

"He already knows his speech," Lili told her husband.

"Does he now?" asked Guy. 20

"We've been at it all afternoon," Lili said. "Why don't you go on and recite
that speech for your father?"

The boy tipped his head towards the rusting tin on the roof as he prepared to
recite his lines.

Lili wiped her hands on an old apron tied around her waist and stopped to
listen.

"Remember what you are," Lili said, "a great rebel leader. Remember, it is the
revolution."

"Do we want him to be all of that?" Guy asked. 25

"He is Boukman," Lili said. "What is the only thing on your mind now,
Boukman?"

"Supper," Guy whispered, enviously eyeing the food cooling off in the middle
of the room. He and the boy looked at each other and began to snicker.

"Tell us the other thing that is on your mind," Lili said, joining in their
laughter.

"Freedom!" shouted the boy, as he quickly slipped into his role.

"Louder!" urged Lili. 30

"Freedom is on my mind!" yelled the boy.

"Why don't you start, son?" said Guy. "If you don't, we'll never get to that
other thing that we have on our minds."

The boy closed his eyes and took a deep breath. At first, his lips parted but
nothing came out. Lili pushed her head forward as though she were holding
her breath. Then like the last burst of lightning out of clearing sky, the boy
began.

*A wall of fire is rising and in the ashes, I see the bones of my people. Not only
those people whose dark hollow faces I see daily in the fields, but all those souls
who have gone ahead to haunt my dreams. At night I relive once more the last
caresses from the hand of a loving father, a valiant love, a beloved friend.*[2]

It was obvious that this was a speech written by a European man, who gave 35
to the slave revolutionary Boukman the kind of European phrasing that might
have sent the real Boukman turning in his grave. However, the speech made
Lili and Guy stand on the tips of their toes from great pride. As their applause
thundered in the small space of their shack that night, they felt as though for a

2. On the night of August 22, 1791, slaves led by a slave foreman named Boukman (who was secretly
a voodoo high priest) built a "wall of fire" that destroyed many plantations in the French colony of
Saint-Domingue, marking the beginning of a mass slave revolt that would lead, fourteen years later,
to the establishment of independent Haiti.

moment they had been given the rare pleasure of hearing the voice of one of the forefathers of Haitian independence in the forced baritone of their only child. The experience left them both with a strange feeling that they could not explain. It left the hair on the back of their necks standing on end. It left them feeling much more love than they ever knew that they could add to their feeling for their son.

"Bravo," Lili cheered, pressing her son into the folds of her apron. "Long live Boukman and long live my boy."

"Long live our supper," Guy said, quickly batting his eyelashes to keep tears from rolling down his face.

The boy kept his eyes on his book as they ate their supper that night. Usually Guy and Lili would not have allowed that, but this was a special occasion. They watched proudly as the boy muttered his lines between swallows of cornmeal.

The boy was still mumbling the same words as the three of them used the last of the rainwater trapped in old gasoline containers and sugarcane pulp from the nearby sugarcane mill to scrub the gourds that they had eaten from.

40   When things were really bad for the family, they boiled clean sugarcane pulp to make what Lili called her special sweet water tea. It was supposed to suppress gas and kill the vermin in the stomach that made poor children hungry. That and a pinch of salt under the tongue could usually quench hunger until Guy found a day's work or Lili could manage to buy spices on credit and then peddle them for a profit at the marketplace.

That night, anyway, things were good. Everyone had eaten enough to put all their hunger vermin to sleep.

The boy was sitting in front of the shack on an old plastic bucket turned upside down, straining his eyes to find the words on the page. Sometimes when there was no kerosene for the lamp, the boy would have to go sit by the side of the road and study under the street lamps with the rest of the neighborhood children. Tonight, at least, they had a bit of their own light.

Guy bent down by a small clump of old mushrooms near the boy's feet, trying to get a better look at the plant. He emptied the last drops of rainwater from a gasoline container on the mushroom, wetting the bulging toes sticking out of his sons' sandals, which were already coming apart around his endlessly growing feet.

Guy tried to pluck some of the mushrooms, which were being pushed into the dust as though they wanted to grow beneath the ground as roots. He took one of the mushrooms in his hand, running his smallest finger over the round bulb. He clipped the stem and buried the top in a thick strand of his wife's hair.

45   The mushroom looked like a dried insect in Lili's hair.

"It sure makes you look special," Guy said, teasing her.

"Thank you so much," Lili said, tapping her husband's arm. "It's nice to know that I deserve these much more than roses."

Taking his wife's hand, Guy said, "Let's go to the sugar mill."

"Can I study my lines there?" the boy asked.

50   "You know them well enough already," Guy said.

"I need many repetitions," the boy said.

Their feet sounded as though they were playing a wet wind instrument as they slipped in and out of the puddles between the shacks in the shantytown. Near the sugar mill was a large television screen in an iron grill cage that the government had installed so that the shantytown dwellers could watch the state-sponsored news at eight o'clock every night. After the news, a gendarme[3] would come and turn off the television set, taking home the key. On most nights, the people stayed at the site long after this gendarme had gone and told stories to one another beneath the big blank screen. They made bonfires with dried sticks, corn husks, and paper, cursing the authorities under their breath.

There was a crowd already gathering for the nightly news event. The sugar mill workers sat in the front row in chairs or on old buckets.

Lili and Guy passed the group, clinging to their son so that in his childhood naïveté he wouldn't accidentally glance at the wrong person and be called an insolent child. They didn't like the ambiance of the nightly news watch. They spared themselves trouble by going instead to the sugar mill, where in the past year they had discovered their own wonder.

Everyone knew that the family who owned the sugar mill were eccentric 55 "Arabs," Haitians of Lebanese or Palestinian descent whose family had been in the country for generations. The Assad family had a son who, it seems, was into all manner of odd things, the most recent of which was a hot-air balloon, which he had brought to Haiti from America and occasionally flew over the shantytown skies.

As they approached the fence surrounding the field where the large wicker basket and deflated balloon rested on the ground, Guy let go of the hands of both his wife and the boy.

Lili walked on slowly with her son. For the last few weeks, she had been feeling as though Guy was lost to her each time he reached this point, twelve feet away from the balloon. As Guy pushed his hand through the barbed wire, she could tell from the look on his face that he was thinking of sitting inside the square basket while the smooth rainbow surface of the balloon itself floated above his head. During the day, when the field was open, Guy would walk up to the basket, staring at it with the same kind of longing that most men display when they admire very pretty girls.

Lili and the boy stood watching from a distance as Guy tried to push his hand deeper, beyond the chain link fence that separated him from the balloon. He reached into his pants pocket and pulled out a small pocketknife, sharpening the edges on the metal surface of the fence. When his wife and child moved closer, he put the knife back in his pocket, letting his fingers slide across his son's tightly coiled curls.

"I wager you I can make this thing fly," Guy said.

"Why do you think you can do that?" Lili asked. 60

"I know it," Guy replied.

He followed her as she circled the sugar mill, leading to their favorite spot under a watch light. Little Guy lagged faithfully behind them. From this distance, the hot-air balloon looked like an odd spaceship.

---

3. Policeman or guard (French).

Lili stretched her body out in the knee-high grass in the field. Guy reached over and tried to touch her between her legs.

"You're not one to worry, Lili," he said. "You're not afraid of the frogs, lizards, or snakes that could be hiding in this grass?"

65   "I am here with my husband," she said. "You are here to protect me if anything happens."

Guy reached into his shirt pocket and pulled out a lighter and a crumpled piece of paper. He lit the paper until it burned to an ashy film. The burning paper floated in the night breeze for a while, landing in fragments on the grass.

"Did you see that, Lili?" Guy asked with a flame in his eyes brighter than the lighter's. "Did you see how the paper floated when it was burned? This is how that balloon flies."

"What did you mean by saying that you could make it fly?" Lili asked.

"You already know all my secrets," Guy said as the boy came charging towards them.

70   "Papa, could you play *Lago* with me?" the boy asked.

Lili lay peacefully on the grass as her son and husband played hide-and-seek. Guy kept hiding and his son kept finding him as each time Guy made it easier for the boy.

"We rest now." Guy was becoming breathless.

The stars were circling the peaks of the mountains, dipping into the cane fields belonging to the sugar mill. As Guy caught his breath, the boy raced around the fence, running as fast as he could to purposely make himself dizzy.

"Listen to what happened today," Guy whispered softly in Lili's ear.

75   "I heard you say that when you walked in the house tonight," Lili said. "With the boy's play, I forgot to ask you."

The boy sneaked up behind them, his face lit up, though his brain was spinning. He wrapped his arms around both their necks.

"We will go back home soon," Lili said.

"Can I recite my lines?" asked the boy.

"We have heard them," Guy said. "Don't tire your lips."

80   The boy mumbled something under his breath. Guy grabbed his ear and twirled it until it was a tiny ball in his hand. The boy's face contorted with agony as Guy made him kneel in the deep grass in punishment.

Lili looked tortured as she watched the boy squirming in the grass, obviously terrified of the crickets, lizards, and small snakes that might be there.

"Perhaps we should take him home to bed," she said.

"He will never learn," Guy said, "if I say one thing and you say another."

Guy got up and angrily started walking home. Lili walked over, took her son's hand, and raised him from his knees.

85   "You know you must not mumble," she said.

"I was saying my lines," the boy said.

"Next time say them loud," Lili said, "so he knows what is coming out of your mouth."

That night Lili could hear her son muttering his lines as he tucked himself in his corner of the room and drifted off to sleep. The boy still had the book with his monologue in it clasped under his arm as he slept.

Guy stayed outside in front of the shack as Lili undressed for bed. She loosened the ribbon that held the old light blue cotton skirt around her waist and let it drop past her knees. She grabbed half a lemon that she kept in the corner by the folded mat that she and Guy unrolled to sleep on every night. Lili let her blouse drop to the floor as she smoothed the lemon over her ashen legs.

Guy came in just at that moment and saw her bare chest by the light of the 90 smaller castor oil lamp that they used for the later hours of the night. Her skin had coarsened a bit over the years, he thought. Her breasts now drooped from having nursed their son for two years after he was born. It was now easier for him to imagine their son's lips around those breasts than to imagine his anywhere near them.

He turned his face away as she fumbled for her nightgown. He helped her open the mat, tucking the blanket edges underneath.

Fully clothed, Guy dropped onto the mat next to her. He laid his head on her chest, rubbing the spiky edges of his hair against her nipples.

"What was it that happened today?" Lili asked, running her fingers along Guy's hairline, an angular hairline, almost like a triangle, in the middle of his forehead. She nearly didn't marry him because it was said that people with angular hairlines often have very troubled lives.

"I got a few hours' work for tomorrow at the sugar mill," Guy said. "That's what happened today."

"It was such a long time coming," Lili said. 95

It was almost six months since the last time Guy had gotten work there. The jobs at the sugar mill were few and far between. The people who had them never left, or when they did they would pass the job on to another family member who was already waiting on line.

Guy did not seem overjoyed about the one day's work.

"I wish I had paid more attention when you came in with the news," Lili said. "I was just so happy about the boy."

"I was born in the shadow of that sugar mill," Guy said. "Probably the first thing my mother gave me to drink as a baby was some sweet water tea from the pulp of the sugarcane. If anyone deserves to work there, I should."

"What will you be doing for your day's work?" 100

"Would you really like to know?"

"There is never any shame in honest work," she said.

"They want me to scrub the latrines."

"It's honest work," Lili said, trying to console him.

"I am still number seventy-eight on the permanent hire list," he said. "I was 105 thinking of putting the boy on the list now, so maybe by the time he becomes a man he can be up for a job."

Lili's body jerked forward, rising straight up in the air. Guy's head dropped with a loud thump onto the mat.

"I don't want him on that list," she said. "For a young boy to be on any list like that might influence his destiny. I don't want him on the list."

"Look at me," Guy said. "If my father had worked there, if he had me on the list, don't you think I would be working?"

"If you have any regard for me," she said, "you will not put him on the list."

110   She groped for her husband's chest in the dark and laid her head on it. She could hear his heart beating loudly as though it were pumping double, triple its normal rate.

"You won't put the boy on any lists, will you?" she implored.

"Please, Lili, no more about the boy. He will not go on the list."

"Thank you."

"Tonight I was looking at that balloon in the yard behind the sugar mill," he said. "I have been watching it real close."

115   "I know."

"I have seen the man who owns it," he said. "I've seen him get in it and put it in the sky and go up there like it was some kind of kite and he was the kite master. I see the men who run after it trying to figure out where it will land. Once I was there and I was one of those men who were running and I actually guessed correctly. I picked a spot in the sugarcane fields. I picked the spot from a distance and it actually landed there."

"Let me say something to you, Guy—"

"Pretend that this is the time of miracles and we believed in them. I watched the owner for a long time, and I think I can fly that balloon. The first time I saw him do it, it looked like a miracle, but the more and more I saw it, the more ordinary it became."

"You're probably intelligent enough to do it," she said.

120   "I am intelligent enough to do it. You're right to say that I can."

"Don't you think about hurting yourself?"

"Think like this. Can't you see yourself up there? Up in the clouds somewhere like some kind of bird?"

"If God wanted people to fly, he would have given us wings on our backs."

"You're right, Lili, you're right. But look what he gave us instead. He gave us reasons to want to fly. He gave us the air, the birds, our son."

125   "I don't understand you," she said.

"Our son, your son, you do not want him cleaning latrines."

"He can do other things."

"Me too. I can do other things too."

A loud scream came from the corner where the boy was sleeping. Lili and Guy rushed to him and tried to wake him. The boy was trembling when he opened his eyes.

130   "What is the matter?" Guy asked.

"I cannot remember my lines," the boy said.

Lili tried to string together what she could remember of her son's lines. The words slowly came back to the boy. By the time he fell back to sleep, it was almost dawn.

The light was slowly coming up behind the trees. Lili could hear the whispers of the market women, their hisses and swearing as their sandals dug into the sharp-edged rocks on the road.

She turned her back to her husband as she slipped out of her nightgown, quickly putting on her day clothes.

135   "Imagine this," Guy said from the mat on the floor. "I have never really seen your entire body in broad daylight."

Lili shut the door behind her, making her way out to the yard. The empty gasoline containers rested easily on her head as she walked a few miles to the public
water fountains. It was harder to keep them steady when the containers were full.
The water splashed all over her blouse and rippled down her back.

The sky was blue as it was most mornings, a dark indigo-shaded turquoise
that would get lighter when the sun was fully risen.

Guy and the boy were standing in the yard waiting for her when she got
back.

"You did not get much sleep, my handsome boy," she said, running her wet
fingers over the boy's face.

"He'll be late for school if we do not go right now," Guy said. "I want to drop   140
him off before I start work."

"Do we remember our lines this morning?" Lili asked, tucking the boy's shirt
down deep into his short pants.

"We just recited them," Guy said. "Even I know them now."

Lili watched them walk down the footpath, her eyes following them until
they disappeared.

As soon as they were out of sight, she poured the water she had fetched into
a large calabash, letting it stand beside the house.

She went back into the room and slipped into a dry blouse. It was never too   145
early to start looking around, to scrape together that night's meal.

"Listen to what happened again today," Lili said when Guy walked through the
door that afternoon.

Guy blotted his face with a dust rag as he prepared to hear the news. After
the day he'd had at the factory, he wanted to sit under a tree and have a leisurely
smoke, but he did not want to set a bad example for his son by indulging his
very small pleasures.

"You tell him, son," Lili urged the boy, who was quietly sitting in a corner,
reading.

"I've got more lines," the boy announced, springing up to his feet. "Papy, do
you want to hear them?"

"They are giving him more things to say in the play," Lili explained, "because   150
he did such a good job memorizing so fast."

"My compliments, son. Do you have your new lines memorized too?" Guy
asked.

"Why don't you recite your new lines for your father?" Lili said.

The boy walked to the middle of the room and prepared to recite. He cleared
his throat, raising his eyes towards the ceiling.

*There is so much sadness in the faces of my people. I have called on their gods,
now I call on our gods. I call on our young. I call on our old. I call on our mighty
and the weak. I call on everyone and anyone so that we shall all let out one piercing cry that we may either live freely or we should die.*

"I see your new lines have as much drama as the old ones," Guy said. He   155
wiped a tear away, walked over to the chair, and took the boy in his arms. He
pressed the boy's body against his chest before lowering him to the ground.

"Your new lines are wonderful, son. They're every bit as affecting as the old."
He tapped the boy's shoulder and walked out of the house.

"What's the matter with Papy?" the boy asked as the door slammed shut behind Guy.

"His heart hurts," Lili said.

After supper, Lili took her son to the field where she knew her husband would be. While the boy ran around, she found her husband sitting in his favorite spot behind the sugar mill.

160   "Nothing, Lili," he said. "Ask me nothing about this day that I have had."

She sat down on the grass next to him, for once feeling the sharp edges of the grass blades against her ankles.

"You're really good with that boy," he said, drawing circles with his smallest finger on her elbow. "You will make a performer of him. I know you will. You can see the best in that whole situation. It's because you have those stars in your eyes. That's the first thing I noticed about you when I met you. It was your eyes, Lili, so dark and deep. They drew me like danger draws a fool."

He turned over on the grass so that he was staring directly at the moon up in the sky. She could tell that he was also watching the hot-air balloon behind the sugar mill fence out of the corner of his eye.

"Sometimes I know you want to believe in me," he said. "I know you're wishing things for me. You want me to work at the mill. You want me to get a pretty house for us. I know you want these things too, but mostly you want me to feel like a man. That's why you're not one to worry about, Lili. I know you can take things as they come."

165   "I don't like it when you talk this way," she said.

"Listen to this, Lili. I want to tell you a secret. Sometimes, I just want to take that big balloon and ride it up in the air. I'd like to sail off somewhere and keep floating until I got to a really nice place with a nice plot of land where I could be something new. I'd build my own house, keep my own garden. Just *be* something new."

"I want you to stay away from there."

"I know you don't think I should take it. That can't keep me from wanting."

"You could be injured. Do you ever think about that?"

170   "Don't you ever want to be something new?"

"I don't like it," she said.

"Please don't get angry with me," he said, his voice straining almost like the boy's.

"If you were to take that balloon and fly away, would you take me and the boy?"

"First you don't want me to take it and now you want to go?"

175   "I just want to know that when you dream, me and the boy, we're always in your dreams."

He leaned his head on her shoulders and drifted off to sleep. Her back ached as she sat there with his face pressed against her collar bone. He drooled and the saliva dripped down to her breasts, soaking her frayed polyester bra. She listened to the crickets while watching her son play, muttering his lines to himself as he went in a circle around the field. The moon was glowing above their heads. Winking at them, as Guy liked to say, on its way to brighter shores.

Opening his eyes, Guy asked her, "How do you think a man is judged after he's gone?"

How did he expect her to answer something like that?

"People don't eat riches," she said. "They eat what it can buy."

"What does that mean, Lili? Don't talk to me in parables. Talk to me honestly."   180

"A man is judged by his deeds," she said. "The boy never goes to bed hungry. For as long as he's been with us, he's always been fed."

Just as if he had heard himself mentioned, the boy came dashing from the other side of the field, crashing in a heap on top of his parents.

"My new lines," he said. "I have forgotten my new lines."

"Is this how you will be the day of this play, son?" Guy asked. "When people give you big responsibilities, you have to try to live up to them."

The boy had relearned his new lines by the time they went to bed.   185

That night, Guy watched his wife very closely as she undressed for bed.

"I would like to be the one to rub that piece of lemon on your knees tonight," he said.

She handed him the half lemon, then raised her skirt above her knees.

Her body began to tremble as he rubbed his fingers over her skin.

"You know that question I asked you before," he said, "how a man is remem-   190
bered after he's gone? I know the answer now. I know because I remember my father, who was a very poor struggling man all his life. I remember him as a man that I would never want to be."

Lili got up with the break of dawn the next day. The light came up quickly above the trees. Lili greeted some of the market women as they walked together to the public water fountain.

On her way back, the sun had already melted a few gray clouds. She found the boy standing alone in the yard with a terrified expression on his face, the old withered mushrooms uprooted at his feet. He ran up to meet her, nearly knocking her off balance.

"What happened?" she asked. "Have you forgotten your lines?"

The boy was breathing so heavily that his lips could not form a single word.

"What is it?" Lili asked, almost shaking him with anxiety.   195

"It's Papa," he said finally, raising a stiff finger in the air.

The boy covered his face as his mother looked up at the sky. A rainbow-colored balloon was floating aimlessly above their heads.

"It's Papa," the boy said. "He is in it."

She wanted to look down at her son and tell him that it wasn't his father, but she immediately recognized the spindly arms, in a bright flowered shirt that she had made, gripping the cables.

From the field behind the sugar mill a group of workers were watching the bal-   200
loon floating in the air. Many were clapping and cheering, calling out Guy's name. A few of the women were waving their head rags at the sky, shouting, "Go! Beautiful, go!"

Lili edged her way to the front of the crowd. Everyone was waiting, watching the balloon drift higher up into the clouds.

"He seems to be right over our heads," said the factory foreman, a short slender mulatto with large buckteeth.

Just then, Lili noticed young Assad, his thick black hair sticking to the beads of sweat on his forehead. His face had the crumpled expression of disrupted sleep.

"He's further away than he seems," said young Assad. "I still don't understand. How did he get up there? You need a whole crew to fly these things."

205   "I don't know," the foreman said. "One of my workers just came in saying there was a man flying above the factory."

"But how the hell did he start it?" Young Assad was perplexed.

"He just did it," the foreman said.

"Look, he's trying to get out!" someone hollered.

A chorus of screams broke out among the workers.

210   The boy was looking up, trying to see if his father was really trying to jump out of the balloon. Guy was climbing over the side of the basket. Lili pressed her son's face into her skirt.

Within seconds, Guy was in the air hurtling down towards the crowd. Lili held her breath as she watched him fall. He crashed not far from where Lili and the boy were standing, his blood immediately soaking the landing spot.

The balloon kept floating free, drifting on its way to brighter shores. Young Assad rushed towards the body. He dropped to his knees and checked the wrist for a pulse, then dropped the arm back to the ground.

"It's over!" The foreman ordered the workers back to work.

Lili tried to keep her son's head pressed against her skirt as she moved closer to the body. The boy yanked himself away and raced to the edge of the field where his father's body was lying on the grass. He reached the body as young Assad still knelt examining the corpse. Lili rushed after him.

215   "He is mine," she said to young Assad. "He is my family. He belongs to me."

Young Assad got up and raised his head to search the sky for his aimless balloon, trying to guess where it would land. He took one last glance at Guy's bloody corpse, then raced to his car and sped away.

The foreman and another worker carried a cot and blanket from the factory.

Little Guy was breathing quickly as he looked at his father's body on the ground. While the foreman draped a sheet over Guy's corpse, his son began to recite the lines from his play.

"A wall of fire is rising and in the ashes, I see the bones of my people. Not only those people whose dark hollow faces I see daily in the fields, but all those souls who have gone ahead to haunt my dreams. At night I relive once more the last caresses from the hand of a loving father, a valiant love, a beloved friend."

220   "Let me look at him one last time," Lili said, pulling back the sheet.

She leaned in very close to get a better look at Guy's face. There was little left of that countenance that she had loved so much. Those lips that curled when he was teasing her. That large flat nose that felt like a feather when rubbed against hers. And those eyes, those night-colored eyes. Though clouded with blood, Guy's eyes were still bulging open. Lili was searching for some kind of sign—a blink, a smile, a wink—something that would remind her of the man that she had married.

"His eyes aren't closed," the foreman said to Lili. "Do you want to close them, or should I?"

The boy continued reciting his lines, his voice rising to a man's grieving roar. He kept his eyes closed, his fists balled at his side as he continued with his newest lines.

"There is so much sadness in the faces of my people. I have called on their gods, now I call on our gods. I call on our young. I call on our old. I call on our mighty and the weak. I call on everyone and anyone so that we shall all let out one piercing cry that we may either live freely or we should die."

"Do you want to close the eyes?" the foreman repeated impatiently.

"No, leave them open," Lili said. "My husband, he likes to look at the sky."

1991

LOUISE ERDRICH
(b. 1954)

Love Medicine

Born in Minnesota of German American and French Chippewa descent, Louise Erdrich grew up in Wahpeton, North Dakota, as a member of the Turtle Mountain Band of Chippewa. She attended Dartmouth College and received an MFA in creative writing from Johns Hopkins University. Her first book, *Love Medicine* (1984), a collection of linked stories, won the National Book Critics Circle Award. In her subsequent publications—*The Beet Queen* (1986), *Tracks* (1988), *The Bingo Palace* (1993), and *Tales of Burning Love* (1996)—she pursued her focus on the lives of Native Americans in contemporary North Dakota. In 1991 she jointly authored the best-selling novel *The Crown of Columbus* with her husband, Michael Dorris. Her recent works include the novels *The Last Report on the Miracles at Little No Horse* (2001), *The Plague of Doves* (2008), *The Round House* (2012), and *LaRose* (2016), as well as *Books and Islands in Ojibwa County: Traveling through the Land of My Ancestors* (2014). The owner of Birchbark Books and Native Arts, Erdrich lives in Minnesota with her family and dogs.

I never really done much with my life, I suppose. I never had a television. Grandma Kashpaw had one inside her apartment at the Senior Citizens, so I used to go there and watch my favorite shows. For a while she used to call me the biggest waste on the reservation and hark back to how she saved me from my own mother, who wanted to tie me in a potato sack and throw me in a slough. Sure, I was grateful to Grandma Kashpaw for saving me like that, for raising me, but gratitude gets old. After a while, stale. I had to stop thanking her. One day I told her I had paid her back in full by staying at her beck and call. I'd do anything for Grandma. She knew that. Besides, I took care of Grandpa like nobody else could, on account of what a handful he'd gotten to be.

But that was nothing. I know the tricks of mind and body inside out without ever having trained for it, because I got the touch. It's a thing you got to be born with. I got secrets in my hands that nobody ever knew to ask. Take Grandma Kashpaw with her tired veins all knotted up in her legs like clumps of blue snails. I take my fingers and I snap them on the knots. The medicine flows out of me. The touch. I run my fingers up the maps of those rivers of veins or I knock very gentle above their hearts or I make a circling motion on their stomachs, and it helps them. They feel much better. Some women pay me five dollars.

I couldn't do the touch for Grandpa, though. He was a hard nut. You know, some people fall right through the hole in their lives. It's invisible, but they come to it after time, never knowing where. There is this woman here, Lulu Lamartine, who always had a thing for Grandpa. She loved him since she was a girl and always said he was a genius. Now she says that his mind got so full it exploded.

How can I doubt that? I know the feeling when your mental power builds up too far. I always used to say that's why the Indians got drunk. Even statistically we're the smartest people on the earth. Anyhow with Grandpa I couldn't hardly believe it, because all my youth he stood out as a hero to me. When he started getting toward second childhood he went through different moods. He would stand in the woods and cry at the top of his shirt. It scared me, scared everyone, Grandma worst of all.

5   Yet he was so smart—do you believe it?—that he *knew* he was getting foolish.

He said so. He told me that December I failed school and come back on the train to Hoopdance. I didn't have nowhere else to go. He picked me up there and he said it straight out: "I'm getting into my second childhood." And then he said something else I still remember: "I been chosen for it. I couldn't say no." So I figure that a man so smart all his life—tribal chairman and the star of movies and even pictured in the statehouse and on cans of snuff—would know what he's doing by saying yes. I think he was called to second childhood like anybody else gets a call for the priesthood or the army or whatever. So I really did not listen too hard when the doctor said this was some kind of disease old people got eating too much sugar. You just can't tell me that a man who went to Washington and gave them bureaucrats what for could lose his mind from eating too much Milky Way. No, he put second childhood on himself.

Behind those songs he sings out in the middle of Mass, and back of those stories that everybody knows by heart, Grandpa is thinking hard about life. I know the feeling. Sometimes I'll throw up a smokescreen to think behind. I'll hitch up to Winnipeg and play the Space Invaders[1] for six hours, but all the time there and back I will be thinking some fairly deep thoughts that surprise even me, and I'm used to it. As for him, if it was just the thoughts there wouldn't be no problem. Smokescreen is what irritates the social structure, see, and Grandpa has done things that just distract people to the point they want to throw him in the cookie jar where they keep the mentally insane. He's far from that, I know for sure, but even Grandma had trouble keeping her patience once he started sneaking off to Lamartine's place. He's not supposed to have his candy, and Lulu feeds it to him. That's *one* of the reasons why he goes.

---

1. Popular 1980s arcade video game.

Grandma tried to get me to put the touch on Grandpa soon after he began stepping out. I didn't want to, but before Grandma started telling me again what a bad state my bare behind was in when she first took me home, I thought I should at least pretend.

I put my hands on either side of Grandpa's head. You wouldn't look at him and say he was crazy. He's a fine figure of a man, as Lamartine would say, with all his hair and half his teeth, a beak like a hawk, and cheeks like the blades of a hatchet. They put his picture on all the tourist guides to North Dakota and even copied his face for artistic paintings. I guess you could call him a monument all of himself. He started grinning when I put my hands on his templates,[2] and I knew right then he knew how come I touched him. I knew the smokescreen was going to fall.

And I was right: just for a moment it fell. 10

"Let's pitch whoopee," he said across my shoulder to Grandma.

They don't use that expression much around here anymore, but for damn sure it must have meant something. It got her goat right quick.

She threw my hands off his head herself and stood in front of him, overmatching him pound for pound, and taller too, for she had a growth spurt in middle age while he had shrunk, so now the length and breadth of her surpassed him. She glared and spoke her piece into his face about how he was off at all hours tomcatting and chasing Lamartine again and making a damn old fool of himself.

"And you got no more whoopee to pitch anymore anyhow!" she yelled at last, surprising me so my jaw just dropped, for us kids all had pretended for so long that those rustling sounds we heard from their side of the room at night never happened. She sure had pretended it, up till now, anyway. I saw that tears were in her eyes. And that's when I saw how much grief and love she felt for him. And it gave me a real shock to the system. You see I thought love got easier over the years so it didn't hurt so bad when it hurt, or feel so good when it felt good. I thought it smoothed out and old people hardly noticed it. I thought it curled up and died, I guess. Now I saw it rear up like a whip and lash.

She loved him. She was jealous. She mourned him like the dead. 15

And he just smiled into the air, trapped in the seams of his mind.

So I didn't know what to do. I was in a laundry then. They was like parents to me, the way they had took me home and reared me. I could see her point for wanting to get him back the way he was so at least she could argue with him, sleep with him, not be shamed out by Lamartine. She'd always love him. That hit me like a ton of bricks. For one whole day I felt this odd feeling that cramped my hands. When you have the touch, that's where longing gets you. I never loved like that. It made me feel all inspired to see them fight, and I wanted to go out and find a woman who I would love until one of us died or went crazy. But I'm not like that really. From time to time I heal a person all up good inside, however when it comes to the long shot I doubt that I got staying power.

And you need that, staying power, going out to love somebody. I knew this quality was not going to jump on me with no effort. So I turned my thoughts back to Grandma and Grandpa. I felt her side of it with my hands and my tangled guts, and I felt his side of it within the stretch of my mentality. He had

2. Blunder for "temples," one of many malapropisms in the story.

gone out to lunch one day and never came back. He was fishing in the middle of Matchimanito. And there was big thoughts on his line, and he kept throwing them back for even bigger ones that would explain to him, say, the meaning of how we got here and why we have to leave so soon. All in all, I could not see myself treating Grandpa with the touch, bringing him back, when the real part of him had chose to be off thinking somewhere. It was only the rest of him that stayed around causing trouble, after all, and we could handle most of it without any problem.

Besides, it was hard to argue with his reasons for doing some things. Take Holy Mass. I used to go there just every so often, when I got frustrated mostly, because even though I know the Higher Power dwells everyplace, there's something very calming about the cool greenish inside of our mission. Or so I thought, anyway. Grandpa was the one who stripped off my delusions in this matter, for it was he who busted right through what Father calls the sacred serenity of the place.

20   We filed in that time. Me and Grandpa. We sat down in our pews. Then the rosary got started up pre-Mass and that's when Grandpa filled up his chest and opened his mouth and belted out them words.

HAIL MARIE FULL OF GRACE.

He had a powerful set of lungs.

And he kept on like that. He did not let up. He hollered and he yelled them prayers, and I guess people was used to him by now, because they only muttered theirs and did not quit and gawk like I did. I was getting red-faced, I admit. I give him the elbow once or twice, but that wasn't nothing to him. He kept on. He shrieked to heaven and he pleaded like a movie actor and he pounded his chest like Tarzan in the Lord I Am Not Worthies. I thought he might hurt himself. Then after a while I guess I got used to it, and that's when I wondered: how come?

So afterwards I out and asked him. "How come? How come you yelled?"

25   "God don't hear me otherwise," said Grandpa Kashpaw.

I sweat. I broke right into a little cold sweat at my hairline because I knew this was perfectly right and for years not one damn other person had noticed it. God's been going deaf. Since the Old Testament, God's been deafening up on us. I read, see. Besides the dictionary, which I'm constantly in use of, I had this Bible once. I read it. I found there was discrepancies between then and now. It struck me. Here God used to raineth bread from clouds, smite the Phillipines,[3] sling fire down on red-light districts where people got stabbed. He even appeared in person every once in a while. God used to pay attention, is what I'm saying.

Now there's your God in the Old Testament and there is Chippewa Gods as well. Indian Gods, good and bad, like tricky Nanabozho or the water monster, Missepeshu, who lives over in Matchimanito. That water monster was the last God I ever heard to appear. It had a weakness for young girls and grabbed one of the Pillagers off her rowboat. She got to shore all right, but only after this monster had its way with her. She's an old lady now. Old Lady Pillager. She still doesn't like to see her family fish that lake.

Our Gods aren't perfect, is what I'm saying, but at least they come around. They'll do a favor if you ask them right. You don't have to yell. But you do have to know, like I said, how to ask in the right way. That makes problems, because

---

3. Blunder for "Philistines."

to ask proper was an art that was lost to the Chippewas once the Catholics gained ground. Even now, I have to wonder if Higher Power turned it back, if we got to yell, or if we just don't speak its language.

I looked around me. How else could I explain what all I had seen in my short life—King smashing his fist in things, Gordie drinking himself down to the Bismarck hospitals, or Aunt June left by a white man to wander off in the snow. How else to explain the times my touch don't work, and farther back, to the old-time Indians who was swept away in the outright germ warfare and dirty-dog killing of the whites. In those times, us Indians was so much kindlier than now.

We took them in.

Oh yes, I'm bitter as an old cutworm just thinking of how they done to us and doing still.

So Grandpa Kashpaw just opened my eyes a little there. Was there any sense relying on a God whose ears was stopped? Just like the government? I says then, right off, maybe we got nothing but ourselves. And that's not much, just person- ally speaking. I know I don't got the cold hard potatoes it takes to understand everything. Still, there's things I'd like to do. For instance, I'd like to help some people like my Grandpa and Grandma Kashpaw get back some happiness within the tail ends of their lives.

I told you once before I couldn't see my way clear to putting the direct touch on Grandpa's mind, and I kept my moral there, but something soon happened to make me think a little bit of mental adjustment wouldn't do him and the rest of us no harm.

It was after we saw him one afternoon in the sunshine courtyard of the Senior Citizens with Lulu Lamartine. Grandpa used to like to dig there. He had his little dandelion fork out, and he was prying up them dandelions right and left while Lamartine watched him.

"He's scratching up the dirt, all right," said Grandma, watching Lamartine watch Grandpa out the window.

Now Lamartine was about half the considerable size of Grandma, but you would never think of sizes anyway. They were different in an even more notice- able way. It was the difference between a house fixed up with paint and picky fence, and a house left to weather away into the soft earth, is what I'm saying. Lamartine was jacked up, latticed, shuttered, and vinyl sided, while Grandma sagged and bulged on her slipped foundations and let her hair go the silver gray of rain-dried lumber. Right now, she eyed the Lamartine's pert flowery dress with such a look it despaired me. I knew what this could lead to with Grandma. Alternating tongue storms and rock-hard silences was hard on a man, even one who didn't notice, like Grandpa. So I went fetching him.

But he was gone when I popped through the little screen door that led out on the courtyard. There was nobody out there either, to point which way they went. Just the dandelion fork quibbling upright in the ground. That gave me an idea. I snookered over to the Lamartine's door and I listened in first, then knocked. But nobody. So I went walking through the lounges and around the card tables. Still nobody. Finally it was my touch that led me to the laundry room. I cracked the door. I went in. There they were. And he was really loving her up good, boy, and she was going hell for leather. Sheets was flapping on the lines above, and washcloths, pillowcases, shirts was also flying through the air, for they was trying to clear out a place for themselves in a high-heaped but shallow laundry cart. The washers and dryers was all on, chock-full of quarters, shaking and moaning. I couldn't hear what Grandpa and the Lamartine was billing and cooing, and they couldn't hear me.

I didn't know what to do, so I went inside and shut the door.

The Lamartine wore a big curly light-brown wig. Looked like one of them squeaky little white-people dogs. Poodles they call them. Anyway, that wig is what saved us from the worse. For I could hardly shout and tell them I was in there, no more could I try and grab him. I was trapped where I was. There was nothing I could really do but hold the door shut. I was scared of somebody else upsetting in and really getting an eyeful. Turned out though, in the heat of the clinch, as I was trying to avert my eyes you see, the Lamartine's curly wig jumped off her head. And if you ever been in the midst of something and had a big change like that occur in the someone, you can't help know how it devastates your basic urges. Not only that, but her wig was almost with a life of its own. Grandpa's eyes were bugging at the change already, and swear to God if the thing didn't rear up and pop him in the face like it was going to start something. He scrambled up, Grandpa did, and the Lamartine jumped up after him all addled looking. They just stared at each other, huffing and puffing, with quizzical expression. The surprise seemed to drive all sense completely out of Grandpa's mind.

40   "The letter was what started the fire," he said. "I never would have done it."

"What letter?" said the Lamartine. She was stiff-necked now, and elegant, even bald, like some alien queen. I gave her back the wig. The Lamartine replaced it on her head, and whenever I saw her after that, I couldn't help thinking of her bald, with special powers, as if from another planet.

"That was a close call," I said to Grandpa after she had left.

But I think he had already forgot the incident. He just stood there all quiet and thoughtful. You really wouldn't think he was crazy. He looked like he was just about to say something important, explaining himself. He said something, all right, but it didn't have nothing to do with anything that made sense.

He wondered where the heck he put his dandelion fork. That's when I decided about the mental adjustment.

45   Now what was mostly our problem was not so much that he was not all there, but that what was there of him often hankered after Lamartine. If we could put a stop to that, I thought, we might be getting someplace. But here, see, my touch was of no use. For what could I snap my fingers at to make him faithful to Grandma? Like the quality of staying power, this faithfulness was invisible. I know it's something that you got to acquire, but I never known where from. Maybe there's no rhyme or reason to it, like my getting the touch, and then again maybe it's a kind of magic.

It was Grandma Kashpaw who thought of it in the end. She knows things. Although she will not admit she has a scrap of Indian blood in her, there's no doubt in my mind she's got some Chippewa. How else would you explain the way she'll be sitting there, in front of her TV story, rocking in her armchair and suddenly she turns on me, her brown eyes hard as lake-bed flint.

"Lipsha Morrissey," she'll say, "you went out last night and got drunk."

How did she know that? I'll hardly remember it myself. Then she'll say she just had a feeling or ache in the scar of her hand or a creak in her shoulder. She is constantly being told things by little aggravations in her joints or by her household appliances. One time she told Gordie never to ride with a crazy Lamartine boy. She had seen something in the polished-up tin of her bread toaster. So he didn't. Sure enough, the time came we heard how Lyman and Henry went out of control in their car, ending up in the river. Lyman swam to the top, but Henry never made it.

Thanks to Grandma's toaster, Gordie was probably spared.

Someplace in the blood Grandma Kashpaw knows things. She also remem- 50 bers things, I found. She keeps things filed away. She's got a memory like them video games that don't forget your score. One reason she remembers so many details about the trouble I gave her in early life is so she can flash back her total when she needs to.

Like now. Take the love medicine. I don't know where she remembered that from. It came tumbling from her mind like an asteroid off the corner of the screen.[4]

Of course she starts out by mentioning the time I had this accident in church and did she leave me there with wet overhalls? No she didn't. And ain't I glad? Yes I am. Now what you want now, Grandma?

But when she mentions them love medicines, I feel my back prickle at the danger. These love medicines is something of an old Chippewa specialty. No other tribe has got them down so well. But love medicines is not for the layman to handle. You don't just go out and get one without paying for it. Before you get one, even, you should go through one hell of a lot of mental condensation. You got to think it over. Choose the right one. You could really mess up your life grinding up the wrong little thing.

So anyhow, I said to Grandma I'd give this love medicine some thought. I knew the best thing was to go ask a specialist like Old Lady Pillager, who lives up in a tangle of bush and never shows herself. But the truth is I was afraid of her, like everyone else. She was known for putting the twisted mouth on people, seizing up their hearts. Old Lady Pillager was serious business, and I have always thought it best to steer clear of that whenever I could. That's why I took the powers in my own hands. That's why I did what I could.

I put my whole mentality to it, nothing held back. After a while I started to 55 remember things I'd heard gossiped over.

I heard of this person once who carried a charm of seeds that looked like baby pearls. They was attracted to a metal knife, which made them powerful. But I didn't know where them seeds grew. Another love charm I heard about I couldn't go along with, because how was I suppose to catch frogs in the act, which it required. Them little creatures is slippery and fast. And then the powerfullest of all, the most extreme, involved nail clips and such. I wasn't anywhere near asking Grandma to provide me all the little body bits that this last love recipe called for. I went walking around for days just trying to think up something that would work.

4. Allusion to Asteroids, another popular 1980s video arcade game.

Well I got it. If it hadn't been the early fall of the year, I never would have got it. But I was sitting underneath a tree one day down near the school just watching people's feet go by when something tells me, look up! Look up! So I look up, and I see two honkers, Canada geese, the kind with little masks on their faces, a bird what mates for life. I see them flying right over my head naturally preparing to land in some slough on the reservation, which they certainly won't get off of alive.

It hits me, anyway. Them geese, they mate for life. And I think to myself, just what if I went out and got a pair? And just what if I fed some part—say the goose heart—of the female to Grandma and Grandpa ate the other heart? Wouldn't that work? Maybe it's all invisible, and then maybe again it's magic. Love is a stony road. We know that for sure. If it's true that the higher feelings of devotion get lodged in the heart like people say, then we'd be home free. If not, eating goose heart couldn't harm nobody anyway. I thought it was worth my effort, and Grandma Kashpaw thought so, too. She had always known a good idea when she heard one. She borrowed me Grandpa's gun.

So I went out to this particular slough, maybe the exact same slough I never got thrown in by my mother, thanks to Grandma Kashpaw, and I hunched down in a good comfortable pile of rushes. I got my gun loaded up. I ate a few of these soft baloney sandwiches Grandma made me for lunch. And then I waited. The cattails blown back and forth above my head. Them stringy blue herons was spearing up their prey. The thing I know how to do best in this world, the thing I been training for all my life, is to wait. Sitting there and sitting there was no hardship on me. I got to thinking about some funny things that happened. There was this one time that Lulu Lamartine's little blue tweety bird, a para-clete, I guess you'd call it, flown up inside her dress and got lost within there. I recalled her running out into the hallway trying to yell something, shaking. She was doing a right good jig there, cutting the rug for sure, and the thing is it *never* flown out. To this day people speculate where it went. They fear she might perhaps of crushed it in her corsets. It sure hasn't ever yet been seen alive. I thought of funny things for a while, but then I used them up, and strange things that happened started weaseling their way into my mind.

60   I got to thinking quite naturally of the Lamartine's cousin named Wristwatch. I never knew what his real name was. They called him Wristwatch because he got his father's broken wristwatch as a young boy when his father passed on. Never in his whole life did Wristwatch take his father's watch off. He didn't care if it worked, although after a while he got sensitive when people asked what time it was, teasing him. He often put it to his ear like he was listening to the tick. But it was broken for good and forever, people said so, at least that's what they thought.

Well I saw Wristwatch smoking in his pickup one afternoon and by nine that evening he was dead.

He died sitting at the Lamartine's table, too. As she told it, Wristwatch had just eaten himself a good-size dinner and she said would he take seconds on the hot dish when he fell over to the floor. They turnt him over. He was gone. But here's the strange thing: when the Senior Citizen's orderly took the pulse he noticed that the wristwatch Wristwatch wore was now working. The moment he died the wristwatch started keeping perfect time. They buried him with the watch still ticking on his arm.

I got to thinking. What if some gravediggers dug up Wristwatch's casket in two hundred years and that watch was still going? I thought what question they would ask and it was this: Whose hand wound it?

I started shaking like a piece of grass at just the thought.

Not to get off the subject or nothing. I was still hunkered in the slough. It was 65 passing late into the afternoon and still no honkers had touched down. Now I don't need to tell you that the waiting did not get to me, it was the chill. The rushes was very soft, but damp. I was getting cold and debating to leave, when they landed. Two geese swimming here and there as big as life, looking deep into each other's little pinhole eyes. Just the ones I was looking for. So I lifted Grandpa's gun to my shoulder and I aimed perfectly, and *blam! Blam!* I delivered two accurate shots. But the thing is, them shots missed. I couldn't hardly believe it. Whether it was that the stock had warped or the barrel got bent someways, I don't quite know, but anyway them geese flown off into the dim sky, and Lipsha Morrissey was left there in the rushes with evening fallen and his two cold hands empty. He had before him just the prospect of another day of bone-cracking chill in them rushes, and the thought of it got him depressed.

Now it isn't my style, in no way, to get depressed.

So I said to myself, Lipsha Morrissey, you're a happy S.O.B. who could be covered up with weeds by now down at the bottom of this slough, but instead you're alive to tell the tale. You might have problems in life, but you still got the touch. You got the power, Lipsha Morrissey. Can't argue that. So put your mind to it and figure out how not to be depressed.

I took my advice. I put my mind to it. But I never saw at the time how my thoughts led me astray toward a tragic outcome none could have known. I ignored all the danger, all the limits, for I was tired of sitting in the slough and my feet were numb. My face was aching. I was chilled, so I played with fire. I told myself love medicine was simple. I told myself the old superstitions was just that—strange beliefs. I told myself to take the ten dollars Mary MacDonald had paid me for putting the touch on her arthritis joint, and the other five I hadn't spent yet from winning bingo last Thursday. I told myself to go down to the Red Owl store.

And here is what I did that made the medicine backfire. I took an evil short-cut. I looked at birds that was dead and froze.

All right. So now I guess you will say, "Slap a malpractice suit on Lipsha 70 Morrissey."

I heard of those suits. I used to think it was a color clothing quack doctors had to wear so you could tell them from the good ones. Now I know better that it's law.

As I walked back from the Red Owl with the rock-hard, heavy turkeys, I argued to myself about malpractice. I thought of faith. I thought to myself that faith could be called belief against the odds and whether or not there's any proof. How does that sound? I thought how we might have to yell to be heard by Higher Power, but that's not saying it's not *there*. And that is faith for you. It's belief even when the goods don't deliver. Higher Power makes promises we all know they can't back up, but anybody ever go and slap an old malpractice suit on God? Or the U.S. government? No they don't. Faith might be stupid, but it gets us through.

So what I'm heading at is this. I finally convinced myself that the real actual power to the love medicine was not the goose heart itself but the faith in the cure.

I didn't believe it, I knew it was wrong, but by then I had waded so far into my lie I was stuck there. And then I went one step further.

The next day, I cleaned the hearts away from the paper packages of gizzards inside the turkeys. Then I wrapped them hearts with a clean hankie and brung them both to get blessed up at the mission. I wanted to get official blessings from the priest, but when Father answered the door to the rectory, wiping his hands on a little towel, I could tell he was a busy man.

75 "Booshoo,[5] Father," I said. "I got a slight request to make of you this afternoon."

"What is it?" he said.

"Would you bless this package?" I held out the hankie with the hearts tied inside it.

He looked at the package, questioning it.

"It's turkey hearts," I honestly had to reply.

80 A look of annoyance crossed his face.

"Why don't you bring this matter over to Sister Martin," he said. "I have duties."

And so, although the blessing wouldn't be as powerful, I went over to the Sisters with the package.

I rung the bell, and they brought Sister Martin to the door. I had her as a music teacher, but I was always so shy then. I never talked out loud. Now, I had grown taller than Sister Martin. Looking down, I saw that she was not feeling up to snuff. Brown circles hung under her eyes.

"What's the matter?" she said, not noticing who I was.

85 "Remember me, Sister?"

She squinted up at me.

"Oh yes," she said after a moment. "I'm sorry, you're the youngest of the Kashpaws. Gordie's brother."

Her face warmed up.

"Lipsha," I said, "that's my name."

90 "Well, Lipsha," she said, smiling broad at me now, "what can I do for you?"

They always said she was the kindest-hearted of the Sisters up the hill, and she was. She brought me back into their own kitchen and made me take a big yellow wedge of cake and a glass of milk.

"Now tell me," she said, nodding at my package. "What have you got wrapped up so carefully in those handkerchiefs?"

Like before, I answered honestly.

"Ah," said Sister Martin. "Turkey hearts." She waited.

95 "I hoped you could bless them."

She waited some more, smiling with her eyes. Kindhearted though she was, I began to sweat. A person could not pull the wool down over Sister Martin. I stumbled through my mind for an explanation, quick, that wouldn't scare her off.

5. Or *boozhoo*: "hello," "greetings" (Ojibwe or Chippewa).

"They're a present," I said, "for Saint Kateri's[6] statue."

"She's not a saint yet."

"I know," I stuttered on. "In the hopes they will crown her."

"Lipsha," she said, "I never heard of such a thing."

So I told her. "Well the truth is," I said, "it's a kind of medicine."

"For what?"

"Love."

"Oh Lipsha," she said after a moment, "you don't need any medicine. I'm sure any girl would like you exactly the way you are."

I just sat there. I felt miserable, caught in my pack of lies.

"Tell you what," she said, seeing how bad I felt, "my blessing won't make any difference anyway. But there is something you can do."

I looked up at her, hopeless.

"Just be yourself."

I looked down at my plate. I knew I wasn't much to brag about right then, and I shortly became even less. For as I walked out the door I stuck my fingers in the cup of holy water that was sacred from their touches. I put my fingers in and blessed the hearts, quick, with my own hand.

I went back to Grandma and sat down in her little kitchen at the Senior Citizens. I unwrapped them hearts on the table, and her hard agate eyes went soft. She said she wasn't even going to cook those hearts up but eat them raw so their power would go down strong as possible.

I couldn't hardly watch when she munched hers. Now that's true love. I was worried about how she would get Grandpa to eat his, but she told me she'd think of something and don't worry. So I did not. I was supposed to hide off in her bedroom while she put dinner on a plate for Grandpa and fixed up the heart so he'd eat it. I caught a glint of the plate she was making for him. She put that heart smack on a piece of lettuce like in a restaurant and then attached to it a little heap of boiled peas.

He sat down. I was listening in the next room.

She said, "Why don't you have some mash potato?" So he had some mash potato. Then she gave him a little piece of boiled meat. He ate that. Then she said, "Why you didn't never touch your salad yet. See that heart? I'm feeding you it because the doctor said your blood needs building up."

I couldn't help it, at that point I peeked through a crack in the door.

I saw Grandpa picking at that heart on his plate with a certain look. He didn't look appetized at all, is what I'm saying. I doubted our plan was going to work. Grandma was getting worried, too. She told him one more time, loudly, that he had to eat that heart.

"Swallow it down," she said. "You'll hardly notice it."

He just looked at her straight on. The way he looked at her made me think I was going to see the smokescreen drop a second time, and sure enough it happened.

6. Kateri Kekakwitha (1656–80), "Lily of the Mohawk," born in what is now upstate New York to a Mohawk father and an Algonquin mother who was a devout Christian. Following the deaths of her parents, Kateri moved to a Jesuit mission near Montreal to spend the rest of her short life in prayer and chastity. Credited with miracles after her death, she was beatified in 1980 and canonized in 1991.

"What you want me to eat this for so bad?" he asked her uncannily.

Now Grandma knew the jig was up. She knew that he knew she was working medicine. He put his fork down. He rolled the heart around his saucer plate.

120   "I don't want to eat this," he said to Grandma. "It don't look good."

"Why it's fresh grade-A," she told him. "One hundred percent."

He didn't ask percent what, but his eyes took on an even more warier look.

"Just go on and try it," she said, taking the salt shaker up in her hand. She was getting annoyed. "Not tasty enough? You want me to salt it for you?" She waved the shaker over his plate.

"All right, skinny white girl!" She had got Grandpa mad. Oopsy-daisy, he popped the heart into his mouth. I was about to yawn loudly and come out of the bedroom. I was about ready for this crash of wills to be over, when I saw he was still up to his old tricks. First he rolled it into one side of his cheek. "Mmmmm," he said. Then he rolled it into the other side of his cheek. "Mmmmmmm," again. Then he stuck his tongue out with the heart on it and put it back, and there was no time to react. He had pulled Grandma's leg once too far. Her goat was got. She was so mad she hopped up quick as a wink and slugged him between the shoulderblades to make him swallow.

125   Only thing is, he choked.

He choked real bad. A person can choke to death. You ever sit down at a restaurant table and up above you there is a list of instructions what to do if something slides down the wrong pipe? It sure makes you chew slow, that's for damn sure. When Grandpa fell off his chair better believe me that little graphic illustrated poster fled into my mind. I jumped out the bedroom. I done everything within my power that I could do to unlodge what was choking him. I squeezed underneath his rib cage. I socked him in the back. I was desperate. But here's the factor of decision: he wasn't choking on the heart alone. There was more to it than that. It was other things that choked him as well. It didn't seem like he wanted to struggle or fight. Death came and tapped his chest, so he went just like that. I'm sorry all through my body at what I done to him with that heart, and there's those who will say Lipsha Morrissey is just excusing himself off the hook by giving song and dance about how Grandpa gave up.

Maybe I can't admit what I did. My touch had gone worthless, that is true. But here is what I seen while he lay in my arms.

You hear a person's life will flash before their eyes when they're in danger. It was him in danger, not me, but it was *his* life come over me. I saw him dying, and it was like someone pulled the shade down in a room. His eyes clouded over and squeezed shut, but just before that I looked in. He was still fishing in the middle of Matchimanito. Big thoughts was on his line and he had half a case of beer in the boat. He waved at me, grinned, and then the bobber went under.

Grandma had gone out of the room crying for help. I bunched my force up in my hands and I held him. I was so wound up I couldn't even breathe. All the moments he had spent with me, all the times he had hoisted me on his shoulders or pointed into the leaves was concentrated in that moment. Time was flashing back and forth like a pinball machine. Lights blinked and balls hopped and rubber bands chirped, until suddenly I realized the last ball had gone down the drain and there was nothing. I felt his force leaving him, flowing out of Grandpa never to return. I felt his mind weakening. The bobber going under in the lake. And I felt the touch retreat back into the darkness inside my body, from where it came.

One time, long ago, both of us were fishing together. We caught a big old 130 snapper what started towing us around like it was a motor. "This here fishline is pretty damn good," Grandpa said. "Let's keep this turtle on and see where he takes us." So we rode along behind that turtle, watching as from time to time it surfaced. The thing was just about the size of a washtub. It took us all around the lake twice, and as it was traveling, Grandpa said something as a joke. "Lipsha," he said, "we are glad your mother didn't want you because we was always looking for a boy like you who would tow us around the lake."

"I ain't no snapper. Snappers is so stupid they stay alive when their head's chopped off," I said.

"That ain't stupidity," said Grandpa. "Their brain's just in their heart, like yours is."

When I looked up, I knew the fuse had blown between my heart and my mind and that a terrible understanding was to be given.

Grandma got back into the room and I saw her stumble. And then she went down too. It was like a house you can't hardly believe has stood so long, through years of record weather, suddenly goes down in the worst yet. It makes sense, is what I'm saying, but you still can't hardly believe it. You think a person you know has got through death and illness and being broke and living on commodity rice will get through anything. Then they fold and you see how fragile were the stones that underpinned them. You see how instantly the ground can shift you thought was solid. You see the stop signs and the yellow dividing markers of roads you traveled and all the instructions you had played according to vanish. You see how all the everyday things you counted on was just a dream you had been having by which you run your whole life. She had been over me, like a sheer overhang of rock dividing Lipsha Morrissey from outer space. And now she went underneath. It was as though the banks gave way on the shores of Matchimanito, and where Grandpa's passing was just the bobber swallowed under by his biggest thought, her fall was the house and the rock under it sliding after, sending half the lake splashing up to the clouds.

Where there was nothing.   135

You play them games never knowing what you see. When I fell into the dream alongside of both of them I saw that the dominions I had defended myself from anciently was but delusions of the screen. Blips of light. And I was scot-free now, whistling through space.

I don't know how I come back. I don't know from where. They was slapping my face when I arrived back at Senior Citizens and they was oxygenating her. I saw her chest move, almost unwilling. She sighed the way she would when somebody bothered her in the middle of a row of beads she was counting. I think it irritated her to no end that they brought her back. I knew from the way she looked after they took the mask off, she was not going to forgive them disturbing her restful peace. Nor was she forgiving Lipsha Morrissey. She had been stepping out onto the road of death, she told the children later at the funeral. I asked was there any stop signs or dividing markers on that road, but she clamped her lips in a vise the way she always done when she was mad.

Which didn't bother me. I knew when things had cleared out she wouldn't have no choice. I was not going to speculate where the blame was put for Grandpa's death. We was in it together. She had slugged him between the shoulders. My touch had failed him, never to return.

All the blood children and the took-ins, like me, came home from Minneapolis and Chicago, where they had relocated years ago. They stayed with friends on the reservation or with Aurelia or slept on Grandma's floor. They were struck down with grief and bereavement to be sure, every one of them. At the funeral I sat down in the back of the church with Albertine. She had gotten all skinny and ragged haired from cramming all her years of study into two or three. She had decided that to be a nurse was not enough for her so she was going to be a doctor. But the way she was straining her mind didn't look too hopeful. Her eyes were bloodshot from driving and crying. She took my hand. From the back we watched all the children and the mourners as they hunched over their prayers, their hands stuffed full of Kleenex. It was someplace in that long sad service that my vision shifted. I began to see things different, more clear. The family kneeling down turned to rocks in a field. It struck me how strong and reliable grief was, and death. Until the end of time, death would be our rock.

140   So I had perspective on it all, for death gives you that. All the Kashpaw children had done various things to me in their lives—shared their folks with me, loaned me cash, beat me up in secret—and I decided, because of death, then and there I'd call it quits. If I ever saw King again, I'd shake his hand. Forgiving somebody else made the whole thing easier to bear.

Everybody saw Grandpa off into the next world. And then the Kashpaws had to get back to their jobs, which was numerous and impressive. I had a few beers with them and I went back to Grandma, who had sort of got lost in the shuffle of everybody being sad about Grandpa and glad to see one another.

Zelda had sat beside her the whole time and was sitting with her now. I wanted to talk to Grandma, say how sorry I was, that it wasn't her fault, but only mine. I would have, but Zelda gave me one of her looks of strict warning as if to say, "I'll take care of Grandma. Don't horn in on the women."

If only Zelda knew, I thought, the sad realities would change her. But of course I couldn't tell the dark truth.

It was evening, late. Grandma's light was on underneath a crack in the door. About a week had passed since we buried Grandpa. I knocked first but there wasn't no answer, so I went right in. The door was unlocked. She was there but she didn't notice me at first. Her hands were tied up in her rosary, and her gaze was fully absorbed in the easy chair opposite her, the one that had always been Grandpa's favorite. I stood there, staring with her, at the little green nubs in the cloth and plastic armrest covers and the sad little hair-tonic stain he had made on the white doily where he laid his head. For the life of me I couldn't figure what she was staring at. Thin space. Then she turned.

145   "He ain't gone yet," she said.

Remember that chill I luckily didn't get from waiting in the slough? I got it now. I felt it start from the very center of me, where fear hides, waiting to attack. It spiraled outward so that in minutes my fingers and teeth were shaking and clattering. I knew she told the truth. She seen Grandpa. Whether or not he had been there is not the point. She had *seen* him, and that meant anybody else could see him, too. Not only that but, as is usually the case with these here ghosts, he had a certain uneasy reason to come back. And of course Grandma Kashpaw had scanned it out.

I sat down. We sat together on the couch watching his chair out of the corner of our eyes. She had found him sitting in his chair when she walked in the door.

"It's the love medicine, my Lipsha," she said. "It was stronger than we thought. He came back even after death to claim me to his side."

I was afraid. "We shouldn't have tampered with it," I said. She agreed. For a while we sat still. I don't know what she thought, but my head felt screwed on backward. I couldn't accurately consider the situation, so I told Grandma to go to bed. I would sleep on the couch keeping my eye on Grandpa's chair. Maybe he would come back and maybe he wouldn't. I guess I feared the one as much as the other, but I got to thinking, see, as I lay there in darkness, that perhaps even through my terrible mistakes some good might come. If Grandpa did come back, I thought he'd return in his right mind. I could talk with him. I could tell him it was all my fault for playing with power I did not understand. Maybe he'd forgive me and rest in peace. I hoped this. I calmed myself and waited for him all night.

He fooled me though. He knew what I was waiting for, and it wasn't what he was looking to hear. Come dawn I heard a blood-splitting cry from the bedroom and I rushed in there. Grandma turnt the lights on. She was sitting on the edge of the bed and her face looked harsh, pinched-up, gray. 150

"He was here," she said. "He came and laid down next to me in bed. And he touched me."

Her heart broke down. She cried. His touch was so cold. She laid back in bed after a while, as it was morning, and I went to the couch. As I lay there, falling asleep, I suddenly felt Grandpa's presence and the barrier between us like a swollen river. I felt how I had wronged him. How awful was the place where I had sent him. Behind the wall of death, he'd watched the living eat and cry and get drunk. He was lonesome, but I understood he meant no harm.

"Go back," I said to the dark, afraid and yet full of pity. "You got to be with your own kind now," I said. I felt him retreating, like a sigh, growing less. I felt his spirit as it shrunk back through the walls, the blinds, the brick courtyard of Senior Citizens. "Look up Aunt June," I whispered as he left.

I slept late the next morning, a good hard sleep allowing the sun to rise and warm the earth. It was past noon when I awoke. There is nothing, to my mind, like a long sleep to make those hard decisions that you neglect under stress of wakefulness. Soon as I woke up that morning, I saw exactly what I'd say to Grandma. I had gotten humble in the past week, not just losing the touch but getting jolted into the understanding that would prey on me from here on out. Your life feels different on you, once you greet death and understand your heart's position. You wear your life like a garment from the mission bundle sale ever after—lightly because you realize you never paid nothing for it, cherishing because you know you won't ever come by such a bargain again. Also you have the feeling someone wore it before you and someone will after. I can't explain that, not yet, but I'm putting my mind to it.

155   "Grandma," I said, "I got to be honest about the love medicine."

She listened. I knew from then on she would be listening to me the way I had listened to her before. I told her about the turkey hearts and how I had them blessed. I told her what I used as love medicine was purely a fake, and then I said to her what my understanding brought me.

"Love medicine ain't what brings him back to you, Grandma. No, it's something else. He loved you over time and distance, but he went off so quick he never got the chance to tell you how he loves you, how he doesn't blame you, how he understands. It's true feeling, not no magic. No supermarket heart could have brung him back."

She looked at me. She was seeing the years and days I had no way of knowing, and she didn't believe me. I could tell this. Yet a look came on her face. It was like the look of mothers drinking sweetness from their children's eyes. It was tenderness.

"Lipsha," she said, "you was always my favorite."

160   She took the beads off the bedpost, where she kept them to say at night, and she told me to put out my hand. When I did this, she shut the beads inside of my fist and held them there a long minute, tight, so my hand hurt. I almost cried when she did this. I don't really know why. Tears shot up behind my eyelids, and yet it was nothing. I didn't understand, except her hand was so strong, squeezing mine.

The earth was full of life and there were dandelions growing out the window, thick as thieves, already seeded, fat as big yellow plungers. She let my hand go. I got up. "I'll go out and dig a few dandelions," I told her.

Outside, the sun was hot and heavy as a hand on my back. I felt it flow down my arms, out my fingers, arrowing through the ends of the fork into the earth. With every root I prized up there was return, as if I was kin to its secret lesson. The touch got stronger as I worked through the grassy afternoon. Uncurling from me like a seed out of the blackness where I was lost, the touch spread. The spiked leaves full of bitter mother's milk. A buried root. A nuisance people dig up and throw in the sun to wither. A globe of frail seeds that's indestructible.

1982

WILLIAM FAULKNER
(1897–1962)

A Rose for Emily

A native of Oxford, Mississippi, William Faulkner left high school without graduating, joined the Royal Canadian Air Force in 1918, and in the mid-1920s lived briefly in New Orleans, where he was encouraged as a writer by Sherwood Anderson. He then spent a few miserable months as a clerk in a New York bookstore; published a collection of poems, *The Marble Faun* (1924); and took a long walking tour of Europe (1925) before returning to Mississippi. With the publication of *Sartoris* in 1929, Faulkner began a cycle of works, featuring recurrent characters and set in fictional Yoknapatawpha County, including *The Sound and the Fury* (1929), *As I Lay Dying* (1930), *Light in August* (1932), *Absalom, Absalom!* (1936), *The Hamlet* (1940), and *Go Down, Moses* (1942). He spent time in Hollywood, writing screenplays for *The Big Sleep* and other films, and lived his last years in Charlottesville, Virginia. Faulkner received the Nobel Prize for Literature in 1950.

I

When Miss Emily Grierson died, our whole town went to her funeral: the men through a sort of respectful affection for a fallen monument, the women mostly out of curiosity to see the inside of her house, which no one save an old manservant— a combined gardener and cook—had seen in at least ten years.

It was a big, squarish frame house that had once been white, decorated with cupolas and spires and scrolled balconies in the heavily lightsome style of the seventies,[1] set on what had once been our most select street. But garages and cotton gins had encroached and obliterated even the august names of that neighborhood; only Miss Emily's house was left, lifting its stubborn and coquettish decay above the cotton wagons and the gasoline pumps—an eyesore among eyesores. And now Miss Emily had gone to join the representatives of those august names where they lay in the cedar-bemused cemetery among the ranked and anonymous graves of Union and Confederate soldiers who fell at the battle of Jefferson.

Alive, Miss Emily had been a tradition, a duty, and a care; a sort of hereditary obligation upon the town, dating from that day in 1894 when Colonel Sartoris, the mayor—he who fathered the edict that no Negro woman should appear on the streets without an apron—remitted her taxes, the dispensation dating from the death of her father on into perpetuity. Not that Miss Emily would have accepted charity. Colonel Sartoris invented an involved tale to the effect that Miss Emily's father had loaned money to the town, which the town, as a matter of business,

---

1. The 1870s, the decade following the Civil War between the "Union and Confederate soldiers" mentioned at the end of the paragraph.

preferred this way of repaying. Only a man of Colonel Sartoris' generation and thought could have invented it, and only a woman could have believed it.

When the next generation, with its more modern ideas, became mayors and aldermen, this arrangement created some little dissatisfaction. On the first of the year they mailed her a tax notice. February came, and there was no reply. They wrote her a formal letter, asking her to call at the sheriff's office at her convenience. A week later the mayor wrote her himself, offering to call or to send his car for her, and received in reply a note on paper of an archaic shape, in a thin, flowing calligraphy in faded ink, to the effect that she no longer went out at all. The tax notice was also enclosed, without comment.

5   They called a special meeting of the Board of Aldermen. A deputation waited upon her, knocked at the door through which no visitor had passed since she ceased giving china-painting lessons eight or ten years earlier. They were admitted by the old Negro into a dim hall from which a stairway mounted into still more shadow. It smelled of dust and disuse—a close, dank smell. The Negro led them into the parlor. It was furnished in heavy, leather-covered furniture. When the Negro opened the blinds of one window, a faint dust rose sluggishly about their thighs, spinning with slow motes in the single sun-ray. On a tarnished gilt easel before the fireplace stood a crayon portrait of Miss Emily's father.

They rose when she entered—a small, fat woman in black, with a thin gold chain descending to her waist and vanishing into her belt, leaning on an ebony cane with a tarnished gold head. Her skeleton was small and spare; perhaps that was why what would have been merely plumpness in another was obesity in her. She looked bloated, like a body long submerged in motionless water, and of that pallid hue. Her eyes, lost in the fatty ridges of her face, looked like two small pieces of coal pressed into a lump of dough as they moved from one face to another while the visitors stated their errand.

She did not ask them to sit. She just stood in the door and listened quietly until the spokesman came to a stumbling halt. Then they could hear the invisible watch ticking at the end of the gold chain.

Her voice was dry and cold. "I have no taxes in Jefferson. Colonel Sartoris explained it to me. Perhaps one of you can gain access to the city records and satisfy yourselves."

"But we have. We are the city authorities, Miss Emily. Didn't you get a notice from the sheriff, signed by him?"

10   "I received a paper, yes," Miss Emily said. "Perhaps he considers himself the sheriff. . . . I have no taxes in Jefferson."

"But there is nothing on the books to show that, you see. We must go by the—"

"See Colonel Sartoris. I have no taxes in Jefferson."

"But, Miss Emily—"

"See Colonel Sartoris." (Colonel Sartoris had been dead almost ten years.) "I have no taxes in Jefferson. Tobe!" The Negro appeared. "Show these gentlemen out."

II

15 So she vanquished them, horse and foot, just as she had vanquished their fathers thirty years before about the smell. That was two years after her father's

death and a short time after her sweetheart—the one we believed would marry her—had deserted her. After her father's death she went out very little; after her sweetheart went away, people hardly saw her at all. A few of the ladies had the temerity to call, but were not received, and the only sign of life about the place was the Negro man—a young man then—going in and out with a market basket.

"Just as if a man—any man—could keep a kitchen properly," the ladies said; so they were not surprised when the smell developed. It was another link between the gross, teeming world and the high and mighty Griersons.

A neighbor, a woman, complained to the mayor, Judge Stevens, eighty years old.

"But what will you have me do about it, madam?" he said.

"Why, send her word to stop it," the woman said. "Isn't there a law?"

"I'm sure that won't be necessary," Judge Stevens said. "It's probably just a 20 snake or a rat that nigger of hers killed in the yard. I'll speak to him about it."

The next day he received two more complaints, one from a man who came in diffident deprecation. "We really must do something about it, Judge. I'd be the last one in the world to bother Miss Emily, but we've got to do something." That night the Board of Aldermen met—three gray-beards and one younger man, a member of the rising generation.

"It's simple enough," he said. "Send her word to have her place cleaned up. Give her a certain time to do it in, and if she don't . . ."

"Dammit, sir," Judge Stevens said, "will you accuse a lady to her face of smelling bad?"

So the next night, after midnight, four men crossed Miss Emily's lawn and slunk about the house like burglars, sniffing along the base of the brickwork and at the cellar openings while one of them performed a regular sowing motion with his hand out of a sack slung from his shoulder. They broke open the cellar door and sprinkled lime there, and in all the outbuildings. As they recrossed the lawn, a window that had been dark was lighted and Miss Emily sat in it, the light behind her, and her upright torso motionless as that of an idol. They crept quietly across the lawn and into the shadow of the locusts that lined the street. After a week or two the smell went away.

That was when people had begun to feel really sorry for her. People in our 25 town, remembering how old lady Wyatt, her great-aunt, had gone completely crazy at last, believed that the Griersons held themselves a little too high for what they really were. None of the young men were quite good enough for Miss Emily and such. We had long thought of them as a tableau; Miss Emily a slender figure in white in the background, her father a spraddled silhouette in the foreground, his back to her and clutching a horsewhip, the two of them framed by the back-flung front door. So when she got to be thirty and was still single, we were not pleased exactly, but vindicated; even with insanity in the family she wouldn't have turned down all of her chances if they had really materialized.

When her father died, it got about that the house was all that was left to her; and in a way, people were glad. At last they could pity Miss Emily. Being left alone, and a pauper, she had become humanized. Now she too would know the old thrill and the old despair of a penny more or less.

The day after his death all the ladies prepared to call at the house and offer condolence and aid, as is our custom. Miss Emily met them at the door, dressed as usual and with no trace of grief on her face. She told them that her father was not dead. She did that for three days, with the ministers calling on her, and the doctors, trying to persuade her to let them dispose of the body. Just as they were about to resort to law and force, she broke down, and they buried her father quickly.

We did not say she was crazy then. We believed she had to do that. We remembered all the young men her father had driven away, and we knew that with nothing left, she would have to cling to that which had robbed her, as people will.

III

She was sick for a long time. When we saw her again, her hair was cut short, making her look like a girl, with a vague resemblance to those angels in colored church windows—sort of tragic and serene.

30   The town had just let the contracts for paving the sidewalks, and in the summer after her father's death they began to work. The construction company came with niggers and mules and machinery, and a foreman named Homer Barron, a Yankee—a big, dark, ready man, with a big voice and eyes lighter than his face. The little boys would follow in groups to hear him cuss the niggers, and the niggers singing in time to the rise and fall of picks. Pretty soon he knew everybody in town. Whenever you heard a lot of laughing anywhere about the square, Homer Barron would be in the center of the group. Presently we began to see him and Miss Emily on Sunday afternoons driving in the yellow-wheeled buggy and the matched team of bays from the livery stable.

At first we were glad that Miss Emily would have an interest, because the ladies all said, "Of course a Grierson would not think seriously of a Northerner, a day laborer." But there were still others, older people, who said that even grief could not cause a real lady to forget *noblesse oblige*—without calling it *noblesse oblige*.[2] They just said, "Poor Emily. Her kinsfolk should come to her." She had some kin in Alabama; but years ago her father had fallen out with them over the estate of old lady Wyatt, the crazy woman, and there was no communication between the two families. They had not even been represented at the funeral.

And as soon as the old people said, "Poor Emily," the whispering began. "Do you suppose it's really so?" they said to one another. "Of course it is. What else could . . ." This behind their hands; rustling of craned silk and satin behind jalousies[3] closed upon the sun of Sunday afternoon as the thin, swift clop-clop-clop of the matched team passed: "Poor Emily."

She carried her head high enough—even when we believed that she was fallen. It was as if she demanded more than ever the recognition of her dignity as the last Grierson; as if it had wanted that touch of earthiness to reaffirm her imperviousness. Like when she bought the rat poison, the arsenic. That was

2. Obligation, coming with noble or upper-class birth, to behave with honor and generosity toward those less privileged.
3. Window blinds made of adjustable horizontal slats.

over a year after they had begun to say "Poor Emily," and while the two female cousins were visiting her.

"I want some poison," she said to the druggist. She was over thirty then, still a slight woman, though thinner than usual, with cold, haughty black eyes in a face the flesh of which was strained across the temples and about the eyesockets as you imagine a lighthouse-keeper's face ought to look. "I want some poison," she said.

"Yes, Miss Emily. What kind? For rats and such? I'd recom—"   35

"I want the best you have. I don't care what kind."

The druggist named several. "They'll kill anything up to an elephant. But what you want is—"

"Arsenic," Miss Emily said. "Is that a good one?"

"Is . . . arsenic? Yes ma'am. But what you want—"

"I want arsenic."   40

The druggist looked down at her. She looked back at him, erect, her face like a strained flag. "Why, of course," the druggist said. "If that's what you want. But the law requires you to tell what you are going to use it for."

Miss Emily just stared at him, her head tilted back in order to look him eye for eye, until he looked away and went and got the arsenic and wrapped it up. The Negro delivery boy brought her the package; the druggist didn't come back. When she opened the package at home there was written on the box, under the skull and bones: "For rats."

IV

So the next day we all said, "She will kill herself"; and we said it would be the best thing. When she had first begun to be seen with Homer Barron, we had said, "She will marry him." Then we said, "She will persuade him yet," because Homer himself had remarked—he liked men, and it was known that he drank with the younger men in the Elk's Club—that he was not a marrying man. Later we said, "Poor Emily," behind the jalousies as they passed on Sunday afternoon in the glittering buggy, Miss Emily with her head high and Homer Barron with his hat cocked and a cigar in his teeth, reins and whip in a yellow glove.

Then some of the ladies began to say that it was a disgrace to the town and a bad example to the young people. The men did not want to interfere, but at last the ladies forced the Baptist minister—Miss Emily's people were Episcopal—to call upon her. He would never divulge what happened during that interview, but he refused to go back again. The next Sunday they again drove about the streets, and the following day the minister's wife wrote to Miss Emily's relations in Alabama.

So she had blood-kin under her roof again and we sat back to watch develop-   45
ments. At first nothing happened. Then we were sure that they were to be married. We learned that Miss Emily had been to the jeweler's and ordered a man's toilet set in silver, with the letters H. B. on each piece. Two days later we learned that she had bought a complete outfit of men's clothing, including a nightshirt, and we said, "They are married." We were really glad. We were glad because the two female cousins were even more Grierson than Miss Emily had ever been.

So we were not surprised when Homer Barron—the streets had been finished some time since—was gone. We were a little disappointed that there was not a public blowing-off, but we believed that he had gone on to prepare for

Miss Emily's coming, or to give her a chance to get rid of the cousins. (By that time it was a cabal, and we were all Miss Emily's allies to help circumvent the cousins.) Sure enough, after another week they departed. And, as we had expected all along, within three days Homer Barron was back in town. A neighbor saw the Negro man admit him at the kitchen door at dusk one evening.

And that was the last we saw of Homer Barron. And of Miss Emily for some time. The Negro man went in and out with the market basket, but the front door remained closed. Now and then we would see her at a window for a moment, as the men did that night when they sprinkled the lime, but for almost six months she did not appear on the streets. Then we knew that this was to be expected too; as if that quality of her father which had thwarted her woman's life so many times had been too virulent and too furious to die.

When we next saw Miss Emily, she had grown fat and her hair was turning gray. During the next few years it grew grayer and grayer until it attained an even pepper-and-salt iron-gray, when it ceased turning. Up to the day of her death at seventy-four it was still that vigorous iron-gray, like the hair of an active man.

From that time on her front door remained closed, save for a period of six or seven years, when she was about forty, during which she gave lessons in china-painting. She fitted up a studio in one of the downstairs rooms, where the daughters and grand-daughters of Colonel Sartoris' contemporaries were sent to her with the same regularity and in the same spirit that they were sent on Sundays with a twenty-five cent piece for the collection plate. Meanwhile her taxes had been remitted.

50   Then the newer generation became the backbone and the spirit of the town, and the painting pupils grew up and fell away and did not send their children to her with boxes of color and tedious brushes and pictures cut from the ladies' magazines. The front door closed upon the last one and remained closed for good. When the town got free postal delivery Miss Emily alone refused to let them fasten the metal numbers above her door and attach a mailbox to it. She would not listen to them.

Daily, monthly, yearly we watched the Negro grow grayer and more stooped, going in and out with the market basket. Each December we sent her a tax notice, which would be returned by the post office a week later, unclaimed. Now and then we would see her in one of the downstairs windows—she had evidently shut up the top floor of the house—like the carven torso of an idol in a niche, looking or not looking at us, we could never tell which. Thus she passed from generation to generation—dear, inescapable, impervious, tranquil, and perverse.

And so she died. Fell ill in the house filled with dust and shadows, with only a doddering Negro man to wait on her. We did not even know she was sick; we had long since given up trying to get any information from the Negro. He talked to no one, probably not even to her, for his voice had grown harsh and rusty, as if from disuse.

She died in one of the downstairs rooms, in a heavy walnut bed with a curtain, her gray head propped on a pillow yellow and moldy with age and lack of sunlight.

V

The Negro met the first of the ladies at the front door and let them in, with their hushed, sibilant voices and their quick, curious glances, and then he disappeared. He walked right through the house and out the back and was not seen again.

The two female cousins came at once. They held the funeral on the second 55 day, with the town coming to look at Miss Emily beneath a mass of bought flowers, with the crayon face of her father musing profoundly above the bier and the ladies sibilant and macabre; and the very old men—some in their brushed Confederate uniforms—on the porch and the lawn, talking of Miss Emily as if she had been a contemporary of theirs, believing that they had danced with her and courted her perhaps, confusing time with its mathematical progression, as the old do, to whom all the past is not a diminishing road, but, instead, a huge meadow which no winter ever quite touches, divided from them now by the narrow bottleneck of the most recent decade of years.

Already we knew that there was one room in that region above stairs which no one had seen in forty years, and which would have to be forced. They waited until Miss Emily was decently in the ground before they opened it.

The violence of breaking down the door seemed to fill this room with pervading dust. A thin, acrid pall as of the tomb seemed to lie everywhere upon this room decked and furnished as for a bridal: upon the valance curtains of faded rose color, upon the rose-shaded lights, upon the dressing table, upon the delicate array of crystal and the man's toilet things backed with tarnished silver, silver so tarnished that the monogram was obscured. Among them lay a collar and tie, as if they had just been removed, which, lifted, left upon the surface a pale crescent in the dust. Upon a chair hung the suit, carefully folded; beneath it the two mute shoes and the discarded socks.

The man himself lay in the bed.

For a long while we just stood there, looking down at the profound and fleshless grin. The body had apparently once lain in the attitude of an embrace, but now the long sleep that outlasts love, that conquers even the grimace of love, had cuckolded him. What was left of him, rotted beneath what was left of the nightshirt, had become inextricable from the bed in which he lay; and upon him and upon the pillow beside him lay that even coating of the patient and biding dust.

Then we noticed that in the second pillow was the indentation of a head. 60 One of us lifted something from it, and leaning forward, that faint and invisible dust dry and acrid in the nostrils, we saw a long strand of iron-gray hair.

1931

CHARLOTTE PERKINS GILMAN
(1860–1935)

The Yellow Wallpaper

Charlotte Anna Perkins was born in Hartford, Connecticut. After a painful, lonely childhood and several years of supporting herself as a governess, art teacher, and designer of greeting cards, Perkins married the artist Charles Stetson. Following her several extended periods of depression, Charles Stetson put his wife in the care of a doctor who, in her own words, "sent me home with the solemn advice to 'live as domestic a life as [. . .] possible,' to 'have but two hours' intellectual life a day,' and 'never to touch pen, brush, or pencil again' as long as I lived." Three months of this regimen brought her "near the borderline of utter mortal ruin" and inspired her masterpiece, "The Yellow Wallpaper." In 1900, she married George Houghton Gilman, having divorced Stetson in 1892. Her nonfiction works, springing from the early women's movement, include *Women and Economics* (1898) and *Man-Made World* (1911). She also wrote several utopian novels, including *Moving the Mountain* (1911) and *Herland* (1915).

I t is very seldom that mere ordinary people like John and myself secure ancestral halls for the summer.

A colonial mansion, a hereditary estate, I would say a haunted house, and reach the height of romantic felicity—but that would be asking too much of fate!

Still I will proudly declare that there is something queer about it.

Else, why should it be let so cheaply? And why have stood so long untenanted?

5   John laughs at me, of course, but one expects that in marriage.

John is practical in the extreme. He has no patience with faith, an intense horror of superstition, and he scoffs openly at any talk of things not to be felt and seen and put down in figures.

John is a physician, and *perhaps*—(I would not say it to a living soul, of course, but this is dead paper and a great relief to my mind—) *perhaps* that is one reason I do not get well faster.

You see he does not believe I am sick!

And what can one do?

10   If a physician of high standing, and one's own husband, assures friends and relatives that there is really nothing the matter with one but temporary nervous depression—a slight hysterical tendency—what is one to do?

My brother is also a physician, and also of high standing, and he says the same thing.

So I take phosphates or phosphites—whichever it is, and tonics, and journeys, and air, and exercise, and am absolutely forbidden to "work" until I am well again.

Personally, I disagree with their ideas.

Personally, I believe that congenial work, with excitement and change, would do me good.

But what is one to do?

I did write for a while in spite of them; but it *does* exhaust me a good deal—having to be so sly about it, or else meet with heavy opposition.

I sometimes fancy that in my condition if I had less opposition and more society and stimulus—but John says the very worst thing I can do is to think about my condition, and I confess it always makes me feel bad.

So I will let it alone and talk about the house.

The most beautiful place! It is quite alone, standing well back from the road, quite three miles from the village. It makes me think of English places that you read about, for there are hedges and walls and gates that lock, and lots of separate little houses for the gardeners and people.

There is a *delicious* garden! I never saw such a garden—large and shady, full of box-bordered paths, and lined with long grape-covered arbors with seats under them.

There were greenhouses, too, but they are all broken now.

There was some legal trouble, I believe, something about the heirs and co-heirs; anyhow, the place has been empty for years.

That spoils my ghostliness, I am afraid, but I don't care—there is something strange about the house—I can feel it.

I even said so to John one moonlight evening, but he said what I felt was a *draught*, and shut the window.

I get unreasonably angry with John sometimes. I'm sure I never used to be so sensitive. I think it is due to this nervous condition.

But John says if I feel so, I shall neglect proper self-control; so I take pains to control myself—before him, at least, and that makes me very tired.

I don't like our room a bit. I wanted one downstairs that opened on the piazza and had roses all over the window, and such pretty old-fashioned chintz hangings! but John would not hear of it.

He said there was only one window and not room for two beds, and no near room for him if he took another.

He is very careful and loving, and hardly lets me stir without special direction.

I have a schedule prescription for each hour in the day; he takes all care from me, and so I feel basely ungrateful not to value it more.

He said we came here solely on my account, that I was to have perfect rest and all the air I could get. "Your exercise depends on your strength, my dear," said he, "and your food somewhat on your appetite; but air you can absorb all the time." So we took the nursery at the top of the house.

It is a big, airy room, the whole floor nearly, with windows that look all ways, and air and sunshine galore. It was nursery first and then playroom and gymnasium, I should judge; for the windows are barred for little children, and there are rings and things in the walls.

The paint and paper look as if a boys' school had used it. It is stripped off—the paper—in great patches all around the head of my bed, about as far as I can reach, and in a great place on the other side of the room low down. I never saw a worse paper in my life.

One of those sprawling flamboyant patterns committing every artistic sin.

It is dull enough to confuse the eye in following, pronounced enough to constantly irritate and provoke study, and when you follow the lame uncertain

curves for a little distance they suddenly commit suicide—plunge off at outrageous angles, destroy themselves in unheard of contradictions.

The color is repellant, almost revolting; a smouldering unclean yellow,
strangely faded by the slow-turning sunlight.

It is a dull yet lurid orange in some places, a sickly sulphur tint in others.

No wonder the children hated it! I should hate it myself if I had to live in this
room long.

There comes John, and I must put this away,—he hates to have me write a
word.

40 We have been here two weeks, and I haven't felt like writing before, since that
first day.

I am sitting by the window now, up in this atrocious nursery, and there is
nothing to hinder my writing as much as I please, save lack of strength.

John is away all day, and even some nights when his cases are serious.

I am glad my case is not serious!

But these nervous troubles are dreadfully depressing.

45 John does not know how much I really suffer. He knows there is no *reason* to
suffer, and that satisfies him.

Of course it is only nervousness. It does weigh on me so not to do my duty in
any way!

I mean to be such a help to John, such a real rest and comfort, and here I am
a comparative burden already!

Nobody would believe what an effort it is to do what little I am able,—to
dress and entertain, and order things.

It is fortunate Mary is so good with the baby. Such a dear baby!

50 And yet I *cannot* be with him, it makes me so nervous.

I suppose John never was nervous in his life. He laughs at me so about this
wallpaper!

At first he meant to repaper the room, but afterwards he said that I was letting it get the better of me, and that nothing was worse for a nervous patient
than to give way to such fancies.

He said that after the wallpaper was changed it would be the heavy bedstead, and then the barred windows, and then that gate at the head of the stairs,
and so on.

"You know the place is doing you good," he said, "and really, dear, I don't care
to renovate the house just for a three months' rental."

55 "Then do let us go downstairs," I said, "there are such pretty rooms there."

Then he took me in his arms and called me a blessed little goose, and said he
would go down cellar, if I wished, and have it whitewashed into the bargain.

But he is right enough about the beds and windows and things.

It is an airy and comfortable room as any one need wish, and, of course, I
would not be so silly as to make him uncomfortable just for a whim.

I'm really getting quite fond of the big room, all but that horrid paper.

60 Out of one window I can see the garden, those mysterious deep-shaded
arbors, the riotous old-fashioned flowers, and bushes and gnarly trees.

Out of another I get a lovely view of the bay and a little private wharf belonging to the estate. There is a beautiful shaded lane that runs down there from

the house. I always fancy I see people walking in these numerous paths and arbors, but John has cautioned me not to give way to fancy in the least. He says that with my imaginative power and habit of story-making, a nervous weakness like mine is sure to lead to all manner of excited fancies, and that I ought to use my will and good sense to check the tendency. So I try.

I think sometimes that if I were only well enough to write a little it would relieve the press of ideas and rest me.

But I find I get pretty tired when I try.

It is so discouraging not to have any advice and companionship about my work. When I get really well, John says we will ask Cousin Henry and Julia down for a long visit; but he says he would as soon put fireworks in my pillow-case as to let me have those stimulating people about now.

I wish I could get well faster.   65

But I must not think about that. This paper looks to me as if it *knew* what a vicious influence it had!

There is a recurrent spot where the pattern lolls like a broken neck and two bulbous eyes stare at you upside down.

I get positively angry with the impertinence of it and the everlastingness. Up and down and sideways they crawl, and those absurd, unblinking eyes are everywhere. There is one place where two breadths didn't match, and the eyes go all up and down the line, one a little higher than the other.

I never saw so much expression in an inanimate thing before, and we all know how much expression they have! I used to lie awake as a child and get more entertainment and terror out of blank walls and plain furniture than most children could find in a toy-store.

I remember what a kindly wink the knobs of our big, old bureau used to   70 have, and there was one chair that always seemed like a strong friend.

I used to feel that if any of the other things looked too fierce I could always hop into that chair and be safe.

The furniture in this room is no worse than inharmonious, however, for we had to bring it all from downstairs. I suppose when this was used as a playroom they had to take the nursery things out, and no wonder! I never saw such ravages as the children have made here.

The wallpaper, as I said before, is torn off in spots, and it sticketh closer than a brother—they must have had perseverance as well as hatred.

Then the floor is scratched and gouged and splintered, the plaster itself is dug out here and there, and this great heavy bed which is all we found in the room, looks as if it had been through the wars.

But I don't mind it a bit—only the paper.   75

There comes John's sister. Such a dear girl as she is, and so careful of me! I must not let her find me writing.

She is a perfect and enthusiastic housekeeper, and hopes for no better profession. I verily believe she thinks it is the writing which made me sick!

But I can write when she is out, and see her a long way off from these windows.

There is one that commands the road, a lovely shaded winding road, and one that just looks off over the country. A lovely country, too, full of great elms and velvet meadows.

80   This wallpaper has a kind of sub-pattern in a different shade, a particularly irritating one, for you can only see it in certain lights, and not clearly then.

But in the places where it isn't faded and where the sun is just so—I can see a strange, provoking, formless sort of figure, that seems to skulk about behind that silly and conspicuous front design.

There's sister on the stairs!

Well, the Fourth of July is over! The people are all gone and I am tired out. John thought it might do me good to see a little company, so we just had mother and Nellie and the children down for a week.

Of course I didn't do a thing. Jennie sees to everything now.

85   But it tired me all the same.

John says if I don't pick up faster he shall send me to Weir Mitchell[1] in the fall.

But I don't want to go there at all. I had a friend who was in his hands once, and she says he is just like John and my brother, only more so!

Besides, it is such an undertaking to go so far.

I don't feel as if it was worth while to turn my hand over for anything, and I'm getting dreadfully fretful and querulous.

90   I cry at nothing, and cry most of the time.

Of course I don't when John is here, or anybody else, but when I am alone.

And I am alone a good deal just now. John is kept in town very often by serious cases, and Jennie is good and lets me alone when I want her to.

So I walk a little in the garden or down that lovely lane, sit on the porch under the roses, and lie down up here a good deal.

I'm getting really fond of the room in spite of the wallpaper. Perhaps *because* of the wallpaper.

95   It dwells in my mind so!

I lie here on this great immovable bed—it is nailed down, I believe—and follow that pattern about by the hour. It is as good as gymnastics, I assure you. I start, we'll say, at the bottom, down in the corner over there where it has not been touched, and I determine for the thousandth time that I *will* follow that pointless pattern to some sort of conclusion.

I know a little of the principle of design, and I know this thing was not arranged on any laws of radiation, or alternation, or repetition, or symmetry, or anything else that I ever heard of.

It is repeated, of course, by the breadths, but not otherwise.

Looked at in one way each breadth stands alone, the bloated curves and flourishes—a kind of "debased Romanesque" with *delirium tremens*—go waddling up and down in isolated columns of fatuity.

100   But, on the other hand, they connect diagonally, and the sprawling outlines run off in great slanting waves of optic horror, like a lot of wallowing seaweeds in full chase.

The whole thing goes horizontally, too, at least it seems so, and I exhaust myself in trying to distinguish the order of its going in that direction.

---

1. Silas Weir Mitchell (1829–1914), American physician, novelist, and specialist in nerve disorders, popularized the rest cure.

They have used a horizontal breadth for a frieze, and that adds wonderfully to the confusion.

There is one end of the room where it is almost intact, and there, when the crosslights fade and the low sun shines directly upon it, I can almost fancy radiation after all,—the interminable grotesque seem to form around a common center and rush off in headlong plunges of equal distraction.

It makes me tired to follow it. I will take a nap I guess.

I don't know why I should write this.   105

I don't want to.

I don't feel able.

And I know John would think it absurd. But I *must* say what I feel and think in some way—it is such a relief!

But the effort is getting to be greater than the relief.

Half the time now I am awfully lazy, and lie down ever so much.   110

John says I mustn't lose my strength, and has me take cod liver oil and lots of tonics and things, to say nothing of ale and wine and rare meat.

Dear John! He loves me very dearly, and hates to have me sick. I tried to have a real earnest reasonable talk with him the other day, and tell him how I wish he would let me go and make a visit to Cousin Henry and Julia.

But he said I wasn't able to go, nor able to stand it after I got there; and I did not make out a very good case for myself, for I was crying before I had finished.

It is getting to be a great effort for me to think straight. Just this nervous weakness I suppose.

And dear John gathered me up in his arms, and just carried me upstairs and   115
laid me on the bed, and sat by me and read to me till it tired my head.

He said I was his darling and his comfort and all he had, and that I must take care of myself for his sake, and keep well.

He says no one but myself can help me out of it, that I must use my will and self-control and not let any silly fancies run away with me.

There's one comfort, the baby is well and happy, and does not have to occupy this nursery with the horrid wallpaper.

If we had not used it, that blessed child would have! What a fortunate escape! Why, I wouldn't have a child of mine, an impressionable little thing, live in such a room for worlds.

I never thought of it before, but it is lucky that John kept me here after all, I   120
can stand it so much easier than a baby, you see.

Of course I never mention it to them any more—I am too wise,—but I keep watch of it all the same.

There are things in that paper that nobody knows but me, or ever will.

Behind that outside pattern the dim shapes get clearer every day.

It is always the same shape, only very numerous.

And it is like a woman stooping down and creeping about behind that pat-   125
tern. I don't like it a bit. I wonder—I begin to think—I wish John would take me away from here!

It is so hard to talk with John about my case, because he is so wise, and because he loves me so.

But I tried it last night.

It was moonlight. The moon shines in all around just as the sun does.

I hate to see it sometimes, it creeps so slowly, and always comes in by one window or another.

130   John was asleep and I hated to waken him, so I kept still and watched the moonlight on that undulating wallpaper till I felt creepy.

The faint figure behind seemed to shake the pattern, just as if she wanted to get out.

I got up softly and went to feel and see if the paper *did* move, and when I came back John was awake.

"What is it, little girl?" he said. "Don't go walking about like that—you'll get cold."

I thought it was a good time to talk, so I told him that I really was not gaining here, and that I wished he would take me away.

135   "Why, darling!" said he, "our lease will be up in three weeks, and I can't see how to leave before.

"The repairs are not done at home, and I cannot possibly leave town just now. Of course if you were in any danger, I could and would, but you really are better, dear, whether you can see it or not. I am a doctor, dear, and I know. You are gaining flesh and color, your appetite is better, I feel really much easier about you."

"I don't weigh a bit more," said I, "nor as much; and my appetite may be better in the evening when you are here, but it is worse in the morning when you are away!"

"Bless her little heart!" said he with a big hug, "she shall be as sick as she pleases! But now let's improve the shining hours by going to sleep, and talk about it in the morning!"

"And you won't go away?" I asked gloomily.

140   "Why, how can I, dear? It is only three weeks more and then we will take a nice little trip of a few days while Jennie is getting the house ready. Really dear you are better!"

"Better in body perhaps—" I began, and stopped short, for he sat up straight and looked at me with such a stern, reproachful look that I could not say another word.

"My darling," said he, "I beg of you, for my sake and for our child's sake, as well as for your own, that you will never for one instant let that idea enter your mind! There is nothing so dangerous, so fascinating, to a temperament like yours. It is a false and foolish fancy. Can you not trust me as a physician when I tell you so?"

So of course I said no more on that score, and we went to sleep before long. He thought I was asleep first, but I wasn't, and lay there for hours trying to decide whether that front pattern and the back pattern really did move together or separately.

On a pattern like this, by daylight, there is a lack of sequence, a defiance of law, that is a constant irritant to a normal mind.

145   The color is hideous enough, and unreliable enough, and infuriating enough, but the pattern is torturing.

You think you have mastered it, but just as you get well underway in following, it turns a back-somersault and there you are. It slaps you in the face, knocks you down, and tramples upon you. It is like a bad dream.

The outside pattern is a florid arabesque, reminding one of a fungus. If you can imagine a toadstool in joints, an interminable string of toadstools, budding and sprouting in endless convolutions—why, that is something like it.

That is, sometimes!

There is one marked peculiarity about this paper, a thing nobody seems to notice but myself, and that is that it changes as the light changes.

When the sun shoots in through the east window—I always watch for that first long, straight ray—it changes so quickly that I never can quite believe it. 150

That is why I watch it always.

By moonlight—the moon shines in all night when there is a moon—I wouldn't know it was the same paper.

At night in any kind of light, in twilight, candlelight, lamplight, and worst of all by moonlight, it becomes bars! The outside pattern I mean, and the woman behind it is as plain as can be.

I didn't realize for a long time what the thing was that showed behind, that dim sub-pattern, but now I am quite sure it is a woman.

By daylight she is subdued, quiet. I fancy it is the pattern that keeps her so 155 still. It is so puzzling. It keeps me quiet by the hour.

I lie down ever so much now. John says it is good for me, and to sleep all I can.

Indeed he started the habit by making me lie down for an hour after each meal.

It is a very bad habit I am convinced, for you see I don't sleep.

And that cultivates deceit, for I don't tell them I'm awake—O no!

The fact is I am getting a little afraid of John. 160

He seems very queer sometimes, and even Jennie has an inexplicable look.

It strikes me occasionally, just as a scientific hypothesis,—that perhaps it is the paper!

I have watched John when he did not know I was looking, and come into the room suddenly on the most innocent excuses, and I've caught him several times *looking at the paper*! And Jennie too. I caught Jennie with her hand on it once.

She didn't know I was in the room, and when I asked her in a quiet, a very quiet voice, with the most restrained manner possible, what she was doing with the paper—she turned around as if she had been caught stealing, and looked quite angry—asked me why I should frighten her so!

Then she said that the paper stained everything it touched, that she had 165 found yellow smooches on all my clothes and John's, and she wished we would be more careful!

Did not that sound innocent? But I know she was studying that pattern, and I am determined that nobody shall find it out but myself!

Life is very much more exciting now than it used to be. You see I have something more to expect, to look forward to, to watch. I really do eat better, and am more quiet than I was.

John is so pleased to see me improve! He laughed a little the other day, and said I seemed to be flourishing in spite of my wallpaper.

I turned it off with a laugh. I had no intention of telling him it was *because* of the wallpaper—he would make fun of me. He might even want to take me away.

170   I don't want to leave now until I have found it out. There is a week more, and I think that will be enough.

I'm feeling ever so much better! I don't sleep much at night, for it is so interesting to watch developments; but I sleep a good deal in the daytime.

In the daytime it is tiresome and perplexing.

There are always new shoots on the fungus, and new shades of yellow all over it. I cannot keep count of them, though I have tried conscientiously.

It is the strangest yellow, that wallpaper! It makes me think of all the yellow things I ever saw—not beautiful ones like buttercups, but old foul, bad yellow things.

175   But there is something else about that paper—the smell! I noticed it the moment we came into the room, but with so much air and sun it was not bad. Now we have had a week of fog and rain, and whether the windows are open or not, the smell is here.

It creeps all over the house.

I find it hovering in the dining-room, skulking in the parlor, hiding in the hall, lying in wait for me on the stairs.

It gets into my hair.

Even when I go to ride, if I turn my head suddenly and surprise it—there is that smell!

180   Such a peculiar odor, too! I have spent hours in trying to analyze it, to find what it smelled like.

It is not bad—at first, and very gentle, but quite the subtlest, most enduring odor I ever met.

In this damp weather it is awful, I wake up in the night and find it hanging over me.

It used to disturb me at first. I thought seriously of burning the house—to reach the smell.

But now I am used to it. The only thing I can think of that it is like is the *color* of the paper! A yellow smell.

185   There is a very funny mark on this wall, low down, near the mopboard. A streak that runs round the room. It goes behind every piece of furniture, except the bed, a long, straight, even *smooch*, as if it had been rubbed over and over.

I wonder how it was done and who did it, and what they did it for. Round and round and round—round and round and round—it makes me dizzy!

I really have discovered something at last.

Through watching so much at night, when it changes so, I have finally found out.

The front pattern *does* move—and no wonder! The woman behind shakes it!

190   Sometimes I think there are a great many women behind, and sometimes only one, and she crawls around fast, and her crawling shakes it all over.

Then in the very bright spots she keeps still, and in the very shady spots she just takes hold of the bars and shakes them hard.

And she is all the time trying to climb through. But nobody could climb through that pattern—it strangles so; I think that is why it has so many heads.

They get through, and then the pattern strangles them off and turns them upside down, and makes their eyes white!

If those heads were covered or taken off it would not be half so bad.

I think that woman gets out in the daytime!   195

And I'll tell you why—privately—I've seen her!

I can see her out of every one of my windows!

It is the same woman, I know, for she is always creeping, and most women do not creep by daylight.

I see her in that long shaded lane, creeping up and down. I see her in those dark grape arbors, creeping all around the garden.

I see her on that long road under the trees, creeping along, and when a car-   200
riage comes she hides under the blackberry vines.

I don't blame her a bit. It must be very humiliating to be caught creeping by daylight!

I always lock the door when I creep by daylight. I can't do it at night, for I know John would suspect something at once.

And John is so queer now, that I don't want to irritate him. I wish he would take another room! Besides, I don't want anybody to get that woman out at night but myself.

I often wonder if I could see her out of all the windows at once.

But, turn as fast as I can, I can only see out of one at one time.   205

And though I always see her, she *may* be able to creep faster than I can turn!

I have watched her sometimes away off in the open country, creeping as fast as a cloud shadow in a high wind.

If only that top pattern could be gotten off from the under one! I mean to try it, little by little.

I have found out another funny thing, but I shan't tell it this time! It does not do to trust people too much.

There are only two more days to get this paper off, and I believe John is   210
beginning to notice. I don't like the look in his eyes.

And I heard him ask Jennie a lot of professional questions about me. She had a very good report to give.

She said I slept a good deal in the daytime.

John knows I don't sleep very well at night, for all I'm so quiet!

He asked me all sorts of questions, too, and pretended to be very loving and kind.

As if I couldn't see through him!   215

Still, I don't wonder he acts so, sleeping under this paper for three months.

It only interests me, but I feel sure John and Jennie are secretly affected by it.

Hurrah! This is the last day, but it is enough. John is to stay in town over night, and won't be out until this evening.

Jennie wanted to sleep with me—the sly thing! but I told her I should undoubtedly rest better for a night all alone.

220   That was clever, for really I wasn't alone a bit! As soon as it was moonlight and that poor thing began to crawl and shake the pattern, I got up and ran to help her.

I pulled and she shook, I shook and she pulled, and before morning we had peeled off yards of that paper.

A strip about as high as my head and half around the room.

And then when the sun came and that awful pattern began to laugh at me, I declared I would finish it to-day!

We go away to-morrow, and they are moving all my furniture down again to leave things as they were before.

225   Jennie looked at the wall in amazement, but I told her merrily that I did it out of pure spite at the vicious thing.

She laughed and said she wouldn't mind doing it herself, but I must not get tired.

How she betrayed herself that time!

But I am here, and no person touches this paper but me,—not *alive!*

She tried to get me out of the room—it was too patent! But I said it was so quiet and empty and clean now that I believed I would lie down again and sleep all I could; and not to wake me even for dinner—I would call when I woke.

230   So now she is gone, and the servants are gone, and the things are gone, and there is nothing left but that great bedstead nailed down, with the canvas mattress we found on it.

We shall sleep downstairs to-night, and take the boat home to-morrow.

I quite enjoy the room, now it is bare again.

How those children did tear about here!

This bedstead is fairly gnawed!

235   But I must get to work.

I have locked the door and thrown the key down into the front path.

I don't want to go out, and I don't want to have anybody come in, till John comes.

I want to astonish him.

I've got a rope up here that even Jennie did not find. If that woman does get out, and tries to get away, I can tie her!

240   But I forgot I could not reach far without anything to stand on!

This bed will *not* move!

I tried to lift and push it until I was lame, and then I got so angry I bit off a little piece at one corner—but it hurt my teeth.

Then I peeled off all the paper I could reach standing on the floor. It sticks horribly and the pattern just enjoys it! All those strangled heads and bulbous eyes and waddling fungus growths just shriek with derision!

I am getting angry enough to do something desperate. To jump out of the window would be admirable exercise, but the bars are too strong even to try.

245   Besides I wouldn't do it. Of course not. I know well enough that a step like that is improper and might be misconstrued.

I don't like to *look* out of the windows even—there are so many of those creeping women, and they creep so fast.

I wonder if they all come out of that wallpaper as I did?

But I am securely fastened now by my well-hidden rope—you don't get *me* out in the road there!

I suppose I shall have to get back behind the pattern when it comes night, and that is hard!

It is so pleasant to be out in this great room and creep around as I please! 250

I don't want to go outside. I won't, even if Jennie asks me to.

For outside you have to creep on the ground, and everything is green instead of yellow.

But here I can creep smoothly on the floor, and my shoulder just fits in that long smooch around the wall, so I cannot lose my way.

Why there's John at the door!

It is no use, young man, you can't open it! 255

How he does call and pound!

Now he's crying for an axe.

It would be a shame to break down that beautiful door!

"John dear!" said I in the gentlest voice, "the key is down by the front steps, under a plantain leaf!"

That silenced him for a few moments. 260

Then he said—very quietly indeed, "Open the door, my darling!"

"I can't," said I. "The key is down by the front door under a plantain leaf!"

And then I said it again, several times, very gently and slowly, and said it so often that he had to go and see, and he got it of course, and came in. He stopped short by the door.

"What is the matter?" he cried. "For God's sake, what are you doing!"

I kept on creeping just the same, but I looked at him over my shoulder. 265

"I've got out at last," said I, "in spite of you and Jane. And I've pulled off most of the paper, so you can't put me back!"

Now why should that man have fainted? But he did, and right across my path by the wall, so that I had to creep over him every time!

1892

ERNEST HEMINGWAY
(1899–1961)

Hills Like White Elephants

Among the most distinctively American of writers, even if he rarely wrote about America, Ernest Hemingway grew up in an upscale Chicago suburb, but spent his summers on Lake Walloon in northern Michigan. Here, his physician father nurtured his love of hunting and fishing. Hemingway graduated from high school just two months after the United States entered World War I. Forbidden to enlist by his parents and uninterested in college, he worked as a reporter for the *Kansas City Star* before volunteering as a Red Cross ambulance driver. Badly wounded on the Italian front, he returned to the States and to journalism. Then, in 1921, he moved to Paris, France, entering the famed expatriate circle that included Ezra Pound, Gertrude Stein, and F. Scott

Fitzgerald. Two volumes of stories, *In Our Time* (1925) and *Men without Women* (1927), and two major novels, *The Sun Also Rises* (1926) and *A Farewell to Arms* (1929), established Hemingway's international reputation as both a masterful literary craftsman and a chief spokesman for the "Lost Generation," while later, less critically acclaimed books on topics such as bullfighting (*Death in the Afternoon*, 1932) and big-game hunting (*Green Hills of Africa*, 1935) helped confirm his status as an almost mythic figure, patron saint of what the *New York Times* called a "cult" of daring and danger. Hemingway supported the Loyalists in the Spanish Civil War—the subject of his novel *For Whom the Bell Tolls* (1940); served as a war correspondent during World War II; and survived two plane crashes and four marriages. Severely depressed and suffering an array of physical ailments, he took his own life shortly before his sixty-second birthday, only a few years after earning both a Pulitzer—for *The Old Man and the Sea* (1952)—and a Nobel (1954).

The hills across the valley of the Ebro[1] were long and white. On this side there was no shade and no trees and the station was between two lines of rails in the sun. Close against the side of the station there was the warm shadow of the building and a curtain, made of strings of bamboo beads, hung across the open door into the bar, to keep out flies. The American and the girl with him sat at a table in the shade, outside the building. It was very hot and the express from Barcelona would come in forty minutes. It stopped at this junction for two minutes and went on to Madrid.

"What should we drink?" the girl asked. She had taken off her hat and put it on the table.

"It's pretty hot," the man said.

"Let's drink beer."

5   "Dos cervezas," the man said into the curtain.

"Big ones?" a woman asked from the doorway.

"Yes. Two big ones."

The woman brought two glasses of beer and two felt pads. She put the felt pads and the beer glasses on the table and looked at the man and the girl. The girl was looking off at the line of hills. They were white in the sun and the country was brown and dry.

"They look like white elephants," she said.

10   "I've never seen one," the man drank his beer.

"No, you wouldn't have."

"I might have," the man said. "Just because you say I wouldn't have doesn't prove anything."

The girl looked at the bead curtain. "They've painted something on it," she said. "What does it say?"

"Anis del Toro. It's a drink."

15   "Could we try it?"

The man called "Listen" through the curtain. The woman came out from the bar.

"Four reales."[2]

"We want two Anis del Toro."

1. River in northern Spain.
2. Spanish coins.

"With water?"

"Do you want it with water?"   20

"I don't know," the girl said. "Is it good with water?"

"It's all right."

"You want them with water?" asked the woman.

"Yes, with water."

"It tastes like licorice," the girl said and put the glass down.   25

"That's the way with everything."

"Yes," said the girl. "Everything tastes of licorice. Especially all the things you've waited so long for, like absinthe."

"Oh, cut it out."

"You started it," the girl said. "I was being amused. I was having a fine time."

"Well, let's try and have a fine time."   30

"All right. I was trying. I said the mountains looked like white elephants. Wasn't that bright?"

"That was bright."

"I wanted to try this new drink. That's all we do, isn't it—look at things and try new drinks?"

"I guess so."

The girl looked across at the hills.   35

"They're lovely hills," she said. "They don't really look like white elephants. I just meant the coloring of their skin through the trees."

"Should we have another drink?"

"All right."

The warm wind blew the bead curtain against the table.

"The beer's nice and cool," the man said.   40

"It's lovely," the girl said.

"It's really an awfully simple operation, Jig," the man said. "It's not really an operation at all."

The girl looked at the ground the table legs rested on.

"I know you wouldn't mind it, Jig. It's really not anything. It's just to let the air in."

The girl did not say anything.   45

"I'll go with you and I'll stay with you all the time. They just let the air in and then it's all perfectly natural."

"Then what will we do afterward?"

"We'll be fine afterward. Just like we were before."

"What makes you think so?"

"That's the only thing that bothers us. It's the only thing that's made us 50
unhappy."

The girl looked at the bead curtain, put her hand out and took hold of two of the strings of beads.

"And you think then we'll be all right and be happy."

"I know we will. You don't have to be afraid. I've known lots of people that have done it."

"So have I," said the girl. "And afterward they were all so happy."

"Well," the man said, "if you don't want to you don't have to. I wouldn't have 55
you do it if you didn't want to. But I know it's perfectly simple."

"And you really want to?"

"I think it's the best thing to do. But I don't want you to do it if you don't really want to."

"And if I do it you'll be happy and things will be like they were and you'll love me?"

"I love you now. You know I love you."

60 "I know. But if I do it, then it will be nice again if I say things are like white elephants, and you'll like it?"

"I'll love it. I love it now but I just can't think about it. You know how I get when I worry."

"If I do it you won't ever worry?"

"I won't worry about that because it's perfectly simple."

"Then I'll do it. Because I don't care about me."

65 "What do you mean?"

"I don't care about me."

"Well, I care about you."

"Oh, yes. But I don't care about me. And I'll do it and then everything will be fine."

"I don't want you to do it if you feel that way."

70 The girl stood up and walked to the end of the station. Across, on the other side, were fields of grain and trees along the banks of the Ebro. Far away, beyond the river, were mountains. The shadow of a cloud moved across the field of grain and she saw the river through the trees.

"And we could have all this," she said. "And we could have everything and every day we make it more impossible."

"What did you say?"

"I said we could have everything."

"We can have everything."

75 "No, we can't."

"We can have the whole world."

"No, we can't."

"We can go everywhere."

"No, we can't. It isn't ours anymore."

80 "It's ours."

"No, it isn't. And once they take it away, you never get it back."

"But they haven't taken it away."

"We'll wait and see."

"Come on back in the shade," he said. "You mustn't feel that way."

85 "I don't feel any way," the girl said. "I just know things."

"I don't want you to do anything that you don't want to do—"

"Nor that isn't good for me," she said. "I know. Could we have another beer?"

"All right. But you've got to realize—"

"I realize," the girl said. "Can't we maybe stop talking?"

90 They sat down at the table and the girl looked across at the hills on the dry side of the valley and the man looked at her and at the table.

"You've got to realize," he said, "that I don't want you to do it if you don't want to. I'm perfectly willing to go through with it if it means anything to you."

"Doesn't it mean anything to you? We could get along."

"Of course it does. But I don't want anybody but you. I don't want any one else. And I know it's perfectly simple."

"Yes, you know it's perfectly simple."

"It's all right for you to say that, but I do know it." 95

"Would you do something for me now?"

"I'd do anything for you."

"Would you please please please please please please please stop talking?"

He did not say anything but looked at the bags against the wall of the station. There were labels on them from all the hotels where they had spent nights.

"But I don't want you to," he said, "I don't care anything about it." 100

"I'll scream," the girl said.

The woman came out through the curtains with two glasses of beer and put them down on the damp felt pads. "The train comes in five minutes," she said.

"What did she say?" asked the girl.

"That the train is coming in five minutes."

The girl smiled brightly at the woman, to thank her. 105

"I'd better take the bags over to the other side of the station," the man said. She smiled at him.

"All right. Then come back and we'll finish the beer."

He picked up the two heavy bags and carried them around the station to the other tracks. He looked up the tracks but could not see the train. Coming back, he walked through the barroom, where people waiting for the train were drinking. He drank an Anis at the bar and looked at the people. They were all waiting reasonably for the train. He went out through the bead curtain. She was sitting at the table and smiled at him.

"Do you feel better?" he asked.

"I feel fine," she said. "There's nothing wrong with me. I feel fine." 110

1927

FRANZ KAFKA

(1883–1924)

A Hunger Artist[1]

Born into a middle-class Jewish family in Prague, Franz Kafka earned a doctorate in law from the German University in that city and held an inconspicuous position in the civil service for many years. Emotionally and physically ill for the last seven or eight years of his short life, he died of tuberculosis in Vienna, never having married (though he was twice engaged to the same woman and lived with an actress in Berlin for some time before he died) and not having published his three major novels, *The Trial* (1925), *The Castle* (1926), and *Amerika* (1927). Indeed, he ordered his friend Max Brod to destroy them and other works he had left in manuscript. Fortunately, Brod did not; and not long after Kafka's death, his sometimes-dreamlike, sometimes-nightmarish work became known and admired all over the world. His stories in English translation are collected in *The Great Wall of China* (1933), *The Penal Colony* (1948), and *The Complete Stories* (1976).

---

1. Translated by Edwin and Willa Muir.

During these last decades the interest in professional fasting has markedly diminished. It used to pay very well to stage such great performances under one's own management, but today that is quite impossible. We live in a different world now. At one time the whole town took a lively interest in the hunger artist; from day to day of his fast the excitement mounted; everybody wanted to see him at least once a day; there were people who bought season tickets for the last few days and sat from morning till night in front of his small barred cage; even in the nighttime there were visiting hours, when the whole effect was heightened by torch flares; on fine days the cage was set out in the open air, and then it was the children's special treat to see the hunger artist; for their elders he was often just a joke that happened to be in fashion, but the children stood openmouthed, holding each other's hands for greater security, marveling at him as he sat there pallid in black tights, with his ribs sticking out so prominently, not even on a seat but down among straw on the ground, sometimes giving a courteous nod, answering questions with a constrained smile, or perhaps stretching an arm through the bars so that one might feel how thin it was, and then again withdrawing deep into himself, paying no attention to anyone or anything, not even to the all-important striking of the clock that was the only piece of furniture in his cage, but merely staring into vacancy with half-shut eyes, now and then taking a sip from a tiny glass of water to moisten his lips.

Besides casual onlookers there were also relays of permanent watchers selected by the public, usually butchers, strangely enough, and it was their task to watch the hunger artist day and night, three of them at a time, in case he should have some secret recourse to nourishment. This was nothing but a formality, instituted to reassure the masses, for the initiates knew well enough that during his fast the artist would never in any circumstances, not even under forcible compulsion, swallow the smallest morsel of food: the honor of his profession forbade it. Not every watcher, of course, was capable of understanding this, there were often groups of night watchers who were very lax in carrying out their duties and deliberately huddled together in a retired corner to play cards with great absorption, obviously intending to give the hunger artist the chance of a little refreshment, which they supposed he could draw from some private hoard. Nothing annoyed the artist more than such watchers; they made him miserable; they made his fast seem unendurable; sometimes he mastered his feebleness sufficiently to sing during their watch for as long as he could keep going, to show them how unjust their suspicions were. But that was of little use; they only wondered at his cleverness in being able to fill his mouth even while singing. Much more to his taste were the watchers who sat close up to the bars, who were not content with the dim night lighting of the hall but focused him in the full glare of the electric pocket torch[2] given them by the impresario. The harsh light did not trouble him at all, in any case he could never sleep properly, and he could always drowse a little, whatever the light, at any hour, even when the hall was thronged with noisy onlookers. He was quite happy at the prospect of spending a sleepless night with such watchers; he was ready to exchange jokes with them, to tell them stories out of his nomadic life, anything at all to keep them awake and demonstrate to them again that he had no eatables in his

2. Flashlight.

cage and that he was fasting as not one of them could fast. But his happiest moment was when the morning came and an enormous breakfast was brought them, at his expense, on which they flung themselves with the keen appetite of healthy men after a weary night of wakefulness. Of course there were people who argued that this breakfast was an unfair attempt to bribe the watchers, but that was going rather too far, and when they were invited to take on a night's vigil without a breakfast, merely for the sake of the cause, they made themselves scarce, although they stuck stubbornly to their suspicions.

Such suspicions, anyhow, were a necessary accompaniment to the profession of fasting. No one could possibly watch the hunger artist continuously, day and night, and so no one could produce first-hand evidence that the fast had really been rigorous and continuous; only the artist himself could know that, he was therefore bound to be the sole completely satisfied spectator of his own fast. Yet for other reasons he was never satisfied; it was not perhaps mere fasting that had brought him to such skeleton thinness that many people had regretfully to keep away from his exhibitions, because the sight of him was too much for them, perhaps it was dissatisfaction with himself that had worn him down. For he alone knew, what no other initiate knew, how easy it was to fast. It was the easiest thing in the world. He made no secret of this, yet people did not believe him, at the best they set him down as modest; most of them, however, thought he was out for publicity or else was some kind of cheat who found it easy to fast because he had discovered a way of making it easy, and then had the impudence to admit the fact, more or less. He had to put up with all that, and in the course of time had got used to it, but his inner dissatisfaction always rankled, and never yet, after any term of fasting—this must be granted to his credit—had he left the cage of his own free will. The longest period of fasting was fixed by his impresario at forty days,[3] beyond that term he was not allowed to go, not even in great cities, and there was good reason for it, too. Experience had proved that for about forty days the interest of the public could be stimulated by a steadily increasing pressure of advertisement, but after that the town began to lose interest, sympathetic support began notably to fall off; there were of course local variations as between one town and another or one country and another, but as a general rule forty days marked the limit. So on the fortieth day the flower-bedecked cage was opened, enthusiastic spectators filled the hall, a military band played, two doctors entered the cage to measure the results of the fast, which were announced through a megaphone, and finally two young ladies appeared, blissful at having been selected for the honor, to help the hunger artist down the few steps leading to a small table on which was spread a carefully chosen invalid repast. And at this very moment the artist always turned stubborn. True, he would entrust his bony arms to the outstretched helping hands of the ladies bending over him, but stand up he would not. Why stop fasting at this particular moment, after forty days of it? He had held out for a long time, an illimitably long time; why stop now, when he was in his best fasting form, or rather, not yet quite in his best fasting form? Why should he be cheated of the fame he would get for fasting longer, for being not only the record hunger artist

3. Common biblical length of time; in the New Testament, Jesus fasts for forty days in the desert and has visions of both God and the devil.

of all time, which presumably he was already, but for beating his own record by a performance beyond human imagination, since he felt that there were no limits to his capacity for fasting? His public pretended to admire him so much, why should it have so little patience with him; if he could endure fasting longer, why shouldn't the public endure it? Besides, he was tired, he was comfortable sitting in the straw, and now he was supposed to lift himself to his full height and go down to a meal the very thought of which gave him a nausea that only the presence of the ladies kept him from betraying, and even that with an effort. And he looked up into the eyes of the ladies who were apparently so friendly and in reality so cruel, and shook his head, which felt too heavy on its strengthless neck. But then there happened yet again what always happened. The impresario came forward, without a word—for the band made speech impossible—lifted his arms in the air above the artist, as if inviting Heaven to look down upon its creature here in the straw, this suffering martyr, which indeed he was, although in quite another sense; grasped him round the emaciated waist, with exaggerated caution, so that the frail condition he was in might be appreciated; and committed him to the care of the blenching ladies, not without secretly giving him a shaking so that his legs and body tottered and swayed. The artist now submitted completely; his head lolled on his breast as if it had landed there by chance; his body was hollowed out; his legs in a spasm of self-preservation clung close to each other at the knees, yet scraped on the ground as if it were not really solid ground, as if they were only trying to find solid ground; and the whole weight of his body, a feather-weight after all, relapsed onto one of the ladies, who, looking round for help and panting a little—this post of honor was not at all what she had expected it to be—first stretched her neck as far as she could to keep her face at least free from contact with the artist, when finding this impossible, and her more fortunate companion not coming to her aid but merely holding extended on her own trembling hand the little bunch of knuckle-bones that was the artist's, to the great delight of the spectators burst into tears and had to be replaced by an attendant who had long been stationed in readiness. Then came the food, a little of which the impresario managed to get between the artist's lips, while he sat in a kind of half-fainting trance, to the accompaniment of cheerful patter designed to distract the public's attention from the artist's condition; after that, a toast was drunk to the public, supposedly prompted by a whisper from the artist in the impresario's ear; the band confirmed it with a mighty flourish, the spectators melted away, and no one had any cause to be dissatisfied with the proceedings, no one except the hunger artist himself, he only, as always.

So he lived for many years, with small regular intervals of recuperation, in visible glory, honored by the world, yet in spite of that troubled in spirit, and all the more troubled because no one would take his trouble seriously. What comfort could he possibly need? What more could he possibly wish for? And if some good-natured person, feeling sorry for him, tried to console him by pointing out that his melancholy was probably caused by fasting, it could happen, especially when he had been fasting for some time, that he reacted with an outburst of fury and to the general alarm began to shake the bars of his cage like a wild animal. Yet the impresario had a way of punishing these outbreaks which he rather enjoyed putting into operation. He would apologize publicly for the artist's behavior, which was only to be excused, he admitted, because of the irritability caused by fasting, a condition hardly to be understood by well-fed people; then by natural transition he went on to mention the artist's equally incomprehensible boast that he could fast for much longer than he was doing; he praised the high ambition, the good will, the great self-denial undoubtedly implicit in such a statement; and then quite simply countered it by bringing out photographs, which were also on sale to the public, showing the artist on the fortieth day of a fast lying in bed almost dead from exhaustion. This perversion of the truth, familiar to the artist though it was, always unnerved him afresh and proved too much for him. What was a consequence of the premature ending of his fast was here presented as the cause of it! To fight against this lack of understanding, against a whole world of non-understanding, was impossible. Time and again in good faith he stood by the bars listening to the impresario, but as soon as the photographs appeared he always let go and sank with a groan back on to his straw, and the reassured public could once more come close and gaze at him.

A few years later when the witnesses of such scenes called them to mind, they ⁵ often failed to understand themselves at all. For meanwhile the aforementioned change in public interest had set in; it seemed to happen almost overnight; there may have been profound causes for it, but who was going to bother about that; at any rate the pampered hunger artist suddenly found himself deserted one fine day by the amusement seekers, who went streaming past him to other more favored attractions. For the last time the impresario hurried him over half Europe to discover whether the old interest might still survive here and there; all in vain; everywhere, as if by secret agreement, a positive revulsion from professional fasting was in evidence. Of course it could not really have sprung up so suddenly as all that, and many premonitory symptoms which had not been sufficiently remarked or suppressed during the rush and glitter of success now came retrospectively to mind, but it was now too late to take any countermeasures. Fasting would surely come into fashion again at some future date, yet that was no comfort for those living in the present. What, then, was the hunger artist to do? He had been applauded by thousands in his time and could hardly come down to showing himself in a street booth at village fairs, and as for adopting another profession, he was not only too old for that but too fanatically devoted to fasting. So he took leave of the impresario, his partner in an unparalleled career, and hired himself to a large circus; in order to spare his own feelings he avoided reading the conditions of his contract.

A large circus with its enormous traffic in replacing and recruiting men, animals and apparatus can always find a use for people at any time, even for a hunger artist, provided of course that he does not ask too much, and in this particular case anyhow it was not only the artist who was taken on but his famous and long-known name as well, indeed considering the peculiar nature of his performance, which was not impaired by advancing age, it could not be objected that here was an artist past his prime, no longer at the height of his professional skill, seeking a refuge in some quiet corner of a circus; on the contrary, the hunger artist averred that he could fast as well as ever, which was entirely credible, he even alleged that if he were allowed to fast as he liked, and this was at once promised him without more ado, he could astound the world by establishing a record never yet achieved, a statement which certainly provoked a smile among the other professionals, since it left out of account the change in public opinion, which the hunger artist in his zeal conveniently forgot.

He had not, however, actually lost his sense of the real situation and took it as a matter of course that he and his cage should be stationed, not in the middle of the ring as a main attraction, but outside, near the animal cages, on a site that was after all easily accessible. Large and gaily painted placards made a frame for the cage and announced what was to be seen inside it. When the public came thronging out in the intervals to see the animals, they could hardly avoid passing the hunger artist's cage and stopping there for a moment, perhaps they might even have stayed longer had not those pressing behind them in the narrow gangway, who did not understand why they should be held up on their way toward the excitements of the menagerie, made it impossible for anyone to stand gazing quietly for any length of time. And that was the reason why the hunger artist, who had of course been looking forward to these visiting hours as the main achievement of his life, began instead to shrink from them. At first he could hardly wait for the intervals; it was exhilarating to watch the crowds come streaming his way, until only too soon—not even the most obstinate self-deception, clung to almost consciously, could hold out against the fact—the conviction was borne in upon him that these people, most of them, to judge from their actions, again and again, without exception, were all on their way to the menagerie. And the first sight of them from the distance remained the best. For when they reached his cage he was at once deafened by the storm of shouting and abuse that arose from the two contending factions, which renewed themselves continuously, of those who wanted to stop and stare at him—he soon began to dislike them more than the others—not out of real interest but only out of obstinate self-assertiveness, and those who wanted to go straight on to the animals. When the first great rush was past, the stragglers came along, and these, whom nothing could have prevented from stopping to look at him as long as they had breath, raced past with long strides, hardly even glancing at him, in their haste to get to the menagerie in time. And all too rarely did it happen that he had a stroke of luck, when some father of a family fetched up before him with his children, pointed a finger at the hunger artist and explained at length what the phenomenon meant, telling stories of earlier years when he himself had watched similar but much more thrilling performances, and the children, still rather uncomprehending, since neither inside nor outside school had they been sufficiently prepared for this lesson—what did they care about fasting?—yet showed by the brightness of their intent eyes that new and better times might be coming. Perhaps, said the hunger artist to himself many a time, things would be a little better if his cage were set not quite so near the menagerie. That made it too easy for people to make their choice, to say nothing of what he suffered from the stench of the menagerie, the animals' restlessness by night, the carrying past of raw lumps of flesh for the beasts of prey, the roaring at feeding times, which depressed him continually. But he did not dare to lodge a complaint with the management; after all, he had the animals to thank for the troops of people who passed his cage, among whom there might always be one here and there to take an interest in him, and who could tell where they might seclude him if he called attention to his existence and thereby to the fact that, strictly speaking, he was only an impediment on the way to the menagerie.

A small impediment, to be sure, one that grew steadily less. People grew familiar with the strange idea that they could be expected, in times like these, to take an interest in a hunger artist, and with this familiarity the verdict went out against him. He might fast as much as he could, and he did so; but nothing could save him now, people passed him by. Just try to explain to anyone the art of fasting! Anyone who has no feeling for it cannot be made to understand it. The fine placards grew dirty and illegible, they were torn down; the little notice board telling the number of fast days achieved, which at first was changed carefully every day, had long stayed at the same figure, for after the first few weeks even this small task seemed pointless to the staff; and so the artist simply fasted on and on, as he had once dreamed of doing, and it was no trouble to him, just as he had always foretold, but no one counted the days, no one, not even the artist himself, knew what records he was already breaking, and his heart grew heavy. And when once in a time some leisurely passer-by stopped, made merry over the old figure on the board and spoke of swindling, that was in its way the stupidest lie ever invented by indifference and inborn malice, since it was not the hunger artist who was cheating; he was working honestly, but the world was cheating him of his reward.

Many more days went by, however, and that too came to an end. An overseer's eye fell on the cage one day and he asked the attendants why this perfectly good cage should be left standing there unused with dirty straw inside it; nobody knew, until one man, helped out by the notice board, remembered about the hunger artist. They poked into the straw with sticks and found him in it. "Are you still fasting?" asked the overseer. "When on earth do you mean to stop?" "Forgive me, everybody," whispered the hunger artist; only the overseer, who had his ear to the bars, understood him. "Of course," said the overseer, and tapped his forehead with a finger to let the attendants know what state the man was in, "we forgive you." "I always wanted you to admire my fasting," said the hunger artist. "We do admire it," said the overseer, affably. "But you shouldn't admire it," said the hunger artist. "Well, then we don't admire it," said the overseer, "but why shouldn't we admire it?" "Because I have to fast, I can't help it," said the hunger artist. "What a fellow you are," said the overseer, "and why can't you help it?" "Because," said the hunger artist, lifting his head a little and speaking, with his lips pursed, as if for a kiss, right into the overseer's ear, so that no syllable might be lost, "because I couldn't find the food I liked. If I had found it, believe me, I should have made no fuss and stuffed myself like you or anyone else." These were his last words, but in his dimming eyes remained the firm though no longer proud persuasion that he was still continuing to fast.

"Well, clear this out now!" said the overseer, and they buried the hunger artist, straw and all. Into the cage they put a young panther. Even the most insensitive felt it refreshing to see this wild creature leaping around the cage that had so long been dreary. The panther was all right. The food he liked was brought him without hesitation by the attendants; he seemed not even to miss his freedom; his noble body, furnished almost to the bursting point with all that it needed, seemed to carry freedom around with it too; somewhere in his jaws it seemed to lurk; and the joy of life streamed with such ardent passion from his throat that for the onlookers it was not easy to stand the shock of it. But they braced themselves, crowded round the cage, and did not want ever to move away.

1924

JAMAICA KINCAID
(b. 1949)
Girl

Raised in poverty by her homemaker mother and carpenter stepfather on the small Caribbean island of
Antigua, Elaine Potter Richardson was sent to the
United States to earn her own living at age seventeen, much like the protagonists of her first novels,
Annie John (1983) and *Lucy* (1990). Working as an au
pair and receptionist, she earned her high-school equivalency degree and studied pho-
tography at the New School for Social Research in New York and, briefly, Franconia
College in New Hampshire. Returning to New York, she took the name of a character in
a George Bernard Shaw play, at least in part out of resentment toward her mother, with
whom she had once been very close. After a short stint as a freelance journalist, Kincaid
worked as a regular contributor to the *New Yorker* from 1976 until 1995, in 1979 marrying its editor's son, composer Allen Shawn, with whom she would eventually move to
Bennington, Vermont, and raise two children. "Girl," her first published story, appeared
in the *New Yorker* in 1978 and was later republished in her first collection, *At the Bottom
of the River* (1983). Subsequent novels include *The Autobiography of My Mother* (1996),
paradoxically the least autobiographical of her books; *Mr. Potter* (2002), a fictionalized
account of her efforts to understand the biological father she never knew; and *See Now
Then* (2013). Kincaid's equally impressive nonfiction includes *My Brother* (1997), a memoir inspired by her youngest brother's death from AIDS, and *A Small Place* (1988), an
essay exploring the profound economic and psychological impact of Antigua's dependence on tourism. Divorced in 2002, Kincaid is currently Professor of African and African American Studies in Residence at Harvard.

W ash the white clothes on Monday and put them on the stone heap; wash
the color clothes on Tuesday and put them on the clothesline to dry; don't
walk barehead in the hot sun; cook pumpkin fritters in very hot sweet oil; soak
your little cloths right after you take them off; when buying cotton to make yourself a nice blouse, be sure that it doesn't have gum on it, because that way it won't
hold up well after a wash; soak salt fish overnight before you cook it; is it true that
you sing benna[1] in Sunday school?; always eat your food in such a way that it
won't turn someone else's stomach; on Sundays try to walk like a lady and not like
the slut you are so bent on becoming; don't sing benna in Sunday school; you
mustn't speak to wharf-rat boys, not even to give directions; don't eat fruits on the
street—flies will follow you; *but I don't sing benna on Sundays at all and never in
Sunday school*; this is how to sew on a button; this is how to make a buttonhole for
the button you have just sewed on; this is how to hem a dress when you see the
hem coming down and so to prevent yourself from looking like the slut I know
you are so bent on becoming; this is how you iron your father's khaki shirt so that
it doesn't have a crease; this is how you iron your father's khaki pants so that they

1. Caribbean folk-music style.

don't have a crease; this is how you grow okra—far from the house, because okra tree harbors red ants; when you are growing dasheen, make sure it gets plenty of water or else it makes your throat itch when you are eating it; this is how you sweep a corner; this is how you sweep a whole house; this is how you sweep a yard; this is how you smile to someone you don't like too much; this is how you smile to someone you don't like at all; this is how you smile to someone you like completely; this is how you set a table for tea; this is how you set a table for dinner; this is how you set a table for dinner with an important guest; this is how you set a table for lunch; this is how you set a table for breakfast; this is how to behave in the presence of men who don't know you very well, and this way they won't recognize immediately the slut I have warned you against becoming; be sure to wash every day, even if it is with your own spit; don't squat down to play marbles—you are not a boy, you know; don't pick people's flowers—you might catch something; don't throw stones at blackbirds, because it might not be a blackbird at all; this is how to make a bread pudding; this is how to make doukona;[2] this is how to make pepper pot; this is how to make a good medicine for a cold; this is how to make a good medicine to throw away a child before it even becomes a child; this is how to catch a fish; this is how to throw back a fish you don't like, and that way something bad won't fall on you; this is how to bully a man; this is how a man bullies you; this is how to love a man, and if this doesn't work there are other ways, and if they don't work don't feel too bad about giving up; this is how to spit up in the air if you feel like it, and this is how to move quick so that it doesn't fall on you; this is how to make ends meet; always squeeze bread to make sure it's fresh; *but what if the baker won't let me feel the bread?*; you mean to say that after all you are really going to be the kind of woman who the baker won't let near the bread?

1978, 1983

JHUMPA LAHIRI
(b. 1967)
Interpreter of Maladies

Born in London and raised in Rhode Island, Jhumpa Lahiri is the daughter of Bengali parents; much of her fiction addresses the difficulty of reconciling an Indian heritage with life in the United States. Lahiri earned a BA from Barnard College and several degrees from Boston University: an MA in English, an MFA in creative writing, an MA in comparative studies in literature and the arts, and a PhD in Renaissance studies. She has published many stories in well-known periodicals such as the *New Yorker* and won the 2000 Pulitzer Prize for her first collection, *Interpreter of Maladies* (1999), a best seller that has been translated into at least twenty-nine languages. Her second collection, *Unaccustomed Earth* (2008), debuted at the top of the *New York Times* best-seller list. Lahiri is also the author of two novels: *The Namesake* (2003) was

2. Spicy pudding, often made from plantain and wrapped in a plantain or banana leaf.

made into a film in 2006; *The Lowland* (2013) was short-listed for both the Man Booker Prize and the National Book Award.

At the tea stall Mr. and Mrs. Das bickered about who should take Tina to the toilet. Eventually Mrs. Das relented when Mr. Das pointed out that he had given the girl her bath the night before. In the rearview mirror Mr. Kapasi watched as Mrs. Das emerged slowly from his bulky white Ambassador, dragging her shaved, largely bare legs across the back seat. She did not hold the little girl's hand as they walked to the rest room.

They were on their way to see the Sun Temple at Konarak.[1] It was a dry, bright Saturday, the mid-July heat tempered by a steady ocean breeze, ideal weather for sightseeing. Ordinarily Mr. Kapasi would not have stopped so soon along the way, but less than five minutes after he'd picked up the family that morning in front of Hotel Sandy Villa, the little girl had complained. The first thing Mr. Kapasi had noticed when he saw Mr. and Mrs. Das, standing with their children under the portico of the hotel, was that they were very young, perhaps not even thirty. In addition to Tina they had two boys, Ronny and Bobby, who appeared very close in age and had teeth covered in a network of flashing silver wires. The family looked Indian but dressed as foreigners did, the children in stiff, brightly colored clothing and caps with translucent visors. Mr. Kapasi was accustomed to foreign tourists; he was assigned to them regularly because he could speak English. Yesterday he had driven an elderly couple from Scotland, both with spotted faces and fluffy white hair so thin it exposed their sunburnt scalps. In comparison, the tanned, youthful faces of Mr. and Mrs. Das were all the more striking. When he'd introduced himself, Mr. Kapasi had pressed his palms together in greeting, but Mr. Das squeezed hands like an American so that Mr. Kapasi felt it in his elbow. Mrs. Das, for her part, had flexed one side of her mouth, smiling dutifully at Mr. Kapasi, without displaying any interest in him.

As they waited at the tea stall, Ronny, who looked like the older of the two boys, clambered suddenly out of the back seat, intrigued by a goat tied to a stake in the ground.

"Don't touch it," Mr. Das said. He glanced up from his paperback tour book, which said "INDIA" in yellow letters and looked as if it had been published abroad. His voice, somehow tentative and a little shrill, sounded as though it had not yet settled into maturity.

5   "I want to give it a piece of gum," the boy called back as he trotted ahead.

Mr. Das stepped out of the car and stretched his legs by squatting briefly to the ground. A clean-shaven man, he looked exactly like a magnified version of Ronny. He had a sapphire blue visor, and was dressed in shorts, sneakers, and a T-shirt. The camera slung around his neck, with an impressive telephoto lens and numerous buttons and markings, was the only complicated thing he wore.

---

1. In paragraphs 91–98, the story provides an accurate history and description of the Sun Temple at Konark (or Konarak), still a pilgrimage as well as tourist site near the east coast in the Orissa region of India. According to legend, the temple was built because Samba, son of Lord Krishna, was cured of leprosy by Surya, the sun god.

He frowned, watching as Ronny rushed toward the goat, but appeared to have no intention of intervening. "Bobby, make sure that your brother doesn't do anything stupid."

"I don't feel like it," Bobby said, not moving. He was sitting in the front seat beside Mr. Kapasi, studying a picture of the elephant god taped to the glove compartment.

"No need to worry," Mr. Kapasi said. "They are quite tame." Mr. Kapasi was forty-six years old, with receding hair that had gone completely silver, but his butterscotch complexion and his unlined brow, which he treated in spare moments to dabs of lotus-oil balm, made it easy to imagine what he must have looked like at an earlier age. He wore gray trousers and a matching jacket-style shirt, tapered at the waist, with short sleeves and a large pointed collar, made of a thin but durable synthetic material. He had specified both the cut and the fabric to his tailor—it was his preferred uniform for giving tours because it did not get crushed during his long hours behind the wheel. Through the windshield he watched as Ronny circled around the goat, touched it quickly on its side, then trotted back to the car.

"You left India as a child?" Mr. Kapasi asked when Mr. Das had settled once again into the passenger seat.

"Oh, Mina and I were both born in America," Mr. Das announced with an air of sudden confidence. "Born and raised. Our parents live here now, in Assansol.[2] They retired. We visit them every couple years." He turned to watch as the little girl ran toward the car, the wide purple bows of her sundress flopping on her narrow brown shoulders. She was holding to her chest a doll with yellow hair that looked as if it had been chopped, as a punitive measure, with a pair of dull scissors. "This is Tina's first trip to India, isn't it, Tina?"

"I don't have to go to the bathroom anymore," Tina announced.

"Where's Mina?" Mr. Das asked.

Mr. Kapasi found it strange that Mr. Das should refer to his wife by her first name when speaking to the little girl. Tina pointed to where Mrs. Das was purchasing something from one of the shirtless men who worked at the tea stall. Mr. Kapasi heard one of the shirtless men sing a phrase from a popular Hindi love song as Mrs. Das walked back to the car, but she did not appear to understand the words of the song, for she did not express irritation, or embarrassment, or react in any other way to the man's declarations.

He observed her. She wore a red-and-white-checkered skirt that stopped above her knees, slip-on shoes with a square wooden heel, and a close-fitting blouse styled like a man's undershirt. The blouse was decorated at chest-level with a calico appliqué in the shape of a strawberry. She was a short woman, with small hands like paws, her frosty pink fingernails painted to match her lips, and was slightly plump in her figure. Her hair, shorn only a little longer than her husband's, was parted far to one side. She was wearing large dark brown sunglasses with a pinkish tint to them, and carried a big straw bag, almost as big as her torso, shaped like a bowl, with a water bottle poking out of it. She walked slowly,

10

2. Or Asonsol, a city in northeastern India, not far from Calcutta and about three hundred miles from Puri, the coastal city in Orissa that the Das family is visiting. Puri is both a tourist resort and a Hindu holy city, said to be dominated by the forces of both the gods and humanity.

carrying some puffed rice tossed with peanuts and chili peppers in a large packet made from newspapers. Mr. Kapasi turned to Mr. Das.

15   "Where in America do you live?"

"New Brunswick, New Jersey."

"Next to New York?"

"Exactly. I teach middle school there."

"What subject?"

20   "Science. In fact, every year I take my students on a trip to the Museum of Natural History in New York City. In a way we have a lot in common, you could say, you and I. How long have you been a tour guide, Mr. Kapasi?"

"Five years."

Mrs. Das reached the car. "How long's the trip?" she asked, shutting the door.

"About two and a half hours," Mr. Kapasi replied.

At this Mrs. Das gave an impatient sigh, as if she had been traveling her whole life without pause. She fanned herself with a folded Bombay film magazine written in English.

25   "I thought that the Sun Temple is only eighteen miles north of Puri," Mr. Das said, tapping on the tour book.

"The roads to Konarak are poor. Actually it is a distance of fifty-two miles," Mr. Kapasi explained.

Mr. Das nodded, readjusting the camera strap where it had begun to chafe the back of his neck.

Before starting the ignition, Mr. Kapasi reached back to make sure the cranklike locks on the inside of each of the back doors were secured. As soon as the car began to move the little girl began to play with the lock on her side, clicking it with some effort forward and backward, but Mrs. Das said nothing to stop her. She sat a bit slouched at one end of the back seat, not offering her puffed rice to anyone. Ronny and Tina sat on either side of her, both snapping bright green gum.

"Look," Bobby said as the car began to gather speed. He pointed with his finger to the tall trees that lined the road. "Look."

30   "Monkeys!" Ronny shrieked. "Wow!"

They were seated in groups along the branches, with shining black faces, silver bodies, horizontal eyebrows, and crested heads. Their long gray tails dangled like a series of ropes among the leaves. A few scratched themselves with black leathery hands, or swung their feet, staring as the car passed.

"We call them the hanuman," Mr. Kapasi said. "They are quite common in the area."

As soon as he spoke, one of the monkeys leaped into the middle of the road, causing Mr. Kapasi to brake suddenly. Another bounced onto the hood of the car, then sprang away. Mr. Kapasi beeped his horn. The children began to get excited, sucking in their breath and covering their faces partly with their hands. They had never seen monkeys outside of a zoo, Mr. Das explained. He asked Mr. Kapasi to stop the car so that he could take a picture.

While Mr. Das adjusted his telephoto lens, Mrs. Das reached into her straw bag and pulled out a bottle of colorless nail polish, which she proceeded to stroke on the tip of her index finger.

The little girl stuck out a hand. "Mine too. Mommy, do mine too."   35

"Leave me alone," Mrs. Das said, blowing on her nail and turning her body slightly. "You're making me mess up."

The little girl occupied herself by buttoning and unbuttoning a pinafore on the doll's plastic body.

"All set," Mr. Das said, replacing the lens cap.

The car rattled considerably as it raced along the dusty road, causing them all to pop up from their seats every now and then, but Mrs. Das continued to polish her nails. Mr. Kapasi eased up on the accelerator, hoping to produce a smoother ride. When he reached for the gearshift the boy in front accommodated him by swinging his hairless knees out of the way. Mr. Kapasi noted that this boy was slightly paler than the other children. "Daddy, why is the driver sitting on the wrong side in this car, too?" the boy asked.

"They all do that here, dummy," Ronny said.   40

"Don't call your brother a dummy," Mr. Das said. He turned to Mr. Kapasi. "In America, you know . . . it confuses them."

"Oh yes, I am well aware," Mr. Kapasi said. As delicately as he could, he shifted gears again, accelerating as they approached a hill in the road. "I see it on *Dallas*, the steering wheels are on the left-hand side."

"What's *Dallas*?" Tina asked, banging her now naked doll on the seat behind Mr. Kapasi.

"It went off the air," Mr. Das explained. "It's a television show."[3]

They were all like siblings, Mr. Kapasi thought as they passed a row of date   45 trees. Mr. and Mrs. Das behaved like an older brother and sister, not parents. It seemed that they were in charge of the children only for the day; it was hard to believe they were regularly responsible for anything other than themselves. Mr. Das tapped on his lens cap, and his tour book, dragging his thumbnail occasionally across the pages so that they made a scraping sound. Mrs. Das continued to polish her nails. She had still not removed her sunglasses. Every now and then Tina renewed her plea that she wanted her nails done, too, and so at one point Mrs. Das flicked a drop of polish on the little girl's finger before depositing the bottle back inside her straw bag.

"Isn't this an air-conditioned car?" she asked, still blowing on her hand. The window on Tina's side was broken and could not be rolled down.

"Quit complaining," Mr. Das said. "It isn't so hot."

"I told you to get a car with air-conditioning," Mrs. Das continued. "Why do you do this, Raj, just to save a few stupid rupees. What are you saving us, fifty cents?"

Their accents sounded just like the ones Mr. Kapasi heard on American television programs, though not like the ones on *Dallas*.

"Doesn't it get tiresome, Mr. Kapasi, showing people the same thing every   50 day?" Mr. Das asked, rolling down his own window all the way. "Hey, do you mind stopping the car. I just want to get a shot of this guy."

Mr. Kapasi pulled over to the side of the road as Mr. Das took a picture of a barefoot man, his head wrapped in a dirty turban, seated on top of a cart of

3. Internationally popular American television show (1978–91) featuring the rich, dysfunctional Ewing family of Dallas.

grain sacks pulled by a pair of bullocks. Both the man and the bullocks were emaciated. In the back seat Mrs. Das gazed out another window, at the sky, where nearly transparent clouds passed quickly in front of one another.

"I look forward to it, actually," Mr. Kapasi said as they continued on their way. "The Sun Temple is one of my favorite places. In that way it is a reward for me. I give tours on Fridays and Saturdays only. I have another job during the week."

"Oh? Where?" Mr. Das asked.

"I work in a doctor's office."

55 "You're a doctor?"

"I am not a doctor. I work with one. As an interpreter."

"What does a doctor need an interpreter for?"

"He has a number of Gujarati patients. My father was Gujarati, but many people do not speak Gujarati in this area,[4] including the doctor. And so the doctor asked me to work in his office, interpreting what the patients say."

"Interesting. I've never heard of anything like that," Mr. Das said.

60 Mr. Kapasi shrugged. "It is a job like any other."

"But so romantic," Mrs. Das said dreamily, breaking her extended silence. She lifted her pinkish brown sunglasses and arranged them on top of her head like a tiara. For the first time, her eyes met Mr. Kapasi's in the rearview mirror: pale, a bit small, their gaze fixed but drowsy.

Mr. Das craned to look at her. "What's so romantic about it?"

"I don't know. Something." She shrugged, knitting her brows together for an instant. "Would you like a piece of gum, Mr. Kapasi?" she asked brightly. She reached into her straw bag and handed him a small square wrapped in green-and-white-striped paper. As soon as Mr. Kapasi put the gum in his mouth a thick sweet liquid burst onto his tongue.

"Tell us more about your job, Mr. Kapasi," Mrs. Das said.

65 "What would you like to know, madame?"

"I don't know," she shrugged, munching on some puffed rice and licking the mustard oil from the corners of her mouth. "Tell us a typical situation." She settled back in her seat, her head tilted in a patch of sun, and closed her eyes. "I want to picture what happens."

"Very well. The other day a man came in with a pain in his throat."

"Did he smoke cigarettes?"

"No. It was very curious. He complained that he felt as if there were long pieces of straw stuck in his throat. When I told the doctor he was able to prescribe the proper medication."

70 "That's so neat."

"Yes," Mr. Kapasi agreed after some hesitation.

"So these patients are totally dependent on you," Mrs. Das said. She spoke slowly, as if she were thinking aloud. "In a way, more dependent on you than the doctor."

"How do you mean? How could it be?"

---

4. Gujarat is a northwestern region of India, on the Arabian Sea. Mr. Kapasi speaks several of India's disparate regional languages—those of Bengal and Orissa, near where he lives, and Gujarati, from the opposite coast—along with the more widespread Hindi and English.

"Well, for example, you could tell the doctor that the pain felt like a burning, not straw. The patient would never know what you had told the doctor, and the doctor wouldn't know that you had told the wrong thing. It's a big responsibility."

"Yes, a big responsibility you have there, Mr. Kapasi," Mr. Das agreed. 75

Mr. Kapasi had never thought of his job in such complimentary terms. To him it was a thankless occupation. He found nothing noble in interpreting people's maladies, assiduously translating the symptoms of so many swollen bones, countless cramps of bellies and bowels, spots on people's palms that changed color, shape, or size. The doctor, nearly half his age, had an affinity for bell-bottom trousers and made humorless jokes about the Congress party.[5] Together they worked in a stale little infirmary where Mr. Kapasi's smartly tailored clothes clung to him in the heat, in spite of the blackened blades of a ceiling fan churning over their heads.

The job was a sign of his failings. In his youth he'd been a devoted scholar of foreign languages, the owner of an impressive collection of dictionaries. He had dreamed of being an interpreter for diplomats and dignitaries, resolving conflicts between people and nations, settling disputes of which he alone could understand both sides. He was a self-educated man. In a series of notebooks, in the evenings before his parents settled his marriage, he had listed the common etymologies of words, and at one point in his life he was confident that he could converse, if given the opportunity, in English, French, Russian, Portuguese, and Italian, not to mention Hindi, Bengali, Orissi, and Gujarati. Now only a handful of European phrases remained in his memory, scattered words for things like saucers and chairs. English was the only non-Indian language he spoke fluently anymore. Mr. Kapasi knew it was not a remarkable talent. Sometimes he feared that his children knew better English than he did, just from watching television. Still, it came in handy for the tours.

He had taken the job as an interpreter after his first son, at the age of seven, contracted typhoid—that was how he had first made the acquaintance of the doctor. At the time Mr. Kapasi had been teaching English in a grammar school, and he bartered his skills as an interpreter to pay the increasingly exorbitant medical bills. In the end the boy had died one evening in his mother's arms, his limbs burning with fever, but then there was the funeral to pay for, and the other children who were born soon enough, and the newer, bigger house, and the good schools and tutors, and the fine shoes and the television, and the countless other ways he tried to console his wife and to keep her from crying in her sleep, and so when the doctor offered to pay him twice as much as he earned at the grammar school, he accepted. Mr. Kapasi knew that his wife had little regard for his career as an interpreter. He knew it reminded her of the son she'd lost, and that she resented the other lives he helped, in his own small way, to save. If ever she referred to his position, she used the phrase "doctor's assistant," as if the process of interpretation were equal to taking someone's temperature, or changing a bedpan. She never asked him about

5. The Indian National Congress party, founded in 1885, led the movement for independence from Britain (gained in 1947) through the successive leadership of Mohandas Gandhi (1869–1948) and Jawaharlal Nehru (1889–1964). The party divided and subdivided, but a faction once led by Indira Gandhi (1917–84) dominated through the 1980s and much of the 1990s, despite being constantly accused of corruption and the use of violent tactics.

the patients who came to the doctor's office, or said that his job was a big responsibility.

For this reason it flattered Mr. Kapasi that Mrs. Das was so intrigued by his job. Unlike his wife, she had reminded him of its intellectual challenges. She had also used the word "romantic." She did not behave in a romantic way toward her husband, and yet she had used the word to describe him. He wondered if Mr. and Mrs. Das were a bad match, just as he and his wife were. Perhaps they, too, had little in common apart from three children and a decade of their lives. The signs he recognized from his own marriage were there—the bickering, the indifference, the protracted silences. Her sudden interest in him, an interest she did not express in either her husband or her children, was mildly intoxicating. When Mr. Kapasi thought once again about how she had said "romantic," the feeling of intoxication grew.

80   He began to check his reflection in the rearview mirror as he drove, feeling grateful that he had chosen the gray suit that morning and not the brown one, which tended to sag a little in the knees. From time to time he glanced through the mirror at Mrs. Das. In addition to glancing at her face he glanced at the strawberry between her breasts, and the golden brown hollow in her throat. He decided to tell Mrs. Das about another patient, and another: the young woman who had complained of a sensation of raindrops in her spine, the gentleman whose birthmark had begun to sprout hairs. Mrs. Das listened attentively, stroking her hair with a small plastic brush that resembled an oval bed of nails, asking more questions, for yet another example. The children were quiet, intent on spotting more monkeys in the trees, and Mr. Das was absorbed by his tour book, so it seemed like a private conversation between Mr. Kapasi and Mrs. Das. In this manner the next half hour passed, and when they stopped for lunch at a roadside restaurant that sold fritters and omelette sandwiches, usually something Mr. Kapasi looked forward to on his tours so that he could sit in peace and enjoy some hot tea, he was disappointed. As the Das family settled together under a magenta umbrella fringed with white and orange tassels, and placed their orders with one of the waiters who marched about in tricornered caps, Mr. Kapasi reluctantly headed toward a neighboring table.

"Mr. Kapasi, wait. There's room here," Mrs. Das called out. She gathered Tina onto her lap, insisting that he accompany them. And so, together, they had bottled mango juice and sandwiches and plates of onions and potatoes deep-fried in graham-flour batter. After finishing two omelette sandwiches Mr. Das took more pictures of the group as they ate.

"How much longer?" he asked Mr. Kapasi as he paused to load a new roll of film in the camera.

"About half an hour more."

By now the children had gotten up from the table to look at more monkeys perched in a nearby tree, so there was a considerable space between Mrs. Das and Mr. Kapasi. Mr. Das placed the camera to his face and squeezed one eye shut, his tongue exposed at one corner of his mouth. "This looks funny. Mina, you need to lean in closer to Mr. Kapasi."

85   She did. He could smell a scent on her skin, like a mixture of whiskey and rosewater. He worried suddenly that she could smell his perspiration, which he

knew had collected beneath the synthetic material of his shirt. He polished off his mango juice in one gulp and smoothed his silver hair with his hands. A bit of the juice dripped onto his chin. He wondered if Mrs. Das had noticed.

She had not. "What's your address, Mr. Kapasi?" she inquired, fishing for something inside her straw bag.

"You would like my address?"

"So we can send you copies," she said. "Of the pictures." She handed him a scrap of paper which she had hastily ripped from a page of her film magazine. The blank portion was limited, for the narrow strip was crowded by lines of text and a tiny picture of a hero and heroine embracing under a eucalyptus tree.

The paper curled as Mr. Kapasi wrote his address in clear, careful letters. She would write to him, asking about his days interpreting at the doctor's office, and he would respond eloquently, choosing only the most entertaining anecdotes, ones that would make her laugh out loud as she read them in her house in New Jersey. In time she would reveal the disappointment of her marriage, and he his. In this way their friendship would grow, and flourish. He would possess a picture of the two of them, eating fried onions under a magenta umbrella, which he would keep, he decided, safely tucked between the pages of his Russian grammar. As his mind raced, Mr. Kapasi experienced a mild and pleasant shock. It was similar to a feeling he used to experience long ago when, after months of translating with the aid of a dictionary, he would finally read a passage from a French novel, or an Italian sonnet, and understand the words, one after another, unencumbered by his own efforts. In those moments Mr. Kapasi used to believe that all was right with the world, that all struggles were rewarded, that all of life's mistakes made sense in the end. The promise that he would hear from Mrs. Das now filled him with the same belief.

When he finished writing his address Mr. Kapasi handed her the paper, but 90 as soon as he did so he worried that he had either misspelled his name, or accidentally reversed the numbers of his postal code. He dreaded the possibility of a lost letter, the photograph never reaching him, hovering somewhere in Orissa, close but ultimately unattainable. He thought of asking for the slip of paper again, just to make sure he had written his address accurately, but Mrs. Das had already dropped it into the jumble of her bag.

They reached Konarak at two-thirty. The temple, made of sandstone, was a massive pyramid-like structure in the shape of a chariot. It was dedicated to the great master of life, the sun, which struck three sides of the edifice as it made its journey each day across the sky. Twenty-four giant wheels were carved on the north and south sides of the plinth. The whole thing was drawn by a team of seven horses, speeding as if through the heavens. As they approached, Mr. Kapasi explained that the temple had been built between A.D. 1243 and 1255, with the efforts of twelve hundred artisans, by the great ruler of the Ganga dynasty, King Narasimhadeva the First, to commemorate his victory against the Muslim army.

"It says the temple occupies about a hundred and seventy acres of land," Mr. Das said, reading from his book.

"It's like a desert," Ronny said, his eyes wandering across the sand that stretched on all sides beyond the temple.

"The Chandrabhaga River once flowed one mile north of here. It is dry now," Mr. Kapasi said, turning off the engine.

95 They got out and walked toward the temple, posing first for pictures by the pair of lions that flanked the steps. Mr. Kapasi led them next to one of the wheels of the chariot, higher than any human being, nine feet in diameter.

"'The wheels are supposed to symbolize the wheel of life,'" Mr. Das read. "'They depict the cycle of creation, preservation, and achievement of realization.' Cool." He turned the page of his book. "'Each wheel is divided into eight thick and thin spokes, dividing the day into eight equal parts. The rims are carved with designs of birds and animals, whereas the medallions in the spokes are carved with women in luxurious poses, largely erotic in nature.'"

What he referred to were the countless friezes of entwined naked bodies, making love in various positions, women clinging to the necks of men, their knees wrapped eternally around their lovers' thighs. In addition to these were assorted scenes from daily life, of hunting and trading, of deer being killed with bows and arrows and marching warriors holding swords in their hands.

It was no longer possible to enter the temple, for it had filled with rubble years ago, but they admired the exterior, as did all the tourists Mr. Kapasi brought there, slowly strolling along each of its sides. Mr. Das trailed behind, taking pictures. The children ran ahead, pointing to figures of naked people, intrigued in particular by the Nagamithunas, the half-human, half-serpentine couples who were said, Mr. Kapasi told them, to live in the deepest waters of the sea. Mr. Kapasi was pleased that they liked the temple, pleased especially that it appealed to Mrs. Das. She stopped every three or four paces, staring silently at the carved lovers, and the processions of elephants, and the topless female musicians beating on two-sided drums.

Though Mr. Kapasi had been to the temple countless times, it occurred to him, as he, too, gazed at the topless women, that he had never seen his own wife fully naked. Even when they had made love she kept the panels of her blouse hooked together, the string of her petticoat knotted around her waist. He had never admired the backs of his wife's legs the way he now admired those of Mrs. Das, walking as if for his benefit alone. He had, of course, seen plenty of bare limbs before, belonging to the American and European ladies who took his tours. But Mrs. Das was different. Unlike the other women, who had an interest only in the temple, and kept their noses buried in a guidebook, or their eyes behind the lens of a camera, Mrs. Das had taken an interest in him.

100 Mr. Kapasi was anxious to be alone with her, to continue their private conversation, yet he felt nervous to walk at her side. She was lost behind her sunglasses, ignoring her husband's requests that she pose for another picture, walking past her children as if they were strangers. Worried that he might disturb her, Mr. Kapasi walked ahead, to admire, as he always did, the three life-sized bronze avatars of Surya, the sun god, each emerging from its own niche on the temple facade to greet the sun at dawn, noon, and evening. They wore elaborate head-dresses, their languid, elongated eyes closed, their bare chests draped with carved chains and amulets. Hibiscus petals, offerings from previous visitors,

were strewn at their gray-green feet. The last statue, on the northern wall of the temple, was Mr. Kapasi's favorite. This Surya had a tired expression, weary after a hard day of work, sitting astride a horse with folded legs. Even his horse's eyes were drowsy. Around his body were smaller sculptures of women in pairs, their hips thrust to one side.

"Who's that?" Mrs. Das asked. He was startled to see that she was standing beside him.

"He is the Astachala-Surya," Mr. Kapasi said. "The setting sun."

"So in a couple of hours the sun will set right here?" She slipped a foot out of one of her square-heeled shoes, rubbed her toes on the back of her other leg.

"That is correct."

She raised her sunglasses for a moment, then put them back on again. "Neat." 105

Mr. Kapasi was not certain exactly what the word suggested, but he had a feeling it was a favorable response. He hoped that Mrs. Das had understood Surya's beauty, his power. Perhaps they would discuss it further in their letters. He would explain things to her, things about India, and she would explain things to him about America. In its own way this correspondence would fulfill his dream, of serving as an interpreter between nations. He looked at her straw bag, delighted that his address lay nestled among its contents. When he pictured her so many thousands of miles away he plummeted, so much so that he had an overwhelming urge to wrap his arms around her, to freeze with her, even for an instant, in an embrace witnessed by his favorite Surya. But Mrs. Das had already started walking.

"When do you return to America?" he asked, trying to sound placid.

"In ten days."

He calculated: A week to settle in, a week to develop the pictures, a few days to compose her letter, two weeks to get to India by air. According to his schedule, allowing room for delays, he would hear from Mrs. Das in approximately six weeks' time.

The family was silent as Mr. Kapasi drove them back, a little past four-thirty, to 110
Hotel Sandy Villa. The children had bought miniature granite versions of the chariot's wheels at a souvenir stand, and they turned them round in their hands. Mr. Das continued to read his book. Mrs. Das untangled Tina's hair with her brush and divided it into two little ponytails.

Mr. Kapasi was beginning to dread the thought of dropping them off. He was not prepared to begin his six-week wait to hear from Mrs. Das. As he stole glances at her in the rearview mirror, wrapping elastic bands around Tina's hair, he wondered how he might make the tour last a little longer. Ordinarily he sped back to Puri using a shortcut, eager to return home, scrub his feet and hands with sandalwood soap, and enjoy the evening newspaper and a cup of tea that his wife would serve him in silence. The thought of that silence, something to which he'd long been resigned, now oppressed him. It was then that he suggested visiting the hills at Udayagiri and Khandagiri, where a number of monastic dwellings were hewn out of the ground, facing one another across a defile. It was some miles away, but well worth seeing, Mr. Kapasi told them.

"Oh yeah, there's something mentioned about it in this book," Mr. Das said. "Built by a Jain king or something."[6]

"Shall we go then?" Mr. Kapasi asked. He paused at a turn in the road. "It's to the left."

Mr. Das turned to look at Mrs. Das. Both of them shrugged.

115   "Left, left," the children chanted.

Mr. Kapasi turned the wheel, almost delirious with relief. He did not know what he would do or say to Mrs. Das once they arrived at the hills. Perhaps he would tell her what a pleasing smile she had. Perhaps he would compliment her strawberry shirt, which he found irresistibly becoming. Perhaps, when Mr. Das was busy taking a picture, he would take her hand.

He did not have to worry. When they got to the hills, divided by a steep path thick with trees, Mrs. Das refused to get out of the car. All along the path, dozens of monkeys were seated on stones, as well as on the branches of the trees. Their hind legs were stretched out in front and raised to shoulder level, their arms resting on their knees.

"My legs are tired," she said, sinking low in her seat. "I'll stay here."

"Why did you have to wear those stupid shoes?" Mr. Das said. "You won't be in the pictures."

120   "Pretend I'm there."

"But we could use one of these pictures for our Christmas card this year. We didn't get one of all five of us at the Sun Temple. Mr. Kapasi could take it."

"I'm not coming. Anyway, those monkeys give me the creeps."

"But they're harmless," Mr. Das said. He turned to Mr. Kapasi. "Aren't they?"

"They are more hungry than dangerous," Mr. Kapasi said. "Do not provoke them with food, and they will not bother you."

125   Mr. Das headed up the defile with the children, the boys at his side, the little girl on his shoulders. Mr. Kapasi watched as they crossed paths with a Japanese man and woman, the only other tourists there, who paused for a final photograph, then stepped into a nearby car and drove away. As the car disappeared out of view some of the monkeys called out, emitting soft whooping sounds, and then walked on their flat black hands and feet up the path. At one point a group of them formed a little ring around Mr. Das and the children. Tina screamed in delight. Ronny ran in circles around his father. Bobby bent down and picked up a fat stick on the ground. When he extended it, one of the monkeys approached him and snatched it, then briefly beat the ground.

"I'll join them," Mr. Kapasi said, unlocking the door on his side. "There is much to explain about the caves."

"No. Stay a minute," Mrs. Das said. She got out of the back seat and slipped in beside Mr. Kapasi. "Raj has his dumb book anyway." Together, through the windshield, Mrs. Das and Mr. Kapasi watched as Bobby and the monkey passed the stick back and forth between them.

"A brave little boy," Mr. Kapasi commented.

6. This site is not a major tourist attraction; "giri" means mountain. Jainism, one of India's several major religions, is an atheist sect that emerged from Hinduism around 580 BCE, at about the same time as Buddhism.

"It's not so surprising," Mrs. Das said.

"No?" 130

"He's not his."

"I beg your pardon?"

"Raj's. He's not Raj's son."

Mr. Kapasi felt a prickle on his skin. He reached into his shirt pocket for the small tin of lotus-oil balm he carried with him at all times, and applied it to three spots on his forehead. He knew that Mrs. Das was watching him, but he did not turn to face her. Instead he watched as the figures of Mr. Das and the children grew smaller, climbing up the steep path, pausing every now and then for a picture, surrounded by a growing number of monkeys.

"Are you surprised?" The way she put it made him choose his words with care. 135

"It's not the type of thing one assumes," Mr. Kapasi replied slowly. He put the tin of lotus-oil balm back in his pocket.

"No, of course not. And no one knows, of course. No one at all. I've kept it a secret for eight whole years." She looked at Mr. Kapasi, tilting her chin as if to gain a fresh perspective. "But now I've told you."

Mr. Kapasi nodded. He felt suddenly parched, and his forehead was warm and slightly numb from the balm. He considered asking Mrs. Das for a sip of water, then decided against it.

"We met when we were very young," she said. She reached into her straw bag in search of something, then pulled out a packet of puffed rice. "Want some?"

"No, thank you." 140

She put a fistful in her mouth, sank into the seat a little, and looked away from Mr. Kapasi, out the window on her side of the car. "We married when we were still in college. We were in high school when he proposed. We went to the same college, of course. Back then we couldn't stand the thought of being separated, not for a day, not for a minute. Our parents were best friends who lived in the same town. My entire life I saw him every weekend, either at our house or theirs. We were sent upstairs to play together while our parents joked about our marriage. Imagine! They never caught us at anything, though in a way I think it was all more or less a setup. The things we did those Friday and Saturday nights, while our parents sat downstairs drinking tea . . . I could tell you stories, Mr. Kapasi."

As a result of spending all her time in college with Raj, she continued, she did not make many close friends. There was no one to confide in about him at the end of a difficult day, or to share a passing thought or a worry. Her parents now lived on the other side of the world, but she had never been very close to them, anyway. After marrying so young she was overwhelmed by it all, having a child so quickly, and nursing, and warming up bottles of milk and testing their temperature against her wrist while Raj was at work, dressed in sweaters and corduroy pants, teaching his students about rocks and dinosaurs. Raj never looked cross or harried, or plump as she had become after the first baby.

Always tired, she declined invitations from her one or two college girlfriends, to have lunch or shop in Manhattan. Eventually the friends stopped calling her, so that she was left at home all day with the baby, surrounded by toys that made her trip when she walked or wince when she sat, always cross and tired. Only occasionally did they go out after Ronny was born, and even more rarely did they entertain. Raj didn't mind; he looked forward to coming home from teaching and watching television and bouncing Ronny on his knee. She had been outraged when Raj told her that a Punjabi friend,[7] someone whom she had once met but did not remember, would be staying with them for a week for some job interviews in the New Brunswick area.

Bobby was conceived in the afternoon, on a sofa littered with rubber teething toys, after the friend learned that a London pharmaceutical company had hired him, while Ronny cried to be freed from his playpen. She made no protest when the friend touched the small of her back as she was about to make a pot of coffee, then pulled her against his crisp navy suit. He made love to her swiftly, in silence, with an expertise she had never known, without the meaningful expressions and smiles Raj always insisted on afterward. The next day Raj drove the friend to JFK.[8] He was married now, to a Punjabi girl, and they lived in London still, and every year they exchanged Christmas cards with Raj and Mina, each couple tucking photos of their families into the envelopes. He did not know that he was Bobby's father. He never would.

145   "I beg your pardon, Mrs. Das, but why have you told me this information?" Mr. Kapasi asked when she had finally finished speaking, and had turned to face him once again.

"For God's sake, stop calling me Mrs. Das. I'm twenty-eight. You probably have children my age."

"Not quite." It disturbed Mr. Kapasi to learn that she thought of him as a parent. The feeling he had had toward her, that had made him check his reflection in the rearview mirror as they drove, evaporated a little.

"I told you because of your talents." She put the packet of puffed rice back into her bag without folding over the top.

"I don't understand," Mr. Kapasi said.

150   "Don't you see? For eight years I haven't been able to express this to anybody, not to friends, certainly not to Raj. He doesn't even suspect it. He thinks I'm still in love with him. Well, don't you have anything to say?"

"About what?"

"About what I've just told you. About my secret, and about how terrible it makes me feel. I feel terrible looking at my children, and at Raj, always terrible. I have terrible urges, Mr. Kapasi, to throw things away. One day I had the urge to throw everything I own out of the window, the television, the children, everything. Don't you think it's unhealthy?"

He was silent.

"Mr. Kapasi, don't you have anything to say? I thought that was your job."

155   "My job is to give tours, Mrs. Das."

"Not that. Your other job. As an interpreter."

"But we do not face a language barrier. What need is there for an interpreter?"

"That's not what I mean. I would never have told you otherwise. Don't you realize what it means for me to tell you?"

7. Person from the Punjab, a northern region of India, near Pakistan.
8. John F. Kennedy International Airport, in New York City.

"What does it mean?"

"It means that I'm tired of feeling so terrible all the time. Eight years, Mr. 160
Kapasi, I've been in pain eight years. I was hoping you could help me feel better,
say the right thing. Suggest some kind of remedy."

He looked at her, in her red plaid skirt and strawberry T-shirt, a woman not
yet thirty, who loved neither her husband nor her children, who had already
fallen out of love with life. Her confession depressed him, depressed him all the
more when he thought of Mr. Das at the top of the path, Tina clinging to his
shoulders, taking pictures of ancient monastic cells cut into the hills to show his
students in America, unsuspecting and unaware that one of his sons was not
his own. Mr. Kapasi felt insulted that Mrs. Das should ask him to interpret her
common, trivial little secret. She did not resemble the patients in the doctor's
office, those who came glassy-eyed and desperate, unable to sleep or breathe
or urinate with ease, unable, above all, to give words to their pains. Still, Mr.
Kapasi believed it was his duty to assist Mrs. Das. Perhaps he ought to tell her
to confess the truth to Mr. Das. He would explain that honesty was the best
policy. Honesty, surely, would help her feel better, as she'd put it. Perhaps he
would offer to preside over the discussion, as a mediator. He decided to begin
with the most obvious question, to get to the heart of the matter, and so he
asked, "Is it really pain you feel, Mrs. Das, or is it guilt?"

She turned to him and glared, mustard oil thick on her frosty pink lips. She
opened her mouth to say something, but as she glared at Mr. Kapasi some certain
knowledge seemed to pass before her eyes, and she stopped. It crushed him; he
knew at that moment that he was not even important enough to be properly
insulted. She opened the car door and began walking up the path, wobbling a
little on her square wooden heels, reaching into her straw bag to eat handfuls of
puffed rice. It fell through her fingers, leaving a zigzagging trail, causing a monkey
to leap down from a tree and devour the little white grains. In search of more, the
monkey began to follow Mrs. Das. Others joined him, so that she was soon being
followed by about half a dozen of them, their velvety tails dragging behind.

Mr. Kapasi stepped out of the car. He wanted to holler, to alert her in some way,
but he worried that if she knew they were behind her, she would grow nervous.
Perhaps she would lose her balance. Perhaps they would pull at her bag or her hair.
He began to jog up the path, taking a fallen branch in his hand to scare away the
monkeys. Mrs. Das continued walking, oblivious, trailing grains of puffed rice.
Near the top of the incline, before a group of cells fronted by a row of squat stone
pillars, Mr. Das was kneeling on the ground, focusing the lens of his camera. The
children stood under the arcade, now hiding, now emerging from view.

"Wait for me," Mrs. Das called out. "I'm coming."

Tina jumped up and down. "Here comes Mommy!" 165

"Great," Mr. Das said without looking up. "Just in time. We'll get Mr. Kapasi
to take a picture of the five of us."

Mr. Kapasi quickened his pace, waving his branch so that the monkeys
scampered away, distracted, in another direction.

"Where's Bobby?" Mrs. Das asked when she stopped.

Mr. Das looked up from the camera. "I don't know. Ronny, where's Bobby?"

Ronny shrugged. "I thought he was right here." 170

"Where is he?" Mrs. Das repeated sharply. "What's wrong with all of you?"

They began calling his name, wandering up and down the path a bit. Because they were calling, they did not initially hear the boy's screams. When they found him, a little farther down the path under a tree, he was surrounded by a group of monkeys, over a dozen of them, pulling at his T-shirt with their long black fingers. The puffed rice Mrs. Das had spilled was scattered at his feet, raked over by the monkeys' hands. The boy was silent, his body frozen, swift tears running down his startled face. His bare legs were dusty and red with welts from where one of the monkeys struck him repeatedly with the stick he had given to it earlier.

"Daddy, the monkey's hurting Bobby," Tina said.

Mr. Das wiped his palms on the front of his shorts. In his nervousness he accidentally pressed the shutter on his camera; the whirring noise of the advancing film excited the monkeys, and the one with the stick began to beat Bobby more intently. "What are we supposed to do? What if they start attacking?"

175   "Mr. Kapasi," Mrs. Das shrieked, noticing him standing to one side. "Do something, for God's sake, do something!"

Mr. Kapasi took his branch and shooed them away, hissing at the ones that remained, stomping his feet to scare them. The animals retreated slowly, with a measured gait, obedient but unintimidated. Mr. Kapasi gathered Bobby in his arms and brought him back to where his parents and siblings were standing. As he carried him he was tempted to whisper a secret into the boy's ear. But Bobby was stunned, and shivering with fright, his legs bleeding slightly where the stick had broken the skin. When Mr. Kapasi delivered him to his parents, Mr. Das brushed some dirt off the boy's T-shirt and put the visor on him the right way. Mrs. Das reached into her straw bag to find a bandage which she taped over the cut on his knee. Ronny offered his brother a fresh piece of gum. "He's fine. Just a little scared, right, Bobby?" Mr. Das said, patting the top of his head.

"God, let's get out of here," Mrs. Das said. She folded her arms across the strawberry on her chest. "This place gives me the creeps."

"Yeah. Back to the hotel, definitely," Mr. Das agreed.

"Poor Bobby," Mrs. Das said. "Come here a second. Let Mommy fix your hair." Again she reached into her straw bag, this time for her hairbrush, and began to run it around the edges of the translucent visor. When she whipped out the hairbrush, the slip of paper with Mr. Kapasi's address on it fluttered away in the wind. No one but Mr. Kapasi noticed. He watched as it rose, carried higher and higher by the breeze, into the trees where the monkeys now sat, solemnly observing the scene below. Mr. Kapasi observed it too, knowing that this was the picture of the Das family he would preserve forever in his mind.

1999

GABRIEL GARCÍA MÁRQUEZ
(1928–2014)
A Very Old Man with Enormous Wings: A Tale for Children[1]

Born in Aracataca, Colombia, a remote town near the Caribbean coast, Gabriel García Márquez studied law at the University of Bogotá and then worked as a journalist in Latin America, Europe, and the United States. In 1967, he took up permanent residence in Barcelona, Spain. His first published book, *Leaf Storm* (1955), set in the fictional small town of Macondo, is based on the myths and legends of his childhood home. His most famous novel, *One Hundred Years of Solitude* (1967), fuses magic, reality, fable, and fantasy to present six generations of one Macondo family, a microcosm of many of the social, political, and economic problems of Latin America. Among his many works are *The Autumn of the Patriarch* (1975), *Chronicle of a Death Foretold* (1981), *Love in the Time of Cholera* (1987), *Of Love and Other Demons* (1994), and *Living to Tell the Tale* (2003), a three-volume set of memoirs. Márquez won the Nobel Prize for Literature in 1982.

O n the third day of rain they had killed so many crabs inside the house that Pelayo had to cross his drenched courtyard and throw them into the sea, because the newborn child had a temperature all night and they thought it was due to the stench. The world had been sad since Tuesday. Sea and sky were a single ashgray thing and the sands of the beach, which on March nights glimmered like powdered light, had become a stew of mud and rotten shellfish. The light was so weak at noon that when Pelayo was coming back to the house after throwing away the crabs, it was hard for him to see what it was that was moving and groaning in the rear of the courtyard. He had to go very close to see that it was an old man, a very old man, lying face down in the mud, who, in spite of his tremendous efforts, couldn't get up, impeded by his enormous wings.

Frightened by that nightmare, Pelayo ran to get Elisenda, his wife, who was putting compresses on the sick child, and he took her to the rear of the courtyard. They both looked at the fallen body with mute stupor. He was dressed like a ragpicker.[2] There were only a few faded hairs left on his bald skull and very few teeth in his mouth, and his pitiful condition of a drenched great-grandfather had taken away any sense of grandeur he might have had. His huge buzzard wings, dirty and half-plucked, were forever entangled in the mud. They looked at him so long and so closely that Pelayo and Elisenda very soon overcame their surprise and in the end found him familiar. Then they dared speak to him, and he answered in an incomprehensible dialect with a strong sailor's voice. That was how they skipped over the inconvenience of the wings and quite intelligently concluded that he was a lonely castaway from some foreign ship wrecked by the

1. Translated by Gregory Rabassa.
2. Someone who earns a living by collecting rags and other refuse.

storm. And yet, they called in a neighbor woman who knew everything about life and death to see him, and all she needed was one look to show them their mistake.

"He's an angel," she told them. "He must have been coming for the child, but the poor fellow is so old that the rain knocked him down."

On the following day everyone knew that a flesh-and-blood angel was held captive in Pelayo's house. Against the judgment of the wise neighbor woman, for whom angels in those times were the fugitive survivors of a celestial conspiracy, they did not have the heart to club him to death. Pelayo watched over him all afternoon from the kitchen, armed with his bailiff's[3] club, and before going to bed he dragged him out of the mud and locked him up with the hens in the wire chicken coop. In the middle of the night, when the rain stopped, Pelayo and Elisenda were still killing crabs. A short time afterward the child woke up without a fever and with a desire to eat. Then they felt magnanimous and decided to put the angel on a raft with fresh water and provisions for three days and leave him to his fate on the high seas. But when they went out into the courtyard with the first light of dawn, they found the whole neighborhood in front of the chicken coop having fun with the angel, without the slightest reverence, tossing him things to eat through the openings in the wire as if he weren't a supernatural creature but a circus animal.

5   Father Gonzaga arrived before seven o'clock, alarmed at the strange news. By that time onlookers less frivolous than those at dawn had already arrived and they were making all kinds of conjectures concerning the captive's future. The simplest among them thought that he should be named mayor of the world. Others of sterner mind felt that he should be promoted to the rank of five-star general in order to win all wars. Some visionaries hoped that he could be put to stud in order to implant on earth a race of winged wise men who could take charge of the universe. But Father Gonzaga, before becoming a priest, had been a robust woodcutter. Standing by the wire, he reviewed his catechism in an instant and asked them to open the door so that he could take a close look at that pitiful man who looked more like a huge decrepit hen among the fascinated chickens. He was lying in a corner drying his open wings in the sunlight among the fruit peels and breakfast leftovers that the early risers had thrown him. Alien to the impertinences of the world, he only lifted his antiquarian eyes and murmured something in his dialect when Father Gonzaga went into the chicken coop and said good morning to him in Latin. The parish priest had his first suspicion of an imposter when he saw that he did not understand the language of God or know how to greet His ministers. Then he noticed that seen close up he was much too human: he had an unbearable smell of the outdoors, the back side of his wings was strewn with parasites and his main feathers had been mistreated by terrestrial winds, and nothing about him measured up to the proud dignity of angels. Then he came out of the chicken coop and in a brief sermon warned the curious against the risks of being ingenuous. He reminded them that the devil had the bad habit of making use of carnival tricks in order to confuse the unwary. He argued that if wings were not the essential element in determining the difference between a hawk and an airplane, they were even less so in the recognition

3. Local government official, usually one employed to make arrests and serve warrants.

of angels. Nevertheless, he promised to write a letter to his bishop so that the latter would write to his primate[4] so that the latter would write to the Supreme Pontiff in order to get the final verdict from the highest courts.

His prudence fell on sterile hearts. The news of the captive angel spread with such rapidity that after a few hours the courtyard had the bustle of a marketplace and they had to call in troops with fixed bayonets to disperse the mob that was about to knock the house down. Elisenda, her spine all twisted from sweeping up so much marketplace trash, then got the idea of fencing in the yard and charging five cents admission to see the angel.

The curious came from far away. A traveling carnival arrived with a flying acrobat who buzzed over the crowd several times, but no one paid any attention to him because his wings were not those of an angel but, rather, those of a sidereal[5] bat. The most unfortunate invalids on earth came in search of health: a poor woman who since childhood had been counting her heartbeats and had run out of numbers; a Portuguese man who couldn't sleep because the noise of the stars disturbed him; a sleepwalker who got up at night to undo the things he had done while awake; and many others with less serious ailments. In the midst of that shipwreck disorder that made the earth tremble, Pelayo and Elisenda were happy with fatigue, for in less than a week they had crammed their rooms with money and the line of pilgrims waiting their turn to enter still reached beyond the horizon.

The angel was the only one who took no part in his own act. He spent his time trying to get comfortable in his borrowed nest, befuddled by the hellish heat of the oil lamps and sacramental candles that had been placed along the wire. At first they tried to make him eat some mothballs, which, according to the wisdom of the wise neighbor woman, were the food prescribed for angels. But he turned them down, just as he turned down the papal lunches[6] that the penitents brought him, and they never found out whether it was because he was an angel or because he was an old man that in the end he ate nothing but egg-plant mush. His only supernatural virtue seemed to be patience. Especially during the first days, when the hens pecked at him, searching for the stellar parasites that proliferated in his wings, and the cripples pulled out feathers to touch their defective parts with, and even the most merciful threw stones at him, trying to get him to rise so they could see him standing. The only time they succeeded in arousing him was when they burned his side with an iron for branding steers, for he had been motionless for so many hours that they thought he was dead. He awoke with a start, ranting in his hermetic language and with tears in his eyes, and he flapped his wings a couple of times, which brought on a whirlwind of chicken dung and lunar dust and a gale of panic that did not seem to be of this world. Although many thought that his reaction had been one not of rage but of pain, from then on they were careful not to annoy him, because the majority understood that his passivity was not that of a hero taking his ease but that of a cataclysm in repose.

4. Highest bishop of a given state.
5. Of, or relating to, the stars.
6. Expensive, elaborately prepared meals.

Father Gonzaga held back the crowd's frivolity with formulas of maidservant inspiration while awaiting the arrival of a final judgment on the nature of the captive. But the mail from Rome showed no sense of urgency. They spent their time finding out if the prisoner had a navel, if his dialect had any connection with Aramaic, how many times he could fit on the head of a pin, or whether he wasn't just a Norwegian with wings. Those meager letters might have come and gone until the end of time if a providential event had not put an end to the priest's tribulations.

10   It so happened that during those days, among so many other carnival attractions, there arrived in town the traveling show of the woman who had been changed into a spider for having disobeyed her parents. The admission to see her was not only less than the admission to see the angel, but people were permitted to ask her all manner of questions about her absurd state and to examine her up and down so that no one would ever doubt the truth of her horror. She was a frightful tarantula the size of a ram and with the head of a sad maiden. What was most heart-rending, however, was not her outlandish shape but the sincere affliction with which she recounted the details of her misfortune. While still practically a child she had sneaked out of her parents' house to go to a dance, and while she was coming back through the woods after having danced all night without permission, a fearful thunderclap rent the sky in two and through the crack came the lightning bolt of brimstone that changed her into a spider. Her only nourishment came from the meatballs that charitable souls chose to toss into her mouth. A spectacle like that, full of so much human truth and with such a fearful lesson, was bound to defeat without even trying that of a haughty angel who scarcely deigned to look at mortals. Besides, the few miracles attributed to the angel showed a certain mental disorder, like the blind man who didn't recover his sight but grew three new teeth, or the paralytic who didn't get to walk but almost won the lottery, and the leper whose sores sprouted sunflowers. Those consolation miracles, which were more like mocking fun, had already ruined the angel's reputation when the woman who had been changed into a spider finally crushed him completely. That was how Father Gonzaga was cured forever of his insomnia and Pelayo's courtyard went back to being as empty as during the time it had rained for three days and crabs walked through the bedrooms.

The owners of the house had no reason to lament. With the money they saved they built a two-story mansion with balconies and gardens and high netting so that crabs wouldn't get in during the winter, and with iron bars on the windows so that angels wouldn't get in. Pelayo also set up a rabbit warren close to town and gave up his job as bailiff for good, and Elisenda bought some satin pumps with high heels and many dresses of iridescent silk, the kind worn on Sunday by the most desirable women in those times. The chicken coop was the only thing that didn't receive any attention. If they washed it down with creolin[7] and burned tears of myrrh inside it every so often, it was not in homage to the angel but to drive away the dungheap stench that still hung everywhere like a ghost and was turning the new house into an old one. At first, when the child learned to walk, they were careful that he not get too close to the chicken coop.

_____

7. Disinfectant.

But then they began to lose their fears and got used to the smell, and before the child got his second teeth he'd gone inside the chicken coop to play, where the wires were falling apart. The angel was no less standoffish with him than with other mortals, but he tolerated the most ingenious infamies with the patience of a dog who had no illusions. They both came down with chicken pox at the same time. The doctor who took care of the child couldn't resist the temptation to listen to the angel's heart, and he found so much whistling in the heart and so many sounds in his kidneys that it seemed impossible for him to be alive. What surprised him most, however, was the logic of his wings. They seemed so natural on that completely human organism that he couldn't understand why other men didn't have them too.

When the child began school it had been some time since the sun and rain had caused the collapse of the chicken coop. The angel went dragging himself about here and there like a stray dying man. They would drive him out of the bedroom with a broom and a moment later find him in the kitchen. He seemed to be in so many places at the same time that they grew to think that he'd been duplicated, that he was reproducing himself all through the house, and the exasperated and unhinged Elisenda shouted that it was awful living in that hell full of angels. He could scarcely eat and his antiquarian eyes had also become so foggy that he went about bumping into posts. All he had left were the bare cannulae of his last feathers. Pelayo threw a blanket over him and extended him the charity of letting him sleep in the shed, and only then did they notice that he had a temperature at night, and was delirious with the tongue twisters of an old Norwegian. That was one of the few times they became alarmed, for they thought he was going to die and not even the wise neighbor woman had been able to tell them what to do with dead angels.

And yet he not only survived his worst winter, but seemed improved with the first sunny days. He remained motionless for several days in the farthest corner of the courtyard, where no one would see him, and at the beginning of December some large, stiff feathers began to grow on his wings, the feathers of a scarecrow, which looked more like another misfortune of decrepitude. But he must have known the reason for those changes, for he was quite careful that no one should notice them, that no one should hear the sea chanteys that he sometimes sang under the stars. One morning Elisenda was cutting some bunches of onions for lunch when a wind that seemed to come from the high seas blew into the kitchen. Then she went to the window and caught the angel in his first attempts at flight. They were so clumsy that his fingernails opened a furrow in the vegetable patch and he was on the point of knocking the shed down with the ungainly flapping that slipped on the light and couldn't get a grip on the air. But he did manage to gain altitude. Elisenda let out a sigh of relief, for herself and for him, when she saw him pass over the last houses, holding himself up in some way with the risky flapping of a senile vulture. She kept watching him even when she was through cutting the onions and she kept on watching until it was no longer possible for her to see him, because then he was no longer an annoyance in her life but an imaginary dot on the horizon of the sea.

1968

ALICE MUNRO

(b. 1931)

Boys and Girls

Described by novelist Jonathan Franzen as having "a strong claim to being the best fiction writer now working in North America" and by the committee that awarded her the 2013 Nobel Prize for Literature as a "master of the contemporary short story," Alice Munro today enjoys an enviably high reputation. That was long in coming and unexpected for a girl raised during the Great Depression and World War II, on a farm in southwestern Ontario—that unglamorous terrain she has since so vividly memorialized in her fiction. She began publishing stories while attending the University of Western Ontario. But when her two-year scholarship ran out, she left the university, married James Munro, and moved first to Vancouver and then to Victoria, where the couple raised three daughters. Though her stories appeared sporadically during the 1950s, it was not until 1968 that then-thirty-eight-year-old Munro published her first book and won the first of multiple Governor General's Awards, Canada's highest literary prize. Divorced and remarried, Munro returned to Ontario and began regularly publishing collections including *Something I've Been Meaning to Tell You* (1974), *The Progress of Love* (1986), *Open Secrets* (1994), the Booker Prize–winning *View from Castle Rock* (2006), and *Dear Life* (2012). One reason Munro has not achieved the wide fame many believe she merits is her focus on short fiction: The one work she published as a novel, *Lives of Girls and Women* (1971), is in fact a series of interlinked stories.

M y father was a fox farmer. That is, he raised silver foxes, in pens; and in the fall and early winter, when their fur was prime, he killed them and skinned them and sold their pelts to the Hudson's Bay Company or the Montreal Fur Traders. These companies supplied us with heroic calendars to hang, one on each side of the kitchen door. Against a background of cold blue sky and black pine forests and treacherous northern rivers, plumed adventurers planted the flags of England or of France; magnificent savages bent their backs to the portage.

For several weeks before Christmas, my father worked after supper in the cellar of our house. The cellar was white-washed, and lit by a hundred-watt bulb over the worktable. My brother Laird and I sat on the top step and watched. My father removed the pelt inside-out from the body of the fox, which looked surprisingly small, mean and rat-like, deprived of its arrogant weight of fur. The naked, slippery bodies were collected in a sack and buried at the dump. One time the hired man, Henry Bailey, had taken a swipe at me with this sack, saying, "Christmas present!" My mother thought that was not funny. In fact she disliked the whole pelting operation—that was what the killing, skinning, and preparation of the furs was called—and wished it did not have to take place in the house. There was the smell. After the pelt had been stretched inside-out on a long board my father scraped away delicately, removing the little clotted webs of blood vessels, the bubbles of fat; the smell of blood and animal fat, with the strong primitive odour of the fox itself, penetrated all parts of the house. I found it reassuringly seasonal, like the smell of oranges and pine needles.

Henry Bailey suffered from bronchial troubles. He would cough and cough until his narrow face turned scarlet, and his light blue, derisive eyes filled up with tears; then he took the lid off the stove, and, standing well back, shot out a great clot of phlegm—hsss—straight into the heart of the flames. We admired him for this performance and for his ability to make his stomach growl at will, and for his laughter, which was full of high whistlings and gurglings and involved the whole faulty machinery of his chest. It was sometimes hard to tell what he was laughing at, and always possible that it might be us.

After we had been sent to bed we could still smell fox and still hear Henry's laugh, but these things, reminders of the warm, safe, brightly lit downstairs world, seemed lost and diminished, floating on the stale cold air upstairs. We were afraid at night in the winter. We were not afraid of *outside* though this was the time of year when snowdrifts curled around our house like sleeping whales and the wind harassed us all night, coming up from the buried fields, the frozen swamp, with its old bugbear chorus of threats and misery. We were afraid of *inside*, the room where we slept. At this time the upstairs of our house was not finished. A brick chimney went up one wall. In the middle of the floor was a square hole, with a wooden railing around it; that was where the stairs came up. On the other side of the stairwell were the things that nobody had any use for any more—a soldiery roll of linoleum, standing on end, a wicker baby carriage, a fern basket, china jugs and basins with cracks in them, a picture of the Battle of Balaclava,[1] very sad to look at. I had told Laird, as soon as he was old enough to understand such things, that bats and skeletons lived over there; whenever a man escaped from the county jail, twenty miles away, I imagined that he had somehow let himself in the window and was hiding behind the linoleum. But we had rules to keep us safe. When the light was on, we were safe as long as we did not step off the square of worn carpet which defined our bedroom-space; when the light was off no place was safe but the beds themselves. I had to turn out the light kneeling on the end of my bed, and stretching as far as I could to reach the cord.

In the dark we lay on our beds, our narrow life rafts, and fixed our eyes on the faint light coming up the stairwell, and sang songs. Laird sang "Jingle Bells," which he would sing any time, whether it was Christmas or not, and I sang "Danny Boy." I loved the sound of my own voice, frail and supplicating, rising in the dark. We could make out the tall frosted shapes of the windows now, gloomy and white. When I came to the part, *When I am dead, as dead I well may be*—a fit of shivering caused not by the cold sheets but by pleasurable emotion almost silenced me. *You'll kneel and say, an Ave there above me*—What was an Ave? Every day I forgot to find out.

Laird went straight from singing to sleep. I could hear his long, satisfied, bubbly breaths. Now for the time that remained to me, the most perfectly private and perhaps the best time of the whole day, I arranged myself tightly under the covers and went on with one of the stories I was telling myself from night to night.

1. **Indecisive Crimean War battle fought on October 25, 1854, famous for the Charge of the Light Brigade.**

These stories were about myself, when I had grown a little older; they took place in a world that was recognizably mine, yet one that presented opportunities for courage, boldness and self-sacrifice, as mine never did. I rescued people from a bombed building (it discouraged me that the real war[2] had gone on so far away from Jubilee). I shot two rabid wolves who were menacing the schoolyard (the teachers cowered terrified at my back). I rode a fine horse spiritedly down the main street of Jubilee, acknowledging the townspeople's gratitude for some yet-to-be-worked-out piece of heroism (nobody ever rode a horse there, except King Billy in the Orangemen's Day[3] parade). There was always riding and shooting in these stories, though I had only been on a horse twice—bareback because we did not own a saddle—and the second time I had slid right around and dropped under the horse's feet; it had stepped placidly over me. I really was learning to shoot, but I could not hit anything yet, not even tin cans on fence posts.

Alive, the foxes inhabited a world my father made for them. It was surrounded by a high guard fence, like a medieval town, with a gate that was padlocked at night. Along the streets of this town were ranged large, sturdy pens. Each of them had a real door that a man could go through, a wooden ramp along the wire, for the foxes to run up and down on, and a kennel—something like a clothes chest with airholes—where they slept and stayed in winter and had their young. There were feeding and watering dishes attached to the wire in such a way that they could be emptied and cleaned from the outside. The dishes were made of old tin cans, and the ramps and kennels of odds and ends of old lumber. Everything was tidy and ingenious; my father was tirelessly inventive and his favourite book in the world was *Robinson Crusoe*.[4] He had fitted a tin drum on a wheelbarrow, for bringing water down to the pens. This was my job in summer, when the foxes had to have water twice a day. Between nine and ten o'clock in the morning, and again after supper, I filled the drum at the pump and trundled it down through the barnyard to the pens, where I parked it, and filled my watering can and went along the streets. Laird came too, with his little cream and green gardening can, filled too full and knocking against his legs and slopping water on his canvas shoes. I had the real watering can, my father's, though I could only carry it three-quarters full.

The foxes all had names, which were printed on a tin plate and hung beside their doors. They were not named when they were born, but when they survived the first year's pelting and were added to the breeding stock. Those my father had named were called names like Prince, Bob, Wally and Betty. Those I had named were called Star or Turk, or Maureen or Diana. Laird named one Maud after a hired girl we had when he was little, one Harold after a boy at school, and one Mexico, he did not say why.

Naming them did not make pets out of them, or anything like it. Nobody but my father ever went into the pens, and he had twice had blood-poisoning from

2. World War II (1939–45).
3. The Orange Society is an Irish Protestant group named after William of Orange, who, as King William III of England, defeated the Catholic James II. The society sponsors an annual procession on July 12 to commemorate the victory of William III at the Battle of the Boyne (1690).
4. Novel (1719) by Daniel Defoe about a man shipwrecked on a desert island; it goes into great detail about the ingenious contraptions he fashions from simple materials.

bites. When I was bringing them their water they prowled up and down on the paths they had made inside their pens, barking seldom—they saved that for nighttime, when they might get up a chorus of community frenzy—but always watching me, their eyes burning, clear gold, in their pointed, malevolent faces. They were beautiful for their delicate legs and heavy, aristocratic tails and the bright fur sprinkled on dark down their backs—which gave them their name—but especially for their faces, drawn exquisitely sharp in pure hostility, and their golden eyes.

Besides carrying water I helped my father when he cut the long grass, and 10 the lamb's quarter and flowering money-musk, that grew between the pens. He cut with the scythe and I raked into piles. Then he took a pitchfork and threw freshcut grass all over the top of the pens, to keep the foxes cooler and shade their coats, which were browned by too much sun. My father did not talk to me unless it was about the job we were doing. In this he was quite different from my mother, who, if she was feeling cheerful, would tell me all sorts of things— the name of a dog she had had when she was a little girl, the names of boys she had gone out with later on when she was grown up, and what certain dresses of hers had looked like—she could not imagine now what had become of them. Whatever thoughts and stories my father had were private, and I was shy of him and would never ask him questions. Nevertheless I worked willingly under his eyes, and with a feeling of pride. One time a feed salesman came down into the pens to talk to him and my father said, "Like to have you meet my new hired man." I turned away and raked furiously, red in the face with pleasure.

"Could of fooled me," said the salesman. "I thought it was only a girl."

After the grass was cut, it seemed suddenly much later in the year. I walked on stubble in the earlier evening, aware of the reddening skies, the entering silences, of fall. When I wheeled the tank out of the gate and put the padlock on, it was almost dark. One night at this time I saw my mother and father standing talking on the little rise of ground we called the gangway, in front of the barn. My father had just come from the meathouse; he had his stiff bloody apron on, and a pail of cut-up meat in his hand.

It was an odd thing to see my mother down at the barn. She did not often come out of the house unless it was to do something—hang out the wash or dig potatoes in the garden. She looked out of place, with her bare lumpy legs, not touched by the sun, her apron still on and damp across the stomach from the supper dishes. Her hair was tied up in a kerchief, wisps of it falling out. She would tie her hair up like this in the morning, saying she did not have time to do it properly, and it would stay tied up all day. It was true, too; she really did not have time. These days our back porch was piled with baskets of peaches and grapes and pears, bought in town, and onions and tomatoes and cucumbers grown at home, all waiting to be made into jelly and jam and preserves, pickles and chili sauce. In the kitchen there was a fire in the stove all day, jars clinked in boiling water, sometimes a cheesecloth bag was strung on a pole between two chairs, straining blue-black grape pulp for jelly. I was given jobs to do and I would sit at the table peeling peaches that had been soaked in the hot water, or cutting up onions, my eyes smarting and streaming. As soon as I was done I ran out of the house, trying to get out of earshot before my mother thought of what she wanted me to do next. I hated the hot dark kitchen in summer, the green blinds and the flypapers, the same old oilcloth table and wavy mirror and bumpy linoleum. My mother was too tired and preoccupied to talk to me, she had no heart to tell about the Normal School Graduation Dance; sweat trickled over her face and she was always counting under her breath, pointing at jars, dumping cups of sugar. It seemed to me that work in the house was endless, dreary and peculiarly depressing; work done out of doors, and in my father's service, was ritualistically important.

I wheeled the tank up to the barn, where it was kept, and I heard my mother saying, "Wait till Laird gets a little bigger, then you'll have a real help."

15   What my father said I did not hear. I was pleased by the way he stood listening, politely as he would to a salesman or a stranger, but with an air of wanting to get on with his real work. I felt my mother had no business down here and I wanted him to feel the same way. What did she mean about Laird? He was no help to anybody. Where was he now? Swinging himself sick on the swing, going around in circles, or trying to catch caterpillars. He never once stayed with me till I was finished.

"And then I can use her more in the house," I heard my mother say. She had a dead-quiet, regretful way of talking about me that always made me uneasy. "I just get my back turned and she runs off. It's not like I had a girl in the family at all."

I went and sat on a feed bag in the corner of the barn, not wanting to appear when this conversation was going on. My mother, I felt, was not to be trusted. She was kinder than my father and more easily fooled, but you could not depend on her, and the real reasons for the things she said and did were not to be known. She loved me, and she sat up late at night making a dress of the difficult style I wanted, for me to wear when school started, but she was also my enemy. She was always plotting. She was plotting now to get me to stay in the house more, although she knew I hated it (*because* she knew I hated it) and keep me from working for my father. It seemed to me she would do this simply out of perversity, and to try her power. It did not occur to me that she could be lonely, or jealous. No grown-up could be; they were too fortunate. I sat and kicked my heels monotonously against a feed bag, raising dust, and did not come out till she was gone.

At any rate, I did not expect my father to pay any attention to what she said. Who could imagine Laird doing my work—Laird remembering the padlock and cleaning out the watering-dishes with a leaf on the end of a stick, or even wheeling the tank without it tumbling over? It showed how little my mother knew about the way things really were.

I have forgotten to say what the foxes were fed. My father's bloody apron reminded me. They were fed horsemeat. At this time most farmers still kept horses, and when a horse got too old to work, or broke a leg or got down and would not get up, as they sometimes did, the owner would call my father, and he and Henry went out to the farm in the truck. Usually they shot and butchered the horse there, paying the farmer from five to twelve dollars. If they had already too much meat on hand, they would bring the horse back alive, and keep it for a few days or weeks in our stable, until the meat was needed. After the war the farmers were buying tractors and gradually getting rid of horses altogether, so it sometimes happened that we got a good healthy horse, that there was just no use for any more. If this happened in the winter we might keep the horse in our stable till spring, for we had plenty of hay and if there was a lot of snow—and the plow did not always get our road cleared—it was convenient to be able to go to town with a horse and cutter.[5]

The winter I was eleven years old we had two horses in the stable. We did 20 not know what names they had had before, so we called them Mack and Flora. Mack was an old black workhorse, sooty and indifferent. Flora was a sorrel mare, a driver. We took them both out in the cutter. Mack was slow and easy to handle. Flora was given to fits of violent alarm, veering at cars and even at other horses, but we loved her speed and high-stepping, her general air of gallantry and abandon. On Saturdays we went down to the stable and as soon as we opened the door on its cosy, animal-smelling darkness Flora threw up her head, rolled her eyes, whinnied despairingly and pulled herself through a crisis of nerves on the spot. It was not safe to go into her stall; she would kick.

This winter also I began to hear a great deal more on the theme my mother had sounded when she had been talking in front of the barn. I no longer felt safe. It seemed that in the minds of the people around me there was a steady undercurrent of thought, not to be deflected, on this one subject. The word *girl* had formerly seemed to me innocent and unburdened, like the world *child*; now it appeared that it was no such thing. A girl was not, as I had supposed, simply what I was; it was what I had to become. It was a definition, always touched with emphasis, with reproach and disappointment. Also it was a joke on me. Once Laird and I were fighting, and for the first time ever I had to use all my strength against him; even so, he caught and pinned my arm for a moment, really hurting me. Henry saw this, and laughed, saying, "Oh, that there Laird's gonna show you, one of these days!" Laird was getting a lot bigger. But I was getting bigger too.

My grandmother came to stay with us for a few weeks and I heard other things. "Girls don't slam doors like that." "Girls keep their knees together when they sit down." And worse still, when I asked some questions, "That's none of girls' business." I continued to slam the doors and sit as awkwardly as possible, thinking that by such measures I kept myself free.

When spring came, the horses were let out in the barnyard. Mack stood against the barn wall trying to scratch his neck and haunches, but Flora trotted up and down and reared at the fences, clattering her hooves against the rails. Snow drifts dwindled quickly, revealing the hard grey and brown earth, the familiar rise and fall of the ground, plain and bare after the fantastic landscape of winter. There was a great feeling of opening-out, of release. We just wore rubbers now, over our shoes; our feet felt ridiculously light. One Saturday we went out to the stable and found all the doors open, letting in the unaccustomed sunlight and fresh air. Henry was there, just idling around looking at his collection of calendars which were tacked up behind the stalls in a part of the stable my mother had probably never seen.

"Come to say goodbye to your old friend Mack?" Henry said. "Here, you give him a taste of oats." He poured some oats into Laird's cupped hands and Laird went to feed Mack. Mack's teeth were in bad shape. He ate very slowly, patiently shifting the oats around in his mouth, trying to find a stump of a molar to grind it on. "Poor old Mack," said Henry mournfully. "When a horse's teeth's gone, he's gone. That's about the way."

5. Small, light sleigh.

25   "Are you going to shoot him today?" I said. Mack and Flora had been in the stable so long I had almost forgotten they were going to be shot.

Henry didn't answer me. Instead he started to sing in a high, trembly, mocking-sorrowful voice, *Oh, there's no more work, for poor Uncle Ned, he's gone where the good darkies go.*[6] Mack's thick, blackish tongue worked diligently at Laird's hand. I went out before the song was ended and sat down on the gangway.

I had never seen them shoot a horse, but I knew where it was done. Last summer Laird and I had come upon a horse's entrails before they were buried. We had thought it was a big black snake, coiled up in the sun. That was around in the field that ran up beside the barn. I thought that if we went inside the barn, and found a wide crack or knothole to look through we would be able to see them do it. It was not something I wanted to see; just the same, if a thing really happened, it was better to see it, and know.

My father came down from the house, carrying the gun.

"What are you doing here?" he said.

30   "Nothing."

"Go on up and play around the house."

He sent Laird out of the stable. I said to Laird, "Do you want to see them shoot Mack?" and without waiting for an answer led him around to the front door of the barn, opened it carefully, and went in. "Be quiet or they'll hear us," I said. We could hear Henry and my father talking in the stable, then the heavy, shuffling steps of Mack being backed out of his stall.

In the loft it was cold and dark. Thin, crisscrossed beams of sunlight fell through the cracks. The hay was low. It was a rolling country, hills and hollows, slipping under our feet. About four feet up was a beam going around the walls. We piled hay up in one corner and I boosted Laird up and hoisted myself. The beam was not very wide; we crept along it with our hands flat on the barn walls. There were plenty of knotholes, and I found one that gave me the view I wanted—a corner of the barnyard, the gate, part of the field. Laird did not have a knothole and began to complain.

I showed him a widened crack between two boards. "Be quiet and wait. If they hear you you'll get us in trouble."

35   My father came in sight carrying the gun. Henry was leading Mack by the halter. He dropped it and took out his cigarette papers and tobacco; he rolled cigarettes for my father and himself. While this was going on Mack nosed around in the old, dead grass along the fence. Then my father opened the gate and they took Mack through. Henry led Mack away from the path to a patch of ground and they talked together, not loud enough for us to hear. Mack again began searching for a mouthful of fresh grass, which was not to be found. My father walked away in a straight line, and stopped short at a distance which seemed to suit him. Henry was walking away from Mack too, but sideways, still negligently holding on to the halter. My father raised the gun and Mack looked up as if he had noticed something and my father shot him.

Mack did not collapse at once but swayed, lurched sideways and fell, first on his side; then he rolled over on his back and, amazingly, kicked his legs for a few seconds in the air. At this Henry laughed, as if Mack had done a trick for him.

6. Lines from the Stephen Foster (1826–64) song "Old Uncle Ned."

Laird, who had drawn a long, groaning breath of surprise when the shot was fired, said out loud, "He's not dead." And it seemed to me it might be true. But his legs stopped, he rolled on his side again, his muscles quivered and sank. The two men walked over and looked at him in a businesslike way; they bent down and examined his forehead where the bullet had gone in, and now I saw his blood on the brown grass.

"Now they just skin him and cut him up," I said. "Let's go." My legs were a little shaky and I jumped gratefully down into the hay. "Now you've seen how they shoot a horse," I said in a congratulatory way, as if I had seen it many times before. "Let's see if any barn cat's had kittens in the hay." Laird jumped. He seemed young and obedient again. Suddenly I remembered how, when he was little, I had brought him into the barn and told him to climb the ladder to the top beam. That was in the spring, too, when the hay was low. I had done it out of a need for excitement, a desire for something to happen so that I could tell about it. He was wearing a little bulky brown and white checked coat, made down from one of mine. He went all the way up, just as I told him, and sat down on the top beam with the hay far below him on one side, and the barn floor and some old machinery on the other. Then I ran screaming to my father, "Laird's up on the top beam!" My father came, my mother came, my father went up the ladder talking very quietly and brought Laird down under his arm, at which my mother leaned against the ladder and began to cry. They said to me, "Why weren't you watching him?" but nobody ever knew the truth. Laird did not know enough to tell. But whenever I saw the brown and white checked coat hanging in the closet, or at the bottom of the rag bag, which was where it ended up, I felt a weight in my stomach, the sadness of unexorcized guilt.

I looked at Laird who did not even remember this, and I did not like the look on this thin, winter-pale face. His expression was not frightened or upset, but remote, concentrating. "Listen," I said, in an unusually bright and friendly voice, "you aren't going to tell, are you?"

"No," he said absently.

"Promise."

40

"Promise," he said. I grabbed the hand behind his back to make sure he was not crossing his fingers. Even so, he might have a nightmare; it might come out that way. I decided I had better work hard to get all thoughts of what he had seen out of his mind—which, it seemed to me, could not hold very many things at a time. I got some money I had saved and that afternoon we went into Jubilee and saw a show, with Judy Canova,[7] at which we both laughed a great deal. After that I thought it would be all right.

Two weeks later I knew they were going to shoot Flora. I knew from the night before, when I heard my mother ask if the hay was holding out all right, and my father said, "Well, after to-morrow there'll just be the cow, and we should be able to put her out to grass in another week." So I knew it was Flora's turn in the morning.

This time I didn't think of watching it. That was something to see just one time. I had not thought about it very often since, but sometimes when I was busy, working at school, or standing in front of the mirror combing my hair and wondering if I would be pretty when I grew up, the whole scene would flash

7. American comedian (1913–83) best known for her yodeling in hillbilly movies of the 1940s.

into my mind: I would see the easy, practised way my father raised the gun, and hear Henry laughing when Mack kicked his legs in the air. I did not have any great feeling of horror and opposition, such as a city child might have had; I was too used to seeing the death of animals as a necessity by which we lived. Yet I felt a little ashamed, and there was a new wariness, a sense of holding-off, in my attitude to my father and his work.

It was a fine day, and we were going around the yard picking up tree branches that had been torn off in winter storms. This was something we had been told to do, and also we wanted to use them to make a teepee. We heard Flora whinny, and then my father's voice and Henry's shouting, and we ran down to the barnyard to see what was going on.

45   The stable door was open. Henry had just brought Flora out, and she had broken away from him. She was running free in the barnyard, from one end to the other. We climbed up on the fence. It was exciting to see her running, whinnying, going up on her hind legs, prancing and threatening like a horse in a Western movie, an unbroken ranch horse, though she was just an old driver, an old sorrel mare. My father and Henry ran after her and tried to grab the dangling halter. They tried to work her into a corner, and they had almost succeeded when she made a run between them, wild-eyed, and disappeared around the corner of the barn. We heard the rails clatter down as she got over the fence, and Henry yelled, "She's into the field now!"

That meant she was in the long L-shaped field that ran up by the house. If she got around the center, heading towards the lane, the gate was open; the truck had been driven into the field this morning. My father shouted to me, because I was on the other side of the fence, nearest the lane, "Go shut the gate!"

I could run very fast. I ran across the garden, past the tree where our swing was hung, and jumped across a ditch into the lane. There was the open gate. She had not got out, I could not see her up on the road; she must have run to the other end of the field. The gate was heavy. I lifted it out of the gravel and carried it across the roadway. I had it half-way across when she came in sight, galloping straight towards me. There was just time to get the chain on. Laird came scrambling through the ditch to help me.

Instead of shutting the gate, I opened it as wide as I could. I did not make any decision to do this, it was just what I did. Flora never slowed down; she galloped straight past me, and Laird jumped up and down, yelling, "Shut it, shut it!" even after it was too late. My father and Henry appeared in the field a moment too late to see what I had done. They only saw Flora heading for the township road. They would think I had not got there in time.

They did not waste any time asking about it. They went back to the barn and got the gun and the knives they used, and put these in the truck; then they turned the truck around and came bouncing up the field toward us. Laird called to them, "Let me go too, let me go too!" and Henry stopped the truck and they took him in. I shut the gate after they were all gone.

50   I supposed Laird would tell. I wondered what would happen to me. I had never disobeyed my father before, and I could not understand why I had done it. Flora would not really get away. They would catch up with her in the truck. Or if they did not catch her this morning somebody would see her and telephone us this afternoon or tomorrow. There was no wild country here for her to run to,

only farms. What was more, my father had paid for her, we needed the meat to feed the foxes, we needed the foxes to make our living. All I had done was make more work for my father who worked hard enough already. And when my father found out about it he was not going to trust me any more, he would know that I was not entirely on his side. I was on Flora's side, and that made me no use to anybody, not even to her. Just the same, I did not regret it; when she came running at me and I held the gate open, that was the only thing I could do.

I went back to the house, and my mother said, "What's all the commotion?" I told her that Flora had kicked down the fence and got away. "Your poor father," she said, "now he'll have to go chasing over the countryside. Well, there isn't any use planning dinner before one." She put up the ironing board. I wanted to tell her, but thought better of it and went upstairs and sat on my bed.

Lately I had been trying to make my part of the room fancy, spreading the bed with old lace curtains, and fixing myself a dressing-table with some leftovers of cretonne for a skirt. I planned to put up some kind of barricade between my bed and Laird's, to keep my section separate from his. In the sunlight, the lace curtains were just dusty rags. We did not sing at night any more. One night when I was singing Laird said, "You sound silly," and I went right on but the next night I did not start. There was not so much need to anyway, we were no longer afraid. We knew it was just old furniture over there, old jumble and confusion. We did not keep to the rules. I still stayed awake after Laird was asleep and told myself stories, but even in these stories something different was happening, mysterious alterations took place. A story might start off in the old way, with a spectacular danger, a fire or wild animals, and for a while I might rescue people; then things would change around, and instead, somebody would be rescuing me. It might be a boy from our class at school, or even Mr. Campbell, our teacher, who tickled girls under the arms. And at this point the story concerned itself at great length with what I looked like—how long my hair was, and what kind of dress I had on; by the time I had these details worked out the real excitement of the story was lost.

It was later than one o'clock when the truck came back. The tarpaulin was over the back, which meant there was meat in it. My mother had to heat dinner up all over again. Henry and my father had changed from their bloody overalls into ordinary working overalls in the barn, and they washed their arms and necks and faces at the sink, and splashed water on their hair and combed it. Laird lifted his arm to show off a streak of blood. "We shot old Flora," he said, "and cut her up in fifty pieces."

"Well I don't want to hear about it," my mother said. "And don't come to my table like that."

My father made him go and wash the blood off. 55

We sat down and my father said grace and Henry pasted his chewing-gum on the end of his fork, the way he always did; when he took it off he would have us admire the pattern. We began to pass the bowls of steaming, overcooked vegetables. Laird looked across the table at me and said proudly, distinctly, "Anyway it was her fault Flora got away."

"What?" my father said.

"She could of shut the gate and she didn't. She just open' it up and Flora run out."

"Is that right?" my father said.

60 Everybody at the table was looking at me. I nodded, swallowing food with great difficulty. To my shame, tears flooded my eyes.

My father made a curt sound of disgust. "What did you do that for?"

I did not answer. I put down my fork and waited to be sent from the table, still not looking up.

But this did not happen. For some time nobody said anything, then Laird said matter-of-factly, "She's crying."

"Never mind," my father said. He spoke with resignation, even good humour, the words which absolved and dismissed me for good. "She's only a girl," he said.

65 I didn't protest that, even in my heart. Maybe it was true.

1968

FLANNERY O'CONNOR

(1925–1964)

A Good Man Is Hard to Find

Mary Flannery O'Connor was born in Savannah, Georgia, studied at the Georgia State College for Women, and won a fellowship to the Writers' Workshop of the University of Iowa, from which she received her MFA. In 1950, she was first diagnosed with lupus, an autoimmune disorder that also afflicted her father and would trouble her for the rest of her brief life. Her first novel, *Wise Blood*, was published in 1952, and her first collection of stories, *A Good Man Is Hard to Find*, in 1955. She was able to complete only one more novel, *The Violent Bear It Away* (1960), and a second collection of stories, *Everything That Rises Must Converge* (1965), before her death. Her posthumously published *Complete Stories* won the National Book Award in 1972. A collection of letters, edited by Sam Fitzgerald under the title *The Habit of Being*, appeared in 1979.

The grandmother didn't want to go to Florida. She wanted to visit some of her connections in east Tennessee and she was seizing at every chance to change Bailey's mind. Bailey was the son she lived with, her only boy. He was sitting on the edge of his chair at the table, bent over the orange sports section of the *Journal*. "Now look here, Bailey," she said, "see here, read this," and she stood with one hand on her thin hip and the other rattling the newspaper at his bald head. "Here this fellow that calls himself The Misfit is aloose from the Federal Pen and headed toward Florida and you read here what it says he did to these people. Just you read it. I wouldn't take my children in any direction with a criminal like that aloose in it. I couldn't answer to my conscience if I did."

Bailey didn't look up from his reading so she wheeled around then and faced the children's mother, a young woman in slacks, whose face was as broad and innocent as a cabbage and was tied around with a green head-kerchief that had two points on the top like a rabbit's ears. She was sitting on the sofa, feeding the baby his apricots out of a jar. "The children have been to Florida before," the old lady said. "You all ought to take them somewhere else for a change so they would see different parts of the world and be broad. They never have been to east Tennessee."

The children's mother didn't seem to hear her but the eight-year-old boy, John Wesley, a stocky child with glasses, said, "If you don't want to go to Florida, why dontcha stay at home?" He and the little girl, June Star, were reading the funny papers on the floor.

"She wouldn't stay at home to be queen for a day," June Star said without raising her yellow head.

"Yes and what would you do if this fellow, The Misfit, caught you?" the   5 grandmother asked.

"I'd smack his face," John Wesley said.

"She wouldn't stay at home for a million bucks," June Star said. "Afraid she'd miss something. She has to go everywhere we go."

"All right, Miss," the grandmother said. "Just remember that the next time you want me to curl your hair."

June Star said her hair was naturally curly.

The next morning the grandmother was the first one in the car, ready to go.   10 She had her big black valise that looked like the head of a hippopotamus in one corner, and underneath it she was hiding a basket with Pitty Sing,[1] the cat, in it. She didn't intend for the cat to be left alone in the house for three days because he would miss her too much and she was afraid he might brush against one of the gas burners and accidentally asphyxiate himself. Her son, Bailey, didn't like to arrive at a motel with a cat.

She sat in the middle of the back seat with John Wesley and June Star on either side of her. Bailey and the children's mother and the baby sat in front and they left Atlanta at eight forty-five with the mileage on the car at 55890. The grandmother wrote this down because she thought it would be interesting to say how many miles they had been when they got back. It took them twenty minutes to reach the outskirts of the city.

The old lady settled herself comfortably, removing her white cotton gloves and putting them up with her purse on the shelf in front of the back window. The children's mother still had on slacks and still had her head tied up in a green kerchief, but the grandmother had on a navy blue straw sailor hat with a bunch of white violets on the brim and a navy blue dress with a small white dot in the print. Her collars and cuffs were white organdy trimmed with lace and at her neckline she had pinned a purple spray of cloth violets containing a sachet. In case of an accident, anyone seeing her dead on the highway would know at once that she was a lady.

She said she thought it was going to be a good day for driving, neither too hot nor too cold, and she cautioned Bailey that the speed limit was fifty-five miles an hour and that the patrolmen hid themselves behind billboards and small clumps of trees and sped out after you before you had a chance to slow down.

---

1. Named after Pitti-Sing, one of the "three little maids from school" in W. S. Gilbert and Arthur Sullivan's operetta *The Mikado* (1885).

She pointed out interesting details of the scenery: Stone Mountain; the blue granite that in some places came up to both sides of the highway; the brilliant red clay banks slightly streaked with purple; and the various crops that made rows of green lace-work on the ground. The trees were full of silver-white sunlight and the meanest of them sparkled. The children were reading comic magazines and their mother had gone back to sleep.

"Let's go through Georgia fast so we won't have to look at it much," John Wesley said.

15   "If I were a little boy," said the grandmother, "I wouldn't talk about my native state that way. Tennessee has the mountains and Georgia has the hills."

"Tennessee is just a hillbilly dumping ground," John Wesley said, "and Georgia is a lousy state too."

"You said it," June Star said.

"In my time," said the grandmother, folding her thin veined fingers, "children were more respectful of their native states and their parents and everything else. People did right then. Oh look at the cute little pickaninny!" she said and pointed to a Negro child standing in the door of a shack. "Wouldn't that make a picture, now?" she asked and they all turned and looked at the little Negro out of the back window. He waved.

"He didn't have any britches on," June Star said.

20   "He probably didn't have any," the grandmother explained. "Little niggers in the country don't have things like we do. If I could paint, I'd paint that picture," she said.

The children exchanged comic books.

The grandmother offered to hold the baby and the children's mother passed him over the front seat to her. She set him on her knee and bounced him and told him about the things they were passing. She rolled her eyes and screwed up her mouth and stuck her leathery thin face into his smooth bland one. Occasionally he gave her a faraway smile. They passed a large cotton field with five or six graves fenced in the middle of it, like a small island. "Look at the graveyard!" the grandmother said, pointing it out. "That was the old family burying ground. That belonged to the plantation."

"Where's the plantation?" John Wesley asked.

"Gone with the Wind,"[2] said the grandmother. "Ha. Ha."

25   When the children finished all the comic books they had brought, they opened the lunch and ate it. The grandmother ate a peanut butter sandwich and an olive and would not let the children throw the box and the paper napkins out the window. When there was nothing else to do they played a game by choosing a cloud and making the other two guess what shape it suggested. John Wesley took one the shape of a cow and June Star guessed a cow and John Wesley said, no, an automobile, and June Star said he didn't play fair, and they began to slap each other over the grandmother.

The grandmother said she would tell them a story if they would keep quiet. When she told a story, she rolled her eyes and waved her head and was very

2. Title of an immensely popular novel, published in 1936, by Margaret Mitchell (1900–49); the novel depicts a large, prosperous Southern plantation, Tara, that is destroyed by Northern troops in the American Civil War.

dramatic. She said once when she was a maiden lady she had been courted by a Mr. Edgar Atkins Teagarden from Jasper, Georgia. She said he was a very good-looking man and a gentleman and that he brought her a watermelon every Saturday afternoon with his initials cut in it, E. A. T. Well, one Saturday, she said, Mr. Teagarden brought the watermelon and there was nobody at home and he left it on the front porch and returned in his buggy to Jasper, but she never got the watermelon, she said, because a nigger boy ate it when he saw the initials, E. A. T.! This story tickled John Wesley's funny bone and he giggled and giggled but June Star didn't think it was any good. She said she wouldn't marry a man that just brought her a watermelon on Saturday. The grandmother said she would have done well to marry Mr. Teagarden because he was a gentleman and had bought Coca-Cola stock when it first came out and that he had died only a few years ago, a very wealthy man.

They stopped at The Tower for barbecued sandwiches. The Tower was a part stucco and part wood filling station and dance hall set in a clearing outside of Timothy. A fat man named Red Sammy Butts ran it and there were signs stuck here and there on the building and for miles up and down the highway saying, TRY RED SAMMY'S FAMOUS BARBECUE. NONE LIKE FAMOUS RED SAMMY'S! RED SAM! THE FAT BOY WITH THE HAPPY LAUGH! A VETERAN! RED SAMMY'S YOUR MAN!

Red Sammy was lying on the bare ground outside The Tower with his head under a truck while a gray monkey about a foot high, chained to a small chinaberry tree, chattered nearby. The monkey sprang back into the tree and got on the highest limb as soon as he saw the children jump out of the car and run toward him.

Inside, The Tower was a long dark room with a counter at one end and tables at the other and dancing space in the middle. They all sat down at a board table next to the nickelodeon[3] and Red Sam's wife, a tall burnt-brown woman with hair and eyes lighter than her skin, came and took their order. The children's mother put a dime in the machine and played "The Tennessee Waltz," and the grandmother said that tune always made her want to dance. She asked Bailey if he would like to dance but he only glared at her. He didn't have a naturally sunny disposition like she did and trips made him nervous. The grandmother's brown eyes were very bright. She swayed her head from side to side and pretended she was dancing in her chair. June Star said play something she could tap to so the children's mother put in another dime and played a fast number and June Star stepped out onto the dance floor and did her tap routine.

"Ain't she cute?" Red Sam's wife said, leaning over the counter. "Would you like to come be my little girl?"   30

"No I certainly wouldn't," June Star said. "I wouldn't live in a broken-down place like this for a million bucks!" and she ran back to the table.

"Ain't she cute?" the woman repeated, stretching her mouth politely.

"Aren't you ashamed?" hissed the grandmother.

Red Sam came in and told his wife to quit lounging on the counter and hurry up with these people's order. His khaki trousers reached just to his hip bones and his stomach hung over them like a sack of meal swaying under his shirt. He came over and sat down at a table nearby and let out a combination sigh and

3. Jukebox.

yodel. "You can't win," he said. "You can't win," and he wiped his sweating red face off with a gray handkerchief. "These days you don't know who to trust," he said. "Ain't that the truth?"

35   "People are certainly not nice like they used to be," said the grandmother.

"Two fellers come in here last week," Red Sammy said, "driving a Chrysler. It was a old beat-up car but it was a good one and these boys looked all right to me. Said they worked at the mill and you know I let them fellers charge the gas they bought? Now why did I do that?"

"Because you're a good man!" the grandmother said at once.

"Yes'm, I suppose so," Red Sam said as if he were struck with this answer.

His wife brought the orders, carrying the five plates all at once without a tray, two in each hand and one balanced on her arm. "It isn't a soul in this green world of God's that you can trust," she said. "And I don't count nobody out of that, not nobody," she repeated, looking at Red Sammy.

40   "Did you read about that criminal, The Misfit, that's escaped?" asked the grandmother.

"I wouldn't be a bit surprised if he didn't attact this place right here," said the woman. "If he hears about it being here, I wouldn't be none surprised to see him. If he hears it's two cent in the cash register, I wouldn't be a tall surprised if he . . ."

"That'll do," Red Sam said. "Go bring these people their Co'-Colas," and the woman went off to get the rest of the order.

"A good man is hard to find," Red Sammy said. "Everything is getting terrible. I remember the day you could go off and leave your screen door unlatched. Not no more."

He and the grandmother discussed better times. The old lady said that in her opinion Europe was entirely to blame for the way things were now. She said the way Europe acted you would think we were made of money and Red Sam said it was no use talking about it, she was exactly right. The children ran outside into the white sunlight and looked at the monkey in the lacy chinaberry tree. He was busy catching fleas on himself and biting each one carefully between his teeth as if it were a delicacy.

45   They drove off again into the hot afternoon. The grandmother took cat naps and woke up every few minutes with her own snoring. Outside of Toombsboro she woke up and recalled an old plantation that she had visited in this neighborhood once when she was a young lady. She said the house had six white columns across the front and that there was an avenue of oaks leading up to it and two little wooden trellis arbors on either side in front where you sat down with your suitor after a stroll in the garden. She recalled exactly which road to turn off to get to it. She knew that Bailey would not be willing to lose any time looking at an old house, but the more she talked about it, the more she wanted to see it once again and find out if the little twin arbors were still standing. "There was a secret panel in this house," she said craftily, not telling the truth but wishing that she were, "and the story went that all the family silver was hidden in it when Sherman came through but it was never found . . ."

"Hey!" John Wesley said. "Let's go see it! We'll find it! We'll poke all the woodwork and find it! Who lives there? Where do you turn off at? Hey Pop, can't we turn off there?"

"We never have seen a house with a secret panel!" June Star shrieked. "Let's go to the house with the secret panel! Hey Pop, can't we go see the house with the secret panel!"

"It's not far from here, I know," the grandmother said. "It wouldn't take over twenty minutes."

Bailey was looking straight ahead. His jaw was as rigid as a horseshoe. "No," he said.

The children began to yell and scream that they wanted to see the house 50 with the secret panel. John Wesley kicked the back of the front seat and June Star hung over her mother's shoulder and whined desperately into her ear that they never had any fun even on their vacation, that they could never do what THEY wanted to do. The baby began to scream and John Wesley kicked the back of the seat so hard that his father could feel the blows in his kidney.

"All right!" he shouted and drew the car to a stop at the side of the road. "Will you all shut up? Will you all just shut up for one second? If you don't shut up, we won't go anywhere."

"It would be very educational for them," the grandmother murmured.

"All right," Bailey said, "but get this: this is the only time we're going to stop for anything like this. This is the one and only time."

"The dirt road that you have to turn down is about a mile back," the grandmother directed. "I marked it when we passed."

"A dirt road," Bailey groaned. 55

After they had turned around and were headed toward the dirt road, the grandmother recalled other points about the house, the beautiful glass over the front doorway and the candle-lamp in the hall. John Wesley said that the secret panel was probably in the fireplace.

"You can't go inside this house," Bailey said. "You don't know who lives there."

"While you all talk to the people in front, I'll run around behind and get in a window," John Wesley suggested.

"We'll all stay in the car," his mother said.

They turned onto the dirt road and the car raced roughly along in a swirl of 60 pink dust. The grandmother recalled the times when there were no paved roads and thirty miles was a day's journey. The dirt road was hilly and there were sudden washes in it and sharp curves on dangerous embankments. All at once they would be on a hill, looking down over the blue tops of trees for miles around, then the next minute, they would be in a red depression with the dust-coated trees looking down on them.

"This place had better turn up in a minute," Bailey said, "or I'm going to turn around."

The road looked as if no one had traveled on it in months.

"It's not much farther," the grandmother said and just as she said it, a horrible thought came to her. The thought was so embarrassing that she turned red in the face and her eyes dilated and her feet jumped up, upsetting her valise in the corner. The instant the valise moved, the newspaper top she had over the basket under it rose with a snarl and Pitty Sing, the cat, sprang onto Bailey's shoulder.

The children were thrown to the floor and their mother, clutching the baby, out the door onto the ground; the old lady was thrown into the front seat. The car turned over once and landed right-side-up in a gulch off the side of the road.

Bailey remained in the driver's seat with the cat—gray-striped with a broad white face and an orange nose—clinging to his neck like a caterpillar.

65   As soon as the children saw they could move their arms and legs, they scrambled out of the car, shouting, "We've had an ACCIDENT!" The grandmother was curled up under the dashboard, hoping she was injured so that Bailey's wrath would not come down on her all at once. The horrible thought she had had before the accident was that the house she had remembered so vividly was not in Georgia but in Tennessee.

Bailey removed the cat from his neck with both hands and flung it out the window against the side of a pine tree. Then he got out of the car and started looking for the children's mother. She was sitting against the side of the red gutted ditch, holding the screaming baby, but she only had a cut down her face and a broken shoulder. "We've had an ACCIDENT!" the children screamed in a frenzy of delight.

"But nobody's killed," June Star said with disappointment as the grandmother limped out of the car, her hat still pinned to her head but the broken front brim standing up at a jaunty angle and the violet spray hanging off the side. They all sat down in the ditch, except the children, to recover from the shock. They were all shaking.

"Maybe a car will come along," said the children's mother hoarsely.

"I believe I have injured an organ," said the grandmother, pressing her side, but no one answered her. Bailey's teeth were clattering. He had on a yellow sport shirt with bright blue parrots designed in it and his face was as yellow as the shirt. The grandmother decided that she would not mention that the house was in Tennessee.

70   The road was about ten feet above and they could see only the tops of the trees on the other side of it. Behind the ditch they were sitting in there were more woods, tall and dark and deep. In a few minutes they saw a car some distance away on top of a hill, coming slowly as if the occupants were watching them. The grandmother stood up and waved both arms dramatically to attract their attention. The car continued to come on slowly, disappeared around a bend and appeared again, moving even slower, on top of the hill they had gone over. It was a big black battered hearselike automobile. There were three men in it.

It came to a stop just over them and for some minutes, the driver looked down with a steady expressionless gaze to where they were sitting, and didn't speak. Then he turned his head and muttered something to the other two and they got out. One was a fat boy in black trousers and a red sweat shirt with a silver stallion embossed on the front of it. He moved around on the right side of them and stood staring, his mouth partly open in a kind of loose grin. The other had on khaki pants and a blue striped coat and a gray hat pulled down very low, hiding most of his face. He came around slowly on the left side. Neither spoke.

The driver got out of the car and stood by the side of it, looking down at them. He was an older man than the other two. His hair was just beginning to gray and he wore silver-rimmed spectacles that gave him a scholarly look. He had a long creased face and didn't have on any shirt or undershirt. He had on blue jeans that were too tight for him and was holding a black hat and a gun. The two boys also had guns.

"We've had an ACCIDENT!" the children screamed.

The grandmother had the peculiar feeling that the bespectacled man was someone she knew. His face was as familiar to her as if she had known him all her life but she could not recall who he was. He moved away from the car and began to come down the embankment, placing his feet carefully so that he wouldn't slip. He had on tan and white shoes and no socks, and his ankles were red and thin. "Good afternoon," he said. "I see you all had you a little spill."

"We turned over twice!" said the grandmother.   75

"Oncet," he corrected. "We seen it happen. Try their car and see will it run, Hiram," he said quietly to the boy with the gray hat.

"What you got that gun for?" John Wesley asked. "Whatcha gonna do with that gun?"

"Lady," the man said to the children's mother, "would you mind calling them children to sit down by you? Children make me nervous. I want all you all to sit down right together there where you're at."

"What are you telling US what to do for?" June Star asked.

Behind them the line of woods gaped like a dark open mouth. "Come here,"   80 said their mother.

"Look here now," Bailey began suddenly, "we're in a predicament! We're in . . ."

The grandmother shrieked. She scrambled to her feet and stood staring. "You're The Misfit!" she said. "I recognized you at once!"

"Yes'm," the man said, smiling slightly as if he were pleased in spite of himself to be known, "but it would have been better for all of you, lady, if you hadn't of reckernized me."

Bailey turned his head sharply and said something to his mother that shocked even the children. The old lady began to cry and The Misfit reddened.

"Lady," he said, "don't you get upset. Sometimes a man says things he don't   85 mean. I don't reckon he meant to talk to you thataway."

"You wouldn't shoot a lady, would you?" the grandmother said and removed a clean handkerchief from her cuff and began to slap at her eyes with it.

The Misfit pointed the toe of his shoe into the ground and made a little hole and then covered it up again. "I would hate to have to," he said.

"Listen," the grandmother almost screamed, "I know you're a good man. You don't look a bit like you have common blood. I know you must come from nice people!"

"Yes mam," he said, "finest people in the world." When he smiled he showed a row of strong white teeth. "God never made a finer woman than my mother and my daddy's heart was pure gold," he said. The boy with the red sweat shirt had come around behind them and was standing with his gun at his hip. The Misfit squatted down on the ground. "Watch them children, Bobby Lee," he said. "You know they make me nervous." He looked at the six of them huddled together in front of him and he seemed to be embarrassed as if he couldn't think of anything to say. "Ain't a cloud in the sky," he remarked, looking up at it. "Don't see no sun but don't see no cloud neither."

"Yes, it's a beautiful day," said the grandmother. "Listen," she said, "you   90 shouldn't call yourself The Misfit because I know you're a good man at heart. I can just look at you and tell."

"Hush!" Bailey yelled. "Hush! Everybody shut up and let me handle this!" He was squatting in the position of a runner about to sprint forward but he didn't move.

"I pre-chate that, lady," The Misfit said and drew a little circle in the ground with the butt of his gun.

"It'll take a half a hour to fix this here car," Hiram called, looking over the raised hood of it.

"Well, first you and Bobby Lee get him and that little boy to step over yonder with you," The Misfit said, pointing to Bailey and John Wesley. "The boys want to ast you something," he said to Bailey. "Would you mind stepping back in them woods there with them?"

95   "Listen," Bailey began, "we're in a terrible predicament! Nobody realizes what this is," and his voice cracked. His eyes were as blue and intense as the parrots in his shirt and he remained perfectly still.

The grandmother reached up to adjust her hat brim as if she were going to the woods with him but it came off in her hand. She stood staring at it and after a second she let it fall on the ground. Hiram pulled Bailey up by the arm as if he were assisting an old man. John Wesley caught hold of his father's hand and Bobby Lee followed. They went off toward the woods and just as they reached the dark edge, Bailey turned and supporting himself against a gray naked pine trunk, he shouted, "I'll be back in a minute, Mamma, wait on me!"

"Come back this instant!" his mother shrilled but they all disappeared into the woods.

"Bailey Boy!" the grandmother called in a tragic voice but she found she was looking at The Misfit squatting on the ground in front of her. "I just know you're a good man," she said desperately. "You're not a bit common!"

"Nome, I ain't a good man," The Misfit said after a second as if he had considered her statement carefully, "but I ain't the worst in the world neither. My daddy said I was a different breed of dog from my brothers and sisters. 'You know,' Daddy said, 'it's some that can live their whole life out without asking about it and it's others has to know why it is, and this boy is one of the latters. He's going to be into everything!'" He put on his black hat and looked up suddenly and then away deep into the woods as if he were embarrassed again. "I'm sorry I don't have on a shirt before you ladies," he said, hunching his shoulders slightly. "We buried our clothes that we had on when we escaped and we're just making do until we can get better. We borrowed these from some folks we met," he explained.

100   "That's perfectly all right," the grandmother said. "Maybe Bailey has an extra shirt in his suitcase."

"I'll look and see terrectly," The Misfit said.

"Where are they taking him?" the children's mother screamed.

"Daddy was a card himself," The Misfit said. "You couldn't put anything over on him. He never got in trouble with the Authorities though. Just had the knack of handling them."

"You could be honest too if you'd only try," said the grandmother. "Think how wonderful it would be to settle down and live a comfortable life and not have to think about somebody chasing you all the time."

The Misfit kept scratching in the ground with the butt of his gun as if he   105
were thinking about it. "Yes'm, somebody is always after you," he murmured.

The grandmother noticed how thin his shoulder blades were just behind his
hat because she was standing up looking down on him. "Do you ever pray?" she
asked.

He shook his head. All she saw was the black hat wiggle between his shoulder blades. "Nome," he said.

There was a pistol shot from the woods, followed closely by another. Then
silence. The old lady's head jerked around. She could hear the wind move through
the tree tops like a long satisfied insuck of breath. "Bailey Boy!" she called.

"I was a gospel singer for a while," The Misfit said. "I been most everything.
Been in the arm service, both land and sea, at home and abroad, been twict
married, been an undertaker, been with the railroads, plowed Mother Earth,
been in a tornado, seen a man burnt alive oncet," and looked up at the children's
mother and the little girl who were sitting close together, their faces white and
their eyes glassy; "I even seen a woman flogged," he said.

"Pray, pray," the grandmother began, "pray, pray. . . ."   110

"I never was a bad boy that I remember of," The Misfit said in an almost
dreamy voice, "but somewheres along the line I done something wrong and got
sent to the penitentiary. I was buried alive," and he looked up and held her
attention to him by a steady stare.

"That's when you should have started to pray," she said. "What did you do to
get sent to the penitentiary that first time?"

"Turn to the right, it was a wall," The Misfit said, looking up again at the
cloudless sky. "Turn to the left, it was a wall. Look up it was a ceiling, look down
it was a floor. I forgot what I done, lady. I set there and set there, trying to
remember what it was I done and I ain't recalled it to this day. Oncet in a while,
I would think it was coming to me, but it never come."

"Maybe they put you in by mistake," the old lady said vaguely.

"Nome," he said. "It wasn't no mistake. They had the papers on me."   115

"You must have stolen something," she said.

The Misfit sneered slightly. "Nobody had nothing I wanted," he said. "It was
a head-doctor at the penitentiary said what I had done was kill my daddy but I
known that for a lie. My daddy died in nineteen ought nineteen of the epidemic
flu and I never had a thing to do with it. He was buried in the Mount Hopewell
Baptist churchyard and you can go there and see for yourself."

"If you would pray," the old lady said, "Jesus would help you."

"That's right," The Misfit said.

"Well then, why don't you pray?" she asked trembling with delight suddenly.   120

"I don't want no hep," he said. "I'm doing all right by myself."

Bobby Lee and Hiram came ambling back from the woods. Bobby Lee was
dragging a yellow shirt with bright blue parrots in it.

"Thow me that shirt, Bobby Lee," The Misfit said. The shirt came flying
at him and landed on his shoulder and he put it on. The grandmother couldn't
name what the shirt reminded her of. "No, lady," The Misfit said while he was
buttoning it up, "I found out the crime don't matter. You can do one thing or you
can do another, kill a man or take a tire off his car, because sooner or later
you're going to forget what it was you done and just be punished for it."

The children's mother had begun to make heaving noises as if she couldn't get her breath. "Lady," he asked, "would you and that little girl like to step off yonder with Bobby Lee and Hiram and join your husband?"

125   "Yes, thank you," the mother said faintly. Her left arm dangled helplessly and she was holding the baby, who had gone to sleep, in the other. "Hep that lady up, Hiram," The Misfit said as she struggled to climb out of the ditch, "and Bobby Lee, you hold onto that little girl's hand."

"I don't want to hold hands with him," June Star said. "He reminds me of a pig."

The fat boy blushed and laughed and caught her by the arm and pulled her off into the woods after Hiram and her mother.

Alone with The Misfit, the grandmother found that she had lost her voice. There was not a cloud in the sky nor any sun. There was nothing around her but woods. She wanted to tell him that he must pray. She opened and closed her mouth several times before anything came out. Finally she found herself saying, "Jesus, Jesus," meaning, Jesus will help you, but the way she was saying it, it sounded as if she might be cursing.

"Yes'm," The Misfit said as if he agreed. "Jesus thown everything off balance. It was the same case with Him as with me except He hadn't committed any crime and they could prove I had committed one because they had the papers on me. Of course," he said, "they never shown me my papers. That's why I sign myself now. I said long ago, you get you a signature and sign everything you do and keep a copy of it. Then you'll know what you done and you can hold up the crime to the punishment and see do they match and in the end you'll have something to prove you ain't been treated right. I call myself The Misfit," he said, "because I can't make what all I done wrong fit what all I gone through in punishment."

130   There was a piercing scream from the woods, followed closely by a pistol report. "Does it seem right to you, lady, that one is punished a heap and another ain't punished at all?"

"Jesus!" the old lady cried. "You've got good blood! I know you wouldn't shoot a lady! I know you come from nice people! Pray! Jesus, you ought not to shoot a lady. I'll give you all the money I've got!"

"Lady," The Misfit said, looking beyond her far into the woods, "there never was a body that give the undertaker a tip."

There were two more pistol reports and the grandmother raised her head like a parched old turkey hen crying for water and called, "Bailey Boy, Bailey Boy!" as if her heart would break.

"Jesus was the only One that ever raised the dead." The Misfit continued, "and He shouldn't have done it. He thown everything off balance. If He did what He said, then it's nothing for you to do but thow away everything and follow Him, and if He didn't, then it's nothing for you to do but enjoy the few minutes you got left the best way you can—by killing somebody or burning down his house or doing some other meanness to him. No pleasure but meanness," he said and his voice had become almost a snarl.

135   "Maybe He didn't raise the dead," the old lady mumbled, not knowing what she was saying and feeling so dizzy that she sank down in the ditch with her legs twisted under her.

"I wasn't there so I can't say He didn't," The Misfit said. "I wisht I had of been there," he said, hitting the ground with his fist. "It ain't right I wasn't there because if I had of been there I would of known. Listen lady," he said in a high voice, "if I had of been there I would of known and I wouldn't be like I am now." His voice seemed about to crack and the grandmother's head cleared for an instant. She saw the man's face twisted close to her own as if he were going to cry and she murmured, "Why you're one of my babies. You're one of my own children!" She reached out and touched him on the shoulder. The Misfit sprang back as if a snake had bitten him and shot her three times through the chest. Then he put his gun down on the ground and took off his glasses and began to clean them.

Hiram and Bobby Lee returned from the woods and stood over the ditch, looking down at the grandmother who half sat and half lay in a puddle of blood with her legs crossed under her like a child's and her face smiling up at the cloudless sky.

Without his glasses, The Misfit's eyes were red-rimmed and pale and defenseless-looking. "Take her off and thow her where you thown the others," he said, picking up the cat that was rubbing itself against his leg.

"She was a talker, wasn't she?" Bobby Lee said, sliding down the ditch with a yodel.

"She would of been a good woman," The Misfit said, "if it had been some- 140 body there to shoot her every minute of her life."

"Some fun!" Bobby Lee said.

"Shut up, Bobby Lee," The Misfit said. "It's no real pleasure in life."

1953

KAREN RUSSELL

(b. 1981)

St. Lucy's Home for Girls Raised by Wolves

Karen Russell's first novel, *Swamplandia!* (2011), details the lives of a family of alligator wrestlers in what she calls "the most bizarre place" on earth—her childhood home of South Florida. After leaving Florida, Russell attended Northwestern University and toyed with the idea of becoming a veterinarian. Deciding that "loving animals and removing deflated basketballs from the intestinal tracts of animals are two very different skill sets," she instead turned to writing, earning an MFA from Columbia University. Just twenty-six when she published her first short-story collection, *St. Lucy's Home for Girls Raised by Wolves* (2006), Russell is almost as renowned for her youth as for her remarkable fiction; both ensured her inclusion on *New York Magazine*'s list of twenty-seven impressive New Yorkers under the age of twenty-six (2005), *Granta*'s Best Young American Novelists (2007), the National Book Foundation's "5 Under 35" (2009), and the *New Yorker*'s "20 under 40" (2010). Since winning a 2013 MacArthur Foundation "genius grant," Russell has published *Vampires in the Lemon Grove: Stories* (2013) and *Sleep Donation: A Novella* (2014). Often blending realism with the totally outlandish, her work has been compared to "slipstream," a genre-bending form of fiction with roots in magical realism. Russell herself, however, often cites "George Saunders's sad/funny ratio" and his work's "deep humility" as her inspirations.

Stage 1: The initial period is one in which everything is new, exciting, and interesting for your students. It is fun for your students to explore their new environment.

—From *The Jesuit Handbook on Lycanthropic Culture Shock*

A t first, our pack was all hair and snarl and floor-thumping joy. We forgot the barked cautions of our mothers and fathers, all the promises we'd made to be civilized and ladylike, couth and kempt. We tore through the austere rooms, overturning dresser drawers, pawing through the neat piles of the Stage 3 girls' starched underwear, smashing lightbulbs with our bare fists. Things felt less foreign in the dark. The dim bedroom was windowless and odorless. We remedied this by spraying exuberant yellow streams all over the bunks. We jumped from bunk to bunk, spraying. We nosed each other midair, our bodies buckling in kinetic laughter. The nuns watched us from the corner of the bedroom, their tiny faces pinched with displeasure.

"*Ay caramba*," Sister Maria de la Guardia sighed. "*Que barbaridad!*"[1] She made the Sign of the Cross. Sister Maria came to St. Lucy's from a halfway home in Copacabana. In Copacabana, the girls are fat and languid and eat pink slivers of guava right out of your hand. Even at Stage 1, their pelts are silky, sunbleached to near invisibility. Our pack was hirsute and sinewy and mostly brunette. We had terrible posture. We went knuckling along the wooden floor on the calloused pads of our fists, baring row after row of tiny, wood-rotted teeth. Sister Josephine sucked in her breath. She removed a yellow wheel of floss from under her robes, looping it like a miniature lasso.

"The girls at our facility are *backwoods*,'" Sister Josephine whispered to Sister Maria de la Guardia with a beatific smile. "You must be patient with them." I clamped down on her ankle, straining to close my jaws around the woolly XXL sock. Sister Josephine tasted like sweat and freckles. She smelled easy to kill.

We'd arrived at St. Lucy's that morning, part of a pack fifteen-strong. We were accompanied by a mousy, nervous-smelling social worker; the baby-faced deacon; Bartholomew, the blue wolfhound; and four burly woodsmen. The deacon handed out some stale cupcakes and said a quick prayer. Then he led us through the woods. We ran past the wild apiary, past the felled oaks, until we could see the white steeple of St. Lucy's rising out of the forest. We stopped short at the edge of a muddy lake. Then the deacon took our brothers. Bartholomew helped him to herd the boys up the ramp of a small ferry. We girls ran along the shore, tearing at our new jumpers in a plaid agitation. Our brothers stood on the deck, looking small and confused.

5   Our mothers and fathers were werewolves. They lived an outsider's existence in caves at the edge of the forest, threatened by frost and pitchforks. They had been ostracized by the local farmers for eating their silled fruit pies and terrorizing the heifers. They had ostracized the local wolves by having sometimes-thumbs, and regrets, and human children. (Their condition skips a generation.) Our pack grew up in a green purgatory. We couldn't keep up with the purebred wolves, but we never stopped crawling. We spoke a slab-tongued pidgin[2] in the

---

1. What barbarity (Spanish). *Ay caramba*: good grief (Spanish).
2. Simplified speech used for communication between speakers of different languages.

cave, inflected with frequent howls. Our parents wanted something better for us; they wanted us to get braces, use towels, be fully bilingual. When the nuns showed up, our parents couldn't refuse their offer. The nuns, they said, would make us naturalized citizens of human society. We would go to St. Lucy's to study a better culture. We didn't know at the time that our parents were sending us away for good. Neither did they.

That first afternoon, the nuns gave us free rein of the grounds. Everything was new, exciting, and interesting. A low granite wall surrounded St. Lucy's, the blue woods humming for miles behind it. There was a stone fountain full of delectable birds. There was a statue of St. Lucy.[3] Her marble skin was colder than our mother's nose, her pupil-less eyes rolled heavenward. Doomed squirrels gamboled around her stony toes. Our diminished pack threw back our heads in a celebratory howl—an exultant and terrible noise, even without a chorus of wolf brothers in the background. There were holes everywhere!

We supplemented these holes by digging some of our own. We interred sticks, and our itchy new jumpers, and the bones of the friendly, unfortunate squirrels. Our noses ached beneath an invisible assault. Everything was smudged with a human odor: baking bread, petrol, the nuns' faint woman-smell sweating out beneath a dark perfume of tallow and incense. We smelled one another, too, with the same astounded fascination. Our own scent had become foreign in this strange place.

We had just sprawled out in the sun for an afternoon nap, yawning into the warm dirt, when the nuns reappeared. They conferred in the shadow of the juniper tree, whispering and pointing. Then they started towards us. The oldest sister had spent the past hour twitching in her sleep, dreaming of fatty and infirm elk. (The pack used to dream the same dreams back then, as naturally as we drank the same water and slept on the same red scree.[4]) When our oldest sister saw the nuns approaching, she instinctively bristled. It was an improvised bristle, given her new, human limitations. She took clumps of her scraggly, nut-brown hair and held it straight out from her head.

Sister Maria gave her a brave smile.

"And what is your name?" she asked.

The oldest sister howled something awful and inarticulate, a distillate of hurt and panic, half-forgotten hunts and eclipsed moons. Sister Maria nodded and scribbled on a yellow legal pad. She slapped on a name tag: HELLO, MY NAME IS _____! "Jeanette it is."

The rest of the pack ran in a loose, uncertain circle, torn between our instinct to help her and our new fear. We sensed some subtler danger afoot, written in a language we didn't understand.

Our littlest sister had the quickest reflexes. She used her hands to flatten her ears to the side of her head. She backed towards the far corner of the garden, snarling in the most menacing register that an eight-year-old wolf-girl can mus-

10

3. Patron saint of the blind, St. Lucy (283–304) either took out her own eyes or was blinded by others, according to legend, defending her vow to remain a virgin and dedicate her life and fortune to God rather than marry a pagan.
4. Loose stones or rocky debris.

ter. Then she ran. It took them two hours to pin her down and tag her: HELLO, MY NAME IS MIRABELLA!

"Stage 1," Sister Maria sighed, taking careful aim with her tranquilizer dart. "It can be a little overstimulating."

> Stage 2: After a time, your students realize that they must work to adjust to the new culture. This work may be stressful and students may experience a strong sense of dislocation. They may miss certain foods. They may spend a lot of time daydreaming during this period. Many students feel isolated, irritated, bewildered, depressed, or generally uncomfortable.

15   Those were the days when we dreamed of rivers and meat. The full-moon nights were the worst! Worse than cold toilet seats and boiled tomatoes, worse than trying to will our tongues to curl around our false new names. We would snarl at one another for no reason. I remember how disorienting it was to look down and see two square-toed shoes instead of my own four feet. Keep your mouth shut, I repeated during our walking drills, staring straight ahead. Keep your shoes on your feet. Mouth shut, shoes on feet. Do not chew on your new penny loafers. Do not. I stumbled around in a daze, my mouth black with shoe polish. The whole pack was irritated, bewildered, depressed. We were all uncomfortable, and between languages. We had never wanted to run away so badly in our lives; but who did we have to run back to? Only the curled black grimace of the mother. Only the father, holding his tawny head between his paws. Could we betray our parents by going back to them? After they'd given us the choicest part of the woodchuck, loved us at our hairless worst, nosed us across the ice floes and abandoned us at St. Lucy's for our own betterment?

Physically, we were all easily capable of clearing the low stone walls. Sister Josephine left the wooden gates wide open. They unslatted the windows at night so that long fingers of moonlight beckoned us from the woods. But we knew we couldn't return to the woods; not till we were civilized, not if we didn't want to break the mother's heart. It all felt like a sly, human taunt.

It was impossible to make the blank, chilly bedroom feel like home. In the beginning, we drank gallons of bathwater as part of a collaborative effort to mark our territory. We puddled up the yellow carpet of old newspapers. But later, when we returned to the bedroom, we were dismayed to find all trace of the pack musk had vanished. Someone was coming in and erasing us. We sprayed and sprayed every morning; and every night, we returned to the same ammonia eradication. We couldn't make our scent stick here; it made us feel invisible. Eventually we gave up. Still, the pack seemed to be adjusting on the same timetable. The advanced girls could already alternate between two speeds: "slouch" and "amble." Almost everybody was fully bipedal.

Almost.

The pack was worried about Mirabella.

20   Mirabella would rip foamy chunks out of the church pews and replace them with ham bones and girl dander. She loved to roam the grounds wagging her invisible tail. (We all had a hard time giving that up. When we got excited, we would fall to the ground and start pumping our backsides. Back in those days we could pump at rabbity velocities. *Que horror!* Sister Maria frowned, looking more than a

little jealous.) We'd give her scolding pinches. "Mirabella," we hissed, imitating the nuns. "No." Mirabella cocked her ears at us, hurt and confused.

Still, some things remained the same. The main commandment of wolf life is Know Your Place, and that translated perfectly. Being around other humans had awakened a slavish-dog affection in us. An abasing, belly-to-the-ground desire to please. As soon as we realized that someone higher up in the food chain was watching us, we wanted only to be pleasing in their sight. Mouth shut, I repeated, shoes on feet. But if Mirabella had this latent instinct, the nuns couldn't figure out how to activate it. She'd go bounding around, gleefully spraying on their gilded statue of St. Lucy, mad-scratching at the virulent fleas that survived all of their powders and baths. At Sister Maria's tearful insistence, she'd stand upright for roll call, her knobby, oddly muscled legs quivering from the effort. Then she'd collapse right back to the ground with an ecstatic *oomph!* She was still loping around on all fours (which the nuns had taught us to see looked unnatural and ridiculous—we could barely believe it now, the shame of it, that we used to locomote like that!), her fists blue-white from the strain. As if she were holding a secret tight to the ground. Sister Maria de la Guardia would sigh every time she saw her. *"Caramba!"* She'd sit down with Mirabella and pry her fingers apart. "You see?" she'd say softly, again and again. "What are you holding on to? Nothing, little one. Nothing."

Then she would sing out the standard chorus, "Why can't you be more like your sister Jeanette?"

The pack hated Jeanette. She was the most successful of us, the one furthest removed from her origins. Her real name was GWARR!, but she wouldn't respond to this anymore. Jeanette spiffed her penny loafers until her very shoes seemed to gloat. (Linguists have since traced the colloquial origins of "goody two-shoes" back to our facilities.) She could even growl out a demonic-sounding precursor to "Pleased to meet you." She'd delicately extend her former paws to visitors, wearing white kid gloves.

"Our little wolf, disguised in sheep's clothing!" Sister Ignatius liked to joke with the visiting deacons, and Jeanette would surprise everyone by laughing along with them, a harsh, inhuman, barking sound. Her hearing was still twig-snap sharp. Jeanette was the first among us to apologize; to drink apple juice out of a sippy cup; to quit eyeballing the cleric's jugular in a disconcerting fashion. She curled her lips back into a cousin of a smile as the traveling barber cut her pelt into bangs. Then she swept her coarse black curls under the rug. When we entered a room, our nostrils flared beneath the new odors: onion and bleach, candle wax, the turnipy smell of unwashed bodies. Not Jeanette. Jeanette smiled and pretended like she couldn't smell a thing.

I was one of the good girls. Not great and not terrible, solidly middle of the pack. But I had an ear for languages, and I could read before I could adequately wash myself. I probably could have vied with Jeanette for the number-one spot, but I'd seen what happened if you gave in to your natural aptitudes. This wasn't like the woods, where you had to be your fastest and your strongest and your bravest self. Different sorts of calculations were required to survive at the home.

The pack hated Jeanette, but we hated Mirabella more. We began to avoid her, but sometimes she'd surprise us, curled up beneath the beds or gnawing on a scapula in the garden. It was scary to be ambushed by your sister. I'd bristle and growl, the way that I'd begun to snarl at my own reflection as if it were a stranger.

"Whatever will become of Mirabella?" we asked, gulping back our own fear. We'd heard rumors about former wolf-girls who never adapted to their new culture. It was assumed that they were returned to our native country, the vanishing woods. We liked to speculate about this before bedtime, scaring ourselves with stories of catastrophic bliss. It was the disgrace, the failure that we all guiltily hoped for in our hard beds. Twitching with the shadow question: *Whatever will become of me?*

We spent a lot of time daydreaming during this period. Even Jeanette. Sometimes I'd see her looking out at the woods in a vacant way. If you interrupted her in the midst of one of these reveries, she would lunge at you with an elder-sister ferocity, momentarily forgetting her human catechism. We liked her better then, startled back into being foamy old Jeanette.

In school, they showed us the St. Francis of Assisi[5] slide show, again and again. Then the nuns would give us bags of bread. They never announced these things as a test; it was only much later that I realized that we were under constant examination. "Go feed the ducks," they urged us. "Go practice compassion for all God's creatures." *Don't pair me with Mirabella,* I prayed, *anybody but Mirabella.* "Claudette"—Sister Josephine beamed—"why don't you and Mirabella take some pumpernickel down to the ducks?"

30   "Ohhkaaythankyou," I said. (It took me a long time to say anything; first I had to translate it in my head from the Wolf.) It wasn't fair. They knew Mirabella couldn't make bread balls yet. She couldn't even undo the twist tie of the bag. She was sure to eat the birds; Mirabella didn't even try to curb her desire to kill things—and then who would get blamed for the dark spots of duck blood on our Peter Pan collars? Who would get penalized with negative Skill Points? Exactly.

As soon as we were beyond the wooden gates, I snatched the bread away from Mirabella and ran off to the duck pond on my own. Mirabella gave chase, nipping at my heels. She thought it was a game. "Stop it," I growled. I ran faster, but it was Stage 2 and I was still unsteady on my two feet. I fell sideways into a leaf pile, and then all I could see was my sister's blurry form, bounding towards me. In a moment, she was on top of me, barking the old word for tug-of-war. When she tried to steal the bread out of my hands, I whirled around and snarled at her, pushing my ears back from my head. I bit her shoulder, once, twice, the only language she would respond to. I used my new motor skills. I threw dirt, I threw stones. "Get away!" I screamed, long after she had made a cringing retreat into the shadows of the purple saplings. "Get away, get away!"

Much later, they found Mirabella wading in the shallows of a distant river, trying to strangle a mallard with her rosary beads. I was at the lake; I'd been sitting there for hours. Hunched in the long cattails, my yellow eyes flashing, shoving ragged hunks of bread into my mouth.

I don't know what they did to Mirabella. Me they separated from my sisters. They made me watch another slide show. This one showed images of former

5. In one of many legends illustrating his special relationship with animals, St. Francis (1181–1226) talks a village out of killing a wolf that has been attacking them and convinces the wolf to stop killing; the villagers then make a pet of the wolf.

wolf-girls, the ones who had failed to be rehabilitated. Long-haired, sad-eyed women, limping after their former wolf packs in white tennis shoes and pleated culottes. A wolf-girl bank teller, her makeup smeared in oily rainbows, eating a raw steak on the deposit slips while her colleagues looked on in disgust. Our parents. The final slide was a bolded sentence in St. Lucy's prim script: DO YOU WANT TO END UP SHUNNED BY BOTH SPECIES?

After that, I spent less time with Mirabella. One night she came to me, holding her hand out. She was covered with splinters, keening a high, whining noise through her nostrils. Of course I understood what she wanted; I wasn't that far removed from our language (even though I was reading at a fifth-grade level, halfway into Jack London's *The Son of the Wolf*).[6]

"Lick your own wounds," I said, not unkindly. It was what the nuns had   35 instructed us to say; wound licking was not something you did in polite company. Etiquette was so confounding in this country. Still, looking at Mirabella— her fists balled together like small, white porcupines, her brows knitted in animal confusion—I felt a throb of compassion. *How can people live like they do?* I wondered. Then I congratulated myself. This was a Stage 3 thought.

> Stage 3: It is common that students who start living in a new and different culture come to a point where they reject the host culture and withdraw into themselves. During this period, they make generalizations about the host culture and wonder how the people can live like they do. Your students may feel that their own culture's lifestyle and customs are far superior to those of the host country.

The nuns were worried about Mirabella, too. To correct a failing, you must first be aware of it as a failing. And there was Mirabella, shucking her plaid jumper in full view of the visiting cardinal. Mirabella, battling a raccoon under the dinner table while the rest of us took dainty bites of peas and borscht. Mirabella, doing belly flops into compost.

"You have to pull your weight around here," we overheard Sister Josephine saying one night. We paused below the vestry window and peered inside.

"Does Mirabella try to earn Skill Points by shelling walnuts and polishing Saint-in-the-Box? No. Does Mirabella even know how to say the word *walnut*? Has she learned how to say anything besides a sinful 'HraaaHA!' as she commits frottage[7] against the organ pipes? No."

There was a long silence.

"Something must be done," Sister Ignatius said firmly. The other nuns nod-   40 ded, a sea of thin, colorless lips and kettle-black brows. "Something must be done," they intoned. That ominously passive construction; a something so awful that nobody wanted to assume responsibility for it.

I could have warned her. If we were back home, and Mirabella had come under attack by territorial beavers or snow-blind bears, I would have warned her. But the truth is that by Stage 3 I wanted her gone. Mirabella's inability to adapt was taking a visible toll. Her teeth were ground down to nubbins; her hair was falling out. She hated the spongy, long-dead foods we were served, and it showed—

6. Short story (1900) about a white settler in the Yukon whose determination to marry an indigenous woman over the objections of her people results in the death of two tribesmen.
7. Rubbing against a person or object for sexual stimulation.

her ribs were poking through her uniform. Her bright eyes had dulled to a sour whiskey color. But you couldn't show Mirabella the slightest kindness anymore—she'd never leave you alone! You'd have to sit across from her at meals, shoving her away as she begged for your scraps. I slept fitfully during that period, unable to forget that Mirabella was living under my bed, gnawing on my loafers.

It was during Stage 3 that we met our first purebred girls. These were girls raised in captivity, volunteers from St. Lucy's School for Girls. The apple-cheeked fourth-grade class came to tutor us in playing. They had long golden braids or short, severe bobs. They had frilly-duvet names like Felicity and Beulah; and pert, bunny noses; and terrified smiles. We grinned back at them with genuine ferocity. It made us nervous to meet new humans. There were so many things that we could do wrong! And the rules here were different depending on which humans we were with: dancing or no dancing, checkers playing or no checkers playing, pumping or no pumping.

The purebred girls played checkers with us.

"These girl-girls sure is dumb," my sister Lavash panted to me between games. "I win it again! Five to none."

45   She was right. The purebred girls were making mistakes on purpose, in order to give us an advantage. "King me," I growled, out of turn. *"I say king me!"* and Felicity meekly complied. Beulah pretended not to mind when we got frustrated with the oblique, fussy movement from square to square and shredded the board to ribbons. I felt sorry for them. I wondered what it would be like to be bred in captivity, and always homesick for a dimly sensed forest, the trees you've never seen.

Jeanette was learning how to dance. On Holy Thursday, she mastered a rudimentary form of the Charleston. *"Brava!"* The nuns clapped. *"Brava!"*

Every Friday, the girls who had learned how to ride a bicycle celebrated by going on chaperoned trips into town. The purebred girls sold seven hundred rolls of gift-wrap paper and used the proceeds to buy us a yellow fleet of bicycles built for two. We'd ride the bicycles uphill, a sanctioned pumping, a grim-faced nun pedaling behind each one of us. "Congratulations!" the nuns would huff. "Being human is like riding this bicycle. Once you've learned how, you'll never forget." Mirabella would run after the bicycles, growling out our old names. HWRAA! GWARR! TRRRRRRR! We pedaled faster.

At this point, we'd had six weeks of lessons, and still nobody could do the Sausalito but Jeanette. The nuns decided we needed an inducement to dance. They announced that we would celebrate our successful rehabilitations with a Debutante Ball. There would be brothers, ferried over from the Home for Man-Boys Raised by Wolves. There would be a photographer from the *Gazette Sophisticate*. There would be a three-piece jazz band from West Toowoomba, and root beer in tiny plastic cups. The brothers! We'd almost forgotten about them. Our invisible tails went limp. I should have been excited; instead, I felt a low mad anger at the nuns. They knew we weren't ready to dance with the brothers; we weren't even ready to talk to them. Things had been so much simpler in the woods. That night I waited until my sisters were asleep. Then I slunk into the closet and practiced the Sausalito two-step in secret, a private mass of twitch and foam. Mouth shut—shoes on feet! Mouth shut—shoes on feet! Mouthshutmouthshut . . .

One night I came back early from the closet and stumbled on Jeanette. She was sitting in a patch of moonlight on the windowsill, reading from one of her library books. (She was the first of us to sign for her library card, too.) Her cheeks looked dewy.

"Why you cry?" I asked her, instinctively reaching over to lick Jeanette's cheek 50 and catching myself in the nick of time.

Jeanette blew her nose into a nearby curtain. (Even her mistakes annoyed us— they were always so well intentioned.) She sniffled and pointed to a line in her book: "The lake-water was reinventing the forest and the white moon above it, and wolves lapped up the cold reflection of the sky." But none of the pack besides me could read yet, and I wasn't ready to claim a common language with Jeanette.

The following day, Jeanette golfed. The nuns set up a miniature putt-putt course in the garden. Sister Maria dug four sandtraps and got old Walter, the groundskeeper, to make a windmill out of a lawn mower engine. The eighteenth hole was what they called a "doozy," a minuscule crack in St. Lucy's marble dress. Jeanette got a hole in one.

On Sundays, the pretending felt almost as natural as nature. The chapel was our favorite place. Long before we could understand what the priest was saying, the music instructed us in how to feel. The choir director—aggressively per-fumed Mrs. Valuchi, gold necklaces like pineapple rings around her neck—taught us more than the nuns ever did. She showed us how to pattern the old hunger into arias. Clouds moved behind the frosted oculus of the nave, glass shadows that reminded me of my mother. The mother, I'd think, struggling to conjure up a picture. A black shadow, running behind the watery screen of pines.

We sang at the chapel annexed to the home every morning. We understood that this was the humans' moon, the place for howling beyond purpose. Not for mating, not for hunting, not for fighting, not for anything but the sound itself. And we'd howl along with the choir, hurling every pitted thing within us at the stained glass. "Sotto voce."[8] The nuns would frown. But you could tell that they were pleased.

> Stage 4: As a more thorough understanding of the host culture is acquired, your students will begin to feel more comfortable in their new environment. Your students feel more at home, and their self-confidence grows. Everything begins to make sense.

"Hey, Claudette," Jeanette growled to me on the day before the ball. "Have 55 you noticed that everything's beginning to make sense?"

Before I could answer, Mirabella sprang out of the hall closet and snapped through Jeanette's homework binder. Pages and pages of words swirled around the stone corridor, like dead leaves off trees.

"What about you, Mirabella?" Jeanette asked politely, stooping to pick up her erasers. She was the only one of us who would still talk to Mirabella; she was high enough in the rankings that she could afford to talk to the scruggliest wolf-girl. "Has everything begun to make more sense, Mirabella?"

Mirabella let out a whimper. She scratched at us and scratched at us, raking her nails along our shins so hard that she drew blood. Then she rolled belly-up

8. In a low voice (Italian).

on the cold stone floor, squirming on a bed of spelling-bee worksheets. Above us, small pearls of light dotted the high, tinted window.

Jeanette frowned. "You are a late bloomer, Mirabella! Usually, everything's begun to make more sense by Month Twelve at the latest." I noticed that she stumbled on the word *bloomer*. HraaaHA! Jeanette could never fully shake our accent. She'd talk like that her whole life, I thought with a gloomy satisfaction, each word winced out like an apology for itself.

60   "Claudette, help me," she yelped. Mirabella had closed her jaws around Jeanette's bald ankle and was dragging her towards the closet. "Please. Help me to mop up Mirabella's mess."

I ignored her and continued down the hall. I had only four more hours to perfect the Sausalito. I was worried only about myself. By that stage, I was no longer certain of how the pack felt about anything.

At seven o'clock on the dot, Sister Ignatius blew her whistle and frog-marched us into the ball. The nuns had transformed the rectory into a very scary place. Purple and silver balloons started popping all around us. Black streamers swooped down from the eaves and got stuck in our hair like bats. A full yellow moon smirked outside the window. We were greeted by blasts of a saxophone, and fizzy pink drinks, and the brothers.

The brothers didn't smell like our brothers anymore. They smelled like pomade and cold, sterile sweat. They looked like little boys. Someone had washed behind their ears and made them wear suspendered dungarees. Kyle used to be a blustery alpha male, BTWWWR!, chewing through rattlesnakes, spooking badgers, snatching a live trout out of a grizzly's mouth. He stood by the punch bowl, looking pained and out of place.

"My stars!" I growled. "What lovely weather we've been having!"

65   "Yeees," Kyle growled back. "It is beginning to look a lot like Christmas." All around the room, boys and girls raised by wolves were having the same conversation. Actually, it had been an unseasonably warm and brown winter, and just that morning a freak hailstorm had sent Sister Josephina to an early grave. But we had only gotten up to Unit 7: Party Dialogue; we hadn't yet learned the vocabulary for Unit 12: How to Tactfully Acknowledge Disaster. Instead, we wore pink party hats and sucked olives on little sticks, inured to our own strangeness.

The nuns swept our hair back into high, bouffant hairstyles. This made us look more girlish and less inclined to eat people, the way that squirrels are saved from looking like rodents by their poofy tails. I was wearing a white organdy dress with orange polka dots. Jeanette was wearing a mauve organdy dress with blue polka dots. Linette was wearing a red organdy dress with white polka dots. Mirabella was in a dark corner, wearing a muzzle. Her party culottes were duct-taped to her knees. The nuns had tied little bows on the muzzle to make it more festive. Even so, the jazz band from West Toowoomba kept glancing nervously her way.

"You smell astoooounding!" Kyle was saying, accidentally stretching the diphthong into a howl and then blushing. "I mean—"

"Yes, I know what it is that you mean," I snapped. (That's probably a little narrative embellishment on my part; it must have been months before I could really "snap" out words.) I didn't smell astounding. I had rubbed a pumpkin muffin all over my body earlier that morning to mask my natural, feral scent. Now I smelled like a purebred girl, easy to kill. I narrowed my eyes at Kyle and flattened my ears, something I hadn't done for months. Kyle looked panicked, trying to remember the words that would make me act like a girl again. I felt hot, oily tears squeezing out of the red corners of my eyes. *Shoesonfeet!* I barked at myself. I tried again. "My! What lovely weather—"

The jazz band struck up a tune.

"The time has come to do the Sausalito," Sister Maria announced, beaming into the microphone. "Every sister grab a brother!" She switched on Walter's industrial flashlight, struggling beneath its weight, and aimed the beam in the center of the room.

Uh-oh. I tried to skulk off into Mirabella's corner, but Kyle pushed me into the spotlight. "No," I moaned through my teeth, "noooooo." All of a sudden the only thing my body could remember how to do was pump and pump. In a flash of white-hot light, my months at St. Lucy's had vanished, and I was just a terrified animal again. As if of their own accord, my feet started to wiggle out of my shoes. *Mouth shut,* I gasped, staring down at my naked toes, *mouthshutmouthshut.*

"Ahem. The time has come," Sister Maria coughed, "to do the Sausalito." She paused. "The Sausalito," she added helpfully, "does not in any way resemble the thing that you are doing."

Beads of sweat stood out on my forehead. I could feel my jaws gaping open, my tongue lolling out of the left side of my mouth. What were the steps? I looked frantically for Jeanette; she would help me, she would tell me what to do.

Jeanette was sitting in the corner, sipping punch through a long straw and watching me pant. I locked eyes with her, pleading with the mute intensity that I had used to beg her for weasel bones in the forest. "What are the steps?" I mouthed.

"The steps!"

"The steps?" Then Jeanette gave me a wide, true wolf smile. For an instant, she looked just like our mother. "Not for you," she mouthed back.

I threw my head back, a howl clawing its way up my throat. I was about to lose all my Skill Points, I was about to fail my Adaptive Dancing test. But before the air could burst from my lungs, the wind got knocked out of me. *Oomph!* I fell to the ground, my skirt falling softly over my head. Mirabella had intercepted my eye-cry for help. She'd chewed through her restraints and tackled me from behind, barking at unseen cougars, trying to shield me with her tiny body. "*Caramba!*" Sister Maria squealed, dropping the flashlight. The music ground to a halt. And I have never loved someone so much, before or since, as I loved my littlest sister at that moment. I wanted to roll over and lick her ears, I wanted to kill a dozen spotted fawns and let her eat first.

But everybody was watching; everybody was waiting to see what I would do. "I wasn't talking to you," I grunted from underneath her. "I didn't want your help. Now you have ruined the Sausalito! You have ruined the ball!" I said more loudly, hoping the nuns would hear how much my enunciation had improved.

"You have ruined it!" my sisters panted, circling around us, eager to close ranks. "Mirabella has ruined it!" Every girl was wild-eyed and itching under her polka dots, punch froth dribbling down her chin. The pack had been waiting for this moment for some time. "Mirabella cannot adapt! Back to the woods, back to the woods!"

80   The band from West Toowoomba had quietly packed their instruments into black suitcases and were sneaking out the back. The boys had fled back towards the lake, bow ties spinning, snapping suspenders in their haste. Mirabella was still snarling in the center of it all, trying to figure out where the danger was so that she could defend me against it. The nuns exchanged glances.

In the morning, Mirabella was gone. We checked under all the beds. I pretended to be surprised. I'd known she would have to be expelled the minute I felt her weight on my back. Walter came and told me this in secret after the ball, "So you can say yer good-byes." I didn't want to face Mirabella. Instead, I packed a tin lunch pail for her: two jelly sandwiches on saltine crackers, a chloroformed squirrel, a gilt-edged placard of St. Bolio. I left it for her with Sister Ignatius, with a little note: "Best wishes!" I told myself I'd done everything I could.

"Hooray!" the pack crowed. "Something has been done!"

We raced outside into the bright sunlight, knowing full well that our sister had been turned loose, that we'd never find her. A low roar rippled through us and surged up and up, disappearing into the trees. I listened for an answering howl from Mirabella, heart thumping—what if she heard us and came back? But there was nothing.

We graduated from St. Lucy's shortly thereafter. As far as I can recollect, that was our last communal howl.

> Stage 5: At this point your students are able to interact effectively in the new cultural environment. They find it easy to move between the two cultures.

85   One Sunday, near the end of my time at St. Lucy's, the sisters gave me a special pass to go visit the parents. The woodsman had to accompany me; I couldn't remember how to find the way back on my own. I wore my best dress and brought along some prosciutto and dill pickles in a picnic basket. We crunched through the fall leaves in silence, and every step made me sadder. "I'll wait out here," the woodsman said, leaning on a blue elm and lighting a cigarette.

The cave looked so much smaller than I remembered it. I had to duck my head to enter. Everybody was eating when I walked in. They all looked up from the bull moose at the same time, my aunts and uncles, my sloe-eyed, lolling cousins, the parents. My uncle dropped a thighbone from his mouth. My littlest brother, a cross-eyed wolf-boy who has since been successfully rehabilitated and is now a dour, balding children's book author, started whining in terror. My mother recoiled from me, as if I was a stranger. TRRR? She sniffed me for a long moment. Then she sank her teeth into my ankle, looking proud and sad. After all the tail wagging and perfunctory barking had died down, the parents sat back on their hind legs. They stared up at me expectantly, panting in the cool gray envelope of the cave, waiting for a display of what I had learned.

"So," I said, telling my first human lie. "I'm home."

2006

DAVID SEDARIS
(b. 1956)
Jesus Shaves

Dubbed by some "the funniest writer alive," David Sedaris uses his own life and the absurdities of the everyday as fodder for stories that often blur the line between fiction and nonfiction. Juxtaposing the high-brow with the lowbrow, they treat everything from his fleeting interests in crystal meth and bee-sized suits of armor to his brother's basement barbecue-sauce business. Sedaris was raised in the suburbs of Raleigh, North Carolina, after his Greek American family moved there from New York. Openly gay, Sedaris points to his inability to play jazz guitar as the source of his father's disappointment—"Fortunately there were six of us [. . .] and it was easy to get lost in the crowd." After graduating from the School of the Art Institute of Chicago, he worked a series of now-well-documented menial jobs in New York City and Chicago before radio host Ira Glass discovered him at a Chicago nightclub, reading from his diary. "Santaland Diaries," which recounts his adventures as a department-store elf, was later featured on National Public Radio, making Sedaris an overnight sensation. Author of multiple *New York Times* best sellers, including *Me Talk Pretty One Day* (2000), *Dress Your Family in Corduroy and Denim* (2004), *When You Are Engulfed in Flames* (2008), and *Let's Explore Diabetes with Owls* (2013), as well as *Squirrel Seeks Chipmunk* (2010), "a collection of fables without morals," Sedaris has also collaborated with his sister, actress-comedian Amy Sedaris, on a number of plays, including *Incident at Cobbler's Knob* (1997) and *The Book of Liz* (2002). As renowned for his voice and comic timing as for his writing, Sedaris draws sellout crowds on his worldwide reading tours.

"And what does one do on the fourteenth of July? Does one celebrate Bastille Day?"

It was my second month of French class, and the teacher was leading us in an exercise designed to promote the use of *one*, our latest personal pronoun.

"Might one sing on Bastille Day?" she asked. "Might one dance in the street? Somebody give me an answer."

Printed in our textbooks was a list of major holidays alongside a scattered arrangement of photos depicting French people in the act of celebration. The object was to match the holiday with the corresponding picture. It was simple enough but seemed an exercise better suited to the use of the word *they*. I didn't know about the rest of the class, but when Bastille Day eventually rolled around, I planned to stay home and clean my oven.

Normally, when working from the book, it was my habit to tune out my fellow 5 students and scout ahead, concentrating on the question I'd calculated might fall to me, but this afternoon, we were veering from the usual format. Questions were answered on a volunteer basis, and I was able to sit back, confident that the same few students would do the talking. Today's discussion was dominated by an Italian nanny, two chatty Poles, and a pouty, plump Moroccan woman who had grown up speaking French and had enrolled in the class to improve her spelling.[1] She'd covered these lessons back in the third grade and took every opportunity to demonstrate her superiority. A question would be asked and she'd give the answer, behaving as though this were a game show and, if quick enough, she might go home with a tropical vacation or a side-by-side refrigerator-freezer. By the end of her first day, she'd raised her hand so many times, her shoulder had given out. Now she just leaned back in her seat and shouted the answers, her bronzed arms folded across her chest like some great grammar genie.

We finished discussing Bastille Day, and the teacher moved on to Easter, which was represented in our textbook by a black-and-white photograph of a chocolate bell lying upon a bed of palm fronds.

"And what does one do on Easter? Would anyone like to tell us?"

The Italian nanny was attempting to answer the question when the Moroccan student interrupted, shouting, "Excuse me, but what's an Easter?"

Despite her having grown up in a Muslim country, it seemed she might have heard it mentioned once or twice, but no. "I mean it," she said. "I have no idea what you people are talking about."

10   The teacher then called upon the rest of us to explain.

The Poles led the charge to the best of their ability. "It is," said one, "a party for the little boy of God who call his self Jesus and . . . oh, shit."

She faltered, and her fellow countryman came to her aid.

"He call his self Jesus, and then he be die one day on two . . . morsels of . . . lumber."

The rest of the class jumped in, offering bits of information that would have given the pope an aneurysm.

15   "He die one day, and then he go above of my head to live with your father."

"He weared the long hair, and after he died, the first day he come back here for to say hello to the peoples."

"He nice, the Jesus."

"He make the good things, and on the Easter we be sad because somebody makes him dead today."

Part of the problem had to do with grammar. Simple nouns such as *cross* and *resurrection* were beyond our grasp, let alone such complicated reflexive phrases as "To give of yourself your only begotten son." Faced with the challenge of explaining the cornerstone of Christianity, we did what any self-respecting group of people might do. We talked about food instead.

20   "Easter is a party for to eat of the lamb," the Italian nanny explained. "One, too, may eat of the chocolate."

"And who brings the chocolate?" the teacher asked.

I knew the word, and so I raised my hand, saying, "The Rabbit of Easter. He bring of the chocolate."

My classmates reacted as though I'd attributed the delivery to the Antichrist. They were mortified.

---

1. France controlled most of Morocco between 1912 and 1956; as a result, though Arabic is now the country's official language, French is still widely taught and serves as the primary language of business and government.

"A rabbit?" The teacher, assuming I'd used the wrong word, positioned her index fingers on top of her head, wiggling them as though they were ears. "You mean one of these? A rabbit rabbit?"

"Well, sure," I said. "He come in the night when one sleep on a bed. With a hand he have the basket and foods." 25

The teacher sadly shook her head, as if this explained everything that was wrong with my country. "No, no," she said. "Here in France the chocolate is brought by the big bell that flies in from Rome."[2]

I called for a time-out. "But how do the bell know where you live?"

"Well," she said, "how does a rabbit?"

It was a decent point, but at least a rabbit has eyes. That's a start. Rabbits move from place to place, while most bells can only go back and forth—and they can't even do that on their own power. On top of that, the Easter Bunny has character; he's someone you'd like to meet and shake hands with. A bell has all the personality of a cast-iron skillet. It's like saying that come Christmas, a magic dustpan flies in from the North Pole, led by eight flying cinder blocks. Who wants to stay up all night so they can see a bell? And why fly one in from Rome when they've got more bells than they know what to do with right here in Paris? That's the most implausible aspect of the whole story, as there's no way the bells of France would allow a foreign worker to fly in and take their jobs. That Roman bell would be lucky to get work cleaning up after a French bell's dog—and even then he'd need papers. It just didn't add up.

Nothing we said was of any help to the Moroccan student. A dead man with 30 long hair supposedly living with her father, a leg of lamb served with palm fronds and chocolate. Confused and disgusted, she shrugged her massive shoulders and turned her attention back to the comic book she kept hidden beneath her binder. I wondered then if, without the language barrier, my classmates and I could have done a better job making sense of Christianity, an idea that sounds pretty far-fetched to begin with.

In communicating any religious belief, the operative word is *faith*, a concept illustrated by our very presence in that classroom. Why bother struggling with the grammar lessons of a six-year-old if each of us didn't believe that, against all reason, we might eventually improve? If I could hope to one day carry on a fluent conversation, it was a relatively short leap to believing that a rabbit might visit my home in the middle of the night, leaving behind a handful of chocolate kisses and a carton of menthol cigarettes. So why stop there? If I could believe in myself, why not give other improbabilities the benefit of the doubt? I accepted the idea that an omniscient God had cast me in his own image and that he watched over me and guided me from one place to the next. The virgin birth, the resurrection, and the countless miracles—my heart expanded to encompass all the wonders and possibilities of the universe.

A bell, though, that's fucked up.

2000

---

2. In remembrance of Jesus's death, bells across France are customarily silenced from the Thursday before Good Friday until Easter morning; children are encouraged to believe that the bells fly to Rome to visit the pope, returning with gifts.

JOHN UPDIKE
(1932–2009)
A & P¹

The man *The Oxford Encyclopedia of American Literature* dubs "perhaps America's most versatile, prolific, and distinguished man of letters of the second half of the twentieth century" spent the early years of his life in Reading and rural Shillington, Pennsylvania. John Updike went on to study English literature at Harvard, where he also contributed cartoons and articles to the famous *Lampoon*. Marrying a Radcliffe fine-arts student in 1953, Updike the next year graduated summa cum laude and sold both his first poem and his first story to the *New Yorker*, whose staff he joined in 1955. Though he would continue to contribute essays, poems, and fiction to that magazine for the rest of his life, in 1957 Updike moved with his young family from Manhattan to rural Massachusetts. In the two years following the move, he published both his first book, a collection of poems (1958), and his first novel (1959). Updike went on to publish some twenty-one novels, thirteen short-story collections, seven volumes of poetry (including *Collected Poems, 1953–1993* [1993]), as well as seven collections of essays, a play, and a memoir. He is best known for the tetralogy tracing the life of high-school basketball star turned car salesman Harry C. Rabbit Angstrom. Begun with *Rabbit, Run* in 1960, the series of novels includes *Rabbit Is Rich* (1981) and *Rabbit at Rest* (1990), both of which won Pulitzer Prizes.

In walks these three girls in nothing but bathing suits. I'm in the third checkout slot, with my back to the door, so I don't see them until they're over by the bread. The one that caught my eye first was the one in the plaid green two-piece. She was a chunky kid, with a good tan and a sweet broad soft-looking can with those two crescents of white just under it, where the sun never seems to hit, at the top of the backs of her legs. I stood there with my hand on a box of HiHo crackers trying to remember if I rang it up or not. I ring it up again and the customer starts giving me hell. She's one of these cash-register-watchers, a witch about fifty with rouge on her cheekbones and no eyebrows, and I know it made her day to trip me up. She'd been watching cash registers for fifty years and probably never seen a mistake before.

By the time I got her feathers smoothed and her goodies into a bag—she gives me a little snort in passing, if she'd been born at the right time they would have burned her over in Salem²—by the time I get her on her way the girls had circled around the bread and were coming back, without a pushcart, back my way along the counters, in the aisle between the checkouts and the Special bins. They didn't even have shoes on. There was this chunky one, with the two-piece—it was bright

1. The Great Atlantic and Pacific Tea Company, so named in 1859, became by the 1930s the leading national chain of supermarkets.
2. The store is located not far from Salem, Massachusetts, where in 1692 nineteen women and men were hanged after being convicted of witchcraft.

green and the seams on the bra were still sharp and her belly was still pretty pale so I guessed she just got it (the suit)—there was this one, with one of those chubby berry-faces, the lips all bunched together under her nose, this one, and a tall one, with black hair that hadn't quite frizzed right, and one of these sunburns right across under the eyes, and a chin that was too long—you know, the kind of girl other girls think is very "striking" and "attractive" but never quite makes it, as they very well know, which is why they like her so much—and then the third one, that wasn't quite so tall. She was the queen. She kind of led them, the other two peeking around and making their shoulders round. She didn't look around, not this queen, she just walked straight on slowly, on these long white prima-donna legs. She came down a little hard on her heels, as if she didn't walk in her bare feet that much, putting down her heels and then letting the weight move along to her toes as if she was testing the floor with every step, putting a little deliberate extra action into it. You never know for sure how girls' minds work (do you really think it's a mind in there or just a little buzz like a bee in a glass jar?) but you got the idea she had talked the other two into coming in here with her, and now she was showing them how to do it, walk slow and hold yourself straight.

She had on a kind of dirty-pink—beige maybe, I don't know—bathing suit with a little nubble all over it and, what got me, the straps were down. They were off her shoulders looped loose around the cool tops of her arms, and I guess as a result the suit had slipped a little on her, so all around the top of the cloth there was this shining rim. If it hadn't been there you wouldn't have known there could have been anything whiter than those shoulders. With the straps pushed off, there was nothing between the top of the suit and the top of her head except just *her*, this clean bare plane of the top of her chest down from the shoulder bones like a dented sheet of metal tilted in the light. I mean, it was more than pretty.

She had sort of oaky hair that the sun and salt had bleached, done up in a bun that was unravelling, and a kind of prim face. Walking into the A & P with your straps down, I suppose it's the only kind of face you *can* have. She held her head so high her neck, coming up out of those white shoulders, looked kind of stretched, but I didn't mind. The longer her neck was, the more of her there was.

She must have felt in the corner of her eye me and over my shoulder Stokesie 5 in the second slot watching, but she didn't tip. Not this queen. She kept her eyes moving across the racks, and stopped, and turned so slow it made my stomach rub the inside of my apron, and buzzed to the other two, who kind of huddled against her for relief, and then they all three of them went up the cat-and-dog-food-breakfast-cereal-macaroni-rice-raisins-seasonings-spreads-spaghetti-soft-drinks-crackers-and-cookies aisle. From the third slot I look straight up this aisle to the meat counter, and I watched them all the way. The fat one with the tan sort of fumbled with the cookies, but on second thought she put the package back. The sheep pushing their carts down the aisle—the girls were walking against the usual traffic (not that we have one-way signs or anything)—were pretty hilarious. You could see them, when Queenie's white shoulders dawned on them, kind of jerk, or hop, or hiccup, but their eyes snapped back to their own baskets and on they pushed. I bet you could set off dynamite in an A & P and the people would by and large keep reaching and checking oatmeal off their lists and muttering "Let me see, there was a third thing, began with A, asparagus, no, ah, yes, applesauce!" or whatever it is they do mutter. But there was no doubt, this jiggled them. A few houseslaves in pin curlers even looked around after pushing their carts past to make sure what they had seen was correct.

You know, it's one thing to have a girl in a bathing suit down on the beach, where what with the glare nobody can look at each other much anyway, and another thing in the cool of the A & P, under the fluorescent lights, against all those stacked packages, with her feet paddling along naked over our checkerboard green-and-cream rubber-tile floor.

"Oh Daddy," Stokesie said beside me. "I feel so faint."

"Darling," I said. "Hold me tight." Stokesie's married, with two babies chalked up on his fuselage already, but as far as I can tell that's the only difference. He's twenty-two, and I was nineteen this April.

"Is it done?" he asks, the responsible married man finding his voice. I forgot to say he thinks he's going to be manager some sunny day, maybe in 1990 when it's called the Great Alexandrov and Petrooshki Tea Company or something.

10   What he meant was, our town is five miles from a beach, with a big summer colony out on the Point, but we're right in the middle of town, and the women generally put on a shirt or shorts or something before they get out of the car into the street. And anyway these are usually women with six children and varicose veins mapping their legs and nobody, including them, could care less. As I say, we're right in the middle of town, and if you stand at our front doors you can see two banks and the Congregational church and the newspaper store and three real-estate offices and about twenty-seven old freeloaders tearing up Central Street because the sewer broke again. It's not as if we're on the Cape; we're north of Boston and there's people in this town haven't seen the ocean for twenty years.

The girls had reached the meat counter and were asking McMahon something. He pointed, they pointed, and they shuffled out of sight behind a pyramid of Diet Delight peaches. All that was left for us to see was old McMahon patting his mouth and looking after them sizing up their joints. Poor kids, I began to feel sorry for them, they couldn't help it.

Now here comes the sad part of the story, at least my family says it's sad, but I don't think it's so sad myself. The store's pretty empty, it being Thursday afternoon, so there was nothing much to do except lean on the register and wait for the girls to show up again. The whole store was like a pinball machine and I didn't know which tunnel they'd come out of. After a while they come around out of the far aisle, around the light bulbs, records at discount of the Caribbean Six or Tony Martin Sings[3] or some such gunk you wonder they waste the wax on, sixpacks of candy bars, and plastic toys done up in cellophane that fall apart when a kid looks at them anyway. Around they come, Queenie still leading the way, and holding a little gray jar in her hand. Slots Three through Seven are unmanned and I could see her wondering between Stokes and me, but Stokesie with his usual luck draws an old party in baggy gray pants who stumbles up with four giant cans

---

3. Typical titles of record albums at the time of the story (1962). Tony Martin (1913–2012), a popular singer and actor, was featured on radio and television in the 1940s and 1950s.

of pineapple juice (what do these bums *do* with all that pineapple juice? I've often asked myself) so the girls come to me. Queenie puts down the jar and I take it into my fingers icy cold. Kingfish Fancy Herring Snacks in Pure Sour Cream: 49¢. Now her hands are empty, not a ring or a bracelet, bare as God made them, and I wonder where the money's coming from. Still with that prim look she lifts a folded dollar bill out of the hollow at the center of her nubbled pink top. The jar went heavy in my hand. Really, I thought that was so cute.

Then everybody's luck begins to run out. Lengel comes in from haggling with a truck full of cabbages on the lot and is about to scuttle into that door marked MANAGER behind which he hides all day when the girls touch his eye. Lengel's pretty dreary, teaches Sunday school and the rest, but he doesn't miss that much. He comes over and says, "Girls, this isn't the beach."

Queenie blushes, though maybe it's just a brush of sunburn I was noticing for the first time, now that she was so close. "My mother asked me to pick up a jar of herring snacks." Her voice kind of startled me, the way voices do when you see the people first, coming out so flat and dumb yet kind of tony, too, the way it ticked over "pick up" and "snacks." All of a sudden I slid right down her voice into her living room. Her father and the other men were standing around in ice-cream coats and bow ties and the women were in sandals picking up her-ring snacks on toothpicks off a big glass plate and they were all holding drinks the color of water with olives and sprigs of mint in them. When my parents have somebody over they get lemonade and if it's a real racy affair Schlitz in tall glasses with "They'll Do It Every Time" cartoons stencilled on.[4]

"That's all right," Lengel said. "But this isn't the beach." His repeating this   15 struck me as funny, as if it had just occurred to him, and he had been thinking all these years the A & P was a great big dune and he was the head lifeguard. He didn't like my smiling—as I say he doesn't miss much—but he concentrates on giving the girls that sad Sunday-school-superintendent stare.

Queenie's blush is no sunburn now, and the plump one in plaid, that I liked better from the back—a really sweet can—pipes up, "We weren't doing any shopping. We just came in for the one thing."

"That makes no difference," Lengel tells her, and I could see from the way his eyes went that he hadn't noticed she was wearing a two-piece before. "We want you decently dressed when you come in here."

"We *are* decent," Queenie says suddenly, her lower lip pushing, getting sore now that she remembers her place, a place from which the crowd that runs the A & P must look pretty crummy. Fancy Herring Snacks flashed in her very blue eyes.

"Girls, I don't want to argue with you. After this come in here with your shoulders covered. It's our policy." He turns his back. That's policy for you. Pol-icy is what the kingpins want. What the others want is juvenile delinquency.

All this while, the customers had been showing up with their carts but, you   20 know, sheep, seeing a scene, they had all bunched up on Stokesie, who shook open a paper bag as gently as peeling a peach, not wanting to miss a word. I could feel in the silence everybody getting nervous, most of all Lengel, who asks me, "Sammy, have you rung up their purchase?"

---

4. Schlitz is an inexpensive brand of beer. The cheap glasses are decorated with a popular saying derived from a syndicated series of single-panel cartoons printed between 1929 and 2008.

I thought and said "No" but it wasn't about that I was thinking. I go through the punches, 4, 9, GROC, TOT—it's more complicated than you think, and after you do it often enough, it begins to make a little song, that you hear words to, in my case "Hello (*bing*) there, you (*gung*) hap-py pee-pul (*splat*)!"—the *splat* being the drawer flying out. I uncrease the bill, tenderly as you may imagine, it just having come from between the two smoothest scoops of vanilla I had ever known were there, and pass a half and a penny into her narrow pink palm, and nestle the herrings in a bag and twist its neck and hand it over, all the time thinking.

The girls, and who'd blame them, are in a hurry to get out, so I say "I quit" to Lengel quick enough for them to hear, hoping they'll stop and watch me, their unsuspected hero. They keep right on going, into the electric eye; the door flies open and they flicker across the lot to their car, Queenie and Plaid and Big Tall Goony-Goony (not that as raw material she was so bad), leaving me with Lengel and a kink in his eyebrow.

"Did you say something, Sammy?"

"I said I quit."

25   "I thought you did."

"You didn't have to embarrass them."

"It was they who were embarrassing us."

I started to say something that came out "Fiddle-de-doo." It's a saying of my grandmother's, and I know she would have been pleased.

"I don't think you know what you're saying," Lengel said.

30   "I know you don't," I said. "But I do." I pull the bow at the back of my apron and start shrugging it off my shoulders. A couple customers that had been heading for my slot begin to knock against each other, like scared pigs in a chute.

Lengel sighs and begins to look very patient and old and gray. He's been a friend of my parents for years. "Sammy, you don't want to do this to your Mom and Dad," he tells me. It's true, I don't. But it seems to me that once you begin a gesture it's fatal not to go through with it. I fold the apron, "Sammy" stitched in red on the pocket, and put it on the counter, and drop the bow tie on top of it. The bow tie is theirs, if you've ever wondered. "You'll feel this for the rest of your life," Lengel says, and I know that's true, too, but remembering how he made that pretty girl blush makes me so scrunchy inside I punch the No Sale tab and the machine whirs "pee-pul" and the drawer splats out. One advantage to this scene taking place in summer, I can follow this up with a clean exit, there's no fumbling around getting your coat and galoshes, I just saunter into the electric eye in my white shirt that my mother ironed the night before, and the door heaves itself open, and outside the sunshine is skating around on the asphalt.

I look around for my girls, but they're gone, of course. There wasn't anybody but some young married screaming with her children about some candy they didn't get by the door of a powder-blue Falcon station wagon. Looking back in the big windows, over the bags of peat moss and aluminum lawn furniture stacked on the pavement, I could see Lengel in my place in the slot, checking the sheep through. His face was dark gray and his back stiff, as if he'd just had an injection of iron, and my stomach kind of fell as I felt how hard the world was going to be to me hereafter.

1962

AUTHORS ON THEIR WORK

JOHN UPDIKE (1932–2009)

From "An Interview with John Updike" (1995)*

There is always some ambiguity or some room for various responses to a story. But I certainly see him [Sammy] as a typical, well-intentioned American male trying to find his way in the society and full of good impulses. I think that he quit his job on a good impulse. [. . .] A kind of feminist protest, in a way, is what he does here. Who knows what his adult life will bring, but I think for the moment he's a boy who's tried to reach out of his immediate environment toward something bigger and better.

*"An Interview with John Updike." Interview by Donald M. Murray, directed by Bruce Schwartz (1995), posted by Murray. *Spike*, 2001.

EUDORA WELTY

(1909–2001)

Why I Live at the P.O.

Known as the "First Lady of Southern Literature," Eudora Welty grew up in Jackson, Mississippi, attended Mississippi State College for Women, and earned a BA from the University of Wisconsin. Among the countless awards she received were two Guggenheim Fellowships, six O. Henry Awards, a Pulitzer Prize, the French Legion of Honor, the National Medal for Literature, and the Presidential Medal of Freedom. Although she wrote five novels, including *The Robber Bridegroom* (1942), *Ponder Heart* (1954), and *The Optimist's Daughter* (1972), Welty is best known for her short stories, many of which appear in *The Collected Stories of Eudora Welty* (1980). Among her nonfiction works are *One Writer's Beginnings* (1984), *A Writer's Eye: Collected Book Reviews* (1994), and five collections of her photographs, including *One Place, One Time* (1978) and *Photographs* (1989). In 1998 the Library of America published a two-volume edition of her selected works, making her the first living author to appear in the series.

I was getting along fine with Mama, Papa-Daddy, and Uncle Rondo until my sister Stella-Rondo just separated from her husband and came back home again. Mr. Whitaker! Of course I went with Mr. Whitaker first, when he first appeared here in China Grove, taking "Pose Yourself" photos, and Stella-Rondo broke us up. Told him I was one-sided. Bigger on one side than the other, which is a deliberate, calculated falsehood: I'm the same. Stella-Rondo is exactly twelve months to the day younger than I am and for that reason she's spoiled.

She's always had anything in the world she wanted and then she'd throw it away. Papa-Daddy give her this gorgeous Add-a-Pearl necklace when she was eight years old and she threw it away playing baseball when she was nine, with only two pearls.

So as soon as she got married and moved away from home the first thing she did was separate! From Mr. Whitaker! This photographer with the popeyes she said she trusted. Came home from one of those towns up in Illinois and to our complete surprise brought this child of two.

Mama said she like to make her drop dead for a second. "Here you had this marvelous blonde child and never so much as wrote your mother a word about it," says Mama. "I'm thoroughly ashamed of you." But of course she wasn't.

5   Stella-Rondo just calmly takes off this *hat*, I wish you could see it. She says, "Why, Mama, Shirley-T.'s adopted, I can prove it."

"How?" says Mama, but all I says was, "H'm!" There I was over the hot stove, trying to stretch two chickens over five people and a completely unexpected child into the bargain without one moment's notice.

"What do you mean—'H'm'?" says Stella-Rondo, and Mama says, "I heard that, Sister."

I said that oh, I didn't mean a thing, only that whoever Shirley-T. was, she was the spit-image of Papa-Daddy if he'd cut off his beard, which of course he'd never do in the world. Papa-Daddy's Mama's papa and sulks.

Stella-Rondo got furious! She said, "Sister, I don't need to tell you you got a lot of nerve and always did have and I'll thank you to make no future reference to my adopted child whatsoever."

10   "Very well," I said. "Very well, very well. Of course I noticed at once she looks like Mr. Whitaker's side too. That frown. She looks like a cross between Mr. Whitaker and Papa-Daddy."

"Well, all I can say is she isn't."

"She looks exactly like Shirley Temple to me," says Mama, but Shirley-T. just ran away from her.

So the first thing Stella-Rondo did at the table was turn Papa-Daddy against me.

"Papa-Daddy," she says. He was trying to cut up his meat. "Papa-Daddy!" I was taken completely by surprise. Papa-Daddy is about a million years old and's got this long-long beard. "Papa-Daddy, Sister says she fails to understand why you don't cut off your beard."

15   So Papa-Daddy l-a-y-s down his knife and fork! He's real rich. Mama says he is, he says he isn't. So he says, "Have I heard correctly? You don't understand why I don't cut off my beard?"

"Why," I says, "Papa-Daddy, of course I understand, I did not say any such a thing, the idea!"

He says, "Hussy!"

I says, "Papa-Daddy, you know I wouldn't any more want you to cut off your beard than the man in the moon. It was the farthest thing from my mind! Stella-Rondo sat there and made that up while she was eating breast of chicken."

But he says, "So the postmistress fails to understand why I don't cut off my beard. Which job I got you through my influence with the government. 'Bird's nest'—is that what you call it?"

20   Not that it isn't the next to smallest P.O. in the entire state of Mississippi.

I says, "Oh, Papa-Daddy," I says, "I didn't say any such a thing, I never dreamed it was a bird's nest, I have always been grateful though this is the next to smallest P.O. in the state of Mississippi, and I do not enjoy being referred to as a hussy by my own grandfather."

But Stella-Rondo says, "Yes, you did say it too. Anybody in the world could of heard you, that had ears."

"Stop right there," says Mama, looking at *me*.

So I pulled my napkin straight back through the napkin ring and left the table.

As soon as I was out of the room Mama says, "Call her back, or she'll starve to death," but Papa-Daddy says, "This is the beard I started growing on the Coast when I was fifteen years old." He would of gone on till nightfall if Shirley-T. hadn't lost the Milky Way she ate in Cairo.

So Papa-Daddy says, "I am going out and lie in the hammock, and you can all sit here and remember my words: I'll never cut off my beard as long as I live, even one inch, and I don't appreciate it in you at all." Passed right by me in the hall and went straight out and got in the hammock.

It would be a holiday. It wasn't five minutes before Uncle Rondo suddenly appeared in the hall in one of Stella-Rondo's flesh-colored kimonos, all cut on the bias, like something Mr. Whitaker probably thought was gorgeous.

"Uncle Rondo!" I says. "I didn't know who that was! Where are you going?"

"Sister," he says, "get out of my way, I'm poisoned."

"If you're poisoned stay away from Papa-Daddy," I says. "Keep out of the hammock. Papa-Daddy will certainly beat you on the head if you come within forty miles of him. He thinks I deliberately said he ought to cut off his beard after he got me the P.O., and I've told him and told him and told him, and he acts like he just don't hear me. Papa-Daddy must of gone stone deaf."

"He picked a fine day to do it then," says Uncle Rondo, and before you could say "Jack Robinson" flew out in the yard.

What he'd really done, he'd drunk another bottle of that prescription. He does it every single Fourth of July as sure as shooting, and it's horribly expensive. Then he falls over in the hammock and snores. So he insisted on zigzagging right on out to the hammock, looking like a half-wit.

Papa-Daddy woke with this horrible yell and right there without moving an inch he tried to turn Uncle Rondo against me. I heard every word he said. Oh, he told Uncle Rondo I didn't learn to read till I was eight years old and he didn't see how in the world I ever got the mail put up at the P.O., much less read it all, and he said if Uncle Rondo could only fathom the lengths he had gone to get me that job! And he said on the other hand he thought Stella-Rondo had a brilliant mind and deserved credit for getting out of town. All the time he was just lying there swinging as pretty as you please and looping out his beard, and poor Uncle Rondo was *pleading* with him to slow down the hammock, it was making him as dizzy as a witch to watch it. But that's what Papa-Daddy likes about a hammock. So Uncle Rondo was too dizzy to get turned against me for the time being. He's Mama's only brother and is a good case of a one-track mind. Ask anybody. A certified pharmacist.

Just then I heard Stella-Rondo raising the upstairs window. While she was married she got this peculiar idea that it's cooler with the windows shut and locked. So she has to raise the window before she can make a soul hear her outdoors.

So she raises the window and says, "*Oh!*" You would have thought she was mortally wounded.

Uncle Rondo and Papa-Daddy didn't even look up, but kept right on with what they were doing. I had to laugh.

I flew up the stairs and threw the door open! I says, "What in the wide world's the matter, Stella-Rondo? You mortally wounded?"

"No," she says, "I am not mortally wounded but I wish you would do me the favor of looking out that window there and telling me what you see."

So I shade my eyes and look out the window.

40   "I see the front yard," I says.

"Don't you see any human beings?"

"I see Uncle Rondo trying to run Papa-Daddy out of the hammock," I says. "Nothing more. Naturally, it's so suffocating-hot in the house, with all the windows shut and locked, everybody who cares to stay in their right mind will have to go out and get in the hammock before the Fourth of July is over."

"Don't you notice anything different about Uncle Rondo?" asks Stella-Rondo.

"Why, no, except he's got on some terrible-looking flesh-colored contraption I wouldn't be found dead in, is all I can see," I says.

45   "Never mind, you won't be found dead in it, because it happens to be part of my trousseau, and Mr. Whitaker took several dozen photographs of me in it," says Stella-Rondo. "What on earth could Uncle Rondo *mean* by wearing part of my trousseau out in the broad open daylight without saying so much as 'Kiss my foot,' *knowing* I only got home this morning after my separation and hung my negligee up on the bathroom door, just as nervous as I could be?"

"I'm sure I don't know, and what do you expect me to do about it?" I says. "Jump out the window?"

"No, I expect nothing of the kind. I simply declare that Uncle Rondo looks like a fool in it, that's all," she says. "It makes me sick to my stomach."

"Well, he looks as good as he can," I says. "As good as anybody in reason could." I stood up for Uncle Rondo, please remember. And I said to Stella-Rondo, "I think I would do well not to criticize so freely if I were you and came home with a two-year-old child I had never said a word about, and no explanation whatever about my separation."

"I asked you the instant I entered this house not to refer one more time to my adopted child, and you gave me your word of honor you would not," was all Stella-Rondo would say, and started pulling out every one of her eyebrows with some cheap Kress tweezers.

50   So I merely slammed the door behind me and went down and made some green-tomato pickle. Somebody had to do it. Of course Mama had turned both the Negroes loose; she always said no earthly power could hold one anyway on the Fourth of July, so she wouldn't even try. It turned out that Jaypan fell in the lake and came within a very narrow limit of drowning.

So Mama trots in. Lifts up the lid and says, "H'm! Not very good for your Uncle Rondo in his precarious condition, I must say. Or poor little adopted Shirley-T. Shame on you!"

That made me tired. I says, "Well, Stella-Rondo had better thank her lucky stars it was her instead of me came trotting in with that very peculiar-looking child. Now if it had been me that trotted in from Illinois and brought a peculiar-looking child of two, I shudder to think of the reception I'd of got, much less controlled the diet of an entire family."

"But you must remember, Sister, that you were never married to Mr. Whitaker in the first place and didn't go up to Illinois to live," says Mama, shaking a spoon in my face. "If you had I would of been just as overjoyed to see you and your little adopted girl as I was to see Stella-Rondo, when you wound up with your separation and came on back home."

"You would not," I says.

"Don't contradict me, I would," says Mama.   55

But I said she couldn't convince me though she talked till she was blue in the face. Then I said, "Besides, you know as well as I do that that child is not adopted."

"She most certainly is adopted," says Mama, stiff as a poker.

I says, "Why, Mama, Stella-Rondo had her just as sure as anything in this world, and just too stuck up to admit it."

"Why, Sister," said Mama. "Here I thought we were going to have a pleasant Fourth of July, and you start right out not believing a word your own baby sister tells you!"

"Just like Cousin Annie Flo. Went to her grave denying the facts of life," I   60
reminded Mama.

"I told you if you ever mentioned Annie Flo's name I'd slap your face," says Mama, and slaps my face.

"All right, you wait and see," I says.

"I," says Mama, "I prefer to take my children's word for anything when it's humanly possible." You ought to see Mama, she weighs two hundred pounds and has real tiny feet.

Just then something perfectly horrible occurred to me.

"Mama," I says, "can that child talk?" I simply had to whisper! "Mama, I won-   65
der if that child can be—you know—in any way? Do you realize?" I says, "that she hasn't spoke one single, solitary word to a human being up to this minute? This is the way she looks," I says, and I looked like this.

Well, Mama and I just stood there and stared at each other. It was horrible!

"I remember well that Joe Whitaker frequently drank like a fish," says Mama. "I believed to my soul he drank *chemicals*." And without another word she marches to the foot of the stairs and calls Stella-Rondo.

"Stella-Rondo? O-o-o-o-o! Stella-Rondo!"

"What?" says Stella-Rondo from upstairs. Not even the grace to get up off the bed.

"Can that child of yours talk?" asks Mama.   70

Stella-Rondo says, "Can she what?"

"Talk! Talk!" says Mama. "Burdyburdyburdyburdy!"

So Stella-Rondo yells back, "Who says she can't talk?"

"Sister says so," says Mama.

"You didn't have to tell me, I know whose word of honor don't mean a thing   75
in this house," says Stella-Rondo.

And in a minute the loudest Yankee voice I ever heard in my life yells out, "OE'm Pop-OE the Sailor-r-r-r Ma-a-an!" and then somebody jumps up and down in the upstairs hall. In another second the house would of fallen down.

"Not only talks, she can tap-dance!" calls Stella-Rondo. "Which is more than some people I won't name can do."

"Why, the little precious darling thing!" Mama says, so surprised. "Just as smart as she can be!" Starts talking baby talk right there. Then she turns on me. "Sister, you ought to be thoroughly ashamed! Run upstairs this instant and apologize to Stella-Rondo and Shirley-T."

"Apologize for what?" I says. "I merely wondered if the child was normal, that's all. Now that she's proved she is, why, I have nothing further to say."

80   But Mama just turned on her heel and flew out, furious. She ran right upstairs and hugged the baby. She believed it was adopted. Stella-Rondo hadn't done a thing but turn her against me from upstairs while I stood there helpless over the hot stove. So that made Mama, Papa-Daddy, and the baby all on Stella-Rondo's side.

Next, Uncle Rondo.

I must say that Uncle Rondo has been marvelous to me at various times in the past and I was completely unprepared to be made to jump out of my skin, the way it turned out. Once Stella-Rondo did something perfectly horrible to him—broke a chain letter from Flanders Field—and he took the radio back he had given her and gave it to me. Stella-Rondo was furious! For six months we all had to call her Stella instead of Stella-Rondo, or she wouldn't answer. I always thought Uncle Rondo had all the brains of the entire family. Another time he sent me to Mammoth Cave with all expenses paid.

But this would be the day he was drinking that prescription, the Fourth of July.

So at supper Stella-Rondo speaks up and says she thinks Uncle Rondo ought to try to eat a little something. So finally Uncle Rondo said he would try a little cold biscuits and ketchup, but that was all. So *she* brought it to him.

85   "Do you think it wise to disport with ketchup in Stella-Rondo's flesh-colored kimono?" I says. Trying to be considerate! If Stella-Rondo couldn't watch out for her trousseau, somebody had to.

"Any objections?" asks Uncle Rondo, just about to pour out all of the ketchup.

"Don't mind what she says, Uncle Rondo," says Stella-Rondo. "Sister has been devoting this solid afternoon to sneering out my bedroom window at the way you look."

"What's that?" says Uncle Rondo. Uncle Rondo has got the most terrible temper in the world. Anything is liable to make him tear the house down if it comes at the wrong time.

So Stella-Rondo says, "Sister says, 'Uncle Rondo certainly does look like a fool in that pink kimono!'"

90   Do you remember who it was really said that?

Uncle Rondo spills out all the ketchup and jumps out of his chair and tears off the kimono and throws it down on the dirty floor and puts his foot on it. It had to be sent all the way to Jackson to the cleaners and re-pleated.

"So that's your opinion of your Uncle Rondo, is it?" he says. "I look like a fool, do I? Well, that's the last straw. A whole day in this house with nothing to do, and then to hear you come out with a remark like that behind my back!"

"I didn't say any such of a thing, Uncle Rondo," I says, "and I'm not saying who did, either. Why, I think you look all right. Just try to take care of yourself and not talk and eat at the same time," I says. "I think you better go lie down."

"Lie down my foot," says Uncle Rondo. I ought to of known by that he was fixing to do something perfectly horrible.

So he didn't do anything that night in the precarious state he was in—just ⁹⁵ played Casino with Mama and Stella-Rondo and Shirley-T. and gave Shirley-T. a nickel with a head on both sides. It tickled her nearly to death, and she called him "Papa." But at 6:30 A.M. the next morning, he threw a whole five-cent package of some unsold one-inch firecrackers from the store as hard as he could into my bedroom and they every one went off. Not one bad one in the string. Anybody else, there'd be one that wouldn't go off.

Well, I'm just terribly susceptible to noise of any kind, the doctor has always told me I was the most sensitive person he had ever seen in his whole life, and I was simply prostrated. I couldn't eat! People tell me they heard it as far as the cemetery, and old Aunt Jep Patterson, that had been holding her own so good, thought it was Judgment Day and she was going to meet her whole family. It's usually so quiet here.

And I'll tell you it didn't take me any longer than a minute to make up my mind what to do. There I was with the whole entire house on Stella-Rondo's side and turned against me. If I have anything at all I have pride.

So I just decided I'd go straight down to the P.O. There's plenty of room there in the back, I says to myself.

Well! I made no bones about letting the family catch on to what I was up to. I didn't try to conceal it.

The first thing they knew, I marched in where they were all playing Old Maid ¹⁰⁰ and pulled the electric oscillating fan out by the plug, and everything got real hot. Next I snatched the pillow I'd done the needlepoint on right off the davenport from behind Papa-Daddy. He went "Ugh!" I beat Stella-Rondo up the stairs and finally found my charm bracelet in her bureau drawer under a picture of Nelson Eddy.¹

"So that's the way the land lies," says Uncle Rondo. There he was, piecing on the ham. "Well, Sister, I'll be glad to donate my army cot if you got any place to set it up, providing you'll leave right this minute and let me get some peace." Uncle Rondo was in France.

"Thank you kindly for the cot and 'peace' is hardly the word I would select if I had to resort to firecrackers at 6:30 A.M. in a young girl's bedroom," I says to him. "And as to where I intend to go, you seem to forget my position as postmistress of China Grove, Mississippi," I says. "I've always got the P.O."

Well, that made them all sit up and take notice.

I went out front and started digging up some four-o'clocks to plant around the P.O.

"Ah-ah-ah!" says Mama, raising the window. "Those happen to be my four- ¹⁰⁵ o'clocks. Everything planted in that star is mine. I've never known you to make anything grow in your life."

"Very well," I says. "But I take the fern. Even you, Mama, can't stand there and deny that I'm the one watered that fern. And I happen to know where I can send in a box top and get a packet of one thousand mixed seeds, no two the same kind, free."

"Oh, where?" Mama wants to know.

1. Opera singer (1901–67) who enjoyed phenomenal popularity in the 1930s and 1940s when he costarred in numerous film musicals with Jeanette MacDonald. The two were known as "America's Singing Sweethearts."

But I says, "Too late. You 'tend to your house, and I'll 'tend to mine. You hear things like that all the time if you know how to listen to the radio. Perfectly marvelous offers. Get anything you want free."

So I hope to tell you I marched in and got that radio, and they could of all bit a nail in two, especially Stella-Rondo, that it used to belong to, and she well knew she couldn't get it back, I'd sue for it like a shot. And I very politely took the sewing-machine motor I helped pay the most on to give Mama for Christmas back in 1929, and a good big calendar, with the first-aid remedies on it. The thermometer and the Hawaiian ukulele certainly were rightfully mine, and I stood on the step-ladder and got all my watermelon-rind preserves and every fruit and vegetable I'd put up, every jar. Then I began to pull the tacks out of the bluebird wall vases on the archway to the dining room.

110   "Who told you you could have those, Miss Priss?" says Mama, fanning as hard as she could.

"I bought 'em and I'll keep track of 'em," I says. "I'll tack 'em up one on each side of the post-office window, and you can see 'em when you come to ask me for your mail, if you're so dead to see 'em."

"Not I! I'll never darken the door to that post office again if I live to be a hundred," Mama says. "Ungrateful child! After all the money we spent on you at the Normal."[2]

"Me either," says Stella-Rondo. "You can just let my mail lie there and *rot*, for all I care. I'll never come and relieve you of a single, solitary piece."

"I should worry," I says. "And who you think's going to sit down and write you all those big fat letters and postcards, by the way? Mr. Whitaker? Just because he was the only man ever dropped down in China Grove and you got him—unfairly—is he going to sit down and write you a lengthy correspondence after you come home giving no rhyme nor reason whatsoever for your separation and no explanation for the presence of that child? I may not have your brilliant mind, but I fail to see it."

115   So Mama says, "Sister, I've told you a thousand times that Stella-Rondo simply got homesick, and this child is far too big to be hers," and she says, "Now, why don't you just sit down and play Casino?"

Then Shirley-T. sticks out her tongue at me in this perfectly horrible way. She has no more manners than the man in the moon. I told her she was going to cross her eyes like that some day and they'd stick.

"It's too late to stop me now," I says. "You should have tried that yesterday. I'm going to the P.O. and the only way you can possibly see me is to visit me there."

So Papa-Daddy says, "You'll never catch me setting foot in that post office, even if I should take a notion into my head to write a letter some place." He says, "I won't have you reachin' out of that little old window with a pair of shears and cuttin' off any beard of mine. I'm too smart for you!"

"We all are," says Stella-Rondo.

120   But I said, "If you're so smart, where's Mr. Whitaker?"

So then Uncle Rondo says, "I'll thank you from now on to stop reading all the orders I get on postcards and telling everybody in China Grove what you think is the matter with them," but I says, "I draw my own conclusions and will continue in the future to draw them." I says, "If people want to write their inner-

2. That is, normal school (teachers' college).

most secrets on penny postcards, there's nothing in the wide world you can do about it, Uncle Rondo."

"And if you think we'll ever *write* another postcard you're sadly mistaken," says Mama.

"Cutting off your nose to spite your face then," I says. "But if you're all determined to have no more to do with the U.S. mail, think of this: What will Stella-Rondo do now, if she wants to tell Mr. Whitaker to come after her?"

"Wah!" says Stella-Rondo. I knew she'd cry. She had a conniption fit right there in the kitchen.

"It will be interesting to see how long she holds out," I says. "And now—I am 125 leaving."

"Good-bye," says Uncle Rondo.

"Oh, I declare," says Mama, "to think that a family of mine should quarrel on the Fourth of July, or the day after, over Stella-Rondo leaving old Mr. Whitaker and having the sweetest little adopted child! It looks like we'd all be glad!"

"Wah!" says Stella-Rondo, and has a fresh conniption fit.

"He left *her*—you mark my words," I says. "That's Mr. Whitaker. I know Mr. Whitaker. After all, I knew him first. I said from the beginning he'd up and leave her. I foretold every single thing that's happened."

"Where did he go?" asks Mama.   130

"Probably to the North Pole, if he knows what's good for him," I says.

But Stella-Rondo just bawled and wouldn't say another word. She flew to her room and slammed the door.

"Now look what you've gone and done, Sister," says Mama. "You go apologize."

"I haven't the time, I'm leaving," I says.

"Well, what are you waiting around for?" asks Uncle Rondo.   135

So I just picked up the kitchen clock and marched off, without saying, "Kiss my foot," or anything, and never did tell Stella-Rondo good-bye.

There was a girl going along on a little wagon right in front.

"Nigger girl," I says, "come help me haul these things down the hill, I'm going to live in the post office."

Took her nine trips in her express wagon. Uncle Rondo came out on the porch and threw her a nickel.

And that's the last I've laid eyes on any of my family or my family laid eyes on 140 me for five solid days and nights. Stella-Rondo may be telling the most horrible tales in the world about Mr. Whitaker, but I haven't heard them. As I tell everybody, I draw my own conclusions.

But oh, I like it here. It's ideal, as I've been saying. You see, I've got everything cater-cornered, the way I like it. Hear the radio? All the war news. Radio, sewing machine, book ends, ironing board and that great big piano lamp—peace, that's what I like. Butter-bean vines planted all along the front where the strings are.

Of course, there's not much mail. My family are naturally the main people in China Grove, and if they prefer to vanish from the face of the earth, for all the mail they get or the mail they write, why, I'm not going to open my mouth. Some of the folks here in town are taking up for me and some turned against me. I know which is which. There are always people who will quit buying stamps just to get on the right side of Papa-Daddy.

But here I am, and here I'll stay. I want the world to know I'm happy.

And if Stella-Rondo should come to me this minute, on bended knees, and *attempt* to explain the incidents of her life with Mr. Whitaker, I'd simply put my fingers in both my ears and refuse to listen.

1941

PART TWO Poetry

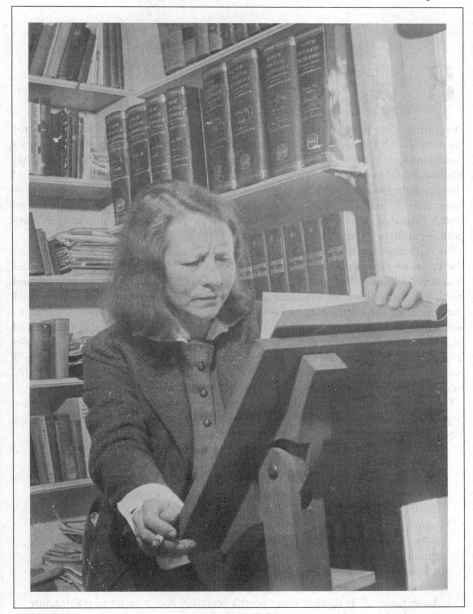

Edna St. Vincent Millay

8 | POETRY: READING, RESPONDING, WRITING

Ways of reading poetry and reasons for doing so differ almost as widely as poems themselves, and in ways we can perhaps best appreciate by considering poetry's functions in other times and places. Though you might be aware, for example, that medieval noblemen paid courtly "bards" to commemorate their achievements and thereby help them to maintain their prestige and power, you might be surprised to learn that since 2007 millions of people across the Middle East have tuned in to watch *Prince of Poets*, a reality show in which poets rather than pop singers compete for audience votes.

Such phenomena might come as a surprise to us simply because today, at least in the West, we don't tend to think of poetry as having great popular appeal or political potency. Millions of us may be moved by the way hip-hop artists use rhyme and rhythm to boast about, or "celebrate and sing," themselves; to show us the danger and excitement of life on the streets; or even to get out the vote. Yet "poetry" seems to many of us a thing apart, something to suffer, to cherish, or to be simply baffled and intimidated by because it seems so arcane, so different and difficult, so essentially irrelevant to the rest of our lives. Though one rarely hears anyone say of all fiction "I hate it" or "I love it" or "I just don't get it," if you're like most people, you've probably said, thought, or heard someone else say at least one of these things about poetry.

This chapter and the ones that follow welcome poetry lovers. But they neither require you to be one nor aim to convert you. They do, we hope, demonstrate a few key points:

- Poetry isn't all one thing: *Poems differ as much as the people who write and read them, or as much as music or movies do.* They can be by turns goofy, sad, or angry; they can tell a story, comment on current events, or simply describe the look of a certain time of day. Deciding that you "love," "hate," "get," or "don't get" all poetry based on your experience of one poem or of one kind of poetry is a little like either deciding you love all music because Mozart moves you or giving up on music entirely because Lady Gaga leaves you cold.
- *A good poem is not a secret message one needs a special decoder ring or an advanced degree to decipher.* Any thoughtful person who's willing to try can make sense of it, though some poems certainly do invite us to rethink our idea of what "making sense" might mean. Poetry has spoken to millions of ordinary people across the centuries and around the world, so at least some poems can speak to us, too, if we give both them and ourselves a chance. By the same token, even the most devoted, experienced poetry lovers among us can become better, more responsive, more thoughtful readers by reading more and different kinds of poetry and by exploring, as the following chapters do, the various elements and techniques with which poetry is made.

- People around the world have often turned to poetry to express their feelings and longings precisely because *poetry is, in certain vital ways, distinct from other forms of writing.* Each genre plays by its own rules and has its own history and traditions, so reading poetry effectively, like succeeding in a video game, does involve learning and playing by certain rules. Any one poem may open itself to multiple responses and interpretations, just as a game may allow you many ways of advancing to the next level. But in both cases there are limits. Neither is a free-for-all in which "anything goes." (In both cases, too, some difficulty can be essential to the fun.) *A poem wouldn't mean anything if it could mean everything.*
- *Yet the questions we ask of a poem and the techniques we use to understand it are simply variations of the same ones we use in reading fiction or drama.* Indeed, some poems narrate action just as a short story does; others work much like scenes from plays.
- Finally, *poems aren't nearly as fragile as we take them to be when we worry about "over-reading" or "analyzing them to death."* You can't kill a poem. But a poem does experience a sort of living death if it's not read, re-read, and pondered over. Poems need you. They can bear the weight of your careful attention, and they deserve it: The best of them are, after all, the result of someone else's. William Wordsworth may have done much to shape our contemporary ideas about poetry when he famously described it as "the spontaneous overflow of powerful feelings," but his own poems were, like most great poems, the result of weeks, even years, of writing and revision.

DEFINING POETRY

But what, after all, is poetry? Trying to define poetry is a bit like trying to catch a snowflake; you can do it, but at the very same moment, the snowflake begins to melt and disappear. With poems, as with fiction, one can always come up with particular examples that don't do what the definition insists they must, as well as numerous writers and readers who will disagree. Yet to claim that poetry eludes all definition is merely to reinforce the idea that it is simply too mysterious for ordinary mortals. Without being all-sufficient or entirely satisfying, a dictionary definition can at least give us a starting point. Here are two such definitions of poetry:

1. Writing that formulates a *concentrated* imaginative awareness of experience in language chosen and *arranged* to create a specific *emotional response* through meaning, sound, and *rhythm*. (*Merriam-Webster*)
2. Composition in verse or some comparable *patterned arrangement* of language in which the expression of *feelings* and ideas is given *intensity* by the use of distinctive style and *rhythm*[. . .] . Traditionally associated with explicit formal departure from the *patterns* of ordinary speech or prose, e.g., in the use of elevated diction, figurative language, and syntactical reordering. (*The Oxford English Dictionary*)

Different as they are, both of these definitions stress four elements: 1) the "patterned arrangement of language" to 2) generate "rhythm" and thereby both 3) express and evoke specific "emotion[s]" or "feelings" in 4) a "concentrated" way, or with "intensity."

But what does all that really mean? To test drive this definition, let's look at an example. And let's pick a tough one: HEAD, HEART, taken from *The Collected Stories of Lydia Davis*, is usually classified as a work of fiction, and it certainly does have the elements of one, including **characters** and some **action** arranged into a **plot** related to us by a **narrator**. Yet one reviewer of Davis's *Collected Stories* tellingly describes this one as "a poem of a story." What specific features of the following story might make it work like a poem? Which, if any, of the features essential to poetry might it lack?

LYDIA DAVIS
Head, Heart

Heart weeps.
Head tries to help heart.
Head tells heart how it is, again:
You will lose the ones you love. They will all go. But even the earth will
    go, someday.
5 Heart feels better, then.
But the words of head do not remain long in the ears of heart.
Heart is so new to this.
I want them back, says heart.
Head is all heart has.
10 Help, head. Help heart.

2007

If difficulty were essential to poetry, "Head, Heart" would not seem to qualify. It's hard to imagine less formal, even less elementary, **diction** or **syntax**. And the whole seems relatively easy to paraphrase (often a helpful thing to do when first encountering a poem): When we're sad about losing someone we love, we reason with ourselves that loss is inevitable because everything earthly, even the earth itself, can't last forever. Such rational explanations give us comfort, but that comfort is itself temporary; we still miss those we've lost and have to keep calling on our heads to help our hearts cope.

We do have emotion here, then, as well as a **conflict** between emotion and reason—and even when they lack plots, most poems do explore conflicts, just as stories and plays do. But do we have a poem? Does it matter that "Head, Heart" depends entirely on two **figures of speech**—**metonymy**, the use of the name of one thing for another closely associated thing (here, "head" for "reason," and "heart" for "emotion"), as well as **personification**, the representation of an object or an abstraction (here, "head" and "heart") as a person (capable of weeping and talking, for example)? Though fiction and drama both use figurative language, we often describe such language as "poetic," even when it occurs in a story or play, because poems do tend to depend much more on it (as we discuss further in ch. 16).

Does it matter that "Head, Heart" is short—just seventy-one words? Though poems come in every size, many poems are short or at least shorter than the typical work of fiction. Brevity is one way that *some* poems achieve the "concentration" and "intensity" the dictionaries take to be essential. Such concentration invites, even requires, ours. As poet Billy Collins puts it, "Poetry offers us the possibility of modulating our pace." The very brevity of a poem can teach us simply to slow down for a moment and pay attention—not only to the details within the poem, but also, through them, to whatever in the world or in ourselves the poem attends to. Sometimes that's all a poem does—simply invites us to pay attention to something we wouldn't notice otherwise.

Regardless of their overall length, moreover, almost all poems concentrate our attention and modulate our pace by doling out words a few at a time, arranging them not just into sentences (as in prose), but into discrete lines. One result is much more blank space and thus more silences and pauses than in prose. For this reason alone, "Head, Heart" looks and works somewhat like a poem. And the deliberateness with which it does so is signaled by the fact that one of its sentences is divided so as to span multiple lines. (Line 3 ends with a colon, not a period.) By arranging words into lines and, often, into **stanzas**, the poet, not a typesetter or printer, determines where words fall on the page. And that perhaps is the most important aspect of that arrangement of language that has differentiated poetry from prose since poetry became a written, as well as spoken, art (an issue discussed further in ch. 17). All printings of a poem, if accurate, reproduce exactly the same breaks and space the words precisely the same way on the page.

AUTHORS ON THEIR CRAFT

BILLY COLLINS ON THE POET AS "LINE-MAKER"

From "A Brisk Walk: An Interview with Billy Collins" (2006)*

I'm a line-maker. I think that's what makes poets different from prose-writers. [. . .] We think not just in sentences the way prose writers do but also in lines. [. . .] When I'm constructing a poem, I'm trying to write one good line after another. [. . .] I'm not thinking of just writing a paragraph and then chopping it up. I'm very conscious of the fact that every line should have a cadence to it. It should contribute to the progress of the poem. And that the ending of the line is a way of turning the reader's attention back into the interior of the poem.

*"A Brisk Walk: An Interview with Billy Collins." Interview by Joel Whitney. *Guernica*, 14 June 2006, www.guernicamag.com/interviews/a_brisk_walk/.

One result is that line endings and beginnings inevitably get more of our attention, bear more oomph and meaning. Notice how many of the lines of "Head, Heart" begin with *head* and *heart* and how these words repeat in a pattern (*Heart, Head, Head, Heart, Heart, Head*—and then *Help*), as if the line beginnings themselves enact the same interplay between "head" and "heart" that the sentences describe. Conversely, certain end words reverberate: *Again*, for example, suggests the repetitive familiarity of this conflict, one that paradoxically seems all the more difficult or poignant because it's both repetitive (each person goes through this again and again) and familiar (all of us go through this); *then* alerts us to the temporariness of the comfort head offers heart, preparing us for the *But* in the next line.

Again and *then* also reverberate in us and with each other because they **rhyme**, just as *head*, *heart*, and *help* **alliterate**. These words share a special aural, as well as spatial and visual, relationship to each other. Though prose writers certainly make their appeal to us in part through sound, poetry remains, as it has been for thousands of years, a more insistently aural form—one that appeals through aural patterning to what Davis here humorously, but not wrongly, calls "the ears of heart" (line 6). As poet Mary Oliver puts it, "To make a poem, we must make sounds. Not random sounds, but chosen sounds."

But are there qualities essential to poetry that "Head, Heart" lacks? Is it, for example, sufficiently aural in its appeal? Does it have genuine rhythm? Perhaps so, perhaps not. As you work your way through the rest of the chapters in this section and read more poems, we encourage you to keep thinking critically about our definitions in order to hone your own sense of just what poetry is, how it works, and what it does.

POETIC SUBGENRES AND KINDS

All poems share some common elements, use some of the same techniques, and thus require us to ask some of the same questions. Later in this chapter, we'll outline some of the steps you can follow and some of the questions you can pose as you read, respond to, and write about any poem. But different sorts of poems also work by slightly different rules and thus invite somewhat different responses and questions.

Poems may be classified into subgenres based on various characteristics, including their length, appearance, and formal features (patterns of rhyme and rhythm, for example); their subject; or even the type of **situation** and **setting** (time and place) they depict. (A **sonnet**, for example, traditionally has fourteen lines. Defined broadly, an **elegy** is a poem about death.) A single poem might well represent multiple subgenres or at least might contain elements of more than one. (One could write an elegy that is also a sonnet, for instance.)

Since Aristotle's time, however, readers and writers have also often divided poems into three broad categories or subgenres—**narrative**, **dramatic**, or **lyric**—based upon their mode of presentation. Put simply, poems that have a plot are either narrative poems (if they feature a narrator) or dramatic poems (if they don't), and many poems that lack a plot are lyrics. The rest of this section describes each of these subgenres in more detail, starting with the one that most resembles fiction and ending with the dramatic monologue, a sort of hybrid that combines features of both dramatic and lyric poetry.

As the dramatic monologue demonstrates, the borders between narrative, dramatic, and lyric poetry are fuzzy, contestable, and shifting. Some poems will cross those borders; others will resist these categories altogether. And the very definition of lyric poetry has not only changed over time, but also remains contested today. The ultimate goal isn't to definitively pigeonhole every poem but rather to develop a language through which to recognize, describe, and explore different poetic modes. Knowing which mode dominates in a particular poem can help ensure that we privilege the right questions as we read and write about it. Learning the **conventions** of particular subgenres and kinds allows us to better adjust to individual poems, to compare them to each other, and to appreciate how each creatively uses, reworks, or even defies or questions generic conventions.

Narrative Poetry

Like a work of prose fiction, a narrative poem tells a story; in other words, it has a plot related by a narrator, though its plot might be based on actual rather than made-up events. Comprising the same elements discussed in the Fiction section of this book, a narrative poem encourages us to ask the same questions—about character, plot, narration, and so on—that we do when reading a short story or novel. (See "Questions about the Elements of Fiction" in chapter 1, p. 19.)

In centuries past, narrative poetry was a—even *the*—dominant subgenre of poetry. As a result, there are many different kinds of narrative poems, including book-length **epics** like Homer's *Iliad*; chivalric **romances** like Thomas Malory's *Le Morte d'Arthur*; grisly murder **ballads**, often rooted in actual events; and a range of harder-to-classify works of varying lengths such as the relatively short but quietly shocking examples below.

EDWIN ARLINGTON ROBINSON
Richard Cory

Whenever Richard Cory went down town,
We people on the pavement looked at him:
He was a gentleman from sole to crown,
Clean favored, and imperially slim.

5   And he was always quietly arrayed,
And he was always human when he talked;
But still he fluttered pulses when he said,
"Good-morning," and he glittered when he walked.

And he was rich—yes, richer than a king—
10 And admirably schooled in every grace:
In fine,[1] we thought that he was everything
To make us wish that we were in his place.

So on we worked, and waited for the light,
And went without the meat, and cursed the bread;
15 And Richard Cory, one calm summer night,
Went home and put a bullet through his head.

1897

- How does the poem characterize Richard Cory? What is the effect of the first-person plural narration?
- What details in the poem's first three stanzas might make its final stanza simultaneously surprising, ironic, and predictable?

---

1. In conclusion, in sum.

ROBERT FROST
"Out, Out—"

The buzz saw snarled and rattled in the yard
And made dust and dropped stove-length sticks of wood,
Sweet-scented stuff when the breeze drew across it.
And from there those that lifted eyes could count
5 Five mountain ranges one behind the other
Under the sunset far into Vermont.
And the saw snarled and rattled, snarled and rattled,
As it ran light, or had to bear a load.
And nothing happened: day was all but done.
10 Call it a day, I wish they might have said
To please the boy by giving him the half hour
That a boy counts so much when saved from work.
His sister stood beside them in her apron
To tell them "Supper." At the word, the saw,
15 As if to prove saws knew what supper meant,
Leaped out at the boy's hand, or seemed to leap—
He must have given the hand. However it was,
Neither refused the meeting. But the hand!
The boy's first outcry was a rueful laugh,
20 As he swung toward them holding up the hand
Half in appeal, but half as if to keep
The life from spilling. Then the boy saw all—
Since he was old enough to know, big boy
Doing a man's work though a child at heart—
25 He saw all spoiled. "Don't let him cut my hand off—
The doctor, when he comes. Don't let him, sister!"
So. But the hand was gone already.
The doctor put him in the dark of ether.
He lay and puffed his lips out with his breath.
30 And then—the watcher at his pulse took fright.
No one believed. They listened at his heart.
Little—less—nothing!—and that ended it.
No more to build on there. And they, since they
Were not the one dead, turned to their affairs.

1916

- What is the effect of Frost's use of a third-person speaker/narrator?
- How does he characterize the poem's central event—the "meeting" between saw and hand (line 18)? What might the poem ask or show us through that event and the characters' responses to it?

Dramatic Poetry

For centuries, plays were written in verse; as a result, drama itself was understood not as a genre in its own right (as we think of it today) but rather as a subgenre of poetry. *Dramatic poetry* thus meant and still can mean actual plays in verse (or *verse drama*). But any poem that consists wholly of dialogue among characters, unmediated by a narrator, counts as a dramatic poem. And we might even apply that label to poems like the following, in which narration is kept to the barest minimum. Indeed, this narrator's only words are "said she," and since every other word in the poem is spoken by one female character to another, the poem essentially reads like a scene from a play. Notice, though, that the poem also depends on techniques of formal organization and patterning unique to poetry: In each of the poem's six stanzas, for example, one woman speaks the first lines, while her companion gets the last line (or two).

THOMAS HARDY
The Ruined Maid

"O 'Melia,[2] my dear, this does everything crown!
Who could have supposed I should meet you in Town?
And whence such fair garments, such prosperi-ty?"—
"O didn't you know I'd been ruined?" said she.

5 —"You left us in tatters, without shoes or socks,
Tired of digging potatoes, and spudding up docks;[3]
And now you've gay bracelets and bright feathers three!"—
"Yes: that's how we dress when we're ruined," said she.

—"At home in the barton[4] you said 'thee' and 'thou,'
10 And 'thik oon,' and 'theäs oon,' and 't'other'; but now
Your talking quite fits 'ee for high compa-ny!"—
"Some polish is gained with one's ruin," said she.

—"Your hands were like paws then, your face blue and bleak
But now I'm bewitched by your delicate cheek,
15 And your little gloves fit as on any la-dy!"—
"We never do work when we're ruined," said she.

—"You used to call home-life a hag-ridden dream,
And you'd sigh, and you'd sock;[5] but at present you seem
To know not of megrims[6] or melancho-ly!"—
20 "True. One's pretty lively when ruined," said she.

—"I wish I had feathers, a fine sweeping gown,
And a delicate face, and could strut about Town!"—

---

2. Short for Amelia.   3. Spading up weeds.   4. Farmyard.   5. Sigh (English dialect).
6. Migraine headaches.

"My dear—a raw country girl, such as you be,
Cannot quite expect that. You ain't ruined," said she.

1866

When we read and write about dramatic poems, we can usefully bring to bear the same questions we do in reading drama. (See "Questions to Ask When Reading a Play" in ch. 18.) But when it comes to short poems like THE RUINED MAID, questions about sets, staging, and even plot will usually be much less relevant than those related to character and conflict, as well as setting, tone, language, symbol, and theme. In Hardy's poem, for example, how are each of the two speakers characterized by *how* they speak, as well as *what* they say? How is our view of them, and especially of 'Melia, "the ruined maid," affected by the formal pattern mentioned earlier, which ensures (among other things) that she gets the last line? How might this pattern, along with rhythm and rhyme, also add **irony** to the poem?

Lyric Poetry

For good historical reasons, lyric poems probably best fulfill your expectations of what poetry should be like. Yet lyric poetry has been and still is defined in myriad ways. The word *lyric* derives from the ancient Greeks, for whom it designated a short poem chanted or sung by a single singer to the accompaniment of a stringed instrument called a lyre (hence, the word *lyric* and the fact that we today also use the word *lyrics* to denote the words of any song). Scholars believe that the earliest "lyrics" in the Greek sense were likely associated with religious occasions and feelings, especially those related to celebration, praise, and mourning. Ever since, the lyric has been associated with brevity, musicality, a single speaker, and the expression of intense feeling. Not surprisingly, at least a few specific kinds of lyric, including the **ode** and the **elegy**, originated in the ancient world.

Over the centuries, the lyric's boundaries have expanded and become fuzzier. Few lyrics are intended to be sung at all, much less to a lyre. But everyone agrees that relatively short poems that focus primarily on the feelings, impressions, and thoughts—that is, on the subjective, inward experience—of a single first-person speaker are lyrics.

Below are two examples very different from each other in subject matter and tone. Yet with these, as with all lyrics, our initial questions in both reading and writing will likely focus on each speaker's situation and inward experience of it. What is each speaker experiencing, feeling, and thinking, and how exactly does the poem make that state of mood and mind at once vivid and relevant to us?

WILLIAM WORDSWORTH
I wandered lonely as a cloud[7]

I wandered lonely as a cloud
That floats on high o'er vales and hills,
When all at once I saw a crowd,

---

7. When any poem lacks a title, it is conventional to substitute the poem's first line, maintaining original capitalization (or lack thereof).

A host, of golden daffodils;
5 Beside the lake, beneath the trees,
Fluttering and dancing in the breeze.

Continuous as the stars that shine
And twinkle on the milky way,
They stretched in never-ending line
10 Along the margin of a bay:
Ten thousand saw I at a glance,
Tossing their heads in sprightly dance.

The waves beside them danced; but they
Out-did the sparkling waves in glee:
15 A poet could not but be gay,
In such a jocund company:
I gazed—and gazed—but little thought
What wealth the show to me had brought:

For oft, when on my couch I lie
20 In vacant or in pensive mood,
They flash upon that inward eye
Which is the bliss of solitude;
And then my heart with pleasure fills,
And dances with the daffodils.

1807

- According to the speaker, what is "the bliss of solitude" (line 22)? Why and how does "solitude" become less "lonely" for him (line 1)?
- What about the relationship between human beings and nature might be implied by the speaker's description of his particular experience?

FRANK O'HARA
Poem

Lana Turner[8] has collapsed!
I was trotting along and suddenly
it started raining and snowing
and you said it was hailing
5 but hailing hits you on the head
hard so it was really snowing and
raining and I was in such a hurry
to meet you but the traffic
was acting exactly like the sky
10 and suddenly I see a headline
LANA TURNER HAS COLLAPSED!
there is no snow in Hollywood
there is no rain in California

8. American actress (1921–95); in 1958, Turner's lover, John Stompanato, Jr., was stabbed to death by her daughter, who was determined to have acted in self-defense.

Lana Turner testifying at the John Stompanato inquest, April 1958

> I have been to lots of parties
> 15 and acted perfectly disgraceful
> but I never actually collapsed
> oh Lana Turner we love you get up
>
>   1962

- What or whom exactly does this poem seem to make fun of? Does the poem also convey more serious sentiments?
- What current celebrity seems to you the best potential substitute for Lana Turner? What about both this celebrity's public persona and the poem itself make your choice seem especially appropriate?

What makes these lyrics different from narrative and dramatic poems? Though both include action ("wander[ing]," "trotting," and so on), that action doesn't quite add up to a plot; what we have might be better described as a situation, scene, or incident. Similarly, though the poems vividly describe external things, from "golden daffodils" to "traffic," greater emphasis ultimately falls on how the "I" experiences and feels about them—the internal, subjective experience or state of mind and mood that those outward things inspire or reflect. Both poems thus encourage us to focus almost exclusively on the complex emotional experience and thoughts of a particular speaker in a specific situation, but ones that we can, if the poem is effective, ultimately understand as having a much wider, sometimes even universal, resonance and relevance.

Most lyrics require us to infer a general theme from a specific experience, but some offer more explicit reflection, commentary, even argument. As you read the following example, notice what happens in line 5 (exactly halfway through the poem), as the speaker turns from personal statements to more impersonal, argumentative ones. How does personal reflection relate to, even enable, argument here?

Frontispiece to Phillis Wheatley's *Poems on Various Subjects, Religious and Moral,* 1773

PHILLIS WHEATLEY
On Being Brought from Africa to America

'Twas mercy brought me from my
    Pagan land,
Taught my benighted soul to
    understand
That there's a God, that there's a
    Saviour too:
Once I redemption neither sought
    nor knew.
5 Some view our sable race with
    scornful eye,
"Their colour is a diabolic die."
Remember, Christians, Negroes,
    black as Cain,[9]
May be refin'd, and join th' angelic
    train.

1773

- What do the poem's first four lines imply about how the speaker feels about "being brought from Africa to America" and about what motivates these feelings?
- What two "view[s]" of Africans are contrasted in the last four lines (line 5)? According to the entire poem, which is the right view, and why and how so?

Descriptive or Observational Lyrics

As Wheatley's poem demonstrates, lyrics come in many varieties. Quite a few are more exclusively descriptive or observational than the examples above, insofar as they describe something or someone to us without bringing much attention to the speaker's personal state of mind or feelings. As we've noted, after all, some poems simply give us the opportunity to look more closely and carefully at something in the world around us. Nineteenth-century poet Percy Bysshe Shelley suggested, in fact, that all poetry's major purpose is just that—helping us see in a new way. Poetry, he said, "strips the veil of familiarity from the world, and lays bare [its] naked and sleeping beauty" and "wonder." Over a century later, American poet James Dickey expressed a similar idea somewhat differently when he defined a poet as "someone who notices and is enormously taken by things that somebody else would walk by."

Obviously, any descriptive poem inevitably reflects its speaker's point of view. Yet lyrics of this type invite us to focus more on what they describe than on the subjective, internal experience or feelings of the speaker doing the describing. As a result, our focus in reading and writing will probably be how the poem characterizes, and encourages us to see, think, and feel about, whatever it describes—whether a

9. One of Adam's sons, who killed his brother Abel. (See Gen. 4.)

moment, a person, an object, or a phenomenon. What is described in each of the poems that follow? What figures of speech are used, and with what implications and effects?

EMILY DICKINSON
The Sky is low—the Clouds are mean

The Sky is low—the Clouds are mean.
A Travelling Flake of Snow
Across a Barn or through a Rut
Debates if it will go—
5 A Narrow Wind complains all Day
How some one treated him
Nature, like Us, is sometimes caught
Without her Diadem—

1866

- Whom does the speaker seem to mean by "Us," and what might this poem imply about the similarity between "Nature" and "Us" (line 7)?

BILLY COLLINS
Divorce

Once, two spoons in bed,
now tined forks

across a granite table
and the knives they have hired.

2008

- This poem consists almost entirely of **metaphor** (implied comparison). What is compared to what here? How would you describe the poem's **tone**? (Is it funny, sad, bitter, or some combination of these?) Why and how so?

The Dramatic Monologue

Finally, we come to the **dramatic monologue**, a subgenre of poem that—by residing somewhere in between lyric and dramatic poetry—can teach us more about both. Robert Browning, the nineteenth-century British poet often credited with inventing this kind of poem, tellingly labeled his own works "dramatic lyrics," describing them as "dramatic in principle," "lyric in expression." On the one hand, the dramatic monologue is "lyric in expression" or like a lyric poem because it features a single speaker who speaks in the first person. On the other hand, it is "dramatic in principle" or resembles a scene from a play for at least two reasons. First, the poem's primary focus is characterization, an obviously fictional or historical speaker's often unintentional revelation of his or her personality, outlook, and values. Such poems tend to offer us a window into an entire, complex psychology and even life history rather than simply one experience or feeling of a speaker we otherwise discover little about (as in lyrics). Often, too, dramatic monologues invite us to see their speakers and situations somewhat differently than the speakers themselves do, much as does fiction narrated by *unreliable narrators*. Second, the speaker of a dramatic monologue conventionally addresses one or more silent **auditors** whose identity we can only infer from the speaker's words *to* them. Often, speaker and auditor are caught in a very specific and "dramatic" moment or situation, one which we also have to tease out from the clues the speaker gives us and which frequently involves some sort of persuasion on the speaker's part. The questions we pose in reading and writing about such poems thus often center on character and characterization and on the comparison of our perception of the speaker and his or her situation with the speaker's own self-representation.

This subgenre remains as popular with contemporary songwriters as with contemporary poets. Bruce Springsteen's albums *Nebraska* (1982) and *The Rising* (2002), for instance, consist mainly of dramatic monologues. Below, you will find the lyrics to one of these, followed by a poem that takes the form of an imaginary letter, thus putting an interesting twist on the conventions regarding "speakers" and "auditors."

BRUCE SPRINGSTEEN
Nebraska

I saw her standin' on her front lawn
   just twirlin' her baton
Me and her went for a ride, sir, and ten
   innocent people died

5 From the town of Lincoln, Nebraska,
   with a sawed-off .410 on my lap
Through the badlands of Wyoming I
   killed everything in my path

I can't say that I'm sorry for the things
10   that we done
At least for a little while, sir, me and
   her we had us some fun

The jury brought in a guilty verdict and
   the judge he sentenced me to death
15 Midnight in a prison storeroom with
   leather straps across my chest

Sheriff, when the man pulls that
   switch, sir, and snaps my poor head back
You make sure my pretty baby is sittin'
20   right there on my lap

They declared me unfit to live, said into
   that great void my soul'd be hurled

They wanted to know why I did what I did
   Well, sir, I guess there's just a meanness in this world[1]
                       1982

- What different motives and explanations for the speaker's actions might
  NEBRASKA provide by means of what he says, how he speaks, and how his
  speech is rendered on the page? Might the song as a whole offer explanations
  that the speaker doesn't offer, at least consciously or directly?

ROBERT HAYDEN

A Letter from Phillis Wheatley

(London, 1773)

Dear Obour[2]
    Our crossing was without
event. I could not help, at times,
reflecting on that first—my Destined—
5 voyage long ago (I yet
have some remembrance of its Horrors)[3]
and marvelling at God's Ways.
    Last evening, her Ladyship[4] presented me
to her illustrious Friends.
10 I scarce could tell them anything
of Africa, though much of Boston
and my hope of Heaven. I read
my latest Elegies to them.
"O Sable Muse!" the Countess cried,
15 embracing me, when I had done.
I held back tears, as is my wont,
and there were tears in Dear
Nathaniel's eyes.
    At supper—I dined apart
20 like captive Royalty—
the Countess and her Guests promised
signatures affirming me
True Poetess, albeit once a slave.[5]

---

1. Allusion to words spoken by a murderer in Flannery O'Connor's "A Good Man Is Hard to Find" (par. 134; p. 366).
2. Obour Tanner, a Rhode Island slave and Wheatley's intimate friend and frequent correspondent.
3. Born in Africa c. 1753–54, Wheatley was taken at around age eight on the slave ship *Phillis* to America, where she was purchased by Boston merchant John Wheatley. In 1773, he sent her to London with his son, Nathaniel, a visit partly motivated by concerns about her health.
4. Selina Hastings, Countess of Huntingdon (1707–91), helped arrange publication of Wheatley's first book of poems, which appeared in London just months after the poet's return to the United States.
5. Wheatley's *Poems on Various Subjects, Religious and Moral* (1773) was prefaced by a letter, signed by seventeen eminent Bostonians, attesting to the poems' authenticity, which had been questioned because of her race.

Indeed, they were most kind, and spoke,
25   moreover, of presenting me
at Court (I thought of Pocahontas)[6]—
an Honor, to be sure, but one,
I should, no doubt, as Patriot decline.
    My health is much improved;
30   I feel I may, if God so Wills,
entirely recover here.
Idyllic England! Alas, there is
no Eden without its Serpent. Beneath
chiming Complaisance I hear him hiss;
35   I see his flickering tongue
when foppish would-be Wits
murmur of the Yankee Pedlar
and his Cannibal Mockingbird.
    Sister, forgive th'intrusion of
40   my Sombreness—Nocturnal Mood
I would not share with any save
your trusted Self. Let me disperse,
in closing, such unseemly Gloom
by mention of an Incident
45   you may, as I, consider Droll:
Today, a little Chimney Sweep,
his face and hands with soot quite Black,
staring hard at me, politely asked:
"Does you, M'lady, sweep chimneys too?"
50   I was amused, but Dear Nathaniel
(ever Solicitous) was not.
    I pray the Blessings of Our Lord
    and Saviour Jesus Christ
    will Abundantly be yours.
55   Phillis
                        1977

- What internal and external conflicts seem to be revealed here? What conflict does Wheatley herself seem aware of? Why might Hayden have chosen both this particular moment in Wheatley's life and this particular addressee (Obour Tanner)?
- How does Hayden's portrayal of both Wheatley's feelings and others' views of her compare to Wheatley's own characterization of these in ON BEING BROUGHT FROM AFRICA TO AMERICA?

6. Daughter of an Algonquian Indian chief (c. 1595–1617), Pocahontas famously befriended Virginia's first English colonists, led by Captain John Smith; she died while visiting England, where she had been presented at the court of King James I.

RESPONDING TO POETRY

Not all poems are as readily accessible as those in this chapter, and even those that are take on additional meanings if we approach them systematically, bringing to bear specific reading habits and skills and some knowledge of poetic genres, conventions, and traditions. Experience will give you a sense of what to expect, but knowing what to expect isn't everything. As a reader of poetry, you should always be open—to new experiences, new feelings, new ideas, new forms of expression. Every poem is a potential new experience, and you will often discover something new with every re-reading.

Steps to Follow, Questions to Ask, and Sample Reading Notes

No one can give you a method that will offer you total experience of all poems. But because individual poems share characteristics with other poems, taking certain steps can prompt you both to ask the right questions and to devise compelling answers. If you are relatively new to poetry, encounter a poem that seems especially difficult, or plan to write about a poem, you may need to tackle the following steps one at a time, pausing to write even as you read and respond. With further experience, you will often find that you can skip some steps or run through them quickly and almost automatically, though your experience and understanding of any poem will be enriched if you slow down and take your time.

Try the first step on your own, then we will both detail and demonstrate the others.

1. **Listen to a poem first.** When you encounter a new poem, read through it once without thinking too much about what it means. Try to simply listen to the poem, even if you read silently, much as you might a song on the radio. Better yet, read it aloud. Doing so will help you hear the poem's sound qualities, get a clearer impression of its **tone**, and start making sense of its **syntax**, the way words combine into sentences.

APHRA BEHN
On Her Loving Two Equally

I

How strongly does my passion flow,
Divided equally twixt[7] two?
Damon had ne'er subdued my heart
Had not Alexis took his part;
5   Nor could Alexis powerful prove,
Without my Damon's aid, to gain my love.

II

When my Alexis present is,
Then I for Damon sigh and mourn;

7. Between.

But when Alexis I do miss,
10 Damon gains nothing but my scorn.
But if it chance they both are by,
For both alike I languish, sigh, and die.

III
Cure then, thou mighty wingèd god,[8]
This restless fever in my blood:
15 One golden-pointed dart take back:
But which, O Cupid, wilt thou take?
If Damon's, all my hopes are crossed;
Or that of my Alexis, I am lost.

1684

Now that you've read Behn's poem, read through the remaining steps and see how one reader used them as a guide for responding. Later, return to these steps as you read and respond to other poems.

2. **Articulate your expectations, starting with the title.** Poets often try to surprise readers, but you can appreciate such surprises only if you first define your expectations. As you read a poem, take note of what you expect and where, when, and how the poem does and doesn't fulfill your expectations.

> The title of Aphra Behn's "On Her Loving Two Equally" makes me think the poem will be about a woman. But can someone really "love two equally"? Maybe this is the question the poem will ask. If so, I expect its answer to be no, because I don't think this is possible. If so, maybe the title is a sort of pun—"On Her Loving *Too* Equally."

3. **Read the syntax literally.** What the sentences literally say is only a starting point, but it is vital. You cannot begin to explore what a poem *means* unless you first know what it *says*. Though poets arrange words into lines and stanzas, they usually write in complete sentences, just as writers in other genres do. At the same time and partly in order to create the sort of aural and visual patterns discussed earlier in this chapter, poets make much more frequent use of **inversion** (a change in normal word order or syntax). To ensure you don't misread, first "translate" the poem rather than fixing on certain words and free-associating or leaping to conclusions. To translate accurately, especially with poems written before the twentieth century, you may need to break this step down into the following smaller steps:

a. *Identify sentences.* For now, ignore the line breaks and look for sentences or independent clauses (word groups that can function as complete sentences). These will typically be preceded and followed by a period (.), a semicolon (;), a colon (:), or a dash (—).

8. Cupid, who, according to myth, shot darts of lead and of gold at the hearts of lovers, corresponding to false love and true love, respectively.

The eighteen lines of Behn's poem can be broken down into nine sentences.

1. How strongly does my passion flow, Divided equally twixt two?
2. Damon had ne'er subdued my heart, Had not Alexis took his part;
3. Nor could Alexis powerful prove, Without my Damon's aid, to gain my love.
4. When my Alexis present is, Then I for Damon sigh and mourn;
5. But when Alexis I do miss, Damon gains nothing but my scorn.
6. But if it chance they both are by, For both alike I languish, sigh, and die.
7. Cure then, thou mighty wingèd god, This restless fever in my blood;
8. One golden-pointed dart take back: But which, O Cupid, wilt thou take?
9. If Damon's, all my hopes are crossed; Or that of my Alexis, I am lost.

b. *Reorder sentences.* Identify the main elements—subject(s), verb(s), object(s)—of each sentence or independent clause, and if necessary rearrange them in normative word order. (In English, this order tends to be subject-verb-object except in the case of a question; in either case, dependent clauses come at the beginning or end of the main clause and next to whatever element they modify.)

c. *Replace each pronoun with the antecedent noun it replaces*; if the antecedent is ambiguous, indicate all the possibilities.

In the following sentences, the reordered words appear in italics, nouns substituted for pronouns appear in parentheses:

1. How strongly does my passion flow, Divided equally twixt two?
2. Damon had ne'er subdued my heart, Had not Alexis took (Alexis's or Damon's) part;
3. Nor could Alexis *prove* powerful *to gain my love* Without my Damon's aid.
4. When my Alexis *is* present, Then I *sigh and mourn* for Damon;
5. But when *I do miss* Alexis, Damon gains nothing but my scorn.
6. But if it chance *both* (Damon and Alexis) are by, *I languish, sigh, and die* For both (Damon and Alexis) alike.
7. *thou mighty wingèd god,* Cure then This restless fever in my blood;
8. *take back* One golden-pointed dart: But which *wilt thou take,* O Cupid?
9. If Damon's, all my hopes are crossed; Or that (dart) of my Alexis, I am lost.

d. *Translate sentences into modern prose.* Use a dictionary to define unfamiliar or ambiguous words or words that seem to be used in an unfamiliar or unexpected way. Add any implied words necessary to link the parts of a sentence to each other and one sentence logically to the next. At this stage, don't move to outright paraphrase; instead, stick closely to the original.

Below, added words appear in brackets, substituted definitions in parentheses:

1. How strongly does my passion flow [when it is] divided equally between two [people]?
2. Damon would never have (*conquered* or *tamed*) my heart if Alexis had not taken (Damon or Alexis's) (*portion*) [of my heart].
3. Nor could Alexis [have] prove[n] powerful [enough] to gain my love without my Damon's aid.
4. When my Alexis is present, then I sigh and mourn for Damon;
5. But when I miss Alexis, Damon doesn't gain anything (*except*) my scorn.
6. But if it (*so happens*) that both (Damon and Alexis) are [near]by [me], I languish, sigh, and die for both (Damon and Alexis) alike.
7. [Cupid], (*you*) mighty god (*with wings*), cure then this restless fever in my blood;
8. Take back one [of your two] darts [with] pointed gold [tips]: But which [of these darts] will you take, O Cupid?
9. If [on the one hand, you take away] Damon's [dart], all my hopes are (*opposed, invalidated, spoiled*); Or [if, on the other hand, you take away] Alexis's [arrow], I am (*desperate, ruined, destroyed; no longer claimed or possessed by anyone; helpless or unable to find my way*).

e. *Note any ambiguities in the original language that you might have ignored in your translation.* For example, look for modifiers that might modify more than one thing; verbs that might have multiple subjects or objects; words that have multiple relevant meanings.

In the second sentence, "his" could refer either to Damon or to Alexis since both names appear in the first part of this sentence; in other words, this could say either "Alexis took Damon's part" or "Alexis took his own part." But what about the word *part*? I translated this as *portion*, and I assumed it referred back to "heart," partly because the two words come at the ends of lines 3 ("heart") and 4 ("part") and also rhyme. But two other definitions of *part* might make sense here: "the role of a character in a play" or "one's . . . allotted task (as in an action)," and "one of the opposing sides in a conflict or dispute," which in this case could be the "conflict" over the speaker's love. On the one hand, then, I could translate this as "Alexis took his own portion of my heart"; "Alexis played his own role in my life or in this three-way courtship drama"; or "Alexis defended his own side in the battle for my love." On the other hand, I could translate it as "Alexis took Damon's part of my heart"; "Alexis played Damon's role"; or even "Alexis defended Damon's side in the battle for my love."

4. Consult reference works. In addition to using a dictionary to define unfamiliar or ambiguous words, look up anything else to which the poem refers that you either don't understand or that you suspect might be ambiguous: a place, a person, a myth, a quotation, an idea, etc.

According to *Britannica.com*, Cupid was the "ancient Roman god of love" and "often appeared as a winged infant carrying a bow and a quiver of arrows whose wounds inspired love or passion in his every victim." It makes sense, then, that the speaker of this poem would think that she might stop loving one of these men if Cupid took back the arrow that made her love him. But the poem wasn't written in ancient Rome (it's dated 1684), so is the speaker just kidding or being deliberately "poetic" when she calls on Cupid? And what about the names "Damon" and "Alexis"? Were those common in the seventeenth century? Maybe so, if a poet could be named Aphra Behn.

5. **Figure out who, where, when, and what happens.** Once you have gotten a sense of the literal meaning of each sentence, ask the following very general factual questions about the whole poem. Remember that not all of the questions will suit every poem. (Which questions apply will depend in part on whether the poem is narrative, dramatic, or lyric.) At this point, stick to the facts. What do you know for sure?

Who?
- Who is, or who are, the poem's **speaker(s)**?
- Who is, or who are, the **auditor(s)**, if any?
- Who are the other **characters**, if any, that appear in the poem?

The title suggests that the speaker is a woman who loves two people. In the poem, she identifies these as two men—Damon and Alexis. The speaker doesn't seem to address anyone in particular (certainly not the two men she talks about) except in the third stanza, when she addresses Cupid—first through the **epithet** "mighty wingèd god" (line 13) and then by name (16). (Because Cupid isn't present, this is an **apostrophe**.)

Where? When?
- Where is the speaker?
- Where and when do any actions described in the poem take place? That is, what is the poem's **setting**?

No place or time is specified in Behn's poem. The poem is dated 1684, and the antiquated diction ("twixt," line 2; "wilt," 16) seems appropriate to that time. But nothing in the poem makes the situation or feelings it describes specific to a time or place. The speaker doesn't say things like "Last Thursday, when Damon and I were hanging out in the garden . . . ," for example. She seems to describe situations that keep happening repeatedly rather than specific incidents.

What?
- What is the **situation** described in the poem?
- What, if anything, literally happens over the course of it, or what **action**, if any, does it describe?
- Or, if the poem doesn't have a **plot**, then how would you describe its internal structure? Even when a poem seems less interested in telling a story than in simply capturing a feeling or describing something or someone, you can still

usually read in it some kind of progression or development or even an argument. When and how does the subject matter or focus or address shift over the course of the poem?

The basic situation is that the speaker loves two men equally. In the second stanza she describes recurring situations—being with one of the men and not the other or being with both of them at once—and the feelings that result. Then, in the third stanza, she imagines what would happen if she stopped loving one of them. The topic or subject essentially remains the same throughout, but there are two subtle shifts. First is the shift from addressing anyone in stanzas one and two to addressing Cupid in stanza three. Second, there are shifts in verb tense and time: the first stanza floats among various tenses ("does," line 1; "took," 4), the second sticks to the present tense ("is," "sigh," "mourn," etc.), and the third shifts to future ("wilt," 16). As a result, I would say that the poem has two parts: in one, the speaker characterizes her situation in the present and recent past; in the other she explores a possible alternative future (that she ends up not liking any better).

6. **Formulate tentative answers to the questions, *Why does it matter? What does it all mean?***

   - Why should the poem matter to anyone other than the poet, or what might the poem show and say to readers?
   - What problems, issues, questions, or **conflicts** does the poem explore that might be relevant to people other than the speaker(s) or the poet—to humanity in general, to the poet's contemporaries, to people of a certain type or in a certain situation, and so forth?
   - How is each problem or conflict developed and resolved over the course of the poem, or how is each question answered? What conclusions does the poem seem to reach about these, or what are its **themes**?

   The title and first two lines pose a question: how strong is our love if we love two people instead of one? We tend to assume that anything that is "divided" is less strong than something unified. The use of the word *flow* in the first line reinforces that assumption because it implicitly compares love to something that flows: a river, for example, "flows," and when a river divides into two streams, each stream is smaller and its flow less strong than the river's. So the way the speaker articulates the question implies an answer: love, like a river, isn't strong and sure when divided.

   But the rest of the poem undermines that answer. In the first stanza, the speaker points out that each lover and his love has "aided" and added to the "power" of the other: neither man would have "gain[ed her] love" if the other hadn't. The second stanza gives a more concrete sense of why: since we tend to yearn for what we don't have at the moment, being with one of these men makes her miss the other one. But if both men are present, she feels the same about both and perhaps even feels *more* complete and satisfied.

As if realizing she can't solve the problem herself, she turns in the third stanza to Cupid and asks him to help by taking away her love for either Damon or Alexis. As soon as she asks for this, though, she indicates the result would be unhappiness. In the end, the poem seems to say (or its theme is) that love *doesn't* flow or work like a river because love can actually be stronger when we love more than one person, as if it's multiplied instead of lessened by division.

Clearly, this is the opposite of what I expected, which was that the poem would ask whether it was possible to love two people and conclude it wasn't. The conflict is also different than I expected—though there's an external conflict between the two men (maybe), the focus is on the speaker's internal conflict, but that conflict isn't over which guy to choose but about how this is actually working (*I love both of them equally; each love reinforces the other*) versus how she thinks things *should* work (*I'm not supposed to love two equally*).

7. **Consider how the poem's form contributes to its effect and meaning.**

    - How is the poem organized on the page, into lines and/or stanzas, for example? (What are the lines and stanzas like in terms of length, shape, and so on? Are they all alike, or do they vary? Are lines **enjambed** or **end-stopped**?)
    - What are the poem's other formal features? (Is there **rhyme** or another form of aural patterning such as **alliteration**? What is the poem's base **meter**, and are there interesting variations? If not, how else might you describe the poem's rhythm?)
    - How do the poem's overall form and its various formal features contribute to its meaning and effect? In other words, what gets lost when you translate the poem into modern prose?

The stanza organization underscores shifts in the speaker's approach to her situation. But organization reinforces meaning in other ways as well. On the one hand, the division into three stanzas and the choice to number them, plus the fact that each stanza has three sentences, mirror the three-way struggle or love triangle described in the poem. On the other hand, because the poem has eighteen *lines* and nine *sentences*, every sentence is "divided equally twixt two" *lines*. Sound and especially rhyme reinforce this pattern, since the two lines that make up one sentence usually rhyme with each other (to form a **couplet**). The only lines that aren't couplets are those that begin the second stanza, where we instead have alternating rhyme—*is* (line 7) rhymes with *miss* (9), *mourn* (8) rhymes with *scorn* (10). But these lines describe how the speaker "miss[es]" one man when the other is "by," a sensation she arguably reproduces in readers by ensuring that we twice "miss" the rhyme that the rest of the poem leads us to expect.

8. **Investigate and consider the ways the poem both uses and departs from poetic conventions, especially those related to form and subgenre.**

• Does the poem use a traditional verse form (such as **blank verse**) or a traditional stanza form (such as **ballad stanza**)? Is it a specific subgenre or kind of poem—a **sonnet**, an **ode**, a **ballad**, for example? If so, how does that affect its meaning?

Over time, stanza and verse forms have been used in certain ways and to certain ends, and particular subgenres have observed certain conventions. As a result, they generate particular expectations for readers familiar with such traditions, and poems gain additional meaning by both fulfilling and defying those expectations. For example, **anapestic** meter (two unstressed syllables followed by a stressed one, as in *Tennessee*) is usually used for comic poems, so when poets use it in a serious poem they are probably making a point.

9. **Argue.** Discussion with others—both out loud and in writing—usually results in clarification and keeps you from being too dependent on personal biases and preoccupations that sometimes mislead even the best readers. Discussing a poem with someone else (especially someone who thinks very differently) or sharing what you've written about the poem can expand your perspective and enrich your experience.

WRITING ABOUT POETRY

If you follow the steps outlined above and keep notes on your personal responses to the poems you read, you will have already begun writing informally. You have also generated ideas and material you can use in more formal writing. To demonstrate how, we conclude this chapter with two examples of such writing. Both grow out of the notes earlier in this chapter. Yet each is quite different in form and content. The first example is a relatively informal response paper that investigates the allusions in Aphra Behn's ON HER LOVING TWO EQUALLY, following up on the discoveries and questions generated by consulting reference works (as in step 4 above). The second example is an essay on the poem that defends and develops as a thesis one answer to the questions *Why does it matter? What does it all mean?* (as in step 6 above) by drawing on discoveries made in earlier and later steps.

As these examples illustrate, there are many different ways to write about poems, just as there are many different things to say about any one. But all such writing begins with a clear sense of the poem itself and your responses to it. Effective writing also depends on a willingness to listen carefully to the poem and to ask genuine questions about how it works, what it says and means, and how it both fulfills and challenges your expectations about life and about poetry.

• • •

From bardic chronicles to imaginary letters, brief introspective lyrics to action-packed epics, "poetry" comes in many sizes, shapes, and varieties; serves myriad purposes for many diverse audiences; and offers pleasures and rewards both like and unlike those we get from fiction, drama, music, or any other art form. In part, though, that's because poetry is something of a trickster and a trespasser, crossing in and out of those other generic domains and trying on their clothes, even as it inhabits and wears very special ones all its own. Poetry speaks to head, as well as heart; ears, as well as eyes. If you keep yours open, it just might speak to you in ways you never expected.

SAMPLE WRITING: RESPONSE PAPER

The following response paper investigates the allusions in Aphra Behn's On Her Loving Two Equally by drawing upon information from reference works. Few response papers involve research, but we have included one that does in order to demonstrate both how you can use information from credible secondary sources to test and deepen your personal response to a poem and how you can develop reading notes like those in chapter 8 into a thoughtful informal response paper.

Names in "On Her Loving Two Equally"

Aphra Behn's "On Her Loving Two Equally" is dated 1684, but refers to an ancient pagan god. That seems weird and made me curious about what he was doing in the poem. According to the *Encyclopedia Britannica Online*, Cupid was the "ancient Roman god of love," "often appeared as a winged infant carrying a bow and a quiver of arrows whose wounds inspired love or passion in his every victim," and "was sometimes portrayed wearing armour like that of Mars, the God of war, perhaps to suggest ironic parallels between warfare and romance" ("Cupid"). It makes sense, then, that the speaker of this poem would think that she might stop loving one of these guys if Cupid took back the arrow that made her love him. And the reference to Cupid also reinforces the association in the poem "between warfare" or at least conflict "and romance." (The speaker is internally conflicted, and there is also an external conflict between the two male lovers.)

I'm still not sure whether the speaker is kidding or being deliberately "poetic" by talking to an ancient Roman god. But either way, this reinforces the idea I had when I was reading, that the poem isn't very specific about time or place. The poem makes the speaker's situation seem like something that has happened or could happen any time, anywhere.

But what about the names Damon and Alexis? Were these real names in seventeenth-century England, which is apparently where Behn was from? According to the Oxford *Dictionary of First Names*, Damon is "a classical Greek name" that was

> made famous in antiquity by the story of Damon and Pythias. In the early 4th century BC Pythias was condemned to death by Dionysius, ruler of Syracuse. His friend Damon offered to stand surety for him, and took his place in the condemned cell while Pythias put his affairs in order. When Pythias duly returned to be executed rather than absconding and leaving his friend to his fate, Dionysius was so impressed by the

trust and friendship of the two young men that he pardoned both of them. ("Damon")

This doesn't tell me for sure whether there were really men named Damon in seventeenth-century England, but it's now clear that using the name "Damon" is another way of alluding to "antiquity" and maybe making this situation and poem seem "antique." But the story of Damon and Pythias seems even more relevant. When I was translating this poem, I noticed that it could imply that Damon and Alexis were actually helping each other, not just fighting over the speaker (especially because "his," in line 4, could refer to either man). Does the fact that the most famous Damon was willing to sit in prison and even be executed to help his best friend give me more evidence that I'm right? On the other hand, does it matter that the name comes from a word meaning " 'to tame, subdue' (often a euphemism for 'kill')" ("Damon")?

I couldn't find anything nearly this interesting about "Alexis," except that it is a Latin form of a Greek name that originally came from a word that means "to defend" ("Alexis").

To sum up, I think two things are important: (1) by referring to Cupid and naming her boyfriends Damon and Alexis, Behn makes her poem and her speaker's situation seem "antique," even for the seventeenth century, and implies her situation could happen any time anywhere; and (2) the fact that the men's names mean "to tame, subdue," even "kill," and "to defend" makes the conflict in the poem more intense, but the fact that the world's most famous Damon sacrificed himself for his friend might add fuel to the idea that these rivals are also friends who are helping each other. Maybe there's even more "loving two equally" going on here than I thought at first? If the speaker loves each of these guys more because she loves the other one, is that true of them, too? This poem is crazy!

WORKS CITED

"Alexis." Hanks et al.

Behn, Aphra. "On Her Loving Two Equally." *The Norton Introduction to Literature*, edited by Kelly J. Mays, shorter 13th ed., W. W. Norton, 2020, pp. 414–15.

"Cupid." *Encyclopaedia Britannica Online*, 5 May 2015, www.britannica.com /topic/Cupid.

"Damon." Hanks et al.

Hanks, Patrick, et al., editors. *A Dictionary of First Names.* 2nd ed., Oxford UP, 2006. *Oxford Reference Online*, doi:10.1093/acref/9780198610601.001.0001.

SAMPLE WRITING: ESSAY

The following sample essay develops the observations about Aphra Behn's ON HER LOVING TWO EQUALLY in chapter 8, demonstrating how you can turn notes about a poem into a coherent, well-structured essay. As this essay also shows, however, you will often discover new ways of looking at a poem (or any literary text) in the very process of writing about it. (For guidelines on correctly quoting and citing poetry, see "Quotation, Citation, and Documentation," chapter 24.)

The writer begins by considering why she is drawn to the poem, even though it does not express her ideal of love. She then uses her personal response to the poem as a starting point for analyzing it in greater depth.

Multiplying by Dividing in Aphra Behn's "On Her Loving Two Equally"

My favorite poem in "Reading, Responding, Writing" is Aphra Behn's "On Her Loving Two Equally"—not because it expresses my ideal of love, but because it challenges conventional ideals. The main ideal or assumption explored in the poem is that true love is exclusive and monogamous, as the very titles of poems like "How Do I [singular] Love Thee [singular]?" or "To My Dear and Loving [and One and Only] Husband" insist (emphasis added). The mere title of Behn's poem upsets that idea by insisting that at least one woman is capable of "Loving Two Equally." In fact, one thing that is immediately interesting about Behn's poem is that, though it poses and explores a question, its question is not "Can a woman love two equally?" The title and the poem take it for granted that she can. Instead, the poem asks whether equally loving two people lessens the power or quality of love—or, as the speaker puts it in the first two lines, "How strongly does my passion flow, / Divided equally twixt two?" Every aspect of this poem suggests that when it comes to love, as opposed to math, division leads to multiplication.

This answer grabs attention because it is so counterintuitive and unconventional. Forget love for just a minute: It's common sense that anything that is divided is smaller and weaker than something unified. In math, for example, division is the opposite of multiplication; if we divide one number by another, we get a number smaller than the first number, if not the second. Although Behn's use of the word *flow* to frame her question compares love to a river instead of a number, the implication is the same: When a river divides into two streams, each of them is smaller than the river, and its flow less strong; as a result, each stream is more easily dammed up or diverted than the undivided river. So the way the speaker initially poses her question seems to support the conventional view: love is stronger when it "flows" toward one person, weaker when divided between two.

As conventional and comforting as that implied answer is, however, it's one the poem immediately rejects. In the remaining lines of the first stanza, the speaker insists that each of her two lovers and the love she feels for him has *not* lessened the strength of her feelings for the other, but the reverse. Each lover and each love has "aid[ed]" (line 6) the other, making him and it more "powerful" (5). Indeed, she says, neither man would have "subdued [her] heart" (3) or "gain[ed her] love" (6) at all if the other hadn't done so as well.

In the second stanza, the speaker gives us a somewhat more concrete sense of why this might be the case. On the one hand, being with either one of these men ("When my Alexis present is," 7) actually makes her both "scorn" him (10) and "miss" (9) the man who's not there ("I for Damon sigh and mourn," 8). This isn't really a paradox; we often yearn more for the person or thing we don't have (the grass is always greener on the *other* side of the fence), and we often lose our appreciation for nearby, familiar things and people. What is far away and inaccessible is often dearer to us because its absence either makes us aware of what it means to us or allows us to forget its flaws and idealize it.

Perhaps because all of this makes the speaker feel that she can't possibly solve the problem by herself, the speaker turns in the third stanza to Cupid—the deity who is supposed to control these things by shooting a "golden-pointed dart" (15) into the heart of each lover. She asks him to solve her dilemma for her by "tak[ing] back" her love for either Damon or Alexis (15). As with her question in the first stanza, however, this plea is revoked as soon as it's formulated, for if she loses Damon, "all [her] hopes are crossed"; if she loses Alexis, she is "lost" (17-18).

Here and throughout the poem, the speaker's main preoccupation seems to be what *she* feels and what this situation is like for *her*—"*my* passion" (1), "*my* heart" (3), "*my* Damon's aid, . . . *my* love" (6), "*my* Alexis" (7), "*I* . . . sigh and mourn" (8), "*I* do miss" (9), "*my* scorn" (10), "*I* languish, sigh, and die" (12), "This restless fever in *my* blood" (14), "*my* hopes" (17), "*my* Alexis" and "*I* am lost" (18). Yet the poem implies that the payoff here is not hers alone and that her feelings are not purely selfish. Both times the word *gain* appears in the poem, for example, her lovers' gains and feelings are the focus—the fact that Alexis is able "to gain [her] love" thanks to "Damon's aid" (6) and that "Damon gains nothing but my scorn" when she is missing Alexis (10). Moreover, ambiguous wording in the first stanza suggests that the men here may be actively, intentionally helping to create this situation and even acting in contradictory, selfish and unselfish, ways. When the speaker says that "Damon had ne'er subdued my heart / Had not Alexis took his part" (3-4), *his* could refer to Alexis or Damon and *part* could mean "a portion" (of her "heart," presumably), "a role" (in her life or in this courtship drama), or a "side in a dispute or conflict" (over her love). Thus, she could be saying that Alexis (unselfishly) defended Damon's suit; (selfishly) fought against Damon or took a share or role that properly belonged to Damon; and/or (neutrally) took his (Alexis's) own share or role or defended his (Alexis's) own cause. Perhaps all of this *has* been the case at various times; people do behave in contradictory ways when they are in love, especially when they perceive that they have a rival. It's also true that men and women alike often more highly prize something or someone that someone else prizes, too. So perhaps each lover's "passion" for her also "flow[s]" more strongly than it would otherwise precisely because he has a rival.

In the end, the poem thus seems to say that love *doesn't* flow or work like a river because love isn't a tangible or quantifiable thing. As a result, love is also different from the sort of battle implied by the martial language of the first stanza in which someone wins only if someone else loses. The poem attributes this to the perversity of the human heart—especially our tendency to yearn for what we can't have and what we think other people want, too.

Through its form, the poem demonstrates that division can increase instead of lessen meaning, as well as love. On the one hand, just as the poem's content stresses the power of the love among *three people*, so the poem's form also stresses "threeness" as well as "twoness." It is after all divided into *three* distinctly numbered stanzas, and each stanza consists of *three* sentences. On the other hand, every *sentence* is "divided equally twixt two" *lines*, just as the speaker's "passion" is divided equally between two men. Formally, then, the poem mirrors the kinds of division it describes. Sound and especially rhyme reinforce this pattern since the two lines that make up one sentence usually rhyme with each other to form a couplet. The only lines that don't conform to this pattern come at the beginning of the second stanza where we instead have alternating rhyme—*is* (7) rhymes with *miss* (9), *mourn* (8) rhymes with *scorn* (10). But here, again, form reinforces content since these lines describe how the speaker "miss[es]" one man when the other is "by," a sensation that she arguably reproduces in us as we read by ensuring we twice "miss" the rhyme that the rest of the poem leads us to expect.

Because of the way it challenges our expectations and our conventional ideas about romantic love, the poem might well make us uncomfortable, per- haps all the more so because the speaker and poet here are female. For though we tend to think all true lovers should be loyal and monogamous, this has been expected even more of women than of men. What the poem says about love might make more sense and seem less strange and even objectionable, how- ever, if we think of other, nonromantic kinds of love: after all, do we really think that our mother and father love us less if their love is "divided equally twixt" ourselves and our siblings, or do we love each of our parents less because there are two of *them*? If we think of these familial kinds of love, it becomes much easier to accept Behn's suggestion that love multiplies when we spread it around.

WORK CITED

Behn, Aphra. "On Her Loving Two Equally." *The Norton Introduction to Literature,* edited by Kelly J. Mays, portable 13th ed., W. W. Norton, 2020, pp. 414–15.

Understanding the Text

9 | SPEAKER: WHOSE VOICE DO WE HEAR?

Poems are personal. The thoughts and feelings they express belong to a specific person, and however general or universal their sentiments seem to be, poems come to us as the expression of an individual human voice. That voice is often a voice of the poet, but not always. Poets sometimes create characters just as writers of fiction or drama do. And the **speaker** of a poem may express ideas or feelings very different from the poet's own and in a distinct voice.

Usually there is much more to a poem than the characterization of the speaker, but often it is necessary first to identify the speaker and determine his or her character before we can appreciate what else goes on in the poem. And sometimes, in looking for the speaker of the poem, we discover the gist of the entire poem.

NARRATIVE POEMS AND THEIR SPEAKERS

In the following narrative poem, the poet relies mainly on one speaker with a highly distinctive voice. This speaker acts as a **narrator**. Generally speaking in the third-person plural, on behalf of a group, however, the speaker sometimes quotes the remarks of individual members of the group (lines 1–2, 16–20), who are thus also speakers in the poem, even if they are never individually identified. As you read the poem, notice how your impressions of Hard Rock and of the group are shaped by both the narrator's words and those of the speakers he quotes.

ETHERIDGE KNIGHT

Hard Rock Returns to Prison from the Hospital for the Criminal Insane

Hard Rock was "known not to take no shit
From nobody," and he had the scars to prove it:
Split purple lips, lumped ears, welts above
His yellow eyes, and one long scar that cut
5 Across his temple and plowed through a thick
Canopy of kinky hair.

The WORD was that Hard Rock wasn't a mean nigger
Anymore, that the doctors had bored a hole in his head,
Cut out part of his brain, and shot electricity
10 Through the rest. When they brought Hard Rock back,
Handcuffed and chained, he was turned loose,

Like a freshly gelded stallion, to try his new status.
And we all waited and watched, like indians at a corral,
To see if the WORD was true.

15   As we waited we wrapped ourselves in the cloak
Of his exploits: "Man, the last time, it took eight
Screws to put him in the Hole."[1] "Yeah, remember when he
Smacked the captain with his dinner tray?" "He set
The record for time in the Hole—67 straight days!"
20   "Ol Hard Rock! man, that's one crazy nigger."
And then the jewel of a myth that Hard Rock had once bit
A screw on the thumb and poisoned him with syphilitic spit.

The testing came, to see if Hard Rock was really tame.
A hillbilly called him a black son of a bitch
25   And didn't lose his teeth, a screw who knew Hard Rock
From before shook him down and barked in his face.
And Hard Rock did *nothing*. Just grinned and looked silly,
His eyes empty like knot holes in a fence.

And even after we discovered that it took Hard Rock
30   Exactly 3 minutes to tell you his first name,
We told ourselves that he had just wised up,
Was being cool; but we could not fool ourselves for long,
And we turned away, our eyes on the ground. Crushed.
He had been our Destroyer, the doer of things
35   We dreamed of doing but could not bring ourselves to do,
The fears of years, like a biting whip,
Had cut grooves too deeply across our backs.

1968

As we might expect, we learn a good deal in this poem about its title character: The first stanza lets us know that he is a black prison inmate and vividly describes his hair and his various "scars" (line 2) as evidence of his fierce, indomitable character, his refusal ever to back down or let anyone treat him badly. In the third stanza we hear about some of his more famous past "exploits" (16). But by the time we get to the third stanza we've been warned that *this* Hard Rock might already be a thing of the past. And the fourth stanza and the first part of the fifth and final one confirm that fear, presenting a man radically transformed and reduced by the lobotomy and electroshock therapy described in stanza two. The poem thus becomes, in part, the tragic tale of Hard Rock's fast, hard fall. And it would be worthwhile to think further about just what other aspects of the poem help to make that fall seem so fast, so hard, so poignant.

One might be the fact that Hard Rock is literally never allowed to speak for himself in the poem. Everything we learn about him comes to us from the narrator and the other speakers whom that narrator quotes—all Hard Rock's fellow inmates. And it is this group, this "we," and its perceptions of Hard Rock even more than the man himself that arguably emerge as HARD ROCK RETURNS's major focus. The

1. Solitary confinement. *Screws*: guards.

poem begins, after all, with what "was 'known'"—and, as the quotation marks here stress, *said*—about Hard Rock by these men (1). It ends with a stanza devoted almost exclusively to their collective reaction to his transformation. How else might the poem work to train our focus on its speakers? How, ultimately, does it characterize them, through how they speak and what they say? What exactly does Hard Rock and Hard Rock's fall mean to these men, and why?

Not all narrative poems are as much *about* their speakers as "Hard Rock Returns" is. Robert Frost's "OUT, OUT—," for instance, features as its main speaker a third-person omniscient narrator, one who isn't a character in the gruesome story he tells and about whom we learn nothing specific. "'Out, Out—'" thereby keeps our attention utterly riveted on the characters and the action themselves. Yet this poem's effect ultimately depends on this very fact and thus, like all narrative poems, on *its* particular narrator and mode of narration, on all its speakers' words. To fully experience and better understand such poems, we can always draw upon the very same concepts and questions about narrators and characters that we draw upon when reading fiction (see chs. 3 and 4).

SPEAKERS IN THE DRAMATIC MONOLOGUE

Like all **dramatic monologues**, the following poem has no narrator. Rather, it consists entirely of the words a single, fictional speaker speaks to a fictional **auditor** in a specific time, place, and dramatic situation, much as would a character in a play. As you read the poem, pay attention to the details that alert you to the time, place, and situation and that help to characterize the speaker, the auditor, and their relationship.

A. E. STALLINGS
Hades[2] Welcomes His Bride

Come now, child, adjust your eyes, for sight
Is here a lesser sense. Here you must learn
Directions through your fingertips and feet
And map them in your mind. I think some shapes
5 Will gradually appear. The pale things twisting
Overhead are mostly roots, although some worms
Arrive here clinging to their dead. Turn here.
Ah.   And in this hall will sit our thrones,
And here you shall be queen, my dear, the queen
10 Of all men ever to be born. No smile?
Well, some solemnity befits a queen.
These thrones I have commissioned to be made
Are unlike any you imagined; they glow
Of deep-black diamonds and lead, subtler
15 And in better taste than gold, as will suit
Your timid beauty and pale throat. Come now,

---

2. Greek god of the underworld (also called Hades) and of death; he married Persephone after abducting her from her mother, Demeter, goddess of corn, grain, and the earth's harvest.

Down these winding stairs, the air more still
And dry and easier to breathe. Here is a room
For your diversions. Here I've set a loom
20 And silk unraveled from the finest shrouds
And dyed the richest, rarest shades of black.
Such pictures you shall weave! Such tapestries!
For you I chose those three thin shadows[3] there,
And they shall be your friends and loyal maids,
25 And do not fear from them such gossiping
As servants usually are wont. They have
Not mouth nor eyes and cannot thus speak ill
Of you. Come, come. This is the greatest room;
I had it specially made after great thought
30 So you would feel at home. I had the ceiling
Painted to recall some evening sky—
But without the garish stars and lurid moon.
What?   That stark shape crouching in the corner?
Sweet, that is to be our bed. Our bed.
35 Ah!   Your hand is trembling! I fear
There is, as yet, too much pulse in it.

1993

So, what do you think of the speaker, his bride (and auditor), and their bower of wormy wedded bliss? Stallings's title alerts us that the former is Hades. If we know our Greek mythology (or simply read the handy footnote), we go into the poem knowing, too, that his bride is also his kidnap victim, Persephone (whose name, interestingly enough, never appears here). Yet HADES WELCOMES HIS BRIDE puts a unique new spin on this old, familiar story by presenting it from the perspective of Hades—or, in Stallings's words, from "the bad guy's point of view"—so as to also make him seem anything but the straightforwardly ghoulish devil or brutish **villain** we might expect. Hades, after all, speaks formally, respectfully, even tenderly to his bride and "queen" from the beginning (line 9), inviting her into a new home to which he recognizes she must "adjust" (1) and offering advice about how to do so (1–5). As he leads her through its rooms and points out its various features, it becomes clear (long before he explicitly says so, in lines 29–30) that he has taken pains to create an environment as tasteful, grand, and hospitable, even homey, as he knows how. He is also sensitive to his bride's reactions, noticing that she isn't smiling (10); that she seems startled by what turns out to be the bed she will share with him; that after he twice utters the words "our bed. Our bed," she "is trembling" (34–35). The fact that he repeats those words also implies that he's eagerly anticipating his wedding night. As the details accumulate, the horrors of this home and of the life and marriage to which this bride is doomed become as palpably apparent to readers as they are to her. Yet Hades's character remains ambiguous: Is he being knowingly malevolent, grandiose, even abusive by arranging and presenting things as he does and by rationalizing his bride's reactions? Is he enjoying scaring the pants off his bride, as it were? Or might he instead be, as one reviewer contends, "engag[ing] in the

---

3. Especially in the sense of "phantoms"; also suggesting *shades*, another word both for "ghost" and for Hades.

same self-deception as" any ordinary "mortal lover" might, so genuinely bent on his bride sharing his delight and so inured to his own literally hellish milieu that he can't or won't see the truth?

Your answers and your interpretation of the speaker here, as in all dramatic monologues, depend entirely on the speaker's own words—on *what* he says and *when* and *how* he says it. The details accumulate into a fairly full, if—in this case—delightfully ambiguous, wonderfully creepy portrait, even though we do not have either a narrator's description or another speaker to give us perspective (as in Knight's "Hard Rock Returns"). As in other dramatic monologues, we do get some hint of another perspective via the reactions of the auditor, but we can only deduce what those reactions might be from what the speaker himself says.

In reading a dramatic monologue aloud, we would want our voice to suggest the feelings, motives, and attitudes the speaker's words imply. Like an actor, we would need to adopt the appropriate tone of voice and emphasis. Conversely, reading a dramatic monologue aloud, trying out various ways of delivering the lines, can help us figure out which interpretation of the speaker's character ultimately seems most faithful to the poem as a whole.

THE LYRIC AND ITS SPEAKER

With narrative poems and dramatic monologues, we are usually in no danger of mistaking the speaker for the poet. Lyrics may present more of a challenge. When there is a pointed discrepancy between the speaker of a **lyric** and what we know of the poet—when the speaker is a woman, for example, and the poet is a man—we know we have a fictional speaker to contend with and that the point (or at least *one* point) of the poem is to observe the characterization carefully.

Sometimes even in lyrics poets "borrow" a character from history and ask readers to factor in historical facts and contexts. In the following poem, for example, the Canadian poet Margaret Atwood draws heavily on facts and traditions about a nineteenth-century émigré from Scotland to Canada. The poem is a lyric spoken in the first person, but its speaker is a fictional character based on a real woman.

The poem comes from a volume called *The Journals of Susanna Moodie: Poems by Margaret Atwood* (1970). A frontier pioneer, Moodie (1803–84) herself wrote two books about Canada, *Roughing It in the Bush* and *Life in the Clearings*, and Atwood found their observations rather stark and disorganized. She wrote her Susanna Moodie poems to refocus the "character" and to reconstruct Moodie's actual geographical exploration and self-discovery. To fully understand these thoughts and meditations, then, we need to know something of the history behind them. Yet even without such knowledge, we can appreciate the poem's powerful evocation of its speaker's situation and feelings.

MARGARET ATWOOD
Death of a Young Son by Drowning

He, who navigated with success
the dangerous river of his own birth
once more set forth

on a voyage of discovery
5 into the land I floated on
but could not touch to claim.

His feet slid on the bank,
the currents took him;
he swirled with ice and trees in the swollen water

10 and plunged into distant regions,
his head a bathysphere;[4]
through his eyes' thin glass bubbles

he looked out, reckless adventurer
on a landscape stranger than Uranus
15 we have all been to and some remember.

There was an accident; the air locked,
he was hung in the river like a heart.
They retrieved the swamped body,

cairn of my plans and future charts,
20 with poles and hooks
from among the nudging logs.

It was spring, the sun kept shining, the new grass
leapt to solidity;
my hands glistened with details.

25 After the long trip I was tired of waves.
My foot hit rock. The dreamed sails
collapsed, ragged.

    I planted him in this country
      like a flag.

                              1970

    Even when poets present themselves as if they were speaking directly to us in their own voices, their poems present only a partial portrait, something considerably less than the full personality and character of the poet. Though there is not an obviously created character—someone with distinct characteristics that are different from those of the poet—strategies of characterization are used to present the person speaking in one way and not another. As a result, you should still differentiate between the speaker and the poet.

4. Manned spherical chamber for deep-sea observation.

AUTHORS ON THEIR CRAFT

BILLY COLLINS AND SHARON OLDS ON "FINDING YOUR OWN VOICE"

From "A Brisk Walk: An Interview with Billy Collins" (2006)*

[. . . T]here's this pet phrase about writing that is bandied around [. . .] "finding your own voice as a poet," which I suppose means that you come out from under the direct influence of other poets and have perhaps found a way to combine those influences so that it appears to be your own voice. But I think you could also put it a different way. You, quote, find your voice, unquote, when you are able to invent this one character who resembles you, obviously, and probably is more like you than anyone else on earth, but is not the equivalent to you.

It is like a fictional character in that it has a very distinctive voice, a voice that seems to be able to accommodate and express an attitude that you are comfortable staying with but an attitude that is flexible enough to cover a number of situations.

. . . .

From "Olds' Worlds" (2008)**

[. . . O]nce a poem is written, and [. . .] it's rewritten, and maybe published, and I'm in front of people, reading it aloud—I'm not too embarrassed by that. [. . .] It doesn't feel personal. It feels like art—a made thing—the "I" in it not myself anymore, but, I'd hope, some pronoun that a reader or hearer could slip into. But how much can a poem reflect or embody a life anyhow? You can want to come close, but it's so profoundly different—the actual body, the flesh, the mortal life.

*"A Brisk Walk: An Interview with Billy Collins." Interview by Joel Whitney. *Guernica*, 14 June 2006, www.guernicamag.com/interviews/a_brisk_walk/.
**"Olds' Worlds." Interview by Marianne Macdonald. *The Guardian*, 26 July 2008, www .theguardian.com/books/2008/jul/26/poetry.

Although the poet is probably writing about a personal, actual experience in the following poem, he is also making a character of himself—that is, characterizing himself in a certain way, emphasizing some parts of himself and not others. We call this character a **persona**.

WILLIAM WORDSWORTH
She Dwelt among the Untrodden Ways

She dwelt among the untrodden ways
   Beside the springs of Dove,[5]
A Maid whom there were none to praise
   And very few to love:

5 A violet by a mossy stone
   Half hidden from the eye!
—Fair as a star, when only one
   Is shining in the sky.

She lived unknown, and few could know
10   When Lucy ceased to be;
But she is in her grave, and, oh,
   The difference to me!

1800

Did Lucy actually live? Was she a friend of the poet? We don't know; the poem doesn't tell us, and even biographers of Wordsworth are unsure. What we do know is that Wordsworth was able to represent grief very powerfully. Whether the speaker is the historical Wordsworth or not, that speaker is a major focus of the poem, and it is his feelings that the poem isolates and expresses. We need to recognize some characteristics of the speaker and be sensitive to his feelings for the poem to work.

Analyzing Speakers: An Exercise

In the following poem, we do not get a full sense of the speaker until well into the poem. As you read, try to imagine the tone of voice you think this person would use. Exactly when do you begin to know what she sounds like?

DOROTHY PARKER
A Certain Lady

Oh, I can smile for you, and tilt my head,
   And drink your rushing words with eager lips,
And paint my mouth for you a fragrant red,
   And trace your brows with tutored finger-tips.
5 When you rehearse your list of loves to me,
   Oh, I can laugh and marvel, rapturous-eyed.
And you laugh back, nor can you ever see
   The thousand little deaths my heart has died.

---

5. Small stream in the Lake District in northern England, near where Wordsworth lived.

And you believe, so well I know my part,
10   That I am gay as morning, light as snow,
And all the straining things within my heart
    You'll never know.
Oh, I can laugh and listen, when we meet,
    And you bring tales of fresh adventurings—
15 Of ladies delicately indiscreet,
    Of lingering hands, and gently whispered things.
And you are pleased with me, and strive anew
    To sing me sagas of your late delights.
Thus do you want me—marveling, gay, and true—
20   Nor do you see my staring eyes of nights.
And when, in search of novelty, you stray,
    Oh, I can kiss you blithely as you go . . .
And what goes on, my love, while you're away,
    You'll never know.

                                        1937

To whom does the speaker seem to be talking? What sort of person is he? How do you feel about him? Which habits and attitudes of his do you like least? How soon can you tell that the speaker is not altogether happy about his conversation and conduct? In what tone of voice would you read the first twenty-two lines aloud? What attitude would you try to express toward the person spoken to? What tone would you use for the last two lines? How would you describe the speaker's personality? What aspects of her behavior are most crucial to the poem's effect?

• • •

The poems we have looked at in this chapter—and those that follow—all suggest the value of beginning the reading of any poem with three simple questions: Who is speaking? What do we know about him or her? What kind of person is she or he? Putting together the evidence that the poem presents in answer to such questions can often take us a long way into the poem. For some poems, such questions won't help a great deal because the speaking voice is too indistinct or the character too scantily presented. But starting with such questions will often lead you toward the central experience the poem offers.

POEMS FOR FURTHER STUDY

WALT WHITMAN
I celebrate myself, and sing myself

I celebrate myself, and sing myself,
And what I assume you shall assume,
For every atom belonging to me as good belongs to you.

I loafe and invite my soul,
5   I lean and loafe at my ease observing a spear of summer grass.

My tongue, every atom of my blood, form'd from this soil, this air,
Born here of parents born here from parents the same, and their parents
      the same,
I, now thirty-seven years old in perfect health begin,
Hoping to cease not till death.

10   Creeds and schools in abeyance,
Retiring back a while sufficed at what they are, but never forgotten,
I harbor for good or bad, I permit to speak at every hazard,
Nature without check with original energy.

                                                                    1855, 1881

• What might be characteristically American about the speaker of this poem?

LANGSTON HUGHES
Ballad of the Landlord

Landlord, landlord,
My roof has sprung a leak.
Don't you 'member I told you about it
Way last week?

5   Landlord, landlord,
These steps is broken down.
When you come up yourself
It's a wonder you don't fall down.

Ten Bucks you say I owe you?
10   Ten Bucks you say is due?
Well, that's Ten Bucks more'n I'll pay you
Till you fix this house up new.

What? You gonna get eviction orders?
You gonna cut off my heat?
15   You gonna take my furniture and
Throw it in the street?

Um-huh! You talking high and mighty.
Talk on—till you get through.
You ain't gonna be able to say a word
20   If I land my fist on you.

Police! Police!
Come and get this man!
He's trying to ruin the government
And overturn the land!

25   Copper's whistle!
Patrol bell!
Arrest.

Precinct Station.
Iron cell.
30   Headlines in press:

MAN THREATENS LANDLORD
TENANT HELD NO BAIL
JUDGE GIVES NEGRO 90 DAYS IN COUNTY JAIL.
1940

• Who are the various speakers in this poem? What is the effect of Hughes's choice not to give us all the words of all the speakers?

E. E. CUMMINGS
next to of course god america i

"next to of course god america i
love you land of the pilgrims' and so forth oh
say can you see by the dawn's early my
country 'tis of centuries come and go
5   and are no more what of it we should worry
in every language even deafanddumb
thy sons acclaim your glorious name by gorry
by jingo by gee by gosh by gum
why talk of beauty what could be more beaut-
10 iful than these heroic happy dead
who rushed like lions to the roaring slaughter
they did not stop to think they died instead
then shall the voice of liberty be mute?"

He spoke. And drank rapidly a glass of water
1926

• Except for the last line, this poem works much like a dramatic monologue. What can you discern about the situation in which the quoted words are spoken? about the speaker and his or her audience? about the poem's attitude toward the speaker?

GWENDOLYN BROOKS
We Real Cool

The Pool Players.
Seven at the Golden Shovel.

We real cool. We
Left school. We

5   Lurk late. We
Strike straight. We

Sing sin. We
Thin gin. We

Jazz June. We
10 Die soon.

                    1950

- Who are "we" in this poem? Do you think that the speaker and the poet share the same idea of what is "cool"?

LUCILLE CLIFTON
cream of wheat

sometimes at night
we stroll the market aisles
ben and jemima and me   they
walk in front   remembering this and
        that
5 i lag behind
trying to remove my chefs cap
wondering about what ever pictured me
then left me personless
Rastus
10 i read in an old paper
i was called rastus
but no mother ever
gave that to her son   toward dawn
we return to our shelves
15 our boxes   ben and jemima and me
we pose and smile   i simmer   what
is my name

                    2008

- At what point and how did you begin to figure out just who the speaker of this poem is? What is the effect of the shifts between plural and singular, "we" and "I"?

SUGGESTIONS FOR WRITING

1. Several of the poems in this chapter create characters and imply situations, as in drama. Write an essay in which you describe and analyze the main speaker of any poem in this chapter.
2. Write an essay in which you compare the speakers in any two poems in this chapter. What kinds of self-image do they have? In each poem, what is the implied distance between the speaker and the poet?
3. Choose any of the poems in this or the previous chapter and write an essay about the way a poet can create irony and humor through the use of a speaker who is clearly distinct from the poet himself or herself.
4. Write a poem, short story, or personal essay in which the speaker or narrator is a character mentioned by a speaker in any of the poems in this chapter—for example, a pre-op Hard Rock, the lover in Dorothy Parker's A CERTAIN LADY, Ben and Jemima in CREAM OF WHEAT, or Persephone in Stallings's HADES WELCOMES HIS BRIDE. How might the same situation, as well as the main speaker of these poems, look and sound different when viewed from another speaker's point of view and described in another speaker's voice?

ELIZABETH BISHOP
Exchanging Hats

Unfunny uncles who insist
in trying on a lady's hat,
—oh, even if the joke falls flat,
we share your slight transvestite twist

5 in spite of our embarrassment.
Costume and custom are complex.
The headgear of the other sex
inspires us to experiment.

Anandrous[6] aunts, who, at the beach
10 with paper plates upon your laps,
keep putting on the yachtsmen's caps
with exhibitionistic screech,

the visors hanging o'er the ear
so that the golden anchors drag,
15 —the tides of fashion never lag.
Such caps may not be worn next year.

Or you who don the paper plate
itself, and put some grapes upon it,
or sport the Indian's feather bonnet,
20 —perversities may aggravate

the natural madness of the hatter.
And if the opera hats collapse
and crowns grow drafty, then, perhaps,
he thinks what might a miter matter?

25 Unfunny uncle, you who wore a
hat too big, or one too many,
tell us, can't you, are there any
stars inside your black fedora?

Aunt exemplary and slim,
30 with avernal[7] eyes, we wonder
what slow changes they see under
their vast, shady, turned-down brim.

1956

• The speaker in this poem uses the first-person plural ("we," line 4; "our," 5; "us," 8). Who might "we" be? How might your response to the poem change if the speaker instead used the first-person singular ("I") or the third-person plural ("they")?

6. Literally, "husbandless."   7. Infernal.

JUDITH ORTIZ COFER
The Changeling

As a young girl
vying for my father's attention,
I invented a game that made him look up
from his reading and shake his head
5   as if both baffled and amused.

In my brother's closet, I'd change
into his dungarees—the rough material
molding me into boy shape; hide
my long hair under an army helmet
10   he'd been given by Father, and emerge
transformed into the legendary Ché[8]
of grown-up talk.

Strutting around the room,
I'd tell of life in the mountains,
15   of carnage and rivers of blood,
and of manly feasts with rum and music
to celebrate victories *para la libertad*.[9]
He would listen with a smile
to my tales of battles and brotherhood
20   until Mother called us to dinner.

She was not amused
by my transformations, sternly forbidding me
from sitting down with them as a man.
She'd order me back to the dark cubicle
25   that smelled of adventure, to shed
my costume, to braid my hair furiously
with blind hands, and to return invisible,
as myself,
to the real world of her kitchen.

1993

• Why do you think the speaker's father is amused by her "transformations" (line 22), and why does her mother forbid them? What does this poem imply about all three characters?

---

8. Ernesto "Che" Guevara (1928–67), Argentinian-born Cuban revolutionary leader.
9. For freedom (Spanish).

10 | SITUATION AND SETTING: WHAT HAPPENS? WHERE? WHEN?

Questions about the **speaker** in a poem (*Who?* questions) lead to questions about *What?* and *Why?* as well as *Where?* and *When?* First you identify the imagined **situation** in the poem: To whom is the speaker speaking? Is there an **auditor** in the poem? Is anyone else present or referred to in the poem? What is happening? Why is this event or communication occurring, and why is it significant? As soon as you zoom in on answers to such questions about persons and actions, you also encounter questions about place and time. (Where and when does the action or communication take place?) In other words, situation entails **setting**.

The place involved in a poem is its *spatial setting*, and the time is its *temporal setting*. The temporal setting may be a specific date or an era, a season of the year or a time of day. Temporal and spatial settings often influence our expectations, although a poet may surprise us by making something very different of what we had thought was familiar. We tend, for example, to think of spring as a time of discovery and growth, and poems set in spring are likely to make use of that association. Similarly, morning usually suggests discovery—beginnings, vitality, the world fresh and new.

Not all poems have an identifiable situation or setting, just as not all poems have a speaker who is easily distinguishable from the author. **Lyrics** that simply present a series of thoughts and feelings directly, in a reflective way, may not present anything resembling a scene with action, dialogue, or description. But many poems depend crucially on a sense of place, a sense of time, and scenes that resemble those in plays or films. And questions about these matters will often lead you to define not only the "facts" but also the feelings central to the design a poem has on its readers.

To understand the dialogue in Thomas Hardy's THE RUINED MAID, for example, we need to recognize that the two women are meeting after an extended period of separation (the situation) and that they meet in a town rather than the rural area in which they grew up together (the setting). We infer (from the opening lines) that the meeting is accidental and that no one else is present for the conversation. The poem's whole "story" depends on their situation: After leading separate lives for a while, they have some catching up to do. We don't know what specific town they are in or what year, season, or time of day it is—and those details are not important to the poem's effect.

More specific settings matter in other poems. Etheridge Knight's HARD ROCK RETURNS TO PRISON FROM THE HOSPITAL FOR THE CRIMINAL INSANE depends entirely on its prison setting, as does A. E. Stallings's HADES WELCOMES HIS BRIDE on all the vividly rendered objects that make up its version of the underworld. Here, the contrast between the actuality of the setting and the alternately matter-of-fact and glowing terms in which the speaker presents it generates **irony**, adds to the overall creepiness, and helps define the ambiguities of the speaker's character.

Situation and setting may be treated in various ways in a poem, ranging from silence to the barest hints of description to full photographic detail. Often it is relatively easy to identify the situation at the beginning of a poem, but the implications of setting, and what happens as the poem unfolds, may be subtler. Poets often rely on readers to fill in the gaps, drawing on their knowledge of circumstances and familiar experiences in the present or in the past. The poem may specify only a few aspects of a *kind* of setting, such as a motel room in the afternoon.

SITUATION

The following poem portrays a situation that should be—at least in some of its aspects—familiar to you. How would you summarize that situation?

RITA DOVE
Daystar

She wanted a little room for thinking:
but she saw diapers steaming on the line,
a doll slumped behind the door.
So she lugged a chair behind the garage
5 to sit out the children's naps.

Sometimes there were things to watch—
the pinched armor of a vanished cricket,
a floating maple leaf. Other days
she stared until she was assured
10 when she closed her eyes
she'd see only her own vivid blood.

She had an hour, at best, before Liza appeared
pouting from the top of the stairs.
And just *what* was mother doing
15 out back with the field mice? Why,
building a palace. Later
that night when Thomas rolled over and
lurched into her, she would open her eyes
and think of the place that was hers
20 for an hour—where
she was nothing,
pure nothing, in the middle of the day.

1986

The mother in Dove's DAYSTAR, overwhelmed by the demands of young children, needs a room of her own. All she can manage, however, is a brief hour of respite. The situation is virtually the whole story here. Nothing really happens except that daily events (washing diapers, picking up toys, explaining the world to children, having sex) that surround her brief private hour and make it precious. Being "nothing" (lines 21 and 22) takes on great value in these circumstances.

Not every poem presents, as Dove's does, familiar and real or realistic situations (any more than all fiction does). Yet even poems that present imaginary or fantastic situations must make them somehow real-seeming and relevant to us. The two poems below are good examples. Both contemplate imaginary situations but of very different kinds. The first works by simply twisting a familiar situation: The poem describes the speaker's experience as a student in a college course, only the course is in Humani*ty*, not Humani*ties*. The second poem is more abstract and speculative: Like the genre of fiction and film to which its title refers (science fiction), it imagines a possible future. As you read the poems, think about what each suggests about real-world situations ("what is") by the way it depicts its wholly imaginary ("what if") one.

DENISE DUHAMEL
Humanity 101

I was on my way to becoming a philanthropist,
or the president, or at least someone who gave a shit,
but I was a nontraditional student
with a lot of catching up to do. I enrolled in Humanity 101
5   (not to be confused with the Humanities,
a whole separate department). When I flunked
the final exam, my professor suggested
I take Remedial Humanity where I'd learn the basics
that I'd missed so far. I may have been a nontraditional student,
10   but I was a traditional person, she said, the way a professor
can say intimate things sometimes, as though
your face and soul are aglow in one of those
magnified (10x) makeup mirrors.

So I took Remedial Humanity, which sounds like an easy A,
15   but, believe me, it was actually quite challenging.
There were analogy questions, such as:
Paris Hilton[1] is to a rich U.S. suburban kid
as a U.S. middle-class kid is to:
1.) a U.S. poverty-stricken kid,
20   2.) a U.S. kid with nothing in the fridge,
or
3.) a Third World kid with no fridge at all.
We were required to write essays about the cause of war—
Was it a phenomenon? Was it our lower animal selves?
25   Was it economics? Was it psychological/sexual/religious
(good vs. evil and all that stuff)? For homework
we had to bend down to talk to a homeless person
slouched against a building. We didn't necessarily have to
give them money or food, but we had to say something like
30   *How are you?* or *What is your favorite color?*
We took field trips to nursing homes, prisons,
day-care centers. We stood near bedsides
or sat on the floor to color with strange little people
who cried and were afraid of us at first.

1. Socialite and media personality (b. 1981), granddaughter of Hilton Hotels founder Conrad Hilton.

35 I almost dropped out. I went to see the professor
during his office hours because I wanted to change my major.
He asked, "Is that because your heart is being smashed?"
He thought I should stick it out, that I could make it,
if I just escaped for an hour a day blasting music
40 into my earbuds or slumping in front of the TV.
I said, "But that's just it. Now I see humanity everywhere,
even on sitcoms, even in pop songs,
even in beer commercials." He closed his door
and showed me the scars under his shirt
45 where he had been stabbed. He said I had to assume
everyone had such a wound, whether I could see it or not.

He assured me that it really did get easier in time,
and that it was hard to make music when you were still
learning how to play the scales. He made me see
50 my potential. He convinced me of my own humanity,
that one day I might even be able to get a PhD. But first
I had to, for extra credit, write a treatise on detachment.

2015

- What does the speaker learn from her Humanity class? Why, according to
  the poem, might we all need one? What aspects of the situation imagined
  here seem especially funny or ironic? How does the poem use specific
  aspects of familiar situations?

TRACY K. SMITH
Sci-Fi

There will be no edges, but curves.
Clean lines pointing only forward.

History, with its hard spine & dog-eared
Corners, will be replaced with nuance,

5 Just like the dinosaurs gave way
To mounds and mounds of ice.

Women will still be women, but
The distinction will be empty. Sex,

Having outlived every threat, will gratify
10 Only the mind, which is where it will exist.

For kicks, we'll dance for ourselves
Before mirrors studded with golden bulbs.

The oldest among us will recognize that glow—
But the word *sun* will have been re-assigned

15 To a Standard Uranium-Neutralizing device
     Found in households and nursing homes.

     And yes, we'll live to be much older, thanks
     To popular consensus. Weightless, unhinged,

     Eons from even our own moon, we'll drift
20   In the haze of space, which will be, once

     And for all, scrutable and safe.

                                        2011

• Does the poem present the future it imagines as positive? negative? both?
  How might this poem's version of the future compare to those conventionally offered up in science fiction and film? Might the poem comment on
  such conventional representations?

SETTING

Frequently a poem's setting draws on common notions of a particular time or place.
Setting a poem in a garden, for example, or writing about apples almost inevitably
reminds readers of the Garden of Eden because it is an important and widely recognized part of the Western heritage. Even people who don't read at all or who lack Judeo-
Christian religious commitments are likely to know about Eden, and poets writing in
Western cultures can count on that knowledge. A reference to something outside the
poem that carries a history of meaning and strong emotional associations is called an
allusion. For example, gardens may carry suggestions of innocence and order, or temptation and the Fall, or both, depending on how the poem handles the allusion.

Specific, well-known places may similarly be associated with particular ideas, values, ways of life, or natural phenomena. The titles of many poems refer, like the following one, directly to specific places or times. As you read the poem, pay attention
to when and where it takes place and to the details of setting, as well as situation.

MATTHEW ARNOLD
Dover Beach[2]

    The sea is calm tonight.
    The tide is full, the moon lies fair
    Upon the straits; on the French coast the light
    Gleams and is gone; the cliffs of England stand,
5   Glimmering and vast, out in the tranquil bay.
    Come to the window, sweet is the night-air!
    Only, from the long line of spray
    Where the sea meets the moon-blanched land,
    Listen! you hear the grating roar
10 Of pebbles which the waves draw back, and fling,
    At their return, up the high strand,

---

2. At the narrowest point on the English Channel. The light on the French coast (lines 3–4) would be
about twenty miles away.

Begin, and cease, and then again begin,
With tremulous cadence slow, and bring
The eternal note of sadness in.

15 Sophocles long ago
Heard it on the Aegean, and it brought
Into his mind the turbid ebb and flow
Of human misery,[3] we
Find also in the sound a thought,
20 Hearing it by this distant northern sea.

The Sea of Faith
Was once, too, at the full, and round earth's shore
Lay like the folds of a bright girdle furled.
But now I only hear
25 Its melancholy, long, withdrawing roar,
Retreating, to the breath
Of the night-wind, down the vast edges drear
And naked shingles[4] of the world.

Ah, love, let us be true
30 To one another! for the world, which seems
To lie before us like a land of dreams,
So various, so beautiful, so new,
Hath really neither joy, nor love, nor light,
Nor certitude, nor peace, nor help for pain;
35 And we are here as on a darkling plain
Swept with confused alarms of struggle and flight,
Where ignorant armies clash by night.

c. 1851   1867

The situation and setting of DOVER BEACH are concrete and specific. It is night by the seashore, and the speaker is gazing at the view from a room with someone he invites to "Come to the window" (line 6) and "Listen" (9); later he says to this person, "Ah, love, let us be true / To one another!" (29–30). Most readers have assumed that the speaker and his companion are about to travel from Dover across the sea to France and that the situation is a honeymoon, or at least that the couple is young and married; after all, the "world [. . .] seems / To lie before us [. . .] / so new" (30–32). Although this poem is not a prayer, it is a kind of plea for hope despite the modern loss of faith. The tide is now full, but the poet hears a destructive repetition of rising and falling waves (the pebbles will be worn down eventually), and he dwells on the "withdrawing" side of this pattern. For centuries, Christian belief, "The Sea of Faith" (21), was at high tide, but now the speaker can only "hear" it "[r]etreating" (24, 26). On the one hand, then, the specifics of setting—the fact that it is night, that the speaker looks out on a stony beach lined with cliffs, and so on—seem to evoke the sense of danger, isolation, and uncertainty the speaker feels as a result of the loss of faith. On the other hand, how might details of setting introduce hope into the poem, especially when we combine them with our knowledge of how tides ebb and flow and how the dark of night gives way to the light of day?

3. In Sophocles's *Antigone* (lines 637–46; pp. 1019–20), the chorus compares the fate of the house of Oedipus to the waves of the sea.   4. Pebble-strewn beaches.

ONE POEM, MULTIPLE SITUATIONS AND SETTINGS

Though many poems depict a single situation and setting, a single poem will sometimes juxtapose multiple "scenes." In such cases, we need both to determine the
situation and setting particular to each scene and to consider how the poem inter-
relates its various scenes to create a singular effect and meaning.

   The following poem describes several scenes. Some seem to have actually occurred
at particular places and times (when the main speaker was "In sixth grade," for
example [line 1]). Others seem hypothetical, abstract, or generic—events that might
or often do happen almost anywhere to almost anybody (like "choos[ing] / persimmons," 6–7). Still others seem indeterminate as to time and/or place (Did "Donna
undres[s]" only once [18]? When?). How many different scenes of each type can you
discern? What connects them to each other? For example, how might at least some
of these scenes demonstrate or discuss various kinds of "precision" (5, 82)? How so,
and what kinds?

LI-YOUNG LEE
Persimmons

In sixth grade Mrs. Walker
slapped the back of my head
and made me stand in the corner
for not knowing the difference
5   between *persimmon* and *precision*.
How to choose
persimmons. This is precision.
Ripe ones are soft and brown-spotted.
Sniff the bottoms. The sweet one
10 will be fragrant. How to eat:
put the knife away, lay down newspaper.
Peel the skin tenderly, not to tear the meat.
Chew the skin, suck it,
and swallow. Now, eat
15 the meat of the fruit,
so sweet,
all of it, to the heart.

Donna undresses, her stomach is white.
In the yard, dewy and shivering
20 with crickets, we lie naked,
face-up, face-down.
I teach her Chinese.
Crickets: *chiu chiu.* Dew: I've forgotten.
Naked: I've forgotten.
25 *Ni, wo:*   you and me.
I part her legs,
remember to tell her
she is beautiful as the moon.

Other words
30   that got me into trouble were
fight and *fright*, *wren* and *yarn*.
Fight was what I did when I was frightened,
fright was what I felt when I was fighting.
Wrens are small, plain birds,
35   yarn is what one knits with.
Wrens are soft as yarn.
My mother made birds out of yarn.
I loved to watch her tie the stuff;
a bird, a rabbit, a wee man.

40   Mrs. Walker brought a persimmon to class
and cut it up
so everyone could taste
a *Chinese apple*. Knowing
it wasn't ripe or sweet, I didn't eat
45   but watched the other faces.

My mother said every persimmon has a sun
inside, something golden, glowing,
warm as my face.

Once, in the cellar, I found two wrapped in newspaper,
50   forgotten and not yet ripe.
I took them and set both on my bedroom windowsill,
where each morning a cardinal
sang, *The sun, the sun.*
Finally understanding
55   he was going blind,
my father sat up all one night
waiting for a song, a ghost.
I gave him the persimmons,
swelled, heavy as sadness,
60   and sweet as love.

This year, in the muddy lighting
of my parents' cellar, I rummage, looking
for something I lost.
My father sits on the tired, wooden stairs,
65   black cane between his knees,
hand over hand, gripping the handle.

He's so happy that I've come home.
I ask how his eyes are, a stupid question.
All gone, he answers.

70   Under some blankets, I find a box.
Inside the box I find three scrolls.
I sit beside him and untie
three paintings by my father:
Hibiscus leaf and a white flower.

75   Two cats preening.
      Two persimmons, so full they want to drop from the cloth.

      He raises both hands to touch the cloth,
      asks, *Which is this?*

      This is persimmons, Father.

80   *Oh, the feel of the wolftail on the silk,*
      the strength, the tense
      precision in the wrist.
      I painted them hundreds of times
      eyes closed. These I painted blind.
85   *Some things never leave a person:*
      scent of the hair of one you love,
      the texture of persimmons,
      in your palm, the ripe weight.

                                                            1986

ONE SITUATION AND SETTING, MULTIPLE POEMS

Careful attention to situation and setting can be helpful not only in understanding how any one poem works and means but also in appreciating the differences
among poems. We can usefully compare *any* two or more poems that focus on a
similar situation or setting. But some poems deliberately invite such comparison by
revisiting precisely the same situation and setting depicted in other, earlier poems.

   The following two poems, by Christopher Marlowe and Sir Walter Raleigh, respectively, provide a famous example of this sort of response. Like all **pastoral** poems,
these are both set in a rural landscape and concerned with the simple life of country
folk, usually (as here) shepherds, who live an outdoor life and tend to basic human
needs. Yet Marlowe's is the more conventional of the two insofar as it presents that
landscape and that life in stylized, idealized terms—as a simple, timeless world of
beauty, music, and love that implicitly operates as a kind of counter to, and interlude
from, the more urbane, adult, complicated, time-bound "real world." Raleigh's poem
is only one of many replies to Marlowe's, which itself indirectly alludes and responds
to countless, even earlier works in the pastoral tradition.

CHRISTOPHER MARLOWE
The Passionate Shepherd to His Love

      Come live with me and be my love,
      And we will all the pleasures prove[5]
      That valleys, groves, hills, and fields,
      Woods, or steepy mountain yields.

5   And we will sit upon the rocks,
      Seeing the shepherds feed their flocks,

5. Experience.

By shallow rivers to whose falls
Melodious birds sing madrigals.

And I will make thee beds of roses
10   And a thousand fragrant posies,
A cap of flowers, and a kirtle[6]
Embroidered all with leaves of myrtle;

A gown made of the finest wool
Which from our pretty lambs we pull;
15   Fair linèd slippers for the cold,
With buckles of the purest gold;

A belt of straw and ivy buds,
With coral clasps and amber studs:
And if these pleasures may thee move,
20   Come live with me, and be my love.

The shepherd swains[7] shall dance and sing
For thy delight each May morning:
If these delights thy mind may move,
Then live with me and be my love.

1600

- What, according to the speaker, are the specific virtues of the ideal world (or setting) and the life to which he invites his "love" (line 1)? How, by implication, might the poem characterize the (real) world he invites her to leave behind?

SIR WALTER RALEIGH
The Nymph's Reply to the Shepherd

If all the world and love were young,
And truth in every shepherd's tongue,
These pretty pleasures might me move
To live with thee and be thy love.

5   Time drives the flocks from field to fold,
When rivers rage, and rocks grow cold,
And Philomel[8] becometh dumb;
The rest complain of cares to come.

The flowers do fade, and wanton fields
10   To wayward winter reckoning yields:
A honey tongue, a heart of gall,
Is fancy's spring, but sorrow's fall.

Thy gowns, thy shoes, thy beds of roses,
Thy cap, thy kirtle, and thy posies
15   Soon break, soon wither, soon forgotten;
In folly ripe, in reason rotten.

6. Gown.   7. Youths.   8. The nightingale.

Thy belt of straw and ivy buds,
Thy coral clasps and amber studs,
All these in me no means can move
20 To come to thee and be thy love.

But could youth last, and love still breed,
Had joys no date,[9] nor age no need,
Then these delights my mind might move
To live with thee and be thy love.

1600

- Raleigh's poem works by presenting the same situation and setting Marlowe's does from a different speaker's perspective and having that speaker, in turn, present a sort of "if/then" scenario (*If* all this were true, *then* I would say yes): For what specific reasons is this nymph *not* going to accept her shepherd's offer? What's the effect of the poem's "if/then" structure?

THE OCCASIONAL POEM

Some subgenres or kinds of poetry are defined mostly, even wholly, by the way they handle situation or setting or by the specific sorts of situation and/or setting they depict, and these will be the major focus of the rest of this chapter. In fact, we've already discussed one: the pastoral poem, which by definition portrays an idyllic rural setting with certain conventional features.

Rather than depicting a particular kind of setting, an **occasional poem** is a poem written about or for a specific real, especially public and ceremonial, occasion. In the past, writing—and often publicly reading—poems in honor of royal birthdays and other state occasions or commemorating military victories and other major national events was considered an obligation of those serving as Poet Laureate. Since 1961, U.S. presidents have sometimes invited poets to recite at their inaugurations poems written for the occasion. (John F. Kennedy was the first to do so, with Robert Frost; Barack Obama was, to date, the last.) But not all poets have needed an invitation to write occasional poems, nor are all occasional poems celebratory: Though written while he was Poet Laureate, Alfred Tennyson's THE CHARGE OF THE LIGHT BRIGADE commemorates an infamously disastrous battle. Occasional poems can even consider much more ordinary, even personal "occasions." Yet the occasional poem and its history are a healthy reminder that, while we often today think of *all* poems as addressing an individual reader and expressing exclusively personal feelings, a good deal of poetry written over the centuries has had a more public, civic focus and purpose, speaking about and to an entire community and its history.

The following, quite modern poem is a good example: an occasional poem that works to capture the significance of a recent public event by considering it in the historical perspective inspired by a very specific setting.

9. End.

MARTÍN ESPADA
Litany at the Tomb of Frederick Douglass[1]

Mount Hope Cemetery, Rochester, New York
November 7, 2008

This is the longitude and latitude of the impossible;
this is the epicenter of the unthinkable;
this is the crossroads of the unimaginable:
the tomb of Frederick Douglass, three days after the election.

5 This is a world spinning away from the gravity of centuries,
where the grave of a fugitive slave has become an altar.
This is the tomb of a man born as chattel, who taught himself to read in
    secret,
scraping the letters in his name with chalk on wood; now on the anvil-flat
    stone
a campaign button fills the O in *Douglass*. The button says: *Obama*.
10 This is the tomb of a man in chains, who left his fingerprints
on the slavebreaker's throat so the whip would never carve his back again;
now a labor union T-shirt drapes itself across the stone, offered up
by a nurse, a janitor, a bus driver. A sticker on the sleeve says: *I Voted*
    Today.
This is the tomb of a man who rolled his call to arms off the press,
15 peering through spectacles at the abolitionist headline; now a newspaper
spreads above his dates of birth and death. The headline says: *Obama Wins.*

This is the stillness at the heart of the storm that began in the body
of the first slave, dragged aboard the first ship to America. Yellow leaves
descend in waves, and the newspaper flutters on the tomb, like the sails
20 Douglass saw in the bay, like the eyes of a slave closing to watch himself
escape with the tide. Believers in spirits would see the pages trembling
on the stone and say: *look how the slave boy teaches himself to read.*
I say a prayer, the first in years: that here we bury what we call
the impossible, the unthinkable, the unimaginable, now and forever. *Amen.*

2008

- Why, according to this poem, was the result of the 2008 presidential election meaningful? Why and how does the poem's particular setting make that occasion's significance especially apparent? In these terms, what details of setting matter most, and why?

---

1. Escaped slave (c. 1818–95) who was involved in the Underground Railroad and became a major spokesman for abolition, especially through his autobiography (1845) and his Rochester-based newspaper, the *North Star.*

AUTHORS ON THEIR WORK

MARTÍN ESPADA (b. 1957)

From "Poetry Month: Martín Espada" (2011)*

While we all have our criticisms of President Obama, we must not forget the history he made in 2008, and the history we all made by voting for him and the feeling behind the making of that history. [. . .] Right after the election, I found myself in Rochester, New York. And it so happens that's where Frederick Douglass is buried, and so this is the poem that came out of it.

First, it's not an Obama poem; it's a Frederick Douglass poem. Second, it's a poem about the making of history; it's about how we felt at the moment that history was made. [. . .] We can't lose that feeling, even as we become frustrated or disillusioned. [. . .] We can't lose the way we felt at that moment [. . .].

*"Poetry Month: Martín Espada." Interview by Brian Lehrer. *The Brian Lehrer Show*, WNYC, 14 Apr. 2011, www.wnyc.org/story/124060-poetry-month-martin-espada/.

THE CARPE DIEM POEM

The following two poems from the 1600s represent similar situations: In each, a male speaker addresses a female auditor whom he desires. The poems belong to the tradition of **carpe diem** (Latin for "seize the day") because the speaker is urging his auditor, his lover, to enjoy pleasures now, before they die. The woman is resisting because of her concern for chastity or social rules. The action of these poems is implied in the shifts in what the speaker is saying. What does the woman do in THE FLEA? Can you imagine the woman's response in TO HIS COY MISTRESS?

JOHN DONNE
The Flea

Mark but this flea, and mark in this,[2]
How little that which thou deny'st me is;
It sucked me first, and now sucks thee,
And in this flea our two bloods mingled be;
5   Thou know'st that this cannot be said
A sin, nor shame, nor loss of maidenhead.
   Yet this enjoys before it woo,
   And pampered[3] swells with one blood made of two,
   And this, alas, is more than we would do.[4]

---

2. Medieval preachers and rhetoricians asked their hearers to "mark" (look at) an object that illustrated a moral or philosophical lesson they wished to emphasize.
3. Fed luxuriously.
4. According to seventeenth-century medical theory, conception involved the literal mingling of the lovers' blood.

10 Oh stay,⁵ three lives in one flea spare,
    Where we almost, yea more than, married are.
    This flea is you and I, and this
    Our marriage bed, and marriage temple is;
    Though parents grudge, and you, we're met
15 And cloistered in these living walls of jet.
       Though use⁶ make you apt to kill me,
       Let not to that, self-murder added be,
       And sacrilege, three sins in killing three.

       Cruel and sudden, hast thou since
20 Purpled thy nail in blood of innocence?
    Wherein could this flea guilty be,
    Except in that drop which it sucked from thee?
    Yet thou triumph'st, and say'st that thou
    Find'st not thyself, nor me, the weaker now;
25   'Tis true; then learn how false fears be;
       Just so much honor, when thou yield'st to me,
       Will waste, as this flea's death took life from thee.

                      1633

• What lines help you imagine what the speaker is doing as he speaks? what the auditor does or says?

ANDREW MARVELL
To His Coy Mistress

    Had we but world enough, and time,
    This coyness,⁷ lady, were no crime.
    We would sit down, and think which way
    To walk, and pass our long love's day.
5 Thou by the Indian Ganges' side
    Shouldst rubies⁸ find: I by the tide
    Of Humber would complain.⁹ I would
    Love you ten years before the Flood,
    And you should if you please refuse
10 Till the conversion of the Jews.¹
    My vegetable love² should grow
    Vaster than empires, and more slow;
    An hundred years should go to praise
    Thine eyes, and on thy forehead gaze;
15 Two hundred to adore each breast,
    But thirty thousand to the rest.

5. Desist. 6. Habit. 7. Hesitancy, modesty (not necessarily suggesting calculation).
8. Talismans believed to preserve virginity.
9. Write love complaints, conventional songs lamenting the cruelty of love. *Humber*: a river and estuary in Marvell's hometown of Hull, England.
1. Which, according to popular Christian belief, will occur just before the end of the world.
2. Which is capable only of passive growth, not of consciousness. The "vegetable soul" is lower than the other two divisions of the soul, "animal" and "rational."

An age at least to every part,
And the last age should show your heart.
For, lady, you deserve this state;[3]
20 Nor would I love at lower rate.
        But at my back I always hear
Time's wingèd chariot hurrying near;
And yonder all before us lie
Deserts of vast eternity.
25 Thy beauty shall no more be found,
Nor, in thy marble vault, shall sound
My echoing song; then worms shall try
That long preserved virginity,
And your quaint honor turn to dust,
30 And into ashes all my lust:
The grave's a fine and private place,
But none, I think, do there embrace.
        Now therefore, while the youthful hue
Sits on thy skin like morning dew,[4]
35 And while thy willing soul transpires[5]
At every pore with instant fires,
Now let us sport us while we may,
And now, like am'rous birds of prey,
Rather at once our time devour
40 Than languish in his slow-chapped[6] pow'r.
Let us roll all our strength and all
Our sweetness up into one ball,
And tear our pleasures with rough strife
Thorough[7] the iron gates of life.
45 Thus, though we cannot make our sun
Stand still,[8] yet we will make him run.[9]

                        1681

• How does each stanza develop the speaker's argument? Is it persuasive?

POEMS FOR FURTHER STUDY

Consider the *Who? What? Why? Where?* and *When?* questions as you read the following poems.

---

3. Dignity.   4. The text reads "glew." "Lew" (warmth) has also been suggested as an emendation.
5. Breathes forth.
6. Slow-jawed. Chronos (Time), ruler of the world in early Greek myth, devoured all of his children except Zeus, who was hidden. Later, Zeus seized power (see line 46 and note).
7. Through.   8. To lengthen his night of love with Alcmene, Zeus made the sun stand still.
9. Each sex act was believed to shorten life by one day.

NATASHA TRETHEWEY
Pilgrimage

Vicksburg, Mississippi[1]

Here, the Mississippi carved
    its mud-dark path, a graveyard

for skeletons of sunken riverboats.
    Here, the river changed its course,

5 turning away from the city
    as one turns, forgetting, from the past—

the abandoned bluffs, land sloping up
    above the river's bend—where now

the Yazoo fills the Mississippi's empty bed.
10   Here, the dead stand up in stone, white

marble, on Confederate Avenue. I stand
    on ground once hollowed by a web of caves;

they must have seemed like catacombs,
    in 1863, to the woman sitting in her parlor,

15 candlelit, underground. I can see her
    listening to shells explode, writing herself

into history, asking *what is to become*
    of all the living things in this place?

This whole city is a grave. Every spring—
20   *Pilgrimage*—the living come to mingle

with the dead, brush against their cold shoulders
    in the long hallways, listen all night

to their silence and indifference, relive
    their dying on the green battlefield.

25 At the museum, we marvel at their clothes—
    preserved under glass—so much smaller

than our own, as if those who wore them
    were only children. We sleep in their beds,

the old mansions hunkered on the bluffs, draped
30   in flowers—funereal—a blur

of petals against the river's gray.
    The brochure in my room calls this

1. On July 4, 1863, the city surrendered to Union forces under Ulysses S. Grant after a forty-day siege; coming just a day after the Confederate defeat at Gettysburg, Vicksburg's surrender is regarded as a major turning point in the Civil War.

living history. The brass plate on the door reads
     Prissy's[2] *Room.* A window frames

35 the river's crawl toward the Gulf. In my dream,
     the ghost of history lies down beside me,

rolls over, pins me beneath a heavy arm.

                          2006

- What different historical times and situations meet in a single place in this poem? Why and how so?

TERRANCE HAYES
Carp Poem

After I have parked below the spray paint caked in the granite
grooves of the Frederick Douglass[3] Middle School sign,

where men-size children loiter like shadows draped in outsize
denim, jerseys, braids, and boots that mean I am no longer young;

5 after I have made my way to the New Orleans Parish Jail down the
     block,
where the black prison guard wearing the same weariness

my prison guard father wears buzzes me in. I follow his pistol and shield
along each corridor trying not to look at the black men

boxed and bunked around me until I reach the tiny classroom
10 where two dozen black boys are dressed in jumpsuits orange as the carp

I saw in a pond once in Japan, so many fat, snaggletoothed fish
ganged in and lurching for food that a lightweight tourist could have
     crossed

the water on their backs so long as he had tiny rice balls or bread
to drop into the mouths below his footsteps, which I'm thinking

15 is how Jesus must have walked on the lake that day, the crackers and
     crumbs
falling from the folds of his robe, and how maybe it was the one fish

so hungry it leaped up his sleeve that he later miraculously changed
into a narrow loaf of bread, something that could stick to a believer's
     ribs,

and don't get me wrong, I'm a believer too, in the power of food at least,
20 having seen a footbridge of carp packed gill to gill, packed tighter

than a room of boy prisoners waiting to talk poetry with a young black
     poet,

---

2. Scarlett O'Hara's maid in Margaret Mitchell's novel *Gone with the Wind* (1936).
3. Prominent African American abolitionist, politician, and former slave (c. 1818–95).

packed so close they'd have eaten each other had there been nothing
    else to eat.

2010

• What is this poem's central setting and situation? How do details of setting
help to define the situation and its significance? What two other situations
and settings appear in the poem, and how so? How does the poem relate
these three scenes?

CATHY SONG
Heaven

He thinks when we die we'll go to China.
Think of it—a Chinese heaven
where, except for his blond hair,
the part that belongs to his father,
5 everyone will look like him.
China, that blue flower on the map,
bluer than the sea
his hand must span like a bridge
to reach it.
10 An octave away.

I've never seen it.
It's as if I can't sing that far.
But look—
on the map, this black dot.
15 Here is where we live,
on the pancake plains
just east of the Rockies,
on the other side of the clouds.
A mile above the sea,
20 the air is so thin, you can starve on it.
No bamboo trees
but the alpine equivalent,
reedy aspen with light, fluttering leaves.
Did a boy in Guangzhou[4] dream of this
25 as his last stop?
I've heard the trains at night
whistling past our yards,
what we've come to own,
the broken fences, the whiny dog, the rattletrap cars.
30 It's still the wild west,
mean and grubby,
the shootouts and fistfights in the back alley.
With my son the dreamer
and my daughter, who is too young to walk,

---

4. Usually called Canton, a seaport city in southeastern China.

35 I've sat in this spot
and wondered why here?
Why in this short life,
this town, this creek they call a river?

He had never planned to stay,
40 the boy who helped to build
the railroads for a dollar a day.
He had always meant to go back.
When did he finally know
that each mile of track led him further away,
45 that he would die in his sleep,
dispossessed,
having seen Gold Mountain,
the icy wind tunneling through it,
these landlocked, makeshift ghost towns?

50 It must be in the blood,
this notion of returning.
It skipped two generations, lay fallow,
the garden an unmarked grave.
On a spring sweater day
55 it's as if we remember him.
I call to the children.
We can see the mountains
shimmering blue above the air.
If you look really hard
60 says my son the dreamer,
leaning out from the laundry's rigging,
the work shirts fluttering like sails,
you can see all the way to heaven.

                                        1988

- Who is "He" in this poem's first line? What family history is recounted in
  the poem? How does the poem make use of contrast?

ADRIENNE SU
Escape from the Old Country

I never had to make one,
no sickening weeks by ocean,

no waiting for the aerogrammes[5]
that gradually ceased to come.

5 Spent the babysitting money
on novels, shoes, and movies,

yet the neighborhood stayed empty.
It had nothing to do with a journey

5. Airmail letters, especially those on specially designed stationery.

not undertaken, nor with dialect,
10 nor with a land that waited

to be rediscovered, then rejected.
As acid rain collected

above the suburban hills, I tried
to imagine being nothing, tried

15 to be able to claim, "I have
no culture," and be believed.

Yet the land occupies the person
even as the semblance of freedom

invites a kind of recklessness.
20 Tradition, unobserved, unasked,

hangs on tight; ancestors roam
into reverie, interfering at the most

awkward moments, first flirtations,
in doorways and dressing rooms—

25 But of course. Here in America,
no one escapes. In the end, each traveler

returns to the town where, everyone
knew, she hadn't even been born.

2006

- To what does "one" refer, in line one? In the context of the rest of the poem, what are the various possible meanings of the sentence "Here in America, / no one escapes" (lines 25–26)?

SUGGESTIONS FOR WRITING

1. Choose one poem in this book in which a single word seems crucial to that poem's total effect and theme. Write an essay in which you work out carefully why and how that's the case.
2. Choose one poem in this book in which syntax (the order of words in sentences) or the placement of words on the page seems especially key to the poem's overall effect and meaning. Write an essay explaining how and why considering word order, in either or both of these senses, might change or deepen a reader's understanding of the poem.
3. Language is a topic of (as well as tool used in) Martha Collins's LIES, A. E. Stall-ings's SHOULDA, WOULDA, COULDA, and even Kay Ryan's BLANDEUR. Write an essay exploring what any of these poems has to say about poetry or language and how word choice, order, and placement help the poem express or illustrate it.

11 | THEME AND TONE

Poetry is full of surprises. Poems express anger or outrage just as effectively as love or sadness, and good poems can be written about going to a rock concert or having lunch or mowing the lawn, as well as about making love or smelling flowers. Even poems on "predictable" subjects can surprise us with unpredicted attitudes or sudden twists. Knowing that a poem is about some particular subject or topic—love, for example, or death—may give us a general idea of what to expect, but it never tells us exactly what we will find in a particular poem. Labeling a poem a "love poem" or a "death poem" is a convenient way to speak of its topic. But poems that may be loosely called "love poems" or "death poems" may have little else in common, may express utterly different attitudes or ideas, and may concentrate on very different aspects of the subject. Letting a poem speak to us means more than merely figuring out its topic; it means listening to *how* the poem says what it says. *What* a poem says about its topic is its **theme**. *How* a poem makes that statement involves its **tone**—the poem's attitude or feelings toward its topic. No two poems on the same subject affect us in exactly the same way; their themes and tones vary, and even similar themes may be expressed in various ways, creating different tones and effects.

TONE

Tone, a term borrowed from acoustics and music, refers to the qualities of the language a speaker uses in social situations or in a poem, and it also refers to a speaker's intended effect. Tone is closely related to style and diction; it is an effect of the speaker's expressions, *as if* showing a real person's feelings, manner, and attitude or relationship to a listener and to the particular subject or situation. Thus, the speaker may use angry or mocking words, may address the listener intimately or distantly, may sincerely confess or coolly observe, may paint a grand picture or narrate a legend.

The following poem describes a romantic encounter of sorts, but its tone may surprise you. As you read the poem, work first to identify its **speaker**, **situation**, and **setting**. Then try both to capture its tone in a single word or two and to figure out which features of the poem most help to create that tone.

W. D. SNODGRASS
Leaving the Motel

Outside, the last kids holler
Near the pool: they'll stay the night.
Pick up the towels; fold your collar
Out of sight.

5 Check: is the second bed
Unrumpled, as agreed?
Landlords have to think ahead
In case of need,

Too. Keep things straight: don't take
10 The matches, the wrong keyrings—
We've nowhere we could keep a keepsake—
Ashtrays, combs, things

That sooner or later others
Would accidentally find.
15 Check: take nothing of one another's
And leave behind

Your license number only,
Which they won't care to trace;
We've paid. Still, should such things get lonely,
20 Leave in their vase

An aspirin to preserve
Our lilacs, the wayside flowers
We've gathered and must leave to serve
A few more hours;

25 That's all. We can't tell when
We'll come back, can't press claims,
We would no doubt have other rooms then,
Or other names.

1968

    The title and details of LEAVING THE MOTEL indicate the situation and setting:
Two secret lovers are at the end of an afternoon sexual encounter in a motel room
(perhaps one is speaking for both of them), reminding themselves not to leave or
take with them any clues for "others" (line 13)—their spouses?—to find.
    Whereas many poems on the topic of love confirm an enduring attachment or
express desire or suggest erotic experience, this poem focuses on the effort to erase a
stolen encounter. The two lovers have no names; indeed, they have registered under
false ones. They have already paid for this temporary shelter, can't stay the night like
other guests or build a home with children of their own, and are running through a
checklist of their agreements and duties ("Check," "Keep things straight," "Check"
[lines 5, 9, 15]). Other than the "wayside" lilacs (line 22), the objects mentioned are
trivial, from matches and keyrings to license numbers. The matter-of-fact but hurried tone suggests that they wish to hide any deep feelings (hinted at in the last two

stanzas in the wish to make "claims" or preserve flowers [26]). The failure to express love—or guilt—enhances the effect when the tone shifts, at the word "still" (19), to the second thoughts about leaving something behind. The poem's short rhyming lines, sounding brisk and somewhat impersonal, contrast with the situation and add to the tone of subdued regret that nothing lasts.

THEME

Our response to the tone of a poem, however it surprises or jars or stirs us, guides us to understand its theme (or themes): what the poem expresses about its topic. A theme is not simply a work's subject or topic; it is a statement *about* that topic. Although we can usually agree on a poem's topic without much difficulty, it is harder to determine how to state a poem's theme. A single theme may be expressed in several different ways, and a single poem may also have more than one theme. Sometimes the poet explicitly states a poem's theme, and such a statement may clarify why the author chose a particular mode of presentation and how the poem fits into the author's own patterns of thinking and growing. However, the author's words may give a misleading view of how most people read the poem, just as a person's self-assessment may not be all we need in order to understand his or her character. Further study of the poem is necessary to understand how it fulfills—or fails to fulfill—the author's intentions. Despite the difficulty of identifying and expressing themes, doing so is an important step in understanding and writing about poetry.

Topic Versus Tone and Theme:
A Comparative Exercise

Reading two or more poems with similar topics side by side may suggest how each is distinctive in what it has to say and how it does so—its theme and tone. The following two poems are about animals, although both of them place their final emphasis on human beings: The animal in each case is only the means to the end of exploring human nature. The poems share the assumption that animal behavior may appear to reflect human habits and conduct and that it may reveal much about us; in each case the character central to the poem is revealed to be surprisingly unlike the way she thinks of herself. But the poems differ in their tones, in the specific relationship between the woman and the animals, and in their themes.

   How would you describe the tone of the following poem? its topic and theme?

MAXINE KUMIN
Woodchucks

Gassing the woodchucks didn't turn out right.
The knockout bomb from the Feed and Grain Exchange
was featured as merciful, quick at the bone
and the case we had against them was airtight,

5 both exits shoehorned shut with puddingstone,[1]
but they had a sub-sub-basement out of range.

Next morning they turned up again, no worse
for the cyanide than we for our cigarettes
and state-store Scotch, all of us up to scratch.
10 They brought down the marigolds as a matter of course
and then took over the vegetable patch
nipping the broccoli shoots, beheading the carrots.

The food from our mouths, I said, righteously thrilling
to the feel of the .22, the bullets' neat noses.
15 I, a lapsed pacifist fallen from grace
puffed with Darwinian pieties for killing,
now drew a bead on the littlest woodchuck's face.
He died down in the everbearing roses.

Ten minutes later I dropped the mother. She
20 flipflopped in the air and fell, her needle teeth
still hooked in a leaf of early Swiss chard.
Another baby next. O one-two-three
the murderer inside me rose up hard,
the hawkeye killer came on stage forthwith.

25 There's one chuck left. Old wily fellow, he keeps
me cocked and ready day after day after day.
All night I hunt his humped-up form. I dream
I sight along the barrel in my sleep.
If only they'd all consented to die unseen
30 gassed underground the quiet Nazi way.

1972

As you read WOODCHUCKS aloud, how does your tone of voice change from beginning to end? What tone do you use to read the ending? How does the hunter feel about her increasing attraction to violence? Why does the poem begin by calling the gassing of the woodchucks "merciful" (line 3) and end by describing it as "the quiet Nazi way" (30)? What names does the hunter call herself? How does the name-calling affect your feelings about her? Exactly when does the hunter begin to *enjoy* the feel of the gun and the idea of killing? How does the poet make that clear? What, ultimately, might the poem as a whole say or show us about ourselves—especially, perhaps, our relation to animals? to violence?

ADRIENNE RICH
Aunt Jennifer's Tigers

Aunt Jennifer's tigers prance across a screen,
Bright topaz denizens of a world of green.

---

1. Mixture of cement, pebbles, and gravel.

> They do not fear the men beneath the tree;
> They pace in sleek chivalric certainty.
>
> 5 Aunt Jennifer's fingers fluttering through her wool
> Find even the ivory needle hard to pull.
> The massive weight of Uncle's wedding band
> Sits heavily upon Aunt Jennifer's hand.
>
> When Aunt is dead, her terrified hands will lie
> 10 Still ringed with ordeals she was mastered by.
> The tigers in the panel that she made
> Will go on prancing, proud and unafraid.
>
> 1951

In this poem, why are tigers a particularly appropriate animal? What words describing the tigers seem especially significant? Why are Aunt Jennifer's hands described as "terrified" (line 9)? What clues does the poem give about why Aunt Jennifer is so afraid? How does the poem make you feel about Aunt Jennifer's life and death? How would you describe the tone of the poem? Why does the poem begin and end with the tigers? Might the poem's theme be a universal one (about all or most people)? Or is the theme more specific (about, say, women versus men or about married people)?

AUTHORS ON THEIR WORK

ADRIENNE RICH (1929–2012)

From "When We Dead Awaken: Writing as Re-Vision" (1971)*

In writing this poem, composed and apparently cool as it is, I thought I was creating a portrait of an imaginary woman. But this woman suffers from the opposition of her imagination, worked out in tapestry, and her lifestyle, "ringed with ordeals she was mastered by." It was important to me that Aunt Jennifer was a person as distinct from myself as possible—distanced by the formalism of the poem, by its objective, observant tone—even by putting the woman in a different generation.

*"When We Dead Awaken: Writing as Re-Vision." Women's Forum of the MLA, Dec. 1971, Chicago. Address.

THEME AND CONFLICT

Since a theme is an idea implied by all of the elements of the poem working together, identifying theme—as opposed to topic and tone—can sometimes be a tough and tricky business. In reading and writing about poetry, then, it often helps to focus first—and most—on conflict. Though we usually think of conflict as an aspect of **plot,** even perfectly plotless poems are almost always organized around and devoted to exploring conflicts and tensions. To begin to identify these, look for contrasts and think about the conflict they imply.

Take, for example, AUNT JENNIFER'S TIGERS. Though it might be hard to say at first just what the theme of Rich's poem might be, it's hard to miss the contrast at its center. Where the tigers Aunt Jennifer embroiders "prance" and "pace" freely, "proud and unafraid," through a world as colorful and as lasting as they are (lines 1, 4, 12), Aunt Jennifer and her world seem just the opposite: Nothing but her fingers and hands move in the poem, and even they are "terrified" and tentative, "fluttering through her wool," "weight[ed]" down by a heavy "wedding band" in life and stilled permanently by death (9, 5, 7). We have, then, not just a contrast but a multifaceted conflict—between imaginary and real worlds, between individual vision and social obligation. What the poem concludes about this conflict is its theme, but starting with questions about conflict often provides not only an easier way into the poem but also a much richer, more textured experience and understanding of it. And very good essays can be written about a poem or poems' conflicts.

The following poem is all about this issue—the role of conflict in poetry. As you read the poem, try to identify the contrasts it sets up, the underlying conflict those contrasts point to, and the theme that ultimately emerges. Then test your own interpretation of the poem against the author's comments about how the poem came to be and what, for her, it's all about.

ADRIENNE SU
On Writing

A love poem risks becoming a ruin,
public, irretrievable, a form of tattooing,

while loss, being permanent,
can sustain a thousand documents.

5 Loss predominates in history,
smorgasbord of death, betrayal, heresy,

crime, contagion, deployment, divorce.
A writer could remain aboard

the ship of grief and thrive, never
10 approaching the shores of rapture.

What can be said about elation
that the elated, seeking consolation

from their joy, will go to books for?
It's wiser and quicker to look for

15 a poem in the dentist's chair
than in the luxury suite where

eternal love, declared, turns out
to be eternal. Who cares about

a stranger's bliss? Thus the juncture
20   where I'm stalled, unaccustomed

to integrity, despite your presence,
our tranquility, and every confidence.

2012

AUTHORS ON THEIR WORK

ADRIENNE SU (b. 1967)

From *The Best American Poetry 2013* (2013)*

When I started assembling my newest manuscript, *The House Unburned*, I found it to be suffering from structural gaps and an excess of grief and regret. [. . .]

To round it out, I needed to come up with some poems of happiness, or at least the absence of unhappiness. This presented a problem, since, as I'm always telling students, successful poems are born of uncertainty, interior conflict, the modes of struggle that lack clear solutions. I went back and forth between two selves: the editor, whose vision for the collection required some happier poems, and the poet, who raged against the affront of an assignment so lacking in ambiguity. How, argued the poet, can happiness, gratification, or success be complex enough to give life to a poem?

Eventually, the answer came with a shift in setting. If the poem could be about writing, conflict would be inherent in the question. So I gave myself permission to write about writing. Now that I had a conflict, the road to the poem appeared. (198)

*The Best American Poetry 2013. Edited by Denise Duhamel, Scribner Poetry, 2013. The Best American Poetry series, edited by David Lehman.

POEMS FOR FURTHER STUDY

PAUL LAURENCE DUNBAR
Sympathy

I know what the caged bird feels, alas!
  When the sun is bright on the upland slopes;
When the wind stirs soft through the springing grass,
And the river flows like a stream of glass;
5   When the first bird sings and the first bud opens,
And the faint perfume from its chalice steals—
I know what the caged bird feels!

I know why the caged bird beats his wing
  Till its blood is red on the cruel bars;

10 For he must fly back to his perch and cling
     When he fain² would be on the bough a-swing;
        And a pain still throbs in the old, old scars
     And they pulse again with a keener sting—
     I know why he beats his wing!

15 I know why the caged bird sings, ah me,
        When his wing is bruised and his bosom sore,—
     When he beats his bars and he would be free;
     It is not a carol of joy or glee,
        But a prayer that he sends from his heart's deep core,
20 But a plea, that upward to Heaven he flings—
     I know why the caged bird sings!

1893

- How might your interpretation of this poem's theme change depending on whether or not you consider the date of its publication and/or the fact that its author was African American?

W. H. AUDEN
Stop all the clocks, cut off the telephone

Stop all the clocks, cut off the telephone,
Prevent the dog from barking with a juicy bone,
Silence the pianos and with muffled drum
Bring out the coffin, let the mourners come.

5 Let aeroplanes circle moaning overhead
Scribbling on the sky the message He Is Dead,
Put crêpe bows round the white necks of the public doves,
Let the traffic policemen wear black cotton gloves.

He was my North, my South, my East and West,
10 My working week and my Sunday rest,
My noon, my midnight, my talk, my song;
I thought that love would last for ever: I was wrong.

The stars are not wanted now: put out every one;
Pack up the moon and dismantle the sun;
15 Pour away the ocean and sweep up the wood;
For nothing now can ever come to any good.

c. 1936

- In what tone of voice would you read line 12? How might you turn this line into a statement of the poem's theme?

2. Gladly.

KAY RYAN
Repulsive Theory

Little has been made
of the soft, skirting action
of magnets reversed,
while much has been
5   made of attraction.
But is it not this pillowy
principle of repulsion
that produces the
doily edges of oceans
10 or the arabesques of thought?
And do these cutout coasts
and incurved rhetorical beaches
not baffle the onslaught
of the sea or objectionable people
15 and give private life
what small protection it's got?
Praise then the oiled motions
of avoidance, the pearly
convolutions of all that
20 slides off or takes a
wide berth; praise every
eddying vacancy of Earth,
all the dimpled depths
of pooling space, the whole
25 swirl set up by fending-off—
extending far beyond the personal,
I'm convinced—
immense and good
in a cosmological sense:
30 unpressing us against
each other, lending
the necessary never
to never-ending.

2003

• What is the "theory" articulated in this poem? Might that theory be the
poem's theme?

SIMON J. ORTIZ
My Father's Song

Wanting to say things,
I miss my father tonight.
His voice, the slight catch,

the depth from his thin chest,
5   the tremble of emotion
in something he has just said
to his son, his song:

We planted corn one Spring at Acu[3]—
we planted several times
10   but this one particular time
I remember the soft damp sand
in my hand.

My father had stopped at one point
to show me an overturned furrow;
15   the plowshare had unearthed
the burrow nest of a mouse
in the soft moist sand.

Very gently, he scooped tiny pink animals
into the palm of his hand
20   and told me to touch them.
We took them to the edge
of the field and put them in the shade
of a sand moist clod.

I remember the very softness
25   of cool and warm sand and tiny alive mice
and my father saying things.

                                        1976

• What are the "things" that the speaker wants to say (line 1)? Are they the
  same "things" he remembers his father saying (26)? Does the poem itself say
  these things?

ROBERT HAYDEN
Those Winter Sundays

Sundays too my father got up early
and put his clothes on in the blueblack cold,
then with cracked hands that ached
from labor in the weekday weather made
5   banked fires blaze. No one ever thanked him.

I'd wake and hear the cold splintering, breaking.
When the rooms were warm, he'd call,
and slowly I would rise and dress,
fearing the chronic angers of that house,

---

3. Alternative name for Acoma village and/or pueblo, about sixty miles west of Albuquerque, New
Mexico. Sometimes translated as "the place that always was," Acu is the oldest continuously inhabited community in the United States.

10   Speaking indifferently to him,
      who had driven out the cold
      and polished my good shoes as well.
      What did I know, what did I know
      of love's austere and lonely offices?

                                                            1966

- Why might the poem begin with the words "Sundays too" (rather than, say, "On Sundays")? What are the "austere and lonely offices" to which the poem's final line refers?

MARTÍN ESPADA
Of the Threads That Connect the Stars

Did you ever see stars? asked my father with a cackle. He was not
speaking of the heavens, but the white flash in his head when a fist burst
between his eyes. In Brooklyn, this would cause men and boys to slap
the table with glee; this might be the only heavenly light we'd ever see.

5   I never saw stars. The sky in Brooklyn was a tide of smoke rolling over us
      from the factory across the avenue, the mattresses burning in the
          junkyard,
      the ruins where squatters would sleep, the riots of 1966[4] that kept me
      locked in my room like a suspect. My father talked truce on the streets.

      My son can see the stars through the tall barrel of a telescope.
10   He names the galaxies with the numbers and letters of astronomy.
      I cannot see what he sees in the telescope, no matter how many eyes
          I shut.
      I understand a smoking mattress better than the language of galaxies.

      My father saw stars. My son sees stars. The earth rolls beneath
      our feet. We lurch ahead, and one day we have walked this far.

                                                            2013

- How does the poem differentiate and connect three generations of one family by describing the stars that each did or didn't, do or don't, see?

---

4. In July 1966, violent conflict repeatedly erupted between blacks and Puerto Ricans in Brooklyn's troubled Bedford-Stuyvesant neighborhood.

SAMPLE WRITING: RESPONSE PAPER

In the response paper below, Stephen Bordland works through W. H. Auden's STOP ALL THE CLOCKS, CUT OFF THE TELEPHONE more or less line by line, writing down whatever ideas come to him—a technique sometimes called **exposition**. The form of this paper is less important than the process of thinking carefully about the poem's music, emotions, and meanings. As you can see, by the time Stephen reaches the end of his response, he has decided on a topic for the more formal essay that he will write later.

Stephen Bordland
Professor O'Connor
English 157
8 January 2019

Response Paper on Auden's "Stop all the clocks, cut off the telephone"

I first heard this poem read aloud when I saw the movie *Four Weddings and a Funeral* on cable. The character who read the poem was reading it at the funeral of his lover. It was perfectly suited to the story and was very moving. I was struck by the actor's reading because the poem seemed to have a steady rhythm for several lines and then suddenly hit what sounded like a dead end— "I thought that love would last for ever: I was wrong" (line 12). Hearing the actor's reading of this poem made me want to read it myself, to see if the poem would still affect me if I read/heard it outside of the context of an emotional scene in a movie. It did, and I think that the "I was wrong" line is the key—a turning point, I guess.

In the anthology, the poem seems to have no actual title, but I did some searching on the Internet and found that this poem was once called "Funeral Blues." If I were reading the poem for the first time under that title, I would at least know that the poem has something to do with death right from the start. But this title makes the poem sound irreverent rather than sincerely painful. I wonder if that would have been true in the 1930s, when Auden wrote the poem. There were lots of blues and jazz songs of that era whose titles ended in "Blues" (like Robert Johnson's "Kind Hearted Woman Blues"), so maybe the title wasn't meant to be read the way that I'm reading it. Anyway, I don't know

---

if Auden himself changed the title, or if there's another story there, but I think it's a better poem without the title.

The poem starts with a request to an unknown person (everyone?) to make some common aspects of daily life go away: "Stop all the clocks" (1) presumably because time seems to be standing still; "cut off the telephone" (1) presumably because the speaker wants to be alone and undisturbed, cut off from human contact. I'm not sure what's implied by "Prevent the dog from barking with a juicy bone" (2) mainly because I'm confused about the literal meaning: Are we supposed to prevent the dog from barking by giving him a juicy bone (one way to interpret "with a juicy bone"), or are we supposed to prevent the dog with a juicy bone in his mouth (another way of interpreting "with a juicy bone") from barking at all? I don't think I really have a handle on what this line means in relation to the other ones, but I'll leave it for now. In the next line, "Silence the pianos" clearly means that the speaker wants no music now that his lover is dead, except for the "muffled drum" (3) that will accompany the coffin and mourners in the fourth line. It's interesting that all of these things so far are sounds—the tick-tock of the clock, the ring of the telephone, a barking dog, music. They all seem to stand in for something, too—for the passing of time, contact with other people (and with pets?), joy as expressed by music.

The image of "aeroplanes" (5) circling overhead (and "moaning" [5]— that's a really good choice of words) writing "He Is Dead" (6) is very strong and would have been a very modern reference at the time of this poem (c. 1936). A *Christian Science Monitor* article about a "skywriting" pilot says that "[s]kywriting's heyday was from the 1930s to the early 1950s when Pepsi Cola used skywriting as its main way of advertising" (Hartill), so the reference here is to a commercial medium being used to make as many people as possible aware of the speaker's loss. If a poet tried to make a reference to something equivalent today, it would have to be a television advertisement or a blog, maybe. I wonder if a modern poet could really pull off a reference to a TV ad and still make it sound sincerely sad.

I'm not sure what the "crêpe bows round the white necks of the public doves" (7) means. Would the bows even be visible? Does "crêpe" imply a color, or is it just a type of fabric? And what is a public dove? I'm not sure I like the repetition in this line of three adjective/noun pairs: "crepe bows," "white necks," "public doves." It seems too precious or "poetic." The "traffic policemen" (8) that I've seen all wear white gloves so that their hand movements can be seen clearly. The speaker wants them all to wear "black cotton gloves," the appropriate color for mourning, but that would probably create real problems for the drivers trying to see what the policemen are directing them to do. So, I wonder if the bows on doves and black gloves on cops are both there to show us that the speaker is feeling not just the sort of grief that moves him to write poetry, but also the sort of intense pain that makes him want to throw the rest of the world into the same confusion and chaos he's experiencing. Or at least, he's not only asking to be alone, but also wanting the rest of the world to share his grief.

In the next four lines, the speaker turns to himself and his lover: "He was my North, my South, my East and West / My working week and my Sunday rest" (9-10). These lines flow so smoothly, with a soothing, regular rhythm; they're almost

Bordland 3

singsongy. But they don't seem sappy or wrong in this poem; they seem painfully sincere. The author uses place (as described by the compass) and time (the whole week, the reference to noon and midnight) to make very clear, in case we hadn't figured it out from the preceding lines, that his lover was everything to him. In the fourth line of this section, this regular rhythm is interrupted, or even stopped dead: "I thought that love would last for ever: I was wrong" (12). This is a very true and moving conclusion to reach, but it also seems ironic, once we read to the end of the poem. If the speaker was wrong to believe (before the death of his lover) that love would last forever, isn't it possible that he's wrong about the conclusion "nothing now can ever come to any good" (16)—that grief will last forever?

I think that Auden probably intended us to be aware of this irony. It seems to me that the poem is broken into three major parts. First, we sympathize with the speaker's grief and sense of loss. Then we're supposed to stop at the point where the speaker makes a judgment about his understanding of the world prior to that loss ("I thought that love would last for ever: I was wrong" [12]) and to spend a moment absorbing the meaning of that judgment. Finally, as we read the most extreme expression of the speaker's loss ("Pack up the moon and dismantle the sun" [14]), we can see that although we sympathize and understand, we also know something that the speaker doesn't know at the moment. Just as his love apparently blinded the speaker to love's inevitable end, so his profound grief is probably blinding him to grief's inevitable end. Also, it may just be me, but it seems that this last part is almost too dramatic or theatrical, as if maybe the speaker has made some sort of transition from being unself-consciously mournful to being self-consciously aware that the way he's expressing himself is poetic.

Back to the idea about the irony: The poem itself seems to be arguing against the notion that love cannot last forever (or, okay, a very long time). After all, people are still reading this poem, and I bet people will continue to read it for as long as people read poetry. That's about as close to forever as we get on this earth, so even though the lovers of this poem are long dead, their love lives on, in a way. Auden must have been aware of this when he was writing the poem. I wonder if he ever said anything in letters, essays, or speeches about art and immortality? If so, I think I'll write a paper on that topic as addressed in this poem.

Bordland 4

WORKS CITED

Auden, W. H. "Stop all the clocks, cut off the telephone." *The Norton Introduction to Literature*, edited by Kelly J. Mays, shorter 13th ed., W. W. Norton, 2020, p. 469.

Hartill, Lane. "Sky Writer." *Christian Science Monitor*, 25 Jan. 2000, www .csmonitor.com/2000/0125/p22s1.html.

12 | LANGUAGE: WORD CHOICE AND ORDER

Fiction and drama depend on language just as poetry does, but in a poem almost everything comes down to the particular meanings and implications, as well as sound and shape, of individual words. When we read stories and plays, we generally focus our attention on character and plot, and although words determine how we imagine those characters and how we respond to what happens to them, we are not as likely to pause over any one word as we may need to when reading a poem, even one with characters and a plot. Because poems are often short and because even long poems are broken up into relatively short lines, much depends on every word in them. Sometimes, as though they were distilled prose, poems contain only the essential words. They say just barely enough to communicate in the most basic way, using elemental signs—each of which is chosen for exactly the right shade of meaning or feeling or both. But elemental does not necessarily mean simple, and these signs may be very rich in their meanings and complex in their effects. The poet's word choice—the **diction** of a poem—determines not only meaning but also just about every effect the poem produces.

PRECISION AND AMBIGUITY

Let's look first at poems that create some of their effects by examining—or playing with—a single word. Here, multiple meanings or the shiftiness, ambiguity, and uncertainty of a word are at issue. The following short poem, for example, depends almost entirely on the ways we use the word "play."

SARAH CLEGHORN
The golf links lie so near the mill

The golf links lie so near the mill
That almost every day
The laboring children can look out
And see the men at play.

1915

While traveling in the American South, Cleghorn had seen, right next to a golf course, a textile mill that employed quite young children. Her poem doesn't *say* that we expect men to work and children to play; it just assumes our expectation and builds an effect of *dramatic irony*—an incongruity between what we expect and what actually occurs—out of the observation. The poem saves almost all of its devastating effect for the final word, after the situation has been carefully described and the irony set up.

In the following poem, a word used over and over acquires multiple meanings and refuses to be limited to a single one. Here, the importance of a word involves its ambiguity (that is, its having more than one possible meaning) rather than its precision or exactness. How many different meanings of the words *lie* and *lay* can you distinguish in the poem?

MARTHA COLLINS
Lies

Anyone can get it wrong, laying low
when she ought to lie, but is it a lie
for her to say she laid him when we know
he wouldn't lie still long enough to let
5   her do it? A good lay is not a song,
not anymore; a good lie is something
else: lyrics, lines, what if you say *dear sister*
when you have no sister, what if you say *guns*
when you saw no guns, though you know
10   they're there? *She laid down her arms; she lay*
down, her arms by her sides. If we don't know,
do we lie if we say? If we don't say, do we lie
down on the job? To arms! in any case
dear friends. If we must lie, let's not lie around.

1999

DENOTATION AND CONNOTATION

Although the unambiguous or "dictionary" meaning of words—that is, their **denotation**—is important, words are more than hard blocks of meaning on whose sense everyone agrees. They also carry emotional force and shades of suggestion. The words we use indicate not only what we mean but also how we feel about it and want to encourage others to feel. A person who holds office is, quite literally (and unemotionally), an *officeholder*—the word denotes what he or she does in a relatively neutral way. But if we want to imply that a particular officeholder is wise, trustworthy, and deserving of political support, we may call that person a *public servant*, a *political leader*, or an *elected official*, whereas if we want to promote distrust or contempt of the same officeholder we might say *politician* or *bureaucrat* or *political hack*. These terms have clear **connotations**—suggestions of emotional coloration that imply our attitude and invite a similar one from our hearers. In poems, as in life, what words connote can be just as important as what they denote.

The following **epitaph**, for example, which describes one person's mixed feelings about another, depends heavily on the connotations of fairly common words.

WALTER DE LA MARE
Slim Cunning Hands

Slim cunning hands at rest, and cozening eyes—
Under this stone one loved too wildly lies;
How false she was, no granite could declare;
   Nor all earth's flowers, how fair.

1950

What the speaker in SLIM CUNNING HANDS remembers about the dead woman—her hands, her eyes—tells part of the story; her physical presence was clearly important to him. The poem's other nouns—*stone, granite, flowers*—all remind us of her death and its finality. All these words denote objects central to the rituals that memorialize a departed life. Granite and stone connote finality as well, while flowers connote fragility and suggest the brevity of life (which is why they have become the symbolic language of funerals). The way the speaker talks about the woman expresses, in just a few words, the complexity of his love for her. She was loved, he says, too "wildly"—by him perhaps, and apparently by others. The excitement she offered is suggested by the word, as is the lack of control. The words *cunning* and *cozening* imply her falsity; they suggest her calculation, cleverness, and untrustworthiness, as well as her skill, persuasiveness, and ability to please. Moreover, coming at the end of the second line, the word *lies* has more than one meaning. The body "lies" under the stone, but falsity has by now become too prominent to ignore as a second meaning. And the word *fair*, a simple yet very inclusive word, suggests how totally attractive the speaker finds her: Her beauty can no more be expressed by flowers than her fickleness can be expressed by something as permanent as words in stone. But the word *fair*, in the emphatic position as the final word, also implies two other meanings that seem to resonate, ironically, with what we have already learned about her from the speaker: "impartial" and "just." "Impartial" she may be in her preferences (as the word *false* suggests), but to the speaker she is hardly "just," and the final defining word speaks both to her appearance and (ironically) to her character. Simple words here tell us perhaps all we need to know of a long story—or at least the speaker's version of it.

Words like *fair* and *cozening* are clearly loaded. They imply more emotionally than they mean literally. They have strong, clear connotations; they tell us what to think, what evaluation to make; and they suggest the basis for the evaluation. Sometimes word choice in poems is less dramatic and less obviously significant. But it is always important. Often simple appropriateness makes the words in a poem work, and words that do not call special attention to themselves can nonetheless be the most effective. Precision of denotation may be just as impressive and productive of specific effects as the resonance or ambiguous suggestiveness of connotation. Often poems achieve their power by a combination of verbal effects, setting off elaborate **figures of speech** or other complicated strategies with simple words chosen to indicate exact actions, moments, or states of mind.

Words are the starting point for all poetry, of course, and almost every word is likely to be significant, either denotatively or connotatively or both. Poets who know their craft pick each word with care to express exactly what needs to be expressed and to suggest every emotional shade that the poem is calculated to evoke in us.

Word Choice: An Example and an Exercise

Before you read the following poem, notice the three words in the title. What do they lead you to expect? What questions do they raise? Jot down your thoughts on a piece of paper. Then, as you read the poem, take note of key words and try to be conscious of the emotional effects and impressions they create.

THEODORE ROETHKE

My Papa's Waltz

The whiskey on your breath
Could make a small boy dizzy;
But I hung on like death:
Such waltzing was not easy.

5 We romped until the pans
Slid from the kitchen shelf;
My mother's countenance
Could not unfrown itself.

The hand that held my wrist
10 Was battered on one knuckle;
At every step you missed
My right ear scraped a buckle.

You beat time on my head
With a palm caked hard by dirt,
15 Then waltzed me off to bed
Still clinging to your shirt.

1948

Exactly how does the situation in My Papa's Waltz and the poem itself fulfill or defy the expectations created by the title? How does the poem answer your questions? How does it characterize the waltz and the speaker's feelings about it? Which words are most suggestive in these terms? What clues are there in the word choice that an adult is remembering a childhood experience? How scared was the boy at the time? How does the grown adult now evaluate the emotions he felt when he was a boy?

WORD ORDER AND PLACEMENT

Individual words qualify and amplify one another—suggestions clarify other suggestions, and meanings grow upon meanings—and thus how words are put together and where individual words are located matters. Notice, for example, that in "Slim Cunning Hands" the final emphasis is on how *fair* in appearance the woman was; the speaker's last word describes the quality he can't forget despite her lack of a different kind of fairness and his distrust of her. Even though it doesn't justify everything else, her beauty mitigates all the disappointment and hurt. Putting the word *fair* at the end of the line and of the poem gives it special emphasis and meaning.

That one word, *fair*, does not stand all by itself, however, any more than any other word in a poem does. Every word exists within larger units of meaning—sentences, patterns of comparison and contrast, the whole poem—and where the word is and how it is used are important. The final word or words may be especially emphatic (as in "Slim Cunning Hands"), and words that are repeated take on a special intensity, as *lie* does in LIES. Certain words may stand out because they are unusual or used in an unusual way (like *unfrown* or *waltzing* in "My Papa's Waltz" (lines 8, 4) or because they are given an artificial prominence—through unusual sentence structure, for example, or because the title calls special attention to them. In a poem, as opposed to a prose work, moreover, the number and placement of words in a line and the spacing of the words and lines stays the same in every printed version. Where words come—in a line, in a stanza—and how they are spatially and visually related to other words also helps to determine their force and meaning.

The subtlety and force of word choice are sometimes strongly affected by **syntax**—the way the sentences are put together. When you find unusual syntax or spacing, you can be pretty sure that something there merits special attention. Notice the odd sentence constructions in the second and third stanzas of "My Papa's Waltz"—the way the speaker talks about the abrasion of buckle on ear in line 12, for example. He does not say that the buckle scraped his ear, as we would expect, but rather "My right ear scraped a buckle." Reversing the expected word order makes a big difference in the effect created; the speaker avoids placing blame and refuses to specify any unpleasant effect. Had he said that the buckle scraped his ear, we would have to worry about the fragile ear. The syntax channels our feeling and helps control what we think of the "waltz."

In the most curious part of the poem, the second stanza, the silent mother appears, and the syntax on both sides of the semicolon is peculiar. In lines 5–6, the connection between the romping and the pans falling is stated oddly: "We romped *until* the pans / Slid from the kitchen shelf" (emphasis added). The speaker does not say that they knocked down the pans or imply awkwardness, but he does suggest energetic activity and duration. He implies intensity, almost intention—as though the romping would not be complete until the pans fell. And the clause about the mother—odd but effective—makes her position clear. A silent bystander in this male ritual, she doesn't seem frightened or angry. She seems to be holding a frown, or to have it molded on her face, as though it were part of her own ritual, and perhaps a facet of her stern character as well. The syntax implies that she *has to* maintain the frown, and the falling of the pans almost seems to be for her benefit. She disapproves, but she remains their audience.

Sometimes poems create, as well, a powerful sense of the way minds and emotions work by varying normal syntactical order in special ways. Listen for and watch, for example, what happens a few lines into the following poem. What does it suggest about what is happening inside the speaker?

SHARON OLDS
Sex without Love

How do they do it, the ones who make love
without love? Beautiful as dancers,
gliding over each other like ice-skaters
over the ice, fingers hooked
5 inside each other's bodies, faces
red as steak, wine, wet as the
children at birth whose mothers are going to
give them away. How do they come to the
come to the   come to the   God   come to the
10 still waters, and not love
the one who came there with them, light
rising slowly as steam off their joined
skin? These are the true religious,
the purists, the pros, the ones who will not
15 accept a false Messiah, love the
priest instead of the God. They do not
mistake the lover for their own pleasure,
they are like great runners: they know they are alone
with the road surface, the cold, the wind,
20 the fit of their shoes, their over-all cardio-
vascular health—just factors, like the partner
in the bed, and not the truth, which is the
single body alone in the universe
against its own best time.

1984

The poem starts calmly enough, with a simple rhetorical question implying that the speaker just cannot understand sex without love. Lines 2–4 carefully compare such sexual activity with two other artful activities, and the speaker—although plainly disapproving—seems coolly in control of the analysis and evaluation. But by the end of the fourth line, something begins to seem odd: "[H]ooked" seems too ugly and extreme a way to characterize the lovers' fingers, however much the speaker may disapprove, and by line 6 the syntax seems to break down. How does "wine" fit the syntax of the line? Is it parallel with "steak," another example of redness? Or is it somehow related to the last part of the sentence, parallel with "faces"? Neither of these possibilities quite works. At best, the punctuation is inadequate; at worst, the speaker's mind is working too fast for the language it generates, scrambling its images. We can't yet be sure what is going on, but by the ninth line the lack of control is manifest with the compulsive repeating (three times) of "come to the" and the interjected "God."

Such verbal behavior—here concretized by the way the poem orders its words and spaces them on the page—invites us to reevaluate the speaker's moralizing relative to her emotional involvement with the issues and with her representation of sexuality itself. The speaker's own values, as well as those who have sex without love, become a subject for evaluation.

Words, the basic materials of poetry, come in many varieties and can be used in many different ways and in myriad—sometimes surprising—combinations. They are seldom simple or transparent, even when we know their meanings and recognize their syntactical combinations as ordinary and conventional. Carefully examining them, individually and collectively, is a crucial part of reading poems, and being able to ask good questions about the words that poems use and the way they use them is one of the most basic, rewarding, and useful skills a reader of poetry can develop.

POEMS FOR FURTHER STUDY

WILLIAM BLAKE
London

> I wander through each chartered[1] street,
> Near where the chartered Thames does flow,
> And mark in every face I meet
> Marks of weakness, marks of woe.
>
> 5 In every cry of every man,
> In every Infant's cry of fear,
> In every voice, in every ban,[2]
> The mind-forged manacles I hear.
>
> How the Chimney-sweeper's cry
> 10 Every black'ning Church appalls;
> And the hapless Soldier's sigh
> Runs in blood down Palace walls.
>
> But most through midnight streets I hear
> How the youthful Harlot's curse
> 15 Blasts the new-born Infant's tear,
> And blights with plagues the Marriage hearse.
>
> 1794

• Does the tone of this poem seem sad, angry, or both? Why and how so? How might the repeated word "chartered" (lines 1, 2) suggest a theme?

GERARD MANLEY HOPKINS
Pied Beauty[3]

> Glory be to God for dappled things—
>   For skies of couple-color as a brinded[4] cow;
>   For rose-moles all in stipple[5] upon trout that swim;

---

1. "Given liberty," but also, ironically, "licensed," "controlled," "preempted as private property."
2. Prohibition, curse, or public condemnation, but also suggesting *banns*, official proclamation of an intended marriage.
3. Particolored beauty: having patches or sections of more than one color.
4. Streaked or spotted.
5. Rose-colored dots or flecks.

Fresh-firecoal chestnut-falls;[6] finches' wings;
5   Landscape plotted and pieced—fold, fallow, and plow;
       And all trades, their gear and tackle and trim.
All things counter, original, spare, strange;
       Whatever is fickle, freckled (who knows how?)
       With swift, slow; sweet, sour; adazzle, dim;
10 He fathers-forth whose beauty is past change;
       Praise him.

                            1887

• How many ways of expressing mixed color can you find in this poem? How does Hopkins expand the meaning of "pied beauty"?

WILLIAM CARLOS WILLIAMS
The Red Wheelbarrow

so much depends
upon

a red wheel
barrow

5 glazed with rain
water

beside the white
chickens.
       1923

• How does setting the words "barrow," "water," and "chickens" on lines of their own help to substantiate the poem's first line?

This Is Just to Say

I have eaten
the plums
that were in
the icebox

5 and which
you were probably
saving
for breakfast

Forgive me
10 they were delicious
so sweet
and so cold
      1934

• What is meant by "This" in the poem's title? What is the apparent occasion for this poem?

6. Fallen chestnuts as red as burning coals.

KAY RYAN
Blandeur

If it please God,
let less happen.
Even out Earth's
rondure, flatten
5 Eiger,[7] blanden
the Grand Canyon.
Make valleys
slightly higher,
widen fissures
10 to arable land,
remand your
terrible glaciers
and silence
their calving,
15 halving or doubling
all geographical features
toward the mean.
Unlean against our hearts.

A. E. STALLINGS
Shoulda, Woulda, Coulda

The mood made him tense—
How she sharpened conditional[8] futures
On strops[9] of might-have-beens,
The butchered present in sutures.

5 He cursed in the fricative,[1]
The way she could not act,
Or live in the indicative,[2]
Only contrary to fact.

Tomorrow should have been vast,
10 Bud-packed, grenade-gravid,[3]
Not just a die miscast.

---

7. Mountain in the Swiss Alps.
8. In grammar, verb mood or tense used in expressing what might happen given the right conditions, as in "She *would eat* if he made her a sandwich."
9. Leather strap or similar device used to sharpen a razor.
1. In phonetics, consonant sound, such as the English *f* or *v*.
2. In grammar, mood of verbs expressing a simple statement of fact.
3. Pregnant, distended with or full of.

It made him sad, it made him livid:
How she construed from the imperfect[4] past
A future less vivid.

2013

- How does this poem end up playing on the various meanings of the words "mood" and "tense" (line 1)? What exactly about the attitude of the woman described in the poem makes her male counterpart first "tense," then "sad" and "livid" (1, 12)?

SUGGESTIONS FOR WRITING

1. Choose one poem in this book in which a single word seems to be especially crucial. Write an essay in which you work out carefully why and how that's the case.
2. Choose one poem in this book in which syntax (the order of words in sentences) or the placement of words on the page seems especially key to the poem's overall effect and meaning. Write an essay explaining how and why considering word order, in either or both of these senses, might change or deepen a reader's understanding of the poem.
3. Language is a topic of (as well as a tool used in) Martha Collins's LIES, A. E. Stallings's SHOULDA, WOULDA, COULDA, and even Kay Ryan's BLANDEUR. Write an essay exploring what any of these poems has to say about poetry or language and how word choice, order, and placement help the poem express or illustrate it.
4. Look up the words *charter* and *ban*, as well as *banns*, in a good online dictionary. Then write an essay explaining how they contribute to the tone and theme of Blake's LONDON. How do all of the varied, even contradictory, meanings of these words matter?

---

4. In grammar, of or relating to a verb tense used to designate a continuing state or incomplete action, especially in the past, as in "We used to speak regularly" and "I was eating."

13 | VISUAL IMAGERY AND FIGURES OF SPEECH

The language of poetry is often visual and pictorial. Rather than depending primarily on abstract ideas and elaborate reasoning, poems depend more on concrete and specific words that create images in our minds. Poems thus help us see things afresh or feel them suggestively through our other physical senses, such as hearing or touch. Sound is, as we will see, a vital aspect of poetry. But most poems use the sense of sight to help us form, in our minds, visual impressions, images that communicate more directly than concepts. We "see" yellow leaves on a branch, a father and son waltzing precariously, or two lovers sitting together on the bank of a stream, so that our response begins from a vivid visual impression of exactly what is happening. Some people think that those media and arts that challenge the imagination of a hearer or reader—radio drama, for example, or poetry—allow us to respond more fully than those (such as television or theater) that actually show things, appealing to our physical senses. Certainly these media leave more to our imagination, to our mind's eye.

Poems are sometimes quite abstract—they can even be *about* abstractions like grandeur or history. But usually they are quite concrete in what they ask us to see. One reason is that they often begin in a poet's mind with a picture or an image: of a person, a place, an event, or any other object of observation. That image may be based on something the poet has actually seen, but it may also be totally imaginary and only based on the "real world" in the sense that it draws on the poet's sense of what the world is like. Even when a poet begins with an idea that draws on visual experience, however, the reader still has to *imagine* (through the poem's words) whatever the poem describes. The poet must rely on words to help the reader flesh out that mental image. In a sense, then, the reader becomes a visual artist, but the poet directs the visualization by evoking specific responses through words. *How* that happens can involve quite complicated verbal strategies—or even *visual* ones that draw on the possibilities of print (see ch. 17).

Seeing in the mind's eye—the re-creation of visual experience—requires different skills from poets and readers. Poets use all the linguistic strategies they can think of to re-create for us something they have already "seen." Poets depend on our having had a rich variety of visual experiences and try to draw on those experiences by using common, evocative words and then refining the process through more elaborate verbal devices. We as readers inhabit the process the other way around, trying to draw on our previous knowledge so that we can "see" by following verbal clues.

The languages of description are quite varied. The visual qualities of poetry result partly from the two aspects of poetic language described in chapter 12: on the one hand, the precision of individual words, and, on the other hand, precision's opposite—the reach, richness, and ambiguity of suggestion that words sometimes accrue. Visualization can also derive from sophisticated rhetorical and literary devices (**figures of speech**, for example, as we will see later in this chapter). But often description begins simply with naming—providing the word (noun, verb, adjective, or adverb) that will trigger images familiar from a reader's own experience. A reader can readily imagine a *dog* or *cat* or *house* or *flower* when each word is named, but not all readers will envision the same kind of dog or flower until the word is qualified in some way. So the poet may specify that the dog is a greyhound or poodle, or that the flower is a daffodil or a lilac; or the poet may indicate colors, sizes, specific movements, or particular identifying features. Such description can involve either narrowing by category (*daffodil* versus *flower*) or expanding through detail ("golden daffodils;/Beside the lake, beneath the trees,"). And often comparisons are either explicitly or implicitly involved. Notice how this works in the three poems below, which move from the least to the most elaborate in their descriptive techniques. As you read each, look for instances of *narrowing by category*, *expanding by detail*, and implicit or explicit *comparing*, and consider how these help to create a vivid, cohesive visual picture of a specific person (in the first two poems) or color and mood (in the third).

DAVID BOTTOMS
Hubert Blankenship

Needing credit, he edges through the heavy door, head down,
and quietly closes the screen behind him.

This is Blankenship, father of five, owner of a plow horse and a cow.

Out of habit he leans against the counter by the stove.
5   He pats the pockets of his overalls

for the grocery list penciled on a torn paper bag,
then rolls into a strip of newsprint

the last of his Prince Albert.[1]
He hardly takes his eyes off his boot, sliced on one side

10   to accommodate his bunion, and hands
the list to my grandfather. Bull of the Woods,[2] three tins

of sardines, Spam, peanut butter, two loaves of bread (Colonial),[3]
then back to the musty feed room

where he ignores the hand truck leaning against the wall

15   and hefts onto his shoulder a hundred-pound bag of horse feed.
He rises to full height, snorting

but hardly burdened,
and parades, head high, to the bed of his pickup.

2015

1. Brand of tobacco, introduced by R. J. Reynolds in 1907, named after the British prince who served as King Edward VII, 1901–10.
2. Brand of chewing tobacco introduced c. 1883.
3. Brand originally introduced by the southern Colonial Baking Company (c. 1928–58).

CLAUDE MCKAY
The Harlem Dancer

Applauding youths laughed with young prostitutes
And watched her perfect, half-clothed body sway;
Her voice was like the sound of blended flutes
Blown by black players upon a picnic day.
5   She sang and danced on gracefully and calm,
The light gauze hanging loose about her form;
To me she seemed a proudly-swaying palm
Grown lovelier for passing through a storm.
Upon her swarthy neck black shiny curls
10 Luxuriant fell; and tossing coins in praise,
The wine-flushed, bold-eyed boys, and even the girls,
Devoured her shape with eager, passionate gaze;
But looking at her falsely-smiling face,
I knew her self was not in that strange place.

                                            1922

LYNN POWELL
Kind of Blue

Not Delft or
delphinium, not Wedgewood[4]
among the knickknacks, not wide-eyed chicory
evangelizing in the devil strip—

5   But way on down in the moonless
            octave below midnight, honey,
            way down where you can't tell cerulean from teal.

Not Mason jars of moonshine, not
waverings of silk, not the long-legged hunger
10 of a heron or the peacock's
iridescent id—

            But Delilahs[5] of darkness, darling,
            and the muscle of the mind
            giving in.

15 Not sullen snow slumped
against the garden, not the first instinct of flame,
not small, stoic ponds, or the cold derangement
of a jealous sea—

---

4. Wedgwood pottery, often of a distinctive blue, manufactured by a company founded in England.
Delft: city in southern Holland renowned for the manufacture of ceramics.
5. Perhaps an allusion to the biblical Delilah, who conspired with the rulers of Philistine to destroy
Samson's strength by seducing him and cutting off his hair.

But bluer than the lips of Lazarus, baby,
20   before Sweet Jesus himself could figure out
what else in the world to do but weep.

2004

More than just a matter of naming, using precise words, and providing basic information, description involves qualification and comparison. Sometimes, as in Lynn Powell's KIND OF BLUE, the poet needs to tell us what *not* to picture, dissociating what the poem describes from other possible images we may have in mind. Different features in the language of description add up to something that describes a whole—a picture or scene—as well as a series of individualized objects.

SIMILE AND ANALOGY

As we've seen, the vividness of the picture writers create in our minds often depends on comparisons. Such comparisons are often made through figures of speech. What we are trying to imagine is pictured in terms of something else familiar to us, and we are asked to think of one thing as if it were something else. Many such comparisons, in which something is pictured or figured forth in terms of something already familiar to us, are taken for granted in daily life. Things we can't see or that aren't familiar to us are imaged as things we already know; for example, God is said to be like a father; Italy is said to be shaped like a boot; life is compared to a forest, a journey, or a sea.

Sometimes, comparisons are made explicitly, as when, in THE HARLEM DANCER, the dancer's "voice" is said to be "like the sound of blended flutes / Blown by black players upon a picnic day" (lines 3–4). Such *explicit* comparisons are called **similes**, and usually (as here) the comparison involves the word *like* or the word *as*. Usually similes are made passingly; they make a quick comparison and usually do not elaborate. Similes sometimes develop into more elaborate comparisons, however, and occasionally, as in the poem below, even govern a poem (in which case they are called **analogies**).

TODD BOSS
My Love for You Is So Embarrassingly

grand . . . would you mind terribly, my groundling,[6]
        if I compared it to the *Hindenburg*[7] (I mean,
    before it burned)—that vulnerable, elephantine

dream of transport, a fabric *Titanic*[8] on an ocean
5   of air? There: with binoculars, dear, you can
    just make me out, in a gondola window, wildly

        flapping both arms as the ship's shadow
        moves like a vagrant country across the
    country where you live in relative safety. I pull

6. Literally, someone on the ground; figuratively, a person of unsophisticated taste, like a spectator who stood in the pit of an Elizabethan theater.
7. German airship destroyed by fire during a failed docking attempt over New Jersey, May 6, 1937.
8. British passenger liner sunk on April 15, 1912, after colliding with an iceberg on its maiden voyage.

10 that oblong shadow along behind me wherever
        I go. It is so big, and goes so slowly, it alters
            ground temperatures noticeably, makes

        housewives part kitchen curtains, wrings
        whimpers from German shepherds. Aren't I
15   ridiculous? Isn't it anachronistic, this

    dirigible devotion, this Zeppelin affection, a moon
        that touches, with a kiss of wheels, the ground
            you take for granted beneath your heels?—

                                                    2011

METAPHOR

When a comparison is implicit, describing something as if it were something else, it
is called a **metaphor**. In the poem that follows, the poet helps us visualize old age
and approaching death through metaphors comparing these with familiar things—
the coming of winter, the approach of sunset, and the dying embers of a fire.

WILLIAM SHAKESPEARE
That time of year thou mayst in me behold

    That time of year thou mayst in me behold
    When yellow leaves, or none, or few, do hang
    Upon those boughs which shake against the cold,
    Bare ruined choirs, where late the sweet birds sang.
5   In me thou see'st the twilight of such day
    As after sunset fadeth in the west;
    Which by and by[9] black night doth take away,
    Death's second self,[1] that seals up all in rest.
    In me thou see'st the glowing of such fire,
10 That on the ashes of his youth doth lie,
    As the deathbed whereon it must expire,
    Consumed with that which it was nourished by.
    This thou perceiv'st, which makes thy love more strong,
    To love that well which thou must leave ere long.

                                                    1609

The first four lines of THAT TIME OF YEAR evoke images of the late autumn, but
notice that the poet does not have the speaker say directly that his physical condition
and age make him resemble autumn. He draws the comparison without stating it as
a comparison: You can see my own state, he says, in the coming of winter, when
almost all the leaves have fallen from the trees. The speaker portrays himself *indirectly* by talking about the passing of the year. Again, then, one thing is pictured *as if*
it were something else. "That time of year" goes on to another metaphor in lines 5–8
and still another in lines 9–12, and each metaphor contributes to our understanding
of the speaker's sense of his old age and approaching death. More important, however, is the way the metaphors give us feelings, an emotional sense of the speaker's
age and of his own attitude toward aging. Through the metaphors we come to under-

9. Shortly.   1. Sleep.

stand, appreciate, and to some extent share the increasing sense of urgency that the poem expresses. Our emotional sense of the poem depends largely on the way each metaphor is developed and by the way each metaphor leads, with its own kind of internal logic, to another, even as later metaphors build on earlier ones. Look back at the poem. What does each metaphor contribute? How does each build on the last?

"That time of year" represents an unusually intricate use of images to organize a poem and focus its emotional impact. Not all poems depend on such a full and varied use of metaphor. Sometimes rather than accumulating metaphors, a poet presents a single metaphor that extends over a section of a poem (in which case it is called an *extended metaphor*) or even over the whole poem (in which case it is called a *controlling metaphor*). The following poem depends from the beginning—even from its title—on a single controlling metaphor.

LINDA PASTAN
Marks

My husband gives me an A
for last night's supper,
an incomplete for my ironing,
a B plus in bed.
5 My son says I am average,
an average mother, but if
I put my mind to it
I could improve.
My daughter believes
10 in Pass/Fail and tells me
I pass. Wait 'til they learn
I'm dropping out.

1978

The speaker in MARKS is obviously less than pleased with the idea of continually being judged, and the metaphor of marks (or grades) as a way of talking about her performance of family duties suggests her irritation. The list of the roles implies the many things expected of her, and the three different systems of marking (letter grades, categories to be checked off on a chart, and pass/fail) detail the difficulties of multiple standards. The poem retains the language of school days all the way to the end ("learn," line 11; "dropping out," 12), and the major effect of the poem depends on the irony of the speaker's surrendering to the metaphor the family has thrust upon her; if she is to be judged as if she were a student, she retains the right to leave the system. Ironically, she joins the system (adopts the metaphor for herself) in order to defeat it.

PERSONIFICATION

Another figure of speech, **personification**, involves treating an abstraction, such as death or justice or beauty, as if it were a person. When "That time of year" talks about the coming of night and of sleep, for example, Sleep is personified as the "second self" of Death (that is, as a kind of "double" for death [line 8]). If personification in this poem is a brief gesture, it proves much more obvious and central in the following poem, though in this case, too, it is death that the poet personifies. How so, and with what implications and effects?

EMILY DICKINSON
Because I could not stop for Death—

Because I could not stop for Death—
He kindly stopped for me—
The Carriage held but just Ourselves—
And Immortality.

5 We slowly drove—He knew no haste
And I had put away
My labor and my leisure too,
For His Civility—

We passed the School, where Children strove
10 At Recess—in the Ring—
We passed the Fields of Gazing Grain—
We passed the Setting Sun—

Or rather—He passed Us—
The Dews drew quivering and chill—
15 For only Gossamer,[2] my Gown—
My Tippet—only Tulle[3]—

We paused before a House that seemed
A Swelling of the Ground—
The Roof was scarcely visible—
20 The Cornice—in the Ground—

Since then—'tis Centuries—and yet
Feels shorter than the Day
I first surmised the Horses' Heads
Were toward Eternity—

c. 1863

METONOMY AND SYNECDOCHE

Simile, analogy, metaphor, and personification all insist on the similarity between two
ostensibly unlike things, things we might normally never think of putting together—a
dancer and a palm tree swaying in the wind, dying and being driven away in a carriage. **Metonymy** instead relies on the fact that we already associate one thing with
another, since it entails referring to a thing by instead naming something else associated with it. Though this sounds complicated, it's not: When you say, "The White
House issued a press release," "Harry and Sally are walking down the aisle this summer," or "The suits disapproved," you aren't speaking literally. Instead you're using
White House as a metonym for the people who work in that building (the U.S. president and his administration); *walking down the aisle* as a metonym for getting married; and *suits* to mean people in authority. The most common type of metonymy—so
common that it is treated as a figure of speech in its own right—is **synecdoche**, which

2. Soft, sheer fabric.   3. Fine net fabric. *Tippet*: shawl.

involves referring to a thing by naming only a part of it, as when we either say that someone has "a lot of mouths to feed" or demand "all hands on deck."

What metonyms can you identify in the following sonnet? What other figures of speech? What does the poet gain from each?

WILLIAM WORDSWORTH
London, 1802

Milton![4] thou should'st be living at this hour:
England hath need of thee: she is a fen
Of stagnant waters: altar, sword and pen,
Fireside, the heroic wealth of hall and bower,
5 Have forfeited their ancient English dower[5]
Of inward happiness.   We are selfish men;
Oh! raise us up, return to us again;
And give us manners, virtue, freedom, power.
Thy soul was like a Star and dwelt apart:
10 Thou hadst a voice whose sound was like the sea;
Pure as the naked heavens, majestic, free,
So didst thou travel on life's common way,
In chearful godliness; and yet thy heart
The lowliest duties on itself did lay.

1807

Figurative Language:
A Comparative Exercise

Indulging in metaphors, personification, and other figures of speech is not the exclusive pastime of poets but something we all do, every day, usually without thinking about it: We "fall head over heels in love" and hope the stock market doesn't "take a dive." Our chairs have "arms" and "legs." We say that the body "houses" the soul. A physician might tell a woman (as one physician did tell a poet whose work appears below) that it's unlikely her "womb could viably house a fetus." Then we look at the house across the street and see a human face staring back at us—with windows for eyes, a door mouth, and so on. One thing poetry can do is to reawaken us to the figures of speech buried in everyday language—to make us see again the visual images they *should* but often no longer do conjure up—and to consider, even feel, their implications.

The two poems below do just that. And both do so by taking as their ostensible subject houses—or rather "house" in general. Yet the two poems are in some ways polar opposites, especially in their use of, and attitude toward, figures of speech. In the first, Tracy K. Smith's ASH, "house" functions as part of

4. Poet John Milton (1608–74), who also wrote pamphlets championing various freedoms, including those of speech and of the press, and backed the anti-royalist cause in the English Civil War.
5. Gift, endowment.

a controlling metaphor, something to which the poem is implicitly comparing another thing that's never named. Identifying that other thing is key to fully experiencing and understanding this riddle-like poem. And doing so will require paying close attention to the specific features, qualities, and actions the poem attributes to "house," in part through yet more figures of speech. The second poem, Emma Bolden's HOUSE IS AN ENIGMA, instead seems to take aim at this very tendency to speak—and even think and *see*—"house" figuratively. What, according to this poem, might be the negative effects of doing so? How does the poem use figures of speech to point out the potential problems with figures of speech—at least or especially those involving "house"?

TRACY K. SMITH
Ash

Strange house we must keep and fill.

House that eats and pleads and kills.

House on legs. House on fire. House infested

With desire. Haunted house. Lonely house.

5 House of trick and suck and shrug.

Give-it-to-me house. *I-need-you-baby* house.

House whose rooms are pooled with blood.

House with hands. House of guilt. House

That other houses built. House of lies

10 And pride and bone. House afraid to be alone.

House like an engine that churns and stalls.

House with skin and hair for walls.

House the seasons singe and douse.

House that believes it is not a house.

2015

EMMA BOLDEN
House Is an Enigma

House is not a metaphor. House has nothing
to do with beak or wing.[6] House is not two

---

6. The phrase *beak and wing* features in many poems, including Christopher Smart's (1722–71) "A Song to David," where it functions as a synecdoche for birds: "every beak and wing / Which cheer the winter, hail the spring" (lines 133–34).

hands held angled towards each other. House is
not its roof or the pine straw on its roof. At night,

5 its windows and doors look nothing like a face.
Its stairs are not vertebrae. Its walls may be

white. They are not pale skin. House does not
appreciate your pun on its panes as pains.

House does not appreciate because house
10 does not have feelings. House has no aesthetic

program. House does what it does, which is
not doing. House does not sit on its foundations.

House exists in its foundations, and when the wind
pushes itself to full gale, house is never the one crying.

2014

ALLUSION

Like many poems, Todd Boss's humorous MY LOVE FOR YOU IS SO EMBARRASSINGLY depends on multiple figures of speech: By comparing his love to the *Hindenburg* and, in turn, the *Hindenburg* (line 2) to the *Titanic* (line 4), the speaker makes use not only of analogy and metaphor but also of **allusion**, a brief reference to a fictitious or actual person, place, or thing and, usually, to the stories or **myth** surrounding it. Like metaphor and simile, allusion allows poets to economically suggest a wealth of sometimes complex images, feelings, and ideas by relying on widely shared literary and cultural knowledge. In this particular case, knowing something about both what happened to the *Hindenburg* and the *Titanic* and what "dream[s]" of human ingenuity and power were destroyed along with them gives us a more specific, vivid picture of how something might be simultaneously "vulnerable" and "elephantine," exhilarating and terrifying, transcendent and potentially disastrous (lines 4, 3).

Sometimes "getting" an allusion or even recognizing one requires us to learn something new. Many of the footnotes in this book aim to help you with that. But whenever you come across a name or other reference in a poem that you don't understand or a phrase that seems oddly familiar, it's well worth your while to consult a reference book or to Google a reliable source. Allusions are one of the ways poems engage with the larger world, participating in a vast conversation they invite and even expect you, too, to be a part of.

Below are two poems that rely on an array of allusions—to everything from historical events, myths, and poems to rock stars. As you read the poems, try not only to spot all the allusions but also to tease out what specifically each contributes to the poem in which it appears.

AMIT MAJMUDAR
Dothead

Well yes, I said, my mother wears a dot.
I know they said "third eye" in class, but it's not

　　　　an *eye* eye, not like that. It's not some freak
　　　　third eye that opens on your forehead like
　5　　on some Chernobyl baby.[7] What it means
　　　　is, what it's *showing* is, there's this unseen
　　　　eye, on the inside. And she's marking it.
　　　　It's how the X that says where treasure's at
　　　　is not the treasure, but as good as treasure.—
10　　All right. What I said wasn't half so measured.
　　　　In fact, I didn't say a thing. Their laughter
　　　　had made my mouth go dry. Lunch was after
　　　　World History; that week was India—myths,
　　　　caste system, suttee,[8] all the Greatest Hits.
15　　The white kids I was sitting with were friends,
　　　　at least as I defined a friend back then.
　　　　So wait, said Nick, does *your* mom wear a dot?
　　　　I nodded, and I caught a smirk on Todd—
　　　　She wear it to the shower? And to bed?—
20　　while Jesse sucked his chocolate milk and Brad
　　　　was getting ready for another stab.
　　　　I said, Hand me that ketchup packet there.
　　　　And Nick said, What? I snatched it, twitched the tear,
　　　　and squeezed a dollop on my thumb and worked
25　　circles till the red planet entered the house of war
　　　　and on my forehead for the world to see
　　　　my third eye burned those schoolboys in their seats,
　　　　their flesh in little puddles underneath,
　　　　pale pools where Nataraja[9] cooled his feet.

　　　　　　　　　　　　　　　　　　　　　　　　　　　2011

PATRICIA LOCKWOOD
What Is the Zoo for What

The word "zoo" is a zoo for the zoo.

A fountain is a zoo for water, the song
is a zoo for sound, the harmonica
is a zoo for the hot breath of Neil Young,[1]
　　　　　vagina is a zoo for baby.

　5　Baby, girl baby, is a zoo for vagina.

7. That is, a baby born with birth defects as a result of the explosion that occurred in April 1986 at the Chernobyl Nuclear Power Plant in Ukraine.
8. Custom of a Hindu widow voluntarily being cremated on her husband's funeral pyre.
9. The Lord of Dancers, an avatar of the Hindu god Shiva, whose ecstatic twirling expresses the cyclic energy of the universe.
1. Influential Canadian singer-songwriter, musician, and activist (b. 1945); though primarily known as a guitarist, Young's only number-one hit, "Heart of Gold" (1972), features one of rock's best-known harmonica solos.

The rose is a zoo for the smell of the rose,
the smell of the rose rattles its cage,
the zookeeper throws something bleeding
to it, the something bleeding is not enough,
10 a toddler fell into the cage of the rose,
the toddler was entirely eaten. His name
was Rilke,[2] it was in all the papers.
A Little Pine Box is a zoo for him now,
                    it said in all the papers.

Then all the kids started doing it. Falling
15 into the violet's cage, approaching the cave
where the smell of violets slept, getting
their whole head clawed off by it.
Neil Young did it to a buttercup
and his face got absolutely mauled.

20 The music that was piped into the zoo
let all the longing escape from it
and it ran riot over the earth, full
of the sight of the smell of a buttercup
rearranging the face of Neil Young,
25 attacking pets at random, attacking
me in my bed as I slept, attacking
the happy wagging ends of my poems.

Can I put Neil Young in a poem.
Will he get trapped in there forever.

30 My voice is a zoo right now for this,
and this paces very much inside it,
it would like very much to escape
and eat hot blood again and go home,
and right down to the restless way
35 I walk I am an argument against zoos.

Zoo is very cruel. Let everything out
and live in the wild. Let it hunt for itself
again. Get the stink of human hand off it.

But the hand is a zoo for hold.

2013

. . .

2. Rainer Maria Rilke (1875–1926), influential German-language poet, known especially for lyrics relying on intensely physical imagery and symbolism. According to one biographer (E. M. Butler), "There is no doubt that roses," in particular, "cast a spell upon Rilke," whose "roses were always explicitly in enclosed spaces: in death-bed chambers, in his study at night, in rose-bowls, bringing summer into a room."

All figurative language involves an attempt to clarify something *and* to prompt readers to feel a certain way about it. Saying that one's love is like a rose implies a delicate and fragile beauty and invites our senses into play so that we can share sensuously a response to appealing fragrance and soft touch, just as the shivering boughs and dying embers in "That time of year" suggest separation and loss at the same time that they invite us to share both the cold sense of loneliness and the warmth of old friendship.

Once you start looking for them, you will find figures of speech in poem after poem; they are among the most common devices through which poets share their visions with us, helping us to see our world and our language anew.

POEMS FOR FURTHER STUDY

WILLIAM SHAKESPEARE
Shall I compare thee to a summer's day?

Shall I compare thee to a summer's day?
Thou art more lovely and more temperate.
Rough winds do shake the darling buds of May,
And summer's lease hath all too short a date.
5   Sometime too hot the eye of heaven shines,
And often is his gold complexion dimmed;
And every fair from fair sometime declines,
By chance or nature's changing course untrimmed.
But thy eternal summer shall not fade,
10   Nor lose possession of that fair thou ow'st,
Nor shall Death brag thou wand'rest in his shade,
When in eternal lines to time thou grow'st.
   So long as men can breathe or eyes can see,
   So long lives this,[3] and this gives life to thee.

1609

- What sort of promise does the speaker make with this poem? Why can he boast that "thy eternal summer shall not fade" (line 9)?

ANONYMOUS
The Twenty-Third Psalm[4]

The Lord is my shepherd; I shall not want.
He maketh me to lie down in green pastures: he leadeth me beside
   the still waters.
He restoreth my soul: he leadeth me in the paths of righteousness
   for his name's sake.

---

3. This poem.
4. Traditionally attributed to King David. This English translation is from the King James Version of the Bible (1611).

Yea, though I walk through the valley of the shadow of death,
    I will fear no evil: for thou art with me;
    thy rod and thy staff they comfort me.
5 Thou preparest a table before me in the presence of mine enemies:
    thou anointest my head with oil; my cup runneth over.
Surely goodness and mercy shall follow me all the days of my life:
    and I will dwell in the house of the Lord for ever.

> • What is the controlling metaphor in this poem? At what point in the psalm
> does the controlling metaphor shift?

JOHN DONNE
Batter my heart, three-personed God[5]

Batter my heart, three-personed God; for You
As yet but knock, breathe, shine, and seek to mend;
That I may rise and stand, o'erthrow me, and bend
Your force, to break, blow, burn, and make me new.
5 I, like an usurped town, to another due,
Labor to admit You, but Oh, to no end!
Reason, Your viceroy[6] in me, me should defend,
But is captived, and proves weak or untrue.
Yet dearly I love You, and would be loved fain,[7]
10 But am betrothed unto Your enemy:
Divorce me, untie or break that knot again,
Take me to You, imprison me, for I,
Except You enthrall me, never shall be free,
Nor ever chaste, except You ravish me.

                                        1633

> • In the poem's controlling metaphor, who is the speaker? Who, or what, is
> God? To whom is the speaker "betrothed" (line 10)?

RANDALL JARRELL
The Death of the Ball Turret Gunner[8]

From my mother's sleep I fell into the State,
And I hunched in its belly till my wet fur froze.
Six miles from earth, loosed from its dream of life,

---

5. From the sequence *Holy Sonnets*.
6. One who rules as the representative of someone of higher rank.   7. Gladly.
8. A ball turret was a Plexiglas sphere set into the belly of a B-17 or B-24 [airplane] and inhabited by two
.50 caliber machine-guns and one man, a short small man. When this gunner tracked with his machine-
guns a fighter attacking his bomber from below, he revolved with the turret; hunched upside-down in his
little sphere, he looked like the foetus in the womb. The fighters which attacked him were armed with
cannon firing explosive shells. The hose was a steam hose [Jarrell's note].

Gunner climbing into ball turret, c. 1942

I woke to black flak and the nightmare fighters.
5   When I died they washed me out of the turret with a hose.

                                                                    1945

• What is meant by "I fell into the State (line 1)"? What do the words "sleep,"
  "dream," and "nightmare" (1, 3, 4) suggest about the situation?

JOY HARJO

The Woman Hanging from the Thirteenth Floor Window

She is the woman hanging from the 13th floor
window. Her hands are pressed white against the
concrete moulding of the tenement building. She
hangs from the 13th floor window in east Chicago,
5   with a swirl of birds over her head. They could
be a halo, or a storm of glass waiting to crush her.

She thinks she will be set free.

The woman hanging from the 13th floor window
on the east side of Chicago is not alone.
10 She is a woman of children, of the baby, Carlos
and of Margaret, and of Jimmy who is the oldest.
She is her mother's daughter and her father's son.

She is several pieces between the two husbands
she has had. She is all the women of the apartment
15 building who stand watching her, watching themselves.

When she was young she ate wild rice on scraped down
plates in warm wood rooms. It was in the farther
north and she was the baby then. They rocked her.

She sees Lake Michigan lapping at the shores of
20 herself. It is a dizzy hole of water and the rich
live in tall glass houses at the edge of it. In some
places Lake Michigan speaks softly, here, it just sputters
and butts itself against the asphalt. She sees
other buildings just like hers. She sees other
25 women hanging from many-floored windows
counting their lives in the palms of their hands
and in the palms of their children's hands.

She is the woman hanging from the 13th floor window
on the Indian side of town. Her belly is soft from
30 her children's births, her worn Levi's swing down below
her waist, and then her feet, and then her heart.
She is dangling.

The woman hanging from the 13th floor hears voices.
They come to her in the night when the lights have gone
35 dim. Sometimes they are little cats mewing and scratching
at the door; sometimes they are her grandmother's voice,
and sometimes they are gigantic men of light whispering
to her to get up, to get up, to get up. That's when she wants
to have another child to hold onto in the night, to be able
40 to fall back into dreams.

And the woman hanging from the 13th floor window
hears other voices. Some of them scream out from below
for her to jump, they would push her over. Others cry softly
from the sidewalks, pull their children up like flowers and gather
45 them into their arms. They would help her, like themselves.
But she is the woman hanging from the 13th floor window,
and she knows she is hanging by her own fingers, her
own skin, her own thread of indecision.

She thinks of Carlos, of Margaret, of Jimmy.
50 She thinks of her father, and of her mother
She thinks of all the women she has been, of all
the men. She thinks of the color of her skin, and
of Chicago streets, and of waterfalls and pines.
She thinks of moonlight nights, and of cool spring storms.
55 Her mind chatters like neon and northside bars.
She thinks of the 4 A.M. lonelinesses that have folded

her up like death, discordant, without logical and
beautiful conclusion. Her teeth break off at the edges.
She would speak.

60 The woman hangs from the 13th floor crying for
the lost beauty of her own life. She sees the
sun falling west over the gray plane of Chicago.
She thinks she remembers listening to her own life
break loose, as she falls from the 13th floor
65 window on the east side of Chicago, or as she
climbs back up to claim herself again.

                                                    1983

• What visual details and figures of speech stand out most in this poem? How
   do they help to characterize the woman, her situation, and her feelings?

14 | SYMBOL

Properly used, the term *symbol* suggests one of the most basic things about poems—their ability to get beyond what words signify and to make larger claims about meanings in the verbal world. All words go beyond themselves. They are not simply a collection of sounds: They signify something beyond their sounds, often things or actions or ideas. Words describe not only a verbal universe but also a world in which actions occur, acts have implications, and events have meaning. Sometimes words signify something beyond themselves, say, *rock* or *tree* or *cloud*, and symbolize something as well, such as solidity or life or dreams. Words can—when their implications are agreed on by tradition, convention, or habit—stand for things beyond their most immediate meanings or significations and become symbols, and even simple words that have accumulated no special power from previous use may be given special significance in special circumstances—in poetry as in life itself.

A **symbol** is, put simply, something that stands for something else. The everyday world is full of examples; a flag, a logo, a trademark, or a skull and crossbones all suggest things beyond themselves, and everyone likely understands what their display indicates, whether or not each viewer shares a commitment to what is thus represented. In common usage a prison symbolizes confinement, constriction, and loss of freedom, and in specialized traditional usage a cross may symbolize oppression, cruelty, suffering, death, resurrection, triumph, or an intersection of some kind (as in *crossroads* and *crosscurrents*). The specific symbolic significance depends on the context; for example, a reader might determine significance by looking at contiguous details in a poem and by examining the poem's attitude toward a particular tradition or body of beliefs. A star means one thing to a Jewish poet and something else to a Christian poet, still something else to a sailor or an actor. In a very literal sense, words themselves are all symbols (they stand for objects, actions, or qualities, not just for letters or sounds), but symbols in poetry are those words and phrases that have a range of reference beyond their literal signification or **denotation**.

THE INVENTED SYMBOL

Poems sometimes create a symbol out of a thing, action, or event that has no previously agreed-upon symbolic significance. Such a symbol is sometimes called an *invented symbol*. The following poem, for example, gives an action symbolic significance.

JAMES DICKEY
The Leap

The only thing I have of Jane MacNaughton
Is one instant of a dancing-class dance.
She was the fastest runner in the seventh grade,
My scrapbook says, even when boys were beginning
5 To be as big as the girls,
But I do not have her running in my mind,
Though Frances Lane is there, Agnes Fraser,
Fat Betty Lou Black in the boys-against-girls
Relays we ran at recess: she must have run

10 Like the other girls, with her skirts tucked up
So they would be like bloomers,
But I cannot tell; that part of her is gone.
What I do have is when she came,
With the hem of her skirt where it should be
15 For a young lady, into the annual dance
Of the dancing class we all hated, and with a light
Grave leap, jumped up and touched the end
Of one of the paper-ring decorations

To see if she could reach it. She could,
20 And reached me now as well, hanging in my mind
From a brown chain of brittle paper, thin
And muscular, wide-mouthed, eager to prove
Whatever it proves when you leap
In a new dress, a new womanhood, among the boys
25 Whom you easily left in the dust
Of the passionless playground. If I said I saw
In the paper where Jane MacNaughton Hill,

Mother of four, leapt to her death from a window
Of a downtown hotel, and that her body crushed-in
30 The top of a parked taxi, and that I held
Without trembling a picture of her lying cradled
In that papery steel as though lying in the grass,
One shoe idly off, arms folded across her breast,
I would not believe myself. I would say
35 The convenient thing, that it was a bad dream
Of maturity, to see that eternal process

Most obsessively wrong with the world
Come out of her light, earth-spurning feet
Grown heavy: would say that in the dusty heels
40 Of the playground some boy who did not depend
On speed of foot, caught and betrayed her.
Jane, stay where you are in my first mind:
It was odd in that school, at that dance.

I and the other slow-footed yokels sat in corners
45   Cutting rings out of drawing paper

Before you leapt in your new dress
And touched the end of something I began,
Above the couples struggling on the floor,
New men and women clutching at each other
50   And prancing foolishly as bears: hold on
To that ring I made for you, Jane—
My feet are nailed to the ground
By dust I swallowed thirty years ago—
While I examine my hands.

1967

Memory is crucial to THE LEAP. The fact that Jane MacNaughton's graceful leap in dancing class has stuck in the speaker's mind all these years means that this leap was important to him, meant something to him, stood for something in his mind. For the speaker, the leap is an "instant" and the "only thing" he has of Jane (lines 2, 1). He remembers its grace and ease, and he struggles at several points to articulate its meaning (16–26, 44–50), but even without articulation or explanation it remains in his head as a visual memory, a symbol of something beyond himself, something he cannot do, something he wanted to be. What that leap stood for, or symbolized, was boldness, confidence, accomplishment, maturity, Jane's ability to go beyond her fellow students in dancing class—the transcending of childhood by someone entering adulthood. Her feet now seem "earth-spurning" (38) in that original leap, and they separate her from everyone else. Jane MacNaughton was beyond the speaker's abilities and any attempt he could make to articulate his hopes, but she was not beyond his dreams. And even before he could say so, she symbolized a dream.

The leap to her death seems cruelly wrong and ironic after the grace of her earlier leap. In memory she is suspended in air, as if there were no gravity, no coming back to earth, as if life could exist as dream. And so the photograph, re-created in precise detail, is a cruel dashing of the speaker's dream—a detailed record of the ending of a leap, a denial of the suspension in which his memory had held her. His dream is grounded; her mortality is insistent. But the speaker still wants to hang on to that symbolic moment (42), which he confronts in a more mature context but will never altogether replace or surrender.

The leap is ultimately symbolic in the *poem*, too, not just in the speaker's mind. In the poem (and for us as readers) its symbolism is double: The first leap symbolizes aspiration, and the second symbolizes the frustration and grounding of high hopes; the two are complementary, one impossible to imagine without the other. The poem is horrifying in some ways, a dramatic reminder that human beings don't ultimately transcend their mortality, their limits, no matter how heroic or unencumbered by gravity they may once have seemed. But the poem is not altogether sad and despairing, partly because it still affirms the validity of the original leap and partly because it creates and elaborates another symbol: the paper chain.

The chain connects Jane to the speaker both literally and figuratively. It is, in part, *his* paper chain that she had leaped to touch in dancing class (18–19), and he thinks of her first leap as "touch[ing] the end of something I began" (47). He and the other earthbound, "slow-footed yokels" (44) made the chain, and it connects them to her original leap, just as a photograph glimpsed in the newspaper connects the speaker to her second leap. And so the paper chain becomes the poem's symbol of linkage, connecting lower accomplishment to higher possibility, the artisan to the artist, material substance to the act of imagination. At the end the speaker examines the hands that made the chain because those hands certify his connection to her and to the imaginative leap she had made for him. The chain thus symbolizes not only the lower capabilities of those who cannot leap like the budding Jane could, but also (later) the connection with her leap as both transcendence and mortality.

Like the leap, the chain is elevated to special meaning, given symbolic significance, only by the poet's treatment of it. A leap and a chain have no necessary significance in themselves—at least no significance that we have all agreed upon—but the poet here makes them significant, symbolic.

THE TRADITIONAL SYMBOL

Some objects and acts have a built-in significance because of past usage in literature, or tradition, or the stories a culture develops to explain itself and its beliefs. Such things have acquired an agreed-upon significance, an accepted value in our minds. They already stand for something before the poet cites them; they are *traditional symbols*. Poets assume that their readers will recognize the traditional meanings of these symbols. Birds, for example, traditionally symbolize flight, freedom from confinement, detachment from earthbound limits, the ability to soar beyond rationality and transcend mortal limits. Traditionally, birds have also been linked with the soul and with imagination, especially poetic imagination, and poets often identify with them as pure and ideal singers of songs.

One traditional symbol, the rose, may be a simple and fairly plentiful flower in its season, but it has so long stood for particular qualities that merely to name it creates predictable expectations. Its beauty, delicacy, fragrance, shortness of life, and depth of color have made it a symbol of the transitoriness of beauty, and countless poets have relied on its accepted symbolism—sometimes to compliment a friend, sometimes to make a point about the nature of symbolism. The following poem draws, in quite a traditional way, on the traditional meanings.

EDMUND WALLER
Song

　　Go, lovely rose!
Tell her that wastes her time and me
　　That now she knows,
When I resemble[1] her to thee,
5　How sweet and fair she seems to be.

　　Tell her that's young,
And shuns to have her graces spied,
　　That hadst thou sprung

1. Compare.

In deserts, where no men abide,
10 Thou must have uncommended died.

    Small is the worth
Of beauty from the light retired;
    Bid her come forth,
Suffer herself to be desired,
15 And not blush so to be admired.

    Then die! that she
The common fate of all things rare
    May read in thee;
How small a part of time they share
20 That are so wondrous sweet and fair!

1645

    The speaker in SONG sends the rose to his love in order to have it speak its traditional meanings of beauty and transitoriness. He counts on accepted symbolism to make his point and hurry her into accepting his advances. The poet does not elaborate or argue these things because he does not need to; he relies on the familiarity of the tradition (though, of course, readers unfamiliar with the tradition will not respond in the same way—that is one reason it is difficult to fully appreciate texts from another linguistic or cultural tradition).

    Poets may use traditional symbols to invoke predictable responses—in effect using shortcuts to meaning by repeating acts of signification sanctioned by time and cultural habit. But often poets examine the tradition even as they employ it, and sometimes they revise or reverse traditional, expected meanings. Symbols do not necessarily stay the same over time, and poets often turn even the most traditional symbols to their own original uses. Knowing the traditions of poetry—reading a lot of poems and observing how they tend to use certain words, metaphors, and symbols—can be very useful in reading new poems, but traditions evolve, and individual poems do highly individual things. Knowing the past never means being able to interpret new texts with certainty. Symbolism makes things happen, but individual poets and texts determine what will happen and how. How does the following poem both draw and comment on the traditional symbolism of roses?

DOROTHY PARKER
One Perfect Rose

A single flow'r he sent me, since we met.
    All tenderly his messenger he chose;
Deep-hearted, pure, with scented dew still wet—
    One perfect rose.

5   I knew the language of the floweret;
    "My fragile leaves," it said, "his heart enclose."
Love long has taken for his amulet
    One perfect rose.

Why is it no one ever sent me yet
10   One perfect limousine, do you suppose?
Ah no, it's always just my luck to get
     One perfect rose.

                                              1937

THE SYMBOLIC POEM

Sometimes symbols—traditional or not—become so insistent in the world of a poem
that the larger referential world is left almost totally behind. In such cases the symbol is everything, and the poem does not just *use* symbols but becomes a symbolic
poem, usually a highly individualized one dependent on a system introduced by the
individual poet. Here is one such poem.

WILLIAM BLAKE
The Sick Rose[2]

O rose, thou art sick.
The invisible worm
That flies in the night
In the howling storm

5   Has found out thy bed
Of crimson joy,
And his dark secret love
Does thy life destroy.
                        1794

William Blake's poem does not seem to be about or refer to a real rose. Rather
the poem is about what the rose represents—not in this case something altogether understandable through the traditional meanings of *rose*.

We usually associate the rose with beauty and love, often with sex; and here several key terms have sexual connotations: "worm," "bed," and "crimson joy" (lines 2,
5, 6). The violation of the rose by the worm is the poem's main concern; the violation seems to have involved secrecy, deceit, and "dark" motives (7), and the result is
sickness rather than the joy of love. The poem is sad; it involves a sense of hurt and
tragedy, nearly of despair. The poem cries out against the misuse of the rose, against
its desecration, implying that instead of a healthy joy in sensuality and sexuality,
there has been in this case destruction and hurt, perhaps because of misunderstanding, repression, and lack of sensitivity.

But to say so much about this poem we have to extrapolate from other poems by
Blake, and we have to introduce information from outside the poem. Fully symbolic
poems often require that we thus go beyond the formal procedures of close reading
that we have discussed so far. As presented in this poem, the rose is not part of the
normal world that we ordinarily see, and it is symbolic in a special sense. The poet

2. In Renaissance emblem books, the scarab beetle, worm, and rose are closely associated: The beetle
feeds on dung, and the smell of the rose is fatal to it.

does not simply take an object from our everyday world and give it special significance, making it a symbol in the same way that James Dickey does with the leap. In
Blake's poem the rose instead seems to belong to its own world, a world made
entirely inside the poem or the poet's head. The rose is not referential, or not primarily so. The whole poem is symbolic; it lives in its own world. But what is the rose
here a symbol of? In general terms, we can say from what the poem tells us; but we
may not be as confident as we can be in the more nearly recognizable world of
"The Leap" or ONE PERFECT ROSE. In THE SICK ROSE, it seems inappropriate to ask
the standard questions: What rose? Where? Which worm? What are the particulars
here? In the world of this poem worms can fly and may be invisible. We are altogether in a world of meanings that have been formulated according to a special
system of knowledge and code of belief. We will feel comfortable and confident in
that world only if we read many poems written by the poet (in this case, William
Blake) within the same symbolic system.

   Negotiation of meanings in symbolic poems can be very difficult indeed. Reading
symbolic poems is an advanced skill that depends on knowledge of context, especially the lives and work of authors and the special literary and cultural traditions
they draw from. But usually the symbols you will find in poems *are* referential of
meanings we all share, and you can readily discover these meanings by carefully
studying the poems themselves.

POEMS FOR FURTHER STUDY

JOHN KEATS
Ode to a Nightingale

I

My heart aches, and a drowsy numbness pains
   My sense, as though of hemlock I had drunk,
Or emptied some dull opiate to the drains
   One minute past, and Lethe-wards[3] had sunk:
5 'Tis not through envy of thy happy lot,
    But being too happy in thine happiness,
      That thou, light-wingèd Dryad[4] of the trees,
        In some melodious plot
   Of beechen green, and shadows numberless,
10   Singest of summer in full-throated ease.

II

O, for a draught of vintage! that hath been
   Cooled a long age in the deep-delvèd earth,
Tasting of Flora[5] and the country green,
   Dance, and Provençal song,[6] and sunburnt mirth!
15 O for a beaker full of the warm South,

3. Toward the river of forgetfulness (Lethe) in Hades, the underworld of classical myth.   4. Wood nymph.
5. Roman goddess of flowers.
6. The medieval troubadours of Provence were famous for their love songs.

Full of the true, the blushful Hippocrene,[7]
  With beaded bubbles winking at the brim,
    And purple-stainèd mouth;
That I might drink, and leave the world unseen,
20 And with thee fade away into the forest dim:

III

Fade far away, dissolve, and quite forget
  What thou among the leaves hast never known,
The weariness, the fever, and the fret
  Here, where men sit and hear each other groan;
25 Where palsy shakes a few, sad, last gray hairs,
  Where youth grows pale, and specter-thin, and dies;
    Where but to think is to be full of sorrow
      And leaden-eyed despairs,
  Where Beauty cannot keep her lustrous eyes,
30 Or new Love pine at them beyond tomorrow.

IV

Away! away! for I will fly to thee,
  Not charioted by Bacchus and his pards,[8]
But on the viewless[9] wings of Poesy,
  Though the dull brain perplexes and retards:
35 Already with thee! tender is the night,
  And haply the Queen-Moon is on her throne,
    Clustered around by all her starry Fays;[1]
      But here there is no light,
  Save what from heaven is with the breezes blown
40 Through verdurous glooms and winding mossy ways.

V

I cannot see what flowers are at my feet,
  Nor what soft incense hangs upon the boughs,
But, in embalmèd[2] darkness, guess each sweet
  Wherewith the seasonable month endows
45 The grass, the thicket, and the fruit-tree wild;
  White hawthorn, and the pastoral eglantine;[3]
    Fast fading violets covered up in leaves;
      And mid-May's eldest child,
  The coming musk-rose, full of dewy wine,
50 The murmurous haunt of flies on summer eves.

VI

Darkling[4] I listen; and, for many a time
  I have been half in love with easeful Death,
Called him soft names in many a musèd rhyme,
  To take into the air my quiet breath;

---

7. Fountain of the Muses on Mt. Helicon, whose waters bring poetic inspiration.
8. The Roman god of wine was sometimes portrayed in a chariot drawn by leopards.
9. Invisible.   1. Fairies.   2. Fragrant, aromatic.   3. Sweetbriar or honeysuckle.   4. In the dark.

55   Now more than ever seems it rich to die,
        To cease upon the midnight with no pain,
            While thou art pouring forth thy soul abroad
                In such an ecstasy!
        Still wouldst thou sing, and I have ears in vain—
60   To thy high requiem become a sod.

                VII
        Thou wast not born for death, immortal Bird!
            No hungry generations tread thee down;
        The voice I hear this passing night was heard
            In ancient days by emperor and clown:
65   Perhaps the selfsame song that found a path
        Through the sad heart of Ruth,[5] when, sick for home,
            She stood in tears amid the alien corn;
                The same that ofttimes hath
        Charmed magic casements, opening on the foam
70   Of perilous seas, in faery lands forlorn.

                VIII
        Forlorn! the very word is like a bell
            To toll me back from thee to my sole self!
        Adieu! the fancy cannot cheat so well
            As she is famed to do, deceiving elf.
75   Adieu! adieu! thy plaintive anthem fades
        Past the near meadows, over the still stream,
            Up the hillside; and now 'tis buried deep
                In the next valley-glades:
        Was it a vision, or a waking dream?
80   Fled is that music:—Do I wake or sleep?

                                                May 1819

• Since birds obviously die, just as humans do, what might the speaker mean
  when he declares, "Thou wast not born for death, immortal Bird!" (line 61)?
  That is, how, according to the poem, is the bird "immortal" in a way the
  speaker isn't? How might this help you begin to understand what the bird
  comes to symbolize in the poem?

ROBERT FROST
The Road Not Taken

Two roads diverged in a yellow wood,
And sorry I could not travel both
And be one traveler, long I stood
And looked down one as far as I could
5   To where it bent in the undergrowth;

---

5. Virtuous Moabite widow who, according to the Old Testament book of Ruth, left her own country to
accompany her mother-in-law, Naomi, back to Naomi's native land. She supported herself as a gleaner.

Then took the other, as just as fair,
And having perhaps the better claim,
Because it was grassy and wanted wear;
Though as for that the passing there
10 Had worn them really about the same,

And both that morning equally lay
In leaves no step had trodden black.
Oh, I kept the first for another day!
Yet knowing how way leads on to way,
15 I doubted if I should ever come back.

I shall be telling this with a sigh
Somewhere ages and ages hence:
Two roads diverged in a wood, and I—
I took the one less traveled by,
20 And that has made all the difference.

                                        1916

• What sort of choices might the fork in the road represent? In these terms,
  what seems most important about the description of the roads? Why and
  how might it matter that the poem's famous last lines (about the great "difference" [line 20] it made to take the road "less traveled by" [19]) are framed
  as something the speaker imagines saying "with a sigh" at some point in the
  distant future (16)?

HOWARD NEMEROV
The Vacuum

The house is so quiet now
The vacuum cleaner sulks in the corner closet,
Its bag limp as a stopped lung, its mouth
Grinning into the floor, maybe at my
5 Slovenly life, my dog-dead youth.

I've lived this way long enough,
But when my old woman died her soul
Went into that vacuum cleaner, and I can't bear
To see the bag swell like a belly, eating the dust
10 And the woolen mice, and begin to howl

Because there is old filth everywhere
She used to crawl, in the corner and under the stair.
I know now how life is cheap as dirt,
And still the hungry, angry heart
15 Hangs on and howls, biting at air.

                                        1955

• What does the vacuum come to symbolize? How might the poem play on
  the various meanings of the word "vacuum"?

ADRIENNE RICH
Diving into the Wreck

First having read the book of myths,
and loaded the camera,
and checked the edge of the knife-blade,
I put on
5   the body-armor of black rubber
the absurd flippers
the grave and awkward mask.
I am having to do this
not like Cousteau[6] with his
10 assiduous team
aboard the sun-flooded schooner
but here alone.

There is a ladder.
The ladder is always there
15 hanging innocently
close to the side of the schooner.
We know what it is for,
we who have used it.
Otherwise
20 it's a piece of maritime floss
some sundry equipment.

I go down.
Rung after rung and still
the oxygen immerses me
25 the blue light
the clear atoms
of our human air.
I go down.
My flippers cripple me,
30 I crawl like an insect down the ladder
and there is no one
to tell me when the ocean
will begin.

First the air is blue and then
35 it is bluer and then green and then
black I am blacking out and yet
my mask is powerful
it pumps my blood with power
the sea is another story
40 the sea is not a question of power
I have to learn alone
to turn my body without force
in the deep element.

6. Jacques-Yves Cousteau (1910–97), French writer and underwater explorer.

And now: it is easy to forget
45   what I came for
among so many who have always
lived here
swaying their crenellated fans
between the reefs
50   and besides
you breathe differently down here.

I came to explore the wreck.
The words are purposes.
The words are maps.
55   I came to see the damage that was done
and the treasures that prevail.
I stroke the beam of my lamp
slowly along the flank
of something more permanent
60   than fish or weed

the thing I came for:
the wreck and not the story of the wreck
the thing itself and not the myth
the drowned face always staring
65   toward the sun
the evidence of damage
worn by salt and sway into this threadbare beauty
the ribs of the disaster
curving their assertion
70   among the tentative haunters.

This is the place.
And I am here, the mermaid whose dark hair
streams black, the merman in his armored body
We circle silently
75   about the wreck
we dive into the hold.
I am she: I am he

whose drowned face sleeps with open eyes
whose breasts still bear the stress
80   whose silver, copper, vermeil cargo lies
obscurely inside barrels
half-wedged and left to rot
we are the half-destroyed instruments
that once held to a course
85   the water-eaten log
the fouled compass

We are, I am, you are
by cowardice or courage
the one who find our way
90   back to this scene

carrying a knife, a camera
a book of myths
in which
our names do not appear.

1972   1973

• What word or phrase first signals that DIVING INTO THE WRECK is to be
understood symbolically, not literally? What are some possible symbolic
interpretations of the wreck and the dive?

ROO BORSON
After a Death

Seeing that there's no other way,
I turn his absence into a chair.
I can sit in it,
gaze out through the window.
5 I can do what I do best
and then go out into the world.
And I can return then with my useless love,
to rest,
because the chair is there.

1989

• Why do you think the speaker chooses to symbolize her absent loved one
with a chair?

BRIAN TURNER
Jundee Ameriki[7]

Many the healers of the body.
Where the healers of the soul?
—AHMAD SHAUQI

At the VA hospital in Long Beach, California,
Dr. Sushruta scores open a thin layer of skin
to reveal an object traveling up through muscle.
It is a kind of weeping the body does, expelling
5 foreign material, sometimes years after injury.
Dr. Sushruta lifts slivers of shrapnel, bits
of coarse gravel, road debris, diamond
points of glass—the minutiae of the story
reconstructing a cold afternoon in Baghdad,
10 November of 2005. The body offers aged cloth
from an *abaya*[8] dyed in blood, shards of bone.
And if he were to listen intently, he might hear

7. American soldier (Arabic).   8. Loose, long robe worn by some Muslim women.

the roughened larynx of this woman calling up
through the long corridors of flesh, saying
15   *Allah al Akbar*,[9] before releasing
her body's weapon, her dark and lasting gift
for this *jundee Ameriki*, who carries fragments
of the war inscribed in scar tissue,
a deep, intractable pain, the dull grief of it
20   the body must learn to absorb.

                                                        2009

• What objects or actions in this poem might operate as symbols, and for what?

AUTHORS ON THEIR WORK

BRIAN TURNER (b. 1967)

From "War and Peace: An Interview with Poet Brian Turner" (2009)*

Iraq will never be finished in our lifetimes—for the veterans who have come back home, for many of them, and then also for the Iraqis, who we can easily forget because we don't have to deal with them. We don't see them, we don't meet them, we don't have to go visit them or help them with anything. They're clear across the horizon in some foreign country. But we are intimately connected.

          • • •

I think people still very much want to talk about these things, but they don't have that avenue. And I do think poetry and art can offer some avenues in, towards the emotional content, not so much the geopolitical possibilities and discussions, but the human content. [. . .] It offers people a way into a moment, and into a world that maybe they've never been a part of or seen and that they can experience a small portion of it and then be reconnected or reengaged to a discussion. I definitely think it's useful.

*"War and Peace: An Interview with Poet Brian Turner." Interview by Stefene Russell. *St. Louis*, 1 Apr. 2009, www.stlmag.com/War-and-Peace-An-Interview-With-Poet-Brian-Turner/.

---

9. Common misrendering of "Allahu akbar," meaning "God is great" or "greatest."

15 | THE SOUNDS OF POETRY

Much of what happens in a poem happens in your mind's eye, but some of it happens in your "mind's ear" and in your voice. Poems are full of meaningful sounds and silences as well as words and sentences. Besides choosing words for their meanings, poets choose words because they have certain sounds, and poems use sound effects to create a mood or establish a tone, just as films do.

Historically, poetry began as an oral phenomenon. Early bards in many cultures chanted or recited their verses, often accompanied by a musical instrument of some kind, and poetry remains a vocal art, dependent on the human voice. Often poems that seem very difficult when looked at silently come alive when read aloud, turned into sound. The music and rhythms become clearer, and saying the words or hearing them spoken is very good practice for learning to hear in your mind's ear when you read silently.

RHYME

Rhyme—repetition or correspondence of the terminal sounds of words—is perhaps the single most familiar sound device poets use, though of course not all poems use it. Early English poetry, in fact, used **alliteration**, instead of rhyming words at the end of the poetic lines, to balance the first and second half of each line, and much, if not most, modern poetry is written in **free verse**—that is, without rhyme or regular **meter**. From the later Middle Ages until the twentieth century, however, the music of rhyme was central to both the sound and the formal conception of most poems in the Western world. Because poetry was originally an oral art (many poems were only later written down, if at all), various kinds of memory devices (sometimes called *mnemonic devices*) were built into poems to help reciters remember them. Rhyme was one such device, and most people still find it easier to memorize poetry that rhymes. The simple pleasure of hearing familiar sounds repeated at regular intervals may help account for the traditional popularity of rhyme. Rhyme also gives poetry a special aural quality that distinguishes it from prose. According to the established taste in eras before our own, there was a decorum or proper behavior in poetry as in other things: A poem should not in any way be mistaken for prose, which was thought to be artistically inferior to poetry and primarily utilitarian.

Some English poets (especially in the Renaissance) did experiment—often very successfully—with unrhymed verse, but the cultural pressure for rhyme was almost constant. Why? Custom, combined with the sense of proper decorum, accounted in part for the assumption that rhyme was necessary to poetry, but there was probably more to it than that. Rather, the poets' sense that poetry was an imitation of larger relationships in the universe made it seem natural to use rhyme to represent or re-create a sense of pattern, harmony, correspondence, symmetry, and order. The sounds of poetry were thus, poets reasoned, reminders of cosmic harmony, of the music of the spheres that animated all creation. In a modern world increasingly perceived as fragmented and chaotic, there may be less of a tendency to assume or assert a sense of harmony and symmetry. It would be too simple to say that rhyme in a poem necessarily means that the poet has a firm sense of cosmic order, or that an unrhymed poem testifies to chaos. But the cultural assumptions of different times have influenced the expectations and practices of both poets and readers.

Rhyme also provides a kind of discipline for the poet, a way of harnessing poetic talents and keeping a rein on the imagination. Robert Frost declared writing free verse pointless, like playing tennis without a net. Frost speaks for many traditional (or so-called *formalist* or *neo-formalist*) poets in suggesting that writing good poetry requires discipline and great care with formal elements such as rhyme or rhythm. Other poets have chosen to play by new rules or to invent their own as they go along, preferring the sparer tones that unrhymed poetry provides. Such poets of course still care about the sounds of their poetry, but they may replace rhyme with other aural devices or mix regular rhyme and meter with more flexible lines, paying tribute to tradition as well as the unexpectedness of experience.

End Rhyme and Rhyme Scheme

When we think of rhyme in poetry, we likely think first of the most common type— *end rhyme*, which occurs when the last words in two or more lines of a poem rhyme with each other. When we speak of a poem's **rhyme scheme**, we refer to its particular pattern of end rhymes. To indicate rhyme scheme, we conventionally assign a different letter of the alphabet to each rhyme sound, reusing the same letter every time the same terminal sound repeats in later lines. Here, for example, are the first two stanzas of Thomas Hardy's THE RUINED MAID, which have a rhyme scheme of *aabb, ccbb* thanks to the way each stanza ends with the very same (long *e*) sound:

"O 'Melia, my dear, this does everything crown!	*a*
Who could have supposed I should meet you in Town?	*a*
And whence such fair garments, such prosperi-ty?"—	*b*
"O didn't you know I'd been ruined?" said she.	*b*
—"You left us in tatters, without shoes or socks,	*c*
Tired of digging potatoes, and spudding up docks;	*c*
And now you've gay bracelets and bright feathers three!"—	*b*
"Yes: that's how we dress when we're ruined," said she.	*b*

Since any two adjacent lines that rhyme form a **couplet**, we could also or instead describe "The Ruined Maid" as a poem comprised entirely of rhyming couplets.

Internal, Slant, and Eye Rhyme

Though end rhyme alone determines a poem's rhyme scheme, it isn't the only kind: *Internal rhyme* occurs when a word within (and thus *internal to*) a line rhymes with another word in the same or adjacent lines, as in the following lines from Samuel Taylor Coleridge's "The Rime of the Ancient Mariner" (internal rhyming words appear in italics):

> In mist or *cloud*, on mast or *shroud*,
> It perched for vespers nine;
> Whiles all the *night*, through fog-smoke *white*,
> Glimmered the *white* moonshine.

Whether end or internal, rhymes differ, too, in type. Technically, rhyme (or what is sometimes called *perfect, true,* or *full rhyme*) requires that words share consonants and vowel sounds, as do "cloud" and "shroud," "night" and "white." When words share one but not the other, we have a version of what's variously called *off, half, near,* or *slant rhyme*—that is, a rhyme slightly "off" or only approximate. (The words *all* and *bowl*, for example, share consonant sounds, but their vowel sounds differ, and the opposite is true of *dark* and *heart*.) Another device more common in poetry written since the later nineteenth century, and (like internal rhyme) ubiquitous in hip-hop lyrics, slant rhyme can produce a variety of effects, all deriving from the poem's failure to provide the sounds our ears expect, whether our brains know it or not. Much the same in reverse is true of *eye rhyme*: As much a visual as an aural device, it occurs, as its name suggests, when words *look* like they should rhyme, but don't, as with *bear* and *ear, Yeats* and *Keats*.

OTHER SOUND DEVICES

Sometimes the sounds in poems just provide special effects, rather like a musical score behind a film, setting the mood and getting us into an appropriate frame of mind. But often sound and meaning go hand in hand, and the poet finds words whose sounds echo the action or make a point by stressing the relationship among words and the things they signify.

A single word that captures or approximates the sound of what it describes, such as *splash* or *squish* or *murmur*, is an *onomatopoeic* word, and the device itself is **onomatopoeia**.

But poets can also turn sound into sense by choosing and ordering words so as to create distinctive, meaningful aural patterns. Rhyme is one such device, but four other important ones are

- **alliteration**—the repetition of usually initial consonant sounds through a sequence of words, as in "In lurid *c*artoon *c*olors, the *b*ig *b*aby / dinosaur steps *b*ackwards" (from Emily Grosholz's "Eden") or "The *W*icked *W*itch of the *W*est";
- **consonance**—the repetition of consonant sounds, especially at the end of words or syllables, without the correspondence of vowel sounds necessary to create rhyme, as in "Abstruser musings" (from Coleridge's FROST AT MIDNIGHT) or "That was a stro*k*e of lu*ck*";
- **assonance**—the repetition of vowel sounds in a sequence of words with different endings, as in "The d*ea*th of the p*oe*t was k*e*pt from his p*oe*ms" (from W. H. Auden's IN MEMORY OF W. B. YEATS); and
- **anaphora**—the repetition of the same word or series of words at or near the beginning of successive sentences or clauses, as in "*It made him* sad, *it made him* livid" (A. E. Stallings's SHOULDA, WOULDA, COULDA). Like the other sound devices here, this one is a favorite of speechwriters as well as poets, as demonstrated by Pat Buchanan's address to the 1992 Republican National Convention: "That's change, all right. But that's *not the kind of*

change America needs. It's *not the kind of change* America wants. And it's *not the kind of change* we can abide in a nation we still call 'God's country.'"

Used effectively, such devices are powerful tools, generating meaning, as well as creating mood or simply providing emphasis. A case in point is the following excerpt from the world's most famous *mock epic*, which describes a scene that may seem at once foreign and familiar to you: A young woman (or "nymph," line 125) sits at a mirrored dressing table (or "toilet," 123), littered with cosmetics and other accoutrements, and, with the help of her lady's maid, prepares herself for the day ahead—fixing her hair, applying makeup, and so on. Given the way these activities are characterized as a distinctly twisted religious ritual (in lines 123–30), what is the effect and significance of alliteration, particularly in line 140 (which here appears in bold)?

ALEXANDER POPE
From The Rape of the Lock

123   And now, unveil'd, the toilet stands displayed,
    Each silver vase in mystic order laid.
125 First, rob'd in white, the nymph intent adores
    With head uncover'd, the cosmetic pow'rs.
    A heav'nly image in the glass appears,
    To that she bends, to that her eyes she rears;
    Th' inferior priestess,[1] at her altar's side,
130 Trembling, begins the sacred rites of pride.
    Unnumber'd treasures ope at once, and here
    The various off'rings of the world appear;
    From each she nicely culls with curious[2] toil,
    And decks the goddess with the glitt'ring spoil.
135 This casket India's glowing gems unlocks,
    And all Arabia breathes from yonder box.
    The tortoise here and elephant unite,
    Transform'd to combs, the speckled and the white.[3]
    Here files of pins extend their shining rows,
140 **Puffs, powders, patches, bibles, billet-doux.**[4]
    Now awful[5] beauty puts on all its arms;
    The fair each moment rises in her charms,
    Repairs her smiles, awakens ev'ry grace,
    And calls forth all the wonders of her face

                            1712, 1714

1. That is, the lady's maid.   2. Strange, unusual.
3. The hair combs, in other words, are made from tortoiseshell (which is "speckled") and ivory from an elephant's tusk (which is "white").
4. Love letter (French). *Patches*: tiny pieces of silk or plaster worn to hide a blemish or heighten one's beauty.   5. Awe-inspiring.

SOUND POEMS

The following poems place especially heavy emphasis on sound and aural patterning. As you read them, try to identify which sound devices they use and with what effects.

HELEN CHASIN
The Word *Plum*

The word *plum* is delicious

pout and push, luxury of
self-love, and savoring murmur

full in the mouth and falling
5 like fruit

taut skin
pierced, bitten, provoked into
juice, and tart flesh

question
10 and reply, lip and tongue
of pleasure.

1968

ALEXANDER POPE
Sound and Sense[6]

337 But most by numbers[7] judge a poet's song,
And smooth or rough, with them, is right or wrong;
In the bright muse though thousand charms conspire,[8]
340 Her voice is all these tuneful fools admire,
Who haunt Parnassus[9] but to please their ear,
Not mend their minds; as some to church repair,
Not for the doctrine, but the music there.
These, equal syllables[1] alone require,
345 Though oft the ear the open vowels tire,
While expletives[2] their feeble aid do join,
And ten low words oft creep in one dull line,
While they ring round the same unvaried chimes,

6. From *An Essay on Criticism*, Pope's poem on the art of poetry and the problems of literary criticism. The passage excerpted here follows a discussion of several common weaknesses of critics—failure to regard an author's intention, for example, or overemphasis on clever metaphors and ornate style.
7. Meter, rhythm, sound. 8. Unite.
9. Mountain in Greece, traditionally associated with the Muses and considered the seat of poetry and music. 1. Regular accents. 2. Filler words, such as "do."

With sure returns of still expected rhymes.
350 Where'er you find "the cooling western breeze,"
In the next line, it "whispers through the trees";
If crystal streams "with pleasing murmurs creep,"
The reader's threatened (not in vain) with "sleep."
Then, at the last and only couplet fraught
355 With some unmeaning thing they call a thought,
A needless Alexandrine[3] ends the song,
That, like a wounded snake, drags its slow length along.
Leave such to tune their own dull rhymes, and know
What's roundly smooth, or languishingly slow;
360 And praise the easy vigor of a line,
Where Denham's strength and Waller's[4] sweetness join.
True ease in writing comes from art, not chance,
As those move easiest who have learned to dance.
'Tis not enough no harshness gives offense,
365 The sound must seem an echo to the sense:
Soft is the strain when Zephyr[5] gently blows,
And the smooth stream in smoother numbers flows;
But when loud surges lash the sounding shore,
The hoarse, rough verse should like the torrent roar.
370 When Ajax[6] strives, some rock's vast weight to throw,
The line too labors, and the words move slow;
Not so, when swift Camilla[7] scours the plain,
Flies o'er th' unbending corn, and skims along the main.
Hear how Timotheus'[8] varied lays surprise,
375 And bid alternate passions fall and rise!
While, at each change, the son of Libyan Jove[9]
Now burns with glory, and then melts with love;
Now his fierce eyes with sparkling fury glow,
Now sighs steal out, and tears begin to flow:
380 Persians and Greeks like turns of nature[1] found,
And the world's victor stood subdued by sound!
The pow'r of music all our hearts allow,
And what Timotheus was, is Dryden now.

1711

Helen Chasin's poem THE WORD *PLUM* savors the sounds of the word as well as the taste and feel of the fruit itself. It is almost as if the poem is tasting the sounds and rolling them slowly on the tongue. The alliterative second and third lines even

---

3. Line of six metrical feet, sometimes used in pentameter poems to vary the pace mechanically. Line 357 is an alexandrine.
4. Sir John Denham and Edmund Waller, seventeenth-century poets credited with perfecting the heroic couplet.   5. The west wind.   6. Greek hero of the Trojan War, noted for his strength.
7. A woman warrior in Virgil's *Aeneid*.
8. Court musician of Alexander the Great, celebrated in a famous poem by John Dryden (see line 383) for the power of his music over Alexander's emotions.
9. In Greek tradition, the chief god of any people was often given the name Zeus (Jove), and the chief god of Libya (the Greek name for all of Africa) was called Zeus Ammon. Alexander visited his oracle and was proclaimed son of the god.   1. Similar alternations of emotion.

replicate the *p*, *l*, *uh*, and *m* sounds of the word while imitating the squishy sounds of eating the fruit. Words like "delicious" and "luxury" sound juicy, and other words, such as "murmur," imitate sounds of satisfaction and pleasure. Even the process of eating is in part re-created aurally. The tight, clipped sounds of "taut skin / pierced" (lines 6–7) suggest the way teeth sharply break the skin and slice quickly into the soft flesh of a plum, and the words describing the tartness ("provoked," "question," 7, 9) force the lips to pucker and the tongue and palate to meet and hold, as if the mouth were savoring a tart fruit. The poet is having fun here refashioning the sensual appeal of a plum, teasing the sounds and meanings out of available words. The words must mean something appropriate and describe something accurately first of all, of course, but when they also imitate the sounds and feel of the process they describe, they do double duty.

Written in a very different era and style, Pope's SOUND AND SENSE uses a number of echoic or onomatopoeic words. In some lines pleasant and unpleasant consonant sounds underline a particular point or emphasize a mood. When the poet talks about a particular weakness in poetry, he illustrates it at the same time—by using open vowels (line 345), expletives (346), monosyllabic words (347), predictable rhymes (350–53), or long, slow lines (357). He similarly illustrates the good qualities of poetry as well (360, for example). But the main effects of the passage come from an interaction of several ingenious strategies at once. In lines 339 and 340, for example, Pope produces complex sound effects in addition to the harmony of a rhyming couplet ("conspire," "admire"). Assonance echoes in the *oo* vowel sounds in "muse," "tuneful," and "fools"; alliteration repeats consonants in "*r*ight or *wr*ong" and "tune*ful fools*." Ironically, the *muse*-ical voice here is a bit out of tune to those who have good poetic taste: Pope intends the *r* and *f* sounds to feel both cute and awkward, as a comment on people who only want easy listening and miss poetry's other "charms," including its meaning (compared to the "doctrine" that is the real purpose of a church service, in line 343).

With a similar technique of demonstrating principles of poetic style and taste, the pace of lines 347, 357, and 359 is controlled by clashing consonant sounds as well as long vowels. Line 347 seems much longer than it is because almost every one-syllable word ends in a consonant that refuses to blend with the beginning of the next word, making the words hard to say without distinct, awkward pauses between them. In lines 357 and 359, long vowels such as those in "wounded," "snake," "slow," "along," "roundly," and "smooth" slow down the pace, and awkward, hard-to-pronounce consonants are again juxtaposed. The commas also provide nearly full stops in the middle of these lines to slow us down still more. Similarly, the harsh lashing of the shore in lines 368–69 is accomplished partly by onomatopoeia and partly by the dominance of rough consonants in line 369. (In Pope's time, the English *r* was still trilled gruffly so that it could be made to sound extremely *rrr*ough and ha*rrrsh*.) Almost every line in this passage demonstrates how to make sound echo sense.

POETIC METER

We can thank the ancient Greeks for systematizing an understanding of meter and providing a vocabulary (including the words *rhythm* and *meter*) that enables us to discuss the art of poetry. *Meter* comes from a Greek word meaning "measure": What we measure in the English language are the patterns of stressed (or accented) syllables that occur naturally when we speak, and, just as when we measure length, the unit we use in measuring poetry is the **foot**. Most traditional poetry in English uses the accentual-syllabic form of meter—meaning that its rhythmic pattern is based on both a set number of syllables per line and a regular pattern of accents in each line. Not all poems have a regular metrical pattern, and not all metered poems follow only one pattern throughout. But like everyday speech, the language of poetry always has *some* accents (as in this italic emphasis on "some"), and poets arrange that rhythm for effect. Thus in nonmetrical as well as metrical poetry, a reader should "listen" for patterns of stress.

The Basic Metrical Feet of Poetry in English

iamb: an unstressed or unaccented syllable followed by a stressed or accented one ("she wént," "belíeve"). This meter is called *iambic*.

trochee: a stressed syllable followed by an unstressed one ("méter," "Hómer"). This meter is called *trochaic*.

anapest: two unstressed syllables followed by a stressed one ("comprehénd," "after yóu"). This meter is called *anapestic*.

dactyl: a stressed syllable followed by two unstressed ones ("róundabout," "dínnertime"). This meter is called *dactylic*.

rising or falling: the above feet either begin or end with the stressed syllable, as if they lose or gain momentum or "height." Hence iambic and anapestic are called rising meters, and trochaic and dactylic are called falling meters.

Other Kinds of Feet

spondee: two stressed syllables. Spondaic feet vary or interrupt the prevailing rhythm, emphasizing a syllable that we would expect to be unstressed ("Lást cáll," "Dón't gó").

pyrrhic: two unstressed syllables. Pyrrhic feet similarly interrupt the expected rising or falling beats, placing an unstressed syllable where we expect an emphasis ("ŭntŏ," "ĭs ă").

Spondees and pyrrhic feet depend on prevailing meter and usually appear singly or only a few times in a row. It is difficult to imagine (or to write or speak) a line or sentence that either has no unstressed syllables—a constant strong beat (spondaic)—or lacks stressed syllables—a rippling monotone (pyrrhic).

Because the concept of meter derives from poetic traditions in Greek and Latin that counted syllables rather than accents, other possible combinations of syllables acquired names, for instance, *amphibrach* (unstressed, stressed, unstressed—noted by Coleridge in his demonstration of meter, METRICAL FEET, below). But since most meter in poetry in English depends on accents rather than the number of syllables, the terms above cover most of the variations that you will encounter.

Counting Feet, or Meter

A line of poetry is subdivided into feet in order to "measure" its meter. The terms are easy enough to understand if you recall geometry or other numeric terminology. Remember that this is a count *not* of the number of syllables but of stresses; thus, for example, monometer could have two or three syllables per line.

monometer:	one foot
dimeter:	two feet
trimeter:	three feet
tetrameter:	four feet
pentameter:	five feet
hexameter:	six feet
heptameter:	seven feet
octameter:	eight feet

Counting the number of feet—that is, the number of accents, stresses, or strong beats per line—helps you identify the *kind* of feet in the line. Thus the terms are combined: *Iambic pentameter* has five iambs per line; *trochaic tetrameter* has four trochees per line, and so on.

Scansion

Scansion is the technique of listening to and marking stressed and unstressed syllables, counting the syllables and feet. Often, you will need to scan several lines before you can be sure of the "controlling" metrical pattern or "base meter" of a poem.

In the following poem, Samuel Taylor Coleridge playfully names and illustrates many types of meter. By marking syllables himself as stressed or unstressed, he also illustrates how scansion works.

SAMUEL TAYLOR COLERIDGE
Metrical Feet

Lesson for a Boy[2]

Trōchĕe trīps frŏm lōng tŏ shōrt;[3]
From long to long in solemn sort
Slōw Spōndēe stālks; strōng fōōt! yet ill able
Ēvĕr tŏ cōme ŭp wĭth Dāctўl trĭsўllăblĕ.
5   Ĭāmbĭcs mārch frŏm shōrt tŏ lōng—
With ă lēāp ănd ă bōūnd thĕ swĭft Ānăpĕsts thrōng;
One syllable long, with one short at each side,
Ămphībrăchўs hāstes wĭth ă stātelў stride—
Fīrst ănd lāst bēĭng lōng, mĭddlĕ shōrt, Amphĭmācer
10   Strīkes hĭs thūndērĭng hōōfs līke ă prōūd hīgh-brĕd Rācer.
If Derwent be innocent, steady, and wise,

2. Written originally for Coleridge's son Hartley, the poem was later adapted for his younger son, Derwent.
3. Long and short marks over syllables are Coleridge's.

And delight in the things of earth, water, and skies;
Tender warmth at his heart, with these meters to show it,
With sound sense in his brains, may make Derwent a poet—
15   May crown him with fame, and must win him the love
Of his father on earth and his Father above.
                    My dear, dear child!
Could you stand upon Skiddaw,[4] you would not from its whole ridge
See a man who so loves you as your fond s. t. coleridge.

                                                          1806

Hearing a poem properly involves practice—listening to others read poetry and especially listening to yourself as you read poems aloud. Your dictionary will show you the stresses for every word of more than one syllable, and the governing stress of individual words will largely control the patterns in a line: If you read a line for its sense (almost as if it were prose), you will usually see the line's basic pattern. But single-syllable words can be a challenge because they may or may not be stressed, depending on their syntactic function and the full meaning of the sentence. Normally, important functional words, such as one-syllable nouns and verbs, are stressed (as in normal conversation or in prose), while conjunctions (such as *and* or *but*), prepositions (such as *on* or *with*), and articles (such as *an* or *the*) are unstressed.

Here are the first two lines of Alexander Pope's "Sound and Sense," marked to show the stressed syllables:

But móst | by núm- | bers júdge | a pó- | et's sóng,
And smóoth | or róugh, | with thém, | is ríght | or wróng.

These lines, like so many in English literature, provide an example of *iambic pentameter*—that is, each line consists of five iambic feet. Notice that there is nothing forced or artificial in the sound of these lines; the words flow easily. In fact, linguists contend that English is naturally iambic, and even the most ordinary, "unpoetic" utterances often fall into this pattern: "Please tell me if you've heard this one before." "They said she had a certain way with words." "The baseball game was televised at nine."

Here are a few more examples of various meters.

iambic pentameter: "In sé- | quent tóil | all fór- | wards dó | conténd" (William Shakespeare, Like as the waves . . .)
trochaic octameter: "Ónce u- | pón a | mídnight | dréary, | whíle I | póndered, | wéak and | wéary" (Edgar Allan Poe, The Raven)
anapestic tetrameter: "There are mán- | y who sáy | that a dóg | has his dáy" (Dylan Thomas, The Song of the Mischievous Dog)

Although scanning lines of poetry by reading them aloud, marking syllables as unstressed or stressed, and adding up feet may seem like a counting game that has little to do with poetry's meaning, it is an important way to understand the sound effects of a poem. Like different styles of music, different meters tend to express different moods or to suit different themes. When you know the basic meter of a poem, you are more alert to subtle variations in the pattern. Poets avoid the predictable or

---

4. Mountain in the lake country of northern England (where Coleridge lived in his early years), near the town of Derwent.

the lulling by using certain "change-ups" in the dominant meter or line length, such as substitution of a different foot (e.g., a trochee or spondee instead of an iamb); **caesura**, a short pause within a line often signaled by punctuation; or **enjambment**, extending the end of the grammatical sentence beyond the end of the poetic line.

Notice that the following example is perfectly regular dactylic hexameter until the final foot, a trochee. Also notice that Longfellow has placed a caesura within a long line.

> "Thís is the | fórest pri- | méval. The | múrmuring | pínes and the | hémlocks" (Henry Wadsworth Longfellow, *Evangeline*)

Substitution of one metrical foot for another—to accommodate idioms and conversational habits or to create a special effect—is quite common, especially in the first foot of a line. Shakespeare often begins an iambic line with a trochee:

> Líke as | the wáves | make towárds | the péb- | bled shóre

Or consider this line from John Milton's *Paradise Lost*, a poem written mainly in iambic pentameter:

> Rócks, cáves, | lákes, féns, | bógs, déns, | and Shádes | of Déath

Here Milton substitutes three spondees for the first three iambs in a pentameter line. John Dryden's "To the Memory of Mr. Oldham" arguably begins with two spondees, a pyrrhic, and an iamb before settling into a regular iambic pentameter:

> Fárewéll, | tóo lít | tle, and | tóo láte | ly knówn

As Dryden's poem shows, meter does leave room for discussion; some readers might read the line above as iambic throughout, and others might read the last three feet as iambic: The natural emphasis on the first word after the caesura, "and," could make the predictable word "too" unstressed. The way you actually read a line, once you have "heard" the basic rhythm, is influenced by two factors: normal pronunciation and prose sense (on the one hand) and the predominant pattern of the poem (on the other). Since these two forces are constantly in tension and are sometimes contradictory, you can almost never fully predict the actual reading of a line, and good reading aloud (like every other art) depends less on formula than on subtlety and flexibility. And, again, very good readers sometimes disagree about whether or not to stress certain syllables. We have noted the use of substitution, and many poems since around 1900 have taken liberties with meter and rhyme. Some poets (such as Marianne Moore) have favored counting syllables rather than accents. Even more widespread is free verse, which does without any governing pattern of stresses or line lengths.

Scansion: An Exercise

Each of the following poems is written in a different meter. Using the terms defined in "Poetic Meter" (on pp. 523–24), as well as in Coleridge's poem "Metrical Feet," pair the following poems with their corresponding meters (e.g., iambic pentameter). (The answers are on p. 529.)

1. ANONYMOUS

There was a young girl from St. Paul

There was a young girl from St. Paul,
Wore a newspaper-dress to a ball.
    The dress caught on fire
    And burned her entire
Front page, sporting section and all.

(Note that this poem is a **limerick** and uses a meter common to this subgenre.)

2. ALFRED, LORD TENNYSON

From The Charge of the Light Brigade[5]

1.

Half a league, half a league,
    Half a league onward,
All in the valley of Death
    Rode the six hundred.
5 "Forward, the Light Brigade!
"Charge for the guns!" he said:
Into the valley of Death
    Rode the six hundred.

2.

    "Forward, the Light Brigade!"
10 Was there a man dismay'd?
Not tho' the soldier knew
    Someone had blunder'd:
Theirs not to make reply,
Theirs not to reason why,
15 Theirs but to do and die:
Into the valley of Death
    Rode the six hundred.

1854

---

5. On October 25, 1854—during the Crimean War—miscommunication among commanders led a British cavalry troop to charge directly into a Russian artillery assault, leading to heavy casualties and an ignominious defeat.

3. JANE TAYLOR

The Star

'Twinkle, twinkle, little star,
How I wonder what you are!
Up above the world so high,
Like a diamond in the sky.

5 When the blazing sun is gone,
When he nothing shines upon,
Then you show your little light,
Twinkle, twinkle, all the night.

Then the trav'ller in the dark,
10 Thanks you for your tiny spark;
He could not see which way to go,
If you did not twinkle so.

In the dark blue sky you keep,
And often through my curtains peep,
15 For you never shut your eye
Till the sun is in the sky.

As your bright and tiny spark
Lights the trav'ller in the dark,
Though I know not what you are,
20 Twinkle, twinkle, little star.

1806

4. ANNE BRADSTREET

To My Dear and Loving Husband

If ever two were one, then surely we.
If ever man were loved by wife, then thee;
If ever wife was happy in a man,
Compare with me ye women if you can.
5 I prize thy love more than whole mines of gold,
Or all the riches that the East doth hold.
My love is such that rivers cannot quench,
Nor aught but love from thee give recompense.
Thy love is such I can no way repay;
10 The heavens reward thee manifold, I pray.
Then while we live, in love let's so persever,
That when we live no more we may live ever.

1678

ANSWERS TO SCANSION EXERCISE: 1. anapestic trimeter (1; 2; 5) and dimeter (3–4),
2. dactylic dimeter, 3. trochaic tetrameter, 4. iambic pentameter

Sound and Sense: A Comparative Exercise

To get a vivid sense of the difference sound can make to the tone and meaning of a poem—and just how you can *use* what you've learned about meter, rhyme, and other sound devices—try comparing the two following poems, both inspired by World War I (1914–18). The first is the most famous of several poems originally published in the British newspaper the *Daily Mail* by Jessie Pope (1868–1941), an English journalist famous, before the war, as a writer of light verse. The second poem is the work of Wilfred Owen (1893–1918), an aspiring English poet who voluntarily enlisted in 1915 (the same year Pope's poem appeared) and, from January 1917, served as an officer on the French front. Begun some nine months later, during Owen's hospitalization for shell shock, and originally entitled "To Jessie Pope," his poem is in some ways as much about traditional poetic representations of war as it is about war itself.

As you read the two poems, pay careful attention to how each uses all of the various sound devices discussed in this chapter, particularly meter and rhyme. How precisely do such sound effects contribute to the poems' very different tones and themes and their very different views of war?

JESSIE POPE
The Call

> Who's for the trench—
>   Are you, my laddie?
> Who'll follow French[6]—
>   Will you, my laddie?
> 5 Who's fretting to begin,
> Who's going out to win?
> And who wants to save his skin—
>   Do you, my laddie?
>
> Who's for the khaki suit—
> 10   Are you, my laddie?
> Who longs to charge and shoot—
>   Do you, my laddie?
> Who's keen on getting fit,
> Who means to show his grit,
> 15 And who'd rather wait a bit—
>   Would you, my laddie?
>
> Who'll earn the Empire's[7] thanks—
>   Will you, my laddie?

6. Field-Marshall John French (1852–1925), commander in chief of the British Expeditionary Force for the first two years of World War I (1914–16).

7. At the start of World War I, the British Empire was the largest in human history, covering over eleven million square miles of the earth's surface; the desire to maintain or expand the empire was one major cause of the war.

Who'll swell the victor's ranks—
20   Will you, my laddie?
When that procession comes,
Banners and rolling drums—
Who'll stand and bite his thumbs—
     Will you, my laddie?

                                    1915

WILFRED OWEN
Dulce et Decorum Est[8]

Bent double, like old beggars under sacks,
Knock-kneed, coughing like hags, we cursed through sludge,
Till on the haunting flares we turned our backs
And towards our distant rest began to trudge.
5 Men marched asleep. Many had lost their boots
But limped on, blood-shod. All went lame; all blind;
Drunk with fatigue; deaf even to the hoots
Of disappointed shells that dropped behind.

Gas! Gas! Quick, boys!—An ecstasy of fumbling,
10 Fitting the clumsy helmets just in time;
But someone still was yelling out and stumbling
And floundering like a man in fire or lime.—
Dim, through the misty panes and thick green light
As under a green sea, I saw him drowning.

15 In all my dreams, before my helpless sight,
He plunges at me, guttering, choking, drowning.

If in some smothering dreams you too could pace
Behind the wagon that we flung him in,
And watch the white eyes writhing in his face,
20 His hanging face, like a devil's sick of sin;
If you could hear, at every jolt, the blood
Come gargling from the froth-corrupted lungs,
Obscene as cancer, bitter as the cud
Of vile, incurable sores on innocent tongues,—
25 My friend, you would not tell with such high zest
To children ardent for some desperate glory,
The old Lie: Dulce et decorum est
Pro patria mori.

                                    1917

8. Part of a phrase from Horace (Roman poet and satirist, 65–68 BCE), quoted in full in the last lines of Owen's poem: "It is sweet and proper to die for one's country" (Latin).

POEMS FOR FURTHER STUDY

WILLIAM SHAKESPEARE
Like as the waves make towards the pebbled shore

Like as the waves make towards the pebbled shore,
So do our minutes hasten to their end,
Each changing place with that which goes before,
In sequent toil all forwards do contend.[9]
5   Nativity, once in the main[1] of light,
Crawls to maturity, wherewith being crowned,
Crooked[2] eclipses 'gainst his glory fight,
And Time that gave doth now his gift confound.[3]
Time doth transfix[4] the flourish set on youth
10 And delves the parallels[5] in beauty's brow,
Feeds on the rarities of nature's truth,
And nothing stands but for his scythe to mow.
And yet to times in hope[6] my verse shall stand,
Praising thy worth, despite his cruel hand.

1609

• Which lines in this poem vary the basic iambic meter? What is the effect of these variations?

GERARD MANLEY HOPKINS
The Windhover[7]

To Christ our Lord

I caught this morning morning's minion,[8] king-
    dom of daylight's dauphin,[9] dapple-dawn-drawn Falcon, in his riding
    Of the rolling level underneath him steady air, and striding
High there, how he rung upon the rein of a wimpling[1] wing
5   In his ecstasy! then off, off forth on swing,
    As a skate's heel sweeps smooth on a bow-bend: the hurl and gliding
    Rebuffed the big wind. My heart in hiding
Stirred for a bird,—the achieve of, the mastery of the thing!

Brute beauty and valor and act, oh, air, pride, plume, here
10   Buckle![2] AND the fire that breaks from thee then, a billion
    Times told lovelier, more dangerous, O my chevalier![3]

---

9. Struggle. *Sequent*: successive.   1. High seas. *Nativity*: newborn life.   2. Perverse.
3. Bring to nothing.   4. Pierce.
5. Lines, wrinkles.   6. The future.
7. Small hawk, the kestrel, which habitually hovers in the air, headed into the wind.
8. Favorite, beloved.   9. Heir to regal splendor.   1. Rippling.
2. Several meanings may apply: to join closely, to prepare for battle, to grapple with, to collapse.
3. Horseman, knight.

No wonder of it: shéer plód makes plow down sillion[4]
Shine, and blue-bleak embers, ah my dear,
   Fall, gall themselves, and gash gold-vermilion.
1877

• What aural devices does Hopkins use here? How do they help him both to
characterize the bird and its flight and to express (even reproduce in us) the
speaker's feeling about them?

WALT WHITMAN
A Noiseless Patient Spider

A noiseless patient spider,
I marked where on a little promontory it stood isolated,
Marked how to explore the vacant vast surrounding,
It launched forth filament, filament, filament, out of itself,
5 Ever unreeling them, ever tirelessly speeding them.

And you O my soul where you stand,
Surrounded, detached, in measureless oceans of space,
Ceaselessly musing, venturing, throwing, seeking the spheres to
    connect them,
Till the bridge you will need be formed, till the ductile anchor hold,
10 Till the gossamer thread you fling catch somewhere, O my soul.
1881

• Like all poems in free verse, Whitman's lacks regular meter and rhyme: By
what other means does he here create meaningful sound effects?

KEVIN YOUNG
Ode to Pork

I wouldn't be here
without you. Without you
I'd be umpteen
pounds lighter & a lot
5 less alive. You stuck
round my ribs even
when I treated you like a dog
dirty, I dare not eat.
I know you're the blues
10 because loving you
may kill me—but still you
rock me down slow
as hamhocks on the stove.
Anyway you come
15 fried, cured, burnt

---

4. Narrow strip of land between furrows in an open field divided for separate cultivation.

to within one inch
of your life I love. Babe,
I revere your every
nickname—bacon, chitlin,
20   cracklin, sin.
Some call you murder,
shame's stepsister—
then dress you up
& declare you white
25   & healthy, but you always
come back, sauced, to me.
Adam himself gave up
a rib to see yours
piled pink beside him.
30   Your heaven is the only one
worth wanting—
you keep me all night
cursing your four-
letter name, the next
35   begging for you again.

                                    2007

• How do sound effects contribute to the tone of ODE TO PORK? to the poem's
  characterization of the speaker's relationship to pork? How might they
  make the poem sound like a blues song?

MARY, LADY CHUDLEIGH
To the Ladies

Wife and servant are the same,
But only differ in the name:
For when that fatal knot is tied,
Which nothing, nothing can divide,
5   When she the word *Obey* has said,
And man by law supreme has made,
Then all that's kind is laid aside,
And nothing left but state[5] and pride.
Fierce as an eastern prince he grows,
10   And all his innate rigor shows:
Then but to look, to laugh, or speak,
Will the nuptial contract break.
Like mutes, she signs alone must make,
And never any freedom take,
15   But still be governed by a nod,
And fear her husband as her god:
Him still must serve, him still obey,
And nothing act, and nothing say,

5. Social position.

But what her haughty lord thinks fit,
20 Who, with the power, has all the wit.
Then shun, oh! shun that wretched state,
And all the fawning flatterers hate.
Value yourselves, and men despise:
You must be proud, if you'll be wise.

1703

- What might the speaker mean when she says a husband "with the power, has all the wit" (line 20)? How might that statement multiply the meanings of the poem's last line?

SUGGESTIONS FOR WRITING

1. Read Pope's Sound and Sense carefully twice—once silently and once aloud—and then mark the stressed and unstressed syllables. Single out all the lines that have major variations from the basic iambic pentameter pattern. Pick out six lines with variations that seem to you worthy of comment, and write a paragraph on each in which you show how the variation contributes to the specific effects achieved in that line and the corresponding point Pope conveys about poetic style.

2. Try your hand at writing limericks in imitation of There was a young girl from St. Paul; study the rhythmic patterns and line lengths carefully, and imitate them exactly in your poem. Begin your limerick with "There once was a _____ from _____" (using a place for which you think you can find a comic rhyme).

3. Write an essay exploring how Wilfred Owen uses meter (including substitutions) and rhyme, as well as other sound devices, in Dulce et Decorum Est both to capture the experience of war and its effects and to respond critically to traditional war poetry, perhaps by comparing this poem to Jessie Pope's The Call. If you choose to draw on Pope's poem, however, you might also want to consider how the poem works and means differently when titled Dulce et Decorum Est rather than (as it originally was) "To Jessie Pope."

4. Pope's Sound and Sense contains this advice for poets: "But when loud surges lash the sounding shore, / The hoarse, rough verse should like the torrent roar" (lines 368–69). In other words, he counsels that the sound of the poet's description should match the sense of what the poem is describing. Write an essay in which you examine the sound and sense in Shakespeare's Like as the waves make towards the pebbled shore or any other poem in this chapter. How does the poem achieve a harmony of meaning and sound?

5. Write an essay in which you discuss any poem in this book in which sound seems a more important element than anything else, even the meaning of words. What is the point of writing and reading this kind of poetry? Can it achieve its effects through silent reading, or must it be experienced aloud?

16 | INTERNAL STRUCTURE

"Proper words in proper places": That is how one great writer of English prose, Jonathan Swift, described good writing. A good poet finds appropriate words, and already we have looked at some implications for readers of the verbal choices a poet makes. But the poet must also decide where to put those words—how to arrange them for maximum semantic, as well as visual and aural, effect—because individual words, figures of speech, symbols, and sounds exist not only within phrases and sentences and rhythmic patterns, but also within the larger whole of the poem. How should the words be arranged and the poem organized? What comes first and what last? What principle or idea of organization will inform the poem? How do the parts combine into a whole? And what is the effect of that arrangement? Considering these questions from the poet's point of view (What is my plan? Where shall I begin? Where do I want to go?) can help us notice the effects of structural choices.

DIVIDING POEMS INTO "PARTS"

It's useful to think of most poems—whether narrative, dramatic, or **lyric**—as informally divisible into parts, distinguished from each other by shifts in subject matter or topic, in **tone**, in address, in tense, or in mode (from narration to reflection or description, for example), and so on. As you read a new poem, look out for such shifts, however subtle, to determine how many parts you think the poem has and how each part relates to, and builds on, the one before. The following lyric, for example, seems to have two parts. How does each part relate to the other? What differentiates and connects them?

PAT MORA
Sonrisas

I live in a doorway
between two rooms, I hear
quiet clicks, cups of black
coffee, *click, click* like facts
5   budgets, tenure, curriculum,
from careful women in crisp beige
suits, quick beige smiles
that seldom sneak into their eyes.

I peek
10 in the other room señoras

in faded dresses stir sweet
milk coffee, laughter whirls
with steam from fresh *tamales*
   sh, sh, mucho ruido,[1]
15 they scold one another,
press their lips, trap smiles
in their dark, Mexican eyes.

1986

This poem's two parts closely resemble each other in that each describes the women who inhabit one of the "two rooms" the speaker "live[s]" "between." Both descriptions include sights ("crisp beige / suits," "faded dresses"), sounds ("quiet clicks," "laughter"), and even the suggestion of tastes ("black / coffee," "sweet / milk coffee"). Yet the relation between the two parts and the two rooms is clearly one of contrast ("crisp [. . .] / suits" *versus* "faded dresses," "quiet clicks" *versus* "laughter," etc.). Here different languages, habits, sights, sounds, and values characterize the worlds symbolized by the two rooms, and the poem is organized around the contrast between them. The meaning of the poem (the difference between the two worlds and the experience of living between them) is very nearly the same as the structure.

To fully understand that meaning and the poem, we would need to tease out all those contrasts and their implications. We would also need to consider the significance of the author's choice not only to make the two parts essentially equal in length, but also to order them as she does. How would the poem and our sense of the speaker's feelings about the two rooms be different if we simply rearranged its **stanzas**, as follows?

I live in a doorway
between two rooms, I hear señoras
in faded dresses stir sweet
milk coffee, laughter whirls
with steam from fresh *tamales*
sh, sh, mucho ruido,
they scold one another,
press their lips, trap smiles
in their dark, Mexican eyes.

I peek
in the other room, I hear
quiet clicks, cups of black
coffee, *click, click* like facts
budgets, tenure, curriculum,
from careful women in crisp beige
suits, quick beige smiles
that seldom sneak into their eyes.

1. A lot of noise (Spanish).

INTERNAL VERSUS EXTERNAL OR FORMAL "PARTS"

In Sonrisas, the internal division created by the speaker's shift in focus (from one room and world to another) corresponds to the poem's formal or "external" division into two stanzas and two sentences. Internal and external or formal divisions need not always coincide with each other, however. Major shifts in a poem can and do occur in the middle of a stanza, a line, even a sentence. Take the following poem. Only one sentence and one stanza long, it has no formal divisions at all. Yet it, too, arguably divides into two parts. As you read the poem, consider whether you agree and, if so, where you think the shift occurs.

GALWAY KINNELL
Blackberry Eating

I love to go out in late September
among the fat, overripe, icy, black blackberries
to eat blackberries for breakfast,
the stalks very prickly, a penalty
5 they earn for knowing the black art
of blackberry-making; and as I stand among them
lifting the stalks to my mouth, the ripest berries
fall almost unbidden to my tongue,
as words sometimes do, certain peculiar words
10 like *strengths* or *squinched*,
many-lettered, one-syllabled lumps,
which I squeeze, squinch open, and splurge well
in the silent, startled, icy, black language
of blackberry-eating in late September.

                                    1980

The poem's first eight lines relate the speaker's experience of just what the title leads us to expect—blackberry eating. But notice what happens in line 9: The speaker's focus shifts from the topic of blackberries to the topic of words, with the word "as" signaling that we're entering the second phase of an **analogy** (or extended **simile**) comparing the experience we've just read about (eating blackberries) to the one we now begin to read about (forming words), with both berries and words "fall[ing] almost unbidden to [the] tongue" (line 8). Here, then, the relation between the poem's two parts and the two objects and experiences they describe is one of likeness rather than contrast (as in "Sonrisas"). Fittingly enough for a poem about connection and comparison, as well as vaguely round "lumps" of things (11), the poem's final line ends with the same words as its first ("in late September"). In a sense, then, the poem might be described as having a circular, as well as two-part (or "bipartite"), structure.

LYRICS AS INTERNAL DRAMAS

Obviously, not all poems consist of only two parts, as do those above. The following poem, for example, arguably divides into three parts. Just as important, in this poem the relationship between the parts seems to be one of development, tracing a change of outlook or attitude *within* the speaker.

SEAMUS HEANEY
Punishment[2]

I can feel the tug
of the halter at the nape
of her neck, the wind
on her naked front.

5   It blows her nipples
to amber beads,
it shakes the frail rigging
of her ribs.

I can see her drowned
10 body in the bog,
the weighing stone,
the floating rods and boughs.

Under which at first
she was a barked sapling
15 that is dug up
oak-bone, brain-firkin:

her shaved head
like a stubble of black corn,
her blindfold a soiled bandage,
20 her noose a ring

to store
the memories of love.
Little adulteress,
before they punished you

25 you were flaxen-haired,
undernourished, and your
tar-black face was beautiful.
My poor scapegoat,

I almost love you
30 but would have cast, I know,
the stones of silence.
I am the artful voyeur

of your brain's exposed
and darkened combs,
35 your muscles' webbing
and all your numbered bones:

2. According to the Roman historian Tacitus (c. 56–120 CE), Germanic peoples punished adulterous women by first shaving their heads and then banishing or killing them. In 1951, in Windeby, Germany, the naked body of a young girl from the first century CE was pulled from the bog where she had been murdered. In modern Ireland, "betraying sisters" (line 38) were sometimes punished by the Irish Republican Army (I.R.A.) for associating with British soldiers.

I who have stood dumb
when your betraying sisters,
cauled[3] in tar,
40   wept by the railings,

who would connive
in civilized outrage
yet understand the exact
and tribal, intimate revenge.
                    1975

In PUNISHMENT, the first shift seems to come in line 23 (again, in the middle of a stanza rather than its beginning): Up to this point, the speaker has described the long-dead girl in the third person (e.g., "*her* neck," "*her* nipples," lines 3, 5; emphasis added). And despite his twice-repeated emphasis on his own perceptions and responses ("*I* can feel," "*I* can see," 1, 9; emphasis added), the girl herself gets most of the attention. Starting in line 23, however, the speaker begins to speak to the girl directly, addressing her in the second person ("you") and through **epithets** ("Little adulteress," "poor scapegoat," 23, 28). Verb tense shifts, too ("were," 25), as the speaker begins to imagine the girl's life "before they punished" her (24). In at least two ways, then, the speaker seems to be coming closer to the girl, now seeing and addressing her as a human being with a history rather than as a thing to be looked at and talked *about*. At the same time, the speaker focuses more on himself as well, expressing his emotions ("I almost love you," 29) and reflecting somewhat critically on the way he looked at the girl's body—and allowed us to—earlier in the poem ("I am the artful voyeur," 32).

Subject matter and tense shift again, however, in line 37: The poem's final two stanzas consider the speaker's behavior toward the "betraying sisters" (38) in an indeterminate past ("I [. . .] have," 37), as if here he describes not one specific experience, but rather a composite of many. Aside from the "your," in line 38, the girl herself seems to have disappeared from the poem (so much so that even that "your" now seems potentially ambiguous: Might it now also refer to someone else?). Though in this poem, unlike BLACKBERRY EATING, we don't have the word *as* to signal an analogy, it seems clear that Heaney's speaker has, over the course of the poem, come to see a similarity between his attitude toward the long-dead girl and the "betraying sisters," the behavior of those responsible for these women's punishments, and even between writing a poem about such women and punishing them. How and why so?

Though "Punishment" is by no means a dramatic poem in the literal sense, it does—like some other lyrics—relate an internal drama of sorts, tracing the process through which its speaker comes to see or accept, as well as share with us, some truth about or insight into the world or himself that he didn't see or accept previously, somewhat as a fictional character might in a dramatic or narrative poem or in a short story. In reading and writing about such poems, a good topic to explore might be what insight the speaker comes to over the course of the poem, and when and why so.

3. Wrapped or enclosed as if in a caul (the inner fetal membrane of higher vertebrates that sometimes covers the head at birth).

Analyzing Internal Structure: An Exercise

Like "Punishment," both of the following poems trace a development in their speakers' perceptions of themselves or the world around them, even if the realizations to which the speakers come and the processes by which they get there differ. As you read each poem, think about where and why the shifts come both in the poem and in the speaker's outlook. In which poem does the change within the speaker seem to happen *during* the poem itself (as in "Punishment"), and which poem might instead depict the change as one that happened at some earlier, unspecified point in time?

SAMUEL TAYLOR COLERIDGE
Frost at Midnight

The frost performs its secret ministry,
Unhelped by any wind. The owlet's cry
Came loud—and hark, again! loud as before.
The inmates of my cottage, all at rest,
5   Have left me to that solitude, which suits
Abstruser musings: save that at my side
My cradled infant slumbers peacefully.
'Tis calm indeed! so calm, that it disturbs
And vexes meditation with its strange
10   And extreme silentness. Sea, hill, and wood,
This populous village! Sea, and hill, and wood,
With all the numberless goings on of life,
Inaudible as dreams! the thin blue flame
Lies on my low burnt fire, and quivers not;
15   Only that film,[4] which fluttered on the grate,
Still flutters there, the sole unquiet thing.
Methinks, its motion in this hush of nature
Gives it dim sympathies with me who live,
Making it a companionable form,
20   Whose puny flaps and freaks the idling Spirit
By its own moods interprets, every where
Echo or mirror seeking of itself,
And makes a toy of Thought.

                        But O! how oft,
How oft, at school, with most believing mind,
25   Presageful, have I gazed upon the bars,
To watch that fluttering stranger! and as oft
With unclosed lids, already had I dreamt

4. In all parts of the kingdom these films are called *strangers* and supposed to portend the arrival of some absent friend [Coleridge's note]. The "film" is a piece of soot fluttering on the bar of the grate.

Of my sweet birth-place, and the old church-tower,
Whose bells, the poor man's only music, rang
30 From morn to evening, all the hot Fair-day,
So sweetly, that they stirred and haunted me
With a wild pleasure, falling on mine ear
Most like articulate sounds of things to come!
So gazed I, till the soothing things I dreamt
35 Lulled me to sleep, and sleep prolonged my dreams!
And so I brooded all the following morn,
Awed by the stern preceptor's face, mine eye
Fixed with mock study on my swimming book:
Save if the door half opened, and I snatched
40 A hasty glance, and still my heart leaped up,
For still I hoped to see the stranger's face,
Townsman, or aunt, or sister more beloved,
My play-mate when we both were clothed alike!⁵

Dear Babe, that sleepest cradled by my side,
45 Whose gentle breathings, heard in this deep calm,
Fill up the interspersed vacancies
And momentary pauses of the thought!
My babe so beautiful! it thrills my heart
With tender gladness, thus to look at thee,
50 And think that thou shalt learn far other lore
And in far other scenes! For I was reared
In the great city, pent 'mid cloisters dim,
And saw nought lovely but the sky and stars.
But thou, my babe! shalt wander like a breeze
55 By lakes and sandy shores, beneath the crags
Of ancient mountain, and beneath the clouds,
Which image in their bulk both lakes and shores
And mountain crags: so shalt thou see and hear
The lovely shapes and sounds intelligible
60 Of that eternal language, which thy God
Utters, who from eternity doth teach
Himself in all, and all things in himself.
Great universal Teacher! he shall mould
Thy spirit, and by giving make it ask.

65   Therefore all seasons shall be sweet to thee,
Whether the summer clothe the general earth
With greenness, or the redbreast sit and sing
Betwixt the tufts of snow on the bare branch
Of mossy apple-tree, while the nigh thatch
70 Smokes in the sun-thaw; whether the eave-drops fall
Heard only in the trances of the blast,

---

5. Late eighteenth-century custom called for all infants to wear dresses, regardless of gender.

Or if the secret ministry of frost
Shall hang them up in silent icicles,
Quietly shining to the quiet Moon.

1798

- Coleridge described some of his poems, including FROST AT MID-
  NIGHT, as having a circular structure. How and why might this poem
  seem circular, or in what way does its end resemble its beginning? In
  what way are the two different? How might the resemblance and difference help us recognize the change in the speaker's outlook?

SHARON OLDS
The Victims

When Mother divorced you, we were glad. She took it and
took it, in silence, all those years and then
kicked you out, suddenly, and her
kids loved it. Then you were fired, and we
5   grinned inside, the way people grinned when
Nixon's helicopter lifted off the South
Lawn for the last time.[6] We were tickled
to think of your office taken away,
your secretaries taken away,
10 your lunches with three double bourbons,
your pencils, your reams of paper. Would they take your
suits back, too, those dark
carcasses hung in your closet, and the black
noses of your shoes with their large pores?
15 She had taught us to take it, to hate you and take it
until we pricked with her for your
annihilation, Father. Now I
pass the bums in doorways, the white
slugs of their bodies gleaming through slits in their
20 suits of compressed silt, the stained
flippers of their hands, the underwater
fire of their eyes, ships gone down with the
lanterns lit, and I wonder who took it and
took it from them in silence until they had
25 given it all away and had nothing
left but this.

1984

- How are the speaker's shifting attitudes toward her father (and the
  poem's parts) both related and differentiated by repetition of the
  word "took"?

---

6. When Richard Nixon resigned the U.S. presidency on August 8, 1974, his exit from the White
House (by helicopter from the lawn) was televised live.

MAKING ARGUMENTS ABOUT STRUCTURE

Dividing a poem into parts and analyzing its internal structure as we have here isn't an exact science: Different readers might well come to slightly different conclusions about the nature, timing, and significance of key shifts and thus about how many parts a poem might be said to have, how one part relates to another, and what sort of whole those parts create. It seems quite possible, for example, to argue that THE VICTIMS has either two parts or three, depending on what you make of lines 15–17 (up to the word "Now"), or that FROST AT MIDNIGHT has three, four, even five parts. In these cases, as in many others, there is no single correct answer. Indeed, ample room for disagreement is in a way precisely the point: Formulating your own ideas about where important shifts come in a poem and why they're important, identifying good evidence to support your conclusions, and considering alternative ways of understanding the poem's structure may take you far down the path to developing your own argument about how the poem as a whole works and means.

POEMS WITHOUT "PARTS"

As we've seen, too, dividing a poem into parts is simply a useful way to *begin* to explore and analyze its structure rather than the entire point or end of such analysis. And this is all the more obviously true with those poems that contain no major shifts and thus no distinct "parts" at all. Such poems nonetheless have a distinct structure; their authors, too, must figure out how to organize their material so as to create something like a beginning, middle, and end. And here, too, such structural choices determine how the poem moves and means. The following poem is a case in point: One sentence and one stanza long, with no major shifts, how does it nonetheless manage both to cohere and to develop? What picture of America results both from its particular details and from the way they are organized?

WALT WHITMAN
I Hear America Singing

I hear America singing, the varied carols I hear,
Those of mechanics, each one singing his as it should be blithe and
    strong,
The carpenter singing his as he measures his plank or beam,
The mason singing his as he makes ready for work, or leaves off work,
5 The boatman singing what belongs to him in his boat, the deckhand
    singing on the steamboat deck,
The shoemaker singing as he sits on his bench, the hatter singing as he
    stands,
The wood-cutter's song, the ploughboy's on his way in the morning, or
    at noon intermission or at sundown,
The delicious singing of the mother, or of the young wife at work, or of
    the girl sewing or washing,
Each singing what belongs to him or her and to none else,

10 The day what belongs to the day—at night the party of young fellows,
        robust, friendly,
     Singing with open mouths their strong melodious songs.

                                                            1860

    By limiting himself to a single sentence and a single stanza, which nonetheless refers to a multitude of people and "songs," Whitman produces a poem that structurally embodies the motto on the U.S. seal—*e pluribus unum*, "Out of many, one." The "many ones" with whom the poem begins are all ordinary men who work with their hands: From "mechanics" (line 2) to a "boatman" (5) and "ploughboy" (7), they work on land and shore, in city and country. Though line 8 doesn't constitute a major shift, it does subtly broaden the poem's picture of America: Women enter the poem; and though they, too, are depicted "at work," the fact that they are identified specifically as a "mother," "young wife," and "girl" introduces, too, the idea both of generations and of family, two important social groups that intervene between many individuals, on the one hand, and an entire country, on the other. Finally, at the poem's end, we move from "day" to "night" and from labor to leisure, in a way that makes clear that these oppositions and time itself have also been structuring principles all along: Line 4, after all, describes the mason as singing "as he makes ready for [. . .] or leaves off work," line 7 the ploughboy and wood-cutter each making "his way in the morning, or at noon intermission or at sundown." By its close, then, the poem has shown us a full day of life in Whitman's version of America and in the lives of those whose various, unique "carols" (1) combine to create a single American song.

POEMS FOR FURTHER STUDY

As you read each of the following poems, consider the following questions: Does the poem seem to divide into internal "parts"? If so, where and why? What are the major shifts? How does each part build on the last? How do the parts combine into a meaningful whole? If the poem doesn't seem divisible into parts, what are its organizing principles? How does the poem build and develop, and what overall picture or even **theme** results?

WILLIAM SHAKESPEARE
Th' expense of spirit in a waste of shame

Th' expense of spirit in a waste[7] of shame
Is lust in action; and, till action, lust
Is perjured, murderous, bloody, full of blame,
Savage, extreme, rude, cruel, not to trust;
5 Enjoyed no sooner but despisèd straight:
Past reason hunted; and no sooner had,
Past reason hated, as a swallowed bait,
On purpose laid to make the taker mad:
Mad in pursuit, and in possession so;
10 Had, having, and in quest to have, extreme;
A bliss in proof,[8] and proved, a very woe;

7. Using up; also, desert. *Expense*: expending.   8. In the act.

Before, a joy proposed; behind, a dream.
All this the world well knows; yet none knows well
To shun the heaven that leads men to this hell.

1609

• Paraphrase this poem. What emotional stages accompany the carrying out
of a violent or lustful act? Is Shakespeare an insightful psychologist? What
is his major insight about how lust works?

PERCY BYSSHE SHELLEY
Ode to the West Wind

I

O wild West Wind, thou breath of Autumn's being,
Thou, from whose unseen presence the leaves dead
Are driven, like ghosts from an enchanter fleeing,

Yellow, and black, and pale, and hectic red,
5 Pestilence-stricken multitudes: O thou,
Who chariotest to their dark wintry bed

The wingèd seeds, where they lie cold and low,
Each like a corpse within its grave, until
Thine azure sister of the Spring shall blow

10 Her clarion[9] o'er the dreaming earth, and fill
(Driving sweet buds like flocks to feed in air)
With living hues and odors plain and hill:

Wild Spirit, which art moving everywhere;
Destroyer and preserver; hear, oh, hear!

II

15 Thou on whose stream, mid the steep sky's commotion,
Loose clouds like earth's decaying leaves are shed,
Shook from the tangled boughs of Heaven and Ocean,

Angels[1] of rain and lightning: there are spread
On the blue surface of thine aëry surge,
20 Like the bright hair uplifted from the head

Of some fierce Maenad,[2] even from the dim verge
Of the horizon to the zenith's height,
The locks of the approaching storm. Thou dirge

Of the dying year, to which this closing night
25 Will be the dome of a vast sepulcher,
Vaulted with all thy congregated might

9. Trumpet call.   1. Messengers.   2. Frenzied female votary of Dionysus, the Greek god of vegetation and fertility who was supposed to die in the fall and rise again each spring.

Of vapors, from whose solid atmosphere
Black rain, and fire, and hail will burst: oh, hear!

III

Thou who didst waken from his summer dreams
30 The blue Mediterranean, where he lay,
Lulled by the coil of his crystàlline streams,

Beside a pumice isle in Baiae's bay,[3]
And saw in sleep old palaces and towers
Quivering within the wave's intenser day,

35 All overgrown with azure moss and flowers
So sweet, the sense faints picturing them! Thou
For whose path the Atlantic's level powers

Cleave themselves into chasms, while far below
The sea-blooms and the oozy woods which wear
40 The sapless foliage of the ocean, know

Thy voice, and suddenly grow gray with fear,
And tremble and despoil themselves:[4] oh, hear!

IV

If I were a dead leaf thou mightest bear;
If I were a swift cloud to fly with thee;
45 A wave to pant beneath thy power, and share

The impulse of thy strength, only less free
Than thou, O uncontrollable! If even
I were as in my boyhood, and could be

The comrade of thy wanderings over Heaven,
50 As then, when to outstrip thy skyey speed
Scarce seemed a vision; I would ne'er have striven

As thus with thee in prayer in my sore need.
Oh, lift me as a wave, a leaf, a cloud!
I fall upon the thorns of life! I bleed!

55 A heavy weight of hours has chained and bowed
One too like thee: tameless, and swift, and proud.

V

Make me thy lyre, even as the forest is:
What if my leaves are falling like its own!
The tumult of thy mighty harmonies

60 Will take from both a deep, autumnal tone,
Sweet though in sadness. Be thou, Spirit fierce,
My spirit! Be thou me, impetuous one!

3. Where Roman emperors had erected villas, west of Naples.
4. The vegetation at the bottom of the sea [. . .] sympathizes with that of the land in the change of
seasons [Shelley's note].

Drive my dead thoughts over the universe
Like withered leaves to quicken a new birth!
65 And, by the incantation of this verse,

Scatter, as from an unextinguished hearth
Ashes and sparks, my words among mankind!
Be through my lips to unawakened earth

The trumpet of a prophecy! O Wind,
70 If Winter comes, can Spring be far behind?

                                                        1820

• What attributes of the West Wind does the speaker want his poetry to
embody? In what ways is this poem like the wind it describes? What is the
effect of its structure?

PHILIP LARKIN
Church Going

Once I am sure there's nothing going on
I step inside, letting the door thud shut.
Another church: matting, seats, and stone,
And little books; sprawlings of flowers, cut
5 For Sunday, brownish now; some brass and stuff
Up at the holy end; the small neat organ;
And a tense, musty, unignorable silence,
Brewed God knows how long. Hatless, I take off
My cycle-clips in awkward reverence,

10 Move forward, run my hand around the font.
From where I stand, the roof looks almost new—
Cleaned, or restored? Someone would know: I don't.
Mounting the lectern, I peruse a few
Hectoring large-scale verses, and pronounce
15 "Here endeth" much more loudly than I'd meant.
The echoes snigger briefly. Back at the door
I sign the book, donate an Irish sixpence,
Reflect the place was not worth stopping for.

Yet stop I did: in fact I often do,
20 And always end much at a loss like this,
Wondering what to look for; wondering, too,
When churches fall completely out of use
What we shall turn them into, if we shall keep
A few cathedrals chronically on show,
25 Their parchment, plate and pyx in locked cases,
And let the rest rent-free to rain and sheep.
Shall we avoid them as unlucky places?

Or, after dark, will dubious women come
To make their children touch a particular stone;

30 Pick simples[5] for a cancer; or on some
    Advised night see walking a dead one?
    Power of some sort or other will go on
    In games, in riddles, seemingly at random;
    But superstition, like belief, must die,
35 And what remains when disbelief has gone?
    Grass, weedy pavement, brambles, buttress, sky,

    A shape less recognizable each week,
    A purpose more obscure. I wonder who
    Will be the last, the very last, to seek
40 This place for what it was; one of the crew
    That tap and jot and know what rood-lofts[6] were?
    Some ruin-bibber,[7] randy for antique,
    Or Christmas-addict, counting on a whiff
    Of gown-and-bands and organ-pipes and myrrh?
45 Or will he be my representative,

    Bored, uninformed, knowing the ghostly silt
    Dispersed, yet tending to this cross of ground
    Through suburb scrub because it held unspilt
    So long and equably what since is found
50 Only in separation—marriage, and birth,
    And death, and thoughts of these—for whom was built
    This special shell? For, though I've no idea
    What this accoutered frowsty barn is worth,
    It pleases me to stand in silence here;

55 A serious house on serious earth it is,
    In whose blent[8] air all our compulsions meet,
    Are recognized, and robed as destinies.
    And that much never can be obsolete,
    Since someone will forever be surprising
60 A hunger in himself to be more serious,
    And gravitating with it to this ground,
    Which, he once heard, was proper to grow wise in,
    If only that so many dead lie round.

                                            1955

• Describe the parts of this poem. How do the first two stanzas differ from the
  rest of the poem? Where and how does the poem shift from the personal to
  the general?

5. Medicinal herbs.
6. Galleries atop the screens (on which crosses ["roods"] are mounted) that divide the naves or main
bodies of churches from the choirs or chancels.
7. Literally, ruin-drinker: someone extremely attracted to antiquarian objects.
8. Blended.

AUTHORS ON THEIR WORK

PHILIP LARKIN (1922–85)

From "A Conversation with Ian Hamilton" (1964)*

It ["Church Going"] is of course an entirely secular poem. I was a bit irritated by an American who insisted to me it was a religious poem. It isn't religious at all. Religion surely means that the affairs of this world are under divine surveillance, and so on, and I go to some pains to point out that I don't bother about that kind of thing. [. . .]

[. . .] the poem is about going to church, not religion—I tried to suggest this by the title—and the union of the important stages of human life—birth, marriage and death—that going to church represents; and my own feeling that when they are dispersed into the registry office and the crematorium chapel life will become thinner in consequence. (22)

From "An Interview with John Haffenden" (1981)**

It ["Church Going"] came from the first time I saw a ruined church in Northern Ireland, and I'd never seen a ruined church before—discarded. It shocked me. Now of course it's commonplace: churches are not so much ruined as turned into bingo-halls, warehouses for refrigerators or split-level houses for architects.

It's not clear in the poem that you began with a ruined church.
No, it wasn't in the poem, but when you go into a church there's a feeling of something . . . well . . . over, derelict.

Some critics have discerned in it a yearning for a latter-day Christian or religious sanction. Is that so?
I suppose so. I'm not someone who's lost faith: I never had it. I was baptized [. . .] but not confirmed. Aren't religions shaped in terms of what people want? No one could help hoping Christianity was true, or at least the happy ending—rising from the dead and our sins forgiven. One longs for these miracles, and so in a sense one longs for religion. But "Church Going" isn't that kind of poem: it's a humanist poem, a celebration of the dignity of . . . well, you know what it says. (56–57)

*"A Conversation with Ian Hamilton." *Further Requirements: Interviews, Broadcasts, Statements and Book Reviews*, edited by Anthony Thwaite, Faber and Faber, 2001, pp. 19–26. Originally published in *London Magazine*, Nov. 1946.
**"An Interview with John Haffenden." *Further Requirements: Interviews, Broadcasts, Statements and Book Reviews*, edited by Anthony Thwaite, Faber and Faber, 2001, pp. 47–62. Originally published in *Viewpoints: Poets in Conversation with John Haffenden*, 1981.

TERRANCE HAYES
Mr. T—[9]

A man made of scrap muscle & the steam
engine's imagination, white feathers
flapping in each lobe for the skull's migration,
should the need arise. Sometimes drugged
5 & duffled (by white men) in a cockpit
bound for the next adventure. And liable
to crush a fool's face like newsprint; headlines
of Hollywood blood and wincing. Half Step 'N Fetchit,[1]
half John Henry. What were we, the skinny B-boys,[2]
10 to learn from him? How to hulk through Chicago
in a hedgerow afro, an ox-grunt kicking dust
behind the teeth; those eighteen glammering
gold chains around the throat of pity,
that fat hollow medallion like the sun on a leash—

2002

- How does the poem characterize Mr. T and the speaker's feelings about
  him? Why might it matter that the speaker uses the first-person plural
  ("we") versus the singular ("I")?

9. Stage name of bodyguard-turned-actor Laurence Tureaud (b. 1952), who first rose to fame as a star
of the 1980s action-adventure series *The A Team* and the film *Rocky III* (1982). His boast "I pity the
fool" became a popular catchphrase.
1. Born Lincoln Theodore Perry (1902–85), "Stepin Fetchit" is widely regarded as the first African
American movie star; he became famous and controversial in the 1930s by repeatedly playing the
same stereotypically simpleminded character.
2. Hip-hop dancers or "breakers." *John Henry*: American folk hero portrayed as an enormously strong
railroad worker who dies from exhaustion after winning a contest against a steam-powered drill.

SAMPLE WRITING: ESSAY IN PROGRESS

The following piece of writing by student Lindsay Gibson was originally just one section of a longer essay on multiple poems by Philip Larkin. Though the beginning and middle of the piece work fine out of that context, you'll notice that we haven't supplied either the title or the real conclusion that the piece needs to have in order to be a complete, effective essay. What should the piece be titled? How might it be brought to a more satisfying conclusion?

You will notice, too, that the essay focuses only partly and somewhat unevenly on issues related to internal structure. How might the essay make more of the poem's structure? More generally, what are the essay's weakest and strongest moments and aspects? How might its argument be improved or expanded? Answering such questions for yourself or discussing them with your classmates can be a useful way to better understand the qualities of a good argument, a good title, and a good conclusion.

Gibson 1

Lindsay Gibson
Dr. Nick Lolordo
Modern British Poetry
27 January 2019

Philip Larkin's "Church Going"

Philip Larkin is one of the semester's most fascinating poets. His use of colloquial language, regular meter, and rhyme sets him slightly apart from other poets of his day, many of whom write in varying forms of verse, use nearly indecipherable language, and rarely, if ever, make use of rhyme at all. Many of his poems are fraught with existential crises, the nature of which only someone living in the postmodern world could understand; consequently, his poems contain a lot of meaning for the contemporary reader.

Larkin's most fascinating poem, "Church Going," embodies many of his best attributes as a poet: it uses everyday, standard English and is therefore easy to read and understand, yet its stanzas contain a real search for meaning that its simple language might not immediately invite the reader to ponder. The poem also addresses one of Larkin's main preoccupations: religion, and specifically the role of religion in a postmodern world. Even with all of this, the most engaging aspect of the poem is the duality reflected in its structure: at

552

first and on the one hand, the speaker makes quiet fun of religion; later and on the other hand, he reveals to us his own search for meaning and the answers that he realizes religion may or may not be able to give him.

The first two stanzas of "Church Going" contain a narrative of a seemingly secular man entering a church he has passed along his way. The speaker observes the layout of the building, the various accoutrements common to a church, and views it all with a mild sense of sarcasm or awkward reverence. His language almost insists on his self-proclaimed ignorance: "Someone would know; I don't" (line 12). And he foreshadows the rest of the poem when appraising the roof of the church as one would an antique: "Cleaned, or restored?" (12). At the end of the second stanza, the speaker reflects that "the place was not worth stopping for" (18). Yet stop he did, and that tells us volumes about what the rest of the poem is about.

In the third stanza, the poem's tone and the speaker's attitude shift as the speaker begins to ponder big questions about religion in today's world: Does it have any meaning left? Should it? The speaker reveals to us that he often stops at churches like these, searching for meaning, yet "Wondering what to look for" (21), not even knowing what the questions are that he wants answered. His use of words like "parchment, plate and pyx" (25) reveals to us that he is not as ignorant about religious liturgy as he would have us believe— which, in turn, is further evidence of the dual nature of the poem: the speaker wants us to believe he doesn't know or care about anything to do with religion, yet he has been on his quest for meaning long enough to know the names of things he claims he does not. The last line of the third stanza poses another compelling question, this time about the future: after churches fall out of use, "Shall we avoid them as unlucky places?" (27). The question of whether, when faith is finally dead, people will still cling to superstitions such as luck and supernatural powers of whatever nature is a fascinating one.

The speaker goes on to explore this question in the next few stanzas by imagining some specific ways in which superstition might persist after religion is gone: women might take their children to "touch a particular stone" (29) or pick herbs around the church to use for medicinal purposes. But in all these imagined examples, no one actually goes to the church to worship anymore. In stanza 4, the speaker presents various tableaus of people using the church for more and more mundane uses, such as a student of architecture, someone else who only likes to see the ruins of old buildings simply because they're old, and finally, and somewhat paradoxically, a "Christmas-addict" (43) who (presumably) wants to see the last religious remnants of his beloved, commoditized, and commercialized holiday. The last person who might visit the church in this post-religion world might even be a doppelganger of the speaker himself, who, though claiming to be "Bored" and "uninformed" (46), visits the church because "it held unspilt / So long and equably what since is found / Only in separation— marriage, and birth, / And death, and thoughts of these" (48-51). Once again the speaker insists that he is ignorant and careless of religion, but goes on to betray the fact that even if he does not believe in the religion itself, he is fascinated by the idea that it held "unspilt" what people now only find in marriages, births, and deaths: meaning. It is at this point that the reader can truly appreciate the point and purpose of this whole poem: meaning, and the search for it. It seems poignant that the speaker realizes there is more *meaning* in the church itself than any other place, whether actual belief in religion is there or not.

The last stanza seems to be an attempt on the speaker's part to reconcile the opposing forces of the poem—the speaker's insistence that he cares nothing for religion and that religion is meaningless anyway versus his existential need to find some kind of meaning that will justify his existence and maybe even the beliefs of others. The speaker finally respects what the church does for people, including himself: one's "compulsions meet, / Are recognized, and robed as destinies" (56-57). When one wonders if compulsions are merely that, one can go to church and be told that he or she is part of a larger whole—one's destiny. And if compulsions can be transformed into destinies, at least in the mind of the wonderer, then there will always be value in such a service: "that much never can be obsolete" (58), according to the speaker of the poem.

The last stanzas of the poem are devoted to a man who gravitates to the church because he "once heard [it] was proper to grow wise in, / If only that so many dead lie round" (62-63). Once again, the speaker shows us that even when belief in the religion associated with the church is completely gone, a sense of reverence, if only for the dead, will remain. The belief may be gone, but the sense of a community among people searching for, and perhaps finding, meaning will remain, and people will always be drawn to that, no matter what their belief system (or lack thereof).

The poem itself has another overarching concern that merits discussion: death. There are many images of or mentions of death throughout the poem: There are "flowers, cut / For Sunday, brownish now" (4-5), the words "Here endeth" (15) echoing through the small church, the possibility of someone seeing a "walking [. . .] dead one" (31), the assertion that "superstition, like belief, must die" (34), talk of the "ghostly silt / Dispersed" (46-47), thoughts of "marriage, and birth, / And death" (50-51). And finally, the last image in the poem is the abandoned church's graveyard in which "so many dead lie round" (63). Throughout the poem there is death: death of people, death of ideas, death of faith. Death's pervasiveness is one more way the poem struggles with its dual nature: the poem narrates a serious search for meaning, yet the very definition of death is that there *is* no meaning. Death is the end, there is nothing more. Any search for meaning is rendered meaningless anyway upon one's death. The speaker implies that there is even an end to the search for meaning itself. The speaker asks in line 35, perhaps the most powerful line of the whole poem, "And what remains when disbelief has gone?" What is left over when even "disbelief" has died? Is it the beginning of another cycle in the search for meaning, or has even the "faith" that there is nothing out there died as well?

The poem "Church Going" is a very layered, intensive look at all the things that matter to us as human beings: meaning, death, hope, hopelessness, and the way all of these things blend together in the perpetual existential crisis that is man's very existence.

WORK CITED

Larkin, Philip. "Church Going." *The Norton Introduction to Literature*, edited by Kelly J. Mays, portable 13th ed., W. W. Norton, 2020, pp. 548–49.

17 | EXTERNAL FORM

The previous chapters have discussed many of the *internal* features of a poem that make it unique: the **tone** and characteristics of its **speaker**; its **situation** and **setting** and its **themes**; its **diction**, **imagery**, and sounds. This chapter ventures into the *external* form of a poem, including its arrangement on the page and into both visual and verbal units. These formal aspects are external in being recognizable; like the fashion and fabric of clothing that expresses the personality of an individual, the external form is an appropriate garb or guise for the unique internal action and meaning of the poem. When reading a poem, you might immediately notice its stanza breaks. Or you might quickly recognize that the poem takes a traditional form such as the sonnet, or that it simply looks odd. These formal features guide readers as well as poets. They help readers feel and appreciate repetitions and connections, changes and gaps, in the language as well as the meaning of the poem.

STANZAS

Most poems of more than a few lines are divided into **stanzas**—groups of lines divided from other groups by white space on the page. Putting some space between groupings of lines has the effect of sectioning a poem, giving its physical appearance a series of divisions that sometimes correspond to turns of thought, changes of scene or image, or other shifts in structure or direction of the kind examined in the last chapter. In Donne's THE FLEA, for example, the stanza divisions mark distinct stages in the action: Between the first and second stanzas, the speaker stops his companion from killing the flea; between the second and third stanzas, the companion follows through on her intention and kills the flea. Any formal division of a poem into stanzas is important to consider; what appear to be gaps or silences may be structural markers.

Historically, stanzas have most often been organized by patterns of **rhyme,** and often of **meter**, too; thus stanza divisions have traditionally been a visual indicator of patterns in sound. In most traditional stanza forms, the pattern of rhyme is repeated in stanza after stanza throughout the poem, until voice and ear become familiar with the pattern and come to expect it. The repetition of pattern allows us to hear deviations from the pattern as well, just as we do in music.

TRADITIONAL STANZA FORMS

As the poems in this anthology demonstrate, stanzas can take myriad forms. Over time, however, certain stanza forms have become traditional, or "fixed." In using such stanza forms, poets thus often implicitly or explicitly allude and even respond to previous poets and poems that have used the same form. Like musicians, they also generate new effects, meanings, and music through meaningful variations on traditional forms.

Terza Rima

In the following poem, the first and third lines in each stanza rhyme, and the middle line then rhymes with the first and third lines of the next stanza.

ROBERT FROST
Acquainted with the Night

I have been one acquainted with the night.
I have walked out in rain—and back in rain.
I have outwalked the furthest city light.

I have looked down the saddest city lane.
5 I have passed by the watchman on his beat
And dropped my eyes, unwilling to explain.

I have stood still and stopped the sound of feet
When far away an interrupted cry
Came over houses from another street,

10 But not to call me back or say good-by;
And further still at an unearthly height,
One luminary clock against the sky

Proclaimed the time was neither wrong nor right.
I have been one acquainted with the night.

                                            1928

In this stanza form, known as **terza rima**, the stanzas are linked to each other by a common sound: one rhyme sound from each stanza is picked up in the next stanza, and so on to the end of the poem (though sometimes poems in this form have sections that use varied rhyme schemes). Most traditional stanza forms involve a metrical pattern as well as a rhyme scheme. Terza rima, like most English fixed stanza and verse forms, involves **iambic** meter (unstressed and stressed syllables alternating regularly), and each line has five beats (**pentameter**).

As the title of the following poem announces, it, too, is written—at least mostly—in terza rima. And it depends, for its full effect, on our knowing not only that this stanza form was used by Dante in *The Divine Comedy*, written in Italian in the early 1300s, but also that this three-book epic depicts the poet's journey through Hell (or the inferno) and Purgatory to Paradise.

RICHARD WILBUR
Terza Rima

In this great form, as Dante proved in Hell,
There is no dreadful thing that can't be said
In passing. Here, for instance, one could tell

How our jeep skidded sideways toward the dead
5 Enemy soldier with the staring eyes,
Bumping a little as it struck his head,

And then flew on, as if toward Paradise[1]

2008

• What might this poem communicate—about, for example, war, poetry,
and/or death—by starting out, but not ending, in terza rima?

Because terza rima requires many rhymes, and thus many different rhyme words,
it is not very common in English, a language less rich in rhyme possibilities than Italian or French because it derives from so many different language families.

Spenserian Stanza

Named for Edmund Spenser, who used it to great effect in his long poem *The Faerie
Queene*, the **Spenserian stanza** is even more rhyme rich than terza rima, using
only three rhyme sounds in nine rhymed lines, as in this stanza from John
Keats's *The Eve of St. Agnes*:

Her falt'ring hand upon the balustrade,	*a*
Old Angela was feeling for the stair,	*b*
When Madeline, St. Agnes' charmèd maid,	*a*
Rose, like a missioned spirit, unaware:	*b*
With silver taper's light, and pious care,	*b*
She turned, and down the agèd gossip led	*c*
To a safe level matting. Now prepare,	*b*
Young Porphyro, for gazing on that bed;	*c*
She comes, she comes again, like ring dove frayed and fled	*c*

Notice that while the first eight lines of a Spenserian stanza are in iambic pentameter, the ninth has one extra foot, making it iambic **hexameter**.

Ballad Stanza

The much more common **ballad stanza** has only one set of rhymes in four lines;
lines 1 and 3 in each stanza do not rhyme at all. And while those lines are in iambic
tetrameter (4 beats/feet), lines 2 and 4 are rhymed iambic **trimeter** (3 beats/feet).
As its name suggests, this stanza form is often used in **ballads** including SIR PAT-
RICK SPENS, which begins with the following stanza:

The king sits in Dumferling toune,	*a*
Drinking the blude-reid wine:	*b*
"O whar will I get guid sailor,	*c*
To sail this ship of mine?"	*b*

TRADITIONAL VERSE FORMS

Stanza forms are not themselves subgenres of poetry, but rather a form that can be
used for various kinds of poems. The same is true of other traditional verse forms—

---

1. Perhaps an allusion, too, to Emily Dickinson's "Because I could not stop for Death—" (p. 492), which
ends with a horse-drawn carriage driven by Death carrying the speaker "toward Eternity—" (line 24).

set patterns of rhythm and rhyme that govern whole poems or parts of them rather than individual stanzas. Three verse forms especially useful to know are the rhyming couplet, blank verse, and free verse.

Any pair of consecutive lines that share *end rhymes* is called a *rhyming couplet*. Andrew Marvell's To His Coy Mistress, for example, consists entirely of iambic tetrameter couplets, beginning with these two:

Had we but world enough, and time,	*a*
This coyness, lady, were no crime.	*a*
We would sit down, and think which way	*b*
To walk, and pass our long love's day.	*b*

A *heroic couplet* requires iambic pentameter, as in Alexander Pope's Sound and Sense:

But most by numbers judge a poet's song,	*a*
And smooth or rough, with them, is right or wrong;	*a*
In the bright muse though thousand charms conspire,	*b*
Her voice is all these tuneful fools admire	*b*

Near the other end of the spectrum from the heroic couplet sits **blank verse**, which consists of lines with regular meter, usually iambic pentameter, but no discernible rhyme scheme, as in these lines, which Adam speaks to Eve in John Milton's *Paradise Lost*:

Well hast thou motioned, well thy thoughts employed,
How we might best fulfil the work which here
God hath assigned us; nor of me shalt pass
Unpraised: for nothing lovelier can be found
In woman, than to study household good,
And good works in her husband to promote.

Though here used by Milton to describe lofty events of cosmic significance, blank verse was among the least formal and most natural of traditional verse forms until the explosion of **free verse** in the twentieth century. Now perhaps the most common of verse forms, free verse is "free" because it lacks both regular meter and rhyme. The wildly different lengths of the following lines from Helen Chasin's The Word *Plum* make its use of free verse especially obvious:

taut skin
pierced, bitten, provoked into
juice, and tart flesh

FIXED FORMS OR FORM-BASED SUBGENRES

Again, all these stanza and verse forms can be used in many different kinds of poems. But some kinds or subgenres of poetry are defined wholly by their use of particular formal patterns. Perhaps the most famous of these are the **sonnet** and the **haiku**, to which we devote the albums that follow this chapter. Others include the **limerick** (see, for example, There was a young girl from St. Paul), the **villanelle** (Do Not Go Gentle into That Good Night, below), the **palindrome** (Myth, below), and the **sestina** (see below). Though relatively rare for much of the twentieth century, such traditional fixed forms have in recent years become increasingly popular once again. *McSweeney's Internet Tendency*, the online version of the eccentric literary magazine edited by novelist Dave Eggers, included no new poetry except sestinas between 2003 and 2006, and you can still find hundreds of examples on its Web site.

You can probably deduce the principles involved in each of these fixed forms by looking carefully at an example; if you have trouble, consult the definitions in the glossary.

TRADITIONAL FORMS: POEMS FOR FURTHER STUDY

DYLAN THOMAS
Do Not Go Gentle into That Good Night[2]

Do not go gentle into that good night,
Old age should burn and rave at close of day;
Rage, rage against the dying of the light.

Though wise men at their end know dark is right,
5 Because their words had forked no lightning they
Do not go gentle into that good night.

Good men, the last wave by, crying how bright
Their frail deeds might have danced in a green bay,
Rage, rage against the dying of the light.

10 Wild men who caught and sang the sun in flight,
And learn, too late, they grieved it on its way,
Do not go gentle into that good night.

Grave men, near death, who see with blinding sight
Blind eyes could blaze like meteors and be gay,
15 Rage, rage against the dying of the light.

And you, my father, there on the sad height,
Curse, bless, me now with your fierce tears, I pray.
Do not go gentle into that good night.
Rage, rage against the dying of the light.

1952

• What do the wise, good, wild, and grave men have in common with the speaker's father? Why do you think Thomas chose such a strict form, the villanelle, for such an emotionally charged subject?

2. Written during the final illness of the poet's father.

NATASHA TRETHEWEY
Myth

I was asleep while you were dying.
It's as if you slipped through some rift, a hollow
I make between my slumber and my waking,

the Erebus[3] I keep you in, still trying
5 not to let go. You'll be dead again tomorrow,
but in dreams you live. So I try taking

you back into morning. Sleep-heavy, turning,
my eyes open, I find you do not follow.
Again and again, this constant forsaking.

10 Again and again, this constant forsaking:
my eyes open, I find you do not follow.
You back into morning, sleep-heavy, turning.

But in dreams you live. So I try taking,
not to let go. You'll be dead again tomorrow.
15 The Erebus I keep you in—still, trying—

I make between my slumber and my waking.
It's as if you slipped through some rift, a hollow.
I was asleep while you were dying.

2007

• How does Trethewey's use of a palindromic structure contribute to the
  poem's evocation of grief? Why do you think the poem is called "Myth"?

---

3. In Greek mythology, the dark region of the underworld through which the dead pass en route to
Hades.

ELIZABETH BISHOP
Sestina

September rain falls on the house.
In the failing light, the old grandmother
sits in the kitchen with the child
beside the Little Marvel Stove,
5 reading the jokes from the almanac,
laughing and talking to hide her tears.

She thinks that her equinoctial tears
and the rain that beats on the roof of the house
were both foretold by the almanac,
10 but only known to a grandmother.
The iron kettle sings on the stove.
She cuts some bread and says to the child,

It's time for tea now; but the child
is watching the teakettle's small hard tears
15 dance like mad on the hot black stove,
the way the rain must dance on the house.
Tidying up, the old grandmother
hangs up the clever almanac

on its string. Birdlike, the almanac
20 hovers half open above the child,
hovers above the old grandmother
and her teacup full of dark brown tears.
She shivers and says she thinks the house
feels chilly, and puts more wood in the stove.

25 *It was to be*, says the Marvel Stove.
I know what I know, says the almanac.
With crayons the child draws a rigid house
and a winding pathway. Then the child
puts in a man with buttons like tears
30 and shows it proudly to the grandmother.

But secretly, while the grandmother
busies herself about the stove,
the little moons fall down like tears
from between the pages of the almanac
35 into the flower bed the child
has carefully placed in the front of the house.

Time to plant tears, says the almanac.
The grandmother sings to the marvellous stove
and the child draws another inscrutable house.

1965

• Try to derive from SESTINA the "rules" that govern the sestina form. Why do
  you think Bishop chose this form for her poem?

A. E. STALLINGS
Sestina: Like

With a nod to Jonah Winter[4]

Now we're all "friends," there is no love but Like,
A semi-demi goddess, something like
A reality-TV star look-alike,
Named Simile or Me Two. So we like
5   In order to be liked. It isn't like
There's Love or Hate now. Even plain "dislike"

Is frowned on: there's no button for it. Like
Is something you can quantify: each "like"
You gather's almost something money-like,
10   Token of virtual support. "Please like
This page to stamp out hunger." And you'd *like*
To end hunger and climate change alike,

But it's unlikely Like does diddly. Like
Just twiddles its unopposing thumbs-ups, like-
15   Wise props up scarecrow silences. *"I'm like,
So OVER him,"* I overhear. "But, like,
He doesn't get it. Like, you know? He's like
It's all OK. Like I don't even LIKE

Him anymore. Whatever. I'm all like . . ."
20   Take "like" out of our chat, we'd all alike
Flounder, agape, gesticulating like
A foreign film sans subtitles, fall like
Dumb phones to mooted desuetude. Unlike
With other crutches, um, when we use "like,"

25   We're not just buying time on credit: Like
Displaces other words; crowds, cuckoo-like,
Endangered hatchlings from the nest.[5] (Click "like"
If you're against extinction!) Like is like
Invasive zebra mussels, or it's like
30   Those nutria-things, or kudzu,[6] or belike

Redundant fast food franchises, each like
(More like) the next. Those poets who dislike
Inversions, archaisms, who just like
Plain English as she's spoke—why isn't "like"

---

4. Poet and children's book author (b. 1962); every line of his breakup poem "Sestina: Bob" (1999) ends with the word *bob*.
5. Some cuckoo species lay their eggs in other birds' nests.
6. Invasive plant of Asian origin, especially ubiquitous in the southern United States. *Nutria*: invasive species of large, semiaquatic rodent, originally from South America.

35 Their (literally) every other word? I'd like
Us just to admit that's what real speech is like.

But as you like, my friend. Yes, we're alike,
How we pronounce, say, lichen, and dislike
Cancer and war. So like this page. Click *Like*.

2013

• How does Stallings here bend sestina conventions to make her point about "real speech" (line 36) and poetry?

THE WAY A POEM LOOKS

Like stanza breaks, other arrangements of print and space help guide the voice and the mind to a clearer sense of sound, meaning, and feeling. But poems are written to be seen as well as heard, and their appearance on the page is crucial to their effect. E. E. Cummings's poem l(a, for example, tries to visualize typographically what the poet asks you to see in your mind's eye.

E. E. CUMMINGS
l(a

l(a
le
af
fa
ll
s)
one
l
iness

1958

The unusual spacing of words in the following poem, with some run together and others widely separated, provides a guide to reading, regulating both speed and sense, so that the poem can capture aloud some of the boy's wide-eyed enthusiasm, remembered now from a later perspective. (Notice how the word "defunct" [line 2] helps establish the time and point of view.)

E. E. CUMMINGS
Buffalo Bill's[7]

Buffalo Bill's
defunct
    who used to
    ride a watersmooth-silver
5   stallion
and break onetwothreefourfive pigeonsjustlikethat
                                       Jesus

he was a handsome man
                    and what i want to know is
how do you like your blueeyed boy
10 Mister Death

                                        1923

Advertising poster, circa 1898. "Buffalo Bill" Cody's "Wild West" shows fascinated crowds across the United States and Europe from 1883 and 1913.

7. From Cummings's *Portraits* XXI.

CONCRETE POETRY

Occasionally, poems are composed in a specific shape so that they resemble physical objects. The idea that poems can be related to the visual arts is an old one. Theodoric in ancient Greece is credited with inventing *technopaegnia*—that is, the construction of poems with visual appeal. Once, the shaping of words to resemble an object was thought to have mystical power, but more recent attempts at **concrete poetry**, or shaped verse, are usually playful exercises that attempt to supplement (or replace) verbal meanings with devices from painting and sculpture. Here are two examples.

GEORGE HERBERT
Easter Wings

Lord, who createdst man in wealth and store,[8]
Though foolishly he lost the same,
Decaying more and more
Till he became
Most poor:
With thee
O let me rise
As larks,[9] harmoniously,
And sing this day thy victories:
Then shall the fall further the flight in me.

My tender age in sorrow did begin;
And still with sicknesses and shame
Thou didst so punish sin,
That I became
Most thin.
With thee
Let me combine,
And feel this day thy victory;
For, if I imp[1] my wing on thine,
Affliction shall advance the flight in me.

1633

- How do this poem's decreasing and increasing line lengths correspond to the meaning of the words? Why do you think Herbert has chosen to present the poem sideways?

8. In plenty.   9. Which herald the morning.
1. Engraft: in falconry, to engraft feathers in a damaged wing, so as to restore the powers of flight.

From *Black, Grey and White: A Book of Visual Sonnets* (2011), by David Miller

The Sonnet

AN ALBUM

The **sonnet**, one of the most persistent and familiar fixed forms, originated in medieval Italy and France. It dominated English poetry in the late sixteenth and early seventeenth centuries and then was revived several times from the late eighteenth century onward. Except for some early experiments with length, the sonnet has always been fourteen lines long, and it usually is written in **iambic pentameter**. It is most often printed as if it were a single stanza, although it actually has formal divisions defined by its various rhyme schemes. For more than four centuries, the sonnet has been surprisingly resilient, and it continues to attract a variety of poets. As a verse form, the sonnet is contained, compact, demanding; whatever it does, it must do concisely. It is best suited to intensity of feeling and concentration of figurative language and expression.

Conventional sonnets are structured according to one of two principles of division. The *English*, or *Shakespearean, sonnet* is divided into three units of four lines each (quatrains) and a final unit of two lines (couplet), and sometimes the line spacing reflects this division. Ordinarily its rhyme scheme reflects the structure: The scheme of *abab cdcd efef gg* is the classic one, but many variations from that pattern still reflect the basic 4-4-4-2 division. In the *Italian*, or *Petrarchan, sonnet* (the Italian poet Francesco Petrarch was an early master of this form), the fundamental break is between the first eight lines (called an octave) and the last six (called a sestet). Its "typical" rhyme scheme is *abbaabba cdecde*, although it, too, produces many variations that still reflect the basic division into two parts, an octave and a sestet.

The two kinds of sonnet structures are useful for different sorts of argument. The 4-4-4-2 structure works very well for a poem that makes a three-step argument (with either a quick summary or a dramatic turn at the end) or for setting up brief, cumulative images. Shakespeare's THAT TIME OF YEAR THOU MAYST IN ME BEHOLD, for example, uses the 4-4-4-2 structure to mark the progressive steps toward death and the parting of lovers by using three distinct metaphors and then summarizing. In the two-part structure of the Italian sonnet, the octave often states a proposition or generalization, and the sestet provides a particular example, consequence, or application of it; alternatively, the second part may turn away from the first to present a new position or response. The final lines may, for example, reverse the first eight and achieve a paradox or irony in the poem, or the poem may nearly balance two comparable arguments or images. Basically, the 8-6 structure lends itself to poems with two points to make, or to those that make one point and then illustrate or complicate it.

During the Renaissance, poets regularly employed the sonnet for love poems; many modern sonnets continue to be about love or private life, and many poets continue to use a personal, apparently open and sincere **tone** in their sonnets. Time, (human) mortality, and (art's) immortality are also conventional topics, reinforced by the form itself: Sonnets are, after all, necessarily brief (just as, they sometimes remind us, all things humans are), yet simultaneously fixed, static, even rigid in somewhat the way monuments are. Today, centuries after the sonnet's introduction, the very fact that the form has endured so long and has been so highly revered can't help but reinforce its association with both immortality and artistic tradition.

But poets often find the sonnet form useful for a variety of other subjects and tones. Sonnets may be about politics, philosophy, motherhood, social media. And their tones vary widely, too, from anger and remorse to tender awe or snark. Sometimes poets take the kind of comfort in the careful limits of the form that William Wordsworth describes in NUNS FRET NOT, finding in its two basic variations, the English sonnet and the Italian sonnet, a wealth of ways to organize their materials into coherent structures. Sometimes a neat and precise structure is instead altered as particular needs or effects may demand. And the two basic structures, Shakespearean and Petrarchan, certainly do not define all the structural possibilities within a fourteen-line poem.

Which of the following sonnets follow the Italian model? the English? In each case, how do form, structure, and content work together? How does each poet adapt the traditional form to his or her particular purpose? Aside from particular patterns of rhyme and meter, what other conventions of the sonnet can you identify? How do individual poems use, rework, even comment on those conventions? (To see how one student answered some of these questions by comparing sonnets by two different writers, read Melissa Makolin's essay OUT-SONNETING SHAKESPEARE . . . .)

HENRY CONSTABLE
My lady's presence makes the roses red

My lady's presence makes the roses red,
Because to see her lips they blush for shame.
The lily's leaves, for envy, pale became,
And her white hands in them this envy bred.
5 The marigold the leaves abroad doth spread,
Because the sun's and her power is the same.
The violet of purple colour came,
Dyed in the blood she made my heart to shed.
In brief: all flowers from her their virtue take;
10 From her sweet breath their sweet smells do proceed;
The living heat which her eyebeams doth make
Warmeth the ground and quickeneth the seed.
The rain, wherewith she watereth the flowers,
Falls from mine eyes, which she dissolves in showers.

                                            1594

- Which type of sonnet is this? How do external form and internal structure here work together?

WILLIAM SHAKESPEARE
My mistress' eyes are nothing like the sun

My mistress' eyes are nothing like the sun;
Coral is far more red than her lips' red;
If snow be white, why then her breasts are dun,[1]

---

1. Mouse-colored.

If hairs be wires, black wires grow on her head.
5 I have seen roses damasked[2] red and white,
But no such roses see I in her cheeks;
And in some perfumes is there more delight
Than in the breath that from my mistress reeks.
I love to hear her speak, yet well I know
10 That music hath a far more pleasing sound;
I grant I never saw a goddess go;[3]
My mistress, when she walks, treads on the ground.
And yet, by heaven, I think my love as rare
As any she belied with false compare.

1609

• How might this poem respond to a sonnet like Constable's My lady's presence . . . and Petrarch's Upon the breeze . . . ?

Not marble, nor the gilded monuments

Not marble, nor the gilded monuments
Of princes, shall outlive this powerful rhyme;
But you shall shine more bright in these contènts
Than unswept stone, besmeared with sluttish time.
5 When wasteful war shall statues overturn,
And broils[4] root out the work of masonry,
Nor Mars his[5] sword nor war's quick fire shall burn
The living record of your memory.
'Gainst death and all-oblivious enmity
10 Shall you pace forth; your praise shall still find room
Even in the eyes of all posterity
That wear this world out to the ending doom.[6]
So, till the judgment that yourself arise,
You live in this, and dwell in lovers' eyes.

1609

• How does each quatrain build on the last?

Let me not to the marriage of true minds

Let me not to the marriage of true minds
Admit impediments.[7] Love is not love
Which alters when it alteration finds,
Or bends with the remover to remove:
5 Oh, no! it is an ever-fixèd mark,

2. Variegated.
3. Walk.
4. Roots of plants.
5. Mars his: Mars's. Nor: neither.
6. Judgment Day.
7. The Church of England's marriage service contains this address to the witnesses: "If any of you
know cause or just impediments why these persons should not be joined together [. . .]."

That looks on tempests and is never shaken;
It is the star to every wandering bark,
Whose worth's unknown, although his height be taken.[8]
Love's not Time's fool, though rosy lips and cheeks
10 Within his bending sickle's compass come;
Love alters not with his brief hours and weeks,
But bears it out even to the edge of doom.
If this be error and upon me proved,
I never writ, nor no man ever loved.

1609

• What might the speaker mean when he says that love doesn't "ben[d] with
the remover to remove" (line 4)? How might the rest of the poem explain
and develop this statement?

JOHN MILTON
When I consider how my light is spent

When I consider how my light is spent,
   Ere half my days, in this dark world and wide,
   And that one talent which is death to hide[9]
Lodged with me useless, though my soul more bent
5 To serve therewith my Maker, and present
   My true account, lest he returning chide;
   "Doth God exact day-labor, light denied?"
I fondly ask; but Patience to prevent[1]
That murmur, soon replies, "God doth not need
10 Either man's work or his own gifts; who best
Bear his mild yoke, they serve him best. His state
Is kingly. Thousands at his bidding speed
   And post o'er land and ocean without rest:
   They also serve who only stand and wait."

c. 1652

• How might the timing of the poem's shift to Patience (in the middle of line
8) be meaningful? Paraphrase the speaker's question and Patience's reply.

WILLIAM WORDSWORTH
Nuns Fret Not

Nuns fret not at their convent's narrow room;
And hermits are contented with their cells;

---

8. That is, measuring the altitude of stars (for purposes of navigation) is not a way to measure value.
9. In the parable of the talents (Matt. 25), the servants who earn interest on their master's money (his
talents) while he is away are called "good and faithful"; the one who simply hides the money and then
returns it is condemned and sent away.
1. Forestall. *Fondly*: foolishly.

And students with their pensive citadels;
Maids at the wheel, the weaver at his loom,
5 Sit blithe and happy; bees that soar for bloom,
High as the highest Peak of Furness-fells,[2]
Will murmur by the hour in foxglove bells:
In truth the prison, unto which we doom
Ourselves, no prison is: and hence for me,
10 In sundry moods, 'twas pastime to be bound
Within the sonnet's scanty plot of ground;
Pleased if some souls (for such there needs must be)
Who have felt the weight of too much liberty,
Should find brief solace there, as I have found.

1807

• What does this poem imply about the sonnet's appeal?

The world is too much with us

The world is too much with us; late and soon,
Getting and spending, we lay waste our powers:
Little we see in Nature that is ours;
We have given our hearts away, a sordid boon![3]
5 This Sea that bares her bosom to the moon;
The winds that will be howling at all hours,
And are up-gathered now like sleeping flowers;
For this, for every thing, we are out of tune;
It moves us not.—Great God! I'd rather be
10 A Pagan suckled in a creed outworn;
So might I, standing on this pleasant lea,
Have glimpses that would make me less forlorn;
Have sight of Proteus rising from the sea;
Or hear old Triton[4] blow his wreathèd horn.

1807

• How does the poem characterize the "Pagan" worldview (line 10) as opposed
to "ou[r]" modern one? What does it mean to "see in Nature" nothing or
"Little [. . .] that is ours" (3)?

ELIZABETH BARRETT BROWNING
How Do I Love Thee?

How do I love thee? Let me count the ways.
I love thee to the depth and breadth and height

2. Mountains in England's Lake District, where Wordsworth lived.
3. Gift. It is the act of giving the heart away that is "sordid."
4. Sea deity, usually represented as blowing on a conch shell. *Proteus*: an old man of the sea who (in
The Odyssey) can assume a variety of shapes.

My soul can reach, when feeling out of sight
For the ends of Being and ideal Grace.
5 I love thee to the level of every day's
Most quiet need, by sun and candlelight.
I love thee freely, as men strive for Right;
I love thee purely, as they turn from Praise;
I love thee with the passion put to use
10 In my old griefs, and with my childhood's faith.
I love thee with a love I seemed to lose
With my lost saints—I love thee with the breath,
Smiles, tears of all my life!—and, if God choose,
I shall but love thee better after death.

1850

• How many "ways" of loving does the speaker "count" in the poem (line 1)?
   How do these ways relate to and build on each other?

CHRISTINA ROSSETTI
In an Artist's Studio

One face looks out from all his canvases,
   One selfsame figure sits or walks or leans;
   We found her hidden just behind those screens,
That mirror gave back all her loveliness.
5 A queen in opal or in ruby dress,
   A nameless girl in freshest summer-greens,
   A saint, an angel—every canvas means
The same one meaning, neither more nor less.
He feeds upon her face by day and night,
10   And she with true kind eyes looks back on him
Fair as the moon and joyful as the light:
   Not wan with waiting, not with sorrow dim;
Not as she is, but was when hope shone bright;
   Not as she is, but as she fills his dream.

1856

• What might this poem suggest about the relationship between painter and
   subject? How might the poem's form encourage us to compare painting to
   poetry?

EDNA ST. VINCENT MILLAY
What lips my lips have kissed, and where, and why

What lips my lips have kissed, and where, and why,
I have forgotten, and what arms have lain

Under my head till morning; but the rain
Is full of ghosts tonight, that tap and sigh
5   Upon the glass and listen for reply,
And in my heart there stirs a quiet pain
For unremembered lads that not again
Will turn to me at midnight with a cry.
Thus in the winter stands the lonely tree,
10   Nor knows what birds have vanished one by one,
Yet knows its boughs more silent than before:
I cannot say what loves have come and gone;
I only know that summer sang in me
A little while, that in me sings no more.

                                        1923

• What are the poem's principal parts? Why does the Italian/Petrarchan model
  suit this sonnet?

Women have loved before as I love now

Women have loved before as I love now;
At least, in lively chronicles of the past—
Of Irish waters by a Cornish prow
Or Trojan waters by a Spartan mast
5   Much to their cost invaded—here and there,
Hunting the amorous line, skimming the rest,
I find some woman bearing as I bear
Love like a burning city in the breast.
I think however that of all alive
10   I only in such utter, ancient way
Do suffer love; in me alone survive
The unregenerate passions of a day
When treacherous queens, with death upon the tread,
Heedless and wilful, took their knights to bed.

                                        1931

• What does this poem imply about the difference between ancient and
  modern ways of loving?

I, being born a woman and distressed

I, being born a woman and distressed
By all the needs and notions of my kind,
Am urged by your propinquity to find
Your person fair, and feel a certain zest
5   To bear your body's weight upon my breast:
So subtly is the fume of life designed,
To clarify the pulse and cloud the mind,
And leave me once again undone, possessed.
Think not for this, however, the poor treason

10   Of my stout blood against my staggering brain,
    I shall remember you with love, or season
    My scorn with pity,—let me make it plain:
    I find this frenzy insufficient reason
    For conversation when we meet again.

1923

• What feelings are expressed here? What does the poem imply about the source or cause of these feelings?

I will put Chaos into fourteen lines

    I will put Chaos[5] into fourteen lines
    And keep him there; and let him thence escape
    If he be lucky; let him twist, and ape
    Flood, fire, and demon—his adroit designs
5 Will strain to nothing in the strict confines
    Of this sweet Order, where, in pious rape,
    I hold his essence and amorphous shape,
    Till he with Order mingles and combines.
    Past are the hours, the years, of our duress,
10 His arrogance, our awful servitude:
    I have him. He is nothing more nor less
    Than something simple not yet understood;
    I shall not even force him to confess;
    Or answer. I will only make him good.

1923

• What might this sonnet suggest about the value or appeal of the sonnet form?

GWENDOLYN BROOKS
First Fight. Then Fiddle.

    First fight. Then fiddle. Ply the slipping string
    With feathery sorcery; muzzle the note
    With hurting love; the music that they wrote
    Bewitch, bewilder. Qualify to sing
5 Threadwise. Devise no salt, no hempen thing
    For the dear instrument to bear. Devote
    The bow to silks and honey. Be remote
    A while from malice and from murdering.
    But first to arms, to armor. Carry hate
10 In front of you and harmony behind.

---

5. In Greek mythology, the formless void preceding creation. But Millay's Chaos recalls another mythological figure, Proteus. A sea god endowed with both a knowledge of all things (past, present, and future) and the ability to assume any form in order to elude humans, he would divulge his knowledge only to a captor able to hold him fast through all his mutations—hence the English term *protean*.

Be deaf to music and to beauty blind.
Win war. Rise bloody, maybe not too late
For having first to civilize a space
Wherein to play your violin with grace.

                                                    1949

• After advising "First fight. Then fiddle," the speaker discusses first music,
  then conflict. Why do you think the poet has arranged her material this way?
  Why a sonnet?

GWEN HARWOOD
In the Park

She sits in the park. Her clothes are out of date.
Two children whine and bicker, tug her skirt.
A third draws aimless patterns in the dirt.
Someone she loved once passes by—too late

5 to feign indifference to that casual nod.
"How nice," et cetera. "Time holds great surprises."
From his neat head unquestionably rises
a small balloon . . . "but for the grace of God . . ."

They stand a while in flickering light, rehearsing
10 the children's names and birthdays. "It's so sweet
to hear their chatter, watch them grow and thrive,"
she says to his departing smile. Then, nursing
the youngest child, sits staring at her feet.
To the Wind she says, "They have eaten me alive."

                                                    1963

• What is the implication of the "small balloon" (line 8) that rises from the
  head of the man who passes by?

BILLY COLLINS
Sonnet

All we need is fourteen lines, well, thirteen now,
and after this one just a dozen
to launch a little ship on love's storm-tossed seas,
then only ten more left like rows of beans.
5 How easily it goes unless you get Elizabethan
and insist the iambic bongos must be played
and rhymes positioned at the ends of lines,
one for every station of the cross.
But hang on here while we make the turn

10   into the final six where all will be resolved,
     where longing and heartache will find an end,
     where Laura will tell Petrarch[6] to put down his pen,
     take off those crazy medieval tights,
     blow out the lights, and come at last to bed.

                                                        1999

• In what respects is Collins's poem a traditional sonnet? In what respects is
  it not? What might it suggest about the relationship between love and
  poetry, especially as conventionally portrayed in sonnets?

HARRYETTE MULLEN
Dim Lady[7]

My honeybunch's peepers are nothing like neon. Today's
special at Red Lobster is redder than her kisser. If Liquid Paper
is white, her racks are institutional beige. If her mop were
Slinkys, dishwater Slinkys would grow on her noggin. I have
5   seen tablecloths in Shakey's Pizza Parlors, red and white, but
no such picnic colors do I see in her mug. And in some minty-
fresh mouthwashes there is more sweetness than in the garlic
breeze my main squeeze wheezes. I love to hear her rap, yet
I'm aware that Muzak has a hipper beat. I don't know any
10 Marilyn Monroes. My ball and chain is plain from head to toe.
And yet, by gosh, my scrumptious Twinkie has as much sex
appeal for me as any lanky model or platinum movie idol
who's hyped beyond belief.

                                                        2002

• How might Mullen's poem essentially "do unto" Shakespeare's MY MIS-
  TRESS' EYES ARE NOTHING LIKE THE SUN much as Shakespeare's poem does
  to earlier, especially Petrarchan sonnets? What is the effect of Mullen's
  diction? her use of brand names? Is DIM LADY a sonnet?

SUGGESTIONS FOR WRITING

1. Consider carefully the structure of, and sequencing in, Brooks's FIRST FIGHT. THEN
   FIDDLE. How do various uses of sound in the poem (**rhyme**, **onomatopoeia**, and
   alliteration, for example) reinforce its themes and tones? Write an essay in which
   you explore the relationship between sound and sense in the poem.
2. Some of the sonnets in this book, including those by Shakespeare, adhere closely to the
   classic English model; others, such as Milton's WHEN I CONSIDER HOW MY LIGHT IS SPENT,
   follow the Italian model; and some, including those by Billy Collins and Harryette
   Mullen, bear only slight resemblance to either of the traditional sonnet models. Take
   any four sonnets in this book as the basis for an essay in which you compare the various ways poets have used the sonnet form to achieve their unique artistic purposes.

6. Italian poet Francesco Petrarch (1304–74), regarded as a father of the sonnet form. Many of his
love poems were inspired by Laura, who may have been the wife of a local nobleman.
7. Shakespeare's sonnets frequently address or refer to the so-called Dark Lady.

3. Several poems in this album are not only sonnets but also commentaries on the sonnet or on certain conventions associated with it such as Petrarchan "conceits" (Shakespeare's My MISTRESS' EYES . . .) or the relation between (male) speaker and (female) subject or love object. Write an essay comparing at least two of these poems. What does each ultimately suggest about the sonnet through both its form and its content?

SAMPLE WRITING: COMPARATIVE ESSAY

The student essay below was written in response to the following assignment (a more elaborate version of the last writing suggestion in ch. 17):

> Your second essay for the course should be 6–9 pages long and should analyze two or more poems included in *The Norton Introduction to Literature*. The poems must be by the same author.
>
> You are *strongly* encouraged to pay attention to how the poems' meaning and effect are shaped by some aspect or aspects of their form. Those aspects might include specific formal features such as rhyme, meter, alliteration, or assonance, and/or external form or subgenre—the fact that a poem is a Shakespearean or Petrarchan sonnet, a haiku, or a dramatic monologue, for example. (In terms of the latter, you might consider how the poem's effect and meaning are shaped by the fact that it takes a particular form.)

In her essay, student writer Melissa Makolin draws on three sonnets by William Shakespeare to argue for the distinctiveness and radicalism of the views expressed in two sonnets by another author, Edna St. Vincent Millay. In a sense, then, Makolin's essay focuses simultaneously on external form (ch. 17) and the author's work, even as it explores gender and engages in a kind of feminist criticism (see "Critical Approaches"). That's a lot to tackle in a relatively short essay, and you will no doubt find things both to admire and to criticize about Makolin's argument. At what points do you find yourself agreeing with her interpretation? disagreeing? wanting more evidence or more analysis of the evidence provided? more contextual information—about literary tradition, the author, or historical and cultural context? Where and how might the essay's logic seem faulty or its claims contradictory? In the end, what might you take away from this sample essay about how to craft an effective, persuasive argument about an author's work?

Makolin 1

Melissa Makolin
Dr. Mays
English 298
15 February 2019

Out-Sonneting Shakespeare: An Examination of
Edna St. Vincent Millay's Use of the Sonnet Form

Edna St. Vincent Millay is known not only for her poetry, but also for the feminist ideals she represents therein. She was an extremely talented poet who turned the sonnet form on its head, using the traditionally restrictive form previously used almost exclusively by male poets to express feminist ideas that were radical for her time. Sonnets, especially as written by Shakespeare and Petrarch, are often about the physical beauty of an idealized but also objectified woman, and they implicitly emphasize the man's dominance over her. Millay uses the sonnet form to assert a much different view of femininity, sexuality, and biological dominance. She uses a form known for its poetic limitations to reject social limitations. She uses a form previously used to objectify women to portray them as sexual beings with power and control over their own bodies and lives. The paradox of Millay's poetry is that she uses a poetically binding, male-dominated form to show that she will not be bound either by literary tradition or societal mores regarding inter-gender relations.

The idea of a woman seeking physical pleasure in defiance of societal constraints is one that was revolutionary when "Women have loved before as I love now" and "I, being born a woman and distressed" were published, in 1931 and 1923 respectively. They are poems about a woman's lust leading her to select a sexual partner based on her physical needs rather than on the desire for love. This is a concept that Shakespeare would have found very contentious for three reasons. First, Shakespeare did not agree with acting on lust of any kind; in fact, this is the topic of his sonnet "Th' expense of spirit in a waste of shame." It is a fourteen-line treatise on the evils that result from acting on lustful urges in which Shakespeare declares,

Th' expense of spirit in a waste of shame
Is lust in action; and, till action, lust
Is perjured, murderous, bloody, full of blame,
Savage, extreme, rude, cruel, not to trust. (lines 1-4)

Lust, sexual or otherwise, is a pathway to a hell both religious and secular. Seventeenth-century society dramatically constricted the liberties of women in particular and didn't encourage sexual freedom for either gender.

Second, the majority of Shakespeare's sonnets simultaneously idealize and trivialize the two things they celebrate: women and love. In poems such as "My mistress' eyes are nothing like the sun," he treats women either as objects of an ordered, almost courtly love or as objects of mild ridicule. In this poem's first twelve lines, he mocks his mistress by describing her halitosis (7-8), referring to her breasts as "dun" (3) and her hair as "black wires" (4), references to all the contemporary conventions of beauty to which she does not conform. He not only tells her what the ideal of feminine beauty is, but also makes light of the various ways in which she does not live up to it. He justifies these hurtful insults by reassuring the poor woman that she is "as rare / As any she belied with false compare" (13-14). He mocks her appearance by telling her that she is special and beautiful in her own way only because he loves her. Insulting someone, breaking down her self-esteem, and convincing her that she could be loved by no one else are tactics used in abusive relationships to subjugate one's partner. This is not love, and the role of women in the traditional Shakespeare sonnet is far from empowered.

Third and finally, in addition to idealizing while simultaneously trivializing women, Shakespeare's sonnets also demean the concept of love. To Shakespeare, a woman is worthy of love either because she is an ideal of physical beauty or because he is noble enough to love her despite her flaws (as in "My mistress' eyes are nothing like the sun"). He takes this warped concept one step further, though, by creating an ideal of love that is egotistical and unhealthy for both parties. In "Shall I compare thee to a summer's day?," he spends the first twelve lines describing the ways in which this particular woman fulfills the contemporary ideals of beauty. It is clear that he ardently reveres her physical appearance, and the poem ends with the kind of declaration of personal devotion consistent with love. The turn, however, exhibits a malignant narcissism when it reassures the beloved that "So long as men can breathe or eyes can see, / So long lives this, and this gives life to thee" (13-14). The object of the speaker's affection is just that, an object that only exists as an appendage to him. Shakespeare makes it clear that it is only because of his poetic greatness that their love will persist through the ages. He uses the poetic form to relegate women to the position of objects.

The sonnets of Edna St. Vincent Millay use Shakespearean and Petrarchan forms to offer quite a different view of the role of women. She sees herself as a liberated woman, and she is not afraid to defy social conventions by taking lovers and discarding them when necessary. In writing sonnets about actively satisfying her lust, she also defies literary conventions, completely changing the male-female power dynamic of past sonnets by male writers. In "Women have loved before as I love now," Millay discusses how women throughout history have felt the same lust that she feels, but unlike other more timid and traditional women, she is willing to join the ranks of the brave women of antiquity and to satisfy her passions despite the potential cost. This poem celebrates the women who choose to act against the standards set for them. Describing them as "treacherous queens, with death upon the tread, / Heedless and wilful, [who] took their knights to bed" makes them sound heroic, and it shifts control in the sexual relationship from the man to the woman (13-14). In Millay's version, the women sexually dominate the men and temporarily free themselves from the constraints of an oppressive society. Further, by alluding to the famous females of the "lively chronicles of the past" (2), she shows not only that this behavior is natural and heroic, but also that it is historically valid. The specific women she alludes to when referring to "Irish waters by a Cornish prow" (3) and "Trojan waters by a Spartan mast" (4) are respectively Iseult, the adulteress of the classic work of medieval passion *The Romance of*

Tristan and Iseult, and Helen of Troy (or any of the other libidinous women) of the Homeric epics.

The fact that Millay uses the sonnet form to illustrate sexual liberation is significant for several reasons. First, it shows that she understands the restrictions placed upon her, both as a poet and as a woman. Second, using the sonnet shows that she can hold her own against the great male poets and write within the boundaries that they have erected; the subject matter of her poetry shows that she chooses not to. Lastly, it is significant because, in using the sonnet form for her own feminist purposes, she directly confronts Shakespeare's one-dimensional portrayal of women by proposing her own view of ideal femininity.

The second of Edna St. Vincent Millay's sonnets that defies the ideals set forth by Shakespeare is "I, being born a woman and distressed." It is a poem about impermanent lust, not eternal love. The speaker tells her lover that her feelings are purely physical ("a certain zest / To bear your body's weight upon my breast," 4-5) and simply arise out of human biology ("the needs and notions of my kind," 2) and close quarters ("propinquity," 3). Emotional and physical needs are two things which need not be dependent on each other, and temporary desire does not have to lead to anything lasting. Consummation of a relationship was never discussed in the time of Shakespeare as a tenet of courtly love because women were supposed to be angelic ideals rather than real people with carnal desires. Millay's speaker defies these unrealistic and unattainable ideals of eternal adoration by warning her lover not to "Think" that "I shall remember you with love" (9, 11), illustrating that desire is impermanent. In fact, it is just a temporary "frenzy" and "insufficient reason" even to have a "conversation when we meet again" (13-14). Lust in Millay's world is fleeting, whereas the love of Shakespeare's world is final and complete once the man conquers all and the woman takes her place on his arm. Millay's poem might seem cynical, but it represents a more realistic view of female and male interactions; life and love are transitory and to be enjoyed in the moment because sexual urges can be sated, are biologically determined, and essential to survival, while emotional ones are (relatively) inconsequential and satisfied in other ways.

Millay draws on Shakespeare as a kind of foil by using the form so associated with his name as a vehicle for her very different views on the same topics. Millay brings sexual relationships to a far more terrestrial level with her assertions that women have primal urges that must be satisfied and that submission to ascribed gender roles is not necessary in order to obtain this satisfaction. She presents a radically modern view of relationships. She lambastes the Shakespearean paradigm of the idealized woman, a traditionally beautiful possession of the egotistical man. By using the Shakespearean sonnet form to propose her own revamped, modern vision of woman, a self-aware person who fearlessly relishes the idea of her own emotional and sexual independence, Millay redefines both "woman" and "love."

Makolin 4

WORKS CITED

Mays, Kelly J., editor. *The Norton Introduction to Literature*. Portable 13th ed.,
W. W. Norton, 2020.

Millay, Edna St. Vincent. "I, being born a woman and distressed." Mays,
p. 573–74.

———. "Women have loved before as I love now." Mays, pp. 573.

Shakespeare, William. "Th' expense of spirit in a waste of shame." Mays, pp. 545–46.

———. "My mistress' eyes are nothing like the sun." Mays, p. 568–69.

———. "Shall I compare thee to a summer's day?" Mays, p. 498.

Reading More Poetry

JULIA ALVAREZ
"Poetry Makes Nothing Happen"?

—W. H. AUDEN[1]

Listening to a poem on the radio,
Mike Holmquist stayed awake on his drive home
from Laramie[2] on Interstate 80,
tapping his hand to the beat of some lines
5 by Longfellow;[3] while overcome by grief
one lonesome night when the bathroom cabinet
still held her husband's meds, May Quinn reached out
for a book by Yeats instead and fell asleep
cradling "When You Are Old," not the poet's best,
10 but still . . . poetry made nothing happen,

which was good, given what May had in mind.
Writing a paper on a Bishop[4] poem,
Jenny Klein missed her ride but arrived home
to the cancer news in a better frame of mind.
15 While troops dropped down into Afghanistan
in the living room, Naomi Stella clapped
to the nursery rhyme her father had turned on,
All the king's horses and all the king's men . . .
If only poetry had made nothing happen!
20 If only the president had listened to Auden!

Faith Chaney, Lulú Pérez, Sunghee Chen—
there's a list as long as an epic poem
of folks who'll swear a poem has never done
a thing for them . . . except . . . perhaps adjust
25 the sunset view one cloudy afternoon,
which made them see themselves or see the world
in a different light—degrees of change so small
only a poem registers them at all.
That's why they can be trusted, why poems might
30 still save us from what happens in the world.

2003

---

1. See "In Memory of W. B. Yeats" (line 36; p. 585).   2. In Wyoming.
3. American poet Henry Wadsworth Longfellow (1807–82).   4. Elizabeth Bishop (1911–79).

- How does this poem answer the question in its title: What, if anything, does poetry "make happen" or keep from happening? What is the effect of the poem's specificity about names and situations? of the way each stanza differently plays on the word "happens?"

ANONYMOUS
Sir Patrick Spens

The king sits in Dumferling toune,[5]
    Drinking the blude-reid[6] wine:
"O whar will I get guid sailor,
    To sail this ship of mine?"

5 Up and spake an eldern knicht,
    Sat at the king's richt knee:
"Sir Patrick Spens is the best sailor
    That sails upon the sea."

The king has written a braid[7] letter
10   And signed it wi' his hand,
And sent it to Sir Patrick Spens,
    Was walking on the sand.

The first line that Sir Patrick read,
    A loud lauch[8] lauched he;
15 The next line that Sir Patrick read,
    The tear blinded his ee.[9]

"O wha is this has done this deed,
    This il deed done to me,
To send me out this time o' the year,
20   To sail upon the sea?

"Make haste, make haste, my merry men all,
    Our guid ship sails the morn."
"O say na sae,[1] my master dear,
    For I fear a deadly storm.

25 "Late, late yestre'en I saw the new moon
    Wi' the auld moon in her arm,
And I fear, I fear, my dear mastér,
    That we will come to harm."

O our Scots nobles were richt laith[2]
30   To weet their cork-heeled shoon,[3]
But lang owre a[4] the play were played
    Their hats they swam aboon.[5]

---

5. Town.   6. Bloodred.   7. Broad: explicit.   8. Laugh.   9. Eye.   1. Not so.   2. Right loath: very reluctant.   3. To wet their cork-heeled shoes. Because cork was expensive, such shoes were a mark of wealth and status.   4. Before all.   5. Above.

O lang, lang, may their ladies sit,
   Wi' their fans into their hand,
35 Or ere they see Sir Patrick Spens
   Come sailing to the land.

O lang, lang, may the ladies stand
   Wi' their gold kems[6] in their hair,
Waiting for their ain[7] dear lords,
40   For they'll see them na mair.

Half o'er, half o'er to Aberdour
   It's fifty fadom deep,
And there lies guid Sir Patrick Spens
   Wi' the Scots lords at his feet.
                              c. 13th century

• Often ballads' plots either involve extraordinary, even violent, events experienced by ordinary folk or center on a conflict between people of different
  social ranks. Is that true of SIR PATRICK SPENS? What might the ballad suggest about "nobles" (line 29) through its form, and especially its "music," as
  well as its content?

W. H. AUDEN
In Memory of W. B. Yeats

(d. January, 1939)

I

He disappeared in the dead of winter:
The brooks were frozen, the airports almost deserted,
And snow disfigured the public statues;
The mercury sank in the mouth of the dying day.
5 What instruments we have agree
The day of his death was a dark cold day.

Far from his illness
The wolves ran on through the evergreen forests,
The peasant river was untempted by the fashionable quays;
10 By mourning tongues
The death of the poet was kept from his poems.

But for him it was his last afternoon as himself,
An afternoon of nurses and rumors;
The provinces of his body revolted,
15 The squares of his mind were empty,
Silence invaded the suburbs,
The current of his feeling failed; he became his admirers.

Now he is scattered among a hundred cities
And wholly given over to unfamiliar affections,

6. Combs.   7. Own.

20 To find his happiness in another kind of wood
   And be punished under a foreign code of conscience.
   The words of a dead man
   Are modified in the guts of the living.

   But in the importance and noise of tomorrow
25 When the brokers are roaring like beasts on the floor of the Bourse,[8]
   And the poor have the sufferings to which they are fairly accustomed,
   And each in the cell of himself is almost convinced of his freedom,
   A few thousand will think of this day
   As one thinks of a day when one did something slightly unusual.
30 What instruments we have agree
   The day of his death was a dark cold day.

             II
   You were silly like us; your gift survived it all:
   The parish of rich women, physical decay,
   Yourself. Mad Ireland hurt you into poetry.
35 Now Ireland has her madness and her weather still,
   For poetry makes nothing happen: it survives
   In the valley of its making where executives
   Would never want to tamper, flows on south
   From ranches of isolation and the busy griefs,
40 Raw towns that we believe and die in; it survives,
   A way of happening, a mouth.

             III
   Earth, receive an honored guest:
   William Yeats is laid to rest.
   Let the Irish vessel lie
45 Emptied of its poetry.

   In the nightmare of the dark
   All the dogs of Europe bark,
   And the living nations wait,
   Each sequestered in its hate;

50 Intellectual disgrace
   Stares from every human face,
   And the seas of pity lie
   Locked and frozen in each eye.

   Follow, poet, follow right
55 To the bottom of the night,
   With your unconstraining voice
   Still persuade us to rejoice;

   With the farming of a verse
   Make a vineyard of the curse,
60 Sing of human unsuccess
   In a rapture of distress;

8. Paris stock exchange.

In the deserts of the heart
Let the healing fountain start,
In the prison of his days
65 Teach the free man how to praise.

1939

• Does Auden's **elegy** as a whole affirm that "poetry makes nothing happen" (line 36)? Why does the death of Yeats seem to inspire the speaker to reflect on this possibility?

W. H. AUDEN
Musée des Beaux Arts[9]

About suffering they were never wrong,
The Old Masters: how well they understood
Its human position; how it takes place
While someone else is eating or opening a window or just walking
    dully along;
5 How, when the aged are reverently, passionately waiting
For the miraculous birth, there always must be
Children who did not specially want it to happen, skating
On a pond at the edge of the wood:
They never forgot

Pieter Bruegel, the Elder, *Landscape with the Fall of Icarus*, circa 1555

9. The Museum of the Fine Arts, in Brussels, Belgium.

10 That even the dreadful martyrdom must run its course
Anyhow in a corner, some untidy spot
Where the dogs go on with their doggy life and the torturer's horse
Scratches its innocent behind on a tree.

In Brueghel's *Icarus*,[1] for instance: how everything turns away
15 Quite leisurely from the disaster; the plowman may
Have heard the splash, the forsaken cry,
But for him it was not an important failure; the sun shone
As it had to on the white legs disappearing into the green
Water; and the expensive delicate ship that must have seen
20 Something amazing, a boy falling out of the sky,
Had somewhere to get to and sailed calmly on.

                                                        1938

BASHŌ[2]

A village without bells—

A village without bells—
    how do they live?
        spring dusk.

This road—

This road—
no one goes down it,
    autumn evening.

WILLIAM BLAKE
The Lamb

    Little Lamb, who made thee?
    Dost thou know who made thee?
Gave thee life, and bid thee feed
By the stream and o'er the mead;
5 Gave thee clothing of delight,
Softest clothing woolly bright;
Gave thee such a tender voice,
Making all the vales rejoice?
    Little Lamb, who made thee?
10   Dost thou know who made thee?

---

1. *Landscape with the Fall of Icarus* by Pieter Bruegel the Elder (1525?–69), located in the Brussels museum. According to Greek myth, Daedalus and his son, Icarus, escaped from imprisonment by using homemade wings of feathers and wax; but when Icarus flew too near the sun, the wax melted, and he fell into the sea and drowned. In the Bruegel painting the central figure is a peasant plowing, and several other figures are more immediately noticeable than Icarus, who, disappearing into the sea, is easy to miss in the lower right-hand corner.
2. Matsuo Bashō (1644–94) is usually considered the first great master of haiku. Translations by Robert Hass.

Little Lamb, I'll tell thee!
Little Lamb, I'll tell thee:
He is calléd by thy name,
For he calls himself a Lamb,
15   He is meek and he is mild;
He became a little child.
I a child and thou a lamb,
We are callèd by his name.
Little Lamb, God bless thee!
20   Little Lamb, God bless thee!

The Tyger

Tyger! Tyger! burning bright
In the forests of the night,
What immortal hand or eye
Could frame thy fearful symmetry?

5   In what distant deeps or skies
Burnt the fire of thine eyes?
On what wings dare he aspire?
What the hand dare seize the fire?

And what shoulder, & what art,
10   Could twist the sinews of thy heart?
And when thy heart began to beat,
What dread hand? & what dread feet?

What the hammer? what the chain?
In what furnace was thy brain?
15   What the anvil? what dread grasp
Dare its deadly terrors clasp?

When the stars threw down their spears
And water'd heaven with their tears,
Did he smile his work to see?
20   Did he who made the Lamb make thee?

Tyger! Tyger! burning bright
In the forests of the night,
What immortal hand or eye
Dare frame thy fearful symmetry?

The Chimney Sweeper

A little black thing among the snow:
Crying weep, weep, in notes of woe!
Where are thy father & mother? say?
They are both gone up to the church to pray.

5   Because I was happy upon the heath,
And smil'd among the winters snow:

They clothed me in the clothes of death,
And taught me to sing the notes of woe.

And because I am happy, & dance & sing,
10 They think they have done me no injury:
And are gone to praise God & his Priest & King
Who make up a heaven of our misery.

ROBERT BROWNING
My Last Duchess

Ferrara[3]

That's my last Duchess painted on the wall,
Looking as if she were alive. I call
That piece a wonder, now: Frà Pandolf's[4] hands
Worked busily a day, and there she stands.
5 Will't please you sit and look at her? I said
"Frà Pandolf" by design, for never read
Strangers like you that pictured countenance,
The depth and passion of its earnest glance,
But to myself they turned (since none puts by
10 The curtain I have drawn for you, but I)
And seemed as they would ask me, if they durst,
How such a glance came there; so, not the first
Are you to turn and ask thus. Sir, 'twas not
Her husband's presence only, called that spot
15 Of joy into the Duchess' cheek: perhaps
Frà Pandolf chanced to say "Her mantle laps
Over my lady's wrist too much," or "Paint
Must never hope to reproduce the faint
Half-flush that dies along her throat": such stuff
20 Was courtesy, she thought, and cause enough
For calling up that spot of joy. She had
A heart—how shall I say?—too soon made glad,
Too easily impressed; she liked whate'er
She looked on, and her looks went everywhere.
25 Sir, 'twas all one! My favor at her breast,
The dropping of the daylight in the West,
The bough of cherries some officious fool
Broke in the orchard for her, the white mule
She rode with round the terrace—all and each
30 Would draw from her alike the approving speech,

3. Alfonso II, Duke of Ferrara in Italy in the mid-sixteenth century, is the presumed speaker of this **dramatic monologue**, which is loosely based on historical events. When the duke's first wife—whom he had married when she was fourteen—died at seventeen under suspicious circumstances, he negotiated through an agent (this poem's **auditor**) for marriage to the niece of the count of Tyrol in Austria.
4. Frà Pandolf is, like Claus (line 56), fictitious.

Or blush, at least. She thanked men,—good! but thanked
Somehow—I know not how—as if she ranked
My gift of a nine-hundred-years-old name
With anybody's gift. Who'd stoop to blame
35 This sort of trifling? Even had you skill
In speech—which I have not—to make your will
Quite clear to such an one, and say, "Just this
Or that in you disgusts me; here you miss,
Or there exceed the mark"—and if she let
40 Herself be lessoned so, nor plainly set
Her wits to yours, forsooth, and made excuse,
—E'en then would be some stooping; and I choose
Never to stoop. Oh sir, she smiled, no doubt,
Whene'er I passed her; but who passed without
45 Much the same smile? This grew; I gave commands;
Then all smiles stopped together. There she stands
As if alive. Will't please you rise? We'll meet
The company below, then. I repeat,
The Count your master's known munificence
50 Is ample warrant that no just pretense
Of mine for dowry will be disallowed;
Though his fair daughter's self, as I avowed
At starting, is my object. Nay, we'll go
Together down, sir. Notice Neptune, though,
55 Taming a sea-horse, thought a rarity,
Which Claus of Innsbruck cast in bronze for me!

                                                          1842

SAMUEL TAYLOR COLERIDGE
Kubla Khan

Or, a Vision in a Dream[5]

In Xanadu did Kubla Khan
A stately pleasure-dome decree:
Where Alph, the sacred river, ran
Through caverns measureless to man
5   Down to a sunless sea.
So twice five miles of fertile ground
With walls and towers were girdled round:
And here were gardens bright with sinuous rills
Where blossomed many an incense-bearing tree;
10 And here were forests ancient as the hills,
Enfolding sunny spots of greenery.
But oh! that deep romantic chasm which slanted

---

5. Coleridge claimed that he wrote this fragment immediately after waking from an opium dream and
that after he was interrupted by a visitor he was unable to finish the poem.

Down the green hill athwart a cedarn cover![6]
A savage place! as holy and enchanted
15 As e'er beneath a waning moon was haunted
By woman wailing for her demon-lover![7]
And from this chasm, with ceaseless turmoil seething,
As if this earth in fast thick pants were breathing,
A mighty fountain momently[8] was forced,
20 Amid whose swift half-intermitted burst
Huge fragments vaulted like rebounding hail,
Or chaffy grain beneath the thresher's flail:
And 'mid these dancing rocks at once and ever
It flung up momently the sacred river.
25 Five miles meandering with a mazy motion
Through wood and dale the sacred river ran,
Then reached the caverns measureless to man,
And sank in tumult to a lifeless ocean:
And 'mid this tumult Kubla heard from far
30 Ancestral voices prophesying war!

    The shadow of the dome of pleasure
    Floated midway on the waves;
    Where was heard the mingled measure
    From the fountain and the caves.
35 It was a miracle of rare device,
    A sunny pleasure-dome with caves of ice!

    A damsel with a dulcimer
    In a vision once I saw:
    It was an Abyssinian maid,
40   And on her dulcimer she played,
    Singing of Mount Abora.
    Could I revive within me
    Her symphony and song,
    To such a deep delight 'twould win me,
45 That with music loud and long,
    I would build that dome in air,
    That sunny dome! those caves of ice!
    And all who heard should see them there,
    And all should cry, Beware! Beware!
50 His flashing eyes, his floating hair!
    Weave a circle round him thrice,
    And close your eyes with holy dread,
    For he on honey-dew hath fed,
    And drunk the milk of Paradise.

                        1798

6. That is, from side to side beneath a cover of cedar trees.
7. In a famous and often-imitated German ballad, the lady Lenore is carried off on horseback by the
specter of her lover and married to him at his grave.   8. Suddenly.

BILLY COLLINS
Introduction to Poetry

I ask them to take a poem
and hold it up to the light
like a color slide

or press an ear against its hive.

5 I say drop a mouse into a poem
and watch him probe his way out,

or walk inside the poem's room
and feel the walls for a light switch.

I want them to water-ski
10 across the surface of a poem
waving at the author's name on the shore.

But all they want to do
is tie the poem to a chair with rope
and torture a confession out of it.

15 They begin beating it with a hose
to find out what it really means.

1988

• Who is "them" (line 1), and what is the effect of the speaker's choice to
  refer to "them" and "they" (12) in this way? What different approaches to
  reading poetry come into conflict here? Why and how?

COUNTEE CULLEN
Yet Do I Marvel

I doubt not God is good, well-meaning, kind,
And did He stoop to quibble could tell why
The little buried mole continues blind,
Why flesh that mirrors Him must some day die,
5 Make plain the reason tortured Tantalus[9]
Is baited by the fickle fruit, declare
If merely brute caprice dooms Sisyphus[1]
To struggle up a never-ending stair.
Inscrutable His ways are, and immune
10 To catechism by a mind too strewn
With petty cares to slightly understand
What awful brain compels His awful hand.

9. Figure in Greek myth condemned, for ambiguous reasons, to stand up to his neck in water he
couldn't drink and to look upon fruit he couldn't reach to eat.
1. King of Corinth who, in Greek myth, was condemned eternally to roll a huge stone uphill.

Yet do I marvel at this curious thing:
To make a poet black, and bid him sing!

1925

E. E. CUMMINGS
in Just-[2]

in Just-
spring   when the world is mud-
luscious the little
lame balloonman

5   whistles   far   and wee

and eddieandbill come
running from marbles and
piracies and it's
spring

10   when the world is puddle-wonderful

the queer
old balloonman whistles
far   and   wee
and bettyandisbel come dancing

15   from hop-scotch and jump-rope and

it's
spring
and
       the
20   goat-footed

balloonMan[3] whistles
far
and
wee

1923

EMILY DICKINSON
Wild Nights—Wild Nights!

Wild Nights—Wild Nights!
Were I with thee
Wild Nights should be
Our luxury!

---

2. First poem in the series *Chansons innocentes* (French for "Songs of Innocence").
3. Pan, whose Greek name means "everything," is traditionally represented with a syrinx (or the pipes of Pan). The upper half of his body is human, the lower half goat; as the father of Silenus he is associated with the spring rites of the god Dionysus.

5 Futile—the Winds—
To a Heart in port—
Done with the Compass—
Done with the Chart!

Rowing in Eden—
10 Ah, the Sea!
Might I but moor—Tonight—
In Thee!

1861

> • Whom might the speaker be addressing? What might it mean to be "Done with the Chart" (line 8)?

"Hope" is the thing with feathers—

"Hope" is the thing with feathers—
That perches in the soul—
And sings the tune without the words—
And never stops—at all—

5 And sweetest—in the Gale—is heard—
And sore must be the storm—
That could abash the little Bird
That kept so many warm—

I've heard it in the chillest land—
10 And on the strangest Sea—
Yet—never—in Extremity,
It asked a crumb—of me.

1862

> • What might be both expected and unexpected or surprising about the poem's controlling metaphor and the way it develops? How might the imagery in this poem compare to that in other Dickinson poems? Or how might the *use* of imagery (rather than the images themselves) compare?

I heard a Fly buzz—when I died—

I heard a Fly buzz—when I died—
The Stillness in the Room
Was like the Stillness in the Air—
Between the Heaves of Storm—

5 The Eyes around—had wrung them dry—
And Breaths were gathering firm
For that last Onset—when the King
Be witnessed—in the Room—

I willed my Keepsakes—Signed away
10 What portion of me be

Assignable—and then it was
There interposed a Fly—

With Blue—uncertain—stumbling Buzz—
Between the light—and me—
15 And then the Windows failed—and then
I could not see to see—

1863

• How would you describe this poem's internal structure? That is, how would
you divide it into parts, and characterize the relationship between them or
the way one part differs from the other? Why a fly?

My Life had stood—a Loaded Gun—

My Life had stood—a Loaded Gun—
In Corners—till a Day
The Owner passed—identified—
And carried Me away—

5 And now We roam in Sovereign Woods—
And now We hunt the Doe—
And every time I speak for Him—
The Mountains straight reply—

And do I smile, such cordial light
10 Upon the Valley glow—
It is as a Vesuvian face
Had let its pleasure through—

And when at Night—Our good Day done—
I guard My Master's Head—
15 'Tis better than the Eider-Duck's
Deep Pillow—to have shared—

To foe of His—I'm deadly foe—
None stir the second time—
On whom I lay a Yellow Eye—
20 Or an emphatic Thumb—

Though I than He—may longer live
He longer must—than I—
For I have but the power to kill,
Without—the power to die—

c. 1863

• How does Dickinson set up and then defy expectations through the poem's
controlling metaphor? How do the poem's quirks (e.g., the jerky rhythm, the
strange syntax, the slant rhymes) contribute to its overall effect?

I stepped from Plank to Plank

I stepped from Plank to Plank
A slow and cautious way
The Stars about my Head I felt
About my Feet the Sea.

5 I knew not but the next
Would be my final inch—
This gave me that precarious Gait
Some call Experience.

1865

• For what does "stepp[ing] from Plank to Plank" become a metaphor in the
poem? Is this experience a positive or a negative one?

Tell all the truth but tell it slant—

Tell all the truth but tell it slant—
Success in Circuit lies
Too bright for our infirm Delight
The Truth's superb surprise
5 As Lightning to the Children eased
With explanation kind
The Truth must dazzle gradually
Or every man be blind—

1872

• What meanings of the word "Circuit" (line 2) seem especially appropriate
and relevant here? Why and how so?

JOHN DONNE

Death, be not proud

Death, be not proud, though some have callèd thee
Mighty and dreadful, for thou art not so;
For those whom thou think'st thou dost overthrow
Die not, poor Death, nor yet canst thou kill me.
5 From rest and sleep, which but thy pictures[4] be,
Much pleasure; then from thee much more must flow,
And soonest[5] our best men with thee do go,
Rest of their bones, and soul's delivery.[6]
Thou art slave to Fate, Chance, kings, and desperate men,
10 And dost with Poison, War, and Sickness dwell;
And poppy or charms can make us sleep as well,

---

4. Likenesses.   5. Most willingly.   6. Deliverance.

And better than thy stroke; why swell'st[7] thou then?
One short sleep past, we wake eternally
And death shall be no more; Death, thou shalt die.

1633

Song

Go, and catch a falling star,
   Get with child a mandrake root,[8]
Tell me, where all past years are,
   Or who cleft the devil's foot,
5 Teach me to hear mermaids singing
Or to keep off envy's stinging,
     And find
     What wind
Serves to advance an honest mind.

10 If thou beest born to strange sights,[9]
   Things invisible to see,
Ride ten thousand days and nights,
   Till age snow white hairs on thee;
Thou, when thou return'st, wilt tell me
15 All strange wonders that befell thee,
     And swear
     No where
Lives a woman true, and fair.

If thou find'st one, let me know:
20   Such a pilgrimage were sweet.
Yet do not, I would not go,
   Though at next door we might meet:
Though she were true when you met her,
And last till you write your letter,
25   Yet she
     Will be
False, ere I come, to two, or three.

1633

A Valediction: Forbidding Mourning

As virtuous men pass mildly away,
   And whisper to their souls to go,
Whilst some of their sad friends do say,
   "The breath goes now," and some say, "No,"

7. Puff with pride.
8. The forked mandrake root looks vaguely like a pair of human legs.
9. That is, if you have supernatural powers.

5 So let us melt, and make no noise,
       No tear-floods, nor sigh-tempests move;
    'Twere profanation of our joys
       To tell the laity our love.

    Moving of the earth[1] brings harms and fears,
10   Men reckon what it did and meant;
    But trepidation of the spheres,[2]
       Though greater far, is innocent.

    Dull sublunary[3] lovers' love
       (Whose soul is sense) cannot admit
15 Absence, because it doth remove
       Those things which elemented[4] it.

    But we, by a love so much refined
       That our selves know not what it is,
    Inter-assured of the mind,
20   Care less, eyes, lips, and hands to miss.

    Our two souls therefore, which are one,
       Though I must go, endure not yet
    A breach, but an expansion,
       Like gold to airy thinness beat.

25 If they be two, they are two so
       As stiff twin compasses are two:
    Thy soul, the fixed foot, makes no show
       To move, but doth, if the other do;

    And though it in the center sit,
30   Yet when the other far doth roam,
    It leans, and hearkens after it,
       And grows erect, as that comes home.

    Such wilt thou be to me, who must,
       Like the other foot, obliquely run;
35 Thy firmness makes my circle[5] just,
       And makes me end where I begun.

                           c. 1611

---

1. Earthquakes.
2. Renaissance theory that the celestial spheres trembled and thus caused unexpected variations in their orbits. Such movements are "innocent" because earthlings do not observe or fret about them.
3. Below the moon—that is, changeable. According to the traditional cosmology that Donne invokes here, the moon is the dividing line between the immutable celestial world and the mutable earthly one.
4. Comprised, made up its elements.   5. Traditional symbol of perfection.

PAUL LAURENCE DUNBAR
We Wear the Mask

We wear the mask that grins and lies,
It hides our cheeks and shades our eyes,—
This debt we pay to human guile;
With torn and bleeding hearts we smile,
5 And mouth with myriad subtleties.

Why should the world be over-wise,
In counting all our tears and sighs?
Nay, let them only see us, while
    We wear the mask.

10 We smile, but, O great Christ, our cries
To thee from tortured souls arise.
We sing, but oh the clay is vile
Beneath our feet, and long the mile;
But let the world dream otherwise,
15   We wear the mask!

                                        1895

T. S. ELIOT
The Love Song of J. Alfred Prufrock

S'io credesse che mia risposta fosse
a persona che mai tornasse al mondo,
questa fiamma staria senza più scosse.
Ma per ciò che giammai di questo fondo
non tornò vivo alcun, s'i'odo il vero,
senza tema d'infamia ti rispondo.[6]

Let us go then, you and I,
When the evening is spread out against the sky
Like a patient etherised upon a table;
Let us go, through certain half-deserted streets,
5 The muttering retreats
Of restless nights in one-night cheap hotels
And sawdust restaurants with oyster-shells:
Streets that follow like a tedious argument
Of insidious intent

6. From Dante, *Inferno* (27.61–66): "If I thought that my reply would be / to one who would ever return to the world, / this flame would stay without further movement; // but since none has ever returned alive from this depth, / if what I hear is true, / I answer you without fear of infamy." The words are spoken by the character Guido da Montefeltro—imprisoned in flame in the depths of hell as a punishment for giving false counsel—to Dante, whom da Montefeltro believes will never return from his journey into the inferno.

10   To lead you to an overwhelming question . . .
　　 Oh, do not ask, "What is it?"
　　 Let us go and make our visit.

　　 In the room the women come and go
　　 Talking of Michelangelo.[7]

15   The yellow fog that rubs its back upon the window-panes,
　　 The yellow smoke that rubs its muzzle on the window-panes,
　　 Licked its tongue into the corners of the evening,
　　 Lingered upon the pools that stand in drains,
　　 Let fall upon its back the soot that falls from chimneys,
20   Slipped by the terrace, made a sudden leap,
　　 And seeing that it was a soft October night,
　　 Curled once about the house, and fell asleep.

　　 And indeed there will be time[8]
　　 For the yellow smoke that slides along the street
25   Rubbing its back upon the window-panes;
　　 There will be time, there will be time
　　 To prepare a face to meet the faces that you meet;
　　 There will be time to murder and create,
　　 And time for all the works and days[9] of hands
30   That lift and drop a question on your plate;
　　 Time for you and time for me,
　　 And time yet for a hundred indecisions,
　　 And for a hundred visions and revisions,
　　 Before the taking of a toast and tea.

35   In the room the women come and go
　　 Talking of Michelangelo.

　　 And indeed there will be time
　　 To wonder, "Do I dare?" and, "Do I dare?"
　　 Time to turn back and descend the stair,
40   With a bald spot in the middle of my hair—
　　 (They will say: "How his hair is growing thin!")
　　 My morning coat, my collar mounting firmly to the chin,
　　 My necktie rich and modest, but asserted by a simple pin—
　　 (They will say: "But how his arms and legs are thin!")
45   Do I dare
　　 Disturb the universe?
　　 In a minute there is time
　　 For decisions and revisions which a minute will reverse.

　　 For I have known them all already, known them all—
50   Have known the evenings, mornings, afternoons,

7. Italian artist Michelangelo Buonarroti (1475–1564).
8. Echo of Andrew Marvell's "To His Coy Mistress" (1681; p. 455), which famously begins, "Had we but world enough, and time / This coyness, lady, were no crime."
9. *Works and Days* is a poem composed about 700 BCE by the Greek writer Hesiod; lamenting the moral decay of the present, it celebrates simple life and hard work, especially agricultural labor.

I have measured out my life with coffee spoons;
I know the voices dying with a dying fall
Beneath the music from a farther room.
    So how should I presume?

55 And I have known the eyes already, known them all—
The eyes that fix you in a formulated phrase,
And when I am formulated, sprawling on a pin,
When I am pinned and wriggling on the wall,
Then how should I begin
60 To spit out all the butt-ends of my days and ways?
    And how should I presume?

And I have known the arms already, known them all—
Arms that are braceleted and white and bare
(But in the lamplight, downed with light brown hair!)
65 Is it perfume from a dress
That makes me so digress?
Arms that lie along a table, or wrap about a shawl.
    And should I then presume?
    And how should I begin?

      . . . . . .

70 Shall I say, I have gone at dusk through narrow streets
And watched the smoke that rises from the pipes
Of lonely men in shirt-sleeves, leaning out of windows? . . .

I should have been a pair of ragged claws
Scuttling across the floors of silent seas.

      . . . . .

75 And the afternoon, the evening, sleeps so peacefully!
Smoothed by long fingers,
Asleep . . . tired . . . or it malingers,
Stretched on the floor, here beside you and me.
Should I, after tea and cakes and ices,
80 Have the strength to force the moment to its crisis?
But though I have wept and fasted, wept and prayed,
Though I have seen my head (grown slightly bald) brought in
    upon a platter,[1]
I am no prophet—and here's no great matter;
I have seen the moment of my greatness flicker,
85 And I have seen the eternal Footman hold my coat, and snicker,
And in short, I was afraid.

And would it have been worth it, after all,
After the cups, the marmalade, the tea,

---

1. Like John the Baptist; at a banquet, King Herod has the prophet's head delivered on a plate to Salome, the woman who requested his execution (Mark 6.17–28; Matt. 14.3–11).

Among the porcelain, among some talk of you and me,
90 Would it have been worth while,
To have bitten off the matter with a smile,
To have squeezed the universe into a ball[2]
To roll it towards some overwhelming question,
To say: "I am Lazarus, come from the dead,[3]
95 Come back to tell you all, I shall tell you all"—
If one, settling a pillow by her head,
    Should say: "That is not what I meant at all.
    That is not it, at all."

And would it have been worth it, after all,
100 Would it have been worth while,
After the sunsets and the dooryards and the sprinkled streets,
After the novels, after the teacups, after the skirts that trail along
    the floor—
And this, and so much more?—
It is impossible to say just what I mean!
105 But as if a magic lantern threw the nerves in patterns on a
    screen:
Would it have been worth while
If one, settling a pillow or throwing off a shawl,
And turning toward the window, should say:
    "That is not it at all,
110   That is not what I meant, at all."

. . . . .

No! I am not Prince Hamlet,[4] nor was meant to be;
Am an attendant lord, one that will do
To swell a progress,[5] start a scene or two,
Advise the prince; no doubt, an easy tool,
115 Deferential, glad to be of use,
Politic, cautious, and meticulous;
Full of high sentence,[6] but a bit obtuse;
At times, indeed, almost ridiculous—
Almost, at times, the Fool.

120 I grow old . . . I grow old . . .
I shall wear the bottoms of my trousers rolled.

Shall I part my hair behind? Do I dare to eat a peach?
I shall wear white flannel trousers, and walk upon the beach.
I have heard the mermaids singing, each to each.

2. Another echo of "To His Coy Mistress": "Let us roll all our strength and all / Our sweetness up into one ball, / And tear our pleasures with rough strife / Thorough the iron gates of life" (lines 41–44; p. 455).
3. The New Testament relates the story of Jesus raising Lazarus from the dead in John 11.1–44.
4. Protagonist of Shakespeare's tragedy *Hamlet* (p. 906), who is indecisive for much of the play.
5. Journey of a royal or noble person, or the representation of such a journey onstage as part of a play (as was common in Shakespeare's age).   6. Sententious; that is, he tends to speak in a pompous, formal manner.

125 I do not think that they will sing to me.

I have seen them riding seaward on the waves
Combing the white hair of the waves blown back
When the wind blows the water white and black.

We have lingered in the chambers of the sea
130 By sea-girls wreathed with seaweed red and brown
Till human voices wake us, and we drown.

1915

ROBERT FROST
Fire and Ice

Some say the world will end in fire,
Some say in ice.
From what I've tasted of desire
I hold with those who favor fire.
5 But if it had to perish twice,
I think I know enough of hate
To say that for destruction ice
Is also great
And would suffice.

1920

Stopping by Woods on a Snowy Evening

Whose woods these are I think I know.
His house is in the village though;
He will not see me stopping here
To watch his woods fill up with snow.

5 My little horse must think it queer
To stop without a farmhouse near
Between the woods and frozen lake
The darkest evening of the year.

He gives his harness bells a shake
10 To ask if there is some mistake.
The only other sound's the sweep
Of easy wind and downy flake.

The woods are lovely, dark, and deep,
But I have promises to keep,
15 And miles to go before I sleep,
And miles to go before I sleep.

1923

ANGELINA GRIMKÉ
Tenebris[7]

There is a tree, by day,
That, at night,
Has a shadow,
A hand huge and black,
5 With fingers long and black.
   All through the dark,
Against the white man's house,
   In the little wind,
The black hand plucks and plucks
10   At the bricks.
The bricks are the color of blood and very small.
      Is it a black hand,
      Or is it a shadow?

1927

Angelina Grimké, circa 1905

SEAMUS HEANEY
Digging

Between my finger and my thumb
The squat pen rests; snug as a gun.

Under my window, a clean rasping sound
When the spade sinks into gravelly ground:
5 My father, digging. I look down

Till his straining rump among the flowerbeds
Bends low, comes up twenty years away
Stooping in rhythm through potato drills[8]
Where he was digging.

10 The coarse boot nestled on the lug, the shaft
Against the inside knee was levered firmly.
He rooted out tall tops, buried the bright edge deep
To scatter new potatoes that we picked
Loving their cool hardness in our hands.

15 By God, the old man could handle a spade.
Just like his old man.

7. In darkness (Latin).
8. Small furrows in which seeds are sown.

My grandfather cut more turf[9] in a day
Than any other man on Toner's bog.
Once I carried him milk in a bottle
20 Corked sloppily with paper. He straightened up
To drink it, then fell to right away
Nicking and slicing neatly, heaving sods
Over his shoulder, going down and down
For the good turf. Digging.

25 The cold smell of potato mould, the squelch and slap
Of soggy peat, the curt cuts of an edge
Through living roots awaken in my head.
But I've no spade to follow men like them.

Between my finger and my thumb
30 The squat pen rests.
I'll dig with it.

1966

GERARD MANLEY HOPKINS
God's Grandeur

The world is charged with the grandeur of God.
    It will flame out, like shining from shook foil;[1]
    It gathers to a greatness, like the ooze of oil
Crushed. Why do men then now not reck his rod?[2]
5 Generations have trod, have trod, have trod;
    And all is seared with trade; bleared, smeared with toil;
    And wears man's smudge and shares man's smell: the soil
Is bare now, nor can foot feel, being shod.

And for all this, nature is never spent;
10   There lives the dearest freshness deep down things;
And though the last lights off the black West went
    Oh, morning, at the brown brink eastward, springs—
Because the Holy Ghost over the bent
    World broods with warm breast and with ah! bright wings.

c. 1877

9. Peat cut into slabs and dried to be used as fuel in stoves and furnaces.
1. "I mean foil in its sense of leaf or tinsel [. . .]. Shaken goldfoil gives off broad glares like sheet lightning and also, and this is true of nothing else, owing to its zig-zag dints and creasings and network of
small many cornered facets, a sort of fork lightning too" (*Letters of Gerard Manley Hopkins to Robert
Bridges*, edited by C. C. Abbott, 1955, p. 169).   2. Heed his authority.

Spring and Fall

to a young child

> Márgarét áre you gríeving[3]
> Over Goldengrove unleaving?
> Leáves, like the things of man, you
> With your fresh thoughts care for, can you?
> 5 Áh! ás the heart grows older
> It will-come to such sights colder
> By and by, nor spare a sigh
> Though worlds of wanwood leafmeal[4] lie;
> And yet you will weep and know why.
> 10 Now no matter, child, the name:
> Sórrow's spríngs áre the same.
> Nor mouth had, no nor mind, expressed
> What heart heard of, ghost[5] guessed:
> It ís the blight man was born for,
> 15 It is Margaret you mourn for.

1880

LANGSTON HUGHES
Harlem

What happens to a dream deferred?

> Does it dry up
> Like a raisin in the sun?
> Or fester like a sore—
> 5 And then run?
> Does it stink like rotten meat?
> Or crust and sugar over—
> Like a syrupy sweet?
> Maybe it just sags
> 10 Like a heavy load.
>
> *Or does it explode?*

1951

Langston Hughes, circa 1925, in a
pastel portrait by Winold Reiss

3. Hopkins's own accent markings.
4. Broken up, leaf by leaf (analogous to "piecemeal"). *Wanwood*: pale, gloomy woods.   5. Soul.

I, Too

I, too, sing America.

I am the darker brother.
They send me to eat in the kitchen
When company comes,
5 But I laugh,
And eat well,
And grow strong.

Tomorrow,
I'll sit at the table.
10 When company comes
Nobody'll dare
Say to me,
"Eat in the kitchen,"
Then.

15 Besides,
They'll see how beautiful I am
And be ashamed—

I, too, am America.

1932

BEN JONSON
On My First Son

Farewell, thou child of my right hand,[6] and joy;
My sin was too much hope of thee, loved boy:
Seven years thou wert lent to me, and I thee pay,
Exacted by thy fate, on the just[7] day.
5 O could I lose all father now! for why
Will man lament the state he should envy,
To have so soon 'scaped world's and flesh's rage,
And, if no other misery, yet age?
Rest in soft peace, and asked, say, "Here doth lie
10 Ben Jonson his[8] best piece of poetry."
For whose sake henceforth all his vows be such
As what he loves may never like too much.

1616

6. Literal translation of the son's name, Benjamin.   7. Exact; the son died on his seventh birthday, in 1603.   8. That is, Ben Jonson's (this was a common Renaissance form of the possessive).

JOHN KEATS
Ode on a Grecian Urn

I

Thou still unravished bride of quietness,
   Thou foster-child of silence and slow time,
Sylvan historian, who canst thus express
   A flowery tale more sweetly than our rhyme:
5 What leaf-fringed legend haunts about thy shape
     Of deities or mortals, or of both,
       In Tempe or the dales of Arcady?[9]
   What men or gods are these? What maidens loath?
     What mad pursuit? What struggle to escape?
10   What pipes and timbrels? What wild
ecstasy?

II

Heard melodies are sweet, but those unheard
   Are sweeter; therefore, ye soft pipes, play on;
Not to the sensual[1] ear, but, more endeared,
   Pipe to the spirit ditties of no tone:
15 Fair youth, beneath the trees, thou canst not leave
     Thy song, nor ever can those trees be bare;
       Bold Lover, never, never canst thou kiss,
   Though winning near the goal—yet, do not grieve;
     She cannot fade, though thou hast not thy bliss,
20   For ever wilt thou love, and she be fair!

III

Ah, happy, happy boughs! that cannot shed
   Your leaves, nor ever bid the Spring adieu;
And, happy melodist, unwearièd,
   For ever piping songs for ever new;
25 More happy love! more happy, happy love!
     For ever warm and still to be enjoyed,
       For ever panting, and for ever young;
All breathing human passion far above,
   That leaves a heart high-sorrowful and cloyed,
30   A burning forehead, and a parching tongue.

IV

Who are these coming to the sacrifice?
   To what green altar, O mysterious priest,
Lead'st thou that heifer lowing at the skies,
   And all her silken flanks with garlands dressed?

9. Arcadia. Tempe is a beautiful valley near Mt. Olympus in Greece, and the valleys ("dales") of Arcadia are a picturesque section of the Peloponnesus; both came to be associated with the pastoral ideal.
1. Of the senses, as distinguished from the "ear" of the spirit or imagination.

Greek vase featuring Hercules driving
a bull to sacrifice, c. 525–520 BCE

35 What little town by river or sea shore,
       Or mountain-built with peaceful citadel,
           Is emptied of its folk, this pious morn?
     And, little town, thy streets for evermore
       Will silent be; and not a soul to tell
40   Why thou art desolate, can e'er return.

                    V
     O Attic shape! Fair attitude! with brede²
       Of marble men and maidens overwrought,³
     With forest branches and the trodden weed;
       Thou, silent form, dost tease us out of thought
45   As doth eternity: Cold Pastoral!
       When old age shall this generation waste,
         Thou shalt remain, in midst of other woe
     Than ours, a friend to man, to whom thou say'st,
       Beauty is truth, truth beauty⁴—that is all
50   Ye know on earth, and all ye need to know.
     May 1819   1820

---

2. Woven pattern. *Attic*: Attica was the district of ancient Greece surrounding Athens.
3. Ornamented all over.
4. In some printings of the poem, "Beauty is truth, truth beauty" is in quotation marks, and in some
texts it is not, leading to critical disagreements about whether the last line and a half are also
inscribed on the urn or spoken by the poem's speaker.

To Autumn

I

Season of mists and mellow fruitfulness,
    Close bosom-friend of the maturing sun;
Conspiring with him how to load and bless
    With fruit the vines that round the thatch-eves run;
5 To bend with apples the mossed cottage-trees,
    And fill all fruit with ripeness to the core;
        To swell the gourd, and plump the hazel shells
With a sweet kernel; to set budding more,
    And still more, later flowers for the bees,
10   Until they think warm days will never cease,
        For Summer has o'er-brimmed their clammy cells.

II

Who hath not seen thee oft amid thy store?
    Sometimes whoever seeks abroad may find
Thee sitting careless on a granary floor,
15   Thy hair soft-lifted by the winnowing wind,[5]
Or on a half-reaped furrow sound asleep,
    Drowsed with the fume of poppies, while thy hook[6]
        Spares the next swath and all its twinèd flowers:
And sometimes like a gleaner thou dost keep
20   Steady thy laden head across a brook;
    Or by a cider-press, with patient look,
        Thou watchest the last oozings hours by hours.

III

Where are the songs of Spring? Ay, where are they?
    Think not of them, thou hast thy music too—
25 While barrèd clouds bloom the soft-dying day,
    And touch the stubble-plains with rosy hue;
Then in a wailful choir the small gnats mourn
    Among the river sallows,[7] borne aloft
        Or sinking as the light wind lives or dies;
30 And full-grown lambs loud bleat from hilly bourn;[8]
    Hedge-crickets sing; and now with treble soft
    The red-breast whistles from a garden-croft;[9]
        And gathering swallows twitter in the skies.
September 19, 1819   1820

5. Which sifts the grain from the chaff.   6. Scythe or sickle.   7. Shallows.   8. Domain.
9. Enclosed garden near a house.

ETHERIDGE KNIGHT
Eastern guard tower

Eastern guard tower
glints in sunset; convicts rest
like lizards on rocks.

The falling snow flakes

The falling snow flakes
Cannot blunt the hard aches nor
Match the steel stillness.

Making jazz swing in

Making jazz swing in
Seventeen syllables AIN'T
No square poet's job.

1960

CLAUDE MCKAY
America

Although she feeds me bread of bitterness,
And sinks into my throat her tiger's tooth,
Stealing my breath of life, I will confess
I love this cultured hell that tests my youth!
5 Her vigor flows like tides into my blood,
Giving me strength erect against her hate.
Her bigness sweeps my being like a flood.
Yet as a rebel fronts a king in state,
I stand within her walls with not a shred
10 Of terror, malice nor even a word of jeer.
Darkly I gaze into the days ahead
To see her might and granite wonders there,
Beneath the touch of Time's unerring hand,
Like ancient treasures buried in the sand.

1921

The White House

Your door is shut against my tightened face,
And I am sharp as steel with discontent;
But I possess the courage and the grace

To bear my anger proudly and unbent.
5 The pavement slabs burn loose beneath my feet,
And passion rends my vitals as I pass,
A chafing savage, down the decent street,
Where boldly shines your shuttered door of glass.
Oh, I must search for wisdom every hour,
10 Deep in my wrathful bosom sore and raw,
And find in it the superhuman power
To hold me to the letter of your law!
Oh, I must keep my heart inviolate
Against the poison of your deadly hate.

1937

PAT MORA

Elena

My Spanish isn't enough.
I remember how I'd smile
listening to my little ones,
understanding every word they'd say,
5 their jokes, their songs, their plots.
    Vamos a pedirle dulces a mamá. Vamos.[1]
But that was in Mexico.
Now my children go to American high schools.
They speak English. At night they sit around
10 the kitchen table, laugh with one another.
I stand by the stove and feel dumb, alone.
I bought a book to learn English.
My husband frowned, drank more beer.
My oldest said, "*Mamá*, he doesn't want you
15 to be smarter than he is." I'm forty,
embarrassed at mispronouncing words,
embarrassed at the laughter of my children,
the grocer, the mailman. Sometimes I take
my English book and lock myself in the bathroom,
20 say the thick words softly,
for if I stop trying, I will be deaf
when my children need my help.

1985

• What does the speaker mean by the first line—"My Spanish isn't enough"?
What other words in the poem address the inadequacy of language?

---

1. Let's go ask mama for sweets. Let's go (Spanish).

Gentle Communion

Even the long-dead are willing to move.
Without a word, she came with me from the desert.
Mornings she wanders through my rooms
making beds, folding socks.

5   Since she can't hear me anymore,
Mamande[2] ignores the questions I never knew
to ask, about her younger days, her red
hair, the time she fell and broke her nose
in the snow. I will never know.

10 When I try to make her laugh,
to disprove her sad album face, she leaves
the room, resists me as she resisted
grinning for cameras, make-up, English.

While I write, she sits and prays,
15 feet apart, legs never crossed,
the blue housecoat buttoned high
as her hair dries white, girlish
around her head and shoulders.

She closes her eyes, bows her head,
20 and like a child presses her hands together,
her patient flesh steeple, the skin
worn, like the pages of her prayer book.

Sometimes I sit in her wide-armed
chair as I once sat in her lap.
25 Alone, we played a quiet I Spy.
She peeled grapes I still taste.

She removes the thin skin, places
the luminous coolness on my tongue.
I know not to bite or chew. I wait
30 for the thick melt,
our private green honey.

1991

• How does this poem draw on the various meanings of the word *communion*? Why might it be significant that the grandmother comes "Without a
word" (line 2)?

2. Child's conflation of *mama grande* (Spanish for "grandmother").

LINDA PASTAN
To a Daughter Leaving Home

When I taught you
at eight to ride
a bicycle, loping along
beside you
5   as you wobbled away
on two round wheels,
my own mouth rounding
in surprise when you pulled
ahead down the curved
10   path of the park,
I kept waiting
for the thud
of your crash as I
sprinted to catch up,
15   while you grew
smaller, more breakable
with distance,
pumping, pumping
for your life, screaming
20   with laughter,
the hair flapping
behind you like a
handkerchief waving
goodbye.

                1988

MARGE PIERCY
Barbie Doll

This girlchild was born as usual
and presented dolls that did pee-pee
and miniature GE stoves and irons
and wee lipsticks the color of cherry candy.
5   Then in the magic of puberty, a classmate said:
You have a great big nose and fat legs.

She was healthy, tested intelligent,
possessed strong arms and back,
abundant sexual drive and manual dexterity.
10   She went to and fro apologizing.
Everyone saw a fat nose on thick legs.

She was advised to play coy,
exhorted to come on hearty,

exercise, diet, smile and wheedle.
15 Her good nature wore out
like a fan belt.
So she cut off her nose and her legs
and offered them up.

In the casket displayed on satin she lay
20 with the undertaker's cosmetics painted on,
a turned-up putty nose,
dressed in a pink and white nightie.
Doesn't she look pretty? everyone said.
Consummation at last.
25 To every woman a happy ending.

1973

SYLVIA PLATH
Daddy

You do not do, you do not do
Any more, black shoe
In which I have lived like a foot
For thirty years, poor and white,
5 Barely daring to breathe or Achoo.

Daddy, I have had to kill you.
You died before I had time—
Marble-heavy, a bag full of God,
Ghastly statue with one gray toe[3]
10 Big as a Frisco seal

And a head in the freakish Atlantic
Where it pours bean green over blue
In the waters off beautiful Nauset.[4]
I used to pray to recover you.
15 Ach, du.[5]

In the German tongue, in the Polish town[6]
Scraped flat by the roller
Of wars, wars, wars.
But the name of the town is common.
20 My Polack friend

Says there are a dozen or two.
So I never could tell where you
Put your foot, your root,

3. Otto Plath, Sylvia's father, lost a toe to gangrene resulting from diabetes.
4. Inlet on Cape Cod, Massachusetts.   5. Oh, you (German).
6. Otto Plath, an ethnic German, was born in Grabow, Poland.

I never could talk to you.
25 The tongue stuck in my jaw.

It stuck in a barb wire snare.
Ich,[7] ich, ich, ich,
I could hardly speak.
I thought every German was you.
30 And the language obscene

An engine, an engine
Chuffing me off like a Jew.
A Jew to Dachau, Auschwitz, Belsen.[8]
I began to talk like a Jew.
35 I think I may well be a Jew.

The snows of the Tyrol, the clear beer of Vienna[9]
Are not very pure or true.
With my gypsy-ancestress and my weird luck
And my Taroc[1] pack and my Taroc pack
40 I may be a bit of a Jew.

I have always been scared of *you*,
With your Luftwaffe,[2] your gobbledygoo.
And your neat moustache
And your Aryan[3] eye, bright blue.
45 Panzer[4]-man, panzer-man, O You—

Not God but a swastika
So black no sky could squeak through.
Every woman adores a Fascist,
The boot in the face, the brute
50 Brute heart of a brute like you.

You stand at the blackboard, daddy,
In the picture I have of you,
A cleft in your chin instead of your foot
But no less a devil for that, no not
55 Any less the black man who

Bit my pretty red heart in two.
I was ten when they buried you.
At twenty I tried to die
And get back, back, back to you.
60 I thought even the bones would do

But they pulled me out of the sack,
And they stuck me together with glue.[5]
And then I knew what to do.

7. German for "I."   8. Sites of World War II Nazi death camps.
9. The snow in the Tyrol (an Alpine region in Austria and northern Italy) is, legendarily, as pure as the beer is clear in Vienna.   1. Tarot, playing cards used mainly for fortune-telling.
2. German air force.   3. People of Germanic lineage, often blond-haired and blue-eyed.
4. Literally "panther" (German), the Nazi tank corps' term for an armored vehicle.
5. Perhaps an allusion to Plath's recovery from her first suicide attempt in 1953.

Sylvia Plath, 1961

I made a model of you,
65   A man in black with a Meinkampf[6] look

And a love of the rack and the screw.
And I said I do, I do.
So daddy, I'm finally through.
The black telephone's off at the root,
70   The voices just can't worm through.

If I've killed one man, I've killed two—
The vampire who said he was you
And drank my blood for a year,
Seven years, if you want to know.
75   Daddy, you can lie back now.

There's a stake in your fat black heart
And the villagers never liked you.
They are dancing and stamping on you.
They always *knew* it was you.
80   Daddy, daddy, you bastard, I'm through.
1962   1965

Lady Lazarus

I have done it again.
One year in every ten
I manage it—

---

6. Title of Adolf Hitler's autobiography and manifesto (1925–27); German for "my struggle."

A sort of walking miracle, my skin
5 Bright as a Nazi lampshade,
My right foot

A paperweight,
My face a featureless, fine
Jew linen.[7]

10 Peel off the napkin
O my enemy.
Do I terrify?—

The nose, the eye pits, the full set of teeth?
The sour breath
15 Will vanish in a day.

Soon, soon the flesh
The grave cave ate will be
At home on me

And I a smiling woman.
20 I am only thirty.
And like the cat I have nine times to die.

This is Number Three.
What a trash
To annihilate each decade.

25 What a million filaments.
The peanut-crunching crowd
Shoves in to see

Them unwrap me hand and foot—
The big strip tease.
30 Gentlemen, ladies

These are my hands
My knees.
I may be skin and bone,

Nevertheless, I am the same, identical woman.
35 The first time it happened I was ten.
It was an accident.

The second time I meant
To last it out and not come back at all.
I rocked shut

40 As a seashell.
They had to call and call
And pick the worms off me like sticky pearls.

Dying
Is an art, like everything else.
45 I do it exceptionally well.

7. During World War II, prisoners in some Nazi camps were gassed to death and their body parts then turned into objects such as lampshades and paperweights.

I do it so it feels like hell.
I do it so it feels real.
I guess you could say I've a call.

It's easy enough to do it in a cell.
50 It's easy enough to do it and stay put.
It's the theatrical

Comeback in broad day
To the same place, the same face, the same brute
Amused shout:

55 "A miracle!"
That knocks me out.
There is a charge

For the eyeing of my scars, there is a charge
For the hearing of my heart—
60 It really goes.

And there is a charge, a very large charge
For a word or a touch
Or a bit of blood

Or a piece of my hair or my clothes.
65 So, so Herr Doktor.
So, Herr Enemy.

I am your opus,
I am your valuable,
The pure gold baby

70 That melts to a shriek.
I turn and burn.
Do not think I underestimate your great concern

Ash, ash—
You poke and stir.
75 Flesh, bone, there is nothing there—

A cake of soap,
A wedding ring,
A gold filling.

Herr God, Herr Lucifer
80 Beware
Beware.

Out of the ash
I rise with my red hair
And I eat men like air.

1965

EDGAR ALLAN POE
The Raven

Once upon a midnight dreary, while I pondered, weak and weary,
Over many a quaint and curious volume of forgotten lore,
While I nodded, nearly napping, suddenly there came a tapping,
As of some one gently rapping, rapping at my chamber door.
5 "'Tis some visitor," I muttered, "tapping at my chamber door—
                    Only this, and nothing more."

Ah, distinctly I remember it was in the bleak December,
And each separate dying ember wrought its ghost upon the floor.
Eagerly I wished the morrow;—vainly I had sought to borrow
10 From my books surcease of sorrow—sorrow for the lost Lenore—
For the rare and radiant maiden whom the angels name Lenore—
                    Nameless here for evermore.

And the silken sad uncertain rustling of each purple curtain
Thrilled me—filled me with fantastic terrors never felt before;
15 So that now, to still the beating of my heart, I stood repeating
"'Tis some visitor entreating entrance at my chamber door;—
Some late visitor entreating entrance at my chamber door;
                    This it is, and nothing more."

Presently my soul grew stronger; hesitating then no longer,
20 "Sir," said I, "or Madam, truly your forgiveness I implore;
But the fact is I was napping, and so gently you came rapping,
And so faintly you came tapping, tapping at my chamber door,
That I scarce was sure I heard you"—here I opened wide the door;—
                    Darkness there, and nothing more.

25 Deep into that darkness peering, long I stood there wondering, fearing,
Doubting, dreaming dreams no mortal ever dared to dream before;
But the silence was unbroken, and the darkness gave no token,
And the only word there spoken was the whispered word, "Lenore!"
This I whispered, and an echo murmured back the word, "Lenore!"—
30   Merely this, and nothing more.

Back into the chamber turning, all my soul within me burning,
Soon I heard again a tapping somewhat louder than before.
"Surely," said I, "surely that is something at my window lattice;
Let me see, then, what thereat is, and this mystery explore—
35 Let my heart be still a moment and this mystery explore;—
                    'Tis the wind and nothing more!"

Open here I flung the shutter, when, with many a flirt and flutter,
In there stepped a stately raven of the saintly days of yore;
Not the least obeisance made he; not an instant stopped or stayed he;
40 But, with mien of lord or lady, perched above my chamber door—
Perched upon a bust of Pallas[8] just above my chamber door—
                    Perched, and sat, and nothing more.

8. Athena, Greek goddess of wisdom.

Then this ebony bird beguiling my sad fancy into smiling,
By the grave and stern decorum of the countenance it wore,
45 "Though thy crest be shorn and shaven, thou," I said, "art sure no craven,
Ghastly grim and ancient raven wandering from the Nightly shore—
Tell me what thy lordly name is on the Night's Plutonian[9] shore!"
Quoth the raven, "Nevermore."

Much I marvelled this ungainly fowl to hear discourse so plainly,
50 Though its answer little meaning—little relevancy bore,
For we cannot help agreeing that no living human being
Ever yet was blessed with seeing bird above his chamber door—
Bird or beast upon the sculptured bust above his chamber door,
With such name as "Nevermore."

55 But the raven, sitting lonely on the placid bust, spoke only
That one word, as if his soul in that one word he did outpour.
Nothing farther then he uttered—not a feather then he fluttered—
Till I scarcely more than muttered "Other friends have flown before—
On the morrow *he* will leave me, as my hopes have flown before."
60   Then the bird said "Nevermore."

Startled at the stillness broken by reply so aptly spoken,
"Doubtless," said I, "what it utters is its only stock and store
Caught from some unhappy master whom unmerciful Disaster
Followed fast and followed faster till his songs one burden bore—
65 Till the dirges of his Hope that melancholy burden bore
Of 'Never—nevermore.'"

But the raven still beguiling all my sad soul into smiling,
Straight I wheeled a cushioned seat in front of bird and bust and door;
Then, upon the velvet sinking, I betook myself to linking
70 Fancy unto fancy, thinking what this ominous bird of yore—
What this grim, ungainly, ghastly, gaunt, and ominous bird of yore
Meant in croaking "Nevermore."

This I sat engaged in guessing, but no syllable expressing
To the fowl whose fiery eyes now burned into my bosom's core;
75 This and more I sat divining, with my head at ease reclining
On the cushion's velvet lining that the lamplight gloated o'er,
But whose velvet violet lining with the lamplight gloating o'er,
She shall press, ah, nevermore!

Then, methought, the air grew denser, perfumed from an unseen censer
80 Swung by angels whose faint foot-falls tinkled on the tufted floor.
"Wretch," I cried, "thy God hath lent thee—by these angels he hath sent
thee
Respite—respite and nepenthe[1] from thy memories of Lenore!
Quaff, oh quaff this kind nepenthe and forget this lost Lenore!"
Quoth the raven, "Nevermore."

85 "Prophet!" said I, "thing of evil!—prophet still, if bird or devil!—
Whether Tempter sent, or whether tempest tossed thee here ashore,

9. Dark; Pluto was the ancient Greek god of the underworld.
1. Drug reputed by the Greeks to cause forgetfulness or sorrow (pronounced "ne-FEN-thee").

Desolate, yet all undaunted, on this desert land enchanted—
On this home by Horror haunted—tell me truly, I implore—
Is there—*is* there balm in Gilead?[2]—tell me—tell me, I implore!"
90   Quoth the raven, "Nevermore."

"Prophet!" said I, "thing of evil—prophet still, if bird or devil!
By that Heaven that bends above us—by that God we both adore—
Tell this soul with sorrow laden if, within the distant Aidenn,[3]
It shall clasp a sainted maiden whom the angels name Lenore—
95 Clasp a rare and radiant maiden whom the angels name Lenore."
                     Quoth the raven, "Nevermore."

"Be that word our sign of parting, bird or fiend!" I shrieked upstarting—
"Get thee back into the tempest and the Night's Plutonian shore!
Leave no black plume as a token of that lie thy soul hath spoken!
100 Leave my loneliness unbroken!—quit the bust above my door!
Take thy beak from out my heart, and take thy form from off my door!"
                     Quoth the raven, "Nevermore."

And the raven, never flitting, still is sitting, still is sitting
On the pallid bust of Pallas just above my chamber door;
105 And his eyes have all the seeming of a demon's that is dreaming,
And the lamp-light o'er him streaming throws his shadow on the floor;
And my soul from out that shadow that lies floating on the floor
                Shall be lifted—nevermore!

                                         1844

EZRA POUND
In a Station of the Metro[4]

The apparition of these faces in the crowd;
Petals on a wet, black bough.
                            1913

The River-Merchant's Wife: A Letter

(after Rihaku)[5]

While my hair was still cut straight across my forehead
I played about the front gate, pulling flowers.
You came by on bamboo stilts, playing horse,
You walked about my seat, playing with blue plums.
5 And we went on living in the village of Chokan:
Two small people, without dislike or suspicion.

At fourteen I married My Lord you.
I never laughed, being bashful.

2. See Jeremiah 8.22. 3. Eden. 4. Paris subway.
5. Japanese name for Li Po, an eighth-century Chinese poet. Pound's poem is based on one by Li Po,
which Pound read in translation.

Lowering my head, I looked at the wall.
10   Called to, a thousand times, I never looked back.

At fifteen I stopped scowling,
I desired my dust to be mingled with yours
For ever and for ever and for ever.
Why should I climb the look out?

15   At sixteen you departed,
You went into far Ku-to-yen, by the river of swirling eddies,
And you have been gone five months.
The monkeys make sorrowful noise overhead.

You dragged your feet when you went out.
20   By the gate now, the moss is grown, the different mosses,
Too deep to clear them away!

The leaves fall early this autumn, in wind.
The paired butterflies are already yellow with August
Over the grass in the West garden;
25   They hurt me. I grow older.
If you are coming down through the narrows of the river Kiang,
Please let me know beforehand,
And I will come out to meet you
       As far as Cho-fu-Sa.

                                                                          1915

DUDLEY RANDALL
Ballad of Birmingham

(On the bombing of a church in Birmingham, Alabama, 1963)[6]

"Mother dear, may I go downtown
Instead of out to play,
And march the streets of Birmingham
In a Freedom March today?"

5   "No, baby, no, you may not go,
For the dogs are fierce and wild,
And clubs and hoses, guns and jails
Aren't good for a little child."

"But, mother, I won't be alone.
10   Other children will go with me,
And march the streets of Birmingham
To make our country free."

---

6. Just before Sunday services on September 15, 1963, a bomb exploded in Birmingham, Alabama's 16th Street Baptist Church, killing four girls, aged eleven to fourteen, and injuring at least twenty-one other members of the predominantly African American congregation.

"No, baby, no, you may not go,
For I fear those guns will fire.
15 But you may go to church instead
And sing in the children's choir."

She has combed and brushed her night-dark hair,
And bathed rose petal sweet,
And drawn white gloves on her small brown hands,
20 And white shoes on her feet.

The mother smiled to know her child
Was in the sacred place,
But that smile was the last smile
To come upon her face.

25 For when she heard the explosion,
Her eyes grew wet and wild.
She raced through the streets of Birmingham
Calling for her child.

She clawed through bits of glass and brick,
30 Then lifted out a shoe.
"Oh, here's the shoe my baby wore,
But, baby, where are you?"

1969

• Compare this poem to other ballads in this volume and elsewhere. Why
is the form appropriate and effective for commemorating this violent
event?

ADRIENNE RICH
At a Bach Concert

Coming by evening through the wintry city
We said that art is out of love with life.
Here we approach a love that is not pity.

This antique discipline, tenderly severe,
5 Renews belief in love yet masters feeling,
Asking of us a grace in what we bear.

Form is the ultimate gift that love can offer—
The vital union of necessity
With all that we desire, all that we suffer.

10 A too-compassionate art is half an art.
Only such proud restraining purity
Restores the else-betrayed, too-human heart.

1951

History[7]

Should I simplify my life for you?
Don't ask how I began to love men.
Don't ask how I began to love women.
Remember the forties songs, the slowdance numbers
5   the small sex-filled gas-rationed Chevrolet?
Remember walking in the snow and who was gay?
Cigarette smoke of the movies, silver-and-gray
profiles, dreaming the dreams of he-and-she
breathing the dissolution of the wisping silver plume?
10 Dreaming that dream we leaned applying lipstick
by the gravestone's mirror when we found ourselves
playing in the cemetery. In Current Events she said
the war in Europe is over, the Allies
and she wore no lipstick have won the war[8]
15 and we raced screaming out of Sixth Period.

Dreaming that dream
we had to maze our ways through a wood
where lips were knives breasts razors and I hid
in the cage of my mind scribbling
20 *this map stops where it all begins*
into a red-and-black notebook.
Remember after the war when peace came down
as plenty for some and they said we were saved
in an eternal present and we knew the world could end?
25 —Remember after the war when peace rained down
on the winds from Hiroshima Nagasaki Utah Nevada?[9]
and the socialist queer Christian teacher jumps from the hotel
        window?[1]
and L.G. saying *I want to sleep with you but not for sex*
and the red-and-black enamelled coffee-pot dripped slow through the
        dark grounds
30 —appetite terror power tenderness
the long kiss in the stairwell the switch thrown
on two Jewish Communists[2] married to each other
the definitive crunch of glass at the end of the wedding?[3]
(When shall we learn, what should be clear as day,
35 *We cannot choose what we are free to love?)*[4]

                                                          1995

---

7. Poem 4 in Rich's sequence "Inscriptions."
8. World War II (1939–45), fought between the Allies or Allied powers (including France, Great Britain, the United States, and the Soviet Union) and the Axis powers (Germany, Japan, Italy).
9. Sites of atomic bomb explosions, the first two in Japan near the end of World War II, the last two at test sites in the American West.
1. Allusion to the critic Francis Otto Matthiessen (1902–50), who taught at Harvard while Rich was an undergraduate there.
2. Julius and Ethel Rosenberg, executed as spies by the United States in 1953.
3. At Jewish weddings the groom breaks a glass to commemorate the loss of Jerusalem and the Temple.
4. Opening lines of W. H. Auden's poem "Canzone" (1942).

WALLACE STEVENS
Anecdote of the Jar

I placed a jar in Tennessee,
And round it was, upon a hill.
It made the slovenly wilderness
Surround that hill.

5   The wilderness rose up to it,
And sprawled around, no longer wild.
The jar was round upon the ground
And tall and of a port in air.

It took dominion everywhere.
10 The jar was gray and bare.
It did not give of bird or bush,
Like nothing else in Tennessee.

1923

The Emperor of Ice-Cream

Call the roller of big cigars,
The muscular one, and bid him whip
In kitchen cups concupiscent curds.[5]
Let the wenches dawdle in such dress
5   As they are used to wear, and let the boys
Bring flowers in last month's newspapers.
Let be be finale of seem.[6]
The only emperor is the emperor of ice-cream.

Take from the dresser of deal,
10 Lacking the three glass knobs, that sheet
On which she embroidered fantails[7] once
And spread it so as to cover her face.
If her horny feet protrude, they come
To show how cold she is, and dumb.
15 Let the lamp affix its beam.
The only emperor is the emperor of ice-cream.

1923

5. "The words 'concupiscent curds' have no genealogy; they are merely expressive: at least, I hope they are expressive. They express the concupiscence of life, but, by contrast with the things in relation to them in the poem, they express or accentuate life's destitution, and it is this that gives them something more than a cheap lustre" (Wallace Stevens, *Letters*. Edited by Holly Stevens, U of California P, 1996, p. 500).
6. "The true sense of Let be be the finale of seem is let being become the conclusion or denouement of appearing to be: in short, ice-cream is an absolute good. The poem is obviously not about icecream, but about being as distinguished from seeming to be" (*Letters* 341).
7. Fantail pigeons.

ALFRED, LORD TENNYSON
Ulysses[8]

    It little profits that an idle king,
By this still hearth, among these barren crags,
Matched with an agèd wife,[9] mete and dole
Unequal laws unto a savage race,
5 That hoard, and sleep, and feed, and know not me.

    I cannot rest from travel; I will drink
Life to the lees.[1] All times I have enjoyed
Greatly, have suffered greatly, both with those
That loved me, and alone; on shore, and when
10 Through scudding drifts the rainy Hyades[2]
Vexed the dim sea. I am become a name;
For always roaming with a hungry heart
Much have I seen and known—cities of men
And manners, climates, councils, governments,
15 Myself not least, but honored of them all—
And drunk delight of battle with my peers,
Far on the ringing plains of windy Troy.
I am a part of all that I have met;
Yet all experience is an arch wherethrough
20 Gleams that untraveled world, whose margin fades
For ever and for ever when I move.
How dull it is to pause, to make an end,
To rust unburnished, not to shine in use!
As though to breathe were life. Life piled on life
25 Were all too little, and of one to me
Little remains; but every hour is saved
From that eternal silence, something more,
A bringer of new things; and vile it were
For some three suns to store and hoard myself,
30 And this gray spirit yearning in desire
To follow knowledge like a sinking star,
Beyond the utmost bound of human thought.

    This is my son, mine own Telemachus,
To whom I leave the scepter and the isle—
35 Well-loved of me, discerning to fulfill
This labor, by slow prudence to make mild
A rugged people, and through soft degrees

8. After the Trojan War ended, Ulysses (or Odysseus), king of Ithaca and one of the war's Greek heroes, returned to his island home (line 34). Homer's account of the situation appears in book 11 of *The Odyssey*, but Dante's account of Ulysses in canto 26 of the *Inferno* is the more immediate background of Tennyson's poem.
9. Penelope.
1. That is, all the way down to the bottom of the cup.
2. Group of stars believed to predict the rain when they rose at the same time as the sun.

Subdue them to the useful and the good.
Most blameless is he, centered in the sphere
40 Of common duties, decent not to fail
In offices of tenderness, and pay
Meet adoration to my household gods,
When I am gone. He works his work, I mine.

There lies the port; the vessel puffs her sail:
45 There gloom the dark, broad seas. My mariners,
Souls that have toiled, and wrought, and thought with me—
That ever with a frolic welcome took
The thunder and the sunshine, and opposed
Free hearts, free foreheads—you and I are old;
50 Old age hath yet his honor and his toil.
Death closes all; but something ere the end,
Some work of noble note, may yet be done,
Not unbecoming men that strove with Gods.
The lights begin to twinkle from the rocks;
55 The long day wanes; the slow moon climbs; the deep
Moans round with many voices. Come, my friends,
'Tis not too late to seek a newer world.
Push off, and sitting well in order smite
The sounding furrows; for my purpose holds
60 To sail beyond the sunset, and the baths
Of all the western stars, until I die.
It may be that the gulfs will wash us down;[3]
It may be we shall touch the Happy Isles,[4]
And see the great Achilles, whom we knew.
65 Though much is taken, much abides; and though
We are not now that strength which in old days
Moved earth and heaven, that which we are, we are:
One equal temper of heroic hearts,
Made weak by time and fate, but strong in will
70 To strive, to seek, to find, and not to yield.

1833

DEREK WALCOTT

A Far Cry from Africa

A wind is ruffling the tawny pelt
Of Africa. Kikuyu,[5] quick as flies,
Batten upon the bloodstreams of the veldt.[6]

---

3. Beyond the Gulf of Gibraltar was supposed to lie a chasm that led to Hades, the underworld.
4. Elysium, the Islands of the Blessed, where heroes like Achilles (line 64) go after death.
5. East African tribe whose members, as Mau Mau fighters, conducted an eight-year insurrection against British colonists in Kenya.
6. Open plains, neither cultivated nor thickly forested (Afrikaans).

Corpses are scattered through a paradise.
5 Only the worm, colonel of carrion, cries:
"Waste no compassion on these separate dead!"
Statistics justify and scholars seize
The salients of colonial policy.
What is that to the white child hacked in bed?
10 To savages, expendable as Jews?

Threshed out by beaters,[7] the long rushes break
In a white dust of ibises whose cries
Have wheeled since civilization's dawn
From the parched river or beast-teeming plain.
15 The violence of beast on beast is read
As natural law, but upright man
Seeks his divinity by inflicting pain.
Delirious as these worried beasts, his wars
Dance to the tightened carcass of a drum,
20 While he calls courage still that native dread
Of the white peace contracted by the dead.

Again brutish necessity wipes its hands
Upon the napkin of a dirty cause, again
A waste of our compassion, as with Spain,[8]
25 The gorilla wrestles with the superman.
I who am poisoned with the blood of both,
Where shall I turn, divided to the vein?
I who have cursed
The drunken officer of British rule, how choose
30 Between this Africa and the English tongue I love?
Betray them both, or give back what they give?
How can I face such slaughter and be cool?
How can I turn from Africa and live?

                                                    1962

• How does the speaker express his divided loyalties in the questions that conclude the poem? What various meanings might the poem's title accrue by the end?

WALT WHITMAN
Facing West from California's Shores

Facing west from California's shores,
Inquiring, tireless, seeking what is yet unfound,

7. In big-game hunting, natives are hired to beat the brush, driving birds—such as ibises—and other animals into the open.
8. Spanish Civil War (1936–39), in which Republican loyalists supported politically by liberals in the West and militarily by Soviet Communists fought Nationalist rebels aided by Nazi Germany and Fascist Italy.

I, a child, very old, over waves, towards the house of maternity,[9] the
    land of migrations, look afar,
Look off the shores of my Western sea, the circle almost circled;
5   For starting westward from Hindustan, from the vales of Kashmere,
From Asia, from the north, from the God, the sage, and the hero,
From the south, from the flowery peninsulas and the spice islands,
Long having wander'd since, round the earth having wander'd,
Now I face home again, very pleas'd and joyous;
10 (But where is what I started for so long ago?
And why is it yet unfound?)

1860

RICHARD WILBUR

Love Calls Us to the Things of This World

    The eyes open to a cry of pulleys,
And spirited from sleep, the astounded soul
Hangs for a moment bodiless and simple
As false dawn.
5   Outside the open window
The morning air is all awash with angels.

    Some are in bed-sheets, some are in blouses,
Some are in smocks: but truly there they are.
Now they are rising together in calm swells
10 Of halcyon[1] feeling, filling whatever they wear
With the deep joy of their impersonal breathing;
    Now they are flying in place, conveying
The terrible speed of their omnipresence, moving
And staying like white water; and now of a sudden
15 They swoon down into so rapt a quiet
That nobody seems to be there.
                  The soul shrinks

    From all that it is about to remember,
From the punctual rape of every blessed day,
20 And cries,
          "Oh, let there be nothing on earth but laundry,
Nothing but rosy hands in the rising steam
And clear dances done in the sight of heaven."

    Yet, as the sun acknowledges
25 With a warm look the world's hunks and colors,
The soul descends once more in bitter love
To accept the waking body, saying now
In a changed voice as the man yawns and rises,
    "Bring them down from their ruddy gallows;

9. Asia, as the supposed birthplace of the human race.
1. Serene.

30 Let there be clean linen for the backs of thieves;
    Let lovers go fresh and sweet to be undone,
    And the heaviest nuns walk in a pure floating
    Of dark habits,
                        keeping their difficult balance."

                                                        1956

W. B. YEATS
All Things Can Tempt Me

All things can tempt me from this craft of verse:
One time it was a woman's face, or worse—
The seeming needs of my fool-driven land;
Now nothing but comes readier to the hand
5 Than this accustomed toil. When I was young,
I had not given a penny for a song
Did not the poet sing it with such airs
That one believed he had a sword upstairs;
Yet would be now, could I but have my wish,
10 Colder and dumber and deafer than a fish.

                                                        1910

• In his commentary on THE LAKE ISLE OF INNISFREE, Yeats suggests that
  over time he abandoned the archaic language and syntax, as well as subject
  matter, of his early verse. How might (or might not) ALL THINGS CAN TEMPT
  ME both exemplify and comment on that shift? How do diction and syntax
  contribute to the poem's effect?

Easter 1916[2]

I have met them at close of day
Coming with vivid faces
From counter or desk among gray
Eighteenth-century houses.
5 I have passed with a nod of the head
Or polite meaningless words,
Or have lingered awhile and said
Polite meaningless words,
And thought before I had done
10 Of a mocking tale or a gibe
To please a companion
Around the fire at the club,
Being certain that they and I
But lived where motley is worn:

---

2. On Easter Monday, 1916, nationalist leaders proclaimed an Irish Republic. After a week of street
fighting, the British government put down the Easter Rebellion and executed a number of prominent
nationalists, including the four mentioned in lines 75–76, all of whom Yeats knew personally.

15 All changed, changed utterly:
    A terrible beauty is born.

    That woman's[3] days were spent
    In ignorant good-will,
    Her nights in argument
20 Until her voice grew shrill.
    What voice more sweet than hers
    When, young and beautiful,
    She rode to harriers?
    This man[4] had kept a school
25 And rode our wingèd horse,[5]
    This other[6] his helper and friend
    Was coming into his force;
    He might have won fame in the end,
    So sensitive his nature seemed,
30 So daring and sweet his thought.
    This other man[7] I had dreamed
    A drunken, vainglorious lout.
    He had done most bitter wrong
    To some who are near my heart,
35 Yet I number him in the song;
    He, too, has resigned his part
    In the casual comedy;
    He, too, has been changed in his turn,
    Transformed utterly:
40 A terrible beauty is born.

    Hearts with one purpose alone
    Through summer and winter seem
    Enchanted to a stone
    To trouble the living stream.
45 The horse that comes from the road,
    The rider, the birds that range
    From cloud to tumbling cloud,
    Minute by minute they change;
    A shadow of cloud on the stream
50 Changes minute by minute;
    A horse-hoof slides on the brim,
    And a horse plashes within it;
    The long-legged moor-hens dive,

3. Countess Constance Georgina Markievicz (1868–1927), a beautiful and well-born young woman from County Sligo who became a vigorous nationalist. She was initially condemned to death, but her sentence was later commuted to life imprisonment, and she was granted amnesty in 1917.
4. Patrick Pearse (1879–1916), who led the assault on the Dublin Post Office, from which the proclamation of a republic was issued. A schoolmaster by profession, he had championed the restoration of the Gaelic language in Ireland and was an active political writer and poet.
5. The mythological Pegasus, a traditional symbol of poetic inspiration.
6. Thomas MacDonagh (1878–1916), also a writer and teacher.
7. Major John MacBride (1868–1916), who had married Yeats's beloved Maud Gonne in 1903 but separated from her two years later.

And hens to moor-cocks call;
55 Minute by minute they live:
The stone's in the midst of all.

Too long a sacrifice
Can make a stone of the heart.
O when may it suffice?
60 That is Heaven's part, our part
To murmur name upon name,
As a mother names her child
When sleep at last has come
On limbs that had run wild.
65 What is it but nightfall?
No, no, not night but death;
Was it needless death after all?
For England may keep faith[8]
For all that is done and said.
70 We know their dream; enough
To know they dreamed and are dead;
And what if excess of love
Bewildered them till they died?
I write it out in a verse—
75 MacDonagh and MacBride
And Connolly[9] and Pearse
Now and in time to be,
Wherever green is worn,
Are changed, changed utterly;
80 A terrible beauty is born.

                                    1916

• The phrase "A terrible beauty is born" becomes a kind of refrain in this
  poem. What does the poem suggest about why the events of Easter 1916
  and the kind of political passion and commitment that went into it were
  simultaneously "terrible" and "beautiful"? What do the stone and the stream
  seem to symbolize?

The Lake Isle of Innisfree[1]

I will arise and go now, and go to Innisfree,
And a small cabin build there, of clay and wattles made,
Nine bean-rows will I have there, a hive for the honey-bee,
And live alone in the bee-loud glade.

5 And I shall have some peace there, for peace comes dropping slow,
Dropping from the veils of the morning to where the cricket sings;
There midnight's all a glimmer, and noon a purple glow,
And evening full of the linnet's wings.

8. Before the uprising, the English had promised eventual home rule to Ireland.
9. James Connolly (1868–1916), leader of the Easter uprising.
1. Island in Lough Gill, County Sligo, Ireland.

I will arise and go now, for always night and day
10   I hear lake water lapping with low sounds by the shore;
While I stand on the roadway, or on the pavements grey,
I hear it in the deep heart's core.

                                                              1890

• Why does the speaker vow to go to Innisfree, and how does the life he imagines living there compare to the one he now lives? In what ways might his
  imagined future seem like a return to the past?

Leda and the Swan[2]

A sudden blow: the great wings beating still
Above the staggering girl, her thighs caressed
By the dark webs, her nape caught in his bill,
He holds her helpless breast upon his breast.

5   How can those terrified vague fingers push
The feathered glory from her loosening thighs?
And how can body, laid in that white rush,
But feel the strange heart beating where it lies?

A shudder in the loins engenders there
10   The broken wall, the burning roof and tower
And Agamemnon dead.
                              Being so caught up,
So mastered by the brute blood of the air,
Did she put on his knowledge with his power
Before the indifferent beak could let her drop?

                                                              1923

• If THE SECOND COMING predicts the end of one historical cycle and its governing (Christian) myth, LEDA AND THE SWAN imagines the beginning of the
  preceding cycle. How does the poem characterize that beginning? Might we
  again have here (as in EASTER 1916) a kind of "terrible beauty"? How would
  you paraphrase the question the speaker poses at the poem's end? Why
  might questions loom so large in this poem?

2. According to Greek myth, Zeus took the form of a swan to rape Leda, who became the mother of
Helen of Troy; of Castor; and also of Clytemnestra, Agamemnon's wife and murderer. Helen's abduc-
tion from her husband, Menelaus, brother of Agamemnon, began the Trojan War (line 10). Yeats
described the visit of Zeus to Leda as an annunciation like that to Mary (see Luke 1.26–38); "I imagine the annunciation that founded Greece as made to Leda" (A Vision, 1937).

The Second Coming[3]

Turning and turning in the widening gyre[4]
The falcon cannot hear the falconer;
Things fall apart; the center cannot hold;
Mere anarchy is loosed upon the world,
5   The blood-dimmed tide is loosed, and everywhere
The ceremony of innocence is drowned;
The best lack all conviction, while the worst
Are full of passionate intensity.

Surely some revelation is at hand;
10   Surely the Second Coming is at hand.
The Second Coming! Hardly are those words out
When a vast image out of *Spiritus Mundi*[5]
Troubles my sight: somewhere in sands of the desert
A shape with lion body and the head of a man,
15   A gaze blank and pitiless as the sun,
Is moving its slow thighs, while all about it
Reel shadows of the indignant desert birds.[6]
The darkness drops again; but now I know
That twenty centuries of stony sleep
20   Were vexed to nightmare by a rocking cradle,
And what rough beast, its hour come round at last,
Slouches towards Bethlehem to be born?

January 1919   1920, 1921

• What vision of the contemporary world is implied by the metaphors in the
  poem's first half? What vision of its future is suggested in the poem's second half?

---

3. The Second Coming of Christ, according to Matthew 24.29–44, will follow a time of "tribula-
tion." In *A Vision* (1937), Yeats describes his view of history as dependent on cycles of about two
thousand years: The birth of Christ had ended the cycle of Greco-Roman civilization, and now the
Christian cycle seemed near an end, to be followed by an antithetical cycle, ominous in its portents.
4. Literally, the widening spiral of a falcon's flight. "Gyre" is Yeats's term for a cycle of history, which
he diagrammed as a series of interpenetrating cones.
5. Or *Anima Mundi* (Latin), the spirit or soul of the world. Yeats considered this universal consciousness or memory a fund from which poets drew their images and symbols.
6. Yeats later wrote of the "brazen winged beast [. . .] described in my poem *The Second Coming*" as
"associated with laughing, ecstatic destruction."

Biographical Sketches: Poets

Sketches are included for all poets represented by two or more poems.

W. H. AUDEN (1907–73)

Wystan Hugh Auden was born in York, England, to a medical officer and a nurse. Intending at first to become a scientist, Auden studied at Oxford University, where he became the center of the "Oxford Group" of poets and leftist intellectuals. His travels during the 1930s led him to Germany, Iceland, China, Spain (where he was an ambulance driver in the civil war), and the United States (where he taught at various universities and, in 1946, became a naturalized citizen). A prolific writer of poems, plays, essays, and criticism, Auden won the Pulitzer Prize in 1948 for his collection of poems *The Age of Anxiety*, set in a New York City bar. Late in life he returned to Christ Church College, Oxford, where he was writer in residence. He is regarded as a masterly poet of political and intellectual conscience as well as one of the twentieth century's greatest lyric craftsmen.

BASHŌ (1644–94)

Born Matsuo Munefusa, the second son of a low-ranking provincial samurai, the haiku poet who came to be known as Bashō at first put aside his literary interests and entered into service with the local ruling military house. In 1666, following the feudal lord's death, Bashō left for Edo (now Tokyo), the military capital of the shogun's new government, to pursue a career as a professional poet. He supported himself as a teacher and editor of other people's poetry but ultimately developed a following and a sizable group of students. A seasoned traveler, Bashō maintained an austere existence on the road and at home, casting himself in travel narratives such as *Oku no hosomichi* (The

Narrow Road to the Interior, 1694) as a pilgrim devoted to nature and Zen.

ELIZABETH BISHOP (1911–79)

Born in Worcester, Massachusetts, Elizabeth Bishop endured the death of her father before she was a year old and the institutionalization of her mother four years later. Bishop was raised first by her maternal grandmother in Nova Scotia, then by her paternal grandparents back in Worcester. At Vassar College she met the poet Marianne Moore, who encouraged her to give up plans for medical school and pursue a career in poetry. Bishop traveled through Canada, Europe, and South America, finally settling in Rio de Janeiro, where she lived for nearly twenty years. Her four volumes of poetry are *North and South* (1946); *A Cold Spring* (1955), which won the Pulitzer Prize; *Questions of Travel* (1965); and *Geography III* (1976), which won the National Book Critics' Circle Award.

WILLIAM BLAKE (1757–1828)

The son of a London haberdasher and his wife, William Blake studied drawing at ten and at fourteen began a seven-year apprenticeship to an engraver. After a first book of poems, *Poetical Sketches* (1783), he began experimenting with what he called "illuminated printing"—the words and pictures of each page were engraved in relief on copper, which was used to print sheets that were then partly colored by hand—a laborious and time-consuming process that resulted in books of singular beauty, no two of which are exactly alike. His great *Songs of Innocence and of Experience* (1794) was produced in this manner, as were his increasingly mythic and prophetic books, including *The Marriage of Heaven and Hell* (1793), *The Four Zoas* (1803), *Milton* (1804), and *Jerusalem* (1809). Blake devoted his later life to pictorial art, illustrating *Chaucer's Canterbury Tales*, the Book of Job, and Dante's *Divine Comedy*, on which he was hard at work when he died.

GWENDOLYN BROOKS (1917–2000)

Gwendolyn Brooks was born in Topeka, Kansas, and raised in Chicago, where she began writing poetry at the age of seven, and where she graduated from Wilson Junior College in 1936. Shortly after beginning her formal study of modern poetry at Chicago's Southside Community Art Center, Brooks produced her first book of poems, *A Street in Bronzeville* (1945). With her second volume, *Annie Allen* (1949), she became the first African American to win the Pulitzer Prize. Though her early work focused on what Langston Hughes called the "ordinary aspects of black life," during the mid-1960s she devoted her poetry to raising African American consciousness and to social activism. In 1968, she was named the Poet Laureate of Illinois; in 1985, she became the first black woman ever to serve as poetry consultant to the Library of Congress.

SAMUEL TAYLOR COLERIDGE (1772–1834)

Born in the small town of Ottery St. Mary in rural Devonshire, England, Samuel Taylor Coleridge is among the greatest and most original of the nineteenth-century Romantic poets. He wrote three of the most haunting and powerful poems in English—*The Rime of the Ancient Mariner* (1798), *Christabel* (1816), and "Kubla Khan" (1816)—as well as immensely influential literary criticism and a treatise on biology. In 1795, in the midst of a failed experiment to establish a "Pantisocracy" (his form of ideal community), he met William Wordsworth, and in 1798 they jointly published their enormously influential *Lyrical Ballads*. Coleridge's physical ailments, addiction to opium, and profound sense of despair made his life difficult and tumultuous and certainly affected his work. Still, he remains a central figure in English literature.

BILLY COLLINS (b. 1941)

Sometimes described as "the most popular poet in America," Billy Collins enjoys the sort of celebrity status usually reserved for Hollywood actors like his friend Bill Murray, reportedly signing six-figure contracts for books in progress. As U.S. Poet Laureate (2001–03), Collins both refused to publish and hence profit from his poem "The Names," written in honor of the victims of the 9/11 attacks, and initiated philanthropic projects like *Poetry 180*, aimed at exciting high schoolers' interest in poetry. Born in New York City, Collins credits his mother with awakening his love of poetry and teaching him the importance of "reading poetry as poetry [. . .] as a set of sounds set to rhythm"—lessons reinforced by his studies at the College of Holy Cross and the University of California–Riverside. Though Collins began publishing his work in the 1980s, it wasn't until 1991 that his book *Questions About Angels* thrust him into the spotlight. Since that time, he has published numerous collections, including *The Art of Drowning* (1995), *Taking off Emily Dickinson's Clothes* (2000), *Ballistics* (2008), and *The Rain in Portugal* (2016). By his own account "unashamedly" "suburban," "domestic," and "middle class," Collins's deceptively simple poetry uses the material of the everyday to, as one reader put it, "help us feel the mystery of being alive."

E. E. CUMMINGS (1894–1962)

Born in Cambridge, Massachusetts, the son of a Congregationalist minister, Edward Estlin Cummings attended Harvard University, where he wrote poetry in the Pre-Raphaelite and Metaphysical traditions. He joined the ambulance corps in France the day after the United States entered World War I but was imprisoned by the French due to his outspoken opposition to the war; he transmuted the experience into his first literary success, the novel *The Enormous Room* (1922). After the war, Cummings established himself as a poet and artist in New York City's Greenwich Village, made frequent trips to France and New Hampshire, and showed little interest in wealth or his growing celebrity. His variety of Modernism is distinguished by its playfulness, its formal experimentation, its lyrical directness, and its celebration of the individual.

EMILY DICKINSON (1830–86)

From childhood on, Emily Dickinson led a sequestered and obscure life. Yet her verse has traveled far beyond the cultured yet relatively circumscribed environment in which she lived: her room, her father's house, her family, a few close friends, and the small town of Amherst, Massachusetts. Indeed, along with Walt Whitman, her far more public contemporary, she all but invented American poetry. Born in Amherst, the daughter of a respected lawyer whom she revered ("His heart was pure and terrible," she once wrote), Dickinson studied for less than a year at the Mount Holyoke Female Seminary, returning permanently to her family home. She became more and more reclusive, dressing only in white, seeing no visitors, yet working ceaselessly at her poems—nearly eighteen hundred in all, only a few of which were published during her lifetime. After her death, her sister Lavinia discovered the rest in a trunk, neatly bound into packets with blue ribbons—among the most important bodies of work in all of American literature.

JOHN DONNE (1572–1631)

The first and greatest of the English writers who came to be known as the Metaphysical poets, John Donne wrote in a revolutionary style that combined highly intellectual conceits with complex, compressed phrasing. Born into an old Roman Catholic family at a time when Catholics were subject to constant harassment and barred from many forms of employment, Donne quietly abandoned his religion and pursued a promising legal career until a politically disastrous marriage ruined his worldly hopes. He struggled for years to support a large family; impoverished and despairing, he even wrote a treatise (*Biathanatos*) on the lawfulness of suicide. King James (who had ambitions for him as a preacher) eventually pressured Donne to take Anglican orders in 1615, and Donne became one of the great sermonizers of his day, rising to the position of dean of St. Paul's Cathedral in 1621. Donne's private devotions (*Meditations*) were published in 1624, and he continued to write poetry until a few years before his death.

PAUL LAURENCE DUNBAR (1872–1906)

The son of former slaves, Paul Laurence Dunbar was born in Dayton, Ohio. He attended a white high school, where he showed an early talent for writing and was elected class president. Unable to afford further education, he then worked as an elevator operator, writing poems and newspaper articles in his spare time. Dunbar took out a loan to subsidize the printing of his first book, *Oak and Ivy* (1893), but with the publication of *Majors and Minors* (1895) and *Lyrics of Lowly Life* (1896), his growing reputation enabled him to support himself by writing and lecturing. Though acclaimed during his lifetime for his lyrical use of rural black dialect in volumes such as *Candle-Lightin' Time* (1902), Dunbar was later criticized for adopting "white" literary conventions and for supposedly pandering to racist images of slaves and ex-slaves. He wrote novels and short stories in addition to poetry and dealt frankly with racial injustice in works such as *The Sport of the Gods* (1903) and *The Fourth of July and Race Outrages* (1903).

MARTÍN ESPADA (b. 1957)

At the age of thirteen, Martín Espada moved with his family to a Long Island neighborhood where they were the only Puerto Ricans, an experience he describes as "more traumatic than anything that ever happened to me on the so-called mean streets" of the racially diverse Brooklyn neighborhood he previously called home. By working everywhere from a bar and a ballpark to a primate lab and a transient hotel, Espada put himself through college, graduating from the University of Wisconsin–Madison with a BA in history. After earning a law degree at Northeastern University, in Boston, he went to work as a lawyer, specializing first in bilingual education, later in housing law. From age twenty, however, Espada was also writing poetry, inspired initially by a family friend's gift of both an anthology of Latin American revolutionary poetry and the prediction that "Tri tambien seras poeta" ("You will also become a poet"). Featuring barrio photos taken by his father, a community activist, Espada's first collection, *The Immigrant Iceboy's Bolero*, appeared in 1982. But it was his third, prize-winning book, *Rebellion Is the*

Circle of a Lover's Hand (1990), that led the *New York Times* to predict he would be "the Latino poet of his generation." In the years since, Espada has done much to earn that title, securing a professorship at the University of Massachusetts–Amherst (in 1993) and publishing not only poetry collections ranging from *City of Coughing and Dead Radiators* (1993) to *The Republic of Poetry* (2006, a finalist for the Pulitzer) but also books of essays including *Zapata's Disciple* (1998), anthologies of Latino and Chicano poetry, and translations. What drives all that work, says Espada, is the same commitment he had as a lawyer: "to speak on behalf of" all those who lack not the ability but the "opportunity" to "speak for themselves."

ROBERT FROST (1874–1963)

Though his poetry identifies Frost with rural New England, he was born and lived to the age of eleven in San Francisco, California. Moving to New England after his father's death, Frost studied classics in high school, entered and dropped out of both Dartmouth and Harvard, and spent difficult years as an unrecognized poet before his first book, *A Boy's Will* (1913), was accepted and published in England. Frost's character was full of contradiction—he held "that we get forward as much by hating as by loving"—yet by the end of his long life he was one of the most honored poets of his time, as well as the most widely read. In 1961, two years before his death, he was invited to read a poem at John F. Kennedy's presidential inauguration ceremony. Frost's poems—masterfully crafted, sometimes deceptively simple—are collected in *The Poetry of Robert Frost* (1969).

ROBERT HAYDEN (1913–80)

Born in a Detroit ghetto, Asa Sheffey became "Robert Hayden" at eighteen months, when he was unofficially adopted by the neighbors who would raise him and whom he would remember in poems such as "Those Winter Sundays." Inspired by the Harlem Renaissance writers he discovered as a teenager, Hayden published his first poem in 1931. Severely nearsighted, he attended Detroit City College (1932–36), thanks only to state rehabilitation grants, and worked for the Federal Writers Project (1936–39), before studying with W. H. Auden at the University of Michigan (MA, 1944). Becoming "a poet who teaches [. . .] so that he can write a poem or two now and then," Hayden held professorships at historically black Fisk University (1946–69) and at the University of Michigan (1969–80). International acclaim came late: In 1966, Langston Hughes and seven other judges unanimously awarded Hayden the Grand Prize for Poetry at the First World Festival of Negro Arts in Senegal, Africa, and in 1976 he became the first African American appointed to the post now known as U.S. Poet Laureate. Like his masterpiece "Middle Passage" (1962), much of Hayden's poetry aims, he said, to "correct the distortions of Afro-American history." Yet he insisted that he was not a "black artist" but an American one. Today he is widely and rightly regarded as among the very best of both.

TERRANCE HAYES (b. 1971)

Born in Columbia, South Carolina, Terrence Hayes attended Coker College on a basketball scholarship, shifting his attention to poetry only in his senior year and going on to earn an MFA from the University of Pittsburgh (1997). His first book of poetry, *Muscular Music* (1999), explores popular culture's impact on African American identity and notions of masculinity. It was followed by *Hip Logic* (2002), a National Poetry Series winner; *Wind in a Box* (2006), listed by *Publishers Weekly* as one of the top 100 books of 2006; and, more recently, *How to Be Drawn* (2015). Characterized as "an elegant and adventurous writer" whose work deftly combines humor and sincerity, Hayes has garnered numerous honors and awards, including a National Book Award for his fourth collection, *Lighthead* (2010), multiple Best American Poetry selections, a Pushcart Prize, and a MacArthur Fellowship. Though he is continually drawn to questions of identity, masculinity, race, culture, and community, he "aspire[s] to a poetic style that resists style"; and indeed, his collections contain poetic forms ranging from pecha kucha, a format for Japanese business presentations, to terza rima, and adopt the voices of poets from Amiri Baraka to Dr. Seuss. Hayes teaches creative writing at the University of Pittsburgh, where he lives with his wife and fellow poet Yona Harvey and their children.

SEAMUS HEANEY (1939–2013)

Considered "the most important Irish poet since Yeats," 1995 Nobel Prize winner Seamus Heaney grew up with his eight siblings on Mossbawm Farm in rural County Derry, Northern Ireland. At twelve, however, scholarships took Heaney first to St. Columb's College and then Queen's University, Belfast, where he studied Irish, Latin, and Old English. Here, too, he discovered the poetry of authors such as Ted Hughes, Patrick Kavanagh, and Robert Frost, which, he said, first taught him to "trust" in the value of that "local" childhood experience that he once "considered archaic and irrelevant to 'the modern world.'" Rural life and labor, as well as the relationship between past and present, the "archaic" and the "modern," loom large from his earliest collection, *Death of a Naturalist* (1966), to later ones such as *District and Circle* (2006). Most famous, perhaps, is *North* (1975), especially its sequence of poems inspired by both the ancient, yet somehow ageless, corpses discovered in Irish and Scandinavian bogs, and by the increasingly violent conflict between Protestants and Catholics in Northern Ireland. Having earned virtually all of the highest honors that a contemporary poet could, Heaney also won acclaim both as a versatile and creative translator, most famously of *Beowulf* (2000) and *Antigone* (*The Burial at Thebes*, 2004), and as an essayist; his *Finders Keepers: Selected Prose, 1971–2001* (2002) won the Truman Capote Award for Literary Criticism, the largest annual prize of its kind. After teaching at Harvard from 1985 until 2006, Heaney lived in Dublin until his death.

GERARD MANLEY HOPKINS (1844–89)

The eldest of the eight children of a marine-insurance adjuster and his wife, Gerard Manley Hopkins attended Oxford University, where his ambition was to become a painter—until, at the age of twenty-two, he converted to Roman Catholicism and burned all his early poetry as too worldly. Not until after his seminary training and ordination as a Jesuit priest, in 1877, did he resume writing poetry, though he made few attempts to publish his verse, which many of his contemporaries found nearly incomprehensible. Near the end of his life, Hopkins was appointed professor of Greek at University College, Dublin, where—out of place, deeply depressed, and all but unknown—he died of typhoid. His poetry, collected and published by his friends, has been championed by modern poets, who admire its controlled tension, strong rhythm, and sheer exuberance.

LANGSTON HUGHES (1902–67)

Born in Joplin, Missouri, Langston Hughes was raised mainly by his maternal grandmother, though he lived intermittently with each of his parents. He studied at Columbia University but left to travel and work at a variety of jobs. Having already published poems in periodicals, anthologies, and his own first collection, *The Weary Blues* (1926), he graduated from Lincoln University; published a successful novel, *Not without Laughter* (1930); and became a major writer of the Harlem Renaissance. During the 1930s, he became involved in radical politics and traveled the world as a correspondent and columnist; during the 1950s, though, the FBI classified him as a security risk and limited his ability to travel. In addition to poems and novels, he wrote essays, plays, screenplays, and an autobiography; he also edited anthologies of literature and folklore.

JOHN KEATS (1795–1821)

Because John Keats was the son of a London livery stable owner and his wife, reviewers would later disparage him as a working-class "Cockney poet." At fifteen he was apprenticed to a surgeon, and at twenty-one he became a licensed pharmacist—in the same year that his first two published poems, including the sonnet "On First Looking into Chapman's Homer," appeared in *The Examiner*, a journal edited by radical critic-poet Leigh Hunt. Hunt introduced Keats to such literary figures as the poet Percy Bysshe Shelley and helped him publish his *Poems by John Keats* (1817). When his second book, the long poem *Endymion* (1818), was fiercely attacked by critics, Keats, suffering from a steadily worsening case of tuberculosis, knew that he would not live to realize his poetic promise. In July 1820, he published *Lamia, Isabella, The Eve of St. Agnes; and Other Poems*, which contained the poignant "To Autumn" and three other great odes: "Ode on a Grecian Urn," "Ode on Melancholy," and "Ode to a Nightingale"; early the next year, he died in Rome. In the years after Keats's death, his letters became almost as famous as his poetry.

ETHERIDGE KNIGHT (1931–91)

A native of Corinth, Mississippi, Etheridge Knight spent much of his adolescence carousing in pool halls, bars, and juke joints, developing a skillful oratorical style in an environment that prized verbal agility. During this time, he also became addicted to narcotics. He served in the U.S. Army from 1947 to 1951; in 1960 he was sentenced to eight years in prison for robbery. At the Indiana State Prison in Michigan City, he began to write poetry and in 1968 published his first collection, *Poems from Prison*. After his release, Knight joined the Black Arts movement, taught at a number of universities, and published works including *Black Voices from Prison* (1970), *Belly Song and Other Poems* (1973), and *Born of a Woman* (1980).

CLAUDE MCKAY (1889–1948)

Festus Claudius McKay was born and raised in Sunny Ville, Clarendon Parish, Jamaica, the youngest of eleven children. He worked as a wheelwright and cabinetmaker, then briefly as a police constable, before writing and publishing two books of poetry in Jamaican dialect. In 1912, he emigrated to the United States, where he attended Booker T. Washington's Tuskegee Institute in Alabama and studied agricultural science at Kansas State College before moving to New York City. McKay supported himself through various jobs while becoming a prominent literary and political figure. The oldest Harlem Renaissance writer, McKay was also the first to publish, with the poetry collection *Harlem Shadows* (1922). His other works include the novels *Home to Harlem* (1928) and *Banana Bottom* (1933) and his autobiography, *A Long Way from Home* (1937).

EDNA ST. VINCENT MILLAY (1892–1950)

Born in Rockland, Maine, Edna St. Vincent Millay published her first poem at twenty, her first poetry collection at twenty-five. After graduating from Vassar College, she moved to New York City's Greenwich Village, where she both gained a reputation as a brilliant poet and became notorious for her bohemian lifestyle and her association with prominent artists, writers, and radicals. In 1923, she won the Pulitzer Prize for her collection *The Ballad of the Harp-Weaver*; in 1925, growing weary of fame, she and her husband moved to Austerlitz, New York, where she lived for the rest of her life. Although her work fell out of favor with mid-twentieth-century Modernists, who rejected her formalism as old-fashioned, her poetry—witty, acerbic, and superbly crafted—has found many new admirers today.

PAT MORA (b. 1942)

Born to Mexican American parents in El Paso, Texas, Pat Mora earned a BA and an MA from the University of Texas at El Paso. She has been a consultant on U.S.-Mexico youth exchanges; a museum director and administrator at her alma mater; and a teacher of English at all levels. Her poetry—collected in *Chants* (1985), *Borders* (1986), *Communion* (1991), *Agua Santa* (1995), *Aunt Carmen's Book of Practical Saints* (1997), and *Adobe Odes* (2006)—reflects and addresses her Chicana and southwestern background. Mora's other publications include *Nepantla: Essays from the Land in the Middle* (1993); a family memoir, *House of Houses* (1997); and many works for children and young adults.

SHARON OLDS (b. 1942)

Born in San Francisco, California; raised in nearby Berkeley by fiercely religious, yet troubled parents; and educated at Stanford (BA, 1964) and Columbia (PhD, 1972) universities (where she wrote a dissertation on Ralph Waldo Emerson), poet Sharon Olds was thirty-seven when she published her first book of poetry, *Satan Says*, in 1981. Since then, she has come to rank as one of America's most important living poets, garnering National Book Critics' Circle Awards for her 1984 collection *The Dead and the Living* and for *Strike Spark: Selected Poems* (2002). In 2013, she became the first woman to win the T. S. Eliot Prize for Poetry, for *Stag's Leap*, a collection that also earned a Pulitzer. Like the work of two writers to whom Olds is often compared, Walt Whitman and Sylvia Plath, however, hers has consistently provoked controversy, thanks mainly to its unflinching attention to, and distinctly female perspective on, the pleasures and pains of both the human body and the family, as well as emotional and physical violence. *The Dead and the Living* is divided between "Poems for the Living," about the poet's experience as daughter and mother, and "Poems for the Dead," about the victims of international conflicts; *The Father* (1992) chronicles her father's death (from cancer), *One Secret Thing* (2008), her mother's. *Stag's Leap* (2013) deals with the disintegration of her thirty-two-year marriage. As famous for her reticence off the page as for her candor on it, Olds teaches creative writing at New York University.

DOROTHY PARKER (1893–1967)

Born in West End, New Jersey, Dorothy Rothschild worked for both *Vogue* and *Vanity Fair* magazines before becoming a freelance writer. In 1917, she married Edwin Pond Parker II, whom she divorced in 1928. Her first book of verse, *Enough Rope* (1926), was a best seller and was followed by *Sunset Gun* (1928), *Death and Taxes* (1931), and *Collected Poems: Not So Deep as a Well* (1936). In 1927, Parker became a book reviewer for the *New Yorker*, to which she contributed for most of her career. In 1933, Parker and her second husband, Alan Campbell, moved to Hollywood, where they collaborated as film writers. In addition, Parker wrote criticism, two plays, short stories, and news reports from the Spanish Civil War. She is probably best remembered, though, as the reigning wit at the "Round Table" at Manhattan's Algonquin Hotel, where, in the 1920s and 1930s, she traded barbs with other prominent writers and humorists.

LINDA PASTAN (b. 1932)

Linda Pastan was born in New York City and raised in nearby Westchester County. After graduating from Radcliffe College, she received an MA in literature from Brandeis University. Although her first published poems appeared in *Mademoiselle* magazine in 1955, Pastan spent many years concentrating on her husband and three children—indeed, much of her poetry deals with her own family life. Her many collections include *A Perfect Circle of Sun* (1971), *The Five Stages of Grief* (1978), American Book Award nominee *PM/AM: New and Selected Poems* (1982), *Carnival Evening: New and Selected Poems 1968–1998* (1998), *Traveling Light* (2011), and *Insomnia* (2015). She lives in Potomac, Maryland.

SYLVIA PLATH (1932–63)

Sylvia Plath was born in Boston, Massachusetts; her father, a Polish immigrant, died when she was eight. After graduating from Smith College, Plath attended Cambridge University on a Fulbright scholarship, and there she met and married English poet Ted Hughes, with whom she had two children. As she documented in her novel *The Bell Jar* (1963), in 1953—between her junior and senior years of college—Plath became seriously depressed, attempted suicide, and was hospitalized. In 1963, the breakup of her marriage led to another suicide attempt, this time successful. Plath has attained cult status as much for her poems as for her "martyrdom" to art and life. In addition to her first volume of poetry, *The Colossus* (1960), Plath's work has been collected in *Ariel* (1966), *Crossing the Water* (1971), and *Winter Trees* (1972). Her selected letters were published in 1975; her expurgated journals in 1983; and her unabridged journals in 2000.

EZRA POUND (1885–1972)

Born in Hailey, Idaho, Ezra Pound studied at the University of Pennsylvania and Hamilton College before traveling to Europe in 1908. He remained there, living in Ireland, England, France, and Italy, for much of his life. Pound's tremendous ambition—to succeed in his own work and to influence the development of poetry and Western culture in general—led him to found the Imagist school of poetry, to advise and assist many great writers (Eliot, Joyce, Williams, Frost, and Hemingway, to name a few), and to write a number of highly influential critical works. His increasingly fiery and erratic behavior led to a charge of treason (he served as a propagandist for Italian Fascist Benito Mussolini during World War II), a diagnosis of insanity, and twelve years at St. Elizabeth's, an institution for the criminally insane.

ADRIENNE RICH (1929–2012)

One of the foremost poets and public intellectuals of her time, Adrienne Rich was born in Baltimore, Maryland, daughter of a former concert pianist and of a renowned Johns Hopkins University pathologist.

Rich's career as a poet began in 1951, when the Radcliffe College senior's first volume, *A Change of World* (1951), was selected by W. H. Auden for the prestigious Yale Younger Poets Award. Two years later, Rich married Harvard economist Alfred Conrad, with whom she had three children. As the 1950s gave way to the 1960s and 1970s, Rich's life and work changed profoundly. Beginning with her 1963 collection, *Snapshots of a Daughter-in-Law*, her poetry became ever less tightly controlled and formal, as it became ever more politically and personally charged, reflecting her deep engagement with the feminist, antiwar, and civil rights movements. After her recently estranged husband's suicide (1970) and publication of the National Book Award–winning *Diving into the Wreck* (1974), Rich began a lifelong partnership with Jamaica-born novelist and editor Michelle Cliff and published her two most influential prose works, *Of Woman Born: Motherhood as Experience and Institution* (1976) and *On Lies, Secrets and Silence* (1979), which includes her landmark essay "Compulsory Heterosexuality and Lesbian Existence." In the decades that followed, Rich never rested on her countless laurels, fiercely pursuing both her craft and her work for social justice. Her thirtieth and last volume of verse, *Tonight No Poetry Will Serve*, came out in 2010, just two years before her death, at age eighty-two, from the rheumatoid arthritis she had battled for decades. In its obituary, the *New York Times* aptly dubbed her "a poet of towering reputation," whose work is "distinguished by an unswerving progressive vision and a dazzling, empathetic ferocity."

KAY RYAN (b. 1945)

Described by poet J. D. McClatchy as "compact, exhilarating, strange affairs" full of sly wordplay and wit, Kay Ryan's poems are often compared to Emily Dickinson's. Like Dickinson, says Jack Foley, "Ryan can certainly be funny, but it is rarely without a sting." Typically less than 20 lines long and with lines often containing six syllables or less, Ryan's poems tend to have what she calls "the most dangerous shape," one in which "nearly every word is on one edge or the other" and "you can't hide anything" because "[a]ny crap is going to show." U.S. Poet Laureate from 2008 to 2010 and winner of both a Pulitzer Prize for Poetry and a MacArthur Fellowship, Ryan earned such accolades the hard way. Raised in California's Mojave Desert and San Joaquin Valley by her oil-well-driller father

and once rejected from the poetry club at UCLA, where she earned both BA (1967) and MA (1968) degrees in English, Ryan began teaching remedial English at the College of Marin in 1971, receiving widespread recognition for her poetry only some twenty years later. "All of us want instant success," she has said. "I'm glad I was on a sort of slow drip." This "drip" has produced over seven volumes, including *Say Uncle* (2000), *The Best of It: New and Selected Poems* (2010), and *Erratic Facts* (2015). In 2009 Ryan was widowed by the death of Carol Adair, her partner of over thirty years. Although she is sometimes accused of being too apolitical by members of the gay community, Ryan's thirty-plus years at Marin have made her a strong and vocal advocate of what she describes as America's "much underpraised and underfunded community colleges."

WILLIAM SHAKESPEARE (1564–1616)

Considering the great fame of his work, surprisingly little is known of William Shakespeare's life. Between 1585 and 1592, he left his birthplace of Stratford-upon-Avon for London to begin a career as playwright and actor. No dates of his professional career are recorded, however, nor can the order in which he composed his plays and poems be determined with absolute certainty. By 1594, he had established himself as a poet with two long works—*Venus and Adonis* and *The Rape of Lucrece*—and his more than 150 sonnets are supreme expressions of the form. His reputation, though, rests on the works he wrote for the theater. Shakespeare produced perhaps thirty-five plays in twenty-five years, proving himself a master of every dramatic genre: tragedy (in works such as *Macbeth*, *Hamlet*, *King Lear*, and *Othello*); historical drama (for example, *Richard III* and *Henry IV*); comedy (*Twelfth Night*, *As You Like It*, and many more); and romance (in plays such as *The Tempest* and *Cymbeline*). Without question, Shakespeare is the most quoted, discussed, and beloved English writer.

TRACY K. SMITH (b. 1972)

Pulitzer Prize–winning poet Tracy K. Smith credits her "love of language" and "sense of [. . .] hearing voices and imagining the lives inside" them to her parents—a mother who was also a teacher with a great "gift for storytelling and mimicry" and an optical-engineer father who "was always reading and pushing us to read." Though raised with her four older siblings mainly in California, Smith has spent much of her life in the Northeast: Born in Massachusetts, she returned there to attend Harvard (BA, 1994), studying with Seamus Heaney, while also—like fellow poets Natasha Trethewey and Kevin Young—participating in the Boston-based writers' group/reading series known as the Dark Room Collective. Grieving her mother's death from cancer, Smith nonetheless moved on to Columbia University, earning her MFA in 1997. Today a mother of three and professor of creative writing at Princeton University, Smith won rave reviews and multiple awards for her first two collections—*The Body's Question* (2003), which she describes as "grappling with the idea of the body as a site for experience, memory, and loss," "discovery and joy," and *Duende* (2007)—and for her 2015 memoir (*Ordinary Light*), which takes its epigraph from James Baldwin's "Sonny's Blues." But what earned her a Pulitzer and secured her reputation as one of America's most innovative and exciting young poets was *Life on Mars* (2011), a collection shaped equally by grief over her father's death, his work on the Hubble Space Telescope, and her interest in exploring (with nods to David Bowie and *2001: A Space Odyssey*) "space" and humans' enduring fascination with—and fantasies about—space "as a kind of metaphor through which to consider some of the facts and problems of life here on Earth." Smith became U.S. Poet Laureate in September 2017.

A. E. STALLINGS (b. 1968)

Alicia Elsbeth Stallings's biography—which could be titled *All the Way from Athens to Athens*—is an unusual one for a contemporary American poet. Admittedly, this daughter of a librarian and a Georgia Tech professor grew up in a bookish home, publishing her first poem—in *Seventeen* magazine—at age sixteen. But at the University of Georgia (in Athens, Georgia) and, later, Oxford University (in England), where she earned her MA, Stallings chose to study not English but ancient Greek and Latin language and literature, inspired, as she explains, both by a love of mythology rooted in a fascination with fairy tales and by her awareness that "the English poets whom [she] admired" most—including T. S. Eliot and A. E. Housman—"had studied the Classics and not English, which wasn't even a discipline then." Unlike most of her peers, moreover, Stallings has taught writing but never

held a full-time academic post. And she has lived abroad—in Athens, Greece—since her 1999 marriage. Published the same year, Stallings's Richard Wilbur Award–winning first collection, *Archaic Smile*, nonetheless assured her reputation as among America's foremost contemporary "New Formalists," a label simultaneously affirmed and greatly complicated by her later collections, *Hapax* (2006) and *Olives* (2012); by essays such as "Crooked Roads without Improvement: Some Thoughts on Formal Verse" (2000); and by her Poetry Foundation–sponsored blog *Harriet* (2007–08). Also a prizewinning translator of poets ranging from Lucretius (99–55 BCE) and Plutarch (46–120 CE) to Angelos Sikelianos (1884–1951), Stallings has garnered numerous highly coveted honors, ranging from a Nemerov Sonnet Award (2004) to a MacArthur Foundation "genius grant" (2011). Despite all that, she is, by her own report, known in Greece simply as "Aliki Psaropoulou, wife of Yannis, mother of Jason and Atalanta," thus enjoying an oddly "freeing" sort of "invisibility."

WALLACE STEVENS (1879–1955)

Born and raised in Reading, Pennsylvania, Wallace Stevens attended Harvard University and New York Law School. In New York City, he worked for a number of law firms, published poems in magazines, and befriended such literary figures as William Carlos Williams and Marianne Moore. In 1916, Stevens moved to Connecticut and began working for the Hartford Accident and Indemnity Company, where he became a vice president in 1934 and where he worked for the rest of his life, writing poetry at night and during vacations. He published his first collection, *Harmonium*, in 1923 and followed it with a series of volumes from 1935 until 1950, establishing himself as one of the twentieth century's most important poets. His lectures were collected in *The Necessary Angel: Essays on Reality and Imagination* (1951); his *Collected Poems* appeared in 1954.

ADRIENNE SU (b. 1967)

Adrienne Su grew up in Atlanta, Georgia, unaware, she says, of the ironies involved in being "viewed as Chinese," while "I knew no Chinese and thrived on the study of Latin." A graduate of Harvard and the University of Virginia, where she studied with Rita Dove, Gregory Orr, and Charles Wright, Su, by her own account, "started writing as soon as I could form a sentence on paper" and "started sending out work" while still in high school. Having worked as a freelance editor and writer, Su is today an associate professor of English and poet in residence at Pennsylvania's Dickinson College; a wife and mother; and the author of poetry collections including *Middle Kingdom* (1997), *Sanctuary* (2006), *Having None of It* (2009), and *Living Quarters* (2015). Crediting her high school Latin teacher and the ancient Roman poet Virgil with first teaching her the art of meter, and her early involvement in poetry slams with bolstering her commitment to writing "poems that on some levels can be read by anyone," Su also, in her words, "prefer[s] the daily to the exotic as subject matter," seeing writing as best when "it's woven into everyday life, as a ritual that fits somewhere between making pancakes for my kids and preparing a class for college students."

NATASHA TRETHEWEY (b. 1966)

Daughter of a social worker and a Canadian poet who met at a Kentucky college, but who had to marry in Ohio because of laws banning interracial unions, Natasha Trethewey was born in her mother's hometown of Gulfport, Mississippi. After her parents' divorce, she lived with her mother in Atlanta, Georgia, summering on the Gulf Coast with both her father and her mother's family. In 1985, Trethewey was just beginning her studies at the University of Georgia when her stepfather murdered her mother. Turning to poetry to deal with her grief, Trethewey earned her BA in 1989; an MA from Virginia's Hollins College, where her father was a professor (1991); and an MFA from the University of Massachusetts at Amherst (1995). After a short stint teaching at Auburn University, Trethewey moved to Emory University and, in 2007, became only the fourth African American poet ever to win the Pulitzer Prize, for *Native Guard*. Her third collection, it explores the problem of individual and collective historical amnesia through elegies to her mother and a ten-sonnet sequence written from the perspective of a soldier in the first all-black regiment to fight on the Union side in the Civil War. The years 2007–08, however, also brought Trethewey loss and hardship when her brother was imprisoned on drug-related

charges and her beloved grandmother died. Interweaving poetry, essays, and letters, her memoir *Beyond Katrina: A Meditation on the Mississippi Gulf Coast* (2010) reflects on both the region and her family's efforts to remember and rebuild. Trethewey's most recent collection is *Thrall* (2012).

WALT WHITMAN (1819–92)

Walt Whitman was born on a farm in West Hills, Long Island, to a British father and a Dutch mother. After working as a journalist throughout New York for many years, he taught for a time and founded his own newspaper, *The Long Islander*, in 1838; he then left journalism to work on *Leaves of Grass*, originally intended as a poetic treatise on American democratic idealism. Published privately in multiple editions from 1855 to 1874, the book of poems at first failed to reach a mass audience. In 1881, Boston's Osgood and Company published another edition of *Leaves of Grass*, which sold well until the district attorney called it "obscene literature" and stipulated that Whitman remove certain poems and phrases. He refused, and it was many years before his works were again published, this time in Philadelphia. By the time Whitman died, his work was revered, as it still is today, for its greatness of spirit and its exuberant American voice.

RICHARD WILBUR (1921–2017)

The son of a painter and a newspaperman's daughter, former U.S. Poet Laureate Richard Wilbur was raised in rural New Jersey, a background that may help to explain his precise imagery and keen interest in nature. Graduating from Amherst College into a world at war, Wilbur in 1942 married the woman who would remain his wife for over sixty years, joined the army, and, by his own account, began to "versify in earnest" because "[o]ne does not use poetry [. . .] as a means to organize oneself and the world, until one's world somehow gets out of hand." The many collections Wilbur published between his first, *The Beautiful Changes and Other Poems* (1947), and *The Nutcracker* (2012) include two Pulitzer Prize winners: *Things of This World* (1956) and *New and Collected Poems* (1988). In recent decades Wilbur's poems have been increasingly lauded for the very qualities that drew criticism in the thirty years between his two Pulitzer Prizes: As critic Gerry Cunningham wittily puts it, "They never raise their voices, put knives to their throats, drink too much, tell dirty jokes, or take their clothes off in public." Using traditional patterns of rhyme and meter, they "acknowledge horror," but remain largely "untouched by it."

WILLIAM CARLOS WILLIAMS (1883–1963)

Born in Rutherford, New Jersey, William Carlos Williams attended school in Switzerland and New York and studied medicine at the University of Pennsylvania and the University of Leipzig in Germany. He spent most of his life in Rutherford, practicing medicine and gradually establishing himself as one of America's great poets. Early in his writing career he left the European-inspired Imagist movement in favor of a more uniquely American poetic style comprised of vital, local language, and "no ideas but in things." His shorter poems have been published in numerous collected editions, including the Pulitzer Prize–winning *Brueghel, and Other Poems* (1963); his five-volume philosophical poem, *Paterson*, was published in 1963. Among his other works are plays such as *A Dream of Love* (1948) and *Many Loves* (1950); a trilogy of novels—*White Mules* (1937), *In the Money* (1940), and *The Build-Up* (1952); his *Autobiography* (1951); his *Selected Essays* (1954); and his *Selected Letters* (1957).

WILLIAM WORDSWORTH (1770–1850)

Regarded by many as the greatest of the Romantic poets, William Wordsworth was born in Cockermouth in the English Lake District, a beautiful, mountainous region that his poetry helped make a pop-ular tourist destination even in his own lifetime. He studied at Cambridge University and then spent a year in France, hoping to witness the French Revolution firsthand; as the revolution's "glorious renovation" dissolved into anarchy and then tyranny, Wordsworth was forced to return to England. Remarkably, he managed to establish "a saving intercourse with my true self" and to write some of his finest poetry, including the early version of his autobiographical masterpiece, *The Prelude*, which first appeared in 1805 and then again, much altered, in 1850. In 1798, Wordsworth and his friend Samuel Taylor Coleridge published *Lyrical Ballads*, which contained many of their greatest poems and is widely considered the founding document of English Romanticism. Revered by the reading public, Wordsworth served as Poet Laureate from 1843 until his death in 1850.

WILLIAM BUTLER YEATS (1865–1939)

William Butler Yeats was born in Dublin, Ireland, and, though he spent most of his youth in London, became the preeminent Irish poet of the twentieth century. Immersed in Irish history, folklore, and politics, as well as spiritualism and the occult, he attended art school for a time but left to devote himself to poetry that was, early in his career, self-consciously dreamy and ethereal. Yeats's poems became tighter and more passionate with his reading of philosophers such as Nietzsche, his involvement (mainly through theater) with the Irish nationalist cause, and his desperate love for the actress and nationalist Maud Gonne. He was briefly a senator in the newly independent Irish government before withdrawing from active public life to Thoor Ballylee, a crumbling Norman tower that Yeats and his wife fashioned into a home. There he developed an elaborate mythology (published as *A Vision* in 1925) and wrote poems that explored fundamental questions of history and identity. He was awarded the Nobel Prize for Literature in 1923.

PART THREE Drama

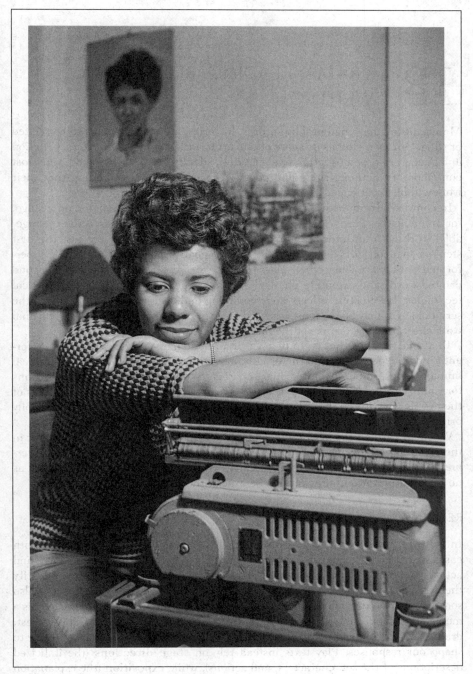

Lorraine Hansberry

18 | DRAMA: READING, RESPONDING, WRITING

Many cultures have had oral literatures: histories, romances, poems to be recited or sung. Our own era has its share of oral art forms, of course, but "literary" fiction and poetry are now most often read privately, silently, from the printed page. Most contemporary fiction writers and poets write with an understanding that their work will be experienced and enjoyed this way.

In contrast, **drama** is written primarily to be performed—by actors, on a stage, for an audience. Playwrights or dramatists (the two terms are used interchangeably) work with an understanding that the words on the page are just the first step—a map of sorts—toward the ultimate goal: a collaborative, publicly performed work of art. They create plays fully aware of the possibilities that go beyond printed words and extend to physical actions, stage devices, and other theatrical techniques for creating effects and modifying audience responses. Although the script of a play may be the most essential piece in the puzzle that makes up the final work of art, the play text is not the final, complete work.

To attend a play—that is, to be part of an audience—represents a very different kind of experience from the usually solitary act of reading. On the stage, real human beings, standing for imaginary characters, deliver lines and perform actions for you to see and hear. In turn, the actors adapt in subtle ways to the reactions of the people who attend the performance and whose responses are no longer wholly private but have become, in part, communal.

When you attend the performance of a play, then, you become a collaborator in the creation of a unique work of art: not the play *text* but instead a specific *interpretation* of that text. No two performances of a play can ever be identical, just as no two interpretations of a play can be exactly the same.

READING DRAMA

In many respects, of course, reading drama is similar to reading fiction. In both cases we anticipate what will happen next; we imagine the characters, settings, and actions; we respond to the symbolic suggestiveness of images; and we identify themes. But because most plays are written to be performed, reading plays is also somewhat different from reading fiction or poetry. In fiction, for example, there is a mediator or **narrator**, someone standing between us and the events. In contrast, drama rarely has such an interpreter or mediator to tell us what is happening or to shape our responses. Play texts instead rely on **stage directions** (the italicized descriptions of the set, characters, and actions), while **exposition** (the explanation of the past and current situation) emerges only here and there through dialogue.

For this reason, reading drama may place a greater demand on the imagination than reading fiction does: The reader must be his or her own narrator and interpreter.

Such exercise for the imagination can prove rewarding, however, for it has much in common with the imaginative work that a director, actors, and other artists involved in a staged production do. In re-creating a play as we read it, we are essentially imagining the play as if it were being performed by live actors in real time. We "cast" the characters, we design the set with its furniture and props, and we choreograph or "block" the physical action, according to the cues in the text.

In reading drama even more than in reading fiction, we construct our ideas of character and personality from what characters say. In some plays, especially those with a modernist or experimental bent, certain lines of dialogue can be mystifying; other characters, as well as the audience or readers, can be left wondering what a speech means. On the one hand, such puzzling lines can become clearer in performance when we see and hear actors deliver them. On the other hand, plays that call for several characters to speak at once or to talk at cross purposes can be much easier to understand when read than they are in performance. In interpreting dialogue, you will naturally draw on your own experiences of comparable situations or similar personalities, as well as your familiarity with other plays or stories.

Questions to Ask When Reading a Play

In reading drama as in reading fiction, you can begin to understand a text by asking some basic questions about the elements of drama.

- **Expectations:** What do you expect
  - from the title? from the first sentence, paragraph, or speech?
  - after the first events or interactions of characters? as the **conflict** is resolved?
- **Characterization:** Who are the characters? Is there a list of characters printed after the title of the play? What do you notice about their names or any identification of their roles, character types, or relationships?
  - Who is/are the **protagonist**(s)?
  - Who is/are the **antagonist**(s) (villain, opponent, obstacle)?
  - Who are the other characters?
  - What does each character know at any moment in the **action**? What does each character expect at any point? What does the audience know or expect that is different from what the characters know or expect?
- **Plot:** What happens in the play?
  - Do the characters or situations change during the play?
  - What are the differences between the beginning, middle, and end of the play? Is it divided into acts? Would there be an intermission in a performance?
  - Can you summarize the plot? Is it a recognizable kind or genre such as **tragedy, comedy, farce**, or mystery?
- **Setting:** What is the setting of the play?
  - *When* does the action occur? Do the stage directions specify a year or era, a day of the week, a season, a time of day?
  - Are there any time changes during the play? Are the scenes in chronological order, or are there any scenes that are supposed to take place earlier or simultaneously? Does the passage of time in the lives of the characters

correspond with the passage of time onstage? Or do we understand that time has passed and events have occurred offstage and between scenes?
- *Where* does it take place? Is it in the United States or another country, or in a specific town or region? Do the stage directions describe the scene that an audience would see onstage, and does this remain the same or change during the play? How many scene changes are there?
- **Style:** What do you notice about how the play is written?
  - What is the style of the dialogue? Are the sentences and speeches short or long? Is the vocabulary simple or complex? Do characters ever speak at the same time, or do they always take turns? Does the play instruct actors to be silent for periods of time? Which characters speak most often? How might their speech patterns differ?
  - Are there any **images** or figures of speech?
  - What is the **tone** or mood? Does the play make the reader or audience feel sad, amused, worried, curious?
- **Theme:** What does the play mean? Can you express its theme or themes?
  - Answers to these big questions may be found in many instances by returning to your answers to the questions above. The play's meaning or theme depends on all its features.

SUSAN GLASPELL
(1876–1948)
Trifles

Though today remembered almost exclusively for her masterful *Trifles* (1916), Susan Glaspell wrote over a dozen plays, fifty short stories, nine novels, and a memoir, in addition to playing a key role in the development of twentieth-century American theater. Born in Davenport, Iowa, she graduated from Drake University in 1899 and spent two years at the *Des Moines Daily News*, where she covered the trial of a fifty-seven-year-old woman accused of murdering her sleeping husband with an axe. When Glaspell's short stories began appearing in magazines, she returned to Davenport. There, she became involved with George Cram Cook, a former English professor and married father of two. The two wed in 1913 and moved east, eventually settling in New York's Greenwich Village and Cape Cod, Massachusetts, where they founded the Provincetown Playhouse (later the Playwright's Theater), an extraordinary gathering of freethinking, Left-leaning actors, directors, and playwrights that included Edna St. Vincent Millay and a then-unknown Eugene O'Neill. Between 1916 and 1922, this pioneering group reportedly staged more plays by women than any other contemporary theater. Among them were eleven by Glaspell, ranging from realistic dramas such as *Trifles* and satirical comedies like *Woman's Honor* (1918) to her expressionistic *The Verge* (1921). Widowed in 1924, Glaspell ended a brief second marriage in 1931, the same year that her last play, *Alison's House*, won the Pulitzer Prize for Drama. Having published her first novel in 1909 and multiple best sellers in the 1920s and 1930s, Glaspell spent the last years of her life writing fiction in Provincetown.

CHARACTERS

SHERIFF	MRS. PETERS, *Sheriff's wife*
COUNTY ATTORNEY	MRS. HALE
HALE	

SCENE: *The kitchen in the now abandoned farmhouse of* JOHN WRIGHT, *a gloomy kitchen, and left without having been put in order—unwashed pans under the sink, a loaf of bread outside the bread-box, a dish-towel on the table—other signs of incompleted work. At the rear the outer door opens and the* SHERIFF *comes in followed by the* COUNTY ATTORNEY *and* HALE. *The* SHERIFF *and* HALE *are men in middle life, the* COUNTY ATTORNEY *is a young man; all are much bundled up and go at once to the stove. They are followed by the two women—the* SHERIFF'S *wife first; she is a slight wiry woman, a thin nervous face.* MRS. HALE *is larger and would ordinarily be called more comfortable looking, but she is disturbed now and looks fearfully about as she enters. The women have come in slowly, and stand close together near the door.*

COUNTY ATTORNEY: [*Rubbing his hands.*] This feels good. Come up to the fire, ladies.

MRS. PETERS: [*After taking a step forward.*] I'm not—cold.

SHERIFF: [*Unbuttoning his overcoat and stepping away from the stove as if to mark the beginning of official business.*] Now, Mr. Hale, before we move things

Marjorie Vonnegut, Elinor Cox, John King, Arthur Hohl, and T. W. Gibson
in a 1916 production of *Trifles*

about, you explain to Mr. Henderson just what you saw when you came here yesterday morning.

COUNTY ATTORNEY: By the way, has anything been moved? Are things just as you left them yesterday?

SHERIFF: [*Looking about.*] It's just the same. When it dropped below zero last night I thought I'd better send Frank out this morning to make a fire for us— no use getting pneumonia with a big case on, but I told him not to touch anything except the stove—and you know Frank.

COUNTY ATTORNEY: Somebody should have been left here yesterday.

SHERIFF: Oh—yesterday. When I had to send Frank to Morris Center for that man who went crazy—I want you to know I had my hands full yesterday. I knew you could get back from Omaha by today and as long as I went over everything here myself—

COUNTY ATTORNEY: Well, Mr. Hale, tell just what happened when you came here yesterday morning.

HALE: Harry and I had started to town with a load of potatoes. We came along the road from my place and as I got here I said, "I'm going to see if I can't get John Wright to go in with me on a party telephone."[1] I spoke to Wright about it once before and he put me off, saying folks talked too much anyway, and all he asked was peace and quiet—I guess you know about how much he talked himself; but I thought maybe if I went to the house and talked about it before his wife, though I said to Harry that I didn't know as what his wife wanted made much difference to John—

COUNTY ATTORNEY: Let's talk about that later, Mr. Hale. I do want to talk about that, but tell now just what happened when you got to the house.

HALE: I didn't hear or see anything; I knocked at the door, and still it was all quiet inside. I knew they must be up, it was past eight o'clock. So I knocked again, and I thought I heard somebody say, "Come in." I wasn't sure, I'm not sure yet, but I opened the door—this door [*Indicating the door by which the two women are still standing.*] and there in that rocker—[*Pointing to it.*] sat Mrs. Wright.

[*They all look at the rocker.*]

COUNTY ATTORNEY: What—was she doing?

HALE: She was rockin' back and forth. She had her apron in her hand and was kind of—pleating it.

COUNTY ATTORNEY: And how did she—look?

HALE: Well, she looked queer.

COUNTY ATTORNEY: How do you mean—queer?

HALE: Well, as if she didn't know what she was going to do next. And kind of done up.

COUNTY ATTORNEY: How did she seem to feel about your coming?

HALE: Why, I don't think she minded—one way or other. She didn't pay much attention. I said, "How do, Mrs. Wright, it's cold, ain't it?" And she said, "Is it?"—and went on kind of pleating at her apron. Well, I was surprised;

---

1. That is, a party line in which a number of households each have extensions, a common arrangement in the early twentieth century, especially in rural areas.

she didn't ask me to come up to the stove, or to set down, but just sat there, not even looking at me, so I said, "I want to see John." And then she—laughed. I guess you would call it a laugh. I thought of Harry and the team outside, so I said a little sharp: "Can't I see John?" "No," she says, kind o' dull like. "Ain't he home?" says I. "Yes," says she, "he's home." "Then why can't I see him?" I asked her, out of patience. "'Cause he's dead," says she. *Dead?*" says I. She just nodded her head, not getting a bit excited, but rockin' back and forth. "Why—where is he?" says I, not knowing what to say. She just pointed upstairs—like that. [*Himself pointing to the room above.*] I got up, with the idea of going up there. I walked from there to here—then I says, "Why, what did he die of?" "He died of a rope round his neck," says she, and just went on pleatin' at her apron. Well, I went out and called Harry. I thought I might—need help. We went upstairs and there he was lyin'—

COUNTY ATTORNEY: I think I'd rather have you go into that upstairs, where you can point it all out. Just go on now with the rest of the story.

HALE: Well, my first thought was to get that rope off. It looked . . . [*Stops, his face twitches.*] . . . but Harry, he went up to him, and he said, "No, he's dead all right, and we'd better not touch anything." So we went back downstairs. She was still sitting that same way. "Has anybody been notified?" I asked. "No," says she, unconcerned. "Who did this, Mrs. Wright?" said Harry. He said it business-like—and she stopped pleatin' of her apron. "I don't know," she says. "You don't *know*?" says Harry. "No," says she. "Weren't you sleepin' in the bed with him?" says Harry. "Yes," says she, "but I was on the inside." "Somebody slipped a rope round his neck and strangled him and you didn't wake up?" says Harry. "I didn't wake up," she said after him. We must 'a looked as if we didn't see how that could be, for after a minute she said, "I sleep sound." Harry was going to ask her more questions but I said maybe we ought to let her tell her story first to the coroner, or the sheriff, so Harry went fast as he could to Rivers' place, where there's a telephone.

COUNTY ATTORNEY: And what did Mrs. Wright do when she knew that you had gone for the coroner?

HALE: She moved from that chair to this one over here [*Pointing to a small chair in the corner.*] and just sat there with her hands held together and looking down. I got a feeling that I ought to make some conversation, so I said I had come in to see if John wanted to put in a telephone, and at that she started to laugh, and then she stopped and looked at me—scared. [*The* COUNTY ATTORNEY, *who has had his notebook out, makes a note.*] I dunno, maybe it wasn't scared. I wouldn't like to say it was. Soon Harry got back, and then Dr. Lloyd came, and you, Mr. Peters, and so I guess that's all I know that you don't.

COUNTY ATTORNEY: [*Looking around.*] I guess we'll go upstairs first—and then out to the barn and around there. [*To the* SHERIFF.] You're convinced that there was nothing important here—nothing that would point to any motive?

SHERIFF: Nothing here but kitchen things.

[*The* COUNTY ATTORNEY, *after again looking around the kitchen, opens the door of a cupboard closet. He gets up on a chair and looks on a shelf. Pulls his hand away, sticky.*]

COUNTY ATTORNEY: Here's a nice mess.

[*The women draw nearer.*]

MRS. PETERS: [*To the other woman.*] Oh, her fruit; it did freeze. [*To the* LAWYER.] She worried about that when it turned so cold. She said the fire'd go out and her jars would break.

SHERIFF: Well, can you beat the women! Held for murder and worryin' about her preserves.

COUNTY ATTORNEY: I guess before we're through she may have something more serious than preserves to worry about.

HALE: Well, women are used to worrying over trifles.

[*The two women move a little closer together.*]

COUNTY ATTORNEY: [*With the gallantry of a young politician.*] And yet, for all their worries, what would we do without the ladies? [*The women do not unbend. He goes to the sink, takes a dipperful of water from the pail and pouring it into a basin, washes his hands. Starts to wipe them on the roller towel, turns it for a cleaner place.*] Dirty towels! [*Kicks his foot against the pans under the sink.*] Not much of a housekeeper, would you say, ladies?

MRS. HALE: [*Stiffly.*] There's a great deal of work to be done on a farm.

COUNTY ATTORNEY: To be sure. And yet [*With a little bow to her.*] I know there are some Dickson county farmhouses which do not have such roller towels. [*He gives it a pull to expose its length again.*]

MRS. HALE: Those towels get dirty awful quick. Men's hands aren't always as clean as they might be.

COUNTY ATTORNEY: Ah, loyal to your sex, I see. But you and Mrs. Wright were neighbors. I suppose you were friends, too.

MRS. HALE: [*Shaking her head.*] I've not seen much of her of late years. I've not been in this house—it's more than a year.

COUNTY ATTORNEY: And why was that? You didn't like her?

MRS. HALE: I liked her all well enough. Farmers' wives have their hands full, Mr. Henderson. And then—

COUNTY ATTORNEY: Yes—?

MRS. HALE: [*Looking about.*] It never seemed a very cheerful place.

COUNTY ATTORNEY: No—it's not cheerful. I shouldn't say she had the home-making instinct.

MRS. HALE: Well, I don't know as Wright had, either.

COUNTY ATTORNEY: You mean that they didn't get on very well?

MRS. HALE: No, I don't mean anything. But I don't think a place'd be any cheer-fuller for John Wright's being in it.

COUNTY ATTORNEY: I'd like to talk more of that a little later. I want to get the lay of things upstairs now. [*He goes to the left, where three steps lead to a stair door.*]

SHERIFF: I suppose anything Mrs. Peters does'll be all right. She was to take in some clothes for her, you know, and a few little things. We left in such a hurry yesterday.

COUNTY ATTORNEY: Yes, but I would like to see what you take, Mrs. Peters, and keep an eye out for anything that might be of use to us.

MRS. PETERS: Yes, Mr. Henderson. [*The women listen to the men's steps on the stairs, then look about the kitchen.*]

MRS. HALE: I'd hate to have men coming into my kitchen, snooping around and criticizing. [*She arranges the pans under the sink which the* LAWYER *had shoved out of place.*]

MRS. PETERS: Of course it's no more than their duty.

MRS. HALE: Duty's all right, but I guess that deputy sheriff that came out to make the fire might have got a little of this on. [*Gives the roller towel a pull.*] Wish I'd thought of that sooner. Seems mean to talk about her for not having things slicked up when she had to come away in such a hurry.

MRS. PETERS: [*Who has gone to a small table in the left rear corner of the room, and lifted one end of a towel that covers a pan.*] She had bread set. [*Stands still.*]

MRS. HALE: [*Eyes fixed on a loaf of bread beside the bread box, which is on a low shelf at the other side of the room. Moves slowly toward it.*] She was going to put this in there. [*Picks up loaf, then abruptly drops it. In a manner of returning to familiar things.*] It's a shame about her fruit. I wonder if it's all gone. [*Gets up on the chair and looks.*] I think there's some here that's all right, Mrs. Peters. Yes—here; [*Holding it toward the window.*] this is cherries, too. [*Looking again.*] I declare I believe that's the only one. [*Gets down, bottle in her hand. Goes to the sink and wipes it off on the outside.*] She'll feel awful bad after all her hard work in the hot weather. I remember the afternoon I put up my cherries last summer. [*She puts the bottle on the big kitchen table, center of the room. With a sigh, is about to sit down in the rocking-chair. Before she is seated realizes what chair it is; with a slow look at it, steps back. The chair, which she has touched, rocks back and forth.*]

MRS. PETERS: Well, I must get those things from the front room closet. [*She goes to the door at the right, but after looking into the other room, steps back.*] You coming with me, Mrs. Hale? You could help me carry them. [*They go in the other room; reappear,* MRS. PETERS *carrying a dress and skirt,* MRS. HALE *following with a pair of shoes.*] My, it's cold in there. [*She puts the clothes on the big table, and hurries to the stove.*]

MRS. HALE: [*Examining the skirt.*] Wright was close. I think maybe that's why she kept so much to herself. She didn't even belong to the Ladies Aid. I suppose she felt she couldn't do her part, and then you don't enjoy things when you feel shabby. She used to wear pretty clothes and be lively, when she was Minnie Foster, one of the town girls singing in the choir. But that—oh, that was thirty years ago. This all you was to take in?

MRS. PETERS: She said she wanted an apron. Funny thing to want, for there isn't much to get you dirty in jail, goodness knows. But I suppose just to make her feel more natural. She said they was in the top drawer in this cupboard. Yes, here. And then her little shawl that always hung behind the door. [*Opens stair door and looks.*] Yes, here it is. [*Quickly shuts door leading upstairs.*]

MRS. HALE: [*Abruptly moving toward her.*] Mrs. Peters?

MRS. PETERS: Yes, Mrs. Hale?

MRS. HALE: Do you think she did it?

MRS. PETERS: [*In a frightened voice.*] Oh, I don't know.

MRS. HALE: Well, I don't think she did. Asking for an apron and her little shawl. Worrying about her fruit.

MRS. PETERS: [*Starts to speak, glances up, where footsteps are heard in the room above. In a low voice.*] Mr. Peters says it looks bad for her. Mr. Henderson is awful sarcastic in a speech and he'll make fun of her sayin' she didn't wake up.

MRS. HALE: Well, I guess John Wright didn't wake when they was slipping that rope under his neck.

MRS. PETERS: No, it's strange. It must have been done awful crafty and still. They say it was such a—funny way to kill a man, rigging it all up like that.

MRS. HALE: That's just what Mr. Hale said. There was a gun in the house. He says that's what he can't understand.

MRS. PETERS: Mr. Henderson said coming out that what was needed for the case was a motive; something to show anger, or—sudden feeling.

MRS. HALE: [*Who is standing by the table.*] Well, I don't see any signs of anger around here. [*She puts her hand on the dish towel which lies on the table, stands looking down at table, one half of which is clean, the other half messy.*] It's wiped to here. [*Makes a move as if to finish work, then turns and looks at loaf of bread outside the bread box. Drops towel. In that voice of coming back to familiar things.*] Wonder how they are finding things upstairs. I hope she had it a little more red-up[2] up there. You know, it seems kind of *sneaking*. Locking her up in town and then coming out here and trying to get her own house to turn against her!

MRS. PETERS: But Mrs. Hale, the law is the law.

MRS. HALE: I s'pose 'tis. [*Unbuttoning her coat.*] Better loosen up your things, Mrs. Peters. You won't feel them when you go out.

[MRS. PETERS *takes off her fur tippet, goes to hang it on hook at back of room, stands looking at the under part of the small corner table.*]

MRS. PETERS: She was piecing a quilt. [*She brings the large sewing basket and they look at the bright pieces.*]

MRS. HALE: It's log cabin pattern. Pretty, isn't it? I wonder if she was goin' to quilt it or just knot it?

[*Footsteps have been heard coming down the stairs. The* SHERIFF *enters followed by* HALE *and the* COUNTY ATTORNEY.]

SHERIFF: They wonder if she was going to quilt it or just knot it!

[*The men laugh, the women look abashed.*]

COUNTY ATTORNEY: [*Rubbing his hands over the stove.*] Frank's fire didn't do much up there, did it? Well, let's go out to the barn and get that cleared up.

[*The men go outside.*]

MRS. HALE: [*Resentfully.*] I don't know as there's anything so strange, our takin' up our time with little things while we're waiting for them to get the evidence. [*She sits down at the big table smoothing out a block with decision.*] I don't see as it's anything to laugh about.

MRS. PETERS: [*Apologetically.*] Of course they've got awful important things on their minds. [*Pulls up a chair and joins* MRS. HALE *at the table.*]

---

2. Tidied up.

MRS. HALE: [*Examining another block.*] Mrs. Peters, look at this one. Here, this is the one she was working on, and look at the sewing! All the rest of it has been so nice and even. And look at this! It's all over the place! Why, it looks as if she didn't know what she was about! [*After she has said this they look at each other, then start to glance back at the door. After an instant* MRS. HALE *has pulled at a knot and ripped the sewing.*]

MRS. PETERS: Oh, what are you doing, Mrs. Hale?

MRS. HALE: [*Mildly.*] Just pulling out a stitch or two that's not sewed very good. [*Threading the needle.*] Bad sewing always made me fidgety.

MRS. PETERS: [*Nervously.*] I don't think we ought to touch things.

MRS. HALE: I'll just finish up this end. [*Suddenly stopping and leaning forward.*] Mrs. Peters?

MRS. PETERS: Yes, Mrs. Hale?

MRS. HALE: What do you suppose she was so nervous about?

MRS. PETERS: Oh—I don't know. I don't know as she was nervous. I sometimes sew awful queer when I'm just tired. [MRS. HALE *starts to say something, looks at* MRS. PETERS, *then goes on sewing.*] Well, I must get these things wrapped up. They may be through sooner than we think. [*Putting apron and other things together.*] I wonder where I can find a piece of paper, and string.

MRS. HALE: In that cupboard, maybe.

MRS. PETERS: [*Looking in cupboard.*] Why, here's a bird-cage. [*Holds it up.*] Did she have a bird, Mrs. Hale?

MRS. HALE: Why, I don't know whether she did or not—I've not been here for so long. There was a man around last year selling canaries cheap, but I don't know as she took one; maybe she did. She used to sing real pretty herself.

MRS. PETERS: [*Glancing around.*] Seems funny to think of a bird here. But she must have had one, or why would she have a cage? I wonder what happened to it.

MRS. HALE: I s'pose maybe the cat got it.

MRS. PETERS: No, she didn't have a cat. She's got that feeling some people have about cats—being afraid of them. My cat got in her room and she was real upset and asked me to take it out.

MRS. HALE: My sister Bessie was like that. Queer, ain't it?

MRS. PETERS: [*Examining the cage.*] Why, look at this door. It's broke. One hinge is pulled apart.

MRS. HALE: [*Looking too.*] Looks as if someone must have been rough with it.

MRS. PETERS: Why, yes. [*She brings the cage forward and puts it on the table.*]

MRS. HALE: I wish if they're going to find any evidence they'd be about it. I don't like this place.

MRS. PETERS: But I'm awful glad you came with me, Mrs. Hale. It would be lonesome for me sitting here alone.

MRS. HALE: It would, wouldn't it? [*Dropping her sewing.*] But I tell you what I do wish, Mrs. Peters. I wish I had come over sometimes when *she* was here. I—[*Looking around the room.*]—wish I had.

MRS. PETERS: But of course you were awful busy, Mrs. Hale—your house and your children.

MRS. HALE: I could've come. I stayed away because it weren't cheerful—and that's why I ought to have come. I—I've never liked this place. Maybe because it's down in a hollow and you don't see the road. I dunno what it is, but it's a lonesome place and always was. I wish I had come over to see Minnie Foster sometimes. I can see now—[*Shakes her head.*]

MRS. PETERS: Well, you mustn't reproach yourself, Mrs. Hale. Somehow we just don't see how it is with other folks until—something comes up.

MRS. HALE: Not having children makes less work—but it makes a quiet house, and Wright out to work all day, and no company when he did come in. Did you know John Wright, Mrs. Peters?

MRS. PETERS: Not to know him; I've seen him in town. They say he was a good man.

MRS. HALE: Yes—good; he didn't drink, and kept his word as well as most, I guess, and paid his debts. But he was a hard man, Mrs. Peters. Just to pass the time of day with him—[*Shivers.*] Like a raw wind that gets to the bone. [*Pauses, her eye falling on the cage.*] I should think she would 'a wanted a bird. But what do you suppose went with it?

MRS. PETERS: I don't know, unless it got sick and died. [*She reaches over and swings the broken door, swings it again, both women watch it.*]

MRS. HALE: You weren't raised round here, were you? [MRS. PETERS *shakes her head.*] You didn't know—her?

MRS. PETERS: Not till they brought her yesterday.

MRS. HALE: She—come to think of it, she was kind of like a bird herself—real sweet and pretty, but kind of timid and—fluttery. How—she—did—change. [*Silence; then as if struck by a happy thought and relieved to get back to every-day things.*] Tell you what, Mrs. Peters, why don't you take the quilt in with you? It might take up her mind.

MRS. PETERS: Why, I think that's a real nice idea, Mrs. Hale. There couldn't possibly be any objection to it, could there? Now, just what would I take? I wonder if her patches are in here—and her things. [*They look in the sewing basket.*]

MRS. HALE: Here's some red. I expect this has got sewing things in it. [*Brings out a fancy box.*] What a pretty box. Looks like something somebody would give you. Maybe her scissors are in here. [*Opens box. Suddenly puts her hand to her nose.*] Why—[MRS. PETERS *bends nearer, then turns her face away.*] There's something wrapped up in this piece of silk.

MRS. PETERS: Why, this isn't her scissors.

MRS. HALE: [*Lifting the silk.*] Oh, Mrs. Peters—it's—

[MRS. PETERS *bends closer.*]

MRS. PETERS: It's the bird.

MRS. HALE: [*Jumping up.*] But, Mrs. Peters—look at it! Its neck! Look at its neck! It's all—other side *to.*

MRS. PETERS: Somebody—wrung—its—neck.

[*Their eyes meet. A look of growing comprehension, of horror. Steps are heard outside.* MRS. HALE *slips box under quilt pieces, and sinks into her chair. Enter* SHERIFF *and* COUNTY ATTORNEY. MRS. PETERS *rises.*]

COUNTY ATTORNEY: [*As one turning from serious things to little pleasantries.*] Well ladies, have you decided whether she was going to quilt it or knot it?

MRS. PETERS: We think she was going to—knot it.

COUNTY ATTORNEY: Well, that's interesting, I'm sure. [*Seeing the bird-cage.*] Has the bird flown?

MRS. HALE: [*Putting more quilt pieces over the box.*] We think the—cat got it.

COUNTY ATTORNEY: [*Preoccupied.*] Is there a cat?

[MRS. HALE *glances in a quick covert way at* MRS. PETERS.]

MRS. PETERS: Well, not *now*. They're superstitious, you know. They leave.

COUNTY ATTORNEY: [*To* SHERIFF PETERS, *continuing an interrupted conversation.*] No sign at all of anyone having come from the outside. Their own rope. Now let's go up again and go over it piece by piece. [*They start upstairs.*] It would have to have been someone who knew just the—

[MRS. PETERS *sits down. The two women sit there not looking at one another, but as if peering into something and at the same time holding back. When they talk now it is in the manner of feeling their way over strange ground, as if afraid of what they are saying, but as if they cannot help saying it.*]

MRS. HALE: She liked the bird. She was going to bury it in that pretty box.

MRS. PETERS: [*In a whisper.*] When I was a girl—my kitten—there was a boy took a hatchet, and before my eyes—and before I could get there—[*Covers her face an instant.*] If they hadn't held me back I would have—[*Catches herself, looks upstairs where steps are heard, falters weakly.*]—hurt him.

MRS. HALE: [*With a slow look around her.*] I wonder how it would seem never to have had any children around. [*Pause.*] No, Wright wouldn't like the bird— a thing that sang. She used to sing. He killed that, too.

MRS. PETERS: [*Moving uneasily.*] We don't know who killed the bird.

MRS. HALE: I knew John Wright.

MRS. PETERS: It was an awful thing was done in this house that night, Mrs. Hale. Killing a man while he slept, slipping a rope around his neck that choked the life out of him.

MRS. HALE: His neck. Choked the life out of him. [*Her hand goes out and rests on the bird-cage.*]

MRS. PETERS: [*With rising voice.*] We don't know who killed him. We don't *know*.

MRS. HALE: [*Her own feeling not interrupted.*] If there's been years and years of nothing, then a bird to sing to you, it would be awful—still, after the bird was still.

MRS. PETERS: [*Something within her speaking.*] I know what stillness is. When we homesteaded in Dakota, and my first baby died—after he was two years old, and me with no other then—

MRS. HALE: [*Moving.*] How soon do you suppose they'll be through, looking for the evidence?

MRS. PETERS: I know what stillness is. [*Pulling herself back.*] The law has got to punish crime, Mrs. Hale.

MRS. HALE: [*Not as if answering that.*] I wish you'd seen Minnie Foster when she wore a white dress with blue ribbons and stood up there in the choir and sang. [*A look around the room.*] Oh, I *wish* I'd come over here once in a while! That was a crime! That was a crime! Who's going to punish that?

MRS. PETERS: [*Looking upstairs.*] We mustn't—take on.

MRS. HALE: I might have known she needed help! I know how things can be— for women. I tell you, it's queer, Mrs. Peters. We live close together and we live far apart. We all go through the same things—it's all just a different kind of the same thing. [*Brushes her eyes, noticing the bottle of fruit, reaches out for it.*] If I was you, I wouldn't tell her her fruit was gone. Tell her it *ain't*. Tell her it's all right. Take this in to prove it to her. She—she may never know whether it was broke or not.

MRS. PETERS: [*Takes the bottle, looks about for something to wrap it in; takes petticoat from the clothes brought from the other room, very nervously begins winding this around the bottle. In a false voice.*] My, it's a good thing the men couldn't hear us. Wouldn't they just laugh! Getting all stirred up over a little thing like a—dead canary. As if that could have anything to do with—with—wouldn't they *laugh!*

[*The men are heard coming down stairs.*]

MRS. HALE: [*Under her breath.*] Maybe they would—maybe they wouldn't.

COUNTY ATTORNEY: No, Peters, it's all perfectly clear except a reason for doing it. But you know juries when it comes to women. If there was some definite thing. Something to show—something to make a story about—a thing that would connect up with this strange way of doing it—

[*The women's eyes meet for an instant. Enter* HALE *from outer door.*]

HALE: Well, I've got the team around. Pretty cold out there.

COUNTY ATTORNEY: I'm going to stay here a while by myself. [*To the* SHERIFF.] You can send Frank out for me, can't you? I want to go over everything. I'm not satisfied that we can't do better.

SHERIFF: Do you want to see what Mrs. Peters is going to take in?

[*The* LAWYER *goes to the table, picks up the apron, laughs.*]

COUNTY ATTORNEY: Oh, I guess they're not very dangerous things the ladies have picked out. [*Moves a few things about, disturbing the quilt pieces which cover the box. Steps back.*] No, Mrs. Peters doesn't need supervising. For that matter, a sheriff's wife is married to the law. Ever think of it that way, Mrs. Peters?

MRS. PETERS: Not—just that way.

SHERIFF: [*Chuckling.*] Married to the law. [*Moves toward the other room.*] I just want you to come in here a minute, George. We ought to take a look at these windows.

COUNTY ATTORNEY: [*Scoffingly.*] Oh, windows!

SHERIFF: We'll be right out, Mr. Hale.

[HALE *goes outside. The* SHERIFF *follows the* COUNTY ATTORNEY *into the other room. Then* MRS. HALE *rises, hands tight together, looking intensely at* MRS. PETERS, *whose eyes make a slow turn, finally meeting* MRS. HALE's. *A moment* MRS. HALE *holds her, then her own eyes point the way to where the box is concealed. Suddenly* MRS. PETERS *throws back quilt pieces and tries to put the box in the bag she is wearing. It is too big. She opens box, starts to take bird out, cannot touch it, goes to pieces, stands there helpless. Sound of a knob turning in the other room.* MRS. HALE *snatches the box and puts it in the pocket of her big coat. Enter* COUNTY ATTORNEY *and* SHERIFF.]

COUNTY ATTORNEY: [*Facetiously.*] Well, Henry, at least we found out that she was not going to quilt it. She was going to—what is it you call it, ladies?

MRS. HALE: [*Her hand against her pocket.*] We call it—knot it, Mr. Henderson.

CURTAIN

1916

QUESTIONS

1. If we were watching a production of TRIFLES and had no cast list, how would we gradually piece together the fact that Mrs. Peters is the sheriff's wife? What are the earliest lines of dialogue that allow an audience to infer this fact?

2. What lines in the play characterize Mrs. Hale's reaction to the men's behavior and attitudes? What lines characterize Mrs. Peters's reaction to the men early in the play, and what lines show her feelings changing later in the play? What might account for the two women's initial differences and their evolving solidarity with Mrs. Wright?

3. What are the "trifles" that the men ignore and the two women notice? Why do the men dismiss them, and why do the women see these things as significant clues? What is the thematic importance of these "trifles"?

4. How would you stage the key moment of the play, Mrs. Hale's discovery of the bird in the sewing basket? What facial expression would she have? What body language? Where would you place Mrs. Peters, and what would she be doing? How would you use lighting to heighten the effectiveness of the scene?

5. If a twenty-first-century playwright were to write an updated version of TRIFLES, what details of plot, character, and setting would be different from those in Glaspell's play? What would be the same? What are some possible "trifles" that might serve the same dramatic functions as those in Glaspell's play?

RESPONDING TO DRAMA

When reading a play in order to write about it, you will need to keep a record of how you respond and what you observe as the action unfolds. Recording your thoughts as you read will help you clarify your expectations and attend to the way the play elicits and manages them. Below you will find examples of two ways of responding to a play. The first shows how you might jot down your initial impressions and questions in the margins as you read. The second shows how one reader used the questions on pages 651–52 to take more comprehensive, methodical notes on the same play. Each of these methods of note-taking has certain advantages, and you may well find that a combination of the two works best.

SAMPLE WRITING: ANNOTATION OF TRIFLES

Though the passage chosen for annotation here is the play's opening, any passage in a play—including stage directions, as well as dialogue—will reward close analysis.

A "trifle" is something unimportant and also a kind of dessert. So is the play going to be about unimportant things? Is it a comedy?

Trifles

CHARACTERS

SHERIFF	MRS. PETERS, *Sheriff's wife*
COUNTY ATTORNEY	MRS. HALE
HALE	

Only character *not* identified either by job or relationship to somebody else. (Why not "Mr. Hale"?)

SCENE: *The kitchen in the now abandoned farmhouse of* JOHN WRIGHT, *a gloomy kitchen, and left without having been put in order—*

Why "now abandoned"? Who's John

Wright? "Gloomy" doesn't sound like a comedy.

Is this a crime scene? Why refer to "work" (not "eating" or something)?

Women described more than men. They look different, but even the "comfortable looking" one (funny expression) isn't comfortable. They stick together.

Why hesitate?

Now attorney gets a name. Sounds like they are in court.

Second mention of things being moved: they're worried about evidence.

So this is "a big case." Is John Wright the criminal or victim?

Everyone knows everyone else. It's very cold, a harsh environment outside this kitchen. And it takes work to make it warm (lighting a fire).

It's a small town (in Nebraska?), but a lot of bad stuff is happening! Sheriff is defensive with attorney—source of conflict?

Again, everybody knows about everybody else.

unwashed pans under the sink, a loaf of bread outside the bread-box, a dish-towel on the table—other signs of incompleted work. At the rear the outer door opens and the SHERIFF *comes in followed by the* COUNTY ATTORNEY *and* HALE. *The* SHERIFF *and* HALE *are men in middle life, the* COUNTY ATTORNEY *is a young man; all are much bundled up and go at once to the stove. They are followed by the two women—the* SHERIFF'*s wife first; she is a slight wiry woman, a thin nervous face.* MRS. HALE *is larger and would ordinarily be called more comfortable looking, but she is disturbed now and looks fearfully about as she enters. The women have come in slowly, and stand close together near the door.*

COUNTY ATTORNEY: [*Rubbing his hands.*] This feels good. Come up to the fire, ladies.

MRS. PETERS: [*After taking a step forward.*] I'm not—cold.

SHERIFF: [*Unbuttoning his overcoat and stepping away from the stove as if to mark the beginning of official business.*] Now, Mr. Hale, before we move things about, you explain to Mr. Henderson just what you saw when you came here yesterday morning.

COUNTY ATTORNEY: By the way, has anything been moved? Are things just as you left them yesterday?

SHERIFF: [*Looking about.*] It's just the same. When it dropped below zero last night I thought I'd better send Frank out this morning to make a fire for us—no use getting pneumonia with a big case on, but I told him not to touch anything except the stove—and you know Frank.

COUNTY ATTORNEY: Somebody should have been left here yesterday.

SHERIFF: Oh—yesterday. When I had to send Frank to Morris Center for that man who went crazy—I want you to know I had my hands full yesterday. I knew you could get back from Omaha by today and as long as I went over everything here myself—

COUNTY ATTORNEY: Well, Mr. Hale, tell just what happened when you came here yesterday morning.

HALE: Harry and I had started to town with a load of potatoes. We came along the road from my place and as I got here I said, "I'm going to see if I can't get John Wright to go in with me on a party telephone." I spoke to Wright about it once before and he put me

Hale assumes most husbands would act differently around their wives, care about what they want—but maybe not Wright.

off, saying folks talked too much anyway, and all he asked was peace and quiet—I guess you know about how much he talked himself; but I thought maybe if I went to the house and talked about it before his wife, though I said to Harry that I didn't know as what his wife wanted made much difference to John—

Attorney is worried about being "official," sticking to facts, actions, "business," and thinks "that" (Wright's personality or feelings?) doesn't count.

COUNTY ATTORNEY: Let's talk about that later, Mr. Hale. I do want to talk about that, but tell now just what happened when you got to the house.

HALE: I didn't hear or see anything; I knocked at the door, and still it was all quiet inside. I knew they must be up, it was past eight o'clock. So I knocked again, and I thought I heard somebody say, "Come in." I wasn't sure, I'm not sure yet, but I opened the door—this door [*Indicating the door by which the two women are still standing.*] and there in that rocker—[*Pointing to it.*] sat Mrs. Wright.

Everyone gets up early—because of all the work they have to do?

Really ordinary things now seem very creepy. Why are the women still standing by the door—because they are afraid? because they aren't part of "official business"? Are they witnesses, too? Why are they here?

She's not listed as character either. What happened?

SAMPLE WRITING: READING NOTES ON *TRIFLES*

Below are examples of the questions an experienced reader might ask when reading the play TRIFLES for the first time, as well as responses to those questions. (See pp. 651–52.) Any of these notes might inspire ideas for essay topics. This is just a selection of the many details that could be observed about this lasting play, in which details certainly matter.

Expectations

Does the title suggest anything? "Trifles" sounds like a comedy (a trifle is something trivial), but it might be ironic. But why does Hale say that "women are used to worrying over trifles"? I expect to find out that the title is significant in some way, even that the theme is somehow connected to "trifles."

Characterization

Who are the characters? What are they like? Three men and two women in the cast of characters. After I read the stage directions and part of the dialogue, I check the list again to keep straight who is who. What kind of situation would bring together a sheriff, a county attorney, a farmer, and two wives? No actors are needed to play either Mr. Wright or Mrs. Wright. Some men who help Mr. Hale (Harry) and Mr. Peters (deputy Frank) are mentioned as coming and going but are never onstage.

The "county attorney" acts like a detective; he seems businesslike and thinks he's smarter than farmers and women. The stage directions specify that he speaks "[w]ith the gallantry of a young politician," but his flattery toward the women doesn't work. We find out his name is Mr. Henderson.

According to the stage directions, Mrs. Peters, the sheriff's wife, is "a slight wiry woman, a thin nervous face"; Mrs. Hale, the farmer's wife, is "larger and would ordinarily be called more comfortable looking." The casting of the two women would be important for contrast; a wider range of physical types would be suitable for the men. Everyone is cold, but only the men take comfort by the fire in the kitchen; the women are upset.

Is there a protagonist, an antagonist, or other types? There isn't a young hero or heroine of this play, and I wouldn't call anyone the villain unless it's the dead man or his murderer. Who the real villain is seems like an important question.

Are the characters' names significant? There's nothing especially meaningful or unusual about the names, although "Hale" means healthy (as in "hale and hearty"), and "Wright" sounds just like "right," though obviously something's wrong in this house. Interesting how "Mrs. Wright" becomes "Minnie Foster" to the women. Think about when. And about why it matters.

Plot

What happens? The big event has already happened; this is the scene of the crime. The men are looking for clues and leave the women in the kitchen, where they discover possible causes or motives for the crime. The women decide not to tell the men about either the evidence they find or their interpretation of it.

Are there scene changes? The whole scene is a fairly short uninterrupted period in one part of a farmhouse. Characters go offstage to other rooms or outdoors to the barn.

How is exposition handled? The county attorney asks Hale to "tell just what happened"; Hale explains what happened before the play started, describing how Mrs. Wright behaved. It comes as a shock to learn that Mrs. Wright told Hale he couldn't see John Wright " 'Cause [he was] dead." Shouldn't she have run to tell someone about the murder or have told Hale as soon as he arrived? When Hale reports that Mrs. Wright said her husband "died of a rope round his neck," it sounds suspicious. Could she have slept so soundly that she didn't realize someone had strangled Mr. Wright?

What events mark the rising action? When the men go upstairs and Mrs. Hale says, "I'd hate to have men coming into my kitchen, snooping around and criticizing," the women have a chance to notice more in the kitchen. Mrs. Hale recalls her relationship to Mrs. Wright, and the women discuss whether the wife really murdered her husband.

The men return to the kitchen on their way out to the barn just after the women discover the quilt pieces with the bad stitching. The next dialogue between the women is more open and brings out Mrs. Hale's regret for not having visited and supported Mrs. Wright in her unhappy marriage. They notice the empty birdcage.

What is the climax? Mrs. Hale finds the dead bird in the pretty box, and the two women understand what it means just before the men return to the kitchen briefly. From then on the women utter small lies to the men. Mrs. Peters for the first time reveals personal memories that suggest she can imagine Mrs. Wright's motives.

What is the resolution? As everyone prepares to leave, Mrs. Peters pretends the bird is insignificant, joining Mrs. Hale in protecting Mrs. Wright and playing along with the men's idea that there's nothing to notice in the kitchen. The women collaborate in hiding the bird.

What kind of play or plot is it? Like some detective stories, the play doesn't ask "whodunnit?" but why the murder was committed. Its mode of representation is a familiar type—domestic realism—in which the places, people, things, and even events are more or less ordinary. (Unfortunately, domestic violence is common.)

Setting

When does the action occur? The play appears to be contemporary with 1916 (a stove heater, party-line telephones, a horse-drawn wagon). It is a winter morning, and the scene takes perhaps an hour.

Where does the action occur? It is obviously farm country, perhaps in the Midwest, where farms are very far apart.

What is the atmosphere? The freezing weather reflects the feeling of the play and gives the characters a motive for gathering in the kitchen. John Wright is described as a chilly wind. The frozen house has ruined Mrs. Wright's preserves. The mess in the kitchen, especially the sticky spill of red fruit in the cupboard, seems related to the unhappiness and horror of the marriage and the crime. Also just shows how hard their lives are maybe.

Are there scene changes? Instead of several scenes over a longer time, showing the deteriorating marriage, the crisis over the bird, the murder itself, Mrs.

Wright's sleepless night, and Mr. Hale's visit, the story unfolds in a single scene, in one room, on the second morning after the murder, between the entrance and exit of Mrs. Hale and Mrs. Peters. It is essential that the play focus on "kitchen things" and what the women visitors notice and think.

Style, Tone, Imagery

What is the style of the dialogue? The dialogue seems similar to everyday speech. There are some differences in speaking style that show the Hales are more rustic than the Peters and the county attorney. Hale has a relaxed way of telling a story: "then I says," etc. Mrs. Hale: "Those towels get dirty awful quick" and "If I was you, I wouldn't tell her her fruit was gone. Tell her it *ain't.*"

How do nonverbal gestures and actions convey meaning? Many specific actions indicated in the stage directions are crucial to the play: everyone looking at the rocking chair, pointing to the room upstairs, looking at the loaf of bread that should have been put back in the bread box, etc.

Do any of the props seem to have symbolic meaning? Some objects in the play are so important they seem symbolic, though the play tries not to be too heavily poetic. All kinds of "trifles" are clues. For instance, the women get Mrs. Wright's clothes to bring to her in jail. "MRS. HALE: [*Examining the skirt.*] Wright was close," meaning stingy. Mrs. Hale's words convey a quick impression: the skirt looks "shabby" because John Wright didn't give his wife any money for clothes (he was "good" but stingy and cold).

There would be some colorful props onstage—the jar of cherries, the red cloth and other quilt material, the pretty box—all of them signs of what has gone wrong. The room itself is "gloomy" and has some dirty and messy things in plain sight; other things in the cupboards are eventually revealed. These props would add to the uncomfortable feeling of the play.

The closest thing to a symbol is the caged songbird. Even the men notice the broken door and missing bird. Mrs. Hale underlines the comparison to Mrs. Wright twice: "she was kind of like a bird," and later, "No, Wright wouldn't like the bird—a thing that sang. She used to sing. He killed that, too."

Theme

What is the theme of the play? The title calls attention to what the play is about. Glaspell didn't call it *The Caged Songbird* or *Murder in the Midwest* or something heavy-handed. The main action is a search for a motive to confirm what everyone believes, that Minnie Wright must have strangled her husband while he was sleeping. But the underlying theme of the play seems to be about men's and women's different perspectives. How can women's everyday things be important? Why would anyone charged with murder worry about preserves? Even the women hope that Mrs. Wright's worry about having her apron and shawl in jail means she didn't commit the crime. The kitchen things—the trifles in her own house—"turn against her," but the women are able to hide evidence that the men consider insignificant.

WRITING ABOUT DRAMA

Writing an essay about drama, like writing about fiction or poetry, can sharpen your responses and focus your reading; at the same time, it can illuminate aspects of the work that other readers may have missed. When you write about drama, in a very real sense you perform the role that directors and actors take on in a stage performance: You offer your "reading" of the text, interpreting it in order to guide other readers' responses. But you also shape and refine your own response by attempting to express it clearly.

Using the notes you have taken while reading a play, try to locate the specific lines and actions that have contributed to your expectations or your discoveries. Are these at the beginning, the middle, or the end of the play? Who gives most of the hints or misleading information? If there is one character who is especially unseeing, especially devious, or especially insightful, you might decide to write an essay describing the function of that character in the play. A good way to undertake such a study of a character in drama (as in fiction) is to imagine the work without that character. Mrs. Hale in *Trifles* is certainly the cleverest "detective," so why do we need Mrs. Peters as well? One obvious answer is that plays need dialogue, and we would find it artificial if Mrs. Hale talked mainly to herself. But a more interesting answer is that in a play the audience learns by witnessing characters with different temperaments responding to the same situation. As these remarks suggest, you can also develop essays that compare characters.

In addition to character studies, essays on drama can focus on the kinds of observations made above: expectations and plot structure; the presence and absence of characters or actions onstage; the different degrees of awareness of characters and audience at various points in the action; titles, stage directions, and other stylistic details, including **metaphors** or other imagery; and, of course, themes. As you write, you will probably discover that you can imagine directing or acting in a performance of the play, and you'll realize that interpreting a play is a crucial step in bringing it to life.

SUGGESTIONS FOR WRITING

1. The action in Glaspell's play unfolds continuously, without interruption, in a single, relatively small room (the kitchen of a farmhouse), with the two female characters never leaving the stage. Write a response paper or essay discussing how these three factors affect your responses to the play, to the crime being investigated, and to the various characters.
2. How do your sympathies for Mrs. Peters change over the course of TRIFLES? What might Mrs. Peters be said to represent in the clash of attitudes at the heart of the play? Write an essay in which you examine both Mrs. Peters's evolving character as it is revealed in TRIFLES and her significance to the play's theme.
3. How would you characterize Susan Glaspell's feminism as revealed in TRIFLES— does it seem radical or moderate? How does it compare to feminist political and social ideas of our own time? (Consult three or more educational or library Web sites for biographical background on Glaspell; there are several sites offering teaching materials on TRIFLES as well. If time allows, you might also pursue sources that provide an overview of women's movements in the United States in the twentieth century.) Write an essay in which you explore the political leanings apparent in TRIFLES, both in the context of Glaspell's play (published in 1916) and in the broader historical context of the struggle for women's rights over the past century.

4. Write an essay in which you propose a production of TRIFLES, complete with details of how you would handle the casting, costumes, set design, lighting, and direction of the actors. What would be your overall controlling vision for the production? Would you attempt to reproduce faithfully the look and feel of the play as it might have been in 1916, or would you introduce innovations, even "update" the play? How would you justify your choices in terms of dramatic effectiveness?

SAMPLE WRITING: RESPONSE PAPER

Response papers are a great way to begin moving from informal notes to a more formal essay. Though many response-paper assignments invite you to respond to any aspect or element of a literary text that grabs your attention, the following example was written in response to a more targeted assignment, one that asked students to "explore something specific about the way TRIFLES handles plot. For example, what are the major internal and/or external conflicts? Or what would you argue is the play's turning point, and why?" Student writer Jessica Zezulka explored the last question. Marginal comments below are the instructor's. But what do you think of this writer's answer? How might she strengthen and develop the argument she begins to make here about the play's turning point? What alternative answers or arguments occur to you?

Zezulka 1

Jessica Zezulka
Professor Mays
English 298
10 January 2019

Trifles Plot Response Paper

While the men dillydally over the facts, the so-called "evidence," the women in *Trifles* discover the missing piece: a motive for murder. The moment Mrs. Hale and Mrs. Peters find the dead canary in the hidden box is the turning point in the play. Up until that instant, their conversation seems trivial, to both a reader and the men involved. Upon discussing the little trifles, the quilt and the sewing, these two women have inadvertently stumbled across what the men are so desperate to find. This turning point changes the way the play is read, as well as the way you view the wife of the dead man.

Mrs. Wright, accused of murdering her husband, appears almost crazy for just up and killing her spouse. The reader is as confused as the men at first, wondering why on earth would she do it? When you realize, along with the two women, that her motive was his brutal killing of the canary, you suddenly become privy to a secret that the men seemingly never learn. The play uses dramatic irony, where the reader knows the truth but the characters in the play are oblivious.

Might it be possible to read their conversation as less trivial (even up to this point) than the male characters do?

Again, though, don't we have relevant evidence before that about the possible state (and effects) of this marriage, which might be just as relevant to motive? If so, what *really* makes this moment stand out?

Interesting! Irony certainly is key to the play, but not all the characters are equally "oblivious," right?

671

Zezulka 2

Susan Glaspell timed this moment perfectly, giving the reader time to be both confused and then suddenly enlightened.

This turning point breeds sympathy for the accused murderess. Mrs. Wright is no longer just a good wife gone bad. You as the reader follow the emotions of the two women in the empty house and can feel their almost immediate comprehension and understanding of both the situation and the woman involved. The wife becomes someone we can relate to, almost having a just cause for murdering her husband. As I said, Glaspell builds the tension to that point perfectly; the reader is all for the law being upheld until you know what led up to the murder. If you asked me, I'd say he deserved it. The women's discussion of *trifles* led to the heart of the matter, a turning point that all but justifies John Wright's death.

So might the play also turn on the conflict—or at least the contrast—between two possible ways of defining "innocence" or even two kinds of "law"?

Zezulka 3

WORK CITED

Glaspell, Susan. *Trifles. The Norton Introduction to Literature*, edited by Kelly J. Mays, portable 13th ed., W. W. Norton, 2020, pp. 652–62.

SAMPLE WRITING: ESSAY

The following sample of student writing demonstrates how you might develop an early response to a play into a more formal and thorough argument about it. In her essay on Susan Glaspell's Trifles, Stephanie Ortega explores the relationship among the female characters in order to offer her own answers to more than one of the questions posed in the previous chapter's "Suggestions for Writing": How does Mrs. Peters's character evolve over the course of *Trifles*? How is that evolution significant to the play's theme, or how might it help to define the play's particular version of feminism?

As always, we encourage you to read the sample with a critical eye, identifying what works and what doesn't so as to discover specific ways to improve your own writing and reading. At what moments in the essay do you find yourself strongly agreeing? discovering something new about or in Glaspell's play? At what moments might you instead find yourself disagreeing or feeling either confused or simply dissatisfied, wanting more? What exactly makes each of these moments especially satisfying, interesting, persuasive, enlightening—or the reverse? If Stephanie Ortega were your classmate, what three specific things would you suggest she do in order to improve the essay in revision? Alternatively, what three qualities or strategies of this essay might you want to emulate in your own work?

Ortega 1

Stephanie Ortega
Professor Mays
English 298
23 January 2019

A Journey of Sisterhood

Trifles begins at the start of a murder investigation. Mrs. Wright has allegedly murdered her harsh husband, John Wright; and the sheriff and his wife, Mrs. Peters; the county attorney; and the neighbors, Mr. and Mrs. Hale, all come to the Wright house to investigate. Throughout the entire play the women are always onstage, whereas the men enter and exit, so the women are the play's focus. But Glaspell's *Trifles* is a feminist play not only because of that, but also because of how it shows two or even three very different women coming together in sisterhood.

Mrs. Peters and Mrs. Hale are first introduced as they stand together by the door of the house where the murder took place, yet though the women stand together, their behavior and views initially seem wide apart. Whereas Mrs. Hale stands up for her counterparts, Mrs. Peters and Mrs. Wright, from the beginning, Mrs. Peters at first tends to stick up more for the men. When the County Attorney makes a remark about Mrs. Wright not having been much of a homemaker and having a dirty home, we see that Mrs. Hale doesn't like men poking in Mrs. Wright's business and having input in the doings of a house. Putting herself in Mrs. Wright's shoes, Mrs. Hale says, "I'd hate to have men coming into *my* kitchen, snooping around and criticizing" (657, emphasis added). But Mrs. Peters states that since it is an investigation, "it's no more than th[e men's] duty" to poke around (657). Later, when Mrs. Hale actually interferes with the investigation by trying to tidy up the place and resew the badly stitched quilt they discover, Mrs. Peters steps in, "*[n]ervously*" saying, "I don't think we ought to touch things" (659). Mrs. Peters's only view is that of her husband; she knows and seems to care very little about Mrs. Wright or her life before marriage, as Minnie Foster. As far as Mrs. Peters is concerned, "the law is the law" (658), and she is "married to" it, as the county attorney will say at the end of the play (662); therefore she must abide by it.

Mrs. Hale's identification with Minnie Foster only intensifies as the play progresses. She remembers Minnie Foster as a carefree woman full of energy and life, bright and cheery like a canary, implying that marriage to John Wright "change[d]" all that (660). Mrs. Hale starts feeling guilty for not visiting Mrs. Wright, telling Mrs. Peters multiple times that she "wish[es she] had come over sometimes when *she* was here," and eventually even suggesting that not coming to see Mrs. Wright was "a crime" (659, 661).

In part because of the way Mrs. Hale talks about her, Minnie Foster's figurative presence becomes ever stronger, bringing Mrs. Hale and Mrs. Peters together as they put themselves into her place, speculating about her feelings and responses to the conditions of her life. When the women come upon a box containing a bird that had its neck wrung, Mrs. Hale associates Mr. Wright's presumed killing of the songbird with his destruction of part of Mrs. Wright, speculating about her feelings: "No, Wright wouldn't like the bird—a thing that sang. She used to sing. He killed that, too" (661). Thus, Mr. Wright's killing of the bird is a symbolic killing of Minnie Foster's spirit. At this point, the women come to understand that Mrs. Wright was indeed the one who killed her husband because when the women realize that Mr. Wright wrung the bird's neck, the women finally know the reason for Mrs. Wright's "funny way" of killing him (658). (It's now that "*Their eyes meet*" with "*[a] look of growing comprehension, of horror*" [660].)

More important, here is where we really start to see a change in Mrs. Peters. For the first time she, too, interferes with the investigators, even though she doesn't actually destroy evidence or lie, when she responds to a question about the cat by simply saying that there is not one "*now*" (661). She expresses sympathy for Minnie Foster and identifies with her, based on her own memories of the way she felt both when her kitten was killed with a hatchet and, much later, when her first baby died, leaving her and her husband alone in the "stillness" of their isolated house (663). Mrs. Peters also states that had she gotten hold of the boy who killed her kitten long ago she would have gotten revenge just as Mrs. Peters and Mrs. Hale now speculate that Minnie Foster Wright did. The women each sympathize with Minnie Foster and the distant person she has become, Mrs. Wright.

By sympathizing with Mrs. Wright and paying attention to the "little things" the men don't consider solid "evidence" (658), the women have single-handedly sorted out a plausible sequence of events and, more importantly, a reason why Mrs. Wright killed her husband the way she did. Yet rather than reveal what they've learned, they slowly, in the silence of mutual sympathy, work together to cover Mrs. Wright's tracks and to protect her. Mrs. Peters is defying the actual law and starting to protect the law of women and sisterhood instead. Mrs. Hale, Mrs. Peters, and Mrs. Wright become one unit, opposing their intuitive feminine selves to the logical and analytical men.

Although Mrs. Wright never once appears onstage, her presence is what brings all three women closer. They are able to attain information that the men simply overlook. And it is this which brings the women forth in the union of sisterhood at the end of the play as they realize that "We [women] all go through the same things—it's all just a different kind of the same thing" (661).

WORK CITED

Glaspell, Susan. *Trifles. The Norton Introduction to Literature,* edited by Kelly J. Mays, portable 13th ed., W. W. Norton, 2020, pp. 652–62.

Understanding the Text

19 | ELEMENTS OF DRAMA

Most of us read more fiction than drama and are likely to encounter drama by watching filmed versions of it. Nonetheless, the skills you have developed in reading stories and poems come in handy when you read plays. And just as with fiction and poetry, you will understand and appreciate drama more fully by becoming familiar with the various elements and conventions of the **genre**.

CHARACTER

Character is possibly the most familiar and accessible of the elements; both fiction and drama feature one or more imaginary persons who take part in the action. The word *character* refers not only to a person represented in an imagined plot, whether narrated or acted out, but also to the unique qualities that make up a personality. From one point of view, "character" as a part in a plot and "character" as a kind of personality are both predictions: This sort of person is likely to see things from a certain angle and behave in certain ways. Notice that the idea of character includes both the individual differences among people and the classification of similar people into types. Whereas much realistic fiction emphasizes unique individuals rather than general character types, drama often compresses and simplifies personalities—a play has only about two hours at the most (sometimes much less) in which to show situations, appearances, and behaviors, without description or background other than **exposition** provided in the dialogue. The advantage of portraying character in broader strokes is that it heightens the contrasts between character types, adding to the drama: Differences provoke stronger reactions.

Plays are especially concerned with character because of the concrete manner in which they portray people on the stage. With a few exceptions (such as experiments in multimedia performance), the only words in the performance of a play are spoken by actors, and usually these actors are *in character*—that is, speaking as though they really are the people they play in the drama. (Rarely, plays have a **narrator** who observes and comments on the action from the sidelines, and in some plays a character may address the audience directly, but even when the actors apparently step outside of the imaginary frame, they are still part of the play and are still playing characters.) In fiction, the narrator's description and commentary can guide a reader's judgment about characters. Reading a play, you will have no such guide because drama relies almost exclusively on *indirect characterization* (see ch. 4). Apart from some clues about characters in the **stage directions**, you will need to imagine the appearance, manners, and movement of someone speaking the lines assigned to any one character. You can do this even as you read through a play for the first time, discovering the characters' attitudes and motivations as the scenes unfold. This ability to predict character and then to revise expectations as situations change is based not only on our experiences of people in real life but also on our familiarity with recurring types of characters or roles.

Consider the patterns of characters in many stories that are narrated or acted out, whether in novels, comic books, television series, Hollywood films, or video games. In many of these forms, there is a leading role, a main character: the **protagonist**. The titles of plays such as HAMLET or ANTIGONE imply that the play will be about a central character, the chief object of the playwright's and the reader's or audience's concern. Understanding the character of the protagonist—often in contrast with an **antagonist**, the opponent of the main character—becomes the consuming interest of such a play. Especially in more traditional or popular genres, the protagonist may be called a **hero** or **heroine**, and the antagonist may be called the **villain**. Most characterization in professional theater, however, avoids depicting pure good and pure evil in a fight to the death. Most characters possess both negative and redeeming qualities.

As in other genres that represent people in action, in drama there are *minor characters* or supporting roles. At least since ancient Rome, romantic comedies have been structured around a leading man and woman, along with a comparable pair (often the "buddies" of the leads) whose problems may be less serious, whose characters may be less complex, or who in other ways support or complicate rather than dominate the action. Sometimes a minor character serves as a **foil**, a character designed to bring out the qualities of another character by means of contrast. The main point to remember is that all the characters in a drama are interdependent and help characterize each other. Through dialogue and behavior, each brings out what is characteristic in the others.

Like movies, plays must respect certain limitations: the time an audience can be expected to sit and watch, the attention and sympathy an audience is likely to give to various characters, the amount of exposition that can be shown rather than spoken aloud. Because of these constraints, playwrights, screenwriters, casting directors, and actors must rely on shortcuts to convey character. Everyone involved, including the audience, consciously or unconsciously relies on stereotypes of various social roles to flesh out the dramatic action. Even a play that seeks to undermine stereotypes must still invoke them. In the United States today, casting—or typecasting—usually relies on an actor's social identity, from gender and race to occupation, region, and age. However, plays that rely too much on stereotypes, positive or negative, may leave everyone disappointed (or offended); a role that defies stereotypes can be more interesting to perform and to watch. Alternatively, a character can be so exceptional and unfamiliar that audiences will fail to recognize any connection to people they might meet, and their responses will fall flat. All dramatic roles, then, must have some connection to types of personality, and good roles modify such types just enough to make the character interesting. Playwrights often overturn or modify expectations of character in order to surprise an audience. So, too, do the actors who play those parts.

Every performance of a given character, like every production of a play, is an interpretation. Not just "adaptations"—Greek or Elizabethan plays set in modern times and performed in modern dress, for example—but even productions that seek to adhere faithfully to the written play are interpretations of what is vital or essential in it. John Malkovich, in the 1983–84 production of Arthur Miller's *Death of a Salesman*, did not portray Biff Loman as the outgoing, successful, hail-fellow-well-met jock the play text might lead us to expect, Instead Malkovich saw Biff as only pretending to be a jock. Big-time athletes, he insisted, don't glad-hand people; they wait for people to come to them. The actor did not change the author's words, but by intonation, body language, and "stage business" (wordless gestures and actions) he suggested his own view of the character. In other words, he broke with the expectations associated with the character's type. As you read and develop your own interpretation of a play, try imagining various interpreta-tions of its characters in order to reveal different possible meanings in the drama.

Questions about Character

- Who is the protagonist? Why and how so? Which other characters, if any, are main or major characters? Which are minor characters?
- What are the protagonist's most distinctive traits, and what is most distinctive about his or her outlook and values? What motivates the character? What is it about the character that creates internal and/or external conflict? Which lines or stage directions reveal most about the character?
- What are the roles of other characters? Which, if any, functions as an antago-nist? Which, if any, serves as a foil? Does any character function as a narrator or **chorus**, providing background information and commentary? Why and how so?
- To what extent are any of the characters in the play "types"? How might this affect an audience's experience of the play? In what ways might a director or actor choose to go against the expected types, and how would this complicate the play's overall effect and meaning?
- Which of the characters, or which aspects of the characters, does the play encourage us to sympathize with or to admire? to view negatively? Why and how so? Are there characters who might be more or less sympathetic, depend-ing on how the role is cast and interpreted?
- If you were directing a production of this play, whom among your friends and acquaintances would you cast in each role, and why? If you were directing a movie version, what professional actors would you cast?

PLOT AND STRUCTURE

An important part of any storyteller's task, whether in narrative or dramatic genres, is the invention, selection, and arrangement of some **action**. Even carefully struc-tured action cannot properly be called a full-scale **plot** without some unifying sense of purpose. That is, what happens should seem to happen for meaningful reasons. This does not mean, of course, that characters or the audience must be satisfied in their hopes or expectations, or that effective plays need to wrap up every loose end. It does mean that a reader or theatergoer should feel that the playwright has com-pleted *this* play—that nothing essential is missing—though the play's outcome or overall effect may be difficult to sum up.

   Conflict is the engine that drives plot, and the presentation of conflict shapes the dramatic structure of a play. A conflict whose outcome is never in doubt may have other kinds of interest, but it is not truly dramatic. In a dramatic conflict, each of the opposing forces must at some point seem likely to triumph or worthy of such triumph—whether conflict is *external* (one character versus another, or one group of characters versus another group, each of whom may represent a different world-view) or *internal* (within a single character torn between competing views, duties, needs, or desires), or even one idea or ideology versus another one. In *Hamlet*, for example, our interest in the struggle between Hamlet and Claudius depends on their being evenly matched. Claudius has possession of the throne and the queen, but Hamlet's role as the heir to the late king and his popularity with the people offset his opponent's strength.

The typical plot in drama, as in fiction, involves five stages: exposition, rising action, climax, falling action, and conclusion. **Exposition**, the first phase of plot, provides essential background information about the characters and situation as they exist at the beginning of a play and perhaps also about the events that got the characters to this point—as when, early in TRIFLES, Mr. Hale describes what happened before the play opens. The second phase, **rising action**, begins when an **inciting incident** leads to conflict—as when, in *Trifles*, the men leave the women alone with what the latter soon discover to be crucial evidence. The moment when the conflict reaches its greatest pitch of intensity and its outcome is decided is the plot's third phase, its **climax** or **turning point**—in *Trifles*, perhaps the discovery of the dead bird and the act of covering up the evidence. The fourth stage, **falling action**, brings a release of emotional tension and moves the characters toward the **resolution** of their conflict and the plot itself toward its fifth and final stage, the **conclusion**. In *Trifles*, the men's return to the kitchen because, they believe, no evidence has been found can be called the falling action. The women's apparent decision to remain mute about what they have discovered can be called the resolution. The play concludes as the characters leave the Wrights' house.

Unlike *Trifles*, some lengthy plays feature more than one plot. In such cases, the plot to which less time and attention is devoted is called the **subplot**.

Many older plays in the Western tradition, such as Shakespeare's, have five acts, each act roughly corresponding to—and thus emphasizing—a particular phase of plot. Acts are often further subdivided into scenes, each of which usually takes place in a somewhat different time and place and features a somewhat different combination of characters. Ancient Greek plays such as ANTIGONE are structured differently, such that individual scenes or *episodes* are separated by choral songs—that is, odes spoken or sung by the group of characters known as the chorus. Modern plays tend to have fewer acts and scenes than those of earlier eras, and plays such as *Trifles*—in which the action unfolds continuously and, usually, in a single time and place—have become so common that they have their own name: the *one-act play*.

In the performance of a play longer than one act, it has become customary to have at least one intermission, in part for the practical reason that the audience may need restrooms or refreshments. Breaks may be signaled by turning down stage lights, turning up the house lights, and lowering the curtain (if there is one).

On rare occasions, very long plays (such as Tony Kushner's *Angels in America* [1992–93]) are performed over more than one evening, with the obvious challenge of finding an audience willing and able to afford tickets and time for more than one performance; those who read such play "cycles" or **sequences** at their own pace at home have a certain advantage.

The key point is that the form of a play and the breaks between scenes or acts result from the nature of the play. Breaks can create suspense—a curtain comes down after an unexplained gunshot—or they can provide relief from tension or an emotional crisis.

Questions about Plot

- Read the first scene or the first few pages and then stop. What potential for conflict do you see here? What do you expect to happen in the rest of the play?
- How is the play divided into acts, scenes, or episodes, if at all? What is the effect of this structure? Does the division of the play correspond at all to the five stages of plot development—exposition, rising action, climax, resolution, conclusion?
- Does the play show a relatively clear progression through the traditional stages of plot development, or does it seem to defy such conventions? If so, how, and what might the playwright achieve through these departures from tradition?
- What is the inciting incident or destabilizing event? How and why does this event destabilize the initial situation? How would you describe the conflict that develops? To what extent is it external, internal, or both?
- What is the climax, or turning point? Why and how so? How is the conflict resolved? How and why might this resolution fulfill or defy your expectations?

STAGES, SETS, AND SETTING

Most of us have been to a theater at one time or another, and we know what a conventional modern stage (the **proscenium stage**) looks like: a room with the wall missing between us and it (the so-called *fourth wall*). So when we read a modern play—that is, one written during the past two or three hundred years—and imagine it taking place before us, we think of it as happening on this kind of stage. Though there are also other modern types of stages—the **thrust stage**, where the audience sits around three sides of the major acting area, and the **arena stage**, where the audience sits all the way around the acting area and players make their entrances and their exits through the auditorium—most plays today are performed on a proscenium stage. Most of the plays in this book can be readily imagined as taking place on such a stage.

Ancient Greek and Elizabethan plays, including those of Shakespeare, were originally staged quite differently from most modern plays, however, and although they may be played today on a proscenium stage, we might be confused as we read if we are unaware of the layout of the theaters for which they were first written. In the Greek theater, the audience sat on a raised semicircle of seats (**amphitheater**) halfway around a circular area (**orchestra**) used primarily for dancing by the chorus. At the back of the orchestra was the **skene**, or stage house, representing the palace or temple before which the action took place. Shakespeare's stage, in contrast, basically involved a rectangular area built inside one end of a large enclosure like a circular walled-in yard; the audience stood on the ground or sat in stacked balconies around three sides of the principal acting area (rather like a thrust stage). There were additional acting areas on either side of this stage, as well as a recessed area at its back (which could represent Gertrude's chamber in *Hamlet*, for example) and an upper acting area (which could serve as Juliet's balcony in *Romeo and Juliet*). A trapdoor in the stage floor was used for occasional effects; the ghost of Hamlet's father probably entered and exited this way. Until three centuries ago—and certainly in Shakespeare's time—plays for large paying audiences were performed outdoors in daylight because of the difficulty and expense of lighting. If you are curious about Shakespeare's stage, you can visit a reconstruction of his Globe Theatre in Southwark, London, England, either in person or online at www.shakespearesglobe.com. Every summer, plays by Shakespeare are performed there for large international audiences willing to sit on hard benches around the arena or to stand as "groundlings" (a lucky few of whom can lean on the stage near the feet of the actors). The walls in the background of the stage are beautifully carved and painted, but there is no painted scenery, minimal furniture, few costume changes, no lighting, and no curtain around the stage (a cloth hanging usually covers the recessed area at the back of the stage). Three or four musicians may play period instruments on the balcony.

As the design of the Globe suggests, the conventions of dramatic writing and stage production have changed considerably over the centuries. Certainly this is true of the way playwrights convey a sense of place—one of the two key ingredients that make up a play's **setting**. Usually the audience is asked to imagine that the featured section of the auditorium is actually a particular place somewhere else. The audience of course knows it is a stage, more or less bare or elaborately disguised, but they accept it as a kitchen, a public square, a wooded park, an open road, or a room in a castle or a hut. *Antigone* takes place entirely before the palace at Thebes. Following the general convention of ancient Greek drama, the play's setting never changes. When the action demands the presence of Teiresias, for example, the scene does not shift to him; instead, an escort brings him to the front of the palace. Similarly, important events that take place elsewhere are described by witnesses who arrive on the scene.

In Shakespeare's theater the conventions of place are quite different: The acting arena does not represent a single specific place but assumes a temporary identity according to the characters who inhabit it, their costumes, and their speeches. At the opening of *Hamlet* we know we are at a sentry station because a man dressed as a soldier challenges two others. By line 15, we know that we are in Denmark because the actors profess to be "liegemen to the Dane." At the end of the scene the actors leave the stage and in a sense take the sentry station with them. Shortly thereafter, a group of people dressed in court costumes and a man and a woman wearing crowns appear. As a theater audience, we must surmise from the costumes and dialogue that the acting area has now become a royal court; when we read the play, the stage directions give us a cue that the place has changed.

In a modern play, there are likely to be several changes of scene, sometimes marked by the lowering of the curtain or the darkening of the stage while different sets and props are arranged. **Sets** (the design, decoration, and scenery) and **props** (articles or objects used onstage) vary greatly in modern productions of plays written in any period. Sometimes space is merely suggested—a circle of sand at one end of the stage, a blank wall behind—to emphasize universal themes or to stimulate the audience's imagination. Often, a set instead uses realistic aids to the imagination. The set of *Trifles*, for example, must include at least a sink, a cupboard, a stove, a small table, a large kitchen table, and a rocking chair, as well as certain props: a birdcage, quilting pieces, and an ornamental box.

Time is the second key ingredient of setting, and conventions for representing time have also altered across the centuries. Three or four centuries ago, European dramatists and critics admired the conventions of classical Greek drama which, they believed, dictated that the action of a play should represent a very short time—sometimes as short as the actual performance time (two or three hours), and certainly no longer than a single day. This unity of time, one of the three so-called **classical unities**, impels a dramatist to select the moment when a stable situation should change and to fill in the necessary prior details by exposition. (These same critics maintained that a play should be unified in place and action as well; the kind of leaping from Denmark to England, or from court to forest, that happens in Shakespeare's plays, as well as subplots, were off-limits according to such standards. In *Trifles*, which observes the three classical unities, all the action before the investigators' visit to the farmhouse is summarized by characters during their brief visit, and the kitchen is the only part of the house seen by the audience.)

When there are gaps and shifts in time, they are often indicated between scenes with the help of scenery, sound effects, stage directions, or notes in the program. An actor must assist in conveying the idea of time if his or her character appears at different ages. Various conventions of classical or Elizabethan drama have also worked effectively to communicate to the audience the idea of the passage of time, from the choral odes in *Antigone* to the breaks between scenes in Shakespeare plays.

Action within a play thus can take place in a wide range of locations and over many years rather than in the one place and the twenty-four-hour period demanded by critics who believed in the classical unities. And we can learn much about how a particular play works and what it means by paying attention to the way it handles setting and sets.

Questions about Setting and Staging

- Does all the action occur in one time and place, or in more than one? If the latter, what are those times and places? How much time tends to pass between scenes or episodes?
- How important do the general time, place, and social milieu seem to be, and in what ways are they important? What about the plot and characters would remain the same if a director chose to set the play in a different time and place? What wouldn't?
- What patterns do you notice regarding where and when things happen? Which characters are associated with each setting? How do different characters relate to the same setting? When, how, and why do scenes change from one setting to another? Are there significant deviations?
- Do the stage directions describe particular settings and props in detail? If so, what seems significant about the details? How might they establish mood, reveal character, and affect individual characters and their interactions with one another? Is there anything in the stage directions that seems to be intended more for readers than for a director staging a production?
- Does the date of the play tell you anything about the way it was originally intended to be staged? Does the representation of time and place in the play implicitly call for a certain type of stage?

  If you were staging the play today, what kind of stage, sets, and props might you use, and why? How might your choices affect how the play works on audiences and what it means to them?

TONE, LANGUAGE, AND SYMBOL

In plays, as in other literary genres, **tone** is difficult to specify or explain. Perhaps tone is especially important in drama because it is, in performance, a spoken form, and vocal tone always affects the meaning of spoken words to some extent, in any culture or language. The actor—and any reader who wishes to imagine a play as spoken aloud—must infer from the written language just how to read a line, what tone of voice to use. The choice of tone must be a negotiation between the words of the playwright and the interpretation and skill of the actor or reader. At times stage directions will specify the tone of a line of dialogue, though even that must be only a hint, since there are many ways of speaking "intensely" or "angrily." Find a line in one of the plays printed here that has a stage direction telling the actor how to deliver it, and with one or two other people take turns saying it that way. If nothing else, such an experiment may help you appreciate the talent of good actors who can put on a certain tone of voice and make it seem natural and convincing. But it will also show you the many options for interpreting tone.

Dramatic irony, in which a character's perception is contradicted by what the audience knows, and even *situational irony*, in which a character's (and the audience's) expectations about what will happen are contradicted by what actually does happen, are relatively easy to detect. But *verbal irony*, in which a statement implies a meaning quite different from its obvious, literal meaning, can be fairly subtle and easy to miss. In the absence of clear stage directions, verbal irony—like other aspects of tone—can also be a matter of interpretation. That is, directors and actors, as well as readers and audiences, will often have to decide which lines in a play should be interpreted ironically. All three types of irony are nonetheless crucial to drama. As the very term *dramatic irony* suggests, drama—even more than fiction—depends for its effects on gaps between what the various characters and the audience know. And situational irony—the gap between expectations and outcomes and even between what characters seem to deserve and what they get—is an especially key component of **tragedy**.

Never hesitate to apply to drama the skills you have developed in interpreting poetry; after all, most early plays were written in some form of verse. Aspects of poetry often emerge in modern plays; for example, **monologues** or extended speeches by one character, while they rarely rhyme or have regular **meter**, may allow greater eloquence than is usual in everyday speech and may include revealing imagery and **figures of speech**. A character in Lorraine Hansberry's A RAISIN IN THE SUN, for example, uses **personification**, as well as **alliteration**, to great effect when she remarks (in act 3) that "death done come in this here house [. . .] Done come walking in my house."

Simple actions or objects, too, often have metaphorical significance or turn into **symbols**. Effective plays often use props in this way, as *Trifles* does with the bird and its cage. And some plays, like some poems, may even be organized around *controlling metaphors*. As you read, pay close attention to metaphors or images, whether in language or in more concrete form.

Allusions, references to other works of literature or art or something else external to the play, can enrich the text in similar ways. The title of Tom Stoppard's comedy *The Real Inspector Hound* (1968), for example, seems to allude to Sir Arthur Conan Doyle's novel *The Hound of the Baskervilles* (1901–02), featuring Sherlock Holmes. Doyle's novel is a classic in the detective fiction genre, which Stoppard's *Inspector Hound* parodies. In a more serious vein, though New Orleans, where Tennessee Williams's *A Streetcar Named Desire* takes place, actually does contain a street called Elysian Fields, the play gets a good deal of symbolic mileage out of using this as a setting thanks to the allusion to Greek mythology (in which the Elysian Fields were the final resting place of heroic and virtuous souls). Awareness of all the stylistic choices in a play can help you reach a clearer, more comprehensive interpretation of it.

Questions about Tone, Language, and Symbol

- Which lines in the play strike you as most ambiguous when it comes to the tone in which they should be spoken? Why and how so? What is the effect of that ambiguity, or how might an actor's or reader's decision about tone here affect the play as a whole?
- How would you describe the overall tone of the whole play? Do any moments or entire scenes or acts in the play seem interestingly different in terms of their tone?
- How do the play's characters differ from one another in terms of their tone? Does any character's tone change over the course of the play?
- Are any details—such as names; actions or statements; references to objects, props, or other details of setting; or allusions, metaphors, or other figures of speech—repeated throughout the play? Do any of these repeated details seem to have special significance? If so, what might that significance be?
- What types of irony, if any, are at work in the play? What is the effect of the irony?

THEME

Theme—a statement a work seems to make about a given issue or subject—is by its very nature the most comprehensive of the elements, embracing the impact of the entire work. Indeed, theme is not part of the work but is abstracted from it by the reader or audience. Since we, as interpreters, infer the theme and put it in our own words, we understandably often disagree about it. To arrive at your own statement of a theme, you need to consider all the elements of a play together: character, structure, setting (including time and place), tone, and other aspects of the style or the potential staging that create the entire effect.

Tips for Identifying Theme

Because theme emerges from a work in its entirety and from all the other elements working together, there's no one-size-fits-all method for discovering theme. Here, however, are some things to look for and consider as you read and re-read a play.

- Pay attention to the title. A title will seldom indicate a play's theme directly, but some titles do suggest a central topic or a key question. Probe the rest of the play to see what insights, if any, about that topic or answers to that question it ultimately seems to offer.

- Identify any statements that the characters make about a general concept, issue, or topic such as human nature, the natural world, and so on, particularly in monologues or in debates between major characters. Look, too, for statements that potentially have a general meaning or application beyond the play, even if they refer to a specific situation. Then consider whether and how the play as a whole corroborates, overturns, or complicates any one such view or statement.
- If a character changes over the course of the play, try to articulate the truth or insight that character seems to discover. Then consider whether and how the play as a whole corroborates or complicates that insight.
- Identify a conflict depicted in the play and state it in general terms or turn it into a general question, leaving out any reference to specific characters, setting, and so on. Then think about the insight or theme that might be implied by the way the conflict is resolved.

• • •

Above all, try to understand a play on its own terms and to separate interpretation from evaluation. You may dislike symbolic or unrealistic drama until you get more used to it; if a play is not supposed to represent what real people would do in everyday life, then it should not be criticized for failing to do so. Alternatively, you may find realistic plays about ordinary adults in middle America in the mid-twentieth century to be lacking in excitement or appeal. Yet if you read carefully, you may discover vigorous, moving portrayals of people trapped in situations all too familiar to them, if alien to you. Tastes may vary as widely as tones of speech, but if you are familiar with the elements of drama and the ways dramatic **conventions** vary over time and across cultures, you can become a good judge of theatrical literature, and you will notice more and more of the fine effects it can achieve. Nothing replaces the exhilaration and immediacy of a live theater performance, but reading and re-reading plays can yield a rich and rewarding appreciation of the dramatic art. A great play is one that works on the page as well as on the stage.

AUGUST WILSON
(1945–2005)

Fences

August Wilson died of liver cancer when he was only sixty. One of the most important dramatists in American theater history, he had come a long way, the hard way. Frederick August Kittel, Jr. (who would later take his mother's maiden name), was the son of a white, German-born baker and his wife, a black cleaning woman who singlehandedly raised their six children in Pittsburgh's down-at-heel Hill District. In 1957, when Wilson was twelve, his mother remarried. Her new husband was an African American sewer-department worker who, as Wilson learned only after his stepfather's death, had been both a high-school football star unable to secure a college scholarship and an ex-convict. After a series of bad experiences, Wilson left school at fifteen. Armed with a tenth-grade education, he took on a number of menial

Denzel Washington as Troy and Viola Davis as Rose in the 2016 film adaptation of *Fences*

jobs, read his way through the public library, and served briefly in the army. In 1968, he returned to the Hill, cofounding the Black Horizon Theater and debuting his first play. Fourteen years later, Wilson struck artistic gold with *Ma Rainey's Black Bottom* (1982), his first Broadway play and the second in what would become a ten-play cycle. Set mostly in the Hill and chronicling African American life in every decade of the twentieth century, the series earned Wilson two Pulitzers (for *Fences*, 1987, and *The Piano Lesson*, 1990); a Tony (for *Fences*); a Grammy (for the *Ma Rainey's* cast album); an Emmy (for his adaption of *Piano Lesson*); and eight Drama Critics Circle awards. Wilson often described *Fences* as his least representative, most conventional play, thanks to the way it revolves around a single "big character." Yet this, his best-known work, is also arguably among his most personal, set in the period of his youth and aimed, he said, at "uncover[ing] the nobility and the dignity" of the adults he grew up around—"that generation, which shielded its children from all of the indignities they went through."

For Lloyd Richards,[1]
who adds to whatever he touches

CHARACTERS

TROY MAXSON
JIM BONO, *Troy's friend*
ROSE, *Troy's wife*
LYONS, *Troy's oldest son by a previous marriage*

GABRIEL, *Troy's brother*
CORY, *Troy and Rose's son*
RAYNELL, *Troy's daughter*

1. Influential Canadian American director-actor (1919–2006) whom August Wilson called his "guide, mentor, and provocateur." The first black director of a Broadway play (Lorraine Hansberry's *A Raisin in the Sun*, 1959, p. 787), artistic director of the Eugene O'Neill Theater Center and the Yale Repertory Theatre, and dean of the Yale School of Drama, Richards oversaw the first productions of all of Wilson's plays, beginning with *Ma Rainey's Black Bottom* (1982).

SETTING: *The setting is the yard which fronts the only entrance to the Maxson household, an ancient two-story brick house set back off a small alley in a big-city neighborhood. The entrance to the house is gained by two or three steps leading to a wooden porch badly in need of paint.*

A relatively recent addition to the house and running its full width, the porch lacks congruence. It is a sturdy porch with a flat roof. One or two chairs of dubious value sit at one end where the kitchen window opens onto the porch. An old-fashioned icebox stands silent guard at the opposite end.

The yard is a small dirt yard, partially fenced (except during the last scene), with a wooden sawhorse, a pile of lumber, and other fence-building equipment off to the side. Opposite is a tree from which hangs a ball made of rags. A baseball bat leans against the tree. Two oil drums serve as garbage receptacles and sit near the house at right to complete the setting.

THE PLAY: *Near the turn of the century, the destitute of Europe sprang on the city with tenacious claws and an honest and solid dream. The city devoured them. They swelled its belly until it burst into a thousand furnaces and sewing machines, a thousand butcher shops and bakers' ovens, a thousand churches and hospitals and funeral parlors and moneylenders. The city grew. It nourished itself and offered each man a partnership limited only by his talent, his guile and his willingness and capacity for hard work. For the immigrants of Europe, a dream dared and won true.*

The descendants of African slaves were offered no such welcome or participation. They came from places called the Carolinas and the Virginias, Georgia, Alabama, Mississippi and Tennessee. They came strong, eager, searching. The city rejected them and they fled and settled along the riverbanks and under bridges in shallow, ramshackle houses made of sticks and tar paper. They collected rags and wood. They sold the use of their muscles and their bodies. They cleaned houses and washed clothes, they shined shoes, and in quiet desperation and vengeful pride, they stole, and lived in pursuit of their own dream. That they could breathe free, finally, and stand to meet life with the force of dignity and whatever eloquence the heart could call upon.

By 1957, the hard-won victories of the European immigrants had solidified the industrial might of America. War had been confronted and won with new energies that used loyalty and patriotism as its fuel. Life was rich, full and flourishing. The Milwaukee Braves won the World Series, and the hot winds of change that would make the sixties a turbulent, racing, dangerous and provocative decade had not yet begun to blow full.

When the sins of our fathers visit us
We do not have to play host.
We can banish them with forgiveness
As God, in His Largeness and Laws.
    —AUGUST WILSON

ACT ONE

Scene 1

It is 1957. Troy and Bono enter the yard, engaged in conversation. Troy is fifty-three years old, a large man with thick, heavy hands; it is this largeness that he strives to fill out and make an accommodation with. Together with his blackness, his largeness informs his sensibilities and the choices he has made in his life.

Of the two men, Bono is obviously the follower. His commitment to their friendship of thirty-odd years is rooted in his admiration of Troy's honesty, capacity for hard work, and his strength, which Bono seeks to emulate.

It is Friday night, payday, and the one night of the week the two men engage in a ritual of talk and drink. Troy is usually the most talkative and at times he can be crude and almost vulgar, though he is capable of rising to profound heights of expression. The men carry lunch buckets and wear or carry burlap aprons and are dressed in clothes suitable to their jobs as garbage collectors.

BONO: Troy, you ought to stop that lying!

TROY: I ain't lying! The nigger had a watermelon this big. (*Indicates with his hands*) Talking about . . . "What watermelon, Mr. Rand?" I like to fell out! "What watermelon, Mr. Rand?" . . . And it sitting there big as life.

BONO: What did Mr. Rand say?

TROY: Ain't said nothing. Figure if the nigger too dumb to know he carrying a watermelon, he wasn't gonna get much sense out of him. Trying to hide that great big old watermelon under his coat. Afraid to let the white man see him carry it home.

BONO: I'm like you . . . I ain't got no time for them kind of people.

TROY: Now what he look like getting mad 'cause he see the man from the union talking to Mr. Rand?

BONO: He come talking to me about . . . "Maxson gonna get us fired." I told him to get away from me with that. He walked away from me calling you a troublemaker. What Mr. Rand say?

TROY: Ain't said nothing. He told me to go down the commissioner's office next Friday. They called me down there to see them.

BONO: Well, as long as you got your complaint filed, they can't fire you. That's what one of them white fellows tell me.

TROY: I ain't worried about them firing me. They gonna fire me 'cause I asked a question? That's all I did. I went to Mr. Rand and asked him, "Why? Why you got the white mens driving and the colored lifting?" Told him, "What's the matter, don't I count? You think only white fellows got sense enough to drive a truck. That ain't no paper job! Hell, anybody can drive a truck. How come you got all whites driving and the colored lifting?" He told me, "Take it to the union." Well, hell, that's what I done! Now they wanna come up with this pack of lies.

BONO: I told Brownie if the man come and ask him any questions . . . just tell the truth! It ain't nothing but something they done trumped up on you 'cause you filed a complaint on them.

TROY: Brownie don't understand nothing. All I want them to do is change the job description. Give everybody a chance to drive the truck. Brownie can't see that. He ain't got that much sense.

BONO: How you figure he be making out with that gal be up at Taylors' all the time . . . that Alberta gal?

TROY: Same as you and me. Getting as much as we is. Which is to say nothing.

BONO: It is, huh? I figure you doing a little better than me . . . and I ain't saying what I'm doing.

TROY: Aw, nigger, look here . . . I know you. If you had got anywhere near that gal, twenty minutes later you be looking to tell somebody. And the first one you gonna tell . . . that you gonna want to brag to . . . is gonna be me.

BONO: I ain't saying that. I see where you be eyeing her.

TROY: I eye all the women. I don't miss nothing. Don't never let nobody tell you Troy Maxson don't eye the women.

BONO: You been doing more than eyeing her. You done bought her a drink or two.

TROY: Hell yeah, I bought her a drink! What that mean? I bought you one, too. What that mean 'cause I buy her a drink? I'm just being polite.

BONO: It's all right to buy her one drink. That's what you call being polite. But when you wanna be buying two or three . . . that's what you call eyeing her.

TROY: Look here, as long as you known me . . . you ever known me to chase after women?

BONO: Hell yeah! Long as I done known you. You forgetting I knew you when.

TROY: Naw, I'm talking about since I been married to Rose?

BONO: Oh, not since you been married to Rose. Now, that's the truth, there. I can say that.

TROY: All right then! Case closed.

BONO: I see you be walking up around Alberta's house. You supposed to be at Taylors' and you be walking up around there.

TROY: What you watching where I'm walking for? I ain't watching after you.

BONO: I seen you walking around there more than once.

TROY: Hell, you liable to see me walking anywhere! That don't mean nothing 'cause you see me walking around there.

BONO: Where she come from anyway? She just kinda showed up one day.

TROY: Tallahassee. You can look at her and tell she one of them Florida gals. They got some big healthy women down there. Grow them right up out the ground. Got a little bit of Indian in her. Most of them niggers down in Florida got some Indian in them.

BONO: I don't know about that Indian part. But she damn sure big and healthy. Woman wear some big stockings. Got them great big old legs and hips as wide as the Mississippi River.

TROY: Legs don't mean nothing. You don't do nothing but push them out of the way. But them hips cushion the ride!

BONO: Troy, you ain't got no sense.

TROY: It's the truth! Like you riding on Goodyears!

(*Rose enters from the house. She is ten years younger than Troy. Her devotion to him stems from her recognition of the possibilities of her life without him: a succession of abusive men and their babies, a life of partying and running the streets, the church, or aloneness with its attendant pain and frustration. She recognizes Troy's spirit as a fine and illuminating one and she either ignores or forgives his faults, only some of which she recognizes. Though she doesn't drink, her presence is an integral part of the Friday*)

*night rituals. She alternates between the porch and the kitchen, where sup-
per preparations are under way.)*

ROSE: What you all out here getting into?

TROY: What you worried about what we getting into for? This is men talk, woman.

ROSE: What I care what you talking about? Bono, you gonna stay for supper?

BONO: No, I thank you, Rose. But Lucille say she cooking up a pot of pigfeet.

TROY: Pigfeet! Hell, I'm going home with you! Might even stay the night if you
got some pigfeet. You got something in there to top them pigfeet, Rose?

ROSE: I'm cooking up some chicken. I got some chicken and collard greens.

TROY: Well, go on back in the house and let me and Bono finish what we was
talking about. This is men talk. I got some talk for you later. You know what
kind of talk I mean. You go on and powder it up.

ROSE: Troy Maxson, don't you start that now!

TROY *(Puts his arm around her)*: Aw, woman . . . come here. Look here, Bono . . . when
I met this woman . . . I got out that place, say, "Hitch up my pony, saddle up my
mare . . . there's a woman out there for me somewhere. I looked here. Looked
there. Saw Rose and latched on to her." I latched on to her and told her—I'm
gonna tell you the truth—I told her, "Baby, I don't wanna marry, I just wanna be
your man." Rose told me . . . tell him what you told me, Rose.

ROSE: I told him if he wasn't the marrying kind, then move out the way so the
marrying kind could find me.

TROY: That's what she told me. "Nigger, you in my way. You blocking the view!
Move out the way so I can find me a husband." I thought it over two or three
days. Come back—

ROSE: Ain't no two or three days nothing. You was back the same night.

TROY: Come back, told her . . . "Okay, baby . . . but I'm gonna buy me a banty
rooster and put him out there in the backyard . . . and when he see a stranger
come, he'll flap his wings and crow . . ." Look here, Bono, I could watch the
front door by myself . . . it was that back door I was worried about.

ROSE: Troy, you ought not talk like that. Troy ain't doing nothing but telling a lie.

TROY: Only thing is . . . when we first got married . . . forget the rooster . . . we
ain't had no yard!

BONO: I hear you tell it. Me and Lucille was staying down there on Logan Street.
Had two rooms with the outhouse in the back. I ain't mind the outhouse none.
But when that goddamn wind blow through there in the winter . . . that's what
I'm talking about! To this day I wonder why in the hell I ever stayed down
there for six long years. But see, I didn't know I could do no better. I thought
only white folks had inside toilets and things.

ROSE: There's a lot of people don't know they can do no better than they doing
now. That's just something you got to learn. A lot of folks still shop at Bella's.

TROY: Ain't nothing wrong with shopping at Bella's. She got fresh food.

ROSE: I ain't said nothing about if she got fresh food. I'm talking about what she
charge. She charge ten cents more than the A&P.[2]

TROY: The A&P ain't never done nothing for me. I spends my money where I'm
treated right. I go down to Bella, say, "I need a loaf of bread, I'll pay you Friday."

2. By the 1930s, the Great Atlantic and Pacific Tea Company, so named in 1859, was the leading
supermarket chain in the United States.

She give it to me. What sense that make when I got money to go and spend it somewhere else and ignore the person who done right by me? That ain't in the Bible.

ROSE: We ain't talking about what's in the Bible. What sense it make to shop there when she overcharge?

TROY: You shop where you want to. I'll do my shopping where the people been good to me.

ROSE: Well, I don't think it's right for her to overcharge. That's all I was saying.

BONO: Look here . . . I got to get on. Lucille be raising all kind of hell.

TROY: Where you going, nigger? We ain't finished this pint. Come here, finish this pint.

BONO: Well, hell, I am . . . if you ever turn the bottle loose.

TROY (*Hands him the bottle*): The only thing I say about the A&P is I'm glad Cory got that job down there. Help him take care of his school clothes and things. Gabe done moved out and things getting tight around here. He got that job . . . He can start to look out for himself.

ROSE: Cory done went and got recruited by a college football team.

TROY: I told that boy about that football stuff. The white man ain't gonna let him get nowhere with that football. I told him when he first come to me with it. Now you come telling me he done went and got more tied up in it. He ought to go and get recruited in how to fix cars or something where he can make a living.

ROSE: He ain't talking about making no living playing football. It's just something the boys in school do. They gonna send a recruiter by to talk to you. He'll tell you he ain't talking about making no living playing football. It's a honor to be recruited.

TROY: It ain't gonna get him nowhere. Bono'll tell you that.

BONO: If he be like you in the sports . . . he's gonna be all right. Ain't but two men ever played baseball as good as you. That's Babe Ruth and Josh Gibson.[3] Them's the only two men ever hit more home runs than you.

TROY: What it ever get me? Ain't got a pot to piss in or a window to throw it out of.

ROSE: Times have changed since you was playing baseball, Troy. That was before the war.[4] Times have changed a lot since then.

TROY: How in hell they done changed?

ROSE: They got lots of colored boys playing ball now. Baseball and football.

BONO: You right about that, Rose. Times have changed, Troy. You just come along too early.

TROY: There ought not never have been no time called too early! Now you take that fellow . . . what's that fellow they had playing right field for the Yankees back then? You know who I'm talking about, Bono. Used to play right field for the Yankees.

---

3. Georgia-born catcher (1911–47) often called "the black Babe Ruth." Hailed by the Baseball Hall of Fame as "the greatest power hitter in black baseball," he died three months before integration of the major leagues. *Babe Ruth*: legendary outfielder, pitcher, and power hitter (1895–1948) for the Boston Red Sox and New York Yankees.
4. World War II (1939–45).

ROSE: Selkirk?[5]

TROY: Selkirk! That's it! Man batting .269, understand? .269. What kind of sense that make? I was hitting .432 with thirty-seven home runs! Man batting .269 and playing right field for the Yankees! I saw Josh Gibson's daughter yesterday. She walking around with raggedy shoes on her feet. Now I bet you Selkirk's daughter ain't walking around with raggedy shoes on her feet! I bet you that!

ROSE: They got a lot of colored baseball players now. Jackie Robinson[6] was the first. Folks had to wait for Jackie Robinson.

TROY: I done seen a hundred niggers play baseball better than Jackie Robinson. Hell, I know some teams Jackie Robinson couldn't even make! What you talking about Jackie Robinson. Jackie Robinson wasn't nobody. I'm talking about if you could play ball then they ought to have let you play. Don't care what color you were. Come telling me I come along too early. If you could play . . . then they ought to have let you play.

(Troy takes a long drink from the bottle.)

ROSE: You gonna drink yourself to death. You don't need to be drinking like that.

TROY: Death ain't nothing. I done seen him. Done wrassled with him. You can't tell me nothing about death. Death ain't nothing but a fastball on the outside corner. And you know what I'll do to that! Lookee here, Bono . . . am I lying? You get one of them fastballs, about waist high, over the outside corner of the plate where you can get the meat of the bat on it . . . and good God! You can kiss it good-bye. Now, am I lying?

BONO: Naw, you telling the truth there. I seen you do it.

TROY: If I'm lying . . . that 450 feet worth of lying! *(Pause)* That's all death is to me. A fastball on the outside corner.

ROSE: I don't know why you want to get on talking about death.

TROY: Ain't nothing wrong with talking about death. That's part of life. Everybody gonna die. You gonna die, I'm gonna die. Bono's gonna die. Hell, we all gonna die.

ROSE: But you ain't got to talk about it. I don't like to talk about it.

TROY: You the one brought it up. Me and Bono was talking about baseball . . . you tell me I'm gonna drink myself to death. Ain't that right, Bono? You know I don't drink this but one night out of the week. That's Friday night. I'm gonna drink just enough to where I can handle it. Then I cuts it loose. I leave it alone. So don't you worry about me drinking myself to death. 'Cause I ain't worried about Death. I done seen him. I done wrestled with him.

   Look here, Bono . . . I looked up one day and Death was marching straight at me. Like Soldiers on Parade! The Army of Death was marching straight at me. The middle of July, 1941. It got real cold just like it be winter. It seem like Death himself reached out and touched me on the shoulder. He touch me just like I touch you. I got cold as ice and Death standing there grinning at me.

ROSE: Troy, why don't you hush that talk.

---

5. George Selkirk (1908–87), Canadian-born player who succeeded Babe Ruth as the New York Yankees right fielder.
6. Brooklyn Dodgers first baseman (1919–72); in 1947, he became the first black player in the major leagues and, in 1949, the first black winner of the National League MVP Award.

TROY: I say . . . What you want, Mr. Death? You be wanting me? You done brought your army to be getting me? I looked him dead in the eye. I wasn't fearing nothing. I was ready to tangle. Just like I'm ready to tangle now. The Bible say be ever vigilant. That's why I don't get but so drunk. I got to keep watch.

FOSE: Troy was right down there in Mercy Hospital. You remember he had pneumonia? Laying there with a fever talking plumb out of his head.

TROY: Death standing there staring at me . . . carrying that sickle in his hand. Finally he say, "You want bound over for another year?" See, just like that . . . "You want bound over for another year?" I told him, "Bound over hell! Let's settle this now!"

It seem like he kinda fell back when I said that, and all the cold went out of me. I reached down and grabbed that sickle and threw it just as far as I could throw it . . . and me and him commenced to wrestling.

We wrestled for three days and three nights. I can't say where I found the strength from. Every time it seemed like he was gonna get the best of me, I'd reach way down deep inside myself and find the strength to do him one better.

ROSE: Every time Troy tell that story he find different ways to tell it. Different things to make up about it.

TROY: I ain't making up nothing. I'm telling you the facts of what happened. I wrestled with Death for three days and three nights and I'm standing here to tell you about it. (Pause) All right. At the end of the third night we done weakened each other to where we can't hardly move. Death stood up, throwed on his robe . . . had him a white robe with a hood on it. He throwed on that robe and went off to look for his sickle. Say, "I'll be back." Just like that. "I'll be back." I told him say, "Yeah, but . . . you gonna have to find me!" I wasn't no fool. I wasn't going looking for him. Death ain't nothing to play with. And I know he's gonna get me. I know I got to join his army . . . his camp followers. But as long as I keep my strength and see him coming . . . as long as I keep up my vigilance . . . he's gonna have to fight to get me. I ain't going easy.

BONO: Well, look here, since you got to keep up your vigilance . . . let me have the bottle.

TROY: Aw hell, I shouldn't have told you that part. I should have left out that part.

ROSE: Troy be talking that stuff and half the time don't even know what he be talking about.

TROY: Bono know me better than that.

BONO: That's right. I know you. I know you got some Uncle Remus[7] in your blood. You got more stories than the devil got sinners.

TROY: Aw hell, I done seen him too! Done talked with the devil.

ROSE: Troy, don't nobody want to be hearing all that stuff.

> (Lyons enters the yard from the street. Thirty-four years old, Troy's son from a previous marriage, he sports a neatly trimmed goatee, sport coat and white shirt, tieless and buttoned at the collar. Though he fancies himself a musician, he is more caught up in the rituals and "idea" of being a musician than in the actual practice of the music. He has come to borrow money from Troy

---

7. African American narrator of the folktales, adapted from African American originals, published by white Georgia journalist Joel Chandler Harris beginning in 1879, and featuring Br'er Rabbit.

and, while he knows he will be successful, he is uncertain as to what extent
his lifestyle will be held up to scrutiny and ridicule.)

LYONS: Hey, Pop.

TROY: What you come "Hey, Popping" me for?

LYONS: How you doing, Rose? (*Kisses her*) Mr. Bono. How you doing?

BONO: Hey, Lyons . . . how you been?

TROY: He must have been doing all right. I ain't seen him around here last week.

ROSE: Troy, leave your boy alone. He come by to see you and you wanna start all
that nonsense.

TROY: I ain't bothering Lyons. (*Offers him the bottle*) Here, get you a drink. We
got an understanding. I know why he come by to see me and he know I know.

LYONS: Come on, Pop . . . I just stopped by to say hi . . . see how you was doing.

TROY: You ain't stopped by yesterday.

ROSE: You gonna stay for supper, Lyons? I got some chicken cooking in the oven.

LYONS: No, Rose . . . thanks. I was just in the neighborhood and thought I'd stop
by for a minute.

TROY: You was in the neighborhood all right, nigger. You telling the truth there.
You was in the neighborhood 'cause it's my payday.

LYONS: Well, hell, since you mentioned it . . . let me have ten dollars.

TROY: I'll be damned! I'll die and go to hell and play blackjack with the devil
before I give you ten dollars.

BONO: That's what I want to know about . . . that devil you done seen.

LYONS: What . . . Pop done seen the devil? You too much, Pops.

TROY: Yeah, I done seen him. Talked to him too!

ROSE: You ain't seen no devil. I done told you that man ain't had nothing to do
with the devil. Anything you can't understand, you want to call it the devil.

TROY: Look here, Bono . . . I went down to see Hertzberger about some furniture. Got three rooms for two-ninety-eight. That what it say on the radio.
"Three rooms . . . two-ninety-eight." Even made up a little song about it. Go
down there . . . man tell me I can't get no credit. I'm working every day and
can't get no credit. What to do? I got an empty house with some raggedy furniture in it. Cory ain't got no bed. He's sleeping on a pile of rags on the floor.
Working every day and can't get no credit. Come back here—Rose'll tell you—
madder than hell. Sit down . . . try to figure what I'm gonna do. Come a knock
on the door. Ain't been living here but three days. Who know I'm here? Open
the door . . . devil standing there bigger than life. White fellow . . . got on good
clothes and everything. Standing there with a clipboard in his hand. I ain't had
to say nothing. First words come out of his mouth was . . . . "I understand you
need some furniture and can't get no credit." I liked to fell over. He say, "I'll
give you all the credit you want, but you got to pay the interest on it." I told
him, "Give me three rooms' worth and charge whatever you want." Next day a
truck pulled up here and two men unloaded them three rooms. Man what
drove the truck give me a book. Say send ten dollars, first of every month to the
address in the book and everything will be all right. Say if I miss a payment the
devil was coming back and it'll be hell to pay. That was fifteen years ago. To
this day . . . the first of the month I send my ten dollars, Rose'll tell you.

ROSE: Troy lying.

TROY: I ain't never seen that man since. Now you tell me who else that could have been but the devil? I ain't sold my soul or nothing like that, you understand. Naw, I wouldn't have truck with the devil about nothing like that. I got my furniture and pays my ten dollars the first of the month just like clockwork.

BONO: How long you say you been paying this ten dollars a month?

TROY: Fifteen years!

BONO: Hell, ain't you finished paying for it yet? How much the man done charged you.

TROY: Aw hell, I done paid for it. I done paid for it ten times over! The fact is I'm scared to stop paying it.

ROSE: Troy lying. We got that furniture from Mr. Glickman, He ain't paying no ten dollars a month to nobody.

TROY: Aw hell, woman. Bono know I ain't that big a fool.

LYONS: I was just getting ready to say . . . I know where there's a bridge for sale.

TROY: Look here, I'll tell you this . . . it don't matter to me if he was the devil. It don't matter if the devil give credit. Somebody has got to give it.

ROSE: It ought to matter. You going around talking about having truck with the devil . . . God's the one you gonna have to answer to. He's the one gonna be at the Judgment.

LYONS: Yeah, well, look here, Pop . . . let me have that ten dollars. I'll give it back to you. Bonnie got a job working at the hospital.

TROY: What I tell you, Bono? The only time I see this nigger is when he wants something. That's the only time I see him.

LYONS: Come on, Pop, Mr. Bono don't want to hear all that. Let me have the ten dollars. I told you Bonnie working.

TROY: What that mean to me? "Bonnie working." I don't care if she working. Go ask her for the ten dollars if she working. Talking about "Bonnie working." Why ain't you working?

LYONS: Aw, Pop, you know I can't find no decent job. Where am I gonna get a job at? You know I can't get no job.

TROY: I told you I know some people down there. I can get you on the rubbish if you want to work. I told you that the last time you came by here asking me for something.

LYONS: Naw, Pop . . . thanks. That ain't for me. I don't wanna be carrying nobody's rubbish. I don't wanna be punching nobody's time clock.

TROY: What's the matter, you too good to carry people's rubbish? Where you think that ten dollars you talking about come from? I'm just supposed to haul people's rubbish and give my money to you 'cause you too lazy to work. You too lazy to work and wanna know why you ain't got what I got.

ROSE: What hospital Bonnie working at? Mercy?

LYONS: She's down at Passavant working in the laundry.

TROY: I ain't got nothing as it is. I give you that ten dollars and I got to eat beans the rest of the week. Naw . . . you ain't getting no ten dollars here.

LYONS: You ain't got to be eating no beans. I don't know why you wanna say that.

TROY: I ain't got no extra money. Gabe done moved over to Miss Pearl's paying her the rent and things done got tight around here. I can't afford to be giving you every payday.

LYONS: I ain't asked you to give me nothing. I asked you to loan me ten dollars. I know you got ten dollars.

TROY: Yeah, I got it. You know why I got it? 'Cause I don't throw my money away out there in the streets. You living the fast life . . . wanna be a musician . . . running around in them clubs and things . . . then, you learn to take care of yourself. You ain't gonna find me going and asking nobody for nothing. I done spent too many years without.

LYONS: You and me is two different people, Pop.

TROY: I done learned my mistake and learned to do what's right by it. You still trying to get something for nothing. Life don't owe you nothing. You owe it to yourself. Ask Bono. He'll tell you I'm right.

LYONS: You got your way of dealing with the world . . . I got mine. The only thing that matters to me is the music.

TROY: Yeah, I can see that! It don't matter how you gonna eat . . . where your next dollar is coming from. You telling the truth there.

LYONS: I know I got to eat. But I got to live too. I need something that gonna help me to get out of the bed in the morning. Make me feel like I belong in the world. I don't bother nobody. I just stay with my music 'cause that's the only way I can find to live in the world. Otherwise there ain't no telling what I might do. Now I don't come criticizing you and how you live. I just come by to ask you for ten dollars. I don't wanna hear all that about how I live.

TROY: Boy, your mama did a hell of a job raising you.

LYONS: You can't change me, Pop. I'm thirty-four years old. If you wanted to change me, you should have been there when I was growing up. I come by to see you . . . ask for ten dollars and you want to talk about how I was raised. You don't know nothing about how I was raised.

ROSE: Let the boy have ten dollars, Troy.

TROY (To Lyons): What the hell you looking at me for? I ain't got no ten dollars. You know what I do with my money. (To Rose) Give him ten dollars if you want him to have it.

ROSE: I will. Just as soon as you turn it loose.

TROY (Handing Rose the money): There it is. Seventy-six dollars and forty-two cents. You see this, Bono? Now, I ain't gonna get but six of that back.

ROSE: You ought to stop telling that lie. Here, Lyons. (Hands him the money)

LYONS: Thanks, Rose. Look . . . I got to run . . . I'll see you later.

TROY: Wait a minute. You gonna say, "Thanks, Rose," and ain't gonna look to see where she got that ten dollars from? See how they do me, Bono?

LYONS: I know she got it from you, Pop. Thanks. I'll give it back to you.

TROY: There he go telling another lie. Time I see that ten dollars . . . he'll be owing me thirty more.

LYONS: See you, Mr. Bono.

BONO: Take care, Lyons!

LYONS: Thanks, Pop. I'll see you again.

(Lyons exits the yard.)

TROY: I don't know why he don't go and get him a decent job and take care of that woman he got.

BONO: He'll be all right, Troy. The boy is still young.

TROY: The *boy* is thirty-four years old.

ROSE: Let's not get off into all that.

BONO: Look here . . . I got to be going. I got to be getting on. Lucille gonna be waiting.

TROY *(Puts his arm around Rose)*: See this woman, Bono? I love this woman. I love this woman so much it hurts. I love her so much . . . I done run out of ways of loving her. So I got to go back to basics. Don't you come by my house Monday morning talking about time to go to work . . .'cause I'm still gonna be stroking!

ROSE: Troy! Stop it now!

BONO: I ain't paying him no mind, Rose. That ain't nothing but gin-talk. Go on, Troy. I'll see you Monday.

TROY: Don't you come by my house, nigger! I done told you what I'm gonna be doing.

> *(The lights fade to black.)*

Scene 2

The lights come up on Rose hanging up clothes. She hums and sings softly to herself. It is the following morning.

ROSE *(Singing)*:
> Jesus, be a fence all around me every day
> Jesus, I want you to protect me as I travel on my way.
> Jesus, be a fence all around me every day.

> *(Troy enters from the house.)*

> Jesus, I want you to protect me
> As I travel on my way.

(To Troy) 'Morning. You ready for breakfast? I can fix it soon as I finish hanging up these clothes?

TROY: I got the coffee on. That'll be all right. I'll just drink some of that this morning.

ROSE: That 651 hit yesterday. That's the second time this month. Miss Pearl hit for a dollar . . . seem like those that need the least always get lucky. Poor folks can't get nothing.

TROY: Them numbers don't know nobody. I don't know why you fool with them. You and Lyons both.

ROSE: It's something to do.

TROY: You ain't doing nothing but throwing your money away.

ROSE: Troy, you know I don't play foolishly. I just play a nickel here and a nickel there.

TROY: That's two nickels you done thrown away.

ROSE: Now I hit sometimes . . . that makes up for it. It always comes in handy when I do hit. I don't hear you complaining then.

TROY: I ain't complaining now. I just say it's foolish. Trying to guess out of six hundred ways which way the number gonna come. If I had all the money niggers, these Negroes, throw away on numbers for one week—just one week—I'd be a rich man.

ROSE: Well, you wishing and calling it foolish ain't gonna stop folks from playing numbers. That's one thing for sure. Besides . . . some good things come from playing numbers. Look where Pope done bought him that restaurant off of numbers.

TROY: I can't stand niggers like that. Man ain't had two dimes to rub together. He walking around with his shoes all run over bumming money for cigarettes. All right. Got lucky there and hit the numbers . . .

ROSE: Troy, I know all about it.

TROY: Had good sense, I'll say that for him. He ain't throwed his money away. I seen niggers hit the numbers and go through two thousand dollars in four days. Man bought him that restaurant down there . . . fixed it up real nice . . . and then didn't want nobody to come in it! A Negro go in there and can't get no kind of service. I seen a white fellow come in there and order a bowl of stew. Pope picked all the meat out the pot for him. Man ain't had nothing but a bowl of meat! Negro come behind him and ain't got nothing but the potatoes and carrots. Talking about what numbers do for people, you picked a wrong example. Ain't done nothing but make a worser fool out of him than he was before.

ROSE: Troy, you ought to stop worrying about what happened at work yesterday.

TROY: I ain't worried. Just told me to be down there at the commissioner's office on Friday. Everybody think they gonna fire me. I ain't worried about them firing me. You ain't got to worry about that. (Pause) Where's Cory? Cory in the house? (Calls) Cory?

ROSE: He gone out.

TROY: Out, huh? He gone out 'cause he know I want him to help me with this fence. I know how he is. That boy scared of work.

(Gabriel enters. He comes halfway down the alley and, hearing Troy's voice, stops.)

He ain't done a lick of work in his life.

ROSE: He had to go to football practice. Coach wanted them to get in a little extra practice before the season start.

TROY: I got his practice . . . running out of here before he get his chores done.

ROSE: Troy, what is wrong with you this morning? Don't nothing set right with you. Go on back in there and go to bed . . . get up on the other side.

TROY: Why something got to be wrong with me? I ain't said nothing wrong with me.

ROSE: You got something to say about everything. First it's the numbers . . . then it's the way the man runs his restaurant . . . then you done got on Cory. What's it gonna be next? Take a look up there and see if the weather suits you . . . or is it gonna be how you gonna put up the fence with the clothes hanging in the yard.

TROY: You hit the nail on the head then.

ROSE: I know you like I know the back of my hand. Go on in there and get you some coffee . . . see if that straighten you up. 'Cause you ain't right this morning.

(Troy starts into the house and sees Gabriel. Gabriel starts singing. Troy's brother, he is seven years younger than Troy. Injured in World War II, he has a metal plate in his head. He carries an old trumpet tied around his waist and believes with every fiber of his being that he is the archangel Gabriel.[8] He carries a chipped basket with an assortment of discarded fruits and vegetables he has picked up in the strip district[9] and which he attempts to sell.)

GABRIEL *(Singing)*:
Yes, ma'am, I got plums
You ask me how I sell them
Oh ten cents apiece
Three for a quarter
Come and buy now
'Cause I'm here today
And tomorrow I'll be gone.

(Rose enters.)

Hey, Rose!
ROSE: How you doing, Gabe?
GABRIEL: There's Troy . . . Hey, Troy!
TROY: Hey, Gabe.

(Troy exits into the kitchen.)

ROSE *(To Gabriel)*: What you got there?
GABRIEL: You know what I got, Rose. I got fruits and vegetables.
ROSE *(Looking in the basket)*: Where's all these plums you talking about?
GABRIEL: I ain't got no plums today, Rose. I was just singing that. Have some tomorrow. Put me in a big order for plums. Have enough plums tomorrow for Saint Peter[1] and everybody.

(Troy reenters from the kitchen and crosses to the steps.)

(To Rose) Troy's mad at me.
TROY: I ain't mad at you. What I got to be mad at you about? You ain't done nothing to me.
GABRIEL: I just moved over to Miss Pearl's to keep out from in your way. I ain't mean no harm by it.
TROY: Who said anything about that? I ain't said anything about that.
GABRIEL: You ain't mad at me, is you?
TROY: Naw . . . I ain't mad at you, Gabe. If I was mad at you I'd tell you about it.

8. Divine messenger in Jewish, Christian, and Islamic traditions. In the Bible, he appears to Daniel (to explain his visions), to Zacharias (to prophesy John the Baptist's birth), and to Mary (to announce that she will bear Jesus). He is also said to be the angelic trumpeter who will announce the arrival of the Last Judgment and Christ's second coming.
9. Market district located on a narrow strip of land northeast of downtown Pittsburgh.
1. Apostle traditionally represented as guardian of heaven's gates because, in Matthew 16.19, Jesus tells him, "I will give unto thee the keys of the kingdom of heaven [. . .]."

GABRIEL: Got me two rooms. In the basement. Got my own door too. Wanna see my key? (Holds up a key) That's my own key! Ain't nobody else got a key like that. That's my key! My two rooms!

TROY: Well, that's good, Gabe. You got your own key . . . that's good.

ROSE: You hungry, Gabe? I was just fixing to cook Troy his breakfast.

GABRIEL: I'll take some biscuits. You got some biscuits? Did you know when I was in Heaven . . . every morning me and Saint Peter would sit down by the Gate and eat some big fat biscuits? Oh, yeah! We had us a good time. We'd sit there and eat us them biscuits and then Saint Peter would go off to sleep and tell me to wake him up when it's time to open the Gates for the Judgment.

ROSE: Well, come on . . . I'll make up a batch of biscuits.

(Rose exits into the house.)

GABRIEL: Troy . . . Saint Peter got your name in the book. I seen it. It say . . . Troy Maxson. I say . . . I know him! He got the same name like what I got. That's my brother!

TROY: How many times you gonna tell me that, Gabe?

GABRIEL: Ain't got my name in the book. Don't have to have my name. I done died and went to Heaven. He got your name though. One morning Saint Peter was looking at his book . . . marking it up for the Judgment . . . and he let me see your name. Got it in there under M. Got Rose's name . . . I ain't seen it like I seen yours . . . but I know it's in there. He got a great big book. Got everybody's name what was ever been born. That's what he told me. But I seen your name. Seen it with my own eyes.

TROY: Go on in the house there. Rose going to fix you something to eat.

GABRIEL: Oh, I ain't hungry. I done had breakfast with Aunt Jemima. She come by and cooked me up a whole mess of flapjacks. Remember how we used to eat them flapjacks?

TROY: Go on in the house and get you something to eat now.

GABRIEL: I got to go sell my plums. I done sold some tomatoes. Got me two quarters. Wanna see? (Shows Troy his quarters) I'm gonna save them and buy me a new horn so Saint Peter can hear me when it's time to open the Gates. (Stops suddenly. Listens) Hear that? That's the hellhounds. I got to chase them out of here. Go on get out of here! Get out! (Exits singing:)

Better get ready for the Judgment
Better get ready for the Judgment
My Lord is coming down.

(Rose enters from the house.)

TROY: He gone off somewhere.

GABRIEL (Offstage):
Better get ready for the Judgment
Better get ready for the Judgment morning
Better get ready for the Judgment
My God is coming down.

ROSE: He ain't eating right. Miss Pearl say she can't get him to eat nothing.

TROY: What you want me to do about it, Rose? I done did everything I can for the man. I can't make him get well. Man got half his head blown away . . . what you expect?

ROSE: Seem like something ought to be done to help him.

TROY: Man don't bother nobody. He just mixed up from that metal plate he got in his head. Ain't no sense for him to go back into the hospital.

ROSE: Least he be eating right. They can help him take care of himself.

TROY: Don't nobody wanna be locked up, Rose. What you wanna lock him up for? Man go over there and fight the war . . . messin' around with them Japs, get half his head blown off . . . and they give him a lousy three thousand dollars. And I had to swoop down on that.

ROSE: Is you fixing to go into that again?

TROY: That's the only way I got a roof over my head . . . 'cause of that metal plate.

ROSE: Ain't no sense you blaming yourself for nothing. Gabe wasn't in no condition to manage that money. You done what was right by him. Can't nobody say you ain't done what was right by him. Look how long you took care of him . . . till he wanted to have his own place and moved over there with Miss Pearl.

TROY: That ain't what I'm saying, woman! I'm just stating the facts. If my brother didn't have that metal plate in his head . . . I wouldn't have a pot to piss in or a window to throw it out of. And I'm fifty-three years old. Now see if you can understand that!

(He gets up from the porch and starts to exit the yard.)

ROSE: Where you going off to? You been running out of here every Saturday for weeks. I thought you was gonna work on this fence?

TROY: I'm gonna walk down to Taylors'. Listen to the ball game. I'll be back in a bit. I'll work on it when I get back.

(He exits the yard. The lights fade to black.)

Scene 3

The lights come up on the yard. It is four hours later. Rose is taking down the clothes from the line. Cory enters carrying his football equipment.

ROSE: Your daddy like to had a fit with you running out of here this morning without doing your chores.

CORY: I told you I had to go to practice.

ROSE: He say you were supposed to help him with this fence.

CORY: He been saying that the last four or five Saturdays, and then he don't never do nothing, but go down to Taylors'. Did you tell him about the recruiter?

ROSE: Yeah, I told him.

CORY: What he say?

ROSE: He ain't said nothing too much. You get in there and get started on your chores before he gets back. Go on and scrub down them steps before he gets back here hollering and carrying on.

CORY: I'm hungry. What you got to eat, Mama?

ROSE: Go on and get started on your chores. I got some meat loaf in there. Go on and make you a sandwich . . . and don't leave no mess in there.

> (*Cory exits into the house. Rose continues to take down the clothes. Troy enters the yard and sneaks up and grabs her from behind.*)

Troy! Go on, now. You liked to scared me to death. What was the score of the game? Lucille had me on the phone and I couldn't keep up with it.

TROY: What I care about the game? Come here, woman. (*Tries to kiss her*)

ROSE: I thought you went down Taylors' to listen to the game. Go on, Troy! You supposed to be putting up this fence.

TROY (*Attempting to kiss her again*): I'll put it up when I finish with what is at hand.

ROSE: Go on, Troy. I ain't studying you.

TROY (*Chasing after her*): I'm studying you . . . fixing to do my homework!

ROSE: Troy, you better leave me alone.

TROY: Where's Cory? That boy brought his butt home yet?

ROSE: He's in the house doing his chores.

TROY (*Calling*): Cory! Get your butt out here, boy!

> (*Rose exits into the house with the laundry. Troy goes over to the pile of wood, picks up a board, and starts sawing. Cory enters from the house.*)

You just now coming in here from leaving this morning?

CORY: Yeah, I had to go to football practice.

TROY: Yeah, what?

CORY: Yessir.

TROY: I ain't but two seconds off you noway. The garbage sitting in there overflowing . . . you ain't done none of your chores . . . and you come in here talking about, "Yeah."

CORY: I was just getting ready to do my chores now, Pop . . .

TROY: Your first chore is to help me with this fence on Saturday. Everything else come after that. Now get that saw and cut them boards.

> (*Cory takes the saw and begins cutting the boards. Troy continues working. There is a long pause.*)

CORY: Hey, Pop . . . why don't you buy a TV?

TROY: What I want with a TV? What I want one of them for?

CORY: Everybody got one. Earl, Ba Bra . . . Jesse!

TROY: I ain't asked you who had one. I say what I want with one?

CORY: So you can watch it. They got lots of things on TV. Baseball games and everything. We could watch the World Series.

TROY: Yeah . . . and how much this TV cost?

CORY: I don't know. They got them on sale for around two hundred dollars.

TROY: Two hundred dollars, huh?

CORY: That ain't that much, Pop.

TROY: Naw, it's just two hundred dollars. See that roof you got over your head at night? Let me tell you something about that roof. It's been over ten years since that roof was last tarred. See now . . . the snow come this winter and sit up there on that roof like it is . . . and it's gonna seep inside. It's just gonna be a little bit . . . ain't gonna hardly notice it. Then the next thing you know, it's gonna be leaking all over the house. Then the wood rot from all that water and you gonna need a whole new roof. Now, how much you think it cost to get that roof tarred?

CORY: I don't know.

TROY: Two hundred and sixty-four dollars . . . cash money. While you thinking about a TV, I got to be thinking about the roof . . . and whatever else go wrong around here. Now if you had two hundred dollars, what would you do . . . fix the roof or buy a TV?

CORY: I'd buy a TV. Then when the roof started to leak . . . when it needed fixing . . . I'd fix it.

TROY: Where are you gonna get the money from? You done spent it for a TV. You gonna sit up and watch the water run all over your brand-new TV.

CORY: Aw, Pop. You got money. I know you do.

TROY: Where I got it at, huh?

CORY: You got it in the bank.

TROY: You wanna see my bankbook? You wanna see that seventy-three dollars and twenty-two cents I got sitting up in there.

CORY: You ain't got to pay for it all at one time. You can put a down payment on it and carry it home with you.

TROY: Not me. I ain't gonna owe nobody nothing if I can help it. Miss a payment and they come and snatch it right out your house. Then what you got? Now, soon as I get two hundred dollars clear, then I'll buy a TV. Right now, as soon as I get two hundred and sixty-four dollars, I'm gonna have this roof tarred.

CORY: Aw . . . Pop!

TROY: You go on and get you two hundred dollars and buy one if ya want it. I got better things to do with my money.

CORY: I can't get no two hundred dollars. I ain't never seen two hundred dollars.

TROY: I'll tell you what . . . you get you a hundred dollars and I'll put the other hundred with it.

CORY: All right, I'm gonna show you.

TROY: You gonna show me how you can cut them boards right now.

(Cory begins to cut the boards. There is a long pause.)

CORY: The Pirates won today. That makes five in a row.

TROY: I ain't thinking about the Pirates. Got an all-white team. Got that boy . . . that Puerto Rican boy . . . Clemente.[2] Don't even half-play him. That boy could be something if they give him a chance. Play him one day and sit him on the bench the next.

CORY: He gets a lot of chances to play.

TROY: I'm talking about playing regular. Playing every day so you can get your timing. That's what I'm talking about.

CORY: They got some white guys on the team that don't play every day. You can't play everybody at the same time.

2. Roberto Clemente (1934–72), Pittsburgh Pirates right fielder (1955–72), four-time National League batting champion, and winner of twelve Gold Gloves.

TROY: If they got a white fellow sitting on the bench . . . you can bet your last dollar he can't play! The colored guy got to be twice as good before he get on the team. That's why I don't want you to get all tied up in them sports. Man on the team and what it get him? They got colored on the team and don't use them. Same as not having them. All them teams the same.

CORY: The Braves got Hank Aaron and Wes Covington.[3] Hank Aaron hit two home runs today. That makes forty-three.

TROY: Hank Aaron ain't nobody. That's what you supposed to do. That's how you supposed to play the game. Ain't nothing to it. It's just a matter of timing . . . getting the right follow-through. Hell, I can hit forty-three home runs right now!

CORY: Not off no major-league pitching, you couldn't.

TROY: We had better pitching in the Negro leagues. I hit seven home runs off of Satchel Paige.[4] You can't get no better than that!

CORY: Sandy Koufax.[5] He's leading the league in strikeouts.

TROY: I ain't thinking of no Sandy Koufax.

CORY: You got Warren Spahn and Lew Burdette.[6] I bet you couldn't hit no home runs off of Warren Spahn.

TROY: I'm through with it now. You go on and cut them boards. (*Pause*) Your mama tell me you done got recruited by a college football team? Is that right?

CORY: Yeah. Coach Zellman say the recruiter gonna be coming by to talk to you. Get you to sign the permission papers.

TROY: I thought you supposed to be working down there at the A&P. Ain't you supposed to be working down there after school?

CORY: Mr. Stawicki say he gonna hold my job for me until after the football season. Say starting next week I can work weekends.

TROY: I thought we had an understanding about this football stuff? You suppose to keep up with your chores and hold that job down at the A&P. Ain't been around here all day on a Saturday. Ain't none of your chores done . . . and now you telling me you done quit your job.

CORY: I'm gonna be working weekends.

TROY: You damn right you are! And ain't no need for nobody coming around here to talk to me about signing nothing.

CORY: Hey, Pop . . . you can't do that. He's coming all the way from North Carolina.

TROY: I don't care where he coming from. The white man ain't gonna let you get nowhere with that football noway. You go on and get your book-learning so you can work yourself up in that A&P or learn how to fix cars or build houses

3. African American fielder (1932–2011) who played for the Milwaukee Braves from 1956 to 1961. *Hank Aaron*: legendary African American batsman (b. 1934) who played twenty-one seasons with the Milwaukee, later Atlanta, Braves (1954–74) and, in 1974–75, broke Babe Ruth's records for most home runs and runs batted in (RBIs).
4. Pitcher (1906–82). Arguably the Negro Leagues' most famous player (1926–47), he pitched in the newly integrated major leagues from age forty-two to sixty (1948–66).
5. Brooklyn, later Los Angeles, Dodgers pitcher (b. 1935), the first player ever to win three Cy Young Awards, and the youngest ever elected to Baseball's Hall of Fame.
6. Like 1957 Cy Young Award winner Warren Spahn (1921–2003), a pitcher for the Boston, later Milwaukee, Braves (1926–2007). Burdette was MVP of the 1957 World Series, the only World Series the Milwaukee Braves ever won and the first, since 1948, won by any non–New York team.

or something, get you a trade. That way you have something can't nobody take away from you. You go on and learn how to put your hands to some good use. Besides hauling people's garbage.

CORY: I get good grades, Pop. That's why the recruiter wants to talk with you. You got to keep up your grades to get recruited. This way I'll be going to college. I'll get a chance . . .

TROY: First you gonna get your butt down there to the A&P and get your job back.

CORY: Mr. Stawicki done already hired somebody else 'cause I told him I was playing football.

TROY: You a bigger fool than I thought . . . to let somebody take away your job so you can play some football. Where you gonna get your money to take out your girlfriend and whatnot? What kind of foolishness is that to let somebody take away your job?

CORY: I'm still gonna be working weekends.

TROY: Naw . . . naw. You getting your butt out of here and finding you another job.

CORY: Come on, Pop! I got to practice. I can't work after school and play football too. The team needs me. That's what Coach Zellman say . . .

TROY: I don't care what nobody else say. I'm the boss . . . you understand? I'm the boss around here. I do the only saying what counts.

CORY: Come on, Pop!

TROY: I asked you . . . did you understand?

CORY: Yeah . . .

TROY: What!?!

CORY: Yessir.

TROY: You go on down there to that A&P and see if you can get your job back. If you can't do both . . . then you quit the football team. You've got to take the crookeds with the straights.

CORY: Yessir. (*Pause*) Can I ask you a question?

TROY: What the hell you wanna ask me? Mr. Stawicki the one you got the questions for.

CORY: How come you ain't never liked me?

TROY: Liked you? Who the hell say I got to like you? What law is there say I got to like you? Wanna stand up in my face and ask a damn fool-ass question like that. Talking about liking somebody. Come here, boy, when I talk to you.

(*Cory comes over to where Troy is working. He stands slouched over and Troy shoves him on his shoulder.*)

Straighten up, goddamn it! I asked you a question . . . what law is there say I got to like you?

CORY: None.

TROY: Well, all right then! Don't you eat every day? (*Pause*) Answer me when I talk to you! Don't you eat every day?

CORY: Yeah.

TROY: Nigger, as long as you in my house, you put that sir on the end of it when you talk to me!

CORY: Yes . . . sir.

TROY: You eat every day.

CORY: Yessir!

TROY: Got a roof over your head.

CORY: Yessir!

TROY: Got clothes on your back.

CORY: Yessir.

TROY: Why you think that is?

CORY: 'Cause of you.

TROY: Aw, hell, I know it's 'cause of me . . . but why do you think that is?

CORY (*Hesitant*): 'Cause you like me.

TROY: Like you? I go out of here every morning . . . bust my butt . . . putting up with them crackers every day . . . 'cause I like you? You about the biggest fool I ever saw. (*Pause*) It's my job. It's my responsibility! You understand that? A man got to take care of his family. You live in my house . . . sleep you behind on my bedclothes . . . fill you belly up with my food . . . 'cause you my son. You my flesh and blood. Not 'cause I like you! 'Cause it's my duty to take care of you. I owe a responsibility to you!

Let's get this straight right here . . . before it go along any further . . . . I ain't got to like you. Mr. Rand don't give me my money come payday 'cause he likes me. He gives me 'cause he owe me. I done give you everything I had to give you. I gave you your life! Me and your mama worked that out between us. And liking your black ass wasn't part of the bargain. Don't you try and go through life worrying about if somebody like you or not. You best be making sure they doing right by you. You understand what I'm saying, boy?

CORY: Yessir.

TROY: Then get the hell out of my face, and get on down to that A&P.

> (*Rose has been standing behind the screen door for much of the scene. She enters as Cory exits.*)

ROSE: Why don't you let the boy go ahead and play football, Troy? Ain't no harm in that. He's just trying to be like you with the sports.

TROY: I don't want him to be like me! I want him to move as far away from my life as he can get. You the only decent thing that ever happened to me. I wish him that. But I don't wish him a thing else from my life. I decided seventeen years ago that boy wasn't getting involved in no sports. Not after what they did to me in the sports.

ROSE: Troy, why don't you admit you was too old to play in the major leagues? For once . . . why don't you admit that?

TROY: What do you mean too old? Don't come telling me I was too old. I just wasn't the right color. Hell, I'm fifty-three years old and can do better than Selkirk's .269 right now!

ROSE: How's was you gonna play ball when you were over forty? Sometimes I can't get no sense out of you.

TROY: I got good sense, woman. I got sense enough not to let my boy get hurt over playing no sports. You been mothering that boy too much. Worried about if people like him.

ROSE: Everything that boy do . . . he do for you. He wants you to say, "Good job, son." That's all.

TROY: Rose, I ain't got time for that. He's alive. He's healthy. He's got to make his own way. I made mine. Ain't nobody gonna hold his hand when he get out there in that world.

ROSE: Times have changed from when you was young, Troy. People change. The world's changing around you and you can't even see it.

TROY (*Slow, methodical*): Woman . . . I do the best I can do. I come in here every Friday. I carry a sack of potatoes and a bucket of lard. You all line up at the door with your hands out. I give you the lint from my pockets. I give you my sweat and my blood. I ain't got no tears. I done spent them. We go upstairs in that room at night . . . and I fall down on you and try to blast a hole into forever. I get up Monday morning . . . find my lunch on the table. I go out. Make my way. Find my strength to carry me through to the next Friday. (*Pause*) That's all I got, Rose. That's all I got to give. I can't give nothing else.

(*Troy exits into the house. The lights fade to black.*)

Scene 4

It is Friday. Two weeks later. Cory starts out of the house with his football equipment. The phone rings.

CORY (*Calling*): I got it! (*Answers the phone, stands in the screen door talking*) Hello? Hey, Jesse. Naw . . . I was just getting ready to leave now.

ROSE (*Calling*): Cory!

CORY: I told you, man, them spikes is all tore up. You can use them if you want, but they ain't no good. Earl got some spikes.

ROSE (*Calling*): Cory!

CORY (*Calling to Rose*): Mam? I'm talking to Jesse. (*Into phone*) When she say that? (*Pause*) Aw, you lying, man. I'm gonna tell her you said that.

ROSE (*Calling*): Cory, don't you go nowhere!

CORY: I got to go to the game, Ma! (*Into the phone*) Yeah, hey, look, I'll talk to you later. Yeah, I'll meet you over Earl's house. Later. Bye, Ma.

(*Cory exits the house and starts out the yard.*)

ROSE: Cory, where you going off to? You got that stuff all pulled out and thrown all over your room.

CORY (*In the yard*): I was looking for my spikes. Jesse wanted to borrow my spikes.

ROSE: Get up there and get that cleaned up before your daddy get back in here.

CORY: I got to go to the game! I'll clean it up *when I get back*.

(*He exits.*)

ROSE: That's all he need to do is see that room all messed up.

(*Rose exits into the house. Troy and Bono enter the yard with a bottle. Troy is dressed in clothes other than his work clothes.*)

BONO: He told him the same thing he told you. Take it to the union.

TROY: Brownie ain't got that much sense. Man wasn't thinking about nothing. He wait until I confront them on it . . . then he wanna come crying seniority. (*Calls*) Hey, Rose!

BONO: I wish I could have seen Mr. Rand's face when he told you.

TROY: He couldn't get it out of his mouth! Liked to bit his tongue! When they called me down there to the commissioner's office . . . he thought they was gonna fire me. Like everybody else.

BONO: I didn't think they was gonna fire you. I thought they was gonna put you on the warning paper.

TROY: Hey, Rose! (*To Bono*) Yeah, Mr. Rand like to bit his tongue.

(*Troy breaks the seal on the bottle, takes a drink, and hands it to Bono.*)

BONO: I see you run right down to Taylors' and told that Alberta gal.

TROY (*Calling*): Hey, Rose! (*To Bono*) I told everybody. Hey, Rose! I went down there to cash my check.

ROSE (*Entering from the house*): Hush all that hollering, man! I know you out here. What they say down there at the commissioner's office?

TROY: You supposed to come when I call you, woman. Bono'll tell you that. (*To Bono*) Don't Lucille come when you call her?

ROSE: Man, hush your mouth. I ain't no dog . . . talk about "come when you call me."

TROY (*Puts his arm around Rose*): You hear this, Bono? I had me an old dog used to get uppity like that. You say, "C'mere, Blue!" . . . and he just lay there and look at you. End up getting a stick and chasing him away trying to make him come.

ROSE: I ain't studying you and your dog. I remember you used to sing that old song.

TROY (*Singing*):
Hear it ring! Hear it ring!
I had a dog his name was Blue.

ROSE: Don't nobody wanna hear you sing that old song.

TROY (*Singing*):
You know Blue was mighty true.

ROSE: Used to have Cory running around here singing that song.

BONO: Hell, I remember that song myself.

TROY (*Singing*):
You know Blue was a good old dog.
Blue treed a possum in a hollow log.

That was my daddy's song. My daddy made up that song.

ROSE: I don't care who made it up. Don't nobody wanna hear you sing it.

TROY (*Makes a song like calling a dog*): Come here, woman.

ROSE: You come in here carrying on, I reckon they ain't fired you. What they say down there at the commissioner's office?

TROY: Look here, Rose . . . Mr. Rand called me into his office today when I got back from talking to them people down there . . . it come from up top . . . he called me in and told me they was making me a driver.

ROSE: Troy, you kidding!

TROY: No I ain't. Ask Bono.

ROSE: Well, that's great, Troy. Now you don't have to hassle them people no more.

(*Lyons enters from the street.*)

TROY: Aw hell, I wasn't looking to see you today. I thought you was in jail. Got it all over the front page of the *Courier* about them raiding Seefus' place . . . where you be hanging out with all them thugs.

LYONS: Hey, Pop . . . that ain't got nothing to do with me. I don't go down there gambling. I go down there to sit in with the band. I ain't got nothing to do with the gambling part. They got some good music down there.

TROY: They got some rogues . . . is what they got.

LYONS: How you been, Mr. Bono? Hi, Rose.

BONO: I see where you playing down at the Crawford Grill tonight.

ROSE: How come you ain't brought Bonnie like I told you. You should have brought Bonnie with you, she ain't been over in a month of Sundays.

LYONS: I was just in the neighborhood . . . thought I'd stop by.

TROY: Here he come . . .

BONO: Your daddy got a promotion on the rubbish. He's gonna be the first colored driver. Ain't got to do nothing but sit up there and read the paper like them white fellows.

LYONS: Hey, Pop . . . if you knew how to read you'd be all right.

BONO: Naw . . . naw . . . you mean if the nigger knew how to *drive* he'd be all right. Been fighting with them people about driving and ain't even got a license. Mr. Rand know you ain't got no driver's license?

TROY: Driving ain't nothing. All you do is point the truck where you want it to go. Driving ain't nothing.

BONO: Do Mr. Rand know you ain't got no driver's license? That's what I'm talking about. I ain't asked if driving was easy. I asked if Mr. Rand know you ain't got no driver's license.

TROY: He ain't got to know. The man ain't got to know my business. Time he find out, I have two or three driver's licenses.

LYONS (*Going into his pocket*): Say, look here, Pop . . .

TROY: I knew it was coming. Didn't I tell you, Bono? I know what kind of "look here, Pop" that was. The nigger fixing to ask me for some money. It's Friday night. It's my payday. All them rogues down there on the avenue . . . the ones that ain't in jail . . . and Lyons is hopping in his shoes to get down there with them.

LYONS: See, Pop . . . if you'd give somebody else a chance to talk sometime, you'd see that I was fixing to pay you back your ten dollars like I told you. Here . . . I told you I'd pay you when Bonnie got paid.

TROY: Naw . . . you go ahead and keep that ten dollars. Put it in the bank. The next time you feel like you wanna come by here and ask me for something . . . you go on down there and get that.

LYONS: Here's your ten dollars, Pop. I told you I don't want you to give me nothing. I just wanted to borrow ten dollars.

TROY: Naw . . . you go on and keep that for the next time you want to ask me.

LYONS: Come on, Pop . . . here go your ten dollars.

ROSE: Why don't you go on and let the boy pay you back, Troy?

LYONS: Here you go, Rose. If you don't take it I'm gonna have to hear about it for the next six months. (*Hands her the money*)

ROSE: You can hand yours over here too, Troy.

TROY: You see this, Bono. You see how they do me.

BONO: Yeah, Lucille do me the same way.

(*Gabriel is heard singing offstage. He enters.*)

GABRIEL: Better get ready for the Judgment! Better get ready for . . . Hey! . . . Hey! There's Troy's boy!

LYONS: How you doing, Uncle Gabe?

GABRIEL: Lyons . . . The King of the Jungle! Rose . . . hey, Rose. Got a flower for you. (*Takes a rose from his pocket*) Picked it myself. That's the same rose like you is!

ROSE: That's right nice of you, Gabe.

LYONS: What you been doing, Uncle Gabe?

GABRIEL: Oh, I been chasing hellhounds and waiting on the time to tell Saint Peter to open the Gates.

LYONS: You been chasing hellhounds, huh? Well . . . you doing the right thing, Uncle Gabe. Somebody got to chase them.

GABRIEL: Oh, yeah . . . I know it. The devil's strong. The devil ain't no pushover. Hellhounds snipping at everybody's heels. But I got my trumpet waiting on the Judgment time.

LYONS: Waiting on the Battle of Armageddon,[7] huh?

GABRIEL: Ain't gonna be too much of a battle when God get to waving that Judgment sword. But the people's gonna have a hell of a time trying to get into Heaven if them Gates ain't open.

LYONS (*Putting his arm around Gabriel*): You hear this, Pop. Uncle Gabe, you all right!

GABRIEL (*Laughing with Lyons*): Lyons! King of the Jungle.

ROSE: You gonna stay for supper, Gabe. Want me to fix you a plate?

GABRIEL: I'll just take a sandwich, Rose. Don't want no plate. Just wanna eat with my hands. I'll take a sandwich.

ROSE: How about you, Lyons? You staying? Got some short ribs cooking.

LYONS: Naw, I won't eat nothing till after we finished playing. (*Pause*) You ought to come down and listen to me play, Pop.

TROY: I don't like that Chinese music. All that noise.

ROSE: Go on in the house and wash up, Gabe . . . I'll fix you a sandwich.

GABRIEL (*As he exits, to Lyons*): Troy's mad at me.

LYONS: What you mad at Uncle Gabe for, Pop.

ROSE: He thinks Troy's mad at him 'cause he moved over to Miss Pearl's.

TROY: I ain't mad at the man. He can live where he want to live at.

LYONS: What he move over there for? Miss Pearl don't like nobody.

ROSE: She don't mind him none. She treats him real nice. She just don't allow all that singing.

TROY: She don't mind that rent he be paying . . . that's what she don't mind.

ROSE: Troy, I ain't going through that with you no more. He's over there 'cause he want to have his own place. He can come and go as he please.

---

7. In Christian tradition, the final, history-ending battle between the armies of good and evil.

TROY: Hell, he could come and go as he please here. I wasn't stopping him. I ain't put no rules on him.

ROSE: It ain't the same thing, Troy. And you know it.

(*Gabriel comes to the screen door.*)

Now, that's the last I wanna hear about that. I don't wanna hear nothing else about Gabe and Miss Pearl. And next week . . .

GABRIEL: I'm ready for my sandwich, Rose.

ROSE: And next week . . . when that recruiter come from that school . . . I want you to sign that paper and go on and let Cory play football. Then that'll be the last I have to hear about that.

TROY (*To Rose as she exits into the house*): I ain't thinking about Cory nothing.

LYONS: What . . . Cory got recruited? What school he going to?

TROY: That boy walking around here smelling his piss . . . thinking he's grown. Thinking he's gonna do what he want, irrespective of what I say. Look here, Bono . . . I left the commissioner's office and went down to the A&P . . . that boy ain't working down there. He lying to me. Telling me he got his job back . . . telling me he working weekends . . . telling me he working after school . . . Mr. Stawicki tell me he ain't working down there at all!

LYONS: Cory just growing up. He's just busting at the seams trying to fill out your shoes.

TROY: I don't care what he's doing. When he get to the point where he wanna disobey me . . . then it's time for him to move on. Bono'll tell you that I bet he ain't never disobeyed his daddy without paying the consequences.

BONO: I ain't never had a chance. My daddy came on through . . . but I ain't never knew him to see him . . . or what he had on his mind or where he went. Just moving on through. Searching out the New Land. That's what the old folks used to call it. See a fellow moving around from place to place . . . woman to woman . . . called it Searching out the New Land. I can't say if he ever found it. I come along, didn't want no kids. Didn't know if I was gonna be in one place long enough to fix on them right as their daddy. I figured I was going searching too. As it turned out I been hooked up with Lucille near about as long as your daddy been with Rose. Going on sixteen years.

TROY: Sometimes I wish I hadn't known my daddy. He ain't cared nothing about no kids. A kid to him wasn't nothing. All he wanted was for you to learn how to walk so he could start you to working. When it come time for eating . . . he ate first. If there was anything left over, that's what you got. Man would sit down and eat two chickens and give you the wing.

LYONS: You ought to stop that, Pop. Everybody feed their kids. No matter how hard times is . . . everybody care about their kids. Make sure they have something to eat.

TROY: The only thing my daddy cared about was getting them bales of cotton in to Mr. Lubin. That's the only thing that mattered to him. Sometimes I used to wonder why he was living. Wonder why the devil hadn't come and got him. "Get them bales of cotton in to Mr. Lubin" and find out he owe him money . . .

LYONS: He should have just went on and left when he saw he couldn't get nowhere. That's what I would have done.

TROY: How he gonna leave with eleven kids? And where he gonna go? He ain't knew how to do nothing but farm. No, he was trapped and I think he knew it. But I'll say this for him . . . he felt a responsibility toward us. Maybe he ain't treated us the way I felt he should have . . . but without that responsibility he could have walked off and left us . . . made his own way.

BONO: A lot of them did. Back in those days what you talking about . . . they walk out their front door and just take on down one road or another and keep on walking.

LYONS: There you go! That's what I'm talking about.

BONO: Just keep on walking till you come to something else. Ain't you never heard of nobody having the walking blues? Well, that's what you call it when you just take off like that.

TROY: My daddy ain't had them walking blues! What you talking about? He stayed right there with his family. But he was just as evil as he could be. My mama couldn't stand him. Couldn't stand that evilness. She run off when I was about eight. She sneaked off one night after he had gone to sleep. Told me she was coming back for me. I ain't never seen her no more. All his women run off and left him. He wasn't good for nobody.

When my turn come to head out, I was fourteen and got to sniffing around Joe Canewell's daughter. Had us an old mule we called Greyboy. My daddy sent me out to do some plowing and I tied up Greyboy and went to fooling around with Joe Canewell's daughter. We done found us a nice spot, got real cozy with each other. She about thirteen and we done figured we was grown anyway . . . so we down there enjoying ourselves . . . ain't thinking about nothing. We didn't know Greyboy had got loose and wandered back to the house and my daddy was looking for me. We down there by the creek enjoying ourselves when my daddy come up on us. Surprised us. He had them leather straps off the mule and commenced to whupping me like there was no tomorrow. I jumped up, mad and embarrassed. I was scared of my daddy. When he commenced to whupping on me . . . quite naturally I run to get out of the way. (*Pause*) Now I thought he was mad 'cause I ain't done my work. But I see where he was chasing me off so he could have the gal for himself. When I see what the matter of it was, I lost all fear of my daddy. Right there is where I become a man . . . at fourteen years of age. (*Pause*) Now it was my turn to run him off. I picked up them same reins that he had used on me. I picked up them reins and commenced to whupping on him. The gal jumped up and run off . . . and when my daddy turned to face me, I could see why the devil had never come to get him . . . 'cause he was the devil himself. I don't know what happened. When I woke up, I was laying right there by the creek, and Blue . . . this old dog we had . . . was licking my face. I thought I was blind. I couldn't see nothing. Both my eyes were swollen shut. I laid there and cried. I didn't know what I was gonna do. The only thing I knew was the time had come for me to leave my daddy's house. And right there the world suddenly got big. And it was a long time before I could cut it down to where I could handle it.

Part of that cutting down was when I got to the place where I could feel him kicking in my blood and knew that the only thing that separated us was the matter of a few years.

(Gabriel enters from the house with a sandwich.)

LYONS: What you got there, Uncle Gabe?

GABRIEL: Got me a ham sandwich. Rose gave me a ham sandwich.

TROY: I don't know what happened to him. I done lost touch with everybody except Gabriel. But I hope he's dead. I hope he found some peace.

LYONS: That's a heavy story, Pop. I didn't know you left home when you was fourteen.

TROY: And didn't know nothing. The only part of the world I knew was the forty-two acres of Mr. Lubin's land. That's all I knew about life.

LYONS: Fourteen's kinda young to be out on your own. *(Phone rings)* I don't even think I was ready to be out on my own at fourteen. I don't know what I would have done.

TROY: I got up from the creek and walked on down to Mobile.[8] I was through with farming. Figured I could do better in the city. So I walked the two hundred miles to Mobile.

LYONS: Wait a minute . . . you ain't walked no two hundred miles, Pop. Ain't nobody gonna walk no two hundred miles. You talking about some walking there.

BONO: That's the only way you got anywhere back in them days.

LYONS: Shhh. Damn if I wouldn't have hitched a ride with somebody!

TROY: Who you gonna hitch it with? They ain't had no cars and things like they got now. We talking about 1918.

ROSE *(Entering)*: What you all out here getting into?

TROY *(To Rose)*: I'm telling Lyons how good he got it. He don't know nothing about this I'm talking.

ROSE: Lyons, that was Bonnie on the phone. She say you supposed to pick her up.

LYONS: Yeah, okay, Rose.

TROY: I walked on down to Mobile and hitched up with some of them fellows that was heading this way. Got up here and found out . . . not only couldn't you get a job . . . you couldn't find no place to live. I thought I was in freedom. Shhh. Colored folks living down there on the riverbanks in whatever kind of shelter they could find for themselves. Right down there under the Brady Street Bridge. Living in shacks made of sticks and tarpaper. Messed around there and went from bad to worse. Started stealing. First it was food. Then I figured, hell, if I steal money I can buy me some food. Buy me some shoes too! One thing led to another. Met your mama. I was young and anxious to be a man. Met your mama and had you. What I do that for? Now I got to worry about feeding you and her. Got to steal three times as much. Went out one day looking for somebody to rob . . . that's what I was, a robber. I'll tell you the truth. I'm ashamed of it today. But it's the truth. Went to rob this fellow . . . pulled out my knife . . . and he pulled out a gun. Shot me in the chest. It felt just like somebody had taken a hot branding iron and laid it on me. When he shot me I jumped at him with my knife. They told me I killed him and they put me in the penitentiary and locked me up for fifteen years. That's where I met Bono. That's where I learned how to play baseball. Got

8. City in southwest Alabama, on the Gulf Coast near the Florida state line.

out that place and your mama had taken you and went on to make life without me. Fifteen years was a long time for her to wait. But that fifteen years cured me of that robbing stuff. Rose'll tell you. She asked me when I met her if I had gotten all that foolishness out of my system. And I told her, "Baby, it's you and baseball all what count with me." You hear me, Bono? I meant it too. She say, "Which one comes first?" I told her, "Baby, ain't no doubt it's baseball . . . but you stick and get old with me and we'll both outlive this baseball." Am I right, Rose? And it's true.

ROSE: Man, hush your mouth. You ain't said no such thing. Talking about, "Baby, you know you'll always be number one with me." That's what you was talking.

TROY: You hear that, Bono. That's why I love her.

BONO: Rose'll keep you straight. You get off the track, she'll straighten you up.

ROSE: Lyons, you better get on up and get Bonnie. She waiting on you.

LYONS (Gets up to go): Hey, Pop, why don't you come on down to the Grill and hear me play?

TROY: I ain't going down there. I'm too old to be sitting around in them clubs.

BONO: You got to be good to play down at the Grill.

LYONS: Come on, Pop . . .

TROY: I got to get up in the morning.

LYONS: You ain't got to stay long.

TROY: Naw, I'm gonna get my supper and go on to bed.

LYONS: Well, I got to go. I'll see you again.

TROY: Don't you come around my house on my payday.

ROSE: Pick up the phone and let somebody know you coming. And bring Bonnie with you. You know I'm always glad to see her.

LYONS: Yeah, I'll do that, Rose. You take care now. See you, Pop. See you, Mr. Bono. See you, Uncle Gabe.

GABRIEL: Lyons! King of the Jungle!

(Lyons exits.)

TROY: Is supper ready, woman? Me and you got some business to take care of. I'm gonna tear it up too.

ROSE: Troy, I done told you now!

TROY (Puts his arm around Bono): Aw hell, woman . . . this is Bono. Bono like family. I done known this nigger since . . . how long I done know you?

BONO: It's been a long time.

TROY: I done known this nigger since Skippy was a pup. Me and him done been through some times.

BONO: You sure right about that.

TROY: Hell, I done know him longer than I known you. And we still standing shoulder to shoulder. Hey, look here, Bono . . . a man can't ask for no more than that. (Drinks to him) I love you, nigger.

BONO: Hell, I love you too . . . but I got to get home see my woman. You got yours in hand. I got to go get mine.

(Bono starts to exit as Cory enters the yard, dressed in his football uniform. He gives Troy a hard, uncompromising look.)

CORY: What you do that for, Pop? (*Throws his helmet down in the direction of Troy*)

ROSE: What's the matter? Cory . . . what's the matter?

CORY: Papa done went up to the school and told Coach Zellman I can't play football no more. Wouldn't even let me play the game. Told him to tell the recruiter not to come.

ROSE: Troy . . .

TROY: What you Troying me for. Yeah, I did it. And the boy know why I did it.

CORY: Why you wanna do that to me? That was the one chance I had.

ROSE: Ain't nothing wrong with Cory playing football, Troy.

TROY: The boy lied to me. I told the nigger if he wanna play football . . . to keep up his chores and hold down that job at the A&P. That was the conditions. Stopped down there to see Mr. Stawicki . . .

CORY: I can't work after school during the football season, Pop! I tried to tell you that Mr. Stawicki's holding my job for me. You don't never want to listen to nobody. And then you wanna go and do this to me!

TROY: I ain't done nothing to you. You done it to yourself.

CORY: Just 'cause you didn't have a chance! You just scared I'm gonna be better than you, that's all.

TROY: Come here.

ROSE: Troy . . .

(*Cory reluctantly crosses over to Troy.*)

TROY: All right! See. You done made a mistake.

CORY: I didn't even do nothing!

TROY: I'm gonna tell you what your mistake was. See . . . you swung at the ball and didn't hit it. That's strike one. See, you in the batter's box now. You swung and you missed. That's strike one. Don't you strike out!

(*The lights go down on the scene.*)

ACT TWO

Scene 1

The following morning. Cory is at the tree hitting the ball with the bat. He tries to mimic Troy, but his swing is awkward, less sure. Rose enters from the house.

ROSE: Cory, I want you to help me with this cupboard.

CORY: I ain't quitting the team. I don't care what Poppa say.

ROSE: I'll talk to him when he gets back. He had to go see about your Uncle Gabe. The police done arrested him. Say he was disturbing the peace. He'll be back directly. Come on in here and help me clean out the top of this cupboard.

(*Cory exits into the house. Rose sees Troy and Bono coming down the alley.*)

Troy . . . what they say down there?

TROY: Ain't said nothing. I give them fifty dollars and they let him go. I'll talk to you about it. Where's Cory?

ROSE: He's in there helping me clean out these cupboards.

TROY: Tell him to get his butt out here.

> (*Troy and Bono go over to the pile of wood. Bono picks up the saw and begins sawing.*)

(*To Bono*) All they want is the money. That makes six or seven times I done went down there and got him. See me coming they stick out their *hands.*

BONO: Yeah, I know what you mean. That's all they care about . . . that money. They don't care about what's right. (*Pause*) Nigger, why you got to go and get some hard wood? You ain't doing nothing but building a little old fence. Get you some soft pine wood. That's all you need.

TROY: I know what I'm doing. This is outside wood. You put pine wood inside the house. Pine wood is inside wood. This here is outside wood. Now you tell me where the fence is gonna be?

BONO: You don't need this wood. You can put it up with pine wood and it'll stand as long as you gonna be here looking at it.

TROY: How you know how long I'm gonna be here, nigger? Hell, I might just live forever. Live longer than old man Horsely.

BONO: That's what Magee used to say.

TROY: Magee's a damn fool. Now you tell me who you ever heard of gonna pull their own teeth with a pair of rusty pliers.

BONO: The old folks . . . my granddaddy used to pull his teeth with pliers. They ain't had no dentists for the colored folks back then.

TROY: Get clean pliers! You understand? Clean pliers! Sterilize them! Besides we ain't living back then. All Magee had to do was walk over to Doc Goldblum's.

BONO: I see where you and that Tallahassee gal . . . that Alberta . . . I see where you all done got tight.

TROY: What you mean "got tight"?

BONO: I see where you be laughing and joking with her all the time.

TROY: I laughs and jokes with all of them, Bono. You know me.

BONO: That ain't the kind of laughing and joking I'm talking about.

> (*Cory enters from the house.*)

CORY: How you doing, Mr. Bono?

TROY: Cory? Get that saw from Bono and cut some wood. He talking about the wood's too hard to cut. Stand back there, Jim, and let that young boy show you how it's done.

BONO: He's sure welcome to it.

> (*Cory takes the saw and begins to cut the wood.*)

Whew-e-e! Look at that. Big old strong boy. Look like Joe Louis.[9] Hell, must be getting old the way I'm watching that boy whip through that wood.

CORY: I don't see why Mama want a fence around the yard noways.

---

9. Alabama-born boxer (1914–81) known as the "Brown Bomber," world heavyweight champion 1937–49.

TROY: Damn if I know either. What the hell she keeping out with it? She ain't got nothing nobody want.

BONO: Some people build fences to keep people out . . . and other people build fences to keep people in. Rose wants to hold on to you all. She loves you.

TROY: Hell, nigger, I don't need nobody to tell me my wife loves me, Cory . . . go on in the house and see if you can find that other saw.

CORY: Where's it at?

TROY: I said find it! Look for it till you find it!

(Cory exits into the house.)

What's that supposed to mean? Wanna keep us in?

BONO: Troy . . . I done known you seem like damn near my whole life. You and Rose both. I done know both of you all for a long time. I remember when you met Rose. When you was hitting them baseball out the park. A lot of them old gals was after you then. You had the pick of the litter. When you picked Rose, I was happy for you. That was the first time I knew you had any sense. I said . . . My man Troy knows what he's doing . . . I'm gonna follow this nigger . . . he might take me somewhere. I been following you too. I done learned a whole heap of things about life watching you. I done learned how to tell where the shit lies. How to tell it from the alfalfa. You done learned me a lot of things. You showed me how to not make the same mistakes . . . to take life as it comes along and keep putting one foot in front of the other. *(Pause)* Rose a good woman, Troy.

TROY: Hell, nigger, I know she a good woman. I been married to her for eighteen years. What you got on your mind, Bono?

BONO: I just say she a good woman. Just like I say anything. I ain't got to have nothing on my mind.

TROY: You just gonna say she a good woman and leave it hanging out there like that? Why you telling me she a good woman?

BONO: She loves you, Troy. Rose loves you.

TROY: You saying I don't measure up. That's what you trying to say. I don't measure up 'cause I'm seeing this other gal. I know what you trying to say.

BONO: I know what Rose means to you, Troy. I'm just trying to say I don't want to see you mess up.

TROY: Yeah, I appreciate that, Bono. If you was messing around on Lucille I'd be telling you the same thing.

BONO: Well, that's all I got to say. I just say that because I love you both.

TROY: Hell, you know me . . . I wasn't out there looking for nothing. You can't find a better woman than Rose. I know that. But seems like this woman just stuck on to me where I can't shake her loose. I done wrestled with it, tried to throw her off me . . . but she just stuck on tighter. Now she's stuck on for good.

BONO: You's in control . . . that's what you tell me all the time. You responsible for what you do.

TROY: I ain't ducking the responsibility of it. As long as it sets right in my heart . . . then I'm okay. 'Cause that's all I listen to. It'll tell me right from wrong every time. And I ain't talking about doing Rose no bad turn. I love Rose. She done carried me a long ways and I love and respect her for that.

BONO: I know you do. That's why I don't want to see you hurt her. But what you gonna do when she find out? What you got then? If you try and juggle both of them . . . sooner or later you gonna drop one of them. That's common sense.

TROY: Yeah, I hear what you saying, Bono. I been trying to figure a way to work it out.

BONO: Work it out right, Troy. I don't want to be getting all up between you and Rose's business . . . but work it so it come out right.

TROY: Aw hell, I get all up between you and Lucille's business. When you gonna get that woman that refrigerator she been wanting? Don't tell me you ain't got no money now. I know who your banker is. Mellon don't need that money bad as Lucille want that refrigerator. I'll tell you that.

BONO: Tell you what I'll do . . . when you finish building this fence for Rose . . . I'll buy Lucille that refrigerator.

TROY: You done stuck your foot in your mouth now!

(Troy grabs up a board and begins to saw. Bono starts to walk out the yard.)

Hey, nigger . . . where you going?

BONO: I'm going home. I know you don't expect me to help you now. I'm protecting my money. I wanna see you put up that fence by yourself. That's what I want to see. You'll be here another six months without me.

TROY: Nigger, you ain't right.

BONO: When it comes to my money . . . I'm as right as fireworks on the Fourth of July.

TROY: All right, we gonna see now. You better get out your bankbook.

(Bono exits, and Troy continues to work. Rose enters from the house.)

ROSE: What they say down there? What's happening with Gabe?

TROY: I went down there and got him out. Cost me fifty dollars. Say he was disturbing the peace. Judge set up a hearing for him in three weeks. Say to show cause why he shouldn't be recommitted.

ROSE: What was he doing that cause them to arrest him?

TROY: Some kids was teasing him and he run them off home. Say he was howling and carrying on. Some folks seen him and called the police. That's all it was.

ROSE: Well, what's you say? What'd you tell the judge?

TROY: Told him I'd look after him. It didn't make no sense to recommit the man. He stuck out his big greasy palm and told me to give him fifty dollars and take him on home.

ROSE: Where's he at now? Where'd he go off to?

TROY: He's gone on about his business. He don't need nobody to hold his hand.

ROSE: Well, I don't know. Seem like that would be the best place for him if they did put him into the hospital. I know what you're gonna say. But that's what I think would be best.

TROY: The man done had his life ruined fighting for what? And they wanna take and lock him up. Let him be free. He don't bother nobody.

ROSE: Well, everybody got their own way of looking at it I guess. Come on and get your lunch. I got a bowl of lima beans and some cornbread in the oven.

Come on get something to eat. Ain't no sense you fretting over Gabe. (*Turns to go in the house*)

TROY: Rose . . . got something to tell you.

ROSE: Well, come on . . . wait till I get this food on the table.

TROY: Rose!

(*She stops and turns around.*)

I don't know how to say this. (*Pause*) I can't explain it none. It just sort of grows on you till it gets out of hand. It starts out like a little bush . . . and the next thing you know it's a whole forest.

ROSE: Troy . . . what is you talking about?

TROY: I'm talking, woman, let me talk. I'm trying to find a way to tell you . . . I'm gonna be a daddy. I'm gonna be somebody's daddy.

ROSE: Troy . . . you're not telling me this? You're gonna be . . . what?

TROY: Rose . . . now . . . see . . .

ROSE: You telling me you gonna be somebody's daddy? You telling your *wife* this?

(*Gabriel enters from the street. He carries a rose in his hand.*)

GABRIEL: Hey, Troy! Hey, Rose!

ROSE: I have to wait eighteen years to hear something like this.

GABRIEL: Hey, Rose . . . I got a flower for you. (*Hands it to her*) That's a rose. Same rose like you is.

ROSE: Thanks, Gabe.

GABRIEL: Troy, you ain't mad at me is you? Them bad mens come and put me away. You ain't mad at me is you?

TROY: Naw, Gabe, I ain't mad at you.

ROSE: Eighteen years and you wanna come with this.

GABRIEL (*Takes a quarter out of his pocket*): See what I got? Got a brand-new quarter.

TROY: Rose . . . it's just . . .

ROSE: Ain't nothing you can say, Troy. Ain't no way of explaining that.

GABRIEL: Fellow that give me this quarter had a whole mess of them. I'm gonna keep this quarter till it stop shining.

ROSE: Gabe, go on in the house there. I got some watermelon in the frigidaire. Go on and get you a piece.

GABRIEL: Say, Rose . . . you know I was chasing hellhounds and them bad mens come and get me and take me away. Troy helped me. He come down there and told them they better let me go before he beat them up. Yeah, he did!

ROSE: You go on and get you a piece of watermelon, Gabe. Them bad mens is gone now.

GABRIEL: Okay, Rose . . . gonna get me some watermelon. The kind with the stripes on it.

(*Gabriel exits into the house.*)

ROSE: Why, Troy? Why? After all these years to come dragging this in to me now. It don't make no sense at your age. I could have expected this ten or fifteen years ago, but not now.

TROY: Age ain't got nothing to do with it, Rose.

ROSE: I done tried to be everything a wife should be. Everything a wife could be. Been married eighteen years and I got to live to see the day you tell me you been seeing another woman and done fathered a child by her. And you know I ain't never wanted no half nothing in my family. My whole family is half. Everybody got different fathers and mothers . . . my two sisters and my brother. Can't hardly tell who's who. Can't never sit down and talk about Papa and Mama. It's your papa and your mama and my papa and my mama . .

TROY: Rose . . . stop it now.

ROSE: I ain't never wanted that for none of my children. And now you wanna drag your behind in here and tell me something like this.

TROY: You ought to know. It's time for you to know.

ROSE: Well, I don't want to know, goddamn it!

TROY: I can't just make it go away. It's done now. I can't wish the circumstance of the thing away.

ROSE: And you don't want to either. Maybe you want to wish me and my boy away. Maybe that's what you want? Well, you can't wish us away. I've got eighteen years of my life invested in you. You ought to have stayed upstairs in my bed where you belong.

TROY: Rose . . . now listen to me . . . we can get a handle on this thing. We can talk this out . . . come to an understanding.

ROSE: All of a sudden it's "we." Where was "we" at when you was down there rolling around with some godforsaken woman? "We" should have come to an understanding before you started making a damn fool of yourself. You're a day late and a dollar short when it comes to an understanding with me.

TROY: It's just . . . She gives me a different idea . . . a different understanding about myself. I can step out of this house and get away from the pressures and problems . . . be a different man. I ain't got to wonder how I'm gonna pay the bills or get the roof fixed. I can just be a part of myself that I ain't never been.

ROSE: What I want to know . . . is do you plan to continue seeing her. That's all you can say to me.

TROY: I can sit up in her house and laugh. Do you understand what I'm saying. I can laugh out loud . . . and it feels good. It reaches all the way down to the bottom of my shoes. (Pause) Rose, I can't give that up.

ROSE: Maybe you ought to go on and stay down there with her . . . if she a better woman than me.

TROY: It ain't about nobody being a better woman or nothing. Rose, you ain't to blame. A man couldn't ask for no woman to be a better wife than you've been. I'm responsible for it. I done locked myself into a pattern trying to take care of you all that I forgot about myself.

ROSE: What the hell was I there for? That was my job, not somebody else's

TROY: Rose, I done tried all my life to live decent . . . to live a clean . . . hard . . . useful life. I tried to be a good husband to you. In every way I knew how. Maybe I come into the world backwards, I don't know. But . . . you born with two strikes on you before you come to the plate. You got to guard it closely . . . always looking for the curveball on the inside corner. You can't afford to let none get past you. You can't afford a call strike. If you going down . . . you going down swinging. Everything lined up against you. What you gonna do. I fooled them,

Rose. I bunted. When I found you and Cory and a halfway decent job . . . I was safe. Couldn't nothing touch me. I wasn't gonna strike out no more. I wasn't going back to the penitentiary, I wasn't gonna lay in the streets with a bottle of wine. I was safe. I had me a family. A job. I wasn't gonna get that last strike. I was on first looking for one of them boys to knock me in. To get me home.

ROSE: You should have stayed in my bed, Troy.

TROY: Then when I saw that girl . . . she firmed up my backbone. And I got to thinking that if I tried . . . I just might be able to steal second. Do you understand, after eighteen years I wanted to steal second.

ROSE: You should have held me tight. You should have grabbed me and held on.

TROY: I stood on first base for eighteen years and I thought . . . well, goddamn it . . . go on for it!

ROSE: We're not talking about baseball! We're talking about you going off to lay in bed with another woman . . . and then bring it home to me. That's what we're talking about. We ain't talking about no baseball.

TROY: Rose, you're not listening to me. I'm trying the best I can to explain it to you. It's not easy for me to admit that I been standing in the same place for eighteen years.

ROSE: I been standing with you! I been right here with you, Troy. I got a life too. I gave eighteen years of my life to stand in the same spot with you. Don't you think I ever wanted other things? Don't you think I had dreams and hopes? What about my life? What about me? Don't you think it ever crossed my mind to want to know other men? That I wanted to lay up somewhere and forget about my responsibilities? That I wanted someone to make me laugh so I could feel good? You not the only one who's got wants and needs. But I held on to you, Troy. I took all my feelings, my wants and needs, my dreams . . . and I buried them inside you. I planted a seed and watched and prayed over it. I planted myself inside you and waited to bloom. And it didn't take me no eighteen years to find out the soil was hard and rocky and it wasn't never gonna bloom.

But I held on to you, Troy. I held you tighter. You was my husband. I owed you everything I had. Every part of me I could find to give you. And upstairs in that room . . . with the darkness falling in on me . . . I gave everything I had to try and erase the doubt that you wasn't the finest man in the world. And wherever you was going . . . I wanted to be there with you. 'Cause you was my husband. 'Cause that's the only way I was gonna survive as your wife. You always talking about what you give . . . and what you don't have to give. But you take too. You take . . . and don't even know nobody's giving!

(*Rose turns to exit into the house; Troy grabs her arm.*)

TROY: You say I take and don't give!

ROSE: Troy! You're hurting me.

TROY: You say I take and don't give.

ROSE: Troy . . . you're hurting my arm! Let go!

TROY: I done give you everything I got. Don't you tell that lie on me.

ROSE: Troy!

TROY: Don't you tell that lie on me!

(*Cory enters from the house.*)

CORY: Mama!

ROSE: Troy, you're hurting me.

TROY: Don't you tell me about no taking and giving.

> (*Cory comes up behind Troy and grabs him. Troy, surprised, is thrown off balance just as Cory throws a glancing blow that catches him on the chest and knocks him down. Troy is stunned, as is Cory.*)

ROSE: Troy. Troy. No!

> (*Troy gets to his feet and starts at Cory.*)
>
> *Troy . . . no. Please! Troy!*
>
> (*Rose pulls on Troy to hold him back. Troy stops himself.*)

TROY (*To Cory*): All right. That's strike two. You stay away from around me, boy. Don't you strike out. You living with a full count. Don't you strike out.

> (*Troy exits out the yard as the lights go down on the scene.*)

Scene 2

It is six months later, early afternoon. Troy enters from the house and starts to exit the yard. Rose enters from the house.

ROSE: Troy, I want to talk to you.

TROY: All of a sudden, after all this time, you want to talk to me, huh? You ain't wanted to talk to me for months. You ain't wanted to talk to me last night. You ain't wanted no part of me then. What you wanna talk to me about now?

ROSE: Tomorrow's Friday.

TROY: I know what day tomorrow is. You think I don't know tomorrow's Friday? My whole life I ain't done nothing but look to see Friday coming and you got to tell me it's Friday.

ROSE: I want to know if you're coming home.

TROY: I always come home, Rose. You know that. There ain't never been a night I ain't come home.

ROSE: That ain't what I mean . . . and you know it. I want to know if you're coming straight home after work.

TROY: I figured I'd cash my check . . . hang out at Taylors' with the boys . . . maybe play a game of checkers . . .

ROSE: Troy, I can't live like this. I won't live like this. You livin' on borrowed time with me. It's been going on six months now you ain't been coming home.

TROY: I be here every night. Every night of the year. That's three hundred sixty-five days.

ROSE: I want you to come home tomorrow after work.

TROY: Rose . . . I don't mess up my pay. You know that now. I take my pay and I give it to you. I don't have no money but what you give me back. I just want to have a little time to myself . . . a little time to enjoy life.

ROSE: What about me? When's my time to enjoy life?

TROY: I don't know what to tell you, Rose. I'm doing the best I can.

ROSE: You ain't come home from work but time enough to change your clothes and run out . . . and you wanna call that the best you can do?

TROY: I'm going over to the hospital to see Alberta. She went into the hospital this afternoon. Look like she might have the baby early. I won't be gone long.

ROSE: Well, you ought to know. They went over to Miss Pearl's and got Gabe today. She said you told them to go ahead and lock him up.

TROY: I ain't said no such thing. Whoever told you that is telling a lie. Pearl ain't doing nothing but telling a big fat lie.

ROSE: She ain't had to tell me. I read it on the papers.

TROY: I ain't told them nothing of the kind.

ROSE: I saw it right there on the papers.

TROY: What it say, huh?

ROSE: It said you told them to take him.

TROY: Then they screwed that up, just the way they screw up everything. I ain't worried about what they got on the paper.

ROSE: Say the government send part of his check to the hospital and the other part to you.

TROY: I ain't got nothing to do with that if that's the way it works. I ain't made up the rules about how it work.

ROSE: You did Gabe just like you did Cory. You wouldn't sign the paper for Cory . . . but you signed for Gabe. You signed that paper.

(The phone is heard ringing inside the house.)

TROY: I told you I ain't signed nothing, woman! The only thing I signed was the release form. Hell, I can't read, I don't know what they had on that paper! I ain't signed nothing about sending Gabe away.

ROSE: I said send him to the hospital . . . you said let him be free . . . now you done went down there and signed him to the hospital for half his money. You went back on yourself, Troy. You gonna have to answer for that.

TROY: See now . . . you been over there talking to Miss Pearl. She done got mad 'cause she ain't getting Gabe's rent money. That's all it is. She's liable to say anything.

ROSE: Troy, I seen where you signed the paper.

TROY: You ain't seen nothing I signed. What she doing got papers on my brother anyway? Miss Pearl telling a big fat lie. And I'm gonna tell her about it too! You ain't seen nothing I signed. Say . . . you ain't seen nothing I signed.

(Rose exits into the house to answer the phone. She returns.)

ROSE: Troy . . . that was the hospital. Alberta had the baby.

TROY: What she have? What is it?

ROSE: It's a girl.

TROY: I better get on down to the hospital to see her.

ROSE: Troy . . .

TROY: Rose . . . I got to go see her now. That's only right . . . what's the matter . . . the baby's all right, ain't it?

ROSE: Alberta died having the baby.

TROY: Died . . . you say she's dead? Alberta's dead?

ROSE: They said they done all they could. They couldn't do nothing for her.

TROY: The baby? How's the baby?

ROSE: They say it's healthy. I wonder who's gonna bury her.

TROY: She had family, Rose. She wasn't living in the world by herself.

ROSE: I know she wasn't living in the world by herself.

TROY: Next thing you gonna want to know if she had any insurance.

ROSE: Troy, you ain't got to talk like that.

TROY: That's the first thing that jumped out your mouth. "Who's gonna bury her?"
Like I'm fixing to take on that task for myself.

ROSE: I am your wife. Don't push me away.

TROY: I ain't pushing nobody away. Just give me some space. That's all. Just give
me some room to breathe.

(*Rose exits into the house. Troy walks about the yard.*)

(*With a quiet rage that threatens to consume him*) All right . . . Mr. Death. See
now . . . I'm gonna tell you what I'm gonna do. I'm gonna take and build me
a fence around this yard. See? I'm gonna build me a fence around what
belongs to me. And then I want you to stay on the other side. See? You stay
over there until you're ready for me. Then you come on. Bring your army.
Bring your sickle. Bring your wrestling clothes. I ain't gonna fall down on my
vigilance this time. You ain't gonna sneak up on me no more. When you ready
for me . . . when the top of your list say "Troy Maxson" . . . that's when you
come around here. You come up and knock on the front door. Ain't nobody
else got nothing to do with this. This is between you and me. Man to man.
You stay on the other side of that fence until you ready for me. Then you come
up and knock on the front door. Anytime you want. I'll be ready for you.

(*The lights fade to black.*)

Scene 3

*The lights come up on the porch. It is late evening three days later. Rose sits lis-
tening to the ball game, waiting for Troy. The final out of the game is made and
Rose switches off the radio. Troy enters the yard carrying an infant wrapped in
blankets. He stands back from the house and calls.*

*Rose enters and stands on the porch. There is a long, awkward silence, the
weight of which grows heavier with each passing second.*

TROY: Rose . . . I'm standing here with my daughter in my arms. She ain't but a
wee bitty little old thing. She don't know nothing about grownups' business.
She innocent . . . and she ain't got no mama.

ROSE: What you telling me for, Troy?

(*She turns and exits into the house.*)

TROY: Well . . . I guess we'll just sit out here on the porch.

(*He sits down on the porch. There is an awkward indelicateness about the
way he handles the baby. His largeness engulfs and seems to swallow her. He
speaks loud enough for Rose to hear:*)

A man's got to do what's right for him. I ain't sorry for nothing I done. It felt right in my heart. (*To the baby*) What you smiling at? Your daddy's a big man. Got these great big old hands. But sometimes he's scared. And right now your daddy's scared 'cause we sitting out here and ain't got no home. Oh, I been homeless before. I ain't had no little baby with me. But I been homeless. You just be out on the road by your lonesome and you see one of them trains coming and you just kinda go like this . . . (*Singing, as a lullaby:*)

> Please, Mr. Engineer, let a man ride the line
> Please, Mr. Engineer, let a man ride the line
> I ain't got no ticket please let me ride the blinds.[1]

(*Rose enters from the house. Troy hearing her steps behind him, stands and faces her.*)

She's my daughter, Rose. My own flesh and blood. I can't deny her no more than I can deny them boys. (*Pause*) You and them boys is my family. You and them and this child is all I got in the world. So I guess what I'm saying is . . . I'd appreciate it if you'd help me take care of her.

ROSE: Okay, Troy . . . you're right. I'll take care of your baby for you . . . 'cause . . . like you say . . . she's innocent . . . and you can't visit the sins of the father upon the child. A motherless child has got a hard time. (*Takes the baby from him*) From right now . . . this child got a mother. But you a womanless man.

(*Rose turns and exits into the house with the baby. The lights fade to black.*)

Scene 4

It is two months later. Lyons enters from the street. He knocks on the door and calls.

LYONS: Hey, Rose! (*Pause*) Rose!

ROSE (*From inside the house*): Stop that yelling. You gonna wake up Raynell. I just got her to sleep.

LYONS: I just stopped by to pay Papa this twenty dollars I owe him. Where's Papa at?

ROSE: He should be here in a minute. I'm getting ready to go down to the church. Sit down and wait on him.

LYONS: I got to go pick up Bonnie over her mother's house.

ROSE: Well, sit it down there on the table. He'll get it.

LYONS: (*Enters the house and sets the money on the table*): Tell Papa I said thanks. I'll see you again.

ROSE: All right, Lyons. We'll see you.

(*Lyons starts to exit as Cory enters.*)

CORY: Hey, Lyons.

1. That is, hitch a free ride on the platform outside a rail car with no door at one end (hence, "blind").

LYONS: What's happening, Cory. Say man, I'm sorry I missed your graduation. You know I had a gig and couldn't get away. Otherwise, I would have been there, man. So what you doing?

CORY: I'm trying to find a job.

LYONS: Yeah, I know how that go, man. It's rough out here. Jobs are scarce.

CORY: Yeah, I know.

LYONS: Look here, I got to run. Talk to Papa . . . he know some people. He'll be able to help get you a job. Talk to him . . . see what he say.

CORY: Yeah . . . all right, Lyons.

LYONS: You take care. I'll talk to you soon. We'll find some time to talk.

> (*Lyons exits the yard. Cory wanders over to the tree, picks up the bat and assumes a batting stance. He studies an imaginary pitcher and swings. Dissatisfied with the result, he tries again. Troy enters. They eye each other for a beat. Cory puts the bat down and exits the yard. Troy starts into the house as Rose exits with Raynell. She is carrying a cake.*)

TROY: I'm coming in and everybody's going out.

ROSE: I'm taking this cake down to the church for the bake sale. Lyons was by to see you. He stopped by to pay you your twenty dollars. It's laying in there on the table.

TROY (*Going into his pocket*): Well . . . here go this money.

ROSE: Put it in there on the table, Troy. I'll get it.

TROY: What time you coming back?

ROSE: Ain't no use in you studying me. It don't matter what time I come back.

TROY: I just asked you a question, woman. What's the matter . . . can't I ask you a question?

ROSE: Troy, I don't want to go into it. Your dinner's in there on the stove. All you got to do is heat it up. And don't you be eating the rest of them cakes in there. I'm coming back for them. We having a bake sale at the church tomorrow.

> (*Rose exits the yard. Troy sits down on the steps, takes a pint bottle from his pocket, opens it and drinks. He begins to sing:*)

TROY:
> Hear it ring! Hear it ring!
> Had an old dog his name was Blue
> You know Blue was mighty true
> You know Blue was a good old dog
> Blue treed a possum in a hollow log
> You know from that he was a good old dog.

> (*Bono enters the yard.*)

BONO: Hey, Troy.

TROY: Hey, what's happening, Bono?

BONO: I just thought I'd stop by to see you.

TROY: What you stop by and see me for? You ain't stopped by in a month of Sundays. Hell, I must owe you money or something.

BONO: Since you got your promotion I can't keep up with you. Used to see you every day. Now I don't even know what route you working.

TROY: They keep switching me around. Got me out in Greentree now . . . hauling white folks' garbage.

BONO: Greentree, huh? You lucky, at least you ain't got to be lifting them barrels. Damn if they ain't getting heavier. I'm gonna put in my two years and call it quits.

TROY: I'm thinking about retiring myself.

BONO: You got it easy. You can *drive* for another five years.

TROY: It ain't the same, Bono. It ain't like working the back of the truck. Ain't got nobody to talk to . . . feel like you working by yourself. Naw, I'm thinking about retiring. How's Lucille?

BONO: She all right. Her arthritis get to acting up on her sometime. Saw Rose on my way in. She going down to the church, huh?

TROY: Yeah, she took up going down there. All them preachers looking for somebody to fatten their pockets. *(Pause)* Got some gin here.

BONO: Naw, thanks. I just stopped by to say hello.

TROY: Hell, nigger . . . you can take a drink. I ain't never known you to say no to a drink. You ain't got to work tomorrow.

BONO: I just stopped by. I'm fixing to go over to Skinner's. We got us a domino game going over his house every Friday.

TROY: Nigger, you can't play no dominoes. I used to whup you four games out of five.

BONO: Well, that learned me. I'm getting better.

TROY: Yeah? Well, that's all right.

BONO: Look here . . . I got to be getting on. Stop by sometime, huh?

TROY: Yeah, I'll do that, Bono. Lucille told Rose you bought her a new refrigerator.

BONO: Yeah, Rose told Lucille you had finally built your fence . . . so I figured we'd call it even.

TROY: I knew you would.

BONO: Yeah . . . okay. I'll be talking to you.

TROY: Yeah, take care, Bono. Good to see you. I'm gonna stop over.

BONO: Yeah. Okay, Troy.

(Bono exits. Troy drinks from the bottle.)

TROY:
Old Blue died and I dug his grave
Let him down with a golden chain
Every night when I hear old Blue bark
I know Blue treed a possum in Noah's Ark.
Hear it ring! Hear it ring!

(Cory enters the yard. Cory and Troy eye each other for a beat. Cory walks over to Troy, who sits in the middle of the steps.)

CORY: I got to get by.

TROY: Say what? What's you say?

CORY: You in my way. I got to get by.

TROY: You got to get by where? This is my house. Bought and paid for. In full. Took me fifteen years. And if you wanna go in my house and I'm sitting on the steps . . . you say excuse me. Like your mama taught you.

CORY: Come on, Pop . . . I got to get by.

(*Cory starts to maneuver his way past Troy. Troy grabs his leg and shoves him back.*)

TROY: You just gonna walk over top of me?

CORY: I live here too!

TROY (*Advancing on him*): You just gonna walk over top of me in my own house?

CORY: I ain't scared of you.

TROY: I ain't asked if you was scared of me. I asked you if you was fixing to walk over top of me in my own house? That's the question. You ain't gonna say excuse me? You just gonna walk over top of me?

CORY: If you wanna put it like that.

TROY: How else am I gonna put it?

CORY: I was walking by you to go into the house 'cause you sitting on the steps drunk, singing to yourself. You can put it like that.

TROY: Without saying excuse me??? (*Cory doesn't respond*) I asked you a question. Without saying excuse me???

CORY: I ain't got to say excuse me to you. You don't count around here no more.

TROY: Oh, I see . . . I don't count around here no more. You ain't got to say excuse me to your daddy. All of a sudden you done got so grown that your daddy don't count around here no more . . . Around here in his own house and yard that he done paid for with the sweat of his brow. You done got so grown to where you gonna take over. You gonna take over my house. Is that right? You gonna wear my pants. You gonna go in there and stretch out on my bed. You ain't got to say excuse me 'cause I don't count around here no more. Is that right?

CORY: That's right. You always talking this dumb stuff. Now, why don't you just get out my way.

TROY: I guess you got someplace to sleep and something to put in your belly. You got that, huh? You got that? That's what you need. You got that, huh?

CORY: You don't know what I got. You ain't got to worry about what I got.

TROY: You right! You one hundred percent right! I done spent the last seventeen years worrying about what you got. Now it's your turn, see? I'll tell you what to do. You grown . . . we done established that. You a man. Now, let's see you act like one. Turn your behind around and walk out this yard. And when you get out there in the alley . . . you can forget about this house. See? 'Cause this is my house. You go on and be a man and get your own house. You can forget about this. 'Cause this is mine. You go on and get yours 'cause I'm through with doing for you.

CORY: You talking about what you did for me . . . what'd you ever give me?

TROY: Them feet and bones! That pumping heart, nigger! I give you more than anybody else is ever gonna give you.

CORY: You ain't never gave me nothing! You ain't never done nothing but hold me back. Afraid I was gonna be better than you. All you ever did was try and make me scared of you. I used to tremble every time you called my name. Every time I heard your footsteps in the house. Wondering all the time . . . what's Papa gonna say if I do this? . . . What's he gonna say if I do that? . . . What's Papa gonna say if I turn on the radio? And Mama, too . . . she tries . . . but she's scared of you.

TROY: You leave your mama out of this. She ain't got nothing to do with this.

CORY: I don't know how she stand you . . . after what you did to her.

TROY: I told you to leave your mama out of this! (*Advances on Cory*)

CORY: What you gonna do . . . give me a whupping? You can't whup me no more. You're too old. You just an old man.

TROY (*Shoves him on his shoulder*): Nigger! That's what you are! You just another nigger on the street to me!

CORY: You crazy! You know that?

TROY: Go on now! You got the devil in you. Get on away from me!

CORY: You just a crazy old man . . . talking about I got the devil in me.

TROY: Yeah, I'm crazy! If you don't get on the other side of that yard . . . I'm gonna show you how crazy I am! Go on . . . get the hell out of my yard.

CORY: It ain't your yard. You took Uncle Gabe's money he got from the Army to buy this house and then you put him out.

TROY (*Advances on Cory*): Get your black ass out of my yard!

(*Troy's advance backs Cory up against the tree. Cory grabs the bat.*)

CORY: I ain't going nowhere! Come on . . . put me out! I ain't scared of you.

TROY: That's my bat!

CORY: Come on!

TROY: Put my bat down!

CORY: Come on, put me out.

(*Cory swings at Troy, who backs across the yard.*)

What's the matter? You so bad . . . put me out!

(*Troy advances on Cory, who backs up.*)

Come on! Come on!

TROY: You're gonna have to use it! You wanna draw that bat back on me . . . you're gonna have to use it.

CORY: Come on! . . . Come on!

(*Cory swings the bat at Troy a second time. He misses. Troy continues to advance on him.*)

TROY: You're gonna have to kill me! You wanna draw that bat back on me. You're gonna have to kill me.

(*Cory, backed up against the tree, can go no farther. Troy taunts him. He sticks out his head and offers him a target.*)

Come on! Come on!

(*Cory is unable to swing the bat. Troy grabs it.*)

Then I'll show you.

(*Cory and Troy struggle over the bat. The struggle is fierce and fully engaged. Troy ultimately is the stronger, and takes the bat from Cory and stands over him ready to swing. He stops himself.*)

Go on and get away from around my house.

(Cory, stung by his defeat, picks himself up, walks slowly out of the yard and up the alley.)

CORY: Tell Mama I'll be back for my things. *(Exits)*

TROY: They'll be on the other side of that fence.

I can't taste nothing. Hallelujah! I can't taste nothing no more. *(Assumes a batting posture and begins to taunt Death, the fastball in the outside corner)* Come on! It's between you and me now! Come on! Anytime you want! Come on! I be ready for you . . . but I ain't gonna be easy.

(The lights go down on the scene.)

Scene 5

The time is 1965. The lights come up in the yard. It is the morning of Troy's funeral. A funeral plaque with a light hangs beside the door. There is a small garden plot off to the side. There is noise and activity in the house as Rose, Gabriel, Lyons and Bono have gathered. The door opens and Raynell, seven years old, enters dressed in a flannel nightgown. She crosses to the garden and pokes around with a stick. Rose calls from the house.

ROSE: Raynell!

RAYNELL: Mam?

ROSE: What you doing out there?

RAYNELL: Nothing.

(Rose comes to the screen door.)

ROSE: Girl, get in here and get dressed. What you doing?

RAYNELL: Seeing if my garden growed.

ROSE: I told you it ain't gonna grow overnight. You got to wait.

RAYNELL: It don't look like it never gonna grow. Dag!

ROSE: I told you a watched pot never boils. Get in here and get dressed.

RAYNELL: This ain't even no pot, Mama.

ROSE: You just have to give it a chance. It'll grow. Now you come on and do what I told you. We got to be getting ready. This ain't no morning to be playing around. You hear me?

RAYNELL: Yes, Mam.

(Rose exits into the house. Raynell continues to poke at her garden with a stick. Cory enters. He is dressed in a Marine corporal's uniform, and carries a duffel bag. His posture is that of a military man, and his speech has a clipped sternness.)

CORY *(To Raynell)*: Hi. *(Pause)* I bet your name is Raynell.

RAYNELL: Uh-huh.

CORY: Is your mama home?

(Raynell runs up on the porch and calls through the screen door:)

RAYNELL: Mama . . . there's some man out here. Mama?

(Rose comes to the screen door.)

ROSE: Cory? Lord have mercy! Look here, you all!

(Rose and Cory embrace in a tearful reunion as Bono and Lyons enter from the house dressed in funeral clothes.)

BONO: Aw, looka here . . .

ROSE: Done got all grown up!

CORY: Don't cry, Mama. What you crying about?

ROSE: I'm just so glad you made it.

CORY: Hey, Lyons. How you doing, Mr. Bono.

(Lyons goes to embrace Cory.)

LYONS: Look at you, man. Look at you. Don't he look good, Rose. Got them corporal stripes.

ROSE: What took you so long.

CORY: You know how the Marines are, Mama. They got to get all their paperwork straight before they let you do anything.

ROSE: Well, I'm sure glad you made it. They let Lyons come. Your Uncle Gabe's still in the hospital. They don't know if they gonna let him out or not. I just talked to them a little while ago.

LYONS: A corporal in the United States Marines.

BONO: Your daddy knew you had it in you. He used to tell me all the time.

LYONS: Don't he look good, Mr. Bono?

BONO: Yeah, he remind me of Troy when I first met him. *(Pause)* Say, Rose, Lucille's down at the church with the choir. I'm gonna go down and get the pallbearers lined up. I'll be back to get you all.

ROSE: Thanks, Jim.

CORY: See you, Mr. Bono.

(Bono exits.)

LYONS *(With his arm around Raynell)*: Cory . . . look at Raynell. Ain't she precious? She gonna break a whole lot of hearts.

ROSE: Raynell, come and say hello to your brother. This is your brother, Cory. You remember Cory.

RAYNELL: No, Mam.

CORY: She don't remember me, Mama.

ROSE: Well, we talk about you. She heard us talk about you. *(To Raynell)* This is your brother Cory. Come on and say hello.

RAYNELL: Hi.

CORY: Hi. So you're Raynell. Mama told me a lot about you.

ROSE: You all come on into the house and let me fix you some breakfast. Keep up your strength.

CORY: I ain't hungry, Mama.

LYONS: You can fix me something, Rose. I'll be in there in a minute.

ROSE: Cory, you sure you don't want nothing. I know they ain't feeding you right.

CORY: No, Mama . . . thanks. I don't feel like eating. I'll get something later.

ROSE: Raynell . . . get on upstairs and get that dress on like I told you.

(Rose and Raynell exit into the house.)

LYONS: So . . . I hear you thinking about getting married.

CORY: Yeah, I done found the right one, Lyons. It's about time.

LYONS: Me and Bonnie been split up about four years now. About the time Papa retired. I guess she just got tired of all them changes I was putting her through. *(Pause)* I always knew you was gonna make something out yourself. Your head was always in the right direction. So . . . you gonna stay in . . . make it a career . . . put in your twenty years?

CORY: I don't know. I got six already, I think that's enough.

LYONS: Stick with Uncle Sam and retire early. Ain't nothing out here. I guess Rose told you what happened with me. They got me down the workhouse I thought I was being slick cashing other people's checks.

CORY: How much time you doing?

LYONS: They give me three years. I got that beat now. I ain't got but nine more months. It ain't so bad. You learn to deal with it like anything else. You got to take the crookeds with the straights. That's what Papa used to say. He used to say that when he struck out. I seen him strike out three times in a row . . . and the next time up he hit the ball over the grandstand. Right out there in Homestead Field.[2] He wasn't satisfied hitting in the seats . . . he wanted to hit it over everything! After the game he had two hundred people standing around waiting to shake his hand. You got to take the crookeds with the straights. Yeah, Papa was something else.

CORY: You still playing?

LYONS: Cory . . . you know I'm gonna do that. There's some fellows down there we got us a band . . . we gonna try and stay together when we get out . . . but yeah, I'm still playing. It still helps me to get out of bed in the morning. As long as it do that I'm gonna be right there playing and trying to make some sense out of it.

ROSE *(Calling)*: Lyons, I got these eggs in the pan.

LYONS: Let me go on and get these eggs, man. Get ready to go bury Papa. *(Pause)* How you doing? You doing all right?

(Cory nods. Lyons touches him on the shoulder and they share a moment of silent grief. Lyons exits into the house. Cory wanders about the yard. Raynell enters.)

RAYNELL: Hi.

CORY: Hi.

RAYNELL: Did you used to sleep in my room?

CORY: Yeah . . . that used to be my room.

RAYNELL: That's what Papa call it. "Cory's room." It got your football in the closet.

(Rose comes to the screen door.)

ROSE: Raynell, get in there and get them good shoes on.

RAYNELL: Mama, can't I wear these? Them other one hurt my feet.

---

2. Among the most renowned teams in the Negro League, the Homestead Grays originated in Homestead, Pennsylvania, just south of Pittsburgh, but moved to Pittsburgh's Forbes Field in the late 1930s.

ROSE: Well, they just gonna have to hurt your feet for a while. You ain't said they hurt your feet when you went down to the store and got them.

RAYNELL: They didn't hurt then. My feet done got bigger.

ROSE: Don't you give me no backtalk now. You get in there and get them shoes on.

(*Raynell exits into the house.*)

Ain't too much changed. He still got that piece of rag tied to that tree. He was out here swinging that bat. I was just ready to go back in the house. He swung that bat and then he just fell over. Seem like he swung it and stood there with this grin on his face . . . and then he just fell over. They carried him on down to the hospital, but I knew there wasn't no need . . . Why don't you come on in the house?

CORY: Mama . . . I got something to tell you. I don't know how to tell you this . . . but I've got to tell you . . . I'm not going to Papa's funeral.

ROSE: Boy, hush your mouth. That's your daddy you talking about. I don't want hear that kind of talk this morning. I done raised you to come to this? You standing there all healthy and grown talking about you ain't going to your daddy's funeral?

CORY: Mama . . . listen . . .

ROSE: I don't want to hear it, Cory. You just get that thought out of your head.

CORY: I can't drag Papa with me everywhere I go. I've got to say no to him. One time in my life I've got to say no.

ROSE: Don't nobody have to listen to nothing like that. I know you and your daddy ain't seen eye to eye, but I ain't got to listen to that kind of talk this morning. Whatever was between you and your daddy . . . the time has come to put it aside. Just take it and set it over there on the shelf and forget about it. Disrespecting your daddy ain't gonna make you a man, Cory. You got to find a way to come to that on your own. Not going to your daddy's funeral ain't gonna make you a man.

CORY: The whole time I was growing up . . . living in his house . . . Papa was like a shadow that followed you everywhere. It weighed on you and sunk into your flesh. It would wrap around you and lay there until you couldn't tell which one was you anymore. That shadow digging in your flesh. Trying to crawl in. Trying to live through you. Everywhere I looked, Troy Maxson was staring back at me . . . hiding under the bed . . . in the closet. I'm just saying I've got to find a way to get rid of that shadow, Mama.

ROSE: You just like him. You got him in you good.

CORY: Don't you tell me that, Mama.

ROSE: You Troy Maxson all over again.

CORY: I don't want to be Troy Maxson. I want to be me.

ROSE: You can't be nobody but who you are, Cory. That shadow wasn't nothing but you growing into yourself. You either got to grow into it or cut it down to fit you. But that's all you got to make life with. That's all you got to measure yourself against that world out there. Your daddy wanted you to be everything he wasn't . . . and at the same time he tried to make you into everything he was. I don't know if he was right or wrong . . . but I do know he meant to do more good than he meant to do harm. He wasn't always right. Sometimes when he touched he bruised. And sometimes when he took me in his arms he cut.

When I first met your daddy I thought, "Here is a man I can lay down with and make a baby." That's the first thing I thought when I seen him. I was thirty years old and had done seen my share of men. But when he walked up to me and said, "I can dance a waltz that'll make you dizzy," I thought, "Rose Lee, here is a man that you can open yourself up to and be filled to bursting. Here is a man that can fill all them empty spaces you been tipping around the edges of." One of them empty spaces was being somebody's mother.

I married your daddy and settle down to cooking his supper and keeping clean sheets on the bed. When your daddy walked through the house he was so big he filled it up. That was my first mistake. Not to make him leave some room for me. For my part in the matter. But at that time I wanted that. I wanted a house that I could sing in. And that's what your daddy gave me. I didn't know to keep up his strength I had to give up little pieces of mine. I did that. I took on his life as mine and mixed up the pieces so that you couldn't hardly tell which was which anymore. It was my choice. It was my life and I didn't have to live it like that. But that's what life offered me in the way of being a woman and I took it. I grabbed hold of it with both hands.

By the time Raynell came into the house, me and your daddy had done lost touch with one another. I didn't want to make my blessing off of nobody's misfortune . . . but I took on to Raynell like she was all them babies I had wanted and never had. (*The phone rings*) Like I'd been blessed to relive a part of my life. And if the Lord see fit to keep up my strength . . . I'm gonna do her just like your daddy did you . . . I'm gonna give her the best of what's in me.

RAYNELL (*Entering, still with her old shoes*): Mama . . . Reverend Tolliver on the phone.

(*Rose exits into the house.*)

Hi.
CORY: Hi.
RAYNELL: You in the Army or the Marines?
CORY: Marines.
RAYNELL: Papa said it was the Army. Did you know Blue?
CORY: Blue? Who's Blue?
RAYNELL: Papa's dog what he sing about all the time.

CORY (*Singing*):
Hear it ring! Hear it ring!
I had a dog his name was Blue
You know Blue was mighty true
You know Blue was a good old dog
Blue treed a possum in a hollow log
You know from that he was a good old dog.
Hear it ring! Hear it ring!

(*Raynell joins in singing.*)

CORY AND RAYNELL:
Blue treed a possum out on a limb

Blue looked at me and I looked at him
Grabbed that possum and put him in a sack
Blue stayed there till I came back
Old Blue's feets was big and round
Never allowed a possum to touch the ground.

Old Blue died and I dug his grave
I dug his grave with a silver spade
Let him down with a golden chain
And every night I call his name
Go on Blue, you good dog you
Go on Blue, you good dog you

RAYNELL:
Blue laid down and died like a man
Blue laid down and died . . .

CORY AND RAYNELL:
Blue laid down and died like a man
Now he's treeing possums in the Promised Land
I'm gonna tell you this to let you know
Blue's gone where the good dogs go
When I hear Old Blue bark
When I hear Old Blue bark
Blue treed a possum in Noah's Ark
Blue treed a possum in Noah's Ark.

(Rose comes to the screen door.)

ROSE: Cory, we gonna be ready to go in a minute.
CORY (To Raynell): You go on in the house and change them shoes like Mama told you so we can go to Papa's funeral.
RAYNELL: Okay, I'll be back.

(Raynell exits into the house. Cory gets up and crosses over to the tree. Rose stands at the screen door watching him. Gabriel enters from the alley.)

GABRIEL (Calling): Hey, Rose!
ROSE Gabe?
GABRIEL: I'm here, Rose. Hey, Rose, I'm here!

(Rose enters from the house.)

ROSE: Lord . . . Look here, Lyons!
LYONS (Enters from the house): See, I told you, Rose . . . I told you they'd let him come.
CORY: How you doing, Uncle Gabe?
LYONS: How you doing, Uncle Gabe?
GABRIEL: Hey, Rose. It's time. It's time to tell Saint Peter to open the Gates. Troy, you ready? You ready, Troy. I'm gonna tell Saint Peter to open the Gates. You get ready now.

(Gabriel, with great fanfare, braces himself to blow. The trumpet is without a mouthpiece. He puts the end of it into his mouth and blows with great force, like a man who has been waiting some twenty-odd years for this single moment. No sound comes out of the trumpet. He braces himself and blows again with the same result. A third time he blows. There is a weight of impossible description that falls away and leaves him bare and exposed to a frightful realization. It is a trauma that a sane and normal mind would be unable to withstand. He begins to dance. A slow, strange dance, eerie and life-giving. A dance of atavistic[3] signature and ritual. Lyons attempts to embrace him. Gabriel pushes Lyons away. Gabriel begins to howl in what is an attempt at song, or perhaps a song turning back into itself in an attempt at speech. He finishes his dance and the Gates of Heaven stand open as wide as God's closet.)

That's the way that go!

(Blackout.)

1987

QUESTIONS

1. In interviews, August Wilson describes FENCES as revolving so completely around its central character that it might "almost" be called "*The Life of Troy Maxson* or just *Troy Maxson.*" To what extent does and doesn't that seem true?
2. Wilson also describes the play as "examin[ing] Troy's life layer by layer [to] find out why he made the choices he made" (see "Authors on Their Work" on p. 737). How do you think the play ultimately answers that question? What does it seem to present as the key to Troy's character or as the thing he values most?
3. According to the play, how have circumstances helped to make Troy the man he is? How might he and his life have been different had he turned fifty-three in either 1947 or 1967? had he been white?
4. Does Troy's character develop over the course of the play or only the way others see him? Why and how so?
5. What is the effect and significance of the fact that the play ends after Troy's death? How would the play work differently and carry a different meaning if its final scene were omitted? if Troy died onstage?
6. What might the fence come to stand for or symbolize in the play? Why might *Fences*, plural, be a more apt title than *The Fence*?
7. How are father-son relationships depicted in the play? How does Troy's relationship with his father compare to and shape his relationship with his sons? Why do you think the play includes Lyons, as well as Cory?
8. How might Rose or your impression of her evolve over the course of the play? Why does she adopt Raynell, and what effect does this choice seem to have? Why might she begin to attend church?
9. What is the significance and effect of Wilson's choice to set the play in the Maxsons' front yard? to punctuate the play with scenes that take place on Friday nights? not to show us Troy at work, Cory playing football, and so on?

---

3. Characterized by a reversion to an ancient or ancestral form.

SUGGESTIONS FOR WRITING

1. Why is Troy Maxson so insistent that his son quit the football team? What about your own cultural and historical context might make his attitude seem surprising? Write a response paper or essay exploring these questions.

2. Write an essay exploring Gabriel's role in the play. What is significant about his injuries and their cause, for example? about his fixation with Judgment Day? about his actions in the play's final scene? What might his final, *"frightful realization"* (736) be, and why, according to Wilson's stage directions, might *"the Gates of Heaven stand open as wide as God's closet"* only after that realization and the *"atavistic"* dance that follows it?

3. Write an essay exploring Wilson's characterization of Rose. What might the play suggest, through her, about the options available to, or conflicts faced by, women in general or African American women in particular in the 1950s? To what extent might Wilson's play reproduce or challenge our preconceptions about such women? Alternatively, consider how FENCES might reproduce or challenge stereotypical views of black men.

4. Research theories of tragedy and the tragic hero. Drawing on both these and evidence from Wilson's play, explain whether and how FENCES might be considered a tragedy or Troy Maxson a tragic hero.

5. Write an epilogue to FENCES, a scene depicting Rose, Lyons, Cory, or Raynell in 1975. What do you imagine has happened to this character, and why and how so? If Cory had a child, for example, what would his relationship with that child be like? What might he say to his child about his father, his mother, and his own childhood?

AUTHORS ON THEIR WORK

AUGUST WILSON (1945–2005)

From Dennis Watlington, "Hurdling Fences" (1989)*

I wanted to explore our commonalities of culture. What you have in *Fences* is a very specific situation, a black family which the forces of racism have molded and shaped, but you also have a husband-wife, father-son. White America looks at black America in this glancing manner. They pass right by the Troy Maxsons of the world and never stop to look at them. They talk about niggers as lazy and shiftless. Well, here's a man with responsibilities as prime to his life. I wanted to examine Troy's life layer by layer and find out why he made the choices he made. (109)

From "Men, Women, and Culture: A Conversation with August Wilson" (1993)**

[INTERVIEWER]: What makes Troy heroic? He's an ex-con, ex-baseball player, now a garbage collector; he exploits his brother and cheats on his wife—what is redeeming about him as an African American man?

WILSON: I think that, for me, this may be nothing more than his willingness to wrestle with his life, his willingness to engage no matter what the circumstances of his life. He hasn't given up despite the twists and turns it's given him. I find that both noble and heroic. (172)

*"Hurdling Fences." Interview by Dennis Watlington. *Vanity Fair*, no. 52, Apr. 1989, pp. 102–13.
**"Men, Women, and Culture: A Conversation with August Wilson." Interview by Nathan L. Grant. *American Drama*, vol. 5, no. 2, Spring 1996, pp. 100–22.

QUIARA ALEGRÍA HUDES
(b. 1977)
Water by the Spoonful

Though she now lives in New York City with her lawyer husband and two small children, Quiara Alegría Hudes hails from Philadelphia, the city that still serves as inspiration and setting for much of her work. The daughter of a Jewish carpenter and a Puerto Rican mother and stepfather, Hudes spent her childhood exploring the city's ethnically and economically diverse neighborhoods, especially the predominantly African American West Philly area she called home and the North Philly barrios where many of her maternal relatives still live. Hudes had her first play produced by Philadelphia Young Playwrights when she was only ten. Yet when she became the first in her family to attend college, at Yale, she majored in music. After graduation, Hudes returned home, launching a successful career as a musician-composer before heading to Brown University. Here she earned an MFA (2003) and completed two plays—the award-winning *Yamaya's Belly* (2005), about a young Cuban boy who dreams of immigrating to the United States, and *The Adventures of Barrio Grrl!*, which she later turned into a children's musical. Hudes received the first of three Pulitzer nominations for her work on another musical, the Tony Award–winning *In the Heights* (2007), featuring music and lyrics by *Hamilton* creator and star Lin-Manuel Miranda. But her real acclaim as a dramatist rests on a trilogy inspired by, and developed partly in collaboration with, her "story-centric family," especially Elliot Ruiz, a cousin wounded in the Iraq War. *Water by the Spoonful* (2011), which won a Pulitzer, is the second play in the sequence that also includes *Elliot, a Soldier's Fugue* (2006) and *The Happiest Song Plays Last* (2012). Together, says Hudes, these plays tell a distinctly "American story" about issues and people we too often "don't talk about," in part by exploiting and exploring diverse, often distinctly twenty-first-century ways of both talking and storytelling.

CHARACTERS

ELLIOT ORTIZ, an Iraq vet with a slight limp, works at Subway sandwich shop, scores an occasional job as a model or actor, Yazmin's cousin, Odessa's birth son, Puerto Rican, twenty-four.

YAZMIN ORTIZ, in her first year as an adjunct professor of music, Odessa's niece and Elliot's cousin, Puerto Rican, twenty-nine.

HAIKUMOM, aka Odessa Ortiz, founder of *www.recover-together.com*, works odd janitorial jobs, lives one notch above squalor, Puerto Rican, thirty-nine.

FOUNTAINHEAD, aka John, a computer programmer and entrepreneur, lives on Philadelphia's Main Line,[1] white, forty-one.

CHUTES&LADDERS, lives in San Diego, has worked a low-level job at the IRS since the Reagan years,[2] his real name is Clayton "Buddy" Wilkie, African American, fifty-six.

ORANGUTAN, a recent community college graduate, her real name is Madeleine Mays and before that Yoshiko Sakai, Japanese by birth, thirty-one.

A GHOST, also plays Professor Aman, an Arabic professor at Swarthmore;[3] also plays a Policeman in Japan.

SETTING: *2009. Six years after Elliot left for Iraq. Philadelphia, San Diego, Japan and Puerto Rico.*

The stage has two worlds. The "real world" is populated with chairs. The chairs are from many locations—living rooms, an office, a seminar room, a church, a diner, internet cafés, etc. They all have the worn-in feel of life. A duct-taped La-Z-Boy. Salvaged trash chairs. A busted-up metal folding chair from a rec center. An Aero chair. An Eames chair.[4] A chair/desk from a college classroom. Diner chairs. A chair from an internet café in Japan. Living room chairs. Library chairs. A church pew. Facing in all different directions.

The "online world" is an empty space. A space that connects the chairs.

MUSIC: *Jazz. John Coltrane.[5] The sublime stuff* (A Love Supreme). *And the noise* (Ascension).

NOTE: *Unless specifically noted, when characters are online, don't have actors typing on a keyboard. Treat it like regular conversation rather than the act of writing or typing. They can be doing things people do in the comfort of their home, like eating potato chips, walking around in jammies, cooking, doing dishes, clipping nails, etc.*

Scene One

Swarthmore College. Elliot and Yaz eat breakfast. Elliot wears a Subway sandwich shop polo shirt.

ELLIOT: This guy ain't coming. How do you know him?

YAZ: We're on a committee together.

ELLIOT: My shift starts in fifteen.

YAZ: All right, we'll go.

ELLIOT: Five more minutes. Tonight on the way home, we gotta stop by Whole Foods.

YAZ: Sure, I need toothpaste.

1. Series of affluent towns in Philadelphia's western suburbs, along the old Main Line of the Pennsylvania Railroad.
2. 1981–89, during the presidency of Ronald Reagan (1911–2004). *IRS:* Internal Revenue Service (acronym).
3. Highly ranked private liberal arts college (founded 1864) located eleven miles southwest of Philadelphia.
4. High-end chair designed in 1956 by renowned husband-and-wife team Charles (1907–78) and Ray Eames (1912–88).
5. American jazz saxophonist and composer (1926–67), pioneer of "free jazz."

Liza Colón-Zayas, Sue Jean Kim, and Frankie R. Faison in the Second Stage Theater production of *Water by the Spoonful*, 2012

ELLIOT: You gotta help me with my mom, Yaz.

YAZ: You said she had a good morning.

ELLIOT: She cooked breakfast.

YAZ: Progress.

ELLIOT: No. The docs said she can't be eating all that junk, it'll mess with her chemo, so she crawls out of bed for the first time in days and cooks eggs for breakfast. In two inches of pork-chop fat. I'm like, Mom, recycle glass and plastic, not grease. She thinks putting the egg on top of a paper towel after you cook it makes it healthy. I told her, Mom, you gotta cook egg whites In Pam spray. But it has to be her way. Like, "That's how we ate them in Puerto Rico and we turned out fine." You gotta talk to her. I'm trying to teach her about quinoa. Broccoli rabe. Healthy shit. So I get home the other day she had made quinoa with bacon. She was like, "It's healthy!"

YAZ: That's Ginny. The more stubborn she's being, the better she's feeling.

ELLIOT: I gave those eggs to the dogs when she went to the bathroom.

YAZ (*Pulls some papers from her purse*): You wanna be my witness?

ELLIOT: To what?

(*Yaz signs the papers.*)

YAZ: My now-legal failure. I'm divorced.

ELLIOT: Yaz. I don't want to hear that.

YAZ: You've been saying that for months and I've been keeping my mouth closed. I just need a John Hancock.

ELLIOT: What happened to "trial separation"?

YAZ: There was a verdict. William fell out of love with me.

ELLIOT: I've never seen you two argue.

YAZ: We did, we just had smiles on our faces.

ELLIOT: That's bullshit. You don't divorce someone before you even have a fight with them. I'm calling him.

YAZ: Go ahead.

ELLIOT: He was just texting me about going to the Phillies game on Sunday.

YAZ: So, go. He didn't fall out of love with the family, just me.

ELLIOT: I'm going to ask him who he's been screwing behind your back.

YAZ: No one, Elliot.

ELLIOT: You were tappin' some extra on the side?

YAZ: He woke up one day and I was the same as any other person passing by on the street, and life is short, and you can only live in mediocrity so long.

ELLIOT: You two are the dog and the owner that look like each other. Ya'll are the *Cosby Show*.[6] Conundrum, Yaz and William make a funny, end-of episode. You show all us cousins, maybe we can't ever do it ourselves, but it *is* possible.

YAZ: Did I ever say, "It's possible"?

ELLIOT: By example.

YAZ: Did I ever say those words?

(*Professor Aman enters.*)

AMAN: Yazmin, forgive me. You must be . . .

ELLIOT: Elliot Ortiz. Nice to meet you, I appreciate it.

AMAN: Professor Aman. (*They shake*) We'll have to make this short and sweet, my lecture begins . . . began . . . well, talk fast.

ELLIOT: Yaz, give us a second?

YAZ: I'll be in the car. (*Exits*)

ELLIOT: I'm late, too, so . . .

AMAN: You need something translated.

ELLIOT: Just a phrase. Thanks, man.

AMAN: Eh, your sister's cute.

ELLIOT: Cousin. I wrote it phonetically. You grow up speaking Arabic?

AMAN: English. What's your native tongue?

ELLIOT: Spanglish. (*Hands Aman a piece of paper*)

AMAN: Mom-ken men fad-luck ted-dini ga-waz saf-far-i. Mom-ken men-fadluck ted-dini gawaz saffari. Am I saying that right?

ELLIOT (*Spooked*): Spot on.

AMAN: You must have some familiarity with Arabic to remember it so clearly.

ELLIOT: Maybe I heard it on TV or something.

AMAN: An odd phrase.

ELLIOT: It's like a song I can't get out of my head.

AMAN: Yazmin didn't tell me what this is for.

ELLIOT: It's not for anything.

AMAN: Do you mind me asking, what's around your neck?

ELLIOT: Something my girl gave me.

AMAN: Can I see? (*Elliot pulls dog tags from under his shirt*) Romantic gift. You were in the army.

6. Television sitcom (1984–92) about a close-knit upper-middle-class African American family starring comedian Bill Cosby (b. 1937).

ELLIOT: Marines.

AMAN: Iraq?

ELLIOT: For a minute.

AMAN: Were you reluctant to tell me that?

ELLIOT: No.

AMAN: Still in the service?

ELLIOT: Honorable discharge. Leg injury.

AMAN: When?

ELLIOT: A few years ago.

AMAN: This is a long time to have a phrase stuck in your head.

ELLIOT: What is this, man?

AMAN: You tell me.

ELLIOT: It's just a phrase. If you don't want to translate, just say so.

AMAN: A college buddy is making a film about Marines in Iraq. Gritty, documentary-style. He's looking for some veterans to interview. Get an authentic point of view. Maybe I could pass your number on to him.

ELLIOT: Nope. No interviews for this guy.

AMAN: You're asking me for a favor. (*Pause*) Yazmin told me you're an actor. Every actor needs a break, right?

ELLIOT: I did enough Q&As about the service. People manipulate you with the questions.

AMAN: It's not just to interview. He needs a right-hand man, an expert to help him. How do Marines hold a gun? How do they kick in civilian doors, this sort of thing. How do they say "Ooh-rah" in a patriotic manner?

ELLIOT: Are you his headhunter or something?

AMAN: I'm helping with the translations, I have a small stake and I want the movie to be accurate. And you seem not unintelligent. For a maker of sandwiches. (*Hands him a business card*) He's in L.A. In case you want a career change. I give you a cup of sugar, you give me a cup of sugar.

ELLIOT: If I have a minute, I'll dial the digits. (*Takes the business card*) So what's it mean?

AMAN: Momken men-fadluck ted-dini gawaz saffari. Rough translation, "Can I please have my passport back?"

Scene Two

Odessa's living room and kitchen. She makes coffee. She goes over to her computer, clicks a button. On a screen we see:

HAIKUMOM, SITEADMIN
STATUS: ONLINE

HAIKUMOM: Rise and shine, kiddos, the rooster's a-crowin', it's a beautiful day to be sober. (*No response*) Your Thursday morning haiku:[7]

   if you get restless

---

7. Originally Japanese poetic form that, in its English-language incarnations, traditionally consists of seventeen syllables divided into three lines of five, seven, and five syllables, respectively.

buy a hydrangea or rose
water it, wait, bloom

(*Odessa continues making coffee. A computer dings and on another screen we see:*)

ORANGUTAN
STATUS: ONLINE

ORANGUTAN: Ninety-one days. Smiley face.

HAIKUMOM (*Relieved*): Orangutan! Jesus, I thought my primate friend had disappeared back to the jungle.

ORANGUTAN: Disappeared? Yes. Jungle? Happily, no.

HAIKUMOM: I'm trying to put a high-five emoticon, but my computer is being a capital B. So, high-five!

(*They high-five in the air. Another computer screen lights up:*)

CHUTES&LADDERS
STATUS: ONLINE

CHUTES&LADDERS: Orangutan? I was about to send a search party after your rear end. Kid, *log on*. No news is bad news.

ORANGUTAN: Chutes&Ladders, giving me a hard time as usual. I'd expect nothing less.

CHUTES&LADDERS: Your last post says: "Day One. Packing bags, gotta run," and then you don't log on for three months?

ORANGUTAN: I was going to Japan, I had to figure out what shoes to bring.

HAIKUMOM: The country?

CHUTES&LADDERS: What happened to Maine?

ORANGUTAN: And I quote, "Get a hobby, find a new job, an exciting city, go teach English in a foreign country." Did you guys think I wouldn't take your seasoned advice? I was batting 0 for ten, and for the first time, guys, I feel fucking free.

HAIKUMOM (*Nonjudgmental*): Censored.

ORANGUTAN: I wake up and I think, What's the world got up its sleeve today? And I look forward to the answer. So, thank you.

CHUTES&LADDERS: We told you so.

ORANGUTAN (*Playful*): Shut up.

HAIKUMOM: You're welcome.

ORANGUTAN: I gave my parents the URL. My username, my password. They logged on and read every post I've ever put on here and for once they said they understood. They had completely cut me off, but after reading this site they bought me the plane ticket. One way. I teach English in the mornings. I have a class of children, a class of teens, and a class of adults, most of whom are older than me. I am free in the afternoons. I have a paycheck which I use for legal things like ice cream, noodles and socks. I walk around feeling like maybe I *am* normal. Maybe, just possibly, I'm not that different. Or maybe it's just homeland delusions.

CHUTES&LADDERS AND HAIKUMOM: Homeland?

HAIKUMOM: You're Japanese?

ORANGUTAN: I *was*, for the first eight days of my life. Yoshiko Sakai. Then on day nine I was adopted and moved to Cape Lewiston, Maine, where I became Ma— M.M., and where in all my days I have witnessed *one* other Asian. In the Superfresh. Deli counter.

CHUTES&LADDERS: Japan . . . Wow, that little white rock sure doesn't discriminate.

HAIKUMOM: Amen.

ORANGUTAN: Mango Internet Café. I'm sitting in an orange plastic chair, a little view of the Hokkaido waterfront.

HAIKUMOM: Japan has a waterfront?

CHUTES&LADDERS: It's an island.

HAIKUMOM: Really? Are there beaches? Can you go swimming?

ORANGUTAN: The ocean reminds me of Maine. Cold water, very quiet, fisherman, boats, the breeze. I wouldn't try swimming. I'm just a looker. I was never one to actually have an experience.

CHUTES&LADDERS: Ah, the ocean . . . There's only one thing on this planet I'm more scared of than that big blue lady.

HAIKUMOM: Let me guess: landing on a sliding board square?[8]

CHUTES&LADDERS: Lol, truer words have never been spoken. You know I was born just a few miles from the Pacific. In the fresh salt air. Back in "those days" I'm at Coronado Beach[9] with a few "friends" doing my "thing" and I get sucked up under this wave. I gasp, I breathe in and my lungs fill with water. I'm like. this is it, I'm going to meet my maker. I had never felt so heavy, not even during my two OD's.[1] I was sinking to the bottom and my head hit the sand like a lead ball. My body just felt like an anvil. The next thing I know there's fingers digging in my ankles. This lifeguard pulls me out, I'm throwing up salt water. I say to him, "Hey blondie, you don't know me from Adam but you are my witness: today's the day I start to *live*." And this lifeguard, I mean he was young with these muscles, this kid looks at me like, "Who is this big black dude who can't even doggy paddle?" When I stand up and brush the sand off me, people *applaud*. An old lady touches my cheek and says, "I thought you were done for." I get back to San Diego that night, make one phone call, the next day I'm in my first meeting, sitting in a folding chair, saying the serenity prayer.[2]

ORANGUTAN: I hate to inflate your already swollen ego, but that was a lucid, touching story. By the way, did you get the lifeguard's name? He sounds hot.

---

8. In Milton Bradley's board game Chutes & Ladders (based on the ancient Indian game Snakes and Ladders), some squares are connected by sliding boards, or "chutes." Players landing on the square picturing the top of the chute advance or "slide" directly to the square picturing the bottom of the chute.

9. On Coronado Island, just off the coast of San Diego, California.

1. Overdoses (acronym).

2. Authored by American theologian Reinhold Niebuhr (1892–1971) and adopted by Alcoholics Anonymous and other twelve-step addiction-recovery programs, it reads, "God, grant me the serenity to accept the things I cannot change, / The courage to change the things I can, / And the wisdom to know the difference."

HAIKUMOM: Hey Chutes&Ladders, it's never too late to learn. Most YMCAs offer adult swimming classes.

CHUTES&LADDERS: I'll do the world a favor and stay out of a speedo.

ORANGUTAN: Sober air toast. To lifeguards.

CHUTES&LADDERS AND HAIKUMOM: To lifeguards.

ORANGUTAN, CHUTES&LADDERS AND HAIKUMOM: Clink.

HAIKUMOM: Chutes&Ladders, I'm buying you a pair of water wings.

Scene Three

John Coltrane's A Love Supreme *plays. A Subway sandwich shop on Philadelphia's Main Line. Elliot sits behind the counter. The phone rings. He gets up, hobbles to it—he walks with a limp.*

ELLIOT: Subway Main Line. Lar! Laaar, what's it doing for you today? Staying in the shade? I got you, how many you need? Listen, the delivery guy's out and my little sports injury is giving me hell so can you pick up? Cool, sorry for the inconvenience. Let me grab a pen. A'ight, pick a hoagie, any hoagie!

> *(Elliot begins writing the order.*
> *Lights rise to a seminar room at Swarthmore College. We find Yaz mid-class. She hits a button on a stereo and the Coltrane stops playing.)*

YAZ: Coltrane's *A Love Supreme*, 1964. Dissonance is still a gateway to resolution. A B-diminished chord is still resolving to? C-major. A tritone is still resolving up to? The major sixth. Diminished chords, tritones, still didn't have the right to be their own independent thought. In 1965 something changed. The ugliness bore no promise of a happy ending. The ugliness became an end in itself. Coltrane democratized the notes. He said, they're all equal. Freedom. It was called Free Jazz but freedom is a hard thing to express musically without spinning into noise. This is from *Ascension*, 1965.

> *(She plays* Ascension. *It sounds uglier than the first sample. In the Subway, a figure comes into view. It is the Ghost.)*

GHOST: Momken men-fadluck ted-dini gawaz saffari?

> *(Elliot tries to ignore the Ghost, reading off the order.)*

ELLIOT: That's three teriyaki onion with chicken. First with hots and onions. Second with everything. Third with extra bacon. Two spicy Italian with American cheese on whole grain. One BMT on flatbread. Good so far?

GHOST: Momken men-fadluck ted-dini gawaz saffari?

ELLIOT: Five chocolate chip cookies, one oatmeal raisin. Three Baked Lay's, three Doritos. Two Sprite Zeros, one Barq's, one Coke, two orange sodas. How'd I do?

GHOST: Momken men-fadluck ted-dini gawaz saffari?

ELLIOT: All right, that'll be ready in fifteen minutes. One sec for your total.

> *(Elliot gets a text message. He reads it; his entire demeanor shifts.)*

Lar, I just got a text. There's a family emergency, I can't do this order right now.

(Elliot hangs up. He exits, limping away.)

YAZ: Oh come on, don't make that face. I know it feels academic. You're going to leave here and become R&B hit makers and Sondheim[3] clones and never think about this noise again. But this is Coltrane, people, this is not Schoenberg.[4] This is jazz, stuff people listen to *voluntarily*. Shopping period is still on—go sit in one session of "Germans and Noise" down the hall and you'll come running back begging for this muzak.

(Yaz turns off the music.)

In fact, change the syllabus. No listening report next week. Instead, I want you to pinpoint the first time you really noticed dissonance. The composer, the piece, the measures. Two pages analyzing the notes and two pages describing the experience personally. This is your creation myth.[5] Before you leave this school you better figure out that story and cling to it for dear life or you'll be a stockbroker within a year.

I was thirteen, I worked in a corrugated box factory all summer, I saved up enough to find my first music teacher—up to that point I was self-taught, playing to the radio. I walked into Don Rappaport's room at Settlement Music School.[6] He was old, he had jowls, he was sitting at the piano and he said, "What do you do?" I said, "I'm a composer, sir." Presumptuous, right? I sat down and played Mr. Rappaport a Yazmin original. He said, "It's pretty, everything goes together. It's like an outfit where your socks are blue and your pants, shirt, hat are all blue." Then he said, "Play an F-sharp major in your left hand." Then he said, "Play a C-major in your right hand." "Now play them together." He asked me, "Does it go together?" I told him, "No, sir." He said, "Now go home and write." My first music lesson was seven minutes long. I had never really heard dissonance before.

(Yaz's phone vibrates. She sees the caller with concern.)

Let's take five.

(As students file out, Yaz makes a phone call. Lights up on Elliot outside the Subway.)

("What's the bad news?") You called three times.
ELLIOT: She's still alive.
YAZ: Okay.

---

3. Stephen Sondheim (b. 1930), multi-award-winning American composer-lyricist best known for hit Broadway musicals including *West Side Story* (1957), for which he wrote the lyrics only; *Sweeney Todd* (1979); and *Into the Woods* (1986).
4. Arnold Schoenberg (1874–1951), influential avant-garde Austrian classical pianist, composer, and music theorist.
5. Narrative recounting a particular culture or religion's understanding of how something (usually the world itself) came to be.
6. Philadelphia institution originally founded (1908) to provide free music instruction to newly arrived immigrants but today offering music, dance, and visual arts classes to children and adults across the city "without regard to age, race or financial circumstances." Hudes is an alumna.

ELLIOT: Jefferson Hospital. They admitted her three hours ago. Pop had the courtesy to text me.

YAZ: Are you still at work?

ELLIOT: Just smashed the bathroom mirror all over the floor. Boss sent me out to the parking lot.

YAZ: Wait there. I'm on my way.

ELLIOT: "Your mom is on breathing machine." Who texts that? Who texts that and then doesn't pick up the phone?

YAZ: I'll be there within twenty.

ELLIOT: Why did I come to work today?

YAZ: She had a good morning. You wanted your thing translated.

ELLIOT: She cooked and I wouldn't eat a bite off the fork. There's a Subway hoagies around the corner and I had to work half an hour away.

YAZ: You didn't want your buddies to see you working a normal job.

ELLIOT: Not normal job. Shit job. I'm a butler. A porter of sandwiches.

YAZ: Ginny's been to Hades and back, stronger each time.

ELLIOT: What is Hades?

YAZ: In Greek mythology, the river through the underworld—

ELLIOT: My mom's on a machine and you're dropping vocab words?!

(*A ding.*)

YAZ: Text message, don't hang up. (*She looks at her phone. A moment, then*) You still there?

ELLIOT: It was my dad wasn't it? Yaz, spit it out.

YAZ: It was your dad.

ELLIOT: And? Yaz, I'm about to start walking down Lancaster Avenue for thirty miles till I get back to Philly and I don't care if I snap every wire out my leg and back—I need to get out of here. I need to see Mom, I need to talk to her!

YAZ: He said, "Waiting for Elliot till we turn off the machine."

Scene Four

The chat room. A screen lights up:

[NO IMAGE]
FOUNTAINHEAD[7]
STATUS: ONLINE

FOUNTAINHEAD: I've uh, wow, hello there everyone. Delete, delete. Good afternoon. Evening. Delete.

(*Deep breath.*)

Things I am taking:

—My life into my own hands.
—My gorgeous, deserving wife out for our seventh anniversary.

---

7. Title of a best-selling 1943 novel by Ayn Rand (1905–82), a famous evocation of her individualist philosophy.

Me: mildly athletic, but work twice as hard. Won state for javelin two years straight. Ran a half marathon last fall. Animated arguer. Two medals for under-grad debate. MBA from Wharton.[8] Beautiful wife, two sons. Built a programming company from the ground up, featured in the *New York Times'* Circuits section, sold it at its peak, bought a yellow Porsche, got a day job to keep myself honest. Salary was 300K, company was run by morons, got laid off, handsome severance, which left me swimming in cash and free time.

Me and crack: long story short, I was at a conference with our CFO and two programmers and a not-unattractive lady in HR.[9] They snorted, invited me to join. A few weeks later that little rock waltzed right into my hand. I've been using off and on since. One eight ball every Saturday, strict rations, portion control. Though the last three or four weeks, it's less like getting high and more like trying to build a time machine. Anything to get back the romance of that virgin smoke.

Last weekend I let myself buy more than my predetermined allotment—I buy in small quantity, because as with my food, I eat what's on my plate. Anyway, I ran over a curb, damaged the underside of my Porsche. Now it's in the shop and I'm driving a rental Mustang. So, not rock bottom but a rental Ford is as close to rock bottom as I'd like to get. Fast forward to tonight. I'm watching my wife's eyelids fall and telling myself, "You are on punishment, Poppa. Daddy's on time out. Do not get out of bed, do not tiptoe down those stairs, do not go down to that basement, do not sit beside that foosball table, do not smoke, and please do not crawl on the carpet looking for one last hit in the fibers."

(Pause.)

In kindergarten my son tested into G and T. Gifted and talented. You meet with the school, they tailor the program to the kid. Math, reading, art, whatever the parent chooses. I said, "Teach my son how to learn. How to use a library. How to find original source material, read a map, track down the experts so he becomes an expert." Which gets me to—

You: the experts. It's the first day of school and I'm knocking at your classroom door. I got my No. 2 pencils, I'll sit in the front row, pay attention, and do my homework. No lesson is too basic. Teach me every technique. Any tip so that Saturday doesn't become every day. Any actions that keep you in the driver seat. Healthy habits and rational thoughts to blot out that voice in the back of my head.

Today, I quit. My wife cannot know, she'd get suspicious if I were at meetings all the time. There can be no medical records, so therapy is out. At least it's not heroin, I'm not facing a physical war. It's a psychological battle and I'm armed with two weapons: willpower and the experts.

I'm taking my wife out tomorrow for our seventh anniversary and little does she know that when we clink glasses, I'll be toasting to Day One.

(Odessa is emotional. Chutes&Ladders and Orangutan seem awestruck.)

---

8. Famed business school (founded 1881) of the University of Pennsylvania, in Philadelphia. *MBA*: master of business administration (acronym).
9. Human resources (acronym). *CFO*: chief financial officer (acronym).

ORANGUTAN (*Clapping*): That was brave.

CHUTES&LADDERS: What. The.

HAIKUMOM: Careful.

CHUTES&LADDERS: Fuck.

HAIKUMOM: Censored.

ORANGUTAN: I'm making popcorn. Oh, this is gonna be fun!

CHUTES&LADDERS: Fountainhead, speaking of experts, I've been meaning to become an asshole. Can you teach me how?

HAIKUMOM: Censored!

ORANGUTAN: "Tips"? This isn't a cooking website. And what is a half marathon?

CHUTES&LADDERS: Maybe it's something like a half crack addict. Or a half husband.

ORANGUTAN: Was that an addiction coming out or an online dating profile? "Married Male Dope Fiend. Smokin' hot."

CHUTES&LADDERS: Fountainhead, you sound like the kind of guy who's read *The 7 Habits of Highly Effective People*[1] cover to cover. Was one of those habits crack? Give the essays a rest and type three words. "I'm. A. Crackhead."

ORANGUTAN: You know, adderall is like totes[2] cool. Us crackheads, we're like yucky and stuff. We're like so nineties. Go try the adderall edge!

HAIKUMOM: Hey.

ORANGUTAN: The guy's a hoax. Twenty bucks says he's pranking. Let's start a new thread.

HAIKUMOM: Hi, Fountainhead, welcome. As the site administrator, I want to honestly congratulate you for accomplishing what so many addicts only hope for: one clean day. Any time you feel like using, log on here instead. It's worked for me. When it comes to junkies, I dug lower than the dungeon. Once upon a time I had a beautiful family, too. Now all I have is six years clean. Don't lose what I lost, what Chutes&Ladders lost.

CHUTES&LADDERS: Excuse me.

HAIKUMOM: Orangutan, I just checked and Fountainhead has no aliases and has never logged onto this site before under a different pseudonym, which are the usual markers of a scam.

ORANGUTAN: I'm just saying. Who toasts to their first day of sobriety?

CHUTES&LADDERS: I hope it's seltzer in that there champagne glass.

ORANGUTAN: Ginger ale, shirley temple.

CHUTES&LADDERS: "A toast, honey. I had that seven-year itch so I became a crackhead."

CHUTES&LADDERS AND ORANGUTAN: Clink.

HAIKUMOM: Hey; kiddos. Your smiley administrator doesn't want to start purging messages. For rules of the forums click on this link. No personal attacks.

ORANGUTAN: We don't come to this site for a pat on the back.

HAIKUMOM: I'm just saying. R-e-s-p-e-c-t.

---

1. Popular business self-help book (1989) by Stephen R. Covey (1932–2012) stressing the principles of independence and self-mastery, interdependence, and continuous improvement.
2. Totally (slang). *Adderall*: stimulant used to treat narcolepsy and attention deficit hyperactivity disorder (ADHD).

CHUTES&LADDERS: I will always give *crack* the respect it deserves. Some pure-bred poodle comes pissing on my tree trunk? Damn straight I'll chase his ass out my forest.

HAIKUMOM: This here is my forest. You two think you were all humble pie when you started out? Check your original posts.

ORANGUTAN: Oh, I know mine. "I-am-scared-I-will-kill-myself-talk-me-off-the-ledge."

HAIKUMOM: So unless someone gets that desperate they don't deserve our noble company? "Suffer like me, or you ain't legit"?

ORANGUTAN: Haikumom's growing claws.

HAIKUMOM: Just don't act entitled because you got so low. *(To Fountainhead)* Sorry. Fountainhead, forgive us. We get very passionate because—

CHUTES&LADDERS: Fountainhead, your Porsche has a massive engine. You got bulging marathon muscles. I'm sure your penis is as big as that javelin you used to throw.

HAIKUMOM: Censored.

CHUTES&LADDERS: But none of those things come close to the size of your ego. If you can put that aside, you may, *may* stand a chance. Otherwise, you're fucked, my friend.

HAIKUMOM: Message purged.

ORANGUTAN: OH MY GOD, WE'RE DYING HERE, DO WE HAVE TO BE SO POLITE ABOUT IT?

HAIKUMOM: Censored.

ORANGUTAN: Oh my G-zero-D. Democracy or dictatorship?

CHUTES&LADDERS: Hey Fountainhead, why the silence?

(Fountainhead logs off.)

HAIKUMOM: Nice work, guys. Congratulations.

CHUTES&LADDERS: You don't suppose he's . . . crawling on the carpet looking for one last rock??

ORANGUTAN: Lordy lord lord, I'm about to go over his house and start looking for one myself!

HAIKUMOM: That's why you're in Japan, little monkey. For now, I'm closing this thread. Fountainhead, if you want to reopen it, email me directly.

Scene Five

A flower shop in Center City[3] Philadelphia. Yaz looks over some brochures. Elliot enters, his limp looking worse.

YAZ: I was starting to get worried. How you holding?

ELLIOT: Joe's Gym, perfect remedy.

YAZ: You went boxing? Really?

ELLIOT: I had to blow off steam. Women don't get it.

YAZ: Don't be a pig. You've had four leg surgeries, no more boxing.

ELLIOT: Did Odessa call?

YAZ: You know how she is. Shutting herself out from the world.

---

3. Downtown district, the city's business and transportation hub.

ELLIOT: We need help this week.

YAZ: And I got your back.

ELLIOT: I'm just saying, pick up the phone and ask, "Do you need anything, Elliot?"

YAZ: I did speak to your dad. Everyone's gathering at the house. People start arriving from PR[4] in a few hours. The next door neighbor brought over two trays of pigs feet.

ELLIOT: I just threw up in my mouth.

YAZ: Apparently a fight broke out over who gets your mom's pocketbooks.

ELLIOT: Those pleather things from the ten-dollar store?

YAZ: Thank you, it's not like she had Gucci purses!

ELLIOT: People just need to manufacture drama.

YAZ: He said they were tearing through Ginny's closets like it was a shopping spree. "I want this necklace!" "I want the photo album!" "Yo, those chancletas[5] are mine!" I'm like, damn, let the woman be buried first.

ELLIOT: Yo, let's spend the day here.

YAZ (*Handing him some papers*): Brochures. I was being indecisive so the florist went to work on a wedding bouquet. I ruled out seven, you make the final call. Celebration of Life, Blooming Garden, Eternity Wreath.

ELLIOT: All of those have carnations. I don't want a carnation within a block of the church.

YAZ: You told me to eliminate seven. I eliminated seven. Close your eyes and point.

ELLIOT: Am I a particularly demanding person?

YAZ: Yes. What's so wrong with a carnation?

ELLIOT: You know what a carnation says to the world? That they were out of roses at the 7-Eleven. It should look something like Mom's garden.

YAZ (*In agreement*): Graveside Remembrances? That looks something like it . . . I'm renominating Graveside Remembrances. Putting it back on the table.

ELLIOT: You couldn't find anything tropical? Yaz, you could find a needle in a damn haystack and you couldn't find a bird of paradise or something?

YAZ: He just shoved some brochures in my hand.

ELLIOT (*Stares her down*): You have an awful poker face.

YAZ: Now, look here.

ELLIOT: You did find something.

YAZ: No. Not exactly.

ELLIOT: How much does it cost? Yaz, this is my mom we're talking about.

YAZ: Five hundred more. Just for the casket piece.

ELLIOT: You can't lie for shit, you never could.

YAZ: Orchid Paradise.

(*Yaz hands him another brochure. They look at it together.*)

ELLIOT: Aw damn. Damn. That looks like her garden.

YAZ: Spitting image.

ELLIOT (*Pointing*): I think she grew those.

YAZ: Right next to the tomatoes.

---

4. Puerto Rico (acronym).
5. Sandals or flip-flops (Spanish slang).

ELLIOT: But hers were yellow. Fuck.

YAZ: It's very odd to order flowers when someone dies. Because the flowers are just gonna die, too. "Would you like some death with your death?"

ELLIOT (*A confession*): I didn't water them.

YAZ (*Getting it*): What, are you supposed to be a gardener all of a sudden?

ELLIOT: It doesn't rain for a month and do I grab the hose and water Mom's garden one time?

YAZ: You were feeding her. Giving her meds. Bathing her. I could've come over and watered a leaf. A single petal.

ELLIOT: The last four days, she'd wake me up in the middle of the night. "Did you water the flowers?" "Yeah, Mom, just like you told me to yesterday." "Carry me out back, I want to see." "Mom, you're too heavy, I can't carry you down those steps one more time today."

YAZ: Little white lies.

ELLIOT: Can you do the sermon?

YAZ: This is becoming a second career.

ELLIOT: Because you're the only one who doesn't cry.

YAZ: Unlike Julia.

ELLIOT (*Imitating*): "¡Ay dios mio![6] ¡Ay! ¡Ay!"

YAZ: I hate public speaking.

ELLIOT: You're a teacher.

YAZ: It's different when it's ideas. Talking about ideas isn't saying something, it's making syllables with your mouth.

ELLIOT: You love ideas. All you ever wanted to do was have ideas.

YAZ: It was an elaborate bait and switch. The ideas don't fill the void, they just help you articulate it.

ELLIOT: You've spoken at city hall. On the radio.

YAZ: You're the face of Main Line Chevrolet. (*Pause*) Can I do it in English?

ELLIOT: You could do it in Russian for all I care. I'll just be in the front row acting like my cheek is itchy so no one sees me crying.

YAZ: The elders want a good Spanish sermon.

ELLIOT: Mami Ginny was it. You're the elder now.

YAZ: I'm twenty-nine.

ELLIOT: But you don't look a day over fifty.

YAZ: You gotta do me a favor in return. I know this is your tragedy but . . . Call William. Ask him not to come to the funeral.

ELLIOT: Oh shit.

YAZ: He saw the obit in the *Daily News*.

ELLIOT: They were close. Mami Ginny loved that blond hair. She was the madrina[7] of your wedding.

YAZ: William relinquished mourning privileges. You fall out of love with me, you lose certain rights. He calls talking about, "I want the condo." Fuck that. Fuck that. Coming from you it won't seem bitter. Wants the fucking condo all for hisself. That I decorated, that I painted. "Oh, and where's the funeral, by the way?" You know, he's been to four funerals in the Ortiz clan and I could feel

---

6. Oh Lord or Oh my God (Spanish).
7. Matron of honor (Spanish).

it, there was a part of him, under it all, that was disgusted. The open casket. The prayers.

ELLIOT: It is disgusting.

YAZ: Sitting in the pew knowing what freaks we are.

ELLIOT: He's good people.

YAZ: I was probably at his side doing the same thing, thinking I'm removed, that I'm somehow different.

ELLIOT: Hey, hey, done.

YAZ: One more condition. I go to Puerto Rico with you. We scatter her ashes together.

ELLIOT: Mami Ginny couldn't be buried in Philly. She had to have her ashes thrown at a waterfall in El Yunque,[8] just to be the most Puerto Rican mother-fucker around.

YAZ: I saw your Colgate ad.

ELLIOT: Dang, cousin Yaz watches Spanish TV?

YAZ: Shut up.

ELLIOT: I walked into the casting office, flashed my pearly whites, showed them my military ID and I charmed them.

YAZ: Do it.

ELLIOT: Give me a dollar.

YAZ: For that big cheeseburger smile?

(She gives him a dollar.)

ELLIOT *(Smiling)*: "Sonrisa,[9] baby!"

(Yaz cracks up laughing, which devolves into tears.)

How we gonna pay for Orchid Paradise?

YAZ: They should have a frequent-flower card. They punch a hole. Buy nine funeral bouquets, get the tenth free. We'd be living in a house full of lilies. Look at that guy. Arranging his daisies like little treasures. What do you think it's like to be him? To be normal?

ELLIOT: Normal? A hundred bucks says that dude has a closet full of animal porno at home.

YAZ: I bet in his family, funerals are rare occasions. I bet he's never seen a cousin get arrested. Let alone one under the age of eighteen. I bet he never saw his eight-year-old cousin sipping rum through a twisty straw or . . . I just remembered this time cousin Maria was babysitting me . . .

ELLIOT: Fat Maria or Buck Tooth Maria?

YAZ: Pig.

ELLIOT: Ah, Fat Maria.

YAZ: I was dyeing her hair. I had never dyed hair before so I asked her to read me the next step and she handed me the box and said, "You read it." And I said, "My rubber gloves are covered in toxic goop, I can't really hold that right now." And so she held it in front of my eyes and said, "You gonna have to read it because I sure as hell can't."

8. Tropical rain forest in Puerto Rico, part of the U.S. National Forest System.
9. Smile (Spanish).

ELLIOT: I been knowed that.

YAZ: I said, "But you graduated from high school." She said, "They just pass you. I just stood in the back." I was in fourth grade. *I could read! (Pause)* I have a degree written in Latin that I don't even understand. I paid seventeen thousand dollars for my piano.

ELLIOT: Oh shit.

YAZ: I have a mortgage on my piano. Drive two miles north? William told me every time I went to North Philly, I'd come back different. His family has Quaker Oats for DNA. They play Pictionary on New Year's. I'd sit there wishing I could scoop the blood out my veins like you scoop the seeds out a pumpkin and he'd be like, "Whatchu thinking about, honey?" And I'd be like, "Nothing. Let's play some Pictionary."

ELLIOT: Yo, being the scholarship case at an all-white prep school really fucked with your head, didn't it?

YAZ: I should've gone to Edison.

ELLIOT: Public school in el barrio.[1] You wouldn't have survived there for a day.

YAZ: Half our cousins didn't survive there.

ELLIOT: True. But you would've pissed your pants. At least their pants was dry when they went down.

YAZ: You're sick.

ELLIOT: And the ladies love me.

YAZ: I thought abuela[2] dying, that would be the end of us. But Ginny grabbed the torch. Christmas, Easter. Now what? Our family may be fucked-up but we had somewhere to go. A kitchen that connected us. Plastic-covered sofas where we could park our communal asses.

ELLIOT: Pop's selling the house. And the plastic-covered sofas. He's moving back to the Bronx, be with his sisters.

YAZ: You going with him? *(Elliot shrugs)* Wow. I mean, once that living room is gone, I may never step foot in North Philly again.

ELLIOT: Washed up at age twenty-four. Disabled vet. Motherless chil'. Working at Subway. Soon-to-be homeless.

YAZ: My couch is your couch.

ELLIOT: Until William takes your couch.

YAZ: My cardboard box is your cardboard box.

ELLIOT: I could go out to L.A. and be a movie star.

YAZ: You need a manager? Shoot I'm coming witchu. Forget Philly.

ELLIOT: Change of scene, baby. Dream team.

YAZ: Probably we should order some flowers first, though. Don'tcha think? *Elliot nods. To the florist)* Sir?

Scene Six

The chat room. Orangutan is online, seems upset.

---

1. Spanish-speaking district or neighborhood.
2. Grandmother (Spanish).

ORANGUTAN: 2:38 A.M. Tuesday. The witching hour.

(Chutes&Ladders logs on.)

CHUTES&LADDERS: 1:38 P.M. Monday. The lunch hour.

ORANGUTAN: I'm in a gay bar slash internet café in the city of Sapporo. Deafening dance music.

CHUTES&LADDERS: Sure you should be in a bar, little monkey?

ORANGUTAN *(Disappointed)*: I flew halfway around the world and guess what? It was still me who got off the plane. *(Taking comfort)* Sapporo is always open. The world turns upside down at night.

CHUTES&LADDERS: You're in a city named after a beer sitting in a bar. Go home.

ORANGUTAN: Everything in this country makes sense but me. The noodles in soup make sense. The woodpecker outside my window every evening? Completely logical. The girls getting out of school in their miniskirts and shy smiles? Perfectly natural. I'm floating. I'm a cloud. My existence is one sustained out-of-body experience. It doesn't matter if I change my shoes, there's not a pair I've ever been able to fill. I'm a baby in a basket on an endless river. Wherever I go I don't make sense there.

CHUTES&LADDERS: Hey, little monkey. How many days you got?

ORANGUTAN: I think day ninety-six is when the demons really come out to play.

CHUTES&LADDERS: Ninety-six? Girl, hang your hat on that.

ORANGUTAN: I really really really want to smoke crack.

CHUTES&LADDERS: Yeah, well *don't.*

ORANGUTAN: Distract me from myself. What do you really really really want, Chutes&Ladders?

CHUTES&LADDERS: I wouldn't say no to a new car—my Tercel is one sorry sight.

ORANGUTAN: What else?

CHUTES&LADDERS: Tuesday's crossword. On Monday I'm done by the time I sit at my desk. I wish every day could be a Tuesday.

ORANGUTAN: What about your son? Don't you really really really want to call him?

CHUTES&LADDERS: By all accounts, having me be a stranger these ten years has given him the best decade of his life.

ORANGUTAN: I've known you for how long?

CHUTES&LADDERS: Three Christmas Eves. When you logged on you were a stone-cold user. We sang Christmas carols online all night. Now you've got ninety days.

ORANGUTAN: Can I ask you a personal question? What's your day job?

CHUTES&LADDERS: IRS. GS4 paper pusher.

ORANGUTAN: Got any vacation days?

CHUTES&LADDERS: A solid collection. I haven't taken a vacation in ten years.

ORANGUTAN: Do you have money?

CHUTES&LADDERS: Enough to eat steak on Friday nights. Enough to buy pay-per-view boxing.

ORANGUTAN: Yeah, I bet that's all the pay-per-view you buy. *(Pause)* Enough money to fly to Japan?

(Pause.)

CHUTES&LADDERS: You should know I'm fifty years old on a good day. I eat three and a half doughnuts for breakfast and save the remaining half for brunch. I have small hands, six toes on my left foot. And my face resembles a corgi.

ORANGUTAN: If I was looking for a hot screw I wouldn't be logging on to this site.

CHUTES&LADDERS: Damn, was it something I said?

ORANGUTAN (*With honest admiration*): I've been on this planet for thirty-one years and you're the only person I've ever met who's more sarcastic than I am yet still believes in God.

CHUTES&LADDERS (*Taking the compliment*): Says the agnostic.

ORANGUTAN: The atheist. Who is very envious of believers. My brain is my biggest enemy—always arguing my soul into a corner. (*Pause*) I like you. Come to Japan. We can go get an ice cream. I can show you the countryside.

CHUTES&LADDERS: I don't have a passport. If my Tercel can't drive there, I generally don't go.

ORANGUTAN: Come save me in Japan. Be my knight in shining armor.

CHUTES&LADDERS: I'll admit, I'm a dashing concept. If you saw my flesh and blood, you'd be disappointed.

ORANGUTAN: I see my flesh and blood every day and I've learned to live with the disappointment.

CHUTES&LADDERS: I'm the squarest of the square. I live in a square house on a square block watching a square box eating square-cut fries.

ORANGUTAN: I get it. You were the kid who colored inside the lines.

CHUTES&LADDERS: No, I was the kid who ate the crayons. *Was.* I went clean and all personality left my life. Flew right out the window. I had to take life on life's terms. Messy, disappointing, bad shit happens to good people, coffee stains on my necktie, boring life.

ORANGUTAN: Maybe we could hang out and have a relationship that has very little to do with crack or addiction or history. We could watch DVDs and microwave popcorn and take walks on the waterfront while we gossip about celebrities. It could be the land of the living.

CHUTES&LADDERS: Stay in the box. Keep things in their place. It's a simple, effective recipe for ten clean years.

ORANGUTAN: Forget simple. I want a goddamn challenge.

CHUTES&LADDERS: You're in recovery and work in a foreign country. That's a challenge.

ORANGUTAN: No. No it's fucking not. Not if I just stay anonymous and alone. Like every day of my shit life so far. A friend, the kind that is nice to you and you are nice to in return. *That* would push the comfort zone. The invitation is open. Come tear my shyness open.

CHUTES&LADDERS: All right, now you're being weird. Can we change the subject?

(*Haikumom appears. She's reading the newspaper.*)

HAIKUMOM: Orangutan, cover your ears.

ORANGUTAN: Big Brother, always watching.

HAIKUMOM: Cover your ears, kiddo.

ORANGUTAN: That doesn't really work online.

HAIKUMOM: Okay, Chutes and Ladders, can we g-chat? One on one?

ORANGUTAN: Come on! No talking behind backs.

HAIKUMOM: Fine. Chutes&Ladders, you listening?

CHUTES&LADDERS: Lord have mercy spit it out.

HAIKUMOM: Orangutan may be immature . . .

ORANGUTAN: Hey.

HAIKUMOM: She may be annoying at times . . .

ORANGUTAN: What the f?

HAIKUMOM: She may be overbearing and self-obsessed and a little bit of a concern troll and she can type faster than she can think which often leads to diarrhea of the keyboard—

CHUTES&LADDERS: Your point?

HAIKUMOM: But she's telling you, "Be my friend." When's the last time someone opened your closet door, saw all them skeletons, and said, "Wassup?! Can I join the party?"

CHUTES&LADDERS: All right, my wrist is officially slapped. Thank you, oh nagging wives.

HAIKUMOM: Internal Revenue Service, 300 North Los Angeles Street 90012? Is that you?

CHUTES&LADDERS: Need my name, too? It's Wilkie. I'll leave it at that.

HAIKUMOM: I'm sending you a care package. Orangutan, you can uncover your ears now. I love you.

ORANGUTAN: Middle finger.

(*Fountainhead's log-on appears.*)

FOUNTAINHEAD: Hey all, thanks for the warm two-by-four to my head.

HAIKUMOM: All right, look who's back.

FOUNTAINHEAD: Knives sharpened? Last night we ran out of butter while my wife was cooking and she sent me to the store and it took every bit of strength I could summon not to make a "wrong turn" to that parking lot I know so well. I got the butter and on the car ride home, I couldn't help it, I drove by the lot, and there was my dealer in the shadows. My brain went on attack. "Use one more time just to prove you won't need another hit tomorrow." I managed to keep on driving and bring the butter home. Major victory. And my wife pulls it out of the plastic bag and says, "This is unsalted. I said salted." Then she feels guilty so she says never mind, never mind, she'll just add a little extra salt to the pie crust but I insist. "No, no, no, my wife deserves the right kind of butter and she's gonna get it!" I mean, I bark it, I'm already halfway out the door, my heart was racing all the way to the parking lot and raced even harder when I sat in the car and smoked. So, Michael Jordan[3] is benched with a broken foot. But he'll come back in the finals.

HAIKUMOM: Thanks for the update, Fountainhead. You may not believe this, but we were missing you and worried about you. Don't beat yourself up about the slip. You had three days clean. This time you'll make it to day four.

FOUNTAINHEAD: Be ambitious. Why not reach for a whopping five?

ORANGUTAN: Maybe you'll make it to day thirty if you tell your wife.

3. American basketball player (b. 1963) named in 1996 one of the fifty greatest players in NBA history.

FOUNTAINHEAD: I told you, I have my reasons, I cannot do that. My wife has some emotional issues.

ORANGUTAN (*Sarcastic*): No!

FOUNTAINHEAD: Listen? Please? Are you capable of that? She's in therapy twice a week. Depression, manic. I don't want to be the reason she goes down a tailspin. I actually have her best interest in mind.

CHUTES&LADDERS: Yawn.

FOUNTAINHEAD: Ah, Chutes&Ladders. I could feel you circling like a vulture. Weigh in, by all means.

CHUTES&LADDERS: And I repeat. Yawn.

FOUNTAINHEAD: Chutes&Ladders, why do I get the feeling you'd be the first in line for tickets to watch me smoke again? That you'd be in the bleachers cheering if I relapse?

CHUTES&LADDERS: How can you relapse when you don't even think you're addicted?

FOUNTAINHEAD: If you read my original post clearly, I wrote that it's a psychological addiction, not like heroin.

CHUTES&LADDERS: Well see then, you're not a junkie after all.

FOUNTAINHEAD: What is this, first-grade recess?

CHUTES&LADDERS: No, this is a site for crackheads trying not to be crackheads anymore. If you're not a crackhead, leave, we don't want you, you are irrelevant, get off my lawn, go.

HAIKUMOM: Chutes&Ladders, please.

CHUTES&LADDERS: I got this.

ORANGUTAN: He's still logged on.

CHUTES&LADDERS: Hey Fountainhead, why did you come to this website?

FOUNTAINHEAD: Because I thoroughly enjoy getting shit on.

HAIKUMOM: Censored.

CHUTES&LADDERS: Why do you want to be here?

FOUNTAINHEAD: Want? The two times I've logged on here I've *wanted* to vomit.

CHUTES&LADDERS: Well? Did you receive some sort of invitation? Did one of us ask you here?

FOUNTAINHEAD: Look, I'm the first to say it. I have a problem.

CHUTES&LADDERS: Adam had problems. Eve had problems. Why are *you here?*

FOUNTAINHEAD: To get information.

CHUTES&LADDERS: Go to Wikipedia. Why are you *here?*

FOUNTAINHEAD: Because I smoke crack.

CHUTES&LADDERS: Go to a dealer. Why are you here?

FOUNTAINHEAD: Because I plan to stop smoking crack.

CHUTES&LADDERS: Fine, when your son has a tummy-ache in the middle of the night and walks in on you tweaking and geeking just tell him, "Don't worry, Junior, Daddy's sucking on a glass dick—"

HAIKUMOM (*Overlaps*): Hey!

CHUTES&LADDERS: "—but Daddy makes 300K and this is all a part of Daddy's Plan!"

FOUNTAINHEAD: I'M A FUCKING CRACKHEAD.

HAIKUMOM (*Apologetic*): Censored.

FOUNTAINHEAD: Fuck you, Chutes&Ladders.

HAIKUMOM: Bleep.

FOUNTAINHEAD: Fuck you . . . Don't talk about my sons. Don't fucking talk about my boys.

HAIKUMOM: Bleep again.

FOUNTAINHEAD: Are you happy, Chutes&Ladders?

CHUTES&LADDERS: Absolutely not, my friend. I'm a crackhead, too, and I wouldn't wish it on my worst enemy.

FOUNTAINHEAD: And I *made* 300K, I'm currently unemployed. An unemployed crackhead. At least I still have all my teeth. *(They laugh)* Better than I can say for my dealer.

CHUTES&LADDERS *(Being a friend)*: Ex-dealer, man.

FOUNTAINHEAD: Ex-dealer. Thank you.

HAIKUMOM: Fountainhead, welcome to the dinner party. Granted, it's a party we never wanted to be invited to, but pull up a chair and pass the salt. Some people here may pour it in your wounds. Just like you, we've all crawled on the floor with a flashlight. We've thrown out the brillo and bought some more. But guess what? You had three days. For three days straight, you didn't try to kill yourself on an hourly basis. Please. Talk to your wife about your addiction. You need every supporting resource. You are in for the fight of your life. You mentioned Wharton. I live in Philly. If you're still in the area and you have an emergency or even a craving, email me directly. Any time of night. Don't take it lightly when I say a sober day for you is a sober day for me. I know you can do this but I know you can't do it alone. So stop being a highly functioning isolator and start being a highly dysfunctional *person*. The only way out it is through it.

ORANGUTAN *(Nostalgic)*: Slogans . . .

HAIKUMOM: Ya'll know I know 'em all.

CHUTES&LADDERS: They saved my life.

ORANGUTAN: Your personal favorite. Go.

HAIKUMOM: "Nothing changes if nothing changes."

(Elliot appears at the boxing gym, punching a bag. The Ghost watches him.)

GHOST: Momken men-fadluck ted-dini gawaz saffari?

ORANGUTAN: "It came to pass, it didn't come to stay."

FOUNTAINHEAD: "I obsessively pursue feeling good, no matter how bad it makes me feel."

CHUTES&LADDERS: Okay, now!

ORANGUTAN: Nice!

HAIKUMOM: Rookie don't play!

GHOST: Momken men-fadluck ted-dini gawaz saffari?

ORANGUTAN: "One hit is too many, one thousand never enough."

HAIKUMOM: "Have an at-ti-tude of gra-ti-tude."

CHUTES&LADDERS: "If you are eating a shit sandwich, chances are you ordered it."

ORANGUTAN: Ding ding ding. We have a winner!

HAIKUMOM: Censored. But good one.

GHOST: Momken men-fadluck ted-dini gawaz saffari?

HAIKUMOM *(Turning a page in the paper)*: Oh shit!

ORANGUTAN: CENSORED!!!!!! YES!!!!!! Whoooooo!

HAIKUMOM: You got me.

ORANGUTAN (*Victorious*): You know how long I've been waiting to do that?!

HAIKUMOM: My sister Ginny's in the *Daily News*! A nice big picture!

GHOST: Momken men-fadluck ted-dini gawaz saffari?

HAIKUMOM: "Eugenia P. Ortiz, A Force For Good In Philadelphia!" Okay, now!

(*Elliot punches harder. His leg is starting to bother him.*)

ELLIOT: Your leg feels great. Your leg feels like a million bucks. No pain. No pain.

HAIKUMOM: "In lieu of flowers contributions may be made to . . ."

(*Haikumom drops the newspaper.*
  The Ghost blows on Elliot, knocking him to the floor.)

GHOST: Momken men-fadluck ted-dini gawaz saffari?

(*Intermission.*)

Scene Seven

A diner. Odessa and John, aka Fountainhead, sit in a booth.

ODESSA: To lapsed Catholics. (*They clink coffee mugs*) And you thought we had nothing in common.

JOHN: When did you become interested in Buddhism?

ODESSA: My older brother used to terrorize me during mass. He would point to a statue, tell me about the evil spirit hiding behind it. Fangs, claws. I thought Saint Lazarus[4] was gonna come to life and suck my eyes out. Buddhism? Not scary. If there's spirits, they're hiding inside you.

JOHN: Aren't those the scariest kind?

ODESSA: So, how many days do you have? It should be two now.

JOHN: I put my sons' picture on my cell phone so if I get the urge, I can just look at them instead.

ODESSA: How many days?

JOHN (*Small talk*): I love Puerto Rico. On my honeymoon we stayed at that hotel in Old San Juan, the old convent. (*Odessa shrugs*) And that Spanish fort at the top of the city? El Morro?

ODESSA: I've always been meaning to make it there.

JOHN: There are these keyholes where the cannons used to fit, and the view of the waves through them, you can practically see the Spanish armada approaching.

ODESSA: I mean, one of these days I've gotta make it to PR.

JOHN: Oh. I just figured . . .

ODESSA: The Jersey Shore. Atlantic City. The Philadelphia airport. Oh, I've been places.

JOHN: On an actual plane?

ODESSA: I only fly first-class, and I'm still saving for that ticket.

(*Odessa's cell phone rings.*)

---

4. In the Gospel of John, Jesus restores Lazarus to life four days after his death.

JOHN: You're a popular lady.

ODESSA (*Into her phone, her demeanor completely changing*): What? I told you, the diner on Spring Garden and Third. I'm busy, come in an hour. One hour. Now stop calling me and asking fucking directions. (*She hangs up*)

JOHN: Says the one who censors.

ODESSA: My sister died.

JOHN: Right. You sure you're okay?

ODESSA: She's dead, ain't nothing left to do. People act like the world is going to fall apart.

JOHN: You write very Zen[5] messages. And yet.

ODESSA: My family knows every button to push.

JOHN: My condolences. (*Pause*) You don't strike me as a computer nerd. I used to employ an entire floor of them.

ODESSA: You should've seen me at first, pecking with two fingers. Now I'm like an octopus with ten little tentacles. In my neck of the woods staying clean is like trying to tap-dance on a minefield. The website fills the hours. So how are we gonna fill yours, huh? When was the last time you picked up a javelin?

JOHN: Senior year of high school.

ODESSA (*Hands him a sheet of paper*): There's a sober softball league. Fairmount Park, games on Sundays. Sober bowling on Thursdays.

JOHN: I lied in my first post. I've been smoking crack for two years. I've tried quitting hundreds of times. Day two? Please, I'm in the seven-hundredth day of hell.

ODESSA: You got it out of your system. Most people lie at one time or another on the site. The good news is, two years in, there's still time. (*Hands him another sheet of paper*) Talbott Recovery Center in Atlanta. It's designed for professionals with addictions. Paradise Recovery in Hawaii. They actually check your income before admitting you. Just for the wealthy. This place in Jersey, it's right over the bridge, they have an outpatient program for professionals like you.

JOHN: I'm tenacious. I'm driven. I love my parents.

ODESSA: Pitchforks against tanks.

JOHN: I relish in paying my taxes.

ODESSA: And you could be dead tomorrow. (*Pause*) Is your dealer male or female?

JOHN: I had a few. Flushed their numbers down the toilet like you suggested.

ODESSA: Your original connection. The one who got you hooked.

JOHN: Female.

ODESSA: Did you have sex with her?

JOHN: You don't beat around the bush do you?

ODESSA: I'll take that as a yes. (*No answer*) Do you prefer sex when you're high to sex when you're sober?

JOHN: I've never really analyzed it.

ODESSA: It can be a dangerous cocktail. Some men get off on smoking and fucking.

JOHN: All men get off on fucking.

---

5. Japanese school of Buddhism stressing the achievement of enlightenment through meditation, often using brief, enigmatic, often paradoxical statements (koans) to transcend rational thought.

ODESSA: Are you scared your wife will find out you're addicted to crack? Or are you scared she'll find out what came of your wedding vows?

JOHN: I should go.

ODESSA: We just ordered.

JOHN: I promised my son. There's a science fair tomorrow. Something about dioramas and crazy glue.

ODESSA: Don't talk about them. Get sober for them.

JOHN: Fuck you.

ODESSA: Leave me three bucks for your coffee cuz I ain't got it.

(*He stands, pulls out three dollars. She throws the money back at him.*)

You picked up the phone and called me.

JOHN (*He sits down again*): I don't know how to do this. I've never done this before.

ODESSA: I have and it usually doesn't end up so good. One in twenty, maybe, hang around. Most people just don't write one day and then thirty days and then you're wondering . . . And sometimes you get the answer. Cuz their wife looks on their computer and sees the website and logs on and writes, "I found him face down in the snow."

JOHN: How many day ones did you have?

ODESSA: Seven years' worth.

JOHN: Do you still crave?

ODESSA: On the good days, only every hour. Would you rather be honest with your wife, or would you rather end up like me? (*Pause*) That wasn't rhetorical.

JOHN: You're not exactly what I wanted to be when I grew up.

ODESSA: Truth. Now we're talking.

(*Elliot and Yaz enter.*)

YAZ: There she is.

(*Elliot and Yaz sit down in the booth.*)

ELLIOT: You were supposed to meet us at the flower place.

YAZ: The deposit was due at nine.

ODESSA: My alarm clock didn't go off.

ELLIOT: Were you up on that chat room all night?

ODESSA (*Ignoring him, to a waiter, off*): Can I get a refill, please?

ELLIOT: Where's the money?

ODESSA: I told you I don't have any money.

ELLIOT: And you think I do? I been paying for Mami Ginny's meds for six months straight—

ODESSA: Well get it from Yaz's mom.

YAZ: My mom put in for the headstone. She got an expensive one.

ODESSA: Headstone? She's getting cremated.

YAZ: She still needs a proper Catholic piece of granite. Right beside abuela, right beside your dad and sister and brother.

ELLIOT: And daughter.

YAZ: Everyone agreed.

ODESSA: No one asked my opinion.

ELLIOT: Everyone who showed up to the family meeting.

ODESSA: I wasn't invited.

YAZ: I texted you twice.

ODESSA: I was out of minutes.

ELLIOT: We just spoke on the phone.

ODESSA: Whatchu want me to do, Elliot, if I say I ain't got no fucking money, I ain't got no money.

JOHN: Hi, I'm John, nice to meet you.

YAZ: Yazmin.

ELLIOT: You one of Mom's rehab buddies?

JOHN: We know each other from work.

ELLIOT: You scrub toilets?

ODESSA (*To John*): I'm a practitioner of the custodial arts.

ELLIOT: Is she your sponsor?

JOHN (*To Odessa*): I thought this was going to be a private meeting.

ELLIOT: I'm her son.

JOHN (*To Odessa*): You must have been young.

ELLIOT: But I was raised by my Aunt Ginny and that particular aunt just died. (*To Odessa*) So now, you got three hours to find some money to pay for one basket of flowers in the funeral of the woman who changed my pampers.

YAZ: We're all supposed to be helping out.

ODESSA: You both know I run out of minutes all the time. No one could be bothered to drive by and tell me face to face?

ELLIOT: Because you always bothered to drive by and say hello to Mami Ginny when you knew she was sick? Because you bothered to hit me up one time this week and say, "Elliot, I'm sorry your mom died."

ODESSA: You still got one mom alive.

ELLIOT: Really? You want to go there?

YAZ: The flower place needs the money today.

ODESSA: She was my sister and you are my son, too.

YAZ: Guys. Two hundred dollars by end of business day.

ODESSA: That's my rent.

ELLIOT: Then fifty.

ODESSA: I just spent fifty getting my phone back on.

ELLIOT: Ten dollars. For the woman who raised your son! Do we hear ten dollars? Going once!

ODESSA: I spent my last ten at the post office.

ELLIOT: Going twice!

(*John goes into his wallet.*)

JOHN: Here's fifty.

(*They all look at him like he's crazy. He pulls out some more money.*)

Two hundred?

(*Elliot pushes the money back to John with one pointer finger, as if the bills might be contaminated.*)

ELLIOT: No offense, I don't take money from users.

JOHN: I'm not . . . I think that was my cue.

ODESSA: Sit down. My son was just going.

ELLIOT: Did World's Best Mom here tell you about her daughter?

ODESSA: I'm about to throw this coffee in your fucking face.

YAZ: Come on, Elliot, I'll pay for the flowers.

> (Elliot doesn't get up.)

ELLIOT: I looked at that chat room once. The woman I saw there? She's literally not the same person I know. (To John) Did she tell you how she became such a saint?

JOHN: We all have skeletons.

ELLIOT: Yeah well she's an archaeological dig. Did she tell you about her daughter?

ODESSA (Suddenly resigned): Go ahead, I ain't got no secrets.

YAZ (Getting up): Excuse me.

ELLIOT: Sit here and listen, Yaz. You were born with a silver spoon and you need to know how it was for me.

YAZ: I said I'd pay for the goddamn flowers so LET'S GO. NOW!

ELLIOT: My sister and I had the stomach flu, right? For a whole day we couldn't keep nothing down.

ODESSA: Three days . . . You were vomiting three days straight.

ELLIOT: Medicine, juice, anything we ate, it would come right back up. (To John) Your co-worker here took us to Children's Hospital.

ODESSA: Jefferson.

ELLIOT: It was wall-to-wall packed. Every kid in Philly had this bug. ERs were turning kids away. They gave us a flier about stomach flu and sent us home. Bright blue paper. Little cartoon diagrams. It said give your kids a spoonful of water every five minutes.

ODESSA: A teaspoon.

ELLIOT: A small enough amount that they can keep it down. Five minutes. Spoon. Five minutes. Spoon. I remember thinking, Wow, this is it. Family time. Quality time. Just the three of us. Because it was gentle, the way you said, "Open up." I opened my mouth, you put that little spoon of water into my mouth. That little bit of relief. And then I watched you do the same thing with my little sister. And I remember being like, "Wow, I love you, Mom. My moms is all right." Five minutes. Spoon. Five minutes. Spoon. But you couldn't stick to something simple like that. You couldn't sit still like that. You had to have your thing. That's where I stop remembering.

ODESSA: I left.

ELLIOT: A Department of Human Services report. That's my memory. Six hours later a neighbor kicks in the door. Me and my sister are lying in a pile of laundry. My shorts was all messed up. And what I really don't remember is my sister. Quote: "Female infant, approximately two years, pamper and tear ducts dry, likely cause of death, dehydration." Cuz when you dehydrate you can't form a single tear.

JOHN (To Elliot): I'm very sorry . . . (He puts some money on the table) For the coffee. (Exits)

ELLIOT: That's some friend you got there.

(*Pause.*)

YAZ: Mary Lou. We can at least say her name out loud. Mary Lou. Mary Lou. (*To Odessa*) One time you came to babysit me, you brought Elliot and Mary Lou—she was still in pampers—and Mary Lou had this soda from 7-Eleven. She didn't want to give me a sip. You yelled at her so bad, you totally cursed her out and I said, "You're not supposed to yell at people like that!" And you said, "No, Yaz, let her cry. She's gotta learn that ya'll are cousins, ya'll are flesh and blood, and we share everything. You hear me, Yaz? In this family we share *everything.*" You walked out of the room, came back from the kitchen with four straws in your hand, sat us down on the floor in a circle, pointed to me and said, "You first." I sipped. "Elliot's turn." He sipped. "Mary Lou's turn." She sipped. Then you sipped. You made us do like that, taking turns, going around the circle, till the cup was empty.

(*Odessa hands Elliot a key.*)

ODESSA: The pawn shop closes at five. Go into my house. Take my computer. Pawn it. However much you get, put towards a few flowers, okay?

(*Odessa exits.*)

Scene Eight

Split scene: Odessa's living room and the chat room.
Chutes&Ladders holds a phone.

ORANGUTAN: Did you hit the call button yet?

CHUTES&LADDERS: I'm working on it.

ORANGUTAN: Where are you? Are you at home?

CHUTES&LADDERS: *Jeopardy!*'s on mute.

ORANGUTAN: Dude, turn off the tube. This is serious. Did you even dial?

CHUTES&LADDERS: Yeah, yeah. (*He does*) All right, it's ringing. What am I going to say?

ORANGUTAN: "Hi, Son, it's Dad."

CHUTES&LADDERS: Wendell. That's his name. (*Hangs up*) No answer.

ORANGUTAN: As in, you hung up?

CHUTES&LADDERS: Yes. I hung up.

ORANGUTAN: Dude, way too quick!

CHUTES&LADDERS: What do you have, a stopwatch? Do you know the average time before someone answers a telephone?

ORANGUTAN: 3.2 rings.

CHUTES&LADDERS: According to . . .

ORANGUTAN: I don't reveal my sources.

CHUTES&LADDERS: Look, my son's a grown man with a good life.

ORANGUTAN: Quit moping and dial Wendell's number.

CHUTES&LADDERS: This Japan thing is cramping my style. Different networks, different time zones. No concurrent *Jeopardy!* watching.

ORANGUTAN: Deflection: nostalgia.

CHUTES&LADDERS: Humor me.

ORANGUTAN (*Humoring him*): How's my little Trebeky[6] doing?

CHUTES&LADDERS: He's had work done. Man looks younger than he did twenty years ago.

ORANGUTAN: Needle or knife?

CHUTES&LADDERS: Needle. His eyes are still in the right place.

ORANGUTAN: Well, it's working. Meow. Purrrrr. Any good categories?

CHUTES&LADDERS: Before and After.

ORANGUTAN: I love Before and After! But I'll go with . . . Quit Stalling for two hundred. (*She hums the* Jeopardy! *theme*)

CHUTES&LADDERS: It's ringing.

ORANGUTAN: My stopwatch is running.

CHUTES&LADDERS: Still ringing.

ORANGUTAN: You're going to be great.

CHUTES&LADDERS: It rang again.

ORANGUTAN: You're a brave soul.

> (*We hear a man's voice at the other end of the line say, "Hello?" Chutes&Ladders hangs up.*)

CHUTES&LADDERS: He must not be around.

ORANGUTAN: Leave a voice mail.

CHUTES&LADDERS: Maybe next time.

> (*Chutes&Ladders logs off.*)

ORANGUTAN: Hey! Don't log off, come on. Chutes&Ladders. Whatever happened to tough love? Log back on, we'll do a crossword. You can't fly before "Final Jeopardy!" Sigh. Anyone else online? Haikumom? I'm still waiting for that daily poem . . . Bueller? Bueller?

> (*In Odessa's living room, Elliot and Yaz enter.*)

YAZ: Wow, look at that computer. Stone age.

ELLIOT: Fred Flinstone shit.

YAZ: Positively Dr. Who.[7]

ELLIOT: Dr. Who?

YAZ: That computer is actually worse than what they give the adjuncts[8] at Swarthmore.

ELLIOT: What does "adjunct" even mean?

YAZ: Exactly. It's the nicest thing she owns.

ELLIOT: Let's not act like this is some heroic sacrifice. Like this makes her the world's martyr.

YAZ: We're not going to get more than fifteen bucks for it.

---

6. Alex Trebek (b. 1940), host of the television game show *Jeopardy!* since 1984.
7. British science-fiction television program (1963–present), a cult classic known for its cheesy props and special effects.
8. College instructors hired on a temporary and usually part-time basis as opposed to permanent, tenure-track faculty.

ELLIOT: Symbols matter, Yaz. This isn't about the money. This is shaking hands. This is tipping your hat. This is holding the door open. This is the bare minimum, the least effort possible to earn the label "person." (*Looks at the screen*) What do you think her password is? (*Types*) "Odessa." Nope. "Odess-aortiz." Nope.

YAZ: It's probably Elliot.

(*He types. Haikumom's log-on appears.*)

ELLIOT: The irony.

YAZ: I think legally that might be like breaking and entering.

ELLIOT (*Typing*): Hello? Oh shit it posted.

ORANGUTAN: Haikumom! Hit me with those seventeen syllables, baby!

YAZ: Haikumom? What the hell is that?

ELLIOT: Her username. She has the whole world thinking she's some Chinese prophet.

YAZ: Haiku are Japanese.

ELLIOT: "Haiku are Japanese." (*Typing*) Hello, Orangutan. How are you?

ORANGUTAN (*Formal*): I am fine. How are you?

ELLIOT (*Typing*): So, I guess you like monkeys, huh?

ORANGUTAN: An orangutan is a primate.

YAZ: Elliot.

ELLIOT: Chill.

ORANGUTAN: And this primate has ninety-eight days. That deserves a poem, don't you think?

ELLIOT (*Typing*): I don't have a poem, but I have a question. What does crack feel like?

ORANGUTAN: What?

YAZ: Elliot, cut it out.

ELLIOT (*Typing*): Sometimes I'm amazed I don't know firsthand.

ORANGUTAN: Who is this?

ELLIOT (*Typing*): How does it make your brain feel?

ORANGUTAN: Like it's flooded with dopamine.[9] Listen, cyber-stalker, if you came here for shits and giggles, we are a sadly unfunny bunch.

ELLIOT (*Typing*): Are you just a smoker or do you inject it right into your eyeballs?

ORANGUTAN: Who the fuck is this?

ELLIOT (*Typing*): Haikumom.

ORANGUTAN: Bullshit, you didn't censor me. Quit screwing around, hacker, who are you?

YAZ: You think Ginny would want you acting this way?

ELLIOT: I think Mami Ginny would want Mami Odessa to pay for a single flower on her fucking casket.

YAZ (*Types*): This is not Haikumom. It's her son.

---

9. A primary neurotransmitter (a chemical used to send signals between nerve cells), affecting motor function, emotions, learning, and behavior, associated especially with pleasure.

ORANGUTAN: Well, if you're looking for the friends and family thread, you have to go to the home page and create a new log-on. This particular forum is for people actually in recovery. Wait, her son the actor? From the Crest ad?

ELLIOT *(Typing)*: Colgate.

ORANGUTAN: "Sonrisa baby!" I saw that on YouTube! Your teeth are insanely white. Ever worked in Hollywood?

ELLIOT *(Typing)*: Psh. I just had this guy begging me to do a feature film. Gritty, documentary-style, about Marines in Iraq. I just don't want to do anything cheesy.

ORANGUTAN: So you're the war hero . . .

ELLIOT *(Typing)*: Haikumom brags.

ORANGUTAN: How's your recovery going? *(No answer)* This is the crack forum, but there's a really good pain-meds forum on this site, too. Link here.

YAZ: What is she talking about?

ORANGUTAN: There's a few war vets on that forum, just like you. You'd be in good company.

YAZ: Pain meds? Elliot? *(He doesn't respond. Yaz types)* What are you talking about?

ORANGUTAN: Haikumom told us about your history.

YAZ *(Typing)*: What history?

ORANGUTAN: Sorry. Maybe she told us in confidence.

ELLIOT: Confidence? They call this shit "world wide" for a reason.

YAZ *(Typing)*: I can search all the threads right now.

ORANGUTAN: That you had a bunch of leg surgeries in Iraq. That if a soldier said they hurt, the docs practically threw pills at them. That you OD'd three times and were in the hospital for it. She was real messed up about it. I guess she had hoped the fruit would fall a little farther from the tree.

YAZ *(To Elliot)*: Is this true?

ELLIOT: I wasn't a soldier. I was a Marine. Soldiers is the army.

YAZ: Oh my god.

ELLIOT *(Takes the keyboard, types)*: What I am: sober. What I am not and never will be: a pathetic junkie like you.

> *(He unplugs the computer. He throws the keyboard on the ground. He starts unplugging cables violently.)*

YAZ: Hold on. Just stop it, Elliot! Stop it!

ELLIOT: The one time I ever reached out to her for anything and she made me a story on a website.

YAZ: Why wouldn't you ask me for help? Why would you deal with that alone?

ELLIOT: The opposite of alone. I seen barracks that looked like dope houses. It was four months in my life, it's over. We've chopped up a lot of shit together, Yaz, but we ain't gonna chop this up. This shit stays in the vault. You got me?

YAZ: No!

ELLIOT: Yaz. *(He looks her straight in the eye)* Please. Please.

YAZ: I want to grab the sky and smash it into pieces. Are you clean?

ELLIOT: The only thing I got left from those days is the nightmares. That's when he came, and some days I swear he ain't never gonna leave.

YAZ: Who?

> (*Elliot tries to walk away from the conversation, but the Ghost is there, blocking his path.*)

Who?!

ELLIOT (*Almost like a child*): Please, Yaz. Please end this conversation. Don't make me beg, Yaz.

YAZ: The pawn shop closes in fifteen minutes. I'll get the monitor, you grab the computer.

Scene Nine

> *Chutes&Ladders is at work, on his desk phone. A bundled pile of mail is on his desk. He takes off the rubber band, browses. Junk, mostly.*

CHUTES&LADDERS (*Into the work phone*): That's right. Three Ws. Dot. Not the word, the punctuation mark. I-R-S. Not "F" like flamingo; "S" like Sam. Dot. Yup, another one. Gov. Grover orange victor.

> (*Orangutan appears, online.*)

ORANGUTAN: I'm doing it. I'm almost there. *And* I can chat! Japan is so advanced. Internet cafes are like parking meters here.

CHUTES&LADDERS: Where are you and what are you doing?

ORANGUTAN: Sapporo train station. Just did some research. Get this: in the early eighties, they straightened all the rivers in Hokkaido.

CHUTES&LADDERS: Why?

ORANGUTAN: To create jobs the government straightened the rivers! Huge bodies of water, manual laborers, scientists, engineers, bulldozers, and the rivers became straight! How nuts is that?

CHUTES&LADDERS: People can't leave good enough alone. Why are humans so damn restless?

ORANGUTAN: It's not restlessness. It's ego. Massive, bizarre ego.

CHUTES&LADDERS: Can't let a river be a river. (*Into the phone*) The forms link is on the left.

ORANGUTAN: Now it's the aughts, people keep being born, jobs still need creating, but there's no curves left to straighten, so, drum roll, the government is beginning a new program to put all the original turns back in the rivers!

CHUTES&LADDERS: Well good luck to them, but no amount of engineering can put a wrinkle back in Nicole Kidman's[1] forehead.

ORANGUTAN: Ever heard of Kushiro?

CHUTES&LADDERS: Is that your new boyfriend's name?

ORANGUTAN: Ha. Ha ha ha. It's home of the hundred-mile-long Kushiro River, which is the pilot project, the first river they're trying to recurve.

---

1. Australian actress (b. 1967) whose adventures in plastic surgery have been the stuff of tabloid rumor since at least 2008.

CHUTES&LADDERS: Kushiro River. Got it. Burned in the brain. One day I'll win a Trivial Pursuit's[2] wedge with that. *(Into the phone)* You, too, ma'am. *(He hangs up)*

ORANGUTAN: My train to Kushiro leaves in twenty minutes. My heart is pounding.

CHUTES&LADDERS: I don't follow.

ORANGUTAN: Kushiro is the town where I was born. I'm going. I'm doing it.

CHUTES&LADDERS: Hold on, now you're throwing curveballs.

ORANGUTAN: In my hand is a sheet of paper. On the paper is the address of the house where my birth parents once lived. I'm going to knock on their door.

(Chutes&Ladder's desk phone rings.)

CHUTES&LADDERS *(Into the phone)*: Help desk, please hold. *(To Orangutan)* How long have you had that address for?

ORANGUTAN: It's been burning a hole in my pocket for two days. I hounded my mom before I left Maine. She finally wrote down the name of the adoption agency. The first clue, the first evidence of who I was I ever had. I made a vow to myself, if I could stay sober for three months, I would track my parents down. So a few days ago class ended early, I went to the agency, showed my passport, and thirty minutes later I had an address on a piece of paper. Ask me anything about Kushiro. All I've done the last two days is research it. I'm an expert. Population, 190,000. There's a tech school, there's an airport.

CHUTES&LADDERS: Why are you telling me this? To get my blessing?

ORANGUTAN: I tell you about the things I do.

CHUTES&LADDERS: You don't want my opinion, you want my approval.

ORANGUTAN: Hand it over.

CHUTES&LADDERS: No.

ORANGUTAN: Don't get monosyllabic.

CHUTES&LADDERS: Take that piece of paper and use it as kindling for a warm winter fire.

ORANGUTAN: Jeez, what did they slip into your Wheaties this morning?

CHUTES&LADDERS: Do a ritual burning and never look back. You have three months. Do you know the worth in gold of three months? Don't give yourself a reason to go back to the shadows.

ORANGUTAN: I'm in recovery. I have no illusions about catharsis. I realize what will most likely happen is nothing. Maybe something tiny. A microscopic butterfly flapping her microscopic wings.

CHUTES&LADDERS: Live in the past, follow your ass.

ORANGUTAN: Don't you have the slightest ambition?

CHUTES&LADDERS: Yes, and I achieve it every day: Don't use and don't hurt anyone. Two things I used to do on a daily basis. I don't do them anymore. Done. Dream realized. No more dreaming.

(His phone rings again.)

(Into the phone) Continue holding, please.

ORANGUTAN: When was the last time you went out on a limb?

2. Board game in which players win wedge-shaped game pieces by correctly answering trivia questions.

CHUTES&LADDERS: Three odd weeks ago.

ORANGUTAN: Did you try hazelnut instead of french roast? Did you listen to *Soul Mornings* instead of NPR?[3]

CHUTES&LADDERS: There's a new secretary down the hall, she's got a nice smile. I decided to go say hello. We had a little back and forth. I said, let's have lunch, she said maybe but meant no, I turned away, looked down and my tie was floating in my coffee cup.

ORANGUTAN: I waited three months to tell you this, every step of the way, the train ride, what the river looks like. What their front door looks like. (*Pause*) I'm quitting this site. I hate this site. I fucking hate this site.

CHUTES&LADDERS: You're already losing it and you haven't even gotten on the train.

ORANGUTAN: Three days ago I suggested you and I meet face to face and you blew a fucking gasket.

CHUTES&LADDERS: That's what this is about?

ORANGUTAN: Don't flatter yourself. This is about me wanting relationships. With humans, not ones and zeroes. So we were once junkies. It's superficial. It's not real friendship.

CHUTES&LADDERS: I beg to differ.

ORANGUTAN: Prove me wrong.

CHUTES&LADDERS: Search down that address and a hundred bucks says your heart comes back a shattered light bulb.

ORANGUTAN: You mean, gasp, I'll actually FEEL something?

CHUTES&LADDERS: What are you going to do if the address is wrong? What if the building's been bulldozed? What if some new tenant lives there? What if the woman who gave you birth then gave you away answers the door?

ORANGUTAN: I DON'T KNOW! A concept you clearly avoid at all costs. Learn how to live, that's all I'm goddamn trying to do!

(*His phone rings. He picks up the receiver and hangs it up.*)

CHUTES&LADDERS: I have three grandsons. You know how I know that? Because I rang my son's doorbell one day. Step 9,[4] make amends. And his wife answered, and I don't blame her for hating me. But I saw three little boys in that living room and one of those boys said, "Daddy, who's that man at the door?" And my son said to *my grandson*, "I don't know. He must be lost." My son came outside, closed the door behind him, exchanged a few cordial words and then asked me to go.

ORANGUTAN: So I shouldn't even try.

CHUTES&LADDERS: I had five years sober until that day.

ORANGUTAN: You really believe in your heart of hearts I should not even try. (*Pause*) Coward.

(*His phone rings. He unplugs the phone line.*)

---

3. National Public Radio (acronym). 4. In the twelve-step addiction-recovery program first pioneered by Alcoholics Anonymous. In their original form, steps 8 and 9 read, "Made a list of all persons we had harmed and became willing to make amends to them all" and "Made direct amends to such people wherever possible, except when to do so would injure them or others."

CHUTES&LADDERS: You think it's easy being your friend?

ORANGUTAN: Sissy. You walk the goddamn earth scared of your own shadow, getting smaller and smaller, until you disappear.

CHUTES&LADDERS: You tease me. You insult me. It's like breathing to you.

ORANGUTAN: You fucking idiot. Why do little girls tease little boys on the playground at recess? Why the fuck were cooties invented? You fucking imbecile!

CHUTES&LADDERS: You disappeared for three months. I couldn't sleep for three months!

ORANGUTAN: I wanted to impress you. I wanted to log on and show you I could be better. And I was an idiot because you're just looking for cowards like you. I'm logging off. This is it. It's over.

CHUTES&LADDERS: Orangutan.

ORANGUTAN: Into the abyss I climb, looking for a flesh-and-blood hand to grasp onto.

CHUTES&LADDERS: Little monkey, stop it.

ORANGUTAN: I'm in the station. My train is in five minutes, you gave me all the motivational speech I need, I'm going to the platform, I'm getting on the train, I'm going to see the house where I was born.

(*She logs off. Chutes&Ladders grabs his phone and hurls it into his wastebasket. He throws his calculator, his mail pile, his pen cup to the ground. Left on his desk is one padded envelope.*)

CHUTES&LADDERS: "To Chutes&Ladders Wilkie." "From Haikumom Ortiz."

(*He rips it open, pulls out a deflated orange water wing, puts it over his hand.*)

Scene Ten

Split scene. Lights rise on a church. Elliot and Yaz stand at the lectern.

YAZ: It is time to honor a woman.[5]

ELLIOT: A woman who built her community with a hammer and nails.

YAZ: A woman who knew her nation's history. Its African roots. European roots. Indigenous roots. A woman who refused to be enslaved but lived to serve.

ELLIOT: A carpenter, a nurse, a comedian, a cook.

YAZ: Eugenia Ortiz.

ELLIOT: Mami Ginny.

(*Lights rise on Odessa's house. She sits on her floor. She scoops a spoonful of water from a mug, pours it onto the floor in a slow ribbon.*)

YAZ: She grew vegetables in her garden lot and left the gate open so anyone could walk in and pick dinner off the vine.

---

5. This eulogy is inspired by and owes much debt to Roger Zepernick's eulogy for Eugenia Burgos [Hudes's note]. Zepernick is an ordained Lutheran minister and onetime director of Centro Pedro Claver, a North Philadelphia social services organization. Eugenia "Ginny" Perez Burgos—Hudes's maternal aunt and a North Philadelphia neighborhood activist and city administrator—died of bone cancer in 2009 at age fifty-nine; obituaries credit her with raising two sons, Shawn Ortiz and Elliot Ruiz.

ELLIOT: She drank beer and told dirty jokes and even the never-crack-a-smile church ladies would be rolling laughing.

YAZ: She told me every time I visited, "Yaz, you're going to Juilliard."[6]

ELLIOT: Every morning when I left for school, "Elliot, nobody can make you invisible but you."

(Lights rise on the Sapporo train station. Orangutan is on the platform.)

LOUDSPEAKER *(An announcement in Japanese)*: 3:00 express to Kushiro now boarding on track one. Please have tickets out and ready for inspection.

YAZ: Zero.

ELLIOT: Birth children.

YAZ: One.

ELLIOT: Adopted son.

(Odessa pours another spoonful of water on the floor. Again, it creates a slow ribbon.)

YAZ: Three.

ELLIOT: Years in the army nurse corps.

YAZ: Three.

ELLIOT: Arrests for civil disobedience. I was in Iraq and she was demonstrating for peace.

YAZ: Forty-seven.

ELLIOT: Wheelchair ramps she installed in homes with disabled children or elderly.

(Odessa pours another spoonful of water on the floor. A small pool is forming.)

YAZ: Twelve.

ELLIOT: Abandoned lots she turned into city-recognized public gardens.

(Another spoonful.)

YAZ: Twenty-two.

ELLIOT: Godchildren recognized by this church.

(Another spoonful.)

YAZ: One hundred and thirty.

ELLIOT: Abandoned homes she refurbished and sold to young families.

LOUDSPEAKER *(Another announcement in Japanese)*: Final boarding call, 3:00 express to Kushiro, track one.

(Orangutan is still on the platform. She seems frozen, like she cannot move.)

YAZ: All while having a fresh pot of rice and beans on the stove every night. For any hungry stranger. And the pilgrims stopped. And they planted roots, because she was here. We are the living, breathing proof.

ELLIOT: I am the . . . Excuse me.

(He exits.)

---

6. Elite performing arts conservatory (founded 1905) housed in New York City's Lincoln Center for the Performing Arts.

YAZ: Elliot is the standing, walking testimony to a life. She. Was. Here.

(*Odessa turns the cup upside down. It is empty.*)

Scene Eleven

Chutes&Ladders at his desk. In front of him: an inflated orange water wing.

CHUTES&LADDERS (*On the phone*): Yeah, it's a 1995 Tercel. Midnight blue. It's got a few miles. A hundred and twenty thousand. But like I said, I'll give it to you for three hundred below Kelley Blue Book. Yup, automatic. Just got new brake pads. Cassette deck, mint condition. I'll even throw in a few tapes. Tina Turner and Lionel Richie.[7] Oh, hold on, call-waiting.

(*He presses mute. Sings to himself:*)

A tisket, a tasket.
A green and yellow basket.
I bought a basket for my mommy.
On the way I dropped it.
Was it red? No no no no!
Was it brown? No no no no![8]

(*Back into the phone*) Sorry about that. I got someone else interested. No, it's all right, I have them on hold. You need to see this thing tonight if you're serious. I put this listing up thirty minutes ago, my phone is ringing off the hook. 6:30? Hey I didn't mention. Little lady has racing stripes.

Scene Twelve

Split scene. Lights rise on the Sapporo train station, same as before. Orangutan has laid down on the platform and fallen asleep, her backpack like a pillow.
Lights rise on Odessa's house, that night. Her phone rings. We hear loud knocking.

ELLIOT (*Offstage*): Mami Odessa! Open the door!

(*More ringing.*)

(*Offstage*) Yo, Mom!
YAZ (*Offstage*): She's not there.
ELLIOT (*Offstage*): Can't you hear her phone ringing? Move out the way.
YAZ (*Offstage*): Be careful, your leg!

(*A few kicks and the door bursts open. Yaz and Elliot enter, switch on the lights. Odessa is in a heap, motionless, on the floor. Yaz runs and holds Odessa in her arms.*)

Oh shit. Odessa! Odessa! Wake up.

---

7. American pop singer-songwriter (b. 1949) popular in the 1980s. *Tina Turner*: singer-actress (b. 1939) widely known as "the Queen of Rock 'n' Roll"; first rocketing to fame in the 1960s (alongside husband Ike), she enjoyed a new wave of international success thanks to her comeback album, *Private Dancer* (1984).
8. Slightly mangled version of "A-Tisket, A-Tasket," a song first recorded in 1938 by jazz legend Ella Fitzgerald (1917–96), based on a traditional nursery rhyme.

(Yaz slaps Odessa's face a few times.)

Her pulse is racing.

(Yaz opens her cell phone, dials.
Elliot finds a spoon on the floor.)

ELLIOT: Oh no. Oh no you fucking didn't! MOM!!! Get up!

YAZ *(Into the phone)*: Hi, I need an ambulance. I have someone unconscious here. I think it's an overdose, crack cocaine. Yes, she has a pulse. 33 Ontario Street. No, no seizures, she's just a lump. Well what should we do while we wait? Okay. Yes. *(She hangs up)* They're on their way. Elevate her feet.

ELLIOT: Help me get her to the sofa. One, two, three.

(Elliot lifts her with Yaz's help. They struggle under her weight. In fact they lift the air. Odessa stands up, lucid, and watches the action: Elliot and Yaz struggling under her invisible weight.)

YAZ: Watch her head.

ELLIOT: Aw, fuck, my leg.

YAZ: Careful.

(They set "Odessa" on the sofa, while Odessa watches, unseen, calm.)

ODESSA: I must be in the terminal. Between flights. The layover.

YAZ: Oh god, not two in one day, please.

ELLIOT: She's been through this shit a million times. She's a survivor! WAKE UP! Call your mom. She'll get here before the ambulance.

(Yaz dials.)

ODESSA: I've been to the airport, one time. My dad flew here from Puerto Rico. First time I met him. We stood by the baggage claim, his flight was late, we waited forever. There was one single, lone suitcase, spinning around a carousel.

YAZ *(To Elliot)*: Voice mail. *(Into the phone)* Mom? Call me back immediately, it's an emergency.

ELLIOT: Give me that. *(Grabs the phone)* Titi,[9] Odessa fucking OD'd and she's dying on her living room floor and I can't take this anymore! COME GET US before I walk off and leave her on the sofa! *(He hangs up)*

YAZ: If you need to, go. No guilt. I got this.

ELLIOT: She's my *mom.* Can I be angry? Can you let me be angry?

YAZ: Why is this family plagued? *(Elliot moves to go)* Where are you going?

ELLIOT: To find something fragile.

(He exits. We hear something shatter.)

ODESSA: Everyone had cleared away from the carousel. Everyone had their bags. But this one was unclaimed. It could still be there for all I know. Spiraling. Spinning. Looking for an owner. Abandoned.

(In the Sapporo station, a Policeman enters with a bright, beaming flashlight and points it at Orangutan.

---

9. Auntie (Spanish).

In Odessa's house, a radiant white light suddenly pours in from above. Odessa looks up, is overwhelmed. It is beautiful. Yaz sees it.)

YAZ: Dear god, do you see that?

(Elliot enters. Watching Yaz, he looks up.)

ELLIOT *(Not seeing it)*: What?

YAZ *(To Odessa)*: It's okay, Odessa, go, go, we love you, I love you Titi, you are good, you *are* good. Oh my god, she's beautiful.

ELLIOT: What are you talking about?

YAZ: It's okay, it's okay. We love you Odessa.

POLICEMAN *(In Japanese)*: Miss, miss, are you okay?

ORANGUTAN *(Waking)*: English, please.

POLICEMAN: No sleeping on the floor.

ORANGUTAN *(Getting up slowly)*: Sorry.

POLICEMAN: Are you sick?

ORANGUTAN: No.

POLICEMAN: Are you intoxicated?

ORANGUTAN: No. I'm very sorry. I just got tired. I'll go. I'm going.

POLICEMAN: Please, can I give you a hand?

ORANGUTAN: No. I got it.

(Orangutan exits. The Policeman turns off his flashlight, exits.
The sound of an ambulance siren. Suddenly the white light disappears. Odessa crawls onto the couch and slips into Yaz's arms, where she's been all along.)

YAZ: Holy shit . . .

ELLIOT: What's happening, Yaz? What the fuck was that?

YAZ: You've got to forgive her, Elliot. You have to.

Scene Thirteen

The chat room.

CHUTES&LADDERS: Oh nagging wives? Orangutan? Hello? Earth to Orangutan. Come on, three days straight I been worrying about you. I have time-sensitive information. Ground control to Major Orangutan.[1]

ORANGUTAN: Ta-da.

CHUTES&LADDERS: Where you been?

ORANGUTAN: Here. There. Morrissey and Nine Inch Nails[2] on loop.

CHUTES&LADDERS: Is that what the kids like these days?

ORANGUTAN *(Rolls eyes)*: That was me rolling my eyes.

CHUTES&LADDERS: Guess what I did.

ORANGUTAN *(Shrugs)*: That was me shrugging.

---

1. David Bowie's 1969 song "Space Oddity" includes the lines "Ground Control to Major Tom: your circuit's dead, there's something wrong."
2. American industrial rock band (founded 1988). *Morrissey*: English singer-songwriter (b. 1959), vocalist of the influential rock band The Smiths (1982–87).

CHUTES&LADDERS: Guess.

ORANGUTAN: Guess what I didn't do?

CHUTES&LADDERS: Meet your birth parents?

ORANGUTAN: Board the train.

CHUTES&LADDERS: Sorry.

ORANGUTAN: Don't apologize. You had my number.

CHUTES&LADDERS: Guess what I did.

ORANGUTAN: Told me so. Had my shit pegged.

CHUTES&LADDERS: I sold my Tercel. My plane lands in Narita Airport a week from this Wednesday.

ORANGUTAN: What?

CHUTES&LADDERS: American Airlines Flight 3312. Arriving 10:01 A.M.

ORANGUTAN: You're a dumbass. Tokyo? Do you have any idea how far that is from Hokkaido? And how much a ticket on the train costs? Oy, and how the hell am I going to get out of teaching that day? Oh, you dollface, you ducky!

CHUTES&LADDERS: I'll be wearing a jean jacket and a Padres cap. That's how you'll know me.

ORANGUTAN: Oh Chutes&Ladders. You old bag of bones, you! You old so-and-so, you mensch,[3] you human being! Why the hell didn't you tell me?

CHUTES&LADDERS: I'm just hoping I have the guts to get on the plane.

ORANGUTAN: Of course you're getting on that damn plane! For me you did this?

(Fountainhead logs on.)

FOUNTAINHEAD: Hey everyone. I managed to find one computer here at the hospital that works. Odessa asked me to post a message on her behalf. She landed on: "Go." Hit reset on the timer. Back to day one.

ORANGUTAN: Who's Odessa?

FOUNTAINHEAD: Sorry. Haikumom.

ORANGUTAN: What? Do you log on here just to mock us?

CHUTES&LADDERS: Hold on, is she okay?

FOUNTAINHEAD: Cardiac arrest. They said she was one hair from a coma. She hadn't used in six years and her system went nuts.

CHUTES&LADDERS: So she's alive?

FOUNTAINHEAD: And just barely ticking. Tubes in and out of her nose. She's responsive, she mumbled a few words.

ORANGUTAN: You can't be serious.

CHUTES&LADDERS: Why are you there? Were you using with her?

FOUNTAINHEAD: No.

CHUTES&LADDERS: Did you sell her the stuff?

FOUNTAINHEAD: No, Jesus, of course not. She gave them my number, I'm her emergency contact. Why, I have no idea, we're practically strangers. Getting here to the hospital, seeing her like that . . . I don't mean this as an insult, but she looked not human. Bones with skin covering. Mummy-like.

ORANGUTAN: Fuck. You.

FOUNTAINHEAD: I'm being descriptive. I'm being honest. The thought of my boys walking in on me like that. My wife finding me . . .

3. Person of great integrity; a really good, stand-up guy (Yiddish).

ORANGUTAN: That woman is the reason I'm. Oh god, you get complacent for one second! One second! You get comfortable for one minute! Fountainhead, go to the stats page. You'll see. There's thousands of members on this site. People she has saved, people she may yet save some day. I am one of them. You are one of them.

CHUTES&LADDERS: Fountainhead, does she have family there? Has anyone come through her room?

FOUNTAINHEAD: Apparently a son and a niece but they had to catch a flight to San Juan.[4]

CHUTES&LADDERS: No parents? No other children? A friend? A neighbor?

FOUNTAINHEAD: None showed up.

CHUTES&LADDERS: Fountainhead. You have a family, I absolutely understand that, and I mean zero disrespect when I say, when I beg of you this: your job on this earth has just changed. It is not to stay clean. It's not to be a husband or a father or a CEO. It's to stay by that woman's side. Make sure she gets home safe. Bathe her. Feed her. Get her checked into a rehab, inpatient. Do not leave her side for a second. Can you do this?

FOUNTAINHEAD: I have one day clean. I'm not meant to be a saint.

CHUTES&LADDERS: Tell me now, swear on your mother's name, otherwise I'm on the first flight to Philadelphia.

FOUNTAINHEAD: I don't know.

CHUTES&LADDERS: Look man, do you believe in God?

FOUNTAINHEAD: Sure, along with unicorns and the boogeyman.

CHUTES&LADDERS: How about miracles?

FOUNTAINHEAD: When the Phils are winning.

CHUTES&LADDERS: How about actions? I bet you believe in those.

FOUNTAINHEAD: Yeah.

CHUTES&LADDERS: Your lifeboat has just arrived. Get on board or get out of the way.

FOUNTAINHEAD: I'll take care of Odessa. You have my word. My solemn word. *(Pause)* She did manage to say one thing: Someone has to take over site admin. She doesn't want the chat room full of curse words.

   (Yaz appears. A screen lights up:)

   FREEDOM&NOISE
   STATUS: ONLINE

FREEDOM&NOISE: I'm good with computers. I'll throw my hat in the ring.

CHUTES&LADDERS: Freedom&Noise, are you new here?

FREEDOM&NOISE: Yes. Very.

   (Fountainhead's phone rings.)

FOUNTAINHEAD: Freedom&Noise, email me offline. Link attached. I gotta go.

CHUTES&LADDERS: You gave us your word. Don't be a stranger.

4. Capital of Puerto Rico.

(Fountainhead logs off. Into the phone:)

FOUNTAINHEAD: Hi, honey, sorry I haven't called sooner. Something came up. Listen, I'm not coming home tonight, just order in. I have a friend who got sick, she's having an emergency. No, it's not a romantic friend. I will tell you about it. When I get home. When I— Honey? Honey . . .

(The call is over. He writes a text message.)

Honey, under my bookmarks, click on "Fantasy Football" link. My username is "Fountainhead." My password is "Porsche71." Log on and read. Send.

Scene Fourteen

Puerto Rico. A hotel room. Yaz is online.

FREEDOM&NOISE: Hello, I am Freedom&Noise, your interim site manager, currently logging on from the Rainforest B&B in Puerto Rico. I am not a user, I've smoked pot twice, both times when I was thirteen, and am therefore unqualified for this position. There was a young woman I once knew. Let's call her "O." My crazy aunt, a fun babysitter, the baddest hide-and-seek player north of Girard Avenue. We played dress-up, built booby traps and forts, and when I was eight, she disappeared. No explanation, no acknowledgment she had ever existed, the grown-ups in the family had taken a vow of silence, and O. had been erased. My freshman year at college, I returned home for Thanksgiving, and thanks to a snow delay I walked into the middle of turkey dinner itself, and there was O., a plate full of food, chowing down. I hadn't seen her in ten years. After dinner she told me to congratulate her, it was her anniversary. I said, "Did you get married?" She pulled a necklace out from under her shirt and said, "You know what these gold letters mean? The 'N' is for narcotics, the 'A' is for anonymous and today is my two-year anniversary of being clean." *(Pause)* A few days ago I met a new woman: Haikumom. A woman who created a living, breathing ecosystem, and since I've never sown a single seed, let alone planted a garden, the least I can do is censor you, fix glitches—and one other thing . . . Formulating first line. Did Haikumom really do these on the fly? Five-seven-five, right? *(Counting the syllables on her fingers)* Box full of ashes . . .

(Elliot enters from the bathroom, freshly showered, pulling on a shirt)

ELLIOT: Whatchu looking at, Willis?[5]
YAZ: Sh. I'm counting syllables.

(Elliot looks over Yaz's shoulder at the computer.)

ELLIOT: Hold up. Don't read that shit, Yaz.
YAZ: You know how Odessa got into haiku in the first place?
ELLIOT: For real, close the computer.

---

5. Play on "Whatchu talkin' about, Willis?," catchphrase of a character (played by diminutive actor Gary Coleman [1968–2010]) on the popular 1980s sitcom *Diff'rent Strokes*.

YAZ: I went through this Japanese minimalist phase freshman year. Rock Gardens, Zen Buddhism, the works. I gave her a haiku collection for Christmas.

ELLIOT: Yeah, and you gave me a midget tree that died by New Year's.

YAZ: Bonsai. You didn't water it.

ELLIOT (*Closing Yaz's laptop*): For the two days I'm away from Philly, let me be away from Philly?

YAZ: You know where I was gonna be by thirty? Two kids. Equal-housework marriage. Tenure, no question. Waaaay tenured, like by the age of twenty-four. Carnegie Hall debuts: Yazmin Ortiz's "Oratorio for Electric Guitar and Children's Choir." I wrote a list on a piece of paper and dug a hole in Fairmount Park and put it in the ground and said, "When I turn thirty, I'll dig it up and cross it all off." And I promise you I'll never have the courage to go to that spot with a shovel and face my list full of crumbs, decoys and bandaids.

ELLIOT: Married with kids, what an awful goal.

YAZ: Odessa's done things.

ELLIOT: Well, when you throw her a parade, don't expect me to come.

YAZ: You've done things.

ELLIOT: I wouldn't come to my own parade, either.

YAZ: Ginny did things. What have I done?

ELLIOT: Second-grade Language Arts. You glued my book report.

YAZ: I couldn't stop your leg from getting chewed up.

ELLIOT: Fairmount little league basketball. You kept score, you brought our equipment.

YAZ: I didn't hold your hand when you were in the desert popping pills trying to make yourself disappear. I didn't keep Odessa away from that needle. I didn't water a single plant in Ginny's garden. We're in PR and I'm gonna dig a new hole and I'm not putting a wish or a list in there, I'm putting a scream in there. And I'm gonna sow it like the ugliest foulest and most necessary seed in the world and it's going to bloom! This time it's going to fucking bloom!

ELLIOT: My eyes just did this weird thing. For a second, it was Mom standing in front of me.

YAZ: Odessa?

ELLIOT: Ginny.

YAZ: Elliot, your birth mother saved your life by giving you away. Tell me I'm wrong.

(*Elliot doesn't respond. Yaz begins gathering her stuff hastily.*)

Now we got some ashes to throw. El Yunque closes in an hour and a half.

ELLIOT: Maybe we should do this tomorrow.

YAZ: I gotta make a call. I'll be in the lobby!

(*She exits.*)

ELLIOT: Yaz?

(*The Ghost appears. He's probably been there the whole time.*)

Yaz!

GHOST: Momken men-fadluck ted-dini gawaz saffari?

(*The Ghost reaches out his hand to touch Elliot.*)

Momken men-fadluck ted-dini gawaz saffari?

(*The second they make contact, Elliot spins on his heels and grabs the Ghost. The Ghost defends himself, pulling away. They start pushing, grabbing, fighting. The Ghost is looking for something—is it Elliot's wallet?*)

Momken men-fadluck ted-dini gawaz saffari?

(*The Ghost finds Elliot's wallet and tears through it, hurling its contents onto the floor. Elliot attacks again, but this time the Ghost reaches out his hand and touches Elliot's face. Elliot freezes, unable to move, as the Ghost's hands glide across his features, considering each one with authority, taking inventory.*)

Momken men-fadluck ted-dini gawaz saffari?

(*The Ghost is gone. Elliot catches his breath, shaken. He reaches into his pocket and pulls out a bottle of pills. He puts one pill in his hand. Then he empties the entire bottle of pills into his hand. He stares at the pills, wanting to throw them away.*)

Scene Fifteen

Split scene. Odessa's bathroom. The bathtub is filled with water. John enters, carrying a very weak Odessa. Odessa is wearing shorts and a bra, a modest outfit for bathing. John lowers her gently into the bathtub.

JOHN: Does that feel okay?

(*Odessa barely nods.*)

It's not too hot or cold?

(*Odessa shakes her head.*)

I don't know how to do this. These are things women do. Take care of sick people. Make the wounds go away.

(*He takes a sponge and starts to bathe her.*)

Is this okay?

(*He lifts her arms and washes her armpits. Embarrassed at first, but quickly gets the swing of it.*)

We check you in at 4:30 so we have plenty of time to clean you up and get you in good clothes, okay? You'll go in there looking like a decent woman.

(*Odessa whispers something inaudible.*)

What was that?

(*She gestures for him to lean in. She whispers into his ear.*)

One more time.

(*She whispers a little louder.*)

Did someone take swimming lessons?

(*She whispers again.*)

Did someone put on water wings?

(*She nods. He continues to bathe her, gently, in silence as:*
    Lights rise on Tokyo. Narita Airport. Orangutan sits on the floor by the luggage carousel. At her feet is a sign that says Chutes&Ladders. She throws the sign like a frisbee across the floor and gets up to leave. Chutes&Ladders enters, rolling a suitcase behind him. He waves to Orangutan.)

CHUTES&LADDERS: Orangutan?

ORANGUTAN: What the holy hell?

CHUTES&LADDERS: Sorry. Sorry. I tried calling but my cell doesn't work here. I told you I'm no good at this fancy kind of living.

ORANGUTAN: You were supposed to land yesterday, you were too scared to get on the plane. You rebook, you were supposed to land today, forty-five minutes ago. Everyone got their luggage already. The last person pulled the last suitcase from the carousel half an hour ago. I thought, Wow, this one sure knows how to play a joke on the ladies. I thought you had left me at the fucking altar.

CHUTES&LADDERS: I got sick on the flight. Totally embarrassing. I had a panic attack as the plane landed and I started tossing into the doggy bag right next to this nice old lady. I've been sitting on the bathroom floor emptying my stomach. Then I had to find a toothbrush and toothpaste and mouthwash because I didn't want to greet you with bad breath and all.

(*She looks skeptical. She sniffs his mouth quickly.*)

ORANGUTAN: Minty. (*Pause*) Oh, you dummy, you big old dummy. COME HERE, you San Diego Padre.

(*They hug. A warm and brief greeting.*)

What's your name?

CHUTES&LADDERS: Clay. Clayton "Buddy" Wilkie.

ORANGUTAN: I'm Madeleine Mays.

CHUTES&LADDERS: It's weird, huh?

ORANGUTAN: Totally weird. The land of the living.

(*They hug. They melt into each other's arms. A hug of basic survival and necessary friendship. Then, they exit, rolling Chutes&Ladders's suitcase off as lights rise in:*
    Puerto Rico. A rock outcropping looking out over a waterfall. Elliot is there, looking down at the water.)

ELLIOT (*Looking down*): Oh shit! Yaz, you gotta see this! Yaz? Fucking Johnny Appleseed of El Yunque.

(*Yaz enters holding a soil-covered flower bulb. She compares the root against a field book.*)

YAZ: I found my spiral ginger! This is going right next to the aloe by the kitchen door, baby!

ELLIOT: Yo, this science experiment ain't getting past security.

YAZ: Experiment my ass. I'm planting these in Ginny's garden.

ELLIOT: Customs gonna sniff that shit from a mile away.

YAZ (*Putting the bulb in a ziploc baggie full of dirt and bulbs*): China rose . . . Sea grape . . . Some kind of fern . . .

ELLIOT: When they cuff those wrists, I don't know you.

YAZ: I'll hide them in my tampon box.

ELLIOT: That don't work. My first trip to PR, Mami Ginny smuggled a coqui[6] back with her kotex and got arrested. Front page of the *Daily News*.

YAZ: Good shit. (*A dirty little secret*) You know what Grandma did?

ELLIOT: Do I want to?

YAZ: She used to smuggle stuff back, too. She'd tuck it below her boobs. She had storage space under there!

ELLIOT: Yeah after she was sixty and had nursed seven kids. Yo you think if I jumped off this rock right now and dove into that water, I'd survive?

YAZ: Just watch out for the huge boulders and the footbridge.

ELLIOT: It's tempting. That spray. (*His phone beeps*) Reception in the rainforest.

YAZ: Kind of ruins the romance.

ELLIOT (*Reads a text message*): Damn, that was fast.

YAZ: What?

ELLIOT: Pop sold the house. Did he even put out a listing?

YAZ: Not that I know of.

ELLIOT: That's like a VW bus going from zero to sixty in three seconds. Don't make no sense.

YAZ: Must have been an inside job.

ELLIOT: I guess so.

YAZ: A way way inside job . . .

ELLIOT: Yaz . . .

YAZ (*Conspiratorially*): Yeeeees?

ELLIOT: What did you do?

YAZ (*Very conspiratorially*): Nothing . . .

ELLIOT: Holy shit!

YAZ: Put my Steinway[7] on craigslist. Got four responses before you made it down to the lobby. My eighty-eight keys are worth more than Ginny's whole house. Sadly. I'll buy an upright.

ELLIOT: You are one crazy motherfucking adjunct! Yo, I don't know if el barrio is ready for you. I don't know if they can handle you!

YAZ: Oh, they gonna handle me.

ELLIOT: Wait wait wait. You need a title.

YAZ: Yaz will do just fine.

---

6. Singing tree frog native to Puerto Rico.
7. Piano made by the legendary German American firm Steinway & Sons (founded 1853).

ELLIOT: Hells no. Command respect. I step on those corners, I'm Big El. *(Pause)* "Professor."

YAZ: "Professor."

ELLIOT: You like that, huh?

YAZ: It'll be the Cousins House. We'll renovate the kitchen. You redo the plumbing, I'll hook up a little tile backsplash.

ELLIOT: I watched Bob Vila[8] with Pop, but I ain't no handyman.

YAZ: Just wait, Mr. Home Depot. You're gonna be like, "Fuacata,[9] fuacata, fuacata," with your power drill and nail gun and vise grips.

ELLIOT: Something like that.

YAZ: Well? Get to it. Toss 'em.

ELLIOT: Me? Why the hell do you think I let you come along?

   (He hands Yaz the box.)

YAZ: Well then say something. Pray.

ELLIOT: I'm all out of prayers.

YAZ: Me, too. Make a toast.

ELLIOT: To LAX. I'm not flying back with you.

YAZ: What do you mean?

ELLIOT: I called from the hotel and changed my flight. One-way ticket. Watch out, Hollywood. *(Pause)* You know how you had to shake me awake last night?

YAZ *(Demeanor shifting)*: You were literally sobbing in your sleep.

ELLIOT: This dream was different than usual. I'm fixing a Subway hoagie, I feel eyes on the back of my neck, I turn around and expect to see him, the first guy I shot down in Iraq. But instead it's Mami Ginny. Standing next to the bread oven, smiling. You know how her eyes smile?

YAZ: Best smile in the world.

ELLIOT: Looking at me, her son. Coming to say good-bye.

YAZ: That's beautiful.

ELLIOT: She puts on her glasses to see my face even better. She squints and something changes. The moment I come into focus, her eyes widen. Her jaw drops, she starts trembling. Then she starts to cry. Something she's seeing scares her. Then she starts to scream. Loud, like, "Ahhh! Ahhh!" She won't stop looking at me, but she's terrified, horrified by what she sees. And I don't know if my lip is bleeding or there's a gash on my forehead or she's looking through my eyes and seeing straight into my fucking soul.

YAZ: Jesus.

ELLIOT: I wanted Mami Odessa to relapse, Yaz. I wanted her to pick up that needle. I knew precisely what to do, what buttons to push, I engineered that shit, I might as well have pushed the thing into her vein. Because I thought, Why would God take the good one? Yo, take the bad mom instead! I was like, Why wouldn't you take the bad fucking mom? If I stay in Philly, I'm gonna turn into it. I'm gonna become one of them. I'm already halfway there. You've got armor, you've got ideas, but I don't.

8. Host (b. 1946) of a series of home-improvement shows, beginning with *This Old House* (1979–89)

9. Onomatopoeic interjection akin to "Wham!" or "Bam!" (Cuban Spanish).

YAZ: Go. Go and don't you ever, ever look back.

(*She takes his hand.*)

But if you do, there will be a plastic-covered sofa waiting for you.

(*Below them, in Philadelphia, John is done bathing Odessa. He lifts her and holds her like an angel above the bathtub. She is dripping wet and seems almost radiant, and yet deeply, deeply sick.*)

I'm the elder now. I stay home. I hold down the fort.

ELLIOT: I'm walking.

YAZ: On three?

YAZ AND ELLIOT: One.

Two.

Three.

(*They toss the ashes. Blackout.*)

2011

QUESTIONS

1. WATER BY THE SPOONFUL features many entirely fictional characters, situations, and events, including the online community created by "Haikumom" and the death of Elliot's infant sister. Yet as the biographical headnote and textual footnotes suggest, the play was also inspired in part by real people and events: Hudes's cousin Elliot Ruiz was raised by their aunt Ginny, who died of cancer; he was wounded in Iraq; Odessa is based in part on a cousin who is a former drug addict; and so on. How, if at all, might this knowledge affect your response to the play and its characters?

2. How do the characters of Elliot and Yaz each develop over the course of the play? What role in that development is played by their experiences in both real and online worlds?

3. As readers or spectators of Hudes's play, we first get to know Odessa via her online interactions, and throughout the play we see much more of these than does Elliott or Yaz. How does that affect how we view and feel about Odessa, Elliott, and their individual and mutual conflicts? Why might Hudes have chosen to structure the play in this way?

4. How would you articulate the main theme of the play? Might it have to do with notions of family? with the ways we help and hurt others? with the process of trauma and recovery? something else entirely?

5. How might Yaz's discussion of musical dissonance provide a language for articulating the play's themes or describing its structure?

6. Especially in terms of conflict or theme, what role is played by Fountainhead, Chutes&Ladders, and Orangutan? How, if at all, might it matter that Fountainhead is the play's only white or upper-middle-class character? that Chutes&Ladders and Orangutan end up meeting in the real world?

SUGGESTIONS FOR WRITING

1. Though WATER BY THE SPOONFUL begins by alternating scenes set entirely in the real world with scenes set wholly in the virtual world, later scenes tend to be more complicated. Scene 10, for example, is a "split scene" that shifts among Ginny's funeral, Odessa's house, and a train station in Sapporo, Japan. Choose one of these "split

scenes" and write an informal response paper about it. How do the various elements of the scene work together and perhaps comment on each other? How might the scene be staged so as to emphasize those connections without confusing the audience?

2. Write an essay exploring what WATER BY THE SPOONFUL seems to suggest about the power and limits of online selves and communities. What might the virtual world allow us to be and do that the real world doesn't, and vice versa?

3. Write an essay exploring the water imagery in Hudes's play. By its end, what various meanings might the phrase "water by the spoonful" accrue?

4. WATER BY THE SPOONFUL features a cast of characters who at first seem very different from each other in terms of their personalities, their backgrounds, their situations in life, and their conflicts. Yet over the course of the play we and they arguably discover just how similar they are. Choose any two characters from the play, perhaps those that initially seem the most different or far removed from each other. Then write an essay comparing the characters and their development over the course of the play. What similarities emerge as the play progresses? To what extent and how do the characters themselves come to appreciate these similarities? What might the play ultimately say or show us through these characters?

5. Charles Isherwood, writing in *The New York Times*, describes WATER BY THE SPOON-FUL's theme as involving "the myriad ways in which human lives can intersect, and the potentially great rewards—or irreparable damage—that can result from the unlikely spark of those connections." Others instead describe the play as exploring the difficulty and importance of forgiving both ourselves and others; the idea "that no one is above reproach—or beyond redemption"; "the true meaning of family" (theatreworks .org); or the "life-affirming message" that "[p]eople instinctively take care of each other" and that "hitting bottom is the start of the trip back up" (Richard Zoglin, in *Time*). Write an essay defending and developing one of these claims.

Reading More Drama

LORRAINE HANSBERRY
(1930–1965)
A Raisin in the Sun

The first African American woman to have a play produced on Broadway, Lorraine Hansberry was born in Chicago to a prominent family and even at a young age showed an interest in writing. She attended the University of Wisconsin, the Art Institute of Chicago, and Roosevelt University, then moved to New York City in order to concentrate on writing for the stage. After extensive fund-raising, Hansberry's play *A Raisin in the Sun* (loosely based on events involving her own family) opened in 1959 at the Ethel Barrymore Theatre on Broadway, received critical acclaim, and won the New York Drama Critics' Circle Award for Best Play. Hansberry's second production, *The Sign in Sidney Brustein's Window*, had a short run on Broadway in 1964. Shortly after, Hansberry died of cancer. *To Be Young, Gifted, and Black*, adapted from her writing, was produced off-Broadway in 1969 and published the next year, when her drama *Les Blancs* was also produced.

What happens to a dream deferred?

Does it dry up
Like a raisin in the sun?
Or fester like a sore—
And then run?
Does it stink like rotten meat?
Or crust and sugar over—
Like a syrupy sweet?
Maybe it just sags
Like a heavy load.

Or does it explode?

—LANGSTON HUGHES[1]

---

1. Hughes's poem, published in 1951, is titled "Harlem (A Dream Deferred)" (p. 607).

CAST OF CHARACTERS

RUTH YOUNGER	JOSEPH ASAGAI
TRAVIS YOUNGER	GEORGE MURCHISON
WALTER LEE YOUNGER (BROTHER)	KARL LINDNER
BENEATHA YOUNGER	BOBO
LENA YOUNGER (MAMA)	MOVING MEN

The action of the play is set in Chicago's Southside, sometime between World War II and the present.

ACT I

Scene One

The Younger living room would be a comfortable and well-ordered room if it were not for a number of indestructible contradictions to this state of being. Its furnishings are typical and undistinguished and their primary feature now is that they have clearly had to accommodate the living of too many people for too many years—and they are tired. Still, we can see that at some time, a time probably no longer remembered by the family (except perhaps for MAMA*), the furnishings of this room were actually selected with care and love and even hope—and brought to this apartment and arranged with taste and pride.*

That was a long time ago. Now the once loved pattern of the couch upholstery has to fight to show itself from under acres of crocheted doilies and couch covers which have themselves finally come to be more important than the upholstery. And here a table or a chair has been moved to disguise the worn places in the carpet; but the carpet has fought back by showing its weariness, with depressing uniformity, elsewhere on its surface.

Weariness has, in fact, won in this room. Everything has been polished, washed, sat on, used, scrubbed too often. All pretenses but living itself have long since vanished from the very atmosphere of this room.

Moreover, a section of this room, for it is not really a room unto itself, though the landlord's lease would make it seem so, slopes backward to provide a small kitchen area, where the family prepares the meals that are eaten in the living room proper, which must also serve as dining room. The single window that has been provided for these "two" rooms is located in this kitchen area. The sole natural light the family may enjoy in the course of a day is only that which fights its way through this little window.

At left, a door leads to a bedroom which is shared by MAMA *and her daughter,* BENEATHA. *At right, opposite, is a second room (which in the beginning of the life of this apartment was probably a breakfast room) which serves as a bedroom for* WALTER *and his wife,* RUTH.

Time: Sometime between World War II and the present.

Place: Chicago's Southside.

At Rise: It is morning dark in the living room. TRAVIS *is asleep on the make-down bed at center. An alarm clock sounds from within the bedroom at right, and presently* RUTH *enters from that room and closes the door behind her. She crosses sleepily*

Ruby Dee as Ruth, Sidney Poitier as Walter, and Diana Sands as Beneatha in the original 1959 Broadway production of *A Raisin in the Sun*

toward the window. As she passes her sleeping son she reaches down and shakes him a little. At the window she raises the shade and a dusky Southside morning light comes in feebly. She fills a pot with water and puts it on to boil. She calls to the boy, between yawns, in a slightly muffled voice.

RUTH *is about thirty. We can see that she was a pretty girl, even exceptionally so, but now it is apparent that life has been little that she expected, and disappointment has already begun to hang in her face. In a few years, before thirty-five even, she will be known among her people as a "settled woman."*

She crosses to her son and gives him a good, final, rousing shake.

RUTH: Come on now, boy, it's seven thirty! [*Her son sits up at last, in a stupor of sleepiness.*] I say hurry up, Travis! You ain't the only person in the world got to use a bathroom! [*The child, a sturdy, handsome little boy of ten or eleven, drags himself out of the bed and almost blindly takes his towels and "today's clothes" from drawers and a closet and goes out to the bathroom, which is in an outside hall and which is shared by another family or families on the same floor.* RUTH

crosses to the bedroom door at right and opens it and calls in to her husband]
Walter Lee! . . . It's after seven thirty! Lemme see you do some waking up in
there now! [*She waits.*] You better get up from there, man! It's after seven thirty
I tell you. [*She waits again.*] All right, you just go ahead and lay there and next
thing you know Travis be finished and Mr. Johnson'll be in there and you'll be
fussing and cussing round here like a mad man! And be late too! [*She waits, at
the end of patience.*] Walter Lee—it's time for you to get up!

> [*She waits another second and then starts to go into the bedroom, but is appar-
> ently satisfied that her husband has begun to get up. She stops, pulls the door
> to, and returns to the kitchen area. She wipes her face with a moist cloth and
> runs her fingers through her sleep-disheveled hair in a vain effort and ties an
> apron around her housecoat. The bedroom door at right opens and her hus-
> band stands in the doorway in his pajamas, which are rumpled and mismated.
> He is a lean, intense young man in his middle thirties, inclined to quick ner-
> vous movements and erratic speech habits—and always in his voice there is a
> quality of indictment.*]

WALTER: Is he out yet?

RUTH: What you mean *out*? He ain't hardly got in there good yet.

WALTER: [*Wandering in, still more oriented to sleep than to a new day.*] Well,
what was you doing all that yelling for if I can't even get in there yet? [*Stopping and thinking.*] Check coming today?

RUTH: They *said* Saturday and this is just Friday and I hopes to God you ain't
going to get up here first thing this morning and start talking to me 'bout no
money—'cause I 'bout don't want to hear it.

WALTER: Something the matter with you this morning?

RUTH: No—I'm just sleepy as the devil. What kind of eggs you want?

WALTER: Not scrambled. [RUTH *starts to scramble eggs.*] Paper come? [RUTH *points
impatiently to the rolled up* Tribune *on the table, and he gets it and spreads it
out and vaguely reads the front page.*] Set off another bomb yesterday.

RUTH: [*Maximum indifference.*] Did they?

WALTER: [*Looking up.*] What's the matter with you?

RUTH: Ain't nothing the matter with me. And don't keep asking me that this
morning.

WALTER: Ain't nobody bothering you. [*Reading the news of the day absently
again.*] Say Colonel McCormick[2] is sick.

RUTH: [*Affecting tea-party interest.*] Is he now? Poor thing.

WALTER: [*Sighing and looking at his watch.*] Oh, me. [*He waits.*] Now what is
that boy doing in that bathroom all this time? He just going to have to start
getting up earlier. I can't be late to work on account of him fooling around
in there.

RUTH: [*Turning on him.*] Oh, no he ain't going to be getting up no earlier no such
thing! It ain't his fault that he can't get to bed no earlier nights 'cause he got
a bunch of crazy good-for-nothing clowns sitting up running their mouths in
what is supposed to be his bedroom after ten o'clock at night . . .

---

2. Robert Rutherford McCormick (1880–1955), owner-publisher of the *Chicago Tribune*.

WALTER: That's what you mad about, ain't it? The things I want to talk about with my friends just couldn't be important in your mind, could they?

[*He rises and finds a cigarette in her handbag on the table and crosses to the little window and looks out, smoking and deeply enjoying this first one.*]

RUTH: [*Almost matter of factly, a complaint too automatic to deserve emphasis.*] Why you always got to smoke before you eat in the morning?

WALTER: [*At the window.*] Just look at 'em down there . . . Running and racing to work . . . [*He turns and faces his wife and watches her a moment at the stove, and then, suddenly.*] You look young this morning, baby.

RUTH: [*Indifferently.*] Yeah?

WALTER: Just for a second—stirring them eggs. It's gone now—just for a second it was—you looked real young again. [*Then, drily.*] It's gone now—you look like yourself again.

RUTH: Man, if you don't shut up and leave me alone.

WALTER: [*Looking out to the street again.*] First thing a man ought to learn in life is not to make love to no colored woman first thing in the morning. You all some evil people at eight o'clock in the morning.

[TRAVIS *appears in the hall doorway, almost fully dressed and quite wide awake now, his towels and pajamas across his shoulders. He opens the door and signals for his father to make the bathroom in a hurry.*]

TRAVIS: [*Watching the bathroom.*] Daddy, come on!

[WALTER *gets his bathroom utensils and flies out to the bathroom.*]

RUTH: Sit down and have your breakfast, Travis.

TRAVIS: Mama, this is Friday. [*Gleefully.*] Check coming tomorrow, huh?

RUTH: You get your mind off money and eat your breakfast.

TRAVIS: [*Eating.*] This is the morning we supposed to bring the fifty cents to school.

RUTH: Well, I ain't got no fifty cents this morning.

TRAVIS: Teacher say we have to.

RUTH: I don't care what teacher say. I ain't got it. Eat your breakfast, Travis.

TRAVIS: I *am* eating.

RUTH: Hush up now and just eat!

[*The boy gives her an exasperated look for her lack of understanding, and eats grudgingly.*]

TRAVIS: You think Grandmama would have it?

RUTH: No! And I want you to stop asking your grandmother for money, you hear me?

TRAVIS: [*Outraged.*] Gaaaleee! I don't ask her, she just gimme it sometimes!

RUTH: Travis Willard Younger—I got too much on me this morning to be—

TRAVIS: Maybe Daddy—

RUTH: *Travis!*

[*The boy hushes abruptly. They are both quiet and tense for several seconds.*]

TRAVIS: [*Presently.*] Could I maybe go carry some groceries in front of the super-market for a little while after school then?

RUTH: Just hush, I said. [TRAVIS *jabs his spoon into his cereal bowl viciously, and rests his head in anger upon his fists.*] If you through eating, you can get over there and make up your bed.

> [*The boy obeys stiffly and crosses the room, almost mechanically, to the bed and more or less carefully folds the covering. He carries the bedding into his mother's room and returns with his books and cap.*]

TRAVIS: [*Sulking and standing apart from her unnaturally.*] I'm gone.

RUTH: [*Looking up from the stove to inspect him automatically.*] Come here. [*He crosses to her and she studies his head.*] If you don't take this comb and fix this here head, you better! [TRAVIS *puts down his books with a great sigh of oppression, and crosses to the mirror. His mother mutters under her breath about his "slubbornness."*] 'Bout to march out of here with that head looking just like chickens slept in it! I just don't know where you get your slubborn ways . . . And get your jacket, too. Looks chilly out this morning.

TRAVIS: [*With conspicuously brushed hair and jacket.*] I'm gone.

RUTH: Get carfare and milk money—[*Waving one finger.*]—and not a single penny for no caps, you hear me?

TRAVIS: [*With sullen politeness.*] Yes'm.

> [*He turns in outrage to leave. His mother watches after him as in his frustra-tion he approaches the door almost comically. When she speaks to him, her voice has become a very gentle tease.*]

RUTH: [*Mocking; as she thinks he would say it.*] Oh, Mama makes me so mad sometimes, I don't know what to do! [*She waits and continues to his back as he stands stock-still in front of the door.*] I wouldn't kiss that woman good-bye for nothing in this world this morning! [*The boy finally turns around and rolls his eyes at her, knowing the mood has changed and he is vindicated; he does not, how-ever, move toward her yet.*] Not for nothing in this world! [*She finally laughs aloud at him and holds out her arms to him and we see that it is a way between them, very old and practiced. He crosses to her and allows her to embrace him warmly but keeps his face fixed with masculine rigidity. She holds him back from her presently and looks at him and runs her fingers over the features of his face. With utter gentleness—*] Now—whose little old angry man are you?

TRAVIS: [*The masculinity and gruffness start to fade at last.*] Aw gaalee—Mama . . .

RUTH: [*Mimicking.*] Aw—gaaaaalleeeee, Mama! [*She pushes him, with rough playfulness and finality, toward the door.*] Get on out of here or you going to be late.

TRAVIS: [*In the face of love, new aggressiveness.*] Mama, could I *please* go carry groceries?

RUTH: Honey, it's starting to get so cold evenings.

WALTER: [*Coming in from the bathroom and drawing a make-believe gun from a make-believe holster and shooting at his son.*] What is it he wants to do?

RUTH: Go carry groceries after school at the supermarket.

WALTER: Well, let him go . . .

TRAVIS: [*Quickly, to the ally.*] I *have* to—she won't gimme the fifty cents . . .

WALTER: [*To his wife only.*] Why not?

RUTH: [*Simply, and with flavor.*] 'Cause we don't have it.

WALTER: [*To* RUTH *only.*] What you tell the boy things like that for? [*Reaching down into his pants with a rather important gesture.*] Here, son—

[*He hands the boy the coin, but his eyes are directed to his wife's.* TRAVIS *takes the money happily.*]

TRAVIS: Thanks, Daddy.

[*He starts out.* RUTH *watches both of them with murder in her eyes.* WALTER *stands and stares back at her with defiance, and suddenly reaches into his pocket again on an afterthought.*]

WALTER: [*Without even looking at his son, still staring hard at his wife.*] In fact, here's another fifty cents . . . Buy yourself some fruit today—or take a taxi-cab to school or something!

TRAVIS: Whoopee—

[*He leaps up and clasps his father around the middle with his legs, and they face each other in mutual appreciation; slowly* WALTER LEE *peeks around the boy to catch the violent rays from his wife's eyes and draws his head back as if shot.*]

WALTER: You better get down now—and get to school, man.

TRAVIS: [*At the door.*] O.K. Good-bye.

[*He exits.*]

WALTER: [*After him, pointing with pride.*] That's *my* boy. [*She looks at him in disgust and turns back to her work.*] You know what I was thinking 'bout in the bathroom this morning?

RUTH: No.

WALTER: How come you always try to be so pleasant!

RUTH: What is there to be pleasant 'bout!

WALTER: You want to know what I was thinking 'bout in the bathroom or not!

RUTH: I know what you thinking 'bout.

WALTER: [*Ignoring her.*] 'Bout what me and Willy Harris was talking about last night.

RUTH: [*Immediately—a refrain.*] Willy Harris is a good-for-nothing loud mouth.

WALTER: Anybody who talks to me has got to be a good-for-nothing loud mouth, ain't he? And what you know about who is just a good-for-nothing loud mouth? Charlie Atkins was just a "good-for-nothing loud mouth" too, wasn't he! When he wanted me to go in the dry-cleaning business with him. And now—he's grossing a hundred thousand a year. A hundred thousand dollars a year! You still call *him* a loud mouth!

RUTH: [*Bitterly.*] Oh, Walter Lee . . .

[*She folds her head on her arms over the table.*]

WALTER: [*Rising and coming to her and standing over her.*] You tired, ain't you? Tired of everything. Me, the boy, the way we live—this beat-up hole—everything. Ain't you? [*She doesn't look up, doesn't answer.*] So tired—moaning and groaning all the time, but you wouldn't do nothing to help, would you? You couldn't be on my side that long for nothing, could you?

RUTH: Walter, please leave me alone.

WALTER: A man needs for a woman to back him up . . .

RUTH: Walter—

WALTER: Mama would listen to you. You know she listen to you more than she do me and Bennie. She think more of you. All you have to do is just sit down with her when you drinking your coffee one morning and talking 'bout things like you do and— [*He sits down beside her and demonstrates graphically what he thinks her methods and tone should be.*] —you just sip your coffee, see, and say easy like that you been thinking 'bout that deal Walter Lee is so interested in, 'bout the store and all, and sip some more coffee, like what you saying ain't really that important to you—And the next thing you know, she be listening good and asking you questions and when I come home—I can tell her the details. This ain't no fly-by-night proposition, baby. I mean we figured it out, me and Willy and Bobo.

RUTH: [*With a frown.*] Bobo?

WALTER: Yeah. You see, this little liquor store we got in mind cost seventy-five thousand and we figured the initial investment on the place be 'bout thirty thousand, see. That be ten thousand each. Course, there's a couple of hundred you got to pay so's you don't spend your life just waiting for them clowns to let your license get approved—

RUTH: You mean graft?

WALTER: [*Frowning impatiently.*] Don't call it that. See there, that just goes to show you what women understand about the world. Baby, don't *nothing* happen for you in this world 'less you pay *somebody* off!

RUTH: Walter, leave me alone! [*She raises her head and stares at him vigorously— then says, more quietly.*] Eat your eggs, they gonna be cold.

WALTER: [*Straightening up from her and looking off.*] That's it. There you are. Man say to his woman: I got me a dream. His woman say: Eat your eggs. [*Sadly, but gaining in power.*] Man say: I got to take hold of this here world, baby! And a woman will say: Eat your eggs and go to work. [*Passionately now.*] Man say: I got to change my life, I'm choking to death, baby! And his woman say— [*In utter anguish as he brings his fists down on his thighs.*] —Your eggs is getting cold!

RUTH: [*Softly.*] Walter, that ain't none of our money.

WALTER: [*Not listening at all or even looking at her.*] This morning, I was lookin' in the mirror and thinking about it . . . I'm thirty-five years old; I been married eleven years and I got a boy who sleeps in the living room— [*Very, very quietly.*] —and all I got to give him is stories about how rich white people live . . .

RUTH: Eat your eggs, Walter.

WALTER: *Damn my eggs . . . damn all the eggs that ever was!*

RUTH: Then go to work.

WALTER: [*Looking up at her.*] See—I'm trying to talk to you 'bout myself— [*Shaking his head with the repetition.*] —and all you can say is eat them eggs and go to work.

RUTH: [*Wearily.*] Honey, you never say nothing new. I listen to you every day, every night and every morning, and you never say nothing new. [*Shrugging.*] So you would rather *be* Mr. Arnold than be his chauffeur. So—I would *rather* be living in Buckingham Palace.[3]

3. London residence of the queen of the United Kingdom of Great Britain and Northern Ireland.

WALTER: That is just what is wrong with the colored woman in this world . . . Don't understand about building their men up and making 'em feel like they somebody. Like they can do something.

RUTH: [*Drily, but to hurt.*] There *are* colored men who do things.

WALTER: No thanks to the colored woman.

RUTH: Well, being a colored woman, I guess I can't help myself none.

[*She rises and gets the ironing board and sets it up and attacks a huge pile of rough-dried clothes, sprinkling them in preparation for the ironing and then rolling them into tight fat balls.*]

WALTER: [*Mumbling.*] We one group of men tied to a race of women with small minds.

[*His sister BENEATHA enters. She is about twenty, as slim and intense as her brother. She is not as pretty as her sister-in-law, but her lean, almost intellectual face has a handsomeness of its own. She wears a bright-red flannel nightie, and her thick hair stands wildly about her head. Her speech is a mixture of many things; it is different from the rest of the family's insofar as education has permeated her sense of English—and perhaps the Midwest rather than the South has finally—at last—won out in her inflection; but not altogether, because over all of it is a soft slurring and transformed use of vowels which is the decided influence of the Southside. She passes through the room without looking at either RUTH or WALTER and goes to the outside door and looks, a little blindly, out to the bathroom. She sees that it has been lost to the Johnsons. She closes the door with a sleepy vengeance and crosses to the table and sits down a little defeated.*]

BENEATHA: I am going to start timing those people.

WALTER: You should get up earlier.

BENEATHA: [*Her face in her hands. She is still fighting the urge to go back to bed.*] Really—would you suggest dawn? Where's the paper?

WALTER: [*Pushing the paper across the table to her as he studies her almost clinically, as though he has never seen her before.*] You a horrible-looking chick at this hour.

BENEATHA: [*Drily.*] Good morning, everybody.

WALTER: [*Senselessly.*] How is school coming?

BENEATHA: [*In the same spirit.*] Lovely. Lovely. And you know, biology is the greatest. [*Looking up at him.*] I dissected something that looked just like you yesterday.

WALTER: I just wondered if you've made up your mind and everything.

BENEATHA: [*Gaining in sharpness and impatience.*] And what did I answer yesterday morning—and the day before that?

RUTH: [*From the ironing board, like someone disinterested and old.*] Don't be so nasty, Bennie.

BENEATHA: [*Still to her brother.*] And the day before that and the day before that!

WALTER: [*Defensively.*] I'm interested in you. Something wrong with that? Ain't many girls who decide—

WALTER AND BENEATHA: [*In unison.*]—"to be a doctor."

[*Silence.*]

WALTER: Have we figured out yet just exactly how much medical school is going to cost?

RUTH: Walter Lee, why don't you leave that girl alone and get out of here to work?

BENEATHA: [*Exits to the bathroom and bangs on the door.*] Come on out of there, please!

　　[*She comes back into the room.*]

WALTER: [*Looking at his sister intently.*] You know the check is coming tomorrow.

BENEATHA: [*Turning on him with a sharpness all her own.*] That money belongs to Mama, Walter, and it's for her to decide how she wants to use it. I don't care if she wants to buy a house or a rocket ship or just nail it up somewhere and look at it. It's hers. Not ours—*hers*.

WALTER: [*Bitterly.*] Now ain't that fine! You just got your mother's interest at heart, ain't you, girl? You such a nice girl—but if Mama got that money she can always take a few thousand and help you through school too—can't she?

BENEATHA: I have never asked anyone around here to do anything for me.

WALTER: No! And the line between asking and just accepting when the time comes is big and wide—ain't it!

BENEATHA: [*With fury.*] What do you want from me, Brother—that I quit school or just drop dead, which!

WALTER: I don't want nothing but for you to stop acting holy 'round here. Me and Ruth done made some sacrifices for you—why can't you do something for the family?

RUTH: Walter, don't be dragging me in it.

WALTER: You are in it—Don't you get up and go work in somebody's kitchen for the last three years to help put clothes on her back?

RUTH: Oh, Walter—that's not fair . . .

WALTER: It ain't that nobody expects you to get on your knees and say thank you, Brother; thank you, Ruth; thank you, Mama—and thank you, Travis, for wearing the same pair of shoes for two semesters—

BENEATHA: [*Dropping to her knees.*] Well—I *do*—all right?—thank everybody . . . and forgive me for ever wanting to be anything at all . . . forgive me, forgive me!

RUTH: Please stop it! Your mama'll hear you.

WALTER: Who the hell told you you had to be a doctor? If you so crazy 'bout messing 'round with sick people—then go be a nurse like other women—or just get married and be quiet . . .

BENEATHA: Well—you finally got it said . . . it took you three years but you finally got it said. Walter, give up; leave me alone—it's Mama's money.

WALTER: *He was my father, too!*

BENEATHA: So what? He was mine, too—and Travis' grandfather—but the insurance money belongs to Mama. Picking on me is not going to make her give it to you to invest in any liquor stores— [*Underbreath, dropping into a chair.*] — and I for one say, God bless Mama for that!

WALTER: [*To* RUTH.] See—did you hear? Did you hear!

RUTH: Honey, please go to work.

WALTER: Nobody in this house is ever going to understand me.

BENEATHA: Because you're a nut.

WALTER: Who's a nut?

BENEATHA: You—you are a nut. Thee is mad, boy.

WALTER: [*Looking at his wife and his sister from the door, very sadly.*] The world's most backward race of people, and that's a fact.

BENEATHA: [*Turning slowly in her chair.*] And then there are all those prophets who would lead us out of the wilderness— [WALTER *slams out of the house.*] — into the swamps!

RUTH: Bennie, why you always gotta be pickin' on your brother? Can't you be a little sweeter sometimes? [*Door opens.* WALTER *walks in.*]

WALTER: [*To* RUTH.] I need some money for carfare.

RUTH: [*Looks at him, then warms; teasing, but tenderly.*] Fifty cents? [*She goes to her bag and gets money.*] Here, take a taxi.

> [WALTER *exits.* MAMA *enters. She is a woman in her early sixties, full-bodied and strong. She is one of those women of a certain grace and beauty who wear it so unobtrusively that it takes a while to notice. Her dark-brown face is surrounded by the total whiteness of her hair, and, being a woman who has adjusted to many things in life and overcome many more, her face is full of strength. She has, we can see, wit and faith of a kind that keep her eyes lit and full of interest and expectancy. She is, in a word, a beautiful woman. Her bearing is perhaps most like the noble bearing of the women of the Hereros of Southwest Africa—rather as if she imagines that as she walks she still bears a basket or a vessel upon her head. Her speech, on the other hand, is as careless as her carriage is precise—she is inclined to slur everything—but her voice is perhaps not so much quiet as simply soft.*]

MAMA: Who that 'round here slamming doors at this hour?

> [*She crosses through the room, goes to the window, opens it, and brings in a feeble little plant growing doggedly in a small pot on the window sill. She feels the dirt and puts it back out.*]

RUTH: That was Walter Lee. He and Bennie was at it again.

MAMA: My children and they tempers. Lord, if this little old plant don't get more sun than it's been getting it ain't never going to see spring again. [*She turns from the window.*] What's the matter with you this morning, Ruth? You looks right peaked. You aiming to iron all them things? Leave some for me. I'll get to 'em this afternoon. Bennie honey, it's too drafty for you to be sitting 'round half dressed. Where's your robe?

BENEATHA: In the cleaners.

MAMA: Well, go get mine and put it on.

BENEATHA: I'm not cold, Mama, honest.

MAMA: I know—but you so thin . . .

BENEATHA: [*Irritably.*] Mama, I'm not cold.

MAMA: [*Seeing the make-down bed as* TRAVIS *has left it.*] Lord have mercy, look at that poor bed. Bless his heart—he tries, don't he?

> [*She moves to the bed* TRAVIS *has sloppily made up.*]

RUTH: No—he don't half try at all 'cause he knows you going to come along behind him and fix everything. That's just how come he don't know how to do nothing right now—you done spoiled that boy so.

MAMA: Well—he's a little boy. Ain't supposed to know 'bout housekeeping. My baby, that's what he is. What you fix for his breakfast this morning?

RUTH: [*Angrily.*] I feed my son, Lena!

MAMA: I ain't meddling— [*Underbreath; busy-bodyish.*] I just noticed all last week he had cold cereal, and when it starts getting this chilly in the fall a child ought to have some hot grits or something when he goes out in the cold—

RUTH: [*Furious.*] I gave him hot oats—is that all right!

MAMA: I ain't meddling. [*Pause.*] Put a lot of nice butter on it? [RUTH *shoots her an angry look and does not reply.*] He likes lots of butter.

RUTH: [*Exasperated.*] Lena—

MAMA: [*To* BENEATHA. MAMA *is inclined to wander conversationally sometimes.*] What was you and your brother fussing 'bout this morning?

BENEATHA: It's not important, Mama.

[*She gets up and goes to look out at the bathroom, which is apparently free, and she picks up her towels and rushes out.*]

MAMA: What was they fighting about?

RUTH: Now you know as well as I do.

MAMA: [*Shaking her head.*] Brother still worrying hisself sick about that money?

RUTH: You know he is.

MAMA: You had breakfast?

RUTH: Some coffee.

MAMA: Girl, you better start eating and looking after yourself better. You almost thin as Travis.

RUTH: Lena—

MAMA: Un-hunh?

RUTH: What are you going to do with it?

MAMA: Now don't you start, child. It's too early in the morning to be talking about money. It ain't Christian.

RUTH: It's just that he got his heart set on that store—

MAMA: You mean that liquor store that Willy Harris want him to invest in?

RUTH: Yes—

MAMA: We ain't no business people, Ruth. We just plain working folks.

RUTH: Ain't nobody business people till they go into business. Walter Lee say colored people ain't never going to start getting ahead till they start gambling on some different kinds of things in the world—investments and things.

MAMA: What done got into you, girl? Walter Lee done finally sold you on investing.

RUTH: No. Mama, something is happening between Walter and me. I don't know what it is—but he needs something—something I can't give him anymore. He needs this chance, Lena.

MAMA: [*Frowning deeply.*] But liquor, honey—

RUTH: Well—like Walter say—I spec people going to always be drinking themselves some liquor.

MAMA: Well—whether they drinks it or not ain't none of my business. But whether I go into business selling it to 'em *is,* and I don't want that on my ledger this late in life. [*Stopping suddenly and studying her daughter-in-law.*] Ruth Younger, what's the matter with you today? You look like you could fall over right there.

RUTH: I'm tired.

MAMA: Then you better stay home from work today.

RUTH: I can't stay home. She'd be calling up the agency and screaming at them, "My girl didn't come in today—send me somebody! My girl didn't come in!" Oh, she just have a fit . . .

MAMA: Well, let her have it. I'll just call her up and say you got the flu—

RUTH: [Laughing.] Why the flu?

MAMA: 'Cause it sounds respectable to 'em. Something white people get, too. They know 'bout the flu. Otherwise they think you been cut up or something when you tell 'em you sick.

RUTH: I got to go in. We need the money.

MAMA: Somebody would of thought my children done all but starved to death the way they talk about money here late. Child, we got a great big old check coming tomorrow.

RUTH: [Sincerely, but also self-righteously.] Now that's your money. It ain't got nothing to do with me. We all feel like that—Walter and Bennie and me—even Travis.

MAMA: [Thoughtfully, and suddenly very far away.] Ten thousand dollars—

RUTH: Sure is wonderful.

MAMA: Ten thousand dollars.

RUTH: You know what you should do, Miss Lena? You should take yourself a trip somewhere. To Europe or South America or someplace—

MAMA: [Throwing up her hands at the thought.] Oh, child!

RUTH: I'm serious. Just pack up and leave! Go on away and enjoy yourself some. Forget about the family and have yourself a ball for once in your life—

MAMA: [Drily.] You sound like I'm just about ready to die. Who'd go with me? What I look like wandering 'round Europe by myself?

RUTH: Shoot—these here rich white women do it all the time. They don't think nothing of packing up they suitcases and piling on one of them big steamships and—swoosh!—they gone, child.

MAMA: Something always told me I wasn't no rich white woman.

RUTH: Well—what are you going to do with it then?

MAMA: I ain't rightly decided. [Thinking. She speaks now with emphasis.] Some of it got to be put away for Beneatha and her schoolin'—and ain't nothing going to touch that part of it. Nothing. [She waits several seconds, trying to make up her mind about something, and looks at RUTH a little tentatively before going on.] Been thinking that we maybe could meet the notes on a little old two-story somewhere, with a yard where Travis could play in the summertime, if we use part of the insurance for a down payment and everybody kind of pitch in. I could maybe take on a little day work again, few days a week—

RUTH: [Studying her mother-in-law furtively and concentrating on her ironing, anxious to encourage without seeming to.] Well, Lord knows, we've put enough rent into this here rat trap to pay for four houses by now . . .

MAMA: [Looking up at the words "rat trap" and then looking around and leaning back and sighing—in a suddenly reflective mood—] "Rat trap"—yes, that's all it is. [Smiling.] I remember just as well the day me and Big Walter moved in here. Hadn't been married but two weeks and wasn't planning on living here no more than a year. [She shakes her head at the dissolved dream.] We was going to set away, little by little, don't you know, and buy a little place out in

Morgan Park. We had even picked out the house. [*Chuckling a little.*] Looks right dumpy today. But Lord, child, you should know all the dreams I had 'bout buying that house and fixing it up and making me a little garden in the back— [*She waits and stops smiling.*] And didn't none of it happen.

[*Dropping her hands in a futile gesture.*]

RUTH: [*Keeps her head down, ironing.*] Yes, life can be a barrel of disappointments, sometimes.

MAMA: Honey, Big Walter would come in here some nights back then and slump down on that couch there and just look at the rug, and look at me and look at the rug and then back at me—and I'd know he was down then . . . really down. [*After a second very long and thoughtful pause; she is seeing back to times that only she can see.*] And then, Lord, when I lost that baby—little Claude—I almost thought I was going to lose Big Walter too. Oh, that man grieved hisself! He was one man to love his children.

RUTH: Ain't nothin' can tear at you like losin' your baby.

MAMA: I guess that's how come that man finally worked hisself to death like he done. Like he was fighting his own war with this here world that took his baby from him.

RUTH: He sure was a fine man, all right. I always liked Mr. Younger.

MAMA: Crazy 'bout his children! God knows there was plenty wrong with Walter Younger—hard-headed, mean, kind of wild with women—plenty wrong with him. But he sure loved his children. Always wanted them to have something—be something. That's where Brother gets all these notions, I reckon. Big Walter used to say, he'd get right wet in the eyes sometimes, lean his head back with the water standing in his eyes and say, "Seem like God didn't see fit to give the black man nothing but dreams—but He did give us children to make them dreams seem worthwhile." [*She smiles.*] He could talk like that, don't you know.

RUTH: Yes, he sure could. He was a good man, Mr. Younger.

MAMA: Yes, a fine man—just couldn't never catch up with his dreams, that's all.

[BENEATHA *comes in, brushing her hair and looking up to the ceiling, where the sound of a vacuum cleaner has started up.*]

BENEATHA: What could be so dirty on that woman's rugs that she has to vacuum them every single day?

RUTH: I wish certain young women 'round here who I could name would take inspiration about certain rugs in a certain apartment I could also mention.

BENEATHA: [*Shrugging.*] How much cleaning can a house need, for Christ's sakes.

MAMA: [*Not liking the Lord's name used thus.*] Bennie!

RUTH: Just listen to her—just listen!

BENEATHA: Oh, God!

MAMA: If you use the Lord's name just one more time—

BENEATHA: [*A bit of a whine.*] Oh, Mama—

RUTH: Fresh—just fresh as salt, this girl!

BENEATHA: [*Drily.*] Well—if the salt loses its savor[4]—

---

4. See Matthew 5.13: "You are the salt of the earth. But if the salt loses its taste, with what can it be seasoned? It is no longer good for anything but to be thrown out and trampled underfoot."

MAMA: Now that will do. I just ain't going to have you 'round here reciting the scriptures in vain—you hear me?

BENEATHA: How did I manage to get on everybody's wrong side by just walking into a room?

RUTH: If you weren't so fresh—

BENEATHA: Ruth, I'm twenty years old.

MAMA: What time you be home from school today?

BENEATHA: Kind of late. [*With enthusiasm.*] Madeline is going to start my guitar lessons today.

[MAMA *and* RUTH *look up with the same expression.*]

MAMA: Your *what* kind of lessons?

BENEATHA: Guitar.

RUTH: Oh, Father!

MAMA: How come you done taken it in your mind to learn to play the guitar?

BENEATHA: I just want to, that's all.

MAMA: [*Smiling.*] Lord, child, don't you know what to do with yourself? How long it going to be before you get tired of this now—like you got tired of that little play-acting group you joined last year? [*Looking at* RUTH.] And what was it the year before that?

RUTH: The horseback-riding club for which she bought that fifty-five-dollar riding habit that's been hanging in the closet ever since!

MAMA: [*To* BENEATHA.] Why you got to flit so from one thing to another, baby?

BENEATHA: [*Sharply.*] I just want to learn to play the guitar. Is there anything wrong with that?

MAMA: Ain't nobody trying to stop you. I just wonders sometimes why you has to flit so from one thing to another all the time. You ain't never done nothing with all that camera equipment you brought home—

BENEATHA: I don't flit! I—I experiment with different forms of expression—

RUTH: Like riding a horse?

BENEATHA: —People have to express themselves one way or another.

MAMA: What is it you want to express?

BENEATHA: [*Angrily.*] Me! [MAMA *and* RUTH *look at each other and burst into raucous laughter.*] Don't worry—I don't expect you to understand.

MAMA: [*To change the subject.*] Who you going out with tomorrow night?

BENEATHA: [*With displeasure.*] George Murchison again.

MAMA: [*Pleased.*] Oh—you getting a little sweet on him?

RUTH: You ask me, this child ain't sweet on nobody but herself— [*Underbreath.*] Express herself!

[*They laugh.*]

BENEATHA: Oh—I like George all right, Mama. I mean I like him enough to go out with him and stuff, but—

RUTH: [*For devilment.*] What does *and stuff* mean?

BENEATHA: Mind your own business.

MAMA: Stop picking at her now, Ruth. [*A thoughtful pause, and then a suspicious sudden look at her daughter as she turns in her chair for emphasis.*] What *does* it mean?

BENEATHA: [*Wearily.*] Oh, I just mean I couldn't ever really be serious about George. He's—he's so shallow.

RUTH: Shallow—what do you mean he's shallow? He's *rich*!

MAMA: Hush, Ruth.

BENEATHA: I know he's rich. He knows he's rich, too.

RUTH: Well—what other qualities a man got to have to satisfy you, little girl?

BENEATHA: You wouldn't even begin to understand. Anybody who married Walter could not possibly understand.

MAMA: [*Outraged.*] What kind of way is that to talk about your brother?

BENEATHA: Brother is a flip—let's face it.

MAMA: [*To* RUTH, *helplessly.*] What's a flip?

RUTH: [*Glad to add kindling.*] She's saying he's crazy.

BENEATHA: Not crazy. Brother isn't really crazy yet—he—he's an elaborate neurotic.

MAMA: Hush your mouth!

BENEATHA: As for George. Well. George looks good—he's got a beautiful car and he takes me to nice places and, as my sister-in-law says, he is probably the richest boy I will ever get to know and I even like him sometimes—but if the Youngers are sitting around waiting to see if their little Bennie is going to tie up the family with the Murchisons, they are wasting their time.

RUTH: You mean you wouldn't marry George Murchison if he asked you someday? That pretty, rich thing? Honey, I knew you was odd—

BENEATHA: No I would not marry him if all I felt for him was what I feel now. Besides, George's family wouldn't really like it.

MAMA: Why not?

BENEATHA: Oh, Mama—The Murchisons are honest-to-God-real-*live*-rich colored people, and the only people in the world who are more snobbish than rich white people are rich colored people. I thought everybody knew that. I've met Mrs. Murchison. She's a scene!

MAMA: You must not dislike people 'cause they well off, honey.

BENEATHA: Why not? It makes just as much sense as disliking people 'cause they are poor, and lots of people do that.

RUTH: [*A wisdom-of-the-ages manner. To* MAMA.] Well, she'll get over some of this—

BENEATHA: Get over it? What are you talking about, Ruth? Listen, I'm going to be a doctor. I'm not worried about who I'm going to marry yet—if I ever get married.

MAMA AND RUTH: *If!*

MAMA: Now, Bennie—

BENEATHA: Oh, I probably will . . . but first I'm going to be a doctor, and George, for one, still thinks that's pretty funny. I couldn't be bothered with that. I am going to be a doctor and everybody around here better understand that!

MAMA: [*Kindly.*] 'Course you going to be a doctor, honey, God willing.

BENEATHA: [*Drily.*] God hasn't got a thing to do with it.

MAMA: Beneatha—that just wasn't necessary.

BENEATHA: Well—neither is God. I get sick of hearing about God.

MAMA: Beneatha!

BENEATHA: I mean it! I'm just tired of hearing about God all the time. What has He got to do with anything? Does He pay tuition?

MAMA: You 'bout to get your fresh little jaw slapped!

RUTH: That's just what she needs, all right!

BENEATHA: Why? Why can't I say what I want to around here, like everybody else?

MAMA: It don't sound nice for a young girl to say things like that—you wasn't brought up that way. Me and your father went to trouble to get you and Brother to church every Sunday.

BENEATHA: Mama, you don't understand. It's all a matter of ideas, and God is just one idea I don't accept. It's not important. I am not going out and be immoral or commit crimes because I don't believe in God. I don't even think about it. It's just that I get tired of Him getting credit for all the things the human race achieves through its own stubborn effort. There simply is no blasted God—there is only man and it is he who makes miracles!

[MAMA *absorbs this speech, studies her daughter and rises slowly and crosses to* BENEATHA *and slaps her powerfully across the face. After, there is only silence and the daughter drops her eyes from her mother's face, and* MAMA *is very tall before her.*]

MAMA: Now—you say after me, in my mother's house there is still God. [*There is a long pause and* BENEATHA *stares at the floor wordlessly.* MAMA *repeats the phrase with precision and cool emotion.*] In my mother's house there is still God.

BENEATHA: In my mother's house there is still God.

[*A long pause.*]

MAMA: [*Walking away from* BENEATHA, *too disturbed for triumphant posture. Stopping and turning back to her daughter.*] There are some ideas we ain't going to have in this house. Not long as I am at the head of this family.

BENEATHA: Yes, ma'am.

[MAMA *walks out of the room.*]

RUTH: [*Almost gently, with profound understanding.*] You think you a woman, Bennie—but you still a little girl. What you did was childish—so you got treated like a child.

BENEATHA: I see. [*Quietly.*] I also see that everybody thinks it's all right for Mama to be a tyrant. But all the tyranny in the world will never put a God in the heavens!

[*She picks up her books and goes out.*]

RUTH: [*Goes to* MAMA'S *door.*] She said she was sorry.

MAMA: [*Coming out, going to her plant.*] They frightens me, Ruth. My children.

RUTH: You got good children, Lena. They just a little off sometimes—but they're good.

MAMA: No—there's something come down between me and them that don't let us understand each other and I don't know what it is. One done almost lost his mind thinking 'bout money all the time and the other done commence to talk about things I can't seem to understand in no form or fashion. What is it that's changing, Ruth?

RUTH: [*Soothingly, older than her years.*] Now . . . you taking it all too seriously. You just got strong-willed children and it takes a strong woman like you to keep 'em in hand.

MAMA: [*Looking at her plant and sprinkling a little water on it.*] They spirited all right, my children. Got to admit they got spirit—Bennie and Walter. Like this little old plant that ain't never had enough sunshine or nothing—and look at it . . .

[*She has her back to* RUTH, *who has had to stop ironing and lean against something and put the back of her hand to her forehead.*]

RUTH: [*Trying to keep* MAMA *from noticing.*] You . . . sure . . . loves that little old thing, don't you? . . .

MAMA: Well, I always wanted me a garden like I used to see sometimes at the back of the houses down home. This plant is close as I ever got to having one. [*She looks out of the window as she replaces the plant.*] Lord, ain't nothing as dreary as the view from this window on a dreary day, is there? Why ain't you singing this morning, Ruth? Sing that "No Ways Tired." That song always lifts me up so— [*She turns at last to see that* RUTH *has slipped quietly into a chair, in a state of semiconsciousness.*] Ruth! Ruth honey—what's the matter with you . . . Ruth!

[CURTAIN.]

Scene Two

It is the following morning; a Saturday morning, and house cleaning is in progress at the Youngers. Furniture has been shoved hither and yon and MAMA is giving the kitchen-area walls a washing down. BENEATHA, in dungarees, with a handkerchief tied around her face, is spraying insecticide into the cracks in the walls. As they work, the radio is on and a Southside disk-jockey program is inappropriately filling the house with a rather exotic saxophone blues. TRAVIS, the sole idle one, is leaning on his arms, looking out of the window.

TRAVIS: Grandmama, that stuff Bennie is using smells awful. Can I go downstairs, please?

MAMA: Did you get all them chores done already? I ain't seen you doing much.

TRAVIS: Yes'm—finished early. Where did Mama go this morning?

MAMA: [*Looking at* BENEATHA.] She had to go on a little errand.

TRAVIS: Where?

MAMA: To tend to her business.

TRAVIS: Can I go outside then?

MAMA: Oh, I guess so. You better stay right in front of the house, though . . . and keep a good lookout for the postman.

TRAVIS: Yes'm. [*He starts out and decides to give his aunt* BENEATHA *a good swat on the legs as he passes her.*] Leave them poor little old cockroaches alone, they ain't bothering you none.

[*He runs as she swings the spray gun at him both viciously and playfully.* WALTER *enters from the bedroom and goes to the phone.*]

MAMA: Look out there, girl, before you be spilling some of that stuff on that child!

TRAVIS: [*Teasing.*] That's right—look out now!

[*He exits.*]

BENEATHA: [*Drily.*] I can't imagine that it would hurt him—it has never hurt the roaches.

MAMA: Well, little boys' hides ain't as tough as Southside roaches.

WALTER: [*Into phone.*] Hello—Let me talk to Willy Harris.

MAMA: You better get over there behind the bureau. I seen one marching out of there like Napoleon yesterday.

WALTER: Hello, Willy? It ain't come yet. It'll be here in a few minutes. Did the lawyer give you the papers?

BENEATHA: There's really only one way to get rid of them, Mama—

MAMA: How?

BENEATHA: Set fire to this building.

WALTER: Good. Good. I'll be right over.

BENEATHA: Where did Ruth go, Walter?

WALTER: I don't know.

[*He exits abruptly.*]

BENEATHA: Mama, where did Ruth go?

MAMA: [*Looking at her with meaning.*] To the doctor, I think.

BENEATHA: The doctor? What's the matter? [*They exchange glances.*] You don't think—

MAMA: [*With her sense of drama.*] Now I ain't saying what I think. But I ain't never been wrong 'bout a woman neither.

[*The phone rings.*]

BENEATHA: [*At the phone.*] Hay-lo . . . [*Pause, and a moment of recognition.*] Well—when did you get back! . . . And how was it? . . . Of course I've missed you—in my way . . . This morning? No . . . house cleaning and all that and Mama hates it if I let people come over when the house is like this . . . You *have*? Well, that's different . . . What is it—Oh, what the hell, come on over . . . Right, see you then.

[*She hangs up.*]

MAMA: [*Who has listened vigorously, as is her habit.*] Who is that you inviting over here with this house looking like this? You ain't got the pride you was born with!

BENEATHA: Asagai doesn't care how houses look, Mama—he's an intellectual.

MAMA: *Who?*

BENEATHA: Asagai—Joseph Asagai. He's an African boy I met on campus. He's been studying in Canada all summer.

MAMA: What's his name?

BENEATHA: Asagai, Joseph. Ah-sah-guy . . . He's from Nigeria.

MAMA: Oh, that's the little country that was founded by slaves way back . . .

BENEATHA: No, Mama—that's Liberia.

MAMA: I don't think I never met no African before.

BENEATHA: Well, do me a favor and don't ask him a whole lot of ignorant questions about Africans. I mean, do they wear clothes and all that—

MAMA: Well, now, I guess if you think we so ignorant 'round here maybe you shouldn't bring your friends here—

BENEATHA: It's just that people ask such crazy things. All anyone seems to know about when it comes to Africa is Tarzan—

MAMA: [*Indignantly.*] Why should I know anything about Africa?

BENEATHA: Why do you give money at church for the missionary work?

MAMA: Well, that's to help save people.

BENEATHA: You mean save them from *heathenism*—

MAMA: [*Innocently.*] Yes.

BENEATHA: I'm afraid they need more salvation from the British and the French.

[RUTH *comes in forlornly and pulls off her coat with dejection. They both turn to look at her.*]

RUTH: [*Dispiritedly.*] Well, I guess from all the happy faces—everybody knows.

BENEATHA: You pregnant?

MAMA: Lord have mercy, I sure hope it's a little old girl. Travis ought to have a sister.

[BENEATHA *and* RUTH *give her a hopeless look for this grandmotherly enthusiasm.*]

BENEATHA: How far along are you?

RUTH: Two months.

BENEATHA: Did you mean to? I mean did you plan it or was it an accident?

MAMA: What do you know about planning or not planning?

BENEATHA: Oh, Mama.

RUTH: [*Wearily.*] She's twenty years old, Lena.

BENEATHA: Did you plan it, Ruth?

RUTH: Mind your own business.

BENEATHA: It is my business—where is he going to live, on the roof? [*There is silence following the remark as the three women react to the sense of it.*] Gee— I didn't mean that, Ruth, honest. Gee, I don't feel like that at all. I—I think it is wonderful.

RUTH: [*Dully.*] Wonderful.

BENEATHA: Yes—really.

MAMA: [*Looking at* RUTH, *worried.*] Doctor say everything going to be all right?

RUTH: [*Far away.*] Yes—she says everything is going to be fine . . .

MAMA: [*Immediately suspicious.*] "She"—What doctor you went to?

[RUTH *folds over, near hysteria.*]

MAMA: [*Worriedly hovering over* RUTH.] Ruth honey—what's the matter with you—you sick?

[RUTH *has her fists clenched on her thighs and is fighting hard to suppress a scream that seems to be rising in her.*]

BENEATHA: What's the matter with her, Mama?

MAMA: [*Working her fingers in* RUTH'S *shoulder to relax her.*] She be all right. Women gets right depressed sometimes when they get her way. [*Speaking softly, expertly, rapidly.*] Now you just relax. That's right . . . just lean back, don't think 'bout nothing at all . . . nothing at all—

RUTH: I'm all right . . .

[*The glassy-eyed look melts and then she collapses into a fit of heavy sobbing. The bell rings.*]

BENEATHA: Oh, my God—that must be Asagai.

MAMA: [*To* RUTH.] Come on now, honey. You need to lie down and rest awhile . . . then have some nice hot food.

[*They exit,* RUTH'S *weight on her mother-in-law.* BENEATHA, *herself profoundly disturbed, opens the door to admit a rather dramatic-looking young man with a large package.*]

ASAGAI: Hello, Alaiyo—

BENEATHA: [*Holding the door open and regarding him with pleasure.*] Hello . . . [*Long pause.*] Well—come in. And please excuse everything. My mother was very upset about my letting anyone come here with the place like this.

ASAGAI: [*Coming into the room.*] You look disturbed too . . . Is something wrong?

BENEATHA: [*Still at the door, absently.*] Yes . . . we've all got acute ghetto-itus. [*She smiles and comes toward him, finding a cigarette and sitting.*] So—sit down! How was Canada?

ASAGAI: [*A sophisticate.*] Canadian.

BENEATHA: [*Looking at him.*] I'm very glad you are back.

ASAGAI: [*Looking back at her in turn.*] Are you really?

BENEATHA: Yes—very.

ASAGAI: Why—you were quite glad when I went away. What happened?

BENEATHA: You went away.

ASAGAI: Ahhhhhhhh.

BENEATHA: Before—you wanted to be so serious before there was time.

ASAGAI: How much time must there be before one knows what one feels?

BENEATHA: [*Stalling this particular conversation. Her hands pressed together, in a deliberately childish gesture.*] What did you bring me?

ASAGAI: [*Handing her the package.*] Open it and see.

BENEATHA: [*Eagerly opening the package and drawing out some records and the colorful robes of a Nigerian woman.*] Oh, Asagai! . . . You got them for me! . . . How beautiful . . . and the records too! [*She lifts out the robes and runs to the mirror with them and holds the drapery up in front of herself.*]

ASAGAI: [*Coming to her at the mirror.*] I shall have to teach you how to drape it properly. [*He flings the material about her for the moment and stands back to look at her.*] Ah—Oh-pay-gay-day, oh-gbah-mu-shay. [*A Yoruba exclamation for admiration.*] You wear it well . . . very well . . . mutilated hair and all.

BENEATHA: [*Turning suddenly.*] My hair—what's wrong with my hair?

ASAGAI: [*Shrugging.*] Were you born with it like that?

BENEATHA: [*Reaching up to touch it.*] No . . . of course not.

[*She looks back to the mirror, disturbed.*]

ASAGAI: [*Smiling.*] How then?

BENEATHA: You know perfectly well how . . . as crinkly as yours . . . that's how.

ASAGAI: And it is ugly to you that way?

BENEATHA: [*Quickly.*] Oh, no—not ugly . . . [*More slowly, apologetically.*] But it's so hard to manage when it's, well—raw.

ASAGAI: And so to accommodate that—you mutilate it every week?

BENEATHA: It's not mutilation!

ASAGAI: [*Laughing aloud at her seriousness.*] Oh . . . please! I am only teasing you because you are so very serious about these things. [*He stands back from her and folds his arms across his chest as he watches her pulling at her hair and frowning in the mirror.*] Do you remember the first time you met me at school? . . . [*He laughs.*] You came up to me and you said—and I thought you were the most serious little thing I had ever seen—you said: [*He imitates her.*] "Mr. Asagai—I want very much to talk with you. About Africa. You see, Mr. Asagai, I am looking for my *identity!*"

[*He laughs.*]

BENEATHA: [*Turning to him, not laughing.*] Yes—

[*Her face is quizzical, profoundly disturbed.*]

ASAGAI: [*Still teasing and reaching out and taking her face in his hands and turning her profile to him.*] Well . . . it is true that this is not so much a profile of a Hollywood queen as perhaps a queen of the Nile— [*A mock dismissal of the importance of the question.*] But what does it matter? Assimilationism is so popular in your country.

BENEATHA: [*Wheeling, passionately, sharply.*] I am not an assimilationist!

ASAGAI: [*The protest hangs in the room for a moment and ASAGAI studies her, his laughter fading.*] Such a serious one. [*There is a pause.*] So—you like the robes? You must take excellent care of them—they are from my sister's personal wardrobe.

BENEATHA: [*With incredulity.*] You—you sent all the way home—for me?

ASAGAI: [*With charm.*] For you—I would do much more . . . Well, that is what I came for. I must go.

BENEATHA: Will you call me Monday?

ASAGAI: Yes . . . We have a great deal to talk about. I mean about identity and time and all that.

BENEATHA: Time?

ASAGAI: Yes. About how much time one needs to know what one feels.

BENEATHA: You never understood that there is more than one kind of feeling which can exist between a man and a woman—or, at least, there should be.

ASAGAI: [*Shaking his head negatively but gently.*] No. Between a man and a woman there need be only one kind of feeling. I have that for you . . . Now even . . . right this moment . . .

BENEATHA: I know—and by itself—it won't do. I can find that anywhere.

ASAGAI: For a woman it should be enough.

BENEATHA: I know—because that's what it says in all the novels that men write. But it isn't. Go ahead and laugh—but I'm not interested in being someone's little episode in America or— [*With feminine vengeance.*] —one of them! [ASAGAI *has burst into laughter again.*] That's funny as hell, huh!

ASAGAI: It's just that every American girl I have known has said that to me. White—black—in this you are all the same. And the same speech, too!

BENEATHA: [*Angrily.*] Yuk, yuk, yuk!

ASAGAI: It's how you can be sure that the world's most liberated women are not liberated at all. You all talk about it too much!

[MAMA *enters and is immediately all social charm because of the presence of a guest.*]

BENEATHA: Oh—Mama—this is Mr. Asagai.

MAMA: How do you do?

ASAGAI: [*Total politeness to an elder.*] How do you do, Mrs. Younger. Please forgive me for coming at such an outrageous hour on a Saturday.

MAMA: Well, you are quite welcome. I just hope you understand that our house don't always look like this. [*Chatterish.*] You must come again. I would love to hear all about— [*Not sure of the name.*] —your country. I think it's so sad the way our American Negroes don't know nothing about Africa 'cept Tarzan and all that. And all that money they pour into these churches when they ought to be helping you people over there drive out them French and Englishmen done taken away your land.

[*The mother flashes a slightly superior look at her daughter upon completion of the recitation.*]

ASAGAI: [*Taken aback by this sudden and acutely unrelated expression of sympathy.*] Yes . . . yes . . .

MAMA: [*Smiling at him suddenly and relaxing and looking him over.*] How many miles is it from here to where you come from?

ASAGAI: Many thousands.

MAMA: [*Looking at him as she would* WALTER.] I bet you don't half look after yourself, being away from your mama either. I spec you better come 'round here from time to time and get yourself some decent home-cooked meals . . .

ASAGAI: [*Moved.*] Thank you. Thank you very much. [*They are all quiet, then—*] Well . . . I must go. I will call you Monday, Alaiyo.

MAMA: What's that he call you?

ASAGAI: Oh—"Alaiyo." I hope you don't mind. It is what you would call a nickname, I think. It is a Yoruba word. I am a Yoruba.

MAMA: [*Looking at* BENEATHA.] I—I thought he was from—

ASAGAI: [*Understanding.*] Nigeria is my country. Yoruba is my tribal origin—

BENEATHA: You didn't tell us what Alaiyo means . . . for all I know, you might be calling me Little Idiot or something . . .

ASAGAI: Well . . . let me see . . . I do not know how just to explain it . . . The sense of a thing can be so different when it changes languages.

BENEATHA: You're evading.

ASAGAI: No—really it is difficult . . . [*Thinking.*] It means . . . it means One for Whom Bread—Food—Is Not Enough. [*He looks at her.*] Is that all right?

BENEATHA: [*Understanding, softly.*] Thank you.

MAMA: [*Looking from one to the other and not understanding any of it.*] Well . . . that's nice . . . You must come see us again—Mr.—

ASAGAI: Ah-sah-guy . . .

MAMA: Yes . . . Do come again.

ASAGAI: Good-bye.

[*He exits.*]

MAMA: [*After him.*] Lord, that's a pretty thing just went out here! [*Insinuatingly, to her daughter.*] Yes, I guess I see why we done commence to get so interested in Africa 'round here. Missionaries my aunt Jenny!

[*She exits.*]

BENEATHA: Oh, Mama! . . .

[*She picks up the Nigerian dress and holds it up to her in front of the mirror again. She sets the headdress on haphazardly and then notices her hair again and clutches at it and then replaces the headdress and frowns at herself. Then she starts to wriggle in front of the mirror as she thinks a Nigerian woman might.* TRAVIS *enters and regards her.*]

TRAVIS: You cracking up?

BENEATHA: Shut up.

[*She pulls the headdress off and looks at herself in the mirror and clutches at her hair again and squinches her eyes as if trying to imagine something. Then, suddenly, she gets her raincoat and kerchief and hurriedly prepares for going out.*]

MAMA: [*Coming back into the room.*] She's resting now. Travis, baby, run next door and ask Miss Johnson to please let me have a little kitchen cleanser. This here can is empty as Jacob's kettle.

TRAVIS: I just came in.

MAMA: Do as you told. [*He exits and she looks at her daughter.*] Where you going?

BENEATHA: [*Halting at the door.*] To become a queen of the Nile!

[*She exits in a breathless blaze of glory.* RUTH *appears in the bedroom doorway.*]

MAMA: Who told you to get up?

RUTH: Ain't nothing wrong with me to be lying in no bed for. Where did Bennie go?

MAMA: [*Drumming her fingers.*] Far as I could make out—to Egypt. [RUTH *just looks at her.*] What time is it getting to?

RUTH: Ten twenty. And the mailman going to ring that bell this morning just like he done every morning for the last umpteen years.

[TRAVIS *comes in with the cleanser can.*]

TRAVIS: She say to tell you that she don't have much.

MAMA: [*Angrily.*] Lord, some people I could name sure is tight-fisted! [*Directing her grandson.*] Mark two cans of cleanser down on the list there. If she that hard up for kitchen cleanser, I sure don't want to forget to get her none!

RUTH: Lena—maybe the woman is just short on cleanser—

MAMA: [*Not listening.*] —Much baking powder as she done borrowed from me all these years, she could of done gone into the baking business!

[*The bell sounds suddenly and sharply and all three are stunned—serious and silent—mid-speech. In spite of all the other conversations and distractions of the morning, this is what they have been waiting for, even* TRAVIS, *who looks helplessly from his mother to his grandmother.* RUTH *is the first to come to life again.*]

RUTH: [*To* TRAVIS.] *Get down them steps, boy!*

[TRAVIS *snaps to life and flies out to get the mail.*]

MAMA: [*Her eyes wide, her hand to her breast.*] You mean it done really come?

RUTH: [*Excited.*] Oh, Miss Lena!

MAMA: [*Collecting herself.*] Well . . . I don't know what we all so excited about 'round here for. We known it was coming for months.

RUTH: That's a whole lot different from having it come and being able to hold it in your hands . . . a piece of paper worth ten thousand dollars . . . [TRAVIS *bursts back into the room. He holds the envelope high above his head, like a little dancer, his face is radiant and he is breathless. He moves to his grandmother with sudden slow ceremony and puts the envelope into her hands. She accepts it, and then merely holds it and looks at it.*] Come on! Open it . . . Lord have mercy, I wish Walter Lee was here!

TRAVIS: Open it, Grandmama!

MAMA: [*Staring at it.*] Now you all be quiet. It's just a check.

RUTH: Open it . . .

MAMA: [*Still staring at it.*] Now don't act silly . . . We ain't never been no people to act silly 'bout no money—

RUTH: [*Swiftly.*] We ain't never had none before—*open it!*

[MAMA *finally makes a good strong tear and pulls out the thin blue slice of paper and inspects it closely. The boy and his mother study it raptly over* MAMA's *shoulders.*]

MAMA: *Travis!* [*She is counting off with doubt.*] Is that the right number of zeros.

TRAVIS: Yes'm . . . ten thousand dollars. Gaalee, Grandmama, you rich.

MAMA: [*She holds the check away from her, still looking at it. Slowly her face sobers into a mask of unhappiness.*] Ten thousand dollars. [*She hands it to* RUTH.] Put it away somewhere, Ruth. [*She does not look at* RUTH; *her eyes seem to be seeing something somewhere very far off.*] Ten thousand dollars they give you. Ten thousand dollars.

TRAVIS: [*To his mother, sincerely.*] What's the matter with Grandmama—don't she want to be rich?

RUTH: [*Distractedly.*] You go on out and play now, baby. [TRAVIS *exits.* MAMA *starts wiping dishes absently, humming intently to herself.* RUTH *turns to her, with kind exasperation.*] You've gone and got yourself upset.

MAMA: [*Not looking at her.*] I spec if it wasn't for you all . . . I would just put that money away or give it to the church or something.

RUTH: Now what kind of talk is that. Mr. Younger would just be plain mad if he could hear you talking foolish like that.

MAMA: [*Stopping and staring off.*] Yes . . . he sure would. [*Sighing.*] We got enough to do with that money, all right. [*She halts then, and turns and looks at her daughter-in-law hard;* RUTH *avoids her eyes and* MAMA *wipes her hands with finality and starts to speak firmly to* RUTH.] Where did you go today, girl?

RUTH: To the doctor.

MAMA: [*Impatiently.*] Now, Ruth . . . you know better than that. Old Doctor Jones is strange enough in his way but there ain't nothing 'bout him make somebody slip and call him "she"—like you done this morning.

RUTH: Well, that's what happened—my tongue slipped.

MAMA: You went to see that woman, didn't you?

RUTH: [*Defensively, giving herself away.*] What woman you talking about?

MAMA: [*Angrily.*] That woman who—

[WALTER *enters in great excitement.*]

WALTER: Did it come?

MAMA: [*Quietly.*] Can't you give people a Christian greeting before you start asking about money?

WALTER: [*To* RUTH.] Did it come? [RUTH *unfolds the check and lays it quietly before him, watching him intently with thoughts of her own.* WALTER *sits down and grasps it close and counts off the zeros.*] Ten thousand dollars— [*He turns suddenly, frantically to his mother and draws some papers out of his breast pocket.*] Mama—look. Old Willy Harris put everything on paper—

MAMA: Son—I think you ought to talk to your wife . . . I'll go on out and leave you alone if you want—

WALTER: I can talk to her later—Mama, look—

MAMA: Son—

WALTER: WILL SOMEBODY PLEASE LISTEN TO ME TODAY!

MAMA: [*Quietly.*] I don't 'low no yellin' in this house, Walter Lee, and you know it— [WALTER *stares at them in frustration and starts to speak several times.*] And there ain't going to be no investing in no liquor stores. I don't aim to have to speak on that again.

[*A long pause.*]

WALTER: Oh—so you don't aim to have to speak on that again? So you have decided . . . [*Crumpling his papers.*] Well, *you* tell that to my boy tonight when you put him to sleep on the living-room couch . . . [*Turning to* MAMA *and speaking directly to her.*] Yeah—and tell it to my wife, Mama, tomorrow when she has to go out of here to look after somebody else's kids. And tell it to *me*, Mama, every time we need a new pair of curtains and I have to watch *you* go out and work in somebody's kitchen. Yeah, you tell me then!

[WALTER *starts out.*]

RUTH: Where you going?

WALTER: I'm going out!

RUTH: Where?

WALTER: Just out of this house somewhere—

RUTH: [*Getting her coat.*] I'll come too.

WALTER: I don't want you to come!

RUTH: I got something to talk to you about, Walter.

WALTER: That's too bad.

MAMA: [*Still quietly.*] Walter Lee— [*She waits and he finally turns and looks at her.*] Sit down.

WALTER: I'm a grown man, Mama.

MAMA: Ain't nobody said you wasn't grown. But you still in my house and my presence. And as long as you are—you'll talk to your wife civil. Now sit down.

RUTH: [*Suddenly.*] Oh, let him go on out and drink himself to death! He makes me sick to my stomach! [*She flings her coat against him.*]

WALTER: [*Violently.*] And you turn mine too, baby! [RUTH *goes into their bedroom and slams the door behind her.*] That was my greatest mistake—

MAMA: [*Still quietly.*] Walter, what is the matter with you?

WALTER: Matter with me? Ain't nothing the matter with *me*!

MAMA: Yes there is. Something eating you up like a crazy man. Something more than me not giving you this money. The past few years I been watching it happen to you. You get all nervous acting and kind of wild in the eyes—[WALTER *jumps up impatiently at her words.*] I said sit there now, I'm talking to you!

WALTER: Mama—I don't need no nagging at me today.

MAMA: Seem like you getting to a place where you always tied up in some kind of knot about something. But if anybody ask you 'bout it you just yell at 'em and bust out the house and go out and drink somewheres. Walter Lee, people can't live with that. Ruth's a good, patient girl in her way—but you getting to be too much. Boy, don't make the mistake of driving that girl away from you.

WALTER: Why—what she do for me?

MAMA: She loves you.

WALTER: Mama—I'm going out. I want to go off somewhere and be by myself for a while.

MAMA: I'm sorry 'bout your liquor store, son. It just wasn't the thing for us to do. That's what I want to tell you about—

WALTER: I got to go out, Mama—

[*He rises.*]

MAMA: It's dangerous, son.

WALTER: What's dangerous?

MAMA: When a man goes outside his home to look for peace.

WALTER: [*Beseechingly.*] Then why can't there never be no peace in this house then?

MAMA: You done found it in some other house?

WALTER: No—there ain't no woman! Why do women always think there's a woman somewhere when a man gets restless. [*Coming to her.*] Mama—Mama—I want so many things . . .

MAMA: Yes, son—

WALTER: I want so many things that they are driving me kind of crazy . . . Mama—look at me.

MAMA: I'm looking at you. You a good-looking boy. You got a job, a nice wife, a fine boy and—

WALTER: A job. [*Looks at her.*] Mama, a job? I open and close car doors all day long. I drive a man around in his limousine and I say, "Yes, sir; no, sir; very good, sir; shall I take the Drive, sir?" Mama, that ain't no kind of job . . . that ain't nothing at all. [*Very quietly.*] Mama, I don't know if I can make you understand.

MAMA: Understand what, baby?

WALTER: [*Quietly.*] Sometimes it's like I can see the future stretched out in front of me—just plain as day. The future, Mama. Hanging over there at the edge of my days. Just waiting for me—a big, looming blank space—full of *nothing*. Just waiting for *me*. [*Pause.*] Mama—sometimes when I'm downtown and I pass them cool, quiet-looking restaurants where them white boys are sitting back and talking 'bout things . . . sitting there turning deals worth millions of dollars . . . sometimes I see guys don't look much older than me—

MAMA: Son—how come you talk so much 'bout money?

WALTER: [*With immense passion.*] Because it is life, Mama!

MAMA: [*Quietly.*] Oh— [*Very quietly.*] So now it's life. Money is life. Once upon a time freedom used to be life—now it's money. I guess the world really do change . . .

WALTER: No—it was always money, Mama. We just didn't know about it.

MAMA: No . . . something has changed. [*She looks at him.*] You something new, boy. In my time we was worried about not being lynched and getting to the North if we could and how to stay alive and still have a pinch of dignity too . . . Now here come you and Beneatha—talking 'bout things we ain't never even thought about hardly, me and your daddy. You ain't satisfied or proud of nothing we done. I mean that you had a home; that we kept you out of trouble till you was grown; that you don't have to ride to work on the back of nobody's streetcar—You my children—but how different we done become.

WALTER: You just don't understand, Mama, you just don't understand.

MAMA: Son—do you know your wife is expecting another baby? [WALTER *stands, stunned, and absorbs what his mother has said.*] That's what she wanted to talk to you about. [WALTER *sinks down into a chair.*] This ain't for me to be telling—but you ought to know. [*She waits.*] I think Ruth is thinking 'bout getting rid of that child.[5]

WALTER: [*Slowly understanding.*] No—no—Ruth wouldn't do that.

MAMA: When the world gets ugly enough—a woman will do anything for her family. *The part that's already living.*

WALTER: You don't know Ruth, Mama, if you think she would do that.

[RUTH *opens the bedroom door and stands there a little limp.*]

RUTH: [*Beaten.*] Yes I would too, Walter. [*Pause.*] I gave her a five-dollar down payment.

[*There is total silence as the man stares at his wife and the mother stares at her son.*]

MAMA: [*Presently.*] Well— [*Tightly.*] Well—son, I'm waiting to hear you say something . . . I'm waiting to hear how you be your father's son. Be the man he was . . . [*Pause.*] Your wife say she going to destroy your child. And I'm

---

5. Abortions were illegal and dangerous in the United States prior to the 1973 *Roe v. Wade* Supreme Court decision.

waiting to hear you talk like him and say we a people who give children life, not who destroys them— [*She rises.*] I'm waiting to see you stand up and look like your daddy and say we done give up one baby to poverty and that we ain't going to give up nary another one . . . I'm waiting.

WALTER: Ruth—

MAMA: If you a son of mine, tell her! [WALTER *turns, looks at her and can say nothing. She continues, bitterly.*] You . . . you are a disgrace to your father's memory. Somebody get me my hat.

[CURTAIN.]

ACT II

Scene One

Time: Later the same day.

   At rise: RUTH *is ironing again. She has the radio going. Presently* BENEATHA'S *bedroom door opens and* RUTH'S *mouth falls and she puts down the iron in fascination.*

RUTH: What have we got on tonight!

BENEATHA: [*Emerging grandly from the doorway so that we can see her thoroughly robed in the costume* ASAGAI *brought.*] You are looking at what a well-dressed Nigerian woman wears— [*She parades for* RUTH, *her hair completely hidden by the headdress; she is coquettishly fanning herself with an ornate oriental fan, mistakenly more like Butterfly*[6] *than any Nigerian that ever was.*] Isn't it beautiful? [*She promenades to the radio and, with an arrogant flourish, turns off the good loud blues that is playing.*] Enough of this assimilationist junk! [RUTH *follows her with her eyes as she goes to the phonograph and puts on a record and turns and waits ceremoniously for the music to come up. Then, with a shout—*] OCOMOGOSIAY!

   [RUTH *jumps. The music comes up, a lovely Nigerian melody.* BENEATHA *listens, enraptured, her eyes far away—"back to the past." She begins to dance.* RUTH *is dumbfounded.*]

RUTH: What kind of dance is that?

BENEATHA: A folk dance.

RUTH: [*Pearl Bailey.*][7] What kind of folks do that, honey?

BENEATHA: It's from Nigeria. It's a dance of welcome.

RUTH: Who you welcoming?

BENEATHA: The men back to the village.

RUTH: Where they been?

BENEATHA: How should I know—out hunting or something. Anyway, they are coming back now . . .

RUTH: Well, that's good.

---

6. Madame Butterfly, a Japanese woman married to, and then abandoned by, an American man in the opera *Madama Butterfly* (1904), by the Italian composer Giacomo Puccini (1858–1924).
7. That is, in the manner of the popular African American singer and entertainer (1918–90).

BENEATHA: [*With the record.*]

> Alundi, alundi
> Alundi alunya
> Jop pu a jeepua
> Ang gu sooooooooooo

> Ai yai yae . . .
> Ayehaye—alundi . . .

[WALTER *comes in during this performance; he has obviously been drinking. He leans against the door heavily and watches his sister, at first with distaste. Then his eyes look off—"back to the past"—as he lifts both his fists to the roof, screaming.*]

WALTER: YEAH . . . AND ETHIOPIA STRETCH FORTH HER HANDS AGAIN! . . .[8]

RUTH: [*Drily, looking at him.*] Yes—and Africa sure is claiming her own tonight. [*She gives them both up and starts ironing again.*]

WALTER: [*All in a drunken, dramatic shout.*] Shut up! . . . I'm digging them drums . . . them drums move me! . . . [*He makes his weaving way to his wife's face and leans in close to her.*] In my heart of hearts— [*He thumps his chest.*] —I am much warrior!

RUTH: [*Without even looking up.*] In your heart of hearts you are much drunkard.

WALTER: [*Coming away from her and starting to wander around the room, shout-ing.*] Me and Jomo . . . [*Intently, in his sister's face. She has stopped dancing to watch him in this unknown mood.*] That's my man, Kenyatta.[9] [*Shouting and thumping his chest.*] FLAMING SPEAR! HOT DAMN! [*He is suddenly in possession of an imaginary spear and actively spearing enemies all over the room.*] OCOMOGOSIAY . . . THE LION IS WAKING . . . OWIMOWEH! [*He pulls his shirt open and leaps up on a table and gestures with his spear. The bell rings.* RUTH *goes to answer.*]

BENEATHA: [*To encourage* WALTER, *thoroughly caught up with this side of him.*] OCOMOGOSIAY, FLAMING SPEAR!

WALTER: [*On the table, very far gone, his eyes pure glass sheets. He sees what we cannot, that he is a leader of his people, a great chief, a descendant of Chaka,[1] and that the hour to march has come.*] Listen, my black brothers—

BENEATHA: OCOMOGOSIAY!

WALTER: —Do you hear the waters rushing against the shores of the coast-lands—

BENEATHA: OCOMOGOSIAY!

WALTER: —Do you hear the screeching of the cocks in yonder hills beyond where the chiefs meet in council for the coming of the mighty war—

BENEATHA: OCOMOGOSIAY!

---

8. See Psalms 68.31: "Princes shall come out of Egypt; Ethiopia shall soon stretch out her hands unto God."

9. Jomo Kenyatta (1893–1978), African political leader and first president of Kenya (1964–78) follow-ing its independence from British colonial rule.

1. Zulu chief (1786–1828), also known as "Shaka" and called "The Black Napoleon" for his strategic and organizational genius.

WALTER: —Do you hear the beating of the wings of the birds flying low over the mountains and the low places of our land—

[RUTH *opens the door.* GEORGE MURCHISON *enters.*]

BENEATHA: OCOMOGOSIAY!

WALTER: —Do you hear the singing of the women, singing the war songs of our fathers to the babies in the great houses . . . singing the sweet war songs? OH, DO YOU HEAR, MY BLACK BROTHERS!

BENEATHA: [*Completely gone.*] We hear you, Flaming Spear—

WALTER: Telling us to prepare for the greatness of the time— [*To* GEORGE.] Black Brother!

[*He extends his hand for the fraternal clasp.*]

GEORGE: Black Brother, hell!

RUTH: [*Having had enough, and embarrassed for the family.*] Beneatha, you got company—what's the matter with you? Walter Lee Younger, get down off that table and stop acting like a fool . . .

[WALTER *comes down off the table suddenly and makes a quick exit to the bathroom.*]

RUTH: He's had a little to drink . . . I don't know what her excuse is.

GEORGE: [*To* BENEATHA.] Look honey, we're going *to* the theatre—we're not going to be *in* it . . . so go change, huh?

RUTH: You expect this boy to go out with you looking like that?

BENEATHA: [*Looking at* GEORGE.] That's up to George. If he's ashamed of his heritage—

GEORGE: Oh, don't be so proud of yourself, Bennie—just because you look eccentric.

BENEATHA: How can something that's natural be eccentric?

GEORGE: That's what being eccentric means—being natural. Get dressed.

BENEATHA: I don't like that, George.

RUTH: Why must you and your brother make an argument out of everything people say?

BENEATHA: Because I hate assimilationist Negroes!

RUTH: Will somebody please tell me what assimila-who-ever means!

GEORGE: Oh, it's just a college girl's way of calling people Uncle Toms—but that isn't what it means at all.

RUTH: Well, what does it mean?

BENEATHA: [*Cutting* GEORGE *off and staring at him as she replies to* RUTH.] It means someone who is willing to give up his own culture and submerge himself completely in the dominant, and in this case, *oppressive* culture!

GEORGE: Oh, dear, dear, dear! Here we go! A lecture on the African past! On our Great West African Heritage! In one second we will hear all about the great Ashanti empires; the great Songhay civilizations; and the great sculpture of Bénin—and then some poetry in the Bantu—and the whole monologue will end with the word *heritage*! [*Nastily.*] Let's face it, baby, your heritage is nothing but a bunch of raggedy-assed spirituals and some grass huts!

BENEATHA: *Grass huts!* [RUTH *crosses to her and forcibly pushes her toward the bedroom.*] See there . . . you are standing there in your splendid ignorance talking about people who were the first to smelt iron on the face of the earth! [RUTH *is pushing her through the door.*] The Ashanti were performing surgical operations when the English— [RUTH *pulls the door to, with* BENEATHA *on the other side, and smiles graciously at* GEORGE. BENEATHA *opens the door and shouts the end of the sentence defiantly at* GEORGE.] —were still tattooing themselves with blue dragons . . . [*She goes back inside.*]

RUTH: Have a seat, George. [*They both sit.* RUTH *folds her hands rather primly on her lap, determined to demonstrate the civilization of the family.*] Warm, ain't it? I mean for September. [*Pause.*] Just like they always say about Chicago weather: If it's too hot or cold for you, just wait a minute and it'll change. [*She smiles happily at this cliché of clichés.*] Everybody say it's got to do with them bombs and things they keep setting off.[2] [*Pause.*] Would you like a nice cold beer?

GEORGE: No, thank you. I don't care for beer. [*He looks at his watch.*] I hope she hurries up.

RUTH: What time is the show?

GEORGE: It's an eight-thirty curtain. That's just Chicago, though. In New York standard curtain time is eight forty.

[*He is rather proud of this knowledge.*]

RUTH: [*Properly appreciating it.*] You get to New York a lot?

GEORGE: [*Offhand.*] Few times a year.

RUTH: Oh—that's nice. I've never been to New York.

[WALTER *enters. We feel he has relieved himself, but the edge of unreality is still with him.*]

WALTER: New York ain't got nothing Chicago ain't. Just a bunch of hustling people all squeezed up together—being "Eastern."

[*He turns his face into a screw of displeasure.*]

GEORGE: Oh—you've been?

WALTER: *Plenty* of times.

RUTH: [*Shocked at the lie.*] Walter Lee Younger!

WALTER: [*Staring her down.*] Plenty! [*Pause.*] What we got to drink in this house? Why don't you offer this man some refreshment. [*To* GEORGE.] They don't know how to entertain people in this house, man.

GEORGE: Thank you—I don't really care for anything.

WALTER: [*Feeling his head; sobriety coming.*] Where's Mama?

RUTH: She ain't come back yet.

WALTER: [*Looking* MURCHISON *over from head to toe, scrutinizing his carefully casual tweed sports jacket over cashmere V-neck sweater over soft eyelet shirt and tie, and soft slacks, finished off with white buckskin shoes.*] Why all you college boys wear them fairyish-looking white shoes?

RUTH: Walter Lee!

[GEORGE MURCHISON *ignores the remark.*]

2. In the 1950s, people commonly blamed weather fluctuations on atomic testing.

WALTER: [*To* RUTH.] Well, they look crazy as hell—white shoes, cold as it is.

RUTH: [*Crushed.*] You have to excuse him—

WALTER: No he don't! Excuse me for what? What you always excusing me for! I'll excuse myself when I needs to be excused! [*A pause.*] They look as funny as them black knee socks Beneatha wears out of here all the time.

RUTH: It's the college *style*, Walter.

WALTER: Style, hell, She looks like she got burnt legs or something!

RUTH: Oh, Walter—

WALTER: [*An irritable mimic.*] Oh, Walter! Oh, Walter! [*To* MURCHISON.] How's your old man making out? I understand you all going to buy that big hotel on the Drive?[3] [*He finds a beer in the refrigerator, wanders over to* MURCHISON, *sipping and wiping his lips with the back of his hand, and straddling a chair backwards to talk to the other man.*] Shrewd move. Your old man is all right, man. [*Tapping his head and half winking for emphasis.*] I mean he knows how to operate. I mean he thinks *big,* you know what I mean, I mean for a *home,* you know? But I think he's kind of running out of ideas now. I'd like to talk to him. Listen, man, I got some plans that could turn this city upside down. I mean I think like he does. *Big.* Invest big, gamble big, hell, lose *big* if you have to, you know what I mean. It's hard to find a man on this whole Southside who understands my kind of thinking—you dig? [*He scrutinizes* MURCHISON *again, drinks his beer, squints his eyes and leans in close, confidential, man to man.*] Me and you ought to sit down and talk sometimes, man. Man, I got me some ideas . . .

GEORGE: [*With boredom.*] Yeah—sometimes we'll have to do that, Walter.

WALTER: [*Understanding the indifference, and offended.*] Yeah—well, when you get the time, man. I know you a busy little boy.

RUTH: Walter, please—

WALTER: [*Bitterly, hurt.*] I know ain't nothing in this world as busy as you colored college boys with your fraternity pins and white shoes . . .

RUTH: [*Covering her face with humiliation.*] Oh, Walter Lee—

WALTER: I see you all the time—with the books tucked under your arms—going to your [*British A—a mimic.*] "clahsses." And for what! What the hell you learning over there? Filling up your heads— [*Counting off on his fingers.*] — with the sociology and the psychology—but they teaching you how to be a man? How to take over and run the world? They teaching you how to run a rubber plantation or a steel mill? Naw—just to talk proper and read books and wear white shoes . . .

GEORGE: [*Looking at him with distaste, a little above it all.*] You're all wacked up with bitterness, man.

WALTER: [*Intently, almost quietly, between the teeth, glaring at the boy.*] And you—ain't you bitter, man? Ain't you just about had it yet? Don't you see no stars gleaming that you can't reach out and grab? You happy?—You contented son-of-a-bitch—you happy? You got it made? Bitter? Man, I'm a volcano. Bitter? Here I am a giant—surrounded by ants! Ants who can't even understand what it is the giant is talking about.

RUTH: [*Passionately and suddenly.*] Oh, Walter—ain't you with nobody!

3. Lake Shore Drive, a scenic thoroughfare along Lake Michigan.

WALTER: [*Violently.*] No! 'Cause ain't nobody with me! Not even my own mother!

RUTH: Walter, that's a terrible thing to say!

[BENEATHA *enters, dressed for the evening in a cocktail dress and earrings.*]

GEORGE: Well—hey, you look great.

BENEATHA: Let's go, George. See you all later.

RUTH: Have a nice time.

GEORGE: Thanks. Good night. [*To* WALTER, *sarcastically.*] Good night, *Prometheus* [4]

[BENEATHA *and* GEORGE *exit.*]

WALTER: [*To* RUTH.] Who is Prometheus?

RUTH: I don't know. Don't worry about it.

WALTER: [*In fury, pointing after* GEORGE.] See there—they get to a point where they can't insult you man to man—they got to go talk about something ain't nobody never heard of!

RUTH: How do you know it was an insult? [*To humor him.*] Maybe Prometheus is a nice fellow.

WALTER: Prometheus! I bet there ain't even no such thing! I bet that simple-minded clown—

RUTH: Walter—

[*She stops what she is doing and looks at him.*]

WALTER: [*Yelling.*] Don't start!

RUTH: Start what?

WALTER: Your nagging! Where was I? Who was I with? How much money did I spend?

RUTH: [*Plaintively.*] Walter Lee—why don't we just try to talk about it . . .

WALTER: [*Not listening.*] I been out talking with people who understand me. People who care about the things I got on my mind.

RUTH: [*Wearily.*] I guess that means people like Willy Harris.

WALTER: Yes, people like Willy Harris.

RUTH: [*With a sudden flash of impatience.*] Why don't you all just hurry up and go into the banking business and stop talking about it!

WALTER: Why? You want to know why? 'Cause we all tied up in a race of people that don't know how to do nothing but moan, pray and have babies!

[*The line is too bitter even for him and he looks at her and sits down.*]

RUTH: Oh, Walter . . . [*Softly.*] Honey, why can't you stop fighting me?

WALTER: [*Without thinking.*] Who's fighting you? Who even cares about you?

[*This line begins the retardation of his mood.*]

RUTH: Well— [*She waits a long time, and then with resignation starts to put away her things.*] I guess I might as well go on to bed . . . [*More or less to herself.*] I don't

---

4. In Greek mythology, Prometheus represented the bold creative spirit; defying the gods, he stole fire from Olympus (the locale of the gods) and gave it to humankind. Though successful, he was harshly punished by Zeus.

know where we lost it . . . but we have . . . [*Then, to him.*] I—I'm sorry about this new baby, Walter. I guess maybe I better go on and do what I started . . . I guess I just didn't realize how bad things was with us . . . I guess I just didn't really realize— [*She starts out to the bedroom and stops.*] You want some hot milk?

WALTER: Hot milk?

RUTH: Yes—hot milk.

WALTER: Why hot milk?

RUTH: 'Cause after all that liquor you come home with you ought to have something hot in your stomach.

WALTER: I don't want no milk.

RUTH: You want some coffee then?

WALTER: No, I don't want no coffee. I don't want nothing hot to drink. [*Almost plaintively.*] Why you always trying to give me something to eat?

RUTH: [*Standing and looking at him helplessly.*] What else can I give you, Walter Lee Younger?

[*She stands and looks at him and presently turns to go out again. He lifts his head and watches her going away from him in a new mood which began to emerge when he asked her "Who cares about you?"*]

WALTER: It's been rough, ain't it, baby? [*She hears and stops but does not turn around and he continues to her back.*] I guess between two people there ain't never as much understood as folks generally thinks there is. I mean like between me and you— [*She turns to face him.*] How we gets to the place where we scared to talk softness to each other. [*He waits, thinking hard himself.*] Why you think it got to be like that? [*He is thoughtful, almost as a child would be.*] Ruth, what is it gets into people ought to be close?

RUTH: I don't know, honey. I think about it a lot.

WALTER: On account of you and me, you mean? The way things are with us. The way something done come down between us.

RUTH: There ain't so much between us, Walter . . . Not when you come to me and try to talk to me. Try to be with me . . . a little even.

WALTER: [*Total honesty.*] Sometimes . . . sometimes . . . I don't even know how to try.

RUTH: Walter—

WALTER: Yes?

RUTH: [*Coming to him, gently and with misgiving, but coming to him.*] Honey . . . life don't have to be like this. I mean sometimes people can do things so that things are better . . . You remember how we used to talk when Travis was born . . . about the way we were going to live . . . the kind of house . . . [*She is stroking his head.*] Well, it's all starting to slip away from us . . .

[MAMA *enters, and* WALTER *jumps up and shouts at her.*]

WALTER: Mama, where have you been?

MAMA: My—them steps is longer than they used to be. Whew! [*She sits down and ignores him.*] How you feeling this evening, Ruth?

[RUTH *shrugs, disturbed some at having been prematurely interrupted and watching her husband knowingly.*]

WALTER: Mama, where have you been all day?

MAMA: [*Still ignoring him and leaning on the table and changing to more comfort-able shoes.*] Where's Travis?

RUTH: I let him go out earlier and he ain't come back yet. Boy, is he going to get it!

WALTER: Mama!

MAMA: [*As if she has heard him for the first time.*] Yes, son?

WALTER: Where did you go this afternoon?

MAMA: I went downtown to tend to some business that I had to tend to.

WALTER: What kind of business?

MAMA: You know better than to question me like a child, Brother.

WALTER: [*Rising and bending over the table.*] Where were you, Mama? [*Bringing his fists down and shouting.*] Mama, you didn't go do something with that insurance money, something crazy?

[*The front door opens slowly, interrupting him, and* TRAVIS *peeks his head in, less than hopefully.*]

TRAVIS: [*To his mother.*] Mama, I—

RUTH: "Mama I" nothing! You're going to get it, boy! Get on in that bedroom and get yourself ready!

TRAVIS: But I—

MAMA: Why don't you all never let the child explain hisself.

RUTH: Keep out of it now, Lena.

[MAMA *clamps her lips together, and* RUTH *advances toward her son menac-ingly.*]

RUTH: A thousand times I have told you not to go off like that—

MAMA: [*Holding out her arms to her grandson.*] Well—at least let me tell him something. I want him to be the first one to hear . . . Come here, Travis. [*The boy obeys, gladly.*] Travis— [*She takes him by the shoulder and looks into his face.*] —you know that money we got in the mail this morning?

TRAVIS: Yes'm—

MAMA: Well—what you think your grandmama gone and done with that money?

TRAVIS: I don't know, Grandmama.

MAMA: [*Putting her finger on his nose for emphasis.*] She went out and she bought you a house! [*The explosion comes from* WALTER *at the end of the revelation and he jumps up and turns away from all of them in a fury.* MAMA *continues, to* TRA-VIS.] You glad about the house? It's going to be yours when you get to be a man.

TRAVIS: Yeah—I always wanted to live in a house.

MAMA: All right, gimme some sugar then— [TRAVIS *puts his arms around her neck as she watches her son over the boy's shoulder. Then, to* TRAVIS, *after the embrace.*] Now when you say your prayers tonight, you thank God and your grandfather—'cause it was him who give you the house—in his way.

RUTH: [*Taking the boy from* MAMA *and pushing him toward the bedroom.*] Now you get out of here and get ready for your beating.

TRAVIS: Aw, Mama—

RUTH: Get on in there— [*Closing the door behind him and turning radiantly to her mother-in-law.*] So you went and did it!

MAMA: [*Quietly, looking at her son with pain.*] Yes, I did.

RUTH: [*Raising both arms classically.*] Praise God! [*Looks at* WALTER *a moment, who says nothing. She crosses rapidly to her husband.*] Please, honey—let me be glad . . . you be glad too. [*She has laid her hands on his shoulders, but he shakes himself free of her roughly, without turning to face her.*] Oh, Walter . . . a home . . . *a home.* [*She comes back to* MAMA.] Well—where is it? How big is it? How much it going to cost?

MAMA: Well—

RUTH: When we moving?

MAMA: [*Smiling at her.*] First of the month.

RUTH: [*Throwing back her head with jubilance.*] Praise God!

MAMA: [*Tentatively, still looking at her son's back turned against her and* RUTH.] It's—it's a nice house too . . . [*She cannot help speaking directly to him. An imploring quality in her voice, her manner, makes her almost like a girl now.*] Three bedrooms—nice big one for you and Ruth . . . Me and Beneatha still have to share our room, but Travis have one of his own—and [*With difficulty.*] I figure if the—new baby—is a boy, we could get one of them double-decker outfits . . . And there's a yard with a little patch of dirt where I could maybe get to grow me a few flowers . . . And a nice big basement . . .

RUTH: Walter honey, be glad—

MAMA: [*Still to his back, fingering things on the table.*] 'Course I don't want to make it sound fancier than it is . . . It's just a plain little old house—but it's made good and solid—and it will be *ours.* Walter Lee—it makes a difference in a man when he can walk on floors that belong to *him* . . .

RUTH: Where is it?

MAMA: [*Frightened at this telling.*] Well—well—it's out there in Clybourne Park[5]—

[RUTH's *radiance fades abruptly, and* WALTER *finally turns slowly to face his mother with incredulity and hostility.*]

RUTH: Where?

MAMA: [*Matter-of-factly.*] Four o six Clybourne Street, Clybourne Park.

RUTH: Clybourne Park? Mama, there ain't no colored people living in Clybourne Park.

MAMA: [*Almost idiotically.*] Well, I guess there's going to be some now.

WALTER: [*Bitterly.*] So that's the peace and comfort you went out and bought for us today!

MAMA: [*Raising her eyes to meet his finally.*] Son—I just tried to find the nicest place for the least amount of money for my family.

RUTH: [*Trying to recover from the shock.*] Well—well—'course I ain't one never been 'fraid of no crackers[6] mind you—but—well, wasn't there no other houses nowhere?

MAMA: Them houses they put up for colored in them areas way out all seem to cost twice as much as other houses. I did the best I could.

RUTH: [*Struck senseless with the news, in its various degrees of goodness and trouble, she sits a moment, her fists propping her chin in thought, and then she starts to*

5. On Chicago's Near North Side.
6. Derogatory term for poor whites.

rise, bringing her fists down with vigor, the radiance spreading from cheek to cheek again.] Well—well!—All I can say is—if this is my time in life—*my time*—to say good-bye— [*And she builds with momentum as she starts to circle the room with an exuberant, almost tearfully happy release.*] —to these God-damned cracking walls!— [*She pounds the walls.*] —and these marching roaches!— [*She wipes at an imaginary army of marching roaches.*] —and this cramped little closet which ain't now or never was no kitchen! . . . then I say it loud and good, *Hallelujah!* and good-bye misery . . . *I don't never want to see your ugly face again!* [*She laughs joyously, having practically destroyed the apartment, and flings her arms up and lets them come down happily, slowly, reflectively, over her abdomen, aware for the first time perhaps that the life therein pulses with happiness and not despair.*] Lena?

MAMA: [*Moved, watching her happiness.*] Yes, honey?

RUTH: [*Looking off.*] Is there—is there a whole lot of sunlight?

MAMA: [*Understanding.*] Yes, child, there's a whole lot of sunlight.

[*Long pause.*]

RUTH: [*Collecting herself and going to the door of the room* TRAVIS *is in.*] Well— I guess I better see 'bout Travis. [*To* MAMA.] Lord, I sure don't feel like whipping nobody today!

[*She exits.*]

MAMA: [*The mother and son are left alone now and the mother waits a long time, considering deeply, before she speaks.*] Son—you—you understand what I done, don't you? [WALTER *is silent and sullen.*] I—I just seen my family falling apart today . . . just falling to pieces in front of my eyes . . . We couldn't of gone on like we was today. We was going backwards 'stead of forwards— talking 'bout killing babies and wishing each other was dead . . . When it gets like that in life—you just got to do something different, push on out and do something bigger . . . [*She waits.*] I wish you say something, son . . . I wish you'd say how deep inside you you think I done the right thing—

WALTER: [*Crossing slowly to his bedroom door and finally turning there and speaking measuredly.*] What you need me to say you done right for? You the head of this family. You run our lives like you want to. It was your money and you did what you wanted with it. So what you need for me to say it was all right for? [*Bitterly, to hurt her as deeply as he knows is possible.*] So you butchered up a dream of mine—you—who always talking 'bout your children's dreams . . .

MAMA: Walter Lee—

[*He just closes the door behind him.* MAMA *sits alone, thinking heavily.*]

[CURTAIN.]

Scene Two

Time: Friday night. A few weeks later.

At rise: Packing crates mark the intention of the family to move. BENEATHA *and* GEORGE *come in, presumably from an evening out again.*

GEORGE: O.K. . . . O.K., whatever you say . . . [*They both sit on the couch. He tries to kiss her. She moves away.*] Look, we've had a nice evening; let's not spoil it, huh? . . .

[*He again turns her head and tries to nuzzle in and she turns away from him, not with distaste but with momentary lack of interest; in a mood to pursue what they were talking about.*]

BENEATHA: I'm *trying* to talk to you.

GEORGE: We always talk.

BENEATHA: Yes—and I love to talk.

GEORGE: [*Exasperated; rising.*] I know it and I don't mind it sometimes . . . I want you to cut it out, see—The moody stuff, I mean. I don't like it. You're a nice-looking girl . . . all over. That's all you need, honey, forget the atmosphere. Guys aren't going to go for the atmosphere—they're going to go for what they see. Be glad for that. Drop the Garbo[7] routine. It doesn't go with you. As for myself, I want a nice— [*Groping.*] —simple [*Thoughtfully.*] — sophisticated girl . . . not a poet— O.K.?

[*She rebuffs him again and he starts to leave.*]

BENEATHA: Why are you angry?

GEORGE: Because this is stupid! I don't go out with you to discuss the nature of "quiet desperation"[8] or to hear all about your thoughts—because the world will go on thinking what it thinks regardless—

BENEATHA: Then why read books? Why go to school?

GEORGE: [*With artificial patience, counting on his fingers.*] It's simple. You read books—to learn facts—to get grades—to pass the course—to get a degree. That's all—it has nothing to do with thoughts.

[*A long pause.*]

BENEATHA: I see. [*A longer pause as she looks at him.*] Good night, George.

[GEORGE *looks at her a little oddly, and starts to exit. He meets* MAMA *coming in.*]

GEORGE: Oh—hello, Mrs. Younger.

MAMA: Hello, George, how you feeling?

GEORGE: Fine—fine, how are you?

MAMA: Oh, a little tired. You know them steps can get you after a day's work. You all have a nice time tonight?

GEORGE: Yes—a fine time. Well, good night.

MAMA: Good night. [*He exits.* MAMA *closes the door behind her.*] Hello, honey. What you sitting like that for?

BENEATHA: I'm just sitting.

MAMA: Didn't you have a nice time?

7. Greta Garbo (1905–90), Swedish-born American film star whose sultry, remote, and European femininity was widely imitated.
8. In *Walden* (1854), Henry Thoreau asserts that "the mass of men lead lives of quiet desperation."

BENEATHA: No.

MAMA: No? What's the matter?

BENEATHA: Mama, George is a fool—honest. [*She rises.*]

MAMA: [*Hustling around unloading the packages she has entered with. She stops.*] Is he, baby?

BENEATHA: Yes.

[BENEATHA *makes up* TRAVIS' *bed as she talks.*]

MAMA: You sure?

BENEATHA: Yes.

MAMA: Well—I guess you better not waste your time with no fools.

[BENEATHA *looks up at her mother, watching her put groceries in the refrigerator. Finally she gathers up her things and starts into the bedroom. At the door she stops and looks back at her mother.*]

BENEATHA: Mama—

MAMA: Yes, baby—

BENEATHA: Thank you.

MAMA: For what?

BENEATHA: For understanding me this time.

[*She exits quickly and the mother stands, smiling a little, looking at the place where* BENEATHA *just stood.* RUTH *enters.*]

RUTH: Now don't you fool with any of this stuff, Lena—

MAMA: Oh, I just thought I'd sort a few things out.

[*The phone rings.* RUTH *answers.*]

RUTH: [*At the phone.*] Hello—Just a minute. [*Goes to door.*] Walter, it's Mrs. Arnold. [*Waits. Goes back to the phone. Tense.*] Hello. Yes, this is his wife speaking . . . He's lying down now. Yes . . . well, he'll be in tomorrow. He's been very sick. Yes—I know we should have called, but we were so sure he'd be able to come in today. Yes—yes, I'm very sorry. Yes . . . Thank you very much. [*She hangs up.* WALTER *is standing in the doorway of the bedroom behind her.*] That was Mrs. Arnold.

WALTER: [*Indifferently.*] Was it?

RUTH: She said if you don't come in tomorrow that they are getting a new man . . .

WALTER: Ain't that sad—ain't that crying sad.

RUTH: She said Mr. Arnold has had to take a cab for three days . . . Walter, you ain't been to work for three days! [*This is a revelation to her.*] Where you been, Walter Lee Younger? [WALTER *looks at her and starts to laugh.*] You're going to lose your job.

WALTER: That's right . . .

RUTH: Oh, Walter, and with your mother working like a dog every day—

WALTER: That's sad too—Everything is sad.

MAMA: What you been doing for these three days, son?

WALTER: Mama—you don't know all the things a man what got leisure can find to do in this city . . . What's this—Friday night? Well—Wednesday I borrowed Willy Harris' car and I went for a drive . . . just me and myself and I drove and drove . . . Way out . . . way past South Chicago, and I parked the car and I sat and looked at the steel mills all day long. I just sat in the car and looked at them big black chimneys for hours. Then I drove back and I went to the Green Hat. [*Pause.*] And Thursday—Thursday I borrowed the car again and I got in it and I pointed it the other way and I drove the other way—for hours—way, way up to Wisconsin, and I looked at the farms. I just drove and looked at the farms. Then I drove back and I went to the Green Hat. [*Pause.*] And today—today I didn't get the car. Today I just walked. All over the Southside. And I looked at the Negroes and they looked at me and finally I just sat down on the curb at Thirty-ninth and South Parkway and I just sat there and watched the Negroes go by. And then I went to the Green Hat. You all sad? You all depressed? And you know where I am going right now—

[RUTH *goes out quietly.*]

MAMA: Oh, Big Walter, is this the harvest of our days?
WALTER: You know what I like about the Green Hat? [*He turns the radio on and a steamy, deep blues pours into the room.*] I like this little cat they got there who blows a sax . . . He blows. He talks to me. He ain't but 'bout five feet tall and he's got a conked head[9] and his eyes is always closed and he's all music—
MAMA: [*Rising and getting some papers out of her handbag.*] Walter—
WALTER: And there's this other guy who plays the piano . . . and they got a sound. I mean they can work on some music . . . They got the best little combo in the world in the Green Hat . . . You can just sit there and drink and listen to them three men play and you realize that don't nothing matter worth a damn, but just being there—
MAMA: I've helped do it to you, haven't I, son? Walter, I been wrong.
WALTER: Naw—you ain't never been wrong about nothing, Mama.
MAMA: Listen to me, now. I say I been wrong, son. That I been doing to you what the rest of the world been doing to you. [*She stops and he looks up slowly at her and she meets his eyes pleadingly.*] Walter—what you ain't never understood is that I ain't got nothing, don't own nothing, ain't never really wanted nothing that wasn't for you. There ain't nothing as precious to me . . . There ain't nothing worth holding on to, money, dreams, nothing else—if it means— if it means it's going to destroy my boy. [*She puts her papers in front of him and he watches her without speaking or moving.*] I paid the man thirty-five hundred dollars down on the house. That leaves sixty-five hundred dollars. Monday morning I want you to take this money and take three thousand dollars and put it in a savings account for Beneatha's medical schooling. The rest you put in a checking account—with your name on it. And from now on any penny that come out of it or that go in it is for you to look after. For you to decide. [*She drops her hands a little helplessly.*] It ain't much, but it's all I

9. Straightened hair.

got in the world and I'm putting it in your hands. I'm telling you to be the head of this family from now on like you supposed to be.

WALTER: [*Stares at the money.*] You trust me like that, Mama?

MAMA: I ain't never stop trusting you. Like I ain't never stop loving you.

[*She goes out, and* WALTER *sits looking at the money on the table as the music continues in its idiom, pulsing in the room. Finally, in a decisive gesture, he gets up, and, in mingled joy and desperation, picks up the money. At the same moment,* TRAVIS *enters for bed.*]

TRAVIS: What's the matter, Daddy? You drunk?

WALTER: [*Sweetly, more sweetly than we have ever known him.*] No, Daddy ain't drunk. Daddy ain't going to never be drunk again. . . .

TRAVIS: Well, good night, Daddy.

[*The father has come from behind the couch and leans over, embracing his son.*]

WALTER: Son, I feel like talking to you tonight.

TRAVIS: About what?

WALTER: Oh, about a lot of things. About you and what kind of man you going to be when you grow up . . . Son—son, what do you want to be when you grow up?

TRAVIS: A bus driver.

WALTER: [*Laughing a little.*] A what? Man, that ain't nothing to want to be!

TRAVIS: Why not?

WALTER: 'Cause, man—it ain't big enough—you know what I mean.

TRAVIS: I don't know then. I can't make up my mind. Sometimes Mama asks me that too. And sometimes when I tell her I just want to be like you—she says she don't want me to be like that and sometimes she says she does . . .

WALTER: [*Gathering him up in his arms.*] You know what, Travis? In seven years you going to be seventeen years old. And things is going to be very different with us in seven years, Travis . . . One day when you are seventeen I'll come home—home from my office downtown somewhere—

TRAVIS: You don't work in no office, Daddy.

WALTER: No—but after tonight. After what your daddy gonna do tonight, there's going to be offices—a whole lot of offices . . .

TRAVIS: What you gonna do tonight, Daddy?

WALTER: You wouldn't understand yet, son, but your daddy's gonna make a transaction . . . a business transaction that's going to change our lives . . . That's how come one day when you 'bout seventeen years old I'll come home and I'll be pretty tired, you know what I mean, after a day of conferences and secretaries getting things wrong the way they do . . . 'cause an executive's life is hell, man— [*The more he talks the farther away he gets.*] And I'll pull the car up on the driveway . . . just a plain black Chrysler, I think, with white walls—no—black tires. More elegant. Rich people don't have to be flashy . . . though I'll have to get something a little sportier for Ruth—maybe a Cadillac convertible to do her shopping in . . . And I'll come up the steps to the house and the gardener will be clipping away at the hedges and he'll say, "Good evening, Mr. Younger." And I'll say, "Hello, Jefferson, how are you this evening?" And I'll go inside and Ruth will come downstairs and meet me at the door and we'll kiss each other and she'll take my arm and we'll go up to your room to see you sitting on the floor with the catalogues of all the great schools in America around you . . . All the great schools in the world. And—and I'll say, all right son—it's your seventeenth birthday, what is it you've decided? . . . Just tell me where you want to go to school and you'll go. Just tell me, what it is you want to be—and you'll *be* it . . . Whatever you want to be—Yessir! [*He holds his arms open for* TRAVIS.] You just name it, son . . . [TRAVIS *leaps into them.*] and I hand you the world!

[WALTER's *voice has risen in pitch and hysterical promise and on the last line he lifts* TRAVIS *high.*]

[BLACKOUT.]

Scene Three

Time: Saturday, moving day, one week later.
    Before the curtain rises, RUTH's *voice, a strident, dramatic church alto, cuts through the silence.*
    It is, in the darkness, a triumphant surge, a penetrating statement of expectation: "Oh, Lord, I don't feel no ways tired! Children, oh, glory hallelujah!"
    As the curtain rises we see that RUTH *is alone in the living room, finishing up the family's packing. It is moving day. She is nailing crates and tying cartons.* BENEATHA *enters, carrying a guitar case, and watches her exuberant sister-in-law.*

RUTH: Hey!
BENEATHA: [*Putting away the case.*] Hi.
RUTH: [*Pointing at a package.*] Honey—look in that package there and see what I found on sale this morning at the South Center. [RUTH *gets up and moves to the package and draws out some curtains.*] Lookahere—hand-turned hems!
BENEATHA: How do you know the window size out there?
RUTH: [*Who hadn't thought of that.*] Oh—Well, they bound to fit something in the whole house. Anyhow, they was too good a bargain to pass up. [RUTH *slaps her head, suddenly remembering something.*] Oh, Bennie—I meant to put a special note on that carton over there. That's your mama's good china and she wants 'em to be very careful with it.
BENEATHA: I'll do it.

[BENEATHA *finds a piece of paper and starts to draw large letters on it.*]

RUTH: You know what I'm going to do soon as I get in that new house?
BENEATHA: What?
RUTH: Honey—I'm going to run me a tub of water up to here . . . [*With her fingers practically up to her nostrils.*] And I'm going to get in it—and I am going to sit . . . and sit . . . and sit in that hot water and the first person who knocks to tell *me* to hurry up and come out—
BENEATHA: Gets shot at sunrise.
RUTH: [*Laughing happily.*] You said it, sister! [*Noticing how large* BENEATHA *is absentmindedly making the note.*] Honey, they ain't going to read that from no airplane.

BENEATHA: [*Laughing herself.*] I guess I always think things have more emphasis if they are big, somehow.

RUTH: [*Looking up at her and smiling.*] You and your brother seem to have that as a philosophy of life. Lord, that man—done changed so 'round here. You know—you know what we did last night? Me and Walter Lee?

BENEATHA: What?

RUTH: [*Smiling to herself.*] We went to the movies. [*Looking at* BENEATHA *to see if she understands.*] We went to the movies. You know the last time me and Walter went to the movies together?

BENEATHA: No.

RUTH: Me neither. That's how long it been. [*Smiling again.*] But we went last night. The picture wasn't much good, but that didn't seem to matter. We went—and we held hands.

BENEATHA: Oh, Lord!

RUTH: We held hands—and you know what?

BENEATHA: What?

RUTH: When we come out of the show it was late and dark and all the stores and things was closed up . . . and it was kind of chilly and there wasn't many people on the streets . . . and we was still holding hands, me and Walter.

BENEATHA: You're killing me.

> [WALTER *enters with a large package. His happiness is deep in him; he cannot keep still with his new-found exuberance. He is singing and wiggling and snapping his fingers. He puts his package in a corner and puts a phonograph record, which he has brought in with him, on the record player. As the music comes up he dances over to* RUTH *and tries to get her to dance with him. She gives in at last to his raunchiness and in a fit of giggling allows herself to be drawn into his mood and together they deliberately burlesque an old social dance of their youth.*]

BENEATHA: [*Regarding them a long time as they dance, then drawing in her breath for a deeply exaggerated comment which she does not particularly mean.*] Talk about—olddddddddddd-fashionedddddddd—Negroes!

WALTER: [*Stopping momentarily.*] What kind of Negroes?

> [*He says this in fun. He is not angry with her today, nor with anyone. He starts to dance with his wife again.*]

BENEATHA: Old-fashioned.

WALTER: [*As he dances with* RUTH.] You know, when these *New Negroes* have their convention— [*Pointing at his sister.*] —that is going to be the chairman of the Committee on Unending Agitation. [*He goes on dancing, then stops.*] Race, race, race! . . . Girl, I do believe you are the first person in the history of the entire human race to successfully brainwash yourself. [BENEATHA *breaks up and he goes on dancing. He stops again, enjoying his tease.*] Damn, even the N double A C P[1] takes a holiday sometimes! [BENEATHA *and* RUTH *laugh. He dances with* RUTH *some more and starts to laugh and stops and*

---

1. National Association for the Advancement of Colored People, civil rights organization founded in 1909.

pantomimes someone over an operating table.] I can just see that chick some-day looking down at some poor cat on an operating table before she starts to slice him, saying . . . [*Pulling his sleeves back maliciously.*] "By the way, what are your views on civil rights down there? . . ."

[*He laughs at her again and starts to dance happily. The bell sounds.*]

BENEATHA: Sticks and stones may break my bones but . . . words will never hurt me!

[BENEATHA *goes to the door and opens it as* WALTER *and* RUTH *go on with the clowning.* BENEATHA *is somewhat surprised to see a quiet-looking middle-aged white man in a business suit holding his hat and a briefcase in his hand and consulting a small piece of paper.*]

MAN: Uh—how do you do, miss. I am looking for a Mrs.— [*He looks at the slip of paper.*] Mrs. Lena Younger?

BENEATHA: [*Smoothing her hair with slight embarrassment.*] Oh—yes, that's my mother. Excuse me [*She closes the door and turns to quiet the other two.*] Ruth! Brother! Somebody's here. [*Then she opens the door. The* MAN *casts a curious quick glance at all of them.*] Uh—come in please.

MAN: [*Coming in.*] Thank you.

BENEATHA: My mother isn't here just now. Is it business?

MAN: Yes . . . well, of a sort.

WALTER: [*Freely, the Man of the House.*] Have a seat. I'm Mrs. Younger's son. I look after most of her business matters.

[RUTH *and* BENEATHA *exchange amused glances.*]

MAN: [*Regarding* WALTER, *and sitting.*] Well—My name is Karl Lindner . . .

WALTER: [*Stretching out his hand.*] Walter Younger. This is my wife— [RUTH *nods politely.*] —and my sister.

LINDNER: How do you do.

WALTER: [*Amiably, as he sits himself easily on a chair, leaning with interest forward on his knees and looking expectantly into the newcomer's face.*] What can we do for you, Mr. Lindner!

LINDNER: [*Some minor shuffling of the hat and briefcase on his knees.*] Well— I am a representative of the Clybourne Park Improvement Association—

WALTER: [*Pointing.*] Why don't you sit your things on the floor?

LINDNER: Oh—yes. Thank you. [*He slides the briefcase and hat under the chair.*] And as I was saying—I am from the Clybourne Park Improvement Association and we have had it brought to our attention at the last meeting that you people—or at least your mother—has bought a piece of residential property at— [*He digs for the slip of paper again.*] —four o six Clybourne Street . . .

WALTER: That's right. Care for something to drink? Ruth, get Mr. Lindner a beer.

LINDNER: [*Upset for some reason.*] Oh—no, really. I mean thank you very much, but no thank you.

RUTH: [*Innocently.*] Some coffee?

LINDNER: Thank you, nothing at all.

[BENEATHA *is watching the man carefully.*]

LINDNER: Well, I don't know how much you folks know about our organization. [*He is a gentle man; thoughtful and somewhat labored in his manner.*] It is one of these community organizations set up to look after—oh, you know, things like block upkeep and special projects and we also have what we call our New Neighbors Orientation Committee . . .

BENEATHA: [*Drily.*] Yes—and what do they do?

LINDNER: [*Turning a little to her and then returning the main force to* WALTER.] Well—it's what you might call a sort of welcoming committee, I guess. I mean they, we, I'm the chairman of the committee—go around and see the new people who move into the neighborhood and sort of give them the low-down on the way we do things out in Clybourne Park.

BENEATHA: [*With appreciation of the two meanings, which escape* RUTH *and* WALTER.] Un-huh.

LINDNER: And we also have the category of what the association calls— [*He looks elsewhere.*] —uh—special community problems . . .

BENEATHA: Yes—and what are some of those?

WALTER: Girl, let the man talk.

LINDNER: [*With understated relief.*] Thank you. I would sort of like to explain this thing in my own way. I mean I want to explain to you in a certain way.

WALTER: Go ahead.

LINDNER: Yes. Well. I'm going to try to get right to the point. I'm sure we'll all appreciate that in the long run.

BENEATHA: Yes.

WALTER: Be still now!

LINDNER: Well—

RUTH: [*Still innocently.*] Would you like another chair—you don't look comfortable.

LINDNER: [*More frustrated than annoyed.*] No, thank you very much. Please. Well—to get right to the point I— [*A great breath, and he is off at last.*] I am sure you people must be aware of some of the incidents which have happened in various parts of the city when colored people have moved into certain areas— [BENEATHA *exhales heavily and starts tossing a piece of fruit up and down in the air.*] Well—because we have what I think is going to be a unique type of organization in American community life—not only do we deplore that kind of thing—but we are trying to do something about it. [BENEATHA *stops tossing and turns with a new and quizzical interest to the man.*] We feel— [*Gaining confidence in his mission because of the interest in the faces of the people he is talking to.*] —we feel that most of the trouble in this world, when you come right down to it— [*He hits his knee for emphasis.*] —most of the trouble exists because people just don't sit down and talk to each other.

RUTH: [*Nodding as she might in church, pleased with the remark.*] You can say that again, mister.

LINDNER: [*More encouraged by such affirmation.*] That we don't try hard enough in this world to understand the other fellow's problem. The other guy's point of view.

RUTH: Now that's right.

[BENEATHA *and* WALTER *merely watch and listen with genuine interest.*]

LINDNER: Yes—that's the way we feel out in Clybourne Park. And that's why I was elected to come here this afternoon and talk to you people. Friendly like, you know, the way people should talk to each other and see if we couldn't find some way to work this thing out. As I say, the whole business is a matter of *caring* about the other fellow. Anybody can see that you are a nice family of folks, hard working and honest I'm sure. [BENEATHA *frowns slightly, quizzically, her head tilted regarding him.*] Today everybody knows what it means to be on the outside of something. And of course, there is always somebody who is out to take the advantage of people who don't always understand.

WALTER: What do you mean?

LINDNER: Well—you see our community is made up of people who've worked hard as the dickens for years to build up that little community. They're not rich and fancy people; just hard-working, honest people who don't really have much but those little homes and a dream of the kind of community they want to raise their children in. Now, I don't say we are perfect and there is a lot wrong in some of the things they want. But you've got to admit that a man, right or wrong, has the right to want to have the neighborhood he lives in a certain kind of way. And at the moment the overwhelming majority of our people out there feel that people get along better, take more of a common interest in the life of the community, when they share a common background. I want you to believe me when I tell you that race prejudice simply doesn't enter into it. It is a matter of the people of Clybourne Park believing, rightly or wrongly, as I say, that for the happiness of all concerned that our Negro families are happier when they live in their *own* communities.

BENEATHA: [*With a grand and bitter gesture.*] This, friends, is the Welcoming Committee!

WALTER: [*Dumfounded, looking at* LINDNER.] Is this what you came marching all the way over here to tell us?

LINDNER: Well, now we've been having a fine conversation. I hope you'll hear me all the way through.

WALTER: [*Tightly.*] Go ahead, man.

LINDNER: You see—in the face of all things I have said, we are prepared to make your family a very generous offer . . .

BENEATHA: Thirty pieces and not a coin less![2]

WALTER: Yeah?

LINDNER: [*Putting on his glasses and drawing a form out of the briefcase.*] Our association is prepared, through the collective effort of our people, to buy the house from you at a financial gain to your family.

RUTH: Lord have mercy, ain't this the living gall!

WALTER: All right, you through?

LINDNER: Well, I want to give you the exact terms of the financial arrangement—

2. See Matthew 26.15, in which Judas Iscariot is paid thirty pieces of silver to betray Jesus.

WALTER: We don't want to hear no exact terms of no arrangements. I want to know if you got any more to tell us 'bout getting together?

LINDNER: [*Taking off his glasses.*] Well—I don't suppose that you feel . . .

WALTER: Never mind how I feel—you got any more to say 'bout how people ought to sit down and talk to each other? . . . Get out of my house, man.

[*He turns his back and walks to the door.*]

LINDNER: [*Looking around at the hostile faces and reaching and assembling his hat and briefcase.*] Well—I don't understand why you people are reacting this way. What do you think you are going to gain by moving into a neighborhood where you just aren't wanted and where some elements—well—people can get awful worked up when they feel that their whole way of life and everything they've ever worked for is threatened.

WALTER: Get out.

LINDNER: [*At the door, holding a small card.*] Well—I'm sorry it went like this.

WALTER: Get out.

LINDNER: [*Almost sadly regarding* WALTER.] You just can't force people to change their hearts, son.

[*He turns and puts his card on a table and exits.* WALTER *pushes the door to with stinging hatred, and stands looking at it.* RUTH *just sits and* BENEATHA *just stands. They say nothing.* MAMA *and* TRAVIS *enter.*]

MAMA: Well—this all the packing got done since I left out of here this morning. I testify before God that my children got all the energy of the dead. What time the moving men due?

BENEATHA: Four o'clock. You had a caller, Mama.

[*She is smiling, teasingly.*]

MAMA: Sure enough—who?

BENEATHA: [*Her arms folded saucily.*] The Welcoming Committee.

[WALTER *and* RUTH *giggle.*]

MAMA: [*Innocently.*] Who?

BENEATHA: The Welcoming Committee. They said they're sure going to be glad to see you when you get there.

WALTER: [*Devilishly.*] Yeah, they said they can't hardly wait to see your face.

[*Laughter.*]

MAMA: [*Sensing their facetiousness.*] What's the matter with you all?

WALTER: Ain't nothing the matter with us. We just telling you 'bout the gentleman who came to see you this afternoon. From the Clybourne Park Improvement Association.

MAMA: What he want?

RUTH: [*In the same mood as* BENEATHA *and* WALTER.] To welcome you, honey.

WALTER: He said they can't hardly wait. He said the one thing they don't have, that they just *dying* to have out there is a fine family of colored people! [*To* RUTH *and* BENEATHA.] Ain't that right!

RUTH AND BENEATHA: [*Mockingly.*] Yeah! He left his card in case—

[*They indicate the card, and* MAMA *picks it up and throws it on the floor—understanding and looking off as she draws her chair up to the table on which she has put her plant and some sticks and some cord.*]

MAMA: Father, give us strength. [*Knowingly—and without fun.*] Did he threaten us?

BENEATHA: Oh—Mama—they don't do it like that anymore. He talked Brotherhood. He said everybody ought to learn how to sit down and hate each other with good Christian fellowship.

[*She and* WALTER *shake hands to ridicule the remark.*]

MAMA: [*Sadly.*] Lord, protect us . . .

RUTH: You should hear the money those folks raised to buy the house from us. All we paid and then some.

BENEATHA: What they think we going to do—eat 'em?

RUTH: No, honey, marry 'em.

MAMA: [*Shaking her head.*] Lord, Lord, Lord . . .

RUTH: Well—that's the way the crackers crumble. Joke.

BENEATHA: [*Laughingly noticing what her mother is doing.*] Mama, what are you doing?

MAMA: Fixing my plant so it won't get hurt none on the way . . .

BENEATHA: Mama, you going to take *that* to the new house?

MAMA: Un-huh—

BENEATHA: That raggedy-looking old thing?

MAMA: [*Stopping and looking at her.*] It expresses *me.*

RUTH: [*With delight, to* BENEATHA.] So there, Miss Thing!

[WALTER *comes to* MAMA *suddenly and bends down behind her and squeezes her in his arms with all his strength. She is overwhelmed by the suddenness of it and, though delighted, her manner is like that of* RUTH *with* TRAVIS.]

MAMA: Look out now, boy! You make me mess up my thing here!

WALTER: [*His face lit, he slips down on his knees beside her, his arms still about her.*] Mama . . . you know what it means to climb up in the chariot?

MAMA: [*Gruffly, very happy.*] Get on away from me now . . .

RUTH: [*Near the gift-wrapped package, trying to catch* WALTER's *eye.*] Psst—

WALTER: What the old song say, Mama . . .

RUTH: Walter—Now?

[*She is pointing at the package.*]

WALTER: [*Speaking the lines, sweetly, playfully, in his mother's face.*]

I got wings . . . you got wings . . .
All God's Children got wings[3] . . .

MAMA: Boy—get out of my face and do some work . . .

WALTER:

When I get to heaven gonna put on my wings,

---

3. Lines from an African American spiritual. Walter's and Beneatha's next lines are also from the song.

Gonna fly all over God's heaven . . .

BENEATHA: [*Teasingly, from across the room.*] Everybody talking 'bout heaven ain't going there!

WALTER: [*To* RUTH, *who is carrying the box across to them.*] I don't know, you think we ought to give her that . . . Seems to me she ain't been very appreciative around here.

MAMA: [*Eying the box, which is obviously a gift.*] What is that?

WALTER: [*Taking it from* RUTH *and putting it on the table in front of* MAMA.] Well—what you all think? Should we give it to her?

RUTH: Oh—she was pretty good today.

MAMA: I'll good you—

[*She turns her eyes to the box again.*]

BENEATHA: Open it, Mama.

[*She stands up, looks at it, turns and looks at all of them, and then presses her hands together and does not open the package.*]

WALTER: [*Sweetly.*] Open it, Mama. It's for you. [MAMA *looks in his eyes. It is the first present in her life without its being Christmas. Slowly she opens her package and lifts out, one by one, a brand-new sparkling set of gardening tools.* WALTER *continues, prodding.*] Ruth made up the note—read it . . .

MAMA: [*Picking up the card and adjusting her glasses.*] "To our own Mrs. Miniver[4]—Love from Brother, Ruth and Beneatha." Ain't that lovely . . .

TRAVIS: [*Tugging at his father's sleeve.*] Daddy, can I give her mine now?

WALTER: All right, son. [TRAVIS *flies to get his gift.*] Travis didn't want to go in with the rest of us, Mama. He got his own. [*Somewhat amused.*] We don't know what it is . . .

TRAVIS: [*Racing back in the room with a large hatbox and putting it in front of his grandmother.*] Here!

MAMA: Lord have mercy, baby. You done gone and bought your grandmother a hat?

TRAVIS: [*Very proud.*] Open it!

[*She does and lifts out an elaborate, but very elaborate, wide gardening hat, and all the adults break up at the sight of it.*]

RUTH: Travis, honey, what is that?

TRAVIS: [*Who thinks it is beautiful and appropriate.*] It's a gardening hat! Like the ladies always have on in the magazines when they work in their gardens.

BENEATHA: [*Giggling fiercely.*] Travis—we were trying to make Mama Mrs. Miniver—not Scarlett O'Hara![5]

MAMA: [*Indignantly.*] What's the matter with you all! This here is a beautiful hat! [*Absurdly.*] I always wanted me one just like it!

---

4. Courageous, charismatic title character of a 1942 film starring Greer Garson.
5. Glamorous, headstrong heroine of Margaret Mitchell's 1936 historical novel *Gone with the Wind*; Vivien Leigh played Scarlett in the 1939 film adaptation.

[*She pops it on her head to prove it to her grandson, and the hat is ludicrous and considerably oversized.*]

RUTH: Hot dog! Go, Mama!

WALTER: [*Doubled over with laughter.*] I'm sorry, Mama—but you look like you ready to go out and chop you some cotton sure enough!

[*They all laugh except* MAMA, *out of deference to* TRAVIS' *feelings.*]

MAMA: [*Gathering the boy up to her.*] Bless your heart—this is the prettiest hat I ever owned— [WALTER, RUTH *and* BENEATHA *chime in—noisily, festively and insincerely congratulating* TRAVIS *on his gift.*] What are we all standing around here for? We ain't finished packin' yet. Bennie, you ain't packed one book.

[*The bell rings.*]

BENEATHA: That couldn't be the movers . . . it's not hardly two good yet—

[BENEATHA *goes into her room.* MAMA *starts for door.*]

WALTER: [*Turning, stiffening.*] Wait—wait—I'll get it.

[*He stands and looks at the door.*]

MAMA: You expecting company, son?

WALTER: [*Just looking at the door.*] Yeah—yeah . . .

[MAMA *looks at* RUTH, *and they exchange innocent and unfrightened glances.*]

MAMA: [*Not understanding.*] Well, let them in, son.

BENEATHA: [*From her room.*] We need some more string.

MAMA: Travis—you run to the hardware and get me some string cord.

[MAMA *goes out and* WALTER *turns and looks at* RUTH. TRAVIS *goes to a dish for money.*]

RUTH: Why don't you answer the door, man?

WALTER: [*Suddenly bounding across the floor to her.*] 'Cause sometimes it hard to let the future begin! [*Stooping down in her face.*]

I got wings! You got wings!
All God's children got wings!

[*He crosses to the door and throws it open. Standing there is a very slight little man in a not too prosperous business suit and with haunted frightened eyes and a hat pulled down tightly, brim up, around his forehead.* TRAVIS *passes between the men and exits.* WALTER *leans deep in the man's face, still in his jubilance.*]

When I get to heaven gonna put on my wings,
Gonna fly all over God's heaven . . .

[*The little man just stares at him.*]

Heaven—

[*Suddenly he stops and looks past the little man into the empty hallway.*] Where's Willy, man?

BOBO: He ain't with me.

WALTER: [*Not disturbed.*] Oh—come on in. You know my wife.

BOBO: [*Dumbly, taking off his hat.*] Yes—h'you, Miss Ruth.

RUTH: [*Quietly, a mood apart from her husband already, seeing* BOBO.] Hello, Bobo.

WALTER: You right on time today . . . Right on time. That's the way! [*He slaps* BOBO *on his back.*] Sit down . . . lemme hear.

[RUTH *stands stiffly and quietly in back of them, as though somehow she senses death, her eyes fixed on her husband.*]

BOBO: [*His frightened eyes on the floor, his hat in his hands.*] Could I please get a drink of water, before I tell you about it, Walter Lee?

[WALTER *does not take his eyes off the man.* RUTH *goes blindly to the tap and gets a glass of water and brings it to* BOBO.]

WALTER: There ain't nothing wrong, is there?

BOBO: Lemme tell you—

WALTER: Man—didn't nothing go wrong?

BOBO: Lemme tell you—Walter Lee. [*Looking at* RUTH *and talking to her more than to* WALTER.] You know how it was. I got to tell you how it was. I mean first I got to tell you how it was all the way . . . I mean about the money I put in, Walter Lee . . .

WALTER: [*With taut agitation now.*] What about the money you put in?

BOBO: Well—it wasn't much as we told you—me and Willy— [*He stops.*] I'm sorry, Walter. I got a bad feeling about it. I got a real bad feeling about it . . .

WALTER: Man, what you telling me about all this for? . . . Tell me what happened in Springfield . . .

BOBO: Springfield.

RUTH: [*Like a dead woman.*] What was supposed to happen in Springfield?

BOBO: [*To her.*] This deal that me and Walter went into with Willy—Me and Willy was going to go down to Springfield and spread some money 'round so's we wouldn't have to wait so long for the liquor license . . . That's what we were going to do. Everybody said that was the way you had to do, you understand, Miss Ruth?

WALTER: Man—what happened down there?

BOBO: [*A pitiful man, near tears.*] I'm trying to tell you, Walter.

WALTER: [*Screaming at him suddenly.*] THEN TELL ME, GODDAMMIT . . . WHAT'S THE MATTER WITH YOU?

BOBO: Man . . . I didn't go to no Springfield, yesterday.

WALTER: [*Halted, life hanging in the moment.*] Why not?

BOBO: [*The long way, the hard way to tell.*] 'Cause I didn't have no reasons to . . .

WALTER: Man, what are you talking about!

BOBO: I'm talking about the fact that when I got to the train station yesterday morning—eight o'clock like we planned . . . Man—*Willy didn't never show up.*

WALTER: Why . . . where was he . . . where is he?

BOBO: That's what I'm trying to tell you . . . I don't know . . . I waited six hours . . . I called his house . . . and I waited . . . six hours . . . I waited in that train station six hours . . . [*Breaking into tears.*] That was all the extra money I had in the world . . . [*Looking up at* WALTER *with the tears running down his face.*] Man, *Willy is gone.*

WALTER: Gone, what you mean Willy is gone? Gone where? You mean he went by himself. You mean he went off to Springfield by himself—to take care of getting the license— [*Turns and looks anxiously at* RUTH.] You mean maybe he didn't want too many people in on the business down there? [*Looks to* RUTH *again, as before.*] You know Willy got his own ways. [*Looks back to* BOBO.] Maybe you was late yesterday and he just went on down there without you. Maybe—maybe—he's been callin' you at home tryin' to tell you what happened or something. Maybe—maybe—he just got sick. He's somewhere—he's got to be somewhere. We just got to find him—me and you got to find him. [*Grabs* BOBO *senselessly by the collar and starts to shake him.*] We got to!

BOBO: [*In sudden angry, frightened agony.*] What's the matter with you, Walter! *When a cat take off with your money he don't leave you no maps!*

WALTER: [*Turning madly, as though he is looking for* WILLY *in the very room.*] Willy! . . . Willy . . . don't do it . . . Please don't do it . . . Man, not with that money . . . Man, please, not with that money . . . Oh, God . . . Don't let it be true . . . [*He is wandering around, crying out for* WILLY *and looking for him or perhaps for help from God.*] Man . . . I trusted you . . . Man, I put my life in your hands . . . [*He starts to crumple down on the floor as* RUTH *just covers her face in horror.* MAMA *opens the door and comes into the room, with* BENEATHA *behind her.*] Man . . . [*He starts to pound the floor with his fists, sobbing wildly.*] *That money is made out of my father's flesh* . . .

BOBO: [*Standing over him helplessly.*] I'm sorry, Walter . . . [*Only* WALTER'S *sobs reply.* BOBO *puts on his hat.*] I had my life staked on this deal, too . . .

   [*He exits.*]

MAMA: [*To* WALTER.] Son— [*She goes to him, bends down to him, talks to his bent head.*] Son . . . Is it gone? Son, I gave you sixty-five hundred dollars. Is it gone? All of it? Beneatha's money too?

WALTER: [*Lifting his head slowly.*] Mama . . . I never . . . went to the bank at all . . .

MAMA: [*Not wanting to believe him.*] You mean . . . your sister's school money . . . you used that too . . . Walter? . . .

WALTER: Yessss! . . . All of it . . . It's all gone . . . [*There is total silence.* RUTH *stands with her face covered with her hands;* BENEATHA *leans forlornly against a wall, fingering a piece of red ribbon from the mother's gift.* MAMA *stops and looks at her son without recognition and then, quite without thinking about it, starts to beat him senselessly in the face.* BENEATHA *goes to them and stops it.*]

BENEATHA: Mama!

   [MAMA *stops and looks at both of her children and rises slowly and wanders vaguely, aimlessly away from them.*]

MAMA: I seen . . . him . . . night after night . . . come in . . . and look at that rug . . . and then look at me . . . the red showing in his eyes . . . the veins moving in his head . . . I seen him grow thin and old before he was forty . . . working and working and working like somebody's old horse . . . killing himself . . . and you—you give it all away in a day . . .

BENEATHA: Mama—

MAMA: Oh, God . . . [*She looks up to Him.*] Look down here—and show me the strength.

BENEATHA: Mama—

MAMA: [*Folding over.*] Strength . . .

BENEATHA: [*Plaintively.*] Mama . . .

MAMA: Strength!

[CURTAIN.]

ACT III

An hour later.

At curtain, there is a sullen light of gloom in the living room, gray light not unlike that which began the first scene of Act I. At left we can see WALTER *within his room, alone with himself. He is stretched out on the bed, his shirt out and open, his arms under his head. He does not smoke, he does not cry out, he merely lies there, looking up at the ceiling, much as if he were alone in the world.*

In the living room BENEATHA *sits at the table, still surrounded by the now almost ominous packing crates. She sits looking off. We feel that this is a mood struck perhaps an hour before, and it lingers now, full of the empty sound of profound disappointment. We see on a line from her brother's bedroom the sameness of their attitudes. Presently the bell rings and* BENEATHA *rises without ambition or interest in answering. It* IS ASAGAI, *smiling broadly, striding into the room with energy and happy expectation and conversation.*

ASAGAI: I came over . . . I had some free time. I thought I might help with the packing. Ah, I like the look of packing crates! A household in preparation for a journey! It depresses some people . . . but for me . . . it is another feeling. Something full of the flow of life, do you understand? Movement, progress . . . It makes me think of Africa.

BENEATHA: Africa!

ASAGAI: What kind of a mood is this? Have I told you how deeply you move me?

BENEATHA: He gave away the money, Asagai . . .

ASAGAI: Who gave away what money?

BENEATHA: The insurance money. My brother gave it away.

ASAGAI: Gave it away?

BENEATHA: He made an investment! With a man even Travis wouldn't have trusted.

ASAGAI: And it's gone?

BENEATHA: Gone!

ASAGAI: I'm very sorry . . . And you, now?

BENEATHA: Me? . . . Me? . . . Me, I'm nothing . . . Me. When I was very small . . . we used to take our sleds out in the wintertime and the only hills we had were the ice-covered stone steps of some houses down the street. And we used to fill them in with snow and make them smooth and slide down them all day . . . and it was very dangerous you know . . . far too steep . . . and sure enough one day a kid named Rufus came down too fast and hit the side-walk . . . and we saw his face just split open right there in front of us . . . And I remember standing there looking at his bloody open face thinking that was the end of Rufus. But the ambulance came and they took him to the hospital and they fixed the broken bones and they sewed it all up . . . and the next time I saw Rufus he just had a little line down the middle of his face . . . I never got over that . . .

> [WALTER sits up, listening on the bed. Throughout this scene it is important that we feel his reaction at all times, that he visibly respond to the words of his sister and ASAGAI.]

ASAGAI: What?

BENEATHA: That that was what one person could do for another, fix him up—sew up the problem, make him all right again. That was the most marvelous thing in the world . . . I wanted to do that. I always thought it was the one concrete thing in the world that a human being could do. Fix up the sick, you know—and make them whole again. This was truly being God . . .

ASAGAI: You wanted to be God?

BENEATHA: No—I wanted to cure. It used to be so important to me. I wanted to cure. It used to matter. I used to care. I mean about people and how their bodies hurt . . .

ASAGAI: And you've stopped caring?

BENEATHA: Yes—I think so.

ASAGAI: Why?

> [WALTER rises, goes to the door of his room and is about to open it, then stops and stands listening, leaning on the door jamb.]

BENEATHA: Because it doesn't seem deep enough, close enough to what ails man-kind—I mean this thing of sewing up bodies or administering drugs. Don't you understand? It was a child's reaction to the world. I thought that doctors had the secret to all the hurts . . . That's the way a child sees things—or an idealist.

ASAGAI: Children see things very well sometimes—and idealists even better.

BENEATHA: I know that's what you think. Because you are still where I left off—you still care. This is what you see for the world, for Africa. You with the dreams of the future will patch up all Africa—you are going to cure the Great Sore of colonialism with Independence—

ASAGAI: Yes!

BENEATHA: Yes—and you think that one word is the penicillin of the human spirit: "Independence!" But then what?

ASAGAI: That will be the problem for another time. First we must get there.

BENEATHA: And where does it end?

ASAGAI: End? Who even spoke of an end? To life? To living?

BENEATHA: An end to misery!

ASAGAI: [*Smiling.*] You sound like a French intellectual.

BENEATHA: No! I sound like a human being who just had her future taken right out of her hands! While I was sleeping in my bed in there, things were happening in this world that directly concerned me—and nobody asked me, consulted me—they just went out and did things—and changed my life. Don't you see there isn't any real progress, Asagai, there is only one large circle that we march in, around and around, each of us with our own little picture—in front of us—our own little mirage that we think is the future.

ASAGAI: That is the mistake.

BENEATHA: What?

ASAGAI: What you just said—about the circle. It isn't a circle—it is simply a long line—as in geometry, you know, one that reaches into infinity. And because we cannot see the end—we also cannot see how it changes. And it is very odd but those who see the changes are called "idealists"—and those who cannot, or refuse to think, they are the "realists." It is very strange, and amusing too, I think.

BENEATHA: You—you are almost religious.

ASAGAI: Yes . . . I think I have the religion of doing what is necessary in the world—and of worshipping man—because he is so marvelous, you see.

BENEATHA: Man is foul! And the human race deserves its misery!

ASAGAI: You see: *you* have become the religious one in the old sense. Already, and after such a small defeat, you are worshipping despair.

BENEATHA: From now on, I worship the truth—and the truth is that people are puny, small and selfish . . .

ASAGAI: Truth? Why is it that you despairing ones always think that only you have the truth? I never thought to see *you* like that. You! Your brother made a stupid, childish mistake—and you are grateful to him. So that now you can give up the ailing human race on account of it. You talk about what good is struggle; what good is anything? Where are we all going? And why are we bothering?

BENEATHA: *And you cannot answer it!* All your talk and dreams about Africa and Independence. Independence and then what? What about all the crooks and petty thieves and just plain idiots who will come into power to steal and plunder the same as before—only now they will be black and do it in the name of the new Independence—You cannot answer that.

ASAGAI: [*Shouting over her.*] *I live the answer!* [*Pause.*] In my village at home it is the exceptional man who can even read a newspaper . . . or who ever *sees* a book at all. I will go home and much of what I will have to say will seem strange to the people of my village . . . But I will teach and work and things will happen, slowly and swiftly. At times it will seem that nothing changes at all . . . and then again . . . the sudden dramatic events which make history leap into the future. And then quiet again. Retrogression even. Guns, murder, revolution. And I even will have moments when I wonder if the quiet was not better than all that death and hatred. But I will look about my village at the illiteracy and disease and ignorance and I will not wonder long. And

perhaps . . . perhaps I will be a great man . . . I mean perhaps I will hold on
to the substance of truth and find my way always with the right course . . .
and perhaps for it I will be butchered in my bed some night by the servants
of empire . . .

BENEATHA: *The martyr!*

ASAGAI: . . . or perhaps I shall live to be a very old man, respected and esteemed
in my new nation . . . And perhaps I shall hold office and this is what I'm trying to tell you, Alaiyo; perhaps the things I believe now for my country will
be wrong and outmoded, and I will not understand and do terrible things to
have things my way or merely to keep my power. Don't you see that there will
be young men and women, not British soldiers then, but my own black countrymen . . . to step out of the shadows some evening and slit my then useless
throat? Don't you see they have always been there . . . that they always will
be. And that such a thing as my own death will be an advance? They who
might kill me even . . . actually replenish me!

BENEATHA: Oh, Asagai, I know all that.

ASAGAI: Good! Then stop moaning and groaning and tell me what you plan to
do.

BENEATHA: Do?

ASAGAI: I have a bit of a suggestion.

BENEATHA: What?

ASAGAI: [*Rather quietly for him.*] That when it is all over—that you come home
with me—

BENEATHA: [*Slapping herself on the forehead with exasperation born of misunderstanding.*] Oh—Asagai—at this moment you decide to be romantic!

ASAGAI: [*Quickly understanding the misunderstanding.*] My dear, young creature
of the New World—I do not mean across the city—I mean across the ocean;
home—to Africa.

BENEATHA: [*Slowly understanding and turning to him with murmured amazement.*] To—to Nigeria?

ASAGAI: Yes! . . . [*Smiling and lifting his arms playfully.*] Three hundred years
later the African Prince rose up out of the seas and swept the maiden back
across the middle passage[6] over which her ancestors had come—

BENEATHA: [*Unable to play.*] Nigeria?

ASAGAI: Nigeria. Home. [*Coming to her with genuine romantic flippancy.*] I will
show you our mountains and our stars; and give you cool drinks from gourds
and teach you the old songs and the ways of our people—and, in time, we
will pretend that— [*Very softly.*] —you have only been away for a day—

[*She turns her back to him, thinking. He swings her around and takes her
full in his arms in a long embrace which proceeds to passion.*]

BENEATHA: [*Pulling away.*] You're getting me all mixed up—

ASAGAI: Why?

BENEATHA: Too many things—too many things have happened today. I must sit
down and think. I don't know what I feel about anything right this minute.

---

6. Term denoting the route traveled by slaves trafficked from Africa to the Americas.

[*She promptly sits down and props her chin on her fist.*]

ASAGAI: [*Charmed.*] All right, I shall leave you. No—don't get up. [*Touching her, gently, sweetly.*] Just sit awhile and think . . . Never be afraid to sit awhile and think. [*He goes to door and looks at her.*] How often I have looked at you and said, "Ah—so this is what the New World hath finally wrought . . ."[7]

[*He exits.* BENEATHA *sits on alone. Presently* WALTER *enters from his room and starts to rummage through things, feverishly looking for something. She looks up and turns in her seat.*]

BENEATHA: [*Hissingly.*] Yes—just look at what the New World hath wrought! . . . Just look! [*She gestures with bitter disgust.*] There he is! *Monsieur le petit bourgeois noir*[8]—himself! There he is—Symbol of a Rising Class! Entrepreneur! Titan of the system! [WALTER *ignores her completely and continues frantically and destructively looking for something and hurling things to the floor and tearing things out of their place in his search.* BENEATHA *ignores the eccentricity of his actions and goes on with the monologue of insult.*] Did you dream of yachts on Lake Michigan, Brother? Did you see yourself on that Great Day sitting down at the Conference Table, surrounded by all the mighty bald-headed men in America? All halted, waiting, breathless, waiting for your pronouncements on industry? Waiting for you—Chairman of the Board? [WALTER *finds what he is looking for—a small piece of white paper—and pushes it in his pocket and puts on his coat and rushes out without ever having looked at her. She shouts after him.*] I look at you and I see the final triumph of stupidity in the world!

[*The door slams and she returns to just sitting again.* RUTH *comes quickly out of* MAMA's *room.*]

RUTH: Who was that?
BENEATHA: Your husband.
RUTH: Where did he go?
BENEATHA: Who knows—maybe he has an appointment at U.S. Steel.
RUTH: [*Anxiously, with frightened eyes.*] You didn't say nothing bad to him, did you?
BENEATHA: Bad? Say anything bad to him? No—I told him he was a sweet boy and full of dreams and everything is strictly peachy keen, as the ofay[9] kids say!

[MAMA *enters from her bedroom. She is lost, vague, trying to catch hold, to make some sense of her former command of the world, but it still eludes her. A sense of waste overwhelms her gait; a measure of apology rides on her shoulders. She goes to her plant, which has remained on the table, looks at it, picks it up and takes it to the window sill and sits it outside, and she stands and looks at it a long moment. Then she closes the window, straightens her body with effort and turns around to her children.*]

MAMA: Well—ain't it a mess in here, though? [*A false cheerfulness, a beginning of something.*] I guess we all better stop moping around and get some work

7. Allusion to the biblical exclamation "What hath God wrought!" (Num. 23.23).
8. Mister Black Middle Class (French).   9. White.

done. All this unpacking and everything we got to do. [RUTH *raises her head slowly in response to the sense of the line; and* BENEATHA *in similar manner turns very slowly to look at her mother.*] One of you all better call the moving people and tell 'em not to come.

RUTH: Tell 'em not to come?

MAMA: Of course, baby. Ain't no need in 'em coming all the way here and having to go back. They charges for that too. [*She sits down, fingers to her brow, thinking.*] Lord, ever since I was a little girl, I always remembers people saying, "Lena—Lena Eggleston, you aims too high all the time. You needs to slow down and see life a little more like it is. Just slow down some." That's what they always used to say down home—"Lord, that Lena Eggleston is a high-minded thing. She'll get her due one day!"

RUTH: No, Lena . . .

MAMA: Me and Big Walter just didn't never learn right.

RUTH: Lena, no! We gotta go. Bennie—tell her . . . [*She rises and crosses to* BENEATHA *with her arms outstretched.* BENEATHA *doesn't respond.*] Tell her we can still move . . . the notes ain't but a hundred and twenty-five a month. We got four grown people in this house—we can work . . .

MAMA: [*To herself.*] Just aimed too high all the time—

RUTH: [*Turning and going to* MAMA *fast—the words pouring out with urgency and desperation.*] Lena—I'll work . . . I'll work twenty hours a day in all the kitchens in Chicago . . . I'll strap my baby on my back if I have to and scrub all the floors in America and wash all the sheets in America if I have to—but we got to move . . . We got to get out of here . . .

[MAMA *reaches out absently and pats* RUTH's *hand.*]

MAMA: No—I sees things differently now. Been thinking 'bout some of the things we could do to fix this place up some. I seen a second-hand bureau over on Maxwell Street[1] just the other day that could fit right there. [*She points to where the new furniture might go.* RUTH *wanders away from her.*] Would need some new handles on it and then a little varnish and then it look like something brand-new. And—we can put up them new curtains in the kitchen . . . Why this place be looking fine. Cheer us all up so that we forget trouble ever came . . . [*To* RUTH.] And you could get some nice screens to put up in your room round the baby's bassinet . . . [*She looks at both of them, pleadingly.*] Sometimes you just got to know when to give up some things . . . and hold on to what you got.

[WALTER *enters from the outside, looking spent and leaning against the door, his coat hanging from him.*]

MAMA: Where you been, son?

WALTER: [*Breathing hard.*] Made a call.

MAMA: To who, son?

WALTER: To The Man.

MAMA: What man, baby?

WALTER: The Man, Mama. Don't you know who The Man is?

1. Street market southwest of the Loop.

RUTH: Walter Lee?

WALTER: *The Man.* Like the guys in the streets say—The Man. Captain Boss—Mistuh Charley . . . Old Captain Please Mr. Bossman . . .

BENEATHA: [*Suddenly.*] Lindner!

WALTER: That's right! That's good. I told him to come right over.

BENEATHA: [*Fiercely, understanding.*] For what? What do you want to see him for!

WALTER: [*Looking at his sister.*] We going to do business with him.

MAMA: What you talking 'bout, son?

WALTER: Talking 'bout life, Mama. You all always telling me to see life like it is. Well—I laid in there on my back today . . . and I figured it out. Life just like it is. Who gets and who don't get. [*He sits down with his coat on and laughs.*] Mama, you know it's all divided up. Life is. Sure enough. Between the takers and the "tooken." [*He laughs.*] I've figured it out finally. [*He looks around at them.*] Yeah. Some of us always getting "tooken." [*He laughs.*] People like Willy Harris, they don't never get "tooken." And you know why the rest of us do? 'Cause we all mixed up. Mixed up bad. We get to looking 'round for the right and the wrong, and we worry about it and cry about it and stay up nights trying to figure out 'bout the wrong and the right of things all the time . . . And all the time, man, them takers is out there operating, just taking and taking. Willy Harris? Shoot—Willy Harris don't even count. He don't even count in the big scheme of things. But I'll say one thing for old Willy Harris . . . he's taught me something. He's taught me to keep my eye on what counts in this world. Yeah— [*Shouting out a little.*] Thanks, Willy!

RUTH: What did you call that man for, Walter Lee?

WALTER: Called him to tell him to come on over to the show. Gonna put on a show for the man. Just what he wants to see. You see, Mama, the man came here today and he told us that them people out there where you want us to move—well they so upset they willing to pay us not to move out there. [*He laughs again.*] And—and oh, Mama—you would of been proud of the way me and Ruth and Bennie acted. We told him to get out . . . Lord have mercy! We told the man to get out. Oh, we was some proud folks this afternoon, yeah. [*He lights a cigarette.*] We were still full of that old-time stuff . . .

RUTH: [*Coming toward him slowly.*] You talking 'bout taking them people's money to keep us from moving in that house?

WALTER: I ain't just talking 'bout it, baby—I'm telling you that's what's going to happen.

BENEATHA: Oh, God! Where is the bottom! Where is the real honest-to-God bottom so he can't go any farther!

WALTER: See—that's the old stuff. You and that boy that was here today. You all want everybody to carry a flag and a spear and sing some marching songs, huh? You wanna spend your life looking into things and trying to find the right and the wrong part, huh? Yeah. You know what's going to happen to that boy someday—he'll find himself sitting in a dungeon, locked in forever—and the takers will have the key! Forget it, baby! There ain't no causes—there ain't nothing but taking in this world, and he who takes most is smartest—and it don't make a damn bit of difference *how*.

MAMA: You making something inside me cry, son. Some awful pain inside me.

WALTER: Don't cry, Mama. Understand. That white man is going to walk in that door able to write checks for more money than we ever had. It's important to him and I'm going to help him . . . I'm going to put on the show, Mama.

MAMA: Son—I come from five generations of people who was slaves and sharecroppers—but ain't nobody in my family never let nobody pay 'em no money that was a way of telling us we wasn't fit to walk the earth. We ain't never been that poor. [*Raising her eyes and looking at him.*] We ain't never been that dead inside.

BENEATHA: Well—we are dead now. All the talk about dreams and sunlight that goes on in this house. All dead.

WALTER: What's the matter with you all! I didn't make this world! It was give to me this way! Hell, yes, I want me some yachts someday! Yes, I want to hang some real pearls 'round my wife's neck. Ain't she supposed to wear no pearls? Somebody tell me—tell me, who decides which women is suppose to wear pearls in this world. I tell you I am a *man*—and I think my wife should wear some pearls in this world!

[*This last line hangs a good while and* WALTER *begins to move about the room. The word "Man" has penetrated his consciousness; he mumbles it to himself repeatedly between strange agitated pauses as he moves about.*]

MAMA: Baby, how you going to feel on the inside?

WALTER: Fine! . . . Going to feel fine . . . a man . . .

MAMA: You won't have nothing left then, Walter Lee.

WALTER: [*Coming to her.*] I'm going to feel fine, Mama. I'm going to look that son-of-a-bitch in the eyes and say— [*He falters.*] —and say, "All right, Mr. Lindner— [*He falters even more.*] —that's your neighborhood out there. You got the right to keep it like you want. You got the right to have it like you want. Just write the check and—the house is yours." And, and I am going to say— [*His voice almost breaks.*] And you—you people just put the money in my hand and you won't have to live next to this bunch of stinking niggers! . . . [*He straightens up and moves away from his mother, walking around the room.*] Maybe—maybe I'll just get down on my black knees . . . [*He does so;* RUTH *and* BENNIE *and* MAMA *watch him in frozen horror.*] Captain, Mistuh, Bossman. [*He starts crying.*] A-hee-hee-hee! [*Wringing his hands in profoundly anguished imitation.*] Yassss-suh! Great White Father, just gi' ussen de money, fo' God's sake, and we's ain't gwine come out deh and dirty up yo' white folks neighborhood . . .

[*He breaks down completely, then gets up and goes into the bedroom.*]

BENEATHA: That is not a man. That is nothing but a toothless rat.

MAMA: Yes—death done come in this here house. [*She is nodding, slowly, reflectively.*] Done come walking in my house. On the lips of my children. You what supposed to be my beginning again. You—what supposed to be my harvest. [*To* BENEATHA.] You—you mourning your brother?

BENEATHA: He's no brother of mine.

MAMA: What you say?

BENEATHA: I said that that individual in that room is no brother of mine.

MAMA: That's what I thought you said. You feeling like you better than he is today? [BENEATHA *does not answer.*] Yes? What you tell him a minute ago?

That he wasn't a man? Yes? You give him up for me? You done wrote his epitaph too—like the rest of the world? Well, who give you the privilege?

BENEATHA: Be on my side for once! You saw what he just did, Mama! You saw him—down on his knees. Wasn't it you who taught me—to despise any man who would do that. Do what he's going to do.

MAMA: Yes—I taught you that. Me and your daddy. But I thought I taught you something else too . . . I thought I taught you to love him.

BENEATHA: Love him? There is nothing left to love.

MAMA: There is always something left to love. And if you ain't learned that, you ain't learned nothing. [*Looking at her.*] Have you cried for that boy today? I don't mean for yourself and for the family 'cause we lost the money. I mean for him; what he been through and what it done to him. Child, when do you think is the time to love somebody the most; when they done good and made things easy for everybody? Well then, you ain't through learning—because that ain't the time at all. It's when he's at his lowest and can't believe in hisself 'cause the world done whipped him so. When you starts measuring somebody, measure him right, child, measure him right. Make sure you done taken into account what hills and valleys he come through before he got to wherever he is.

[TRAVIS *bursts into the room at the end of the speech, leaving the door open.*]

TRAVIS: Grandmama—the moving men are downstairs! The truck just pulled up.

MAMA: [*Turning and looking at him.*] Are they, baby? They downstairs?

[*She sighs and sits.* LINDNER *appears in the doorway. He peers in and knocks lightly, to gain attention, and comes in. All turn to look at him.*]

LINDNER: [*Hat and briefcase in hand.*] Uh—hello . . . [RUTH *crosses mechanically to the bedroom door and opens it and lets it swing open freely and slowly as the lights come up on* WALTER *within, still in his coat, sitting at the far corner of the room. He looks up and out through the room to* LINDNER.]

RUTH: He's here.

[*A long minute passes and* WALTER *slowly gets up.*]

LINDNER: [*Coming to the table with efficiency, putting his briefcase on the table and starting to unfold papers and unscrew fountain pens.*] Well, I certainly was glad to hear from you people. [WALTER *has begun the trek out of the room, slowly and awkwardly, rather like a small boy, passing the back of his sleeve across his mouth from time to time.*] Life can really be so much simpler than people let it be most of the time. Well—with whom do I negotiate? You, Mrs. Younger, or your son here? [MAMA *sits with her hands folded on her lap and her eyes closed as* WALTER *advances.* TRAVIS *goes close to* LINDNER *and looks at the papers curiously.*] Just some official papers, sonny.

RUTH: Travis, you go downstairs.

MAMA: [*Opening her eyes and looking into* WALTER'S.] No. Travis, you stay right here. And you make him understand what you doing, Walter Lee. You teach him good. Like Willy Harris taught you. You show where our five generations done come to. Go ahead, son—

WALTER: [*Looks down into his boy's eyes.* TRAVIS *grins at him merrily and* WALTER *draws him beside him with his arm lightly around his shoulders.*] Well, Mr. Lindner. [BENEATHA *turns away.*] We called you— [*There is a profound, simple groping quality in his speech.*] —because, well, me and my family [*He looks around and shifts from one foot to the other.*] Well—we are very plain people . . .

LINDNER: Yes—

WALTER: I mean—I have worked as a chauffeur most of my life—and my wife here, she does domestic work in people's kitchens. So does my mother. I mean—we are plain people . . .

LINDNER: Yes, Mr. Younger—

WALTER: [*Really like a small boy, looking down at his shoes and then up at the man.*] And—uh—well, my father, well, he was a laborer most of his life.

LINDNER: [*Absolutely confused.*] Uh, yes—

WALTER: [*Looking down at his toes once again.*] My father almost beat a man to death once because this man called him a bad name or something, you know what I mean?

LINDNER: No, I'm afraid I don't.

WALTER: [*Finally straightening up.*] Well, what I mean is that we come from people who had a lot of pride. I mean—we are very proud people. And that's my sister over there and she's going to be a doctor—and we are very proud—

LINDNER: Well—I am sure that is very nice, but—

WALTER: [*Starting to cry and facing the man eye to eye.*] What I am telling you is that we called you over here to tell you that we are very proud and that this is—this is my son, who makes the sixth generation of our family in this country, and that we have all thought about your offer and we have decided to move into our house because my father—my father—he earned it. [MAMA *has her eyes closed and is rocking back and forth as though she were in church, with her head nodding the amen yes.*] We don't want to make no trouble for nobody or fight no causes—but we will try to be good neighbors. That's all we got to say. [*He looks the man absolutely in the eyes.*] We don't want your money.

[*He turns and walks away from the man.*]

LINDNER: [*Looking around at all of them.*] I take it then that you have decided to occupy.

BENEATHA: That's what the man said.

LINDNER: [*To* MAMA *in her reverie.*] Then I would like to appeal to you, Mrs. Younger. You are older and wiser and understand things better I am sure . . .

MAMA: [*Rising.*] I am afraid you don't understand. My son said we was going to move and there ain't nothing left for me to say. [*Shaking her head with double meaning.*] You know how these young folks is nowadays, mister. Can't do a thing with 'em. Good-bye.

LINDNER: [*Folding up his materials.*] Well—if you are that final about it . . . There is nothing left for me to say. [*He finishes. He is almost ignored by the family, who are concentrating on* WALTER LEE. *At the door* LINDNER *halts and looks around.*] I sure hope you people know what you're doing.

[*He shakes his head and exits.*]

RUTH: [*Looking around and coming to life.*] Well, for God's sake—if the moving men are here—LET'S GET THE HELL OUT OF HERE!

MAMA: [*Into action.*] Ain't it the truth! Look at all this here mess. Ruth, put Travis' good jacket on him . . . Walter Lee, fix your tie and tuck your shirt in, you look just like somebody's hoodlum. Lord have mercy, where is my plant? [*She flies to get it amid the general bustling of the family, who are deliberately trying to ignore the nobility of the past moment.*] You all start on down . . . Travis child, don't go empty-handed . . . Ruth, where did I put that box with my skillets in it? I want to be in charge of it myself . . . I'm going to make us the biggest dinner we ever ate tonight . . . Beneatha, what's the matter with them stockings? Pull them things up, girl . . .

[*The family starts to file out as two moving men appear and begin to carry out the heavier pieces of furniture, bumping into the family as they move about.*]

BENEATHA: Mama, Asagai—asked me to marry him today and go to Africa—

MAMA: [*In the middle of her getting-ready activity.*] He did? You ain't old enough to marry nobody— [*Seeing the moving men lifting one of her chairs precariously.*] Darling, that ain't no bale of cotton, please handle it so we can sit in it again. I had that chair twenty-five years . . .

[*The movers sigh with exasperation and go on with their work.*]

BENEATHA: [*Girlishly and unreasonably trying to pursue the conversation.*] To go to Africa, Mama—be a doctor in Africa . . .

MAMA: [*Distracted.*] Yes, baby—

WALTER: Africa! What he want you to go to Africa for?

BENEATHA: To practice there . . .

WALTER: Girl, if you don't get all them silly ideas out your head! You better marry yourself a man with some loot . . .

BENEATHA: [*Angrily, precisely as in the first scene of the play.*] What have you got to do with who I marry!

WALTER: Plenty. Now I think George Murchison—

[*He and* BENEATHA *go out yelling at each other vigorously;* BENEATHA *is heard saying that she would not marry* GEORGE MURCHISON *if he were Adam and she were Eve, etc. The anger is loud and real till their voices diminish.* RUTH *stands at the door and turns to* MAMA *and smiles knowingly.*]

MAMA: [*Fixing her hat at last.*] Yeah—they something all right, my children . . .

RUTH: Yeah—they're something. Let's go, Lena.

MAMA: [*Stalling, starting to look around at the house.*] Yes—I'm coming. Ruth—

RUTH: Yes?

MAMA: [*Quietly, woman to woman.*] He finally come into his manhood today, didn't he? Kind of like a rainbow after the rain . . .

RUTH: [*Biting her lip lest her own pride explode in front of* MAMA.] Yes, Lena.

[WALTER'S *voice calls for them raucously.*]

MAMA: [*Waving* RUTH *out vaguely.*] All right, honey—go on down. I be down directly.

[RUTH *hesitates, then exits.* MAMA *stands, at last alone in the living room, her plant on the table before her as the lights start to come down. She looks around at all the walls and ceilings and suddenly, despite herself, while the children call below, a great heaving thing rises in her and she puts her fist to her mouth, takes a final desperate look, pulls her coat about her, pats her hat and goes out. The lights dim down. The door opens and she comes back in, grabs her plant, and goes out for the last time.*]

[CURTAIN.]

1959

JANE MARTIN
Two Monologues from *Talking With . . .*

The true identity of the award-winning playwright known as "Jane Martin" has been the subject of widespread speculation and debate since 1982, when her *Talking With . . .* debuted to great acclaim at the sixth annual Humana Festival in Louisville, Kentucky, and then went on to win the 1982 American Theatre Critics Association (ATCA) principal citation for most outstanding script of the season. Composed of eleven monologues by a diverse array of female characters, the play established Martin as a master of the monologue form and earned her comparisons to Flannery O'Connor, thanks not least to its bizarre, even grotesque, and obsessive characters, its deft rendering of their distinctive speech patterns, its often darkly religious undertones, and its fascination with physical and psychological violence. In the years since, Martin's work has included two other monologue-based plays, *Vital Signs* (1990) and *Sez She* (2006); comedies such as *Cementville* (1991) and *Criminal Hearts* (1992); the theater satire *Anton in Show Business* (2000), about three Texas actresses who mount a disastrous production of Anton Chekhov's *The Three Sisters*; the parody *Flaming Guns of the Purple Sage* (2001); and three highly topical plays: *Keely and Du* (1993), about a working-class rape victim held captive by pro-life terrorists bent on preventing her from having an abortion; *Mr. Bundy* (1998), in which the parents of an eleven-year-old discover that a convicted child molester lives next door; and *Flags* (2005), which focuses on a father's extreme reaction to the death of his soldier-son in Iraq. Prior to 2001, almost all of Martin's plays debuted at the Humana Festival under the direction of its founder, Jon Jory (b. 1938). As a result, and despite the director's demurrals, many believe Jane Martin is in fact either Jory himself or a team of writers that includes him.

The play Talking With . . . *consists of eleven monologues delivered by a diverse array of female characters. We here include two, "Handler" and "French Fries."*

Handler

A young woman in a simple, country-print dress. On the floor before her is a handmade wooden box about two feet long and eighteen inches high with a sliding wire screen top.

CARO: My Dada [Pronounced *"Dád-aw."*] was gonna do this tonight but the Lord froze his face so he sent me. I learned this from my Dada and he learned it up from great Gran, who took it on from the Reverend Soloman Bracewood, who had him a mule ministry[1] 'round these parts way back when. Dada taught Miss Ellie, my ma, and my brother Jamie . . . he was in it too, 'fore he went for Detroit.

See, what I got in here is snakes. Lotta people don't like snakes. Gives it its nature, I guess. This here is water mocs. Jamie, he said they got the dirtiest, nastiest bite of all . . . well, rattlers is yer biggest. Lotta venom. You milk you a rattler, you can half fill up a juice glass. Dada said Jamie should do rattlers, but he never. Did 'heads, copperheads. Now they're slower and safer but it ain't such a good show. You know those dang snakes smell like cucumbers? Well, they do. Miss Ellie, she favored moccasins. Dada too . . . well, Dada he did all kinds, all ways. Your moccasin now, he's your good ol' boy snake. Flat out mean an' lots of get up n' go. Heck, they'll chase ya. They will. Ol' Dada he didn't like Miss Ellie doin' 'em. "You lay off them mocs 'fore they lay you down." Made Miss Ellie laugh. Lotta handlers think moccasins are slimy. Couldn't get me to touch one. They'll do rattlers . . . got him a nice dry feel. Little bit sandpapery. Rattler can find ya in the pitch dark though. They git on to yer body heat. Snake handlin'. *All* my blood does it. Only Dada an' me now though. Snake handlin', with the Holiness Church. Down where I come from we take God pretty serious. If you got the spirit, snake don't bite. If he bites you, you know you ain't got the spirit. Makes the difference real clear, don't it?

It's right there in the scripture . . . Mark, Chapter 16, verses 17 and 18, "And these signs shall follow them that believe. In my name they shall cast out devils; they shall speak in new tongues; they shall take up serpents; and if they shall drink any deadly thing, it shall not hurt them; they shall lay hands on the sick and they shall recover." Don't figure it could be much clearer than that. There's some churches don't use snakes, use strychnine, powdered poison, same idea though. They mix it with Cherry kool-ade, sing 'em a hymn, drink it off, and then just stand around waitin' to see if they fall over. Ain't much of a show. Not like snakes. Dada does fire but I can't do it. Pours some kerosene in a coke bottle, sticks a rag in the top and lights it up. Holds that fire under his chin, passes it down the arm, puts his hand in it, you know, that kind of stuff. He says there's people do blow torches down to Tennessee. I don't know. Jamie give it a try 'fore he went to Detroit. Just about burned his ass off. Sorry.

When I handle, I keep 'em in this box. Dada gimme this and some Heidi[2] doll on my ninth birthday. Sometimes I'll just open up the lid and put my foot in or, uh, maybe stick it open side to my chest. There's some lay it to their face. I don't. Scares my eyes. Durin' service we take 'em right out, pass 'em around. It's more dangerous than a single handler. Snake gets to comparin' who got the spirit a whole lot an' who jes got it some. Somebody's jes about bound to come in second. Don't get me wrong now. Y' don't die everytime yer

---

1. That is, he was a traveling preacher who traveled by mule.
2. Protagonist of two Swiss children's books published in 1880 by Johanna Spyri and of many subsequent films.

bit. I been bit seven times. Four times by the same serpent. Dada says he got the sweet tooth for me. Dada been bit thirty-two times an' never saw him a doctor. Used to let me kiss him on the marks. Last one got him here.

(*Points to eye.*) Froze him right up. Dada says he'll thaw but I don't know.

Day after Jamie took off Miss Ellie did moccasins standin' in the back of the pickup over to Hard Burley. Shouldn't ought to 'cause her mind weren't there. Coal truck backfired and she got bit. Snake bit her three more times 'fore she hit the ground. Dada layed hands on her but she died anyway. There was ten of us handled right there at the funeral. Snake handlin'.

Snake knows what you feel. You can fool a person but you can't fool a snake. You got the spirit, God locks their jaws. Keeps you safe. Tell you what though . . . I don't believe in a God. Left me. Gone with Miss Ellie. I was handlin' when I knew it sure. Snake was jes comin' on down the line. Marita she yells out, "The Lord. Lord's in me and with me. In me and with me." Noah he was ululatin', talkin' in tongues. Couple of folks was rollin' and singing. Dada was doin' switch grips. Had Miss Ellie's weddin' ring on his little finger. And it came on me, heck, there ain't no God in here. There's just a bunch of shouters gettin' tranced. There ain't no God in here at all. 'Bout that time they layed that serpent to me. Felt fussy. Nasty. Just lookin' for an excuse y'know? An' I was an empty vessel, worse nor a pharasee,[3] grist for the mill. My blood went so cold I coulda crapped ice-cubes. Snake knew. Started to get leverage. So I said, "Snake. You Satan's hand-maiden. You're right, there ain't no God in me. I'm just a woman, but I'm the only woman in my Dada's house and he needs me home. Outta his faith and his need, you lock yer jaws." I let that snake feel a child's pure love and it sponged it up offa my hands and then ol'wiggley went limp. I tranced it. It was a real good service. Didn't nobody handlin' get bit.

(*Takes snake out of the box.*) Yes, you got to believe. Holiness Church is dead right about that. Make me wonder, you know? I git to lookin' at people and wonderin' if they got anything in 'em could lock a serpent's jaws. Any power or spirit or love or whatever. I look at 'em and I wonder, could they handle? Tell you what though, you can see it in a face. You can read it. You look me full in the face it don't take me 30 seconds. It's like I was the snake, some ol' pit viper, an' I can read yer heart. Maybe you could handle and maybe you can't, but there's but one sure thing in this world . . . yer empty, yer gonna get bit.

[*Fade out.*]

French Fries

An old woman in a straight-back chair holding a McDonald's cup. She is surrounded by several bundles of newspapers. She wears thick glasses that distort her eyes to the viewer.

ANNA MAE: If I had one wish in my life, why I'd like to live in McDonald's. Right there in the restaurant. 'Stead of in this old place. I'll come up to the brow of the hill, bowed down with my troubles, hurtin' under my load and I'll see

3. In Matthew 23, Jesus represents the Pharisees, a Jewish sect, as "hypocrites" who do not practice as they preach.

that yellow horseshoe, sort of like part of a rainbow, and it gives my old spirit a lift. Lord, I can sit in a McDonald's all day. I've done it too. Walked the seven miles with the sun just on its way, and then sat on the curb till five minutes of seven. First one there and the last to leave. Just like some ol' french fry they forgot.

I like the young people workin' there. Like a team of fine young horses when I was growin' up. All smilin'. Tell you what I really like though is the plastic. God gave us plastic so there wouldn't be no stains on his world. See, in the human world of the earth it all gets scratched, stained, tore up, faded down. Loses its shine. All of it does. In time. Well, God he gave us the idea of plastic so we'd know what the everlasting really was. See if there's plastic then there's surely eternity. It's God's hint.

You ever watch folks when they come on in the McDonald's? They always speed up, almost run the last few steps. You see if they don't. Old Dobbin[1] with the barn in sight. They know it's safe in there and it ain't safe outside. Now it ain't safe outside and you know it.

I've seen a man healed by a Big Mac. I have. I was just sittin' there. Last summer it was. Oh, they don't never move you on. It's a sacred law in McDonald's, you can sit for a hundred years. Only place in the world. Anyway, a fella, maybe thirty-five, maybe forty, come on in there dressed real nice, real bright tie, bran' new baseball cap, nice white socks and he had him that disease. You know the one I mean, Cerebral Walrus[2] they call it. Anyway, he had him a cock leg. His poor old body had it two speeds at the same time. Now he got him some coffee, with a lid on, and sat him down and Jimmy the tow-head[3] cook knew him, see, and he brought over a Big Mac. Well, the sick fella ate maybe half of it and then he was just sittin', you know, suffering those tremors, when a couple of *ants* come right out of the burger. Now there ain't no ants in McDonald's no way. Lord sent those ants, and the sick fella he looked real sharp at the burger and a bunch *more* ants marched on out nice as you please and his head lolled right over and he pitched himself out of that chair and banged his head on the floor, loud. Thwack! Like a bowling ball dropping. Made you half sick to hear it. We jump up and run over but he was cold out. Well those servin' kids, so cute, they watered him, stuck a touch pepper up his nostril, slapped him right smart, and bang, up he got. Standin' an' blinkin'. "Well, how are you?," we say. An he looks us over, looks right in our eyes, and he say, "I'm fine." And he was. He was fine! Tipped his Cincinnati Reds baseball cap, big "us'-swallowed-the-canary" grin, paraded out of there clean, straight like a pole-bean poplar, walked him a plumb line without no trace of the "walrus." Got outside, jumped up, whooped, hollered, sang him the National Anthem, flagged down a Circle Line bus, an' rode off up Muhammad Ali Boulevard wavin' an' smilin' like the King of the Pharoahs. Healed by a Big Mac. I saw it.

McDonald's. You ever see anybody die in a McDonald's? No sir. No way. Nobody ever has died in one. Shoot, they die in Burger Kings all the time. Kentucky Fried Chicken's got their own damn ambulances. Noooooooooooo, you

---

1. Traditional name for a horse, especially a working farm horse.
2. Cerebral palsy.   3. Someone with extremely blond, even white, hair.

Laura Saladino in a scene from *Talking with . . .* at Theatre TCU, directed by Blake Robertson

can't die in a McDonald's no matter how hard you try. It's the spices. Seals you safe in this life like it seals in the flavor. Yesssssss, yes!

I asked Jarrell could I live there. See they close up around ten, and there ain't a thing goin' on in 'em till seven a.m. I'd just sit in those nice swingy chairs and lean forward. Rest my head on those cool, cool, smooth tables, sing me a hymn and sleep like a baby. Jarrell, he said he'd write him a letter up the chain of command and see would they let me. Oh, I got my bid in. Peaceful and clean.

Sometimes I see it like the last of a movie. You know how they start the picture up real close and then back it off steady and far? Well, that's how I dream it. I'm living in McDonald's and it's real late at night and you see me up close, smiling, and then you see the whole McDonald's from the outside, lit up and friendly. And I get smaller and smaller, like they do, and then it's just a light in the darkness, like a star, and I'm in it. I'm part of that light, part of the whole sky, and it's all McDonald's, but part of something even bigger, something fixed and shiny . . . like plastic.

I know. I know. It's just a dream. Just a beacon in the storm. But you got to have a dream. It's our dreams make us what we are.

[*Blackout.*]

1980

HENRIK IBSEN
(1828–1906)

A Doll House[1]

Born in Skien, Norway, Henrik Ibsen was apprenticed to an apothecary until 1850, when he left for Oslo and published his first play, *Catilina*, a verse tragedy. By 1857 Ibsen was director of Oslo's Norwegian Theater, but his early plays, such as *Love's Comedy* (1862), were poorly received. Disgusted with what he saw as Norway's backwardness, Ibsen left in 1864 for Rome, where he wrote two more verse plays, *Brand* (1866) and *Peer Gynt* (1867), before turning to the realistic style and harsh criticism of traditional social mores for which he is best known. *The League of Youth* (1869), *Pillars of Society* (1877), *A Doll House* (1879), *Ghosts* (1881), *An Enemy of the People* (1882), *The Wild Duck* (1884), and *Hedda Gabler* (1890) won him a reputation throughout Europe as a controversial and outspoken advocate of moral and social reform. Near the end of his life, Ibsen explored the human condition in the explicitly symbolic terms of *The Master Builder* (1892) and *When We Dead Awaken* (1899). Ibsen's works had enormous influence on twentieth-century drama.

CHARACTERS

TORVALD HELMER, *a lawyer*
NORA, *his wife*
DR. RANK
MRS. LINDE
NILS KROGSTAD, *a bank clerk*

THE HELMERS' THREE SMALL CHILDREN
ANNE-MARIE, *their nurse*
HELENE, *a maid*
A DELIVERY BOY

The action takes place in HELMER's *residence.*

ACT I

A comfortable room, tastefully but not expensively furnished. A door to the right in the back wall leads to the entryway; another to the left leads to HELMER's *study. Between these doors, a piano. Midway in the left-hand wall a door, and further back a window. Near the window a round table with an armchair and a small sofa. In the right-hand wall, toward the rear, a door, and nearer the foreground a porcelain stove with two armchairs and a rocking chair beside it. Between the stove and the side door, a small table. Engravings on the walls. An etagère with china figures and other small art objects; a small bookcase with richly bound books; the floor carpeted; a fire burning in the stove. It is a winter day.*

1. Translated by Rolf Fjelde.

A bell rings in the entryway; shortly after we hear the door being unlocked. NORA *comes into the room, humming happily to herself; she is wearing street clothes and carries an armload of packages, which she puts down on the table to the right. She has left the hall door open; and through it a* DELIVERY BOY *is seen, holding a Christmas tree and a basket, which he gives to the* MAID *who let them in.*

NORA: Hide the tree well, Helene. The children mustn't get a glimpse of it till this evening, after it's trimmed. [*To the* DELIVERY BOY, *taking out her purse.*] How much?

DELIVERY BOY: Fifty, ma'am.

NORA: There's a crown. No, keep the change. [*The* BOY *thanks her and leaves.* NORA *shuts the door. She laughs softly to herself while taking off her street things. Drawing a bag of macaroons from her pocket, she eats a couple, then steals over and listens at her husband's study door.*] Yes, he's home. [*Hums again as she moves to the table right.*]

HELMER: [*From the study.*] Is that my little lark twittering out there?

NORA: [*Busy opening some packages.*] Yes, it is.

HELMER: Is that my squirrel rummaging around?

NORA: Yes!

HELMER: When did my squirrel get in?

NORA: Just now. [*Putting the macaroon bag in her pocket and wiping her mouth.*] Do come in, Torvald, and see what I've bought.

HELMER: Can't be disturbed. [*After a moment he opens the door and peers in, pen in hand.*] Bought, you say? All that there? Has the little spendthrift been out throwing money around again?

NORA: Oh, but Torvald, this year we really should let ourselves go a bit. It's the first Christmas we haven't had to economize.

HELMER: But you know we can't go squandering.

NORA: Oh yes, Torvald, we can squander a little now. Can't we? Just a tiny, wee bit. Now that you've got a big salary and are going to make piles and piles of money.

HELMER: Yes—starting New Year's. But then it's a full three months till the raise comes through.

NORA: Pooh! We can borrow that long.

HELMER: Nora! [*Goes over and playfully takes her by the ear.*] Are your scatter-brains off again? What if today I borrowed a thousand crowns, and you squandered them over Christmas week, and then on New Year's Eve a roof tile fell on my head, and I lay there—

NORA: [*Putting her hand on his mouth.*] Oh! Don't say such things!

HELMER: Yes, but what if it happened—then what?

NORA: If anything so awful happened, then it just wouldn't matter if I had debts or not.

HELMER: Well, but the people I'd borrowed from?

NORA: Them? Who cares about them! They're strangers.

HELMER: Nora, Nora, how like a woman! No, but seriously, Nora, you know what I think about that. No debts! Never borrow! Something of freedom's lost—and something of beauty, too—from a home that's founded on borrowing and debt. We've made a brave stand up to now, the two of us; and we'll go right on like that the little while we have to.

NORA: [*Going toward the stove.*] Yes, whatever you say, Torvald.

HELMER: [*Following her.*] Now, now, the little lark's wings mustn't droop. Come on, don't be a sulky squirrel. [*Taking out his wallet.*] Nora, guess what I have here.

NORA: [*Turning quickly.*] Money!

HELMER: There, see. [*Hands her some notes.*] Good grief, I know how costs go up in a house at Christmastime.

NORA: Ten—twenty—thirty—forty. Oh, thank you, Torvald; I can manage no end on this.

HELMER: You really will have to.

NORA: Oh yes, I promise I will. But come here so I can show you everything I bought. And so cheap! Look, new clothes for Ivar here—and a sword. Here a horse and a trumpet for Bob. And a doll and a doll's bed here for Emmy; they're nothing much, but she'll tear them to bits in no time anyway. And here I have dress material and handkerchiefs for the maids. Old Anne-Marie really deserves something more.

HELMER: And what's in that package there?

NORA: [*With a cry.*] Torvald, no! You can't see that till tonight!

HELMER: I see. But tell me now, you little prodigal, what have you thought of for yourself?

NORA: For myself? Oh, I don't want anything at all.

HELMER: Of course you do. Tell me just what—within reason—you'd most like to have.

NORA: I honestly don't know. Oh, listen, Torvald—

HELMER: Well?

NORA: [*Fumbling at his coat buttons, without looking at him.*] If you want to give me something, then maybe you could—you could—

HELMER: Come, on, out with it.

NORA: [*Hurriedly.*] You could give me money, Torvald. No more than you think you can spare; then one of these days I'll buy something with it.

HELMER: But Nora—

NORA: Oh, please, Torvald darling, do that! I beg you, please. Then I could hang the bills in pretty gilt paper on the Christmas tree. Wouldn't that be fun?

HELMER: What are those little birds called that always fly through their fortunes?

NORA: Oh yes, spendthrifts; I know all that. But let's do as I say, Torvald; then I'll have time to decide what I really need most. That's very sensible, isn't it?

HELMER: [*Smiling.*] Yes, very—that is, if you actually hung onto the money I give you, and you actually used it to buy yourself something. But it goes for the house and for all sorts of foolish things, and then I only have to lay out some more.

NORA: Oh, but Torvald—

HELMER: Don't deny it, my dear little Nora. [*Putting his arm around her waist.*] Spendthrifts are sweet, but they use up a frightful amount of money. It's incredible what it costs a man to feed such birds.

NORA: Oh, how can you say that! Really, I save everything I can.

HELMER: [*Laughing.*] Yes, that's the truth. Everything you can. But that's nothing at all.

NORA: [*Humming, with a smile of quiet satisfaction.*] Hm, if you only knew what expenses we larks and squirrels have, Torvald.

HELMER: You're an odd little one. Exactly the way your father was. You're never at a loss for scaring up money; but the moment you have it, it runs right out through your fingers; you never know what you've done with it. Well, one takes you as you are. It's deep in your blood. Yes, these things are hereditary, Nora.

NORA: Ah, I could wish I'd inherited many of Papa's qualities.

HELMER: And I couldn't wish you anything but just what you are, my sweet little lark. But wait; it seems to me you have a very—what should I call it?—a very suspicious look today—

NORA: I do?

HELMER: You certainly do. Look me straight in the eye.

NORA: [*Looking at him.*] Well?

HELMER: [*Shaking an admonitory finger.*] Surely my sweet tooth hasn't been running riot in town today, has she?

NORA: No. Why do you imagine that?

HELMER: My sweet tooth really didn't make a little detour through the confectioner's?

NORA: No, I assure you, Torvald—

HELMER: Hasn't nibbled some pastry?

NORA: No, not at all.

HELMER: Not even munched a macaroon or two?

NORA: No, Torvald, I assure you, really—

HELMER: There, there now. Of course I'm only joking.

NORA: [*Going to the table, right.*] You know I could never think of going against you.

HELMER: No, I understand that; and you *have* given me your word. [*Going over to her.*] Well, you keep your little Christmas secrets to yourself, Nora darling. I expect they'll come to light this evening, when the tree is lit.

NORA: Did you remember to ask Dr. Rank?

HELMER: No. But there's no need for that; it's assumed he'll be dining with us. All the same, I'll ask him when he stops by here this morning. I've ordered some fine wine. Nora, you can't imagine how I'm looking forward to this evening.

NORA: So am I. And what fun for the children, Torvald!

HELMER: Ah, it's so gratifying to know that one's gotten a safe, secure job, and with a comfortable salary. It's a great satisfaction, isn't it?

NORA: Oh, it's wonderful!

HELMER: Remember last Christmas? Three whole weeks before, you shut yourself in every evening till long after midnight, making flowers for the Christmas tree, and all the other decorations to surprise us. Ugh, that was the dullest time I've ever lived through.

NORA: It wasn't at all dull for me.

HELMER: [*Smiling.*] But the outcome *was* pretty sorry, Nora.

NORA: Oh, don't tease me with that again. How could I help it that the cat came in and tore everything to shreds.

HELMER: No, poor thing, you certainly couldn't. You wanted so much to please us all, and that's what counts. But it's just as well that the hard times are past.

NORA: Yes, it's really wonderful.

HELMER: Now I don't have to sit here alone, boring myself, and you don't have to tire your precious eyes and your fair little delicate hands—

NORA: [*Clapping her hands.*] No, is it really true, Torvald, I don't have to? Oh, how wonderfully lovely to hear! [*Taking his arm.*] Now I'll tell you just how I've thought we should plan things. Right after Christmas—[*The doorbell rings.*] Oh, the bell. [*Straightening the room up a bit.*] Somebody would have to come. What a bore!

HELMER: I'm not at home to visitors, don't forget.

MAID: [*From the hall doorway.*] Ma'am, a lady to see you—

NORA: All right, let her come in.

MAID: [*To* HELMER.] And the doctor's just come too.

HELMER: Did he go right to my study?

MAID: Yes, he did.

[HELMER *goes into his room. The* MAID *shows in* MRS. LINDE, *dressed in traveling clothes, and shuts the door after her.*]

MRS. LINDE: [*In a dispirited and somewhat hesitant voice.*] Hello, Nora.

NORA: [*Uncertain.*] Hello—

MRS. LINDE: You don't recognize me.

NORA: No, I don't know—but wait, I think—[*Exclaiming.*] What! Kristine! Is it really you?

MRS. LINDE: Yes, it's me.

NORA: Kristine! To think I didn't recognize you. But then, how could I? [*More quietly.*] How you've changed, Kristine!

MRS. LINDE: Yes, no doubt I have. In nine—ten long years.

NORA: Is it so long since we met! Yes, it's all of that. Oh, these last eight years have been a happy time, believe me. And so now you've come in to town, too. Made the long trip in the winter. That took courage.

MRS. LINDE: I just got here by ship this morning.

NORA: To enjoy yourself over Christmas, of course. Oh, how lovely! Yes, enjoy ourselves, we'll do that. But take your coat off. You're not still cold? [*Helping her.*] There now, let's get cozy here by the stove. No, the easy chair there! I'll take the rocker here. [*Seizing her hands.*] Yes, now you have your old look again; it was only in that first moment. You're a bit more pale, Kristine—and maybe a bit thinner.

MRS. LINDE: And much, much older, Nora.

NORA: Yes, perhaps a bit older; a tiny, tiny bit; not much at all. [*Stopping short; suddenly serious.*] Oh, but thoughtless me, to sit here, chattering away. Sweet, good Kristine, can you forgive me?

MRS. LINDE: What do you mean, Nora?

NORA: [*Softly.*] Poor Kristine, you've become a widow.

MRS. LINDE: Yes, three years ago.

NORA: Oh, I knew it, of course; I read it in the papers. Oh, Kristine, you must believe me; I often thought of writing you then, but I kept postponing it, and something always interfered.

MRS. LINDE: Nora dear, I understand completely.

NORA: No, it was awful of me, Kristine. You poor thing, how much you must have gone through. And he left you nothing?

MRS. LINDE: No.

NORA: And no children?

MRS. LINDE: No.

NORA: Nothing at all, then?

MRS. LINDE: Not even a sense of loss to feed on.

NORA: [Looking incredulously at her.] But Kristine, how could that be?

MRS. LINDE: [Smiling wearily and smoothing her hair.] Oh, sometimes it happens, Nora.

NORA: So completely alone. How terribly hard that must be for you. I have three lovely children. You can't see them now; they're out with the maid. But now you must tell me everything—

MRS. LINDE: No, no, no, tell me about yourself.

NORA: No, you begin. Today I don't want to be selfish. I want to think only of you today. But there is something I must tell you. Did you hear of the wonderful luck we had recently?

MRS. LINDE: No, what's that?

NORA: My husband's been made manager in the bank, just think!

MRS. LINDE: Your husband? How marvelous!

NORA: Isn't it? Being a lawyer is such an uncertain living, you know, especially if one won't touch any cases that aren't clean and decent. And of course Torvald would never do that, and I'm with him completely there. Oh, we're simply delighted, believe me! He'll join the bank right after New Year's and start getting a huge salary and lots of commissions. From now on we can live quite differently—just as we want. Oh, Kristine, I feel so light and happy! Won't it be lovely to have stacks of money and not a care in the world?

MRS. LINDE: Well, anyway, it would be lovely to have enough for necessities.

NORA: No, not just for necessities, but stacks and stacks of money!

MRS. LINDE: [Smiling.] Nora, Nora, aren't you sensible yet? Back in school you were such a free spender.

NORA: [With a quiet laugh.] Yes, that's what Torvald still says. [Shaking her finger.] But "Nora, Nora" isn't as silly as you all think. Really, we've been in no position for me to go squandering. We've had to work, both of us.

MRS. LINDE: You too?

NORA: Yes, at odd jobs—needlework, crocheting, embroidery, and such—[Casually.] and other things too. You remember that Torvald left the department when we were married? There was no chance of promotion in his office, and of course he needed to earn more money. But that first year he drove himself terribly. He took on all kinds of extra work that kept him going morning and night. It wore him down, and then he fell deathly ill. The doctors said it was essential for him to travel south.

MRS. LINDE: Yes, didn't you spend a whole year in Italy?

NORA: That's right. It wasn't easy to get away, you know. Ivar had just been born. But of course we had to go. Oh, that was a beautiful trip, and it saved Torvald's life. But it cost a frightful sum, Kristine.

MRS. LINDE: I can well imagine.

NORA: Four thousand, eight hundred crowns it cost. That's really a lot of money.

MRS. LINDE: But it's lucky you had it when you needed it.

NORA: Well, as it was, we got it from Papa.

MRS. LINDE: I see. It was just about the time your father died.

NORA: Yes, just about then. And, you know, I couldn't make that trip out to nurse him. I had to stay here, expecting Ivar any moment, and with my poor sick Torvald to care for. Dearest Papa, I never saw him again, Kristine. Oh, that was the worst time I've known in all my marriage.

MRS. LINDE: I know how you loved him. And then you went off to Italy?

NORA: Yes. We had the means now, and the doctors urged us. So we left a month after.

MRS. LINDE: And your husband came back completely cured?

NORA: Sound as a drum!

MRS. LINDE: But—the doctor?

NORA: Who?

MRS. LINDE: I thought the maid said he was a doctor, the man who came in with me.

NORA: Yes, that was Dr. Rank—but he's not making a sick call. He's our closest friend, and he stops by at least once a day. No, Torvald hasn't had a sick moment since, and the children are fit and strong, and I am, too. [*Jumping up and clapping her hands.*] Oh, dear God, Kristine, what a lovely thing to live and be happy! But how disgusting of me—I'm talking of nothing but my own affairs. [*Sits on a stool close by* KRISTINE, *arms resting across her knees.*] Oh, don't be angry with me! Tell me, is it really true that you weren't in love with your husband? Why did you marry him, then?

MRS. LINDE: My mother was still alive, but bedridden and helpless—and I had my two younger brothers to look after. In all conscience, I didn't think I could turn him down.

NORA: No, you were right there. But was he rich at the time?

MRS. LINDE: He was very well off, I'd say. But the business was shaky, Nora. When he died, it all fell apart, and nothing was left.

NORA: And then—?

MRS. LINDE: Yes, so I had to scrape up a living with a little shop and a little teaching and whatever else I could find. The last three years have been like one endless workday without a rest for me. Now it's over, Nora. My poor mother doesn't need me, for she's passed on. Nor the boys, either; they're working now and can take care of themselves.

NORA: How free you must feel—

MRS. LINDE: No—only unspeakably empty. Nothing to live for now. [*Standing up anxiously.*] That's why I couldn't take it any longer out in that desolate hole. Maybe here it'll be easier to find something to do and keep my mind occupied. If I could only be lucky enough to get a steady job, some office work—

NORA: Oh, but Kristine, that's so dreadfully tiring, and you already look so tired. It would be much better for you if you could go off to a bathing resort.

MRS. LINDE: [*Going toward the window.*] I have no father to give me travel money, Nora.

NORA: [*Rising.*] Oh, don't be angry with me.

MRS. LINDE: [*Going to her.*] Nora dear, don't you be angry with me. The worst of my kind of situation is all the bitterness that's stored away. No one to work for, and yet you're always having to snap up your opportunities. You have to live; and so you grow selfish. When you told me the happy change in your lot, do you know I was delighted less for your sakes than for mine?

NORA: How so? Oh, I see. You think maybe Torvald could do something for you.

MRS. LINDE: Yes, that's what I thought.

NORA: And he will, Kristine! Just leave it to me; I'll bring it up so delicately— find something attractive to humor him with. Oh, I'm so eager to help you.

MRS. LINDE: How very kind of you, Nora, to be so concerned over me—doubly kind, considering you really know so little of life's burdens yourself.

NORA: I—? I know so little—?

MRS. LINDE: [*Smiling.*] Well, my heavens—a little needlework and such—Nora, you're just a child.

NORA: [*Tossing her head and pacing the floor.*] You don't have to act so superior.

MRS. LINDE: Oh?

NORA: You're just like the others. You all think I'm incapable of anything serious—

MRS. LINDE: Come now—

NORA: That I've never had to face the raw world.

MRS. LINDE: Nora dear, you've just been telling me all your troubles.

NORA: Hm! Trivia! [*Quietly.*] I haven't told you the big thing.

MRS. LINDE: Big thing? What do you mean?

NORA: You look down on me so, Kristine, but you shouldn't. You're proud that you worked so long and hard for your mother.

MRS. LINDE: I don't look down on a soul. But it *is* true: I'm proud—and happy, too—to think it was given to me to make my mother's last days almost free of care.

NORA: And you're also proud thinking of what you've done for your brothers.

MRS. LINDE: I feel I've a right to be.

NORA: I agree. But listen to this, Kristine—I've also got something to be proud and happy for.

MRS. LINDE: I don't doubt it. But whatever do you mean?

NORA: Not so loud. What if Torvald heard! He mustn't, not for anything in the world. Nobody must know, Kristine. No one but you.

MRS. LINDE: But what is it, then?

NORA: Come here. [*Drawing her down beside her on the sofa.*] It's true—I've also got something to be proud and happy for. I'm the one who saved Torvald's life.

MRS. LINDE: Saved—? Saved how?

NORA: I told you about the trip to Italy. Torvald never would have lived if he hadn't gone south—

MRS. LINDE: Of course; your father gave you the means—

NORA: [*Smiling.*] That's what Torvald and all the rest think, but—

MRS. LINDE: But—?

NORA: Papa didn't give us a pin. I was the one who raised the money.

MRS. LINDE: You? That whole amount?

NORA: Four thousand, eight hundred crowns. What do you say to that?

MRS. LINDE: But Nora, how was it possible? Did you win the lottery?

NORA: [*Disdainfully.*] The lottery? Pooh! No art to that.

MRS. LINDE: But where did you get it from then?

NORA: [*Humming, with a mysterious smile.*] Hmm, tra-la-la-la.

MRS. LINDE: Because you couldn't have borrowed it.

NORA: No? Why not?

MRS. LINDE: A wife can't borrow without her husband's consent.

NORA: [*Tossing her head.*] Oh, but a wife with a little business sense, a wife who knows how to manage—

MRS. LINDE: Nora, I simply don't understand—

NORA: You don't have to. Whoever said I *borrowed* the money? I could have gotten it other ways. [*Throwing herself back on the sofa.*] I could have gotten it from some admirer or other. After all, a girl with my ravishing appeal—

MRS. LINDE: You lunatic.

NORA: I'll bet you're eaten up with curiosity, Kristine.

MRS. LINDE: Now listen here, Nora—you haven't done something indiscreet?

NORA: [*Sitting up again.*] Is it indiscreet to save your husband's life?

MRS. LINDE: I think it's indiscreet that without his knowledge you—

NORA: But that's the point: he mustn't know! My Lord, can't you understand? He mustn't ever know the close call he had. It was to *me* the doctors came to say his life was in danger—that nothing could save him but a stay in the south. Didn't I try strategy then! I began talking about how lovely it would be for me to travel abroad like other young wives; I begged and I cried; I told him please to remember my condition, to be kind and indulge me; and then I dropped a hint that he could easily take out a loan. But at that, Kristine, he nearly exploded. He said I was frivolous, and it was his duty as man of the house not to indulge me in whims and fancies—as I think he called them. Aha, I thought, now you'll just have to be saved—and that's when I saw my chance.

MRS. LINDE: And your father never told Torvald the money wasn't from him?

NORA: No, never. Papa died right about then. I'd considered bringing him into my secret and begging him never to tell. But he was too sick at the time— and then, sadly, it didn't matter.

MRS. LINDE: And you've never confided in your husband since?

NORA: For heaven's sake, no! Are you serious? He's so strict on that subject. Besides—Torvald, with all his masculine pride—how painfully humiliating for him if he ever found out he was in debt to me. That would just ruin our relationship. Our beautiful, happy home would never be the same.

MRS. LINDE: Won't you ever tell him?

NORA: [*Thoughtfully.*] Yes—maybe sometime years from now, when I'm no longer so attractive. Don't laugh! I only mean when Torvald loves me less than now, when he stops enjoying my dancing and dressing up and reciting for him. Then it might be wise to have something in reserve—[*Breaking off.*] How ridiculous! That'll never happen—Well, Kristine, what do you think of my big secret? I'm capable of something too, hm? You can imagine, of course, how this thing hangs over me. It really hasn't been easy meeting the payments on time. In the business world there's what they call quarterly interest and what they call amortization, and these are always so terribly hard to manage. I've had to skimp a little here and there, wherever I could, you know. I could hardly spare anything from my house allowance, because Torvald has to live well. I couldn't let the children go poorly dressed; whatever I got for them, I felt I had to use up completely—the darlings!

MRS. LINDE: Poor Nora, so it had to come out of your own budget, then?

NORA: Yes, of course. But I was the one most responsible, too. Every time Torvald gave me money for new clothes and such, I never used more than half; always bought the simplest, cheapest outfits. It was a godsend that everything looks so well on me that Torvald never noticed. But it did weigh me down at times, Kristine. It *is* such a joy to wear fine things. You understand.

MRS. LINDE: Oh, of course.

NORA: And then I found other ways of making money. Last winter I was lucky enough to get a lot of copying to do. I locked myself in and sat writing every evening till late in the night. Ah, I was tired so often, dead tired. But still it was wonderful fun, sitting and working like that, earning money. It was almost like being a man.

MRS. LINDE: But how much have you paid off this way so far?

NORA: That's hard to say, exactly. These accounts, you know, aren't easy to figure. I only know that I've paid out all I could scrape together. Time and again I haven't known where to turn. [*Smiling.*] Then I'd sit here dreaming of a rich old gentleman who had fallen in love with me—

MRS. LINDE: What! Who is he?

NORA: Oh, really! And that he'd died, and when his will was opened, there in big letters it said, "All my fortune shall be paid over in cash, immediately, to that enchanting Mrs. Nora Helmer."

MRS. LINDE: But Nora dear—who *was* this gentleman?

NORA: Good grief, can't you understand? The old man never existed; that was only something I'd dream up time and again whenever I was at my wits' end for money. But it makes no difference now; the old fossil can go where he pleases for all I care; I don't need him or his will—because now I'm free. [*Jumping up.*] Oh, how lovely to think of that, Kristine! Carefree! To know you're carefree, utterly carefree; to be able to romp and play with the children, and to keep up a beautiful, charming home—everything just the way Torvald likes it! And think, spring is coming, with big blue skies. Maybe we can travel a little then. Maybe I'll see the ocean again. Oh yes, it *is* so marvelous to live and be happy!

[*The front doorbell rings.*]

MRS. LINDE: [*Rising.*] There's the bell. It's probably best that I go.

NORA: No, stay. No one's expected. It must be for Torvald.

MAID: [*From the hall doorway.*] Excuse me, ma'am—there's a gentleman here to see Mr. Helmer, but I didn't know—since the doctor's with him—

NORA: Who is the gentleman?

KROGSTAD: [*From the doorway.*] It's me, Mrs. Helmer.

[MRS. LINDE *starts and turns away toward the window.*]

NORA: [*Stepping toward him, tense, her voice a whisper.*] You? What is it? Why do you want to speak to my husband?

KROGSTAD: Bank business—after a fashion. I have a small job in the investment bank, and I hear now your husband is going to be our chief—

NORA: In other words, it's—

KROGSTAD: Just dry business, Mrs. Helmer. Nothing but that.

NORA: Yes, then please be good enough to step into the study. [*She nods indifferently as she sees him out by the hall door, then returns and begins stirring up the stove.*]

MRS. LINDE: Nora—who was that man?

NORA: That was a Mr. Krogstad—a lawyer.

MRS. LINDE: Then it really was him.

NORA: Do you know that person?

MRS. LINDE: I did once—many years ago. For a time he was a law clerk in our town.

NORA: Yes, he's been that.

MRS. LINDE: How he's changed.

NORA: I understand he had a very unhappy marriage.

MRS. LINDE: He's a widower now.

NORA: With a number of children. There now, it's burning. [*She closes the stove door and moves the rocker a bit to one side.*]

MRS. LINDE: They say he has a hand in all kinds of business.

NORA: Oh? That may be true; I wouldn't know. But let's not think about business. It's so dull.

[DR. RANK *enters from* HELMER'S *study.*]

RANK: [*Still in the doorway.*] No, no, really—I don't want to intrude, I'd just as soon talk a little while with your wife. [*Shuts the door, then notices* MRS. LINDE.] Oh, beg pardon. I'm intruding here too.

NORA: No, not at all. [*Introducing him.*] Dr. Rank, Mrs. Linde.

RANK: Well now, that's a name much heard in this house. I believe I passed the lady on the stairs as I came.

MRS. LINDE: Yes, I take the stairs very slowly. They're rather hard on me.

RANK: Uh-hm, some touch of internal weakness?

MRS. LINDE: More overexertion, I'd say.

RANK: Nothing else? Then you're probably here in town to rest up in a round of parties?

MRS. LINDE: I'm here to look for work.

RANK: Is that the best cure for overexertion?

MRS. LINDE: One has to live, Doctor.

RANK: Yes, there's a common prejudice to that effect.

NORA: Oh, come on, Dr. Rank—you really do want to live yourself.

RANK: Yes, I really do. Wretched as I am, I'll gladly prolong my torment indefinitely. All my patients feel like that. And it's quite the same, too, with the morally sick. Right at this moment there's one of those moral invalids in there with Helmer—

MRS. LINDE: [*Softly.*] Ah!

NORA: Who do you mean?

RANK: Oh, it's a lawyer, Krogstad, a type you wouldn't know. His character is rotten to the root—but even he began chattering all-importantly about how he had to *live*.

NORA: Oh? What did he want to talk to Torvald about?

RANK: I really don't know. I only heard something about the bank.

NORA: I didn't know that Krog—that this man Krogstad had anything to do with the bank.

RANK: Yes, he's gotten some kind of berth down there. [*To* MRS. LINDE.] I don't know if you also have, in your neck of the woods, a type of person who scuttles about breathlessly, sniffing out hints of moral corruption, and then maneuvers his victim into some sort of key position where he can keep an eye on him. It's the healthy these days that are out in the cold.

MRS. LINDE: All the same, it's the sick who most need to be taken in.

RANK: [*With a shrug.*] Yes, there we have it. That's the concept that's turning society into a sanatorium.

[NORA, *lost in her thoughts, breaks out into quiet laughter and claps her hands.*]

RANK: Why do you laugh at that? Do you have any real idea of what society is?

NORA: What do I care about dreary old society? I was laughing at something quite different—something terribly funny. Tell me, Doctor—is everyone who works in the bank dependent now on Torvald?

RANK: Is that what you find so terribly funny?

NORA: [*Smiling and humming.*] Never mind, never mind [*Pacing the floor.*] Yes, that's really immensely amusing: that we—that Torvald has so much power now over all those people. [*Taking the bag out of her pocket.*] Dr. Rank, a little macaroon on that?

RANK: See here, macaroons! I thought they were contraband here.

NORA: Yes, but these are some that Kristine gave me.

MRS. LINDE: What? I—?

NORA: Now, now, don't be afraid. You couldn't possibly know that Torvald had forbidden them. You see, he's worried they'll ruin my teeth. But hmp! Just this once! Isn't that so, Dr. Rank? Help yourself! [*Puts a macaroon in his mouth.*] And you too, Kristine. And I'll also have one, only a little one—or two, at the most. [*Walking about again.*] Now I'm really tremendously happy. Now there's just one last thing in the world that I have an enormous desire to do.

RANK: Well! And what's that?

NORA: It's something I have such a consuming desire to say so Torvald could hear.

RANK: And why can't you say it?

NORA: I don't dare. It's quite shocking.

MRS. LINDE: Shocking?

RANK: Well, then it isn't advisable. But in front of us you certainly can. What do you have such a desire to say so Torvald could hear?

NORA: I have such a huge desire to say—to hell and be damned!

RANK: Are you crazy?

MRS. LINDE: My goodness, Nora!

RANK: Go on, say it. Here he is.

NORA: [*Hiding the macaroon bag.*] Shh, shh, shh!

[HELMER *comes in from his study, hat in hand, overcoat over his arm.*]

NORA: [*Going toward him.*] Well, Torvald dear, are you through with him?

HELMER: Yes, he just left.

NORA: Let me introduce you—this is Kristine, who's arrived here in town.

HELMER: Kristine—? I'm sorry, but I don't know—

NORA: Mrs. Linde, Torvald dear. Mrs. Kristine Linde.

HELMER: Of course. A childhood friend of my wife's, no doubt?

MRS. LINDE: Yes, we knew each other in those days.

NORA: And just think, she made the long trip down here in order to talk with you.

HELMER: What's this?

MRS. LINDE: Well, not exactly—

NORA: You see, Kristine is remarkably clever in office work, and so she's terribly eager to come under a capable man's supervision and add more to what she already knows—

HELMER: Very wise, Mrs. Linde.

NORA: And then when she heard that you'd become a bank manager—the story was wired out to the papers—then she came in as fast as she could and— Really, Torvald, for my sake you can do a little something for Kristine, can't you?

HELMER: Yes, it's not at all impossible. Mrs. Linde, I suppose you're a widow?

MRS. LINDE: Yes.

HELMER: Any experience in office work?

MRS. LINDE: Yes, a good deal.

HELMER: Well, it's quite likely that I can make an opening for you—

NORA: [*Clapping her hands.*] You see, you see!

HELMER: You've come at a lucky moment, Mrs. Linde.

MRS. LINDE: Oh, how can I thank you?

HELMER: Not necessary. [*Putting his overcoat on.*] But today you'll have to excuse me—

RANK: Wait, I'll go with you. [*He fetches his coat from the hall and warms it at the stove.*]

NORA: Don't stay out long, dear.

HELMER: An hour; no more.

NORA: Are you going too, Kristine?

MRS. LINDE: [*Putting on her winter garments.*] Yes, I have to see about a room now.

HELMER: Then perhaps we can all walk together.

NORA: [*Helping her.*] What a shame we're so cramped here, but it's quite impossible for us to—

MRS. LINDE: Oh, don't even think of it! Good-bye, Nora dear, and thanks for everything.

NORA: Good-bye for now. Of course you'll be back this evening. And you too, Dr. Rank. What? If you're well enough? Oh, you've got to be! Wrap up tight now.

[*In a ripple of small talk the company moves out into the hall; children's voices are heard outside on the steps.*]

NORA: There they are! There they are! [*She runs to open the door. The children come in with their nurse,* ANNE-MARIE.] Come in, come in! [*Bends down and kisses them.*] Oh, you darlings—! Look at them, Kristine. Aren't they lovely!

RANK: No loitering in the draft here.

HELMER: Come, Mrs. Linde—this place is unbearable now for anyone but mothers.

[DR. RANK, HELMER, *and* MRS. LINDE *go down the stairs.* ANNE-MARIE *goes into the living room with the children.* NORA *follows, after closing the hall door.*]

NORA: How fresh and strong you look. Oh, such red cheeks you have! Like apples and roses. [*The children interrupt her throughout the following.*] And it was so much fun? That's wonderful. Really? You pulled both Emmy and Bob on the sled? Imagine, all together! Yes, you're a clever boy, Ivar. Oh, let me hold her a bit, Anne-Marie. My sweet little doll baby! [*Takes the smallest from the nurse and dances with her.*] Yes, yes, Mama will dance with Bob as well. What? Did you throw snowballs? Oh, if I'd only been there! No, don't bother, Anne-Marie—I'll undress them myself. Oh yes, let me. It's such fun. Go in and rest; you look half frozen. There's hot coffee waiting for you on the stove. [*The nurse goes into the room to the left.* NORA *takes the children's winter things off, throwing them about, while the children talk to her all at once.*] Is that so? A big dog chased you? But it didn't bite? No, dogs never bite little, lovely doll babies. Don't peek in the packages, Ivar! What is it? Yes, wouldn't you like to know. No, no, it's an ugly something. Well? Shall we play? What shall we play? Hide-and-seek? Yes, let's play hide-and-seek. Bob must hide first. I must? Yes, let me hide first. [*Laughing and shouting, she and the children play in and out of the living room and the adjoining room to the right. At last* NORA *hides under the table. The children come storming in, search, but cannot find her, then hear her muffled laughter, dash over to the table, lift the cloth up and find her. Wild shouting. She creeps forward as if to scare them. More shouts. Meanwhile, a knock at the hall door; no one has noticed it. Now the door half opens, and* KROGSTAD *appears. He waits a moment; the game goes on.*]

KROGSTAD: Beg pardon, Mrs. Helmer—

NORA: [*With a strangled cry, turning and scrambling to her knees.*] Oh! What do you want?

KROGSTAD: Excuse me. The outer door was ajar; it must be someone forgot to shut it—

NORA: [*Rising.*] My husband isn't home, Mr. Krogstad.

KROGSTAD: I know that.

NORA: Yes—then what do you want here?

KROGSTAD: A word with you.

NORA: With—? [*To the children, quietly.*] Go in to Anne-Marie. What? No, the strange man won't hurt Mama. When he's gone, we'll play some more. [*She leads the children into the room to the left and shuts the door after them. Then, tense and nervous:*] You want to speak to me?

KROGSTAD: Yes, I want to.

NORA: Today? But it's not yet the first of the month—

KROGSTAD: No, it's Christmas Eve. It's going to be up to you how merry a Christmas you have.

NORA: What is it you want? Today I absolutely can't—

KROGSTAD: We won't talk about that till later. This is something else. You do have a moment to spare, I suppose?

NORA: Oh yes, of course—I do, except—

KROGSTAD: Good. I was sitting over at Olsen's Restaurant when I saw your husband go down the street—

NORA: Yes?

KROGSTAD: With a lady.

NORA: Yes. So?

KROGSTAD: If you'll pardon my asking: wasn't that lady a Mrs. Linde?

NORA: Yes.

KROGSTAD: Just now come into town?

NORA: Yes, today.

KROGSTAD: She's a good friend of yours?

NORA: Yes, she is. But I don't see—

KROGSTAD: I also knew her once.

NORA: I'm aware of that.

KROGSTAD: Oh? You know all about it. I thought so. Well, then let me ask you short and sweet: is Mrs. Linde getting a job in the bank?

NORA: What makes you think you can cross-examine me, Mr. Krogstad—you, one of my husband's employees? But since you ask, you might as well know— yes, Mrs. Linde's going to be taken on at the bank. And I'm the one who spoke for her, Mr. Krogstad. Now you know.

KROGSTAD: So I guessed right.

NORA: [Pacing up and down.] Oh, one does have a tiny bit of influence, I should hope. Just because I am a woman, don't think it means that—When one has a subordinate position, Mr. Krogstad, one really ought to be careful about pushing somebody who—hm—

KROGSTAD: Who has influence?

NORA: That's right.

KROGSTAD: [In a different tone.] Mrs. Helmer, would you be good enough to use your influence on my behalf?

NORA: What? What do you mean?

KROGSTAD: Would you please make sure that I keep my subordinate position in the bank?

NORA: What does that mean? Who's thinking of taking away your position?

KROGSTAD: Oh, don't play the innocent with me. I'm quite aware that your friend would hardly relish the chance of running into me again; and I'm also aware now whom I can thank for being turned out.

NORA: But I promise you—

KROGSTAD: Yes, yes, yes, to the point: there's still time, and I'm advising you to use your influence to prevent it.

NORA: But Mr. Krogstad, I have absolutely no influence.

KROGSTAD: You haven't? I thought you were just saying—

NORA: You shouldn't take me so literally. I! How can you believe that I have any such influence over my husband?

KROGSTAD: Oh, I've known your husband from our student days. I don't think the great bank manager's more steadfast than any other married man.

NORA: You speak insolently about my husband, and I'll show you the door.

KROGSTAD: The lady has spirit.

NORA: I'm not afraid of you any longer. After New Year's, I'll soon be done with the whole business.

KROGSTAD: [*Restraining himself.*] Now listen to me, Mrs. Helmer. If necessary, I'll fight for my little job in the bank as if it were life itself.

NORA: Yes, so it seems.

KROGSTAD: It's not just a matter of income; that's the least of it. It's something else—All right, out with it! Look, this is the thing. You know, just like all the others, of course, that once, a good many years ago, I did something rather rash.

NORA: I've heard rumors to that effect.

KROGSTAD: The case never got into court; but all the same, every door was closed in my face from then on. So I took up those various activities you know about. I had to grab hold somewhere; and I dare say I haven't been among the worst. But now I want to drop all that. My boys are growing up. For their sakes, I'll have to win back as much respect as possible here in town. That job in the bank was like the first rung in my ladder. And now your husband wants to kick me right back down in the mud again.

NORA: But for heaven's sake, Mr. Krogstad, it's simply not in my power to help you.

KROGSTAD: That's because you haven't the will to—but I have the means to make you.

NORA: You certainly won't tell my husband that I owe you money?

KROGSTAD: Hm—what if I told him that?

NORA: That would be shameful of you. [*Nearly in tears.*] This secret—my joy and my pride—that he should learn it in such a crude and disgusting way—learn it from you. You'd expose me to the most horrible unpleasantness—

KROGSTAD: Only unpleasantness?

NORA: [*Vehemently.*] But go on and try. It'll turn out the worse for you, because then my husband will really see what a crook you are, and then you'll *never* be able to hold your job.

KROGSTAD: I asked if it was just domestic unpleasantness you were afraid of?

NORA: If my husband finds out, then of course he'll pay what I owe at once, and then we'd be through with you for good.

KROGSTAD: [*A step closer.*] Listen, Mrs. Helmer—you've either got a very bad memory, or else no head at all for business. I'd better put you a little more in touch with the facts.

NORA: What do you mean?

KROGSTAD: When your husband was sick, you came to me for a loan of four thousand, eight hundred crowns.

NORA: Where else could I go?

KROGSTAD: I promised to get you that sum—

NORA: And you got it.

KROGSTAD: I promised to get you that sum, on certain conditions. You were so involved in your husband's illness, and so eager to finance your trip, that

I guess you didn't think out all the details. It might just be a good idea to remind you. I promised you the money on the strength of a note I drew up.

NORA: Yes, and that I signed.

KROGSTAD: Right. But at the bottom I added some lines for your father to guarantee the loan. He was supposed to sign down there.

NORA: Supposed to? He did sign.

KROGSTAD: I left the date blank. In other words, your father would have dated his signature himself. Do you remember that?

NORA: Yes, I think—

KROGSTAD: Then I gave you the note for you to mail to your father. Isn't that so?

NORA: Yes.

KROGSTAD: And naturally you sent it at once—because only some five, six days later you brought me the note, properly signed. And with that, the money was yours.

NORA: Well, then; I've made my payments regularly, haven't I?

KROGSTAD: More or less. But—getting back to the point—those were hard times for you then, Mrs. Helmer.

NORA: Yes, they were.

KROGSTAD: Your father was very ill, I believe.

NORA: He was near the end.

KROGSTAD: He died soon after?

NORA: Yes.

KROGSTAD: Tell me, Mrs. Helmer, do you happen to recall the date of your father's death? The day of the month, I mean.

NORA: Papa died the twenty-ninth of September.

KROGSTAD: That's quite correct; I've already looked into that. And now we come to a curious thing—[Taking out a paper.] which I simply cannot comprehend.

NORA: Curious thing? I don't know—

KROGSTAD: This is the curious thing: that your father co-signed the note for your loan three days after his death.

NORA: How—? I don't understand.

KROGSTAD: Your father died the twenty-ninth of September. But look. Here your father dated his signature October second. Isn't that curious, Mrs. Helmer? [NORA is silent.] Can you explain it to me? [NORA remains silent.] It's also remarkable that the words "October second" and the year aren't written in your father's hand, but rather in one that I think I know. Well, it's easy to understand. Your father forgot perhaps to date his signature, and then someone or other added it, a bit sloppily, before anyone knew of his death. There's nothing wrong in that. It all comes down to the signature. And there's no question about that, Mrs. Helmer. It really was your father who signed his own name here, wasn't it?

NORA: [After a short silence, throwing her head back and looking squarely at him.] No, it wasn't. I signed papa's name.

KROGSTAD: Wait, now—are you fully aware that this is a dangerous confession?

NORA: Why? You'll soon get your money.

KROGSTAD: Let me ask you a question—why didn't you send the paper to your father?

NORA: That was impossible. Papa was so sick. If I'd asked him for his signature, I also would have had to tell him what the money was for. But I couldn't tell him, sick as he was, that my husband's life was in danger. That was just impossible.

KROGSTAD: Then it would have been better if you'd given up the trip abroad.

NORA: I couldn't possibly. The trip was to save my husband's life. I couldn't give that up.

KROGSTAD: But didn't you ever consider that this was a fraud against me?

NORA: I couldn't let myself be bothered by that. You weren't any concern of mine. I couldn't stand you, with all those cold complications you made, even though you knew how badly off my husband was.

KROGSTAD: Mrs. Helmer, obviously you haven't the vaguest idea of what you've involved yourself in. But I can tell you this: it was nothing more and nothing worse that I once did—and it wrecked my whole reputation.

NORA: You? Do you expect me to believe that you ever acted bravely to save your wife's life?

KROGSTAD: Laws don't inquire into motives.

NORA: Then they must be very poor laws.

KROGSTAD: Poor or not—if I introduce this paper in court, you'll be judged according to law.

NORA: This I refuse to believe. A daughter hasn't a right to protect her dying father from anxiety and care? A wife hasn't a right to save her husband's life? I don't know much about laws, but I'm sure that somewhere in the books these things are allowed. And you don't know anything about it—you who practice the law? You must be an awful lawyer, Mr. Krogstad.

KROGSTAD: Could be. But business—the kind of business we two are mixed up in—don't you think I know about that? All right. Do what you want now. But I'm telling you *this*: if I get shoved down a second time, you're going to keep me company. [*He bows and goes out through the hall.*]

NORA: [*Pensive for a moment, then tossing her head.*] Oh, really! Trying to frighten me! I'm not so silly as all that. [*Begins gathering up the children's clothes, but soon stops.*] But—? No, but that's impossible! I did it out of love.

THE CHILDREN: [*In the doorway, left.*] Mama, that strange man's gone out the door.

NORA: Yes, yes, I know it. But don't tell anyone about the strange man. Do you hear? Not even Papa!

THE CHILDREN: No, Mama. But now will you play again?

NORA: No, not now.

THE CHILDREN: Oh, but Mama, you promised.

NORA: Yes, but I can't now. Go inside; I have too much to do. Go in, go in, my sweet darlings. [*She herds them gently back in the room and shuts the door after them. Settling on the sofa, she takes up a piece of embroidery and makes some stitches, but soon stops abruptly.*] No! [*Throws the work aside, rises, goes to the hall door and calls out.*] Helene! Let me have the tree in here. [*Goes to the table, left, opens the table drawer, and stops again.*] No, but that's utterly impossible!

MAID: [*With the Christmas tree.*] Where should I put it, ma'am?

NORA: There. The middle of the floor.

MAID: Should I bring anything else?

NORA: No, thanks. I have what I need.

[*The* MAID, *who has set the tree down, goes out.*]

NORA: [*Absorbed in trimming the tree.*] Candles here—and flowers here. That terrible creature! Talk, talk, talk! There's nothing to it at all. The tree's going to be
lovely. I'll do anything to please you, Torvald. I'll sing for you, dance for you—

[HELMER *comes in from the hall, with a sheaf of papers under his arm.*]

NORA: Oh! You're back so soon?

HELMER: Yes. Has anyone been here?

NORA: Here? No.

HELMER: That's odd. I saw Krogstad leaving the front door.

NORA: So? Oh yes, that's true. Krogstad was here a moment.

HELMER: Nora, I can see by your face that he's been here, begging you to put in
a good word for him.

NORA: Yes.

HELMER: And it was supposed to seem like your own idea? You were to hide it
from me that he'd been here. He asked you that, too, didn't he?

NORA: Yes, Torvald, but—

HELMER: Nora, Nora, and you could fall for that? Talk with that sort of person
and promise him anything? And then in the bargain, tell me an untruth.

NORA: An untruth—?

HELMER: Didn't you say that no one had been here? [*Wagging his finger.*] My little
songbird must never do that again. A songbird needs a clean beak to warble
with. No false notes. [*Putting his arm about her waist.*] That's the way it should
be, isn't it? Yes, I'm sure of it. [*Releasing her.*] And so, enough of that. [*Sitting
by the stove.*] Ah, how snug and cozy it is here. [*Leafing among his papers.*]

NORA: [*Busy with the tree, after a short pause.*] Torvald!

HELMER: Yes.

NORA: I'm so much looking forward to the Stenborgs' costume party, day after
tomorrow.

HELMER: And I can't wait to see what you'll surprise me with.

NORA: Oh, that stupid business!

HELMER: What?

NORA: I can't find anything that's right. Everything seems so ridiculous, so inane.

HELMER: So my little Nora's come to *that* recognition?

NORA: [*Going behind his chair, her arms resting on its back.*] Are you very busy,
Torvald?

HELMER: Oh—

NORA: What papers are those?

HELMER: Bank matters.

NORA: Already?

HELMER: I've gotten full authority from the retiring management to make all
necessary changes in personnel and procedure. I'll need Christmas week for
that. I want to have everything in order by New Year's.

NORA: So that was the reason this poor Krogstad—

HELMER: Hm.

NORA: [*Still leaning on the chair and slowly stroking the nape of his neck.*] If you
weren't so very busy, I would have asked you an enormous favor, Torvald.

HELMER: Let's hear. What is it?

NORA: You know, there isn't anyone who has your good taste—and I want so much to look well at the costume party. Torvald, couldn't you take over and decide what I should be and plan my costume?

HELMER: Ah, is my stubborn little creature calling for a lifeguard?

NORA: Yes, Torvald, I can't get anywhere without your help.

HELMER: All right—I'll think it over. We'll hit on something.

NORA: Oh, how sweet of you. [*Goes to the tree again. Pause.*] Aren't the red flowers pretty—? But tell me, was it really such a crime that this Krogstad committed?

HELMER: Forgery. Do you have any idea what that means?

NORA: Couldn't he have done it out of need?

HELMER: Yes, or thoughtlessness, like so many others. I'm not so heartless that I'd condemn a man categorically for just one mistake.

NORA: No, of course not, Torvald!

HELMER: Plenty of men have redeemed themselves by openly confessing their crimes and taking their punishment.

NORA: Punishment—?

HELMER: But now Krogstad didn't go that way. He got himself out by sharp practices, and that's the real cause of his moral breakdown.

NORA: Do you really think that would—?

HELMER: Just imagine how a man with that sort of guilt in him has to lie and cheat and deceive on all sides, has to wear a mask even with the nearest and dearest he has, even with his own wife and children. And with the children, Nora—that's where it's most horrible.

NORA: Why?

HELMER: Because that kind of atmosphere of lies infects the whole life of a home. Every breath the children take in is filled with the germs of something degenerate.

NORA: [*Coming closer behind him.*] Are you sure of that?

HELMER: Oh, I've seen it often enough as a lawyer. Almost everyone who goes bad early in life has a mother who's a chronic liar.

NORA: Why just—the mother?

HELMER: It's usually the mother's influence that's dominant, but the father's works in the same way, of course. Every lawyer is quite familiar with it. And still this Krogstad's been going home year in, year out, poisoning his own children with lies and pretense; that's why I call him morally lost. [*Reaching his hands out toward her.*] So my sweet little Nora must promise me never to plead his cause. Your hand on it. Come, come, what's this? Give me your hand. There, now. All settled. I can tell you it'd be impossible for me to work alongside of him. I literally feel physically revolted when I'm anywhere near such a person.

NORA: [*Withdraws her hand and goes to the other side of the Christmas tree.*] How hot it is here! And I've got so much to do.

HELMER: [*Getting up and gathering his papers.*] Yes, and I have to think about getting some of these read through before dinner. I'll think about your costume, too. And something to hang on the tree in gilt paper, I may even see about that. [*Putting his hand on her head.*] Oh you, my darling little songbird. [*He goes into his study and closes the door after him.*]

NORA: [*Softly, after a silence.*] Oh, really! it isn't so. It's impossible. It must be impossible.

ANNE-MARIE: [*In the doorway, left.*] The children are begging so hard to come in to Mama.

NORA: No, no, no, don't let them in to me! You stay with them, Anne-Marie.

ANNE-MARIE: Of course, ma'am. [*Closes the door.*]

NORA: [*Pale with terror*]. Hurt my children—! Poison my home? [*A moment's pause; then she tosses her head.*] That's not true. Never. Never in all the world.

ACT II

Same room. Beside the piano the Christmas tree now stands stripped of orna-ment, burned-down candle stubs on its ragged branches. NORA's *street clothes lie on the sofa.* NORA, *alone in the room, moves restlessly about; at last she stops at the sofa and picks up her coat.*

NORA: [*Dropping the coat again.*] Someone's coming! [*Goes toward the door, listens.*] No—there's no one. Of course—nobody's coming today, Christmas Day—or tomorrow, either. But maybe—[*Opens the door and looks out.*] No, nothing in the mailbox. Quite empty. [*Coming forward.*] What nonsense! He won't do anything serious. Nothing terrible could happen. It's impossible. Why, I have three small children.

[ANNE-MARIE, *with a large carton, comes in from the room to the left.*]

ANNE-MARIE: Well, at last I found the box with the masquerade clothes.

NORA: Thanks. Put it on the table.

ANNE-MARIE: [*Does so.*] But they're all pretty much of a mess.

NORA: Ahh! I'd love to rip them in a million pieces!

ANNE-MARIE: Oh, mercy, they can be fixed right up. Just a little patience.

NORA: Yes, I'll go get Mrs. Linde to help me.

ANNE-MARIE: Out again now? In this nasty weather? Miss Nora will catch cold— get sick.

NORA: Oh, worse things could happen—How are the children?

ANNE-MARIE: The poor mites are playing with their Christmas presents, but—

NORA: Do they ask for me much?

ANNE-MARIE: They're so used to having Mama around, you know.

NORA: Yes, but Anne-Marie, I *can't* be together with them as much as I was.

ANNE-MARIE: Well, small children get used to anything.

NORA: You think so? Do you think they'd forget their mother if she was gone for good?

ANNE-MARIE: Oh, mercy—gone for good!

NORA: Wait, tell me, Anne-Marie—I've wondered so often—how could you ever have the heart to give your child over to strangers?

ANNE-MARIE: But I had to, you know, to become little Nora's nurse.

NORA: Yes, but how could you *do* it?

ANNE-MARIE: When I could get such a good place? A girl who's poor and who's gotten in trouble is glad enough for that. Because that slippery fish, he didn't do a thing for me, you know.

NORA: But your daughter's surely forgotten you.

ANNE-MARIE: Oh, she certainly has not. She's written to me, both when she was confirmed and when she was married.

NORA: [Clasping her about the neck.] You old Anne-Marie, you were a good mother for me when I was little.

ANNE-MARIE: Poor little Nora, with no other mother but me.

NORA: And if the babies didn't have one, then I know that you'd—What silly talk! [Opening the carton.] Go in to them. Now I'll have to—Tomorrow you can see how lovely I'll look.

ANNE-MARIE: Oh, there won't be anyone at the party as lovely as Miss Nora. [She goes off into the room, left.]

NORA: [Begins unpacking the box, but soon throws it aside.] Oh, if I dared to go out. If only nobody would come. If only nothing would happen here while I'm out. What craziness—nobody's coming. Just don't think. This muff—needs a brushing. Beautiful gloves, beautiful gloves. Let it go. Let it go! One, two, three, four, five, six—[With a cry.] Oh, there they are! [Poises to move toward the door, but remains irresolutely standing. MRS. LINDE enters from the hall, where she has removed her street clothes.]

NORA: Oh, it's you, Kristine. There's no one else out there? How good that you've come.

MRS. LINDE: I hear you were up asking for me.

NORA: Yes, I just stopped by. There's something you really can help me with. Let's get settled on the sofa. Look, there's going to be a costume party tomorrow evening at the Stenborgs' right above us, and now Torvald wants me to go as a Neapolitan peasant girl and dance the tarantella[2] that I learned in Capri.

MRS. LINDE: Really, are you giving a whole performance?

NORA: Torvald says yes, I should. See, here's the dress. Torvald had it made for me down there; but now it's all so tattered that I just don't know—

MRS. LINDE: Oh, we'll fix that up in no time. It's nothing more than the trimmings—they're a bit loose here and there. Needle and thread? Good, now we have what we need.

NORA: Oh, how sweet of you!

MRS. LINDE: [Sewing.] So you'll be in disguise tomorrow, Nora. You know what? I'll stop by then for a moment and have a look at you all dressed up. But listen, I've absolutely forgotten to thank you for that pleasant evening yesterday.

NORA: [Getting up and walking about.] I don't think it was as pleasant as usual yesterday. You should have come to town a bit sooner, Kristine—Yes, Torvald really knows how to give a home elegance and charm.

MRS. LINDE: And you do, too, if you ask me. You're not your father's daughter for nothing. But tell me, is Dr. Rank always so down in the mouth as yesterday?

2. Lively folk dance of southern Italy, thought to cure the bite of the tarantula.

NORA: No, that was quite an exception. But he goes around critically ill all the time—tuberculosis of the spine, poor man. You know, his father was a disgusting thing who kept mistresses and so on—and that's why the son's been sickly from birth.

MRS. LINDE: [*Lets her sewing fall to her lap.*] But my dearest Nora, how do you know about such things?

NORA: [*Walking more jauntily.*] Hmp! When you've had three children, then you've had a few visits from—from women who know something of medicine, and they tell you this and that.

MRS. LINDE: [*Resumes sewing; a short pause.*] Does Dr. Rank come here every day?

NORA: Every blessed day. He's Torvald's best friend from childhood, and *my* good friend, too. Dr. Rank almost belongs to this house.

MRS. LINDE: But tell me—is he quite sincere? I mean, doesn't he rather enjoy flattering people?

NORA: Just the opposite. Why do you think that?

MRS. LINDE: When you introduced us yesterday, he was proclaiming that he'd often heard my name in this house; but later I noticed that your husband hadn't the slightest idea who I really was. So how could Dr. Rank—?

NORA: But it's all true, Kristine. You see, Torvald loves me beyond words, and, as he puts it, he'd like to keep me all to himself. For a long time he'd almost be jealous if I even mentioned any of my old friends back home. So of course I dropped that. But with Dr. Rank I talk a lot about such things, because he likes hearing about them.

MRS. LINDE: Now listen, Nora; in many ways you're still like a child. I'm a good deal older than you, with a little more experience. I'll tell you something: you ought to put an end to all this with Dr. Rank.

NORA: What should I put an end to?

MRS. LINDE: Both parts of it, I think. Yesterday you said something about a rich admirer who'd provide you with money—

NORA: Yes, one who doesn't exist—worse luck. So?

MRS. LINDE: Is Dr. Rank well off?

NORA: Yes, he is.

MRS. LINDE: With no dependents?

NORA: No, no one. But—

MRS. LINDE: And he's over here every day?

NORA: Yes, I told you that.

MRS. LINDE: How can a man of such refinement be so grasping?

NORA: I don't follow you at all.

MRS. LINDE: Now don't try to hide it, Nora. You think I can't guess who loaned you the forty-eight hundred crowns?

NORA: Are you out of your mind? How could you think such a thing! A friend of ours, who comes here every single day. What an intolerable situation that would have been!

MRS. LINDE: Then it really wasn't him.

NORA: No, absolutely not. It never even crossed my mind for a moment—And he had nothing to lend in those days; his inheritance came later.

MRS. LINDE: Well, I think that was a stroke of luck for you, Nora dear.

NORA: No, it never would have occurred to me to ask Dr. Rank—Still, I'm quite sure that if I had asked him—

MRS. LINDE: Which you won't, of course.

NORA: No, of course not. I can't see that I'd ever need to. But I'm quite positive that if I talked to Dr. Rank—

MRS. LINDE: Behind your husband's back?

NORA: I've got to clear up this other thing; *that's* also behind his back. I've *got* to clear it all up.

MRS. LINDE: Yes, I was saying that yesterday, but—

NORA: [*Pacing up and down.*] A man handles these problems so much better than a woman—

MRS. LINDE: One's husband does, yes.

NORA: Nonsense. [*Stopping.*] When you pay everything you owe, then you get your note back, right?

MRS. LINDE: Yes, naturally.

NORA: And can rip it into a million pieces and burn it up—that filthy scrap of paper!

MRS. LINDE: [*Looking hard at her, laying her sewing aside, and rising slowly.*] Nora, you're hiding something from me.

NORA: You can see it in my face?

MRS. LINDE: Something's happened to you since yesterday morning. Nora, what is it?

NORA: [*Hurrying toward her.*] Kristine! [*Listening.*] Shh! Torvald's home. Look, go in with the children a while. Torvald can't bear all this snipping and stitching. Let Anne-Marie help you.

MRS. LINDE: [*Gathering up some of the things.*] All right, but I'm not leaving here until we've talked this out. [*She disappears into the room, left, as* TORVALD *enters from the hall.*]

NORA: Oh, how I've been waiting for you, Torvald dear.

HELMER: Was that the dressmaker?

NORA: No, that was Kristine. She's helping me fix up my costume. You know, it's going to be quite attractive.

HELMER: Yes, wasn't that a bright idea I had?

NORA: Brilliant! But then wasn't I good as well to give in to you?

HELMER: Good—because you give in to your husband's judgment? All right, you little goose, I know you didn't mean it like that. But I won't disturb you. You'll want to have a fitting, I suppose.

NORA: And you'll be working?

HELMER: Yes. [*Indicating a bundle of papers.*] See. I've been down to the bank. [*Starts toward his study.*]

NORA: Torvald.

HELMER: [*Stops.*] Yes.

NORA: If your little squirrel begged you, with all her heart and soul, for something—?

HELMER: What's that?

NORA: Then would you do it?

HELMER: First, naturally, I'd have to know what it was.

NORA: Your squirrel would scamper about and do tricks, if you'd only be sweet and give in.

HELMER: Out with it.

NORA: Your lark would be singing high and low in every room—

HELMER: Come on, she does that anyway.

NORA: I'd be a wood nymph and dance for you in the moonlight.

HELMER: Nora—don't tell me it's that same business from this morning?

NORA: [*Coming closer.*] Yes, Torvald, I beg you, please!

HELMER: And you actually have the nerve to drag that up again?

NORA: Yes, yes, you've got to give in to me; you *have* to let Krogstad keep his job in the bank.

HELMER: My dear Nora, I've slated his job for Mrs. Linde.

NORA: That's awfully kind of you. But you could just fire another clerk instead of Krogstad.

HELMER: This is the most incredible stubbornness! Because you go and give an impulsive promise to speak up for him, I'm expected to—

NORA: That's not the reason, Torvald. It's for your own sake. That man does writing for the worst papers; you said it yourself. He could do you any amount of harm. I'm scared to death of him—

HELMER: Ah, I understand. It's the old memories haunting you.

NORA: What do you mean by that?

HELMER: Of course, you're thinking about your father.

NORA: Yes, all right. Just remember how those nasty gossips wrote in the papers about Papa and slandered him so cruelly. I think they'd have had him dismissed if the department hadn't sent you up to investigate, and if you hadn't been so kind and open-minded toward him.

HELMER: My dear Nora, there's a notable difference between your father and me. Your father's official career was hardly above reproach. But mine is; and I hope it'll stay that way as long as I hold my position.

NORA: Oh, who can ever tell what vicious minds can invent? We could be so snug and happy now in our quiet, carefree home—you and I and the children, Torvald! That's why I'm pleading with you so—

HELMER: And just by pleading for him you make it impossible for me to keep him on. It's already known at the bank that I'm firing Krogstad. What if it's rumored around now that the new bank manager was vetoed by his wife—

NORA: Yes, what then—?

HELMER: Oh yes—as long as our little bundle of stubbornness gets her way—! I should go and make myself ridiculous in front of the whole office—give people the idea I can be swayed by all kinds of outside pressure. Oh, you can bet I'd feel the effects of that soon enough! Besides—there's something that rules Krogstad right out at the bank as long as I'm the manager.

NORA: What's that?

HELMER: His moral failings I could maybe overlook if I had to—

NORA: Yes, Torvald, why not?

HELMER: And I hear he's quite efficient on the job. But he was a crony of mine back in my teens—one of those rash friendships that crop up again and again to embarrass you later in life. Well, I might as well say it straight out: we're on a first-name basis. And that tactless fool makes no effort at all to hide it in front of others. Quite the contrary—he thinks that entitles him to take a familiar air around me, and so every other second he comes booming out with his "Yes, Torvald!" and "Sure thing, Torvald!" I tell you, it's been excruciating for me. He's out to make my place in the bank unbearable.

NORA: Torvald, you can't be serious about all this.

HELMER: Oh no? Why not?

NORA: Because these are such petty considerations.

HELMER: What are you saying? Petty? You think I'm petty!

NORA: No, just the opposite, Torvald dear. That's exactly why—

HELMER: Never mind. You call my motives petty; then I might as well be just that. Petty! All right! We'll put a stop to this for good. [*Goes to the hall door and calls.*] Helene!

NORA: What do you want?

HELMER: [*Searching among his papers.*] A decision. [*The* MAID *comes in.*] Look here; take this letter; go out with it at once. Get hold of a messenger and have him deliver it. Quick now. It's already addressed. Wait, here's some money.

MAID: Yes, sir. [*She leaves with the letter.*]

HELMER: [*Straightening his papers.*] There, now, little Miss Willful.

NORA: [*Breathlessly.*] Torvald, what was that letter?

HELMER: Krogstad's notice.

NORA: Call it back, Torvald! There's still time. Oh, Torvald, call it back! Do it for my sake—for your sake, for the children's sake! Do you hear, Torvald; do it! You don't know how this can harm us.

HELMER: Too late.

NORA: Yes, too late.

HELMER: Nora dear, I can forgive you this panic, even though basically you're insulting me. Yes, you are! Or isn't it an insult to think that *I* should be afraid of a courtroom hack's revenge? But I forgive you anyway, because this shows so beautifully how much you love me. [*Takes her in his arms.*] This is the way it should be, my darling Nora. Whatever comes, you'll see: when it really counts, I have strength and courage enough as a man to take on the whole weight myself.

NORA: [*Terrified.*] What do you mean by that?

HELMER: The whole weight, I said.

NORA: [*Resolutely.*] No, never in all the world.

HELMER: Good. So we'll share it, Nora, as man and wife. That's as it should be. [*Fondling her.*] Are you happy now? There, there, there—not these frightened dove's eyes. It's nothing at all but empty fantasies—Now you should run through your tarantella and practice your tambourine. I'll go to the inner office and shut both doors, so I won't hear a thing; you can make all the noise you like. [*Turning in the doorway.*] And when Rank comes, just tell him where he can find me. [*He nods to her and goes with his papers into the study, closing the door.*]

NORA: [*Standing as though rooted, dazed with fright, in a whisper.*] He really could do it. He will do it. He'll do it in spite of everything. No, not that, never, never! Anything but that! Escape! A way out—[*The doorbell rings.*] Dr. Rank! Anything but that! *Anything*, whatever it is! [*Her hands pass over her face, smoothing it; she pulls herself together, goes over and opens the hall door.* DR. RANK *stands outside, hanging his fur coat up. During the following scene, it begins getting dark.*]

NORA: Hello, Dr. Rank. I recognized your ring. But you mustn't go in to Torvald yet; I believe he's working.

RANK: And you?

NORA: For you, I always have an hour to spare—you know that. [*He has entered, and she shuts the door after him.*]

RANK: Many thanks. I'll make use of these hours while I can.

NORA: What do you mean by that? While you can?

RANK: Does that disturb you?

NORA: Well, it's such an odd phrase. Is anything going to happen?

RANK: What's going to happen is what I've been expecting so long—but I honestly didn't think it would come so soon.

NORA: [*Gripping his arm.*] What is it you've found out? Dr. Rank, you have to tell me!

RANK: [*Sitting by the stove.*] It's all over with me. There's nothing to be done about it.

NORA: [*Breathing easier.*] Is it you—then—?

RANK: Who else? There's no point in lying to one's self. I'm the most miserable of all my patients, Mrs. Helmer. These past few days I've been auditing my internal accounts. Bankrupt! Within a month I'll probably be laid out and rotting in the churchyard.

NORA: Oh, what a horrible thing to say.

RANK: The thing itself is horrible. But the worst of it is all the other horror before it's over. There's only one final examination left; when I'm finished with that, I'll know about when my disintegration will begin. There's something I want to say. Helmer with his sensitivity has such a sharp distaste for anything ugly. I don't want him near my sickroom.

NORA: Oh, but Dr. Rank—

RANK: I won't have him in there. Under no condition. I'll lock my door to him—As soon as I'm completely sure of the worst, I'll send you my calling card marked with a black cross, and you'll know then the wreck has started to come apart.

NORA: No, today you're completely unreasonable. And I wanted you so much to be in a really good humor.

RANK: With death up my sleeve? And then to suffer this way for somebody else's sins. Is there any justice in that? And in every single family, in some way or another, this inevitable retribution of nature goes on—

NORA: [*Her hands pressed over her ears.*] Oh, stuff! Cheer up! Please—be gay!

RANK: Yes, I'd just as soon laugh at it all. My poor, innocent spine, serving time for my father's gay army days.

NORA: [*By the table, left.*] He was so infatuated with asparagus tips and *pâté de foie gras*, wasn't that it?

RANK: Yes—and with truffles.

NORA: Truffles, yes. And then with oysters, I suppose?

RANK: Yes, tons of oysters, naturally.

NORA: And then the port and champagne to go with it. It's so sad that all these delectable things have to strike at our bones.

RANK: Especially when they strike at the unhappy bones that never shared in the fun.

NORA: Ah, that's the saddest of all.

RANK: [*Looks searchingly at her.*] Hm.

NORA: [*After a moment.*] Why did you smile?

RANK: No, it was you who laughed.

NORA: No, it was you who smiled, Dr. Rank!

RANK: [*Getting up.*] You're even a bigger tease than I'd thought.

NORA: I'm full of wild ideas today.

RANK: That's obvious.

NORA: [*Putting both hands on his shoulders.*] Dear, dear Dr. Rank, you'll never die for Torvald and me.

RANK: Oh, that loss you'll easily get over. Those who go away are soon forgotten.

NORA: [*Looks fearfully at him.*] You believe that?

RANK: One makes new connections, and then—

NORA: Who makes new connections?

RANK: Both you and Torvald will when I'm gone. I'd say you're well under way already. What was that Mrs. Linde doing here last evening?

NORA: Oh, come—you can't be jealous of poor Kristine?

RANK: Oh yes, I am. She'll be my successor here in the house. When I'm down under, that woman will probably—

NORA: Shh! Not so loud. She's right in there.

RANK: Today as well. So you see.

NORA: Only to sew on my dress. Good gracious, how unreasonable you are. [*Sitting on the sofa.*] Be nice now, Dr. Rank. Tomorrow you'll see how beautifully I'll dance; and you can imagine then that I'm dancing only for you—yes, and of course for Torvald, too—that's understood. [*Takes various items out of the carton.*] Dr. Rank, sit over here and I'll show you something.

RANK: [*Sitting.*] What's that?

NORA: Look here. Look.

RANK: Silk stockings.

NORA: Flesh-colored. Aren't they lovely? Now it's so dark here, but tomorrow—No, no, no, just look at the feet. Oh well, you might as well look at the rest.

RANK: Hm—

NORA: Why do you look so critical? Don't you believe they'll fit?

RANK: I've never had any chance to form an opinion on that.

NORA: [*Glancing at him a moment.*] Shame on you. [*Hits him lightly on the ear with the stockings.*] That's for you. [*Puts them away again.*]

RANK: And what other splendors am I going to see now?

NORA: Not the least bit more, because you've been naughty. [*She hums a little and rummages among her things.*]

RANK: [*After a short silence.*] When I sit here together with you like this, completely easy and open, then I don't know—I simply can't imagine—whatever would have become of me if I'd never come into this house.

NORA: [*Smiling.*] Yes, I really think you feel completely at ease with us.

RANK: [*More quietly, staring straight ahead.*] And then to have to go away from it all—

NORA: Nonsense, you're not going away.

RANK: [*His voice unchanged.*]—and not even be able to leave some poor show of gratitude behind, scarcely a fleeting regret—no more than a vacant place that anyone can fill.

NORA: And if I asked you now for—? No—

RANK: For what?

NORA: For a great proof of your friendship—

RANK: Yes, yes?

NORA: No, I mean—for an exceptionally big favor—

RANK: Would you really, for once, make me so happy?

NORA: Oh, you haven't the vaguest idea what it is.

RANK: All right, then tell me.

NORA: No, but I can't, Dr. Rank—it's all out of reason. It's advice and help, too—and a favor—

RANK: So much the better. I can't fathom what you're hinting at. Just speak out. Don't you trust me?

NORA: Of course. More than anyone else. You're my best and truest friend, I'm sure. That's why I want to talk to you. All right, then, Dr. Rank: there's something you can help me prevent. You know how deeply, how inexpressibly dearly Torvald loves me; he'd never hesitate a second to give up his life for me.

RANK: [*Leaning close to her.*] Nora—do you think he's the only one—

NORA: [*With a slight start.*] Who—?

RANK: Who'd gladly give up his life for you.

NORA: [*Heavily.*] I see.

RANK: I swore to myself you should know this before I'm gone. I'll never find a better chance. Yes, Nora, now you know. And also you know now that you can trust me beyond anyone else.

NORA: [*Rising, natural and calm.*] Let me by.

RANK: [*Making room for her, but still sitting.*] Nora—

NORA: [*In the hall doorway.*] Helene, bring the lamp in. [*Goes over to the stove.*] Ah, dear Dr. Rank, that was really mean of you.

RANK: [*Getting up.*] That I've loved you just as deeply as somebody else? Was *that* mean?

NORA: No, but that you came out and told me. That was quite unnecessary—

RANK: What do you mean? Have you known—?

[*The* MAID *comes in with the lamp, sets it on the table, and goes out again.*]

RANK: Nora—Mrs. Helmer—I'm asking you: have you known about it?

NORA: Oh, how can I tell what I know or don't know? Really, I don't know what to say—Why did you have to be so clumsy, Dr. Rank! Everything was so good.

RANK: Well, in any case, you now have the knowledge that my body and soul are at your command. So won't you speak out?

NORA: [*Looking at him.*] After that?

RANK: Please, just let me know what it is.

NORA: You can't know anything now.

RANK: I have to. You mustn't punish me like this. Give me the chance to do whatever is humanly possible for you.

NORA: Now there's nothing you can do for me. Besides, actually, I don't need any help. You'll see—it's only my fantasies. That's what it is. Of course! [*Sits in the rocker, looks at him, and smiles.*] What a nice one you are, Dr. Rank. Aren't you a little bit ashamed, now that the lamp is here?

RANK: No, not exactly. But perhaps I'd better go—for good?

NORA: No, you certainly can't do that. You must come here just as you always have. You know Torvald can't do without you.

RANK: Yes, but *you?*

NORA: You know how much I enjoy it when you're here.

RANK: That's precisely what threw me off. You're a mystery to me. So many times I've felt you'd almost rather be with me than with Helmer.

NORA: Yes—you see, there are some people that one loves most and other people that one would almost prefer being with.

RANK: Yes, there's something to that.

NORA: When I was back home, of course I loved Papa most. But I always thought it was so much fun when I could sneak down to the maids' quarters, because they never tried to improve me, and it was always so amusing, the way they talked to each other.

RANK: Aha, so it's *their* place that I've filled.

NORA: [*Jumping up and going to him.*] Oh, dear, sweet Dr. Rank, that's not what I meant at all. But you can understand that with Torvald it's just the same as with Papa—

[*The* MAID *enters from the hall.*]

MAID: Ma'am—please! [*She whispers to* NORA *and hands her a calling card.*]

NORA: [*Glancing at the card.*] Ah! [*Slips it into her pocket.*]

RANK: Anything wrong?

NORA: No, no, not at all. It's only some—it's my new dress—

RANK: Really? But—there's your dress.

NORA: Oh, that. But this is another one—I ordered it—Torvald mustn't know—

RANK: Ah, now we have the big secret.

NORA: That's right. Just go in with him—he's back in the inner study. Keep him there as long as—

RANK: Don't worry. He won't get away. [*Goes into the study.*]

NORA: [*To the* MAID.] And he's standing waiting in the kitchen?

MAID: Yes, he came up by the back stairs.

NORA: But didn't you tell him somebody was here?

MAID: Yes, but that didn't do any good.

NORA: He won't leave?

MAID: No, he won't go till he's talked with you, ma'am.

NORA: Let him come in, then—but quietly. Helene, don't breathe a word about this. It's a surprise for my husband.

MAID: Yes, yes, I understand—[*Goes out.*]

NORA: This horror—it's going to happen. No, no, no, it can't happen, it mustn't.

[*She goes and bolts* HELMER'S *door. The* MAID *opens the hall door for* KROGSTAD *and shuts it behind him. He is dressed for travel in a fur coat, boots, and a fur cap.*]

NORA: [*Going toward him.*] Talk softly. My husband's home.

KROGSTAD: Well, good for him.

NORA: What do you want?

KROGSTAD: Some information.

NORA: Hurry up, then. What is it?

KROGSTAD: You know, of course, that I got my notice.

NORA: I couldn't prevent it, Mr. Krogstad. I fought for you to the bitter end, but nothing worked.

KROGSTAD: Does your husband's love for you run so thin? He knows everything I can expose you to, and all the same he dares to—

NORA: How can you imagine he knows anything about this?

KROGSTAD: Ah, no—I can't imagine it either, now. It's not at all like my fine Torvald Helmer to have so much guts—

NORA: Mr. Krogstad, I demand respect for my husband!

KROGSTAD: Why, of course—all due respect. But since the lady's keeping it so carefully hidden, may I presume to ask if you're also a bit better informed than yesterday about what you've actually done?

NORA: More than you ever could teach me.

KROGSTAD: Yes, I *am* such an awful lawyer.

NORA: What is it you want from me?

KROGSTAD: Just a glimpse of how you are, Mrs. Helmer. I've been thinking about you all day long. A cashier, a night-court scribbler, a—well, a type like me also has a little of what they call a heart, you know.

NORA: Then show it. Think of my children.

KROGSTAD: Did you or your husband ever think of mine? But never mind. I simply wanted to tell you that you don't need to take this thing too seriously. For the present, I'm not proceeding with any action.

NORA: Oh no, really! Well—I knew that.

KROGSTAD: Everything can be settled in a friendly spirit. It doesn't have to get around town at all; it can stay just among us three.

NORA: My husband must never know anything of this.

KROGSTAD: How can you manage that? Perhaps you can pay me the balance?

NORA: No, not right now.

KROGSTAD: Or you know some way of raising the money in a day or two?

NORA: No way that I'm willing to use.

KROGSTAD: Well, it wouldn't have done you any good, anyway. If you stood in front of me with a fistful of bills, you still couldn't buy your signature back.

NORA: Then tell me what you're going to do with it.

KROGSTAD: I'll just hold onto it—keep it on file. There's no outsider who'll even get wind of it. So if you've been thinking of taking some desperate step—

NORA: I have.

KROGSTAD: Been thinking of running away from home—

NORA: I have!

KROGSTAD: Or even of something worse—

NORA: How could you guess that?

KROGSTAD: You can drop those thoughts.

NORA: How could you guess I was thinking of *that*?

KROGSTAD: Most of us think about *that* at first. I thought about it too, but I discovered I hadn't the courage—

NORA: [*Lifelessly.*] I don't either.

KROGSTAD: [*Relieved.*] That's true, you haven't the courage? You too?

NORA: I don't have it—I don't have it.

KROGSTAD: It would be terribly stupid, anyway. After that first storm at home blows out, why, then—I have here in my pocket a letter for your husband—

NORA: Telling everything?

KROGSTAD: As charitably as possible.

NORA: [*Quickly.*] He mustn't ever get that letter. Tear it up. I'll find some way to get money.

KROGSTAD: Beg pardon, Mrs. Helmer, but I think I just told you—

NORA: Oh, I don't mean the money I owe you. Let me know how much you want from my husband, and I'll manage it.

KROGSTAD: I don't want any money from your husband.

NORA: What do you want, then?

KROGSTAD: I'll tell you what. I want to recoup, Mrs. Helmer; I want to get on in the world—and there's where your husband can help me. For a year and a half I've kept myself clean of anything disreputable—all that time struggling with the worst conditions; but I was satisfied, working my way up step by step. Now I've been written right off, and I'm just not in the mood to come crawling back. I tell you, I want to move on. I want to get back in the bank—in a better position. Your husband can set up a job for me—

NORA: He'll never do that!

KROGSTAD: He'll do it. I know him. He won't dare breathe a word of protest. And once I'm in there together with him, you just wait and see! Inside of a year, I'll be the manager's right-hand man. It'll be Nils Krogstad, not Torvald Helmer, who runs the bank.

NORA: You'll never see the day!

KROGSTAD: Maybe you think you can—

NORA: I have the courage now—for *that*.

KROGSTAD: Oh, you don't scare me. A smart, spoiled lady like you—

NORA: You'll see; you'll see!

KROGSTAD: Under the ice, maybe? Down in the freezing, coal-black water? There, till you float up in the spring, ugly, unrecognizable, with your hair falling out—

NORA: You don't frighten me.

KROGSTAD: Nor do you frighten me. One doesn't do these things, Mrs. Helmer. Besides, what good would it be? I'd still have him safe in my pocket.

NORA: Afterwards? When I'm no longer—?

KROGSTAD: Are you forgetting that *I'll* be in control then over your final reputation? [NORA *stands speechless, staring at him.*] Good; now I've warned you. Don't do anything stupid. When Helmer's read my letter, I'll be waiting for his reply. And bear in mind that it's your husband himself who's forced me back to my old ways. I'll never forgive him for that. Good-bye, Mrs. Helmer. [*He goes out through the hall.*]

NORA: [*Goes to the hall door, opens it a crack, and listens.*] He's gone. Didn't leave the letter. Oh no, no, that's impossible too! [*Opening the door more and more.*] What's that? He's standing outside—not going downstairs. He's thinking it over? Maybe he'll—? [*A letter falls in the mailbox; then* KROGSTAD's *footsteps are heard, dying away down a flight of stairs.* NORA *gives a muffled cry and runs over toward the sofa table. A short pause.*] In the mailbox. [*Slips warily over to the hall door.*] It's lying there. Torvald, Torvald—now we're lost!

MRS. LINDE: [*Entering with the costume from the room, left.*] There now, I can't see anything else to mend. Perhaps you'd like to try—

NORA: [*In a hoarse whisper.*] Kristine, come here.

MRS. LINDE: [*Tossing the dress on the sofa.*] What's wrong? You look upset.

NORA: Come here. See that letter? *There!* Look—through the glass in the mailbox.

MRS. LINDE: Yes, yes, I see it.

NORA: That letter's from Krogstad—

MRS. LINDE: Nora—it's Krogstad who loaned you the money!

NORA: Yes, and now Torvald will find out everything.

MRS. LINDE: Believe me, Nora, it's best for both of you.

NORA: There's more you don't know. I forged a name.

MRS. LINDE: But for heaven's sake—?

NORA: I only want to tell you that, Kristine, so that you can be my witness.

MRS. LINDE: Witness? Why should I—?

NORA: If I should go out of my mind—it could easily happen—

MRS. LINDE: Nora!

NORA: Or anything else occurred—so I couldn't be present here—

MRS. LINDE: Nora, Nora, you aren't yourself at all!

NORA: And someone should try to take on the whole weight, all of the guilt, you follow me—

MRS. LINDE: Yes, of course, but why do you think—?

NORA: Then you're the witness that it isn't true, Kristine. I'm very much myself; my mind right now is perfectly clear; and I'm telling you: nobody else has known about this; I alone did everything. Remember that.

MRS. LINDE: I will. But I don't understand all this.

NORA: Oh, how could you ever understand it? It's the miracle now that's going to take place.

MRS. LINDE: The miracle?

NORA: Yes, the miracle. But it's so awful, Kristine. It mustn't take place, not for anything in the world.

MRS. LINDE: I'm going right over and talk with Krogstad.

NORA: Don't go near him; he'll do you some terrible harm!

MRS. LINDE: There was a time once when he'd gladly have done anything for me.

NORA: He?

MRS. LINDE: Where does he live?

NORA: Oh, how do I know? Yes. [*Searches in her pocket.*] Here's his card. But the letter, the letter—!

HELMER: [*From the study, knocking on the door.*] Nora!

NORA: [*With a cry of fear.*] Oh! What is it? What do you want?

HELMER: Now, now, don't be so frightened. We're not coming in. You locked the door—are you trying on the dress?

NORA: Yes, I'm trying it. I'll look just beautiful, Torvald.

MRS. LINDE: [*Who has read the card.*] He's living right around the corner.

NORA: Yes, but what's the use? We're lost. The letter's in the box.

MRS. LINDE: And your husband has the key?

NORA: Yes, always.

MRS. LINDE: Krogstad can ask for his letter back unread; he can find some excuse—

NORA: But it's just this time that Torvald usually—

MRS. LINDE: Stall him. Keep him in there. I'll be back as quick as I can. [*She hurries out through the hall entrance.*]

NORA: [*Goes to* HELMER's *door, opens it, and peers in.*] Torvald!

HELMER: [*From the inner study.*] Well—does one dare set foot in one's own living room at last? Come on, Rank, now we'll get a look—[*In the doorway.*] But what's this?

NORA: What, Torvald dear?

HELMER: Rank had me expecting some grand masquerade.

RANK: [*In the doorway.*] That was my impression, but I must have been wrong.

NORA: No one can admire me in my splendor—not till tomorrow.

HELMER: But Nora dear, you look so exhausted. Have you practiced too hard?

NORA: No, I haven't practiced at all yet.

HELMER: You know, it's necessary—

NORA: Oh, it's absolutely necessary, Torvald. But I can't get anywhere without your help. I've forgotten the whole thing completely.

HELMER: Ah, we'll soon take care of that.

NORA: Yes, take care of me, Torvald, please! Promise me that? Oh, I'm so nervous. That big party—You must give up everything this evening for me. No business—don't even touch your pen. Yes? Dear Torvald, promise?

HELMER: It's a promise. Tonight I'm totally at your service—you little helpless thing. Hm—but first there's one thing I want to—[*Goes toward the hall door.*]

NORA: What are you looking for?

HELMER: Just to see if there's any mail.

NORA: No, no, don't do that, Torvald!

HELMER: Now what?

NORA: Torvald, please. There isn't any.

HELMER: Let me look, though. [*Starts out.* NORA, *at the piano, strikes the first notes of the tarantella.* HELMER, *at the door, stops.*] Aha!

NORA: I can't dance tomorrow if I don't practice with you.

HELMER: [*Going over to her.*] Nora dear, are you really so frightened?

NORA: Yes, so terribly frightened. Let me practice right now; there's still time before dinner. Oh, sit down and play for me, Torvald. Direct me. Teach me, the way you always have.

HELMER: Gladly, if it's what you want. [*Sits at the piano.*]

NORA: [*Snatches the tambourine up from the box, then a long, varicolored shawl, which she throws around herself, whereupon she springs forward and cries out:*] Play for me now! Now I'll dance!

[HELMER *plays and* NORA *dances.* RANK *stands behind* HELMER *at the piano and looks on.*]

HELMER: [*As he plays.*] Slower. Slow down.

NORA: Can't change it.

HELMER: Not so violent, Nora!

NORA: Has to be just like this.

HELMER: [*Stopping.*] No, no, that won't do at all.

NORA: [*Laughing and swinging her tambourine.*] Isn't that what I told you?

RANK: Let me play for her.

HELMER: [*Getting up.*] Yes, go on. I can teach her more easily then.

[RANK *sits at the piano and plays;* NORA *dances more and more wildly.* HELMER *has stationed himself by the stove and repeatedly gives her directions; she seems not to hear them; her hair loosens and falls over her shoulders; she does not notice, but goes on dancing.* MRS. LINDE *enters.*]

MRS. LINDE: [*Standing dumbfounded at the door.*] Ah—!

NORA: [*Still dancing.*] See what fun, Kristine!

HELMER: But Nora darling, you dance as if your life were at stake.

NORA: And it is.

HELMER: Rank, stop! This is pure madness. Stop it, I say!

[RANK *breaks off playing, and* NORA *halts abruptly.*]

HELMER: [*Going over to her.*] I never would have believed it. You've forgotten everything I taught you.

NORA: [*Throwing away the tambourine.*] You see for yourself.

HELMER: Well, there's certainly room for instruction here.

NORA: Yes, you see how important it is. You've got to teach me to the very last minute. Promise me that, Torvald?

HELMER: You can bet on it.

NORA: You mustn't, either today or tomorrow, think about anything else but me; you mustn't open any letters—or the mailbox—

HELMER: Ah, it's still the fear of that man—

NORA: Oh yes, yes, that too.

HELMER: Nora, it's written all over you—there's already a letter from him out there.

NORA: I don't know. I guess so. But you mustn't read such things now; there mustn't be anything ugly between us before it's all over.

RANK: [*Quietly to* HELMER.] You shouldn't deny her.

HELMER: [*Putting his arm around her.*] The child can have her way. But tomorrow night, after you've danced—

NORA: Then you'll be free.

MAID: [*In the doorway, right.*] Ma'am, dinner is served.

NORA: We'll be wanting champagne, Helene.

MAID: Very good, ma'am. [*Goes out.*]

HELMER: So—a regular banquet, hm?

NORA: Yes, a banquet—champagne till daybreak! [*Calling out.*] And some maca-roons, Helene. Heaps of them—just this once.

HELMER: [*Taking her hands.*] Now, now, now—no hysterics. Be my own little lark again.

NORA: Oh, I will soon enough. But go on in—and you, Dr. Rank. Kristine, help me put up my hair.

RANK: [*Whispering, as they go.*] There's nothing wrong—really wrong, is there?

HELMER: Oh, of course not. It's nothing more than this childish anxiety I was telling you about. [*They go out, right.*]

NORA: Well?

MRS. LINDE: Left town.

NORA: I could see by your face.

MRS. LINDE: He'll be home tomorrow evening. I wrote him a note.

NORA: You shouldn't have. Don't try to stop anything now. After all, it's a wonderful joy, this waiting here for the miracle.

MRS. LINDE: What is it you're waiting for?

NORA: Oh, you can't understand that. Go in to them; I'll be along in a moment.

[MRS. LINDE *goes into the dining room.* NORA *stands a short while as if composing herself; then she looks at her watch.*]

NORA: Five. Seven hours to midnight. Twenty-four hours to the midnight after, and then the tarantella's done. Seven and twenty-four? Thirty-one hours to live.

HELMER: [*In the doorway, right.*] What's become of the little lark?

NORA: [*Going toward him with open arms.*] Here's your lark!

ACT III

Same scene. The table, with chairs around it, has been moved to the center of the room. A lamp on the table is lit. The hall door stands open. Dance music drifts down from the floor above. MRS. LINDE *sits at the table, absently paging through a book, trying to read, but apparently unable to focus her thoughts. Once or twice she pauses, tensely listening for a sound at the outer entrance.*

MRS. LINDE: [*Glancing at her watch.*] Not yet—and there's hardly any time left. If only he's not—[*Listening again.*] Ah, there he is. [*She goes out in the hall and cautiously opens the outer door. Quiet footsteps are heard on the stairs. She whispers:*] Come in. Nobody's here.

KROGSTAD: [*In the doorway.*] I found a note from you at home. What's back of all this?

MRS. LINDE: I just *had* to talk to you.

KROGSTAD: Oh? And it just *had* to be here in this house?

MRS. LINDE: At my place it was impossible; my room hasn't a private entrance. Come in; we're all alone. The maid's asleep, and the Helmers are at the dance upstairs.

KROGSTAD: [*Entering the room.*] Well, well, the Helmers are dancing tonight? Really?

MRS. LINDE: Yes, why not?

KROGSTAD: How true—why not?

MRS. LINDE: All right, Krogstad, let's talk.

KROGSTAD: Do we two have anything more to talk about?

MRS. LINDE: We have a great deal to talk about.

KROGSTAD: I wouldn't have thought so.

MRS. LINDE: No, because you've never understood me, really.

KROGSTAD: Was there anything more to understand—except what's all too common in life? A calculating woman throws over a man the moment a better catch comes by.

MRS. LINDE: You think I'm so thoroughly calculating? You think I broke it off lightly?

KROGSTAD: Didn't you?

MRS. LINDE: Nils—is that what you really thought?

KROGSTAD: If you cared, then why did you write me the way you did?

MRS. LINDE: What else could I do? If I had to break off with you, then it was my job as well to root out everything you felt for me.

KROGSTAD: [*Wringing his hands.*] So that was it. And this—all this, simply for money!

MRS. LINDE: Don't forget I had a helpless mother and two small brothers. We couldn't wait for you, Nils; you had such a long road ahead of you then.

KROGSTAD: That may be; but you still hadn't the right to abandon me for somebody else's sake.

MRS. LINDE: Yes—I don't know. So many, many times I've asked myself if I did have that right.

KROGSTAD: [*More softly.*] When I lost you, it was as if all the solid ground dissolved from under my feet. Look at me; I'm a half-drowned man now, hanging onto a wreck.

MRS. LINDE: Help may be near.

KROGSTAD: It was near—but then you came and blocked it off.

MRS. LINDE: Without my knowing it, Nils. Today for the first time I learned that it's you I'm replacing at the bank.

KROGSTAD: All right—I believe you. But now that you know, will you step aside?

MRS. LINDE: No, because that wouldn't benefit you in the slightest.

KROGSTAD: Not "benefit" me, hm! I'd step aside anyway.

MRS. LINDE: I've learned to be realistic. Life and hard, bitter necessity have taught me that.

KROGSTAD: And life's taught me never to trust fine phrases.

MRS. LINDE: Then life's taught you a very sound thing. But you do have to trust in actions, don't you?

KROGSTAD: What does that mean?

MRS. LINDE: You said you were hanging on like a half-drowned man to a wreck.

KROGSTAD: I've good reason to say that.

MRS. LINDE: I'm also like a half-drowned woman on a wreck. No one to suffer with; no one to care for.

KROGSTAD: You made your choice.

MRS. LINDE: There wasn't any choice then.

KROGSTAD: So—what of it?

MRS. LINDE: Nils, if only we two shipwrecked people could reach across to each other.

KROGSTAD: What are you saying?

MRS. LINDE: Two on one wreck are at least better off than each on his own.

KROGSTAD: Kristine!

MRS. LINDE: Why do you think I came into town?

KROGSTAD: Did you really have some thought of me?

MRS. LINDE: I have to work to go on living. All my born days, as long as I can remember, I've worked, and it's been my best and my only joy. But now I'm completely alone in the world; it frightens me to be so empty and lost. To work for yourself—there's no joy in that. Nils, give me something—someone to work for.

KROGSTAD: I don't believe all this. It's just some hysterical feminine urge to go out and make a noble sacrifice.

MRS. LINDE: Have you ever found me to be hysterical?

KROGSTAD: Can you honestly mean this? Tell me—do you know everything about my past?

MRS. LINDE: Yes.

KROGSTAD: And you know what they think I'm worth around here.

MRS. LINDE: From what you were saying before, it would seem that with me you could have been another person.

KROGSTAD: I'm positive of that.

MRS. LINDE: Couldn't it happen still?

KROGSTAD: Kristine—you're saying this in all seriousness? Yes, you are! I can see it in you. And do you really have the courage, then—?

MRS. LINDE: I need to have someone to care for; and your children need a mother. We both need each other. Nils, I have faith that you're good at heart—I'll risk everything together with you.

KROGSTAD: [Gripping her hands.] Kristine, thank you, thank you—Now I know I can win back a place in their eyes. Yes—but I forgot—

MRS. LINDE: [Listening.] Shh! The tarantella. Go now! Go on!

KROGSTAD: Why? What is it?

MRS. LINDE: Hear the dance up there? When that's over, they'll be coming down.

KROGSTAD: Oh, then I'll go. But—it's all pointless. Of course, you don't know the move I made against the Helmers.

MRS. LINDE: Yes, Nils, I know.

KROGSTAD: And all the same, you have the courage to—?

MRS. LINDE: I know how far despair can drive a man like you.

KROGSTAD: Oh, if I only could take it all back.

MRS. LINDE: You easily could—your letter's still lying in the mailbox.

KROGSTAD: Are you sure of that?

MRS. LINDE: Positive. But—

KROGSTAD: [Looks at her searchingly.] Is that the meaning of it, then? You'll save your friend at any price. Tell me straight out. Is that it?

MRS. LINDE: Nils—anyone who's sold herself for somebody else once isn't going to do it again.

KROGSTAD: I'll demand my letter back.

MRS. LINDE: No, no.

KROGSTAD: Yes, of course. I'll stay here till Helmer comes down; I'll tell him to give me my letter again—that it only involves my dismissal—that he shouldn't read it—

MRS. LINDE: No, Nils, don't call the letter back.

KROGSTAD: But wasn't that exactly why you wrote me to come here?

MRS. LINDE: Yes, in that first panic. But it's been a whole day and night since then, and in that time I've seen such incredible things in this house. Helmer's got to learn everything; this dreadful secret has to be aired; those two have to come to a full understanding; all these lies and evasions can't go on.

KROGSTAD: Well, then, if you want to chance it. But at least there's one thing I can do, and do right away—

MRS. LINDE: [*Listening.*] Go now, go, quick! The dance is over. We're not safe another second.

KROGSTAD: I'll wait for you downstairs.

MRS. LINDE: Yes, please do; take me home.

KROGSTAD: I can't believe it; I've never been so happy. [*He leaves by way of the outer door; the door between the room and the hall stays open.*]

MRS. LINDE: [*Straightening up a bit and getting together her street clothes.*] How different now! How different! Someone to work for, to live for—a home to build. Well, it is worth the try! Oh, if they'd only come! [*Listening.*] Ah, there they are. Bundle up. [*She picks up her hat and coat.* NORA'S *and* HELMER'S *voices can be heard outside; a key turns in the lock, and* HELMER *brings* NORA *into the hall almost by force. She is wearing the Italian costume with a large black shawl about her; he has on evening dress, with a black domino*[3] *open over it.*]

NORA: [*Struggling in the doorway.*] No, no, no, not inside! I'm going up again. I don't want to leave so soon.

HELMER: But Nora dear—

NORA: Oh, I beg you, please, Torvald. From the bottom of my heart, *please*— only an hour more!

HELMER: Not a single minute, Nora darling. You know our agreement. Come on, in we go; you'll catch cold out here. [*In spite of her resistance, he gently draws her into the room.*]

MRS. LINDE: Good evening.

NORA: Kristine!

HELMER: Why, Mrs. Linde—are you here so late?

MRS. LINDE: Yes, I'm sorry, but I did want to see Nora in costume.

NORA: Have you been sitting here, waiting for me?

MRS. LINDE: Yes. I didn't come early enough; you were all upstairs; and then I thought I really couldn't leave without seeing you.

HELMER: [*Removing* NORA'S *shawl.*] Yes, take a good look. She's worth looking at, I can tell you that, Mrs. Linde. Isn't she lovely?

MRS. LINDE: Yes, I should say—

HELMER: A dream of loveliness, isn't she? That's what everyone thought at the party, too. But she's horribly stubborn—this sweet little thing. What's to be done with her? Can you imagine, I almost had to use force to pry her away.

NORA: Oh, Torvald, you're going to regret you didn't indulge me, even for just a half hour more.

HELMER: There, you see. She danced her tarantella and got a tumultuous hand— which was well earned, although the performance may have been a bit too naturalistic—I mean it rather overstepped the proprieties of art. But never

---

3. Hood worn by members of some religious orders.

mind—what's important is, she made a success, an overwhelming success. You think I could let her stay on after that and spoil the effect? Oh no; I took my lovely little Capri girl—my capricious little Capri girl, I should say—took her under my arm; one quick tour of the ballroom, a curtsy to every side, and then—as they say in novels—the beautiful vision disappeared. An exit should always be effective, Mrs. Linde, but that's what I can't get Nora to grasp. Phew, it's hot in here. [*Flings the domino on a chair and opens the door to his room.*] Why's it dark in here? Oh yes, of course. Excuse me. [*He goes in and lights a couple of candles.*]

NORA: [*In a sharp, breathless whisper.*] So?

MRS. LINDE: [*Quietly.*] I talked with him.

NORA: And—?

MRS. LINDE: Nora—you must tell your husband everything.

NORA: [*Dully.*] I knew it.

MRS. LINDE: You've got nothing to fear from Krogstad, but you have to speak out.

NORA: I won't tell.

MRS. LINDE: Then the letter will.

NORA: Thanks, Kristine. I know now what's to be done. Shh!

HELMER: [*Reentering.*] Well, then, Mrs. Linde—have you admired her?

MRS. LINDE: Yes, and now I'll say good night.

HELMER: Oh, come, so soon? Is this yours, this knitting?

MRS. LINDE: Yes, thanks. I nearly forgot it.

HELMER: Do you knit, then?

MRS. LINDE: Oh yes.

HELMER: You know what? You should embroider instead.

MRS. LINDE: Really? Why?

HELMER: Yes, because it's a lot prettier. See here, one holds the embroidery so, in the left hand, and then one guides the needle with the right—so—in an easy, sweeping curve—right?

MRS. LINDE: Yes, I guess that's—

HELMER: But, on the other hand, knitting—it can never be anything but ugly. Look, see here, the arms tucked in, the knitting needles going up and down—there's something Chinese about it. Ah, that was really a glorious champagne they served.

MRS. LINDE: Yes, good night, Nora, and don't be stubborn anymore.

HELMER: Well put, Mrs. Linde!

MRS. LINDE: Good night, Mr. Helmer.

HELMER: [*Accompanying her to the door.*] Good night, good night. I hope you get home all right. I'd be very happy to—but you don't have far to go. Good night, good night. [*She leaves. He shuts the door after her and returns.*] There, now, at last we got her out the door. She's a deadly bore, that creature.

NORA: Aren't you pretty tired, Torvald?

HELMER: No, not a bit.

NORA: You're not sleepy?

HELMER: Not at all. On the contrary, I'm feeling quite exhilarated. But you? Yes, you really look tired and sleepy.

NORA: Yes, I'm very tired. Soon now I'll sleep.

HELMER: See! You see! I was right all along that we shouldn't stay longer.

NORA: Whatever you do is always right.

HELMER: [*Kissing her brow.*] Now my little lark talks sense. Say, did you notice what a time Rank was having tonight?

NORA: Oh, was he? I didn't get to speak with him.

HELMER: I scarcely did either, but it's a long time since I've seen him in such high spirits. [*Gazes at her a moment, then comes nearer her.*] Hm—it's marvelous, though, to be back home again—to be completely alone with you. Oh, you bewitchingly lovely young woman!

NORA: Torvald, don't look at me like that!

HELMER: Can't I look at my richest treasure? At all that beauty that's mine, mine alone—completely and utterly.

NORA: [*Moving around to the other side of the table.*] You mustn't talk to me that way tonight.

HELMER: [*Following her.*] The tarantella is still in your blood, I can see—and it makes you even more enticing. Listen. The guests are beginning to go. [*Dropping his voice.*] Nora—it'll soon be quiet through this whole house.

NORA: Yes, I hope so.

HELMER: You do, don't you, my love? Do you realize—when I'm out at a party like this with you—do you know why I talk to you so little, and keep such a distance away; just send you a stolen look now and then—you know why I do it? It's because I'm imagining then that you're my secret darling, my secret young bride-to-be, and that no one suspects there's anything between us.

NORA: Yes, yes; oh, yes, I know you're always thinking of me.

HELMER: And then when we leave and I place the shawl over those fine young rounded shoulders—over that wonderful curving neck—then I pretend that you're my young bride, that we're just coming from the wedding, that for the first time I'm bringing you into my house—that for the first time I'm alone with you—completely alone with you, your trembling young beauty! All this evening I've longed for nothing but you. When I saw you turn and sway in the tarantella—my blood was pounding till I couldn't stand it—that's why I brought you down here so early—

NORA: Go away, Torvald! Leave me alone. I don't want all this.

HELMER: What do you mean? Nora, you're teasing me. You will, won't you? Aren't I your husband—?

[*A knock at the outside door.*]

NORA: [*Startled.*] What's that?

HELMER: [*Going toward the half.*] Who is it?

RANK: [*Outside.*] It's me. May I come in a moment?

HELMER: [*With quiet irritation.*] Oh, what does he want now? [*Aloud.*] Hold on. [*Goes and opens the door.*] Oh, how nice that you didn't just pass us by!

RANK: I thought I heard your voice, and then I wanted so badly to have a look in. [*Lightly glancing about.*] Ah, me, these old familiar haunts. You have it snug and cozy in here, you two.

HELMER: You seemed to be having it pretty cozy upstairs, too.

RANK: Absolutely. Why shouldn't I? Why not take in everything in life? As much as you can, anyway, and as long as you can. The wine was superb—

HELMER: The champagne especially.

RANK: You noticed that too? It's amazing how much I could guzzle down.

NORA: Torvald also drank a lot of champagne this evening.

RANK: Oh?

NORA: Yes, and that always makes him so entertaining.

RANK: Well, why shouldn't one have a pleasant evening after a well-spent day?

HELMER: Well spent? I'm afraid I can't claim that.

RANK: [*Slapping him on the back.*] But I can, you see!

NORA: Dr. Rank, you must have done some scientific research today.

RANK: Quite so.

HELMER: Come now—little Nora talking about scientific research!

NORA: And can I congratulate you on the results?

RANK: Indeed you may.

NORA: Then they were good?

RANK: The best possible for both doctor and patient—certainty.

NORA: [*Quickly and searchingly.*] Certainty?

RANK: Complete certainty. So don't I owe myself a gay evening afterwards?

NORA: Yes, you're right, Dr. Rank.

HELMER: I'm with you—just so long as you don't have to suffer for it in the morning.

RANK: Well, one never gets something for nothing in life.

NORA: Dr. Rank—are you very fond of masquerade parties?

RANK: Yes, if there's a good array of odd disguises—

NORA: Tell me, what should we two go as at the next masquerade?

HELMER: You little featherhead—already thinking of the next!

RANK: We two? I'll tell you what: you must go as Charmed Life—

HELMER: Yes, but find a costume for *that!*

RANK: Your wife can appear just as she looks every day.

HELMER: That was nicely put. But don't you know what you're going to be?

RANK: Yes, Helmer, I've made up my mind.

HELMER: Well?

RANK: At the next masquerade I'm going to be invisible.

HELMER: That's a funny idea.

RANK: They say there's a hat—black, huge—have you never heard of the hat that makes you invisible? You put it on, and then no one on earth can see you.

HELMER: [*Suppressing a smile.*] Ah, of course.

RANK: But I'm quite forgetting what I came for. Helmer, give me a cigar, one of the dark Havanas.

HELMER: With the greatest pleasure. [*Holds out his case.*]

RANK: Thanks. [*Takes one and cuts off the tip.*]

NORA: [*Striking a match*] Let me give you a light.

RANK: Thank you. [*She holds the match for him; he lights the cigar.*] And now good-bye.

HELMER: Good-bye, good-bye, old friend.

NORA: Sleep well, Doctor.

RANK: Thanks for that wish.

NORA: Wish me the same.

RANK: You? All right, if you like—Sleep well. And thanks for the light. [*He nods to them both and leaves.*]

HELMER: [*His voice subdued.*] He's been drinking heavily.

NORA: [*Absently.*] Could be. [HELMER *takes his keys from his pocket and goes out in the hall.*] Torvald—what are you after?

HELMER: Got to empty the mailbox; it's nearly full. There won't be room for the morning papers.

NORA: Are you working tonight?

HELMER: You know I'm not. Why—what's this? Someone's been at the lock.

NORA: At the lock—?

HELMER: Yes, I'm positive. What do you suppose—? I can't imagine one of the maids—? Here's a broken hairpin. Nora, it's yours—

NORA: [*Quickly.*] Then it must be the children—

HELMER: You'd better break them of that. Hm, hm—well, opened it after all. [*Takes the contents out and calls into the kitchen.*] Helene! Helene, would you put out the lamp in the hall. [*He returns to the room, shutting the hall door, then displays the handful of mail.*] Look how it's piled up. [*Sorting through them.*] Now what's this?

NORA: [*At the window.*] The letter! Oh, Torvald, no!

HELMER: Two calling cards—from Rank.

NORA: From Dr. Rank?

HELMER: [*Examining them.*] "Dr. Rank, Consulting Physician." They were on top. He must have dropped them in as he left.

NORA: Is there anything on them?

HELMER: There's a black cross over the name. See? That's a gruesome notion. He could almost be announcing his own death.

NORA: That's just what he's doing.

HELMER: What! You've heard something? Something he's told you?

NORA: Yes. That when those cards came, he'd be taking his leave of us. He'll shut himself in now and die.

HELMER: Ah, my poor friend! Of course I knew he wouldn't be here much longer. But so soon—And then to hide himself away like a wounded animal.

NORA: If it has to happen, then it's best it happens in silence—don't you think so, Torvald?

HELMER: [*Pacing up and down.*] He'd grown right into our lives. I simply can't imagine him gone. He with his suffering and loneliness—like a dark cloud setting off our sunlit happiness. Well, maybe it's best this way. For him, at least. [*Standing still.*] And maybe for us too, Nora. Now we're thrown back on each other, completely. [*Embracing her.*] Oh you, my darling wife, how can I hold you close enough? You know what, Nora—time and again I've wished you were in some terrible danger, just so I could stake my life and soul and everything, for your sake.

NORA: [*Tearing herself away, her voice firm and decisive.*] Now you must read your mail, Torvald.

HELMER: No, no, not tonight. I want to stay with you, dearest.

NORA: With a dying friend on your mind?

HELMER: You're right. We've both had a shock. There's ugliness between us— these thoughts of death and corruption. We'll have to get free of them first. Until then—we'll stay apart.

NORA: [*Clinging about his neck.*] Torvald—good night! Good night!

HELMER: [*Kissing her on the cheek.*] Good night, little songbird. Sleep well, Nora. I'll be reading my mail now. [*He takes the letters into his room and shuts the door after him.*]

NORA: [*With bewildered glances, groping about, seizing* HELMER'S *domino, throwing it around her, and speaking in short, hoarse, broken whispers.*] Never see him again. Never, never. [*Putting her shawl over her head.*] Never see the children either—them, too. Never, never. Oh, the freezing black water! The depths—down—Oh, I wish it were over—He has it now; he's reading it—now. Oh no, no, not yet. Torvald, good-bye, you and the children—[*She starts for the hall; as she does,* HELMER *throws open his door and stands with an open letter in his hand.*]

HELMER: Nora!

NORA: [*Screams.*] Oh—!

HELMER: What is this? You know what's in this letter?

NORA: Yes, I know. Let me go! Let me out!

HELMER: [*Holding her back.*] Where are you going?

NORA: [*Struggling to break loose.*] You can't save me, Torvald!

HELMER: [*Slumping back.*] True! Then it's true what he writes? How horrible! No, no, it's impossible—it can't be true.

NORA: It *is* true. I've loved you more than all this world.

HELMER: Ah, none of your slippery tricks.

NORA: [*Taking one step toward him.*] Torvald—!

HELMER: What *is* this you've blundered into!

NORA: Just let me loose. You're not going to suffer for my sake. You're not going to take on my guilt.

HELMER: No more playacting. [*Locks the hall door.*] You stay right here and give me a reckoning. You understand what you've done? Answer! You understand?

NORA: [*Looking squarely at him, her face hardening.*] Yes. I'm beginning to understand everything now.

HELMER: [*Striding about.*] Oh, what an awful awakening! In all these eight years—she who was my pride and joy—a hypocrite, a liar—worse, worse—a criminal! How infinitely disgusting it all is! The shame! [NORA *says nothing and goes on looking straight at him. He stops in front of her.*] I should have suspected something of the kind. I should have known. All your father's flimsy values—Be still! All your father's flimsy values have come out in you. No religion, no morals, no sense of duty—Oh, how I'm punished for letting him off! I did it for your sake, and you repay me like this.

NORA: Yes, like this.

HELMER: Now you've wrecked all my happiness—ruined my whole future. Oh, it's awful to think of. I'm in a cheap little grafter's hands; he can do anything he wants with me, ask for anything, play with me like a puppet—and I can't breathe a word. I'll be swept down miserably into the depths on account of a featherbrained woman.

NORA: When I'm gone from this world, you'll be free.

HELMER: Oh, quit posing. Your father had a mess of those speeches too. What good would that ever do me if you were gone from this world, as you say? Not the slightest. He can still make the whole thing known; and if he does, I could be falsely suspected as your accomplice. They might even think that I was behind it—that I put you up to it. And all that I can thank you for—you that I've coddled the whole of our marriage. Can you see now what you've done to me?

NORA: [*Icily calm.*] Yes.

HELMER: It's so incredible, I just can't grasp it. But we'll have to patch up whatever we can. Take off the shawl. I said, take it off! I've got to appease him somehow or other. The thing has to be hushed up at any cost. And as for you and me, it's got to seem like everything between us is just as it was—to the outside world, that is. You'll go right on living in this house, of course. But you can't be allowed to bring up the children; I don't dare trust you with them—Oh, to have to say this to someone I've loved so much, and that I still—! Well, that's done with. From now on happiness doesn't matter; all that matters is saving the bits and pieces, the appearance—[*The doorbell rings.* HELMER *starts.*] What's that? And so late. Maybe the worst—? You think he'd—? Hide, Nora! Say you're sick. [NORA *remains standing motionless.* HELMER *goes and opens the door.*]

MAID: [*Half dressed, in the hall.*] A letter for Mrs. Helmer.

HELMER: I'll take it. [*Snatches the letter and shuts the door.*] Yes, it's from him. You don't get it; I'm reading it myself.

NORA: Then read it.

HELMER: [*By the lamp.*] I hardly dare. We may be ruined, you and I. But—I've got to know. [*Rips open the letter, skims through a few lines, glances at an enclosure, then cries out joyfully.*] Nora! [NORA *looks inquiringly at him.*] Nora! Wait—better check it again—Yes, yes, it's true. I'm saved. Nora, I'm saved!

NORA: And I?

HELMER: You too, of course. We're both saved, both of us. Look. He's sent back your note. He says he's sorry and ashamed—that a happy development in his life—oh, who cares what he says! Nora, we're saved! No one can hurt you. Oh, Nora, Nora—but first, this ugliness all has to go. Let me see—[*Takes a look at the note.*] No, I don't want to see it; I want the whole thing to fade like a dream. [*Tears the note and both letters to pieces, throws them into the stove and watches them burn.*] There—now there's nothing left—He wrote that since Christmas Eve you—Oh, they must have been three terrible days for you, Nora.

NORA: I fought a hard fight.

HELMER: And suffered pain and saw no escape but—No, we're not going to dwell on anything unpleasant. We'll just be grateful and keep on repeating: it's over now, it's over! You hear me, Nora? You don't seem to realize—it's over. What's it mean—that frozen look? Oh, poor little Nora, I understand. You can't believe I've forgiven you. But I have, Nora; I swear I have. I know that what you did, you did out of love for me.

NORA: That's true.

HELMER: You loved me the way a wife ought to love her husband. It's simply the means that you couldn't judge. But you think I love you any the less for not knowing how to handle your affairs? No, no—just lean on me; I'll guide you and teach you. I wouldn't be a man if this feminine helplessness didn't make you twice as attractive to me. You mustn't mind those sharp words I said— that was all in the first confusion of thinking my world had collapsed. I've forgiven you, Nora; I swear I've forgiven you.

NORA: My thanks for your forgiveness. [*She goes out through the door, right.*]

HELMER: No, wait—[*Peers in.*] What are you doing in there?

NORA: [*Inside.*] Getting out of my costume.

HELMER: [*By the open door.*] Yes, do that. Try to calm yourself and collect your thoughts again, my frightened little songbird. You can rest easy now; I've got wide wings to shelter you with. [*Walking about close by the door.*] How snug and nice our home is, Nora. You're safe here; I'll keep you like a hunted dove I've rescued out of a hawk's claws. I'll bring peace to your poor, shuddering heart. Gradually it'll happen, Nora; you'll see. Tomorrow all this will look different to you; then everything will be as it was. I won't have to go on repeating I forgive you; you'll feel it for yourself. How can you imagine I'd ever conceivably want to disown you—or even blame you in any way? Ah, you don't know a man's heart, Nora. For a man there's something indescribably sweet and satisfying in knowing he's forgiven his wife—and forgiven her out of a full and open heart. It's as if she belongs to him in two ways now: in a sense he's given her fresh into the world again, and she's become his wife and his child as well. From now on that's what you'll be to me—you little, bewildered, helpless thing. Don't be afraid of anything, Nora; just open your heart to me, and I'll be conscience and will to you both—[NORA *enters in her regular clothes.*] What's this? Not in bed? You've changed your dress?

NORA: Yes, Torvald, I've changed my dress.

HELMER: But why now, so late?

NORA: Tonight I'm not sleeping.

HELMER: But Nora dear—

NORA: [*Looking at her watch.*] It's still not so very late. Sit down, Torvald; we have a lot to talk over. [*She sits at one side of the table.*]

HELMER: Nora—what is this? That hard expression—

NORA: Sit down. This'll take some time. I have a lot to say.

HELMER: [*Sitting at the table directly opposite her.*] You worry me, Nora. And I don't understand you.

NORA: No, that's exactly it. You don't understand me. And I've never understood you either—until tonight. No, don't interrupt. You can just listen to what I say. We're closing out accounts, Torvald.

HELMER: How do you mean that?

NORA: [*After a short pause.*] Doesn't anything strike you about our sitting here like this?

HELMER: What's that?

NORA: We've been married now eight years. Doesn't it occur to you that this is the first time we two, you and I, man and wife, have ever talked seriously together?

HELMER: What do you mean—seriously?

NORA: In eight whole years—longer even—right from our first acquaintance, we've never exchanged a serious word on any serious thing.

HELMER: You mean I should constantly go and involve you in problems you couldn't possibly help me with?

NORA: I'm not talking of problems. I'm saying that we've never sat down seriously together and tried to get to the bottom of anything.

HELMER: But dearest, what good would that ever do you?

NORA: That's the point right there: you've never understood me. I've been wronged greatly, Torvald—first by Papa, and then by you.

HELMER: What! By us—the two people who've loved you more than anyone else?

NORA: [*Shaking her head.*] You never loved me. You've thought it fun to be in love with me, that's all.

HELMER: Nora, what a thing to say!

NORA: Yes, it's true now, Torvald. When I lived at home with Papa, he told me all his opinions, so I had the same ones too; or if they were different I hid them, since he wouldn't have cared for that. He used to call me his doll-child, and he played with me the way I played with my dolls. Then I came into your house—

HELMER: How can you speak of our marriage like that?

NORA: [*Unperturbed.*] I mean, then I went from Papa's hands into yours. You arranged everything to your own taste, and so I got the same taste as you—or I pretended to; I can't remember. I guess a little of both, first one, then the other. Now when I look back, it seems as if I'd lived here like a beggar—just from hand to mouth. I've lived by doing tricks for you, Torvald. But that's the way you wanted it. It's a great sin what you and Papa did to me. You're to blame that nothing's become of me.

HELMER: Nora, how unfair and ungrateful you are! Haven't you been happy here?

NORA: No, never. I thought so—but I never have.

HELMER: Not—not happy!

NORA: No, only lighthearted. And you've always been so kind to me. But our home's been nothing but a playpen. I've been your doll-wife here, just as at home I was Papa's doll-child. And in turn the children have been my dolls. I thought it was fun when you played with me, just as they thought it fun when I played with them. That's been our marriage, Torvald.

HELMER: There's some truth in what you're saying—under all the raving exaggeration. But it'll all be different after this. Playtime's over; now for the schooling.

NORA: Whose schooling—mine or the children's?

HELMER: Both yours and the children's, dearest.

NORA: Oh, Torvald, you're not the man to teach me to be a good wife to you.

HELMER: And you can say that?

NORA: And I—how am I equipped to bring up children?

HELMER: Nora!

NORA: Didn't you say a moment ago that that was no job to trust me with?

HELMER: In a flare of temper! Why fasten on that?

NORA: Yes, but you were so very right. I'm not up to the job. There's another job I have to do first. I have to try to educate myself. You can't help me with that. I've got to do it alone. And that's why I'm leaving you now.

HELMER: [*Jumping up.*] What's that?

NORA: I have to stand completely alone, if I'm ever going to discover myself and the world out there. So I can't go on living with you.

HELMER: Nora, Nora!

NORA: I want to leave right away. Kristine should put me up for the night—

HELMER: You're insane! You've no right! I forbid you!

NORA: From here on, there's no use forbidding me anything. I'll take with me whatever is mine. I don't want a thing from you, either now or later.

HELMER: What kind of madness is this!

NORA: Tomorrow I'm going home—I mean, home where I came from. It'll be easier up there to find something to do.

HELMER: Oh, you blind, incompetent child!

NORA: I must learn to be competent, Torvald.

HELMER: Abandon your home, your husband, your children! And you're not even thinking what people will say.

NORA: I can't be concerned about that. I only know how essential this is.

HELMER: Oh, it's outrageous. So you'll run out like this on your most sacred vows.

NORA: What do you think are my most sacred vows?

HELMER: And I have to tell you that! Aren't they your duties to your husband and children?

NORA: I have other duties equally sacred.

HELMER: That isn't true. What duties are they?

NORA: Duties to myself.

HELMER: Before all else, you're a wife and a mother.

NORA: I don't believe in that anymore. I believe that, before all else, I'm a human being, no less than you—or anyway, I ought to try to become one. I know the majority thinks you're right, Torvald, and plenty of books agree with you, too. But I can't go on believing what the majority says, or what's written in books. I have to think over these things myself and try to understand them.

HELMER: Why can't you understand your place in your own home? On a point like that, isn't there one everlasting guide you can turn to? Where's your religion?

NORA: Oh, Torvald, I'm really not sure what religion is.

HELMER: What—?

NORA: I only know what the minister said when I was confirmed. He told me religion was this thing and that. When I get clear and away by myself, I'll go into that problem too. I'll see if what the minister said was right, or, in any case, if it's right for me.

HELMER: A young woman your age shouldn't talk like that. If religion can't move you, I can try to rouse your conscience. You do have some moral feeling? Or, tell me—has that gone too?

NORA: It's not easy to answer that, Torvald. I simply don't know. I'm all confused about these things. I just know I see them so differently from you. I find out, for one thing, that the law's not at all what I'd thought—but I can't get it through my head that the law is fair. A woman hasn't a right to protect her dying father or save her husband's life! I can't believe that.

HELMER: You talk like a child. You don't know anything of the world you live in.

NORA: No, I don't. But now I'll begin to learn for myself. I'll try to discover who's right, the world or I.

HELMER: Nora, you're sick; you've got a fever. I almost think you're out of your head.

NORA: I've never felt more clearheaded and sure in my life.

HELMER: And—clearheaded and sure—you're leaving your husband and children?

NORA: Yes.

HELMER: Then there's only one possible reason.

NORA: What?

HELMER: You no longer love me.

NORA: No. That's exactly it.

HELMER: Nora! You can't be serious!

NORA: Oh, this is so hard, Torvald—you've been so kind to me always. But I can't help it. I don't love you anymore.

HELMER: [Struggling for composure.] Are you also clearheaded and sure about that?

NORA: Yes, completely. That's why I can't go on staying here.

HELMER: Can you tell me what I did to lose your love?

NORA: Yes, I can tell you. It was this evening when the miraculous thing didn't come—then I knew you weren't the man I'd imagined.

HELMER: Be more explicit; I don't follow you.

NORA: I've waited now so patiently eight long years—for, my Lord, I know miracles don't come every day. Then this crisis broke over me, and such a certainty filled me: *now* the miraculous event would occur. While Krogstad's letter was lying out there, I never for an instant dreamed that you could give in to his terms. I was so utterly sure you'd say to him: go on, tell your tale to the whole wide world. And when he'd done that—

HELMER: Yes, what then? When I'd delivered my own wife into shame and disgrace—!

NORA: When he'd done that, I was so utterly sure that you'd step forward, take the blame on yourself and say: I am the guilty one.

HELMER: Nora—!

NORA: You're thinking I'd never accept such a sacrifice from you? No, of course not. But what good would my protests be against you? That was the miracle I was waiting for, in terror and hope. And to stave that off, I would have taken my life.

HELMER: I'd gladly work for you day and night, Nora—and take on pain and deprivation. But there's no one who gives up honor for love.

NORA: Millions of women have done just that.

HELMER: Oh, you think and talk like a silly child.

NORA: Perhaps. But you neither think nor talk like the man I could join myself to. When your big fright was over—and it wasn't from any threat against me, only for what might damage you—when all the danger was past, for you it was just as if nothing had happened. I was exactly the same, your little lark, your doll, that you'd have to handle with double care now that I'd turned out so brittle and frail. [Gets up.] Torvald—in that instant it dawned on me that for eight years I've been living here with a stranger, and that I'd even conceived three children—oh, I can't stand the thought of it! I could tear myself to bits.

HELMER: [Heavily.] I see. There's a gulf that's opened between us—that's clear. Oh, but Nora, can't we bridge it somehow?

NORA: The way I am now, I'm no wife for you.

HELMER: I have the strength to make myself over.

NORA: Maybe—if your doll gets taken away.

HELMER: But to part! To part from you! No, Nora, no—I can't imagine it.

NORA: [*Going out, right.*] All the more reason why it has to be. [*She reenters with her coat and a small overnight bag, which she puts on a chair by the table.*]

HELMER: Nora, Nora, not now! Wait till tomorrow.

NORA: I can't spend the night in a strange man's room.

HELMER: But couldn't we live here like brother and sister—

NORA: You know very well how long that would last. [*Throws her shawl about her.*] Good-bye, Torvald. I won't look in on the children. I know they're in better hands than mine. The way I am now, I'm no use to them.

HELMER: But someday, Nora—someday—?

NORA: How can I tell? I haven't the least idea what'll become of me.

HELMER: But you're my wife, now and wherever you go.

NORA: Listen, Torvald—I've heard that when a wife deserts her husband's house just as I'm doing, then the law frees him from all responsibility. In any case, I'm freeing you from being responsible. Don't feel yourself bound, any more than I will. There has to be absolute freedom for us both. Here, take your ring back. Give me mine.

HELMER: That too?

NORA: That too.

HELMER: There it is.

NORA: Good. Well, now it's all over. I'm putting the keys here. The maids know all about keeping up the house—better than I do. Tomorrow, after I've left town, Kristine will stop by to pack up everything that's mine from home. I'd like those things shipped up to me.

HELMER: Over! All over! Nora, won't you ever think about me?

NORA: I'm sure I'll think of you often, and about the children and the house here.

HELMER: May I write you?

NORA: No—never. You're not to do that.

HELMER: Oh, but let me send you—

NORA: Nothing. Nothing.

HELMER: Or help you if you need it.

NORA: No. I accept nothing from strangers.

HELMER: Nora—can I never be more than a stranger to you?

NORA: [*Picking up the overnight bag.*] Ah, Torvald—it would take the greatest miracle of all—

HELMER: Tell me the greatest miracle!

NORA: You and I both would have to transform ourselves to the point that—Oh, Torvald, I've stopped believing in miracles.

HELMER: But I'll believe. Tell me! Transform ourselves to the point that—?

NORA: That our living together could be a true marriage. [*She goes out down the hall.*]

HELMER: [*Sinks down on a chair by the door, face buried in his hands.*] Nora! Nora! [*Looking about and rising.*] Empty. She's gone. [*A sudden hope leaps in him.*] The greatest miracle—?

[*From below, the sound of a door slamming shut.*]

1879

WILLIAM SHAKESPEARE
(1564–1616)

Considering the great and well-deserved fame of his work, surprisingly little is known of William Shakespeare's life. Between 1585 and 1592, he left his birthplace of Stratford-upon-Avon for London to begin a career as a playwright and actor. No dates of his professional career are recorded, however, nor can the order in which he composed his plays and poetry be determined with certainty. By 1594, he had established himself as a poet with two long works—*Venus and Adonis* and *The Rape of Lucrece*; his more than 150 sonnets are supreme expressions of the form. His matchless reputation, though, rests on his works for the theater. Shakespeare produced perhaps thirty-five plays in twenty-five years, proving himself a master of every dramatic genre: tragedy (in works such as *Macbeth*, *Hamlet*, *King Lear*, and *Othello*); historical drama (for example, *Richard III* and *Henry IV*); comedy (*A Midsummer Night's Dream*, *Twelfth Night*, *As You Like It*, and many more); and romance or "tragi-comedy" (in plays such as *The Tempest* and *Cymbeline*). Without question, Shakespeare is the most quoted, discussed, and beloved writer in English literature.

Hamlet[1]

CHARACTERS

CLAUDIUS, *King of Denmark*
HAMLET, *son of the former king and*
    nephew to the present king
POLONIUS, *Lord Chamberlain*
HORATIO, *friend of Hamlet*
LAERTES, *son of Polonius*
VOLTEMAND ⎫
CORNELIUS ⎪
ROSENCRANTZ ⎬ *courtiers*
GUILDENSTERN ⎪
OSRIC ⎪
A GENTLEMAN ⎭
A PRIEST

MARCELLUS ⎫ *officers*
BERNARDO ⎭
FRANCISCO, *a soldier*
REYNALDO, *servant to Polonius*
PLAYERS
TWO CLOWNS, *gravediggers*
FORTINBRAS, *Prince of Norway*
A NORWEGIAN CAPTAIN
ENGLISH AMBASSADORS
GERTRUDE, *Queen of Denmark, and*
    mother of Hamlet
OPHELIA, *daughter of Polonius*
GHOST OF HAMLET'S FATHER

LORDS, LADIES, OFFICERS, SOLDIERS, SAILORS, MESSENGERS, AND ATTENDANTS

SCENE: *The action takes place in or near the royal castle of Denmark at Elsinore.*

---

1. Glosses and notes are loosely based on those in *The Norton Shakespeare*, 3rd ed., edited by Stephen Greenblatt.

ACT I

Scene 1

A guard station atop the castle. Enter BERNARDO *and*
FRANCISCO, *two sentinels.*

BERNARDO: Who's there?

FRANCISCO: Nay, answer me. Stand and unfold° yourself.   *identify*

BERNARDO: Long live the king!

FRANCISCO: Bernardo?

BERNARDO: He.   5

FRANCISCO: You come most carefully° upon your hour.   *dutifully; cautiously*

BERNARDO: 'Tis now struck twelve. Get thee to bed, Francisco.

FRANCISCO: For this relief much thanks. 'Tis bitter cold,
      And I am sick at heart.

BERNARDO: Have you had quiet guard?

FRANCISCO: Not a mouse stirring.   10

BERNARDO: Well, good night.
      If you do meet Horatio and Marcellus,
      The rivals° of my watch, bid them make haste.   *partners*

      [*Enter* HORATIO *and* MARCELLUS.]

FRANCISCO: I think I hear them. Stand, ho! Who is there?

HORATIO: Friends to this ground.°   *country*

MARCELLUS: And liegemen° to the Dane.²   *sworn servants* 15

FRANCISCO: Give° you good night.   *God give or grant*

MARCELLUS: O, farewell, honest soldier!
      Who hath relieved you?

FRANCISCO: Bernardo hath my place.
      Give you good night.   [*Exit* FRANCISCO.]

MARCELLUS: Holla, Bernardo!

BERNARDO: Say—
      What, is Horatio there?

HORATIO: A piece of him.

BERNARDO: Welcome, Horatio. Welcome, good Marcellus.   20

HORATIO: What, has this thing appeared again tonight?

BERNARDO: I have seen nothing.

MARCELLUS: Horatio says 'tis but our fantasy,
      And will not let belief take hold of him
      Touching° this dreaded sight twice seen of us.   *Concerning* 25
      Therefore I have entreated him along
      With us to watch the minutes of this night,
      That if again this apparition come,
      He may approve° our eyes and speak to it.   *confirm the testimony of*

HORATIO: Tush, tush, 'twill not appear.

BERNARDO: Sit down awhile,   30

---

2. The king of Denmark, who is also called "Denmark" (as in line 48). In line 61 a similar reference is
used for the king of Norway.

And let us once again assail your ears,
That are so fortified against our story,
What we have two nights seen.

HORATIO: Well, sit we down.
And let us hear Bernardo speak of this.

35 BERNARDO: Last night of all,°   *Just last night*
When yond same star that's westward from the pole°   *polestar*
Had made his° course t' illume that part of heaven   *its*
Where now it burns, Marcellus and myself,
The bell then beating one—

[*Enter* GHOST.]

40 MARCELLUS: Peace, break thee off. Look where it comes again.
BERNARDO: In the same figure like the king that's dead.
MARCELLUS: Thou art a scholar; speak to it, Horatio.
BERNARDO: Looks 'a° not like the king? Mark it, Horatio.   *he*
HORATIO: Most like. It harrows me with fear and wonder.
BERNARDO: It would° be spoke to.   *wishes to*
45 MARCELLUS: Speak to it, Horatio.
HORATIO: What art thou that usurp'st[3] this time of night
Together with that fair and warlike form
In which the majesty of buried Denmark
Did sometimes march? By heaven I charge thee, speak.
MARCELLUS: It is offended.
50 BERNARDO: See, it stalks away.
HORATIO: Stay. Speak, speak. I charge thee, speak. [*Exit* GHOST.]
MARCELLUS: 'Tis gone and will not answer.
BERNARDO: How now, Horatio! You tremble and look pale.
Is not this something more than fantasy?
55   What think you on't?
HORATIO: Before my God, I might not this believe
Without the sensible° and true avouch°   *sensory / testimony*
Of mine own eyes.
MARCELLUS: It is not like the king?
HORATIO: As thou art to thyself.
60   Such was the very armor he had on
When he the ambitious Norway combated.
So frowned he once when, in an angry parle,°   *parley; encounter*
He smote the sledded Polacks[4] on the ice.
'Tis strange.
65 MARCELLUS: Thus twice before, and jump° at this dead hour,   *precisely*
With martial stalk° hath he gone by our watch.   *walk; gait*
HORATIO: In what particular thought to work° I know not,   *theory to follow*
But in the gross and scope of mine opinion,[5]
This bodes some strange eruption° to our state.   *calamity*

---

3. Wrongfully seizes (both the night and the king's shape).
4. Poles traveling by sled.   5. But in my general opinion.

MARCELLUS: Good now,[6] sit down, and tell me he that knows,   70
    Why this same strict and most observant watch
    So nightly toils the subject of the land,[7]
    And why such daily cast of brazen cannon
    And foreign mart° for implements of war;   *trade*
    Why such impress° of shipwrights, whose sore task   *impressment; drafting* 75
    Does not divide the Sunday from the week.
    What might be toward° that this sweaty haste   *impending*
    Doth make the night joint-laborer with the day?
    Who is't that can inform me?
HORATIO: That can I.
    At least, the whisper goes so. Our last king,   80
    Whose image even but now appeared to us,
    Was as you know by Fortinbras of Norway,
    Thereto pricked° on by a most emulate° pride,   *spurred / rivalrous*
    Dared to the combat; in which our valiant Hamlet
    (For so this side of our known world esteemed him)   85
    Did slay this Fortinbras; who by a sealed compact[8]
    Well ratified by law° and heraldry,°   *civil law / the law of arms*
    Did forfeit, with his life, all those his lands
    Which he stood seized° of, to the conqueror;   *possessed*
    Against the which a moiety° competent°   *portion / equal* 90
    Was gagèd° by our king; which had° returned   *staked / would have*
    To the inheritance° of Fortinbras,   *ownership*
    Had he been vanquisher; as, by the same covenant
    And carriage of the article designed,[9]
    His fell to Hamlet. Now, sir, young Fortinbras,   95
    Of unimprovèd° mettle hot and full,   *untested; untrained*
    Hath in the skirts° of Norway here and there   *outskirts*
    Sharked up a list[1] of lawless resolutes
    For food and diet to some enterprise[2]
    That hath a stomach[3] in't; which is no other,   100
    As it doth well° appear unto our state,   *obviously*
    But to recover of us by strong hand[4]
    And terms compulsatory, those foresaid lands
    So by his father lost; and this, I take it,
    Is the main motive of our preparations,   105
    The source of this our watch, and the chief head°   *source*
    Of this post-haste° and romage° in the land.   *feverish activity / commotion*
BERNARDO: I think it be no other but e'en so.
    Well may it sort° that this portentous figure   *chance*
    Comes armèd through our watch so like the king   110
    That was and is the question° of these wars.   *cause*

6. Good sir, now: an entreaty.　7. Requires the country's subjects to toil every night.　8. Contract to
which each set his seal.　9. And execution of the contract's provisions.
1. Indiscriminately gathered together a band ("list"), as a shark takes prey.　2. The men will "feed" his
enterprise and be fed in return for their service.　3. Courageous action; challenge to the pride (of both
the prince and his men).　4. Main force (punning on the name "Fortinbras," literally "strong arm").

HORATIO: A mote° it is to trouble the mind's eye.   *speck of dust*
          In the most high and palmy° state of Rome,   *flourishing*
          A little ere the mightiest Julius⁵ fell,
115   The graves stood tenantless, and the sheeted° dead   *shrouded*
          Did squeak and gibber in the Roman streets;
          As stars with trains of fire, and dews of blood,
          Disasters in the sun; and the moist star,⁶
          Upon whose influence Neptune's empire stands,
120   Was sick almost to doomsday with eclipse.⁷
          And even the like precurse° of feared events,   *precursor; forerunner*
          As harbingers preceding still° the fates   *always*
          And prologue to the omen° coming on,   *disastrous event*
          Have heaven and earth together demonstrated
125   Unto our climatures° and countrymen.   *regions*

          [*Enter* GHOST.]

          But soft,° behold, lo where it comes again!   *hush*
          I'll cross it⁸ though it blast me.—Stay, illusion.

          [*It spreads (its) arms.*]

          If thou hast any sound or use of voice,
          Speak to me.
130   If there be any good thing to be done,
          That may to thee do ease, and grace to me,
          Speak to me.
          If thou art privy to thy country's fate,
          Which happily° foreknowing may avoid,   *perhaps; fortunately*
135   O, speak!
          Or if thou hast uphoarded in thy life
          Extorted treasure in the womb of earth,
          For which, they say, you spirits oft walk in death,

          [*The cock crows.*]

          Speak of it. Stay, and speak. Stop it, Marcellus.
140 MARCELLUS: Shall I strike at it with my partisan?°   *halberd*
     HORATIO: Do, if it will not stand.
     BERNARDO: 'Tis here.
     HORATIO: 'Tis here.
     MARCELLUS: 'Tis gone.   [*Exit* GHOST.]
          We do it wrong, being so majestical,
          To offer it the show of violence;
145   For it is as the air, invulnerable,
          And our vain blows malicious mockery.
     BERNARDO: It was about to speak when the cock crew.

---

5. Julius Caesar, Roman consul assassinated in 44 BCE.   6. The moon, which controls the tides of the sea ("Neptune's empire," line 119). *Disasters:* malevolent influences (astrological term).   7. Solar and lunar eclipses would accompany Christ's return to earth on Judgment Day (see Rev. 6.12).   8. Move across the ghost's path, confront; also, make the sign of the cross (to counter its evil influence).

HORATIO: And then it started like a guilty thing
    Upon a fearful summons. I have heard
    The cock, that is the trumpet to the morn,   150
    Doth with his lofty and shrill-sounding throat
    Awake the god of day,[9] and at his warning,
    Whether in sea or fire, in earth or air,
    Th' extravagant and erring° spirit hies°   *wandering / hurries*
    To his confine°; and of the truth herein   *enclosure; proper place* 155
    This present object° made probation.°   *example / proof*
MARCELLUS: It faded on the crowing of the cock.
    Some say that ever 'gainst° that season comes   *always when*
    Wherein our Savior's birth is celebrated,
    This bird of dawning singeth all night long,   160
    And then, they say, no spirit dare stir abroad,
    The nights are wholesome, then no planets strike,[1]
    No fairy takes,° nor witch hath power to charm,   *bewitches*
    So hallowed and so gracious° is that time.   *full of God's grace*
HORATIO: So have I heard and do in part believe it.   165
    But look, the morn in russet mantle clad
    Walks o'er the dew of yon high eastward hill.
    Break we our watch up, and by my advice
    Let us impart what we have seen tonight
    Unto young Hamlet, for upon my life   170
    This spirit, dumb to us, will speak to him.
    Do you consent we shall acquaint him with it,
    As needful in our loves,[2] fitting our duty?
MARCELLUS: Let's do't, I pray, and I this morning know
    Where we shall find him most conveniently. [*Exeunt.*]   175

Scene 2

A chamber of state. Enter KING CLAUDIUS, QUEEN GERTRUDE,
HAMLET, POLONIUS, LAERTES, VOLTEMAND, CORNELIUS
and other members of the court.

KING: Though yet of Hamlet our[3] dear brother's death
    The memory be green, and that it us befitted
    To bear our hearts in grief, and our whole kingdom
    To be contracted in one brow of woe,
    Yet so far hath discretion fought with nature°   *natural love* 5
    That we with wisest sorrow think on him,
    Together with remembrance of ourselves.[4]
    Therefore our sometime° sister, now our queen,   *former*

9. Phoebus Apollo, the sun god in classical mythology.   1. Heavenly bodies were thought to exercise
a negative influence on earthly events when in certain unfavorable astrological positions.
2. As necessary because of the love we have for him.
3. My. The king uses the traditional royal "we," though he may also speak here of all Danes.
4. Recalls the proverbial expression "He is not wise that is not wise for himself."

Th' imperial jointress[5] to this warlike state,
10   Have we, as 'twere with a defeated joy,
With an auspicious and a dropping eye,[6]
With mirth in funeral, and with dirge in marriage,
In equal scale weighing delight and dole,°   *sorrow; dolor*
Taken to wife; nor have we herein barred°   *excluded; contradicted*
15   Your better wisdoms, which have freely gone
With this affair along. For all, our thanks.
Now follows that you know° young Fortinbras,   *that which you should know*
Holding a weak supposal° of our worth,   *poor opinion*
Or thinking by our late dear brother's death
20   Our state to be disjoint° and out of frame,°   *fractured / order*
Colleaguèd° with this dream of his advantage,   *Reinforced; buoyed up*
He hath not failed to pester us with message
Importing° the surrender of those lands   *Concerning*
Lost by his father, with all bonds of law,
25   To our most valiant brother. So much for him.
Now for ourself, and for this time of meeting,
Thus much the business is: we have here writ
To Norway, uncle of young Fortinbras—
Who, impotent and bedrid, scarcely hears
30   Of this his nephew's purpose—to suppress
His further gait° herein, in that the levies,   *progress*
The lists, and full proportions are all made
Out of his subject;° and we here dispatch   *subjects; peoples*
You, good Cornelius, and you, Voltemand,
35   For bearers of this greeting to old Norway,
Giving to you no further personal power
To business° with the king, more than the scope   *do business*
Of these dilated° articles allow.   *spelled out; specific*
Farewell, and let your haste commend° your duty.°   *demonstrate / dutifulness*
40 CORNELIUS: ⎫
    VOLTEMAND: ⎬ In that, and all things will we show our duty.
KING: We doubt it nothing,° heartily farewell.   *not at all*
            [*Exeunt* VOLTEMAND *and* CORNELIUS.]
And now, Laertes, what's the news with you?
You told us of some suit.° What is't, Laertes?   *petition; request*
You cannot speak of reason to the Dane
45   And lose your voice. What wouldst thou beg, Laertes,
That shall not be my offer, not thy asking?[7]
The head is not more native° to the heart,   *naturally connected*
The hand more instrumental° to the mouth,   *serviceable*
Than is the throne of Denmark to thy father.
What wouldst thou have, Laertes?

---

5. Widow who holds a *jointure* or life interest in the estate of her deceased husband; also, joint possessor (with her new husband, Claudius).   6. One eye ("auspicious") looking hopefully, the other downcast, or "dropping" tears.   7. That I would not offer before you asked.

LAERTES: My dread° lord,   *revered* 50
    Your leave° and favor° to return to France,   *permission / approval*
    From whence, though willingly, I came to Denmark
    To show my duty in your coronation,
    Yet now I must confess, that duty done,
    My thoughts and wishes bend again toward France,   55
    And bow them to your gracious leave and pardon.
KING: Have you your father's leave? What says Polonius?
POLONIUS: He hath, my lord, wrung from me my slow leave
    By laborsome petition, and at last
    Upon his will° I sealed my hard° consent.   *desire / reluctant* 60
    I do beseech you give him leave to go.
KING: Take thy fair hour,[8] Laertes. Time be thine,
    And thy best graces spend it at thy will.[9]
    But now, my cousin[1] Hamlet, and my son—
HAMLET: [*Aside.*] A little more than kin, and less than kind.[2]   65
KING: How is it that the clouds still hang on you?
HAMLET: Not so, my lord. I am too much in the sun.[3]
QUEEN: Good Hamlet, cast thy nighted color[4] off,
    And let thine eye look like a friend on Denmark.°   *King and country of Denmark*
    Do not for ever with thy vailèd lids°   *downcast eyes* 70
    Seek for thy noble father in the dust.
    Thou know'st 'tis common—all that lives must die,
    Passing through nature to eternity.
HAMLET: Ay, madam, it is common.°   *commonplace; crude*
QUEEN: If it be,
    Why seems it so particular° with thee?   *personal* 75
HAMLET: Seems, madam? Nay, it is. I know not "seems."
    'Tis not alone my inky cloak, good mother,
    Nor customary suits of solemn black,
    Nor windy suspiration° of forced breath,   *sigh*
    No, nor the fruitful river in the eye,   80
    Nor the dejected havior° of the visage,   *expression*
    Together with all forms, moods, shapes of grief,
    That can denote me truly. These indeed seem,
    For they are actions that a man might play,
    But I have that within which passes show—   85
    These but the trappings and the suits of woe.
KING: 'Tis sweet and commendable in your nature, Hamlet,
    To give these mourning duties to your father,
    But you must know your father lost a father,
    That father lost, lost his, and the survivor bound   90
    In filial obligation for some term

---

8. Opportune moment (while you are young).   9. And you should use time ("it") as your best qualities dictate.   1. "Cousin" is used here as a general term of kinship.   2. Play on the proverbial expression "The nearer in kin the less in kindness."   3. Sunshine of the king's favor; also, punning on
"son."   4. Black mourning clothes and melancholic demeanor.

To do obsequious[5] sorrow. But to persever
In obstinate condolement° is a course   *lamenting*
Of impious stubbornness. 'Tis unmanly grief.
95   It shows a will most incorrect to° heaven,   *unsubmissive toward*
A heart unfortified, a mind impatient,
An understanding simple° and unschooled.   *childish*
For what we know must be, and is as common
As any the most vulgar thing to sense,[6]
100   Why should we in our peevish opposition
Take it to heart? Fie, 'tis a fault to heaven,
A fault against the dead, a fault to nature,
To reason most absurd, whose common theme
Is death of fathers, and who still° hath cried,   *always*
105   From the first corse° till he that died today,   *corpse*
"This must be so." We pray you throw to earth
This unprevailing° woe, and think of us   *unavailing*
As of a father, for let the world take note
You are the most immediate° to our throne,   *next in succession*
110   And with no less nobility° of love   *purity; generosity*
Than that which dearest father bears his son
Do I impart toward you. For your intent
In going back to school in Wittenberg,[7]
It is most retrograde° to our desire,   *contrary*
115   And we beseech you, bend you° to remain   *agree*
Here in the cheer and comfort of our eye,
Our chiefest courtier, cousin, and our son.
QUEEN: Let not thy mother lose her prayers, Hamlet.
I pray thee stay with us, go not to Wittenberg.
120   HAMLET: I shall in all my best obey you, madam.
KING: Why, 'tis a loving and a fair reply.
Be as ourself in Denmark. Madam, come.
This gentle and unforced accord of Hamlet
Sits smiling to° my heart, in grace° whereof,   *Pleases / honor*
125   No jocund health° that Denmark drinks today   *toast*
But the great cannon to the clouds shall tell,°   *sound*
And the king's rouse° the heaven shall bruit° again,   *bout of drinking / echo*
Respeaking earthly thunder. Come away.
                    [*Flourish. Exeunt all but* HAMLET.]
HAMLET: O, that this too too solid flesh would melt,
130   Thaw, and resolve° itself into a dew,   *dissolve*
Or that the Everlasting had not fixed
His canon° 'gainst self-slaughter. O God, God,   *law*
How weary, stale, flat, and unprofitable
Seem to me all the uses° of this world!   *customs; business*
135   Fie on't, ah, fie, 'tis an unweeded garden

5. Suitable for funeral obsequies or ceremonies.   6. As the most obvious and ordinary thing perceived by our senses.   7. University of both Martin Luther (1483–1546), the father of Protestantism,
and the legendary Faustus or Doctor Faust; many Danes attended there.

That grows to seed. Things rank and gross in nature
Possess it merely.° That it should come to this,   *entirely*
But two months dead, nay, not so much, not two.
So excellent a king, that was to this
Hyperion to a satyr,[8] so loving to my mother,   140
That he might not beteem° the winds of heaven   *permit*
Visit her face too roughly. Heaven and earth,
Must I remember? Why, she would hang on him
As if increase of appetite had grown
By what it fed on, and yet, within a month—   145
Let me not think on't. Frailty, thy name is woman—
A little month, or ere those shoes were old
With which she followed my poor father's body
Like Niobe,[9] all tears, why she, even she—
O God, a beast that wants discourse° of reason   *lacks the faculty* 150
Would have mourned longer—married with my uncle,
My father's brother, but no more like my father
Than I to Hercules.[1] Within a month,
Ere yet the salt of most unrighteous tears
Had left the flushing in her gallèd° eyes,   *irritated* 155
She married. O, most wicked speed, to post°   *hurry*
With such dexterity to incestuous sheets!
It is not, nor it cannot come to good.
But break my heart, for I must hold my tongue.

[*Enter* HORATIO, MARCELLUS, *and* BERNARDO.]

HORATIO: Hail to your lordship!
HAMLET: I am glad to see you well.   160
      Horatio—or I do forget myself.
HORATIO: The same, my lord, and your poor servant ever.
HAMLET: Sir, my good friend, I'll change° that name with you.   *exchange*
      And what make you from[2] Wittenberg, Horatio?
      Marcellus?   165
MARCELLUS: My good lord!
HAMLET: I am very glad to see you. [*To* BERNARDO.] Good
      even, sir.—
      But what, in faith, make you from Wittenberg?
HORATIO: A truant disposition, good my lord.
HAMLET: I would not hear your enemy say so,   170
      Nor shall you do my ear that violence
      To make it truster° of your own report   *believer*
      Against yourself. I know you are no truant.

8. Hyperion, a Greek sun god, stands here for beauty and greatness in contrast to the monstrous
satyr, a lecherous creature, half man and half goat.
9. In Greek mythology, Niobe was turned to stone after a tremendous fit of weeping over the death of
her fourteen children, a punishment for her boasting about them.
1. Demigod of classical myth, renowned for his strength, as demonstrated in a series of spectacular labors.
2. What are you doing away from.

But what is your affair in Elsinore?
175   We'll teach you to drink deep ere you depart.
HORATIO: My lord, I came to see your father's funeral.
HAMLET: I prithee° do not mock me, fellow-student,   *pray thee*
    I think it was to see my mother's wedding.
HORATIO: Indeed, my lord, it followed hard upon.°   *quickly thereafter*
180 HAMLET: Thrift, thrift, Horatio. The funeral-baked meats
    Did coldly° furnish forth the marriage tables.   *when cold*
    Would I had met my dearest° foe in heaven   *bitterest*
    Or ever° I had seen that day, Horatio!   *Before*
    My father—methinks I see my father.
HORATIO: Where, my lord?
185 HAMLET: In my mind's eye, Horatio.
HORATIO: I saw him once, 'a° was a goodly king.   *he*
HAMLET: 'A was a man, take him for all in all,
    I shall not look upon his like again.
HORATIO: My lord, I think I saw him yesternight.
190 HAMLET: Saw who?
HORATIO: My lord, the king your father.
HAMLET: The king my father?
HORATIO: Season° your admiration° for a while   *Moderate / amazement*
    With an attent° ear till I may deliver°   *attentive / relate*
    Upon the witness of these gentlemen
    This marvel to you.
195 HAMLET: For God's love, let me hear!
HORATIO: Two nights together had these gentlemen,
    Marcellus and Bernardo, on their watch
    In the dead waste and middle of the night
    Been thus encountered. A figure like your father,
200   Armèd at point° exactly, cap-a-pe,°   *in readiness / head to toe*
    Appears before them, and with solemn march
    Goes slow and stately by them. Thrice he walked
    By their oppressed and fear-surprisèd eyes
    Within his truncheon's° length, whilst they, distilled   *officer's baton's*
205   Almost to jelly with the act° of fear,   *effect*
    Stand dumb and speak not to him. This to me
    In dreadful secrecy impart they did,
    And I with them the third night kept the watch,
    Where, as they had delivered,° both in time,   *reported*
210   Form of the thing, each word made true and good,
    The apparition comes. I knew your father.
    These hands are not more like.°   *alike*
HAMLET: But where was this?
MARCELLUS: My lord, upon the platform where we watch.
HAMLET: Did you not speak to it?
HORATIO: My lord, I did,
215   But answer made it none. Yet once methought
    It lifted up it° head and did address   *its*
    Itself to motion,° like as it would° speak;   *start to move / as if it wanted to*

But even° then the morning cock crew loud,   *just*
And at the sound it shrunk in haste away
And vanished from our sight.
HAMLET: 'Tis very strange.   220
HORATIO: As I do live, my honored lord, 'tis true,
And we did think it writ down° in our duty   *prescribed*
To let you know of it.
HAMLET: Indeed, sirs, but
This troubles me. Hold you the watch tonight?
ALL: We do, my lord.
HAMLET: Armed, say you?
ALL: Armed, my lord.   225
HAMLET: From top to toe?
ALL: My lord, from head to foot.
HAMLET: Then saw you not his face.
HORATIO: O yes, my lord, he wore his beaver° up.   *helmet face guard*
HAMLET: What, looked he frowningly?
HORATIO: A countenance more in sorrow than in anger.   230
HAMLET: Pale or red?
HORATIO: Nay, very pale.
HAMLET: And fixed his eyes upon you?
HORATIO: Most constantly.
HAMLET: I would I had been there.
HORATIO: It would have much amazed you.
HAMLET: Very like.
Stayed it long?   235
HORATIO: While one with moderate haste might tell° a   *count*
hundred.
BOTH: Longer, longer.
HORATIO: Not when I saw't.
HAMLET: His beard was grizzled,° no?   *gray*
HORATIO: It was as I have seen it in his life,
A sable silvered.
HAMLET: I will watch tonight.   240
Perchance 'twill walk again.
HORATIO: I warr'nt° it will.   *warrant; guarantee*
HAMLET: If it assume my noble father's person,
I'll speak to it though hell itself should gape
And bid me hold my peace. I pray you all,
If you have hitherto concealed this sight,   245
Let it be tenable° in your silence still,   *held*
And whatsomever else shall hap° tonight,   *happen; occur*
Give it an understanding but no tongue.
I will requite your loves. So fare you well.
Upon the platform 'twixt eleven and twelve   250
I'll visit you.
ALL: Our duty to your honor.
HAMLET: Your loves, as mine to you. Farewell.
                    [*Exeunt all but* HAMLET.]

My father's spirit in arms? All is not well.
I doubt° some foul play. Would the night were come!   *suspect*
255 Till then sit still, my soul. Foul deeds will rise,
Though all the earth o'erwhelm them, to men's eyes.

                                                    [*Exit.*]

Scene 3

The dwelling of POLONIUS. *Enter* LAERTES *and* OPHELIA.

LAERTES: My necessaries are embarked.° Farewell.   *aboard ship*
      And, sister, as the winds give benefit
      And convoy° is assistant,° do not sleep,   *transportation / available*
      But let me hear from you.
OPHELIA: Do you doubt that?
5 LAERTES: For Hamlet, and the trifling of his favor,
      Hold it a fashion and a toy in blood,
      A violet in the youth of primy nature,³
      Forward,° not permanent, sweet, not lasting,   *Early blooming*
      The perfume and suppliance° of a minute,   *diversion*
      No more.
OPHELIA: No more but so?
10 LAERTES: Think it no more.
      For nature crescent° does not grow alone   *growing*
      In thews° and bulk, but as this temple° waxes   *muscles / body*
      The inward service° of the mind and soul   *responsibility*
      Grows wide withal.° Perhaps he loves you now,   *along with it*
15 And now no soil° nor cautel° doth besmirch   *stain / deception*
      The virtue of his will,° but you must fear,   *intentions*
      His greatness weighted,° his will is not his own,   *rank considered*
      For he himself is subject to his birth.
      He may not, as unvalued° persons do,   *common*
20 Carve for himself, for on his choice depends
      The safety and health of this whole state,
      And therefore must his choice be circumscribed
      Unto the voice° and yielding° of that body°   *assent / consent / state*
      Whereof he is the head. Then if he says he loves you,
25 It fits° your wisdom so far to believe it   *befits*
      As he in his particular act° and place°   *power of action / social position*
      May give his saying deed,⁴ which is no further
      Than the main° voice of Denmark goes withal.   *collective*
      Then weigh what loss your honor may sustain
30 If with too credent° ear you list° his songs,   *trusting / listen to*
      Or lose your heart, or your chaste treasure open
      To his unmastered° importunity.   *uncontrolled*
      Fear it, Ophelia, fear it, my dear sister,

3. A flower of his natural impulses in their prime.   4. May act on his promise.

And keep you in the rear of your affection,[5]
Out of the shot and danger of desire.   35
The chariest° maid is prodigal° enough   *most circumspect / risk-taking*
If she unmask her beauty to the moon.
Virtue itself scapes not calumnious strokes.
The canker galls the infants[6] of the spring
Too oft before their buttons° be disclosed,°   *buds / opened* 40
And in the morn and liquid dew of youth
Contagious blastments° are most imminent.   *blights*
Be wary then; best safety lies in fear.
Youth to itself rebels, though none else near.[7]

OPHELIA: I shall the effect of this good lesson keep   45
As watchman to my heart. But, good my brother,
Do not as some ungracious pastors do,
Show me the steep and thorny way to heaven,
Whiles like a puffed° and reckless libertine   *proud*
Himself the primrose path of dalliance treads   50
And recks° not his own rede.°   *heeds / advice*

LAERTES: O, fear me not.°   *fear not for me*

[*Enter* POLONIUS.]

I stay too long. But here my father comes.
A double blessing is a double grace;
Occasion smiles upon a second leave.[8]

POLONIUS: Yet here, Laertes? Aboard, aboard, for shame!   55
The wind sits in the shoulder° of your sail,   *at the back*
And you are stayed° for. There—my blessing with thee,   *waited*
And these few precepts in thy memory
Look thou character.° Give thy thoughts no tongue,   *inscribe*
Nor any unproportioned° thought his act.   *unruly* 60
Be thou familiar,° but by no means vulgar.°   *friendly / indiscriminately*
Those friends thou hast, and their adoption tried,[9]   *social*
Grapple them unto thy soul with hoops of steel;
But do not dull° thy palm with entertainment°   *callous / greetings*
Of each new-hatched, unfledged comrade. Beware   *(handshakes)* 65
Of entrance to a quarrel, but being in,
Bear't that th' opposèd[1] may beware of thee.
Give every man thy ear, but few thy voice;
Take each man's censure,° but reserve thy judgment.   *opinion*
Costly thy habit° as thy purse can buy,   *dress* 70
But not expressed in fancy;° rich not gaudy,   *showiness*
For the apparel oft proclaims the man,
And they in France of the best rank and station

---

5. And be restrained, despite the forward march of your feelings.   6. The cankerworm injures the
shoots.   7. Young people are naturally rebellious, even without provocation.
8. Favorable circumstances allow us a second farewell.   9. Those friends of yours who have proven
true and reliable.   1. Conduct it so that the opponent.

Are of a most select and generous chief in that.[2]
75   Neither a borrower nor a lender be,
      For loan oft loses both itself and friend,
      And borrowing dulls th' edge of husbandry.°   *economy; thrift*
      This above all, to thine own self be true,
      And it must follow as the night the day
80   Thou canst not then be false to any man.
      Farewell. My blessing season° this in thee!   *mature*
LAERTES: Most humbly do I take my leave, my lord.
POLONIUS: The time invests° you. Go, your servants tend.°   *presses / wait*
LAERTES: Farewell, Ophelia, and remember well
      What I have said to you.
85 OPHELIA: 'Tis in my memory locked,
      And you yourself shall keep the key of it.
LAERTES: Farewell.   [*Exit.*]
POLONIUS: What is't, Ophelia, he hath said to you?
OPHELIA: So please you, something touching the Lord Hamlet.
90 POLONIUS: Marry,[3] well bethought.
      'Tis told me he hath very oft of late
      Given private time to you, and you yourself
      Have of your audience° been most free and bounteous.   *attention*
      If it be so—as so 'tis put on° me,   *suggested to*
95   And that in way of caution—I must tell you,
      You do not understand yourself so clearly
      As it behooves my daughter and your honor.
      What is between you? Give me up the truth.
OPHELIA: He hath, my lord, of late made many tenders°   *offers, as of money*
100   Of his affection to me.
POLONIUS: Affection? Pooh! You speak like a green girl,
      Unsifted° in such perilous circumstance.   *Inexperienced*
      Do you believe his tenders, as you call them?
OPHELIA: I do not know, my lord, what I should think.
105 POLONIUS: Marry, I will teach you. Think yourself a baby
      That you have ta'en these tenders for true pay
      Which are not sterling. Tender° yourself more dearly,   *Value; protect*
      Or (not to crack the wind of the poor phrase,
      Running it thus)[4] you'll tender me a fool.[5]
110 OPHELIA: My lord, he hath importuned me with love
      In honorable fashion.
POLONIUS: Ay, fashion° you may call it. Go to,[6] go to.   *conventional flattery*
OPHELIA: And hath given countenance° to his speech, my lord, *authority*
      With almost all the holy vows of heaven.
115 POLONIUS: Ay, springes° to catch woodcocks.[7] I do know, *traps*

2. Are of all people the most adept at displaying rank in fine appearance.   3. By the Virgin Mary, a mild oath.   4. The metaphor compares an overworked phrase to an overworked (broken-winded) horse. The phrase comes at the end of line 109.   5. A multiple pun: render or make me look like a fool; give me a fool, by being one yourself; give me a (grand)baby (idiomatically, a "fool").   6. That's enough; come, come.   7. Proverbially gullible birds.

When the blood burns, how prodigal° the soul   *lavishly*
Lends the tongue vows. These blazes, daughter,
Giving more light than heat, extinct° in both   *extinguished*
Even in their promise, as it is a-making,
You must not take for fire. From this time   120
Be something scanter of your maiden presence.
Set your entreatments⁸ at a higher rate
Than a command° to parle.° For Lord Hamlet,   *request / speak (with you)*
Believe so much in° him that he is young,   *concerning*
And with a larger tether may he walk   125
Than may be given you. In few,° Ophelia,   *brief*
Do not believe his vows, for they are brokers,
Not of that dye which their investments° show,   *clerical vestments*
But mere implorators° of unholy suits,   *solicitors*
Breathing° like sanctified and pious bawds,   *Speaking* 130
The better to beguile. This is for all:
I would not, in plain terms, from this time forth
Have you so slander° any moment leisure   *disgrace*
As to give words or talk with the Lord Hamlet.
Look to't, I charge you. Come your ways.°   *Come along* 135
OPHELIA: I shall obey, my lord.   [*Exeunt.*]

Scene 4

The guard station. Enter HAMLET, HORATIO *and* MARCELLUS.

HAMLET: The air bites shrewdly;° it is very cold.   *sharply*
HORATIO: It is a nipping and an eager° air.   *a keen; bitter*
HAMLET: What hour now?
HORATIO: I think it lacks of twelve.
MARCELLUS: No, it is struck.
HORATIO: Indeed? I heard it not.
It then draws near the season°   *time* 5
Wherein the spirit held his wont° to walk.   *was accustomed*

[*A flourish of trumpets, and two pieces go off.*]

What does this mean, my lord?
HAMLET: The king doth wake tonight and takes his rouse,
Keeps wassail, and the swagg'ring up-spring reels,⁹
And as he drains his draughts of Rhenish° down,   *Rhine wine* 10
The kettledrum and trumpet thus bray out
The triumph of his pledge.¹
HORATIO: Is it a custom?
HAMLET: Ay, marry, is't,
But to my mind, though I am native here
And to the manner° born, it is a custom   *custom* 15
More honored in the breach° than the observance.°   *when broken / when observed*

8. Negotiations before a surrender.   9. Has a drinking party ("wassail") and staggers ("reels")
through a wild German dance.   1. His success at draining his cup after making a toast ("pledge").

This heavy-headed revel east and west
Makes us traduced and taxed of other nations.
They clepe° us drunkards, and with swinish phrase   call
20   Soil our addition,° and indeed it takes   reputation
From our achievements, though performed at height,°   excellently
The pith and marrow of our attribute.°   honor
So oft it chances in particular men,
That for some vicious mole° of nature in them,   blemish
25   As in their birth,° wherein they are not guilty   parentage
(Since nature cannot choose his° origin),   its
By their o'ergrowth of some complexion,[2]
Oft breaking down the pales° and forts of reason,   fences; boundaries
Or by some habit that too much o'er-leavens
30   The form of plausive° manners—that these men,   pleasing
Carrying, I say, the stamp of one defect,
Being nature's livery or fortune's star,[3]
His virtues else, be they as pure as grace,
As infinite as man may undergo,°   sustain
35   Shall in the general censure° take corruption   public opinion
From that particular fault. The dram° of evil   tiny amount (eighth of an ounce)
Doth all the noble substance often doubt
To his own scandal.°   shame

[*Enter* GHOST.]

HORATIO: Look, my lord, it comes.
HAMLET: Angels and ministers of grace defend us!
40   Be thou a spirit of health or goblin damned,
Bring with thee airs° from heaven or blasts from hell,   gentle breezes
Be thy intents wicked or charitable,
Thou com'st in such a questionable shape
That I will speak to thee. I'll call thee Hamlet,
45   King, father, royal Dane. O, answer me!
Let me not burst in ignorance, but tell
Why thy canonized° bones, hearsèd° in death,   consecrated ; coffined
Have burst their cerements;° why the sepulchre   graveclothes
Wherein we saw thee quietly inurned
50   Hath oped his ponderous and marble jaws
To cast thee up again. What may this mean
That thou, dead corse, again in complete steel°   armor
Revisits thus the glimpses of the moon,
Making night hideous, and we fools of nature°   mere mortals
55   So horridly to shake our disposition°   mental foundations
With thoughts beyond the reaches of our souls?
Say, why is this? Wherefore? What should we do?

2. Humor. The body was believed to contain various humors such as blood and choler, with good
health and temperament depending on their balance, as opposed to the "o'ergrowth" of any one.
3. Being a congenital defect ("nature's livery" or clothing) or a blemish caused by fortune (the influence of chance astrological events).

[GHOST *beckons.*]

HORATIO: It beckons you to go away with it,
    As if it some impartment° did desire   *communication*
    To you alone.
MARCELLUS: Look with what courteous action   60
    It waves° you to a more removèd ground.   *beckons*
    But do not go with it.
HORATIO: No, by no means.
HAMLET: It will not speak; then I will follow it.
HORATIO: Do not, my lord.
HAMLET: Why, what should be the fear?
    I do not set my life at a pin's fee,°   *value* 65
    And for my soul, what can it do to that,
    Being a thing immortal as itself?
    It waves me forth again. I'll follow it.
HORATIO: What if it tempt you toward the flood,° my lord,   *sea*
    Or to the dreadful summit of the cliff   70
    That beetles° o'er his base into the sea,   *juts out*
    And there assume some other horrible form,
    Which might deprive your sovereignty of reason
    And draw you into madness? Think of it.
    The very place puts toys of desperation,°   *desperate fancies* 75
    Without more motive,° into every brain   *cause*
    That looks so many fathoms to the sea
    And hears it roar beneath.
HAMLET: It wafts me still.
    Go on. I'll follow thee.
MARCELLUS: You shall not go, my lord.
HAMLET: Hold off your hands.   80
HORATIO: Be ruled. You shall not go.
HAMLET: My fate cries out
    And makes each petty artere° in this body   *artery*
    As hardy as the Nemean lion's[4] nerve.
    Still am I called. Unhand me, gentlemen.
    By heaven, I'll make a ghost of him that lets° me.   *hinders* 85
    I say, away! Go on. I'll follow thee.
                   [*Exeunt* GHOST *and* HAMLET.]
HORATIO: He waxes desperate with imagination.
MARCELLUS: Let's follow. 'Tis not fit thus to obey him.
HORATIO: Have after.° To what issue° will this come?   *Go on / end; result*
MARCELLUS: Something is rotten in the state of Denmark.   90
HORATIO: Heaven will direct it.
MARCELLUS: Nay, let's follow him.
                          [*Exeunt.*]

---

4. Mythological monster slain by Hercules as one of his twelve labors.

Scene 5

Near the guard station. Enter GHOST *and* HAMLET.

HAMLET: Whither wilt thou lead me? Speak. I'll go no
    further.
GHOST: Mark me.
HAMLET: I will.
GHOST: My hour is almost come,
    When I to sulph'rous and tormenting flames
    Must render up myself.
HAMLET: Alas, poor ghost!
5 GHOST: Pity me not, but lend thy serious hearing
    To what I shall unfold.
HAMLET: Speak. I am bound to hear.
GHOST: So art thou to revenge, when thou shalt hear.
HAMLET: What?
GHOST: I am thy father's spirit,
10   Doomed for a certain term to walk the night,   *do penance*
    And for the day confined to fast° in fires,
    Till the foul crimes done in my days of nature°   *my natural life*
    Are burnt and purged away. But that I am forbid
    To tell the secrets of my prison house,
15   I could a tale unfold whose lightest word
    Would harrow up° thy soul, freeze thy young blood,   *torment*
    Make thy two eyes like stars start from their spheres,
    Thy knotted and combinèd° locks to part,   *tangled*
    And each particular hair to stand an end,
20   Like quills upon the fretful porpentine.°   *porcupine*
    But this eternal blazon⁵ must not be
    To ears of flesh and blood. List, list, O, list!
    If thou didst ever thy dear father love—
HAMLET: O God!
25 GHOST: Revenge his foul and most unnatural murder.
HAMLET: Murder!
GHOST: Murder most foul, as in the best it is,
    But this most foul, strange, and unnatural.
HAMLET: Haste me to know't, that I, with wings as swift
30   As meditation or the thoughts of love,
    May sweep to my revenge.
GHOST: I find thee apt.
    And duller shouldst thou be than the fat° weed   *gross*
    That rots itself in ease on Lethe⁶ wharf,—
    Wouldst thou not stir in this. Now, Hamlet, hear.
35   'Tis given out° that, sleeping in my orchard,   *said*
    A serpent stung me. So the whole ear of Denmark

5. Description of eternity or the afterlife.
6. River of the classical underworld; its waters induced forgetfulness. *Rots:* "roots," in some versions
of the play.

Is by a forgèd process° of my death   *fabricated account*
Rankly abused.° But know, thou noble youth,   *deceived*
The serpent that did sting thy father's life
Now wears his crown.

HAMLET: O my prophetic soul!   40
    My uncle!

GHOST: Ay, that incestuous, that adulterate° beast,   *adulterous*
    With witchcraft of his wits, with traitorous gifts°—   *abilities; presents*
    O wicked wit and gifts that have the power
    So to seduce!—won to his shameful lust   45
    The will of my most seeming virtuous queen.
    O Hamlet, what a falling off was there,
    From me, whose love was of that dignity
    That it went hand in hand even with the vow
    I made to her in marriage, and to decline°   *sink down* 50
    Upon a wretch whose natural gifts were poor
    To° those of mine!   *Compared to*
    But virtue, as it never will be moved,
    Though lewdness court it in a shape of heaven,
    So lust, though to a radiant angel linked,   55
    Will sate itself in a celestial bed
    And prey on garbage.
    But soft, methinks I scent the morning air.
    Brief let me be. Sleeping within my orchard,
    My custom always of the afternoon,   60
    Upon my secure hour thy uncle stole,
    With juice of cursed hebona[7] in a vial,
    And in the porches of my ears did pour
    The leperous distilment,° whose effect   *distillation*
    Holds such an enmity with blood of man   65
    That swift as quicksilver° it courses through   *liquid mercury*
    The natural gates and alleys of the body,
    And with a sudden vigor it doth posset°   *coagulate*
    And curd,° like eager° droppings into milk,   *curdle / acid*
    The thin and wholesome blood. So did it mine,   70
    And a most instant tetter barked about[8]
    Most lazar-like° with vile and loathsome crust   *leper-like*
    All my smooth body.
    Thus was I sleeping by a brother's hand
    Of life, of crown, of queen at once dispatched,°   *deprived* 75
    Cut off even in the blossoms of my sin,
    Unhouseled, disappointed, unaneled,[9]
    No reck'ning made, but sent to my account
    With all my imperfections on my head.
    O, horrible! O, horrible, most horrible!   80

7. A poison, possibly henbane.
8. Covered like bark. *Tetter*: a skin disease.
9. Without the customary rites of the Church; that is, without receiving the Sacrament, without confession and absolution, and without ritual anointing.

If thou hast nature in thee, bear it not.
Let not the royal bed of Denmark be
A couch of luxury° and damnèd incest.   *lechery*
But howsomever thou pursues this act,
85   Taint not thy mind, nor let thy soul contrive
Against thy mother aught.° Leave her to heaven,   *anything*
And to those thorns that in her bosom lodge
To prick and sting her. Fare thee well at once.
The glowworm shows the matin° to be near,   *morning*
90   And gins° to pale his uneffectual fire.   *begins*
Adieu, adieu, adieu. Remember me.   [*Exit.*]
   HAMLET: O all you host of heaven! O earth! What else?
And shall I couple° hell? O, fie! Hold, hold, my heart,   *add*
And you, my sinews, grow not instant old,
95   But bear me stiffly up. Remember thee?
Ay, thou poor ghost, whiles memory holds a seat
In this distracted globe.[1] Remember thee?
Yea, from the table° of my memory   *tablet; book*
I'll wipe away all trivial fond° records,   *foolish*
100   All saws of books, all forms, all pressures past[2]
That youth and observation copied there,
And thy commandment all alone shall live
Within the book and volume of my brain,
Unmixed with baser matter. Yes, by heaven!
105   O most pernicious woman!
O villain, villain, smiling, damnèd villain!
My tables—meet it is I set it down
That one may smile, and smile, and be a villain.
At least I am sure it may be so in Denmark.
110   So, uncle, there you are. Now to my word:°   *for my motto or watchword*
It is "Adieu, adieu. Remember me."
I have sworn't.

   [*Enter* HORATIO *and* MARCELLUS.]

   HORATIO: My lord, my lord!
   MARCELLUS: Lord Hamlet!
   HORATIO: Heavens secure him!
   HAMLET: So be it!
115 MARCELLUS: Illo, ho, ho,[3] my lord!
   HAMLET: Hillo, ho, ho, boy! Come, bird, come.
   MARCELLUS: How is't, my noble lord?
   HORATIO: What news, my lord?
   HAMLET: O, wonderful!
   HORATIO: Good my lord, tell it.

---

1. Skull or head, but also world and, perhaps, an allusion to the Globe Theatre.
2. All adages or old "saws" from books, all images or customs, all previous impressions.
3. Falconer's cry; hence the reference to a "bird" in the next line.

HAMLET: No, you will reveal it.

HORATIO: Not I, my lord, by heaven.

MARCELLUS: Nor I, my lord.   120

HAMLET: How say you then, would heart of man once think it?
    But you'll be secret?

BOTH: Ay, by heaven, my lord.

HAMLET: There's never a villain dwelling in all Denmark
    But he's an arrant knave.

HORATIO: There needs no ghost, my lord, come from the grave   125
    To tell us this.

HAMLET: Why, right, you are in the right,
    And so without more circumstance° at all   *elaborate speech*
    I hold it fit that we shake hands and part,
    You, as your business and desire shall point you,
    For every man hath business and desire   130
    Such as it is, and for my own poor part,
    Look you, I'll go pray.

HORATIO: These are but wild and whirling words, my lord.

HAMLET: I am sorry they offend you, heartily;
    Yes, faith, heartily.

HORATIO: There's no offence, my lord.   135

HAMLET: Yes, by Saint Patrick, but there is, Horatio,
    And much offence too. Touching° this vision here,   *Concerning*
    It is an honest ghost, that let me tell you.
    For your desire to know what is between us,
    O'ermaster't as you may. And now, good friends,   140
    As you are friends, scholars, and soldiers,
    Give° me one poor request.   *Grant*

HORATIO: What is't, my lord? We will.

HAMLET: Never make known what you have seen tonight.

BOTH: My lord, we will not.

HAMLET: Nay, but swear't.

HORATIO: In faith,   145
    My lord, not I.

MARCELLUS: Nor I, my lord, in faith.

HAMLET: Upon my sword.

MARCELLUS: We have sworn, my lord, already.

HAMLET: Indeed, upon my sword, indeed.

    [GHOST *cries under the stage.*]

GHOST: Swear.

HAMLET: Ha, ha, boy, say'st thou so? Art thou there, truepenny?°   *trusty fellow*
    Come on. You hear this fellow in the cellarage.°   *cellars* 150
    Consent to swear.

HORATIO: Propose the oath, my lord.

HAMLET: Never to speak of this that you have seen,
    Swear by my sword.

GHOST: [*Beneath.*] Swear.

155 HAMLET: Hic et ubique?⁴ Then we'll shift our ground.
Come hither, gentlemen,
And lay your hands again upon my sword.
Swear by my sword
Never to speak of this that you have heard.
160 GHOST: [*Beneath.*] Swear by his sword.
HAMLET: Well said, old mole! Canst work i' th' earth so fast?
A worthy pioneer!⁵ Once more remove,° good friends.   *move*
HORATIO: O day and night, but this is wondrous strange!
HAMLET: And therefore as a stranger° give it welcome.   *guest*
165 There are more things in heaven and earth, Horatio,
Than are dreamt of in your⁶ philosophy.
But come.
Here as before, never, so help you mercy,
How strange or odd some'er° I bear myself   *so ever*
170 (As I perchance hereafter shall think meet
To put an antic° disposition on),   *a mad; crazy*
That you, at such times, seeing me, never shall,
With arms encumbered° thus, or this head-shake,   *folded*
Or by pronouncing of some doubtful phrase,
175 As "Well, we know," or "We could, an if° we would"   *an if = if*
Or "If we list° to speak," or "There be, and if they might"   *liked*
Or such ambiguous giving out, to note
That you know aught of me—this do swear,
So grace and mercy at your most need help you.
180 GHOST: [*Beneath.*] Swear.   [*They swear.*]
HAMLET: Rest, rest, perturbèd spirit! So, gentlemen,
With all my love I do commend me to you,
And what so poor a man as Hamlet is
May do t'express his love and friending° to you,   *friendship*
185 God willing, shall not lack.° Let us go in together,   *be lacking or undone*
And still your fingers on your lips, I pray.
The time is out of joint. O cursèd spite
That ever I was born to set it right!
Nay, come,⁷ let's go together.   [*Exeunt.*]

ACT II

Scene 1

The dwelling of POLONIUS. *Enter* POLONIUS *and* REYNALDO.

POLONIUS: Give him this money and these notes, Reynaldo.
REYNALDO: I will, my lord.
POLONIUS: You shall do marvellous wisely, good Reynaldo,

---

4. Here and everywhere? (Latin).
5. Soldier who digs trenches.
6. Some versions of the play have "our," not "your."
7. The others politely wait for Hamlet to lead the way, but he insists otherwise.

Before you visit him, to make inquire
Of his behavior.
REYNALDO: My lord, I did intend it.   5
POLONIUS: Marry, well said, very well said. Look you, sir.
    Enquire me° first what Danskers° are in Paris,   *for me / Danes*
    And how, and who, what means,° and where they keep,°   *income / lodge*
    What company, at what expense; and finding
    By this encompassment° and drift of question   *indirect means* 10
    That they do know my son, come you more nearer
    Than your particular demands° will touch it.   *direct questions*
    Take you° as 'twere some distant knowledge of him,   *Pretend*
    As thus, "I know his father and his friends,
    And in part him." Do you mark this, Reynaldo?   15
REYNALDO: Ay, very well, my lord.
POLONIUS: "And in part him, but," you may say, "not well,
    But if't be he I mean, he's very wild,
    Addicted so and so." And there put on him
    What forgeries° you please; marry, none so rank°   *lies / foul* 20
    As may dishonor him. Take heed of that.
    But, sir, such wanton, wild, and usual slips
    As are companions noted and most known
    To youth and liberty.
REYNALDO: As gaming, my lord.
POLONIUS: Ay, or drinking, fencing, swearing,   25
    Quarrelling, drabbing°—you may go so far.   *whoring*
REYNALDO: My lord, that would dishonor him.
POLONIUS: Faith, no, as you may season it in the charge.°   *soften the accusation*
    You must not put another scandal on him,
    That he is open° to incontinency.°   *inclined / sexual excess* 30
    That's not my meaning. But breathe his faults so quaintly°   *delicately*
    That they may seem the taints of liberty,°   *faults of freedom*
    The flash and outbreak of a fiery mind,
    A savageness in unreclaimèd° blood,   *untamed*
    Of general assault.°   *Touching everyone*
REYNALDO: But, my good lord—   35
POLONIUS: Wherefore should you do this?
REYNALDO: Ay, my lord,
    I would know that.
POLONIUS: Marry, sir, here's my drift,
    And I believe it is a fetch of warrant.°   *permissible trick*
    You laying these slight sullies on my son,
    As 'twere a thing a little soiled wi' th' working,[8]   40
    Mark you,
    Your party° in converse, him you would sound,   *partner*
    Having° ever seen in the prenominate° crimes   *If he has / already named*
    The youth you breathe of guilty, be assured
    He closes with you in this consequence,°   *to this effect* 45

8. Stained by education in the ways of the world, "shop-soiled."

"Good sir," or so, or "friend," or "gentleman,"
According to the phrase° or the addition°   *expression / title of address*
Of man and country.

REYNALDO: Very good, my lord.

POLONIUS: And then, sir, does 'a° this—'a does—What   *he*
      was I about to say?
50   By the mass, I was about to say something.
      Where did I leave?

REYNALDO: At "closes in the consequence."

POLONIUS: At "closes in the consequence"—ay, marry,
      He closes thus: "I know the gentleman.
55   I saw him yesterday, or th' other day,
      Or then, or then, with such, or such, and as you say,
      There was 'a gaming, there o'ertook in's rouse,
      There falling out at tennis," or perchance
      "I saw him enter such a house of sale,"
60   Videlicet,° a brothel, or so forth.   *That is to say (Latin)*
      See you, now—
      Your bait of falsehood takes this carp of truth,
      And thus do we of wisdom and of reach,°   *ability*
      With windlasses° and with assays of bias,°   *roundabout paths / indirect tests*
65   By indirections find directions° out;   *tendencies*
      So by my former lecture and advice
      Shall you my son.⁹ You have me, have you not?

REYNALDO: My lord, I have.

POLONIUS: God b'wi' ye; fare ye well.

REYNALDO: Good my lord.

70 POLONIUS: Observe his inclination in° yourself.   *for*

REYNALDO: I shall, my lord.

POLONIUS: And let him ply° his music.   *practice*

REYNALDO: Well, my lord.

POLONIUS: Farewell.   [*Exit* REYNALDO.]

      [*Enter* OPHELIA.]

                    How now, Ophelia, what's the matter?

OPHELIA: O my lord, my lord, I have been so affrighted!

75 POLONIUS: With what, i' th' name of God?

OPHELIA: My lord, as I was sewing in my closet,°   *private chamber*
      Lord Hamlet with his doublet° all unbraced,°   *jacket / unfastened*
      No hat upon his head, his stockings fouled,
      Ungartered and down-gyvèd¹ to his ankle,
80   Pale as his shirt, his knees knocking each other,
      And with a look so piteous in purport
      As if he had been loosèd out of hell
      To speak of horrors—he comes before me.

9. Shall you make discoveries about my son.
1. Fallen down like fetters ("gyves").

POLONIUS: Mad for thy love?

OPHELIA: My lord, I do not know,
    But truly I do fear it.

POLONIUS: What said he?   85

OPHELIA: He took me by the wrist, and held me hard,
    Then goes he to the length of all his arm,
    And with his other hand thus o'er his brow,
    He falls to such perusal of my face
    As 'a° would draw it. Long stayed he so.   *As if he* 90
    At last, a little shaking of mine arm,
    And thrice his head thus waving up and down,
    He raised a sigh so piteous and profound
    As it did seem to shatter all his bulk,°   *body*
    And end his being. That done, he lets me go,   95
    And with his head over his shoulder turned
    He seemed to find his way without his eyes,
    For out adoors he went without their helps,
    And to the last bended° their light on me.   *directed*

POLONIUS: Come, go with me. I will go seek the king.   100
    This is the very ecstasy° of love,   *insanity*
    Whose violent property° fordoes° itself,   *character / destroys*
    And leads the will to desperate undertakings
    As oft as any passion under heaven
    That does afflict our natures. I am sorry.   105
    What, have you given him any hard words of late?

OPHELIA: No, my good lord, but as you did command
    I did repel his letters, and denied
    His access to me.

POLONIUS: That hath made him mad.
    I am sorry that with better heed and judgment   110
    I had not quoted° him. I feared he did but trifle,   *observed*
    And meant to wrack[2] thee; but beshrew° my jealousy.°   *curse / suspicion*
    By heaven, it is as proper to our age
    To cast beyond ourselves in our opinions
    As it is common for the younger sort   115
    To lack discretion. Come, go we to the king.
    This must be known, which being kept close,° might   *secret*
    move
    More grief to hide than hate to utter love.[3]
    Come.   [*Exeunt.*]

Scene 2

A public room. Enter KING, QUEEN, ROSENCRANTZ *and*
GUILDENSTERN.

---

2. Harm; ruin (through seduction).
3. Polonius suggests that although it will cause trouble ("grief") to reveal the secret of Hamlet's "love"
(for Ophelia), "to hide" it would incur greater suffering.

KING: Welcome, dear Rosencrantz and Guildenstern.
    Moreover that[4] we much did long to see you,
    The need we have to use you did provoke
    Our hasty sending.° Something have you heard   *summons*
5   Of Hamlet's transformation—so call it,
    Sith nor° th' exterior nor the inward man   *Since neither*
    Resembles that it was. What it should be,
    More than his father's death, that thus hath put him
    So much from th' understanding of himself,
10   I cannot deem of. I entreat you both
    That, being of so young days° brought up with him,   *from childhood*
    And sith so neighbored° to his youth and havior,   *familiar*
    That you vouchsafe your rest° here in our court   *agree to stay*
    Some little time, so by your companies
15   To draw him on to pleasures, and to gather
    So much as from occasion° you may glean,   *opportunity*
    Whether aught to us unknown afflicts him thus,
    That opened° lies within our remedy.   *if disclosed*
QUEEN: Good gentlemen, he hath much talked of you,
20   And sure I am two men there are not living
    To whom he more adheres.° If it will please you   *is attached*
    To show us so much gentry° and good will   *courtesy*
    As to expend your time with us awhile
    For the supply and profit of our hope,
25   Your visitation shall receive such thanks
    As fits a king's remembrance.
ROSENCRANTZ: Both your majesties
    Might, by the sovereign power you have of° us,   *over*
    Put your dread° pleasures more into command   *reverend*
    Than to entreaty.
GUILDENSTERN: But we both obey,
30   And here give up ourselves in the full bent°   *completely*
    To lay our service freely at your feet,
    To be commanded.
KING: Thanks, Rosencrantz and gentle Guildenstern.
QUEEN: Thanks, Guildenstern and gentle Rosencrantz.
35   And I beseech you instantly to visit
    My too much changed son. Go, some of you,
    And bring these gentlemen where Hamlet is.
GUILDENSTERN: Heavens make our presence and our practices
    Pleasant and helpful to him!
QUEEN: Ay, amen!
        [*Exeunt* ROSENCRANTZ *and* GUILDENSTERN.]

      [*Enter* POLONIUS.]

40 POLONIUS: Th' ambassadors from Norway, my good lord,
    Are joyfully returned.

---

4. In addition to the fact that.

KING: Thou still° hast been the father of good news.   *always*
POLONIUS: Have I, my lord? I assure you, my good liege,
   I hold my duty as I hold my soul,
   Both to my God and to my gracious king;   45
   And I do think—or else this brain of mine
   Hunts not the trail of policy° so sure   *statecraft*
   As it hath used to do—that I have found
   The very cause of Hamlet's lunacy.
KING: O, speak of that, that do I long to hear.   50
POLONIUS: Give first admittance to th' ambassadors.
   My news shall be the fruit° to that great feast.   *dessert*
KING: Thyself do grace to them, and bring them in.
                    [Exit POLONIUS.*]*
   He tells me, my dear Gertrude, he hath found
   The head° and source of all your son's distemper.   *origin* 55
QUEEN: I doubt° it is no other but the main,   *fear*
   His father's death and our o'erhasty marriage.
KING: Well, we shall sift° him.   *examine*

*[Enter Ambassadors (*VOLTEMAND *and* CORNELIUS*) with*
POLONIUS.*]*

              Welcome, my good friends,
   Say, Voltemand, what from our brother° Norway?   *fellow monarch*
VOLTEMAND: Most fair return of greetings and desires.°   *good wishes* 60
   Upon our first,[5] he sent out to suppress
   His nephew's levies,° which to him appeared   *raising of troops*
   To be a preparation 'gainst the Polack,°   *king of Poland*
   But better looked into, he truly found
   It was against your highness, whereat grieved,   65
   That so his sickness, age, and impotence
   Was falsely borne in hand, sends out arrests[6]
   On Fortinbras, which he in brief obeys,
   Receives rebuke from Norway, and in fine,°   *short; the end*
   Makes vow before his uncle never more   70
   To give th' assay° of arms against your majesty.   *trial*
   Whereon old Norway, overcome with joy,
   Gives him three thousand crowns in annual fee,°   *income*
   And his commission to employ those soldiers,
   So levied as before, against the Polack,   75
   With an entreaty, herein further shown,
               [Gives CLAUDIUS *a paper.]*
   That it might please you to give quiet pass°   *safe conduct*
   Through your dominions for this enterprise,
   On such regards of safety and allowance
   As therein are set down.
KING: It likes° us well,   *pleases* 80
   And at our more considered time[7] we'll read,

---

5. That is, first appearance.   6. Orders to stop. *Falsely borne in hand*: disloyally taken advantage of.
7. That is, when we have more time for consideration.

Answer, and think upon this business.
Meantime we thank you for your well-took° labor.   *successful*
Go to your rest; at night we'll feast together.
Most welcome home!   [*Exeunt* AMBASSADORS.]
85   POLONIUS: This business is well ended.
My liege and madam, to expostulate°   *discuss*
What majesty should be, what duty is,
Why day is day, night night, and time is time,
Were nothing but to waste night, day, and time.
90   Therefore, since brevity is the soul of wit,
And tediousness the limbs and outward flourishes,°   *adornments*
I will be brief. Your noble son is mad.
Mad call I it, for to define true madness,
What is't but to be nothing else but mad?
But let that go.
95   QUEEN: More matter with less art.
POLONIUS: Madam, I swear I use no art at all.
That he is mad, 'tis true: 'tis true 'tis pity,
And pity 'tis 'tis true. A foolish figure,°   *figure of speech*
But farewell it, for I will use no art.
100 Mad let us grant him, then, and now remains
That we find out the cause of this effect,
Or rather say the cause of this defect,
For this effect defective comes by cause.
Thus it remains, and the remainder thus.
105 Perpend.°   *Consider*
I have a daughter—have while she is mine—°   *until she marries*
Who in her duty and obedience, mark,
Hath given me this. Now gather, and surmise.
[*Reads*] *the letter.*
"To the celestial, and my soul's idol, the most beauti-
110 fied Ophelia."—That's an ill phrase, a vile phrase, "beauti-
fied" is a vile phrase. But you shall hear. Thus:
"In her excellent white bosom, these, etc."
QUEEN: Came this from Hamlet to her?
POLONIUS: Good madam, stay° awhile. I will be faithful.[8]   *wait*

115   "Doubt thou the stars are fire,
             Doubt that the sun doth move;
           Doubt° truth to be a liar;   *Suspect*
             But never doubt I love.

           O dear Ophelia, I am ill at these numbers.° I have not   *verses*
120   art to reckon° my groans, but that I love thee best, O   *count*
           most best, believe it. Adieu.
             Thine evermore, most dear lady,
               whilst this machine is° to him, Hamlet."   *body belongs*
This in obedience hath my daughter shown me,

8. That is, read the letter faithfully or accurately.

125 And more above,° hath his solicitings,   *in addition*
As they fell out° by time, by means, and place,   *occurred*
All given to mine ear.

KING: But how hath she
Received his love?

POLONIUS: What do you think of me?

KING: As of a man faithful and honorable.

POLONIUS: I would fain° prove so. But what might you think,   *hope to* 130
When I had seen this hot love on the wing.
(As I perceived it, I must tell you that,
Before my daughter told me), what might you,
Or my dear majesty your queen here, think,
If I had played the desk or table-book,[9]   135
Or given my heart a winking, mute and dumb,[1]
Or looked upon this love with idle sight,
What might you think? No, I went round° to work,   *directly*
And my young mistress thus I did bespeak:°   *address*
"Lord Hamlet is a prince out of thy star.°   *sphere* 140
This must not be." And then I prescripts° gave her,   *instructions*
That she should lock herself from his resort,°   *visits*
Admit no messengers, receive no tokens.
Which done, she took the fruits of my advice;
And he repelled, a short tale to make,   145
Fell into a sadness, then into a fast,
Thence to a watch,° thence into a weakness,   *insomnia*
Thence to a lightness,° and by this declension,°   *dizziness / decline*
Into the madness wherein now he raves,
And all we mourn for.

KING: Do you think 'tis this?   150

QUEEN: It may be, very like.

POLONIUS: Hath there been such a time—I would fain know
        that—
That I have positively said "'Tis so,"
When it proved otherwise?

KING: Not that I know.

POLONIUS: [*Pointing to his head and shoulder.*] Take this
        from this, if this be otherwise.   155
If circumstances lead me, I will find
Where truth is hid, though it were hid indeed
Within the centre.°   *earth's center*

KING: How may we try° it further?   *test*

POLONIUS: You know sometimes he walks four hours together
        Here in the lobby.

QUEEN: So he does, indeed.   160

POLONIUS: At such a time I'll loose my daughter to him.
        Be you and I behind an arras° then.   *wall tapestry*

9. If I had recorded the perception (in my memory) but kept it hidden.
1. Or made my heart effectively silent.

Mark the encounter. If he love her not,
And be not from his reason fall'n thereon,°   on that account
Let me be no assistant for a state,
165   But keep a farm and carters.°   cart drivers
KING: We will try it.

[Enter HAMLET reading a book.]

QUEEN: But look where sadly the poor wretch comes reading.
POLONIUS: Away, I do beseech you both away,
I'll board° him presently.   [Exeunt KING and QUEEN.]   accost
                                 O, give me leave.°   excuse me
170   How does my good Lord Hamlet?
HAMLET: Well, God-a-mercy.[2]
POLONIUS: Do you know me, my lord?
HAMLET: Excellent well, you are a fishmonger.
POLONIUS: Not I, my lord.
175   HAMLET: Then I would you were so honest a man.
POLONIUS: Honest, my lord?
HAMLET: Ay, sir, to be honest as this world goes, is to be one
    man picked out of ten thousand.
POLONIUS: That's very true, my lord.
180   HAMLET: For if the sun breed maggots in a dead dog, being
    a god kissing carrion[3]—Have you a daughter?
POLONIUS: I have, my lord.
HAMLET: Let her not walk i' th' sun.° Conception[4] is a bless-   out in public
    ing, but as your daughter may conceive—friend, look to't.°   take care
185   POLONIUS: How say you by that? [Aside.] Still harping on my
    daughter. Yet he knew me not at first. 'A° said I was a fish-   He
    monger. 'A is far gone. And truly in my youth I suffered
    much extremity for love. Very near this. I'll speak to him
    again.—What do you read, my lord?
190   HAMLET: Words, words, words.
POLONIUS: What is the matter,[5] my lord?
HAMLET: Between who?
POLONIUS: I mean the matter that you read, my lord.
HAMLET: Slanders, sir; for the satirical rogue says here that
195   old men have grey beards, that their faces are wrinkled,
    their eyes purging° thick amber° and plumtree gum, and   discharging / resin
    that they have a plentiful lack of wit,° together with most   intellect
    weak hams°—all which, sir, though I most powerfully   thighs
    and potently believe, yet I hold it not honesty° to have it   honorable
200   thus set down, for yourself, sir, shall grow old as I am, if
    like a crab you could go backward.
POLONIUS: [Aside.] Though this be madness, yet there is
    method in't.—Will you walk out of the air, my lord?
HAMLET: Into my grave?

2. Thank you (used with inferiors).   3. Reference to the belief that maggots were produced spontane-
ously by the action of sunshine on carrion.   4. Ability to form ideas; pregnancy.
5. Content, subject, although Hamlet deliberately interprets it as "subject of a quarrel."

POLONIUS: [*Aside.*] Indeed, that's out of the air.° How preg-   drafts (perhaps)   205
nant sometime his replies are! a happiness° that often   an appropriateness
madness hits on, which reason and sanity could not so
prosperously° be delivered of. I will leave him, and sud-   successfully
denly° contrive the means of meeting between him and   immediately
my daughter.—My honorable lord. I will most humbly   210
take my leave of you.

HAMLET: You cannot take from me anything that I will
more willingly part withal°—except my life, except my   with
life, except my life.

      [*Enter* GUILDENSTERN *and* ROSENCRANTZ.]

POLONIUS: Fare you well, my lord.   215
HAMLET: These tedious old fools!
POLONIUS: You go to seek the Lord Hamlet. There he is.
ROSENCRANTZ: [*To* POLONIUS.] God save you, sir!
                              [*Exit* POLONIUS.]
GUILDENSTERN: My honored lord!
ROSENCRANTZ: My most dear lord!   220
HAMLET: My excellent good friends! How dost thou,
    Guildenstern?
    Ah, Rosencrantz! Good lads, how do you both?
ROSENCRANTZ: As the indifferent° children of the earth.   ordinary
GUILDENSTERN: Happy° in that we are not over-happy;   Fortunate   225
    On Fortune's cap we are not the very button.°   highest point
HAMLET: Nor the soles of her shoe?
ROSENCRANTZ: Neither, my lord.
HAMLET: Then you live about her waist, or in the middle of
    her favors?   230
GUILDENSTERN: Faith, her privates[6] we.
HAMLET: In the secret parts of Fortune? O, most true, she
    is a strumpet.° What news?   whore
ROSENCRANTZ: None, my lord, but that the world's grown
    honest.   235
HAMLET: Then is doomsday near. But your news is not true.
Let me question more in particular. What have you, my
good friends, deserved at the hands of Fortune, that she
sends you to prison hither?
GUILDENSTERN: Prison, my lord?   240
HAMLET: Denmark's a prison.
ROSENCRANTZ: Then is the world one.
HAMLET: A goodly° one, in which there are many confines,°   spacious / enclosures
wards° and dungeons. Denmark being one o' th' worst.   cells
ROSENCRANTZ: We think not so, my lord.   245
HAMLET: Why then 'tis none to you; for there is nothing
either good or bad, but thinking makes it so. To me it is a
prison.

6. A triple pun: private persons (who hold no public office); intimate friends; private parts, genitalia.

ROSENCRANTZ: Why then your ambition makes it one. 'Tis
250   too narrow for your mind.
HAMLET: O God, I could be bounded in a nutshell and count
      myself a king of infinite space, were it not that I have bad
      dreams.
GUILDENSTERN: Which dreams indeed are ambition; for the
255   very substance of the ambitious is merely the shadow of a
      dream.
HAMLET: A dream itself is but a shadow.
ROSENCRANTZ: Truly, and I hold ambition of so airy and
      light a quality that it is but a shadow's shadow.
260   HAMLET: Then are our beggars bodies, and our monarchs and
      outstretched heroes the beggars' shadows. Shall we to th'
      court? for, by my fay,° I cannot reason.   *faith*
BOTH: We'll wait upon° you.   *accompany*
HAMLET: No such matter.° I will not sort° you with the rest   *Certainly not / class*
265   of my servants; for to speak to you like an honest man, I
      am most dreadfully attended.° But in the beaten° way of   *waited upon /*
      friendship, what make you at Elsinore?[7]   *well-worn track*
ROSENCRANTZ: To visit you, my lord; no other occasion.
HAMLET: Beggar that I am, I am even poor in thanks, but I
270   thank you; and sure, dear friends, my thanks are too dear
      a halfpenny.[8] Were you not sent for? Is it your own inclin-
      ing? Is it a free° visitation? Come, come, deal justly with   *voluntary*
      me. Come, come, nay speak.
GUILDENSTERN: What should we say, my lord?
275   HAMLET: Anything but to th' purpose. You were sent for,
      and there is a kind of confession in your looks, which your
      modesties° have not craft enough to color.° I know the   *senses of decency / disguise*
      good king and queen have sent for you.
ROSENCRANTZ: To what end, my lord?
280   HAMLET: That you must teach me. But let me conjure° you by   *solemnly request*
      the rights of our fellowship, by the consonancy° of our   *harmonious friendship*
      youth, by the obligation of our ever preserved love, and by
      what more dear a better proposer can charge you withal, be
      even° and direct with me whether you were sent for or no.   *level*
285   ROSENCRANTZ: [*Aside to* GUILDENSTERN.] What say you?
HAMLET: [*Aside.*] Nay, then, I have an eye of° you.—If you   *on*
      love me, hold not off.
GUILDENSTERN: My lord, we were sent for.
HAMLET: I will tell you why; so shall my anticipation prevent°   *forestall*
290   your discovery,° and your secrecy to the king and queen   *disclosure*
      moult no feather.[9] I have of late—but wherefore I know
      not—lost all my mirth, forgone all custom of exercises; and
      indeed it goes so heavily with my disposition, that this

7. What are you doing at Elsinore.   8. Not worth a halfpenny.
9. Remain unimpaired, as a bird that has lost no feathers.

goodly frame° the earth seems to me a sterile promontory,   *structure*
this most excellent canopy the air, look you, this brave   295
o'er-hanging firmament,[1] this majestical roof fretted° with   *adorned*
golden fire, why it appeareth nothing to me but a foul and
pestilent congregation° of vapors. What a piece of work is a   *mass*
man, how noble in reason, how infinite in faculties, in form
and moving, how express° and admirable in action, how   *precise; expressive* 300
like an angel in apprehension, how like a god: the beauty of
the world, the paragon of animals. And yet to me, what is
this quintessence of dust? Man delights not me, nor woman
neither, though by your smiling you seem to say so.

ROSENCRANTZ: My lord, there was no such stuff in my   305
    thoughts.

HAMLET: Why did ye laugh, then, when I said "Man delights
    not me"?

ROSENCRANTZ: To think, my lord, if you delight not in man,
    what lenten[2] entertainment° the players shall receive   *welcome* 310
    from you. We coted° them on the way, and hither are   *passed*
    they coming to offer you service.

HAMLET: He that plays the king shall be welcome—his maj-
    esty shall have tribute of me; the adventurous knight shall
    use his foil° and target;° the lover shall not sigh gratis;° the   *sword / shield / for free* 315
    humorous[3] man shall end° his part in peace; the clown   *play out*
    shall make those laugh whose lungs are tickle o' th' sere;°   *primed to laugh*
    and the lady shall say her mind freely, or the blank verse
    shall halt° for't. What players are they?   *limp (fail to scan)*

ROSENCRANTZ: Even those you were wont to take such delight   320
    in, the tragedians° of the city.   *actors*

HAMLET: How chances it they travel? Their residence,° both   *(in the city)*
    in reputation and profit, was better both ways.

ROSENCRANTZ: I think their inhibition° comes by the   *hindrance (to staying*
    means of the late innovation.[4]   *in the city)* 325

HAMLET: Do they hold the same estimation° they did when   *esteem; reputation*
    I was in the city? Are they so followed?

ROSENCRANTZ: No, indeed, are they not.

HAMLET: How comes it? Do they grow rusty?

ROSENCRANTZ: Nay, their endeavor keeps° in the wonted°   *continues / accustomed* 330
    pace; but there is, sir, an eyrie° of children, little eyases,   *nest for a bird of prey*
    that cry out on the top of question,[5] and are most tyran-
    nically clapped for't. These are now the fashion, and so
    berattle° the common° stages (so they call them) that   *noisily abuse / public*

---

1. Heavens overhead, but also, perhaps, referring to the roof or "heavens" overhanging the Elizabethan stage and decorated with stars.
2. Meager. Lent is a period of penitence and fasting.
3. Eccentric, governed by excess of one of the bodily humors. (See 1.4.27 and note.)   4. Latest fashion, perhaps the rage for companies of boy actors, the "little eyases" or hawks alluded to in line 331.
Such a company flourished at the Blackfriars Theatre from 1600–08.   5. With a loud, high delivery.

335   many wearing rapiers are afraid of goose quills[6] and dare
      scarce come thither.

HAMLET: What, are they children? Who maintains 'em?
      How are they escoted?° Will they pursue the quality° no   *supported / profession*
      longer than they can sing?[7] Will they not say afterwards,
340   if they should grow themselves to common players (as it
      is most like,° if their means° are no better), their writers   *likely / financial options*
      do them wrong to make them exclaim against their own
      succession?°   *later employment*

ROSENCRANTZ: Faith, there has been much todo on both
345   sides; and the nation° holds it no sin to tarre° them to   *populace / goad*
      controversy. There was for a while no money bid for argu-
      ment,[8] unless the poet and the player went to cuffs in°   *came to blows over*
      the question.

HAMLET: Is't possible?
350   GUILDENSTERN: O, there has been much throwing about of
      brains.°   *battle of wits*

HAMLET: Do the boys carry it° away?   *(the victory)*

ROSENCRANTZ: Ay, that they do, my lord. Hercules and his
      load too.[9]

355   HAMLET: It is not very strange, for my uncle is King of Den-
      mark, and those that would make mouths° at him while   *grimaces*
      my father lived give twenty, forty, fifty, a hundred ducats
      apiece for his picture in little.° 'Sblood,° there is some-   *miniature /*
      thing in this more than natural, if philosophy could find   *By God's blood*
360   it out.

      [*A flourish.*]

GUILDENSTERN: There are the players.

HAMLET: Gentlemen, you are welcome to Elsinore. Your
      hands. Come then, th' appurtenance° of welcome is fash-   *fitting accompaniment*
      ion and ceremony. Let me comply with° you in this garb,°   *welcome / fashion*
365   lest my extent° to the players, which I tell you must show   *offering (of welcome)*
      fairly outwards should more appear like entertainment°   *(warm) welcome*
      than yours. You are welcome. But my uncle-father and
      aunt-mother are deceived.

GUILDENSTERN: In what, my dear lord?

370   HAMLET: I am but mad north-north-west; when the wind is
      southerly I know a hawk° from a handsaw.   *plasterer's tool*

      [*Enter* POLONIUS.]

POLONIUS: Well be with you, gentlemen.

HAMLET: Hark you, Guildenstern—and you too—at each
      ear a hearer. That great baby you see there is not yet out
375   of his swaddling clouts.°   *clothes*

---

6. Pens of satirical writers.   7. Until their voices break (at puberty).   8. Paid for a play plot.
9. During one of his labors Hercules assumed for a time the burden of the Titan Atlas, who supported
the world on his shoulders. Hercules bearing the world was the sign of the Globe Theatre.

ROSENCRANTZ: Happily° he is the second time come to ⟨Perhaps⟩
    them, for they say an old man is twice a child.
HAMLET: I will prophesy he comes to tell me of the players.
    Mark it.—You say right, sir, a Monday morning, 'twas then
    indeed.   380
POLONIUS: My lord, I have news to tell you.
HAMLET: My lord, I have news to tell you. When Roscius
    was an actor in Rome¹—
POLONIUS: The actors are come hither, my lord.
HAMLET: Buzz, buzz.   385
POLONIUS: Upon my honor—
HAMLET: Then came each actor on his ass—
POLONIUS: The best actors in the world, either for tragedy,
    comedy, history, pastoral, pastoral-comical, historical-
    pastoral, tragical-historical, tragical-comical historical-   390
    pastoral, scene individable,² or poem unlimited. Seneca
    cannot be too heavy nor Plautus³ too light. For the law of
    writ and the liberty, these are the only men.
HAMLET: O Jephtha, judge of Israel, what a treasure hadst
    thou!⁴   395
POLONIUS: What a treasure had he, my lord?
HAMLET: Why—

    "One fair daughter, and no more,
    The which he loved passing° well."   ⟨surpassing⟩

POLONIUS: [Aside.] Still on my daughter.   400
HAMLET: Am I not i' th' right, old Jephtha?
POLONIUS: If you call me Jephtha, my lord, I have a daughter
    that I love passing well.
HAMLET: Nay, that follows not.⁵
POLONIUS: What follows then, my lord?   405
HAMLET: Why—

    "As by lot,° God wot"°   ⟨chance / knows⟩

and then, you know,

    "It came to pass, as most like° it was."   ⟨likely⟩

The first row° of the pious chanson° will show you more,   ⟨stanza / song⟩ 410
for look where my abridgement⁶ comes.

1. Roscius was the most famous actor of ancient Rome; hence this would be old news.
2. Play without breaks or divisions, or play observing the three classical unities—hence, following "the
law of writ," unlike plays "unlimited" by such rules or laws or taking "liberty" with them (lines 391–
93). Essentially, Hamlet thus refers here to every contemporary kind or category of drama.
3. Seneca and Plautus were ancient Roman writers of tragedy and comedy, respectively.
4. To ensure victory, Jephtha promises to sacrifice the first creature to meet him on his return.
Unfortunately, his only daughter is the victim of his vow (Judg. 11). Jephtha, Judge of Israel was the
title of a popular ballad, the "pious chanson" (line 410) from which Hamlet subsequently sings.
5. Polonius's having a daughter is not a logical consequence of Hamlet calling him Jephtha.
6. That which cuts short by interrupting.

[*Enter the* PLAYERS.]

You are welcome, masters; welcome, all.—I am glad to
see thee well.—Welcome, good friends.—O, old friend!
Why, thy face is valanced° since I saw thee last. Com'st   *fringed (with a beard)*
415   thou to beard° me in Denmark?—What, my young lady   *defy*
and mistress?[7] By'r lady, your ladyship is nearer to heaven
than when I saw you last by the altitude of a chopine.°   *high platform shoe*
Pray God your voice, like a piece of uncurrent gold, be
not cracked within the ring.[8]—Masters, you are all wel-
420   come. We'll e'en to't° like French falconers, fly at any-   *go to work at once*
thing we see. We'll have a speech straight.° Come give us   *right away*
a taste of your quality,° come a passionate speech.   *professional skill*

FIRST PLAYER: What speech, my good lord?

HAMLET: I heard thee speak me a speech once, but it was
425   never acted, or if it was, not above once, for the play, I
remember, pleased not the million; 'twas caviary° to the   *caviar*
general.° But it was—as I received it, and others whose   *masses*
judgments in such matters cried in the top of° mine—an   *outweighed*
excellent play, well digested° in the scenes, set down with   *arranged*
430   as much modesty as cunning. I remember one said there
were no sallets[9] in the lines to make the matter savory, nor
no matter in the phrase that might indict the author of
affectation, but called it an honest method, as wholesome
as sweet, and by very much more handsome° than fine.°   *well-crafted / showy*
435   One speech in't I chiefly loved. 'Twas Æneas' tale to Dido,
and thereabout of it especially where he speaks of Priam's
slaughter.[1] If it live in your memory, begin at this line—let
me see, let me see:

   "The rugged° Pyrrhus, like th' Hyrcanian beast"°—   *savage / tiger*

440   'tis not so; it begins with Pyrrhus—

   "The rugged Pyrrhus, he whose sable arms,
   Black as his purpose, did the night resemble
   When he lay couchéd in th' ominous horse,[2]
   Hath now this dread and black complexion smeared
445   With heraldry° more dismal; head to foot   *heraldic colors*
   Now is he total gules,° horridly tricked°   *all red / adorned*
   With blood of fathers, mothers, daughters, sons,
   Baked and impasted with° the parching° streets,   *encrusted by / burning*
   That lend a tyrannous and a damnèd light
450   To their lord's murder. Roasted in wrath and fire,

7. Boy who played female roles.
8. A coin was no longer legal tender if the circle or ring enclosing the monarch's head was broken.
9. Salads; seasoned dishes. I.e., deliberate attempts to embellish the style in order to make the lines
more pleasing ("savory").
1. Aeneas, fleeing with his band from fallen Troy ("Ilium," line 463), arrives in Carthage, where he
tells Dido, the queen of Carthage, of Troy's fall and the death of Priam, the aged king of Troy, at the
hands of Pyrrhus, the son of the slain Achilles.   2. That is, the Trojan horse.

And thus o'er-sizèd[3] with coagulate° gore,   *clotted*
With eyes like carbuncles,° the hellish Pyrrhus   *glowing gems*
Old grandsire Priam seeks."

So proceed you.

POLONIUS: Fore God, my lord, well spoken, with good   455
accent and good discretion.

FIRST PLAYER: "Anon he finds him[4]
Striking too short at Greeks. His antique sword,
Rebellious to his arm, lies where it falls,
Repugnant° to command. Unequal matched,   *Resistant*   460
Pyrrhus at Priam drives, in rage strikes wide.
But with the whiff and wind of his fell° sword   *fierce*
Th' unnervèd° father falls. Then senseless Ilium,   *strengthless*
Seeming to feel this blow, with flaming top
Stoops to his° base, and with a hideous crash   *its*   465
Takes prisoner Pyrrhus' ear. For, lo! his sword,
Which was declining° on the milky° head   *descending / white*
Of reverend Priam, seemed i' th' air to stick.
So as a painted tyrant[5] Pyrrhus stood,
And like a neutral to his will and matter,[6]   470
Did nothing.
But as we often see, against° some storm,   *before*
A silence in the heavens, the rack° stand still,   *clouds*
The bold winds speechless, and the orb° below   *earth*
As hush as death, anon the dreadful thunder   475
Doth rend the region;° so, after Pyrrhus' pause,   *sky*
A rousèd vengeance sets him new awork
And never did the Cyclops' hammers fall
On Mars's armor, forged for proof eterne,[7]
With less remorse than Pyrrhus' bleeding sword   480
Now falls on Priam.
Out, out, thou strumpet, Fortune! All you gods,
In general synod take away her power,
Break all the spokes and fellies[8] from her wheel,
And bowl the round nave° down the hill of heaven°   *wheel hub / Mount Olympus* 485
As low as to the fiends."

POLONIUS: This is too long.

HAMLET: It shall to the barber's with your beard.—Prithee
say on. He's for a jig,[9] or a tale of bawdry, or he sleeps. Say
on; come to Hecuba.[1]   490

3. As though coated with sizing, thick liquid used to prepare a canvas for painting.
4. Soon, that is, Pyrrhus finds Priam.   5. That is, like a tyrant in a painting, hence unmoving.
6. As one indifferent to his intention and the action at hand.
7. Mars, as befits a Roman war god, had armor made by the blacksmith god Vulcan and his assistants,
the Cyclopes. It was suitably impenetrable (of "proof eterne").   8. The power of Fortune's ever-turn-
ing wheel, raising and lowering men in succession, was proverbial. *Fellies*: curved parts of the wheel's
rim.   9. Ridiculous verse, or the dance that followed many plays.
1. Wife of Priam and queen of Troy. Her "loins" are described below as "o'erteemèd" because of her
unusual fertility. The number of her children varies in different accounts, but twenty is a safe minimum.

FIRST PLAYER: "But who, ah woe! had seen the moblèd°   *veiled; muffled (in a hood)*
    queen—"
HAMLET: "The moblèd queen"?
POLONIUS: That's good. "Moblèd queen" is good.
FIRST PLAYER: "Run barefoot up and down, threat'ning the
    flames
495   With bisson rheum,° a clout° upon that head   *blinding tears / cloth*
    Where late the diadem stood, and for a robe,
    About her lank and all o'er-teemèd loins,
    A blanket, in the alarm of fear caught up—
    Who this had seen, with tongue in venom steeped,
500   'Gainst Fortune's state° would treason have pronounced.   *rule*
    But if the gods themselves did see her then,
    When she saw Pyrrhus make malicious sport
    In mincing with his sword her husband's limbs,
    The instant burst of clamor that she made,
505   Unless things mortal move them not at all,
    Would have made milch° the burning eyes of heaven,   *milky; moist*
    And passion° in the gods."   *suffering; pity*
POLONIUS: Look whe'r° he has not turned his color, and has   *whether*
    tears in's eyes. Prithee no more.
510 HAMLET: 'Tis well. I'll have thee speak out the rest of this
    soon.—Good my lord, will you see the players well
    bestowed?° Do you hear, let them be well used,° for they   *lodged / treated*
    are the abstract° and brief chronicles of the time; after   *summary*
    your death you were better have a bad epitaph than their
515   ill report while you live.
POLONIUS: My lord, I will use them according to their desert.
HAMLET: God's bodkin,° man, much better. Use every man   *By God's dear body*
    after° his desert, and who shall 'scape whipping? Use them   *according to*
    after your own honor and dignity. The less they deserve,
520   the more merit is in your bounty. Take them in.
POLONIUS: Come, sirs.
HAMLET: Follow him, friends. We'll hear a play tomorrow.
                    [*Aside to* FIRST PLAYER.]
    Dost thou hear me, old friend, can you play "The Mur-
    der of Gonzago"?
525 FIRST PLAYER: Ay, my lord.
HAMLET: We'll ha't° tomorrow night. You could for a   *have it*
    need° study a speech of some dozen or sixteen lines   *if necessary*
    which I would set down and insert in't, could you not?
FIRST PLAYER: Ay, my lord.
530 HAMLET: Very well. Follow that lord, and look you mock him
    not.
                    [*Exeunt* POLONIUS *and* PLAYERS.]
    My good friends, I'll leave you till night. You are wel-
    come to Elsinore.
ROSENCRANTZ: Good my lord.
                    [*Exeunt* ROSENCRANTZ *and* GUILDENSTERN.]

HAMLET: Ay, so God b'wi'ye. Now I am alone.   535
    O, what a rogue and peasant slave am I!
    Is it not monstrous that this player here,
    But° in a fiction, in a dream of passion,   *Merely*
    Could force his soul so to his own conceit°   *imagined situation*
    That from her° working all his visage wanned;°   *(his soul's) / grew pale* 540
    Tears in his eyes, distraction in his aspect
    A broken voice, and his whole function suiting
    With forms to his conceit? And all for nothing,
    For Hecuba!
    What's Hecuba to him or he to Hecuba,   545
    That he should weep for her? What would he do
    Had he the motive and the cue for passion
    That I have? He would drown the stage with tears,
    And cleave the general ear° with horrid speech,   *the ears of people generally*
    Make mad the guilty, and appal the free,°   *innocent*
    Confound the ignorant, and amaze° indeed   *bewilder* 550
    The very faculties of eyes and ears.
    Yet I,
    A dull and muddy-mettled° rascal peak°   *dull-spirited / mope*
    Like John-a-dreams,° unpregnant of² my cause,   *a man dreaming*
    And can say nothing; no, not for a king   555
    Upon whose property° and most dear life   *rightful sovereignty*
    A damned defeat³ was made. Am I a coward?
    Who calls me villain, breaks my pate° across,   *head*
    Plucks off my beard and blows it in my face,
    Tweaks me by the nose, gives° me the lie i' th' throat   *attributes to* 560
    As deep as to the lungs? Who does me this?
    Ha, 'swounds,° I should take it; for it cannot be   *by God's wounds*
    But I am pigeon-livered and lack gall⁴
    To make oppression bitter, or ere this
    I should 'a fatted all the region kites⁵   565
    With this slave's offal. Bloody, bawdy villain!
    Remorseless, treacherous, lecherous, kindless° villain!   *unnatural*
    O, vengeance!
    Why, what an ass am I! This is most brave,°   *fine*
    That I, the son of a dear father murdered,   570
    Prompted to my revenge by heaven and hell,
    Must like a whore unpack my heart with words,
    And fall a-cursing like a very drab,°   *whore*
    A scullion!° Fie upon't! foh!   *menial kitchen servant*
    About,° my brains. Hum—I have heard   *Into action* 575
    That guilty creatures sitting at a play,
    Have by the very cunning° of the scene   *artfulness*
    Been struck so to the soul that presently

2. Not quickened to action by.   3. An overthrow worthy of damnation
4. Bitter fluid (humor) produced by the liver and the supposed source of anger. Pigeons were thought
not to secrete gall.   5. Birds of prey in the sky ("region").

580

They have proclaimed° their malefactions;   *admitted*
For murder, though it have no tongue, will speak
With most miraculous organ. I'll have these players
Play something like the murder of my father
Before mine uncle. I'll observe his looks.
I'll tent° him to the quick. If 'a do blench,°   *probe / blanch; grow pale*

585

I know my course. The spirit that I have seen
May be a devil, and the devil hath power
T' assume a pleasing shape, yea, and perhaps
Out of my weakness and my melancholy,
As he is very potent with° such spirits,[6]   *powerful over*

590

Abuses me to damn me. I'll have grounds
More relative° than this. The play's the thing   *relevant; conclusive*
Wherein I'll catch the conscience of the king.   [*Exit.*]

ACT III

Scene 1

A room in the castle. Enter KING, QUEEN, POLONIUS,
OPHELIA, ROSENCRANTZ *and* GUILDENSTERN.

KING: And can you by no drift of conference[7]
    Get from him why he puts on this confusion,
    Grating so harshly all his days of quiet
    With turbulent and dangerous lunacy?
5 ROSENCRANTZ: He does confess he feels himself distracted,°   *confused; agitated*
    But from what cause 'a will by no means speak.
GUILDENSTERN: Nor do we find him forward° to be sounded,°   *eager / questioned*
    But with a crafty madness keeps aloof
    When we would bring him on to some confession
    Of his true state.
10 QUEEN: Did he receive you well?
ROSENCRANTZ: Most like a gentleman.
GUILDENSTERN: But with much forcing of his disposition.°   *mood*
ROSENCRANTZ: Niggard of question,[8] but of our demands[8]
    Most free in his reply.
QUEEN: Did you assay° him   *tempt*
15   To any pastime?
ROSENCRANTZ: Madam, it so fell out that certain players
    We o'er-raught° on the way. Of these we told him,   *passed*
    And there did seem in him a kind of joy
    To hear of it. They are here about the court,
20   And as I think, they have already order
    This night to play before him.

6. Those afflicted with too much bile, a humor or "spirit" (distillation), were believed to suffer melancholy and to be prone to hallucinations, thus being easily tricked ("Abuse[d]," line 590) by the devil.   7. Carefully directed conversation.   8. Reluctant to offer conversation, but to our questions.

POLONIUS: 'Tis most true,
    And he beseeched me to entreat your majesties
    To hear and see the matter.°   *performance*
KING: With all my heart, and it doth much content me
    To hear him so inclined.   25
    Good gentlemen, give him a further edge,°   *stimulus; appetite*
    And drive his purpose into these delights.
ROSENCRANTZ: We shall, my lord.
                    [*Exeunt* ROSENCRANTZ *and* GUILDENSTERN.]
KING: Sweet Gertrude, leave us
        too,
    For we have closely° sent for Hamlet hither,   *privately*
    That he, as 'twere by accident, may here   30
    Affront° Ophelia.   *Confront*
    Her father and myself (lawful espials°)   *spies*
    Will so bestow ourselves that, seeing unseen,
    We may of their encounter frankly judge,
    And gather by him, as he is behaved,   35
    If't be th' affliction of his love or no
    That thus he suffers for.
QUEEN: I shall obey you.—
    And for your part, Ophelia, I do wish
    That your good beauties be the happy cause
    Of Hamlet's wildness. So shall I hope your virtues   40
    Will bring him to his wonted° way again,   *accustomed*
    To both your honors.
OPHELIA: Madam, I wish it may.
                                                        [*Exit* QUEEN.]
POLONIUS: Ophelia, walk you here.—Gracious,° so please you,   *Your grace*
    We will bestow ourselves.—[*To* OPHELIA.] Read on
        this book,[9]
    That show of such an exercise° may color°   *(of devotion) / explain* 45
    Your loneliness.—We are oft to blame in this,
    'Tis too much proved, that with devotion's visage
    And pious action we do sugar o'er
    The devil himself.
KING: [*Aside*.]   O, 'tis too true.
    How smart° a lash that speech doth give my conscience!   *sharp* 50
    The harlot's cheek, beautied with plast'ring° art,   *cosmetic*
    Is not more ugly to the thing that helps it
    Than is my deed to my most painted word.
    O heavy burden!
POLONIUS: I hear him coming. Let's withdraw, my lord.   55
                    [*Exeunt* KING *and* POLONIUS.]

    [*Enter* HAMLET.]

9. A prayer book or devotional text, as the lines below make clear.

HAMLET: To be, or not to be, that is the question:
Whether 'tis nobler in the mind to suffer
The slings and arrows of outrageous fortune,
Or to take arms against a sea of troubles,
60   And by opposing end them. To die, to sleep—
No more; and by a sleep to say we end
The heartache, and the thousand natural shocks
That flesh is heir to. 'Tis a consummation
Devoutly to be wished—to die, to sleep—
65   To sleep, perchance to dream, ay there's the rub;°   obstacle; impediment
For in that sleep of death what dreams may come
When we have shuffled° off this mortal coil°   cast / turmoil; flesh
Must give us pause—there's the respect°   consideration
That makes calamity of so long life.[1]
70   For who would bear the whips and scorns of time,
Th' oppressor's wrong, the proud man's contumely,°   insulting behavior
The pangs of despised° love, the law's delay,   scorned
The insolence of office,° and the spurns°   bureaucrats / spurnings; rejections
That patient merit of° th' unworthy takes,   from
75   When he himself might his quietus[2] make
With a bare bodkin?° Who would fardels° bear,   mere dagger / burdens
To grunt and sweat under a weary life,
But that the dread of something after death,
The undiscovered country, from whose bourn°   border
80   No traveller returns, puzzles the will,
And makes us rather bear those ills we have
Than fly to others that we know not of?
Thus conscience[3] does make cowards of us all;
And thus the native hue° of resolution   natural complexion
85   Is sicklied o'er with the pale cast° of thought,   tint
And enterprises of great pitch° and moment°   height / importance
With this regard° their currents turn awry   consideration
And lose the name of action.—Soft you now°   Wait a moment
The fair Ophelia.—Nymph, in thy orisons°   prayers
Be all my sins remembered.
90 OPHELIA: Good my lord,
How does your honor for this many a day?
HAMLET: I humbly thank you, well, well, well.
OPHELIA: My lord, I have remembrances of yours
That I have longèd long to re-deliver.
I pray you now receive them.
95 HAMLET: No, not I,
I never gave you aught.

---

1. That makes adversity so long-lived (as opposed to quickly ended in suicide).   2. Settlement; a paid-off account was marked "Quietus est" (Latin: It is laid to rest).   3. Both moral conscience and consciousness.

OPHELIA: My honored lord, you know right well you did,
And with them words of so sweet breath composed
As made the things more rich. Their perfume lost,
Take these again, for to the noble mind   100
Rich gifts wax° poor when givers prove unkind.   *grow*
There, my lord.
HAMLET: Ha, ha! are you honest?°   *chaste; truthful*
OPHELIA: My lord?
HAMLET: Are you fair?   105
OPHELIA: What means your lordship?
HAMLET: That if you be honest and fair, your honesty should
admit no discourse to° your beauty.   *familiar conversation with*
OPHELIA: Could beauty, my lord, have better commerce°   *dealings*
than with honesty?   110
HAMLET: Ay, truly, for the power of beauty will sooner
transform honesty from what it is to a bawd than the
force of honesty can translate beauty into his likeness.
This was sometimes a paradox,° but now   *formerly an uncredited opinion*
the time gives it proof. I did love you once.   115
OPHELIA: Indeed, my lord, you made me believe so.
HAMLET: You should not have believed me, for virtue cannot
so inoculate our old stock° but we shall relish° of it. I   *sinful nature / taste*
loved you not.
OPHELIA: I was the more deceived.   120
HAMLET: Get thee to a nunnery.⁴ Why wouldst thou be a
breeder of sinners? I am myself indifferent° honest, but   *moderately*
yet I could accuse me of such things that it were better
my mother had not borne me: I am very proud, revenge-
ful, ambitious, with more offences at my beck° than I   *command* 125
have thoughts to put them in, imagination to give them
shape, or time to act them in. What should such fellows
as I do crawling between earth and heaven? We are
arrant° knaves all; believe none of us. Go thy ways to a   *complete*
nunnery. Where's your father?   130
OPHELIA: At home, my lord.
HAMLET: Let the doors be shut upon him, that he may play
the fool nowhere but in's own house. Farewell.
OPHELIA: O, help him, you sweet heavens!
HAMLET: If thou dost marry, I'll give thee this plague for thy   135
dowry: be thou as chaste as ice, as pure as snow, thou shalt
not escape calumny. Get thee to a nunnery, farewell. Or if
thou wilt needs marry, marry a fool, for wise men know
well enough what monsters⁵ you° make of them. To a nun-   *(women)*
nery, go, and quickly too. Farewell.   140

---

4. Here used in both its literal senses and as a slang term for brothel.
5. Alluding to the belief that cuckolds grew horns, but Hamlet may mean a more spiritual or psychological transformation as well.

OPHELIA: Heavenly powers, restore him!

HAMLET: I have heard of your paintings,° too, well enough.   *cosmetics*
God hath given you one face, and you make yourselves
another. You jig, you amble, and you lisp;⁶ you nickname
145   God's creatures, and make your wantonness your igno-
rance.⁷ Go to, I'll no more on't,° it hath made me mad. I   *of it*
say we will have no more marriage. Those that are married
already, all but one, shall live. The rest shall keep as they
are. To a nunnery, go.   [*Exit.*]

150 OPHELIA: O, what a noble mind is here o'erthrown!
The courtier's, soldier's, scholar's, eye, tongue, sword,
Th' expectancy° and rose° of the fair state,   *hope / ornament*
The glass° of fashion and the mould of form,⁸   *mirror image*
Th' observed of all observers, quite quite down!
155   And I of ladies most deject and wretched,
That sucked the honey of his music° vows,   *musical*
Now see that noble and most sovereign reason
Like sweet bells jangled, out of time and harsh;
That unmatched form and feature of blown° youth   *full-blown*
160   Blasted with ecstasy.° O, woe is me   *madness*
T' have seen what I have seen, see what I see!

[*Enter* KING *and* POLONIUS.]

KING: Love! His affections° do not that way tend,   *feelings*
Nor what he spake, though it lacked form a little,
Was not like madness. There's something in his soul
165   O'er which his melancholy sits on brood,⁹
And I do doubt° the hatch and the disclose°   *fear / public disclosure*
Will be some danger; which to prevent,
I have in quick determination
Thus set it down:° he shall with speed to England   *resolved*
170   For the demand of our neglected tribute.
Haply° the seas and countries different,   *Perhaps*
With variable objects,° shall expel   *different sights or objects*
This something-settled° matter in his heart   *somewhat rooted*
Whereon his brains still° beating puts him thus   *constantly*
175   From fashion of himself.¹ What think you on't?
POLONIUS: It shall do well. But yet do I believe
The origin and commencement of his grief
Sprung from neglected° love.—How now, Ophelia?   *unrequited*
You need not tell us what Lord Hamlet said,
180   We heard it all.—My lord, do as you please,
But if you hold it fit, after the play

6. Dance (or sing), walk, and talk affectedly.
7. You call things by fashionable (not God-given) names, and you blame your affectation on ignorance, or "play dumb."   8. Pattern or model of decorum.   9. That is, like a hen whose egg will soon
"hatch" (line 166).   1. That is, "puts him" in a state unlike his normal self.

Let his queen-mother all alone entreat him
To show his grief. Let her be round° with him,   *blunt*
And I'll be placed, so please you, in the ear°   *earshot*
Of all their conference. If she find him not,[2]   185
To England send him; or confine him where
Your wisdom best shall think.

KING: It shall be so.
Madness in great ones must not unwatched go.

                                          [*Exeunt.*]

Scene 2

A public room in the castle. Enter HAMLET *and three of the*
PLAYERS.

HAMLET: Speak the speech, I pray you, as I pronounced it to
you, trippingly on the tongue; but if you mouth° it as   *speak*
many of our players do, I had as lief the town-crier spoke
my lines. Nor do not saw the air too much with your hand
thus, but use all gently, for in the very torrent, tempest,   5
and as I may say, whirlwind of your passion, you must
acquire and beget a temperance that may give it smooth-
ness. O, it offends me to the soul to hear a robustious°   *bombastic*
periwig-pated° fellow tear a passion to tatters, to very rags,   *bewigged*
to split the ears of the groundlings,[3] who for the most part   10
are capable of nothing but inexplicable dumb shows° and   *pantomimes*
noise. I would have such a fellow whipped for o'erdoing
Termagant. It out-herods Herod.[4] Pray you avoid it.

FIRST PLAYER: I warrant° your honor.   *assure; guarantee*

HAMLET: Be not too tame neither, but let your own discretion   15
be your tutor. Suit the action to the word, the word to the
action, with this special observance, that you o'erstep not
the modesty° of nature; for anything so o'erdone is from°   *moderation / contrary to*
the purpose of playing, whose end both at the first, and
now, was and is, to hold as 'twere the mirror up to nature,   20
to show virtue her own feature, scorn her own image, and
the very age and body of the time his form° and pressure.°   *shape / image*
Now this overdone, or come tardy° off, though it makes the   *faultily*
unskilful° laugh, cannot but make the judicious grieve, the *undiscriminating*
censure of the which one must in your allowance o'erweigh   25
a whole theatre of others. O, there be players that I have
seen play—and heard others praise, and that highly—not
to speak it profanely,[5] that neither having th' accent of
Christians, nor the gait of Christian, pagan, nor man, have
so strutted and bellowed that I have thought some of   30

2. Does not discover his problem.   3. Spectators who paid least and had to stand.   4. Termagant, a
"Saracen" deity, and the biblical Herod were stock characters in popular drama noted for their
excesses of sound and fury.   5. To speak blasphemy (in what he is about to say).

nature's journeymen[6] had made men, and not made them
well, they imitated humanity so abominably.

FIRST PLAYER: I hope we have reformed that indifferently°   *somewhat*
  with us, sir.

35 HAMLET: O, reform it altogether. And let those that play
  your clowns speak no more than is set down for them, for
  there be of° them that will themselves laugh, to set° on   *some of / urge*
  some quantity of barren° spectators to laugh too, though   *unthinking*
  in the meantime some necessary question of the play be
40 then to be considered. That's villainous, and shows a
  most pitiful ambition in the fool that uses it. Go, make
  you ready.   [*Exeunt* PLAYERS.]

  [*Enter* POLONIUS, GUILDENSTERN, *and* ROSENCRANTZ.]

  How now, my lord? Will the king hear this piece of work?
POLONIUS: And the queen too, and that presently.
45 HAMLET: Bid the players make haste.   [*Exit* POLONIUS.]
  Will you two help to hasten them?
ROSENCRANTZ: Ay, my lord.   [*Exeunt they two.*]
HAMLET: What, ho, Horatio!

  [*Enter* HORATIO.]

HORATIO: Here, sweet lord, at your service.
50 HAMLET: Horatio, thou art e'en as just° a man   *honest; balanced*
  As e'er my conversation coped° withal.   *encountered*
HORATIO: O my dear lord!
HAMLET: Nay, do not think I flatter,
  For what advancement may I hope from thee,
  That no revenue hast but thy good spirits
55 To feed and clothe thee? Why should the poor be
      flattered?
  No, let the candied° tongue lick absurd pomp,   *flattering*
  And crook the pregnant° hinges of the knee   *quick (to bow)*
  Where thrift° may follow fawning. Dost thou hear?   *prosperity*
  Since my dear soul was mistress of her choice
60 And could of° men distinguish her election,   *between*
  S'hath sealed thee for herself,[7] for thou hast been
  As one in suff'ring all that suffers nothing,
  A man that Fortune's buffets and rewards
  Hast ta'en with equal thanks; and blest are those
65 Whose blood° and judgment are so well commingled   *passion*
  That they are not a pipe for Fortune's finger
  To sound what stop° she please. Give me that man   *finger hole; musical note*
  That is not passion's slave, and I will wear him
  In my heart's core, ay, in my heart of heart.
70 As I do thee. Something too much of this.

---

6. Craftsmen who are not yet masters of a craft.   7. She has marked you as her own.

There is a play tonight before the king.
One scene of it comes near the circumstance
Which I have told thee of my father's death.
I prithee, when thou seest that act afoot,
Even with the very comment° of thy soul   *keenest observation* 75
Observe my uncle. If his occulted° guilt   *hidden*
Do not itself unkennel° in one speech,   *break loose*
It is a damnèd ghost that we have seen,
And my imaginations are as foul
As Vulcan's stithy.[8] Give him heedful note,°   *careful attention* 80
For I mine eyes will rivet to his face,
And after we will both our judgments join
In censure° of his seeming.°   *judgment / outward appearance*
HORATIO: Well, my lord.
If 'a steal aught the whilst this play in playing,
And 'scape detecting, I will pay the theft.[9]   85

[*Enter Trumpets and Kettledrums,* KING, QUEEN, POLO-
NIUS, OPHELIA, ROSENCRANTZ, GUILDENSTERN, *and
other* LORDS *attendant.*]

HAMLET: They are coming to the play. I must be idle.°   *unoccupied; mad*
Get you a place.
KING: How fares our cousin° Hamlet?   *kinsman*
HAMLET: Excellent, i' faith, of the chameleon's dish. I eat
the air, promise-crammed.[1] You cannot feed capons° so.   *fattened chickens*
KING: I have nothing with this answer, Hamlet. These words   *for slaughter* 90
are not mine.
HAMLET: No, nor mine now. [*To* POLONIUS.] My lord, you
played once i' th' university, you say?
POLONIUS: That did I, my lord, and was accounted a good
actor.   95
HAMLET: What did you enact?
POLONIUS: I did enact Julius Cæsar. I was killed i' th' Capi-
tol; Brutus killed me.
HAMLET: It was a brute part of him to kill so capital a calf°   *fool*
there. Be the players ready?   100
ROSENCRANTZ: Ay, my lord, they stay° upon your patience.°   *wait / leisure*
QUEEN: Come hither, my dear Hamlet, sit by me.
HAMLET: No, good mother, here's metal more attractive.
POLONIUS: [*To the* KING.] O, ho! do you mark that?
HAMLET: Lady, shall I lie in your lap?   105

[*Lying down at* OPHELIA's *feet.*]

OPHELIA: No, my lord.

8. Anvil; in classical mythology, the god Vulcan is a blacksmith.   9. And escape (my) detection, I will
repay the theft (you can hold me accountable).   1. Chameleons were believed to survive on air alone.
Hamlet also puns on "heir," referring to Claudius's insubstantial promises regarding succession.

HAMLET: I mean, my head upon your lap?

OPHELIA: Ay, my lord.

HAMLET: Do you think I meant country matters?[2]

110 OPHELIA: I think nothing, my lord.

HAMLET: That's a fair thought to lie between maids' legs.

OPHELIA: What is, my lord?

HAMLET: Nothing.

OPHELIA: You are merry, my lord.

115 HAMLET: Who, I?

OPHELIA: Ay, my lord.

HAMLET: O God, your only° jig-maker! What should a man   *unrivaled*
do but be merry? For look you how cheerfully my mother
looks, and my father died within's° two hours.   *within these*

120 OPHELIA: Nay, 'tis twice two months, my lord.

HAMLET: So long? Nay then, let the devil wear black, for I'll
have a suit of sables.[3] O heavens! die two months ago, and
not forgotten yet? Then there's hope a great man's memory
may outlive his life half a year, but by'r lady 'a must build

125 churches then, or else shall 'a suffer not thinking on,° with   *not being thought about*
the hobby-horse, whose epitaph is "For O, for O, the hobby-
horse is forgot!"[4]

> *The trumpets sound. Dumb Show follows. Enter a* KING
> *and a* QUEEN *very lovingly; the* QUEEN *embracing him
> and he her. She kneels, and makes show of protestation
> unto him. He takes her up, and declines his head upon
> her neck. He lies him down upon a bank of flowers; she,
> seeing him asleep, leaves him. Anon come in another
> man, takes off his crown, kisses it, pours poison in the
> sleeper's ears, and leaves him. The* QUEEN *returns, finds
> the* KING *dead, makes passionate action. The* POISONER
> *with some three or four come in again, seem to condole
> with her. The dead body is carried away. The* POISONER
> *woos the* QUEEN *with gifts; she seems harsh awhile, but
> in the end accepts love.*   [*Exeunt.*]

OPHELIA: What means this, my lord?

HAMLET: Marry, this is miching mallecho;[5] it means mischief.

130 OPHELIA: Belike this show imports° the argument° of the play.   *explains / plot*

[*Enter* PROLOGUE.]

HAMLET: We shall know by this fellow. The players cannot
keep counsel°; they'll tell all.   *a secret*

---

2. Presumably, rustic misbehavior, but here and elsewhere in this exchange Hamlet treats Ophelia to
some ribald puns. "Nothing" (line 110), for example, suggests female genitalia, "thing" male.
3. Expensive furs, but also meaning "black." Hamlet simultaneously forswears his ascetic mourning
and vows to keep it.   4. In traditional games and dances, the hobbyhorse was a man with a mock
horse's body strapped around his waist. "The hobbyhorse is forgot" seems to have been a ballad refrain.
5. Sneaking crime (from the Spanish *malhecho*, "evil deed").

OPHELIA: Will 'a tell us what this show meant?

HAMLET: Ay, or any show that you will show him. Be not you
    ashamed to show, he'll not shame to tell you what it means.   135

OPHELIA: You are naught,° you are naught. I'll mark° the play.   *obscene / attend to*

PROLOGUE: *For us, and for our tragedy,*
        Here stooping to your clemency,
        We beg your hearing patiently.   [*Exit.*]

HAMLET: Is this a prologue, or the posy⁶ of a ring?   140

OPHELIA: 'Tis brief, my lord.

HAMLET: As woman's love.

[*Enter the* PLAYER KING *and* QUEEN.]

PLAYER KING: *Full thirty times hath Phœbus' cart⁷ gone round*
        Neptune's salt wash and Tellus' orbèd ground,
        And thirty dozen moons with borrowed sheen°   *reflected light* 145
        About the world have times twelve thirties been,
        Since love our hearts and Hymen did our hands
        Unite comutual° in most sacred bands.   *mutually*

PLAYER QUEEN: *So many journeys may the sun and moon*
        Make us again count o'er ere love be done!   150
        But woe is me, you are so sick of late,
        So far from cheer and from your former state,
        That I distrust° you. Yet though I distrust,   *fear for*
        Discomfort you, my lord, it nothing must.
        For women's fear and love hold quantity,°   *are in equal proportions* 155
        In neither aught,° or in extremity.°   *nothing / a lot; too much*
        Now what my love is proof° hath made you know,   *experience*
        And as my love is sized,° my fear is so.°   *in size / also*
        Where love is great, the littlest doubts are fear;
        Where little fears grow great, great love grows there.   160

PLAYER KING: *Faith, I must leave thee, love, and shortly too;*
        My operant° powers their functions leave° to do.   *vital / cease*
        And thou shalt live in this fair world behind,
        Honored, beloved, and haply° one as kind   *perhaps*
        For husband shalt thou—

PLAYER QUEEN: *O, confound the rest!*   165
        Such love must needs be treason in my breast.
        In second husband let me be accurst!
        None wed the second but who killed the first.

HAMLET: That's wormwood.°   *bitter medicine*

PLAYER QUEEN: *The instances° that second marriage move°*   *motives / prompt* 170
        Are base respects of thrift,° but none of love.   *economic considerations*
        A second time I kill my husband dead,
        When second husband kisses me in bed.

---

6. Motto engraved inside.   7. The speech contains several references to Greek mythology. Phoebus
was the sun god, and his chariot or "cart" is the sun. The "salt wash" of Neptune is the ocean; Tellus
was an earth goddess, and her "orbed ground" is the earth or globe. Hymen was the god of marriage.

PLAYER KING: *I do believe you think what now you speak,*
175   *But what we do determine oft we break.*
    Purpose° is but the slave to memory,   intention
    Of violent birth, but poor validity;°   enduring strength
    Which now, like fruit unripe, sticks on the tree,
    But fall unshaken when they mellow be.
180   *Most necessary 'tis that we forget*
    To pay ourselves what to ourselves is debt.[8]
    What to ourselves in passion we propose,
    The passion ending, doth the purpose lose.
    The violence of either grief or joy
185   *Their own enactures with themselves destroy.*[9]
    Where joy most revels, grief doth most lament;
    Grief joys, joy grieves, on slender accident.°   small, unforeseen event
    This world is not for aye,° nor 'tis not strange   always; eternity
    That even our loves should with our fortunes change;
190   *For 'tis a question left us yet to prove,*
    Whether love lead fortune, or else fortune love.
    The great man down, you mark his favorite flies;
    The poor advanced° makes friends of enemies;   promoted (man)
    And hitherto° doth love on fortune tend,°   to this extent / attend
195   *For who not needs shall never lack a friend,*
    And who in want a hollow friend doth try,°   test
    Directly seasons him° his enemy.   ripens him into
    But orderly to end where I begun,
    Our wills and fates do so contrary run
200   *That our devices still° are overthrown;*   plans always
    Our thoughts are ours, their ends° none of our own.   results
    So think thou wilt no second husband wed,
    But die thy thoughts when thy first lord is dead.
PLAYER QUEEN: *Nor earth to me give food, nor heaven light,*
205   *Sport and repose lock from me day and night,*
    To desperation turn my trust and hope,
    An anchor's cheer° in prison be my scope,   anchorite's (hermit's) food
    Each opposite° that blanks° the face of joy   opposing force / blanches
    Meet what I would have well, and it destroy,
210   *Both here and hence pursue me lasting strife,*
    If once a widow, ever I be wife!
HAMLET: *If she should break it now!*
PLAYER KING: *'Tis deeply sworn. Sweet, leave me here awhile.*
    My spirits grow dull, and fain° I would beguile   gladly
    The tedious day with sleep.   [*Sleeps.*]
215 PLAYER QUEEN: *Sleep rock thy brain,*
    And never come mischance between us twain!   [*Exit.*]
HAMLET: Madam, how like you this play?
QUEEN: The lady doth protest too much, methinks.

---

8. That is, to fulfill those promises made to ourselves.   9. Destroy themselves and the motive for
action they provided.

HAMLET: O, but she'll keep her word.

KING: Have you heard the argument?° Is there no offence in't? *plot* 220

HAMLET: No, no, they do but jest, poison in jest; no offence i' th' world.

KING: What do you call the play?

HAMLET: "The Mouse-trap." Marry, how? Tropically.[1] This 225
play is the image of a murder done in Vienna. Gonzago is
the duke's name; his wife, Baptista. You shall see anon.
'Tis a knavish piece of work, but what of that? Your maj-
esty, and we that have free° souls, it touches° us not. Let *guiltless / wounds; concerns*
the galled jade wince, our withers are unwrung.[2] 230

[*Enter* LUCIANUS.]

This is one Lucianus, nephew to the king.

OPHELIA: You are as good as a chorus,[3] my lord.

HAMLET: I could interpret between you and your love, if I
could see the puppets dallying.[4]

OPHELIA: You are keen,° my lord, you are keen. *sharply satirical* 235

HAMLET: It would cost you a groaning to take off mine edge.[5]

OPHELIA: Still better,° and worse.° *wittier / more obscene*

HAMLET: So you mistake your husbands.[6]—Begin, murderer. Leave thy damnable° faces and begin. Come, the *grimacing*
croaking raven doth bellow for revenge. 240

LUCIANUS: *Thoughts black, hands apt, drugs fit, and time*
  agreeing,
  Confederate season,° else no creature seeing, *Opportune time*
  Thou mixture rank,° of midnight weeds collected, *foul*
  With Hecate's ban[7] thrice blasted, thrice infected,
  Thy natural magic and dire property° *quality* 245
  On wholesome life usurp immediately. [*Pours the poi-*
  son in his ears.]

HAMLET: 'A poisons him i' th' garden for his estate.° His *position; state*
name's Gonzago. The story is extant, and written in very
choice Italian. You shall see anon how the murderer gets
the love of Gonzago's wife. 250

OPHELIA: The king rises.

HAMLET: What, frighted with false fire?° *fireworks; blanks*

QUEEN: How fares my lord?

POLONIUS: Give o'er the play.

KING: Give me some light. Away! 255

---

1. Figuratively; involving a rhetorical trope, with a possible pun on "trap." 2. A "galled jade" is a
horse with a sore back. The "withers" are the ridge between a horse's shoulders; "unwrung withers"
are not chafed by the harness. 3. Character(s) who explain, "interpret" (line 233), or comment on
the action, as in ancient Greek drama and Elizabethan puppet shows.
4. Flirting. Hamlet (also) uses "interpret" here in the sense of acting as a go-between for two lovers.
5. It would cost you a groaning (as in sexual intercourse or childbirth) to take the "edge" off my ("keen" or
sharp) wit or sexual appetite. 6. With these false promises ("for better and for worse"), you take your husbands in marriage and cheat on them. 7. Curse of Hecate, the goddess of witchcraft in classical myth.

POLONIUS: Lights, lights, lights! [*Exeunt all but* HAMLET *and* HORATIO.]

HAMLET:

> Why, let the strucken deer go weep,[8]
>   The hart ungallèd° play.   *uninjured*
> For some must watch° while some must sleep;   *stay awake*
260   Thus runs the world away.[9]
> Would not this,° sir, and a forest of feathers°—if the rest of   (*The Mousetrap* / *plumes*
> my fortunes turn Turk° with me—with two Provincial roses   *renegade*
> on my razed shoes,[1] get me a fellowship in a cry of players?[2]

HORATIO: Half a share.

265 HAMLET: A whole one, I.

> For thou dost know, O Damon dear,[3]
>   This realm dismantled was
> Of Jove himself, and now reigns here
>   A very, very—peacock.

270 HORATIO: You might have rhymed.[4]

HAMLET: O good Horatio, I'll take the ghost's word for a thousand pound. Didst perceive?

HORATIO: Very well, my lord.

HAMLET: Upon the talk of the poisoning.

275 HORATIO: I did very well note° him.   *observe*

HAMLET: Ah, ha! Come, some music. Come, the recorders.

> For if the king like not the comedy.
> Why then, belike he likes it not, perdy.[5]

Come, some music.

[*Enter* ROSENCRANTZ *and* GUILDENSTERN.]

280 GUILDENSTERN: Good my lord, vouchsafe me a word with you.

HAMLET: Sir, a whole history.

GUILDENSTERN: The king, sir—

HAMLET: Ay, sir, what of him?

GUILDENSTERN: Is in his retirement° marvellous   *withdrawal*
285   distempered.°   *vexed*

HAMLET: With drink, sir?

GUILDENSTERN: No, my lord, with choler.[6]

HAMLET: Your wisdom should show itself more richer° to sig-   *resourceful*
nify this to the doctor, for for me to put him to his purga-
290 tion[7] would perhaps plunge him into more choler.

---

8. Deer were thought to weep when mortally wounded.   9. That's the way of the world.   1. Decorated with slashes. *Provincial roses*: large rosettes concealing shoelaces.   2. Pack or troupe of actors. *Fellowship*: profit-sharing partnership (such as Shakespeare had in the Lord Chamberlain's Men). 3. Damon and Pythias were legendary ideals of friendship.   4. The expected rhyme word (for "was," line 267) would be "ass."   5. *Par Dieu* (French for "by God").   6. Bile, the bodily humor or fluid believed, in too great a quantity, to produce both anger and indigestion. "Choler" can thus also mean both "anger" and "indigestion."   7. A multiple pun: bloodletting (a medical treatment); spiritual purging (confession and absolution); legal purging (clearing oneself of a crime).

GUILDENSTERN: Good my lord, put your discourse into some
    frame,° and start° not so wildly from my affair.   *order / jump away*
HAMLET: I am tame, sir. Pronounce.
GUILDENSTERN: The queen your mother, in most great
    affliction of spirit, hath sent me to you.   295
HAMLET: You are welcome.
GUILDENSTERN: Nay, good my lord, this courtesy is not of the
    right breed. If it shall please you to make me a wholesome°   *reasonable; sane*
    answer, I will do your mother's commandment. If not, your
    pardon° and my return shall be the end of my business.   *permission to go* 300
HAMLET: Sir, I cannot.
ROSENCRANTZ: What, my lord?
HAMLET: Make you a wholesome answer; my wit's diseased.
    But, sir, such answer as I can make, you shall command,
    or rather, as you say, my mother. Therefore no more, but   305
    to the matter. My mother, you say—
ROSENCRANTZ: Then thus she says: your behavior hath
    struck her into amazement and admiration.°   *bewilderment*
HAMLET: O wonderful son, that can so stonish a mother!
    But is there no sequel at the heels of his mother's admira-   310
    tion? Impart.°   *Do tell*
ROSENCRANTZ: She desires to speak with you in her closet
    ere you go to bed.
HAMLET: We shall obey, were she ten times our mother.
    Have you any further trade with us?   315
ROSENCRANTZ: My lord, you once did love me.
HAMLET: And do still, by these pickers and stealers.[8]
ROSENCRANTZ: Good my lord, what is your cause of distem-
    per? You do surely° bar the door upon your own liberty, if   *securely*
    you deny your griefs to your friend.   320
HAMLET: Sir, I lack advancement.
ROSENCRANTZ: How can that be, when you have the voice
    of the king himself for your succession in Denmark?
HAMLET: Ay, sir, but "while the grass grows"—the proverb[9]
    is something° musty.   *somewhat* 325

    [*Enter the* PLAYERS *with recorders.*]

    O, the recorders! Let me see one. To withdraw° with you   *step aside; speak privately*
        —why do you go about to recover the wind of me, as if
        you would drive me into a toil?[1]
GUILDENSTERN: O my lord, if my duty be too bold, my love
    is too unmannerly.[2]   330

---

8. Hands. (The Anglican catechism includes a promise to "keep my hands from picking and stealing,
and my tongue from evil speaking, lying, and slandering.")   9. The proverb ends "the horse
starves."   1. The simile refers to hunting. Hamlet asks why Guildenstern is attempting to get wind-
ward of him, as if he would drive him into a net ("toil").   2. If I have been discourteous in doing my
duty, my love (for you) is to blame.

HAMLET: I do not well understand that. Will you play upon
this pipe?

GUILDENSTERN: My lord, I cannot.

HAMLET: I pray you.

335 GUILDENSTERN: Believe me, I cannot.

HAMLET: I do beseech you.

GUILDENSTERN: I know no touch of it, my lord.

HAMLET: It is as easy as lying. Govern these ventages° with   *finger holes*
your fingers and thumb, give it breath with your mouth,

340 and it will discourse most eloquent music. Look you,
these are the stops.°   *finger holes; notes*

GUILDENSTERN: But these cannot I command to any
utt'rance of harmony. I have not the skill.

HAMLET: Why, look you now, how unworthy a thing you

345 make of me! You would play upon me, you would seem to
know my stops, you would pluck out the heart of my mys-
tery, you would sound° me from my lowest note to the   *fathom; play*
top of my compass;° and there is much music, excellent   *limit*
voice, in this little organ, yet cannot you make it speak.

350 'Sblood, do you think I am easier to be played on than a
pipe? Call me what instrument you will, though you can
fret³ me, you cannot play upon me.

[*Enter* POLONIUS.]

God bless you, sir!

POLONIUS: My lord, the queen would speak with you, and

355 presently.°   *immediately*

HAMLET: Do you see yonder cloud that's almost in shape of
a camel?

POLONIUS: By th' mass, and 'tis like a camel indeed.

HAMLET: Methinks it is like a weasel.

360 POLONIUS: It is backed like a weasel.

HAMLET: Or like a whale.

POLONIUS: Very like a whale.

HAMLET: Then I will come to my mother by and by. [*Aside.*]
They fool me to the top of my bent.⁴—I will come by and

365 by.

POLONIUS: I will say so.   [*Exit.*]

HAMLET: "By and by" is easily said. Leave me, friends.
          [*Exeunt all but* HAMLET.]
'Tis now the very witching time of night,
When churchyards yawn, and hell itself breathes out

370 Contagion to this world. Now could I drink hot blood,
And do such bitter business as the day
Would quake to look on. Soft, now to my mother.

---

3. A pun: annoy and play a guitar or similar instrument using the "frets" or small bars on the
neck.   4. They treat me as an utter fool or they go along with my foolishness to its limit or to the
limit of my endurance.

O heart, lose not thy nature;° let not ever   *natural affection*
The soul of Nero⁵ enter this firm° bosom.   *resolute*
Let me be cruel, not unnatural;   375
I will speak daggers to her, but use none.
My tongue and soul in this be hypocrites—
How in my words somever⁶ she be shent,°   *rebuked*
To give them seals° never, my soul, consent!   [*Exit.*]   *fulfillment in action*

Scene 3

A room in the castle. Enter KING, ROSENCRANTZ, *and*
GUILDENSTERN.

KING: I like him not,° nor stands it safe with us   *distrust him*
   To let his madness range. Therefore prepare you.
   I your commission will forthwith dispatch,
   And he to England shall along with you.
   The terms° of our estate° may not endure   *responsibilities / position* 5
   Hazard so near's as doth hourly grow
   Out of his brows.⁷
GUILDENSTERN: We will ourselves provide,°   *equip (for the journey)*
   Most holy and religious fear° it is   *care*
   To keep those many many bodies safe
   That live and feed upon your majesty.   10
ROSENCRANTZ: The single and peculiar° life is bound   *individual; private*
   With all the strength and armor of the mind
   To keep itself from noyance,° but much more   *harm*
   That spirit upon whose weal° depends and rests   *well-being*
   The lives of many. The cess° of majesty   *cessation; decease* 15
   Dies not alone, but like a gulf° doth draw   *whirlpool*
   What's near it with it. It is a massy° wheel   *massive*
   Fixed on the summit of the highest mount,
   To whose huge spokes ten thousand lesser things
   Are mortised° and adjoined, which° when it falls,   *affixed / so that* 20
   Each small annexment, petty consequence,
   Attends° the boist'rous ruin. Never alone   *Accompanies*
   Did the king sigh, but with a general groan.
KING: Arm° you, I pray you, to this speedy voyage,   *Prepare*
   For we will fetters put about this fear,   25
   Which now goes too free-footed.
ROSENCRANTZ: We will haste us.
         [*Exeunt* ROSENCRANTZ *and* GUILDENSTERN.]

   [*Enter* POLONIUS.]

POLONIUS: My lord, he's going to his mother's closet.
   Behind the arras I'll convey° myself   *station; put*

5. The Roman emperor Nero, known for his excesses, was believed to have murdered his mother.
6. However much by my words.   7. An ambiguous term suggesting "brain," "expressions," or "effrontery."

To hear the process.° I'll warrant she'll tax° him home,°   *proceedings / rebuke /*
30   And as you said, and wisely was it said,   *sharply*
  'Tis meet that some more audience than a mother,
  Since nature makes them partial, should o'erhear
  The speech, of vantage.[8] Fare you well, my liege.
  I'll call upon you ere you go to bed,
  And tell you what I know.
35 KING: Thanks, dear my lord.
                          [*Exit* POLONIUS.]
  O, my offence is rank, it smells to heaven;
  It hath the primal eldest curse[9] upon't,
  A brother's murder. Pray can I not,
  Though inclination be as sharp as will.
40   My stronger guilt defeats my strong intent,
  And like a man to double business[1] bound,
  I stand in pause where I shall first begin,
  And both neglect. What if this cursèd hand
  Were thicker than itself with brother's blood,
45   Is there not rain enough in the sweet heavens
  To wash it white as snow? Whereto serves mercy
  But to confront the visage of offence?[2]
  And what's in prayer but this twofold force,
  To be forestallèd° ere we come to fall,   *prevented*
50   Or pardoned being down? Then I'll look up.
  My fault is past, But, O, what form of prayer
  Can serve my turn? "Forgive me my foul murder"?
  That cannot be, since I am still possessed
  Of those effects° for which I did the murder—   *gains*
55   My crown, mine own ambition, and my queen.
  May one be pardoned and retain th' offence?[3]
  In the corrupted currents of this world
  Offence's gilded[4] hand may shove by justice,
  And oft 'tis seen the wicked prize[5] itself
60   Buys out the law. But 'tis not so above.
  There is no shuffling;° there the action lies   *evasion*
  In his true nature,[6] and we ourselves compelled,
  Even to the teeth and forehead of° our faults,   *face-to-face with*
  To give in evidence.° What then? What rests?°   *testify / remains to be done*
65   Try what repentance can. What can it not?
  Yet what can it when one cannot repent?
  O wretched state! O bosom black as death!
  O limèd[7] soul, that struggling to be free

---

8. In addition, or from an advantageous position. 9. That of Cain, who murdered his brother, Abel (Gen. 4.10–12). 1. Two mutually opposed goals. 2. What purpose has mercy if not to confront or oppose sin face-to-face. 3. That is, benefits of the offense or crime. 4. Bearing gold as a bribe. 5. Prize gained by wickedness. 6. There the deed (the original crime or sin) appears in its true form, and the trial, or legal proceedings, are properly conducted. 7. Caught as with birdlime, a sticky substance smeared on twigs to catch birds.

Art more engaged!° Help, angels! Make assay.°   *entangled / some attempt*
Bow, stubborn knees, and heart with strings of steel,   70
Be soft as sinews of the new-born babe.
All may be well.   [*He kneels.*]

[*Enter* HAMLET.]

HAMLET: Now might I do it pat,° now 'a is a-praying,   *easily*
And now I'll do't—and so 'a goes to heaven,
And so am I revenged. That would be scanned.⁸   75
A villain kills my father, and for that,
I, his sole son, do this same villain send
To heaven.
Why, this is hire and salary, not revenge.
'A took my father grossly, full of bread,⁹   80
With all his crimes broad blown,° as flush° as May;   *full-blown / vigorous*
And how his audit° stands who knows save heaven?   *spiritual account*
But in our circumstance and course of thought
'Tis heavy with him;¹ and am I then revenged
To take him° in the purging of his soul,   *(Claudius)* 85
When he is fit and seasoned° for his passage?   *ready; prepared*
No.
Up, sword, and know thou a more horrid hent.°   *design; occasion*
When he is drunk, asleep, or in his rage,
Or in th' incestuous pleasure of his bed,   90
At game a-swearing, or about some act
That has no relish° of salvation in't—   *flavor; trace*
Then trip him, that his heels may kick at heaven,
And that his soul may be as damned and black
As hell, whereto it goes. My mother stays.°   *waits* 95
This physic° but prolongs thy sickly days.   [*Exit.*]   *medicine*
KING: [*Rising.*] My words fly up, my thoughts remain below.
Words without thoughts never to heaven go.   [*Exit.*]

Scene 4

The Queen's chamber. Enter QUEEN *and* POLONIUS.

POLONIUS: 'A will come straight.° Look you lay home to him.²   *immediately*
Tell him his pranks have been too broad° to bear with,   *outrageous*
And that your grace hath screen'd and stood between
Much heat and him. I'll silence me even here.
Pray you be round° with him.   *blunt* 5
HAMLET: [*Within.*] Mother, mother, mother!
QUEEN: I'll warrant you. Fear° me not.   *Doubt*

8. That deserves careful evaluation.   9. In a state of sin and without fasting.
1. Hamlet suggests that from "our"—human, earthly—perspective, as opposed to that of "heaven"
(line 82), his father's spiritual account seems to be heavily weighted against him.
2. Be sure that you are sharp with him.

Withdraw, I hear him coming.

[POLONIUS *goes behind the arras. Enter* HAMLET.]

HAMLET: Now, mother, what's the matter?
10 QUEEN: Hamlet, thou hast thy father much offended.
HAMLET: Mother, you have my father much offended.
QUEEN: Come, come, you answer with an idle tongue.
HAMLET: Go, go, you question with a wicked tongue.
QUEEN: Why, how now,° Hamlet?   *what's this*
HAMLET: What's the matter now?
QUEEN: Have you forgot me?³
15 HAMLET: No, by the rood,° not so.   *cross of Christ*
      You are the queen, your husband's brother's wife,
      And would it were not so, you are my mother.
QUEEN: Nay, then I'll set those to you that can speak.⁴
HAMLET: Come, come, and sit you down. You shall not budge.
20   You go not till I set you up a glass°   *mirror*
      Where you may see the inmost part of you.
QUEEN: What wilt thou do? Thou wilt not murder me?
      Help, ho!
POLONIUS: [*Behind.*] What, ho! help!
25 HAMLET: [*Draws.*] How now, a rat?
      Dead for a ducat, dead!⁵

[*Kills* POLONIUS *with a pass through the arras.*]

POLONIUS: [*Behind.*] O, I am slain!
QUEEN: O me, what hast thou done?
HAMLET: Nay, I know not.
      Is it the king?
30 QUEEN: O, what a rash and bloody deed is this!
HAMLET: A bloody deed!—almost as bad, good mother,
      As kill a king and marry with his brother.
QUEEN: As kill a king?
HAMLET: Ay, lady, it was my word.
                          [*Parting the arras.*]
      Thou wretched, rash, intruding fool, farewell!
35   I took thee for thy better. Take thy fortune.
      Thou find'st to be too busy° is some danger.—   *nosy; officious*
      Leave wringing of your hands. Peace, sit you down
      And let me wring your heart, for so I shall
      If it be made of penetrable stuff,
40   If damnèd custom° have not brazed it⁶ so   *sinful habit*
      That it be proof° and bulwark against sense.°   *armor / natural feeling*
QUEEN: What have I done that thou dar'st wag thy tongue
      In noise so rude against me?

---

3. Forgotten the respect you owe to me as your mother.   4. That is, those who can deal with someone
as impossibly rude as you.   5. I bet a ducat I have killed it.   6. Plated it with brass.

HAMLET: Such an act
          That blurs the grace and blush of modesty,
          Calls virtue hypocrite, takes off the rose   45
          From the fair forehead of an innocent love.
          And sets a blister° there, makes marriage-vows   brand
          As false as dicers' oaths. O, such a deed
          As from the body of contraction° plucks   marriage contract
          The very soul, and sweet religion makes   50
          A rhapsody° of words. Heaven's face does glow°   meaningless jumble / blush
          O'er this solidity and compound mass°   solid earth
          With heated visage, as against the doom°—   Judgement Day
          Is thought-sick at the act.
QUEEN: Ay me, what act
          That roars so loud and thunders in the index?°   table of contents 55
HAMLET: Look here upon this picture and on this,
          The counterfeit presentment° of two brothers.   painted portrayal
          See what a grace was seated on this brow:
          Hyperion's[7] curls, the front° of Jove himself,   forehead
          An eye like Mars, to threaten and command,   60
          A station° like the herald Mercury   bearing
          New lighted° on a heaven-kissing hill—   Newly alighted
          A combination and a form indeed
          Where every god did seem to set his seal,°   mark of approval
          To give the world assurance of a man.   65
          This was your husband. Look you now what follows.
          Here is your husband, like a mildewed ear°   (of grain)
          Blasting° his wholesome brother. Have you eyes?   Infecting
          Could you on this fair mountain leave° to feed,   cease
          And batten° on this moor? Ha! have you eyes?   feed greedily 70
          You cannot call it love, for at your age
          The heyday in the blood[8] is tame, it's humble,
          And waits upon the judgment, and what judgment
          Would step from this to this? Sense° sure you have   Sensation
          Else could you not have motion, but sure that sense   75
          Is apoplexed° for madness would not err,   paralyzed
          Nor sense° to ecstasy° was ne'er so thralled   reason / madness
          But it reserved some quantity° of choice   power
          To serve in such a difference.[9] What devil was't
          That thus hath cozened° you at hoodman-blind?[1]   cheated 80
          Eyes without feeling, feeling without sight,
          Ears without hands or eyes, smelling sans[2] all,
          Or but a sickly part of one true sense

---

7. These lines refer to various figures from classical myth: Hyperion, titan of heavenly light; Jove (or Jupiter), the god of sky and thunder and king of the gods; Mars, god of war; and Mercury, messenger or "herald" of the gods.   8. The excitement of sexual passion.   9. To make such a distinction.
1. Blindman's buff, traditional game, a variant of tag, in which the seeker is blindfolded.   2. Without (French). Compare Psalm 115. 5–6 on idolators: "Eyes have they, but they see not: They have ears, but they hear not: noses have they, but they smell not."

Could not so mope.³ O shame! where is thy blush?
85   Rebellious hell,
If thou canst mutine° in a matron's bones,   *mutiny*
To flaming youth let virtue be as wax
And melt in her° own fire. Proclaim no shame   *(youth's)*
When the compulsive ardor gives the charge,°   *order to attack*
90   Since frost itself as actively doth burn,
And reason panders° will.   *pimps for*
QUEEN: O Hamlet, speak no more!
Thou turn'st my eyes into my very soul;
And there I see such black and grainèd° spots   *engrained*
As will not leave° their tinct.°   *lose / color, tincture*
HAMLET: Nay, but to live
95   In the rank sweat of an enseamèd° bed,   *greasy*
Stewed in curruption, honeying and making love
Over the nasty sty—
QUEEN: O, speak to me no more!
These words like daggers enter in my ears;
No more, sweet Hamlet.
HAMLET: A murderer and a villain,
100   A slave that is not twentieth part the tithe
Of your precedent° lord, a vice⁴ of kings,   *previous*
A cutpurse° of the empire and the rule,   *pickpocket*
That from a shelf the precious diadem stole
And put it in his pocket—
105   QUEEN: No more.

[*Enter* GHOST.]

HAMLET: A king of shreds and patches—⁵
Save me and hover o'er me with your wings,
You heavenly guards! What would your gracious figure?
QUEEN: Alas, he's mad.
110   HAMLET: Do you not come your tardy son to chide,
That lapsed in time and passion⁶ lets go by
Th' important° acting of your dread command?   *urgent*
O, say!
GHOST: Do not forget. This visitation
115   Is but to whet thy almost blunted purpose.
But look, amazement on thy mother sits.
O, step between her and her fighting soul!
Conceit° in weakest bodies strongest works.   *Imagination*
Speak to her, Hamlet.
HAMLET: How is it with you, lady?
120   QUEEN: Alas, how is't with you,
That you do bend your eye on vacancy,

3. Could not be so obtuse or stupid.   4. The "Vice" in morality plays was a clown or buffoon who
personified evil.   5. Motley, the costume of a jester.   6. That allowed time to pass and the passion
(for revenge) to fade.

And with th' incorporal° air do hold discourse? *bodiless*
Forth at your eyes your spirits wildly peep,
And as the sleeping soldiers in th' alarm,
Your bedded° hairs like life in excrements[7] *(formerly) flat* 125
Start up and stand an end. O gentle son,
Upon the heat and flame of thy distemper
Sprinkle cool patience. Whereon do you look?
HAMLET: On him, on him! Look you how pale he glares.
His form° and cause conjoined,° preaching to stones, *appearance / collaborating* 130
Would make them capable.—Do not look upon me,
Lest with this piteous action you convert
My stern effects.° Then what I have to do *intended acts*
Will want true color—tears perchance for blood.[8]
QUEEN: To whom do you speak this? 135
HAMLET: Do you see nothing there?
QUEEN: Nothing at all, yet all that is I see.
HAMLET: Nor did you nothing hear?
QUEEN: No, nothing but ourselves.
HAMLET: Why, look you there. Look how it steals away. 140
My father, in his habit° as° he lived! *dress and bearing / as if*
Look where he goes even now out at the portal.
                              [*Exit* GHOST.]
QUEEN: This is the very coinage of your brain.
This bodiless creation ecstasy
Is very cunning° in. *skilled*
HAMLET: Ecstasy? 145
My pulse as yours doth temperately keep time,
And makes as healthful music. It is not madness
That I have uttered. Bring me to the test,
And I the matter will re-word,° which madness *repeat exactly*
Would gambol° from. Mother, for love of grace, *skitter away* 150
Lay not that flattering unction° to your soul, *ointment*
That not your trespass but my madness speaks.
It will but skin° and film the ulcerous place *cover*
Whiles rank corruption, mining° all within, *undermining*
Infects unseen. Confess yourself to heaven, 155
Repent what's past, avoid what is to come.
And do not spread the compost on the weeds,
To make them ranker. Forgive me this my virtue,° *virtuous exhortation*
For in the fatness of these pursy° times *bloated*
Virtue itself of vice must pardon beg, 160
Yea, curb° and woo for leave° to do him good. *bow / permission*
QUEEN: O Hamlet, thou hast cleft my heart in twain.
HAMLET: O, throw away the worser part of it,
And live the purer with the other half.

---

7. In insensate outgrowths (a term used of nails and hair).   8. That is, he might shed (colorless) tears
instead of blood.

165　　Good night—but go not to my uncle's bed.
　　　Assume a° virtue, if you have it not.　　　　　　　　　　　*Put on*
　　　That monster custom° who all sense doth eat　　　　　　　　*habit*
　　　Of habits devil,° is angel yet in this,　　　　　　　　　　*devilish*
　　　That to the use° of actions fair and good　　　　　　*habitual practice*
170　　He likewise gives a frock or livery
　　　That aptly° is put on. Refrain tonight,　　　　　　　　　　*easily*
　　　And that shall lend a kind of easiness
　　　To the next abstinence; the next more easy;
　　　For use almost can change the stamp of nature,
175　　And either curb the devil, or throw him out
　　　With wondrous potency. Once more, good night,
　　　And when you are desirous to be blest,
　　　I'll blessing beg of you. For this same lord
　　　I do repent; but heaven hath pleased it so,
180　　To punish me with this, and this with me,
　　　That I must be their scourge and minister.
　　　I will bestow° him and will answer well°　　*dispose of / take responsibility for*
　　　The death I gave him. So, again, good night.
　　　I must be cruel only to be kind.
185　　Thus bad begins and worse remains behind.°　　　　　　*to follow*
　　　One word more, good lady.
QUEEN:　　　　　　　　　　　　What shall I do?
HAMLET: Not this, by no means, that I bid you do:
　　　Let the bloat° king tempt you again to bed,　　　　　　*bloated*
　　　Pinch wanton° on your cheek, call you his mouse,　　　　*lewdly*
190　　And let him, for a pair of reechy° kisses,　　　　　　　　*filthy*
　　　Or paddling in° your neck with his damned fingers,　　*fondling*
　　　Make you to ravel° all this matter out,　　　　　　　　*reveal*
　　　That I essentially am not in madness,
　　　But mad in craft. 'Twere good you let him know,
195　　For who that's but° a queen, fair, sober, wise,　　　　　*only*
　　　Would from a paddock,° from a bat, a gib,°　　　*toad / tom cat*
　　　Such dear concernings° hide? Who would so do?　　*vital affairs*
　　　No, in despite of sense and secrecy,
　　　Unpeg the basket on the house's top,
200　　Let the birds fly, and like the famous ape,
　　　To try conclusions,° in the basket creep　　　　　　　*test results*
　　　And break your own neck down.⁹
QUEEN: Be thou assured, if words be made of breath
　　　And breath of life, I have no life to breathe
205　　What thou hast said to me.
HAMLET: I must to England; you know that?
QUEEN:　　　　　　　　　　　　　Alack,
　　　I had forgot. 'Tis so concluded on.

---

9. Apparently a reference to a now-lost fable in which an ape opens a cage of birds on a rooftop. Seeing the birds fly away and thinking that if he were in the basket he, too, could fly, the ape tries the
experiment and breaks his neck.

HAMLET: There's letters sealed, and my two school-fellows,
    Whom I will trust as I will adders fanged,
    They bear the mandate; they must sweep° my way   *prepare* 210
    And marshal me to knavery. Let it work,°   *proceed*
    For 'tis the sport to have the enginer
    Hoist with his own petard;[1] and't shall go hard
    But I will delve one yard below their mines
    And blow them at the moon. O, 'tis most sweet   215
    When in one line two crafts directly meet.
    This man shall set me packing.
    I'll lug the guts into the neighbor room.
    Mother, good night. Indeed, this counsellor
    Is now most still, most secret, and most grave,   220
    Who was in life a foolish prating knave.
    Come sir, to draw toward an end with you.
    Good night, mother.

                [Exit the QUEEN. *Then exit* HAMLET
                      tugging POLONIUS.]

ACT IV

Scene 1

A room in the castle. Enter KING, QUEEN, ROSENCRANTZ
and GUILDENSTERN.

KING: There's matter in these sighs, these profound heaves,
    You must translate;° 'tis fit we understand them.   *explain*
    Where is your son?
QUEEN: Bestow this place on us a little while.
            [Exeunt ROSENCRANTZ *and* GUILDENSTERN.]
    Ah, mine own lord, what have I seen tonight!   5
KING: What, Gertrude? How does Hamlet?
QUEEN: Mad as the sea and wind when both contend
    Which is the mightier. In his lawless fit,
    Behind the arras hearing something stir,
    Whips out his rapier, cries "A rat, a rat!"   10
    And in this brainish apprehension° kills   *brain-sick notion*
    The unseen good old man.
KING: O heavy deed!
    It had been so with us° had we been there.   *me (royal "we")*
    His liberty is full of threats to all—
    To you yourself, to us, to every one.   15

---

1. The "enginer," or creator of military "engines" or devices, is here described as being blown up
("hoist") by a bomb of his own construction ("his own petard"). The military imagery continues in the
succeeding lines where Hamlet describes himself as digging ("delving") a countermine or tunnel
beneath the one Claudius is digging to defeat Hamlet. In line 216, the two tunnels and devious plots
("crafts") unexpectedly meet.

HAMLET: Compounded it with dust, whereto 'tis kin.

ROSENCRANTZ: Tell us where 'tis, that we may take it thence
    And bear it to the chapel.

HAMLET: Do not believe it.

ROSENCRANTZ: Believe what?   10

HAMLET: That I can keep your counsel and not mine own.[3]
    Besides, to be demanded of° a sponge—what replication°   *questioned by / reply*
    should be made by the son of a king?

ROSENCRANTZ: Take you me for a sponge, my lord?

HAMLET: Ay, sir, that soaks up the king's countenance,° his   *favor* 15
    rewards, his authorities. But such officers do the king
    best service in the end. He keeps them like an apple in
    the corner of his jaw, first mouthed to be last swallowed.
    When he needs what you have gleaned, it is but squeez-
    ing you and, sponge, you shall be dry again.   20

ROSENCRANTZ: I understand you not, my lord.

HAMLET: I am glad of it. A knavish speech sleeps in a foolish
    ear.

ROSENCRANTZ: My lord, you must tell us where the body is,
    and go with us to the king.   25

HAMLET: The body is with the king, but the king is not with
    the body.[4]
        The king is a thing—

GUILDENSTERN: A thing, my lord!

HAMLET: Of nothing. Bring me to him. Hide fox, and all   30
    after.[5]   *[Exeunt.]*

Scene 3

A room in the castle. Enter KING.

KING: I have sent to seek him, and to find the body.
    How dangerous is it that this man goes loose!
    Yet must not we put the strong law on him.
    He's loved of° the distracted° multitude,   *by / confused; unreasonable*
    Who like not in their judgment but their eyes,[6]   5
    And where 'tis so, th' offender's scourge° is weighed,   *punishment*
    But never the offence. To bear° all smooth and even,   *manage*
    This sudden sending him away must seem
    Deliberate pause.° Diseases desperate grown   *Careful planning*
    By desperate appliance° are relieved,   *remedy* 10
    Or not at all.

[Enter ROSENCRANTZ, GUILDENSTERN, *and all the rest.]*

3. Hamlet plays on two senses of "counsel": that I can follow your advice and not keep my secret.
4. A riddle. Hamlet may mean that Polonius is gone to the afterlife with King Hamlet but King
Claudius is still alive; or he may refer to the legal theory of the "king's two bodies" (one the king's literal, physical, mortal body; the other the figurative, immortal body of the state).   5. Apparently a reference to a children's game like hide-and-seek.   6. Who choose not by reason but by external appearance.

How now! what hath befall'n?

ROSENCRANTZ: Where the dead body is bestowed, my lord,
    We cannot get from him.

KING: But where is he?

ROSENCRANTZ: Without,° my lord; guarded, to know° your   *Outside / await*
    pleasure.

KING: Bring him before us.

15 ROSENCRANTZ: Ho! bring in the lord.

[*They enter with* HAMLET.]

KING: Now, Hamlet, where's Polonius?

HAMLET: At supper.

KING: At supper? Where?

HAMLET: Not where he eats, but where 'a is eaten. A certain
20 convocation of politic° worms are e'en° at him. Your worm   *scheming / now*
    is your only emperor for diet. We fat all creatures else° to   *besides ourselves*
    fat us, and we fat ourselves for maggots. Your fat king and
    your lean beggar is but variable service°—two dishes, but   *different courses*
    to one table. That's the end.

25 KING: Alas, alas!

HAMLET: A man may fish with the worm that hath eat of a
    king, and eat of the fish that hath fed of that worm.

KING: What dost thou mean by this?

HAMLET: Nothing but to show you how a king may go a
30 progress° through the guts of a beggar.   *royal procession*

KING: Where is Polonius?

HAMLET: In heaven. Send thither to see. If your messenger
    find him not there, seek him i' th' other place yourself.
    But if, indeed, you find him not within this month, you
35 shall nose° him as you go up the stairs into the lobby.   *smell*

KING: [*To* ATTENDANTS.] Go seek him there.

HAMLET: 'A will stay till you come.   [*Exeunt* ATTENDANTS.]

KING: Hamlet, this deed, for thine especial safety—
    Which we do tender,° as we dearly° grieve   *value / deeply*
40 For that which thou hast done—must send thee hence
    With fiery quickness. Therefore prepare thyself.
    The bark° is ready, and the wind at help,   *ship*
    Th' associates tend,° and everything is bent°   *companions wait / poised*
    For England.

HAMLET: For England?

KING: Ay, Hamlet.

HAMLET: Good.

45 KING: So it is, if thou knew'st our purposes.

HAMLET: I see a cherub⁷ that sees them. But come, for England!
    Farewell, dear mother.

KING: Thy loving father, Hamlet.

7. The keen-sighted second order of angels, cherubim symbolized heavenly knowledge.

HAMLET: My mother. Father and mother is man and wife,
   man and wife is one flesh.[8] So, my mother. Come, for
   England.   [*Exit.*]   50
KING: Follow him at foot;° tempt him with speed aboard.   *his heel*
   Delay it not; I'll have him hence tonight.
   Away! for everything is sealed and done
   That else leans° on th' affair. Pray you make haste.   *bears*
   [*Exeunt all but the* KING.]
   And, England,° if my love thou hold'st at aught°—   *King of England / any value* 55
   As my great power thereof may give thee sense,
   Since yet thy cicatrice° looks raw and red   *scar*
   After the Danish sword, and thy free awe
   Pays homage to us—thou mayst not coldly set°   *set aside*
   Our sovereign process,° which imports at full   *mandate* 60
   By letters congruing to° that effect   *according with*
   The present° death of Hamlet. Do it, England,   *immediate*
   For like the hectic° in my blood he rages,   *fever*
   And thou must cure me. Till I know 'tis done,
   Howe'er my haps,° my joys were ne'er begun.   [*Exit.*]   *fortunes* 65

Scene 4

Near Elsinore. Enter FORTINBRAS *with his army.*

FORTINBRAS: Go, captain, from me greet the Danish king.
   Tell him that by his license° Fortinbras   *permission*
   Craves the conveyance of° a promised march   *escort for*
   Over his kingdom. You know the rendezvous.
   If that his majesty would aught with us,   5
   We shall express our duty in his eye,°   *presence*
   And let him know so.
CAPTAIN: I will do't, my lord.
FORTINBRAS: Go softly° on.   [*Exeunt all but the* CAPTAIN.]   *slowly; circumspectly*

   [*Enter* HAMLET, ROSENCRANTZ, GUILDENSTERN, *and*
   OTHERS.]

HAMLET: Good sir, whose powers° are these?   *forces; troops*
CAPTAIN: They are of Norway, sir.   10
HAMLET: How purposed, sir, I pray you?
CAPTAIN: Against some part of Poland.
HAMLET: Who commands them, sir?
CAPTAIN: The nephew to old Norway, Fortinbras.
HAMLET: Goes it against the main° of Poland, sir,   *heart* 15
   Or for some frontier?
CAPTAIN: Truly to speak, and with no addition,°   *exaggeration*
   We go to gain a little patch of ground

8. As stated in Genesis 2.23–24 and the marriage rite of the Anglican Book of Common Prayer.

That hath in it no profit but the name.
20   To pay five ducats, five, I would not farm° it;   *lease*
Nor will it yield to Norway or the Pole
A ranker rate° should it be sold in fee.°   *higher return / outright*
HAMLET: Why, then the Polack never will defend it.
CAPTAIN: Yes, it is already garrisoned.
25   HAMLET: Two thousand souls and twenty thousand ducats
Will not debate the question of this straw.°   *trifle*
This is th' imposthume° of much wealth and peace,   *abscess*
That inward breaks, and shows no cause° without   *symptom*
Why the man dies. I humbly thank you, sir.
CAPTAIN: God b'wi'ye, sir.   [*Exit.*]
30   ROSENCRANTZ: Will't please you go, my lord?
HAMLET: I'll be with you straight. Go a little before.
                    [*Exeunt all but* HAMLET.]
How all occasions do inform against° me,   *accuse*
And spur my dull revenge! What is a man,
If his chief good and market° of his time   *occupation; profit*
35   Be but to sleep and feed? A beast, no more.
Sure he that made us with such large discourse,°   *reasoning power*
Looking before and after, gave us not
That capability° and godlike reason   *intelligence*
To fust° in us unused. Now, whether it be   *grow moldy*
40   Bestial oblivion, or some craven scruple
Of thinking too precisely on th' event—
A thought which, quartered, hath but one part wisdom
And ever three parts coward—I do not know
Why yet I live to say "This thing's to do,"
45   Sith° I have cause, and will, and strength, and means,   *Since*
To do't. Examples gross as earth exhort me.
Witness this army of such mass and charge,°   *cost*
Led by a delicate and tender° prince,   *young*
Whose spirit, with divine ambition puffed,
50   Makes mouths at° the invisible event,°   *Scorns / unforeseeable outcome*
Exposing what is mortal and unsure
To all that fortune, death, and danger dare,
Even for an eggshell. Rightly to be great
Is not to stir without great argument,
55   But greatly to find quarrel in a straw
When honor's at the stake. How stand I then,
That have a father killed, a mother stained,
Excitements° of my reason and my blood,   *Urgings*
And let all sleep, while to my shame I see
60   The imminent death of twenty thousand men
That for a fantasy and trick° of fame   *fragile trifle*
Go to their graves like beds, fight for a plot
Whereon the numbers cannot try the cause,

Which is not tomb enough and continent
To hide the slain?⁹ O, from this time forth,   65
My thoughts be bloody, or be nothing worth!   [*Exit.*]

Scene 5

A room in the castle. Enter QUEEN, HORATIO *and a* GENTLEMAN.

QUEEN: I will not speak with her.
GENTLEMAN: She is importunate, indeed distract.°   *deranged*
    Her mood will needs to be pitied.
QUEEN: What would she have?
GENTLEMAN: She speaks much of her father, says she hears
    There's tricks i' th' world, and hems, and beats her heart,   5
    Spurns enviously at straws,¹ speaks things in doubt°   *obscurely*
    That carry but half sense. Her speech is nothing,
    Yet the unshapèd use° of it doth move   *incoherent manner*
    The hearers to collection;° they yawn° at it,   *inference / gape*
    And botch° the words up fit to° their own thoughts,   *patch / to match* 10
    Which,° as her winks and nods and gestures yield them,   *(words)*
    Indeed would make one think there might be thought,
    Though nothing sure, yet much unhappily.²
HORATIO: 'Twere good she were spoken with, for she may strew
    Dangerous conjectures in ill-breeding minds.   15
QUEEN: Let her come in.   [*Exit* GENTLEMAN.]
    [*Aside.*] To my sick soul, as sin's true nature is,
    Each toy° seems prologue to some great amiss.°   *triviality / calamity*
    So full of artless jealousy° is guilt,   *suspicion*
    It spills itself in fearing to be spilt.   20

    [*Enter* OPHELIA *distracted.*]

OPHELIA: Where is the beauteous majesty of Denmark?
QUEEN: How now,° Ophelia!   *What's this*
OPHELIA:

      [*Sings.*]

    How should I your true love know
      From another one?
    By his cockle hat³ and staff,   25
    And his sandal shoon.°   *shoes*

QUEEN: Alas, sweet lady, what imports° this song?   *means*

9. The plot of ground involved is so small that it cannot contain the number of men fighting or the
corpses of those who die fighting.   1. Takes offense at trifles.   2. Though they reveal nothing for
certain, her words provoke disturbing inferences.   3. A hat decorated with a cockle shell indicated
that its wearer had made a pilgrimage to the shrine of St. James at Compostela in Spain. A pilgrim
often carried a staff.

OPHELIA: Say you? Nay, pray you mark.°   *listen; pay attention*

    [*Sings.*]

He is dead and gone, lady,
30   He is dead and gone;
At his head a grass-green turf,
   At his heels a stone.

  O, ho!
QUEEN: Nay, but Ophelia—
OPHELIA: Pray you mark.

    [*Sings.*]

White his shroud as the mountain snow—

    [*Enter* KING.]

35 QUEEN: Alas, look here, my lord.
OPHELIA:

    [*Sings.*]

Larded° all with sweet flowers;   *Garnished*
Which bewept to the grave did not go
With true-love showers.°   *tears*

KING: How do you, pretty lady?
40 OPHELIA: Well, God dild° you! They say the owl was a baker's   *yield (reward)*
daughter.[4] Lord, we know what we are, but know not what
we may be. God be at your table!
KING: Conceit° upon her father.   *Brooding imagination*
OPHELIA: Pray let's have no words of this, but when they
45 ask you what it means, say you this:

    [*Sings.*]

Tomorrow is Saint Valentine's day,
   All in the morning betime,°   *early*
And I a maid at your window,
   To be your Valentine.

50 Then up he rose, and donn'd his clo'es,
   And dupped° the chamber-door,   *opened*
Let in the maid, that out a maid
   Never departed more.

KING: Pretty Ophelia!
55 OPHELIA: Indeed, without an oath, I'll make an end on't.°   *of it*

    [*Sings.*]

---

4. Reference to a folktale about a young woman transformed into an owl when she fails to offer generosity to Jesus, who had asked for bread in her mother's shop.

> By Gis° and by Saint Charity,   *Jesus*
>   Alack, and fie for shame!
> Young men will do't, if they come to't;
>   By Cock,⁵ they are to blame.
> Quoth she "before you tumbled me,   60
>   You promised me to wed."
>
> He answers:
>
> "So would I'a done, by yonder sun,
> An° thou hadst not come to my bed."   *If*

KING: How long hath she been thus?   65

OPHELIA: I hope all will be well. We must be patient, but I cannot choose but weep to think they would lay him i' th' cold
ground. My brother shall know of it, and so I thank you for
your good counsel. Come, my coach! Good night, ladies,
good night. Sweet ladies, good night, good night.   [*Exit.*]   70

KING: Follow her close; give her good watch, I pray you.

          [*Exeunt* HORATIO *and* GENTLEMAN.]

> O, this is the poison of deep grief; it springs
> All from her father's death, and now behold!
> O Gertrude, Gertrude!
> When sorrows come, they come not single spies,°   *scouts* 75
> But in battalions: first, her father slain;
> Next, your son gone, and he most violent author
> Of his own just remove; the people muddied,°   *confused; disturbed*
> Thick and unwholesome in their thoughts and whispers
> For good Polonius' death; and we have done but greenly°   *naively* 80
> In hugger-mugger° to inter him; poor Ophelia   *haste; secrecy*
> Divided from herself and her fair judgment,
> Without the which we are pictures, or mere beasts;
> Last, and as much containing° as all these,   *and as important*
> Her brother is in secret come from France,   85
> Feeds on his wonder, keeps himself in clouds,°   *his intentions obscure*
> And wants° not buzzers° to infect his ear   *lacks / scandalmongers*
> With pestilent speeches of his father's death,
> Wherein necessity, of matter beggared,°   *short on facts*
> Will nothing stick° our person to arraign°   *Will not hesitate / accuse* 90
> In ear and ear. O my dear Gertrude, this,
> Like to a murd'ring piece,⁶ in many places
> Gives me superfluous° death.   *redundant*
>
> [*A noise within.*]

QUEEN: Alack, what noise is this?

KING: Attend!   95

> Where are my Switzers?° Let them guard the door.   *Swiss guards*
> What is the matter?

---

5. Corruption of "God," with a sexual pun.   6. Weapon designed to scatter its shot.

MESSENGER: Save yourself, my lord.
The ocean, overpeering of his list,°   *rising above its limits*
Eats not the flats with more impiteous° haste   *pitiless*
100   Than young Laertes, in a riotous head,°   *insurrection; tidal wave*
O'erbears your officers. The rabble call him lord,
And as° the world were now but° to begin,   *as = as if / only now*
Antiquity forgot, custom not known,
The ratifiers and props of every word,[7]
105   They cry "Choose we, Laertes shall be king."
Caps, hands, and tongues, applaud it to the clouds,
"Laertes shall be king, Laertes king."
QUEEN: How cheerfully on the false trail they cry![8]

[*A noise within.*]

O, this is counter,° you false Danish dogs!   *backward; wrong*
110   KING: The doors are broke.

[*Enter* LAERTES, *with* OTHERS.]

LAERTES: Where is this king?—Sirs, stand you all without.
ALL: No, let's come in.
LAERTES: I pray you give me leave.
ALL: We will, we will.
LAERTES: I thank you. Keep° the door.   [*Exeunt his followers.*]   *Guard*
                                   O thou vile king,
115   Give me my father!
QUEEN: Calmly, good Laertes.
LAERTES: That drop of blood that's calm proclaims me
        bastard,
        Cries cuckold to my father, brands the harlot
        Even here between the chaste unsmirchèd brow
        Of my true mother.
KING: What is the cause, Laertes,
120   That thy rebellion looks so giant-like?
        Let him go, Gertrude. Do not fear° our person.   *fear for*
        There's such divinity doth hedge a king
        That treason can but peep to° what it would,°   *at / would do*
        Acts little of his will. Tell me, Laertes,
125   Why thou art thus incensed. Let him go, Gertrude.
        Speak, man.
LAERTES: Where is my father?
KING: Dead.
QUEEN: But not by him.°   *(the king)*
KING: Let him demand his fill.
LAERTES: How came he dead? I'll not be juggled° with.   *fooled*
        To hell allegiance, vows to the blackest devil,
130   Conscience and grace to the profoundest pit!

---

7. Agreement or contract (sworn "word"); language itself.   8. As if following the wrong scent like
hunting dogs.

I dare damnation. To this point° I stand,   *resolve*
That both the worlds I give to negligence,[9]
Let come what comes, only I'll be revenged
Most throughly° for my father.   *thoroughly*
KING: Who shall stay° you?   *prevent*   135
LAERTES: My will, not all the world's.
And for my means, I'll husband° them so well   *manage*
They shall go far with little.
KING: Good Laertes,
If you desire to know the certainty°   *truth (about the death)*
Of your dear father, is't writ in your revenge
That, swoopstake,[1] you will draw° both friend and foe,   *take from*   140
Winner and loser?
LAERTES: None but his enemies.
KING: Will you know them, then?
LAERTES: To his good friends thus wide I'll ope my arms,
And like the kind life-rend'ring pelican,
Repast them with my blood.[2]   145
KING: Why, now you speak
Like a good child and a true gentleman.
That I am guiltless of your father's death,
And am most sensibly° in grief for it,   *sympathetically*
It shall as level° to your judgment 'pear   *plain*
As day does to your eye.   150

[*A noise within:* "Let her come in."]

LAERTES: How now? What noise is that?

[*Enter* OPHELIA.]

O, heat dry up my brains! tears seven times salt
Burn out the sense and virtue° of mine eye!   *natural power*
By heaven, thy madness shall be paid with weight
Till our scale turn the beam.[3] O rose of May,   155
Dear maid, kind sister, sweet Ophelia!
O heavens, is't possible a young maid's wits
Should be as mortal as an old man's life?
Nature is fin° in love, and where 'tis fine   *refined*
It sends some precious instances° of itself   *tokens*   160
After the thing it loves.[4]
OPHELIA:

        [*Sings.*]

        They bore him barefac'd on the bier;
            Hey non nonny, nonny, hey nonny;
            And in his grave rain'd many a tear—

9. That both this world and the next I disregard.   1. Indiscriminately. (The winner of a sweepstakes
gained the stakes of all other players.)   2. The pelican was believed to feed ("repast") her young with
her own blood.   3. Until vengence outweighs the injury, tilting the "scale" of justice.   4. Laertes suggests that Ophelia, because of her love for her dead father, gave up her sanity as a token of grief.

165   Fare you well, my dove!

LAERTES: Hadst thou thy wits, and didst persuade° revenge,   *argue for*
    It could not move thus.

OPHELIA: You must sing "A-down, a-down, and you call him
    a-down-a." O, how the wheel⁵ becomes it! It is the false
170   steward, that stole his master's daughter.

LAERTES: This nothing's more than matter.⁶

OPHELIA: There's a rosemary, that's for remembrance. Pray
    you, love, remember. And there is pansies, that's for
    thoughts.

175 LAERTES: A document° in madness, thoughts and remem-   *An object lesson*
    brance fitted.

OPHELIA: There's fennel for you, and columbines. There's
    rue for you, and here's some for me. We may call it herb
    of grace a Sundays. O, you must wear your rue with a dif-
180   ference.° There's a daisy. I would give you some violets,⁷   *for a different reason (?)*
    but they withered all when my father died. They say 'a
    made a good end.

      [*Sings.*]

     For bonny sweet Robin is all my joy.

LAERTES: Thought and affliction, passion, hell itself,
185   She turns to favor° and to prettiness.   *beauty*

OPHELIA:

      [*Sings.*]

     And will 'a not come again?
     And will 'a not come again?
       No, no, he is dead,
       Go to thy death-bed,
190   He never will come again.

     His beard was as white as snow,
     All flaxen° was his poll;°   *white / head*
       He is gone, he is gone,
       And we cast away moan:
195   God-a-mercy on his soul!

    And of all Christian souls, I pray God. God b'wi'you.

                     [*Exit.*]

LAERTES: Do you see this, O God?

KING: Laertes, I must commune with your grief,
    Or you deny me right. Go but apart,
200   Make choice of whom° your wisest friends you will,   *whichever of*

5. Refrain of a song, in this case "A-down, a-down, and you call him a-down-a" but also suggesting
the Wheel of Fortune or a spinning wheel to whose rhythm such songs were sung.   6. This nonsense
signifies more than coherent speech ("matter").   7. Here (as in lines 172–74), Ophelia apparently
distributes flowers to the other characters, referring to the well-known "language of flowers." According to it, fennel symbolizes or is associated with flattery; columbines with ingratitude or marital infi-
delity; rue with repentance, as is the "herb of grace" (wormwood); daisies with dissembling seduction
(perhaps); and violets with faithfulness.

And they shall hear and judge 'twixt you and me.
If by direct or by collateral° hand   *indirect*
They find us touched,° we will our kingdom give,   *involved in guilt*
Our crown, our life, and all that we call ours,
To you in satisfaction;° but if not,   *recompense* 205
Be you content to lend your patience to us,
And we shall jointly labor with your soul
To give it due content.
LAERTES: Let this be so.
His means of death, his obscure funeral—
No trophy,° sword, nor hatchment,° o'er his bones,   *memorial / coat of arms* 210
No noble rite nor formal ostentation°—   *(funereal) pomp*
Cry to be heard, as 'twere from heaven to earth,
That I must call't in question.°   *demand an explanation*
KING: So you shall;
And where th' offence is, let the great axe fall.
I pray you go with me.   [*Exeunt.*]   215

Scene 6

Another room in the castle. Enter HORATIO *and a* GENTLEMAN.

HORATIO: What are they that would speak with me?
GENTLEMAN: Sea-faring men, sir. They say they have letters
    for you.
HORATIO: Let them come in.   [*Exit* GENTLEMAN.]
    I do not know from what part of the world   5
    I should be greeted, if not from Lord Hamlet.

    [*Enter* SAILORS.]

SAILOR: God bless you, sir.
HORATIO: Let him bless thee too.
SAILOR: 'A shall, sir, an't° please him. There's a letter for you,   *if it*
    sir—it came from th' ambassador that was bound for Eng-   10
    land—if your name be Horatio, as I am let to know it is.
HORATIO: [*Reads.*] "Horatio, when thou shalt have over-
    looked° this, give these fellows some means° to the king.   *read / access*
    They have letters for him. Ere we were two days old at
    sea, a pirate of very warlike appointment° gave us chase.   *equipment* 15
    Finding ourselves too slow of sail, we put on a compelled
    valor, and in the grapple I boarded them. On the instant
    they got clear of our ship, so I alone became their pris-
    oner. They have dealt with me like thieves of mercy, but
    they knew what they did;[8] I am to do a good turn for   20
    them. Let the king have the letters I have sent, and repair
    thou° to me with as much speed as thou wouldest fly   *come*

8. They have been merciful, but with the expectation of a return. Hamlet recalls the thieves crucified
next to Christ and Christ's plea for forgiveness for those who "know not what they do" (Luke 23.34–43).

death. I have words to speak in thine ear will make thee
dumb; yet are they much too light for the bore of the
25   matter.[9] These good fellows will bring thee where I am.
Rosencrantz and Guildenstern hold their course for
England. Of them I have much to tell thee. Farewell.
        He that thou knowest thine, Hamlet."
        Come, I will give you way° for these your letters,   *means of delivery*
30   And do't the speedier that you may direct me
        To him from whom you brought them.   [*Exeunt.*]

Scene 7

Another room in the castle. Enter KING *and* LAERTES.

KING: Now must your conscience my acquittance seal,°   *innocence affirm.*
        And you must put me in your heart for friend,
        Sith° you have heard, and with a knowing ear,   *Since*
        That he which hath your noble father slain
        Pursued my life.
5 LAERTES: It well appears. But tell me
        Why you proceeded not against these feats,°   *acts*
        So criminal and so capital° in nature,   *punishable by death.*
        As by your safety, greatness, wisdom, all things else,
        You mainly° were stirred up.   *greatly*
        KING: O, for two special reasons,
10   Which may to you, perhaps, seem much unsinewed,°   *very weak*
        But yet to me th' are strong. The queen his mother
        Lives almost by his looks, and for myself—
        My virtue or my plague, be it either which—
        She is so conjunctive° to my life and soul   *closely joined*
15   That, as the star moves not but in his sphere,[1]
        I could not but by her. The other motive,
        Why to a public count° I might not go,   *accounting; reckoning*
        Is the great love the general gender° bear him,   *common people*
        Who, dipping all his faults in their affection,
20   Work like the spring that turneth wood to stone,[2]
        Convert his gyves[3] to graces; so that my arrows,
        Too slightly timbered° for so loud a wind,   *shafted*
        Would have reverted to my bow again,
        But not where I had aimed them.
25 LAERTES: And so have I a noble father lost,
        A sister driven into desp'rate terms,
        Whose worth, if praises may go back again,[4]

---

9. Metaphor from gunnery, referring to shot too small for the weapons to be fired.
1. Reference to the Ptolemaic cosmology, in which planets and stars were believed to revolve in crystalline spheres concentrically about the earth. (Two planets were said to be "in conjunction" when
they appeared close, as if traveling in the same sphere or "conjunct.")   2. Certain springs contain so
much lime that they can petrify absorbent objects (like a piece of wood).   3. Literally, fetters; figuratively (as here), faults, shortcomings.   4. That is, "back again" in time, to what once was.

Stood challenger on mount of all the age
For her perfections.⁵ But my revenge will come.

KING: Break not your sleeps for that. You must not think   30
That we are made of stuff so flat and dull
That we can let our beard be shook with danger,⁶
And think it pastime. You shortly shall hear more.
I loved your father, and we love our self,
And that, I hope, will teach you to imagine—   35

[*Enter a* MESSENGER *with letters.*]

How now? What news?

MESSENGER: Letters, my lord, from Hamlet.
These to your majesty; this to the queen.

KING: From Hamlet! Who brought them?

MESSENGER: Sailors, my lord, they say. I saw them not.
They were given me by Claudio; he received them   40
Of him that brought them.

KING: Laertes, you shall hear them.—
Leave us.   [*Exit* MESSENGER.]
[*Reads.*] "High and mighty, you shall know I am set
naked° on your kingdom. Tomorrow shall I beg leave to   destitute
see your kingly eyes; when I shall, first asking your par-   45
don° thereunto, recount the occasion of my sudden and   permission
more strange return.
        Hamlet."
What should this mean? Are all the rest come back?
Or is it some abuse,° and no such thing?   deception 50

LAERTES: Know you the hand?

KING: 'Tis Hamlet's character.° "Naked"!   handwriting
And in a postscript here, he says "alone."
Can you devise° me?   explain it to; direct

LAERTES: I am lost in it, my lord. But let him come.   55
It warms the very sickness in my heart
That I shall live and tell him to his teeth
"Thus didest thou."⁷

KING: If it be so, Laertes—
As how should it be so, how otherwise?—⁸
Will you be ruled by me?   60

LAERTES: Ay, my lord,
So° you will not o'errule me to a peace.   Provided that

KING: To thine own peace. If he be now returned,
As checking at° his voyage, and that he means   turning aside from
No more to undertake it, I will work him
To an exploit now ripe in my device,°   planning 65
Under the which he shall not choose but fall;
And for his death no wind of blame shall breathe

5. Conspicuously challenged the world to match her perfections.   6. That I can allow anyone to endanger me with contemptuous behavior.   7. This which I do now to you, you did to my father.
8. How could Hamlet be returning, and yet how else could he have sent this letter?

But even his mother shall uncharge° the practice°   *not accuse / connivance*
And call it accident.

LAERTES: My lord, I will be ruled;
70   The rather if you could devise it so
That I might be the organ.°   *instrument; agent*

KING: It falls right.
You have been talked of since your travel much,
And that in Hamlet's hearing, for a quality
Wherein they say you shine. Your sum of parts°   *abilities*
75   Did not together pluck such envy from him
As did that one, and that, in my regard,
Of the unworthiest siege.°   *lowest rank*

LAERTES: What part is that, my lord?

KING: A very riband in the cap of youth,
Yet needful too, for youth no less becomes
80   The light and careless livery that it wears
Than settled age his sables and his weeds,
Importing° health and graveness. Two months since   *Suggesting*
Here was a gentleman of Normandy.
I have seen myself, and served against, the French,
85   And they can° well on horseback, but this gallant   *perform*
Had witchcraft in't. He grew unto his seat,
And to such wondrous doing brought his horse,
As had he been incorpsed and demi-natured[9]
With the brave beast. So far he topped° my thought°   *surpassed / expectation*
90   That I, in forgery° of shapes and tricks,   *my imaginings*
Come short of what he did.

LAERTES: A Norman was't?

KING: A Norman.

LAERTES: Upon my life, Lamord.

KING: The very same.

LAERTES: I know him well. He is the brooch° indeed   *ornament*
95   And gem of all the nation.

KING: He made confession° of you,   *testimonial*
And gave you such a masterly report
For art and exercise in your defence,
And for your rapier most especial,
100   That he cried out 'twould be a sight indeed
If one could match you. The scrimers° of their nation   *fencers*
He swore had neither motion, guard, nor eye,
If you opposed them. Sir, this report of his
Did Hamlet so envenom with his envy
105   That he could nothing do but wish and beg
Your sudden° coming o'er, to play with you.   *immediate*
Now out of this—

---

9. As if he had been in the same body and had half the nature of. The image recalls the centaur of classical myth.

LAERTES: What out of this, my lord?
KING: Laertes, was your father dear to you?
         Or are you like the painting of a sorrow,
         A face without a heart?   110
LAERTES: Why ask you this?
KING: Not that I think you did not love your father,
         But that I know love is begun by time,°   circumstance
         And that I see in passages of proof,°   tests of experience
         Time qualifies° the spark and fire of it.   moderates
         There lives within the very flame of love   115
         A kind of wick or snuff that will abate it,
         And nothing is at a like° goodness still,°   an equal / always
         For goodness, growing to a plurisy,[1]
         Dies in his own too much.° That we would do,   excess
         We should do when we would; for this "would" changes,   120
         And hath abatements and delays as many
         As there are tongues, are hands, are accidents,
         And then this "should" is like a spendthrift's sigh
         That hurts by easing.[2] But to the quick° of th' ulcer—   center
         Hamlet comes back; what would you undertake   125
         To show yourself in deed your father's son
         More than in words?
LAERTES: To cut his throat i' th' church.
KING: No place indeed should murder sanctuarize;[3]
         Revenge should have no bounds. But, good Laertes,
         Will you do this? Keep close within your chamber.   130
         Hamlet returned shall know you are come home.
         We'll put on those shall[4] praise your excellence,
         And set a double varnish on the fame
         The Frenchman gave you, bring you in fine° together,   short
         And wager on your heads. He, being remiss,°   unwary 135
         Most generous, and free from all contriving,
         Will not peruse° the foils, so that with ease,   examine
         Or with a little shuffling, you may choose
         A sword unbated,[5] and in a pass of practice
         Requite him for your father.
LAERTES: I will do't,   140
         And for that purpose I'll anoint my sword.
         I bought an unction° of a mountebank°   ointment / quack
         So mortal that but dip a knife in it,
         Where it draws blood no cataplasm° so rare,   poultice
         Collected from all simples° that have virtue°   herbs / potency 145
         Under the moon, can save the thing from death
         That is but scratched withal.° I'll touch my point   with it

1. Chest inflammation, metaphorically like a fire in the heart.   2. A sigh was believed to draw a drop
of blood from the heart and thus to "hurt" by "easing" sadness.   3. Provide sanctuary for a murderer.   4. I shall incite some people to.   5. Not blunted, as an actual practice foil would be.

With this contagion, that if I gall° him slightly,   *prick*
It may be death.

KING: Let's further think of this,
150   Weigh what convenience both of time and means
May fit us to our shape.° If this should fail,   *purpose; plot; roles*
And that our drift look° through our bad performance,   *our intention be seen*
'Twere better not assayed. Therefore this project
Should have a back or second that might hold
155   If this did blast in proof.[6] Soft, let me see.
We'll make a solemn wager on your cunnings°—   *skills*
I ha't.
When in your motion° you are hot and dry—   *exercise*
As make your bouts more violent to that end—
160   And that he calls for drink, I'll have prepared him
A chalice for the nonce,° whereon but sipping,   *occasion*
If he by chance escape your venomed stuck,°   *thrust*
Our purpose may hold there.—But stay, what noise?

[*Enter* QUEEN.]

QUEEN: One woe doth tread upon another's heel,
165   So fast they follow. Your sister's drowned, Laertes.
LAERTES: Drowned? O, where?
QUEEN: There is a willow grows aslant the brook
That shows his hoar leaves[7] in the glassy stream.
Therewith fantastic garlands did she make
170   Of crowflowers, nettles, daisies, and long purples[8]
That liberal shepherds give a grosser name,
But our cold° maids do dead men's fingers call them.   *chaste*
There on the pendent boughs her coronet weeds
Clamb'ring to hang, an envious sliver° broke,   *a malicious twig*
175   When down her weedy trophies and herself
Fell in the weeping brook. Her clothes spread wide,
And mermaid-like awhile they bore her up,
Which time she chanted snatches of old tunes,
As one incapable° of her own distress,   *unaware*
180   Or like a creature native and indued°   *habituated*
Unto that element. But long it could not be
Till that her garments, heavy with their drink,
Pulled the poor wretch from her melodious lay°   *song*
To muddy death.

LAERTES: Alas, then she is drowned?
185 QUEEN: Drowned, drowned.
LAERTES: Too much of water hast thou, poor Ophelia,
And therefore I forbid my tears; but yet

6. Fail when tried; literally, explode when put to the test (like a cannon).   7. Willow leaves are gray-white ("hoary") on the underside (reflected from below by the "glassy," mirror-like water). The willow was an emblem of mourning and of forsaken love.   8. Purple orchises, a type of orchid known by the coarser ("grosser") name of "dog's cullions" (testicles) or "goat's cullions." *Crowflowers*: wildflowers.

It is our trick;° nature her custom holds,   *characteristic way*
Let shame say what it will. When these° are gone,   *(his tears)*
The woman will be out.[9] Adieu, my lord.   190
I have a speech o' fire that fain° would blaze   *gladly*
But that this folly drowns it.   [*Exit.*]
KING: Let's follow, Gertrude.
How much I had to do to calm his rage!
Now fear I this will give it start again;
Therefore let's follow.   [*Exeunt.*]   195

ACT V

Scene 1

A churchyard. Enter two CLOWNS.°   *rustics; peasants*

CLOWN: Is she to be buried in Christian burial when she
   wilfully seeks her own salvation?[1]
OTHER: I tell thee she is. Therefore make her grave straight.°   *right away*
   The crowner° hath sat on her,° and finds it Christian burial.[2]   *coroner / held an inquest*
CLOWN: How can that be, unless she drowned herself in her   5
   own defence?
OTHER: Why, 'tis found so.
CLOWN: It must be "se offendendo";[3] it cannot be else. For
   here lies the point: if I drown myself wittingly, it argues
   an act, and an act hath three branches—it is to act, to   10
   do, to perform; argal,[4] she drowned herself wittingly.
OTHER: Nay, but hear you, Goodman Delver.°   *Master Digger*
CLOWN: Give me leave. Here lies the water; good. Here stands
   the man; good. If the man go to this water and drown him-
   self, it is, will he, nill he, he goes—mark you that. But if   15
   the water come to him and drown him, he drowns not
   himself. Argal, he that is not guilty of his own death short-
   ens not his own life.
OTHER: But is this law?
CLOWN: Ay, marry, is't; crowner's quest° law.   *inquest* 20
OTHER: Will you ha' the truth on't? If this had not been a
   gentlewoman, she should have been buried out o' Christian burial.
CLOWN: Why, there thou say'st.° And the more pity that great   *how right you are*
   folk should have count'nance° in this world to drown   *privilege* 25
   or hang themselves more than their even-Christen.°   *fellow Christian*
   Come, my spade. There is no ancient gentlemen but
   gard'ners, ditchers, and grave-makers. They hold up° Adam's   *carry on*
   profession.

9. The woman (Ophelia) or the feminine side of my nature will be gone with them.   1. Probably a
mistake for "damnation." Because suicide was a mortal sin, suicides were not ordinarily permitted
"Christian burial" (in consecrated ground with the church's blessing and ritual).   2. And has given the
verdict that she is eligible for Christian burial (in effect, a determination that Ophelia did not kill herself).   3. Error for *se defendendo*, killing in self-defense (Latin).   4. Error for "ergo," therefore (Latin).

30 OTHER: Was he a gentleman?

CLOWN: 'A was the first that ever bore arms.[5]

OTHER: Why, he had none.

CLOWN: What, art a heathen? How dost thou understand the
Scripture? The Scripture says Adam digged. Could he dig
35 without arms? I'll put another question to thee. If thou
answerest me not to the purpose, confess thyself—[6]

OTHER: Go to.[7]

CLOWN: What is he that builds stronger than either the
mason, the shipwright, or the carpenter?

40 OTHER: The gallows-maker, for that frame outlives a thousand tenants.

CLOWN: I like thy wit well, in good faith. The gallows does°   serves
well. But how does it well? It does well to those that do
ill. Now thou dost ill to say the gallows is built stronger
45 than the church. Argal, the gallows may do well to thee.
To't again, come.

OTHER: Who builds stronger than a mason, a shipwright, or
a carpenter?

CLOWN: Ay tell me that, and unyoke.[8]

50 OTHER: Marry, now I can tell.

CLOWN: To't.

OTHER: Mass,° I cannot tell.   By the mass

CLOWN: Cudgel thy brains no more about it, for your dull ass
will not mend° his pace with beating. And when you are   improve
55 asked this question next, say "a grave maker." The houses
he makes lasts till doomsday. Go, get thee in, and fetch me
a stoup° of liquor.   [Exit OTHER CLOWN.]   flagon

[Enter HAMLET and HORATIO as CLOWN digs and sings.]

In youth, when I did love, did love,
Methought it was very sweet,
60 To contract° the time for-a my behove,°   shorten / advantage
O, methought there-a was nothing-a meet.[9]

HAMLET: Has this fellow no feeling of his business, that 'a
sings in grave-making?

HORATIO: Custom hath made it in him a property of easiness.[1]

65 HAMLET: 'Tis e'en so. The hand of little employment hath
the daintier sense.°   more delicate feeling

CLOWN:

[Sings.]

5. Those bearing a family coat of arms were officially recognized as gentlemen, but the clown here
takes the word "arm" literally.   6. "Confess thyself and be hanged" was a proverbial expression.
7. Expression of impatience.   8. Rest your wits from work (like draft animals).
9. Suitable. The gravedigger's song is a free version of the poem "The aged lover renounceth love" by
Thomas, Lord Vaux, published in Tottel's Miscellany (1557). The extra-metrical "a"s are probably
grunts while digging.   1. Something (a "property") he can do easily, without distress.

But age, with his stealing steps,
   Hath clawed me in his clutch,
And hath shipped me into the land,°   *earth*
   As if I had never been such.   70

[*Throws up a skull.*]

HAMLET: That skull had a tongue in it, and could sing once.
How the knave jowls° it to the ground, as if 'twere Cain's   *slams*
jawbone, that did the first murder! This might be the
pate of a politician,[2] which this ass now o'erreaches;° one   *gets the better of*
that would circumvent God, might it not?   75

HORATIO: It might, my lord.

HAMLET: Or of a courtier, which could say, "Good morrow,
sweet lord! How does thou, sweet lord?" This might be
my Lord Such-a-one, that praised my Lord Such-a-one's
horse, when 'a meant to beg it, might it not?   80

HORATIO: Ay, my lord.

HAMLET: Why, e'en so, and now my Lady Worm's, chapless,° *lacking a lower jaw*
and knock'd about the mazzard° with a sexton's spade.   *head*
Here's fine revolution,[3] an° we had the trick° to see't. Did   *if / ability*
these bones cost no more the breeding but to play at   85
loggets with them?[4] Mine ache to think on't.

CLOWN:

   [*Sings.*]

A pick-axe and a spade, a spade,
   For and° a shrouding sheet: *And also*
O, a pit of clay for to be made
   For such a guest is meet.   90

[*Throws up another skull.*]

HAMLET: There's another. Why may not that be the skull of a
lawyer? Where be his quiddities[5] now, his quillets,° his   *quibbles*
cases, his tenures,° and his tricks? Why does he suffer   *property titles*
this mad knave now to knock him about the sconce°   *head*
with a dirty shovel, and will not tell him of his action° of *legal prosecution* 95
battery? Hum! This fellow might be in's time a great buyer
of land, with his statutes, his recognizances, his fines, his
double vouchers, his recoveries.[6] Is this the fine° of his   *end*
fines, and the recovery of his recoveries, to have his fine°   *subtle*
pate full of fine° dirt? Will his vouchers vouch° him no *fine-grained / guarantee* 100
more of his purchases, and double ones too, than the

2. Schemer for political advantage.
3. Reversal of fortune (literally, the turning of Fortune's revolving wheel).   4. Was it so easy and
inexpensive to bring these bones to maturity that they can be treated as "loggets" (small wooden clubs
thrown as part of a game).   5. Subtle distinctions.   6. In this speech Hamlet reels off a list of legal
terms relating to property transactions. "Statutes" were mortgages, often linked with "recognizances,"
bonds acknowledging a particular debt. "Fines" and "recoveries" were both kinds of lawsuits regarding
land ownership. The "double voucher" summoned two witnesses to testify in such cases.

length and breadth of a pair of indentures?[7] The very con-
veyances° of his lands will scarcely lie in this box,° and   *deeds / deed-box; coffin*
must th' inheritor° himself have no more, ha?   *owner*

105   HORATIO: Not a jot more, my lord.

HAMLET: Is not parchment made of sheepskins?

HORATIO: Ay, my lord, and of calves' skins too.

HAMLET: They are sheep and calves° which seek out assur-   *simpletons and fools*
ance in that. I will speak to this fellow. Whose grave's

110   this, sirrah?[8]

CLOWN: Mine, sir.

[*Sings.*]

O, a pit of clay for to be made
For such a guest is meet.

HAMLET: I think it be thine indeed, for thou liest in't.

115   CLOWN: You lie out on't, sir, and therefore 'tis not yours. For
my part, I do not lie in't, yet it is mine.

HAMLET: Thou dost lie in't, to be in't and say it is thine.
'Tis for the dead, not for the quick;° therefore thou liest.   *living*

CLOWN: 'Tis a quick° lie, sir; 'twill away again from me to you.   *nimble*

120   HAMLET: What man dost thou dig it for?

CLOWN: For no man, sir.

HAMLET: What woman, then?

CLOWN: For none neither.

HAMLET: Who is to be buried in't?

125   CLOWN: One that was a woman, sir; but, rest her soul, she's dead.

HAMLET: How absolute° the knave is! We must speak by the   *precise*
card,° or equivocation will undo us. By the Lord, Horatio,   *exactly*
this three years I have took note of it, the age is grown so

130   picked° that the toe of the peasant comes so near the heel   *refined; punctilious*
of the courtier, he galls° his kibe.° How long hast thou   *chafes / heel*
been a grave-maker?

CLOWN: Of all the days i' th' year, I came to't that day that
our last King Hamlet overcame Fortinbras.

135   HAMLET: How long is that since?

CLOWN: Cannot you tell that? Every fool can tell that. It was
that very day that young Hamlet was born—he that is
mad, and sent into England.

HAMLET: Ay, marry, why was he sent into England?

140   CLOWN: Why, because 'a was mad. 'A shall recover his wits
there; or, if 'a do not, 'tis no great matter there.

HAMLET: Why?

CLOWN: 'Twill not be seen in him there. There the men are
as mad as he.

145   HAMLET: How came he mad?

CLOWN: Very strangely, they say.

---

7. Two copies of a document. The dead man's property (his grave) is hardly bigger than these.
8. Form of address used with social inferiors.

HAMLET: How strangely?

CLOWN: Faith, e'en with losing his wits.

HAMLET: Upon what ground?⁹

CLOWN: Why, here in Denmark. I have been sexton here,   150
man and boy, thirty years.

HAMLET: How long will a man lie i' th' earth ere he rot?

CLOWN: Faith, if 'a be not rotten before 'a die—as we have
many pocky¹ corses now-a-days that will scarce hold the
laying in²—'a will last you some eight year or nine year. A   155
tanner will last you nine year.

HAMLET: Why he more than another?

CLOWN: Why, sir, his hide is so tanned with his trade that 'a
will keep out water a great while; and your water is a sore
decayer of your whoreson° dead body. Here's a skull now   *vile* 160
hath lien you° i' th' earth three and twenty years.   *lain*

HAMLET: Whose was it?

CLOWN: A whoreson mad fellow's it was. Whose do you
think it was?

HAMLET: Nay, I know not.   165

CLOWN: A pestilence on him for a mad rogue! 'A poured a
flagon of Rhenish° on my head once. This same skull, sir,   *Rhine wine*
was, sir, Yorick's skull, the king's jester.

HAMLET: [*Takes the skull.*] This?

CLOWN: E'en that.   170

HAMLET: Alas, poor Yorick! I knew him, Horatio—a fellow
of infinite jest, of most excellent fancy. He hath bore me
on his back a thousand times, and now how abhorred° in   *disgusting*
my imagination it is! My gorg° rises at it. Here hung those   *gorge*
lips that I have kissed I know not how oft. Where be   175
your gibes now, your gambols, your songs, your flashes of
merriment that were wont to set the table on a roar? Not
one now to mock your own grinning? Quite chap-fall'n?°   *dejected*
Now get you to my lady's chamber, and tell her, let her
paint an inch thick, to this favor° she must come. Make   *appearance* 180
her laugh at that. Prithee, Horatio, tell me one thing.

HORATIO: What's that, my lord?

HAMLET: Dost thou think Alexander³ looked o' this fashion
i' th' earth?

HORATIO: E'en so.   185

HAMLET: And smelt so? Pah!   [*Throws down the skull.*]

HORATIO: E'en so, my lord.

HAMLET: To what base uses we may return, Horatio! Why
may not imagination trace the noble dust of Alexander
till 'a find it stopping a bung-hole?°   *opening of a cask* 190

HORATIO: 'Twere to consider too curiously° to consider so.   *precisely*

9. From what cause, but the clown takes him to mean "In what country."   1. Corrupted by syphi-
lis.   2. That is, hold together during burial rites.   3. Alexander the Great (356–23 BCE), king of the
ancient Greek kingdom of Macedon. By the age of thirty he had created one of the ancient world's
largest empires, stretching from Greece to northwest India.

HAMLET: No, faith, not a jot, but to follow him thither with
modesty° enough, and likelihood to lead it. Alexander died,   *reasonable speculation*
Alexander was buried, Alexander returneth to dust; the
195   dust is earth; of earth we make loam;[4] and why of that loam
whereto he was converted might they not stop a beerbarrel?

      Imperious Cæsar, dead and turned to clay,
      Might stop a hole to keep the wind away.
      O, that that earth which kept the world in awe
200   Should patch a wall t'expel the winter's flaw!°   *squall; gusty wind*

But soft, but soft awhile! Here comes the king,
The queen, the courtiers.

[*Enter* KING, QUEEN, LAERTES, *and the Corse*° *with a*   *Corpse*
PRIEST *and* LORDS *attendant.*]
               Who is this they follow?
And with such maimèd° rites? This doth betoken   *truncated*
The corse they follow did with desperate hand
205   Fordo° its own life. 'Twas of some estate.°   *Destroy / rank*
Couch we° awhile and mark.   *Conceal ourselves*
             [*Retires with* HORATIO.]
LAERTES: What ceremony else?°   *more*
HAMLET: That is Laertes, a very noble youth. Mark.
LAERTES: What ceremony else?
210   PRIEST: Here obsequies have been as far enlarged°   *extended*
      As we have warranty.° Her death was doubtful,°   *sanction for / suspicious*
      And but that great command° o'ersways the order,°   *royal authority / usual rules*
      She should in ground unsanctified been lodged
      Till the last trumpet. For° charitable prayers,   *Rather than*
215   Shards, flints, and pebbles, should be thrown on her.
      Yet here she is allowed her virgin crants,°   *garlands*
      Her maiden strewments,[5] and the bringing home°   *(to the grave)*
      Of bell and burial.[6]
LAERTES: Must there no more be done?
PRIEST: No more be done.
220   We should profane the service of the dead
To sing a requiem and such rest to her
As to peace-parted° souls.   *peacefully departed*
LAERTES: Lay her i' th' earth,
And from her fair and unpolluted flesh
May violets spring! I tell thee, churlish priest,
225   A minist'ring angel shall my sister be
When thou liest howling.°   *(in hell)*
HAMLET: What, the fair Ophelia!
QUEEN: Sweets to the sweet. Farewell!   [*Scatters flowers.*]
I hoped thou shouldst have been my Hamlet's wife.

4. Mixture of clay and straw used as plaster.
5. Flowers strewn on the grave.   6. That is, in the customary way, with funeral bells and burial service.

I thought thy bride-bed to have decked, sweet maid,
And not t' have strewed thy grave.

LAERTES: O, treble woe   230
  Fall ten times treble on that cursèd head
  Whose wicked deed thy most ingenious sense°   quick, perceptive intelligence
  Deprived thee of! Hold off the earth awhile,[7]
  Till I have caught her once more in mine arms.
                          [*Leaps into the grave.*]
  Now pile your dust upon the quick and dead,   235
  Till of this flat a mountain you have made
  T' o'er-top old Pelion or the skyish head
  Of blue Olympus.[8]

HAMLET: [*Coming forward.*] What is he whose grief
  Bears such an emphasis, whose phrase° of sorrow   *rhetoric*
  Conjures° the wand'ring stars,° and makes them stand   *Enchants / planets* 240
  Like wonder-wounded° hearers? This is I,   *awestruck*
  Hamlet the Dane.[9]

  [HAMLET *leaps into the grave and they grapple.*]

LAERTES: The devil take thy soul!
HAMLET: Thou pray'st not well.
  I prithee take thy fingers from my throat,
  For though I am not splenitive[1] and rash,   245
  Yet have I in me something dangerous,
  Which let thy wisdom fear. Hold off thy hand.
KING: Pluck them asunder.
QUEEN: Hamlet! Hamlet!
ALL: Gentlemen!   250
HORATIO: Good my lord, be quiet.

  [*The* ATTENDANTS *part them, and they come out of the
  grave.*]

HAMLET: Why, I will fight with him upon this theme
  Until my eyelids will no longer wag.°   *blink*
QUEEN: O my son, what theme?
HAMLET: I loved Ophelia. Forty thousand brothers   255
  Could not with all their quantity of love
  Make up my sum. What wilt thou do for her?
KING: O, he is mad, Laertes.
QUEEN: For love of God, forbear° him.   *bear with*
HAMLET: 'Swounds,° show me what th'owt do.   *By Christ's wounds* 260
  Woo't° weep, woo't fight, woo't fast, woo't tear thyself,   *Will you*
  Woo't drink up eisel,° eat a crocodile?   *vinegar*

---

7. Stop filling the grave for a moment.   8. The rivalry between Laertes and Hamlet in this scene
extends to their rhetoric. Pelion and Olympus, mentioned here by Laertes, and Ossa, mentioned
below by Hamlet, are Greek mountains noted in mythology for their height. Olympus was the home
of the gods, and the other two were piled one on top of the other by giants attempting to reach Olympus's summit and overthrow the gods.   9. Normally the title of Denmark's king.   1. Hot-tempered
(literally, full of spleen, one of the humors).

I'll do't. Dost come here to whine?
To outface° me with leaping in her grave?   *outdo*
265   Be buried quick° with her, and so will I.   *alive*
And if thou prate of mountains, let them throw
Millions of acres on us, till our ground,
Singeing his pate° against the burning zone,°   *head / sun's sphere*
Make Ossa like a wart! Nay, an° thou'lt mouth,   *if*
I'll rant as well as thou.
270   QUEEN: This is mere madness
And thus awhile the fit will work on him.
Anon,° as patient as the female dove   *Soon*
When that her golden couplets° are disclosed,°   *chicks / hatched*
His silence will sit drooping.
HAMLET: Hear you, sir.
275   What is the reason that you use° me thus?   *treat*
I loved you ever. But it is no matter.
Let Hercules himself do what he may,
The cat will mew, and dog will have his day.   [*Exit.*]
KING: I pray thee, good Horatio, wait upon° him.   *attend*

        [*Exit* HORATIO.]

280   [*To* LAERTES.] Strengthen your patience in° our last   *with*
        night's speech.
We'll put the matter to the present push.°—   *immediate trial*
Good Gertrude, set some watch over your son.—
This grave shall have a living monument.[2]
An hour of quiet shortly shall we see;
285   Till then in patience our proceeding be.   [*Exeunt.*]

Scene 2

A hall or public room. Enter HAMLET *and* HORATIO.

HAMLET: So much for this, sir; now shall you see the other.°   *other matter*
        You do remember all the circumstance?
HORATIO: Remember it, my lord!
HAMLET: Sir, in my heart there was a kind of fighting
5   That would not let me sleep. Methought I lay
Worse than the mutines° in the bilboes.° Rashly,   *mutineers / stocks*
And praised be rashness for it—let us know,°   *acknowledge*
Our indiscretion° sometime serves us well,   *unreasoned action*
When our deep plots do pall;° and that should learn° us   *prove ineffectual / teach*
10   There's a divinity that shapes our ends,
Rough-hew them how we will—
HORATIO: That is most certain.
HAMLET: Up from my cabin,
My sea-gown scarfed° about me, in the dark   *wrapped*

2. Lasting memorial, but perhaps also referring to Hamlet, now "living" but seen to be sacrified in
requital of Ophelia (and her father)—hence, a "monument."

Groped I to find out them, had my desire,
Fingered° their packet, and in fine° withdrew   *Stole / finally; quickly* 15
To mine own room again, making so bold,
My fears forgetting manners, to unseal
Their grand commission; where I found, Horatio—
Ah, royal knavery!—an exact° command,   *a precisely worded*
Larded° with many several° sorts of reasons,   *Garnished / different* 20
Importing° Denmark's health, and England's too,   *Concerning*
With, ho! such bugs and goblins in my life,[3]
That on the supervise,° no leisure bated,°   *reading / allowed*
No, not to stay° the grinding of the axe,   *await*
My head should be struck off.

HORATIO: Is't possible?   25

HAMLET: Here's the commission; read it at more leisure.
    But wilt thou hear now how I did proceed?

HORATIO: I beseech you.

HAMLET: Being thus benetted round with villainies,
    Ere I could make a prologue to my brains,   30
    They° had begun the play. I sat me down,   *(Hamlet's brains)*
    Devised a new commission, wrote it fair.°   *legibly, in a learned manner*
    I once did hold it, as our statists° do,   *statesmen*
    A baseness to write fair, and labored much
    How to forget that learning; but sir, now   35
    It did me yeoman's service.[4] Wilt thou know
    Th' effect° of what I wrote?   *contents*

HORATIO: Ay, good my lord.

HAMLET: An earnest conjuration° from the king,   *appeal*
    As England was his faithful tributary,°   *payer of tribute*
    As love between them like the palm might flourish,
    As peace should still her wheaten garland wear   40
    And stand a comma 'tween their amities[5]
    And many such like as's of great charge,[6]
    That on the view and knowing of these contents,
    Without debatement further more or less,   45
    He should those bearers put to sudden death,
    Not shriving-time allowed.[7]

HORATIO: How was this sealed?

HAMLET: Why, even in that was heaven ordinant,°   *guiding*
    I had my father's signet in my purse,
    Which was the model of that Danish seal,   50
    Folded the writ up in the form of th' other,
    Subscribed° it, gave't th' impression,° placed it safely,   *Signed / (of the seal)*
    The changeling[8] never known. Now, the next day

---

3. Such fanciful horrors to result if I remained alive.   4. It served me well, like a yeoman. English
yeomen (free landholders) were renowned for their good service and valor, especially in war.
5. Interests. A comma separates things but keeps them connected, in friendship or "amity," unlike a
period.   6. Weighty clauses beginning with "as."   7. Without time for confession ("shriving") and
absolution, as would be usual with legal executions.   8. Malicious elf child substituted for an infant,
as Hamlet swaps his counterfeit letter for the authentic one.

Was our sea-fight, and what to this was sequent°   *subsequent*
55   Thou knowest already.
HORATIO: So Guildenstern and Rosencrantz go to't.
HAMLET: Why, man, they did make love to this employment.
     They are not near° my conscience; their defeat°   *do not touch / destruction*
     Does by their own insinuation grow.
60   'Tis dangerous when the baser nature comes
     Between the pass and fell incensèd points⁹
     Of mighty opposites.°   *opponents*
HORATIO: Why, what a king is this!
HAMLET: Does it not, think thee, stand me now upon—¹
     He that hath killed my king and whored my mother,
65   Popped in between th' election and my hopes,
     Thrown out his angle° for my proper° life,   *fishhook / own*
     And with such coz'nage°—is't not perfect conscience   *trickery*
     To quit° him with this arm? And is't not to be damned   *requite; repay*
     To let this canker of our nature come
70   In° further evil?   *Into*
HORATIO: It must be shortly known to him from England
     What is the issue° of the business there.   *outcome*
HAMLET: It will be short;° the interim is mine.   *soon*
     And a man's life's no more than to say "one."²
75   But I am very sorry, good Horatio,
     That to Laertes I forgot myself;
     For by the image° of my cause I see   *mirror image*
     The portraiture of his. I'll court his favors.
     But sure the bravery° of his grief did put me   *ostentation*
     Into a tow'ring passion.
80 HORATIO: Peace; who comes here?

     [*Enter* OSRIC.]

OSRIC: Your lordship is right welcome back to Denmark.
HAMLET: I humbly thank you, sir. [*Aside to* HORATIO.] Dost
     know this water-fly?
HORATIO: [*Aside to* HAMLET.] No, my good lord.
85 HAMLET: [*Aside to* HORATIO.] Thy state is the more gra-
     cious,° for 'tis a vice to know him. He hath much land,   *blessed*
     and fertile. Let a beast be lord of beasts, and his crib°   *manger*
     shall stand at the king's mess.° 'Tis a chough,° but as I   *table / jackdaw*
     say, spacious in the possession of dirt.
90 OSRIC: Sweet lord, if your lordship were at leisure, I should
     impart a thing to you from his majesty.
HAMLET: I will receive it, sir, with all diligence of spirit. Put
     your bonnet° to his right use. 'Tis for the head.³   *hat*
OSRIC: I thank your lordship, it is very hot.

9. Fencing language: the thrust ("pass") and cruel ("fell") rapiers ("points").   1. Rest incumbent upon
me.   2. That is, a man's life lasts no longer than the time it takes to say "one."
3. Osric has evidently removed his hat in deference to the prince.

HAMLET: No, believe me, 'tis very cold; the wind is northerly. 95

OSRIC: It is indifferent° cold, my lord, indeed. *moderately*

HAMLET: But yet methinks it is very sultry and hot for my
  complexion.° *constitution*

OSRIC: Exceedingly, my lord; it is very sultry, as 'twere—I
  cannot tell how. My lord, his majesty bade me signify to 100
  you that 'a° has laid a great wager on your head. Sir, this *he*
  is the matter—

HAMLET: I beseech you, remember.[4] [*Moves him to put on
  his hat.*]

OSRIC: Nay, good my lord; for my ease, in good faith.
  Sir, here is newly come to court Laertes; believe me, 105
  an absolute gentleman, full of most excellent
  differences° of very soft° society and great showing.° *qualities / pleasing / appearance*
  Indeed, to speak feelingly° of him, he is the card° or *appreciatively / chart; map*
  calendar° of gentry, for you shall find in him the *directory*
  continent° of what part a gentleman would see. *embodiment* 110

HAMLET: Sir, his definement° suffers no perdition in you, *description*
  though I know to divide him inventorially would
  dozy° th' arithmetic of memory, and yet but yaw *dizzy*
  neither in respect of his quick sail.[5] But in the verity of
  extolment,° I take him to be a soul of great article, and *in truthful praise* 115
  his infusion° of such dearth° and rareness as, to make *inborn essence / preciousness*
  true diction° of him, his semblage is his mirror,[6] and *speak truly*
  who else would trace him, his umbrage, nothing more.[7]

OSRIC: Your lordship speaks most infallibly of him.

HAMLET: The concernancy,° sir? Why do we wrap the *relevance (to us)* 120
  gentleman in our more rawer breath?[8]

OSRIC: Sir?

HORATIO: Is't not possible to understand in another tongue?
  You will to't, sir, really.[9]

HAMLET: What imports the nomination° of this gentleman? *naming; mention* 125

OSRIC: Of Laertes?

HORATIO: [*Aside.*] His purse is empty already. All's golden
  words are spent.

HAMLET: Of him, sir.

OSRIC: I know you are not ignorant— 130

HAMLET: I would you did, sir; yet, in faith, if you did, it
  would not much approve° me. Well, sir. *commend*

OSRIC: You are not ignorant of what excellence Laertes is—

4. "Remember your courtesy," conventional expression inviting a subordinate to put his hat back on.
In the next line, Osric declines the invitation, using an equally conventional expression.   5. To list
his (Laertes's) qualities individually would confuse the memory's reckoning up, and yet only steer
erratically ("yaw") around Laertes's skills—that is, the description would only approximate his virtues.   6. His likeness ("semblage") is (only) his own mirror image; he is unrivaled.   7. And whoever
would imitate ("trace") him is like his shadow ("umbrage"), not the real thing at all.   8. Cruder words
(since we are so much inferior to Laertes).   9. Can't he understand his words in another man's
mouth—that is, when someone speaks as affectedly as he does? You will have your joke, sir, truly.

HAMLET: I dare not confess that, lest I should compare° *compare myself*
135   with him in excellence; but to know a man well were° to *requires one*
      know himself.
OSRIC: I mean, sir, for his weapon; but in the imputation laid
      on him by them, in his meed° he's unfellowed.° *merit / unmatched*
HAMLET: What's his weapon?
140 OSRIC: Rapier and dagger.
HAMLET: That's two of his weapons—but well.
OSRIC: The king, sir, hath wagered with him six Barbary
      horses, against the which he has impawned,° as I take it, *staked*
      six French rapiers and poniards, with their assigns,[1] as
145   girdle, hangers, and so. Three of the carriages, in faith,
      are very dear to fancy, very responsive to the hilts, most
      delicate carriages, and of very liberal conceit.[2]
HAMLET: What call you the carriages?
HORATIO: [*Aside to* HAMLET.] I knew you must be edified by
150   the margent[3] ere you had done.
OSRIC: The carriages, sir, are the hangers.
HAMLET: The phrase would be more germane to the matter
      if we could carry a cannon by our sides.[4] I would it might
      be hangers till then. But on! Six Barbary horses against
155   six French swords, their assigns, and three liberal con-
      ceited carriages; that's the French bet against the Dan-
      ish. Why is this all impawned, as you call it?
OSRIC: The king, sir, hath laid,° sir, that in a dozen passes *wagered*
      between yourself and him he shall not exceed you three
160   hits; he° hath laid on twelve for nine, and it would come *(Laertes, presumably)*
      to immediate trial if your lordship would vouchsafe the
      answer.° *accept the challenge*
HAMLET: How if I answer no?
OSRIC: I mean, my lord, the opposition of your person in trial.
165 HAMLET: Sir, I will walk here in the hall. If it please his maj-
      esty, it is the breathing° time of day with me. Let the *exercising*
      foils be brought, the gentleman willing, and the king
      hold his purpose; I will win for him an° I can. If not, I *if*
      will gain nothing but my shame and the odd hits.
170 OSRIC: Shall I deliver you so?
HAMLET: To this effect, sir, after what flourish your nature will.
OSRIC: I commend my duty° to your lordship. *dedicate my service*
HAMLET: Yours, yours. [*Exit* OSRIC.] He does well to com-
      mend° it himself; there are no tongues else for's turn.° *praise; recommend / purpose*
175 HORATIO: This lapwing runs away with the shell on his head.[5]

---

1. Accessories, which Osric goes on to list: sword belt ("girdle"), attaching straps ("hangers").
2. Osric's language is again elaborate: The "carriages," he says, capture the imagination ("fancy") and
match or echo (are "responsive to") the ornamentation on the rapiers' hilts; they are finely wrought
("delicate") and of an elaborate ("liberal") design ("conceit"). As subsequent lines make clear, even the
term "carriage" is over-fancy and obscure.   3. Marginal gloss (as in a book).   4. A common definition
of "carriage" was a mount for a cannon.   5. The lapwing (or plover) was thought to be so precocious
that it could run immediately after being hatched, even, as here, with bits of the shell still on its head.

HAMLET: 'A did comply,° sir, with his dug° before 'a sucked
it. Thus has he, and many more of the same bevy that I
know the drossy° age dotes on, only got the tune of the
time; and out of an habit of encounter, a kind of yesty collection which carries them through and through the most
fanned and winnowed opinions; and do but blow them to
their trial, the bubbles are out.[6]

deal / mother's breast

worthless

180

[*Enter a* LORD.]

LORD: My lord, his majesty commended him to you by young
Osric, who brings back to him that you attend° him in
the hall. He sends to know if your pleasure hold to play
with Laertes, or that you will take longer time.

await

185

HAMLET: I am constant to my purposes; they follow the
king's pleasure. If his fitness speaks, mine is ready; now or
whensoever, provided I be so able as now.

LORD: The king and queen and all are coming down.

190

HAMLET: In happy time.

LORD: The queen desires you to use some gentle entertain-
ment° to Laertes before you fall to play.

cordiality

HAMLET: She well instructs me.   [*Exit* LORD.]

HORATIO: You will lose this wager, my lord.

195

HAMLET: I do not think so. Since he went into France I have
been in continual practice. I shall win at the odds. But
thou wouldst not think how ill° all's here about my heart.
But it's no matter.

uneasy

HORATIO: Nay, good my lord—

200

HAMLET: It is but foolery, but it is such a kind of gaingiving°
as would perhaps trouble a woman.

misgiving

HORATIO: If your mind dislike anything, obey it. I will forestall their repair° hither, and say you are not fit.

coming

HAMLET: Not a whit, we defy augury. There is special
providence[7] in the fall of a sparrow. If it be now, 'tis not to
come; if it be not to come, it will be now; if it be not now,
yet it will come. The readiness is all. Since no man of
aught he leaves knows, what is't to leave betimes?° Let be.

205

early

[*A table prepared. Enter* TRUMPETS, DRUMS, *and* OFFI-
CERS *with cushions;* KING, QUEEN, OSRIC *and* ATTEN-
DANTS *with foils, daggers, and* LAERTES.]

KING: Come, Hamlet, come and take this hand from me.

210

6. And from the formulas of courteous conversation ("habit of encounter"), they make a frothy and
inflated repertoire of speech and behavior ("yesty collection"), which gets them through or passes for
the most carefully considered wisdom ("fanned and winnowed opinions"); and if you test them by
merely blowing on them—as Hamlet does in speaking to Osric—they pop and dissolve like "bubbles."
7. God's direction for a specific event (over and above "general providence," the whole shape of God's
design). Compare Matthew 10.29: "Are not two sparrows sold for a farthing? and one of them shall
not fall on the ground without your Father."

[The KING *puts* LAERTES' *hand into* HAMLET's.]

HAMLET: Give me your pardon, sir. I have done you wrong,
But pardon 't as you are a gentleman.
This presence° knows, and you must needs have heard,   royal company
How I am punished with a sore distraction.°   agitation; insanity
215   What I have done
That might your nature, honor, and exception,°   disapproval; resentment
Roughly awake, I here proclaim was madness.
Was 't Hamlet wronged Laertes? Never Hamlet.
If Hamlet from himself be ta'en away,
220   And when he's not himself does wrong Laertes,
Then Hamlet does it not, Hamlet denies it.
Who does it then? His madness. If't be so,
Hamlet is of the faction that is wronged;
His madness is poor Hamlet's enemy.
225   Sir, in this audience,
Let my disclaiming from° a purposed evil   disavowal of
Free me so far in your most generous thoughts
That I have shot my arrow o'er the house
And hurt my brother.
LAERTES: I am satisfied in nature,
230   Whose motive in this case should stir me most
To my revenge. But in my terms of honor[8]
I stand aloof, and will no reconcilement
Till by some elder masters of known honor
I have a voice° and precedent of peace   authority
235   To keep my name ungored.° But till that time   unsullied
I do receive your offered love like love,
And will not wrong it.·
HAMLET: I embrace it freely,
And will this brother's wager frankly° play.   freely
Give us the foils. Come on.
LAERTES: Come, one for me.
240 HAMLET: I'll be your foil° Laertes. In mine ignorance   contrast
Your skill shall, like a star i' th' darkest night,
Stick° fiery off indeed.   Sparkle; jab
LAERTES: You mock me, sir.
HAMLET: No, by this hand.
KING: Give them the foils, young Osric. Cousin Hamlet,
You know the wager?
245 HAMLET: Very well, my lord;
Your Grace has laid the odds o' th' weaker side.
KING: I do not fear it, I have seen you both;
But since he is bettered° we have therefore odds.°   favored / handicapping
LAERTES: This is too heavy; let me see another.
250 HAMLET: This likes° me well. These foils have all a° length?   pleases; suits / the same

---

8. But where my social standing as a man of honor (versus "nature," line 229) is concerned.

[*They prepare to play.*]

OSRIC: Ay, my good lord.

KING: Set me the stoups° of wine upon that table.   *flagons*
    If Hamlet give the first or second hit,
    Or quit in answer of the third exchange,⁹
    Let all the battlements their ordnance° fire.   *cannons* 255
    The king shall drink to Hamlet's better breath,°   *energy*
    And in the cup an union° shall he throw,   *a pearl*
    Richer than that which four successive kings
    In Denmark's crown have worn. Give me the cups,
    And let the kettle° to the trumpet speak,   *kettledrum* 260
    The trumpet to the cannoneer without,
    The cannons to the heavens, the heaven to earth,
    "Now the king drinks to Hamlet." Come, begin—

[*Trumpets the while.*]

    And you, the judges, bear a wary eye.

HAMLET: Come on, sir.

LAERTES: Come, my lord.

    [*They play.*]

HAMLET: One.

LAERTES: No.

HAMLET: Judgment?

OSRIC: A hit, a very palpable hit.   265

[*Drums, trumpets, and shot. Flourish; a piece° goes off.*]   *cannon*

LAERTES: Well, again.

KING: Stay,° give me drink. Hamlet, this pearl is thine.   *Stop*
    Here's to thy health. Give him the cup.

HAMLET: I'll play this bout first; set it by awhile.   270
    Come.

    [*They play.*]

    Another hit; what say you?

LAERTES: A touch, a touch, I do confess't.

KING: Our son shall win.

QUEEN: He's fat,° and scant of breath.   *sweaty*
    Here, Hamlet, take my napkin,° rub thy brows.   *handkerchief* 275
    The queen carouses° to thy fortune, Hamlet.   *drinks*

HAMLET: Good madam!

KING: Gertrude, do not drink.

QUEEN: I will, my lord; I pray you pardon me.

KING: [*Aside.*] It is the poisoned cup; it is too late.   280

HAMLET: I dare not drink yet, madam; by and by.

QUEEN: Come, let me wipe thy face.

LAERTES: My lord, I'll hit him now.

---

9. Or repay Laertes's victories by winning the third bout.

KING: I do not think't.
LAERTES: [*Aside.*] And yet it is almost against my conscience.
285 HAMLET: Come, for the third, Laertes. You do but dally.
  I pray you pass° with your best violence;   *thrust*
  I am afeard you make a wanton of me.°   *trifle with me*
LAERTES: Say you so? Come on.

  [*They play.*]

OSRIC: Nothing, neither way.
290 LAERTES: Have at you now!

  [LAERTES *wounds* HAMLET: *then, in scuffling, they*
  change rapiers, and HAMLET *wounds* LAERTES.]

KING: Part them. They are incensed.
HAMLET: Nay, come again.

  [*The* QUEEN *falls.*]

OSRIC: Look to the queen there, ho!
HORATIO: They bleed on both sides. How is it, my lord?
295 OSRIC: How is't, Laertes?
LAERTES: Why, as a woodcock to mine own springe,° Osric.   *snare*
  I am justly killed with mine own treachery.
HAMLET: How does the queen?
KING: She swoons to see them bleed.
QUEEN: No, no, the drink, the drink! O my dear Hamlet!
300   The drink, the drink! I am poisoned.   [*Dies.*]
HAMLET: O, villainy! Ho! let the door be locked.
  Treachery! seek it out.
LAERTES: It is here, Hamlet. Hamlet, thou art slain;
  No med'cine in the world can do thee good.
305   In thee there is not half an hour's life.
  The treacherous instrument is in thy hand,
  Unbated° and envenomed. The foul practice   *Unblunted*
  Hath turned itself on me. Lo, here I lie,
  Never to rise again. Thy mother's poisoned.
310   I can no more. The king, the king's to blame.
HAMLET: The point envenomed too?
  Then, venom, to thy work.   [*Hurts the* KING.]
ALL: Treason! treason!
KING: O, yet defend me, friends. I am but hurt.
315 HAMLET: Here, thou incestuous, murd'rous, damnèd Dane,
  Drink off this potion. Is thy union[1] here?
  Follow my mother.

  [*The* KING *dies.*]

LAERTES: He is justly served.
  It is a poison tempered° by himself.   *mixed*

---

1. Referring to both the pearl and his incestuous marriage to Gertrude.

Exchange forgiveness with me, noble Hamlet.
Mine and my father's death come not upon thee,[2]   320
Nor thine on me!   [*Dies.*]
HAMLET: Heaven make thee free of it! I follow thee.
I am dead, Horatio. Wretched queen, adieu!
You that look pale and tremble at this chance,
That are but mutes° or audience to this act,   *nonspeaking actors* 325
Had I but time, as this fell sergeant Death
Is strict in his arrest, O, I could tell you—
But let it be. Horatio, I am dead:
Thou livest; report me and my cause aright
To the unsatisfied.°   *uninformed*
HORATIO: Never believe it.   330
I am more an antique Roman than a Dane.[3]
Here's yet some liquor left.
HAMLET: As th'art a man,
Give me the cup. Let go. By heaven, I'll ha't.
O God, Horatio, what a wounded name,
Things standing thus unknown, shall live behind me!   335
If thou didst ever hold me in thy heart,
Absent thee from felicity awhile,
And in this harsh world draw thy breath in pain,
To tell my story.

[*A march afar off.*]
                    What warlike noise is this?
OSRIC: Young Fortinbras, with conquest come from Poland,   340
To th' ambassadors of England gives
This warlike volley.°   *military salute*
HAMLET: O, I die, Horatio!
The potent poison quite o'er-crows° my spirit.   *triumphs over*
I cannot live to hear the news from England,
But I do prophesy th' election lights   345
On Fortinbras. He has my dying voice.[4]
So tell him, with th' occurrents,° more and less,   *occurrences*
Which have solicited[5]—the rest is silence.   [*Dies.*]
HORATIO: Now cracks a noble heart. Good night, sweet prince,
And flights of angels sing thee to thy rest!   350

[*March within.*]

Why does the drum come hither?

2. May your soul not be judged accountable for my death or my father's.   3. Ancient ("antique")
Romans generally preferred suicide to dishonor and believed that servants or retainers should not
outlive their master's overthrow.   4. Vote. Because Denmark is an elective monarchy, Fortinbras can
only become king by receiving the "voice," or vote, of electors such as Hamlet.
5. Some editors assume that the sentence is grammatically incomplete, broken off by death. Hamlet
seems to refer to the events ("occurrences") that have led to this moment and moved ("solicited") him
to give his support to Fortinbras.

[*Enter* FORTINBRAS, *with the* AMBASSADORS *and with drum, colors, and* ATTENDANTS.]

FORTINBRAS: Where is this sight?

HORATIO: What is it you would see?
If aught of woe or wonder, cease your search.

FORTINBRAS: This quarry cries on havoc.[6] O proud death,
355   What feast is toward° in thine eternal cell   *preparing*
That thou so many princes at a shot
So bloodily hast struck?

AMBASSADORS: The sight is dismal;
And our affairs from England come too late.
The ears are senseless° that should give us hearing   *unhearing*
360   To tell him° his commandment is fulfilled,   *(Claudius)*
That Rosencrantz and Guildenstern are dead.
Where should we have our thanks?

HORATIO: Not from his mouth,
Had it th' ability of life to thank you.
He never gave commandment for their death.
365   But since, so jump° upon this bloody question,°   *immediately / matter*
You from the Polack wars, and you from England,
Are here arrived, give orders that these bodies
High on a stage be placèd to the view,
And let me speak to th' yet unknowing world
370   How these things came about. So shall you hear
Of carnal, bloody, and unnatural acts;
Of accidental judgments,° casual° slaughters;   *retributions / chance*
Of deaths put on° by cunning and forced cause;   *instigated*
And, in this upshot,° purposes mistook   *result*
375   Fall'n on th' inventors' heads. All this can I
Truly deliver.

FORTINBRAS: Let us haste to hear it,
And call the noblest to the audience.°   *hearing*
For° me, with sorrow I embrace my fortune.   *As for*
I have some rights of memory° in this kingdom,   *remembered*
380   Which now to claim my vantage° doth invite me.   *favorable opportunity*

HORATIO: Of that I shall have also cause to speak,
And from his mouth whose voice will draw on more.
But let this same be presently performed,
Even while men's minds are wild, lest more mischance
On° plots and errors happen.   *On top of*

385 FORTINBRAS: Let four captains
Bear Hamlet like a soldier to the stage,
For he was likely, had he been put on,°   *put to the test*
To have proved most royal; and for his passage
The soldier's music and the rite of war
390   Speak loudly for him.

6. All this slaughtered game ("quarry") proclaims a massacre.

Take up the bodies. Such a sight as this
Becomes the field,° but here shows° much amiss.   *battlefield / appears*
Go, bid the soldiers shoot.
  [Exeunt marching. A peal of ordnance shot off.]

c. 1600

SOPHOCLES
(496–406 BCE)
Antigone[1]

Sophocles lived at a time when Athens and Greek
civilization were at the peak of their power and influence. He served as a general under Pericles, played a
prominent role in the city's affairs, and was arguably
the greatest of the Greek tragic playwrights, winning
the annual dramatic competition about twenty times,
a feat unmatched by even his great contemporaries, Aeschylus and Euripides. An innovator, Sophocles fundamentally changed the nature of dramatic performance by adding
a third actor, enlarging the chorus, and introducing the use of painted scenery. Aristotle
held that Sophocles's *Oedipus the King* (c. 429 BCE) was the perfect tragedy and used
it as his model when he discussed the nature of tragedy in his *Poetics*. Today only seven
of Sophocles's tragedies survive—the Oedipus trilogy (*Oedipus the King, Oedipus at
Colonus,* and *Antigone*), *Philoctetes, Ajax, Trachiniae,* and *Electra*—though he is believed
to have written as many as 123 plays.

CHARACTERS

ANTIGONE	HAEMON
ISMENE	TEIRESIAS
CHORUS OF THEBAN ELDERS	A MESSENGER
CREON	EURYDICE
A SENTRY	SECOND MESSENGER

The two sisters ANTIGONE *and* ISMENE *meet in front of the palace gates in
Thebes.*

ANTIGONE: Ismene, my dear sister,
  whose father was my father, can you think of any
  of all the evils that stem from Oedipus[2]

1. Translated by David Grene.
2. In Greek legend, Oedipus became king of Thebes by inadvertently fulfilling the prophecy that he
was destined to kill his father and marry his mother (as depicted in Sophocles's *Oedipus the King*); for
these offenses against nature and the gods, Creon sent Oedipus, along with his daughters Antigone
and Ismene, into exile at Colonus. Oedipus's sons, Eteocles and Polyneices, agreed to take turns
ruling Thebes. But when Eteocles refused to give up the throne at the end of his first allotted
year, Polyneices gathered an "Argive army" (line 17) and attacked the city.

that Zeus does not bring to pass for us, while we yet live?
5   No pain, no ruin, no shame, and no dishonor
but I have seen it in our mischiefs,
yours and mine.
And now what is the proclamation that they tell of
made lately by the commander, publicly,
10   to all the people? Do you know it? Have you heard it?
Don't you notice when the evils due to enemies
are headed towards those we love?

ISMENE: Not a word, Antigone, of those we love,
either sweet or bitter, has come to me since the moment
15   when we lost our two brothers,
on one day, by their hands dealing mutual death.
Since the Argive[3] army fled in this past night,
I know of nothing further, nothing
of better fortune or of more destruction.

20 ANTIGONE: *I* knew it well; that is why I sent for you
to come outside the palace gates
to listen to me, privately.

ISMENE: What is it? Certainly your words
come of dark thoughts.

25 ANTIGONE: Yes, indeed; for those two brothers of ours, in burial
has not Creon honored the one, dishonored the other?
Eteocles, they say he has used justly
with lawful rites and hid him in the earth
to have his honor among the dead men there.
30   But the unhappy corpse of Polyneices
he has proclaimed to all the citizens,
they say, no man may hide
in a grave nor mourn in funeral,
but leave unwept, unburied, a dainty treasure
35   for the birds that see him, for their feast's delight.
That is what, they say, the worthy Creon
has proclaimed for you and me—for me, I tell you—
and he comes here to clarify to the unknowing
his proclamation; he takes it seriously;
40   for whoever breaks the edict death is prescribed,
and death by stoning publicly.
There you have it; soon you will show yourself
as noble both in your nature and your birth,
or yourself as base, although of noble parents.

45 ISMENE: If things are as you say, poor sister, how
can I better them? how loose or tie the knot?

ANTIGONE: Decide if you will share the work, the deed.

ISMENE: What kind of danger is there? How far have your thoughts gone?

ANTIGONE: Here is this hand. Will you help it to lift the dead man?

---

3. From Argos, a rival Greek city-state.

ISMENE: Would you bury him, when it is forbidden the city? 50
ANTIGONE: At least he is my brother—and yours, too,
    though you deny him. *I* will not prove false to him.
ISMENE: You are so headstrong. Creon has forbidden it.
ANTIGONE: It is not for him to keep me from my own.
ISMENE: O God! 55
    Consider, sister, how our father died,
    hated and infamous; how he brought to light
    his own offenses; how he himself struck out
    the sight of his two eyes;
    his own hand was their executioner. 60
    Then, mother and wife, two names in one, did shame
    violently on her life, with twisted cords.
    Third, our two brothers, on a single day,
    poor wretches, themselves worked out their mutual doom.
    Each killed the other, hand against brother's hand. 65
    Now there are only the two of us, left behind,
    and see how miserable our end shall be
    if in the teeth of law we shall transgress
    against the sovereign's decree and power.
    You ought to realize we are only women, 70
    not meant in nature to fight against men,
    and that we are ruled, by those who are stronger,
    to obedience in this and even more painful matters.
    I do indeed beg those beneath the earth
    to give me their forgiveness, 75
    since force constrains me,
    that I shall yield in this to the authorities.
    Extravagant action is not sensible.
ANTIGONE: I would not urge you now; nor if you wanted
    to act would I be glad to have you with me. 80
    Be as you choose to be; but for myself
    I myself will bury him. It will be good
    to die, so doing. I shall lie by his side,
    loving him as he loved me; I shall be
    a criminal—but a religious one. 85
    The time in which I must please those that are dead
    is longer than I must please those of this world.
    For there I shall lie forever. You, if you like,
    can cast dishonor on what the gods have honored.
ISMENE: I will not put dishonor on them, but 90
    to act in defiance of the citizenry,
    my nature does not give me means for that.
ANTIGONE: Let that be your excuse. But I will go
    to heap the earth on the grave of my loved brother.
ISMENE: How I fear for you, my poor sister! 95
ANTIGONE: Do not fear for me. Make straight your own path to destiny.
ISMENE: At least do not speak of this act to anyone else;

bury him in secret; I will be silent, too.
ANTIGONE: Oh, oh, no! shout it out. I will hate you still worse
100   for silence—should you not proclaim it,
      to everyone.
ISMENE: You have a warm heart for such chilly deeds.
ANTIGONE: I know I am pleasing those I should please most.
ISMENE: *If* you can do it. But you are in love
105   with the impossible.
ANTIGONE: No. When I can no more, then I will stop.
ISMENE: It is better not to hunt the impossible
      at all.
ANTIGONE: If you will talk like this I will loathe you,
110   and you will be adjudged an enemy—
      justly—by the dead's decision. Let me alone
      and my folly with me, to endure this terror.
      No suffering of mine will be enough
      to make me die ignobly.
115 ISMENE: Well, if you will, go on.
      Know this; that though you are wrong to go, your friends
      are right to love you.
CHORUS: Sun's beam, fairest of all
      that ever till now shone
120   on seven-gated Thebes;
      O golden eye of day, you shone
      coming over Dirce's stream;[4]
      You drove in headlong rout
      the whiteshielded man from Argos,
125   complete in arms;
      his bits rang sharper
      under your urging.

      Polyneices brought him here
      against our land, Polyneices,
130   roused by contentious quarrel;
      like an eagle he flew into our country,
      with many men-at-arms,
      with many a helmet crowned with horsehair.

      He stood above the halls, gaping with murderous lances,
135   encompassing the city's
      seven-gated mouth[5]
      But before his jaws would be sated
      with our blood, before the fire,
      pine fed, should capture our crown of towers,
140   he went hence—

4. River near Thebes.
5. Thebes was known throughout the ancient world for having seven gateways through the walls protecting the city.

such clamor of war stretched behind his back,
from his dragon foe, a thing he could not overcome.

For Zeus, who hates the most
the boasts of a great tongue,
saw them coming in a great tide,   145
insolent in the clang of golden armor.
The god struck him down with hurled fire,
as he strove to raise the victory cry,
now at the very winning post.

The earth rose to strike him as he fell swinging.   150
In his frantic onslaught, possessed, he breathed upon us
with blasting winds of hate.
Sometimes the great god of war was on one side,
and sometimes he struck a staggering blow on the other;
the god was a very wheel horse[6] on the right trace.   155

At seven gates stood seven captains,
ranged equals against equals, and there left
their brazen suits of armor
to Zeus, the god of trophies.
Only those two wretches born of one father and mother   160
set their spears to win a victory on both sides;
they worked out their share in a common death.

Now Victory, whose name is great, has come
to Thebes of many chariots
with joy to answer her joy,   165
to bring forgetfulness of these wars;
let us go to all the shrines of the gods
and dance all night long.
Let Bacchus lead the dance,
shaking Thebes to trembling.   170

But here is the king of our land,
Creon,[7] son of Menoeceus;
in our new contingencies with the gods,
he is our new ruler.
He comes to set in motion some design—   175
what design is it? Because he has proposed
the convocation of the elders.
He sent a public summons for our discussion.

CREON: Gentlemen: as for our city's fortune,
the gods have shaken her, when the great waves broke,   180
but the gods have brought her through again to safety.
For yourselves, I chose you out of all and summoned you

6. Strongest and ablest horse in a team pulling a vehicle, harnessed nearest the front wheels "on the right trace."
7. Brother of Jocasta, mother and wife of Oedipus; he became king of Thebes after the deaths of Oedipus's sons.

to come to me, partly because I knew you
as always loyal to the throne—at first,
185   when Laïus[8] was king, and then again
when Oedipus saved our city and then again
when he died and you remained with steadfast truth
to their descendants,
until they met their double fate upon one day,
190   striking and stricken, defiled each by a brother's murder.
Now here I am, holding all authority
and the throne, in virtue of kinship with the dead.
It is impossible to know any man—
I mean his soul, intelligence, and judgment—
195   until he shows his skill in rule and law.
I think that a man supreme ruler of a whole city,
if he does not reach for the best counsel for her,
but through some fear, keeps his tongue under lock and key,
him I judge the worst of any;
200   I have always judged so; and anyone thinking
another man more a friend than his own country,
I rate him nowhere. For my part, God is my witness,
who sees all, always, I would not be silent
if I saw ruin, not safety, on the way
205   towards my fellow citizens. I would not count
any enemy of my country as a friend—
because of what I know, that she it is
which gives us our security. If she sails upright
and we sail on her, friends will be ours for the making.
210   In the light of rules like these, I will make her greater still.

In consonance with this, I here proclaim
to the citizens about Oedipus' sons.
For Eteocles, who died this city's champion,
showing his valor's supremacy everywhere,
215   he shall be buried in his grave with every rite
of sanctity given to heroes under earth.
However, his brother, Polyneices, a returned exile,
who sought to burn with fire from top to bottom
his native city, and the gods of his own people;
220   who sought to taste the blood he shared with us,
and lead the rest of us to slavery—
I here proclaim to the city that this man
shall no one honor with a grave and none shall mourn.
You shall leave him without burial; you shall watch him
225   chewed up by birds and dogs and violated.
Such is my mind in the matter; never by me
shall the wicked man have precedence in honor

8. Father of Oedipus.

over the just. But he that is loyal to the state
in death, in life alike, shall have my honor.
CHORUS: Son of Menoeceus, so it is your pleasure   230
to deal with foe and friend of this our city.
To use any legal means lies in your power,
both about the dead and those of us who live.
CREON: I understand, then, you will do my bidding.
CHORUS: Please lay this burden on some younger man.   235
CREON: Oh, watchers of the corpse I have already.
CHORUS: What else, then, do your commands entail?
CREON: That you should not side with those who disagree.
CHORUS: There is none so foolish as to love his own death.
CREON: Yes, indeed those are the wages, but often greed   240
has with its hopes brought men to ruin.

[*The* SENTRY *whose speeches follow represents a remarkable experiment in
Greek tragedy in the direction of naturalism of speech. He speaks with
marked clumsiness, partly because he is excited and talks almost colloquially.
But also the royal presence makes him think apparently that he should be
rather grand in his show of respect. He uses odd bits of archaism or somewhat
stale poetical passages, particularly in catch phrases. He sounds something
like lower-level Shakespearean characters, e.g. Constable Elbow, with his
uncertainty about benefactor and malefactor.*]

SENTRY: My lord, I will never claim my shortness of breath
is due to hurrying, nor were there wings in my feet.
I stopped at many a lay-by in my thinking;
I circled myself till I met myself coming back.   245
My soul accosted me with different speeches.
"Poor fool, yourself, why are you going somewhere
when once you get there you will pay the piper?"
"Well, aren't you the daring fellow! stopping again?
and suppose Creon hears the news from someone else—   250
don't you realize that you will smart for that?"
I turned the whole matter over. I suppose I may say
"I made haste slowly" and the short road became long.
However, at last I came to a resolve:
I must go to you; even if what I say   255
is nothing, really, still I shall say it.
I come here, a man with a firm clutch on the hope
that nothing can betide him save what is fated.
CREON: What is it then that makes you so afraid?
SENTRY: No, I want first of all to tell you my side of it.   260
I didn't do the thing; I never saw who did it.
It would not be fair for me to get into trouble.
CREON: You hedge, and barricade the thing itself.
Clearly you have some ugly news for me.
SENTRY: Well, you know how disasters make a man   265

hesitate to be their messenger.

CREON: For God's sake, tell me and get out of here!

SENTRY: Yes, I *will* tell you. Someone just now
buried the corpse and vanished. He scattered on the skin

270 some thirsty dust; he did the ritual,
duly, to purge the body of desecration.

CREON: What! Now who on earth could have done that?

SENTRY: I do not know. For there was there no mark
of axe's stroke nor casting up of earth

275 of any mattock; the ground was hard and dry,
unbroken; there were no signs of wagon wheels.
The doer of the deed had left no trace.
But when the first sentry of the day pointed it out,
there was for all of us a disagreeable

280 wonder. For the body had disappeared;
not in a grave, of course; but there lay upon him
a little dust as of a hand avoiding
the curse of violating the dead body's sanctity.
There were no signs of any beast nor dog

285 that came there; he had clearly not been torn.
There was a tide of bad words at one another,
guard taunting guard, and it might well have ended
in blows, for there was no one there to stop it.
Each one of us was the criminal but no one

290 manifestly so; all denied knowledge of it.
We were ready to take hot bars in our hands
or walk through fire,[9] and call on the gods with oaths
that we had neither done it nor were privy
to a plot with anyone, neither in planning

295 nor yet in execution.
At last when nothing came of all our searching,
there was one man who spoke, made every head
bow to the ground in fear. For we could not
either contradict him nor yet could we see how

300 if we did what he said we would come out all right.
His word was that we must lay information
about the matter to yourself; we could not cover it.
This view prevailed and the lot of the draw chose me,
unlucky me, to win that prize. So here

305 I am. I did not want to come,
and you don't want to have me. I know that.
For no one likes the messenger of bad news.

CHORUS: My lord: I wonder, could this be God's doing?
This is the thought that keeps on haunting me.

9. Ancient legal custom required an accused person to undergo a "trial by ordeal," such as walking
through fire; if the resulting injuries were not serious, the person was considered innocent and therefore divinely protected.